This page has been designed to fold out for easy reference, particularly when using the maps.

GW00467462

SYMBOLS USED ON THE MAPS

The roads

Freeway with Route Number	
Freeway under construction	
Highway, sealed, with National Route Number	
Highway, sealed, with State Route Number (Tasmania only)	
Highway, unsealed	
Highway under construction	
Major road, sealed, with Metropolitan Route Number	
Major road, sealed	
Major road, unsealed	
Major road, unsealed	
Major road under construction	
Other road	
Vehicular track	
Vehicular track	
Metropolitan and suburban minor road	
One way street	
Bridge	
Ferry	Fy

Other features

Total kilometres between two main points	30
Intermediate kilometres	5
Kilometres from GPO (Suburb maps)	16
Railway with station	Newcastle
Railway with town	Eudlo
Railway, disused / abandoned	+ + + + + +
State boundary	
Walking track	
Aboriginal land	
Park, recreational area	
Built-up area	
Homestead	Mooloogoolo
Area of interest	
Building of interest	
Place of interest	Caravan Park ■
Other landmark	Tower ■
Airport, landing ground	✈
River	
Lake	
Intermittent lake	
Swamp	
Area subject to flooding	
Conduit, aquaduct	
Canal, drain, pipeline, channel	
Lighthouse	★
Hill, mountain	Mt. Dandenong + 633m
Text entry in A-Z listing	➊

How to use this book

Explore Australia begins with an Australia-wide introduction giving detailed information on planning a trip, accommodation, driving in outback conditions, breakdowns and travelling with children. From page 37 both text and maps are colour coded on a state-by-state basis.

The text

Each state section begins with a general introduction, a detailed description of the capital city and suggested tours. This is followed by an A–Z listing of towns. Each town description includes:
- a population figure (taken from the most recent Census statistics available and intended to provide only an approximate idea of the size of the town)
- a listing of what is of interest in the town and in the surrounding area
- an address for the local tourist information centre (where available)
- a guide to the minimum family accommodation available
- a reference to the map/s on which the town appears

The maps

Every part of Australia is mapped in *Explore Australia*, from cities to the outback. Heavily-populated areas are mapped in greater detail. Distance is shown by black and red markers on the maps and a scale bar at the top of each map. A ➊ symbol alongside a town name indicates there is a description of the town in the A–Z listing for that state.

Continuation of maps: For easy continuation from one map to another there is always some overlap when maps are at the same scale. The symbol on the edges of the map pages indicates the next map page that should be turned to.

Feature maps of holiday regions: Holiday regions are mapped to show tourist highlights in detail. These maps accompany the feature on the region in the text.

Intercity route maps: These maps have been designed to help you plan your route between major cities. Information is given on distances between the towns along each route, roadside rest areas and road conditions where relevant.

Cross-references

Text to maps: Each town described in the A–Z listings includes a reference to the map/s on which the town appears.

Maps to text: The ➊ symbol alongside a town name on the maps indicates there is a description of that town in the text.

The gazetteer

To find out about a particular place mentioned in the text or shown on a map, it is essential to use the index references in the gazetteer. For example:

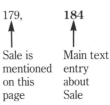

ROAD DISTANCES BETWEEN MAIN CITIES

This distance chart shows distances by road between cities. The distances shown are in kilometres and are based on the most direct route, not necessarily the most practical.

	Adelaide	Brisbane	Canberra	Darwin	Melbourne	Perth	Sydney
Adelaide		2062	1204	3024	725	2707	1424
Albury	913	1545	343	3937	310	3620	563
Alice Springs	1534	2946	2680	1490	2259	3933	2958
Ballarat	616	1765	762	3640	109	3323	982
Bendigo	641	1632	642	3665	149	3348	862
Birdsville	1202	1619	2153	2246	2470	3293	2129
Brisbane	2062		1268	3399	1686	4363	982
Broken Hill	509	1553	1073	3127	820	2810	1174
Broome	4271	4646	4975	1875	4996	2258	5112
Cairns	3384	1697	2922	2885	3008	6050	2679
Canberra	1204	1268		3917	653	3911	286
Darwin	3024	3399	4170		3749	4163	3994
Geelong	862	1760	727	3852	74	3410	947
Geraldton	3131	4787	4335	3739	3856	424	4555
Kalgoorlie	2188	3634	3392	4760	2913	597	3465
Katherine	2710	3085	3856	314	3435	3718	3588
Mackay	2666	979	2204	2913	2290	5275	1941
Melbourne	725	1686	653	3749		3432	873
Mildura	397	1671	807	3421	554	3104	1027
Mount Gambier	454	2071	1068	3478	482	3161	1288
Newcastle	1599	807	461	3819	1048	4159	175
Perth	2707	4363	3911	4163	3432		3984
Port Augusta	308	1754	1512	2716	1037	2399	1585
Port Hedland	4831	5178	5536	2482	5057	1625	5609
Rockhampton	2329	642	1867	2954	1953	5199	1624
Sydney	1424	982	286	3994	873	4131	
Tennant Creek	2040	2440	3186	984	2765	4622	3010
Townsville	3038	1351	2576	2541	2662	5911	2313
Wagga Wagga	959	1285	245	3672	438	3666	465

Hobart to Launceston **200 kilometres**

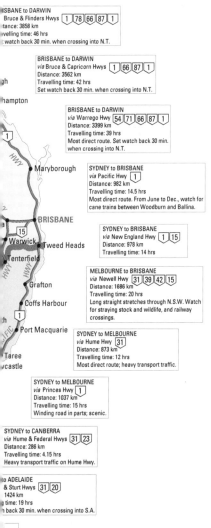

ISBANE to DARWIN
Bruce & Flinders Hwys [1] [78] [66] [87] [1]
stance: 3858 km
velling time: 46 hrs
watch back 30 min. when crossing into N.T.

BRISBANE to DARWIN
via Bruce & Capricorn Hwys [1] [66] [87] [1]
Distance: 3562 km
Travelling time: 42 hrs
Set watch back 30 min. when crossing into N.T.

BRISBANE to DARWIN
via Warrego Hwy [54] [71] [66] [87] [1]
Distance: 3399 km
Travelling time: 39 hrs
Most direct route. Set watch back 30 min. when crossing into N.T.

SYDNEY to BRISBANE
via Pacific Hwy [1]
Distance: 982 km
Travelling time: 14.5 hrs
Most direct route. From June to Dec., watch for cane trains between Woodburn and Ballina.

SYDNEY to BRISBANE
via New England Hwy [1] [15]
Distance: 978 km
Travelling time: 14 hrs

MELBOURNE to BRISBANE
via Newell Hwy [31] [39] [42] [15]
Distance: 1686 km
Travelling time: 20 hrs
Long straight stretches through N.S.W. Watch for straying stock and wildlife, and railway crossings.

SYDNEY to MELBOURNE
via Hume Hwy [31]
Distance: 873 km
Travelling time: 12 hrs
Most direct route; heavy transport traffic.

SYDNEY to MELBOURNE
via Princes Hwy [1]
Distance: 1037 km
Travelling time: 15 hrs
Winding road in parts; scenic.

SYDNEY to CANBERRA
via Hume & Federal Hwys [31] [23]
Distance: 286 km
Travelling time: 4.15 hrs
Heavy transport traffic on Hume Hwy.

to ADELAIDE
& Sturt Hwys [31] [20]
1424 km
g time: 19 hrs
h back 30 min. when crossing into S.A.

Maryborough
hampton
BRISBANE
Warwick Tweed Heads
Tenterfield
Grafton
Coffs Harbour
Port Macquarie
Taree
castle

COPYRIGHT, PENGUIN BOOKS AUSTRALIA LTD

Warning

Driving in northern and outback Australia can be extremely hazardous. During the wet season from October to March torrential rains frequently flood large areas, making roads impassable for weeks on end. When planning journeys into these areas read carefully the section on Outback Motoring in this book. Always:

- Check the road conditions before departure.
- Notify a responsible person of your planned route.
- Check that your car is in good mechanical order.
- Carry plenty of water and supplies of food.
- Stay with the car in case of breakdown.

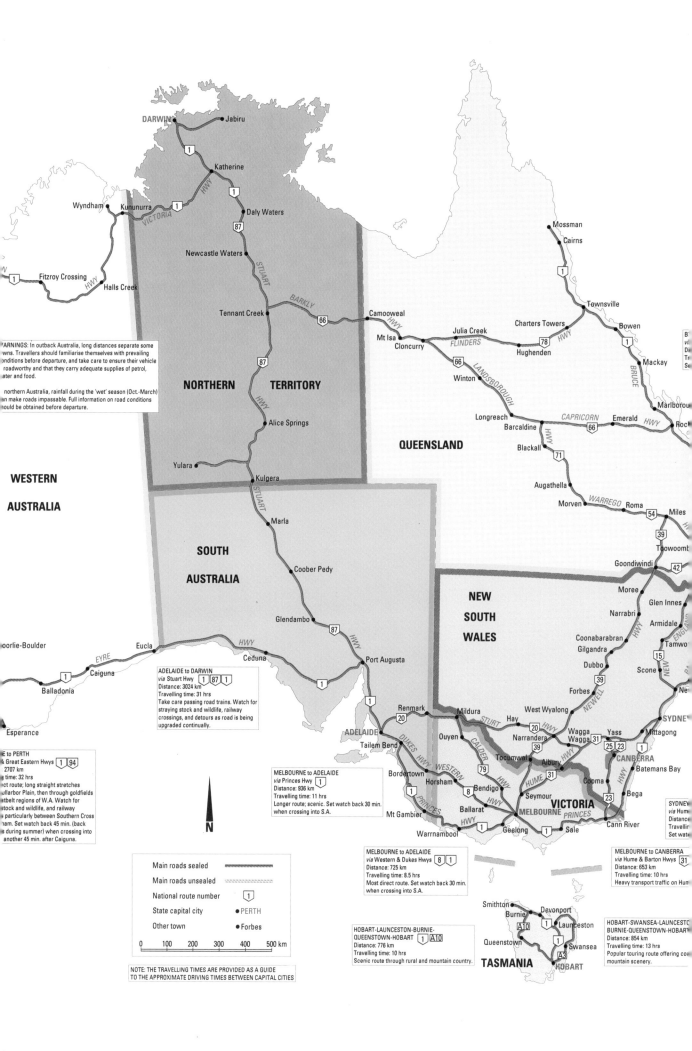

EXPLORE AUSTRALIA

Robert Hale Ltd
Clerkenwell House
Clerkenwell Green
London EC1R 0HT

This twelfth edition published in Great Britain by Robert Hale Ltd, 1993
First published by George Philip & O'Neil Pty Ltd, 1980
Second edition 1981
Third edition 1983
Reprinted 1984
Fourth edition 1985
Fifth edition 1986
Sixth edition published by Penguin Books Australia, 1987
Seventh edition 1988
Eighth edition 1989
Ninth edition 1990
Tenth edition 1991
Eleventh edition 1992
Copyright © Concept, text and index:
Penguin Books Australia Ltd, 1993
Copyright © Maps: (as designated) BP Australia, 1993;
Penguin Books Australia Ltd, 1993

ISBN 0 7090 5193 X

Printed and bound in Hong Kong through Bookbuilders Ltd

Disclaimer: The publisher cannot accept responsibility for any errors or
omissions. The representation on the maps of any road or track is not
necessarily evidence of public right of way.
The population figures given in *Explore Australia* have been taken from
the most recent Census results available. They are intended to
provide only an approximate idea of the size of the various cities and
towns.
Accommodation listed is a guide to the minimum available family accommodation
in each town.

HALF-TITLE PAGE: Uluru (Ayers Rock), Northern Territory (Richard I'anson)
TITLE PAGE: Bondi Beach, New South Wales (Richard I'anson)

EXPLORE AUSTRALIA

THE COMPLETE TOURING COMPANION

ROBERT HALE • LONDON

ACKNOWLEDGEMENTS

Editor Fran Church
Cartographic co-ordinator Colin Critchell AMAIC
State cartographic consultants
Australian Capital Territory: Paul Sjoberg
Queensland: Bruno Scaggiante, MID (Aust.), MAIC
New South Wales: Bruce Vaughan
Northern Territory: Len Carter, AMAIC
South Australia: George Ricketts, MAIC
Tasmania: Phil Broughton, FAIC
Victoria: Tim Corr, B.App.Sc (Cartog.)
Western Australia: Peter Rose, AMAIC
Cartographic assistant Bruce McGurty, B.A. (Geog.)
Desk-top publishing Claire Kirkwood
Editorial assistants Astrid Browne, Elizabeth O'Brien, Ian Sibley, Barbara Whiter
Cover design Smartworks, Melbourne
Research EdInk, Melbourne; George Ricketts
Motoring consultant Peter Wherrett

Photographers Australian Picture Library: John Carnemolla; Richard I'Anson, Gary Lewis, Peter McNeill, P.D. Munchenberg, Photo Index, Segments Photo Library, Don Skirrow, Robin Smith, Ken Stepnell, Stock Photos: Rick Altman, Bill Bachman, Diana Calder, Brian Carroll, Allan Dodds, Peter Elliston, L.A. Frances, Gary Hall, Darrell Jones, Noeline Kelly, Gary Lewis, James Lauritz, Tony Martorano, Lance Nelson, Otto Rogge, Paul Steel, Ken Stepnell, Ken Straiton; Thunderhead Photographics: Peter Jarver.

The revision of this edition could not have occurred without the assistance of the following organisations, some of whom also supplied photographs:
New South Wales NSW Tourism Commission; Ballina Tourist Information Centre; Bathurst and District Tourism; Bombala Tourist Information; Cobar Tourist Information; Coffs Harbour Tourist Information Centre; Cooma Tourist Information Centre; Cootamundra Business Enterprise Centre; Dubbo Tourist Information Centre; Goulburn Tourist Information Centre; Lismore Tourist Information Centre; Macarthur Country Tourist Association; Merriwa Tourist Information Centre; Moree Tourist Information Centre; Mudgee Tourist Information Centre; Mullumbimby Neighbourhood Centre; Murrurundi Museum; Murwillumbah Tourist Information Centre; Narrandera Tourist Information Centre; Port Stephens Tourist Organisation; Sydney Convention and Visitors Bureau; Tumut Tourist Information Centre; Warren Shire Council; Wentworth Tourist Information Centre; White Cliffs Tourist Association.
Australian Capital Territory ACT Tourism Commission.
Victoria Apollo Bay Tourist Centre; Avoca Tourist Information Centre; Bairnsdale Tourist Information Centre; Ballarat Tourist Association Inc.; Bellarine Peninsula Tourism; Benalla Tourist Information Centre; Bendigo Tourism; Birchip Shire; Bright Tourist Information Centre; Broadford Shire; Camperdown Tourist Information Centre; Cann River Department of Conservation and Environment Information Centre; Casterton Tourist Association; Chiltern Shire; Clunes (Talbot and Clunes Shire); Colac Apex Tourist Information Centre; Cowes/Phillip Island Information Centre; Creswick Shire; Donald Shire; Echuca–Moama and District Tourism Development; Edenhope Shire; GO Tourism, Geelong; Glenrowan Tourist Information Centre; Goulburn Tourist Association; Nagambie; Grampians and Wimmera Tourism, Horsham; Hamilton and District Tourist Information Centre; Lakes Entrance Tourist Information Centre; Lorne Tourist Information Centre; Mansfield Visitors Centre; Marysville Information Centre; Mornington Peninsula Vignerons Association; Myrtleford Information Centre; Sale Information Centre; Seymour Shire; West Gippsland Tourism; Wodonga Gateway Tourist Information Centre; Yarra Valley Wine Growers' Association; and tourist information outlets at Ararat, Bacchus Marsh, Beechworth, Buchan, Castlemaine, Coleraine, Corryong, Daylesford, Dunkeld, Emerald, Euroa, Harrietville and Healesville.
South Australia Tourism South Australia; Balaklava District Council; Burra Tourist Information Office; Clare Tourist Information Office; Cowell Information Centre (District Council of Franklin Harbour); Crystal Brook Tourist Information Centre; Gawler Tourist Information Centre; Goolwa Tourist Information Centre; Kingscote, Kangaroo Island, Tourist Information (National Parks and Wildlife Service); Melrose Tourist Information (District Council of Mt Remarkable); Minlaton District Council; Morgan District Council; Mount Gambier Tourist Information Office; Penola Tourist Office; Pinnaroo District Council; Port Augusta Tourist Office; Quorn District Council; Renmark Tourist Office; Robe Library and Tourist Information Centre; Strathalbyn Tourist Office; Victor Harbor Tourist Office; Yankalilla District Council; and tourist information outlets at Kimba and Wilmington.
Western Australia Western Australian Tourism Commission; Augusta-Margaret River Tourist Bureau; Boyup Brook Tourism Association; Bunbury Tourist Bureau; Busselton Tourist Bureau; Central South Region; Collie Tourist and Travel Bureau; Donnybrook-Balingup Tourist Information; Gascoyne Region; Goldfields Region; Great Southern Region; Harvey Districts Tourist Bureau; Kimberley Region; Mandurah Tourist Bureau; Manjimup Tourist Bureau; Midlands Region; Mid West Region; Nannup Tourist Information Centre; Northcliffe Tourist Centre; Perth Region; Pilbara Region; Department of Conservation and Land Management; Rottnest Island Authority; South West Tourism.
Northern Territory Northern Territory Tourist Commission; Conservation Commission; National Parks and Wildlife Service.
Queensland Brisbane Visitors & Convention Bureau; Atherton Tableland Promotions Bureau; Biloela Tourist Information Centre; Bowen Chamber of Commerce; Caloundra Tourist Information Centre; Capricorn Tourism Development Organisation; Charters Towers Tourist Information Centre; Clermont Shire; Emerald Tourist Information Centre; Far North Queensland Promotion Bureau; Gold Coast Visitors and Convention Bureau; Goondiwindi Tourist Information Centre; Logan City Shire; Longreach Tourist Association; Mission Beach Tourist Information Centre, Wongaling; Normanton Shire; Oakey Tourist Information Centre; Proserpine Shire; Roma Tourist Information Centre; Southern Downs Tourist Association; Stanthorpe Tourist Information Centre; Tourism Sunshine Coast; Townsville North Queensland Tourism Authority Information Centre; Whitsunday Tourism Association.
Tasmania Tourism Tasmania; Tasmanian Travel Centres (Hobart, Launceston, Burnie, Devonport); Central Tourism Association; Circular Head Tourist Authority; Department of Parks Wildlife and Heritage; Department of Tourism, Sport and Recreation; Hydro-electric Commission of Tasmania; MidNorth Regional Tourism Association; National Trust of Australia (Tasmania); Wilderness Gateway Tourism Association; various municipal councils and tourism outlets throughout the state.

The publisher wishes to acknowledge the contribution of the founding editors, Sue Donovan and Celia Pollock, and the assistance given them by the team of researchers, writers, designers, illustrators, research assistants, tourist authorities, shire councils and municipalities, and corporations.

CONTENTS

Tasmania

Lake Jindabyne, Snowy Mountains, NSW

CALENDAR OF EVENTS

Note: The information given here was accurate at the time of printing. However, as the timing of events held annually is subject to change and some events may extend into the following month, it is best to check with the local tourism authority or event organisers to confirm the details. The calendar is not exhaustive. Most towns and regions throughout Australia hold sporting competitions, regattas and rodeos, arts and craft, and trade exhibitions, agricultural and flower shows, music festivals and other such events annually. Details of these events are available from tourism outlets in each state.

JANUARY

ALL STATES Public holidays: New Year's Day; Australia Day.
NSW Sydney: Festival of Sydney. **Manly:** Iron Man Gold. **Bowral:** Horse Show. **Brunswick Heads:** Festival of Fish and Chips. **Corowa:**Federation Festival. **Culburra–Orient Point:** Open Fishing Carnival. **Deniliquin:** Sun Festival. **Forbes:** Australian Flatlands Hang Gliding Titles. **Guyra:** Lamb and Potato Festival. **Tamworth:** Australasian Country Music Festival; Akubra National Finals Rodeo. **Wentworth Falls:** Australia Day Regatta.
ACT Canberra: Australia Day in the National Capital; Australia Day Cup; Embassies Open Day; Multicultural Festival.
VIC. Melbourne: Australian Open (tennis championships); Summer in the City. **Eltham:** Montsalvat Jazz Festival. **Cobram:** 'Peaches and Cream' Festival (biennial). **Hanging Rock:** New Year's Day Picnic Race Meeting. **Heyfield:** Timber Festival. **Inverloch:** Fun Festival. **Mount Beauty:** Conquestathon (race to summit of Mt Bogong). **Natimuk:** Tractor Pull. **Orbost:** Snowy Mountain Country Music Festival. **Port Fairy:** Moyneyana Festival. **Portland:** Country and Western Music Festival; Fishing Carnival. **Yackandandah:** Country Music Festival.
SA Adelaide: Sheffield Shield Cricket. **Glenelg:** Greek Blessing of the Waters. **Hahndorf:** Founders Day; Schutzenfest German Festival. **Kingston:**Yachting Regatta. **Loxton:** Apex Fisherama. **Murray Bridge:** State Championship Swimming. **Port Germein:** Festival of the Crab. **Port Lincoln:** Port Lincoln Rodeo; Lincoln Week Regatta; Tunarama Festival. **Port**

Lizard races, Harts Range, NT

Vincent: Gala Day; Birdman Event; Classic Yacht Race. **Robe** Beer Can Regatta. **Streaky Bay:** Aquatic Sports Day and Mardi Gras; Family Fish Day Contest and Sailboat Regatta; Perlubie Beach Sports and Race Day. **Tanunda:** Oom Pah Festival.
WA Perth: Hopman Cup (tennis); Matilda Festival; Perth Cup (horse racing); Vines Golf Classic. **Albany:** Wittenoom Cup (golf). **Busselton:** Festival of Busselton. **Denmark:** Rainbow Festival. **Esperance:** Oz Rock Festival. **Mandurah:** Kanyana Carnival. **Narrogin:** State Gliding Championships. **Rockingham:** Cockburn Yachting Regatta.
QLD Clermont: Beef 'N Beer Festival. **Gold Coast:** Carrara: Albert Aussie Weekend. **Hervey Bay:** Hervey Bay Rodeo. **Redcliffe:** Blessing of the Waters Theophania. **Stanthorpe:** Agricultural Show.
TAS. Hobart: Summer Festival. **Burnie:** New Year's Day Athletic Carnival. **Cygnet:** Huon Folk Festival. **Triabunna:** Spring Bay Crayfish Derby.

FEBRUARY

NSW Sydney: Gay and Lesbian Mardi Gras. **Bungendore:** Country Music Muster. **Gosford:**Agricultural Show. **Jamberoo:** Folk Festival. **Kiama:** Jazz

Festival. **Mittagong:** Dahlia Festival. **Nelson Bay:** Game Fishing Championships. **Orange:** Banjo Paterson Festival. **Tenterfield:** Highland Gathering. **Ulladulla:** Open Game Fishing Tournament. **Wagga Wagga:** Gumi Festival.
ACT Canberra: Royal Canberra Show; St Valentine's Day Jazz Festival, Australian National University; Canberra Symphony Orchestra at Government House, Annual Prom Concert.
VIC. Melbourne: Australian Masters Golf Tournament; Formula 5000 (motor racing). **Chinatown:** Chinese New Year Festival. **St Kilda:** St Kilda Festival. **Bacchus Marsh:** Apple Valley Festival (biennial). **Bendigo:** Go-Cart Grand Prix. **Buninyong:** Gold King Festival. **Camperdown:** Leura Festival. **Clunes:** Golden Pyramid Festival. **Coal Creek:** Twilight Music and Theatre Festival. **Edenhope:** Henley-on-Lake Wallace. **Geelong:** National Aquatic Festival; Pako Festa. **Kyneton:** Food and Wine Festival. **Maldon:** Camp Draft. **Torrumbarry:** Southern 80 (ski-race to Echuca). **Warrnambool:** Wunta Fiesta. **Werribee:** Harvest Picnic.
SA Adelaide: Adelaide Festival Fringe (biennial). **Berri:** Speedboat Spectacular. **Kadina:** Miners Ball. **Kingscote:** Kangaroo Island Racing Carnival. **Loxton:** Mardi Gras. **Millicent:** Radiata Festival. **Mount Compass:** Compass Cup Cow Race. **Port Lincoln:** Adelaide to Lincoln Yacht Race. **Tailem Bend:** Gumi Racing Festival. **Waikerie:** Rotary International Food Fair.
WA Perth: Chinese New Year Festival; Festival of Perth; Kyana Aboriginal Festival; Moon Chow Festival. **Margaret River:** Leeuwin Estate Concert.
QLD Yepoon: Surf Life Saving Championships.
TAS. Public holidays: Hobart Cup Day and Hobart Regatta Day (S. Tas. only); Launceston Cup Day (N. Tas. only). **Hobart:** Hobart Cup; Royal Hobart Regatta. **Devonport:** Food and Wine Fun Festival. **Evandale:** Village Fair, incorporating Penny Farthing Championships. **Fingal:** Fingal Valley Festival, incorporating Coal Shovelling Championships and Roof Bolting Championships. **Golconda:** Tasmanian Circus Festival. **Launceston:** Great Tasmanian Bike Ride (biennial). **New Norfolk:** Soroptimists Duck Race. **Oatlands:** Rodeo. **Richmond:** Country Music Festival.

MARCH

NSW Albury: World Cup Festival of Sport; **Coonabarabran:** Warrumbungle Arts and Crafts Exhibition. **Dubbo:** Orana Country Music Festival. **Moree:** NSW Mud Trials Championship. **Moss Vale:** Agricultural Show: **Myall Lakes:** Prawn Festival. Robertson: Agricultural Show. **Wellington:** Wellington Boot.
ACT Public holiday: Canberra Day. **Canberra:** Black Opal Stakes; Canberra Festival;, Autumn Flower Show; Jewish Food Fair; Antique Fair.
VIC. Public holiday: Labour Day. **Melbourne:** Autumn Racing Carnival; International Dragon Boat Festival; Moomba and Comedy Festival. **Bairnsdale:** Riviera Festival. **Ballan:** Arcadian Festival. **Ballarat:** Antique Fair; Begonia Festival; Super Southern Swap Meet. **Bendigo:** Eaglehawk Dahlia and Arts Festival. **Branxholm:** Bushwackers Carnival. **Cavendish:** Wannon River Regatta. **Colac:** Kana Festival. **Corryong:** High Country Festival. **Daylesford:** Highland Gathering. **Dooen:** Wimmera Machinery Field Days. **Geelong:** Highland Gathering. **Hamilton:** Pastoral Museum Pioneer Day. **Horsham:** Apex Fishing Contest. **Koo-wee-rup:** Potato Festival. **Korumburra:** Karmai (Giant Worm) Festival. **Kyabram:** Rodeo. **Latrobe Valley:** Latrobe Valley Festival. **Maffra:** Mardi Gras. **Mildura:** Great Mildura Paddleboat Race. **Mount Beauty:** The Conquestathon, footrace. **Myrtleford:** Tobacco, Hops and Timber Festival. Port Albert: Seabank Fishing Competition. **Port Fairy:** Folk Festival. **Portland:** Dahlia Festival. **Rutherglen:** Tastes of Rutherglen. **Seymour:** Rafting Festival. **Warragul:** Gippsland Field Days. **Yarra Valley:** Grape Grazing Festival.
SA Adelaide: Adelaide Festival of Arts (biennial, even years). **Thebarton:** Glendi Greek Festival. **Coonawarra:** Centenary Festival. **Lucindale:** Field Days and Tractor Pull. **Strathalbyn:** International Penny Farthing Challenge Cup and Colonial Street Fair. **Streaky Bay:** Streaky Bay Cup Race Meeting. **Tanunda:** Essenfest. **Wudinna:** Street Party and Annual Keg Roll.
WA Brookton: Old Time Motor Show. **Geraldton:** Kite Festival and Wind on Water. **Greenough:** Wind on Water Day (can-boat regatta/kite flying). **Kalbarri:** Sports Fishing Classic. **Kambalda:** Rock Drilling Competition. **Kununurra:** Dam to Dam Regatta. **Margaret River:** Drug Offensive Masters (surfing). **Mount Barker:** The Field Day. **Narrogin:** Agrolympics; Narrogin Speed Classic (vintage car rally). **Pemberton:** King Karri Karnival. **Wagin:** Woolorama.

QLD Burketown: Barramundi Competition. **Einasleigh:** Races and Rodeo. **Emerald:** Sunflower Festival. **Gold Coast (Surfers Paradise):** Grand Prix. **Gympie:** Spring Valley Fair. **Kingaroy:** Peanut Festival (biennial). **Logan City:** Command Performance. **Stanthorpe:** Apple and Grape Harvest Festival (biennial). **Warwick:** Agricultural Show.
TAS. Public holiday: Eight Hours Day. **Hobart:** Garden Week. **Cygnet:** Port Cygnet Fishing Carnival. **Kingsborough:** Kingsborough Festival. **Longford:** Targa Tasmania. **New Norfolk:** Hop Festival. **St Helens/Port Arthur:** Tasmanian Sport and Game Fishing Festival.

EASTER

ALL STATES Public holidays: Good Friday; Easter Monday; Easter Tuesday (Tas. and Vic. only).
NSW Sydney: Royal Easter Show. **Bathurst:** James Hardie 12 hour car race. **Bingara:** Easterfish. **Bourke:** Festival of Sport. **Cowra:** Easter Golf Classic; Festival of Lachlan Valley. **Deniliquin:** Jazz Festival. **Griffith:** Wine and Food Festival (biennial). **Kempsey:** Cavalcade of Sport. **Maclean:** Highland Gathering. **Oxley:** Gymkhana. **Ulladulla:** Blessing of the Fleet. **Wentworth:** Henley on the Darling Rowing Regatta.
VIC. Easterbike (various locations). **Alexandra:** Easter Art Show. **Ballarat:** Eureka Jazz Festival; Opera Festival. **Beechworth:** Golden Horseshoes Festival. **Bendigo:** Easter Fair and Chinese Dragon Procession. **Dargo:** Walnut Festival. **Echuca:** Tisdalls Winery Vintage Festival and Grape Stomp. **Kyabram:** Antique Aeroplane Fly-in. **Kyneton:** Antique Fair; Autumn Flower Show. **Lake Bolac:** Easter Yachting Regatta. **Maldon:** Easter Fair. **Mallacoota:** Carnival in 'Coota. **Numurkah:** Rose Festival. **Quambatook:** Australian Tractor Pull Championships. **Stawell:** Easter Gift (professional footrace). **Torquay:** Bells Beach Easter Surfing Classic. **Warracknabeal:** Wheatlands Easter Carnival. **Wonthaggi:** Easter Carnival. **Yarram:** Tarra Valley Festival.
SA Berri: Easter Carnival and Rodeo. **Clare:** Clare Valley Easter Festival; Racing Carnival. **Coober Pedy:** Opal Festival; Outback Festival. **Oakbank:** Easter Racing Carnival (picnic race meeting). **Port Victoria:** Annual Fishing Competition. **Waikerie:** Horse and Pony Club.
WA Perth: BMX National Championships. **Donnybrook:** Apple Festival (biennial). **Guilderton:** King of the River. **Lancelin:** National Beach Buggy Championships. **Nannup:** Folk Festival. **Northcliffe:** Forest Festival.
NT Borroloola: Fishing Classic.
QLD Brisbane: Brisbane – Gladstone

Yacht Race. **Boulia:** Rodeo/gymkhana. **Bundaberg:** Easter Roundup. **Burketown:** World Barramundi Handline — Rod Fishing Championships. **Gladstone:** Harbour Festival. **Hamilton Island:** Race Week. **Roma:** Easter in the Country. **Scarness (Hervey Bay):** Yachting Regatta. **Tin Can Bay:** Easter Parade. **Townsville:** Gamefishing Club Easter Classic. **Warwick:** Easter Rock Swap.
TAS. Hobart/Devonport/Pipers River: Tazz Jazz.

APRIL

ALL STATES Heritage Week. Public holiday: Anzac Day.
NSW Sydney: AJC Racing Carnival; Australian International Dragon Boat Festival; finish of Great NSW Bike Ride; Sydney Cup Week. **Armidale:** New England Wool Expo. **Broken Hill:** St Patricks Races. **Bowral:** Southern Highlands Antique Fair. **Bundanoon:** Brigadoon at Bundanoon (Highland Gathering). **Cooma:** Man From Snowy River Marathon. **Leeton:** Sunwhite Rice Festival (biennial, even years). **Lightning Ridge:** Great Goat Race. **Tumut:** Tumut Valley Festival of the Falling Leaf. **Wee Waa:** Cotton Festival (biennial).
ACT Canberra: Marathon; Anzac Day Service, Australian War Memorial.
VIC: Barmah: Barmah Muster. **Bright:** Autumn Festival; Heritage Festival. **Lake Goldsmith (Beaufort):** Steam Rally.
SA Aldgate: Autumn Leaves Festival. **Barossa Valley:** Vintage Festival (biennial, odd years). **Burra:** Three Days Orienteering. **Goolwa:** Boat Rally and Picnic Races. **Kimba:** Yeltana Horse Spectacular. **Laura:** Folk Fair. **Stansbury:** Oyster Festival.
WA Perth: National Trust Heritage Week. **Albany:** Yachting Masters Australia. **Balingup:** Small Farm Field Day. **Northam:** Blue Gum Camel Farm Races.
NT Darwin: Barra Classic.
QLD Comet: Rodeo. **Kingaroy:** Peanut Festival (biennial). **Manly:** XXXX Gold Cup Regatta. **Mount Isa:** Country Music Festival. **Rockhampton:** Beef Exposition. **Surfers Paradise:** Gold Coast Cup.
TAS. Hobart: Three Peaks Race (Mts Strzelecki/Freycinet/Wellington). **Launceston:** Targa Tasmania (car rally).

MAY

NSW Boggabri: Wean Picnic Races. **Casino:** Beef Week and Rural Trade Expo. **Dangar Island:** Bridge to Bridge Power Boat Race. **Liverpool:** Sydney–Melbourne Marathon. **Scone:** Horse Week. **Tweed Heads:** Wintersun Carnival. **Wagga Wagga:** Winfield Gold Cup; Golden Gown Fashion Awards.
ACT Canberra: Rock Eisteddfod.

VIC. Melbourne: Next Wave Festival. State-wide: Victoria's Garden Scheme closes. **Bendigo:** Gold Rush Fun Day. **Kalorama:** Chestnut Festival. **Warrnambool:** Southern right whales due at Logans Beach; 3-day May Racing Carnival.
SA Public holiday: Adelaide Cup Day. **Adelaide:** Adelaide Cup Carnival; Come Out Youth Festival (biennial, odd numbered years). **Ceduna:** Regional 'Come Out' Week. **Clare Valley:** Clare Valley Gourmet Weekend. **Mannum:** Houseboat Hirers Open Days. **Nuriootpa:** Hot Air Balloon Regatta. **Yorke Peninsula: (Kadina/Moonta/Wallaroo):** Kernewek Lowender (Cornish Festival, biennial, odd years). **Yunta:** Races.
WA Carnarvon: Mirari Festival. **Fremantle:** Fremantle – Exmouth Yachting Classic. **Toodyay:** Moondyne (Colonial and Convict) Festival. **York:** Theatre Festival (biennial); Winter Music Festival (biennial).
NT Darwin: Bougainvillea Festival; Expo NT; On the Beach Day. **Alice Springs:** Bangtail Muster; Camel Cup; Food and Wine Festival. **Katherine:** Rel Week (parachuting). **Tennant Creek:** Goldrush Festival; Tennant Creek Cup Day.
QLD Public holiday: Labour Day. **Charters Towers:** Country Music Festival. **Chinchilla:** May Day Spectacular. **Dimbulah:** Tobacco Festival. **Dysart:** Coal and Country Festival. **Fraser Island:** Orchid Beach Fishing Expo. **Hervey Bay:** Bay Carna. **Julia Creek:** Rodeo. **Kuranda:** Folk Festival. **Laidley:** Clydesdale Society Show and Field Day. **Mingeba:** Rodeo and Picnic Race Meeting. **Normanton:** Show, Rodeo and Gymkhana. **Noosa:** Festival of the Arts. **Port Douglas:** Reef and Rainforest Festival. **Richmond:** Rodeo. **Thursday Island:** Cultural Festival. **Warwick:** Bush Week.
TAS. Carrick: Agfest. **Glenorchy:** City to Casino Fun Run. **Stanley:** Literature Fair.

JUNE

ALL STATES Public holiday: Queen's Birthday (except WA).
NSW Sydney: Sydney Film Festival. **Manly:** Food and Wine Festival. **Albury:** Woolcraft and Sheep Show. **Blue Mountains:** Yulefest. **Bourke:** Bourke to B — Bash (charity car rally). **Dubbo:** Stampede. **Grenfell:** Henry Lawson Festival of Arts. **Gulgong:** Henry Lawson Birthday Celebrations. **Lake Keepit:** Keepit Kool Regatta. **Narrabri:** Cotton Fibre Exhibition. **Snowy Mtns:** Opening of Ski Season (long weekend). **Southern Highlands:** Christmas in June.
ACT Canberra: Embassies Open Day;

National Eisteddford. **Duntroon:** Trooping the Colour.
VIC. Melbourne: Melbourne International Film Festival. **Echuca - Moama:** Steam, Horse and Vintage Car Rally. **Hamilton:** Eisteddfod. **Rutherglen:** Winery Walkabout Weekend. **Sea Lake:** Mallee Desert Car Rally.
SA Barmera: SA Country Music Festival. **Gawler:** Gawler 3 Day Event (dressage, cross-country riding and showjumping). **Kingscote:** Half Marathon. **McLaren Vale:** Sip'N Savour Festival. **Renmark:** Riverland Citrus Week.
WA Public holiday: Foundation Day. West Week (week-long celebration of foundation of state). **Broome:** Fringe Arts Festival. **Cossack:** Cossack Fair and Yachting Regatta. **Kambalda:** Sky Diving Gathering. **Manjimup:** 15 000 Motocross. **Northam:** Soiree Avon Valley Arts Society. **Pannawonica:** Panna Regatta. **Wyndham:** Parrys Creek Picnic (Foundation Day bush carnival). **York:** Theatre Festival.
NT Darwin: Bougainvillea Festival; Darwin Cup Carnival; City to Surf Fun Run. **Adelaide River:** Bush Race Meeting. **Alice Springs:** Finke Desert Race. **Katherine:** Barunga Sport and Cultural Festival; Katherine Cup; Canoe Marathon. **Lake Bennett:** Birdman Rally. **Tennant Creek:** Brunette Downs Races.
QLD Brisbane: Eagle Farm: QTC Sires Produce Stakes. **Birdsville:** Gymkhana. **Blackall:** Race Meeting. **Cardwell:** Coral Sea Crab Racing Championships. **Cloncurry:** Agricultural Show. **Cooktown:** Discovery Festival. **Croydon:** Rodeo. **Gayndah:** Orange Festival (biennial). **Georgetown:** Rodeo. **Longreach:** Hall of Fame Race Meeting. **Magnetic Island:** Rediscovery Weekend. **Monto:** Dairy Festival (biennial). **Mossman:** Bavarian Festival. **Mount Surprise:** Rodeo. **Rockhampton:** Agricultural Show. **Taldora Station:** Saxby Roundup. **Whitsunday:** Festival of Sail.
TAS. St Helens: Suncoast Jazz Festival.

JULY

NSW Barraba: Frost Over Barraba Art Show. **Blue Mountains:** Yulefest. **Cowra:** Wine Show. **Grafton:** Racing Carnival. **Gunnedah:** Dorothea MacKellar Anniversary Day. **Port Macquarie:** Life Style Expo. **Stroud:** International Brick and Rolling-pin Throwing Contest. **Sussex Inlet:** Fishing Carnival.
VIC. Bendigo: Wine Festival. **Daylesford:** Mid-Winter Festival. **Hamilton:** Wool Heritage Week. **Swan Hill:** Italian Festa.
SA Cowell: Jade Marathon. **Morgan:** Fun Run, Walk, Cyclathon. **Willunga:** Almond Blossom Festival.

WA Perth: Perth Marathon. **Broome:** Broome Cup. **Carnarvon:** Tropical Festival and Rodeo. **Denmark:** Winter Festival. **Derby:** Boab Festival; Country and Western Music Festival. **Exmouth:** Gala Week; Independence Day Celebrations. **Kalgoorlie:** Great Gold Festival. **Marble Bar:** Marble Bar Cup Race Weekend. **Wickham:** Cossack–Wickham Fun Run.
NT Darwin: Agricultural Show (regional public holiday). **Alice Springs:** Agricultural Show (regional public holiday). **Katherine:** Agricultural Show (regional public holiday). **Tennant Creek:** Agricultural Show (regional public holiday). **Wauchope:** Wauchope v. the World Cricket Match.
QLD Brisbane: Jumbo Tennis Day. **Atherton:** Agricultural Show. **Broadbeach:** Gold Coast International Marathon. **Burketown:** Rodeo and Races. **Cairns:** Agricultural Show. **Chinchilla:** Polocrosse Carnival. **Cleveland:** Flinders Day (enactment of landing on Coochiemudlo Island). **Ipswich:** Limelight Festival. **Laura:** Cape York Aboriginal Dance Festival. **Mackay:** Festival of the Arts. **Mareeba:** Rodeo. **Mission Beach:** Banana Festival. **Pomona:** King of the Mountain Festival. **Stanthorpe:** Brass Monkey Month. **Texas:** Agricultural Show. **Townsville:** Turf Club Winter Carnival.
TAS. Hobart: Brighton Craft Fair.

AUGUST

NSW Sydney: Sun City to Surf (fun run to Bondi Beach). **Bellingen:** Jazz Festival. **Blue Mountains:** Yulefest. **Bourke:** Picnic Races. **Brewarrina:** Rodeo. **Cootamundra:** Wattle Time. **Euston:** Polocross Carnival. **Inverell:** Grafton to Inverell International Cycle Classic. **Junee:** Art & Crafts Festival. **Leeton:** Edisteddfod. **Murwillumbah:** Tweed Banana Festival. **Narrandera:** Camellia Show. **Quirindi:** Polo Carnival. **Thredbo:** FIS Australian Championships and Continental Cup (snow skiing).
VIC. State-wide: Victoria's Garden Scheme opens. **Bendigo:** Biennial Red Ribbon Rebellion Re-enactment at Sandhurst Town. **Falls Creek:** International Ski Marathon Kangaroo Hoppet. **Mt Buller/Mt Hotham:** FIS Australian Championships and Continental Cup (snow skiing).
SA Adelaide: Festival City Marathon. **Barossa Valley:** Classic Gourmet Weekend. **Cleve:** Eyre Peninsula Field Days (biennial). **Kadina:** Agricultural Show. **Mt Gambier:** Eisteddfod. **Paringa:** Billy Boiling Championships and Bush Picnic. **Whyalla:** Harrier's Show; King and Queen of the Mountain.
WA Perth: City to Surf Fun Run.

Broome: Shinju Matsuri (Festival of the Pearl). **Carnarvon:** Dry River Regatta. **Dampier/Karratha:** FeNaCLNG Festival, incorporating Dampier Game Fishing Classic. **Dowerin:** Machinery Field Days. **Fitzroy Crossing:** Fun Run; Race Meeting and Rodeo. **Kununurra:** Ord River Festival. **Newman:** Fortescue Festival. **Northam:** Avon Descent (white-water raft race) and Festival. **Onslow:** Bougainvillea Festival. **Tom Price:** Nameless Festival. **Pingelly:** Tulip and Art Festival. **Port Hedland:** Spinifex Spree. **Wyndham:** Top of the West Festival and Race Meeting.
NT Public holiday: Picnic Day. **Darwin:** Australian Safari; Darwin Cup; Darwin Rodeo; Mud Crab Tying Competition. **Alice Springs:** Harts Range Races; Yuendumu Aboriginal Sports Carnival. **Tennant Creek:** Goldrush Folk Festival; Tennant Creek Rodeo.
QLD Public holiday: Brisbane Show Day. **Brisbane:** Royal Brisbane National Show (Ekka). **Anakie:** Gemfest Festival of Gems. **Cloncurry:** Merry Muster Rodeo. **Cunnamulla/Eulo:** Opal Festival. **Eulo:** World Lizard Racing Championships. **Gympie:** Country Music Muster. **Hervey Bay:** Whale Festival. **Ingham:** Herbert River Rodeo. **Innisfail:** Sugar Festival. **Jondaryan:** Australian Heritage Festival. **Malanda:** Dairy Festival. **Mount Isa:** Rotary Rodeo. **Moura:** Coal and Country Festival. **Tin Can Bay:** Country Music Muster. **Tully:** Rain Festival.

SEPTEMBER

NSW Sydney: Carnivale; Rugby League Grand Final. **Bondi:** Festival of the Winds (kite flying). **Bellingen:** Azalea Festival. **Boggabri:** Gum Tree Clay Pigeon Shoot. **Bourke:** Engonnia Picnic Races; Police Outback Trek. **Bowral:** Tulip Time Festival. **Brewarrina:** Festival of Fisheries. **Canowindra:** Ballooning Festival. **Coffs Harbour:** Buttercup Buskers Festival. **Glen Innes:** Minerama Gem Festival. **Hay:** Festival of the Plains (biennial). **Henty:** Machinery Field Days. **Maclean:** Cane Harvest Festival. **Mudgee:** Wine Festival. **Mullumbimby:** Chincogan Fiesta. Oberon: Daffodil Festival. **Tibooburra:** Gymkhana and Rodeo. **Walcha:** Spring Art Festival. **Wauchope:** Colonial Week. **Wollongong:** Festival of Wollongong. **Yamba:** Leisure Spectacular.
ACT Canberra: Floriade Spring Festival; Spring Bulb and Camelia Show; Red Cross Embassy Open Days.
VIC. Public holiday: Show Day. Springbike (various locations). **Melbourne:** Antiquarian Book Fair; Australian Football

League and Association Finals; Fringe Arts Festival; International Festival of the Arts; Royal Melbourne Show. **Anglesea – Aireys Inlet:** Angair Festival. **Bendigo:** Monster Antique Fair. **Halls Gap:** Wildflower Exhibition, Grampians National Park. **Kyneton:** Daffodil and Arts Festival. **Leongatha:** Daffodil and Floral Festival. **Little Desert:** Wildflower Exhibition, Little Desert Lodge. **Maryborough:** Golden Wattle Festival. **Olinda:** Rhododendron Festival (3 months). **Rutherglen:** Spring Wine and Art Show. **Shepparton:** Shepptember Festival. **Silvan:** Tulip Festival. **Yarrawonga:** Ice Breaker Yacht Regatta.
SA Adelaide: Royal Adelaide Show. **Adelaide Hills:** Spring Festival; Handmade in the Hills. **Beltana:** Picnic Races and Gymkhana. **Glenelg:** Bay to Birdwood Run (vintage car rally; biennial). **Hawker:** Art Show; Photographic Show. **Loxton:** Historical Village Fair. **Paskeville:** Yorke Peninsula Field Days. **Port Pirie:** Blessing of the Fleet. **Renmark:** Spring Family Festival. **Robe:** Blessing of the Fleet. **Stirling:** Food and Wine Affair.
WA Perth: Football League Finals; Kings Park Wildflower Festival; Perth Royal Show; Rally Australia. **Bencubbin:** WA State Marbles Championships. **Coolgardie:** Camel Races; Coolgardie Day. **Cranbrook:** Wildflower Show. **Kalgoorlie:** Kalgoorlie Cup; Spring Festival. **Mount Magnet:** Fun Day. **Port Hedland:** All Can Regatta. **Stirling Range National Park:** Awareness Week. **Three Springs:** White Rock Stakes Wheelbarrow Relay. **Toodyay:** Folk Festival. **York:** Jazz Festival.
NT National Aboriginal Week (statewide). **Darwin:** Beer Can Regatta. **Alice Springs:** Alice Springs Rodeo; Henley-on-Todd. **Bathurst Island:** NT Barra Classic. **Katherine:** Caulfield Cup. **Tennant Creek:** Mary Ann Dam Yacht Regatta.
QLD Brisbane: City of Brisbane Chelsea Flower Show; Spring Hill Festival; Warana Festival. **Airlie Beach:** Fun Race. **Atherton:** Maize Festival. **Biggenden:** Rose Festival (biennial). **Birdsville:** Birdsville Races. **Boonah:** Potato Festival. **Caboolture:** Historical Village Open Day. **Charleville:** Booga Woongaroo Festival. **Dunk Island:** Billfish Classic. **Herberton:** Tin Festival. **Hervey Bay:** Pier Festival. **Laidley:** Tourist Festival. **Logan City:** Spring Fair. **Mackay:** Sugartime Festival. **Maryborough:** Heritage Festival. **Miles:** Wildflower Festival. **Redland Bay:** Strawberry Festival. **Rockhampton:** Capricana (Springtime Festival). **Sunshine Coast:** Festival of the Gardens. **Toowoomba:** Carnival of Flowers. **Townsville:** Pacific Festival.

Winton: Outback Festival (biennial). **Yeppoon:** Pineapple Festival.
TAS. Hobart: Film Festival; TFL Grand Final; Tasmanian Tulip Festival. **Burnie:** Burnie Festival. **Sheffield:** Daffodil Festival. **Stanley:** Circular Head Arts Festival.

OCTOBER

NSW Albury: Agricultural Spring Show. **Balranald:** Flower Show. **Bathurst:** Mt Panorama Tooheys 1000 car races. **Batlow:** Apple Blossom Festival. **Bourke:** Outback Surf Classic. **Casino:** Agricultural Show. **Cowra:** Sakura Bonsai and Japanese Cultural Exhibition. **Forster–Tuncurry:** Oyster Festival. **Gilgandra:** Cooee Festival. **Glen Innes:** Australian Bush Music Festival. **Gosford:** Mangrove Mountain District Country Fair. **Goulburn:** Lilac City Festival. **Grafton:** Jacaranda Festival. **Inverell:** Sapphire City Floral Festival. **Kempsey:** Country Truck Show. **Leura:** Gardens Festival. **Lord Howe Island:** Lion IslandLord Howe Island Yacht Race. **Narrabri:** Spring Festival. **Newcastle:** Folk Festival. **Parkes:** Country Music Spectacular. **Port Kembla:** Put Into Port Festival. **Port Macquarie:** Carnival of the Pines. **Walcha:** Timber Expo (biennial). **Wentworth:** Country and Western Festival. **West Wyalong:** Highway Festival. **Windsor/Richmond:** Macquarie Towns Festival. **Young:** Cherry Festival.
ACT Canberra: Canberra Cup; Canberra Quilters Exhibition of Work; Embassies Open Day; Floriade Spring Festival; Oktoberfest; Winery Walkabout.
VIC. Melbourne: Fantastic Entertainment in Public Places (FEIPP) summer program begins; Oktoberfest; Spring Racing Carnival, including Caulfield Cup; Sun Tour of Victoria. **Chinatown:** Autumn Moon Lantern Festival. **Ararat:** Golden Gateway Festival. **Avoca:** Wool and Wine Festival. **Ballarat:** Kite Festival. **Bendigo:** Mandurang Arts and Orchid Festival. **Bright:** Springtime in Bright. **Dunolly:** Gold Rush Festival. **Echuca–Moama:** Rich River Festival, including Tisdall Winery Fine Food and Wine Day and Jazz Night. **Eildon:** Water Festival. **Euroa:** Wool Week. **Geelong:** Spring Festival. **Hamilton:** Spring Flower Show. **Marysville:** Wirreanda Festival. **Melton:** Djerriwarrh Festival. **Mildura:** Bottlebrush Festival. **Tallangatta:** Arts Festival. **Wangaratta:** Wangaratta Festival. **Warrnambool:** Melbourne – Warrnambool Cycling Classic.
SA Adelaide: League Football Finals. **Andamooka:** Opal Festival. **Balaklava:** Festival of Wineries and Galleries. **Barmera:** Show. **Barossa Valley:** Music Festival. **Berri:** Multicultural Festival.

Bordertown: Clayton Farm Vintage Field Day. **Goolwa:** Folk and Steam Festival. **Kingscote:** Blessing of the Fleet. **Koppio:** Smithy Museum Open Day. **Loxton:** Show. **Mannum:** River Festival. **Marrabel:** Rodeo. **McLaren Vale:** Bushing Festival. **Naracoorte:** Show. **Penola:** Petticoat Lane Street Party. **Port Pirie:** Festival of Country Music. **Renmark:** Show. **Strathalbyn:** Glenbarr Scottish Festival. **Wellington:** Strawberry Fair. **Yorke Peninsula: (Ardrossan, Maitland, Port Victoria)** Barley Festival. **Yorketown:** Picnic races and Gymkhana. **WA** Perth: Spring in the (Swan) Valley Festival. **Bridgetown:** Blackwood Classic (powerboat race); Blackwood Marathon Relay. **Bunbury:** Octoberfest. **Dunsborough:** Naturaliste Triangle Funfest. **Eucla:** Eucla Shoot. **Exmouth:** Game Fishing Competitions. **Geraldton:** Blessing of the Fleet; Geraldton – Batavia Coast Sunshine Festival. **Kukerin:** Trach Mach Vintage Fair. **Manjimup:** Timber Festival. **Margaret River:** Margaret River Masters (windsurfing/surfing competitions); Spring Festival. **Morawa:** Music Spectacular. **Mount Barker:** Wine Show. **Nannup:** Jarrah Jerker's Jog (railway-sleeper teams race). **York:** Flying 50 (vintage car rally; biennial, even years).
NT Darwin: Octoberfest. **Alice Springs:** Beerfest; Central Australian Masters Olympic Games (biennial).
QLD Brisbane: Colonial George Street Festival. **Ayr:** Water Festival. **Bowen:** Coral Coast Festival. **Cairns:** Fun in the Sun Festival. **Dalby:** Harvest Festival. **Gatton:** Potato Carnival. **Gold Coast:** Tropicarnival. **Goondiwindi:** Spring Festival. **Gympie:** Gold Rush Festival. **Hervey Bay:** Hervey Bay - Fraser Island Sailboard Marathon. **Ingham:** Maraka Festival. **Ipswich:** Goodna and District Jacaranda Festival. **Lake Tinnaburra:** Tablelands Water Sports Festival. **Mapleton:** Yarn Festival. **Mount Isa:** Oktoberfest. **Mount Tamborine:** Avocado and Rhubarb Festival. **Nanango:** Mardi Gras. **Noosa:** Festival of the Waters. **Normanton:** Races and B & S Ball. **Ravenshoe:** Torimba Forest Festival. **Stanthorpe:** Granite Belt Spring Wine Festival. **Thangool:** Arts Festival. **Townsville:** Aquatic Festival. **Warwick:** Rose and Rodeo Festival. **Yandina:** Spring Flower and Ginger Festival. **TAS.** Public holidays: Hobart Show Day (S. Tas. only); Launceston Show Day (N. Tas. only). **Hobart:** Royal Hobart Agricultural Show. **Burnie:** Rhododendron Festival. **Deloraine:** Tasmanian Cottage Industry Exhibition and Craft Fair. **Derby:** Derby Day. **Great Lake:** Tasmanian Trout Fishing Championships. **Kingston:** Oliebollen Festival. **Launceston:** Garden Festival; Royal National Show; Tasmanian Poetry

Festival. **Richmond:** Village Fair. **Wynyard:** Tulip Festival.

NOVEMBER

NSW Campbelltown: Fishers Ghost Festival. **Carcoar:** Ben Hall Festival. **Glen Innes:** Land of the Beardies Bush Festival. **Kyogle:** Fairmont Festival. **Lithgow:** Festival of the Valley. **Moree:** Carnival of the Golden Grain. **Narrandera:** Country Music Festival. **Newcastle:** Surfest. **Nowra:** Shoalhaven Fun Festival Triathalon. **Penrith:** City Jazz Festival. **Rylstone:** Village Festival. **Shoalhaven:** Fun Festival. **Windsor:** Bridge to Bridge Water Ski Classic. **Young:** Cherry Festival.
ACT Canberra: Horticultural Society, Annual Spring Show; Wine Show; Australian Craft Show.
VIC. Public holiday: Melbourne Cup Day. **Melbourne:** Spring Racing Carnival, including Melbourne Cup and Oaks Day. **Carlton:** Melbourne Lygon Arts Festival. **Ballarat:** Rowing Regatta. **Benalla:** Rose Festival. **Bendigo:** National Swap Meet (vintage cars/bikes). **Castlemaine:** State Festival (biennial, even years); Spring Garden Festival (odd years). **Harrow:** National Bush Billycart Championships. **Lake Goldsmith:** Steam Rally. **Macedon:** Mt Macedon Festival. **Maldon:** Folk Festival. **Mansfield:** Mountain Country Festival. **Port Fairy:** Heritage Discovery Weekend. **Portland:** Pioneer Week. **Wandin:** Victorian Cherry Festival. **Wangaratta:** Festival of Jazz.
SA Adelaide: Australian Formula One Grand Prix; Christmas Pageant. **Ardrossan:** Wine and Cheese Tasting. **Bordertown:** Camel Race Festival. **Ceduna:** Grand Prix Sailing Carnival. **Hahndorf:** Blumenfest (Festival of Flowers). **Mount Gambier:** Blue Lake Festival. **Murray Bridge:** Big River Challenge Festival. **Riverland:** Multicultural Festival (biennial, even years); Wine Festival (biennial, odd years). **Streaky Bay:** Snapper Fishing Contest.
WA Albany: Perth – Albany Ocean Yacht Race. **Broome:** Mango Festival. **Bunbury:** Pram Race. **Denison:** Blessing of the Fleet. **Exmouth:** Gamex, world class game fishing. **Fremantle:** Fremantle Festival. **Kambalda:** Raft Regatta. **Manjimup:** Timber Festival. **Mount Barker:** Agricultural Show. **Northam:** Avon Valley Country Music Festival.
QLD Atherton: Tablelands Band Festival. **Bribie Island:** Bribie Cup Yacht Race. **Heron Island:** Dive Festival. **Home Hill:** Harvest Festival. **Logan City:** River Festival and Raft Race. **Whitsunday Passage and Outer Reef:** Game Fishing Championships.
Tas. Public holiday: Recreation Day

(N. Tas. only). **Hobart:** North Hobart Fiesta. **Battery Point:** Salamanca's Writers Weekend. **Campbell Town:** Country Music Festival. **Penguin:** Town Fiesta. **Ross:** Rodeo. **Westbury:** Maypole Festival. **Zeehan:** King of the Mountain Fun Run.

DECEMBER

ALL STATES Public holidays: Christmas Day; Boxing Day.
Carols by Candlelight (various locations).
NSW Sydney: Hot Summer Festival; Scottish Week; Sydney – Hobart Yacht Race. **Manly:** Summer Festival. **Abaercrombie Caves:** Underground music in caves. **Coffs Harbour:** South Pittwater – Coffs Harbour Race Series. **Cowra:** International Motor Boat and Ski Challenge. **Mulwala:** Red Cross Murray River Canoe Marathon. **The Entrance:** Tuggerah Lakes Mardi Gras Festival. **Yass:** Warrambalulah Festival.
ACT Canberra: Street Machine Summernats (national hot-rod exhibition and races); Fiesta Capitale.
VIC. Melbourne: Finish of Great Victorian Bike Ride. **Bendigo:** Tram Spectacular (procession). **Corryong:** Nariel Creek Folk Music Festival. **Daylesford:** Highland Gathering; New Year's Eve Festival. **Gisborne:** Gisborne Festival. **Horsham:** Kannamaroo Festival. **Moyston:** World Rabbit Skinning Championships. **Nagambie:** Rowing Regatta.
SA Public holiday: Proclamation Day. **Adelaide:** Christmas Pageant. **Barmera:** Christmas Pageant. **Berri:** Rowing Regatta. **Glenelg:** Proclamation Day Celebrations. **Naracoorte:** Street Traders Party; Carols by Candlelight. **Renmark:** Christmas Pageant; Rowing Regatta. **Streaky Bay:** Carols by the Sea.
WA Perth: Australian Derby; Christmas Pageant; Tennis, Hopman Cup; City Beach Fun Run. **Derby:** Kimberley Boxing Day Sports (cockroach and frog races, egg and nose race, seed spit competition, etc.).
NT Darwin: Darwin–Adelaide World Solar Challenge Race for Solar-powered Vehicles (biennial).
QLD Beaudesert: Lions Christmas Carnival. **Innisfail:** Opera Festival. **Karumba:** Fisherman's Ball. **Logan City:** Christmas Spectacular. **Maleny:** Folk Festival. **Whitsunday:** Festival of Sail.
TAS. Hobart: Brighton Craft Fair; Christmas Pageant; Summer Festival; Sydney–Hobart/Melbourne–Hobart Yacht Races. **Battery Point:** Salamanca's All Ears World Music Festival. **Burnie:** Christmas Festival. **Latrobe:** Latrobe Wheel Race and Latrobe Gift. **Port Arthur:** Chopping Carnival. **Triabunna:** Tandara Woodchoppers Classic. **Ulverstone:** Ulvertone Fiesta.

INTRODUCTION

Exploring Australia by motor vehicle provides the traveller with the opportunity to venture into remote areas, tropical rainforests and inland deserts; to visit large cosmopolitan cities and tiny outback settlements.

Australia's deserts are as vast as the Sahara; its snowfields rival those of Switzerland; its surfing beaches are among the best in the world. The entire continent is criss-crossed by a combination of bitumen highways and rough bush tracks, almost all navigable in the modern motor car, although some demand 4WD vehicles.

Australia comprises an area of some 8.5 million square kilometres; it covers a distance of 3700 kilometres from north to south, and 4000 kilometres east to west. Within these boundaries there is an extraordinary range of flora and fauna, a variety of climatic extremes and a host of geological wonders.

Australia's temperatures vary from an average 30°C in the mid-summer of the Centre to an average of 6°C in the highlands in winter.

It is a land of extremes; the parched deserts of central Australia may be totally dry for years until flooding rains produce a short-term sea. Sydney has a population of around 4 million, whereas Innamincka in South Australia, near the New South Wales and Queensland borders, has only ten permanent residents.

The predominant colours of Australia are red, blue and green; inland, the stark red of the Simpson Desert sand-dunes contrasts dramatically with the deep azure blue of the noonday sky. Dotted here and there are clumps of velvet-green scrub and, after recent rains, Sturt's desert pea blooms scarlet.

Australia has been the home of Aboriginal tribes for a period in excess of 40 000 years and evidence of their occupation abounds. Many cave paintings and rock carvings made thousands of years ago are found at Ayers Rock, that superb monolith sited almost in the centre of this island continent.

Despite its name, the so-called 'Dead Centre' is far from dead, even in times of drought, and the moonscapes of sand and rocky tors and hardy bush scrub have a forbidding beauty all their own.

Across the 'Far North', from the Cape York Peninsula in the east to the Kimberleys in the west, tropical rainforests are so lush in parts as to be impenetrable and of a green so green as to rival the colour from an artist's paint-box.

Almost all of Australia is accessible to the explorer. It is possible to drive from Melbourne at the base of the mainland to Cairns in the Far North.

The intrepid explorer can plan a trip from the Pacific to the Indian Ocean; from the rainforest in the north, to the temperate, breeze-washed beaches of the southern coast. And for the traveller seeking peace and tranquillity, there is the further, ever-beckoning green pasturelands and rugged mountainous interior of Tasmania, the Island State.

Simply put, all Australia is a wonderland. And in order to discover what it has to offer, either for a one-day tour or as a full-year once-in-a-lifetime adventure, *Explore Australia* is an invaluable travelling companion. It is designed to be of assistance with every facet of your travel itinerary. It is an encouragement and an almanac; a manual and a tour guide. It is recommended that you read it as part of your travel planning, particularly for long-distance journeys. For experienced road travellers, it will reinforce knowledge acquired in the past; for 'new chums', it can ensure the utmost pleasure from the holiday you have planned and help to make it trouble-free.

Have a good trip — and drive carefully!

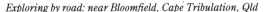

Exploring by road: near Bloomfield, Cape Tribulation, Qld

PLANNING AHEAD

There is so much of Australia to see and so many ways to see it. Today, even the most remote sections of this vast continent are accessible, particularly to 4WD vehicles designed for use on bush tracks and unmade roads.

For some, exploring Australia will mean touring the made highways and staying in motels and hotels. Others will tow their accommodation behind them in the form of a caravan or camper and, probably, as a result, also stay mainly on made roads. Still others will fit out a commercial van with sleeping and cooking facilities and produce a mobile home, and yet another group, perhaps the true adventurers, will load a tent, a mobile fridge and a barbecue unit into the back of a 4WD stationwagon and 'go bush'. To each his own. The country is there to be seen and enjoyed, whatever the style and method of travel, but in all cases, careful planning will enhance the journey immeasurably.

Obviously, a one-, two- or three-day tour will not require the time and effort necessary for a 'round Australia' jaunt, but in any case, route pre-planning, an estimate of travel time and, where appropriate, use of overnight accommodation will need to be considered. So, indeed, will the roadworthiness of the vehicle. While it is reasonable to expect that all vehicles are properly maintained and in reliable condition, some extra attention will not go astray, and more particularly for long journeys. More of that later.

Advance Information

Any journey will benefit from careful **advance planning**. The idea of 'throwing a bag in the back and taking off' is attractive in theory but creates complications in practice.

Do try to gather as much information as possible as far ahead of your planned departure as you can. Remember, the planning is half the fun. Research will confirm, or perhaps deny, your original choice of destination; it also will reveal ways and means, and problems involved, where such exist. And bear in mind that although the information sources available are extensive, there is nothing like local knowledge. So, remember to re-check everything you have learned as you go.

The first places to contact to obtain information are the relevant **state tourist bureaus** and **motoring organisations (see:** Useful Information). They are excellent sources for travel brochures, regional maps and accommodation guides, and they usually have up-to-date knowledge of current local conditions. For details on specific areas, they can put you in touch with the appropriate tourist authority.

If you are planning a fly/drive holiday, or intend to combine rail and motor travel, the various **travel agencies, airline travel centres** and the **main railway booking offices** in each state can provide both advice and information.

Also, read this book. The introductions to each state provide basic information on main tourist areas. Once you have made a decision on your destination, check it out by consulting the gazetteer entries for specific towns and other points of interest. Do note that while the capital cities and towns have been covered quite comprehensively, the fine detail will be available locally.

On arrival, visit a local newsagent or bookshop and see what is available. Reading a history of the area will reveal a great deal to enhance your visit and all cities and most major towns will have a pocket-sized guide, detailing points of interest and listing sporting events and local entertainment venues.

How Far Ahead to Start

It can be a major disappointment to decide upon a certain destination and then discover that all motels, caravan parks and camping-grounds in the area are booked out. In some regions at certain times of the year — Christmas, Easter, school holiday periods — accommodation can be booked out a year in advance. Explore all possibilities and, on long journeys, remember the travel time factor. When booking accommodation in advance, allow enough time to travel comfortably to your destination. Your trip will lose a great deal of its charm if you have to rush from one point to the next (**see:** Itineraries).

While all tourist centres are particularly busy at the obvious peak times, some others will be booked out around the time of special events: Melbourne at Melbourne Cup time; Adelaide at the time of the Australian Formula One Grand Prix, for example (**see:** Calendar of Events). Check ahead for the timing of local special events.

If you wish to return to a favourite hotel or try a special type of accommodation — a farm homestead, a house-boat or charter boat — book well ahead. Others will have the same interests.

And remember, most national parks require advance notice to give prior permission, if you wish to camp within their boundaries.

When to Go

With a few exceptions, you can travel Australia at any time of the year. The exceptions include the Far North, between October and May, in the 'wet' or tropical monsoon season (this applies particularly if you plan to use bush tracks and unmade roads, many of which are impassable for months). Tropical cyclones are random summer hazards between November and March. In the NSW and Victorian high country, from about May to August, many roads will be snowbound. The 'Centre' is not especially inviting in mid-summer, when daytime temperatures can reach 45°C plus, while it can be bitterly cold at night.

Otherwise, remember the **holiday peaks.** If you can avoid the dense traffic during the major vacation periods, do so.

Which Way to Go

If you quail at the thought of driving seemingly endless kilometres, you should consider an alternative: both fly/drive packages and MotoRail facilities eliminate time-consuming travel and allow for concentration on areas of particular interest. Given fuel costs, both these are not necessarily extravagances. Cost them out against the expenses involved in using your own car for the entire trip.

MotoRail: For information on this easy and non-tiring way of covering long distances, contact the state tourist bureaus or the main state railway offices. Enquire about **CAPER fares**: a reduction in rail fare is available on some services if travel is booked and paid for in advance.

For rail enquiries in each state, contact:

New South Wales
Country Link Travel Centre,
Wynyard Station
11 - 31 York St, Sydney 2000
(02) 224 4744, (008) 043 126

Victoria
V/Line Transport House
589 Collins St, Melbourne 3000
(03) 619 5000, (008) 136 109

South Australia

Australian National Passenger
Reservations and Enquiries
1 Richmond Rd, Keswick 5035
(08) 231 7699, (008) 888 417

The Ghan

Western Australia
Westrail Centre
West Pde, East Perth 6000
(09) 326 2222

Queensland
Queensland Railways
305 Edward St, Brisbane 4000
(07) 235 2222

The MotoRail services available are:

Perth – Sydney – Perth
Indian-Pacific
Two services a week each way;
66 hours.

Perth – Adelaide – Perth
Indian-Pacific
Two services a week each way; 38 hours. This service connects with *The Overland* to Melbourne.

Melbourne – Adelaide – Melbourne
The Overland
Daily, each way; (overnight) 12 hours.

Melbourne – Mildura – Melbourne
The Vinelander
Four services a week each way; (overnight) 10 hours.

Adelaide – Alice Springs – Adelaide
The Ghan
May – October, 2 services a week each way; November – April, 1 service a week each way; 23 hours.

Brisbane – Townsville – Cairns – Townsville – Brisbane
The Queenslander
One service a week each way; 33 hours. One extra service each way a week including Proserpine stop; check frequency.

There are no MotoRail services between Melbourne – Sydney and Sydney – Brisbane.

Other Touring Possibilities

The **Abel Tasman** car and passenger ferry makes three return voyages weekly between Melbourne and Devonport in northern Tasmania. Bookings can be made through the TT-Line Tasmania at Port Melbourne and Dockside, Devonport, or through your local Tasmanian Travel Centre. The **Starship SeaCat Tasmania** ferries passengers and vehicles between Port Welshpool, Victoria and George Town in northern Tasmania, a 4.5 hour journey. Coach services from Melbourne and Launceston connect with terminals. The *Starship SeaCat* operates from the end of November through to the beginning of May, with six return voyages weekly (daily during peak periods). One warning: if you are prone to sea-sickness, Bass Strait is often a rough crossing and you may not enjoy even this relatively short voyage. An option to explore Tasmania is a **fly/drive holiday**, with a rental car awaiting your aircraft.

Campervan rental is available in all states and most cities and major towns. Campervans are fully equipped and vary in size and level of luxury. Costs vary accordingly and also with the season. There are often restrictions on where you can take a campervan. Check first.

If you are interested in a 'full-on' **adventure tour,** but are intimidated by the thought of doing it alone, motoring organisations and many private tour operators provide escorted group trips into more remote areas, Cape York for example. These tag-along tours save you the worry of navigation and pre-planning (except for your vehicle) and also mean expert help and back-up in case of a mechanical breakdown.

You also could leave your vehicle behind and **tour** in a large 4WD coach, or take a **camel trek** or try a **canoe adventure** — in fact almost anything your heart desires. Check with your travel agent or Government tourist bureau (**see:** Useful Information).

For the young at heart, there are over 100 **youth hostels** throughout Australia. For information, contact the main headquarters of the Australian Youth Hostels Association, 10 Mallett St, Camperdown, NSW 2050; (02) 565 1699.

If you are planning a stay in a city or at a resort area for any length of time, a sensible family alternative to motel or hotel accommodation is a **serviced** or **self-service flat**. The relevant tourist bureau (**see:** Useful Information) will provide details.

House swapping is yet another possibility for a lengthy stay. Advertisements for those seeking a house-swapping holiday often appear in the classified sections of the newspapers. Make sure you are totally satisfied with the arrangements made concerning your commitments and with the people with whom you are dealing. Also check that your householder's insurance covers you in such circumstances (**see:** Insurance).

A **host farm** can make a refreshing change from the norm. Such accommodation varies from spartan to luxurious and, in some cases, guests are invited to take part in farm life. Associations in each state (**see:** Farm Holidays) or tourist authorities will provide details.

If you would prefer **bed and breakfast** accommodation only in a 'homestay' or 'farmstay' environment throughout Australia, contact: Bed & Breakfast, PO Box 408, Gordon NSW 2072; (02) 498 5344, 498 1539 (AH).

Not to be confused with bushwalking, **backpacking** is a mode of travel using accommodation provided at budget rates in a communal environment. Note, however, the accommodation offered is not always suitable for children. During the high season, resort hostels may not accept telephone reservations without payment and it is advisable to book well in advance. For information on the range of accommodation available, contact: The Secretary, Backpackers Resorts of Australia Pty Ltd, PO Box 1000, Byron Bay NSW 2481; (018) 66 6888 (9-5, M-F). Backpackers VIP Discount Kit $15; accommodation guide to 93 hostels Australia-wide free; both plus $2 postage and handling.

If you are into **staying afloat**, consider hiring a paddle-wheeler on the Murray or a houseboat on the Hawkesbury or Eildon Weir, or even chartering a yacht to cruise in the Whitsundays. Check with your travel agent or government tourist bureau (**see:** Useful Information).

FARM HOLIDAYS

The following is a list of contact addresses in each state if you wish to arrange a farm holiday.

New South Wales
Farm Hosts & Farm Holidays
PO Box 65, Culcairn 2660
(060) 29 8621
(Properties available Australia-wide)

Victoria
Host Farms Association Inc.
332 Banyule Rd, View Bank 3084
(03) 457 5413

South Australia
The United Farms & Stock Owners
122 Frome St, Adelaide 5000
(08) 232 5555

Western Australia
WA Farm and Country Holidays
Association
Munaleeun Farm
Jackson Road
Albany via Narrikup 6326
(098) 53 2091

Northern Territory
Northern Territory Government
Tourist Bureau in any state

Queensland
Queensland Host Farm Association
C/o RACQ Travel Service
GPO Box 1403
Fortitude Valley 4001
(07) 361 2390, (008) 77 7888

Tasmania
Homehost Tasmania Pty Ltd
PO Box 780, Sandy Bay 7005
(002) 24 1612

Campervan at Ayers Rock, Uluru National Park, NT

Dividing Up the Dollars

Very few people can afford the 'money-no-object' approach to holidays, no matter what the length of stay. Part of your planning should include some time spent on budgeting. You will need to consider accommodation, food, fuel and entertainment principally, although emergency funds should not be forgotten. **Travel insurance** is a possible precaution to be considered also (**see**: Insurance). Accommodation costs can be estimated when you pre-book, but you might simply average the figure. If you do, estimate high rather than low. **Food** is a matter of personal choice: you may eat out every night or prepare all or some of your meals yourself. Eating out can be averaged at around $35 per head per day; preparing your own meals, at $15 per day per person.

You can work out your **fuel** costs in advance. If you do not already know your vehicle's fuel consumption, find out before you leave. The usual method is based on a litres per 100 kilometres base. If your vehicle uses, say, 16 litres per 100 km and your journey distance works out around 5000 km, you will use 50 times 16 litres of fuel or 800 litres. Allow for rises in petrol and charges and also for the fact that fuel is more expensive in remote areas.

When budgeting, remember also that accommodation, travel and rental charges tend to rise during peak periods.

Carrying large amounts of **cash** with you is not a good idea, which is why travellers cheques were invented. Use them, but also make arrangements with your bank to enable you to draw from the bank's branches on your route as you travel.

Car Maintenance Courses

If you plan to tour in the remoter areas, it is of advantage to acquire basic mechanical skills. Car-care and/or basic car-maintenance courses are provided by Adult Education centres, TAFE Colleges and automobile clubs in all states of Australia. The courses vary widely in content and length. A call to these organisations will ascertain what course is available and appropriate to your needs.

Insurance

The benefits of a comprehensive insurance policy on your vehicle, caravan or trailer are obvious. Apart from cover against loss or damage due to accident, theft or vandalism, your personal effects are covered against loss or damage when they are in the insured vehicle. Additional policies will cover such eventualities as the cost of temporary accommodation should your caravan become uninhabitable, for example. Some companies provide short-term (maximum 6 weeks) travel insurance, for example to cover loss of luggage or the cancellation of accommodation bookings. Information and advice can be obtained from the various motoring organisations and insurance companies.

Itineraries

Some people make them and stick to them. Others do not. At the very least, a rough schedule to ensure a mixture of travel and sight-seeing time is essential. And allow some flexibility. You never know what might detain you: the weather for example (rest breaks are necessary in extreme heat) or children, who tend to have a low tolerance for long stretches of driving without a break (**see**: Child's Play).

MOTORING ORGANISATIONS

There are motoring organisations in all Australian states and territories (**see**: Useful Information). All are affiliated under the Australian Automobile Association and reciprocal rights are available to their members. Membership can consist of service and social membership or service membership only.

When planning a trip, it would be advisable for you to take out **service membership** of the motoring organisation in your home state. Not only will this ensure that you receive service in that state, but by producing your membership card you also can request assistance from the equivalent organisation in other states.

The advantages of service membership of a motoring organisation are wide-ranging: emergency breakdown and towing services, vehicle inspection and 'approved repairer' services; tuition in safe and defensive driving for licensed drivers; legal advice on such matters as the procedure to be followed after motor vehicle accidents or traffic charges, and the possible penalties; motor vehicle insurance cover; and touring information and advice for motoring holidays, including guides, maps and reports on road conditions, accommodation and travel bookings, and special tours, package holidays and accommodation at concessional rates. **Social or 'club' membership** entitles members to the use of club facilities and accommodation, including reciprocal use in some 50 clubs throughout Australia.

Houseboat, Richmond River, Ballina, NSW

BUDGET BITERS

- Admission charges
- Theatre or cinema tickets
- Souvenirs and gifts
- Postcards and stamps
- Snacks and drinks
- Camera film and accessories
- Chemist and medical expenses
- Tips
- Garage repairs and replacement of parts
- Bridge tolls

Clothing

Be very strict with yourself and the family when you are packing and travel as lightly as you can. It is better to spend an hour at a laundromat washing a selection of non-irons than overburden your vehicle with clothing you probably will not wear.

Essentials are a warm **sweater**, even in summer, sensible **comfortable shoes** and a **wide-brimmed hat** to protect yourself from the sun at all times. Carry items like swimwear, towels, spare socks and sweaters in a loose bag, which can be kept within easy reach. **Gumboots** are a handy item also.

First-aid Kit

A first-aid kit is essential. Include band-aids, antiseptic, bandages, headache tablets, sunburn cream, insect repellent and a soothing lotion for bites. Eye-drops are a good idea, as is a thermometer and a tourniquet. A range of such kits is available from the St John Ambulance Service, which also conducts basic courses in first aid. As **car sickness** is often a problem on long journeys, particularly with young children, do not forget to include medication to counter this. Your local chemist or a doctor will advise you on what is available.

Useful Extras

Depending on the length and nature of your tour, some items are valuable, some essential (**see:** Tools and Spare Parts). Carry picnic and barbecue equipment, tissues, toilet paper and a container or plastic bag for rubbish — and take it with you rather than leaving it behind, at least until you can find a legitimate rubbish-tip. Rugs or blankets are a necessary extra (**see:** Natural Hazards: Bushfire), as is a large sheet of plastic, which can be used as an emergency windscreen (**see also:** How to Obtain Water). If you are going outback, some type of shade cover, such as a tarpaulin, as sun protection is a necessary item in case of an emergency stop (**see:** Surviving in the Outback).

On the road: between Ivanhoe and Menindee, NSW

PETS

Don't forget: whether you are leaving your pets behind or taking them with you, you will need to make a booking for them also.

Leaving them behind:
- Pet care services (Yellow Pages): These provide care of pets in their own environment. They also will care for plants and property, etc.
- Dog boarding kennels and catteries (Yellow Pages): Provide care and accommodation; some have pickup and delivery services.
- Animal welfare organisations/veterinary surgeons (Yellow Pages): For advice and information.

Taking them with you:
- Make sure, in advance, that the accommodation or mode of travel booked permits animals. Many caravan parks and most national parks do not admit animals.
- During the trip, carry additional water and stop at regular intervals to give opportunity for toiletting and exercise.
- Do not leave an animal unattended in a vehicle for any length of time; always provide a source of fresh air.
- Allow sufficient room in the vehicle to comfortably accommodate the animal.
- Do not transport an animal in a moving caravan.

TIME ZONES

Australia has 3 time zones:
- **Eastern Standard Time** (EST) In Queensland, New South Wales, Victoria and Tasmania.
- **Central Standard Time** (CST is a half-hour behind EST) In South Australia and Northern Territory.
- **Western Standard Time** (WST is 2 hours behind EST) In Western Australia.

Daylight saving is adopted by some states in the summer months. In New South Wales, Victoria, Tasmania, Australian Capital Territory and South Australia, clocks are put forward one hour at the beginning of summer. Western Australia, Northern Territory and Queensland do not have daylight saving.

INTER CAPITAL CITY ROUTE MAPS

The following intercity route maps will help you to plan your route between major cities. As well, you can use the individual maps while undertaking your journey, since they provide information on distances between all towns along the route, roadside rest areas and road conditions, where relevant.

*Road sign beside Eyre Highway
Nullarbor Plain, SA*

LOCATION MAP

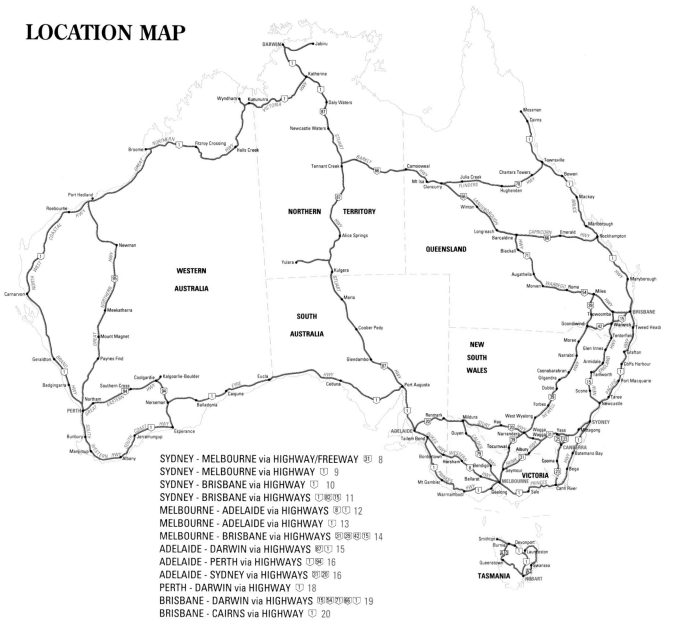

SYDNEY - MELBOURNE via HIGHWAY/FREEWAY ③① 8
SYDNEY - MELBOURNE via HIGHWAY ① 9
SYDNEY - BRISBANE via HIGHWAY ① 10
SYDNEY - BRISBANE via HIGHWAYS ① ⑧② ⑮ 11
MELBOURNE - ADELAIDE via HIGHWAYS ⑧ ① 12
MELBOURNE - ADELAIDE via HIGHWAY ① 13
MELBOURNE - BRISBANE via HIGHWAYS ③① ③⑨ ④② ⑮ 14
ADELAIDE - DARWIN via HIGHWAYS ⑧⑦ ① 15
ADELAIDE - PERTH via HIGHWAYS ① ⑨④ 16
ADELAIDE - SYDNEY via HIGHWAYS ③① ②⓪ 16
PERTH - DARWIN via HIGHWAY ① 18
BRISBANE - DARWIN via HIGHWAYS ⑮ ⑤④ ⑦① ⑥⑥ ① 19
BRISBANE - CAIRNS via HIGHWAY ① 20

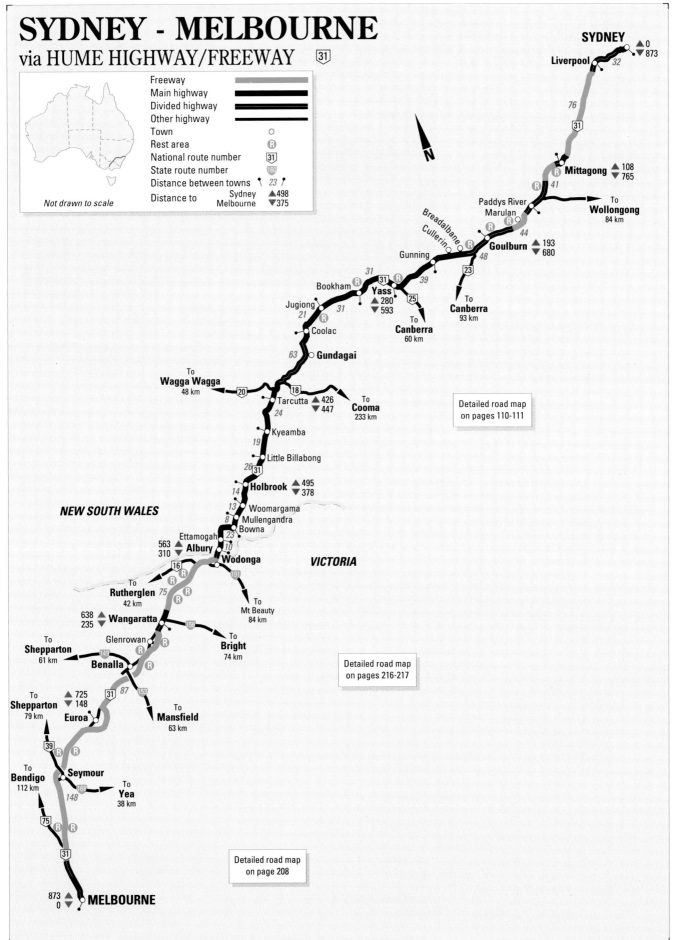

SYDNEY - MELBOURNE
via HUME HIGHWAY/FREEWAY 31

SYDNEY - MELBOURNE
via PRINCES HIGHWAY ①

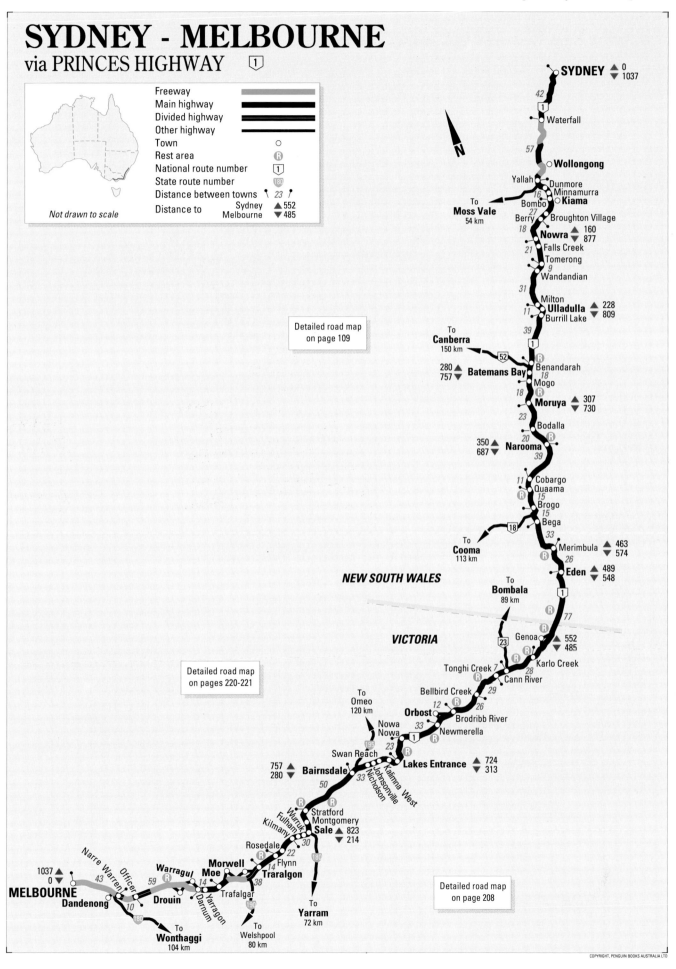

Freeway	
Main highway	
Divided highway	
Other highway	
Town	○
Rest area	ⓡ
National route number	①
State route number	⑱⓪
Distance between towns	↖ *23* ↘
Distance to	Sydney ▲552
	Melbourne ▼485

Not drawn to scale

Detailed road map
on page 109

Detailed road map
on pages 220-221

Detailed road map
on page 208

SYDNEY ▲ 0 ▼ 1037

42

Waterfall

57

Wollongong

Yallah
Dunmore
Minnamurra
16 Bombo **Kiama**
To *27* Berry Broughton Village
Moss Vale
54 km *18* **Nowra** ▲160 ▼877
21 Falls Creek
Tomerong
9 Wandandian
31 Milton
11 **Ulladulla** ▲228 ▼809
Burrill Lake

To *39*
Canberra
150 km ⑤② Benandarah
280▲ *18* Mogo
757▼ **Batemans Bay** *18*
Moruya ▲307 ▼730
23 Bodalla
350▲ *20* ⓡ
687▼ **Narooma**
39

11 Cobargo
Quaama
ⓡ *15* Brogo
15 Bega
To ⑱ *33*
Cooma Merimbula ▲463 ▼574
113 km ⓡ *26*
NEW SOUTH WALES **Eden** ▲489 ▼548
To ①
Bombala ⓡ *77*
89 km ⓡ
VICTORIA ㉓ Genoa ▲552 ▼485
ⓡ Karlo Creek
Tonghi Creek *7* *28*
ⓡ *29* Cann River
Bellbird Creek
To *12* ⓡ *26*
Omeo **Orbost** Brodribb River
120 km *33* Newmerella
Nowa ①
Nowa ⓡ
⑲⑤ *23*
Swan Reach
757▲ **Bairnsdale** Kalimna West **Lakes Entrance** ▲724 ▼313
280▼ *50* *33* Johnsonville
Nicholson
ⓡ ⓡ Stratford
Wurruk Montgomery
Fulham **Sale** ▲823 ▼214
Kilmany *30* ⑱⓪
Rosedale *22*
ⓡ Flynn
Morwell *14*
Warragul **Moe** ⓡ To
1037▲ Narre Warren *59* ⓡ *14* **Traralgon** **Yarram**
0▼ *43* Officer Drouin Yarragon *38* 72 km
MELBOURNE Trafalgar ⑲⓪
Dandenong *10*
⑱⓪ To
To Welshpool
Wonthaggi 80 km
104 km

SYDNEY - BRISBANE
via PACIFIC HIGHWAY ①

QUEENSLAND

Detailed road map on page 435

BRISBANE ▲0 ▼982

24

Slacks Creek Loganholme
Beenleigh Yatala
Stapylton Ormeau
Pimpama
Oxenford Coomera

50

Worongary **Southport**
Mudgeeraba **Surfers Paradise**
Reedy Creek

25 **Coolangatta** ▲99 ▼883

Condong *31* **Tweed Heads**
Chinderah
Murwillumbah Tumbulgum

15 Burringbar

17

Brunswick Heads ▲162 ▼820

21

To **Lismore** 35 km *26* Bangalow

44 **Ballina** ▲209 ▼773

9 *18*
12 Wardell
Broadwater
Woodburn

NEW SOUTH WALES

① *74*

To **Glen Innes** 159 km

38 *13* *9*
Cowper
Ulmarra

344 ▲ **Sth Grafton**
638 ▼ *29*

Halfway Creek
16
13 Corindi

25 **Woolgoolga** ▲402 ▼580

Korora
Boambee **Coffs Harbour** ▲427 ▼555

23
36 Raleigh

486 ▲ **Macksville** **Nambucca Heads**
496 ▼
17
Eungai Creek
29
Frederickton ①
7 **Kempsey** ▲539 ▼443

To **Walcha** 172 km *31*
Telegraph Point
34 *42*
Port Macquarie

Kew
22
Johns River
27 Moorland
661 ▲ **Taree** Coopernook
321 ▼ Purfleet

45

Coolongolook
11 Wootton
20
43 **Bulahdelah** ▲737 ▼245

Karuah
To **Maitland** 18 km *37*
15 **Kurri Kurri** *23*
Pelaw Main **Raymond Terrace** ▲807 ▼175
Brunkerville Hexham

① To **Newcastle** 49 km
142
Gosford

Detailed road map on page 111

SYDNEY ▲982 ▼0

Freeway	
Main highway	
Divided highway	
Other highway	
Town	○
Rest area	Ⓡ
National route number	①
State route number	160
Distance between towns	23
Distance to	Brisbane ▲539
	Sydney ▼443

Not drawn to scale

COPYRIGHT, PENGUIN BOOKS AUSTRALIA LTD

SYDNEY - BRISBANE
via NEW ENGLAND HIGHWAY ① 82 15

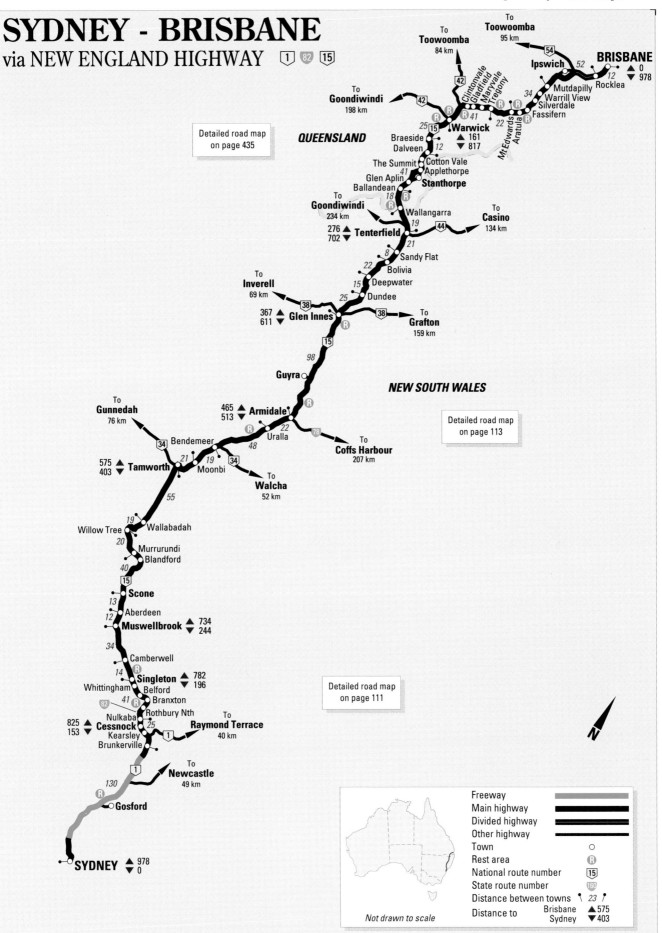

To Toowoomba 84 km

To Toowoomba 95 km

54

BRISBANE ▲ 0 ▼ 978

Ipswich 52

12 Rocklea

Mutdapilly
Warrill View
Silverdale
Fassifern

34

Clintonvale
Gladfield
Maryvale
Tregony

42

To Goondiwindi 198 km

42

QUEENSLAND

41

25 15 **Warwick** ▲ 161 ▼ 817

22 Mt Edwards
Aratula

Braeside
Dalveen

12

Cotton Vale
Applethorpe

The Summit 41

Stanthorpe

Glen Aplin
Ballandean

18

To Goondiwindi 234 km

Wallangarra

To Casino 134 km

276 ▲ 702 ▼ **Tenterfield**

19

44

21

8 Sandy Flat

22 Bolivia

15 Deepwater

To Inverell 69 km

25 Dundee

38

38

To Grafton 159 km

367 ▲ 611 ▼ **Glen Innes**

15

98

Guyra

NEW SOUTH WALES

465 ▲ 513 ▼ **Armidale**

To Gunnedah 76 km

Detailed road map on page 113

34 Bendemeer

22 Uralla

48

78

To Coffs Harbour 207 km

21 19 34

575 ▲ 403 ▼ **Tamworth**

Moonbi

To **Walcha** 52 km

55

19 Willow Tree

Wallabadah

20

Murrurundi
Blandford

40

15

Scone

13

12 Aberdeen

Muswellbrook ▲ 734 ▼ 244

34

Camberwell

14

Singleton ▲ 782 ▼ 196

Whittingham Belford

82 41 Branxton

Rothbury Nth

Nulkaba

825 ▲ 153 ▼ **Cessnock**

25

1

To **Raymond Terrace** 40 km

Kearsley
Brunkerville

Detailed road map on page 111

1

To **Newcastle** 49 km

130

Gosford

SYDNEY ▲ 978 ▼ 0

Detailed road map on page 435

	Freeway
	Main highway
	Divided highway
	Other highway
○	Town
Ⓡ	Rest area
15	National route number
160	State route number
`23`	Distance between towns
Distance to	Brisbane ▲ 575 / Sydney ▼ 403

Not drawn to scale

N

MELBOURNE - ADELAIDE
via WESTERN & DUKES HIGHWAYS 〔8〕〔1〕

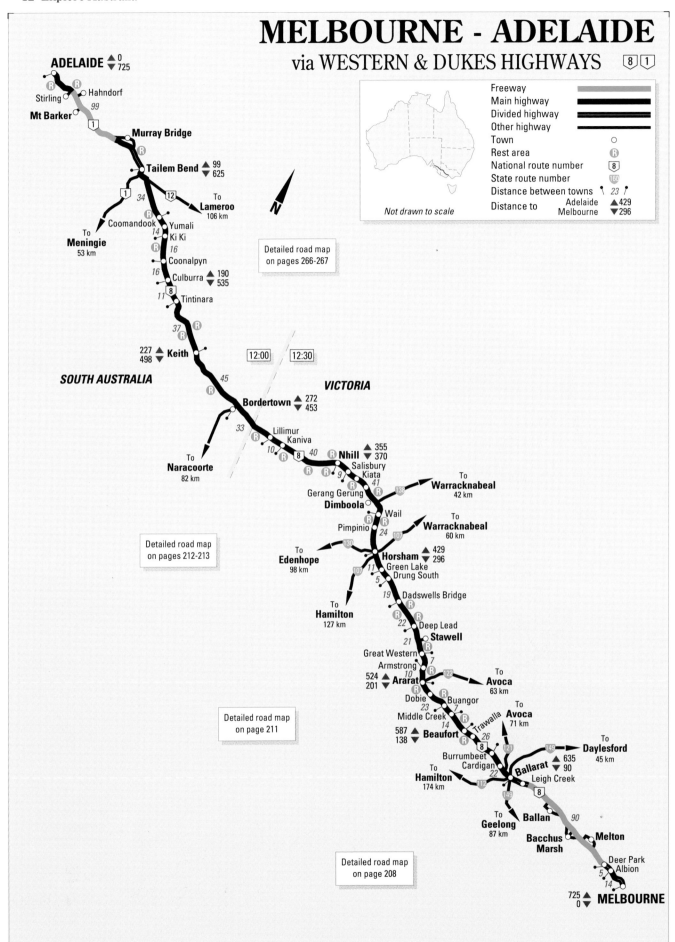

ADELAIDE ▲ 0 ▼ 725

Stirling Hahndorf
Mt Barker 99
〔1〕
Murray Bridge
Tailem Bend ▲ 99 ▼ 625

〔1〕 34 〔12〕
To Lameroo 106 km
Coomandook Yumali
14 Ki Ki
To Meningie 53 km 16
Coonalpyn
16 Culburra ▲ 190 ▼ 535
11 〔8〕 Tintinara
37

227 ▲ Keith
498 ▼

12:00   12:30

SOUTH AUSTRALIA 45 VICTORIA

Bordertown ▲ 272 ▼ 453

33 Lillimur
Kaniva
10 40 〔8〕 Nhill ▲ 355 ▼ 370
Salisbury
9 Kiata
41
To Naracoorte 82 km
To Warracknabeal 42 km
Gerang Gerung 〔138〕
Dimboola Wail
Pimpinio 24 〔107〕 To Warracknabeal 60 km
〔130〕
Horsham ▲ 429 ▼ 296
To Edenhope 98 km 〔107〕 11 Green Lake
Drung South
5
19 Dadswells Bridge
To Hamilton 127 km 22 Deep Lead
Stawell
21
Great Western
Armstrong 7
524 ▲ 10 〔127〕
201 ▼ Ararat
Dobie Buangor To Avoca 63 km
23 7
Middle Creek
14 Trawalla To Avoca 71 km
587 ▲ 26 〔121〕
138 ▼ Beaufort 〔8〕 〔149〕 To Daylesford 45 km
Burrumbeet
Cardigan ▲ 635
To Hamilton 174 km 22 Ballarat ▼ 90
Leigh Creek
〔12〕
〔149〕 〔8〕
To Geelong 87 km Ballan 90
Bacchus Marsh Melton
Deer Park
Albion
5
14
725 ▲ MELBOURNE
0 ▼

Detailed road map on pages 266-267

Detailed road map on pages 212-213

Detailed road map on page 211

Detailed road map on page 208

Freeway	
Main highway	
Divided highway	
Other highway	
Town	○
Rest area	Ⓡ
National route number	〔8〕
State route number	〔160〕
Distance between towns	↖ 23 ↗
Distance to	Adelaide ▲ 429
	Melbourne ▼ 296

Not drawn to scale

N

COPYRIGHT, PENGUIN BOOKS AUSTRALIA LTD

MELBOURNE - ADELAIDE
via PRINCES HIGHWAY ①

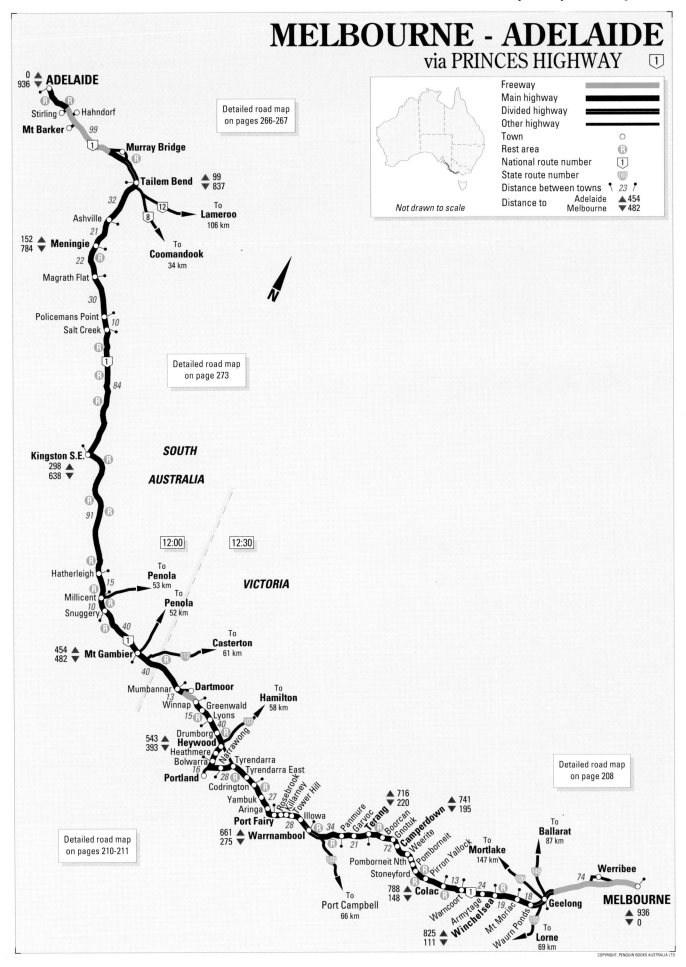

Legend:

(grey line)	Freeway
(black line)	Main highway
(double line)	Divided highway
(line)	Other highway
○	Town
Ⓡ	Rest area
①	National route number
160	State route number
↖ 23 ↗	Distance between towns
Adelaide ▲454	Distance to
Melbourne ▼482	

Not drawn to scale

Detailed road map on pages 266-267

Detailed road map on page 273

Detailed road map on page 208

Detailed road map on pages 210-211

Route (Adelaide to Melbourne):

- 0 / 936 ▲▼ **ADELAIDE**
- Ⓡ Stirling ○ ○ Hahndorf Ⓡ
- **Mt Barker** ○
- 99
- ① **Murray Bridge** Ⓡ
- **Tailem Bend** ▲ 99 ▼ 837
- 32
- ⑧ ⑫ To **Lameroo** 106 km
- Ashville
- 21
- 152 / 784 ▲▼ **Meningie** Ⓡ
- To **Coomandook** 34 km
- 22
- Magrath Flat Ⓡ
- 30
- Policemans Point
- Salt Creek 10
- Ⓡ
- ① 84
- Ⓡ
- **SOUTH AUSTRALIA**
- **Kingston S.E.** 298 ▲ 638 ▼ Ⓡ
- 91 Ⓡ
- 12:00 12:30
- **VICTORIA**
- Hatherleigh Ⓡ
- 15 To **Penola** 53 km
- Millicent Ⓡ
- 10 To **Penola** 52 km
- Snuggery Ⓡ
- 40 ①
- 454 / 482 ▲▼ **Mt Gambier** Ⓡ ⑰ To **Casterton** 61 km
- 40
- Mumbannar ○ **Dartmoor**
- 13 To **Hamilton** 58 km
- Winnap Greenwald
- 15 Lyons Ⓡ
- 40 Narrawong ⑩
- 543 / 393 ▲▼ **Heywood** Drumborg
- Heathmere
- Bolwarra Tyrendarra
- 16 Tyrendarra East
- **Portland** 28 Ⓡ
- Codrington
- Yambuk 27
- Aringa Rosebrook Killarney Tower Hill
- **Port Fairy** 28
- 661 / 275 ▲▼ **Warrnambool** Ⓡ 34 Illowa
- 21 Panmure Garvoc
- 100 **Terang** ▲ 716 ▼ 220
- Boorcan Gnotuk
- Weerite **Camperdown** ▲ 741 ▼ 195
- Pomborneit
- Pomborneit Nth 72 Pirron Yallock To **Mortlake** 147 km
- Stoneyford Ⓡ 106 149
- 788 / 148 ▲▼ **Colac** Ⓡ 13 Ⓡ To **Ballarat** 87 km
- To **Port Campbell** 66 km
- Warncoort 24 Ⓡ 18 **Werribee** 74
- 825 / 111 ▲▼ Armytage ① **Winchelsea** 19 Mt Moriac 100 **Geelong**
- Waurn Ponds To **Lorne** 69 km
- **MELBOURNE** ▲ 936 ▼ 0

MELBOURNE - BRISBANE
via NEWELL HIGHWAY 31 39 42 15

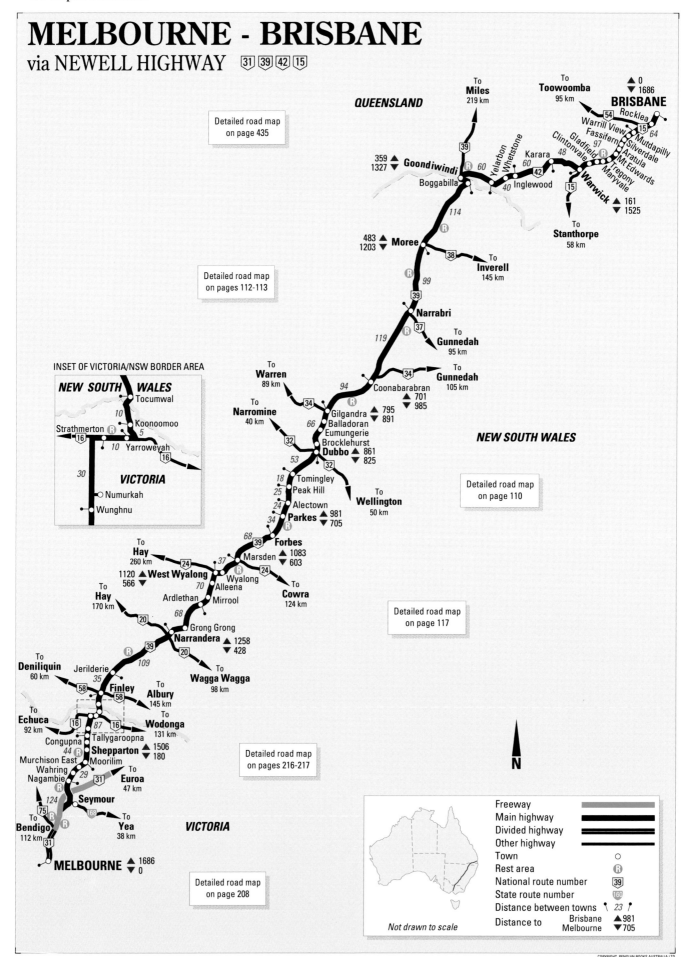

QUEENSLAND

To
Miles
219 km

To
Toowoomba
95 km

▲ 0
▼ 1686

BRISBANE

Rocklea
54
Warrill View
Mutdapilly
15 64
Fassifern
Silverdale
Gladfield
97
Clintonvale
Aratula
48
Tregony
Mt Edwards
Maryvale

Yelarbon
Whetstone
Karara

359 ▲
1327 ▼ **Goondiwindi**
60 R
60
42
Warwick

Boggabilla
40
Inglewood
15

114

161
1525

To
Stanthorpe
58 km

483 ▲
1203 ▼ **Moree**
38
To
Inverell
145 km

R
99

39
Narrabri
37

NEW SOUTH WALES

119
To
Gunnedah
95 km

34
To
Gunnedah
105 km

To
Warren
89 km

94
Coonabarabran
701
985

34

R
Narromine
40 km
Gilgandra
Balladoran
795
891

32
66
Eumungerie
Brocklehurst
Dubbo ▲ 861
▼ 825

53
32

18 Tomingley
25 Peak Hill
To
Wellington
50 km

24 Alectown
34 **Parkes** ▲ 981
▼ 705

INSET OF VICTORIA/NSW BORDER AREA

NEW SOUTH WALES
Tocumwal
10
Koonoomoo
Strathmerton R 5
16
10 Yarroweyah
16

30

VICTORIA
Numurkah

Wunghnu

68
39 **Forbes** ▲ 1083
▼ 603

37 Marsden
24

To
Hay
260 km
24
1120 ▲ **West Wyalong**
566 ▼
70 Wyalong
Alleena
To
Cowra
124 km

To
Hay
170 km
Ardlethan Mirrool

20
68

To
Deniliquin
60 km
39
Grong Grong
Narrandera ▲ 1258
▼ 428

109
20

Jerilderie
To
Wagga Wagga
98 km

35
58
Finley
58
To
Albury
145 km

To
Echuca
92 km
16
87
16
To
Wodonga
131 km

Congupna
44 Tallygaroopna
1506
180
Shepparton ▼
Murchison East
Moorilim
Wahring
29
To
Euroa
47 km
Nagambie
R
31
124
75 **Seymour**
R
168

To
Bendigo
112 km
31
To
Yea
38 km

VICTORIA

MELBOURNE ▲ 1686
▼ 0

Detailed road map on page 435

Detailed road map on pages 112-113

Detailed road map on page 110

Detailed road map on page 117

Detailed road map on pages 216-217

Detailed road map on page 208

N

Legend	
Freeway	
Main highway	
Divided highway	
Other highway	
Town	○
Rest area	R
National route number	39
State route number	160
Distance between towns	23
Distance to	Brisbane ▲ 981
	Melbourne ▼ 705

Not drawn to scale

COPYRIGHT, PENGUIN BOOKS AUSTRALIA LTD

ADELAIDE-DARWIN
via STUART HIGHWAY `87` `1`

Freeway	
Main highway	
Divided highway	
Other highway	
Town	○
Rest area	Ⓡ
National route number	`87`
State route number	`160`
Distance between towns	`↖ 23 ↗`
Distance to	Darwin ▲ 1490
	Adelaide ▼ 1531

Not drawn to scale

N

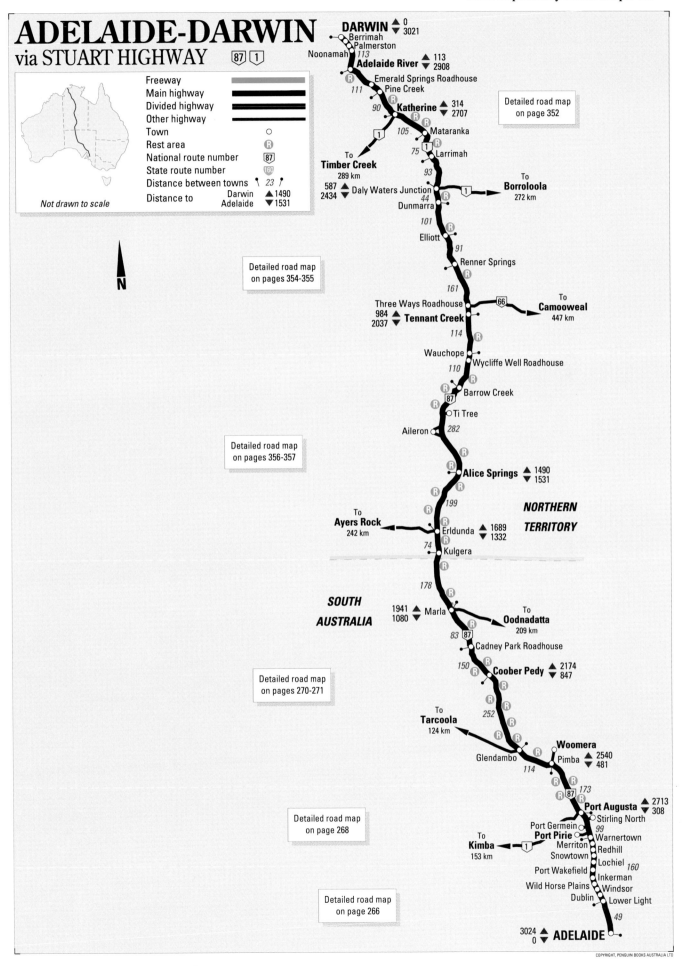

DARWIN ▲ 0 ▼ 3021
Berrimah
Palmerston
Noonamah *113*
Adelaide River ▲ 113 ▼ 2908
111 Emerald Springs Roadhouse
Ⓡ Pine Creek
90 **Katherine** ▲ 314 ▼ 2707
`1` *105* Mataranka
Ⓡ *75* Larrimah
93
To Timber Creek 289 km *587* Daly Waters Junction
2434 *44* Dunmarra Ⓡ
101 Ⓡ
Elliott
91
Ⓡ Renner Springs
161
Three Ways Roadhouse `66`
984 ▲ **Tennant Creek**
2037 ▼ *114* Ⓡ
Wauchope
110 Wycliffe Well Roadhouse
`87` Barrow Creek
Ⓡ ○ Ti Tree
Aileron *282*
Ⓡ
Ⓡ **Alice Springs** ▲ 1490 ▼ 1531
Ⓡ
Ⓡ *199*
To Ayers Rock 242 km Erlunda ▲ 1689 ▼ 1332
74 Kulgera

Detailed road map on page 352

Detailed road map on pages 354-355

Detailed road map on pages 356-357

NORTHERN TERRITORY

To Borroloola 272 km `1`

To Camooweal 447 km

SOUTH AUSTRALIA

178 Ⓡ
1941 ▲ Marla
1080 ▼
83 `87` Cadney Park Roadhouse
Ⓡ
150 **Coober Pedy** ▲ 2174 ▼ 847
Ⓡ
Ⓡ
252 Ⓡ
Ⓡ
To Tarcoola 124 km Ⓡ
Ⓡ **Woomera**
Glendambo Pimba ▲ 2540 ▼ 481
114
Ⓡ *173*
Ⓡ `87` **Port Augusta** ▲ 2713 ▼ 308
Stirling North
Port Germein *99*
Port Pirie Warnertown
To Kimba 153 km `1` Merriton Redhill
Snowtown Lochiel *160*
Port Wakefield Inkerman
Wild Horse Plains Windsor
Dublin Lower Light
49
3024 ▲ **ADELAIDE**
0 ▼

To Oodnadatta 209 km

Detailed road map on pages 270-271

Detailed road map on page 268

Detailed road map on page 266

ADELAIDE - PERTH
via EYRE & GREAT EASTERN HIGHWAYS

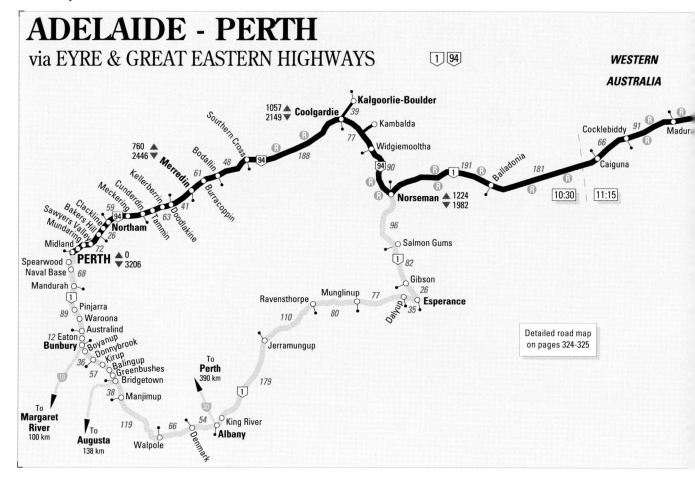

ADELAIDE - SYDNEY
via HUME & STURT HIGHWAYS

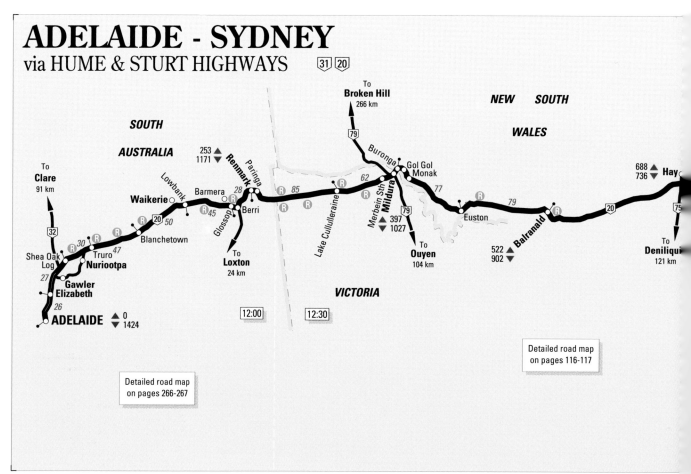

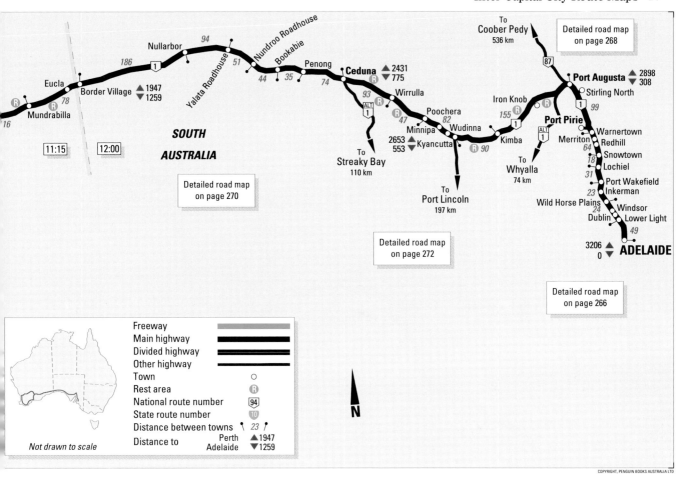

To
Coober Pedy
536 km

Detailed road map
on page 268

87

Port Augusta ▲ 2898
▼ 308

Stirling North

Nullarbor
94

186

Yalata Roadhouse

51

Nundroo Roadhouse

Bookabie

Penong

Eucla

Border Village ▲ 1947
▼ 1259

78

Mundrabilla

16

11:15   12:00

**SOUTH
AUSTRALIA**

44 *35*

74

Ceduna ▲ 2431
▼ 775

93

ALT
1

Wirrulla

47

Minnipa

2653 ▲
553 ▼ Kyancutta

Poochera

82

Wudinna

To
Streaky Bay
110 km

To
Port Lincoln
197 km

Detailed road map
on page 270

Detailed road map
on page 272

Iron Knob

155

Kimba

1

R *90*

To
Whyalla
74 km

ALT
1

Port Pirie

Merriton

64

Warnertown
Redhill
Snowtown
Lochiel

18

31

Port Wakefield
Inkerman

23

Wild Horse Plains

24

Windsor
Lower Light

Dublin

49

3206 ▲
0 ▼ **ADELAIDE**

1   *99*

Detailed road map
on page 266

Freeway
Main highway
Divided highway
Other highway
Town   ○
Rest area   Ⓡ
National route number   94
State route number   10
Distance between towns   *23*
Distance to   Perth   ▲ 1947
                     Adelaide   ▼ 1259

Not drawn to scale

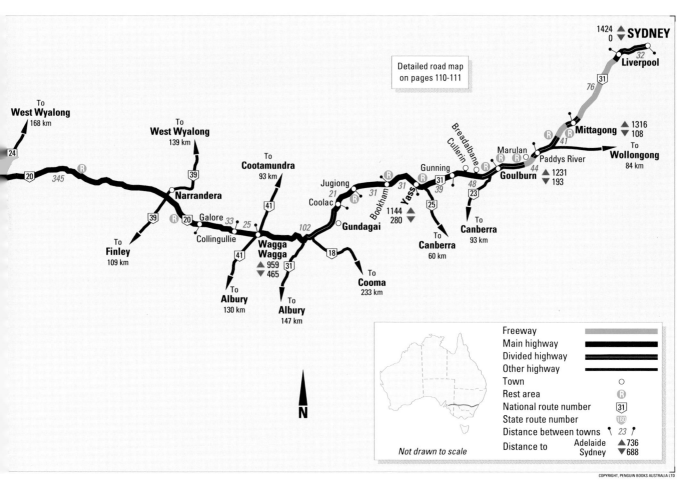

1424 ▲ **SYDNEY**
0 ▼

32

Liverpool

Detailed road map
on pages 110-111

76

31

To
West Wyalong
168 km

24

345

20

To
West Wyalong
139 km

39

Narrandera

39   Ⓡ   20

Galore *33*

Collingullie

To
Finley
109 km

41

To
Cootamundra
93 km

41

25

Jugiong

21

Coolac

102

Gundagai

Bookham

Yass

31

Gunning

Breadalbane

Cullerin

39

Marulan

Paddys River

Goulburn ▲ 1231
▼ 193

44

41

48

23

To
Canberra
93 km

Mittagong ▲ 1316
▼ 108

To
Wollongong
84 km

25

1144 ▲
280 ▼

To
Canberra
60 km

18

**Wagga
Wagga**
▲ 959
▼ 465

31

To
Cooma
233 km

To
Albury
130 km

To
Albury
147 km

Freeway
Main highway
Divided highway
Other highway
Town   ○
Rest area   Ⓡ
National route number   31
State route number   160
Distance between towns   *23*
Distance to   Adelaide   ▲ 736
                     Sydney   ▼ 688

Not drawn to scale

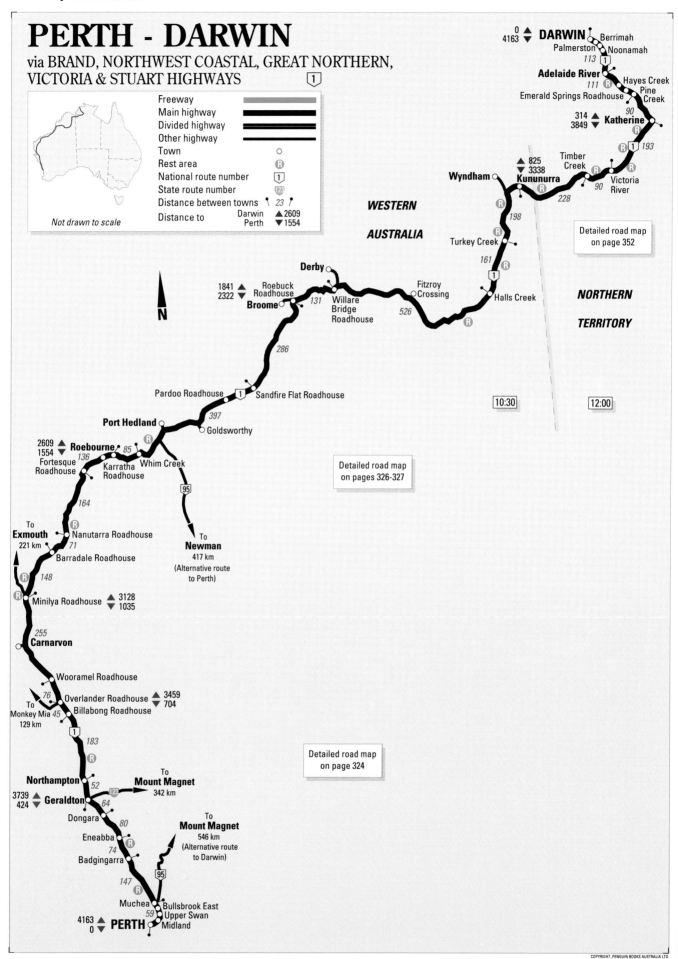

PERTH - DARWIN
via BRAND, NORTHWEST COASTAL, GREAT NORTHERN, VICTORIA & STUART HIGHWAYS ①

Legend

Freeway	
Main highway	
Divided highway	
Other highway	
Town	○
Rest area	®
National route number	①
State route number	123
Distance between towns	23
Distance to	Darwin ▲ 2609
	Perth ▼ 1554

Not drawn to scale

DARWIN 0 / 4163 Berrimah
Palmerston Noonamah
113
Adelaide River Hayes Creek
111 Pine Creek
Emerald Springs Roadhouse 90
314 / 3849 Katherine
193
WESTERN 825 / 3338
Timber Creek
AUSTRALIA Wyndham Kununurra
198 90 Victoria River
228
Turkey Creek
161
Detailed road map on page 352
Derby
1841 / 2322 Roebuck Roadhouse
131 Fitzroy Crossing
Broome Willare Bridge Roadhouse 526 Halls Creek
NORTHERN
TERRITORY
286

Pardoo Roadhouse ① Sandfire Flat Roadhouse
397
Port Hedland Goldsworthy

10:30   12:00

2609 / 1554 Roebourne 85
136 Whim Creek
Fortescue Roadhouse Karratha Roadhouse
164 95
To Exmouth Nanutarra Roadhouse
221 km 71
Barradale Roadhouse To Newman
148 417 km (Alternative route to Perth)
Minilya Roadhouse ▲ 3128 / ▼ 1035
255
Carnarvon

Detailed road map on pages 326-327

Wooramel Roadhouse
76 Overlander Roadhouse ▲ 3459 / ▼ 704
To Monkey Mia 45 Billabong Roadhouse
129 km ①
183

Detailed road map on page 324

Northampton
52 124 To Mount Magnet
3739 / 424 Geraldton 64 342 km
Dongara
80 To Mount Magnet
Eneabba 546 km (Alternative route to Darwin)
74
Badgingarra
147 95
Muchea Bullsbrook East
59 Upper Swan
4163 / 0 PERTH Midland

COPYRIGHT, PENGUIN BOOKS AUSTRALIA LTD

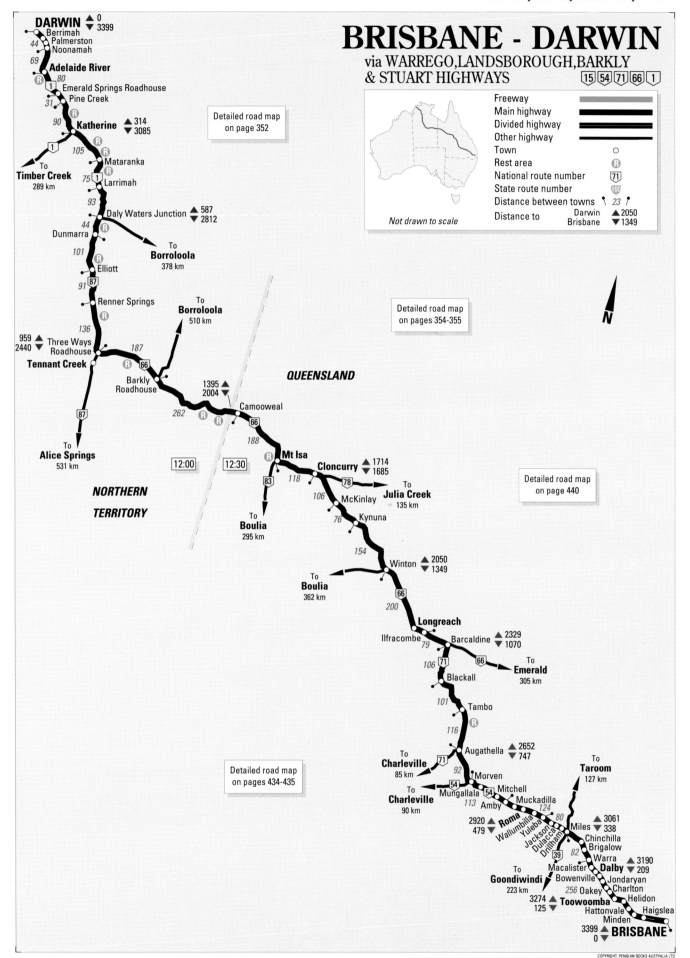

BRISBANE - DARWIN
via WARREGO, LANDSBOROUGH, BARKLY & STUART HIGHWAYS

15 54 71 66 1

Freeway	
Main highway	
Divided highway	
Other highway	
Town	○
Rest area	R
National route number	71
State route number	160
Distance between towns	23
Distance to	Darwin ▲2050
	Brisbane ▼1349

Not drawn to scale

DARWIN ▲0 ▼3399
Berrimah
Palmerston
Noonamah
44
69
Adelaide River
R 80
Emerald Springs Roadhouse
Pine Creek
31
R
90 Katherine ▲314 ▼3085
R
105
R
R Mataranka
To 75 R Larrimah
Timber Creek
289 km 93
Daly Waters Junction ▲587 ▼2812
44
R
Dunmarra
101
R
Elliott
91 87
Renner Springs
R
136
959 ▲ Three Ways
2440 ▼ Roadhouse 187
Tennant Creek R 66
Barkly
Roadhouse
87 262 R R
To
Alice Springs
531 km

NORTHERN

TERRITORY

Detailed road map
on page 352

Detailed road map
on pages 354-355

QUEENSLAND

Borrooloola
378 km

To
Borrooloola
510 km

1395 ▲ 2004 ▼
Camooweal
66
188
12:00 12:30
R Mt Isa ▲1714 ▼1685
83 118 Cloncurry
106 McKinlay 78
To Julia Creek
76 Kynuna 135 km
To
Boulia
295 km
154
Winton ▲2050 ▼1349
To 66
Boulia 200
362 km
Longreach
Ilfracombe ▲2329
79 Barcaldine ▼1070
106 71 66
Blackall To Emerald
305 km
101
Tambo
R
116
▲2652 ▼747
Augathella
To 71
Charleville 92 Morven
85 km 54
To 54 Mitchell
Charleville Mungallala Muckadilla
90 km 113 Amby 124
2920 ▲ Roma 80
479 ▼ Wallumbilla Yuleba Jackson
Dulacca
Drillham 39 82
To Macalister
Goondiwindi Bowenville
223 km 256 Oakey
3274 ▲ Toowoomba
125 ▼ Hattonvale
Minden
3399 ▲
0 ▼ BRISBANE

Detailed road map
on page 440

Detailed road map
on pages 434-435

To
Taroom
127 km

▲3061
Miles ▼338
Chinchilla
Brigalow
Warra ▲3190
Dalby ▼209
Jondaryan
Charlton
Helidon
Haigslea

N

BRISBANE - CAIRNS
via BRUCE HIGHWAY

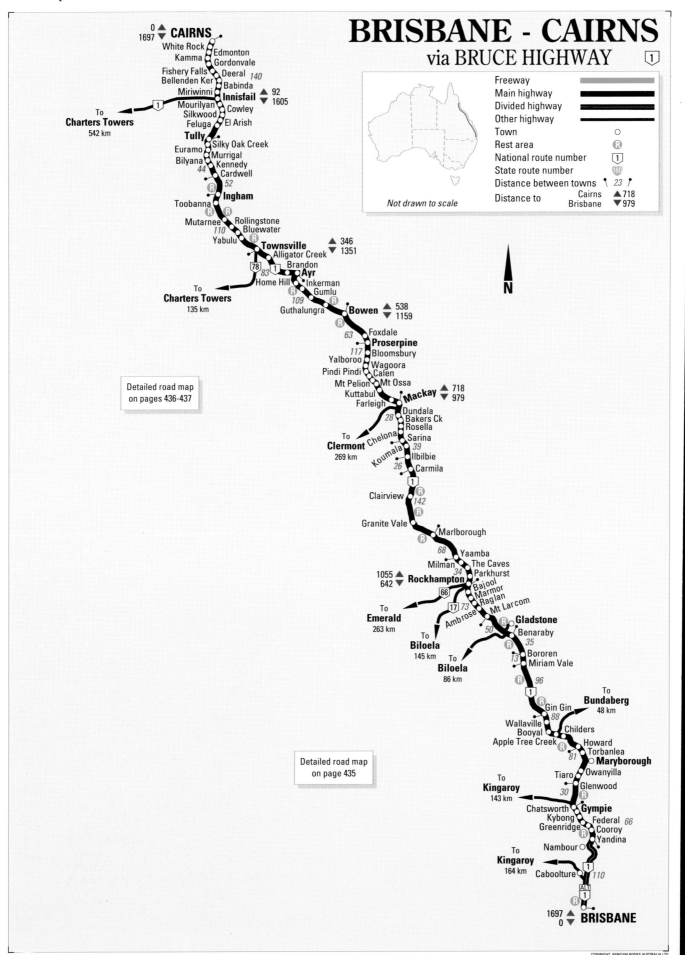

Legend

Freeway	
Main highway	
Divided highway	
Other highway	
Town	○
Rest area	R
National route number	1
State route number	160
Distance between towns	23
Distance to Cairns	▲718
Brisbane	▼979

Not drawn to scale

N

0 ▲ / 1697 ▼ **CAIRNS**
White Rock
Edmonton
Kamma
Gordonvale
Fishery Falls
Deeral 140
Bellenden Ker
Babinda
Miriwinni
92 / 1605
Innisfail
Mourilyan
Cowley
Silkwood
El Arish
Feluga
Tully
Euramo
Silky Oak Creek
Murrigal
Bilyana
Kennedy
44
Cardwell
52
Ingham
Toobanna
Mutarnee
Rollingstone
Bluewater
110
Yabulu
Townsville ▲346 / ▼1351
Alligator Creek
Brandon
78 / 83 / **Ayr**
Home Hill
Inkerman
Gumlu
109
Bowen ▲538 / ▼1159
Guthalungra
63
Foxdale
Proserpine
117
Bloomsbury
Yalboroo
Wagoora
Pindi Pindi
Calen
Mt Pelion
Mt Ossa
Kuttabul
Mackay ▲718 / ▼979
Farleigh
Dundala
28
Bakers Ck
Rosella
Chelona
Sarina
39
Koumala
Ilbilbie
26
Carmila
1
Clairview
142
Granite Vale
Marlborough
68
Yaamba
Milman
The Caves
34
Parkhurst
1055 ▲ / 642 ▼ **Rockhampton**
Bajool
66
Marmor
Raglan
17 / 73
Mt Larcom
Ambrose
Gladstone
50
Benaraby
35
Bororen
13
Miriam Vale
96
1
Gin Gin
88
Wallaville
Childers
Booyal
Apple Tree Creek
Howard
Torbanlea
81
Maryborough
Tiaro
Owanyilla
Glenwood
30
R
Chatsworth
Gympie
Kybong
Federal 66
Greenridge
Cooroy
Yandina
Nambour
1
Caboolture
110
ALT 1
1697 ▲ / 0 ▼ **BRISBANE**

To **Charters Towers** 542 km

To **Charters Towers** 135 km

Detailed road map on pages 436-437

To **Clermont** 269 km

To **Emerald** 263 km

To **Biloela** 145 km

To **Biloela** 86 km

To **Bundaberg** 48 km

Detailed road map on page 435

To **Kingaroy** 143 km

To **Kingaroy** 164 km

HAVE A GOOD TRIP

Checking the Car

All the care that you devote to your own comfort can be for nothing if you do not make sure that the car checks out, too.

For a one-, two- or three-day tour, you could simply fuel up, check the tyre pressures, clean all the windows and head off, and if you maintain your vehicle at all times in reasonable condition — as indeed you should — probably little further preparation is required. However, a vacation of a week or more, or any time long-distance driving is involved, will require more thorough preparation. If you intend travelling through remote areas, for example, you first should check that your vehicle is able to handle 'off road' conditions. The service department of your state motoring organisations (**see:** Motoring Organisations) will give advice and carry out a preliminary inspection of your vehicle.

Unless you are a capable mechanic and able to undertake the necessary servicing of your vehicle yourself, this preparation should be left in the hands of your garage. You will be particularly concerned to avoid breakdowns and to confirm the reliability of safety-related items, therefore your instructions (**see:** checklist below) will include a check of the fuel supply, electrics, brakes, tyres and certain ancillary equipment.

- **Fuel supply** Check fuel-pump for quantity and flow. Check carburettor for wear and potential blockages *or* check condition of electronic or mechanical fuel injection. When the tank is almost empty, remove the drain plug and drain the tank, to check that the remaining fuel is perfectly clean. Check fuel-supply lines for cracks and poor connections, and make sure no fuel line is exposed to damage by rocks or low-clearance projections.
- **Electrics** Check battery output and condition (including terminals), alternator/generator output and condition, spark plugs, condenser, coil, distributor and all terminals and cables. If the vehicle is fitted with electronic ignition, have it checked in the prescribed manner.

  Check all lights, not just to see that they work, but to make sure that they are likely to continue to work. It is very, very dark at night in outback Australia.
- **Brakes** Check wear of pads and/or linings and check discs for runout and drums for scoring. (Ask the mechanic

to clean off any brake dust also.) Check brake lines and hoses for cracks and wear. Make sure brake lines are not liable to be damaged by rocks or low projections. Check parking brake for adjustment and cable stretch.

- **Tyres** Check for uneven or excessive wear. Check walls for cracks and stone or kerb fractures. Check pressures. Include spare (or spares) in all checks.
- **Other items** Check windscreen-wiper blades for wear and proper contact and washers for direction and effectiveness. Include rear wiper and washer, where fitted.
- Check **windscreen glass** for cracks and replace if necessary.
- Check **seat mountings and adjustments.**
- Check all **lubricants levels** (including brake and clutch fluid) and either top up or drain and refill.
- Check **wheel bearings** for play and adjust or replace.
- Check **universal and constant velocity joints,** where appropriate, and replace if necessary.
- Check **dust and water sealing.** (A pre-run test in appropriate conditions will reveal any problems. What you do not need is dust, exhaust fumes or water inside the vehicle.)
- If you carry a **roof-rack**, check mounts and welds for weaknesses and cracks.
- Check all **seat-belts** for tears or sun-hardening. Replace if necessary.

Also check inertia reels.
- Check **radiator water level and condition.** Drain and flush, if necessary. Check radiator for leaks and radiator pressure cap for pressure release accuracy. Check water-pump operation. Check radiator and heater hoses for cracks and general condition, and replace if necessary. Check hose clamps.
- Check **fan-belt** for tension and fraying.
- Check anything else you might think is worthwhile.
- Do all this as near as possible to your departure date and *do not overlook anything* — lives may be at stake.

Packing the Car

Firstly, and most importantly, you should carry only those items that are absolutely necessary with you in the passenger compartment. In a sedan, this is not difficult. You have a boot, and that is where most items should be carried; but in a station sedan or wagon, it is much more difficult to isolate everything. This is important, because loose items in the passenger compartment get under your feet (fatal for the driver), interfere with your comfort and will become potentially dangerous projectiles in the event of a collision. So for your station-wagon, buy or rig up a 'safety net', which can be fitted at the back of the rear seat and separates you from the extraneous odds and sods that otherwise could harm you.

This rule applies also to food and drink.

Prior to departure, a thorough inspection of the vehicle is advisable

Empty bottles and cartons should be stowed out of the way in a small carry-bag for rubbish, until you are able to dispose of them.

And if you are short of space, cull some non-essential items.

In order to provide extra space, many drivers fix a **roof-rack** to their vehicle. This is not recommended. Laden roof-racks upset the balance of the vehicle by changing its centre of gravity, making it top-heavy. They disturb the air-flow, which can destabilise the vehicle, and they certainly increase fuel consumption by interfering with the aerodynamics. In some circumstances, they can snag on overhanging limbs of trees.

If you must use a roof-rack, carry as little on it as possible and keep the maximum loading height as low as you can. Protect the load by wrapping it in a tarpaulin or ground-sheet and, if possible, create a sharp (aerofoil) leading edge on the load to improve air-flow.

A better alternative to a roof-rack is a small, strong, lightweight **trailer,** but there are times when this will be a disadvantage also.

If you are towing a **caravan,** some items can be carried inside the van, on the floor, preferably strapped down and located over the axle/s. In some states, caravans must be fitted with a fire extinguisher. (And remember, no people or animals are to be transported in a towed caravan.)

Once your vehicle is loaded, and preferably with the passengers aboard (yes, even as you leave home on day one), check the **tyre pressures**. The additional load will mean higher pressures are needed. The tyre placard or owner's handbook can be used as a guideline, but in reality modern steel radials, fully laden, should be inflated to around 242 kilopascals (36 psi). (*This is not too high.*) The tyre will bag if it is under-inflated and destabilise the car. It also will offer a baggy sidewall to rocks and stones, and encourage wall fractures and potential blow-outs. Laden tyre pressure requirements vary with tyre size and design, but the pressure is important. If you are in any doubt, contact the tyre manufacturer and ask.

When to Set Off

There is evidence to suggest that people drive best during the hours in which they are accustomed to being awake, and probably at work. As drowsiness is deadly in drivers, this finding is worth noting. Leaving home, for example, at 1 a.m. might beat the traffic and the heat of the day to a large extent, but somewhere between 3 and 5 a.m. you may find yourself wanting to doze off again.

Touring by caravan: near Mossman, Qld

Plan to share long-distance driving as much as possible and depart around or just before sun-up and stop no later than sundown. Allow regular stops, not just to stretch your legs but to take nourishment as well. Food helps keep the energy levels up. You might care to leave later, if you are travelling east, to avoid the rising sun, and finish earlier if you are travelling west, for the converse reason.

Leaving Home

Everyone knows the feeling — which usually comes when you are a good distance from home: did I lock all the windows, turn off the electricity at the meter...? Usually all is well, but it never hurts to double-check everything before you leave.

CHECKLIST BEFORE DEPARTURE

- Cancel newspapers and mail deliveries.
- Make arrangements for the garden to be watered and the lawns mowed. Board out your indoor plants, or if this is not possible, place the pots in the sink, surround them with damp peat and water thoroughly. Encasing each in a sealed polythene bag also helps during summer months.
- If you have a pet, arrange for its safe keeping well in advance (**see:** Pets).
- Arrange for a neighbour to keep an eye on the house. Your local police will co-operate. Alternatively, consult a professional home security service (Yellow Pages).
- Valuable items, such as jewellery, are best left for safe keeping at your bank.
- Before leaving, turn the electricity off at the mains, but leave the fridge door open. Make sure that everything else that should be turned off is off.
- Check that all windows and doors are locked; then check again.
- Make sure you leave a contact address with a friend or neighbour.

BETTER DRIVING

The two most important ingredients in skilful driving are **concentration** and **smoothness.**

To facilitate the first, get comfortable and stay comfortable. Discomfort destroys concentration. Lack of concentration is the biggest single cause of road accidents.

Wear the right clothes: loose-fitting, cool or warm as appropriate, but capable of being changed (not while you are driving!) as temperatures change. Light-weight shoes are better than boots. (There are such things as driving shoes, which are excellent.) Wear good quality anti-glare sun-glasses. Sit comfortably: neither too close to the steering-wheel and cramped, nor too far back and stretching, and be sure you can reach the foot controls through the entire length of their movement. Drive with both hands all the time. No one can control a car properly with one hand. Driving gloves are recommended. Make all seat, belt and rear-view mirror adjustments before you drive off. (This is especially relevant if you share the driving with someone not your size.)

Concentration means *no distractions*. It is probably idealistic to suggest no conversation takes place while you are driving, but do not allow this to interfere with your concentration. And aim to keep the children quiet and amused (**see:** Child's Play)**. If an important issue needs to be resolved, first stop the car and then sort it out.**

Smoothness is vital for the vehicle's safe, effective operation, but unfortunately many people are not smooth drivers. A vehicle in motion is a tonne or so of iron, steel and plastic sitting atop a set of springs. It is inherently unstable and prone to influences such as pitch and roll. This is difficult enough to control in normal motion, but worse when the driver exaggerates these instabilities by stabbing at the brakes, jerking the steering-wheel and crashing the gears. Two things derive from being a smooth driver: the first is passenger comfort. On a long trip, everyone will arrive much fresher and more relaxed if the driver has provided a smooth and therefore pleasant journey. The second is increased safety. The vehicle will react better to smooth, controlled input than it will to hamfisted driving. Smooth driving could bring even further benefits: less wear and tear and lower fuel consumption.

However, to define better driving as a combination of concentration and smoothness only would not be wholly accurate.

There are other factors:
- **Know your vehicle.** Understand its capacities: to brake, especially in emergencies—some cars move around a lot; or become directionally unstable under harsh braking. Be aware of its usable power and its limitations. And drive well within the cornering and road-holding limits of the vehicle's suspension and tyre combination.
- **Drive defensively.** Assume all other drivers are asleep, inattentive or devoid of skill. It is remarkable how such an attitude will increase driving awareness.

- **Do not be impatient.** Pre-planning should have provided you with ample time for the day's journey.
- **Do not drive with an incapacitating illness or injury.** Something as simple as a bruised elbow might restrict rapid arm movement when you most need it.

Emergencies

Of course, the best way to handle emergencies is to avoid them. However, to suggest one problem or another will never occur is unrealistic. (A course in defensive driving is of advantage. **See:** Motoring Organisations.)

Take care when driving in bad weather conditions

IN CASE OF ACCIDENT

In all states of Australia, any accident in which someone is injured or killed *must* be reported to police at once, or within 24 hours. In Western Australia, any accident involving a car must be reported.

In any case, it is highly advisable to report to police any accident that involves substantial property damage. Police may or may not decide to attend the scene, but they at least will have your report on record, which may well be useful should there be legal proceedings or insurance claims.

When involved in an accident and if required by police, you *must* give your name and address and produce your driver's licence. If you do not have it with you, you may be liable to an on-the-spot fine. It is advisable also to obtain the insurance details of the other parties involved.

All parties involved in the accident should exchange names and addresses and insurance details.

Do not volunteer any other information. In particular, do not discuss the accident. Should court action result, you may find something said in the stress of the aftermath of the accident used against you. Above all, **do not admit you are at fault in any way,** even if you think you may be.

You are not obliged to make a statement to police. If you are disturbed and upset, it is better to wait until you can think clearly.

An accident that involves damage to persons or property should be reported to your insurance company as soon as possible.

See also: Accident Action.

The possibility of **skidding** worries most drivers, as well it should. There are a number of root causes of a skid, some of them composite. Essentially, skidding occurs when the tyres lose their grip on the road. The most common form is a front-wheel (or sometimes all-wheel) skid caused by over-braking. When the wheels stop rolling, the vehicle will no longer react to steering input. If you do not 'jump' on the brake pedal, then such a skid will not occur (i.e. 'smoothness' in driving). However, if it does, try, quickly, to ease just sufficient pressure off the brake pedal to allow the wheels to roll again and the steering will come back, which at least will allow you to take avoiding action, as well as slow down. A rear-wheel skid also may occur as a result of harsh braking, usually while turning at the same time (e.g. corner entry speed too high, braking too harsh). In slippery conditions, the tail of the car also may fish-tail because of excessive speed of entry into a corner or, in RWD vehicles, because too much power has been applied too soon, causing the rear tyres to break traction. A rear-wheel skid of any kind requires some reverse steering, often only briefly. It is not enough to say: turn the steering in the direction of the skid. By how much? Turn the steering wheels to point them in the direction you wish to travel and, at the same time, try to recognise what you did to cause the skid in the first place. If it was because of excessive acceleration, back off a little and re-apply the accelerator more gently. If it was because of excessive speed of entry into the corner and/or braking at the same time, ease the brakes and let your corrective steering realign the car and then, smoothly, increase the power again.

Skids can be complex and difficult to control. Over-correction is common, with the result that the vehicle swings into another skid in the opposite direction. Do not panic and be smooth in your reaction. Easy to say — not so easy to do.

Aquaplaning is a form of skidding where the tyres roll a layer of water up in front of the vehicle and then ride on to it, breaking contact with the adhesive road surface. What you sense is a sudden loss of driving 'feel'. Slow down, very smoothly, until the tyres come off the layer of water and then proceed more carefully. Watch out for deep puddles. They are the danger.

Driving in snow, ice and mud also produces adhesion problems. Once again, smooth, steady progress, while 'feeling' the vehicle and staying on top of its movements, is the only answer.

When planning a visit to the **snow,** your vehicle should be fitted with chains. If it is not and the car's back wheels begin to spin wildly on packed and rutted snow or ice:

- Stop the car.
- Look for and remove any obstructions under the car.
- Pack loose gravel, sticks or vegetation under the driving wheels.
- Remember that on a level surface, a gentle push sometimes will get the car going.
- Because it cannot be seen, ice can be more dangerous than snow.

When driving in **fog:**

- Switch on dipped headlights, or foglights if your car is fitted with them.
- Use front and back demisters.
- If visibility is reduced to such an extent that driving becomes an ordeal, pull as far off the road as you can and wait until you feel you are able to continue.

The above applies equally to driving either in the cities or the outback. The techniques are the same, only the conditions vary. (**See:** Outback Motoring for more detail on bush driving.)

POSITIONING

Positioning is vital on any road.
- Try to stagger the position of your car in the line of traffic so that you can see well ahead.

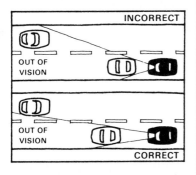

- When turning right on a two-lane highway, do not angle the car; keep it square to the other traffic so cars can pass on the left.

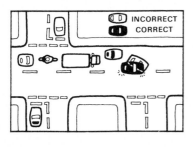

BASIC TRAFFIC LAWS

There are variations in road traffic laws from state to state throughout Australia. Some affect the traveller, some do not. Drivers are expected to know and observe those rules that apply to a vehicle's operation; however, specific state laws that affect the registration of vehicles, trailers or caravans for example are not enforced between states.

In Victoria until March 1993, the law regarding **right and lefthand turns** required that where opposing traffic was turning from one street into another, the vehicle turning left had to give way to the vehicle turning right. Take care until Victorian drivers become accustomed to this change which has brought Victoria in line with the other states.

The city of Melbourne, which is the last stronghold of the tram, has its unique **hook turn**, where at some inner-city intersections a vehicle making a righthand turn must move to the far left of the intersection and wait until the traffic clears and the traffic lights change before completing the turn. Overtaking on the right of a tram is forbidden and no vehicle may pass a stationary tram at a recognised tram stop.

Drink driving laws are extremely strict in all states and drivers can be pulled up at random and be required to take a blood alcohol test.

Speed regulations vary in each state. In some states, the use of **cameras** to 'catch' speeding drivers, both in the city and country, is widespread; as well, cameras are positioned at traffic lights on many intersections to 'record' drivers who do not stop at the red light.

In most other respects, the road traffic laws are essentially the same from state to state. However, legislation is subject to change and the cautious driver will check first with the relevant state motoring organisation (see: Motoring Organisations) before driving interstate for answers to any questions raised on specific regulations.

TOWING

Towing your accommodation behind you will provide the advantage of low-budget touring and flexibility as to stop-overs. However, it can be a disadvantage also, in that it may restrict access to some areas and locations. You can, however, use the caravan for most sections of your journey and park it on-site somewhere while you go off and explore the more difficult 4WD tracks.

If you are new to towing, the first thing you must do is to get expert advice on your **towing hitch** (see: Motoring Organisations). It is very important that **the rig** (i.e. car and caravan, boat or trailer) is balanced and the weight over the tow ball is not excessive. An adjust-able height hitch with spring bars is best.

Once you have decided on the hitch, and you have learned how to hook up and un-hook, you must learn to **reverse** the rig. Find a wide open area, an empty car-park for example, and practise. Get the feel of the rig and aim to be proficient before you depart.

On the road, remember to make allowances for the added overall length and give yourself extra space turning and extra distance for overtaking. The added weight obviously will affect the towing vehicle's performance in acceleration and braking.

In most states, there are **speed limits** on articulated vehicles and you should know what they are and abide by them (**see**: Basic Traffic Laws). High-speed towing of vans and trailers can cause major difficulties, magnifying driving problems substantially.

Cross-winds can be a problem when towing a caravan, the van's slab sides acting like sails. The combination of high speed and cross-winds can cause **'trailer-sway'**, a dangerous characteristic that dramatically destabilises both towing vehicle and caravan. You probably will feel it happening before you see it, but the rear-view mirrors will confirm it very effectively indeed. Should the trailer begin to move about, ease back on your speed, braking if necessary, but very gently. Harsh or sudden braking will compound the problem. When the caravan stabilises, resume speed, perhaps less rapidly, if you are continuing in a cross-wind area.

Fit good quality towing mirrors on your vehicle. It is very important that your rear view down both sides of the trailer or caravan is not obscured.

If, because of the relative slowness of your progress, you find a line of vehicles banking up behind you, be courteous and pull over when and where you can, to allow the bank-up of vehicles to overtake.

The carrying of goods and equipment in a caravan has been mentioned, but it is worth repeating that if you do, locate such items as much as possible over and just to the front of the caravan axle/s, never behind, which will lift the front of the caravan and the tow ball.

Before setting off and every day of the trip, whatever the vehicle, always **check and double check that the hitch is secure,** that the **safety chains are correctly fitted** and that the **electrical connections are working,** so that indicator lights function at the rear of the towed vehicle.

Finally, when towing remember to allow extra time for each day's travel, and remain alert.

CHECKLIST

When towing anything:
- Check the hitch for security. The law in most states demands that tow bars are fitted with safety chains.
- Check that the tail and stop lights, marker lights and signal lights are working.
- Remember to check the air in the caravan or trailer tyres.
- If towing a boat, check the lashings.
- Check that caravan doors, windows and roof vents are closed before departure.
- If the caravan or trailer is fitted with separate brakes, check these as soon as you start to move.

On the Stuart Highway near Elliott, NT

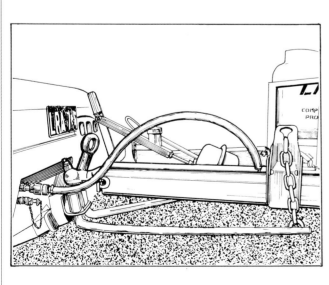

Make sure all parts of the hitch are connected properly, including safety chains, brakes and electrical connections.

NATURAL HAZARDS

Flood
In some remote areas, floods can occur without warning. Do not camp in dry river beds or close to the edges of creeks or streams. Always exercise extreme caution when approaching flooded roads or bridges. Floodwaters are deceptive; always check the depth before attempting to cross. If you do find yourself stranded in deep water:
- Do not panic.
- Wind up all the windows, to slow down or prevent water entering. (You should have closed all the windows before you tried to cross.)
- When the car has stabilised, undo the seatbelts.
- Turn the headlights on to help rescuers locate the car.
- If the car does not sink, but drifts (which is often the case with a well-sealed car), wait until it reaches shallow water or is close to the bank, then open the door or windows and climb out.
- Form a human chain and help children to keep their heads above water.
- If the car is sinking, it will be necessary to wait for the water pressure to equalise before you can open the doors or windows. As a last resort, kick out the windscreen or rear window.

Bushfire
If you have to travel on days of critical fire danger (i.e. total fire ban days), make sure you carry some woollen blankets and a filled water container. If you are trapped as a bushfire approaches:
- Do not panic.
- Stop the car in the nearest cleared area.
- Wind up all the windows.
- Turn on the hazard lights to warn any other traffic.
- DO NOT GET OUT OF YOUR CAR. The temperature may become unbearably hot, but it is still safer to stay in the car.
- Lay on the car floor, below window level, to avoid radiant heat.
- Cover yourself and your passengers with blankets.
- The car will not explode, or catch on fire, and a fast-moving wildfire will pass quickly overhead.

ANIMAL HAZARDS

Although some species of Australia's unique wildlife are immensely appealing, some species are extremely dangerous.

Marine life
Box jellyfish (or sea wasps) are found in the coastal waters of Queensland and northern Australia in the summer months (end November – end April). A sting from their many long tentacles can be lethal, and for that reason swimming on coastal beaches north of Rockhampton is prohibited at this time. Also, walking barefoot at the water's edge in this region in summer is not advisable.

Among Australia's several species of poisonous stinging fish, the **stonefish**, found all around the northern coastline, is best avoided.

The small **blue-ringed octopus** is common in Australian coastal waters. Its bite can paralyse in 15 minutes. Do not handle in any circumstances.

Sharks are common in Australian waters. Avoid swimming in deep water and do not swim where sharks have been seen.

Freshwater and saltwater crocodiles are found in north and northwestern Australia. Both species can be dangerous, particularly the saltwater crocodile, which may be found in both salt water and fresh water. Heed local warning signs and do not swim or paddle in natural waterways or allow children or animals near the water's edge.

Snakes
Snakes are timid and generally do not attack unless threatened. However, several species are highly venomous.

Spiders
The bite from both the funnel-web and red-back spider can be deadly. The funnel-web is found in and around Sydney. The red-back is widespread.

Insects
Wasps, bees, ticks, ants (particularly the bull-ant), scorpions and centipedes are found throughout Australia. Their sting or bite normally is not harmful, except to those people who are allergy prone.

Study Australia's wildlife and learn to identify dangerous species. Remember also that some plant species are poisonous. When visiting a new area, check with local authorities to ascertain which dangerous species, if any, are found there.

OUTBACK MOTORING

Australia is a vast country and all areas are worth visiting. The most remote areas are spectacularly beautiful and unspoiled. Australia's very size and remoteness, however, inhibits many people from exploring it. Nevertheless, properly set up and equipped, and armed with common sense and a little background knowledge, there is no reason why every intending traveller should not take the opportunity to explore the country's huge open spaces.

If you intend to undertake a trip into the outback, planning ahead will be even more important than it is for a holiday in more populated regions. It is worth remembering that it is possible to travel in some sections of the Australian outback and not see another vehicle or person for two or three days. (The Canning Stock Route is a good example.)

It is possible to travel in some areas of the outback in a 2WD vehicle, but it is safer and much more practical to do so in a 4WD vehicle suited to off-road conditions (**see:** Checking the Car).

Your vehicle should be fitted with **air-conditioning,** not only to counteract very high inland daytime temperatures but also to make it possible to drive with all the windows closed through what might be kilometre after kilometre of dust.

You should be able to carry out, at the very least, **small running repairs** and for this reason, you must carry a workshop manual for the vehicle and some tools and appropriate spare parts (**see:** Tools and Spare Parts).

Outback **driving conditions** vary greatly according to location and the time of year. The deserts are usually dry; but after rain, conditions will be totally different. The tropics are only accessible in the 'dry' season, and even then there are usually streams to ford and, often, washaways to contend with. It is always tough, but it is equally rewarding.

Pre-reading **road conditions** is vital. Learning to recognise that a patch of different colour may represent a dramatic change in surface is an example. Sand often gives way to rock; rock may lead to mud; hard surfaces become soft bulldust with little warning.

Soft **sand, bulldust and mud** are best negotiated at the highest reasonable speed and in the highest possible gear *and* in 4WD. However, it pays to stop and examine the road surface first. Do not enter deep mud or mud covered with

SHARING THE OUTBACK

As you travel through the outback, **remember:** You are sharing the land with its traditional Aboriginal owners, pastoralists, other tourists—even nature itself—so in order to protect and preserve the outback for future visitors:

- Respect Aboriginal sacred and cultural sites, heritage buildings and pioneer relics.
- Protect native flora and fauna: take photographs not specimens.
- Follow restrictions on the use of firearms and shooting, which protect wildlife and stock.
- Carry your own fuel source (e.g. portable gas stove), to avoid lighting fires in fire-sensitive areas.
- When lighting a campfire (if you must), keep it small and use any fallen wood sparingly. Never leave a fire unattended and extinguish completely, covering the remains.
- Do not camp immediately near to water sources (e.g. on riverbanks or by dams). Allow access for stock and native animals.
- Do not bury your rubbish: carry out everything you take in.
- Dispose of faecal waste by burial.
- Leave gates as you find them: open or shut.
- Do not ignore signs warning of dangers or entry restrictions. These have been erected for your protection.

OUTBACK ADVICE SERVICE

The Royal Flying Doctor Service of Australia offers a service to tourists who plan to tour the outback. RFDS bases and Visitors Centres provide advice on outback touring and on proper emergency procedures. Bases at Broken Hill (NSW), Charleville (Qld) and Jandakot (WA) also hire out transceiver sets, with a fixed emergency call button in case of accident or sickness, at a very reasonable cost. Those bases, that do not hire out sets, can suggest local outlets for them.

NSW
***Broken Hill:** Airport, Broken Hill 2880; (080) 88 0777
SA
***Port Augusta:** 4 Vincent St, Port Augusta 5700; (086) 42 2044
WA
Carnarvon: 29 Douglas St, Carnarvon 6701; (099) 41 1758
***Derby:** Clarendon St, Derby 6728; (091) 91 1211
***Jandakot:** 3 Eagle Dr, Jandakot Airport 6164; (09) 332 7733
***Kalgoorlie:** 46 Picadilly St,

Kalgoorlie 6430; (090) 21 2211
Meekatharra: Main St, Meekatharra 6642; (099) 81 1107
Port Hedland: The Esplanade, Port Hedland 6721; (091) 73 1386
NT
***Alice Springs:** Stuart Tce, Alice Springs 0870; (089) 52 1033
Qld
***Cairns:** 1 Junction St, Cairns 4870; (070) 53 1952
***Charleville:** Old Cunnamulla Rd, Charleville 4470; (076) 54 1233
***Mount Isa:** Barkly Highway, Mount Isa 4825; (077) 43 2800
Tas.
Launceston: 9 Adelaide St, Launceston 7250; (003) 31 2121

For general information regarding the services offered by the RFDS, contact: The Australian Council of the Royal Flying Doctor Service of Australia, PO Box 345, Hurstville NSW 2220; (02) 241 2411.

*These bases have Visitors Centres; check opening times.

DIRECTION FINDING

If you cannot read a map or use a compass — or if you do not have one or the other with you — it is vital to have some means of orientating yourself if you are lost.

A simple method of finding north is to use a conventional wrist-watch.

Place the 12 on the watch in line with the sun and bisect the angle between it and the hour-hand. This will give a fairly accurate indication of north.

At night, the Southern Cross can be used to determine south.

When exploring a side track off the main road, make a rough sketch of the route you are following, noting all turn-offs, and distances between them, on the speedometer, together with any prominent landmarks. Reconcile your return route with the sketch, point by point.

water without first establishing the depth of either or both.

Deep **sand** will require low tyre pressures. Carry a tyre pressure gauge in the glove compartment and drop pressures to about 10 psi. You will need to reinflate as soon as possible once on gravel or bitumen roads again, because the soft tyres will perform very badly and may blow out as a result of stone fractures on hard surfaces.

When **crossing a creek or stream,** stop and check the track across first for clear passage and water depth. If the water is deep enough to make a bow wave across the bonnet or radiator, cover the front of the vehicle with a plastic or canvas tarpaulin and remove the fan-belt to stop water being sprayed over the engine electrics. Once you have determined that passage is possible, drive through in low range, second gear or high range, first gear and clear the opposite embankment before stopping again. If it has recently rained, or is still raining, beware of flash flooding.

HOW TO OBTAIN WATER

Less than 24 hours without water can be fatal in outback heat.

It is essential to conserve body moisture. Take advantage of any shade that can be found.

Do not leave your vehicle. It may be the only effective shade available.

Ration your drinking water. **Do not drink radiator coolant.**

Although a river or creek bed may be dry, there is often an underground source of water. A hole dug about a metre deep may produce a useful soak.

Where there is vegetation, it is possible to extract water from it using an **'Arizona still'**.

- Dig a hole about one metre across and a little more than half as deep. Put a vessel of some kind in the hole's centre to collect the water.
- Surround the vessel with cut vegetation. (Fleshy plants, such as succulents, will hold more moisture that drier saltbush.)
- Cover the hole with a plastic sheet held down by closely packed rocks, so that the hole is sealed off. Put a small stone in the centre of the sheet, directly above the collection vessel.

The sun's heat will evaporate moisture from the plants. This moisture will condense on the inside of the plastic, run down the cone formed by the weight of the stone and drip off into the vessel.

In uninterrupted sunlight, with suitable plants, about one litre of water should be collected about every six hours.

The still takes about three hours to start producing and it will become less efficient as the ground moisture dries out. A new hole will need to be dug at intervals.

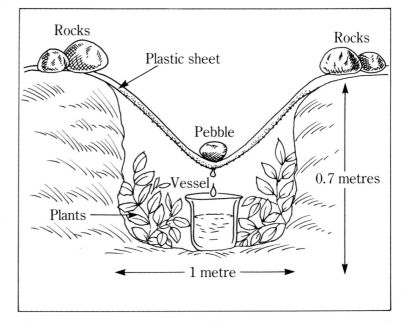

CRITICAL RULES FOR OUTBACK MOTORING

- Check intended routes carefully.
- Check the optimum time of year to travel.
- Check that your vehicle is suited to the conditions.
- Check your load; keep it to a minimum.
- Check ahead for local road conditions, weather forecasts and fuel availability.
- Check that you have advised someone of your route, destination and arrival time, particularly if you intend travelling off the main roads.
- Check that you have essential supplies: water, food, fuel, spare parts, detailed maps; carry one week's extra supply of food and water in case of emergency.
- **Always remain with your vehicle if it breaks down.**

WARNING: WHEN DRIVING ON DESERT ROADS
- There is no water, except after rains.
- Unmade roads can be extremely hazardous, especially when wet.
- Traffic is almost non-existent, except on main roads.

Dips are common on outback roads and can break suspension components if you enter too fast. The technique for crossing a dip is to: brake on entry, to drop the vehicle's nose, and hold the brake on until momentarily before the bottom of the depression. Then accelerate again, to lift the nose, and therefore the suspension, as you exit. This will prevent the springs from bottoming out and give maximum clearance.

Cattle-grids are another potential hazard. They are often neglected, with broken approaches and exits. If a grid appears to be in disrepair, stop and take a look first, before attempting to cross.

Road-trains operate in many parts of outback Australia. These long, multi-trailered trucks are very difficult and sometimes dangerous to overtake. On dusty roads, they will produce a dust-cloud impossible to see through and, therefore, it is equally im-

possible for their drivers to see you. Wait for an opprtunity to get the front of your vehicle out to a position where the road-truck driver can see you in the rear-view mirror, but even then do not try to overtake until he has signalled that he knows you are there. Usually, he will slow down for you to overtake him.

Sometimes it is prudent to stop and take a break, rather than try to overtake a road-train.

If you meet an oncoming road-train, pull over and stop until it has passed.

Animals present hazards on outback roads, particularly the larger variety. In the outback, there are vast areas of unfenced property where stock roams free. A bullock or a large kangaroo can do considerable damage to your vehicle. Be especially wary around sunrise and sunset when animals are more active. A bull-bar or roo-bar gives limited protection. They are effective only at low speeds, especially against larger animals.

Despite the spacious loneliness of the outback, driver concentration levels should be maintained at as high a level as in city peak hours.

Surviving in the Outback

Possibly the only reason why you might find yourself stranded in a remote area is either a major mechanical breakdown or if your vehicle becomes hopelessly bogged. Should either occur, you should be properly equipped to be able to wait where you are until you are found.

Always carry a week's supply of spare water with you. The minimum is 20 litres per head. **Do not use this for any other reason than an emergency.**

Iron rations consisting of dry biscuits and some canned food will keep hunger at bay, but body evaporation and consequent thirst is the vital factor. Do not drink radiator coolant. Often it is not water but a chemical compound, and even if it is water, usually it has been treated with chemicals.

Do not try to walk out of a remote area. You are going to survive only if you wait by the car. And you are much more likely to be found if someone knows where you are. Before entering a remote area, check the route first with police or a local authority at the point of departure, and tell them where and when you are going and when you expect to arrive. When you reach your destination, telephone and advise of your arrival.

If you are stranded and you have no choice but to wait where you are, set up some type of shelter such as a tarpaulin and, in the heat of the day, remain in its shade as motionless as possible. Movement accelerates fluid loss. (**See also:** How to Obtain Water.)

CARRYING A CAMERA

If you are making a 'once in a lifetime' trip, you probably will want to preserve the highlights on film, so it is wise to check a few points before setting out.

- If you have recently purchased or hired a camera, take one 'test' film so that you know how the equipment reacts to different light conditions.
- As weather conditions may vary on your trip, it is a good idea to carry film with a range of different speeds. If you are not an expert, talk to your local dealer about the varieties of film available.
- Before you leave, ensure that you have a good supply of film, batteries, a lens brush, a flash holder and spare bulbs. Other useful accessories are a close-up lens, exposure meter, lens hood and filters.
- To safeguard your equipment from damage by water, heat, sand and dust, protect it in a camera bag. It can get very hot in a closed car, so always keep the camera in the shade. The best place is on the floor, on the opposite side to the exhaust pipe. Make sure, however, that the bag is secured.
- High temperatures and humidity can damage colour film. Store your film in the coolest spot available and do not break the watertight vapour seal until just before use. Once the film is used, remove it from the camera and send it for processing as soon as possible.
- Even with automatic exposure, when filming in hot conditions it probably will be necessary to allow one stop or one-half of a stop down to compensate for the brilliance of light. If in doubt, consult the instruction sheet included with the film.
- Personal property insurance covers the loss of cameras and photographic equipment while travelling (**see:** Insurance).

QUARANTINE REGULATIONS

Throughout Australia, state quarantine regulations prohibit the transport by travellers of certain plants and foods, and even soil, across state borders. Further information is available from offices of agricultural departments in all states.

BREAKDOWNS

There are many causes of breakdowns that can be cured by the amateur 'street-wise' mechanic; there are others that require both mechanical expertise and the right tools and, perhaps, location; and there are those that can be repaired only in the workshop. The advice that follows applies to the former and it is essentially basic.

Proper **vehicle preparation and maintenance** should prevent the possibility of roadside breakdowns and, on long journeys, the regular vehicle service schedule should be maintained.

In areas where you have access to service through a motoring organisation, do not attempt to carry out roadside repairs yourself, unless you are fully equipped (with tools, parts and knowledge) to do so. (Remember to carry your membership card, which entitles you to assistance in other states. **See:** Motoring Organisations.)

If you are driving a **rental car**, most rental companies list their recognised repair organisations in the manual supplied. (You should check that these details are provided when collecting the car.) If you find that the rental vehicle cannot be repaired immediately, you

Bulldust, a hazard of outback driving

should request an exchange vehicle.

If you plan to journey into remote areas, it is a good idea to first take a basic course in vehicle maintenance (**see:** Car Maintenance Courses). As well, you should carry a range of tools and spares (**see:** Tools and Spare Parts).

Many modern cars are fitted with electronic engine management systems, or with electronic ignition and fuel injection. Generally, these are more reliable than older systems and often, in case of partial failure of the system, they have a 'limp home' mode, which enables travelling a limited distance at limited speed. However, total failure of such a system is difficult, perhaps impossible, to remedy at the roadside without expert knowledge and equipment. It may seem extreme, but in such a vehicle, travel into genuinely remote areas is rendered much safer by the installation or hire of an appropriate long-range radio — the reasons are obvious.(See: Outback Advice Service.)

For those who drive earlier-model vehicles with less complex electrics and fuel systems, the trouble-shooting flow-charts are designed to be of assistance. But first, always remember to:

TROUBLE SHOOTING

ENGINE WILL NOT TURN OVER	If flat . . .	If battery OK . . .
Check battery for charge.	recharge or replace, or tow-start (if manual transmission vehicle) until next service opportunity. (If automatic, check handbook. Most autos cannot be tow- or clutch-started.)	check if battery terminals and straps are loose, broken or dirty. If so, clean, repair or replace.

- **Watch warning gauges:** These have been installed to serve as a warning that things *may* be going wrong. A flickering battery warning light will suggest all is not well with the generator/ alternator charge rate and should be attended to. A fluctuating temperature gauge *may* suggest the onset of a problem with the cooling system. And so on.
- **Make a daily check** of levels of fuel, water and oil (including that in spare containers). Also check fan-belt tension and condition.
- **Strange sounds:** If the vehicle develops an unexplained sound, move to the side of the road as soon as possible. Park on flat ground, if you can; you may have to spend some time under the bonnet, so look for shade or shelter from sun and rain. A loud, 'serious' sound usually indicates a major problem. Try to locate the source of the sound. If it is coming from the engine, do nothing and seek help.

When the Engine Stops

When the engine either splutters to a stop, constantly misfires or stops suddenly but was otherwise running smoothly, the problem is probably in one of two areas: fuel supply or electrics. Read the flow-charts before unpacking your tool-kit, to establish where the problem lies. If the problem is within the drive-train—gearbox, drive-shaft or differential—once again, seek help.

TOOLS AND SPARE PARTS

Travelling in remote areas requires that someone in the vehicle knows, at least, the basics of breakdown repairs (**see**: Breakdowns). This in turn means carrying emergency tools and spare parts, and spare fuel. The following is a guide:

Tools
- Set of screwdrivers
- Small set of sockets
- Set of open-end/ring combination spanners
- Small ball pein (engineer's) hammer
- Pliers
- Small and medium adjustable wrenches
- Hand drill and bits
- Workshop scissors
- Wire-cutters
- Tyre-pressure gauge
- Wheel brace
- Jack with supplementary wide base for soft sand or mud
- Battery-operated soldering-iron
- Jumper leads
- Small backpackers shovel
- Pair of vice grips
- Small bolt-cutters
- Good quality tow-rope

- Heavy duty torch (and spare batteries)

Spare Parts
- Epoxy resin bonding 'goo'
- Plastic insulating tape
- Roll of cloth adhesive tape
- 1 metre fuel line (reinforced plastic)
- Spare electrical connections (range)
- Spare hose-clips (range)
- Distributor cap
- Set of high tension leads
- Condenser (where appropriate)
- Rotor
- Set of spark plugs
- Set of points
- Coil
- Spare fuel filters (replace daily in areas of constant dust)
- Fuel pump kit
- Water pump kit
- Set of assorted nuts, bolts, washers, split pins
- At least one spare tyre, mounted, in good condition and over-inflated (to allow for some air loss)

Fuel
- Spare fuel (40 litres minimum) in steel jerry cans. (Do *not* use plastic containers; some plastics 'react' with fuel.) Check fuel range and distance between re-fuelling points.

If terminals OK . . .

check for jammed starter motor. For manual vehicle, put in top gear and rock back and forth to try to free pinion. An indication that starter may be jammed is an audible click when you try to start the engine and it will not turn over. With an automatic vehicle, try to turn engine back and forth with a spanner on crankshaft pulley to free pinion. Put gearbox into 'N' first.

If the starter motor is free . . .

it is possible a solenoid has failed. Unless you are an auto electrician *and* carry a spare, seek help.

STARTER MOTOR WHIRRS BUT WILL NOT TURN ENGINE

Very likely, you have stripped a starter ring-gear, which means major repair work. But check to see that the starter motor is fully bolted to its mounting bracket, and tighten if not.

ENGINE TURNS OVER BUT WILL NOT FIRE, OR FIRES BUT WILL NOT RUN CLEANLY, OR MIS-FIRES REGULARLY, OR RUNS AND STOPS

Problem may be electrics or fuel supply. If unsure, begin with **electrics**.

Electrics

1 Check that spark is getting to spark plugs. Remove high tension (HT) lead from No. 1 plug and remove No. 1 plug. Reattach HT lead to plug and hold plug body with pliers 1 mm from cylinder-head bolt or similar and turn engine over. Plug should produce strong blue spark at regular intervals.

2 If not . . .

the simplest and fastest way to deal with an electrical problem is to replace parts, either at once or progressively, with spares (**see:** Tools and Spare Parts). Replace coil and all HT leads and try engine. If problem persists, remove distributor cap and replace condenser and points. Re-set points and fit new rotor and distributor cap. Engine should start and run cleanly.

2 If accelerator and choke cables are operating correctly . . .

do not replace air cleaner; remove fuel line to carburettor and turn engine over. Fuel should flow freely. If so, check it is not contaminated by pumping small amount into clear glass or plastic container and examine for water and/or dirt.

3 If water or dirt are apparent . . .

check and replace fuel filter and remove and check fuel pump. Examine glass for contamination. If none or very little, replace fuel line to carburettor and try engine again.

OVERHEATING IN A WATER-COOLED ENGINE
(Occurs when coolant level falls or circulation is interrupted. Dash gauge gives warning, but vehicle also will lose power.)

1 Stop vehicle. DO NOT REMOVE RADIATOR CAP. Check hoses and hose connections for signs of leakage — steam if system is boiling. Any identified leak can be cured temporarily with spare hoses or binding with cloth tape.

2 If no sign of leakage . . .

After about 10 minutes and holding radiator cap with a thick cloth, slowly remove cap, letting out steam under pressure at same time. Top up radiator and fill with engine running and car's heater on hot setting. Do not add cold water until engine is running and then mix cold with hot water.

3 If you carry no spare parts, you can still confirm electrics as the problem by a process of elimination. If there is no spark at the spark plugs, the problem has to be between battery and plug. Check that low tension lead at side of distributor is connected properly and tightly mounted. If so, remove distributor cap and check for cracks. If there is a crack, repair with an epoxy glue/filler until it can be replaced. Check that condenser is tightly mounted and its LT wire is connected. Check that points open and close properly by turning engine over by hand slowly and watching for a spark between points. Points may be burned or deeply pitted. If so, remove points and use nail-file to clean up faces, then replace and re-set. If, however, you have established an electrical problem and you have no spares, seek assistance.

4 If you have a spark at the plugs, most likely you have a fuel-supply problem.

Fuel supply

Check fuel tank for fuel, despite gauge reading. (It may be faulty.)

1 If fuel OK . . .

Check accelerator cable connection and for free operation *and* check choke cable and operation. For vehicle with automatic choke, remove air-cleaner carrier and element and look down choke tube. If choke butterfly is not fully open, open it and check to see if it stays open. If it closes again, engine is flooding, and may not run for that reason. A faulty auto choke cannot be repaired at the roadside.

4 If there is substantial contamination . . .

it may be coming from fuel tank. Tank will need to be drained and perhaps flushed. Drained fuel should be saved and strained back. If you are travelling a long way before next fuel stop, be careful not to waste fuel.

5 If no fuel at fuel line and no apparent blockage . . .

fuel pump has failed for some reason. If you are carrying a spare, replace pump. If not, seek assistance.

6 If fuel is clean and running freely . . .

blockage may be inside carburettor. Carefully remove top and then main jet and float. Clear main jet and clean out float bowl. Be careful not to interfere with float level. Replace parts and try engine again.

3 Check again for leaks.

4 If there is a slow drip from radiator core itself . . .

fix with an internal chemical sealant or externally with an epoxy filler or adhesive.

5 If no leak is apparent . . .

check fanbelt for tension. It may be slipping and not driving water pump. If so, tighten by releasing bolts on generator/alternator and increasing tension and re-tightening.

6 If you cannot account for overheating by any of the preceding, you may have a failed water-pump, a blocked system, a failed pressure cap or a combination of all three. Seek help as soon as possible, but you may drive on if you can continue topping up.

CHILD'S PLAY

Everyone in the family looks forward to a holiday, but most parents dread a long car trip, when children travelling in the back seat can become bored and irritable passengers.

Most children are good travellers, but there are some car journeys that are inappropriate for small children (say, under the age of 10). Usually, though, children will consider every trip as an adventure, looking forward to it for weeks ahead. A little thought and planning by parents will avoid the boredom of a long drive and ease the strain on all concerned, and particularly the driver, who needs to be able to apply total concentration.

Dos and Donts

Several days before setting out, make a list of 'dos' and 'donts' for the children and explain, seriously, why their co-operation is necessary. Make it quite clear that you expect them to observe the rules because they are safety measures, and reinforce this message at the time of departure. For example:

- DO NOT fight or yell loudly while the car is in motion. This distracts the driver and can cause a collision or a bad incident, which might bring the holiday to an abrupt end.
- DO NOT play with door handles or locks. (Set the child-proof locks on rear doors before departure.)
- DO keep head, arms and hands inside the car. DO NOT lean out of the windows, ever.
- DO NOT unbuckle seat-belts or restraints while the car is in motion.

Handy Hints

- Any long car trip, even with frequent stops, can be tiring. Make sure the children are as cool and comfortable as possible. Curtains (or substitutes, e.g. a towel) or sun screens on rear windows are advisable. Babies and pre-school children may need their security blankets or favourite soft toy. These items can save the day if the children are upset or sleepy.
- Pack a small bag — a cosmetic bag is ideal — with packets of moist towelettes or a damp face-cloth.
- Make sure your first-aid kit contains some junior aspirin or a similar dosage, and also supplies of any other medication taken by the children. It is wise to carry some insect repellent and sunblock or suntan lotion, since children

tend to get bitten and sunburnt easily. Also bring a mosquito net to cover your baby's basinet when you are outdoors.
- Make up a 'busy box' for the children to take on the trip. Use a small box — a shoe box is best — and keep it on the back seat where the children can reach it easily. Fill the box with small notepads, crayons or felt-tipped pens (pencils break and need to be sharpened) and activity books. Choose activity books for each child's age group. Do not forget to include your children's favourite story-books.
- If your car does not have a radio, take along a transistor. If it has a cassette deck, include some tapes of stories and children's songs for 'quiet times'. Music soothes and lulls children to sleep.
- Although your main concern will be to keep the children happy and occupied during the car trip, it is also important to take along some games, such as snakes and ladders or Monopoly, or a pack of cards, to keep them amused in the motel in the evenings and on rainy days. Encourage older children to keep a diary. A rubber ball and skipping-rope will be welcomed by young children who like to play outdoors.
- If you have room, breakfast trays can be used as book supports for colouring-in or drawing. If not, a clipboard will serve as well.
- When travelling with young children, make sure that you stop the car every hour or so, so they can stretch their legs and let off steam. Try to stop at a park or an area with some play equipment. If it is raining, stop at a newsagent or bookshop where the children can browse and perhaps buy something to read.
- If children complain of feeling sick, stop the car as soon as possible and let them out for some fresh air. Sit with them for a while and persuade them to take a sip of water before continuing the trip.
- When approaching a rest area or a small town, ask the children if they want to go to the toilet. Do not delay until they get desperate and cannot wait.
- Even though you plan to stop for meals and snacks on your journey, you should still pack some food and drink. Children become very hungry and thirsty when travelling and it is important that they eat little but often. Pack small snacks in their own lunch-boxes. Avoid

chocolate, which is messy and tends to make children feel sick. Good for snacks are sultanas, nuts (for older children only), bananas, seedless grapes, cheese cubes, celery and carrot sticks, boiled sweets. Potato chips make a mess and encourage thirst. Avoid greasy foods. For lunches, pack easy-to-eat meals like chicken drumsticks or bite-size rolled-up pieces of cold meat with buttered bread on the side. Children can find large sandwiches difficult to handle, so remember to cut their sandwiches into small squares. Sandwich fillings require some thought: avoid anything moist or runny.
- Avoid flasks and cups for children's drinks. Purchase milk or fruit juice in small cartons and make sure you have a good supply of drinking straws. If you use a flask, take training cups for younger children and use paper or styrofoam cups with tight-fitting lids and straws for the older ones. Further supplies can be purchased at milk bars and take-away food places.
- Do not forget to pack a supply of small plastic garbage bags for waste paper and empty drink cartons.
- When eating out, choose those places that have fast service, or have meals sent to your room.

Games

To while away the long hours you will spend in the car with your children, here are some games for them to play.

For younger children

Colour contest: Each child selects one colour, then tries to spot cars of that colour. The first with ten cars wins.

Spot the mistake in the story: Either you or an older child tells a story with obvious mistakes. For example, 'Once upon a time, there was a boy called Goldilocks, and he visited the house of the seven dwarfs.'

Scavenger: Make a list of 10 things you are likely to come across during your trip, e.g. farmhouse, bus stop, cow, lamb, chemist shop, man with a hat. Ask the children to spot them, one at a time. Older children cross the objects off the list as they are seen.

Alphabet game: Select a letter and ask the children to spot as many things as possible beginning with that particular initial.

For older children

Rhyme stories: One child starts a story, and the next has to take up the story with a line that rhymes. The second child also continues the story with a line of new rhyme. For example:

1st child: 'I know a man called Sam.'
2nd child: 'He loves to eat ham.
 The more he eats the more he wants.'

Cliff-hangers: One child begins a story and stops at the most exciting part, leaving the next child to continue.

I packed my bag . . .(a good memory game): Each player has to name one object he or she puts into a bag. As each child takes a turn, he or she lists all the objects in order and adds a new item to the list. For example:

1st child: 'I packed my bag and put an apple in it.'
2nd child: 'I packed my bag and put an apple and a comb in it.'
3rd child: 'I packed my bag and put an apple, a comb and a key in it.'

What am I? This is an old favourite. One player thinks of an object or an animal and keeps it secret. The others take turns to ask questions, which must be answered only by 'Yes' or 'No', for clues to the player's identity.

Number-plate messages: Take the letters of a number plate on a nearby car and ask the children to make up a message from them. For example:
WFL: What's for lunch?
EYH: Eat your hat.

Navigation: Older children enjoy this game very much. All you need is a spare road-map covering the route you are taking. The children can follow your progress with a coloured marker.

The following games take only a few minutes to prepare:

Word scramble: Prepare a list of words with jumbled-up letters and get the children to unscramble them.

Crossword: Draw crossword squares on several notepads. During the trip, play the crossword game by calling out letters at random. The children write the letters in any square they wish and try to make up words.

SAFE BOATING

- Tell someone where you are going.
- Carry adequate equipment.
- Carry effective life jackets.
- Carry enough fuel and water.
- Ensure engine reliability.
- Guard against fire.
- Do not overload the craft.
- Know the boating rules and local regulations; also distress signals.
- Watch the weather.
- Do not drink alcohol while boating.

SAFE SKIING

Skiing is fun, but like any other sport, there is the risk of injury. It is also a strenuous sport. Avoid overdoing it when you go on the slopes. All ski resorts have instructors if you need to take lessons. Choose slopes that suit your ability. Wear clothing suited to the conditions. Check equipment before setting out. Avoid skiing alone. If you must, then tell someone where you are going. If lost, stay where you are or retrace your tracks. **Cross-country skiing** requires careful planning. Tell someone in authority of your intended route; travel in a group; take plenty of food and adequate equipment for your survival; protect yourself against sunburn; and watch the weather. Be alert for signs of exposure (hypothermia) — tiredness, reluctance to carry on, clumsiness, loss of judgement and collapse.

SAFE SWIMMING AND SURFING

- Swim or surf only at those beaches patrolled by lifesavers.
- Swim or surf within the safe swimming area indicated by the red and yellow flags.
- An amber flag indicates the surf is dangerous.
- A red flag and sign 'Danger — closed to bathing' indicates the beach is unsafe. Do not swim or surf in this area.
- Do not enter the water directly after a meal or under the influence of alcohol.
- If you are caught in a rip or strong current, swim diagonally across it. If you tire or cannot avoid the current, do not panic. Straighten and raise one arm as a distress signal and float until help arrives.
- If seized with a cramp, keep the affected part perfectly still, raise one arm as before and float until help arrives.

Red and yellow flags indicate safe swimming area

NEW SOUTH WALES

Founding State

In 1770 Captain Cook took possession for the British of all Australian territories east of the 135th meridian of east longitude and named them New South Wales. Today the founding state has shrunk somewhat and occupies just ten per cent of the continent. It is a state of contrasts, covering an area of 801 428 square kilometres, with extremes of country ranging from subtropical to alpine.

The state's capital, Sydney, is Australia's largest city. Established as the site of a penal colony in 1788, the settlement at Sydney Cove was developed under the guiding hand of Governor Arthur Phillip. Following his departure in 1792, however, much of Arthur's initial planning was negated owing to the influence of the infamous NSW Corps, until 1810 heralded the arrival of the redoubtable Governor Macquarie.

In 1813 Blaxland, Lawson and Wentworth discovered the lands to the west of the Blue Mountains. Further exploration quickly followed and settlement fanned out from Sydney. Sydney itself thrived and its citizens agitated against the stigma of the penal presence, with the result that transportation of convicts ended in 1840. The gold-rushes of the 1850s swelled the population and led to much development throughout the state. With the granting of responsible government in 1856, the founding state was well on its way.

Today New South Wales is the most populous state and its central region, around Sydney, Newcastle and Wollongong-Port Kembla, has been described as 'the heart of industrial Australia'. New South Wales produces two-thirds of the nation's black coal from huge deposits in the Hunter Valley, the Blue Mountains and the Illawarra Region. Its other main source of mineral wealth is the silver-lead-zinc mines of Broken Hill. Primary production is diversified and thriving — New South Wales is the nation's main wheat producer and has more than one-third of the nation's sheep population.

The state is divided naturally into four regions — the sparsely populated western plains, which take up two-thirds of the

The Three Sisters, Blue Mountains

state; the high tablelands and peaks of the Great Dividing Range; the pastoral and farming country of the Range's western slopes; and the fertile coastal region.

The climate varies with the landscape: subtropical along the north coast; temperate all year round on the south coast. The north-west has fearsome dry summers; and the high country has brisk winters with extremes of cold in the highest alpine areas. Sydney has a midsummer average of 25.7°C, a midwinter average of 15.8°C and boasts sunshine for 342 days a year.

Lively and sophisticated, Sydney offers the shopping, restaurants and nightlife expected of a great cosmopolitan city, yet within a 200 kilometre radius is much of the best country in New South Wales: superb beaches, the myriad of intricate bays and inlets of Pittwater, the Hawkesbury

and Tuggerah Lakes and the breathtaking Illawarra coastline. The scenic Blue Mountains and the Jenolan Caves can be reached in a day trip. Most of the state's highways lead out from the capital. The Pacific Highway runs north to Port Macquarie and the industrial city of Newcastle. Inland, you can sample the products of the rich Hunter Valley vineyards. Further north, the country becomes hilly and subtropical, with irresistible golden beaches, and the New England tablelands inland — high mountain and grazing country, at its best in autumn.

The state's extreme north and west is still frontier territory, with limited tourist facilities. If you enjoy getting off the beaten track, and if you and your car are well-prepared, the region can be very rewarding. Highlights include the spectacular Nandewar and Warrumbungle Ranges, Lightning Ridge and the green oasis of Broken Hill, the state's storehouse of mineral wealth.

Many relics of the early gold mining and agricultural history of the rich central tablelands and plains region can be seen in and around such towns as Bathurst, Dubbo, Wellington, Griffith and Wagga Wagga. Towards the Victorian border, where the Murray River forms a natural state boundary, irrigation greens the countryside and supports many vineyards and citrus groves. The Murray River towns retain much of the history of the riverboat era when the Murray was a major transport route.

The Princes Highway leads south from Sydney down the Illawarra Coast, famous for its panoramic views, excellent beaches and numerous national parks. Good fishing of all kinds can be enjoyed and there is splendid bushwalking and climbing in the nearby foothills of the southern highlands.

The Snowy Mountains area includes the natural grandeur of the Kosciusko National Park and the man-assisted grandeur of the Snowy Mountains hydro-electric scheme.

Linked by a network of freeways, highways and roads, New South Wales offers a wide variety of regions to explore.

SYDNEY

Australia's First City

Sydney, a thriving harbourside metropolis populated by more than 3.5 million people, is Australia's largest and probably best-known city. It was the first site of European settlement on the Australian continent, a settlement vastly different from today's cosmopolitan showcase.

As Captain Cook sailed up the east coast of Australia in 1770, he noted the entrance to what is now Sydney Harbour and named the craggy headland Port Jackson, in honour of the then Secretary of the British Admiralty, Sir George Jackson.

'New Holland', as the continent was known, was deemed a perfect spot for a penal colony, providing also a reason for a British presence in the South Pacific. Command of the first colonial expedition was entrusted to Captain Arthur Phillip. On his arrival at Botany Bay in 1788, Phillip was not impressed with this proposed settlement site. Looking further afield, on January 26 he sailed into a beautiful natural harbour, where he dropped anchor, named the area Sydney Cove, hoisted the flag and proclaimed the colony of New South Wales.

Sydney Cove, now **Circular Quay**, saw those first fleet convicts toiling to clear a site for the settlement that was to become the city of Sydney. Testament to their endeavours is **The Rocks**, an area of winding lanes and sandstone buildings situated near the **Harbour Bridge**. An integral part of Sydney's history, providing rich memories of how the city was forged, today The Rocks features outdoor cafes, art and craft centres, curio shops, and a retinue of rollicking pubs. The **Sydney Observatory**, a group of colonial buildings, houses a museum of astronomy with some hands-on displays. Another attraction with interactive exhibits at The Rocks is the **Earth Exchange** (formerly the Geological and Mining Museum), 18 Hickson Road, where visitors can journey across millions of years from the creation of our earth to the present. Nearby, **The Story of Sydney**, a walkthrough sound and cinematic heritage experience, contains high-tech computerised models.

Sydney Cove has remained the gateway

Sydney Tower

to Australia, situated in calm waters some eleven kilometres from the towering bluffs that flank the harbour mouth: North Head and **South Head**. Both headlands command a breathtaking view back along the harbour to the city, automatically drawing the focus to the shimmering city skyline which highlights the **Harbour Bridge**, the **Opera House** and **Sydney Tower**.

While these three structures may be the city's best known landmarks, it is the harbour itself that is Sydney's pride and joy. Its innumerable waterways extend in all directions, the product of a drowned valley system that finds bottom in the depths of the Pacific. Its surface, however, is a glistening blue aquatic playground for Sydneysiders.

With the harbour as its heart, the city proper is bounded by water to the north and west and fringed to the east by the green parklands of the Botanic Gardens and the Domain. **Hyde Park**, sitting in the middle of the city, provides areas of tranquil, verdant delight in a bustling

central business district.

Within these boundaries, Sydney is an exciting and rewarding city to explore — elegant, lively, relaxed, solemn, Georgian, Edwardian, Victorian and dazzlingly contemporary; a perfect blend of historic bedrock and futuristic planning.

Where Phillip's First Fleet dropped anchor, the shoreline has become a neat U-shaped area, with major wharves on either arm and harbour ferry terminals at its base. **Circular Quay** is the hub of Sydney's water traffic and a bright, colourful part of town where buskers play amid strolling lunchtime shoppers.

The Quay was built in the nineteenth century to handle overseas shipping and, in the final great era of sail, the days of the superb clipper ships, Sydney Cove was a forest of majestic masts. Today it boasts a huge international shipping terminal with anchorage for ships of 40 000 tonnes. Nearby are several five-star restaurants where patrons dine while overlooking the harbour lights and the luxurious **Park Hyatt** hotel.

In the sandstone building alongside the Sydney Cove Passenger Terminal is the **Museum of Contemporary Art**, which houses the J.W. Power Collection of some 4500 works of art, including Australian and Aboriginal art. It is Australia's first major museum dedicated to the contemporary visual arts.

Across the water from the Quay, the Harbour Bridge disgorges its congested traffic into Sydney's mini-twin — **North Sydney**, a high-rise, high-density satellite of the 1960s. The **Harbour Tunnel** is designed to take Sydney into the next century with fewer traffic problems.

Under the shadow of the Bridge to the west of the harbour is **Pier One**, a complex of shops, restaurants (specialising in seafood) and a tavern decorated in Old Sydney style. Once a disembarkation point for immigrants, Pier One has been remodelled to reflect its original purpose.

In keeping with the maritime atmosphere is nearby **Pier Four**, which has been converted into a permanent home for the Sydney Theatre Company. The Wharf Theatre is a modern, yet moody,

Sydney Opera House and city skyline

venue for the STC's year-round calendar, while the Wharf Restaurant, with award-winning cuisine, commands one of Sydney's best views.

Standing sentinel at the eastern end of Sydney Cove is the **Sydney Opera House**, a building whose aspect is breath-taking against the blue of the harbour. Its white arches seem to flow out of the water, just as designer Joern Utzon intended, like sails scudding up from the waves. At weekends, the Opera House promenade is alive with audiences listening to free outdoor concerts.

In line with Sydney's boundaries, the city's bus services terminate at three main points: **Circular Quay** in the north, **Wynyard Square** in the west and, in the south, **Central Railway Station**, the grand, domed building that is the outlet for all country and interstate train services. An underground train service goes aboveground outside the central business area and connects the city with outlying suburbs. The **Sydney Explorer** tourist bus loops around twenty kilometres of the city, stopping at twenty-two leading attractions and allowing passengers to alight and rejoin following buses at will.

While around the Central Railway area has a slightly seedy downtown feeling about it, at the Quay it is typically waterfront. **Circular Quay Plaza** and the Rocks area are the home of some of the city's oldest pubs, many of which are 'early openers' catering for night-shift workers from 6 a.m.

Detached from these, and from its high-rise neighbours, in the centre of the Plaza the old **Customs House** continues to preside over the scene, a monument in sandstone to nineteenth-century Sydney. Its time-honoured clock is surrounded by tridents and dolphins, and the coat of arms above the entrance is one of the best stone carvings in Australia.

Immediately behind Circular Quay Plaza, a series of maritime-flavoured laneways and narrow streets culminates in **Macquarie Place** and its sheltering canopies of giant Moreton Bay fig trees. An anchor and a cannon from Phillip's flagship HMS *Sirius* are preserved in the park, which they share with gas lamps, an 1857 drinking fountain, an ornate Victorian 'gents' (classified by the National Trust) and a weathered obelisk from which distances to all points in the colony used to be measured.

In the surrounding laneways look for one of the world's smallest churches, the tiny **Marist Chapel** at 5 Young Street, run by the Marist Fathers.

Government House is an imposing neo-Gothic sandstone mansion of the 1840s, not open to the public but easily

---

Hotels
Hotel Intercontinental
117 Macquarie St, Sydney
(02) 230 0200
Park Hyatt
7 Hickson Rd, The Rocks
(02) 241 1234
Park Lane
161 Elizabeth St, Sydney
(02) 286 6000
Ramada Renaissance
30 Pitt St, Sydney
(02) 259 7000
Sebel Town House
23 Elizabeth Bay Rd, Elizabeth Bay
(02) 358 3244
Ritz Carlton
93 Macquarie St, Sydney
(02) 252 4600
Sydney Hilton
259 Pitt St, Sydney
(02) 266 0610
Sydney Regent
199 George St, Sydney
(02) 238 0000

Family and Budget
Russell
143a George St, Sydney
(02) 241 3543
Jackson
94 Victoria St, Potts Point
(02) 358 5144
YWCA
5–11 Wentworth Ave, Darlinghurst
(02) 264 2451
York Apartments
5 York St, Sydney
(02) 210 5000

Motel Groups: Bookings
Flag (008) 01 1177
Best Western (008) 22 2166
Travelodge (008) 22 2446
Golden Chain (008) 02 3966

This list is for information only; inclusion is not necessarily a recommendation.

Archibald Fountain, Hyde Park

admired from the adjacent Botanic Gardens. Between the entrances to both, the fortress-like lines of the **NSW Conservatorium of Music** successfully conceal the building's origin as stables, designed in 1816 by the renowned convict architect Francis Greenway, and completed in 1821 as part of an earlier Government House on the site.

The Royal Botanic Gardens, more than twenty-four hectares of formal landscaping, were originally dedicated in 1816. Today they are a perennial landscape of colour where more than 4000 native and exotic plants bloom throughout the year. In one small corner there is a stone wall, over 200 years old, marking the original plot of the colony's first vegetable garden, planted at the direction of Governor Phillip. The Pyramid greenhouse contains Australian tropical plants, and nearby is the elegant glass Ark, a major tropical plant centre housing some of the world's rarest plants.

An imposing sandstone building on the western side of **Macquarie Street**, the **State Library of New South Wales**, overlooks the Botanic Gardens. In the library's Mitchell and Dixson wings is one of the world's great repositories of national archives and memorabilia, a priceless collection of Australiana and historical records. The new wing of the State

Library is sited between the old building and Parliament House. This high-tech building features the latest technology, including study aids for the disabled. A brochure for a self-guided tour of the library is available.

Adjacent to the Library are two of Sydney's oldest buildings, the **New South Wales Parliament** and the **Colonial Mint** (now a museum). Between them, in all its dour Victorian splendour, is **Sydney Hospital**, a city institution, which opened in 1879.

Parliament House and the former Mint were once a part of the original colonial hospital, which was known as the Rum Hospital. When there was a shortage of coinage in the colony and rum was the currency, the builders were paid in casks of the spirit. Behind the buildings, the **Domain** — a Sunday afternoon forum for 'soap-box' orators — separates the rear of Macquarie Street from the **Art Gallery of New South Wales.**

During January, when the annual **Festival of Sydney** is in full swing, the Domain becomes a giant outdoor concert hall where hundreds of thousands of Sydneysiders flock to hear jazz, opera and symphonies in the park.

Macquarie Street finally leads into **Queens Square**, arguably one of Sydney's most elegant precincts. The

square is encircled by Hyde Park, the towering **Law Courts** building and Francis Greenway's pre-1820 masterpieces, **St James's Church** and **Hyde Park Barracks** (now a social history museum with unique relics from Sydney's convict origins). Flowing harmoniously on from the old barracks are two great neo-Gothic triumphs of the nineteenth century: the **Registrar-General's Building** and **St Mary's Roman Catholic Cathedral**.

Hyde Park is divided into two sections by **Park Street**. One half is dominated by the **Archibald Fountain** — a legacy to the city from the first publisher of the *Bulletin* — and the other by a **Pool of Remembrance** and the **Anzac War Memorial.** At night, Hyde Park's avenues of trees are lit with thousands of fairy-lights. On the eastern boundary of the park, in **College Street**, stand the **Australian Museum**; one of Sydney's oldest colleges, **Sydney Grammar School**; and two high-rise neighbours, the **Returned Servicemen's League** headquarters and the **NSW Police Department** administration building.

On the city side of Hyde Park runs **Elizabeth Street.** No longer the major city artery it once was, now it serves as a vital, almost continuous, bus feeder route, particularly where two underground

CITY ON THE WATER

In the arid continent of Australia, Sydney is a cosmopolitan subtropical oasis, set around the bays and inlets of Port Jackson, where some 250 kilometres of unspoiled foreshore is scalloped with white sandy beaches. The southern Pacific Ocean caresses the shores in sheltered coves and thunders in on some of the best surf beaches in the country. The climate is mild, the water warm enough for swimming nine months of the year.

Australia's best-known city sits majestically on the shores of its beautiful natural harbour — a harbour bustling with commuter ferries and hydrofoils, small tugs and massive container ships, and visiting luxury liners. Sydneysiders are rightly proud of their city. It is the cradle of Australian history and, industrially and commercially, the focal-point of the South Pacific. The people are relaxed yet sophisticated. The water that surrounds them has a major impact on their lifestyle; many office workers commute by ferry and spend their lunch hours by the foreshore, enjoying the cool sea breeze in hot summer months. At weekends Sydneysiders collectively stretch out on the beaches, set sail, swim or surf. Year-round, Sydneysiders ensure their harbour is a hub of activity.

Sydney owes a lot to its harbour, first discovered in 1770 by Captain James Cook, who named it Port Jackson. In 1788, Captain Arthur Phillip declared it 'the finest harbour in the world'. Today, due to its vast size, its protection from storms, its uniform depth, small tides, freedom from silting, and lack of navigational hazards, together with its wharves, conveniently situated close to the city's business centre, it is arguably the world's best natural harbour. It embraces more than fifty-five square kilometres of water and caters for more than 4000 vessels each year.

Sydneysiders take delight in the water and at weekends sailboats, speedboats, yachts and launches join the busy harbour traffic. Sydney Harbour is also the venue of many boating classics, including the Festival of Sydney's Ferry Boat Race in January and the classic Sydney to Hobart Yacht Race, which sets out from Sydney on

Sydney Harbour

Boxing Day each year, escorted to the Heads by a colourful fleet of pleasure boats.

Between Sydney's two most famous landmarks, the Opera House and the Harbour Bridge, is Sydney Cove — the birthplace of city, state and nation. In 1788, Captain Arthur Phillip chose this inlet to establish the first colony because of its deep bay and running stream of fresh water. Its foreshore, now Circular Quay, in the heart of the city, is dwarfed by skyscrapers, with the City Circle Railway passing immediately overhead and the Cahill Expressway forming a canopy over the railway.

Circular Quay is the nucleus of a network of ferry services that links the city to its suburbs (Manly, Mosman, Neutral Bay, Balmain), popular beaches and Taronga Zoo. Most ferry routes pass close to Fort Denison, also known as 'Pinchgut', where convicts were once imprisoned on a diet of bread and water. Today this fortress island can be hired as a perfect festive location for special functions. It is possible also to hire an aqua cab (water taxi) to take you to any point around the harbour, while special cruises go to Middle Harbour, the Lane Cove and Parramatta Rivers, and up the coast to Broken Bay and the Hawkesbury River.

The ferry service to Manly dates back to 1854. This resort suburb took as its slogan around the turn of the century: 'seven miles from Sydney and a thousand miles from care' and it stands as true today. Named by Captain Phillip after the 'manly' behaviour of the Aborigines, this suburb can be reached by

a 35-minute ferry ride, a 13-minute journey in a hydrofoil or an even quicker trip in a UTA catamaran. Manly stands at the gateway to Sydney Harbour, and each summer its population doubles due to the mild climate and the popularity of the eighteen harbour and ocean beaches nearby. Manly Oceanarium enables visitors to 'walk under the ocean' to view the amazing marine life.

Between Grotto Point and Middle Head is the fishing and boating haven of Middle Harbour. Here the Spit Bridge opens for vessels visiting the area's many channels and bays, which are rich in small coves and beaches.

Along the northern shore of Port Jackson are several well-known beaches: Chowder Bay, where American whalers concocted their famous dish using Sydney rock oysters; Neutral Bay, where ships from foreign countries once anchored; and the picturesque Mosman Bay and Chinamans Beach, a favourite haunt of artists.

On the southern foreshore, almost 100 hectares of parkland in the Domain and Royal Botanic Gardens beckons office workers, who flock to the gardens for a quiet lunch break, a stroll or a jog along the foreshore or a quick game of cricket.

Sydney is also renowned for its fine surf beaches. The scenic northern beaches stretch from Manly to Palm Beach. To the south, Bondi, just seven kilometres from the General Post Office, is the most popular and most famous metropolitan beach. Coogee and Cronulla are also popular. The smaller beaches at Clovelly, Tamarama and Bronte offer quiet seclusion from crowds. Sydney's thirty-four surfing beaches are patrolled by volunteer lifesavers, who stage colourful large-scale carnivals throughout the summer months to test their mettle against other clubs. Lady Jane and Reef beaches on the harbour cater to nude sunbathers.

Shark scares are not uncommon in Sydney and some beaches are protected with shark-proof enclosures. Surfers should take heed of warning flags placed on the sand, which mark the areas safe for surfing on that day. Rock-pools are abundant and are ideal for children. It is not advisable to swim in the harbour.

Queen Victoria building, George Street

railway stations, **St James** and **Museum**, disgorge. It is still, however, noteworthy for the headquarters of one of Australia's great retailing empires, **David Jones**, and another of Sydney's historic buildings, the **Great Synagogue**.

David Jones, with its marble floors, liveried doormen and title of 'the most beautiful store in the world', stands on the corner of Elizabeth Street and Market Street and is a Sydney landmark. 'I'll see you on DJ's corner' was, and still is, a regular Sydney rendezvous. From here, Elizabeth Street continues north to the spacious semicircle of Chifley Square, named in honour of former Prime Minister J.B. Chifley.

In a wedge-shaped sector of blocks made by Bent, Bridge, Young, Phillip and Loftus Streets stand the office buildings of colonial New South Wales, elaborately constructed from Sydney's superb Hawkesbury sandstone, on which the city is built. Mostly late Victorian, the buildings still serve their original purpose as housing for state departments, such as Education and Agriculture.

All are massively solid and ornamented with either statues, gargoyles, handsomely worked-stone, or all three. Within them, cedar-lined offices open on to marbled corridors with staircases with wrought-iron balustrades and ceilings so high and arched as to be almost vault-like. The ministerial offices still within are treasure-troves of priceless colonial artefacts, from grandfather clocks to richly panelled fireplaces.

The disordered pattern of the surrounding streets is a product of the complete lack of planning that occurred once Governor Phillip was recalled from Sydney. Bullock-tracks and wandering cow-paths determined the town plan until Governor Macquarie attempted to impose order some twenty years later. Today the result contributes to Sydney's charm.

Castlereagh Street, parallel to Elizabeth Street, also loses itself in the tangle of colonial office blocks above the

Quay. In **Martin Place**, a traffic-free plaza running from Elizabeth Street through Castlereagh and Pitt Streets and finishing at George Street, lunchtime office-workers attend outdoor concerts in the amphitheatre, flower-sellers hawk their wares from colourful barrows and cut-price theatre and concert tickets are on sale at a Halftix booth. The **GPO** sits in Martin Place, between Pitt and George Streets. It is undergoing extensive renovations to maintain its spectacular architecture, which includes a grand clock atop its column-held rooftop. South of Martin Place the character of the area changes from a merchant belt to a shopping mecca. The **MLC Centre** dominates almost a whole block and contains suites of luxurious offices above and, at ground level, some exclusive and very expensive shops, mostly jewellers and fashionable boutiques. The complex also houses a convenient fast-food area, the Australia Tavern, a cinema (the Dendy) and, for the theatre-goer, Sydney's prestigious **Theatre Royal**. The King and Castlereagh Streets crossroads, with its collection of elite retail traders such as Chanel and Gucci, has been compared to New York's Fifth Avenue and London's Bond Street.

There are more cinemas nearby and a less expensive shopping complex: **Centrepoint.** Here you can visit the 270-metre-high golden **Sydney Tower**, with its two revolving restaurants. From the observation decks at the summit, high-powered binoculars and a video television camera offer spectacular views of Sydney landmarks.

Only two of Sydney's north–south arteries actually make a complete journey from Circular Quay to Central Railway Station: **Pitt Street and George Street.** As Pitt Street between King and Market Streets is a pedestrian mall, traffic must make this journey using George Street only. Of the two, Pitt Street is probably the more exciting in terms of shops, cafes and street hawkers. On carnival-thronged evenings along George Street's entertainment section, cinema complexes, fast-food houses and pin-ball alleys, all-night bookshops and erotic movie houses all compete for the jostling crowd's attention. The monorail beside Pitt Street worms through the city above street level, linking it to the **Darling Harbour Complex.**

In both Pitt and George Streets there is little trace of colonial Sydney, although handsome turn-of-the-century commercial buildings are carefully watched over by devoted citizens and the National Trust, lest developers' ambitions exceed their sense of history and good taste.

Between King and Park Streets, Pitt Street comes into its own: department stores, including Grace Bros and Centre-point; another popular sporting club, **City Tattersalls**; the Pitt Street side of the Methodist Church's Wesley headquarters; cinemas, one a complex of several choices; and, dominating the two blocks, the sumptuous **Sydney Hilton Hotel**, now out-stripped by its soaring neighbour, Sydney Tower, Sydney's tallest building.

Pitt Street becomes rather nondescript as it heads south towards Central Railway Station, with some secondhand stores, places offering cheap accommodation, and a laneway that leads to a nineteenth-century police headquarters building, now more a city watch-house and serving as cells for the grim **Central Criminal Court** building on one of the cross streets, Liverpool Street.

Further west is **Darling Harbour**, an ambitious public centre, opened on Australia Day 1988, which has become an entertainment centre for Sydneysiders. This impressive complex features the **Chinese 'Garden of Friendship'**, an exhibition and convention centre, waterside walks, a variety of eating places, seven-day-a-week shopping, and splendid parklands around a busy harbour inlet that was once a dull industrial port. At the western end of the National Trust classified **Pyrmont Bridge** is the National **Maritime Museum** and near the eastern end of this one-time traffic carrier, now used as a walkway, is the **Sydney Aquarium.**

Not far from Darling Harbour is Australia's largest fish market, the **Sydney Fish Market** at **Pyrmont;** it has retail stores, coffee shops, souvenir outlets and Australia's first seafood school.

The **Powerhouse Museum** on the southern edge of the Darling Harbour Complex is also well worth a visit. Its size is such that it can exhibit aeroplanes, trams, boats and steam-engines, as well as many equally fascinating smaller exhibits. Opposite is the **Sydney Entertainment Centre,** a major venue for concerts and conventions. Nearby lies **Dixon Street**, the pedestrianised heart of **Sydney's China Town**, a traditional area of restaurants, warehouses, specialty stores and Chinese grocers, where even the banks and service stations are labelled in Chinese script.

Apart from its entertainment area that makes its nights so boisterous, by day George Street boasts a number of Sydney's most important and interesting buildings, both old and new. Until a few years ago, Sydney's and Australia's tallest building was the **Australia Square Tower**. Tall and circular in shape, it has an observation platform on the forty-eighth floor and a revolving restaurant,

Sydney's most famous beach, Bondi

the 'Summit'. These days, the tower is dwarfed by the AMP and MLC buildings on Sydney's rocketing skyline, and now more recently by the **Sheraton Wentworth Hotel**, situated opposite on Phillip Street. Tours of the city's historic **Tank Stream** are offered by the Sydney Water Board every Sunday; access to the Tank Stream is from the basement of the Plaza Building in Australia Square.

South from here are Wynyard underground railway station, the GPO, Sydney's Victorian massif, and the remarkable **Queen Victoria Building**, which monopolises an entire block. The latter has been restored by the Sydney City Council, in conjunction with an Asian consortium, including the reburnishing of its enormous copper dome, which once loomed over the older city skyline. The building now houses over 160 shops. A landmark of the city's earlier days is to be found opposite the Queen Victoria building, through the George Street entrance to the Hilton Hotel. In the hotel's basement, restored to its original ornate detail, is the superb **Marble Bar** of the old **Adams Hotel**, which once stood on the site of the Hilton. On the next corner stands one of Sydney's most recent and talked-about buildings, the spiralling blue **Coopers and Lybrand tower**. With its art deco design, it has

been dubbed the 'Superman' building because of its similarity to the fictitious *Daily Planet* building of comic-strip fame.

Sydney has several shopping arcades that run off Pitt and George Streets. One of these, **the Strand**, is particularly noteworthy, having been restored to its 1892 splendour, and housing some of Australia's leading fashion designers, jewellers and crafts people.

The **Town Hall**, now dwarfed but not overshadowed by a modern council administration block, is Italian Renaissance in style. Built of mellow brown sandstone, it was completed in 1874. A graceful, shaded pedestrian plaza, **Sydney Square,** is located around the Town Hall and separates it from Sydney's Anglican Cathedral, **St Andrew's.** Erected in stages from 1839 onwards, it was not until the final additions and alterations were completed that the present main entrance on to George Street finally was opened in 1919.

Of the city's cross-streets, two handsome boulevards are noteworthy: Park Street and Martin Place. The authentic heart of the city, **Martin Place**, with its memorial **Cenotaph** to Australia's war dead, is the annual stage for the city's Anzac Day March on April 25.

Park Street ambles east, its footpaths splitting Hyde Park in two and providing a

A COLONIAL PAST

At the first settlement at Sydney Cove, Captain Watkin Tench of the Marines wrote that 'to proceed on a narrow, confined scale in a country of the extensive limits we possess, would be unpardonable . . . extent of Empire demands grandeur of design'.

Such 'grand design' began in 1810, when the vision of the new Governor, Lachlan Macquarie, was put into practice by the convict architect Francis Greenway, giving us a heritage of splendid buildings, many of which are landmarks today. It continued through nearly a century of growth and lofty ideals to create a prosperous and busy metropolis — a great symbol of colonial aspirations.

As it developed, **Sydney** was both 'mean and princely', a mixture of broad, tree-lined avenues and narrow streets and alleys, grand buildings and crowded cottages and terraces. Its switchback, craggy hills around the sprawling indented harbour made orderly Georgian-style planning impossible, and the grand outlines of earlier days soon became blurred by the city's growth from first settlement to colonial seat, to state capital, to modern city.

In modern Sydney, however, with its gleaming towers, its crowds and its traffic, substantial and fascinating remnants of old Sydney can still be seen. Some parts of the city, such as the Rocks area, adjacent to Circular Quay, are almost pure history. The old pubs and bandstands, sandstone cottages and terrace houses, the Argyle Cut and Agar Steps, the Garrison Church and the village green are an oasis separated from the bustling city by Flagstaff Hill, where the old Observatory stands, and the approaches to the Harbour Bridge are seen.

There are many other inner suburban areas that are reminiscent of the feeling of old Sydney. Paddington is the show-place historic suburb, with its picturesque terraces and cottages, many of them superbly restored by proud owners. The narrow streets of this once working-class suburb provide an intimate, neighbourly feeling. Balmain, Leichhardt and Redfern are becoming popular as the advantages of inner-suburban living attract owners who are conscious of the aesthetic quality of the old sandstone cottages.

In the city itself, the street that best reflects the past is probably Macquarie Street, which overlooks both the Botanic Gardens and the Domain, where Government House, the Conservatorium of Music, the State Library and Art Gallery of NSW are situated. Governor Macquarie planned for the east side of the street to be occupied by official buildings and for the west to contain the town houses of wealthy citizens, which are now occupied mainly by members of the medical profession.

Among other interesting buildings in Macquarie Street are: Parliament House (1816), a verandahed sandstone building, originally one wing of the Rum Hospital; the adjoining Mint Building, restored from the other wing of the original Rum Hospital; Sydney Hospital: these sandstone buildings replaced the central block of the Rum Hospital; the Royal College of Physicians; and the Hyde Park Barracks (1819), now a museum. In nearby Queens Square is the classically designed St James's Church.

At the harbour end of Mrs Macquarie's Road is a natural reminder of the Macquarie era — a sandstone shell known as Mrs Macquarie's Chair. The Governor's wife is said to have sat here and gazed out upon the great harbour, now one of the world's busiest and most picturesque waterways.

There are a number of other major buildings in or near the city: such buildings as Elizabeth Bay House, in Regency style, now beautifully restored and a show-place for the rich furnishings of the time when it looked out over a harbour verged by cliff and woodland; the General Post Office in Martin Place, completed in 1887 in

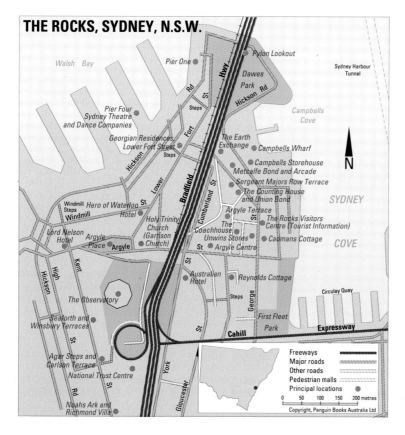

THE ROCKS, SYDNEY, N.S.W.

Walsh Bay
Pier One
Pylon Lookout
Sydney Harbour Tunnel
Dawes Park
Hickson Rd
Pier Four
Sydney Theatre and Dance Companies
Campbells Cove
Georgian Residences
Lower Fort Street
The Earth Exchange
Campbells Wharf
Campbells Storehouse
Metcalfe Bond and Arcade
Sergeant Majors Row Terrace
The Counting House and Union Bond
Windmill Steps
Hero of Waterloo Hotel
Windmill
SYDNEY
Argyle Terrace
The Rocks Visitors Centre (Tourist Information)
Holy Trinity Church (Garrison Church)
The Coachhouse
Unwins Stores
Lord Nelson Hotel
Argyle Place
Argyle
Cadmans Cottage
COVE
Argyle Centre
Australian Hotel
Reynolds Cottage
High
Kent
The Observatory
Steps
Circular Quay
First Fleet Park
Seaforth and Winsbury Terraces
Cahill
Expressway
Agar Steps and Carlson Terrace
National Trust Centre
York
Gloucester
Noahs Ark and Richmond Villa

Freeways
Major roads
Other roads
Pedestrian malls
Principal locations
0   50   100   150   200 metres
Copyright, Penguin Books Australia Ltd

classic Renaissance style; the Great Hall of Sydney University, and St Andrew's Cathedral, both designed by Edmund Blacket; St Mary's Cathedral, designed by William Wardell; the Greek Revival court-house in Taylor Square, designed by Mortimer Lewis; and Vaucluse House, the former home of William Charles Wentworth, father of the NSW Constitution. But perhaps the most striking example of colonial architecture in Sydney is Victoria Barracks in Darlinghurst. This two-storeyed sandstone building of severe Georgian style, seventy-four metres long, with white-painted upper and lower verandahs, is a model of elegance. (Visit on Tuesday at 10 a.m., watch the changing of the guard and be taken on a tour of the barracks.)

As settlement extended from the harbourside colony, villages were established, first in the upper **Hawkesbury region** to the north-west, then to the south and, finally, as the Blue Mountains were breached, out to the western plains and throughout New South Wales.

In the upper Hawkesbury valley are the sister towns of Windsor and Richmond, two of the Macquarie Towns, beautifully sited on the river and retaining the peaceful charm and many of the buildings of earlier days. Windsor has a number of fine buildings: Claremont Cottage, St Matthew's Anglican Church, the Macquarie Arms, Tebbutt's Observatory, the Doctor's House, the Toll House, and the court-house, to name but a few. At Richmond are the mansion Hobartville, Toxana House, St Peter's Anglican Church, the School of Arts and Belmont.

In the **Southern Highlands**, the settlements of Mittagong, Moss Vale, Berrima and Bowral are full of historic interest. The Berrima Village Trust is responsible for its preservation as it was in the nineteenth century. Sited in a valley, Berrima contains a number of fine sandstone buildings grouped around a central common, among them the gaol and court-house, the Surveyor-General Inn, the Church of the Holy Trinity, Harper's Mansion and Allington. Throughout New South Wales, there are many other historic towns and properties bearing the hallmarks of the nation's foundation.

See also: Individual entries in A–Z listing.

The Rocks

Vaucluse House, Vaucluse

pleasant walk before turning into **William Street,** which inevitably leads to **Kings Cross,** Sydney's version of Soho and Greenwich Village. The Cross, though, has its own unique flavour: the breath of a Sydney Harbour breeze and a glimpse of blue water are a delight. Whatever the Cross has borrowed from other cities in its strip joints, gaudy night-spots and colourful characters, it has its own bohemian traditions to draw on. In its backyard are **Garden Island** dockyard, where the Fleet is nearly always in, and the encircling apartment houses of select **Elizabeth Bay**. On its boundaries are Darlinghurst and Woolloomooloo.

The once notorious **Darlinghurst,** a long-time haunt of pimps, prostitutes and gangsters, boasts the historic Darlinghurst Gaol (where bushrangers were hanged) as one of its attractions. Today, however, the face of Darlinghurst has changed dramatically and it is now the home of artists and poets. Its main artery, **Oxford Street**, with its 'adult' bookshops, pubs, clothing stores and restaurants is the 'gay' capital of Australia.

Woolloomooloo (the famous Loo) has seen its cramped houses and narrow streets predictably skyrocket in price as the desire for trendy inner-city living escalates.

Individual restaurants and bars are many and various — too numerous to list — but among the major hotels around the Cross are the Sebel Town House, the Crest, the Hyatt, the Boulevard and the Gazebo. Trendy brasseries compete amid the leftovers of 'sleaze' on Bayswater Road and Kellett Street, where the gentrification of the Cross is most apparent. But, even so, there are a great number of erotic movie-houses and specialty

bookshops — with the red-light-district flavour that seems to go with them — still left in the Cross. A less controversial landmark is the dandelion-shaped **El Alamein Fountain** commemorating the World War II battle.

In the other direction, Darlinghurst Road and Bayswater Road lead to Sydney's 'trendiest' area, **Paddington**, a suburb of steep hills, unplanned streets and picturesque terrace houses, hardly one without ornate Victorian wrought-iron railings and fences and lots of trees. The old-fashioned pubs are now terribly chic; well-spoken children and large dogs exercise on streets once the domain of street-urchins before Paddington underwent its fashionable revival back in the late fifties. Next door to 'Paddo' is **Centennial Park**, Sydney's equivalent to New York's Central and London's Regent Park, where horseriding, cycling and picnicking are weekend activities.

Paddington's counterpart on the other side of Sydney, **Glebe** (bordering historic **Sydney University**) is not quite so leafy or picturesque, and certainly not as expensive but is seeing a revival. Nearby **Balmain** with its harbour frontage also has undergone a fashionable revival.

At every turn of a corner these three suburbs reveal something old and handsome in weathered sandstone: a church, a cottage, a school from Sydney's past. They also have given rise to a Sydney phenomenon: the advent of the 'Church Bazaar'. These village markets, usually held on Saturdays, feature colourful identities plying their wares at open-air stalls in the grounds of schools or churches. For this reason alone, the suburbs are worth a visit.

So is the rest of Australia's first city: from

Paddington's neighbours, **Woollahra** and **Rushcutters Bay** through the harbourside suburbs of exclusive **Double Bay**, **Rose Bay** and **Vaucluse** to **The Gap** and **South Head**; or across the harbour by the ferry, hydrofoil or Harbour Bridge to **Manly** and the long line of beaches stretching north to **Palm Beach**, competing in terms of wealth and privilege with the precipitous bush gorges and superior heights of the elegant **North Shore** suburbs. Beyond all that again lies the metropolitan heartland of Sydney's great urban sprawl — seventy-five kilometres from the harbour across the vast, flat western suburbs to the foothills of the **Blue Mountains** that once hemmed in the first settlers but are no longer a barrier to modern Sydney's unbounded ambition.

A floatplane service at **Rose Bay** has flights between Sydney and Palm Beach, Gosford and Newcastle; and the Manly Ferry *Collaroy* offers cruises from Circular Quay up the coast into Broken Bay and the Hawkesbury River. Near the Hawkesbury at **Berowra** is the famous Berowra Waters Inn, ranked as one of the best restaurants in Australia.

It is not possible to list all of Sydney's restaurants. In Sydney one can dine out on the cuisines of virtually every nation in the world. However, it should be mentioned that Sydney is famous for its rock oyster and the Balmain Bug — an odd-looking but tasty crustacean. The choice of cinema, live theatre and live theatre restaurants is just as comprehensive.

For further information, contact the NSW Travel Centre, 19 Castlereagh St, Sydney 2000; (02) 231 4444.

Bi-centennial monument, Centennial Park

TOURS FROM SYDNEY

Sydney's range of available day-tours out and about is almost unrivalled for the variety of scenic and recreational attractions on offer.

In the frantic rush to get out of the city, however, it is easy to overlook two of Sydney's greatest assets: **Royal National Park**, little more than an hour's drive south from the GPO, and **Ku-ring-gai Chase National Park**, forty kilometres north.

Harbour Cruises from Circular Quay

An ideal way to view Sydney and its harbour is by boat. Several cruises are available. State Transit run three daily: a two-and-a-half hour harbour sights or harbour history cruise, and a one-and-a-half hour harbour lights cruise. Harbour lights does not run on Sunday evening. No bookings needed; for further information: (02) 247 4738.

'Coffee cruises' operated by Captain Cook Cruises run twice daily through Main and Middle Harbours and the same company's luncheon cruises travel up the Parramatta and Lane Cove Rivers daily. The *John Cadman* makes a 'dinner cruise' daily. The 38-metre cruise ship *Proud Sydney* offers overnight harbour cruises.

Experience the thrill of sailing on a harbour luncheon cruise aboard the *Solway Lass,* a restored sailing ship.

Captain Cook Cruises also conducts tours to Fort Denison, one of the most historic relics in Australia, from Tuesday to Sunday.

Taronga Zoo, 12 minutes by ferry from Circular Quay, Wharf 5

Taronga is set in thirty hectares of harbourside bushland, giving it a magnificent and unique setting: the views back to the city are splendid. Of particular interest are the displays of Australian native animals and the nocturnal house. Children will enjoy meeting the tame animals at the Friendship Farm (open daily).

Palm Beach, 48 km from Sydney via Pittwater Road

This beautiful beach in bush surroundings offers swimming and boating facilities and a choice of ocean or Pittwater beaches. The drive from Sydney reveals many of Sydney's lovely northern beaches and it is tempting to stop at every one. The Mona Vale Road provides a shorter route if you are based in the northern suburbs;

allow time for a visit to the fauna reserve Waratah Park at Terrey Hills.

Captain Cook's Landing Place, Kurnell, about 35 km from Sydney via the Princes Highway and Captain Cook Bridge

The site of the first recorded landing by Europeans on the east coast of Australia in 1770 is set aside as a historic site on a pleasantly laid-out reserve. An excellent museum displays items related to Captain James Cook's life and discoveries. A short 'historical walk' takes visitors past several interesting points. There are picnic and barbecue facilities in the grounds.

Parramatta, 22 km from Sydney via the Great Western Highway

Although it has now become a city within Sydney, Parramatta retains its individuality and has some interesting buildings. Pick up a Historic Houses self-guiding leaflet from the tourist centre in Prince Alfred Park ((02) 630 3703). Elizabeth Farm, in Alice St, (1793) contains part of the oldest surviving building in Australia and, as the home of Elizabeth and John Macarthur, was for the first 40 years of the colony the social, political and

Experiment Farm Cottage, Parramatta

THE BLUE MOUNTAINS

The Blue Mountains have been a favourite holiday resort for Sydney-siders for more than a century. Rising from the coastal plain sixty-five kilometres west of Sydney, they combine a unique blend of superb mountain scenery and outstanding geographical features with a plethora of highly developed tourist attractions.

The towering cliffs of the Blue Mountains presented a seemingly impassable barrier to the early settlers until Blaxland, Lawson and Wentworth made their historic crossing in 1813 — thus opening up much-needed pastureland beyond.

In the late 1870s, the well-to-do of Sydney discovered the area's charms as a resort, and started to build elaborate holiday houses to escape the summer heat of the coast. At first they travelled by Cobb & Co. coach, later by train. Now the mountains are less than two hours from Sydney by road or rail. One-day round-trip coach tours run daily between Sydney and Katoomba.

The Blue Mountains are justly famous for their spectacular scenery of high precipices rising from densely wooded valleys. Their highest point is about 1100 metres above sea-level. Although the area has been developed for tourism, deep gorges and high rocks make much of the terrain inaccessible, except to skilled bushwalkers and mountaineers. Climbing schools offer rock-climbing weekends for beginners, and there are day courses in beginners' abseiling.

The panoramic **Blue Mountains National Park**, which covers an area of 216 000 hectares, is the fourth largest national park in the state.

The City of Blue Mountains incorporates over twenty towns and villages, including the main towns of **Katoomba**, **Blackheath**, **Wentworth Falls**, **Springwood** and **Glenbrook**. All these towns depend on tourism and are geared for the holiday trade. They offer a wide range of accommodation from cottages and guest-houses to luxurious hotels and motels, and sporting facilities of all kinds. The area is famous for its bushwalking, bicycle and horse-riding trails. In spring, many superb private gardens in the Blue Mountains are open to the public. Of special renown is the Leura Gardens Festival held annually in early October.

For further information, contact the Blue Mountains Tourism Authority on (047) 39 6266 or visit the Information Centres at Echo Point, Katoomba or Glenbrook on the Great Western Highway.

Why are the Blue Mountains so blue? The whole area is heavily timbered with eucalypts which constantly disperse fine droplets of oil into the atmosphere. These droplets cause the blue light-rays of the sun to be scattered more effectively, thus intensifying the usual light refraction phenomenon (known as Rayleigh Scattering) which causes distant objects to appear blue.

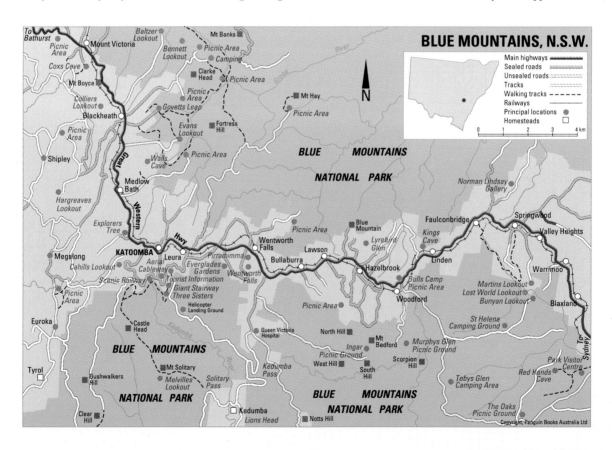

agricultural centre. Don't miss the audio-visual and period (1830s) gardens. Experiment Farm Cottage in Ruse St was the site of James Ruse's 'experiment' to support himself from the land in the early years of the colony: hence its name. Closer to the centre of the city are two historic sites: Old Government House in attractive Parramatta Park has been beautifully restored and maintained by the National Trust from its 1799 (enlarged 1815) beginnings. Take the guided tour to learn more. A guide will show the significance of St John's Church (1850s) in the heart of the shopping district too. St John's cemetery is now a block away from the church itself and contains the oldest headstone in the colony, dated January 1791.

Windsor and Richmond, 60 km from Sydney via the Great Western Highway and Windsor Road

These two towns on the Hawkesbury River are reminders of the earliest days of settlement in New South Wales. In Windsor, there are many historic buildings in George Street and Thompson Square. The Doctor's House, Thompson Square, built in 1844, is one of the most impressive, but the court-house and the many churches and hotels in both towns are all of interest. The Hawkesbury Museum at 7 Thompson Square, Windsor, is housed in an old colonial build-

ing. It contains various items of historic interest relating to pioneer days. **See also:** Entries in the A–Z listing.

Historic Camden and Campbelltown, 60 km from Sydney via Liverpool, on the Hume Highway

Liverpool, situated 32 km from Sydney and a major retail and commercial centre, has many historic buildings of interest: St Luke's Church (1818), Liverpool Hospital (1825–30), designed by Francis Greenway and now the Liverpool College of TAFE, and Glenfield Farm (1817). The ultra-modern Liverpool Museum, built as a bicentennial project, fronts Collingwood Cottage, built in 1810 for a whaling captain. A good stopping-point is Chipping Norton Lakes, a reclaimed area with picnic and barbecue facilities, and walking-tracks. Further down the highway, lovers of history can enjoy a relaxed stroll around the streets of two early towns of New South Wales, Camden and Campbelltown. (**See:** Entries in A–Z listing.) Although most of the historic buildings are not open for inspection, a pleasant day can be spent just taking in the atmosphere. A self-guided walking-tour booklet is available from the Macarthur Country Tourist Association, Liverpool. Between Camden and Campbelltown, off Narellan Road, is the 400-hectare Mt Annan Botanic Garden, the native plant garden of the Royal Botanic Gardens, Sydney, opened in 1988.

Skyway, Blue Mountains

Katoomba and the Blue Mountains via Penrith, 104 km from Sydney via the Great Western Highway (or by mini-fare excursion, State Rail)

The historic town of Penrith, 57 km from Sydney, dates back to the opening of the Blue Mountains road in 1815 when a court-house and a small gaol were built there. Today it makes a pleasant stop-over en route to the Blue Mountains. Penrith's attractions include the Museum of Fire in Castlereagh St, the *Nepean Belle* paddleboat, which cruises the Nepean Gorge, Vicary's Winery south of town and the Lewers Regional Art Gallery at Emu Plains. **See also:** The Blue Mountains; and Katoomba entry in A–Z listing.

The Hunter Valley Vineyards, 160 km from Sydney via the Pacific Highway

Although it is possible to do this trip in a day, this certainly would not do the area justice — and it is definitely not a good idea if you plan to do any wine-tasting!

The best time to visit the Hunter Valley is at vintage time, when you can see the grapes being fermented in great open vats. Picking starts any time from the end of January, but this can vary considerably, and sometimes does not start until well into February.

Most of the forty-plus wineries welcome visitors. It is well worth while visiting a few of the smaller wineries. Tyrrell's and Drayton's wineries were established within a few years of each other in the 1850s and at Tyrrell's you can still see the classic hand presses being used during vintage and fermentation.

Most of the wineries are open every day. Inspections can be arranged with the wineries direct or by calling at the Tourist Information Centre, cnr Mt View and Wollombi Rds, Cessnock; (049) 90 4477. **See also:** Wineries of New South Wales.

Hunter Valley vineyards

NEW SOUTH WALES   from A to Z

Adaminaby   Population 283

This small town on the Snowy Mountains Hwy is renowned as a base for cross-country skiers and the ski area of Mt Selwyn is nearby. It is the stepping-off point for Lake Eucumbene, which has five holiday resorts around its shores. These offer varied accommodation, including caravan and camping parks, cottages and units. Fishing is excellent and boats may be hired. Providence Portal is the only place in the Snowy Mountains where water can be seen gushing from one of the giant tunnels into the lake. **In the area:** Cruisers for hire at Buckenderra, 44 km south. Yarrangobilly Caves and thermal pool, off Snowy Mountains Hwy, 53 km north. Horseriding and alpine horse-back safaris. Farm holidays available. **Tourist information:** Lake Eucumbene and North Snowfields Visitors Centre, Adaminaby Real Estate, Denison St; (064) 54 2435. **Accommodation:** 1 hotel, 2 motels, 1 caravan/camping park. MAP REF. 109 D8, 110 E13

Adelong   Population 855

Fossickers and historians will find plenty to interest them in this picturesque tablelands town on the Snowy Mountains Hwy. In the mid-1850s it produced 200 tonnes of gold and attracted 29 000 hopeful miners. **Of interest:** Main street, Tumut St, from Campbell to Neil Sts, classified by National Trust; some buildings such as Bank of NSW rated as being of great historic interest. Also in Tumut St, Gold Fields Galleries art and craft centre and restored Old Pharmacy with Old Prison Clock (over 125 years old), originally from Kiandra court-house. **In the area:** Adelong Falls 2 km north, on Tumblong–Gundagai Rd; scenic picnic area; also gold-fossicking. Oasis coloured sheep farm, 8 km along same road; spinning, shearing and sales of wool and garments. **Tourist information:** York's Newsagency, Tumut St; (069) 46 2051. **Accommodation:** 1 hotel, 1 motel, 1 caravan park. MAP REF. 109 B6, 110 C11, 117 R11

Albury   Population 37 164

Albury–Wodonga is situated on the Murray River, 572 km from Sydney. The Albury region was a meeting-place for five local Aboriginal tribes, but today it makes a convenient stop-over point for motorists driving via the Hume Hwy between Sydney and Melbourne. The building of the Hume Weir in 1936 created Lake Hume, one of the most extensive and beautiful man-made lakes in Australia. This huge expanse of water is a paradise for swimmers, sailors, canoeists, water-skiers, speedboat enthusiasts, windsurfers and anglers. **Of interest:** Albury Regional Museum, in what was Turk's Head Hotel, Wodonga Pl, adjacent to tourist centre. Botanical Gardens (1871), cnr Wogonga Pl and Dean St. The Parklands, comprising Noreuil and Australia Parks and Hovell Tree Reserve, on western side of Wodonga Pl at entrance to town. Riverside walks, river swimming, kiosk and picnic areas. Both PS *Cumberoona* and MV *Discover* offer Murray River cruises; embarkation points within parks. Albury Regional Art Centre, Dean St. Performing Arts Centre, Civic Centre, Swift St. 360° views of surrounding area from Albury Monument Hill at end of Dean St. Frog Hollow Leisure Park, Olive St; maze, theatre, minigolf. Haberfield's Milk Dairy Shop, Hovell St; sales of local dairy products. **In the area:** Ettamogah Wildlife Sanctuary, 12 km north-east on Hume Hwy. Cartoonist Ken Maynard's Ettamogah Pub, worth photographing. Cooper's Ettamogah Winery, 3 km further along hwy. Jindera Pioneer Museum, 14 km north-west; former general store. Hume Weir Trout Farm, 14 km east; trout feeding, fishing and tastings. Bogong Mountains, gateway to Victorian snowfields and high country, 130 km south. Day trips to wineries of Rutherglen, 47 km west, and into Mad Dan Morgan country, 200 km round trip north. Hume and Hovell Walking Track from Albury to Gunning, over 300 km north-east. Farm holidays available. **Tourist information:** Crossing Place Visitors Centre, Hume Hwy; (060) 21 2655. **Accommodation:** Albury–Wodonga, 2 hotels, 55 motels, 13 caravan/camping parks. MAP REF. 110 A13, 117 P13, 217 R4, 219 B4

Alstonville   Population 3266

The village of Alstonville nestles at the top of the Ballina Cutting between Ballina and Lismore. Surrounding properties produce potatoes, sugarcane, tropical fruits, macadamia nuts and avocados. **Of interest:** Town has won prizes each year in 'Tidy Towns' competition since 1986. Lumley Park, Bruxner Hwy; open-air pioneer transport museum. **In the area:** House With No Steps, 10 km south; nursery, crafts, fruit sales and tearooms run by disabled. **Tourist information:** Ballina Tourist Information Centre, Las Balsas Plaza, Ballina; (066) 86 3484. **Accommodation:** 1 hotel, 1 motel. MAP REF. 113 Q3

Ettamogah Pub, Table Top, near Albury

Armidale   Population 19 525

Situated midway between Sydney and Brisbane in the New England Ranges (altitude 900 m), this important city is the centre of the New England district and an attractive tourist centre. **Of interest:** New England Regional Art Museum, Kentucky St; contains Hinton Collection, most valuable provincial art collection in Australia. Also in Kentucky St, Aboriginal Centre and Keeping Place; museum and education centre. Folk Museum with display of pioneer relics, in classified National Trust building, cnr Faulkner and Rusden Sts. In Dangar St, St Mary's Roman Catholic Cathedral (1912), magnificent Gothic revival structure, and St Peter's Anglican Cathedral (1875), made from 'Armidale blues' bricks. The Stables (1872), Moore St, now craft shop. Court House (1860), Imperial Hotel (1889), both in Beardy St. Central Park, Dangar St; pleasant city park with useful relief map of area. **In the area:** University of New England, 5 km north-west, with historic Booloominbah homestead, now administration building, and kangaroo and deer park. National Trust-owned Saumarez Homestead (1888), 6 km south. Rural Life and Industry Museum at ghost town of Hillgrove, 27 km east; exhibits of gold-mining equipment. Oxley Wild Rivers National Park, 39 km east, includes Wollomombi Falls, highest falls in Australia, plunging 457 m. Fine views from Point Lookout (1500 m) in New England National Park, 80 km east. **Tourist information:** Visitors Centre and Coach Station, cnr Marsh and Dumaresq Sts; (067) 73 8527. **Accommodation:** 5 hotels, 22 motels, 2 caravan/camping parks.
MAP REF. 113 L8

Ashford   Population 602

This small New England town is the centre of a tobacco-growing district. **In the area:** Network of limestone caves and spectacular Macintyre Falls, 36 km north-west. Pindari Dam, 20 km south; bushwalking, swimming, fishing, camping, barbecue facilities. **Tourist information:** Water Towers Complex, Campbell St, Inverell; (067) 22 1693. **Accommodation:** 1 hotel, 1 caravan/camping park.
MAP REF. 113 K4, 435 N13

Ballina   Population 12 398

A fishing town at the mouth of the Richmond River in northern NSW, Ballina's ideal year-round temperatures, picturesque farmlands, golden beaches and a friendly rural atmosphere make the area a popular family holiday destination. Cedar-cutters were among the first settlers, attracted by the red cedar trees along the shores of the river. Farmers followed and by the turn of the century the dairy-farming industry was firmly established alongside sugarcane plantations. **Of interest:** Ballina Maritime Museum, in Tourist Information Centre; steam riverboat exhibit and restored Las Balsas Expedition rafts that sailed from South America in 1973. Framed Gallery, River St. Opal and Gem Museum, Pine St. Quilts and Collectables, Martin St. Balina Outdoor Entertainment Reserve, Canal Rd. The Big Prawn, Pacific Hwy; fresh seafood, antiques, arts and crafts. *Richmond Princess* river cruises. **In the area:** MacKay Harrison Galleries, 2 km north on Lennox Head Rd. Freshwater Lake Ainsworth, 12 km north, at Lennox Head. Macadamia Land, 17 km north at Knockrow; entertainment park. Broadwater Sugar Mill, on Pacific Hwy at Broadwater, 19 km south; inspection tours during sugar season; covered shoes must be worn. Thursday Plantation Tea Tree Oil, 3 km west; guided tours. Macadamia Magic at Alphadale, 25 km west; processing and packaging of nuts. **Tourist information:** Las Balsas Plaza; (066) 86 3484. **Accommodation:** 14 motels, 8 caravan/camping parks.
MAP REF. 113 Q3, 435 Q13

Balranald   Population 1398

On the Murrumbidgee River, 438 km from Melbourne, in a wool, cattle, wheat, fruit and timber area. **Of interest:** Historic Homebush Hotel (1878), former Bank of NSW, Historical Museum and Heritage Park. Lions Park has barbecue facilities and children's playground. **In the area:** Balranald (low-level) Weir for picnics, barbecues and fishing. Yanga Lake, 7 km south-east; good fishing and water sports. Mungo National Park, 150 km north-west. **Tourist information:** Market St; (050) 20 1599. **Accommodation:** 1 hotel/motel, 4 motels, 1 caravan/camping park.
MAP REF. 116 H9, 215 O6

Bangalow   Population 677

Discover the rustic charm of this delightful village, set amidst magnificent scenery. **Of interest:** Many art, craft and antique shops. Colourful market, held every fourth Sun. **In the area:** Byron Creek walking-track, passing through splendid rainforest to picnic area. Beaches at Byron Bay, 12 km east. **Tourist information:** Byron Tourist Information Office, 69 Jonson St, Byron Bay; (066) 85 8050. **Accommodation:** 1 hotel, 1 motel.
MAP REF. 113 Q2, 435 Q12

Barham–Koondrook

Population 1041

These twin towns, situated on either side of the Murray River, are centres for the timber, fat lamb, cattle, dairying and tourism industries. **Of interest:** Barham Lakes Complex, Murray St; man-made lakes, 4 km walking track, picnic/barbecue areas, swimming, paddle-boats and canoes for hire. Bonum Red Gum Saw Mill, Moulamein Rd. **In the area:** Gannawarra Wetlander Cruises, 15 km south via Koondrook. Barbecue cruises. Houseboats for hire. Shannkirst Cashmere Stud, Koondrook. **Tourist information:** 25 Murray St, Barham; (054) 53 3100. **Accommodation:** 2 hotels, 6 motels, 3 caravan/camping parks.
MAP REF. 116 I12, 215 R13

Barooga   Population 710

A small, but rapidly growing town near the Victorian town of Cobram, Barooga's beautiful setting and abundant wildlife make it a popular holiday resort. **Of interest:** Sandy beaches along Murray River. Barooga Sportsmen's Club, with poker machines, and Cobram–Barooga Golf Club; both offer entertainment and restaurants. Binghi Boomerang Factory, Tocumwal Rd. **In the area:** Kramner Cellars (Seppelts Vineyards), Mulwala Rd, 2 km east. Brentwood Fruit Juices, 6 km east. Drop-irrigation junction. Citrus and grape growing. **Tourist information:** The Old Grain Shed, cnr Station St and Punt Rd, Cobram; (058) 72 2132. **Accommodation:** 1 hotel, 6 motels, 2 caravan/camping parks.
MAP REF. 117 M13, 217 K3

Barraba   Population 1498

Surrounded by magnificent mountain scenery on the Manilla River in the Nandewar Ranges, Barraba is the centre for an agricultural and pastoral area and an ideal base for exploring the eastern part of the Nandewar Mountains. **Of interest:** Nandewar Historical Museum; open by request. Clay Pan Fuller Gallery, Queen St. **In the area:** Adam's Lookout, 4 km north. Breathtaking views from Mt Kaputar's summit, reached by good road from Narrabri. Horton River Falls and Horton Valley, 38 km north-west towards Mt Kaputar National Park; picnic/barbecue facilities. **Tourist information:** 116 Queen St; (067) 82 1255. **Accommodation:** 3 hotels, 1 motel, 2 caravan/camping parks. **See also:** New England.
MAP REF. 113 J7

Batemans Bay   Population 6492

Crayfish and oysters are the specialty of this attractive resort town on the Princes Hwy. The charming site, at the estuary of

THE SOUTH COAST

The southern coast of New South Wales — from Batemans Bay down to the Victorian border — is a fisherman's paradise. Hemmed in by the Great Dividing Range, it is one of the finest areas for fishing in southern Australia. It is also a haven for anyone who enjoys swimming, surfing or bushwalking in an unspoiled setting.

One of the attractions of this stretch of coast is the variety of country to be seen: superb white surf beaches, and crystal-clear blue sea against a backdrop of craggy mountains, gentle hills, lakes, inlets and forests. The coast is dotted with quaint little fishing and holiday resorts, which have a wide range of hotel, motel and holiday flat accommodation, as well as many caravan parks. These towns are not highly commercialised, although many of them triple their population in the peak summer months. Boats of all kinds can be hired at the major resorts.

Peaceful **Batemans Bay**, at the estuary of the Clyde River, has become very popular with Canberra people since the road linking the Monaro and Princes Highways was updated. **Narooma**, **Montague Island** and **Bermagui** are famous for their big-game fishing. Black marlin, blue fin and hammerhead sharks are the main catch. Narooma also boasts an eighteen-hole cliff-side golf course where you tee off from the third hole across a narrow canyon.

Bega, to the south, is the unofficial capital of the area and is an important dairying and cheese-making centre. As Bega is about ten minutes inland from the coast and two hours from the snowfields, the town's proud boast is that you can ski in the Snowies and surf in the Pacific on the same day. Further south is the popular holiday resort of **Merimbula** and its sister village of **Pambula**.

The southernmost town of the region is the quaint old fishing village of **Eden**, and its former rival settlement, **Boydtown**, both reminders of the colourful whaling days of the last century.

Fishing is excellent all along the coast. You can catch a wide variety of fish, including rock cod, bream and jewfish, from the beach or net crayfish off the rockier parts of the coast. Prawning is good in the scattered inlets; and trout and perch can be caught in the many rivers draining from the mountains.

Because of its position, the South Coast attracts tourists from Victoria and Canberra, as well as from other parts of New South Wales. The region's all-year-round mild climate has made it a favourite with visitors, but you must book well ahead in the peak holiday period.

For further information, contact the Sapphire Coast Tourist Association, PO Box 424, Bega; (064) 92 3313.

Excellent surfing beaches line the South Coast

the Clyde River, 294 km south of Sydney, makes it an ideal picnic and bushwalking spot. **Of interest:** Birdland Animal Park, Beach Rd; native and exotic birds, wildlife, rainforest trail, picnic areas and barbecues. Excellent swimming, surfing and fishing; outstanding bowling club. **In the area:** Shell Museum, Batehaven, 1 km east; shells from all over world. Mogo Goldfields Park, Mogo, 8 km south; features working gold-mine. Surfing at Malua Bay, 10 km south-east. Durras and Durras Lake, 10 km north, for fishing, swimming and varied wildlife; houseboats for hire. Murramarang National Park, 10 km north; rainforest and popular swimming beaches. Nelligen, 10 km north-west, on Clyde River, for picnics, water-skiing and cruises. Araluen, old gold-mining town, 82 km north-west. **Tourist information:** Eurobodalla Coast Visitors Centre, Princes Hwy; (044) 72 6900. **Accommodation:** 16 motels, 4 caravan/camping parks. **See also:** The South Coast.
MAP REF. 109 G7, 110 H12

Bathurst Population 22 237

This sedate old city, 209 km west of Sydney on the Macquarie River, has many historic connections. It is the centre of a pastoral and fruit- and grain-growing district, and the birthplace of former Prime Minister, J.B. Chifley, although today it is possibly better known for its famous motor racing circuit, Mount Panorama. **Of interest:** Self-guiding Historic Walking Tour. Ben Chifley's Cottage, Busby St. Historical Society Museum in East Wing of court-house, Russell St. Miss Traill's house (c. 1845), 321 Russell St; contents, collected by one family over 100 years, record history of town and reflect family's passion for horse-breeding and racing. Bathurst Regional Art Gallery, Keppel St. **In the area:** Fossicker's Self-drive Tour of Bathurst (60–90 min.) South of town, on Panorama Ave, Mt Panorama: Bathurst Gold Diggings, Karingal Village; reconstruction of gold-mining era. Motor races held at Mt Panorama Circuit in Oct. Bathurst Motor Racing Museum nearby. Magnificent views from lookout at summit of Mt Panorama; picnic area in McPhillamy Park. Sir Joseph Banks Nature Reserve in park. Bathurst Sheep and Cattle Drome at Rossmore Park, 6 km north-east on Limekilns Rd, Kelso; performing sheep and cattle. Milking, shearing, sheep-dog demonstrations. Abercrombie Caves, 72 km south, via Trunkey, on Bathurst–Goulburn Rd; limestone cave system containing spectacular Arch Cave, considered one of finest natural arches in world and larger than Grand Arch at Jenolan Caves. Kanangra-Boyd National Park;

Kangaroos, Pebbly Beach, near Batemans Bay

major access off Oberon–Jenolan Caves Rd, 5 km south of caves. Abercrombie House (1870s), 6 km west, on Ophir Rd; baronial-style Gothic mansion. Hill End Historic Site, 86 km north-west; former goldfield, many original buildings, some restored. Visitor Centre in old Hill End Hospital. Equipment for panning and fossicking for hire in village. Other old gold towns nearby include Rockley, O'Connell, Trunkey Creek and Sofala. Newhaven Park, Georges Plains; Yarrabin Guest Property, O'Connell; and Chesleigh Homestead, Sofala; offer farm holidays. **Tourist information:** East Wing, Court-house Building, Russell St; (063) 33 6288. **Accommodation:** 7 hotels, 13 motels, 1 caravan/camping park.
MAP REF. 110 G5

Batlow Population 1227

This timber-milling and former gold-mining town in the Great Dividing Range south of Tumut is situated in a district renowned for its apples, pears and berry fruits. **Of interest:** Granny Smith's Country Cottage, Pioneer St; arts, crafts, teas and tourist information. Museum, Mayday Rd. Mountain Maid Cannery, off Kurrajong Ave, and Batlow Fruit Packing Complex, Forest Rd; seasonal tours. Superb town views from Weemala Lookout Flora and Fauna Reserve, H.V. Smith Dr. Apple Blossom Festival held in Oct. **In the area:** Hume and Hovell's Lookout, 6 km east; views over Blowering Reservoir and picnic area at site where explorers paused in 1824. Blowering Reservoir, 53 km east; picnic/barbecue areas. Bush-walks and drives through scenic areas on south-west slopes of Bago State Forest. Access points to 370 km

Hume and Hovell Walking Trail, which runs from Yass to Albury. Several farms on Tumut Rd offer pick-your-own berry fruits and cherries. **Tourist information:** Pioneer St; (069) 49 1447. **Accommodation:** 1 hotel, 1 motel, 1 caravan park.
MAP REF. 109 B6, 110 D11, 117 R11, 219 H1

Bega Population 4294

It is possible to swim and ski on the same day when staying at Bega, set as it is between the beach and the best Kosciusko snow resorts. This town, at the junction of the Princes and Snowy Mountains Hwys, which link Sydney, Melbourne and Canberra, is important for its position. **Of interest:** Bega Family Historical Museum, cnr Bega and Auckland Sts. Grevillea Estate Winery, Buckajo Rd; open daily for tastings and sales. Inspection of Bega Cheese Factory, North Bega (well signposted). **In the area:** Bega Valley Lookout (2 km north) and Dr George Lookout (8 km north-east) for fine views. Brogo Valley Rotolactor, 18 km north; see cows being milked. Tathna, 18 km east; beautiful beaches and historic wharf. Mimosa Rocks National Park, 17 km north of Tathra, offers swimming, fishing and bushwalking. Water sports on Wallagoot Lake, 10 km south of Tathra. Bushwalking, fishing and canoeing at Bournda National Park, 20 km south-east of Bega. Historic village of Candelo, 23 km south-west, untouched by time; art gallery and monthly market. **Tourist information:** Gipps St; (064) 92 2045. **Accommodation:** 5 hotels, 5 motels, 2 caravan/camping parks. **See also:** The South Coast.
MAP REF. 109 F10

Bellingen   Population 1834

Attractive tree-lined town on the banks of the Bellinger River in the rich dairylands of the Bellinger Valley. In pioneer days it was a timber-getting and shipbuilding centre. **Of interest:** Much of town classified by Heritage Commission. Restored Hammond and Wheatley Emporium. **In the area:** River walks. Scenic island in river. Picnicking at Thora, 14 km west, at foot of Mt Dorrigo. State forests for bush-walking and horseriding. Trout fishing in streams on Dorrigo Plateau. **Tourist information:** Yellow Shed, cnr High and Prince Sts; (066) 55 1189. **Accommodation:** 1 hotel, 1 motel, 1 caravan/camping park.
MAP REF. 113 P8

Bermagui   Population 995

Fishing in all forms — lake, estuary, deep-sea and big-game — is excellent in this delightful small port, 13 km from the Princes Hwy. It was much publicised for its fishing by American novelist-sportsman Zane Grey in the 1930s. **Of interest:** Beautiful rock-pools, rugged coastline and unspoiled countryside. **In the area:** Wallaga Lake National Park, 8 km north; boating, fishing, swimming, bushwalking and picnicking. Montague Island, 23 km north; mecca for big-game fishermen from all over world. Cobargo, on Princes Hwy, 19 km west; unspoiled old town with several art galleries, wood and leather crafts, pottery and tearooms. **Tourist information:** Newsagency, 5 Coluga St; (064) 93 4240. **Accommodation:** Bermagui, 1 hotel, 4 motels, 5 caravan/camping parks. Cobargo, 1 motel. **See also:** The South Coast.
MAP REF. 109 G9

Berridale   Population 670

Berridale is a rural town near Lake Eucumbene, Lake Jindabyne and the southern ski-fields. **Of interest:** In Exchange Sq., Berridale Pottery and Peels Inn (1863). Snowy River Ag Barn and Fibre Centre, and Snowy River Winery, on road south to Dalgety. **Tourist information:** Snowy River Shire Council, 2 Myack St; (064) 56 3251. **Accommodation:** 1 hotel, 5 motels, 1 caravan/camping park.
MAP REF. 109 D9

Berrigan   Population 993

A traditional country town with many old buildings reflecting a bygone era, Berrigan is the headquarters of the Berrigan Shire Council and is best known for its connections with horseracing. **Of interest:** Historic buildings. Berrigan Racecourse and Kilfenora Racing Stables. Sojourn Station Art Studio. Golf course and other sports amenities. **Tourist in-**

formation: Tocumwal Tourist Information Centre, Tocumwal River Foreshore, Tocumwal; (058) 74 2131. **Accommodation:** 3 hotels, 1 hotel/ motel, 1 motel, 1 caravan/camping park.
MAP REF. 117 M12, 217 L1

Berrima   Population 654

A superbly preserved 1830s Australian town. **Of interest:** Many old buildings restored as craft and antique shops, restaurants and galleries. Australia's oldest licensed hotel, the Surveyor General (1834), still operating. Harper's Mansion (1834), Historical Museum and gaol (1839) once used to house convicts. Court-house; excellent video of early Berrima. **Tourist information:** Winifred West Park, Old Hume Hwy, Mittagong; (048) 71 2888. **Accommodation:** 2 motels.
MAP REF. 109 G3, 110 I8

Berry   Population 1375

Old English trees add to the charm of this picturesque township on the Princes Hwy, 18 km north of Nowra. In the midst of rich dairying country, it was founded by David Berry, whose brother Alexander was the first settler in the Shoalhaven area. **Of interest:** Several buildings with National Trust classifications, including Historical Museum. **In the area:** Cambewarra Lookout, 14 km west. Coolangatta, 11 km south-east, on site of first settlement in area in 1822; group of convict-built cottages, restored and converted into historic village and resort. **Tourist information:** Princes Hwy, Bomaderry; (044) 21 0778. **Accommodation:** 1 hotel, 2 motels.
MAP REF. 107 E10, 109 H4, 111 J9

Bingara   Population 1363

Diamonds, sapphires, tourmalines and gold may be found in the local creeks and rivers of this fascinating little town. **Of interest:** All Nations Gold Mine, top of Hill St. Historical Society Museum (1860), in slab building thought to be town's first hotel and classified by National Trust; houses collection of old furniture and photographs depicting early days of district. Murray Cod Hatchery, Bandalong St; open by request. Good fishing in town's rivers and creeks. **In the area:** Upper Bingara goldfields, 24 km south; remains of old gold and copper mines, also Chinese cemetery. Glacial area at Rocky Creek, 37 km south-west; good spot for gold-panning. Copeton Dam, 42 km east, for fishing and boating. **Tourist information:** Shire Offices, 33 Maitland St; (067) 24 1505. **Accommodation:** 2 hotels, 1 motel, 1 caravan/ camping park. **See also:** New England.
MAP REF. 113 J5

Blayney   Population 2593

On the Mid Western Hwy between Cowra and Bathurst, Blayney is a rural town close to the historic villages of Carcoar and Millthorpe. **Of interest:** Holly Folly craft shop, Adelaide Rd. **In the area:** Taroona Wool Pack, 8 km east, on Bathurst Rd. Cottesbrook Galleries, on Mid Western Hwy, 15 km east. Carcoar, 14 km south-west, reminiscent of English village and scene of NSW's first bank hold-up in 1863; many delightful buildings and shops, pleasant picnic areas and Stokes Stable Museum. Carcoar Dam, 15 km south; picnic areas, fishing, water sports and overnight camping. Golden Memories Museum and Millthorpe Crafts and Book Store at Millthorpe, 13 km north. **Tourist information:** Bathurst and District Tourism, East Wing, Courthouse Building, Russell St; (063) 33 6288. **Accommodation:** 4 hotels, 1 motel, 1 caravan park.
MAP REF. 110 F5

Boggabri   Population 967

Situated 115 km north-west of Tamworth, farming pursuits such as shearing, cotton growing and wheat harvesting are a feature of the area. Farm visits and accommodation are available and can be arranged through the Visitor Information Centre at Narrabri. **Of interest:** Historical Museum, Brent St. Honey factory, Lynn St; inspection by appointment. Wean Picnic Races held in May. Gum Tree Clay Pigeon Shoot, Oct. Labour Day weekend. **In the area:** Gemstone fossicking. Fishing. Gin's Leap, rock formation, 4 km north. Dripping Rock waterfall, on Manilla Rd, 35 km east. **Tourist information:** Newell Hwy, Narrabri; (067) 92 3583. **Accommodation:** 3 hotels, 1 motel, 1 caravan/camping park.
MAP REF. 112 H8

Bombala   Population 1458

This small town on the Monaro Hwy, 89 km south of Cooma, supports wool, beef cattle, sheep, vegetables and timber-milling and is a rich trout-fishing area. **Of interest:** Historical Walk (1 hr) around town includes Old Mechanics Institute and court-house; self-guided leaflet available. White House Gallery, (c.1835) Caveat St. **In the area:** Historic homestead, Burnima, 6 km north on Monaro Hwy; open by arrangement. Coolumbooka Nature Reserve, 15 km north-east. Gold-mines at Craigie, 33 km south-west. Scenic drive to Bendoc Mines, 57 km south-west into Vic.; gold fossicking along route, with landowners' permission. **Tourist information:** The White House, 34 Caveat St; (064) 58 3751.

Accommodation: 3 hotels, 1 motel, 1 caravan/ camping park.
MAP REF. 109 E11, 221 N2

Bourke Population 3018
Anything 'Back o' Bourke is the real outback. Bourke itself is the service centre of a vast area of sheep country which produces up to 55 000 bales of wool a year. It is claimed to be the largest centre for wool shipment in the world. **Of interest:** Fishing for cod in Darling River. Annual events include: Festival of Sport at Easter, Breakaway to Bourke and Bourke to B— (a different destination each year, but always a name starting with 'B') Bash in June, picnic races in Aug. and Sept., Outback Trek in Sep. and Outback Surf Classic in Oct. Annual Explorers Trial car rally leaves Bourke for Warrumbungle National Park each Easter. **In the area:** Mt Gunderbooka, 74 km south, has caves with Aboriginal art. Fort Bourke Stockade, 20 km south-west; testament to early explorer Major Thomas Mitchell. Mt Oxley, 40 km east, for superb views of plains. **Tourist information:** 45 Mitchell Street; (068) 72 2280. **Accommodation:** 4 hotels, 4 motels, 3 caravan/camping parks.
MAP REF. 115 M6

Bowral Population 7390
The friendly township of Bowral nestles below Mount Gibraltar, 114 km south of Sydney. Originally a popular summer retreat for wealthy Sydney residents, who left a legacy of stately mansions and beautiful gardens, Bowral today is a thriving town with a harmonious blending of modern and colonial architecture. **Of interest:** Corbett Gardens, Merigang St, showpiece of Tulip Time Festival held in Sept., as are Milton Park Gardens, Horderns Rd. Bradman Oval, near house where cricketer Sir Donald Bradman spent his youth, and the Bradman Museum, St Jude St. Specialty shopping in antiques, especially Bong Bong St. Bowral also has many restaurants and a variety of accommodation, from country resorts to guest-houses and bed and breakfast cottages. **In the area:** Lookout on Mt Gibraltar, 2 km north. **Tourist information:** Winifred West Park, Old Hume Hwy, Mittagong; (048) 71 2888. **Accommodation:** 2 hotels, 6 motels.
MAP REF. 107 A6, 109 H3, 110 I8

Braidwood Population 958
This old town, 84 km south of Goulburn, has been declared a historic village by the National Trust. Gold was discovered in the area in 1852 and Braidwood developed as the principal town of the southern goldfields. Much of the architecture

BACK O'BOURKE

Once you go beyond Bourke you are off the beaten tourist track, and for a very good reason; the far west of New South Wales is one of the state's most fascinating and uniquely Australian areas. It is the real outback of Australian folklore, depicted so graphically in the stories of Henry Lawson.

The far west of New South Wales is an area of vast red plains, dotted with rock ranges and small creeks. The area boasts a variety of native flora and fauna. For most of the year Bourke itself offers a pleasant climate, but the summer can be very hot, into the 40s. If you prepare for your trip carefully and stay on gazetted roads, you will have a fascinating holiday. But before you venture on to secondary roads, consult the locals about road conditions. **See also:** Outback Motoring.

Cameron Corner, junction of the NSW, SA and Qld borders

from this period has survived. **Of interest:** Museum, churches, old hotels, restaurants, galleries, craft and antique shops. Self-guiding leaflet describing many of town's historic buildings available. **Tourist information:** Museum, Wallace St; (048) 42 2310. **Accommodation:** 2 hotels, 1 motel.
MAP REF. 109 F6, 110 G11

Brewarrina Population 1166
Located 95 km east of Bourke, this town takes its name from an Aboriginal word for 'good fishing', which is still very appropriate. Pastoral activities include grazing and wheat production. **Of interest:** Aboriginal fisheries in bed of Darling River. Aboriginal Cultural Museum presents aspects of Aboriginal life from the Dreamtime to present. Festival of Fisheries held early Sept. Wildlife park in Doyle St. **In the area:** Narran Lake, 40 km east, for native birdlife and other fauna. **Tourist information:** Shire Offices, Bathurst St; (068) 39 2308. **Accommodation:** 2 hotels, 1 motel, 1 caravan/camping park.
MAP REF. 112 A6, 115 O6

Broken Hill Population 24 460
This artificial oasis in the vast arid lands of far western NSW was created to serve the miners in the incredibly rich silver-lead-zinc mines of the Barrier Range. The green parks and colourful gardens of this city, 1170 km west of Sydney, seem unreal in the setting of the surrounding semi-desert. The city's water supply comes from local water-storage schemes and from the Menindee Lakes on the Darling River. The mines produce 2 million tonnes of ore annually. Note that Broken Hill operates on Central Standard Time, that is half an hour behind the rest of NSW. **Of interest:** Self-guided Heritage Trails. Historic streetscape in Argent St classified by National Trust. Railway,

Mineral and Train Museum, cnr Blende and Bromide Sts, Bond Store Museum, cnr Crystal and Bromide Sts. White's Mineral Art and Mining Museum, Allendale St. Many art galleries, including Entertainment Centre, cnr Blende and Chloride Sts, featuring Silver Tree, commissioned by Charles Rasp, discoverer of Broken Hill ore-body in 1883. Broken Hill is home of legendary Brushmen of the Bush, group of artists that includes Pro Hart and Jack Absalom. Inspection of School of the Air, cnr McCulloch and Lane Sts. Underground mine tours to Delprat's Mine, off Crystal St. Moslem Mosque (1891), Buck St; built by Afghan community who then lived in town. **In the area:** Inspection of Royal Flying Doctor Service, 10 km east at airport. Zinc Twin Lakes, off Wentworth Rd, South Broken Hill. Water sports, fishing and camping at Menindee Lakes, 110 km south-east. Sundown Nature Trail, 9 km north on Tibooburra Rd. Silverton, 24 km north-west, where silver chlorides were discovered in 1883. Town used as location for such films as *Wake in Fright, Mad Max 2* and *A Town Like Alice*. Within town: tours of Day Dream Mine; Heritage Walking Trail; Peter Browne's Art Gallery; Horizon Gallery; Silverton Hotel; Silverton Gaol Museum; camel rides. Mundi Mundi Plains Lookout, 4 km further north, and Umberumberka Reservoir Lookout, 39 km north-west. Mootwingee National Park, 130 km north-east of Broken Hill; magnificent scenery and rich in Aboriginal relics. Visitors are advised to be fully self-sufficient in food, water and fuel. **Tourist information:** Cnr Blende and Bromide Sts; (080) 87 6077. **Accommodation:** 12 hotels, 13 motels, 3 caravan/camping parks.
MAP REF. 114 B12, 116 B1

Brunswick Heads

Population 1585
This small town at the mouth of the Brunswick River is renowned for its outstanding fishing and a large commercial fishing fleet is based here. Boats and canoes can be hired; also good for surfing, swimming and water-skiing. **Of interest:** Annual events: Fish and Chips (wood chop) Festival in Jan.; Blessing of the Fleet and Fishing Festival at Easter; River Festival in Nov. Popular Brunswick Heads Markets held first Sat. of every month. **In the area:** New Brighton Hotel, old pub with 'character', at Billinudgel, 7 km north. Pioneer Plantation at Mooball, 14 km north, offers guided tours of banana farm and walk-through wildlife habitat. Crystal Castle, outside Mullumbimby, 10 km west; collection of crystal. Cape Byron lighthouse at Byron Bay, 19 km south.

Minyon Falls, 50 km south-west; picnic area in Rummery Park, with walking tracks. **Tourist information:** Byron Tourist Information Office, 69 Jonson St, Byron Bay; (066) 85 8050. **Accommodation:** 1 hotel, 4 motels, 3 caravan/camping parks.
MAP REF. 113 R2, 435 Q12

Bulahdelah   Population 1098

Situated on the Pacific Hwy at the foot of Alum Mountain, Bulahdelah is a good base for a bushwalking or houseboating holiday. **Of interest:** Mountain, which has huge alum deposits, also well known for its rare varieties of rock orchids. **In the area:** Bulahdelah Logging Railway, 19 km north; full-size steam tourist train, runs Fri., Sat. and school holidays. Myall Lakes National Park, 12 km east, one of the state's largest networks (10 000 ha) of coastal lakes; where water is basis of activity; bushwalking and camping in rainforest. **Tourist information:** Great Lakes Tourist Board, Little St, Forster; (065) 54 8799. **Accommodation:** 4 motels, 1 caravan/camping park.
MAP REF. 111 N2

Bundanoon   Population 1291

This charming township is located 32 km south of Mittagong. The area is renowned for its deep gullies and magnificent views over the rugged mountains and gorges of the Morton National Park. While many of the lookouts can be reached by car, some visitors prefer to walk. In April, when the mists roll in from the gullies, Bundanoon becomes Brigadoon for a day and celebrates with spectacular highland games. Bundanoon was once well known as a honeymoon resort: today it boasts an English-style pub, delightful guesthouses and a health resort. The train stops in the heart of the town. **Tourist information:** Winifred West Park, Old Hume Hwy, Mittagong; (048) 71 2888. **Accommodation:** 1 hotel, 5 motels, 2 caravan/camping parks.
MAP REF. 109 G4, 110 I9

Byron Bay   Population 3730

Surfers from near and far gravitate to Wategos Beach, on Cape Byron. Due to its northerly aspect, it is one of the best beaches for surfboard riding on the east coast. Dairy products, bacon, beef and tropical fruits are produced locally. Visitors can go bushwalking, horseriding, fishing, swimming, scuba-diving or paragliding, or just do absolutely nothing while enjoying the delightful climate and relaxing lifestyle of this idyllic spot. **In the area:** Australia's most powerful lighthouse, 3 km south-east at Cape Byron, most easterly point on Australian mainland; walking trail and lookout.

Award-winning Wheel Resort, 3 km south; caters especially for disabled visitors. The Everglades, Suffolk Park, 6 km south. **Tourist information:** 69 Jonson St; (066) 85 8050. **Accommodation:** 2 hotels, 18 motels, 4 caravan/camping parks.
MAP REF. 113 R2, 435 Q12

Camden   Population 10 065

In 1805 John Macarthur was granted 5000 acres at what was known as the Cowpastures, where he began his famous sheep-breeding experiments. The township of Camden dates from 1840, and is located 60 km south-west of Sydney on the Camden Valley Way. **Of interest:** Many historic buildings, including Belgenny (1819) and Camden Park House (1834), both part of Macarthur's Camden Estate, Elizabeth Macarthur Dr; Church of St John the Evangelist (1840–49), John St; Camelot, designed by J. Horbury Hunt, and Kirkham Stables (1816) both in Kirkham Lane. Camden History Museum, John St. **In the area:** El Caballo Blanco, featuring famous dancing Andalusian horses; also antique horse-drawn carriage museum, large wildlife reserve and fun park. Historic Gledswood homestead and winery, next door to El Caballo Blanco; both at Catherine Field, 10 km north. Museum of Aviation at Narellan, 3 km north-east. Mt Annan Botanic Garden on Narellan Rd. Hot-air balloon flights, gliding and skydiving. **Tourist information:** Macarthur Country Tourist Assocn, cnr Hume Hwy and Congressional Dr, Liverpool; (02) 821 2311. **Accommodation:** 3 motels, 1 caravan park. **See also:** Wineries of New South Wales.
MAP REF. 101 K12, 109 H2, 111 J7

Camden Haven   Population 3524

A fisherman's dream, consisting of the villages Laurieton, North Haven and Dunbogan, all less than 3 km apart, 44 km south of Port Macquarie; Camden Haven has a tidal inlet for estuary fishing. **Of interest:** Oysters, lobsters, crabs, bream and flathead, in local rivers and lakes. Seafront well-known fishing spot. Delightful bushwalks along seafront and around lakes. Panoramic views from North Brother Mountain. **Tourist information:** Pacific Hwy, Kew; (065) 59 4400. **Accommodation:** Laurieton, 1 hotel, 3 motels, 2 caravan/camping parks. North Haven, 2 motels, 3 caravan/camping parks.
MAP REF. 113 O11

Campbelltown   Population 37 140

Named by Governor Macquarie in 1820 after his wife's maiden name, Campbelltown is now a rapidly growing city. It is

also the location for the legend of Fisher's ghost: the ghost of a murdered convict is alleged to have pointed to the place where his body was subsequently found and as a result the murderer was brought to justice. **Of interest:** Campbelltown City Bicentennial Art Gallery and Japanese Gardens, Art Gallery Rd, cnr Camden and Appin Rds. Historic buildings include Glenalvon (1840), and Richmond Villa (1830–40) in Lithgow St; Colonial Houses at 284–298 Queen St; St Peter's Church (1823), Cordeaux St; Old St John's Church, cnr Broughton and George Sts, with grave of James Ruse; Emily Cottage (1840), cnr Menangle and Camden Rds; and Campbelltown Art and Craft Society (licensed as Farrier's Arms Inn in 1843), and Fisher's Ghost Restaurant, formerly Kendall's Millhouse (1844), both in Queen St. Annual Festival of Fisher's Ghost held in Nov. **In the area:** Mount Annan Botanic Garden, 10 km west, on Narellan Rd. Menangle House (1839) and St James's Church at Menangle, 9 km south-west. **Tourist information:** Macarthur Country Tourist Assocn, cnr Hume Hwy and Congressional Dr, Liverpool; (02) 821 2311. **Accommodation:** 4 motels.
MAP REF. 101 L12, 109 I2, 111 J7

Canowindra   Population 1717
Bushranger Ben Hall and his gang commandeered this township in 1863. Canowindra today is known as the 'Balloon Capital of Australia'; hot-air balloons fly every weekend from April to October. Situated on the Belubula River, Canowindra is noted for its unusual curving main street and notable buildings; the entire commercial section has been classified by the National Trust as a Heritage Conservation Area. **Of interest:** Museum, antique shops and display gallery for the Knitters Guild of NSW. **Accommodation:** 3 hotels, 1 motel, 1 caravan/camping park.
MAP REF. 110 E5

Casino   Population 10 067
This important commercial centre on the Richmond River could be dubbed the city of parks. There are about 20 in all, most with good picnic facilities. **Of interest:** Casino Folk Museum, Walker St. Freshwater fishing on Cooke's Weir and Richmond River. **In the area:** Aboriginal rock carvings, 20 km west on Tenterfield Rd. **Tourist information:** Memorial Baths Centre, Centre St; (066) 62 3566. **Accommodation:** 3 hotels, 5 motels, 2 caravan/camping parks.
MAP REF. 113 P3, 435 Q13

Cessnock   Population 17 506
Many of the excellent Hunter River table wines are produced in the Cessnock district. The economy of the city, formerly based on coal-mining, is now centred on both wine and tourism. **In the area:** Hot-air ballooning at Rothbury, 11 km north. 'Rusa Park', Exotic Wildlife Park, at Nulkaba, 7 km north-west. Peppers guesthouse resort at Pokolbin, 14 km north-west. Over 40 quality wineries open for tastings and sales in Pokolbin area. At Pelaw Main, 17 km east, Richmond Main Mining Museum; steam train rides. Picturesque village of Wollombi, 29 km south-west, with wealth of historic buildings, including beautiful St John's Anglican Church, court-house (now Endeavour Museum) and old-style general store/post office. Also horseriding. Watagan Mountains and State Forest, 33 km south-east; picnic/barbecue facilities at Heaton, Hunter's and McLean's Lookouts. **Tourist information:** cnr Mt View and Wollombi Rds; (049) 90 4477. **Accommodation:** 11 hotels, 28 motels, 3 caravan/camping parks.
MAP REF. 104 C5, 111 K3

Cobar   Population 4287
A progressive copper, gold, silver, lead and zinc mining town with wide tree-lined streets, Cobar is 723 km north-west of Sydney. The town is on the Barrier Hwy, used by travellers to visit outback areas of NSW, Qld and NT. Since the opening of the CSA Copper Mine in the mid-1960s, and the introduction of a channel water-supply, the town has been transformed

from an arid landscape to a green oasis. The CSA Mine, which is the most highly mechanised mine in Australia, has an annual output of 600 000 tonnes of copper and copper-zinc ores. The Elura silver-lead-zinc mine opened in 1983 and the Peak gold mine in 1992. Wool is the main local primary industry. **Of interest:** Regional Museum, Barrier Hwy; pastoral, mining and technological displays. Fine early architecture, including court-house and police station, Barton St; St Laurence O'Toole Catholic Church, Prince St; and Great Western Hotel, Marshall St, with longest iron-lace verandah in state. Above-ground tours of CSA Mine on Fri. aftn, or by special arrangement. **In the area:** Commonwealth Meteorological Station, 4 km north-west; inspection by appointment. Mt Grenfell Aboriginal cave paintings, turn-off 40 km west on Barrier Hwy, near Mt Grenfell homestead; human and animal figures densely cover walls of rock shelters; picnic area nearby. **Tourist information:** Cobar Regional Museum, Barrier Hwy; (068) 36 2448. **Accommodation:** 2 hotels, 1 hotel/motel, 6 motels, 1 caravan/camping park.
MAP REF. 115 M10

Coffs Harbour   Population 18 074
One of the larger centres on the Holiday Coast, this popular subtropical resort town is 580 km north of Sydney on the Pacific Hwy. The surrounding districts produce timber, bananas, vegetables, dairy products and fish. Coffs Harbour is really two towns — one on the highway and the other near the artificial harbour

Bellbird Hotel, Cessnock

and railway station. **Of interest:** Historic buildings around harbour area include Pier Hotel (rebuilt 1920s) and jetty (1892). Coffs Harbour Museum, High St. Pet Porpoise Pool, Orlando St; sea circus with performing porpoises and seals, also research and nursery facilities. Aquajet Waterslide, Park Beach Rd. Mutton Bird Island National Park, 1 km walk across sea wall. North Coast Regional Botanical Gardens complex, Hardacre St. **In the area:** Clog-making and Dutch village at Clog Barn on Pacific Hwy, 2 km north. The Big Banana, 4 km north along Pacific Hwy; unusual concrete landmark in form of huge banana has displays inside illustrating banana industry; Big Banana Theme Park includes Aboriginal Dreamtime Cave experience and 'realistic' bunyip; World of Horticulture, with monorail, is nearby; all open daily. Coastline views from surrounding area. Nude bathing at Little Digger Beach, 4 km north. Coffs Harbour Zoo, 14 km north; koalas, kangaroos, deer and wombats; also Devonshire teas. Bruxner Park Flora Reserve, Korora, 9 km north-west; dense tropical jungle area of vines, ferns and orchids; bushwalking tracks and picnic area at Park Creek. Georges Gold Mine tours, 38 km west. Canoeing, game fishing and scuba-diving. **Tourist information:** Orara Pk, Pacific Hwy; (066) 52 1522. **Accommodation:** 9 hotels, 25 motels, 6 caravan/camping parks.
MAP REF. 113 P7

Tourist resorts, Coffs Harbour

Coleambally   Population 5622
This, the state's newest town, officially opened in June 1968 and the centre of the Coleambally Irrigation Area, is south of the Murrumbidgee River. Rice is the main crop of the 87 600 ha under irrigation; vegetables, grain, sorghum, safflower and soya beans also are grown. The town has a modern shopping centre and a rice mill. **Of interest:** Wineglass Water Tower. **Tourist information:** cnr Banna and Jondaryan Aves, Griffith; (069) 62 4145. **Accommodation:** 1 hotel, 1 motel.
MAP REF. 117 M9

Condobolin   Population 3229
On the Lachlan River, 475 km west of Sydney, Condobolin is the centre of a red-soil plains district producing wool, fat lambs, fruit and mixed farm products. **Of interest:** Community Centre, housed in old hotel, cnr Bathurst and Dennison Sts. Gum Bend Lake and olympic swimming pool. **In the area:** Aboriginal relics, 40 km west, including monument marking burial-place of one of last Lachlan tribal elders. Agricultural Research Station, 10 km east. Mt Tilga, 8 km north, said to be geographic centre of NSW; stiff climb to

summit but view is worth it. **Accommodation:** 4 hotels, 3 motels, 1 caravan/camping park.
MAP REF. 110 A4, 117 P4

Cooma   Population 7406
This lively, modern tourist centre at the junction of the Monaro and Snowy Mountains Hwys, on the Southern Tablelands of NSW, was once dubbed Australia's most cosmopolitan town. Thousands of migrants from many different countries worked here on the Snowy Mountains Scheme. Today it is a busy tourist centre all year round, and the jumping-off point for the Snowies. (Motorists are advised to check their tyres and stock up on petrol and provisions before setting off for the snow country.) **Of interest:** Lambie St Walk; introduces historic buildings classified by National Trust. Old Gaol Museum, Vale St. Clog Maker, Sharp St; clog-making demonstration by Dutch craftsman. International Avenue of Flags, Centennial Park, Sharp St; flags of 27 countries, unfurled in 1959 to commemorate 10th anniversary of Snowy Mountains Hydro-electric Authority, in recognition of varied nationalities of people who worked on project. The Time Walk, also in park; Bicentennial project presenting history of district in 40 ceramic mosaics. Snowy Mountains Authority information centre, Monaro Hwy; displays, tours. Dodgem City Entertainment, Commissioner St. **In the area:** Southern Cloud Park, on Snowy Mountains Hwy, 1 km west; display (with audio tape) of remains of *Southern Cloud* aircraft, which crashed here in 1931 but was not found until 1958. Llama Farm, 13 km west on Snowy Mountains Hwy. Cloyne Rose Gardens, 4 km north. **Tourist information:** 119 Sharp St; (064) 50 1742. **Accommodation:** 7 hotels, 19 motels, 1 caravan park, 2 caravan/camping parks.
MAP REF. 109 D8

Coonabarabran   Population 3033
A tourist-conscious town in the Warrumbungle Mountains on the Castlereagh River, 465 km north-west of Sydney, near

CAVES AND CAVERNS

Minaret formation in the River Cave, Jenolan Caves

Magical underground limestone caves are one of the geographical wonders of New South Wales. Glittering limestone stalactites and stalagmites, caused by the ceaseless dripping of limestone-impregnated water over tens of thousands of years, glow eerily in cathedral-like caves. These incredibly delicate formations of ribbed columns, frozen cascades and waterfalls and delicate 'tapestries' and 'shawls' look like part of a subterranean fairyland.

The **Jenolan Caves** are the most famous. Since they were first opened in 1866, several million people have visited them. Situated on a spur of the Great Dividing Range, a few kilometres to the south-west of the Blue Mountains, they are open daily for guided tours. The caves are surrounded by a 2430 hectare flora and fauna reserve with walking-trails, kiosk, licensed café and picnic facilities. The charming tudor-style guest-house, Jenolan Caves

House provides accommodation, as do Binda Bush Cabins.

The **Wombeyan Caves** are set in a pleasant valley in the Southern Highlands, 193 km south-west of Sydney. They can be reached from the Wombeyan turn-off, 60 kilometres north-west of Mittagong. From here a well-surfaced but narrow road winds through spectacular mountain scenery. The alternate route (and the one recommended for caravanners) is via Goulburn, Taralga and Richlands. Five of the caves are open for inspection and are easily accessible by graded paths. They are fully developed for visitors, with steps and handrails, and are open daily or on demand for self-guided tours, historical and adventure caving tours. Displays at Visitors Centre; caravan park, camping areas and family/ group accommodation available. Three walking tracks lead from reserve to attractions in area.

The **Yarrangobilly Caves**, 6.5 km

off the Snowy Mountains Highway, 109 km north of Cooma, are open daily (subject to winter road conditions) for self-guided or guided tours. On weekends, school and public holidays, additional tours are available, subject to demand. Among some 60 caves in the area only four have been developed and are open for inspection (one with wheelchair access). An added attraction here is a thermal pool. Originally a mineral spring, the pool is heated to a constant temperature of 27°C all the year round, and the water is slightly mineralised. Tours include the History Walk and the Adventure Cave Walk. The reserve surrounding the caves contains some of the most beautiful unspoiled country in the state. But bring your own food and drink; there is no kiosk in the area.

For further information, contact Jenolan Caves Reserve Trust, (063) 59 3311; Wombeyan Caves, (048) 43 5976; and Yarrangobilly Caves, (064) 54 9597.

Warrumbungle National Park. **Of interest:** Crystal Kingdom, Oxley Hwy, with unique collection of minerals found in Warrumbungle Range; open daily. **In the area:** At Miniland, 8 km west, life-size models of prehistoric animals displayed in bushland setting; also children's fun park, kiosk, picnic and barbecue facilities and historical museum. Siding Spring Observatory, 24 km west, has largest optical telescope in southern hemisphere. Warrumbungle National Park, 35 km west; bushwalking, rock-climbing, nature study, photography. Pilliga Scrub at Baradine, 44 km north-west; 390 000 ha forest consisting mainly of white cypress pine and broom plains of dense heath and scrub; location of picnic areas from Baradine Forestry Office. **Tourist information:** Bicentennial Centre, Newell Hwy; (068) 42 1441. **Accommodation:** 3 hotels, 12 motels, 3 caravan/camping parks. **See also:** The Newell.
MAP REF. 112 F10

Coonamble   Population 3058

This town on the Castlereagh Hwy is situated on the Western Plains, 518 km north-west of Sydney. It serves a district which produces wheat, wool, lamb, beef, cypress pine and hardwood timber. **Of interest:** Historical Museum, former police station and stables, Aberfond St. **In the area:** Youie Bore, 20 km north on Castlereagh Hwy; water from bore is hot and supplies five properties with stock water. Macquarie Marshes, 80 km north-west; breeding ground for waterbirds. Warrana Creek Weir for boating and swimming. Farm holidays available. **Tourist information:** Coonamble Motel, Castlereagh St; (068) 22 1400. **Accommodation:** 5 hotels, 3 motels, 1 caravan/camping park.
MAP REF. 112 D9

Cootamundra   Population 6314

This town on the Olympic Way, 427 km from Sydney, is less than 2 hours' drive from Canberra, and is well known for the Cootamundra wattle (Acacia baileyana). It has a strong retail sector and is a large stock-selling centre for the surrounding pastoral and agricultural rural holdings. **Of interest:** Self-guiding 'Two Foot Tour' leaflet leads visitors on walk around town, taking in historic buildings, many restored. Birthplace of Sir Donald Bradman, town's most famous son, at 89 Adams St; open daily. Cootamundra Public School Museum, Cooper St. **In the area:** Tours of Yandilla Mustard Seed Oil, 26 km north. Merriwonga sheep and grain property and Old Nubba Schoolhouse offer farm holidays. **Tourist information:** Business Enterprise Centre, Hovell St (at railway station); (069) 42 1400. **Accommodation:** 7 hotels, 4 motels, 1 caravan/camping park.
MAP REF. 109 B4, 110C9, 117R9A

Court-house, Coonabarabran

Corowa   Population 4315

Birthplace of Australia's Federation, Corowa took its name from 'Currawa', an Aboriginal word describing pine trees that once grew there in profusion. A typical Australian country town, Corowa's wide main street, Sanger St, lined with turn-of-the-century verandahed buildings, runs down to the banks of the Murray River. The town offers visitors opportunities for tennis, swimming, water-skiing, river cruising, bird-watching and bushwalking. Tom Roberts' painting *Shearing of the Rams*, in the National Gallery of Victoria, was completed nearby in 1889. **Of interest:** Federation Museum, Queen St. National Federation Festival held in Jan. **In the area:** Rutherglen wineries, only a short drive or bicycle ride away. **Tourist information:** Railway Station Building, John St; (060) 33 3221. **Accommodation:** 14 motels, 4 caravan/camping parks.
MAP REF. 117 N13, 217 O4

Cowra   Population 8207 (shire)

The peaceful air of this busy country town on the Lachlan River belies its dramatic recent history. On 5 August 1944, over 1000 Japanese prisoners attempted to escape from a nearby POW camp. Four Australian soldiers and 231 Japanese prisoners were killed in the ensuing struggle. **Of interest:** Cowra Rose Garden, adjacent to tourist information centre. **In the area:** Australian and Japanese War Cemeteries, 5 km north, beside Cowra–Canowindra Rd. Australian soldiers who died are buried in Australian War Cemetery. Japanese soldiers who died during escape, as well as Japanese internees who died elsewhere in Australia, are buried in Japanese cemetery. Sakura Ave, 5 km of flowering cherry trees, links site with that of POW camp, with Breakout Walking Track, and Japanese Garden and Cultural Centre. Gardens cover 5 ha; traditional teahouse, bonsai house and pottery complement Cultural Centre, which houses display of Japanese art and crafts. Quarry Cellars, 4 km south, on Boorowa Rd; wine tastings and sales. Conimbla National Park, 27 km west. Wyangala State Recreation Area, 40 km south-east, mecca for water sports and fishing enthusiasts. **Tourist information:** Mid Western Hwy, near Boorowa turn-off; (063) 42 4333. **Accommodation:** 3 hotels, 2 hotel/motels, 5 motels, 3 caravan/camping parks.
MAP REF. 109 D1, 110 E6

Crookwell   Population 1966

Located 45 km north-west of Goulburn, Crookwell is the centre of a rich agricultural and pastoral district, producing

top-quality apples, pears and cherries, and is the state's major supplier of certified seed potatoes. **Of interest:** Crookwell Potato Co-operative, where modern potato-grading machinery can be seen in operation. Crookwell Memorial Park. **In the area:** Redground Lookout, 8 km north-east. Many quaint historic villages associated with gold and copper mining and bushranging: Tuena, Peelwood, Laggan, Bigga, Binda (all north of town) and Roslyn (south, and birthplace of poet Dame Mary Gilmore). Upper reaches of Lake Wyangala and Grabine State Recreation Area, 65 km north-west; waterskiing, picnicking, fishing, sailing, bushwalking and camping. Abercrombie Caves 64 km further north along Bathurst Rd; guided tours. Farm holidays and farm tours. **Tourist information:** 44 Goulburn St; (048) 32 1988. **Accommodation:** 2 hotels, 2 motels, 1 caravan/camping park.
MAP REF. 109 E3, 110 G8

Culburra–Orient Point

Population 2525
Famous for its prawning, this unspoiled resort is situated east of Nowra on a magnificent ocean beach near Wollumboola Lake. **Of interest:** Surfing, swimming, lake, shore and rock fishing. Beach is patrolled in summer holidays. **Tourist information:** Shoalhaven Tourist Centre, 254 Princes Hwy, Bomaderry; (044) 21 0778. **Accommodation:** 1 motel, 1 caravan/camping park.
MAP REF. 107 F13, 111 J10

Culcairn   Population 1138

Dating back to 1880 and planned to service the railway between Sydney and Melbourne, the township today reflects the district's rural prosperity. Bushranger Dan Morgan started his life of crime at Round Hill Station, one of the noted stations in the Culcairn district, with a holdup at the station on 19 June 1864. Once known as the oasis of the Riverina because of its unlimited underground watersupply (discovered in 1926), the town owes its picturesque tree-lined streets and parks to this artesian water. **Of interest:** Historic Culcairn Hotel (1891), Railway Pde. Many buildings in Railway Pde and on Olympic Way classified by National Trust. Centenary Mural, Main St. Artesian pumping station, Gordon St. **In the area:** John McLean's Grave, 3 km east; a price was put on Morgan's head after he shot McLean. Round Hill Station, on Holbrook Rd. At Walla Walla, 18 km west, Old Schoolhouse (1875) Museum; and 4 km north, Morgan's Lookout. Premier Yabbies, 7 km south of Culcairn; farm and catch-out. Pioneer Museum at

Jindera, 42 km south. **Tourist information:** Railway Pde; (060) 29 6136. **Accommodation:** 1 hotel, 1 motel, 1 caravan/camping park.
MAP REF. 110 A12, 117 P12, 217 R1, 219 B1

Deniliquin   Population 7566

At the centre of the largest irrigation complex in Australia, on the Edward River, 750 km south-west of Sydney, Deniliquin has the largest rice mill in the southern hemisphere. The northern part of the district is famed for merino sheep studs such as Wanganella and Boonoke. **Of interest:** Tours of rice mill, Saleyard Rd. Peppin Heritage Centre (1879), former school, George St. Waring Gardens, in town centre. Island Sanctuary, off Cressy St footbridge; free-range animals and birds. River beaches, including McLean and Willoughby's Beaches. Sun Festival held in Jan. Jazz Festival each Easter. **In the area:** Pioneer Tourist Park and Garden Centre, 6 km north; antique steam and pump display. Bird Observatory Tower at Mathoura, 34 km south. Irrigation works include Lawsons Syphon, 6 km east and Stevens Weir, 26 km west. **Tourist information:** Cressy St; (058) 81 2878. **Accommodation:** 4 hotels, 3 hotel/motels, 7 motels, 5 caravan parks.
MAP REF. 117 K12

Dorrigo   Population 1167

Magnificent river, mountain and forest scenery is a feature of this important timber town. **Of interest:** Calico Cottage, Hickory St; crafts and Devonshire teas. Dorrigo Pottery, Tyringham Rd. **In the area:** Dangar Falls, 2 km north. Dorrigo National Park, 5 km east; birds' eye views over canopy of World Heritage-listed rainforest from Skywalk leading from Rainforest Centre. Excellent trout fishing in district. Dutton Trout Hatchery at Ebor, 49 km west. **Tourist information:** Dorrigo Hotel, Hickory St; (066) 57 2486. **Accommodation:** 2 hotels, 3 motels, 1 caravan/camping park.
MAP REF. 113 O7

Dubbo   Population 25 796

This pleasant city lies on the banks of the Macquarie River, 420 km north-west of Sydney, and is recognised as the regional capital of western NSW and supports many agricultural and secondary industries. **Of interest:** Old Dubbo Gaol, Macquarie St, with original gallows and solitary confinement cells; animatronic robots tell story of convicts. Dubbo Museum, Macquarie St. Dubbo Regional Art Gallery, Darling St. **In the area:** Western Plains Zoo, 5 km south, Australia's first open-range zoo with over 300 ha of landscaped exhibits; animals from 6 continents, some roaming free in natural surroundings. Military Museum, 8 km south; open-air exhibits. Yarrabar Pottery, 4 km further south. Restored Dundullimal Homestead (1840s), 7 km south-east, on Obley Rd. Jinchilla Gardens and Gallery, 12 km north, off Gilgandra Rd. **Tourist information:** cnr

Japanese Gardens, Cowra

THE SNOWY MOUNTAINS

The Snowy Mountains are a magnet to tourists all year round. The combination of easily accessible mountains, alpine heathlands, forests, lakes, streams and dams is hard to beat. In winter, skiers flock to the snug, well-equipped snow resorts in the area. As the snow melts, anglers, bushwalkers, water-skiers and boating enthusiasts move in. Almost as many holiday-makers stay at the ski resorts in summer as in winter.

The creation of the Snowy Mountains Hydro-electric Scheme was indirectly responsible for boosting tourism. The roads built for the Scheme through the previously inaccessible mountain country helped to open up the area, which is now used for winter sports.

All the snow resorts of the Snowy Mountains are within Kosciusko National Park, which is the largest national park in the state and includes the highest plateau in the Australian continent. Mount Kosciusko (2228 m) is its highest peak.

Perisher Valley

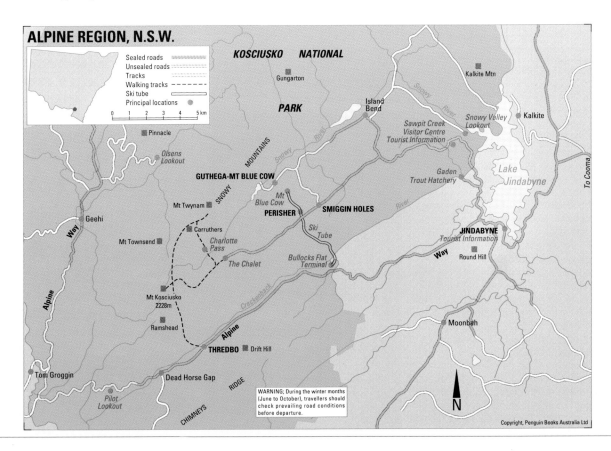

ALPINE REGION, N.S.W.

Sealed roads
Unsealed roads
Tracks
Walking tracks
Ski tube
Principal locations

0 1 2 3 4 5 km

KOSCIUSKO   NATIONAL

PARK

Kalkite Mtn

Gungarton

Island
Bend

Pinnacle

Olsens
Lookout

Sawpit Creek
Visitor Centre
Tourist Information

Snowy Valley
Lookout

Kalkite

GUTHEGA-MT BLUE COW

Gaden
Trout Hatchery

Lake
Jindabyne

Mt Twynam

Mt
Blue Cow

Geehi

PERISHER

SMIGGIN HOLES

Carruthers

Charlotte
Pass

Ski
Tube

JINDABYNE
Tourist Information

Mt Townsend

The Chalet

Bullocks Flat
Terminal

Round Hill

Mt Kosciusko
2228m

Ramshead

Moonbah

Alpine

THREDBO   Drift Hill

Tom Groggin

Dead Horse Gap

Pilot
Lookout

RIDGE

CHIMNEYS

N

WARNING; During the winter months (June to October), travellers should check prevailing road conditions before departure.

The major ski areas are: Thredbo, Perisher Valley, Smiggin Holes, Mt Blue Cow/Guthega, and Charlotte Pass in the southern part of the Kosciusko National Park, and Mt Selwyn in the north.

The resorts are easily accessible and the major centres have first-class amenities such as chair-lifts, ski-tows, motels, hotels, restaurants, lodges, apres-ski entertainment, and expert instruction. The snow sports season officially begins on the long weekend in June and continues until mid- or late October.

Thredbo Village, 96 km from Cooma at the foot of the Crackenback Range. This world-class resort has the only giant slalom course in Australia approved by the world skiing control board. It is the site for international skiing events. There is a wide range of facilities for skiers at all levels. The chair-lift to the summit of Mt Crackenback operates through the summer. Thredbo has a wide range of amenities, restaurants and entertainment, including year-round paragliding. Ski hire and instruction.

Charlotte Pass, 98 km from Cooma and 8 km from the summit of Mt Kosciusko. A convenient base for ski tours to some of Australia's highest peaks and most spectacular ski runs.

Perisher Valley, 90 km from Cooma. One of the highest and most popular ski resorts in the area; caters for downhill and cross-country skiers. Ski hire and instruction.

Smiggin Holes, 89 km from Cooma. Linked to Perisher by ski-lifts and a free shuttle bus service. Ski hire and instruction.

Mt Selwyn, at the northern end of Kosciusko National Park, has been designed for beginners, families and school groups. Mt Selwyn is one of the main centres for cross-country skiing. No overnight accommodation. Ski hire and instruction.

Mt Blue Cow/Guthega can only be reached by the Skitube underground railway which runs from Bullocks Flat terminal near Jindabyne up to Perisher Valley and on to Mt Blue Cow. No overnight accommodation. Ski hire and instruction.

For further information on the Snowy Mountains, contact the Visitors Centre at Sawpit Creek; (064) 56 2102. **See also:** Safe Skiing.

Darling and Erskine Sts; (068) 84 1422. **Accommodation:** 6 hotels, 29 motels, 5 caravan parks. **See also:** The Newell. MAP REF. 110 E1, 112 E13

Dungog　Population 2106

These days an ideal base for bushwalking enthusiasts, Dungog was established in 1838 as a military post to prevent bushranging in the area. Situated on the upper reach of the Williams River, it is on one of the main access routes to Barrington Tops National Park. **In the area:** Chichester Dam, 23 km north, in picturesque mountain setting; Duncan Park within is ideal spot for barbecue. Telegherry Forest Park, 30 km north; walking trails to waterfalls along Telegherry River; picnic, swimming and camping spots. Barrington Tops National Park, 40 km north; Barrington Brush noted for its unusual native flora and rich variety of wildlife. Superb views from Mt Allyn (1100 m), 40 km north-west. Clarence Town historic village, 25 km south. **Tourist information:** Shire Offices, (049) 92 1224; or Information and Neighbourhood Service, (049) 92 1133. **Accommodation:** 2 hotels, 1 motel. MAP REF. 111 L2

Eden　Population 3248

Quiet former whaling town on Twofold Bay, 512 km south of Sydney, with an outstanding natural harbour. Today fishing and timber-getting are the main industries. **Of interest:** Whaling Museum, Imlay St; exhibits include skeleton of notorious 'Tom the killer whale' and 70-million-year-old snail fossils. **In the area:** Ben Boyd National Park, extending 8 km north and 19 km south of Eden; outstanding scenery and ideal for fishing, swimming, camping and bushwalking. Prominent park feature, Boyd's Tower (1840s), at Red Point. On perimeter of park, at Nullica Bay, 9 km south, former rival settlement of Boydtown, including convict-built Sea Horse Inn, still licensed; safe beach and excellent fishing. Davidson Whaling Station Historic Site on Kiah Inlet. Good fishing at Wonboyn Lake Resort, 40 km south, surrounded by Ben Boyd National Park and Nadgee Nature Reserve. Harris Daishowa Chipmill visitors centre at Jews Head, 26 km south; video and static display on logging and milling operations. **Tourist information:** Princes Hwy; (064) 96 1953. **Accommodation:** 1 hotel, 10 motels, 6 caravan/camping parks. **See also:** The South Coast. MAP REF. 109 F11, 221 P3

Eugowra　Population 579

'The great gold-escort robbery' occurred near this small town on the Orange–Forbes road in 1862. **Of interest:** Eugowra Museum exhibits Aboriginal skeleton and artefacts, gemstone collection and early farm equipment and wagons. **In the area:** Escort Rock, 3 km east, where bushranger Frank Gardiner and his gang hid before ambushing the Forbes gold-escort. Rock is on private property, but plaque on road gives details and unlocked gate allows entry to visitors. Picnic facilities. **Tourist information:** Visitors Centre, Civic Gardens, Byng St, Orange; (063) 61 5226. **Accommodation:** 2 hotels. MAP REF. 110 D5

Evans Head　Population 1903

This holiday and fishing resort, and centre of the NSW prawning industry, is situated off the Pacific Hwy via Woodburn. It has safe surf beaches and sandy river-flats. Rock, beach and ocean fishing, boating, windsurfing. **Of interest:** Highly recommended seafood restaurant, run by trawler fishermen. **In the area:** Broadwater National Park, 5 km north, between Evans Head and Broadwater; bushwalking, birdwatching, fishing and swimming. Bundjalung National Park, on southern edge of Evans Head; Aboriginal relics, varied wildlife, canoeing. **Tourist information:** Grafton Information Centre, Pacific Hwy, Grafton; (066) 42 4677. **Accommodation:** 1 hotel, 1 motel, 1 caravan park, 1 caravan/camping park. MAP REF. 113 Q4

Finley　Population 2216

This town on the Newell Hwy 20 km from the Victorian border, is the centre of the Berriquin irrigation scheme. North of the town is the Finley Lake for boating and sailing, with picnic areas on its banks. **Tourist information:** River Foreshore, Tocumwal; (058) 74 2131. **Accommodation:** 3 hotels, 5 motels, 1 caravan/camping park. MAP REF. 117 M12, 217 J1

Forbes　Population 7915

Bushranger Ben Hall is buried in the cemetery at this former gold-mining town, 386 km west of Sydney, on the Lachlan River. He was shot by police just outside the town in 1865. Today the town's industries include an abattoir and a flour mill. **Of interest:** Many historic buidings, especially in Camp and Lachlan Sts. Historical museum, Cross St; relics associated with Ben Hall, most noted bushranger of Lachlan River district. Forbes Cemetery, Bogan Gate Rd; contains graves of Ben Hall and Ned Kelly's sister, Kate Foster. Historical sites include memorial in King George V Park, where 'German Harry'

discovered gold in 1861. Another memorial, marking the spot where explorer John Oxley first passed through Forbes, in small park in Dowling St. **In the area:** Lachlan Vintage Village, re-creation of gold-rush era, 1 km south; 73 ha site with restaurant and picnic facilities. Sandhills Vineyard, 6 km east on Eugowra Rd; tastings and sales and picnic facilities. **Tourist information:** 89 Lachlan St; (068) 52 1822. **Accommodation:** 9 hotels, 6 motels, 4 caravan/camping parks. **See also:** The Newell.
MAP REF. 110 C5, 117 R5

Forster–Tuncurry

Population 11 239
Twin towns on opposite sides of Wallis Lake, a holiday area in the Great Lakes district, Forster and Tuncurry are connected by a bridge. Launches and boats may be hired for lake and deep-sea fishing. The area is renowned for its good fishing, including flathead, bream and whiting, as well as oysters and prawns. **Of interest:** Forster Art and Craft Centre. Oyster Festival held in Oct. **In the area:** Curtis Collection, 3 km south; vintage cars. The Green Cathedral, at Tiona on shores of Wallis Lake, 13 km south, unusual open-air 'cathedral'. Booti Booti State Recreation Area, 17 km south. Sugar Creek Toymakers at Bungwahl, 22 km south. Wallingat State Forest, 25 km south. Myall Lakes National Park, 35 km south; houseboats for hire. Camping and beaches at Seal Rocks, 40 km south. The Grandis, accessed from The Lakes Way, 48 km south in Bulahdelah State Forest, tallest tree in NSW. **Tourist information:** Great Lakes Tourist Board, Little St; (065) 54 8799. **Accommodation:** 2 hotels, 19 motels, 9 caravan/camping parks.
MAP REF. 111 N2, 113 N13

Gerringong

Population 2326
Spectacular views of white sand and rolling breakers can be seen from this resort, 11 km south of Kiama on the lovely Illawarra coast. **Of interest:** Surfing, fishing and swimming at local beaches (Werri, Gerroa, Seven Mile). Memorial to pioneer aviator Sir Charles Kingsford Smith at northern end of Seven Mile Beach, site of his take-off to New Zealand in the Southern Cross in 1933. Wild Country Park at Fox Ground, 6 km south. Bushwalks through Seven Mile Beach National Park, 13 km south; camping and picnic areas. **Tourist information:** Visitors Centre, Blowhole Pt, Kiama; (042) 32 3322. **Accommodation:** 1 hotel, 3 motels, 3 caravan/camping parks.
MAP REF. 107 G10, 109 I4, 111 J9

Gilgandra

Population 2713
Gilgandra is a historic town at the junction of the three highways, in timber, wool and farming country. It is the home of the famous 'Coo-ee March', which left from Gilgandra for Sydney in 1915 in a drive to recruit more soldiers to fight in World War I. It is also known for its windmills, which once provided residents with sub-artesian water. **Of interest:** The Observatory and Display Centre, cnr Wamboin and Willie Sts, with 300 mm (12 inch) telescope. Museum, Warner Rd; displays of memorabilia from Coo-ee March. Film *The Chant of Jimmy Blacksmith* was based on Breelong Massacre, which took place near Gilgandra, and related items can be seen in museum. Orana Cactus World, Newell Hwy. **In the area:** Australian Collection, 2 km north. Gilgandra Flora Reserve, 14.5 km north; wildflowers in spring. Warrumbungle National Park, 82 km north-east. **Tourist information:** Coo-ee March Memorial Park, Newell Hwy; (068) 47 2045. **Accommodation:** 2 hotels, 6 motels, 3 caravan/camping park.
MAP REF. 112 E11

Glen Innes

Population 5971
Gazetted in 1852, this mountain town was the scene of many bushranging exploits last century. In a beautiful setting, at an altitude of 1073 m, it is now the progressive centre of a lush farming district, where sapphire mining is an important industry. Tin is also mined. **Of interest:** Many original public buildings, particularly in Grey St, some restored; self-guiding leaflets available. Centennial Parklands with Martin's Lookout, now site of Australian Standing Stones, celtic monument. Land of the Beardies History House, cnr Ferguson St and West Ave, folk museum housed in town's first hospital and set in extensive grounds; features reconstructed slab hut, period room settings and pioneer relics. Minerama Gem Festival held in Sept.; Australian Bush Music Festival on Oct. long weekend; Land of the Beardies Bush Festival in Nov. **In the area:** Gibraltar Range National Park, 70 km north-east; impressive Dandahra Falls and The Needles and Anvil Rock, famous granite formations. World Heritage-listed Washpool National Park 75 km north-east; rainforest wilderness area. Mushroom Rock, near Backwater, 47 km south-east; unique rock formation with fossicking areas for garnets, zircons, topaz and sapphires nearby. Guy Fawkes River National Park, 77 km south-east; wild river area for bushwalking, canoeing and fishing. Convict-carved tunnel, halfway between Glen Innes and Grafton, on road east, passing through scenic mountain and riverside country. **Tourist information:** Church St (New England Hwy); (067) 32 2397. **Accommodation:** 4 hotels, 10 motels, 5 caravan/camping parks. **See also:** New England.
MAP REF. 113 M5

Gloucester

Population 2397
This quiet town lies at the foot of a range of monolithic hills called 'the Bucketts'. It is at the junction of three tributaries of the Manning River, the upper reaches of which are excellent for trout and perch fishing. **Of interest:** Folk Museum in Church St. The Bucketts Walk, immediately west of town. Gloucester Park, outstanding sporting complex. **In the area:** Scenic views from Mograni Lookout (5 km east), Kia-ora Lookout (7 km north) and Berrico Trig Station (14 km west). Mountain Maid Gold Mine at Copeland, 16 km west. Altamira Holiday Ranch, 18 km east. **Tourist information:** Gloucester Caravan Park; (065) 58 1720. **Accommodation:** 2 motels, 1 caravan/camping park.
MAP REF. 111 M1, 113 M12

Gosford

Population 38 205
Gosford is 85 km north of Sydney on beautiful Brisbane Water. **Of interest:** Henry Kendall Cottage, built as inn in 1838, where poet lived (1874–5); picnic facilities in pleasant grounds. **In the area:** Australian Reptile Park and Wildlife Sanctuary, Pacific Hwy north; taipans, pythons, goannas and platypuses. Old Sydney Town, 9 km west; reconstruction of early pioneer settlement, recreated from carefully researched pre-1810 material. Somersby Falls, near Old Sydney Town; ideal picnic spot. Central Park Family Fun Centre at Forresters Beach, 31 km east. The Ferneries, Oak Rd, Matcham, 11 km north-east; rainforest area with picnic/barbecue facilities, paddle-boats and children's playground, and Devonshire teas. Bouddi National Park, 17 km south-east; bushwalking, camping, fishing and swimming. Brisbane Water National Park, 10 km south-west; spectacular displays of waratahs in spring. **Tourist information:** 200 Mann St; (043) 25 2835. **Accommodation:** 3 hotels, 9 motels, 1 caravan/camping parks.
MAP REF. 101 Q1, 104 E13, 111 K5

Goulburn

Population 21 552
This provincial city, steeped in early colonial history (it was proclaimed a town in 1833), is on the Hume Hwy 209 km south-west of Sydney. It is the centre of a wealthy farming district (including wool, wheat, stud cattle and horses) at the

Old Sydney Town, Gosford

junction of the Wollondilly and Mulwarry Rivers beyond the Southern Highlands. **Of interest:** Riversdale (1840), Maud St; National Trust classified coaching house. St Clair History House (c.1843), Sloane St; 20-room mansion, restored by local historical society. Regional Art Gallery, Bourke St. Garroorigang and Hume Dairy, South Goulburn (1857), in almost original condition; private home, open by appointment. Old Goulburn Brewery Hotel, Bungonia Rd. Goulburn court-house, Montague St. Cathedral of St Saviour, Bourke St. Cathedral of St Peter and St Paul, cnr Bourke and Verner Sts. Sun. afternoon concerts at The Towers (c.1842) guest-house, Braidwood Rd. Farm holidays at historic Lansdowne Park, Bungonia Rd. Gulfon's Craft Village, Common St, housed in old brick-works (1884); working displays and sales. Goulburn Yurt Works, Copford Rd; inspection tours of factory making prefabricated round houses. The Big Merino, a 15-m-high sculptured relief, Hume Hwy; displays of wool products and Australiana. Goulburn Steam Museum, Fitzroy St; rides on 'Leisureland Express'. Barbecue facilities by Wollondilly River at nearby Marsden Weir. Rocky Hill War Memorial, Memorial Dr; city's best-known landmark, built in memory of local

men who served in World War I. **In the area:** Pelican Sheep Station, 10 km south; shearing and sheepdog demonstrations. Farm holidays at Avago Lodge, near Taralga, 45 km north. **Tourist information:** 2 Montague St; (048) 21 5343. **Accommodation:** 7 hotels, 13 motels, 3 caravan/camping parks.
MAP REF. 109 F4, 110 G9

Grafton   Population 16 647

A garden city, famous for the magnificent jacaranda, wheel- and flame-trees lining its wide streets, Grafton is situated on the Pacific Hwy at its junction with the Gwydir Hwy, 665 km north of Sydney. A colourful Jacaranda Festival is held annually in the last week of October and first week of November. **Of interest:** Numerous National Trust buildings. Schaeffer House (1900), Fitzroy St; now district historical museum. Picturesque riverbank parks and gardens are city feature. Stately Prentice House, Fitzroy St; one of Australia's finest small provincial art galleries. Susan Island in Clarence River; recreation reserve covered with rainforest and home to large fruit-bat colony; access by hired canoe. **In the area:** Weekend gliding at Merino Mac's Australian Agradome, 25 km south. Canoeing

and rafting on wild-river systems in surrounding shires such as Nymboida; also many scenic drives. Ulmarra village, 12 km north, classified by National Trust and a fine example of turn-of-the-century river port; art, craft and antique shops. Houseboats for hire at Brushgrove, 20 km northeast. Four major national parks within hour's drive: Yuraygir (70 km east) and Bundjalung (70 km north) coastal parks, and Washpool (88 km) and Gibraltar Range (92 km) to west. World Heritage-listed rainforest in Washpool National Park offers excellent walking tracks and abundant wildlife. **Tourist information:** Pacific Hwy; (066) 42 4677. **Accommodation:** 17 hotels, 14 motels, 2 caravan parks.
MAP REF. 113 P5

Grenfell   Population 1986

The birthplace of famous poet and short-story writer Henry Lawson, and the background for many of his verses and stories, this small town on the Mid Western Hwy, 377 km west of Sydney, is also famous for the Guinea Pig Races held on Easter Sunday and during the Henry Lawson Festival of Arts held every June. **Of interest:** Grenfell Museum, Camp St. O'Brien's Lookout, where gold was discovered.

WINERIES OF NEW SOUTH WALES

A vineyard holiday takes you through peaceful, ordered countryside and gives you the chance to learn more about wine and its making at first hand. It also gives you a perfect excuse for wine tasting and, later, sampling the local wines with a meal in a first-class restaurant in the area. The obvious place to head for in New South Wales is the famous **Hunter Valley**. It is not far from Sydney (two hours' drive each way) and, with more than forty wineries, must rate as one of the most important wine-growing districts in Australia. Although it is just possible to do a day-trip from Sydney to the Hunter, it is well worth booking into a motel in the area for at least one night, to do justice to it. Mid-week is the best time to visit, with lower tariffs and fewer crowds.

The Hunter is Australia's oldest commercial wine-producing area, wine having first been made there in the 1830s. The Hunter's table wines, both red and white, still rank as among the best in Australia.

Most of the early colonial vineyards have vanished and all but two or three family concerns have been taken over by the larger companies with such well-known names as Lindemans and McWilliams.

The high reputation of the district is maintained by such well-known properties as Mount Pleasant, Oakvale, Drayton's Bellevue, Tyrrell's and Tulloch's Glen Elgin.

Most wineries welcome visitors and are open for inspection and wine tastings daily. Several of them have picnic grounds, barbecue facilities and high-class restaurants.

There are many restaurants in the area, including the Pokolbin Cellars at Hungerford Hill, Blaxland's at Pokolbin and the Casuarina at North Pokolbin.

The Hungerford Hill Wine Village at Pokolbin has wine tastings, wine sales, a gallery, accommodation at the Quality Pokolbin Resort, specialty shops, a restaurant, kiosk and picnic facilities, an adventure playground for children, plus an aquagolf driving range and clay pigeon shooting with laser beams.

It is best to go at vintage time — usually around February in the Hunter — if you want to see a vineyard in full swing. However, this is the most hectic time of year for vignerons, so do not expect their undivided attention. For an idea of the range of wineries in the district, try Tyrrell's and Drayton's wineries for a glimpse of the more

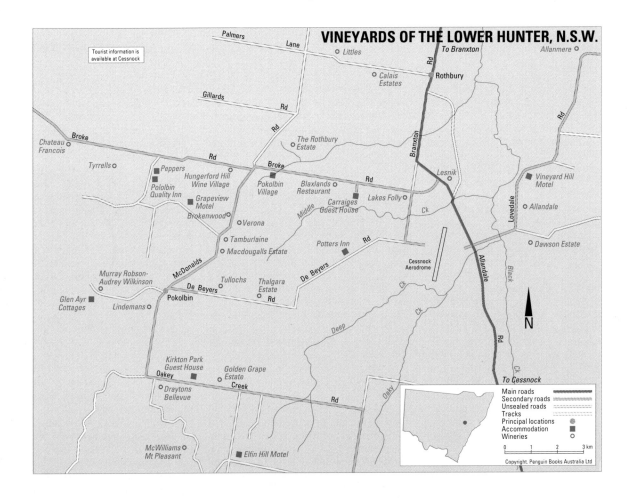

VINEYARDS OF THE LOWER HUNTER, N.S.W.

traditional family approach, and Lindeman or Hunter Estate for the modern 'big company' style.

South of Sydney at **Camden** is Gledswood, birthplace of Australia's wine industry. The first vines were planted in 1827 and the winery was re-established as Gledswood Cellars in 1970. The winery offers wine tastings and purchases, an art gallery and shearing demonstrations. Barbecue facilities are available. Hay-rides and candle-lit dinners can be arranged for parties.

You could have an equally enjoyable wine-tasting holiday in the Riverina towns of **Griffith** and **Leeton**, in the other main wine-growing area of the state. Griffith, Leeton and **Narrandera** are the main towns in the **Murrumbidgee Irrigation Area**, which grows eighty per cent of the state's wine-producing grapes. Well-known wineries such as McWilliam's, de Bortoli and Rosetto & Sons are open to visitors who wish to taste the wines of the Riverina. In Leeton, visitors are welcome to sample the vintages at Toorak Winery and Lillypilly Estate. **Mudgee**, 261 kilometres north-west of Sydney, is also in an area where fine wines are produced from around a dozen wineries. Other smaller vineyards are scattered throughout the state — some of them quite close to Sydney.

See also: Individual entries in A–Z listing.

Pokolbin Winery, Hunter Valley

Henry Lawson Obelisk, next to Lawson Park, on site of house where poet is believed to have been born. **In the area:** Weddin Mountains National Park, 18 km south-west; bushwalking, camping and picnicking. Area was used as hideout by bushrangers Ben Hall, Frank Gardiner, Johnnie Gilbert and others. Easy walk to Ben Hall's Cave. **Accommodation:** 5 hotels, 1 motel, 1 caravan park.
MAP REF. 109 B1, 110 D6

Griffith   Population 13 630

A thriving country city which developed as a result of the introduction of irrigation, Griffith was designed by Walter Burley Griffin, architect of Canberra, and named after Sir Arthur Griffith, the first Minister for Public Works in the NSW government. A diversity of industries surround the city, with rice being the biggest profit-maker, followed by citrus fruits, grapes, vegetables and eggs and poultry. Griffith is well known as a wine-producing area; there are 17 wineries in the district. The Murrumbidgee Irrigation Area produces 80 per cent of the state's wines. The Griffith Wine and Food Festival is held over Easter. **Of interest:** Tours of rice mill, Viticultural Research Station, agricultural, horticultural and viticultural farms, and various food-processing factories. Regional Theatre, Banna Ave; stage curtain designed and created by combined efforts of 300 residents of Griffith to give visual overview of city, surrounding villages and industries. Regional Art Gallery, Banna Ave; monthly exhibitions. Griffith Cottage Gallery and Crafty Spot, Benerembah St. **In the area:** Many wineries open for tastings and/or guided tours. Pioneer Park Museum, set in 18 ha of bushland, 2 km north; drop-log buildings and collection of memorabilia from early 20th century. Bagtown village recreated here to give insight into development of area. Bagtown Cemetery, 5 km south; reminder of pioneering days. Lake Wyangan, 10 km north-west; water-sports and picnic facilities. Cocoparra National Park, 19 km north-east. **Tourist information:** cnr Banna and Jondaryan Aves; (069) 62 4145. **Accommodation:** 2 hotels, 2 hotel/motel, 7 motels, 2 caravan/camping parks. **See also:** Wineries of New South Wales.
MAP REF. 117 N8

Gulgong   Population 1988

This fascinating old gold-mining town, 29 km north-west of Mudgee, is known as 'the town on the $10 note'. In its heyday in the 1870s it was packed with fortune hunters from all over the world. Some of its former glory remains in the form of many restored buildings, but none of

those depicted on the $10 note. The town's narrow streets are lined with clapboard and iron buildings decorated in their original iron lace. **Of interest:** Henry Lawson Centre, Mayne St; largest collection of Lawson memorabilia outside Sydney's Mitchell Library. Historic buildings to note on 'Town Trail' include Prince of Wales Opera House, Mayne St; Ten Dollar Town Motel (formerly Royal Hotel), cnr Mayne and Medley Sts; American Tobacco Warehouse and Fancy Goods Emporium, Mayne St; and Gulgong Pioneers Museum, cnr Herbert and Bayly Sts. **Tourist information:** 64 Market St, Mudgee; (063) 72 5874/5. **Accommodation:** 4 hotels, 3 motels, 1 caravan/camping park.
MAP REF. 110 G2, 112 G13

Gundagai   Population 2124

Much celebrated in song and verse, this prosperous town on the Murrumbidgee River at the foot of Mt Parnassus, 398 km south-west of Sydney, has become part of Australian folklore. Its rich history includes Australia's worst flood disaster in 1852, when 89 people drowned, nearby gold-rushes and many bushranging attacks. Today it is the centre of a rich pastoral and agricultural district which produces wool, wheat, fruit and vegetables, and is a convenient overnight stopping-place for motorists along the Hume Hwy. **Of interest:** Marble carving of cathedral, comprising over 20 000 pieces, by Frank Rusconi, sculptor of tuckerbox dog, on display in Tourist Information Centre, Sheridan St. Outstanding collection of early photographs with letters and possessions of poet Henry Lawson at Gabriel Gallery, Sheridan St. Historical museum, Homer St. Court-house (built 1859 and still in use), classified by National Trust as building of great architectural merit; scene of many historic trials, including that of notorious bushranger, Captain Moonlite. St John's Anglican Church (1861), cnr Otway and Punch Sts, and Prince Albert bridge (1866), longest timber viaduct in Australia, classified by National Trust. Views from Mt Parnassus Lookout, Otway St, and Rotary Lookout, South Gundagai. Spring Flower Show held in Oct. **In the area:** Dog on the Tuckerbox at 'Snake Gully' Caltex service station, 'five miles from' or 8 km north; monument to pioneer teamsters and their dogs, celebrated in song by Jack O'Hagan. Larger-than-life copper statues of *Dad and Dave* characters at 'Snake Gully'. Nearby kiosk, fern-house and ruins of Five Mile Pub, where teamsters and gold-miners once broke their journeys. **Tourist information:** Sheridan St; (069) 44 1341. **Accommodation:** 2 hotels, 7 motels, 2 caravan parks.
MAP REF. 109 B5, 110 C10, 117 R10

Gunnedah   Population 9144
A prosperous town on the banks of the Namoi River, Gunnedah is recognised as the centre of rich pastoral and agricultural country, and is one of the largest stock-marketing and killing centres in NSW. Other industries include a brickworks, a tannery, flour mills and some coal mining. **Of interest:** Water Tower Museum, Anzac Park. Dorothea MacKellar Memorial statue in park. Rural Museum, Mullaley Rd. Red Chief Memorial, State Office building, Abbott St. Old Bank Gallery, Conadilly St. Creative Arts Centre, Chandos St. 8th Division Memorial Avenue of flowering gums. Self-drive town tour and self-guiding Bindea Town Walk. **In the area:** Porcupine Lookout, 3 km south-east; picnic spot. 150° East Time Meridian, 28 km west. Lake Keepit Dam and State Recreation Centre, 34 km north-east, for water sports, bushwalking, picnicking and camping; caravan park and gliding club. **Tourist information:** Anzac Park; (067) 42 1564. **Accommodation:** 6 hotels, 6 motels, 1 caravan/camping park.
MAP REF. 112 I9

Gunning   Population 424
In the centre of lush pastoral country on the Hume Hwy between Goulburn and Yass. **Of interest:** Pye Cottage, a slab-style pioneer cottage, post office, Royal Hotel, old court-house (now church), Do Duck Inn, Caxton House and Cottage, police station—all in main street, Hume Hwy. Still Light Gallery, Warrataw St. **In the area:** Greendale Pioneer Cemetery, Gunning–Boorowa Rd. Hume and Hovell Walking Track extends from Gunning to Albury. **Tourist information:** Yass Information Centre, Coronation Park, Cooma St, Yass; (06) 226 2557. **Accommodation:** 1 hotel, 1 motel.
MAP REF. 109 E4, 110 F9

Guyra   Population 1999
Guyra is Aboriginal for 'fish may be caught', and the local streams are excellent for fishing, including trout and eels. At 1300 m, this small town in the Great Dividing Range is one of the highest in NSW, with occasional snowfalls in winter. Guyra is the centre of a highly productive rural area known for lambs, wool and potatoes. **Of interest:** Historical Society Museum, Bradley St. Waterbirds at Mother of Ducks Lagoon. Lamb and Potato Festival held in Jan. **In the area:** Chandler's Peak for spectacular views. Thunderbolt's Cave, 10 km south. Llangothlin Handcraft Hall on hwy, 13 km north. Unusual balancing rock formation and gem fossicking at Backwater, 34 km north-east. Ebor Falls and picnic reserve,

75 km east. Copeton Dam, 90 km west; fishing, boating and camping. Farm holidays at Wattleridge, Mosgiel, Milani Trout Cottage and Cabar Feidh. **Tourist information:** Guyra Nursery, Nincoola St; (067) 79 1420. **Accommodation:** 2 hotels, 3 motels, 1 caravan park.
MAP REF. 113 L7

Harden–Murrumburrah

Population 2070
Twin towns, 357 km south-west of Sydney. Settled in 1830, the area is rich grain and stock producing country. **Of interest:** Harden–Murrumburrah Historical Museum and Witch Craft and Coffee Cottage, both in Albury St. Newson Park, in Harden, with picnic/barbecue area. **In the area:** Barwang Vineyard, 20 km north. Asparagus plantation at Jugiong, 30 km south. **Tourist information:** Shire Offices; (063) 86 2305. **Accommodation:** 4 hotels, 1 motel, 1 caravan/camping park.
MAP REF. 109 C3, 110 D8

Hartley   Population under 200
This historic village just off the Great Western Hwy, 134 km west of Sydney, used to be an important stop-over for travellers in the early colonial days. Situated in the Hartley Valley, it is now administered by the National Parks and Wildlife Service. **Of interest:** Self-guided leaflet introduces historic buildings, including: convict-built court-house (1837), designed by colonial architect Mortimer Lewis, Royal Hotel (early 1840s), Old Trahlee Cottage, post office (1846), St Bernard's Church and Presbytery (1842), Farmer's Inn, Ivy Cottage and Shamrock Inn. **In the area:** Craftwork at Hartley Vale, 15 km north-east. **Tourist information:** 285 Main St, Lithgow; (063) 51 2307. **Accommodation:** None.
MAP REF. 100 D5, 109 G1, 110 H6

Hay   Population 2961
Hay serves as the commercial centre for the huge area of semi-arid grazing country on the Murrumbidgee River at the junction of the Cobb, Mid Western and Sturt Hwys. Increasing irrigation from the Murrumbidgee has led to an expansion in vegetable and fruit growing. Many world-famous sheep studs are in the area. **Of interest:** Historic buildings in Lachlan St. Witcombe Memorial Fountain (1883) and plaque in Lachlan St to commemorate epic journey of explorer Charles Sturt along Murrumbidgee and Murray rivers in 1829–30. Hay Gaol Museum, Church St; pioneer relics. Coachhouse in main shopping area that houses original Cobb & Co. coach that plied

Deniliquin–Hay–Wilcannia run until 1901. Hay Park, with picnic/barbecue areas and children's playgrounds. Country Tram Stop Art and Craft Centre. Sandy river beaches along Murrumbidgee for swimming, boating and fishing; Sandy Point Beach venue for Australia Day 'Surf' Carnival. Birdwatching area close to town, breeding-ground for inland species. Bishop's Lodge, South Hay (1888); restored as museum, exhibition gallery and conference centre. **In the area:** Ruberto's Winery, Sturt Hwy, South Hay. Weir on Murrumbidgee River, 12 km west. Sunset viewing area, 16 km north on Booligal Rd. Famous sheep studs of Mungadal, Uardry and Cedar Grove. **Tourist information:** 407 Moppett St; (069) 93 1003. **Accommodation:** 7 hotels, 6 motels, 2 caravan/camping parks.
MAP REF. 117 K8

Henty   Population 880
The historic pastoral township of Henty, the 'Home of the Header', is in the heart of 'Morgan Country', so called because of the famous but ill-fated bushranger Dan Morgan. Almost midway between Albury–Wodonga and Wagga Wagga, Henty can be reached by the Olympic Way or by the Hume Hwy and Boomerang Way. **Of interest:** Headlie Taylor Header Memorial, Henty Park, off Allen St; tribute to machine (invented 1914) that revolutionised grain industry. Annual Henty Field Days held in Sept. **In the area:** Sergeant Smith Memorial Stone, 2 km west on Pleasant Hills Rd, marks site where Dan Morgan fatally wounded a policeman. Doodle Cooma Swamp (2000 ha), breeding area for waterbirds, visible from memorial stone. Built of chocks and logs (no nails), Buckarginga Woolshed, on Cookardinia Rd, 11 km east. Squatters Arms Inn (1848) at Cookardinia, 24 km east. **Tourist information:** Railway Pde, Culcairn; (060) 29 6136. **Accommodation:** 1 hotel, 1 motel, 1 caravan/camping park.
MAP REF. 117 P11

Holbrook   Population 1354
This small town, 521 km south-west of Sydney on the Hume Hwy, is a noted stock-breeding centre. **Of interest:** Commander Holbrook submarine in Holbrook Park, Hume Hwy; replica of submarine in which Commander N. D. Holbrook won VC early in World War I. Town (formerly Germanton) was renamed in his honour. Woolpack Inn Museum, located in former hotel built in 1860; exhibits include complete plant of old cordial factory, bakery, horse-drawn vehicles and farm equipment. **In the**

area: Ultralight Centre at Holbrook airport. Glenfalloch for farm holidays. **Tourist information:** Woolpack Inn Museum, Albury St (Hume Hwy); (060) 36 2131. **Accommodation:** 2 hotels, 6 motels, 1 caravan/camping park.
MAP REF. 110 B12, 117 Q12, 219 D2

Iluka
Population 1484
Iluka is a coastal resort on the Clarence River, famous for its fishing. A deep-sea fishing fleet operates from the harbour. **Of interest:** Daily passenger ferry services to Yamba. River cruises. Iluka Amateur Fishing Classic held in July. **In the area:** Woombah Coffee Plantation, 14 km south, world's southernmost coffee plantation. Bundjalung National Park and the World Heritage-listed Iluka Rainforest border northern edge of town. Houseboats for hire at Brushgrove, 33 km west. **Tourist information:** Pacific Hwy, Grafton; (066) 42 4677. **Accommodation:** 1 motel, 3 caravan parks.
MAP REF. 113 Q4

Inverell
Population 9693
Known as 'Sapphire City', this interesting town, 69 km west of Glen Innes, is in the midst of fertile farming land also rich in minerals. Industrial diamonds, zircons, tin and 75% of the world's sapphires are mined in the area. **Of interest:** Courthouse, Otho St, classified by National Trust. Pioneer Village, Tingha Rd; buildings dating from 1840, moved from their original sites, include Grove Homestead, Paddy's Pub and Mt Drummond Woolshed. Tour Centre/Mining Museum in Water Towers Complex, Campbell St. Art Society Gallery, Evans St. Gem Centre, Byron St. Sapphire City Floral Festival, Art Exhibition, and Collectables and Bottle Show, all held in Oct. **In the area:** Lake Inverell Reserve, 3 km east. DeJon Sapphire Centre, 19 km east on Glen Ennis Rd; inspection of working sapphire mine. Honey Farm and Bottle Museum, 8 km west. Gwydir Ranch 4WD Park, 28 km west. Goonoowigall Bushland Reserve, 5 km south. Gilgai Winery, 12 km south; tastings and sales. Conrad and Kin Conrad Silver Mine, 29 km south; inspection tours. Green Valley Farm, 35 km south, with museum. Copeton Dam State Recreation Area, 40 km south-west; boating, water-skiing, swimming and fishing, bushwalking, rock-climbing, children's adventure playgrounds, picnic/barbecue facilities. Whole area renowned for fossicking. **Tourist information:** Water Towers Complex, Campbell St; (067) 22 1693. **Accommodation:** 4 hotels, 6 motels, 3 caravan/ camping parks. **See also:** New England.
MAP REF. 113 K5

Jamberoo
Population 482
Jamberoo is one of the most picturesque areas of the NSW coast with lush pastures surrounded by towering escarpments. The district has been famous for the quality of its dairy products since the early settlement days. **Of interest:** Jamberoo Hotel, Allowrie St; bush bands Sun. aftn. Jamberoo Valley Folk Festival held end Feb. **In the area:** Jamberoo Recreation and Grass Ski Park, 3 km north. Breathtaking Minnamurra Rainforest, 4 km west. **Tourist information:** Kiama Visitors Centre, Blowhole Point, Kiama; (042) 32 3322. **Accommodation:** 1 hotel, 1 motel/lodge, 1 guest-house.
MAP REF. 107 O8, 109 I4, 111 J9

Jerilderie
Population 954
This small town on the Newell Hwy was held by the Kelly gang for two days in 1879 when they captured the police, cut the telegraph-wires and robbed the bank. Today it is the centre of the largest merino stud area in NSW and also supports an expanding vegetable industry. **Of interest:** Telegraph Office Museum, Powell St; next door The Willows historic home offers crafts, Devonshire teas and tourist information. Court-house. Lake Jerilderie for watersports; adjacent Lake Park features 'Steel Wings', one of largest windmills in southern hemisphere, also shady picnic areas. **Tourist information:** The Willows, Powell St; (058) 86 1666. **Accommodation:** 1 hotel/motel, 4 motels, 1 caravan/camping park.
MAP REF. 117 M11

Jindabyne
Population 1733
Now situated on the shores of Lake Jindabyne at the foothills of the Snowy Mountains, the original township was located on the banks of the Snowy River. From 1962, residents of the old town progressively moved up to the site chosen by the Snowy Mountains Hydro-electric Authority to relocate the town. This made way for the damming of the Snowy River to form a water storage as part of the Snowy Mountains Scheme. At an altitude of 930 m and situated in the 'Heart of the Snowy Mountains', Jindabyne attracts snow skiers in winter and fishermen, watersports enthusiasts and bushwalkers in summer. An outdoor ice-skating rink

Witcombe Memorial Fountain, Lachlan St, Hay

NATIONAL PARKS OF NEW SOUTH WALES

The coastal edge of Ben Boyd National Park, near Merimbula

The national parks of New South Wales encompass areas ranging from World Heritage-listed rainforests to unspoiled beaches. Tourists return time and time again to these popular scenic retreats, which offer a wide range of activities for holiday-makers.

Many of the state's parks are found along the coast, their rugged headlands, quiet inlets and sweeping beaches pounded by the crashing surf. The easy accessibility of these coastal parks accounts for their popularity.

Among the seventy-five parks proclaimed in New South Wales is Australia's first, the Royal National Park, just 32 kilometres south of Sydney. Established in 1879, **Royal National Park** has 15 069 hectares of heath-covered sandstone plateau country, broken here and there by fine surf beaches, including Wattamolla and Garie. From August to November, the area is ablaze with the colourful wildflowers. More than 700 plant species in the park in turn attract over 250 species of birds. Visitors to the park can enjoy picnicking at many picturesque spots along the coast. Activities are mainly for sun-lovers: surfing, swimming, canoeing, beach fishing and bushwalking. The Hacking River runs through almost the entire length of the park. Boats may be hired at Audley and visitors can row leisurely up the river, following its twisting course under a canopy of figs and coachwoods decked with tree-ferns.

Also south of Sydney is **Botany Bay National Park** in two sections: the northern section contains the sandy beaches of La Perouse and features a maritime museum, while the southern section at Kurnell protects the site of Captain Cook's first Australian landing in 1770. Here a staffed Discovery Centre has exhibitions on the history of the area.

Just north of Sydney are two prominent national parks, on the southern and northern shores of the Hawkesbury River: **Ku-ring-gai Chase** and **Brisbane Water National Parks,** which are renowned for their sheltered creeks and inlets and bushland walking-tracks adorned with wildflowers.

Ku-ring-gai Chase, established in 1894 and only 24 km from Sydney, hugs the shores of the Hawkesbury, Broken Bay and Pitt Water. Comprising 15 000 hectares of open rainforest, eucalypt forests, scrub and heath, it is the home of a wide range of birdlife, including the elusive lyrebird, honeyeaters, waterbirds, colourful parrots and lorikeets. A small colony of koalas dwells in the eucalypt forest. Aboriginal cave painting galleries and rock engravings are accessed by a network of walking tracks.

Brisbane Water also has sandstone landscapes rich in Aboriginal art. There are scenic views from Warrah Trig and Staples Lookout, while Somersby Falls and Girakool picnic area mark the beginning of rainforest walks.

Nearby is **Dharug National Park**, its sandstone cliffs rising high above the meandering Hawkesbury River. This park houses magnificent waterfalls set in forests of coachwood, sassafras and eucalypts and framed by colourful wildflowers in spring, including Christmas bells, spider flowers and boronias. A network of walking tracks includes a section of the convict-built Great North Road.

Further inland, to the west of Sydney, are splendid parks nestling in mountains that overawed the early explorers. Year after year, innumerable visitors return to the **Blue Mountains National Park**, where mysterious blue mists shroud the immense valleys of the Grose River, creating ever-changing patterns of colours: green, blue and purple.

At Katoomba, pillars of weathered sandstone rise abruptly like isolated church spires: these are the Three Sisters, the most popular tourist attraction in the Blue Mountains. The 247 021 hectare park is also a sanctuary for grey kangaroos, wallabies, platypuses and many species of birds, including the unique rock warbler.

The **New England National Park**, which preserves one of the largest remaining areas of rainforest in New South Wales, is 576 kilometres northeast of Sydney. Its 29 985 hectares cover three distinct zones: subalpine with tall snow gums, temperate forests of ancient Antarctic beeches and true subtropical rainforests, rich in ferns and orchids. The park has a diverse range of flora and fauna. Some 20 kilometres of walking-tracks reveal to visitors the silent charm of the rainforest while the trackless wilderness attracts more experienced bushwalkers. **Yuraygir National Park**, on the far north coast, is a water wonderland with isolated beaches, quiet lakes and striking scenery. The park deserves its reputation as a prime area for fishing; surfing is popular; its waterways invite exploration by canoe; and the estuaries offer safe swimming. Beachwalking is an excellent and easy way to explore Yuraygir.

In the far north of the state, **Border Ranges** and **Mount Warning National Parks** both offer the visitor vistas of World Heritage-listed rainforst. The 31 508 hectare Border Ranges includes the rim of the ancient volcano once centred on Mt Warning to the east. The western section is difficult wilderness terrain. Stunning escarpments, waterfalls, scenic drives and walking tracks from picnic areas abound in the eastern part.

Known to the Aborigines as 'Wollumbin', the cloud-catcher, Mt Warning (1157 metres) dominates the landscape and catches the first rays of the rising sun on the continent. A walk through Breakfast Creek rainforest leads to a steep climb and the summit viewing platform.

One park popular throughout the year is **Warrumbungle National Park**, located on the western slopes of the Great Divide, 491 kilometres northwest of Sydney. Here is some of the most spectacular scenery in the nation: sheltered gorges, rocky spires, permanent freshwater springs.

At Warrumbungle, east meets west: the dry western plains and moist eastern coast combine to give high peaks covered with snow gums and lower forests filled with fragrant native trees and shrubs. Walking trails lead to lookout points where hikers are rewarded with the fascinating colours of sunrise and sunset. In the spring and summer months, the colourful displays of wildflowers and the calls of brightly plumaged birds lure many visitors.

Mount Kaputar National Park, near Narrabri, is one of Australia's most accessible wilderness areas. Its vegetation ranges from rainforest to subalpine, and the park is rich in flora and fauna. One of the highlights in the park is Sawn Rocks, a 40-metre-high rock formation resembling a series of organ pipes.

The largest coastal lake system in New South Wales is protected by the **Myall Lakes National Park**, an important waterbird habitat. Water is the focus of tourist activities: sailing and canoeing on the quiet lake waters; surfing and beach fishing off the shores of the Pacific Ocean.

The largest national park in New South Wales is **Kosciusko**, with its 690 000 hectares of glacial lakes, limestone caves, grasslands, heaths and woodlands. Situated 450 kilometres south-west of Sydney, this park is of particular significance because it embraces a large area of the continent's only extensive alpine region and contains Australia's highest mountains as well as the sources of the important Murray, Snowy and Murrumbidgee Rivers. Here are the most extensive snowfields of the nation, housing developed ski resorts, including the famous Thredbo, Perisher Valley, Smiggin Holes, Guthega, Mt Blue Cow, Mt Selwyn and Charlotte Pass. There are easy grades for beginners and slopes for expert skiers. Although Kosciusko is associated with winter

sports, it is also a superb summer retreat with its crisp, clean air, crystal-clear lakes and a wonderful display of alpine wildflowers. This is a popular venue for those who enjoy camping, fishing, boating and bushwalking.

Over 9000 hectares of rocky but beautiful coastline flanking Twofold Bay make up **Ben Boyd National Park**. Flowering heaths and colourful banksias add to the area's attraction. Boyd's Tower, constructed in the 1840s, is a prominent feature of the park.

In the far west of New South Wales are four outstanding national parks. **Kinchega**, 110 kilometres south-east of Broken Hill, contains the beautiful saucer-shaped overflow lakes of the Darling River. The lakes provide a most important breeding ground for a wide variety of waterbirds, including herons, ibises, spoonbills and black swans. Walking-tracks through forests of river red gums and scenic drives follow the course of the river and the lake shores.

North-east of Wentworth is the World Heritage-listed **Mungo National Park**. The shores of the now dry lake hold a continuous record of Aboriginal life dating back 40 000 years. The remarkable 'Walls of China' a great crescent-shaped dune, stretches along the eastern shore of the lake-bed.

Mootwingee National Park, covering an area of 68 912 hectares and 130 kilometres north-east of Broken Hill, offers breathtaking scenery and a rich heritage of Aboriginal art.

The most remote national park in the state is **Sturt**, 1400 kilometres from Sydney and 330 kilometres north of Broken Hill. This is an ideal place for those who want to get away from it all and experience the real Australian outback. The park's 310 634 hectares comprise scenic open deserts, red sand dunes, rocky ridges, lakes and billabongs.Visitors must come well prepared but may camp within the park and enjoy bushwalking over the sandplains. Wildflowers, which include the scarlet and black blooms of Sturt's desert rose are abundant. Fort Grey, where Sturt and his party built a stockade to protect their supplies, is worth a visit.

For more information about national parks of New South Wales, contact the National Parks and Wildlife Service, 43 Bridge St (PO Box 1967), Hurstville, NSW 2220; (02) 585 6333.

Trout fishing near Jindabyne

converts to a mini-golf course in summer. **Of interest:** Lake Jindabyne is well stocked with trout and is ideal for boating and water-skiing. **In the area:** Kosciusko National Park Headquarters and Information Centre, Sawpit Creek, 20 km west, on Mt Kosciusko Rd. Winter shuttle-bus service to Perisher Valley and Smiggin Holes. After snow has melted, 50-min. drive west from Jindabyne leads to Charlotte Pass, where there is choice of 300 m boardwalk to view main range or 16 km round trip to summit of Mt Kosciusko. At Thredbo, 28 km west, chair-lift operates all year and in summer provides easy access over steel-mesh track to summit of Mt Kosciusko, 13 km round trip. Eagles Range for farm holidays. **Tourist information:** Snowy River Information Centre, Petamin Plaza; (064) 56 2444. **Accommodation:** 3 motels/hotels, 4 motels, 1 caravan/camping park.
MAP REF. 109 C9

Junee   Population 3720

Junee is an important railhead town and commercial centre, 482 km south-west of Sydney. **Of interest:** Historic buildings include Monte Cristo (1884), restored Victorian homestead overlooking town; afternoon teas and luncheons by arrangement;

(069) 24 1637. 'Woodoak', reconstructed church interior made of oak, with other wood carvings, on display. **In the area:** Scenic road to Mt Ulandra, 45 km east. **Tourist information:** Tarcutta St, Wagga Wagga; (069) 23 5402. **Accommodation:** 4 hotels, 1 motel, 1 caravan/camping park.
MAP REF. 109 A4, 110 B9, 117 Q9

Katoomba–Wentworth Falls

Population 15 627
Visitors are big business in Katoomba, the highly developed tourism centre of the magnificent Blue Mountains. At least 3 million people visit the area each year. Katoomba and the smaller towns of Leura and Wentworth Falls have many interesting features as well as the superb mountain scenery for which they are famous. Originally developed as a coal-mine last century, it was not long before Katoomba was attracting wealthy Sydney holiday-makers. Word of the area's attractions spread and guest and holiday houses sprang up almost overnight. The coal-mine foundered, but Katoomba continued to develop as a tourist resort. The Blue Mountains region abounds in natural and man-made attractions: the Blue Mountains National Park, historic sites,

art galleries, gift, craft and antique shops, as well as cosy tea-rooms and fine restaurants. **Of interest:** Scenic Skyway and Railway Complex, Violet St/Cliff Dr; first horizontal passenger-carrying ropeway in Australia, the Scenic Skyway travels about 350 m across mountain gorge above Cooks Crossing, giving magnificent views of Katoomba Falls, Orphan Rock and Jamison Valley. Built in 1880s by founder of Katoomba coal-mine to bring out coal and transport miners, and reputed to be world's steepest railway, the Scenic Railway descends into Jamison Valley at average incline of 45°, through sunlit, tree-clad gorge approximately 445 m in length. Famous rock formations (The Three Sisters and Orphan Rock) and Katoomba Falls are floodlit at night. At Wentworth Falls, Yester Grange (1870s), 73-sq. house, on 4.7 ha site; restored and furnished to late-Victorian splendour. Everglades Garden, cnr Denson Rd and Fitzroy St in Leura, one of Australia's great gardens. Leuralla, Olympian Pde; historic art deco mansion in Leura, houses major collection of 19th-century Australian art and memorial museum to Dr H. V. Evatt. Cliff Drive follows cliff-tops around Katoomba–Leura, offering spectacular views at many lookouts and picnic spots. Walking-tracks along cliff-tops and descending into Jamison Valley offer chance to experience delights of heathland and rainforest. Wide selection of accommodation available from such superb resorts as Fairmont Resort at Leura, luxurious guest-houses, modern motels, holiday cottages and cabins. Visitors can enjoy horseriding, four-wheel driving, cycling and walking. **In the area:** Dramatic views from Sublime Point (on Blue Mountains Scenic Drive from Leura) and Hanging Rock (north of Blackheath on 4WD track). Jemby-Rinjah Lodge at Blackheath, 12 km north, has environmental studies centre set on edge of Blue Mountains National Park. Govett's Leap and Evans Point Lookouts in park. Hydro Majestic Hotel at Medlow Bath, 7 km north; health resort dating from around turn of century. Norman Lindsay Gallery and Museum at Springwood, 32 km east. Mount Victoria, 18 km north, National Trust classified village with craft shops and museum; nearby waterfalls, Pulpit Rock reserve and Mount York Historic Site. Yerranderie, abandoned old silver-mining town, 70 km south of Blackheath, surrounded by 2430 ha wildlife reserve. Jenolan Caves, containing some of most splendid underground caves and above-ground arches in Australia, in recreation reserve 80 km south of Katoomba. **Tourist information:** Echo Point, Katoomba; (047) 82 0756; or the Blue Mountains

Information Centre, Gt Western Hwy, Glenbrook; (047) 39 6266. **Accommodation:** 6 hotels, 13 motels, 3 caravan/camping parks. **See also:** The Blue Mountains.
MAP REF. 100 E7, 109 G1, 110 I6

Kempsey   Population 9335

Kempsey is situated in the Macleay River Valley, 480 km north of Sydney, and is the commercial centre of a growing district of dairying, tourism and light industry, including the Akubra hat factory. The town celebrated its sesquicentenary in 1986. **Of interest:** Macleay River Historical Society Museum, Pacific Hwy, South Kempsey. Number of 19th-century buildings in Kemp, Elbow, Sea and Belgrave Sts, West Kempsey. **In the area:** Trial Bay Gaol, 5 km north-east; built by prisoners in 1880s. South West Rocks, 32 km north-east, beach resort; river cruises. Bellbrook, 47 km north-west; village classified by National Trust. Crescent Head, 20 km southeast. Limeburners Creek Nature Reserve, further 20 km south of village. Hat Head National Park, 25 km east. Fish Rock and cave, noted for scuba-diving, 5 km off Smoky Cape, in park. **Tourist information:** Pacific Hwy; (065) 62 5444. **Accommodation:** 6 hotels, 10 motels, 5 caravan parks.
MAP REF. 113 O10

Khancoban   Population 481

Situated in the lush green Murray Valley at the western end of the Alpine Way, 109 km north-west of Jindabyne, this small modern town was built by the Snowy Mountains Authority and is now an administrative centre. Khancoban offers a variety of accommodation from a luxurious alpine retreat to a caravan park. **In the area:** Inspections of Murray 1 Power Station; trout fishing, water sports, whitewater rafting. Excellent picnic and rest areas along Alpine Way and spectacular mountain views from Olsen's and Scammel's Spur Lookouts. Brilliant roadside displays of wildflowers in spring and autumn. **Tourist information:** National Parks and Wildlife Service, Scott St; (060) 76 9373. **Accommodation:** 2 motels, 1 caravan park.
MAP REF. 109 B8, 110 D13, 219 H6

Kiama   Population 9184

The spectacular Blowhole is the best-known attraction of this resort town. Discovered by explorer George Bass in 1797, it sprays water up to heights of 60 m. It is floodlit until 9.30 p.m. each evening. Kiama is the centre of a prosperous dairying and mixed farming district. **Of interest:** Kiama Beach for surfing,

The Blowhole, Kiama

swimming and fishing. Pilots Cottage historical museum, beside Kiama Visitors Centre and restaurant at Blowhole Point. Terrace houses, specialty and craft shops in Collins St. Family History Centre, Railway Pde; worldwide collection of records for tracing family history. **In the area:** Little Blowhole, 2 km south, off Tingira Cres; although smaller, sometimes outblows its famous brother. Cathedral Rocks, 3 km north, at Jones Beach; scenic rocky outcrop, best viewed at dawn. **Tourist information:** Blowhole Point; (042) 32 3322. **Accommodation:** 2 hotels, 6 motels, 4 caravan/camping parks. **See also:** The Illawarra Coast.
MAP REF. 107 G8, 109 I4, 111 J9

Kyogle   Population 2983

Kyogle makes a good base for exploring the mountains nearby. It is also the centre of a lush dairy and mixed farming area on the upper reaches of the Richmond River near the Qld border. **In the area:** World Heritage-listed Border Ranges National Park, 35 km north; Tweed Range Scenic Drive (64 km), through eastern section, takes in pristine rainforest and deep gorges with waterfalls plunging into crystal-clear creeks. Magnificent views from Mt Lindesay, 45 km north-west, on NSW/Qld border. Wiangaree State Forest, 30 km north; rainforest with elevated coastal views. Toonumbar Dam, 31 km west, offers bushwalking and picnic/barbecue areas; freshwater fishing and camping at Bell's Bay. Picnic spots include Roseberry Nursery and Moore Park (23 km and 27 km north), Tooloom Falls (95 km north-west) and scenic area at Nimbin Rocks (32 km east). **Tourist information:** 29 Summerland Way; (066) 32 1044. **Accommodation:** 1 hotel, 1 motel, 1 caravan/camping park.
MAP REF. 113 P2, 435 Q12

Lake Cargelligo   Population 1206

A small township, 586 km west of Sydney, of the same name as the lake, which serves the surrounding agricultural and pastoral district. **Of interest:** Fishing, boating, water-skiing and swimming on lake; picnic facilities. Lake is home to many species of birds, including pelicans, wild ducks, geese and black swans, galahs, cockatoos and, at times, the rare black cockatoo. **Accommodation:** 1 hotel, 2 motels, 1 caravan/camping park.
MAP REF. 117 N5

Lake Macquarie
Population (est.) 158 300

Lake Macquarie is a city without a town centre, but boasts the largest saltwater coastal lake in Australia as its hub. The

northern shore townships of Lake Macquarie such as Toronto, Speers Point, Belmont and Boolaroo contain many restaurants and sailing clubs. The lake is excellent for swimming, sailing, fishing and associated water sports. **Of interest:** Lake cruises on MV *Wangi Queen* and MV *Macquarie Lady*, both leaving from Toronto Wharf and Belmont. Dobell House, 47 Dobell Dr., Wangi Wangi; home of great Australian artist Sir William Dobell, with collection of his work and memorabilia. Eraring Power Station; inspection tours. **Tourist information:** Tourism Lake Macquarie, Council Chambers, Main Rd, Speers Point; (049) 21 0221. **Accommodation:** Belmont: 2 hotels, 10 motels, 9 caravan/camping parks. Charlestown: 4 hotels, 5 motels. Toronto: 3 hotels, 3 motels, 6 caravan/camping parks.
MAP REF. 104 G8, 111 L4

Leeton Population 6421
Located 560 km south-west of Sydney, Leeton is the first of the planned towns in the Murrumbidgee Irrigation Area and was designed by American architect Walter Burley Griffin. The town is an important administrative and processing centre for this intensive fruit, rice and winegrape growing area. **Of interest:** Historic Hydro Hotel (1919), Chelmsford Pl. Letona Fruit Cannery, Wamoon Ave; Sunwhite Rice Mill, Yanco Ave; Quelch Juice Factory, Brady Way; and Tavella Cheese Factory, Massey Ave; guided tours weekdays. Leeton Sunwhite Rice Festival held every even year for 11 days, including Easter. **In the area:** Toorak and Lillypilly Estate Wineries, both close to town. Fivebough Swamp, 2 km north; famous waterbird sanctuary. Yanco Agricultural High School, 10 km south. Murrumbidgee State Forests, 12 km south. Gogeldrie Weir, 23 km south-west. Yanco Weir, 25 km south-east. Aquatic Park near Yanco. Whitton Court-house Museum, 23 km west. Gliding and hot-air ballooning. **Tourist information:** Chelmsford Pl.; (069) 53 2832. **Accommodation:** 3 hotels, 4 motels, 2 caravan parks. **See also:** Wineries of New South Wales.
MAP REF. 117 N8

Lennox Head Population 1854
Just north of Ballina, Lennox Head has retained its charming seaside village atmosphere. The area is famous for its surfing beaches. **Of interest:** Freshwater Lake Ainsworth, 50 m from surfing beach; popular with windsurfers. **In the area:** Swimming, surfing, snorkelling. Many scenic walks and rainforests are short drive away. **Tourist information:** Ballina Tourist Information Centre, Las Balsas Plaza, Ballina; (066) 86 3484.

Accommodation: 3 motels, 1 caravan/camping park.
MAP REF. 113 R3

Lightning Ridge Population 1292
Small opal-mining township in the famous Lightning Ridge opal fields, 74 km north of Walgett, via the Castlereagh Hwy. The extremely valuable black opal found in the area attracts gem enthusiasts from all over Australia and overseas. **Of interest:** Bowling Club and Diggers Rest Hotel, Morilla St, share township's social life. Underground mine tours, opal-cutting demonstrations; museums, potteries, and displays of local art and craft, including opal jewellery and gem opals. **In the area:** Cactus Nursery, 2 km north, off Bald Hill Rd. Fauna Orphanage, Opal St, 3 km south. Hot Artesian Bore Baths (free), 2 km north-east. Nature reserves and fossicking. **Tourist information:** Walgett Shire Council, 77 Fox St, Walgett; (068) 28 1399. **Accommodation:** 3 motels, 5 caravan/camping parks.
MAP REF. 112 C4, 115 R4, 435 J13

Lismore Population 24 896
Regional centre of the Northern Rivers district of NSW, a closely settled and intensively cultivated rural area producing dairy products, tropical fruits, beef, timber and fodder crops, Lismore is situated on Wilsons River (formerly the north arm of the Richmond River), 821 km from Sydney. It is best known for its rainforest heritage, including the Rotary Rainforest Reserve, situated within the residential area of the city, Wilsons Park and the Boatharbour Reserve. **Of interest:** Lismore Information and Heritage Centre, and surrounding Heritage Park (picnic areas), cnr Ballina and Molesworth Sts. Cedar Log Memorial, Ballina St. Richmond River Historical Museum and Lismore Regional Art Gallery, both in Molesworth St. Robinson's Lookout, Robinson Ave. Claude Riley Memorial Lookout, New Ballina Rd. River cruises on MV *Bennelong*, The Wharf, Magellan St. **In the area:** Macadamia Magic at Alphadale, 11 km east; macadamia-processing plant and tourist complex. Rocky Creek Dam, 25 km north. Minyon Falls and Peates Mountain Lookout, in Whian Whian State Forest, 25 km north. Spectacular volcanic Nimbin Rocks, 3 km south of Nimbin (29 km north). World Heritage-listed Border Ranges National Park, 25 km north of Nimbin, and Nightcap National Park, 25 km north of Lismore. Lismore Lake, 3 km south; picnic/barbecue facilities, pleasant lagoon for swimming and children's adventure park. Tucki Tucki Koala Reserve, 15 km south, adjacent to Lismore–Woodburn Rd;

Aboriginal ceremonial ground nearby. **Tourist information:** Cnr Ballina and Molesworth Sts; (066) 22 0122. **Accommodation:** 9 hotels, 12 motels, 4 caravan/camping parks.
MAP REF. 113 Q3, 435 Q13

Lithgow Population 12 369
This important coal-mining city on the north-west fringes of the Blue Mountains is a must for railway enthusiasts. The city itself is highly industrialised with two power-stations and several large factories, but the surrounding countryside is beautiful. **Of interest:** Eskbank House, Bennett St, built in 1841 by Thomas Brown, who discovered Lithgow coal seam; now museum with fine collection of 19th-century furniture and vehicles, and displays depicting industrial history of area. Blast Furnace Park, off Inch St; ruins of Australia's first blast furnace complex. **In the area:** Zig Zag Steam Railway, 10 km east, via Bells Line of Road; breathtaking stretch of railway, regarded as engineering masterpiece when built in 1869, and restored by enthusiasts; train trips and picnic facilities. Sweeping views from Hassan Walls Lookout, 5 km south, off Great Western Hwy. Historic village of Hartley, 12 km south-east, off Great Western Hwy, has convict-built court-house (1837) of outstanding architectural and historic interest. Jenolan Caves, 60 km south-east. Wallerawang Power Station, 13 km north-west; guided tours. **Tourist information:** 285 Main Street; (063) 51 2307. **Accommodation:** 6 hotels, 5 motels, 1 caravan/camping park.
MAP REF. 100 C4, 110 H5

Lockhart Population 910
This pleasant historic town, situated 65 km south-west of Wagga, was originally known as Green's Gunyah and was renamed Lockhart in 1897. A distinctive feature of the commercial centre is the wide, shady shopfront verandahs, a fine example of a turn-of-the-century streetscape, for which it received a classified listing by the National Trust. **Tourist information:** Tarcutta St, Wagga Wagga; (069) 23 5402. **Accommodation:** 1 hotel, 1 motel, 1 caravan park.
MAP REF. 117 O10

Macksville Population 2811
This is an attractive town on the Nambucca River, south of Nambucca Heads. **Of interest:** Mary Boulton Pioneer Cottage, River St; charming replica of pioneer home, includes furniture, costumes and museum of horsedrawn vehicles in its collection. **In the area:** Cosmopolitan Hotel (1903), the 'Pub with No Beer', made famous by song, at Taylors Arm,

26 km west; surrounded by lawns and trees, with barbecue/picnic area. Joseph and Eliza Newman Folk Museum at unspoiled Bowraville (the 'Verandah Post Town'), 16 km north-west. **Accommodation:** 2 hotels, 3 motels, 2 caravan parks. MAP REF. 113 P8

Maclean   Population 2681
Fishing and river prawning fleets are based at Maclean, known as 'the Scottish town in Australia', on the Clarence River, about 740 km north of Sydney. Fishermen from here and from the nearby towns of Yamba and Iluka catch about 20% of the state's seafood. Sugarcane, maize and mixed farm crops are grown in the area. **Of interest:** Scottish Corner, River St; shop with tourist information. Bicentennial Museum and adjoining Stone Cottage (1879), Wharf St. Maclean Lookout and Pinnacle Rocks. Rainforest walking track from High School. Maclean Highland Gathering held at Easter. Cane Harvest Festival in Sept. **In the area:** Houseboats for hire at Brushgrove, 21 km south-west. Yuraygir National Park, 24 km south-east. **Tourist information:** Shire Offices; (066) 43 1927. **Accommodation:** 3 hotels, 2 motels, 3 caravan parks. MAP REF. 113 P5

Maitland   Population 43 247
On the Hunter River, 28 km from Newcastle, Maitland dates back to the early days of the colony. The city's winding High St has been recorded by the National Trust as a Conservation Area and over 90% of the buildings date back to the 1800s. First settled in 1818, when convicts were put to work as cedar-getters, it was a flourishing township by the 1840s. Today it is a thriving city. **Of interest:** National Trust properties Grossman House, Georgian-style folk museum, and Brough House (1870), containing city's art collection, in Church St, are mirror images of each other. Cintra, Regent St; Victorian mansion offering b & b accommodation. Self-guiding Heritage Walk of East Maitland and Morpeth. **In the area:** Walka Waterworks, 3 km north; former pumping station, now excellent picnic site. At Morpeth, 5 km north-east: historic buildings with superb iron lace and many specialty craft shops. At Lochinvar, 13 km west: Windermere Colonial Museum, built of sandstone brick by convict labour in 1820s, later occupied by William Charles Wentworth; also NSW Equestrian Centre. **Tourist information:** Hew Cottage, cnr Banks St and New England Hwy; (049) 33 2611. **Accommodation:** 4 hotels, 6 motels, 1 caravan/camping park. MAP REF. 104 F3, 111 L3

Manilla   Population 2017
This small town, set in beautiful countryside, boasts Dutton's Meadery, one of only two meaderys in the state. Visitors can sample and buy fresh honey and mead. **Of interest:** Picturesque street setting with antique stores and coffee shops. Royce Cottage Historical Museum, Manilla St. **In the area:** Manilla Ski Gardens on Lake Keepit, 20 km south-west. Muluerindie Country Holidays, 22 km east. Warrabah National Park, 40 km north, peaceful riverside retreat; fishing, swimming and canoeing on Namoi River **Tourist information:** Visitors Information Centre, Kable Ave, Tamworth; (067) 68 4462. **Accommodation:** 1 motel, 1 caravan/camping park. **See also:** New England. MAP REF. 113 J8

Menindee   Population 406
It was at this small township, 110 km south-east of Broken Hill, which now serves the surrounding country population, that the ill-fated Burke and Wills stayed in 1860 on their journey north. **Of interest:** Maiden's Hotel (where they lodged). Ah Chung's Bakehouse Gallery, Menindee St. Menindee Lakes Lookout. Menindee Lakes, upstream from township; water-storage scheme that guarantees an unfailing water supply to Broken Hill. Yachting, fishing and swimming on lakes; nearby Copi Hollow attracts water-skiers and powerboat enthusiasts. Kinchega National Park, 1 km west; emus, red kangaroos and waterbirds abound. **Tourist information:** Broken Hill Tourist Information Centre, cnr Blende and Bromide Sts, Broken Hill; (080) 87 6077. **Accommodation:** 2 hotels, 1 motel, 2 caravan/camping parks. MAP REF. 114 E13, 116 E2

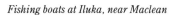

Fishing boats at Iluka, near Maclean

Merimbula   Population 3278

Excellent surfing, fishing and prawning make this small sea and lake town a popular holiday resort. Its sister village of Pambula also offers fine fishing and surfing. **Of interest:** Aquarium at Merimbula Wharf, Lake St. Old School Museum, Main St. Magic Mountain Family Recreation Park, Sapphire Coast Dr. Seafood Festival held in May; Jazz Festival in June. **In the area:** Cruises on lakes. Boats for hire. Tura Beach, 2 km north. Pambula Beach, 10 km south, with walking track and lookout. Ben Boyd National Park, 13 km south. **Tourist information:** Beach St; (064) 95 1129. **Accommodation:** 16 motels, 4 caravan/camping parks. **See also:** The South Coast.
MAP REF. 109 F10, 221 P2

Merriwa   Population 961

This small township in the western Hunter region is noted for its many historic buildings. **Of interest:** Self-guiding Historic Walks; buildings of note in Vennacher, Bay and McCartney Sts. Historical Museum housed in stone cottage (1857), Bettington St. Bottle Museum in Tourist Information Centre, Vennacher St. **In the area:** Convict-built Flags Rd, runs from town to Gungal, 25 km southeast. The Drip picnic area, at Goulburn River National Park, 35 km south. Official gem-fossicking area 27 km south-west. Cassilis, 45 km north-west; small town noted for its historic sandstone buildings. Aboriginal hands painted on rocks in caves just off Mudgee Rd, 32 km southwest of Cassilis. Ulan coal-mine, further 8 km south-west, largest open-cut mine in southern hemisphere; viewing area. **Tourist information:** Vennacher St; (065) 48 2505. **Accommodation:** 1 motel, 1 caravan/camping park.
MAP REF. 110 I1, 112 I13

Mittagong   Population 4828

The gateway to the Southern Highlands, Mittagong is 110 km south of Sydney. **Of interest:** Butterfly House and The Maze, Bessemer St. Natural wonders of Lake Alexandra, Queen St; mecca for children. **In the area:** Well-planned walks through nearby hills, include Box Vale and Natural Arch Walks; follow Hume Fwy from Mittagong to Berrima turnoff, 15 km south-west. **Tourist information:** Winifred West Park, Old Hume Hwy; (048) 71 2888. **Accommodation:** 2 hotels, 6 motels, 1 caravan/camping park.
MAP REF. 107 A6, 109 H3, 110 I8

Moama–Echuca   Population 8409

Moama and its twin city Echuca, on the Victorian side of the Murray River,

Fitzroy Falls, Morton National Park, near Moss Vale

embody the age of the paddle-steamer, when the port of Echuca was a major outlet for agricultural products. **Of interest:** Visitors can recapture the spirit of the paddle-steamer era at the restored port at Echuca. **In the area:** Murray River tours aboard cruise boats or paddle-steamers. Moira and Barmah redgum forests, 35 km south-east. **Tourist information:** Cobb Hwy; (054) 82 6001. **Accommodation:** 1 hotel/motel, 6 motels, 4 caravan/ camping parks.
MAP REF. 117 K13, 216 F4

Molong   Population 1400

The grave of Yaranigh, the faithful Aboriginal guide of explorer Sir Thomas Mitchell, is 2 km east of this Mitchell Hwy town. Yaranigh was buried there in 1850, according to the rites of his tribe. The grave is marked by a headstone which pays tribute to his courage and fidelity. Four trees, one dead but preserved for its Aboriginal carvings, mark the four corners of the burial ground. **Of interest:** Yarn Market, Craft Cottage and Coach House Gallery, Bank St. Annual sheepdog trials held in March. **In the area:** Mitchell's Monument, 21 km south, marks site of explorer's base camp. **Tourist information:** Civic Centre, Byne St, Orange; (063) 61 5226. **Accommodation:** 2 hotels, 1 motel, 1 caravan/camping park.
MAP REF. 110 E4

Moree   Population 10 215

Situated on the Mehi River, 640 km from Sydney, this town is the nucleus of a large beef, wool, cotton and wheat producing region. It is best known for its artesian spa baths, said to relieve arthritis and rheumatism. **Of interest:** Spa complex, Anne St; with olympic swimming pool. Mary Brand Park, Gwydir St. Meteorological station, Jones Ave. Moree Lands Office (1894), National Trust classified, cnr Frome and Heber Sts; self-guiding leaflet on Mehi River Walking Track. Moree Plains Regional Gallery, Heber St. Yurundiali Aboriginal Corporation, Endeavour Lane; screen printing clothing factory. **In the area:** Pecan Nut Farm, 35 km east; tours in season. Inspection of cotton gins during harvesting season. **Tourist information:** Lyle Houlihan Park, Alice St;

(067) 52 9559. **Accommodation:** 6 hotels, 1 hotel/motel, 13 motels, 3 caravan/camping parks. **See also:** The Newell.
MAP REF. 112 H4

Moruya
Population 2386

Many famous old dairying estates were founded near this town, which was once a gateway to the Araluen and Braidwood goldfields. Situated on the Moruya River, 322 km from Sydney, it is now a dairying, timber and oyster-farming centre. Granite used in the pylons of the Sydney Harbour Bridge was quarried in the district. **Of interest:** Eurobodalla Historic Museum, in town centre, depicts discovery of gold at Mogo and general history of district. **In the area:** Mort Memorial Church and historic cemetery at Moruya Heads, 7 km east. Coomerang House at Bodalla, 24 km south; home of 19th-century industrialist and dairy farmer Thomas Sutcliffe Mort. Nerrigundah, 44 km south-west; former gold-mining town. Fishing, surfing and water sports. **Tourist information:** Eurobodalla Coast Visitors Centres on Princes Hwy at Batemans Bay, (044) 72 6900, and Narooma, (044) 76 2881. **Accommodation:** 1 hotels, 2 motels, 2 caravan/camping parks.
MAP REF. 109 G8

Moss Vale
Population 5016

The industrial and agricultural centre of the Southern Highlands, the town stands on part of the 1000 acre parcel of land granted to Charles Throsby in 1819. **Of interest:** Leighton Park running almost half length of main street. Cecil Hoskins Reserve with abundance of birdlife. Historic Throsby Park, on northern edge of town; open to public on special occasions. **In the area:** At township of Sutton Forest, 6 km south on Illawarra Hwy, Old Butcher Shop Gallery has items ranging from shortbread to antiques. Exeter, 4 km further south. Fitzroy Falls in Morton National Park, 20 km south-east. **Tourist information:** Winifred West Park, Hume Hwy, Mittagong; (048) 71 2888. **Accommodation:** 2 hotels, 2 motels, 2 caravan/camping parks.
MAP REF. 107 A7, 109 H4, 110 I9

Moulamein
Population 425

This is the oldest town in the Riverina, already well established in the 1870s as a prosperous inland port on the Edward River. Today the town is renowned for its fishing. **Of interest:** Old wharf, Main St. Restored court-house. Riverside picnic areas. Lake Moulamein and nearby state forests. **Tourist information:** Golden

THE NEWELL

With its excellent bitumen surface and long, straight stretches, the Newell provides fast and easy driving right across New South Wales. Driving time between Melbourne and Brisbane is up to six hours quicker by this route. The time you save could be put to good use enjoying the many interesting towns and attractions along the way.

From the Murray River town of **Tocumwal** to the Queensland border town of **Goondiwindi**, the highway runs through a wide range of scenery and is well served with motels, roadside cafes and service stations.

Tocumwal, with sandy beaches on the Murray, offers swimming and fishing as well as boating. At **Jerilderie**, 57 km further north, visit the tiny restored post office held up by the Kelly gang in 1879. In **Narrandera** there is an excellent caravan park on the shore of Lake Talbot, a popular water sports centre. Beyond **West Wyalong** to the north is Lake Cowal, the largest natural lake in New South Wales and an important bird sanctuary; further north out of **Forbes** is a major tourist attraction — the Lachlan Vintage Village, a re-creation of a nineteenth-century gold-mining town.

There is plenty to see in **Parkes,** including a vintage car museum and the Henry Parkes Museum. The fa-mous radio telescope is on the highway, north of the town. **Dubbo** boasts what is probably the most popular tourist attraction on the Newell — the superb Western Plains Zoo, claimed to be the best open-range wildlife park in Australia.

From Dubbo the highway passes through the spectacular volcanic Warrumbungle National Park, which is ideal for bushwalking. If you have children aboard, do not miss the award-winning fantasy park, 'Miniland', with its life-size prehistoric animals, just west of **Coonabarabran**. Once you get beyond the Warrumbungle Ranges the scenery changes dramatically to the vast Pilliga scrub country. **Narrabri**, in the heart of 'Cotton Country', offers a diversity of attractions, including Mt Kaputar National Park, Sawn Rocks, the Australia Telescope and gemstone fossicking. The northern town of **Moree**, not far from the Queensland border, is famed for its artesian baths and pecan nut farm.

For further information, contact the Newell Highway Promotion Committee, PO Box 532, Parkes 2870; (068) 62 4365. A booklet on the Newell is available at tourist information centres, motoring organisations and NSW Travel Centres.

Western Plains Zoo, Dubbo

PORT STEPHENS

Port Stephens

The white volcanic sand and aquamarine waters of the beaches of Port Stephens have a distinctly tropical look, and the annual average temperature is within about 2°C of that of the Gold Coast. This large deepwater port, less than an hour's drive from Newcastle, is one of the most unspoiled and attractive seaside holiday areas on the New South Wales coast. Two-and-a-half times the size of Sydney Harbour, and almost enclosed by two volcanic headlands, the large harbour is fringed by sheltered white sandy beaches backed by stretches of natural bushland. In spring, wildflowers grow in profusion.

The deep, calm waters of the harbour are ideal for boating and offer excellent fishing. A wide range of boats, from aquascooters and catamarans to sailing and power boats, can be hired. Various cruises that explore the harbour and Myall River are available. Big-game fishing waters are within reach outside the harbour, but local fishing clubs warn against leaving the heads unless you are an experienced sailor with a two-motor boat. The best way to reach these waters is aboard one of the many charter boats licensed to take fishermen and sight-seers outside the heads. Early in the afternoon you can watch the local fishing fleet coming into **Nelson Bay**, the main anchorage of the port.

Restaurants in the area — not surprisingly — offer fresh seafood as a specialty. You can sample a superb lobster supreme, washed down by a fine Hunter Valley wine. What more could you ask? For dedicated oyster lovers, a trip to Moffat's Oyster Barn, Swan Bay, is a must. As well as seeing oysters

under cultivation and learning about their four-year life cycle, you can enjoy a delicious meal of oysters, plus other seafood (bookings, (049) 97 5433). If you go by boat, make sure you do not run aground on an oyster lease!

You can hire almost anything in the area: bicycles (how about a tandem?), beach umbrellas, fishing tackle; there are also golf courses, bowling greens and all the other usual sporting facilities.

For surfing, you can visit the spectacular ocean beaches which stretch in both directions outside the harbour. Within about six kilometres from Nelson Bay are Zenith, Wreck and Box Beaches, Fingal Bay and One Mile Beach.

Other local attractions include art galleries, craft markets on each first and third Sunday of the month; Aussie Ewe and Lamb Centre, Anna Bay; toboggan run at Tomaree Leisure Park, Salamander Bay; Oakvale Farm and Fauna World; Fighter World, RAAF Base Williamtown. Accommodation, including hotels, motels and modern holiday flats, is available throughout the area and there are caravan and camping parks. The main resorts, apart from Nelson Bay, are **Shoal Bay**, **Fingal Bay**, **Anna Bay**, **Tanilba Bay**, **Salamander Bay**, **Soldiers Point** and **Lemon Tree Passage** on the south shore, and **Tea Gardens** and **Hawks Nest** on the north.

For more detailed information about the area, including nearby attractions such as the Myall Lakes, contact the Tourist Information Centre, Victoria Pde, Nelson Bay; (049) 81 1579.

Rivers Tourism, 25 Murray St, Barham; (054) 53 3100. **Accommodation:** 1 hotel, 1 caravan/camping park.
MAP REF. 116 I10, 215 R9

Mudgee   Population 6576
This attractively laid-out town is the centre of a productive agricultural area on the Cudgegong River, 264 km north-west of Sydney. Wine grapes, fine wool, sheep, cattle and honey are among the local produce. There are horse studs in the area. **Of interest:** Many fine buildings in town centre, including St John's Church of England (1860), St Mary's Roman Catholic Church, railway station, town hall and Colonial Inn Museum, all in Market St. Mt Vincent Meadery, Common Rd. Honey Haven, cnr Hill End and Gulgong Rds, and Mudgee Honey, Robertson St. **In the area:** Henry Lawson's boyhood home memorial; plaque on remains of demolished cottage, 6 km north. Cudgegong River Park, 14 km west, on eastern foreshores of Burrendong Dam; water sports and excellent fishing. Windamere Dam, 24 km east, with camping facilities. Local wineries, including Craigmoor, Montrose, Huntington Estate, Botobolar; tasting and sales. **Tourist information:** 64 Market St; (063) 72 5874. **Accommodation:** 5 hotels, 8 motels, 3 caravan/camping parks. **See also:** Wineries of New South Wales.
MAP REF. 110 G3

Mullumbimby   Population 2453
Situated in lush subtropical country, Mullumbimby is approximately 850 km north-east of Sydney. **Of interest:** Art Gallery, cnr Burringbar and Stuart Sts. Restored Cedar House, Dalley St; classified by National Trust, with antiques gallery. Brunswick Valley Historical Museum, in old post office (1907), Stuart St. Brunswick Valley Heritage Park, Tyagarah St. **In the area:** Nightcap National Park to north, and Tuntable Falls to south. Sakura Farm, 15 km west, in hills at Mullum; run by Buddhist monk, it offers unique retreat-style holidays. Crystal Castle, 7 km north; large display of natural quartz. Wanganui Gorge and rainforest walking-track, 20 km west. Skydiving and paragliding at airstrip at Tyagarah, on Pacific Hwy, 13 km southeast. **Tourist information:** Neighbourhood Centre, Dalley St; (066) 84 1286. **Accommodation:** 2 hotels, 2 motels.
MAP REF. 113 Q2, 435 Q12

Mulwala   Population 1330
On the foreshores of Lake Mulwala, the town is a major aquatic centre. Lake Mulwala is a man-made lake of over 6000 ha,

formed by the damming of the Murray River at Yarrawonga Weir in 1939 to provide water for irrigation. **Of interest:** Yachting, water-skiing, sail-boarding, swimming, canoeing and fishing. Tunzafun Amusement Park offers entertainment for young. Bowlers and golfers are well catered for in area with excellent facilities and licensed clubs. Cruise boats operate scenic tours on Lake Mulwala. **Tourist information:** Irvine Pde, Yarrawonga; (057) 44 1989. **Accommodation:** 2 hotels, 9 motels, 6 caravan/camping parks.
MAP REF. 117 N13, 217 M4

Murrurundi   Population 878
This picturesque town on the New England Hwy, set in a lush valley on the Pages River, is overshadowed by the Liverpool Ranges. **Of interest:** St Joseph's Catholic Church, Polding St; contains 1000 pieces of Italian marble. Murrurundi Museum, Main St. Paradise Park, Paradise Rd; horseshoe-shaped, surrounded by mountains; visits by wildlife in evening. **In the area:** Chillot's Creek, 15 km north, where huge diprotodon remains, now in Sydney Museum, were found. Burning Mountain at Wingen, 20 km south. Timor Limestone Caves, 43 km east. **Tourist information:** Council Offices, 47 Mayne St; (065) 46 6205. **Accommodation:** 2 motels, 1 caravan/camping park.
MAP REF. 113 J11

Murwillumbah   Population 7678
Situated on the banks of the Tweed River, 31 km south of the Qld border in the beautiful Tweed Valley, Murwillumbah's local industries include cattle-raising and the growing of sugarcane, bananas, tea and coffee. **Of interest:** Tweed River Historical Society Museum, Tumblegum Rd. **In the area:** Tweed River House-boats for hire, on Pacific Hwy, 1 km north of Visitors Centre. Condong sugar mill, 5 km north; inpections July–Dec. Avocadoland, 15 km north. Griffith Tablecraft, 8 km north-east. World Heritage-listed areas within radius of 50 km include Mt Warning, Nightcap and Border Ranges National Parks. Madura Tea Estates, 12 km north-east. Hare Krishna Community Farm, Eungella, 10 km west; visitors welcome. Farm holidays specialty of area; at Attunga Park Resort, Crystal Creek Rainforest Retreat, Midginbil Hill, Bushranger Resort, Mt Warning Forest Hideaway, Mt Warning Lodge and Tyalgum Tops. **Tourist information:** Cnr Pacific Hwy and Alma St; (066) 72 1340. **Accommodation:** 6 hotels, 8 motels, 7 caravan/camping parks.
MAP REF. 113 Q1, 429 P11, 435 Q12

Muswellbrook   Population 9988
In the Upper Hunter Valley, Muswellbrook is the centre of pastoral enterprises, including fodder crops, stud cattle and horses, wineries, sheep and dairy products. There is also a large open-cut coal-mining industry. **Of interest:** Muswellbrook Art Gallery in old town hall. **In the area:** Matt Peel's Quarter Horse Stud and Rural Museum, 12 km west. Bayswater Power Station, 16 km south; inspection tours. Wollemi National Park, 30 km south-west. Eight local wineries open daily for tastings and sales. **Tourist information:** Sheridan Winery (065) 43 3800. **Accommodation:** 1 hotel, 8 motels, 1 caravan/camping park.
MAP REF. 111 J2, 113 J13

Nambucca Heads   Population 4923
At the mouth of the Nambucca River, 552 km north of Sydney, this beautifully sited town is ideal for boating, fishing and swimming. **Of interest:** Nambucca Historical Museum, Headland Reserve; many old photographs. Orana Mineral and Art Museum, Seaview St; 1500 items on display. Breathtaking views from several local lookouts. River cruises on *Nambucca Princess*. **Tourist information:** Ridge St; (065) 68 6954. **Accommodation:** 1 hotel, 9 motels, 6 caravan/camping parks.
MAP REF. 113 P8

Rolling green hills, Central Tilba

Narooma   Population 2864
This popular fishing resort at the mouth of the Wagonga River on the Princes Hwy, 360 km south of Sydney, is well known for its rock oysters. **Of interest:** Tuross and other nearby lakes and inlets. Mystery Bay near Lake Corunna, famous for coloured sands and strange rock formations, and other inlets and lakes north and south of town. Cruises on Wagunga Princess. **In the area:** Montague Island, wildlife sanctuary 5.7 nautical miles offshore, may be visited but prebookings necessary. Historic village of Central Tilba, 17 km south of Narooma, just off Princes Hwy, classified as 'unusual mountain village' by National Trust; founded in 1894 and virtually unchanged since 1904 (excluding cheese factory), with buildings in original 19th-century condition. **Tourist information:** Eurobodalla Coast Visitors Centre, Princes Hwy; (044) 76 2881. **Accommodation:** 1 hotel, 10 motels, 4 caravan/camping parks. **See also:** The South Coast.
MAP REF. 109 G9

Narrabri   Population 7246
Situated between the spectacular Nandewar Range, including Mt Kaputar National Park and the extensive Pilliga scrub country, this town has become a phenomenally successful cotton-producing centre. **Of interest:** Historic buildings include court-house (1886), Maitland St. Self-guiding town tour

leaflet available. Riverside picnic area, Tibbereena St. Agricultural show held in April and Spring Festival on Oct. long weekend. **In the area:** Guided tours of cotton-fields and gins, Apr.–June. Plant Breeding Institute, 9 km north, on Newell Hwy. Australia Telescope, 25 km west. Yarrie Lake, 32 km west. Pilliga State Forest, 23 km south-west. Sawn Rocks, 35 km north-east, on Bingara Rd within park; spectacular basaltic formation. Mt Kaputar National Park, 53 km east; 360° views from peak take in one-tenth of NSW: spectacular volcanic blue mountain country. **Tourist information:** Newell Hwy; (067) 92 3583. **Accommodation:** 6 hotels, 2 hotel/motels, 8 motels, 3 caravan/camping parks. **See also:** National Parks of New South Wales; The Newell.
MAP REF. 112 H7

Narrandera   Population 4835
This historic town on the Murrumbidgee River, at the junction of the Newell and Sturt Hwys, has been declared an urban conservation area with buildings classified/listed by the National Trust. Located 580 km south-west of Sydney, it is the gateway to the Murrumbidgee Irrigation Area. **Of interest:** Lake Talbot Aquatic Playground and caravan/camping complex; 100 m waterslide, 3 pools, ski area, fishing, bushwalking tracks and koala reserve. Antique Corner, Larmer St. NSW Forestry Tree Nursery, Branch St. Tiger Moth Memorial, Narrandera Park, Newell Hwy. Parkside Cottage Museum and Narrandera Park and Miniature Zoo, Newell Hwy. **In the area:** Inland Fisheries Research Station (with star, Percy the Murray Cod) and John Lake Centre, 6 km south-east. Berembed Weir, 40 km south-east. Pine Hill Nursery, 5 km north-east. Robertson Gladioli Farm, 8 km west. Alabama Ostrich Farm, 30 km north. **Tourist information:** Narrandera Park, Newell Hwy; (069) 59 1766. **Accommodation:** 5 hotels, 10 motels, 2 caravan/camping parks. **See also:** The Newell; Wineries of New South Wales.
MAP REF. 117 O9

Narromine   Population 3205
On the Macquarie River, 457 km from Sydney, renowned for quality agricultural products, including citrus fruit, tomatoes, sheep, cattle and cotton. **In the area:** Gin Gin Weir. Gliding at airport. Trangie Agricultural and Yates Research Stations. Swane's Rose Production Nursery, 5 km west. **Tourist information:** 84/86 Dandaloo St. **Accommodation:** 4 hotels, 3 motels, 3 caravan/camping parks.
MAP REF. 110 D1, 112 D13

Nelson Bay   Population 9376
The beautiful bay on which this town is sited is the main anchorage of Port Stephens, about 60 km north of Newcastle. **Of interest:** Restored Inner Lighthouse, Nelson Head. Self-guiding Heritage Walk, from Dutchmans Bay to Little Beach. Native Flora Reserve at Little Beach. Cruises on harbour and Myall River; also boats for hire. **In the area:** Gan Gan Lookout, 2 km south-west on Nelson Bay Rd. Tomaree Leisure Park at Salamander Bay, 5 km south-west. Gemstone House, on Shoal Bay Rd, 8 km south-west. Oakvale Farm and Fauna World, 16 km south-west on Nelson Bay Rd at Salt Ash. Fighter World, displays of modern and historic aircraft, at RAAF base, Williamtown, 35 km west. Convict-built Tanilba House (1831), 37 km west. Tomaree National Park, 50 km west; nude bathing at Sumurai Beach, within park. Festival of Port Stephens held Feb.–March. **Tourist information:** Victoria Pde; (049) 81 1579. **Accommodation:** 11 motels, 1 caravan/camping park. **See also:** Port Stephens.
MAP REF. 111 M3

Newcastle   Population 255 787
Australia's largest industrial city has created international interest by wiping clean its previously grimy, polluted reputation. Encircled by some of the finest surfing beaches in the world, overlooking a huge, spectacular harbour, Newcastle, just 158 km north of Sydney, was always uniquely positioned to claim the image of an aquatic playground. While modern technology successfully tackled pollution, the City Fathers of Australia's sixth largest city called for a plan to ensure residents and visitors could take full advantage of its superb location. The $13-million answer was a brilliant foreshore redevelopment scheme. Rebuilding also has occurred in some areas following an earthquake that struck the city in December 1989. **Of interest:** Queens Wharf, colourful and cosmopolitan centrepoint of foreshore redevelopment, with everything from an ice-cream parlour to indoor and outdoor restaurants, 'boutique' brewery, brewing range of specialty beers, and observation tower; linked by walkway to City Mall, part of Hunter St. Scenic walks along foreshore with its sweeping lawns and swaying palms, and along nearby city streets lined with Sydney-style terrace houses. City parks and gardens. Art gallery, Laman St. Maritime and military museums, Fort Scratchley, Nobbys Rd. City Hall, Laman St. Many fine surf beaches. River and harbour cruises. **In the area:** Hexham Swamp Nature Reserve within Shortland Wetlands, 15 km west; bird

habitat with other wildlife and canoe trail. Fighter Aviation museum and high-tech exhibition at Williamtown RAAF base, 20 km north. Lake Macquarie, 27 km south, huge aquatic playground with well-maintained parks lining foreshore; picnic/barbecue facilities. About 50 km north-west is Australia's famous wine region, the Hunter Valley. Yuelarbah Track, part of Great North Walk from Sydney to Newcastle, covers 25 km from Lake Macquarie to Newcastle harbour. **Tourist information:** Queens Wharf; (049) 29 9299. **Accommodation:** 27 hotels, 30 motels, 13 caravan/camping parks.
MAP REF. 103 , 104 I5, 111 L4

Nowra–Bomaderry
Population 19 553
Rapidly becoming a popular tourist centre, Nowra is the principal town of the Shoalhaven River district. Bomaderry is directly opposite on the northern side of the river. **Of interest:** Meroogal (1885), cnr Worrigee and West Sts; Historic House Trust property open to public. Shoalhaven Historical Museum, cnr Plunkett and Kinghorn Sts, in old police station. Fishing, water-skiing, canoeing and sailing on Shoalhaven River. Hanging Rock, via Junction St, for fine views. Riverside Animal Park, Rockhill Rd; native fauna and peacocks in rainforest setting. **In the area:** HMAS *Albatross* Naval Air Station, South Nowra; two hangars converted to navy museum. Kangaroo Valley, 23 km north-west; many old buildings, including Friendly Inn (classified by National Trust) and Pioneer Farm Museum, reconstruction of typical dairy farm of 1880s. Fitzroy Falls in Morton National Park, 38 km north-west. Many beautiful beaches within 30 km radius of town. **Tourist information:** Shoalhaven Tourist Centre, 254 Princes Hwy, Bomaderry; (044) 21 0778. **Accommodation:** Nowra: 9 motels, 1 caravan/camping park. Bomaderry: 1 hotel, 2 motels, 1 caravan/camping park. **See also:** The Illawarra Coast.
MAP REF. 107 D12, 109 H5, 110 I10

Nundle   Population 265
The history of this small town began in the early gold-rush era during the 1850s. Renowned for its fishing, Nundle is situated 60 km south-east of Tamworth, at the foot of the Great Dividing Range, in a district that produces sheep, cattle, wheat and timber. **Of interest:** Court-house and Historical Museum, old bakery store and historic Peel Inn (1860s), all in Jenkins St. Goldmining display in restored coffin factory, Gill St. **In the area:** Hanging Rock and Sheba Dams, picnic and camping area, 11 km east. Chaffey Dam, 11 km

north. Fossicking at Hanging Rock and gold-panning on Peel River. **Tourist information:** Shire Offices; (067) 69 3205. **Accommodation:** 1 hotel, 1 motel, 1 caravan/camping park.
MAP REF. 113 K11

Nyngan   Population 2502
The centre of a wool-growing district on the Bogan River, 603 km north-west of Sydney. **Of interest:** Historic buildings, especially in Cobar and Bogar Sts. **In the area:** Cairn marking geographic centre of NSW, 65 km south. Grave of Richard Cunningham, botanist with Major Mitchell's party, speared by Aborigines in 1835, on private property, 70 km south. Bird sanctuary in Macquarie Marshes, 64 km north. **Tourist information:** Country Collection, Pangee St; (068) 32 1503. **Accommodation:** 3 hotels, 2 hotel/motels, 3 motels, 2 caravan/camping parks.
MAP REF. 112 A11, 115 P11

Orange   Population 28 935
A prosperous old city set in rich red volcanic soil, famous for its apples, Orange is situated 264 km north-west of Sydney on the slopes of Mt Canobolas. An obelisk marks the birthplace of the city's most famous citizen, poet A. B. (Banjo) Paterson; his birthday is celebrated with activities from mid-Feb. to mid-March. **Of interest:** Historic Cook Park Museum, McNamara St. Summer St; begonia conservatory (begonias flower Feb.–May), duck ponds, fernery and picnic area. Orange Civic Centre, Byng St; $5-million complex comprising a theatre, Regional Art Gallery, exhibition rooms, bar and restaurant. **In the area:** Campbell's Corner, 8 km south on Pinnacle Rd, attractive roadside picnic/barbecue spot. Agriculture Research Centre, 5 km north; field days held in Nov. Ophir goldfields, 27 km north, site of first discovery of payable gold in Australia in 1851; still fossicking centre with picnic area and walking-trails to historic gold tunnels. Gallery of Minerals, 1 km east; mineral and fossil collection. Apple Stop Antiques at Lucknow Village, 10 km east. Golden Memories Museum at Millthorpe, 22 km south-east; over 5000 exhibits, including grandma's kitchen, blacksmith's shop and art and craft centre. Lake Canobolas Park, 8 km south-west via Cargo Rd; recreation and camping area with deer park, children's playground and barbecues; also trout-fishing. Mt Canobolas Park, 1500 ha bird and animal sanctuary, 14 km south-west. **Tourist information:** Civic Gardens, Byng St; (063) 61 5226. **Accommodation:** 10 hotels, 10 motels, 3 caravan/camping parks.
MAP REF. 110 F5

Parkes   Population 8739
Situated 364 km west of Sydney on the Newell Hwy, and often referred to as the 'gateway to the stars', Parkes is the commercial and industrial centre of an important agricultural area. **Of interest:** Motor Museum, cnr Bogar and Dalton Sts; vintage and veteran vehicles, and local art and craft. Henry Parkes Museum, Clarinda St; memorabilia and library of 1000 volumes. Pioneer Park Museum, Pioneer St, in historic school and church; displays of early farm machinery and transport. Kelly Reserve, on northern outskirts of town; picnics and barbecues in bush setting. Imposing views from Shrine of Remembrance at eastern end of Bushman St. Annual marbles tournament held in Apr. at Parkes Golf Club. **In the area:** Mugincoble Wheat Sub-terminal, 8 km south-east. CSIRO Radio Telescope Visitors Centre, 23 km north; many educational aids explain use of giant saucer-shaped telescope. Peak Hill, 48 km north; open-cut gold mine, flora and fauna park, and accommodation. **Tourist information:** Kelly Reserve, Newell Hwy; (068) 62 4365. **Accommodation:** 8 hotels, 11 motels, 5 caravan/camping parks. **See also:** The Newell.
MAP REF. 110 D4

Picton   Population 1975
Picton, named after Sir Thomas Picton, hero of Waterloo, is 80 km south-west of Sydney on Remembrance Drive (former Hume Hwy). The old buildings and quiet hills of this small town seem to echo the past. **Of interest:** Historic buildings include: old railway viaduct (1862) over Stonequarry Creek, seen from Showgrounds, off Menangle St; St Mark's Church (1848), Menangle St; George IV Inn which incorporates Scharer's Little Brewery, Argyle St. **In the area:** Jarvisfield (1865), family home of pioneer landholders, now clubhouse of Antill Park Golf Club, 2 km north, on Old Hume Hwy. Wollondilly Heritage Centre and slab-built St Matthew's Church (1838) at The Oaks, 21 km north. Burragorang Lookout, 15 km west of The Oaks. Railway Museum at Thirlmere, 5 km south. Wirrimbirra Sanctuary, 13 km south; National Trust sanctuary for native flora and fauna, with cabins for overnight visitors. Mowbray Park, 8 km north-west, for farm holidays. **Tourist information:** Macarthur Country Tourist Assocn, cnr Hume Hwy and Congressional Dr., Liverpool; (02) 821 2311. **Accommodation:** 1 hotel, 1 motel, 1 caravan park.
MAP REF. 107 C1, 109 H2, 110 I7

Radio Telescope, Parkes

Pitt Town
Population 496

One of the five Macquarie Towns, Pitt Town was named after William Pitt the elder, and marked out on a site to the east of the present village in January 1811. The surrounding rich alluvial river flats provided early Sydney with almost 50% of its food supply, which was transported by boat down the Hawkesbury River and around to Sydney Town. Pitt Town did not develop a 20th-century town centre and thus remains more modest in architectural style than Windsor. *A Country Practice* television producers use this village for location filming. **Of interest:** Curious reminder of importance of river for life in Pitt Town lies at end of Bathurst St, overlooking Pitt Town Bottoms. Old Manse, belonging to oldest Presbyterian (now Uniting) Church in Australia, 8 km north at Ebenezer. **Tourist information:** Hawkesbury Regional Tourist Centre, Windsor Rd, Vineyard; (045) 87 7388. **See also:** The Hawkesbury
MAP REF. 101 L4, 111 J6

Port Macquarie
Population 22 884

Founded as a convict settlement in 1821, and one of the oldest towns in the state, Port Macquarie (known locally as 'Port') is now a major holiday resort, situated at the mouth of the Hastings River, 423 km north of Sydney. **Of interest:** Award-winning Hastings Historical Museum, Clarence St, housed in 15 rooms of commercial building, built 1835–40; convict and pioneer relics. St Thomas's (1824), Church St; convict-built church designed by convict architect Thomas Owen. Historic cemetery, Horton St; graves dating

Mouth of the Hastings River, Port Macquarie

from 1842. Roto House and Macquarie Nature Reserve, Lord St; koala hospital and study centre. Port Macquarie Observatory, William St. Fantasy Glades, Pacific Dr; re-creation of story of Snow White and other fairytale characters, with birds, animals, bushwalks, children's playground and kiosk. Billabong and Kingfisher Parks offer close-up look at Australian animals. Town Beach has surf at one end and sheltered coves at other. Kooloonbung Creek Nature Reserve offers 50 ha of natural bushland, with walking trails. Peppermint Park has slides, skateboard areas and roller-skating. River cruises daily. Orchid World, Ocean Dr.; Australian and exotic plants, also camel rides and safaris. Old World Timber Art on Hastings River Dr. **In the area:** Exceptionally good fishing and all water sports. Charter fishing available, including reef fishing. Shelly Beach Resort, 3 km south-east on Pacific Dr. The Big Bull at Redbank Farm, working dairy farm, 20 km west, via Wauchope. Sea Acres Rainforest Centre, Pacific Drive, 5 km south; some 30 ha of rainforest, multilevel boardwalk allows viewing of flora and fauna. Cassegrain Winery, 12 km west; tastings and sales. The Banksias, recreational nature reserve, 13 km north, towards Crescent Head. **Tourist information:** Horton St; (065) 83 1293. **Accommodation:** 2 hotels, 40 motels, 18 caravan/camping parks.
MAP REF. 113 P11

Queanbeyan
Population 19 383

Adjoining Canberra, Queanbeyan has a special relationship with the Australian capital. The town, proclaimed in 1838, is named from a squattage held by an ex-convict innkeeper, Timothy Beard, on the Molonglo River called 'Quinbean' (which means 'clear waters'). **Of interest:** Queanbeyan History Museum. Rehwinkel's Animal Farm. Byrne's Mill. Mill House Gallery. **In the area:** At Bungendore, 26 km north-east, historic village square and exhibition depicting story of 'Jacky Jacky', Aboriginal bushranger; also wood-turning, antiques and herbal farm. Bywong Mining Town, 31 km north-east. **Tourist information:** Queanbeyan Information Centre, cnr Farrer Place and Lowe St; (06) 298 0241. **Accommodation:** 4 hotels, 18 motels, 2 caravan/camping parks.
MAP REF. 109 E6, 110 F11, 127 G4

Quirindi
Population 2812

Appropriately named after an Aboriginal word meaning 'nest in the hills', this town in the Liverpool Ranges was proclaimed in 1856. **Of interest:** Historical Cottage and Museum. One of the first towns in Australia to organise the game of polo, it still holds an annual polo carnival in first week of Aug. **In the area:** Who'd-A-Thought-It Lookout, 2 km north-east. Many properties offer farm holidays. **Tourist information:** Sports Centre, 248 George St; (067) 46 2128. **Accommodation:** 5 hotels, 2 motels, 1 caravan/camping park.
MAP REF. 113 J11

Raymond Terrace
Population 8793

Several historic buildings remain in this town, which was an important wool-shipping centre in the 1840s. **Of interest:** Heritage Town Walk takes in significant buildings, including court-house (1838), still in use; Irrawang (1830), homestead of pioneer James King; Church of England and rectory, built of hand-hewn sandstone in 1830s; and Sketchley Cottage, once sited at Seaham, 8 km north. **In the area:** Hunter Region Botanic Gardens, on Pacific Hwy at Motto Farm, 2 km south. Fighter World, RAAF Base Williamtown, 16 km east. **Tourist information:** Neighbourhood Centre, 13 King St; (049) 87 1331. **Accommodation:** 4 motels, 2 caravan/camping parks.
MAP REF. 104 H3, 111 L3

Richmond
Population 15 490

One of the five Macquarie towns and sister town to Windsor, 5 km away, Richmond was proclaimed a town in 1810. **Of interest:** Hobartville, Castlereagh Rd. Toxana (1841), Windsor St. St Peter's Church (1841), Windsor St; graveyard where many notable pioneers, including William Cox and Australia's convict

THE HAWKESBURY

The Hawkesbury River, one of the most attractive rivers in Australia, is located north of Sydney. The river and its surrounds played an important role in Sydney's early colonial history. The first settlers arrived in the area in 1794 to establish farming settlements to help feed the starving colony. In 1810 Governor Macquarie founded the towns of **Windsor**, **Richmond**, **Castlereagh**, **Wilberforce** and **Pitt Town** in the upper Hawkesbury valley. Today much of this land is still used for agriculture and there are many oyster leases on the lower river.

Although farming has been pursued since the late eighteenth century, the charm of the Hawkesbury lies mainly in the fact that the river is still surrounded by large areas of untouched bushland. Two major national parks front the river: upstream the Dharug National Park, noted for its Aboriginal rock carvings, and downstream the Ku-ring-gai Chase National Park.

The Hawkesbury River is a popular recreational waterway, particularly at its lower and wider reaches between Brooklyn and Pittwater.

One of the best ways of exploring the Hawkesbury is by boat. Craft of all types from small rowing dinghies to cruisers and houseboats are available for hire at **Brooklyn**, a small town near the Hawkesbury River Bridge, and also at **Bobbin Head**, **Berowra Waters** and **Wisemans Ferry**. (Before hiring a boat, read the section on Safe Boating.) A delightful way to see the river is to join the river mail-boat run which leaves Brooklyn on weekdays and takes three hours. Cruises on the river are also available, from 2 hours to 2 days, on the luxury catamaran *Windsor Princess*.

If you are travelling north from Sydney by road, the Newcastle–Sydney Freeway crosses the Hawkesbury and its tributary, Mooney Mooney Creek. This section of the freeway cuts through sandstone cliffs and offers spectacular views.

For further information, contact the Hawkesbury Regional Tourist Centre, Windsor Rd, Vineyard; (045) 87 7388.

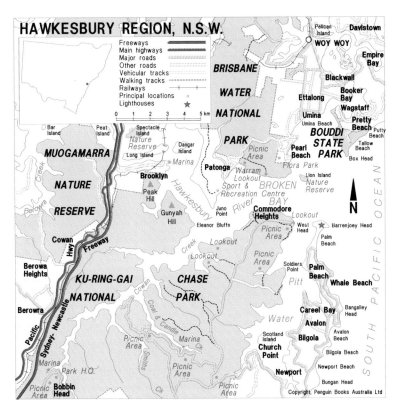

Riverside cottages on the Hawkesbury

NEW ENGLAND

If you pull over for a rest in the New England area, it is worth keeping your eyes on the ground, despite the lovely scenery. Some of the best fossicking specimens in the district have been found by the roadside. Jaspers, serpentine, all kinds of quartz, crystal and chalcedony are found right throughout this area — not to mention sapphires, diamonds and gold, though these require a little more effort to find.

The round trip from Nundle, through Tamworth, Manilla, Barraba, Bingara, Warialda, then on to the New England towns of **Inverell** and **Glen Innes** and back, is known as 'The Fossickers' Way' and tourist signs have been placed at intervals to guide the motorist. Nearby is the Copeton Dam, which holds two-and-a-half times as much water as Sydney Harbour, with part of its foreshores forming Copeton State Recreational Area.

Glen Innes and Inverell have nearby sapphire reserves where fossickers may hire tools and try their luck. Anything you find is yours; but remember, you must have a fossicker's licence, available from all New South Wales court-houses, tourist centres, and some sporting stores. The largest find in the Nullamanna Fossicking Reserve, near Inverell, to date is a 70-carat blue, valued at $3000.

The New England district is the largest area of highlands in Australia, and has plenty to offer besides gemstones. The countryside is varied and lovely, with magnificent mountains, and streams cascading into spectacular gorges, contrasting with the rich black-soil plains of wheat and cotton to the west. Some of the state's most outstanding national parks and world heritage features are found in New England, and the southern hemisphere's largest granite monolith, Bald Rock, is near **Tenterfield**.

Fishing is excellent, with trout in the streams of the tablelands and cod and yellow-belly in the lower New England rivers to the west. You can also fish, picnic, swim, sail or water-ski at Pindari and Copeton Dam; try whitewater rafting with 'Wildwater Adventures' or horseriding with Steve Langley's renowned 'Pub Crawls on Horseback'.

Other towns in New England are **Ashford**, **Delungra**, **Guyra**, **Tingha**, **Walcha**, **Uralla**, **Deepwater** and the city of **Armidale**.

For further information, contact the New England Tourism Development Authority, 215 Beardy St, Armidale; (067) 72 8155.

Bald Rock, near Tenterfield

chronicler Margaret Catchpole are buried. **In the area:** RAAF base, 3 km east on Windsor–Richmond Rd; oldest Air Force establishment in Australia, used for civilian flying from 1915. University of Western Sydney, 3 km south; foundation-stone laid in 1895. **Tourist information:** Hawkesbury Regional Tourist Centre, Windsor Rd, Vineyard; (045) 87 7388. **Accommodation:** 2 hotels, 3 motels. **See also:** The Hawkesbury.
MAP REF. 101 J5, 109 I1, 111 J6

Robertson   Population 273
The link between the Southern Highlands and the coast, Robertson sits at the top of the Macquarie Pass and vantage-points offer spectacular views of the coast. It is the centre of the largest potato-growing district in NSW. **In the area:** Fitzroy, Belmore and Carrington Falls, all in Morton National Park, 10 km south. **Tourist information:** Tourist Centre, Winifred West Park, Hume Hwy, Mittagong; (048) 71 2888. **Accommodation:** 1 hotel, 1 motel.
MAP REF. 107 C8, 109 H4, 110 I9

Rylstone/Kandos   Population 654
Aboriginal hand-paintings on a sandstone rock overhang are a feature of the region, which is west of the Great Dividing Range on the Cudgegong River, north-east of Bathurst. **Of interest:** Industrial Museum at Kandos. **In the area:** Fern Tree Gully, 16 km north; magnificent tree-ferns in subtropical forest. Glen Davis, 56 km south-east on Capertee River, surrounded by sheer cliff-faces. Many camping spots and fishing areas on Capertee, Cudgegong and Turon rivers. **Tourist information:** 64 Market St, Mudgee; (063) 72 5874. **Accommodation:** 4 hotels, 1 motel, 1 caravan/camping park.
MAP REF. 110 H3

Sawtell   Population 7905
This peaceful family holiday resort, 8 km south of Coffs Harbour, has safe beaches and tidal creeks for fishing, swimming and surfing. There are enchanting walks and drives in the surrounding bush and mountains, including Sawtell Reserve. **In the area:** Whitewater rafting on Nymboida, Gwydir and Murray rivers. **Accommodation:** 2 hotels, 2 motels, 1 caravan/camping park.
MAP REF. 113 P7

Scone   Population 4272
This pleasant town set in beautiful country on the New England Hwy 280 km north of Sydney, is the second largest thoroughbred and horse-breeding centre in the world. **Of interest:** Scone Historical Society Museum, Kingdon St.

Grassroot art gallery and restaurant, part of well-equipped tourist information centre in Elizabeth Park near to mare and foal sculpture. **In the area:** Glenbawn Dam, 15 km east; water sports and picnic/barbecue facilities. Hunter Valley Museum of Rural Life, 2 km west of dam. Burning Mountain at Wingen, 20 km north; deep coal-seam that has been smouldering for at least 1000 years. Barrington Tops National Park, 80 km northeast, for scenic drives and walks. **Tourist information:** Kelly St, New England Hwy; (065) 45 1526, (065) 45 2907. **Accommodation:** 1 hotel, 5 motels, 2 caravan parks, 1 caravan/camping park. MAP REF. 111 J1, NSW113 J12

Shellharbour   Population 1754

This attractive holiday resort south of Lake Illawarra is one of the oldest settlements on the south coast. It was a thriving port in the 1830s, but its importance declined once the south coast railway opened. Today it is a residential and seaside holiday town. **In the area:** Bass Point Headland and Marine Reserve, 3 km south; picnic area with views. Lake Illawarra, 7 km north; boats for hire. Fine beaches for fishing, surfing and boating on Windang Peninsula, 10 km north. Jamberoo Valley and Minnamurra Rainforest Centre, 20 km south-west. **Tourist information:** 93 Crown St, Wollongong; (042) 28 0300. **Accommodation:** 1 hotels, 1 motels, 1 caravan/camping park. **See also:** The Illawarra Coast. MAP REF. 107 G7, 109 I4, 111 J9

Singleton   Population 10 990

Located beside the Hunter River amid rich grazing land, Singleton is the geographical heart of the Hunter Valley. New wealth in the form of huge open-cut coal mines has joined the traditional rural industry and transformed Singleton into one of the most progressive country centres in the state. **Of interest:** Built as Bicentennial project, monolithic sundial, largest in southern hemisphere, located along banks of river, in James Cook Park. Gardens of historic home, Townhead; sales of herbs. **In the area:** Nearby Lake St Clair, with magnificent views of Mt Royal Range; extensive recreational and waterway facilities, including camping. Township is home of Singleton Army Camp, whose Royal Australian Infantry Corps Museum of Small Arms, 5 km south, traces development of firearms from 15th century. On New England Hwy between Singleton and Muswellbrook, 26 km north-west, Bayswater Power Station, biggest thermal power-station in southern hemisphere. Singleton is central location for visits to wineries of upper and lower Hunter Valley. **Tourist information:** Shire Offices; (065) 72 1866. **Accommodation:** 6 hotels, 2 hotel-motels, 5 motels, 2 caravan/camping parks. MAP REF. 104 A1, 111 K3

Stroud   Population 484

There are many historic buildings in this small country town, 75 km north of Newcastle. One of the finest is the convict-built Anglican Church of St John, built in 1833 of local clay bricks, with its beautiful stained-glass windows and cedar furnishings. **Of interest:** Rectory of St John's (1836), Stroud House (1832), Parish House (1837), court-house, post office and Quambi House. Underground silo (one of 8 built in 1841) at Silo Hill Reserve. Heritage Tour self-guiding leaflet available. **Tourist information:** Great Lakes Tourist Board, Little St, Forster; (065) 54 8799. **Accommodation:** Limited. MAP REF. 111 M2

Tamworth   Population 30 729

This progressive, prosperous city at the junction of the New England and Oxley Hwys is the country music capital of Australasia, as well as being the heart of many other cultural and musical activities. Many thousands of fans flock here for the 10-day Australasian Country Music Festival, which has been held each January since 1973. Tamworth, with its attractive public buildings and beautiful parks and gardens, is the commercial and entertainment capital of northern NSW. **Of interest:** Country Music Hands of Fame cornerstone at CWA park, Kable St (outside tourist centre), has hand imprints of cream of Australasia's country music stars, including Tex Morton, Slim Dusty and Smoky Dawson. Country music Roll of Renown at Radio Centre, Calala, dedicated to country music artists who have contributed to Australia's heritage. Calala Cottage, Denison St, home of Tamworth's first mayor, classified by National Trust and restored by Tamworth Historical Society. Tamworth City Gallery, Marius St, houses works by Turner, Hans Heysen and Will Ashton, and is home of National Fibre Collection. Oxley Gallery, Peel St (specialising in gemstones), Weswal Gallery, Brisbane St, and Tininburra Gallery, Moore Creek Rd. Country Collection on New England Hwy features fascinating gemstone collection, Gallery of Stars Wax Museum, Great Australian Ice-creamery and famous Longyard Hotel. Oxley Park Wildlife Sanctuary north off Brisbane St; bushwalks, picnic/barbecue facilities and friendly kangaroos. Oxley Lookout for panoramic views of city and rich Peel Valley. Power-station Museum traces Tamworth's history as first city in southern hemisphere to have electric street lighting. **In the area:** Lake Keepit State Recreation Area, 57 km north-west; ideal for water sports and has excellent visitor facilities. Warrabah National Park, 75 km north-east. Historic gold-mining township of Nundle nestled in 'Hills of Gold', a 63 km scenic drive south-east. Chaffey Dam, 45 km south-east, for sailing; Dulegal Arboretum on foreshore. **Tourist information:** Kable Ave; (067) 68 4462. **Accommodation:** 7 hotels, 2 hotel/motels, 28 motels, 4 caravan/camping parks. MAP REF. 113 K9

Taree   Population 15 994

Attractively laid out, Taree serves as the manufacturing and commercial centre of the Manning River district, on the Pacific Hwy, 320 km north of Sydney. **Of interest:** Manning River cruises. The Big Oyster. **In the area:** Easy access by car to top of Ellenborough Falls, on Bulga Plateau, 50 km north-west. Crowdy Bay National Park, 40 km north-east; wildflowers in spring, fishing, swimming, bushwalking. The Bird Tree, 50 km north. Forest drives and walking-trails in Manning Valley. Taree–Forster Grass Ski Park. Farm holidays at Clarendon beef-cattle property. Fine surfing beaches on coast 13 km east. Upland streams liberally stocked with rainbow and brown trout. **Tourist information:** Manning Valley Tourist Information Centre, Pacific Hwy, Taree North; (065) 52 1900. **Accommodation:** 5 hotels, 27 motels, 3 caravan/camping parks. MAP REF. 111 N1, 113 N12

Tathra   Population 1249

Tathra is a relaxed seaside township, centrally located on the south coast of NSW, 18 km east of Bega and midway between Merimbula and Bermagui. Tathra is an ideal place for a family holiday, with its patrolled 3 km long surf beach, safe swimming for small children at Mogareka Inlet (the sandy mouth of the Bega River), and good fishing spots. **Of interest:** Sea Wharf, classified by National Trust. **In the area:** Bournda State Recreation Area, immediately south of town; camping and bushwalking. Fishing and water sports on Lake Wallagoot. Mimosa Rocks National Park, 17 km north. Diving and deep-sea fishing charters at Kianniny Bay. **Tourist information:** Beachhouse Gallery, Andy Poole Drive; (064) 94 1483. **Accommodation:** 1 motel, 1 hotel/motel, 4 caravan/camping parks. MAP REF. 109 F10

Temora   Population 4295

Commercial centre for the rich wheat district of the northern and western Riverina, which also produces oats, barley, fat

lambs, pigs and cattle. **Of interest:** Temora Rural Museum with large number of working displays; also rock and mineral collection. **In the area:** Lake Centenary, 3 km north. Paragon Gold Mine at Gidginbung, 15 km north. **Tourist information:** White Rose Cafe, 186 Hoskins St; (069) 77 2131. **Accommodation:** 2 hotels, 3 motels, 1 caravan/camping park.
MAP REF. 110 B8, 117 Q8

Tenterfield   Population 3370
Tenterfield sits astride the Great Dividing Range at the northern end of the New England Highlands in northern NSW and offers a contrast of rugged mountains and serene rural landscapes. Autumn in Tenterfield is particularly spectacular. Primarily a sheep and cattle grazing area, the district also has a variety of other industries, including orchards, logging and sawmilling, a silica mine, a gold-mine, various farm crops and the growing industry of tourism. **Of interest:** Centenary Cottage (1871), Logan St; local history collection. Logan St historic walk. Sir Henry Parkes Library and Museum in School of Arts (1876), Rouse St; displays relics relating to Sir Henry Parkes, who made his famous Federation speech in this building in 1889. Tenterfield Saddler (1860s), High St. **In the area:** Mt McKenzie Granite Drive, 30 km circular route west of town, includes Ghost Gully. Bluff Rock, 10 km south on New England Hwy; unusual granite outcrop. Thunderbolt's Hideout, 11 km north-east. Bald Rock National Park, 35 km north-east;

panoramic views from summit of Bald Rock, large granite monolith. Spectacular Boonoo Boonoo Falls, within Boonoo Boonoo National Park, 32 km north. **Tourist information:** Rouse St; (067) 36 1082. **Accommodation:** 3 hotels, 2 hotel/motels, 6 motels, 3 caravan parks. **See also:** New England.
MAP REF. 113 M3, 435 O13

Terrigal–Wamberal
Population 7453
Excellent surfing is one of the main attractions of this popular holiday resort on the Central Coast. **In the area:** Bouddi National Park, 17 km south; bushwalking, camping, fishing and swimming. **Tourist information:** Terrigal Dr, Terrigal; (043) 84 6577. **Accommodation:** 1 hotel, 5 motels, 2 caravan/camping parks.
MAP REF. 101 R1, 104 F13

The Entrance   Population 37 831
Blessed with clear, clean beaches, this beautiful lakeside and ocean resort, only $1^1/_2$ hours from both Sydney and Newcastle, is the family holiday playground of these two cities. **Of Interest:** Daily pelican feeding in Memorial Park. 'Concerts by the Sea', bi-monthly events, starting in Jan. each year with 'Country by the Sea'. Annual Tuggerah Lakes Mardi Gras Festival held first weekend in Dec. **In the area:** Fishing on lakes—Tuggerah, Budgewoi and Munmorah—and ocean beach. During summer months, prawning on lakes. Water sports on Lake Tuggerah. Lake cruises depart from The

Entrance public wharf. **Tourist information:** Tuggerah Lakes Tourist Assocn, Memorial Pk, Marine Pde; (043) 32 9282. **Accommodation:** 3 hotels, 10 motels, 12 caravan parks.
MAP REF. 104 F12, 111 L5

The Rock   Population 768
This small township, 32 km south-west of Wagga Wagga, is noted for its unusual scenery. Walking-trails through a flora and fauna reserve lead to the summit of The Rock (about 365 m). One species, the groundsel plant, is believed to be unique to the area. **Accommodation:** 1 motel.
MAP REF. 110 A11, 117 P11

Tibooburra   Population 134
The name of this former gold town, 337 km north of Broken Hill, comes from an Aboriginal word meaning 'heaps of boulders'. The town is surrounded by granite outcrops and was known as The Granites. **Of interest:** Buildings of local stone, including court-house (1888), Family Hotel (1888) and Tibooburra Hotel (1890). Gymkhana and rodeo held in Oct. on NSW Labour Day weekend. **In the area:** Self-guiding Golden Gully Scenic Walk, 3 km north. Nearby goldfields. Sturt National Park, 20 km north; semi-desert area, noted for its wildlife and geological features. Pastoral Museum at Mt Wood, 27 km east, within park. Former gold township of Milparinka, 42 km south; restored court-house, together with remains of old police station, bank, general store and post office, still to be seen, but Albert Hotel is town's only active

Peppers-on-Sea Resort Hotel, Terrigal

concern. Further 11 km north-west of Milparinka are Mt Poole Homestead and Mt Poole, where cairn commemorates Charles Sturt's expedition. Cameron's Corner, 150 km north-west, where three states meet. **Tourist information:** National Parks and Wildlife Service, Tibooburra; (080) 91 3308. **Accommodation:** 2 hotels, 1 motel, 1 caravan/camping park.
MAP REF. 114 C4, 435 A13, 441 H13

Tingha Population 837
This small tin-mining town, 28 km south-east of Inverell, is known for its outstanding museum. **Of interest:** Campbells Honey Farm, Swimming Pool Rd. Nucoorilma Aboriginal Arts and Crafts. **In the area:** Smith's Mining and Natural History Museum at Green Valley Farm, 10 km south; Aboriginal artefacts, antiques, mineral and gemstone collection; also cabin accommodation. Fossicking for gems. Water sports on Copeton Dam, 15 km west. **Tourist information:** Shire Offices, Bradley St, Guyra; (067) 79 1577. **Accommodation:** 1 hotel, 1 caravan park.
MAP REF. 113 K6

Tocumwal Population 1273
This peaceful Murray River town on the Newell Hwy is ideal for swimming, fishing and boating. **Of interest:** Huge fibreglass codfish in town square represents Aboriginal legend about giant Murray cod that lived in nearby blowhole. Picnic area with lawns and sandy river beach, 200 m from town square. **In the area:** River Murray Heritage Centre, 3 km north. Aerodrome, 5 km north-east, largest RAAF base in Australia during World War II, now houses world-renowned Sportavia Soaring Centre. The Rocks, 11 km north-east; once stone quarry, now popular picnic spot. Binghi Boomerang Factory at Barooga, 19 km east. Several golf courses. Ulupna Island flora and fauna reserve. **Tourist information:** Tocumwal River Foreshore; (058) 74 2131. **Accommodation:** 3 hotels, 1 hotel/motel, 10 motels, 3 caravan/camping parks. **See also:** The Newell.
MAP REF. 117 M12, 217 J2

Tooleybuc Population under 200
A quiet, tranquil, riverside town with a village atmosphere, Tooleybuc's social centre is its Sporting Club. The town boasts a range of recreational facilities, including fishing, bowls, picnicking and riverside walks. **Of interest:** The Opal Shack; demonstrations of opal cutting. **Tourist information:** 25 Murray St,

Barham; (054) 53 3100. **Accommodation:** 1 hotel, 3 motels, 1 caravan/camping park.
MAP REF. 116 G10, 215 N8

Toukley Population 6520
Situated on the peninsula between Tuggerah and Budgewoi Lakes, this delightful coastal hamlet offers a holiday experience with pollution-free beaches and breathtaking scenery. **Of interest:** Toukley open-air markets, every Sun. at shopping centre carpark. Shark-free lakes provide venue for all forms of water sports. During summer months prawning from lake foreshores. **In the area:** Rockpool at Cabbage Tree Bay. Norah Head Lighthouse, 5 km east; inpections restricted to certain days and times. Many bushwalking trails in magnificent Munmorah State Recreation Area, 10 km north, or Red Gum Forest in Wyrrabalong National Park, 4 km south. **Tourist information:** Tuggerah Lakes Tourist Assocn, Wallarah Point Pk, Gorokan; (043) 92 4666. **Accommodation:** 1 hotel/resort, 6 motels, 4 caravan/camping parks.
MAP REF. 104 G11

Tumbarumba Population 1603
A former gold-mining town situated in the western foothills of the Snowy Mountains, 504 km south-west of Sydney, Tumbarumba has much to offer the visitor who prefers to get off the beaten track. It is an ideal base for day-trips to the Snowy Mountains. **Of interest:** Historical Society Museum, Bridge St; working model of water-powered timber mill. **In the area:** Henry Angel Trackhead on Hume and Hovell Walking Track has facilities for campers and picnickers and is starting-point for many bushwalks. Site of old Union Jack Mine, 3 km north. Pioneer Women's Museum, 5 km west. William's mini hydro-electric scheme and Lake Mannus, 7 km south. Paddy's River Falls, 16 km south, where spectacular cascades drop 60 m; walking-track and picnic area. Tooma, 34 km south; historic hotel and store. Mt Selwyn Ski Resort, 70 km south-east. **Tourist information:** Tumbarumba Wool and Craft Centre, 10 Bridge St; (069) 48 2805. **Accommodation:** 2 hotels, 1 motel, 2 caravan/camping parks.
MAP REF. 109 B7, 110 C12, 117 R12, 219 H2

Tumut Population 6099
Situated on the Snowy Mountains Hwy, 424 km from Sydney, Tumut attracts visitors all year round. Close to ski resorts and the great dams of the Snowy Mountains Hydro-electric Scheme, it is

renowned also for spectacular mountain scenery. **Of interest:** Inspections of local power-station, marble and millet broom factories. Old Butter Factory Complex, Adelong Rd, includes: Tumut Valley Whip Works and Saddlery, and Don's Woodcraft. Festival of the Falling Leaf held Apr.–May. **In the area:** Largest African violet farm in Australia, 7 km south on Tumut Plains Rd. Blowering Lake, 10 km south, major centre for water sports; fishing for rainbow trout, brown trout and perch. Talbingo Dam and Reservoir, 40 km south; second tallest rock-filled dam in Australia, set in steep wooded country and renowned for large trout. Excellent fishing on Tumut and Goobraganda Rivers; whitewater rafting, canoeing and horseriding. **Tourist information:** Fitzroy St (Snowy Mountains Hwy); (069) 47 1849. **Accommodation:** 2 hotels, 6 motels, 2 caravan/camping parks.
MAP REF. 109 B6, 110 D11

Tweed Heads Population 5120
This exciting town on the NSW/Qld border combines the attraction of being a comprehensive shopping venue with the pleasurable entertainment provided by its licensed clubs. **Of interest:** World's first laser-beam lighthouse sits atop Point Danger, one half in NSW and other in Qld. **In the area:** Tweed Endeavour cruise boats, operating from River Tce, visit locations along Tweed River. Minjungbal Museum and Resource Centre, just over Boyds Bay Bridge; Aboriginal ceremonial bora ring, museum and nature walk through sections of mangroves and rainforest. Avocadoland, 15 km south on Pacific Hwy. Cabarita Gardens Lake Resort, 20 km south on Tweed Coast Rd. **Tourist information:** Cnr Pacific Hwy and Alma St, Murwillumbah; (066) 72 1340. **Accommodation:** 2 hotels, 22 motels, 9 caravan/camping parks.
MAP REF. 113 R1, 429 R8, 435 Q12

Ulladulla Population 7408
Ulladulla, a picturesque fishing town, and nearby Milton are at the northern end of a stretch of beautiful coastal lakes and lagoons with white sandy beaches. **Of interest:** Ulladulla Wildflower Reserve, cnr Green and Warden Sts. Colourful Blessing of the Fleet ceremony held each Easter. **In the area:** Mollymook, 2 km north, for surfing, excellent fishing and golf. Narrawallee Beach, 4 km north, for surfing; but nearby Narrawallee Inlet has calm shallow water ideal for children. Bendalong, 36 km north, for surfing and swimming. Sussex Inlet, 47 km north; fishing carnival in May. Lakes Conjola,(23 km north) and Burrill (5 km south-west); swimming, fishing and

water-skiing. Views from summit of Pigeon House Mountain in Morton National Park, 25 km west. **Tourist information:** Shoalhaven Tourist Information Centre, Princes Hwy; (044) 55 1269. **Accommodation:** 1 hotel, 7 motels, 1 caravan park, 4 caravan/camping parks. **See also:** The Illawarra Coast. MAP REF. 109 H6, 110 I11,

Uralla   Population 2250

'Gentleman' bushranger Captain Thunderbolt was shot dead by a local policeman in 1870, in the swampy country south-east of this New England town. Rich gold discoveries were made in the vicinity in the 1850s. **Of interest:** Heritage Walking Tour; self-guiding leaflets detail over 30 historic buildings in town. McCrossin's Mill (1870), Salisbury St; goldfields history exhibits, including Joss House. Statue of Thunderbolt in Bridge St and grave in Uralla Cemetery. **In the area:** Fossicking at Old Rocky River diggings, 5 km west; pleasant picnic spot. Gostwyck, 11 km south-east; one of oldest properties in area; inspection of private chapel by appointment. **Tourist information:** Shire Offices, Bridge St; (067) 78 4496. **Accommodation:** 2 hotels, 2 motels, 2 caravan/camping parks. MAP REF. 113 L8

Urunga   Population 2336

One of the best fishing spots on the north coast, 32 km south of Coffs Harbour at the mouth of the Bellinger River, the town is separated from the ocean by a broad lagoon. **Of interest:** Safe river swimming-pool for children, with picnic reserve. **Tourist information:** The Honey Place, Pacific Hwy; (066) 55 6160. **Accommodation:** 1 hotel, 4 motels, 1 caravan park, 4 caravan/camping parks. MAP REF. 113 P8

Wagga Wagga   Population 37 577

Often referred to simply as Wagga, this prosperous city on the Murrumbidgee River, 517 km from Sydney, is a service centre for agriculture, including agricultural and soil conservation research, commerce and retailing. **Of interest:** Botanic Gardens and Zoo on Willans Hill; miniature railway runs through gardens. Historical Museum, adjacent to gardens; indoor and outdoor exhibits. City Art Gallery, Gurwood St, with Studio Glass movement collection. Gumi Festival (rubber craft race) held in Feb. **In the area:** Lake Albert, 7 km south, for water sports. Murray Cod Hatcheries and Fauna Park, 8 km east. Charles Sturt University–Riverina, 10 km north-west, includes Charles Sturt Winery on campus; tastings and sales. Wagga Wagga Winery, 15 km north-east has early Australiana theme

and restaurant. Tours of military base at Kapooka, 10 km south-west. **Tourist information:** Tarcutta St; (069) 23 5402. **Accommodation:** 12 hotels, 24 motels, 6 caravan/camping parks. MAP REF. 110 B10, 117 Q10

Walcha   Population 1639

This small town on the Oxley Hwy on the eastern slopes of the Great Dividing Range was first settled in 1832. **Of interest:** Pioneer Cottage and Museum, Derby St; includes Tiger Moth plane, first to be used for crop-dusting in Australia, and replica of blacksmith's shop. Fenwicke House, 19th-century terrace in Fitzroy St; art gallery and b & b accommodation. Spring Art Festival held in Sept. **In the area:** Ohio homestead (1842), 4 km east; open by appointment. Oxley Wild Rivers National Park, 20 km east; areas around Oxley, Tia and Wollomombi Falls developed for picnicking and camping. Several properties offer farm holidays. Trout fishing in many streams (with access to private property by request). **Tourist information:** Craft Centre, Fitzroy St (Oxley Hwy); (067) 77 2802. **Accommodation:** 2 hotels, 2 motels, 1 caravan/camping park. MAP REF. 113 L9

Walgett   Population 2151

A small rural community situated at the junction of the Barwon and Namoi Rivers, 300 km north of Dubbo. **Of interest:** Barwon Aboriginal Community, Fox St. First settler's grave. Good fishing all year. **In the area:** Grawin, Glengarry and Sheepyard opal-fields, 70 km west. (Motorists are warned water is scarce; adequate supply should be carried.) Narran Lake, 96 km west via Cumborah Rd, one of largest

Morton National Park, near Ulladulla

inland lakes in Australia; wildlife sanctuary, with no facilities for private visits, but tours in light aircraft can be arranged through Walgett Aero Club, (068) 28 1344. **Tourist information:** Shire Offices, 77 Fox St; (068) 28 1399. **Accommodation:** 2 hotel/motels, 3 motels, 1 caravan/camping park. MAP REF. 112 D6, 115 R6

Warialda   Population 1335

Small town on Gwydir Hwy west of Inverell, in a stud farm district. **Of interest:** Historical buildings, especially along Stephen and Hope Sts. Pioneer Cemetery, Queen and Stephen Sts; graves date from 1850s. Well's Family Gem and Mineral Collection, Hope St; also Aboriginal artefacts and bottle display. **In the area:** Fossicking, bushwalking, wildflowers. Picnic spots at Cranky Rock Reserve, 8 km east. Lowe's Animal Kingdom, 4 km north-west; free-ranging Australian animals. **Tourist information:** Shire Offices, Hope St; (067) 29 1016. **Accommodation:** 1 hotel, 1 motel, 1 caravan/camping park. MAP REF. 113 J4

Warren   Population 2030

In a wool and cotton-growing district on the Macquarie River, this Oxley Hwy town offers excellent fishing. **Of interest:** Macquarie Park, on banks of river, and Tiger Bay Wildlife Park. **In the area:** Austcott Cotton Farm, 10 km south-west; inspection tours late Apr.–June. Warren Weir, 5 km south-east. Visits to merino studs. **Tourist information:** Shire Offices, Dubbo St; (068) 47 4606; Craft Shop, Burton St; (068) 47 3181. **Accommodation:** 2 hotels, 2 motels, 2 caravan/camping parks. MAP REF. 112 C11, 115 R11

Wauchope   Population 4181

Nearby Timbertown, a major re-creation of a typical timber town of the 1880s, has put Wauchope on the tourist map. The town itself is the centre of a timber-getting, dairying, beef cattle and mixed farming area on the Oxley Hwy, 19 km from the mouth of the Hastings River. **Of interest:** Hastings Dairy Co-operative, Randall St; demonstrations of cheese production. Train Meadows, King Creek Rd; model train display. **In the area:** Timbertown, recreated village with shops and school on edge of Broken Bago State Forest, 3 km west; attractions include working bullock-team, horse-drawn wagons, smithy, steam-powered train and sleeper-cutting demonstrations. Small weatherboard church adjacent houses Historical Society Museum. **Accommodation:** 2 hotels, 2 motels. MAP REF. 113 O11

THE ILLAWARRA COAST

The magnificent panoramic views along the rugged Illawarra coast more than compensate for the sometimes winding route of the Princes Highway, which runs the length of it. 'Illawarra' is a corruption of an Aboriginal word appropriately meaning 'high and pleasant place by the sea'. Stretching from Sydney south to Batemans Bay, the Illawarra coast is bounded on the west by the Southern Highlands.

Fine surf beaches stretch along Illawarra's craggy coastline, which is liberally dotted with mountain streams, waterfalls, inlets and lakes — ideal for prawning and water sports. Wildflowers and fauna abound in the many reserves along the coast, and the distinctive vegetation includes cabbagepalms, tree-ferns and giant fig trees. This is the setting for the state's third largest city — **Wollongong**, which has many tourist attractions, scenic lookouts and beautiful beaches.

The other main towns on the coast are **Shellharbour**, a popular holiday resort and residential town south of Lake Illawarra; **Kiama**, the centre of a prosperous dairying and mixed-farming district; **Nowra**, the main town of the fascinating Shoalhaven River district; and **Ulladulla**, a picturesque little fishing town and popular summer holiday resort.

For further information, contact the Leisure Coast Tourist Association, 93 Crown St, Wollongong; (042) 28 0300.

View of Wollongong from Sublime Point

Wee Waa
Population 2106

This small town near the Namoi River is the centre of a cotton-growing district producing the highest cotton yield in Australia. **Of interest:** Guided tours from Namoi Cotton Co-op, Short St, to Merah North Cotton Gin (9 km), Apr.–Aug. Agricultural Show held in Apr. Cotton Festival held biennially in May. **In the area:** Yarrie Lake, 24 km south, for boating and birdwatching. Cuttabri Wine Shanty, 25 km south-west; original Cobb & Co. coaching stop between Wee Waa and Pilliga. Cubbaroo Winery, 45 km west; tastings and sales. **Tourist information:** Newell Hwy, Narrabri; (067) 92 3583. **Accommodation:** 1 hotel, 2 motels, 2 caravan parks.
MAP REF. 112 G7

Wellington
Population 5277

Limestone caves are one of the interesting features of this town at the junction of the Macquarie and Bell Rivers, 362 km north-west of Sydney. **Of interest:** Historical Museum in old bank (1883), cnr Percy and Warne Sts. From Mt Arthur Reserve, 3 km west of town, walking trails to Mt Binjang with lookout at summit. Maps available from Visitors Centre in Cameron Park, attractive area on western side of main street (Mitchell Hwy). **In the area:** Wellington Caves, 9 km south; guided tours of Cathedral Cave, and smaller Garden Cave with its rare cave coral; picnic/barbecue facilities, kiosk, aviary and animal enclosure, fossil and clock museum; horseriding available nearby. Wellington Golf Club (18 hole) next to caves open to public. Glenfinlass Wines, 8 km south-west on Parkes Rd; Markeita Cellars, 16 km south in village of Neurea. Burrendong Dam, 32 km east; panoramic views from spillway. Areas for waterskiing, sailing, power-boating and fishing nearby; camping facilities and cabin accommodation. **Tourist information:** Cameron Park, Nanima Cr.; (068) 45 2001. **Accommodation:** 7 hotels, 4 motels, 4 caravan/camping parks.
MAP REF. 110 F2

Wentworth
Population 1352

Wentworth is a historic town at the junction of the Murray and Darling Rivers. At one time a busy riverboat and customs port, today it is a quiet holiday town. **Of interest:** Rotary Folk Museum and Old Wentworth Gaol (1881), both in Beverly St. Court-house (1870s), Darling St. Apphara Art Gallery, Adams St. Historic PS Ruby, Fotherby Park, Wentworth St. Riverboat cruises on PS Loyalty. Lock 10, weir and park, for picnics. **In the area:** Houseboats for hire. Model aircraft display at Yelta, 12 km east. Orange World and Stanley Wine Co. on Silver City Hwy, 26 km east, at Buronga, and Gol Gol Fisheries, 2 km further east. Mungo National Park, 157 km

north-east, via Pooncarie. **Tourist information:** Shop 4, Adams St; (050) 27 3624. **Accommodation:** 3 hotels, 6 motels, 2 caravan parks.
MAP REF. 116 D7, 214 F2

West Wyalong   Population 3700

This former gold-mining town, at the junction of the Mid Western and Newell Hwys, which celebrates its centenary in 1994, is now the business centre of a prosperous wheat, wool and mixed-farming area. **Of interest:** Aboriginal Artefacts Gallery, Newell Hwy. Bland District Historical Museum, Newell Hwy; scale model of gold-mine, historical displays and archives. Highways Festival held long weekend in Oct. **In the area:** Lake Cowal, 48 km north-east, via Clear Ridge, largest natural lake in NSW; also important bird sanctuary and popular fishing spot. Weethalle Whistlestop, 65 km west, on Hay Rd; Devonshire teas and art and crafts. At Barmedman, 32 km south-east, Mineral Spring Pool, believed to provide relief from arthritis and rheumatism. **Tourist information:** McCann Park, Newell Hwy; (069) 72 3645. **Accommodation:** 7 hotels, 11 motels, 2 caravan/ camping parks. **See also:** The Newell.
MAP REF. 110 A6, 117 P7

White Cliffs   Population 207

White Cliffs Pioneer Opal Fields, 97 km north-west of Wilcannia, is a town where pioneering is a way of life. The opal fields were the first commercial fields in NSW; the first lease was granted in 1890, and by 1899 the fields were supporting 4500 people. Precious opal is still mined today, while the town area is powered by a solar power station. Jewelled opal 'pineapples' are found only in this area. **Of interest:** Underground Art Gallery; Eagles Gallery Pottery; Rosavilla with antiques and rock and mineral collections; Jock's Dugout Museum. Historic buildings include the now restored police station (1897), post office (1900), public school (1900). Pioneer children's cemetery. Unique underground dugout homes. Many opal showrooms where opal cutting and polishing can be seen. Fossicking for opal in old field. Experimental solar power station. Unique underground motel. Camping, barbecues and swimming-pool in Town Reserve. **In the area:** Mootwingee National Park, 90 km south-west; guided tours of Aboriginal rock art sites in cooler months (extremely hot in summer). **Tourist information:** Association Secretary; (080) 91 6611. **Accommodation:** 1 hotel, 1 motel, 1 caravan/camping park.
MAP REF. 114 F9

Whitton   Population 369

Whitton, 35 km south-east of Griffith, is the oldest town in the Murrumbidgee Irrigation Area and has large rice and grain storage facilities. **Of interest:** Whitton Court-house and Gaol Museum. **In the area:** Gogeldrie Weir, 14 km south-east. **Tourist information:** Chelmsford Pl, Leeton; (067) 53 2832. **Accommodation:** 1 hotel.
MAP REF. 117 N8

Wilcannia   Population 1048

Once the 'queen city of the west', this quaint township still has many impressive sandstone buildings. It was proclaimed a town in 1864 and was once a key inland port in the days of paddle-steamers. Gradually declining in the early 1920s with the advent of the car, today it is the service centre for a far-flung rural population. **Of interest:** Self-guiding leaflet of Historic Town Tour introduces several fine stone buildings, including post office, prison and court-house (1880) and Athenaeum Chambers (1890), which houses Tourist Information Centre; also opening bridge (1895) across Darling River and paddle-steamer wharf upstream. **In the area:** Opal fields at White Cliffs, 97 km north-west. **Tourist information:** Central Darling Shire, Athenaeum Chambers, Reid St; (080) 91 5909. **Accommodation:** 2 hotels, 2 motels, 1 caravan/camping park.
MAP REF. 114 G11

Windsor   Population 13 490

An exciting town for lovers of history and early architecture, Windsor is one of the oldest towns in Australia, situated 56 km

Opal mining, White Cliffs

north-west of Sydney. **Of interest:** St Matthew's Church, Moses St, oldest Church of England church in Australia, designed by Francis Greenway and convict-built in 1817. Nearby graveyard is even older. Court-house, Court St, another Greenway building. The Doctor's House (1844), Thompson Sq.; privately owned. Many other fine buildings in historic George St and Thompson Sq. Hawkesbury Museum, Thompson Sq.; formerly Daniel O'Connell Inn, built in 1843. **In the area:** Australiana Pioneer Village, 6 km north; features Rose Cottage, oldest timber dwelling in Australia, wagon and buggy collection, picnic/barbecue facilities and lake with paddleboats. Tizzana Winery, 14 km north at Ebenezer; tastings and sales of fortified wines and barbecue facilities. Ebenezer Uniting Church (1809), claimed to be oldest church in Australia still holding regular services. Nearby, old cemetery and schoolhouse (1817). Cattai Park State Recreation Area, 14 km north-east, offers historic homestead, friendship farm, horse and pony rides, canoe hire, picnic/barbeque facilities and camping area. **Tourist information:** Hawkesbury Regional Tourist Centre, Windsor Rd, Vineyard; (045) 87 7388. **Accommodation:** 1 hotel, 4 motels. **See also:** The Hawkesbury.
MAP REF. 101 K5, 109 I1, 111 J6,

Wingham   Population 4297

The oldest town on the Manning River, 13 km north-west of Taree, Wingham was established in 1843. **Of interest:** Manning Valley Historical Museum, part of attractive 'Village Square' with several prominent historic buildings, bounded by Isabella, Bert, Farquhar and Wynter Sts. The Brush, close to town centre (via Isabella St); unusual park consisting of dense rainforest with orchids, ferns, Moreton Bay fig trees and subtropical flowers. From Sept. to May each year thousands of flying foxes migrate here from Qld. **Tourist information:** Tourist Information Centre, Pacific Hwy, Taree North; (065) 52 1900. **Accommodation:** 2 hotels, 1 motel.
MAP REF. 113 N12

Wisemans Ferry

Population under 200
Situated on the southern side of the Hawkesbury River, 66 km north-west of Sydney, Wisemans Ferry is an important recreational area for those interested in water sports. Two vehicular ferries provide transport across the river. **Of interest:** Wisemans Ferry Inn, named after founder of original ferry service and innkeeper; said to be haunted by his wife, whom he allegedly pushed down front

steps of inn to her death. Dharug National Park, on northern side of river, named after local Aboriginal tribe, is important for its wealth of Aboriginal rock engravings. Convict-built Old Great North Road in park one of great engineering feats of early colony; walk or cycle along lower section (closed to vehicles) from ferry. **Tourist information:** Windsor Rd, Vineyard; (045) 87 7388. **Accommodation:** 2 hotels, 2 caravan/camping parks. **See also:** The Hawkesbury.
MAP REF. 101 M1, 111 J5

Wollongong   Population 206 803
The third largest city in NSW. Clustered around Port Kembla Harbour is the highly automated steel mill operated by BHP, an export coal loader and the largest grain handling facility in NSW. The area surrounding the city contains some of the South Coast's most spectacular scenery. **Of interest:** Illawarra Historical Society Museum, Market St; includes handicraft room and furnished Victorian parlour. Wollongong City Gallery, cnr Burrelli and Kiera Sts. Spectacular mall shopping area with soaring steel arches and water displays. Botanic Gardens and Rhododendron Park. Surfing beaches and rock-pools, to north and south. Foreshore parks for picnicking. Wollongong Harbour, fishing fleet and fish market. Historic lighthouse (1872). **In the area:** Lake Illawarra, 5 km south, stretching from South Pacific Ocean to foothills of Illawarra Range, for prawning, fishing and sailing; boats for hire. Seaside village of Shellharbour, 22 km south; walking trails in nearby Blackbutt Reserve. Many lookouts with superb views of coast, including Bald Hill Lookout, 36 km north; site of aviator Lawrence Hargrave's first attempt at flight in early 1900s, now favourite spot for hang-gliding. Symbio Animal Gardens, 44 km north at Helensburgh; free-roaming wombats, kangaroos, donkeys and other animals. Mt Kembla Village, 15 km west, scene of tragic mining disaster in 1902; features monument in church; original miners' huts; and several historic buildings, including Historical Museum housed in former post office, with pioneer kitchen, blacksmith's shop and reconstruction of Mt Kembla disaster. **Tourist information:** 93 Crown St; (042) 28 0300. **Accommodation:** 2 hotels, 5 motels. **See also:** The Illawarra Coast.
MAP REF. 106, 107 G5, 109 I3, 111 J8

Woodburn   Population 602
Woodburn is a pleasant town on the Pacific Hwy, astride the Richmond River. **Of interest:** Riverside Park. Monument and remains of settlement at New Italy, result

of ill-fated Marquis de Rays' expedition in 1880. Houseboats for hire. **Tourist information:** Wilsons River Heritage Centre, cnr Ballina and Molesworth Sts, Lismore; (066) 22 0122. **Accommodation:** 1 motel.
MAP REF. 113 Q3, 435 Q13

Woolgoolga   Population 2346
This charming seaside town on the Pacific Hwy, 26 km north of Coffs Harbour, is excellent for crabbing, prawning and whiting fishing. Good surf beach. **Of interest:** Guru Nanak Sikh Temple, River St, place of worship for town's Indian population. Raj Mahal Indian Cultural Centre. Woolgoolga Art Gallery on Turon Parade; paintings, pottery, workshops. **In the area:** Sam's Place, 5 km north at Mullaway; pottery demonstrations and restaurant. Yuraygir National Park, 10 km north, offers bushwalking, canoeing, fishing, surfing, swimming, and picnic and camping areas on beautiful stretch of unspoiled coastline. Wedding Bells State Forest. **Accommodation:** 6 motels, 3 caravan/camping parks.
MAP REF. 113 P7

Woy Woy   Population 12 206
Situated 90 km north of Sydney and 6 km south of Gosford. **Of interest:** Boating, fishing and swimming on Brisbane Water, Broken Bay and Hawkesbury River. Centre for Brisbane Water National Park, 3 km south-west, noted for

spring wildflowers, bushwalking, birdwatching and Aboriginal rock art sites. **Tourist information:** Umina Visitors Centre and Tea Rooms, cnr Bullion and West Sts, Umina; (043) 43 2200. **Accommodation:** On peninsula: 3 hotels, 2 motels, 3 caravan/camping parks.
MAP REF. 101 Q2

Wyong   Population 3902
Wyong is pleasantly situated on the Pacific Hwy between the Tuggerah Lakes and the State Forests of Watagan, Olney and Ourimbah. **Of interest:** Many sports catered for, including golf, swimming, most water sports, horse and dog racing and trotting. Festival of Arts held in Mar. Historical Bush Picnic in Oct. **In the area:** Hinterland popular for bushwalking and camping. Wyong District Museum, Anzac Rd, Tuggerah, 5 km south; recalls early ferry services across lakes and forest logging. Also at Tuggerah: Burbank Nursery, Japanese gardens and Plantarium. Award-winning Forest of Tranquillity at Ourimbah, 12 km south. **Tourist information:** Tuggerah Lakes Tourist Assocn, Memorial Park, Marine Pde, The Entrance; (043) 32 9282. **Accommodation:** 2 hotels, 2 motel, 2 caravan/camping parks.
MAP REF. 104 E11, 111 L5

Yamba   Population 2880
This prawning and fishing town at the mouth of the Clarence River offers sea,

Stanwell Tops, near Wollongong

lake and river fishing. It is the largest coastal resort in the Clarence Valley. Of interest: Story House Museum, River St; historical records of early Yamba. Views from base of lighthouse, reached via steep Pilot St. **In the area:** Daily passenger ferry services to Iluka. River cruises. Lake Wooloweyah, 4 km south, for fishing and prawning. Yuraygir National Park, 5 km south; swimming, fishing and bushwalking in area dominated by sand ridges and banksia heath. The Blue Pool at Angourie, 5 km south; only 50 m from ocean, freshwater pool of unknown depth and origin; popular swimming and picnic spot. Houseboats for hire at Brushgrove, 35 km south-west. **Tourist information:** Pacific Hwy, Grafton; (066) 42 4677. **Accommodation:** 1 hotel, 8 motels, 3 caravan parks.
MAP REF. 113 Q5

Yanco
Population 408

Located 8 km south of Leeton, this is where Sir Samuel McCaughey developed his own irrigation scheme, which led to the establishment of the Murrumbidgee Irrigation Area. His mansion is now an agricultural high school and with the nearby Yanco Agricultural Institute is open to public viewing. Yanco Powerhouse Museum has interesting displays and the Yanco Aquatic Park is nearby. There are extensive redgumforestsalongtheMurrumbidgee River and well-marked forest drives lead to sandy beaches and fishing spots.
MAP REF. 117 N9

Yass
Population 4529

Close to the junction of two major highways (the Hume and the Barton), this interesting old town is on the Yass River, surrounded by beautiful, rich, rolling country, 280 km south-west of Sydney and 55 km from Canberra. Of interest: Grave of Hamilton Hume, who discovered Yass Plains in 1824, in Yass Cemetery, signposted from Ross St. He lived at Cooma Cottage (1830), 3 km east, for 40 years; cottage classified by National Trust and open for inspection. Hamilton Hume Museum, Comur St, with wool and wealth theme. Many old buildings in town relate to Australia's heritage; self-guiding leaflet available. **In the area:** Burrinjuck State Recreation Area, 54 km south-west off Hume Hwy; bushwalking, water sports and fishing. At Wee Jasper, 53 km south-west: Goodradigbee River for trout fishing, Micalong Creek, Carey's Cave, with superb limestone formations, and Hume and Hovell Walking Track. **Tourist information:** Coronation Park, Cooma St; (06) 226 2557. **Accommodation:** 4 hotels, 6 motels.
MAP REF. 109 D4, 110 E9

Young
Population 6797

Attractive former gold-mining town in the western foothills of the Great Dividing Range, 395 km west-south-west of Sydney. Today cherries and prunes are the area's best-known exports, as well as flour, steel, tiles and magnesium oxide. **Of interest:** Lambing Flat Historic Museum, Campbell St; fascinating reminders of town's colourful history, including 'roll-up' flag carried by gold-miners during infamous anti-Chinese Lambing Flat riots of 1861. Art Gallery, cnr Short St and Olympic Way. Backguard Gully with historic Pug-mill, on Boorowa Rd; reconstruction showing early gold-mining methods. **In the area:** Chinaman's Dam, 4 km south-east, recreation area with picnic/barbecue facilities, children's playground and scenic walks. At Murringo Village, 24 km east; several historic buildings and home of crystal designer and engraver Helmut Heibel. Five wineries in area, all open for tastings and sales. **Tourist information:** cnr Campbell St and Olympic Way; (063) 82 3394. **Accommodation:** 6 hotels, 5 motels, 1 hotel/motel, 1 caravan/camping park.
MAP REF. 109 C3, 110 D8

Yuraygir National Park, near Yamba

Maps of New South Wales

Location Map

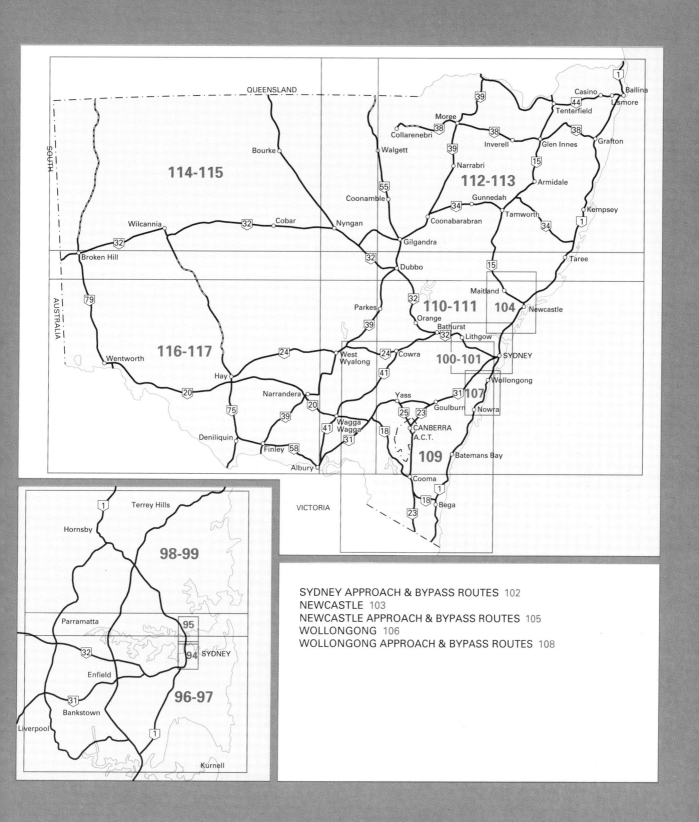

SYDNEY APPROACH & BYPASS ROUTES 102
NEWCASTLE 103
NEWCASTLE APPROACH & BYPASS ROUTES 105
WOLLONGONG 106
WOLLONGONG APPROACH & BYPASS ROUTES 108

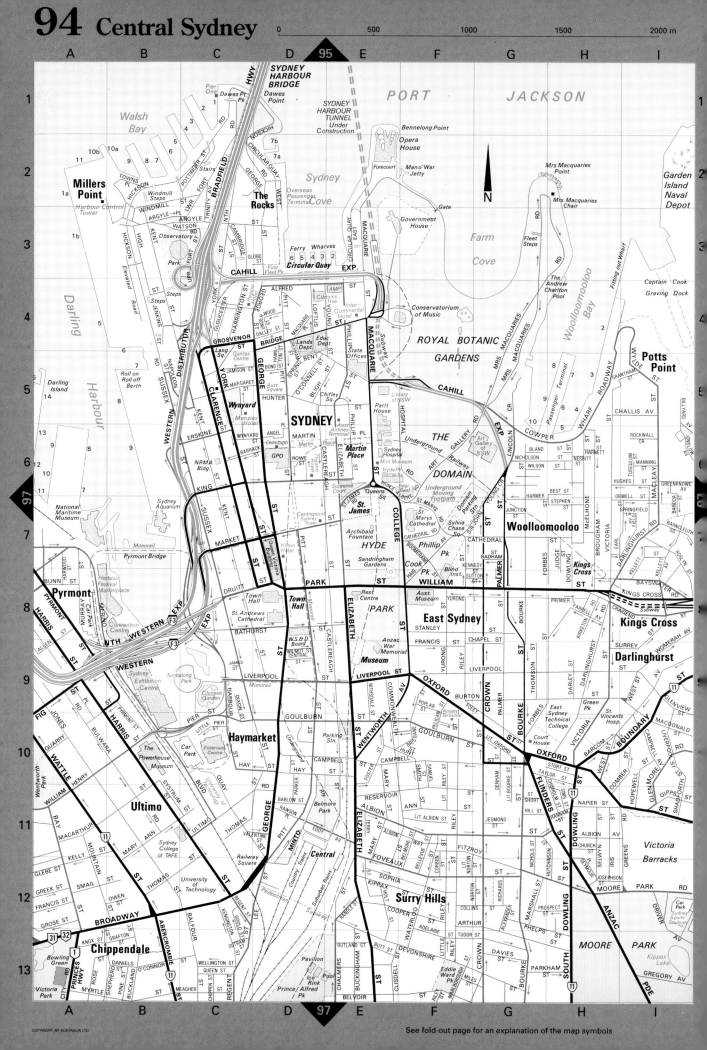

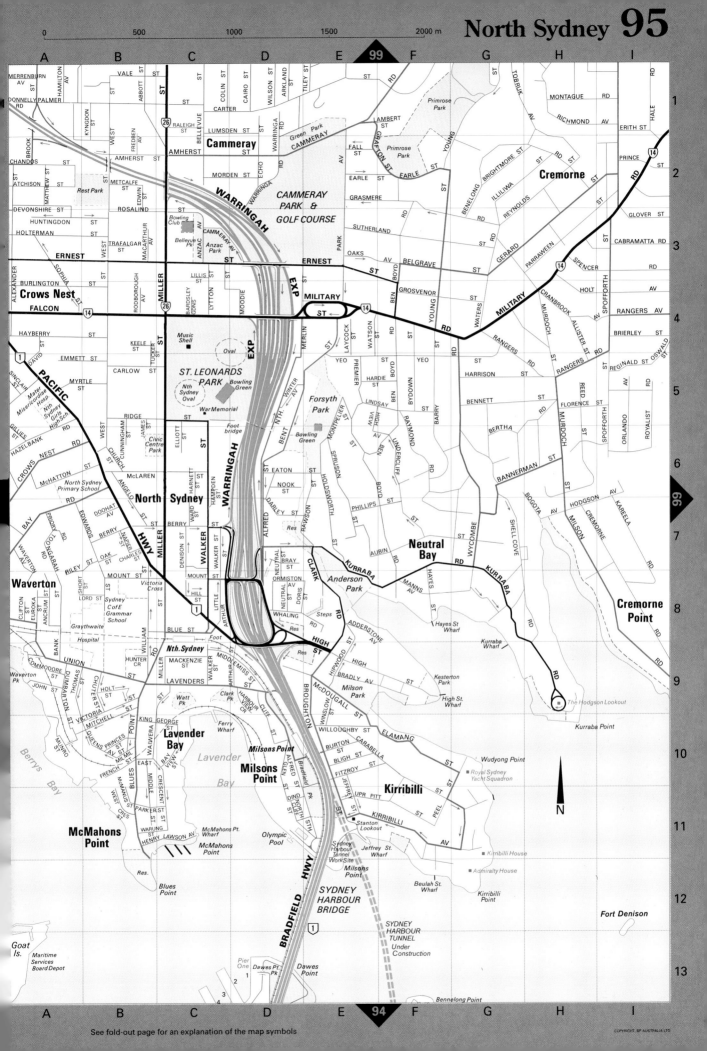

See fold-out page for an explanation of the map symbols

COPYRIGHT. BP AUSTRALIA LTD.

A B C D 98 E F G H I

1 Cumberland Hwy · 77 · Briens Rd · Redbank Rd · Westmead Hospital · Psychiatric Centre · Tramway Museum · North Parramatta · Church St · Pennant · James Ruse · Gladstone St · Isabella St · Pennant St · Kissing Point · Dundas · Bishop · Drive-in Res · Victoria · Spurway · Kissing Pt Whf · 40 · West Ryde · G.C. · Bennett St · Adelaide St · Parkes St · Ryde · 33 · Buffalo · Pidding · Higginbotham · Cem.

Wentworthville · Westmead · Parramatta Park · Victoria · George · Macquarie · Hassall St · Harris Park · Victoria · Rydalmere · South · Hosp. · Victoria · Ermington · Patterson · River Rd · Borona Res. · Meadowbank · Melrose Park · Constitution · Church St · Morrison · Putney · Pellisier Rd · Acacia · Ryde · 40 · Pitt Rd · 10

2 Great Western Hwy · 25 · Parramatta · Harris Park · Camellia · Rosehill Racecourse · Rosehill · Grand Av · Durham St · Devon St · Unwin St · Silverwater Bridge · Parramatta River · Silverwater Corrective Centre · Jamieson · Walker St · Homebush Bay · Brays Bay · Conv. Hosp. · Mortlake · Pt. Ferry · Raven · Mortlake · Cabarita · Pt. · Tennyson

3 Granville · William St · Clyde · Clyburn · Parramatta Gt · Western · 32 · 20 · Showgnd · Duck · Newton · Carnarvon · Alberta · Wetherill St · Western · Silverwater · 45 · Holker Park · Haslams · Powells · Victoria · Bicentennial Park · Concord Golf Course · Concord · Correys Av · Smythes · Ian Pde · Exile Bay · Abb · Hen and Chicken

4 Sherwood Rd · Merrylands · South Granville · Mona · Mary St · Auburn · Queen St · Olympic · Western · 45 · John St · Delhi · Boorea · Mons St · Birnie Av · Marlborough · Bachell Av · North Strathfield · 15 Rd · Flemington · Homebush · Hume · Concord · 33 · Paterson · Gipps · Canada Bay · King · Queens St · Harris Rd

5 Guildford · Rhodes Av · Clyde · Wellington Rd · Cumberland Rd · Vaughan St · Lidcombe · Rookwood · Mt. Auburn · St. Johns · Chisholm · Berala · Victoria St · Rookwood Cemetery · Joseph St · Arthur St · Pemberton · Barker St · Newton Av · Ada St · Wallis St · Strathfield · The Boulevarde · Enfield · Hume Rd · Burwood · Victoria St · Burwood · Croydon · Fitzroy St

6 The Horsley Dr · 101 · Fairfield · Yennora · Fairfield · The Promenade · Barbers Rd · Woodville Rd · Gurney · Miowera · Leightonfield · Curtis · Campbell St · Munro · Helen St · Amy St · Regents Park · Golf Course · Hospital · Strathfield · 15 · Liverpool Rd · Hume Hwy · Coronation Pde · Homebush · Mitchell St · Croydon River · Croydon Park · Hume Rd · 10 · 31 · Milton

7 Carramar · Horsley · Mitchell · Liverpool River · Belar Av · Hume Hwy · Villawood · 55 · Chester Hill · Sefton · Jocelyn · Rodd St · Birrong · Marks St · Hector · Spencer St · Rose St · Brunker · Chullora · Rookwood Rd · 45 · Cardigan Rd · Rawson · Greenacre · Boronia · Juno · Roberts · Wentworth St · Burwood · Georges River · Belfield · Lees · Ashbury · Race course

8 Hume Hwy · Lansvale · Lansdowne · Lansdowne Park · Miram-Jeena Regl Res · Bass Hill · 31 · 20 · Glassop · William St · Highland · Allum St · Yagoona · Greenacre · Jacobs St · Chapel Rd · Waterloo Rd · Mt. Lewis · Wattle · King · Punchbowl · Railway · Lakemba · Boulevarde · Haldon · Lakemba · 15 · Campsie · 54 · Belmore · Bexley Rd · Clem Park

9 Norton Av · Charlton Av · Ernest St · Riverside · Georges Hall · Bankstown Aerodrome · Riverwood Golf Course · 55 · Babaul St · Haigh Av · Marion St · Wren St · Condell Park · Norman St · Cambridge St · Lancelot St · Augusta · Bankstown · Chapel Rd S · Stacey St · Griffiths St · Scott St · Wiley Pk · Punchbowl · 54 · Georges Rd · Moorefields · G.C. · Kingsgrove · Bexley Nth · Homer · Moorefields

10 Newbridge Rd · 54 · Dredge Av · Moorebank · Chipping Norton · 25 · Milperra · 54 · Bankstown Golf Course · Milperra · Horsley · Bullecourt Av · Carrington · Showgnd · 20 · Canterbury Rd · Gow St · Bryant · 45 · Fairford Av · Turvey St · Wiggs Rd · Kentucky Rd · Hannans · Shorter · Grove Av · Graham St · Narwee · Penshurst · 33 · Beverly Hills · Vanessa · Morgan · Shaw · Bexley · G.C. · Croydon · Kingsgrove

11 61 · Hammondville · New Brighton Golf Course · Henry · East Hills Golf Course · Maxwell Rd · Poziers Av · Bullecourt Av · Ashford Av · Beaconsfield · Bransgrove · Horsley Rd · Panania · Weston St · The River · Polo · Sphinx · Padstow · Watson Av · Ronald St · Banks Rd · Davies Rd · Coleridge St · Webb St · Clarendon St · Riverwood · Broad Arrow · Mount View · Peakhurst · Forest Rd · 20 · Stoney · Penshurst · King Georges Rd · 33 · Carrington Av · Hurstville · Forest

12 Heathcote · Stewart Av · Holdsworthy · Military Enquiry Centre · Georges · 55 · East Hills · Lawson · Kelso Park · Weston · Tower · Malvern · Picnic Point · Paul St · Prince · Kennedy · Ferndale St · Neptune St · Alma St · Faraday · Clancy · Villiers · Salt Pan Ck · Lawson · Duke St · N.Pk. · Evans St · Belmore Rd · Barry Av · Isaac St · Golf Course · Balmoral · Acacia · Forest Rd · Lorraine · Gungah Bay · Mortdale · Hurstville · Laycock · Railway · Oxford · Victoria · Hurstville Grove · Oatley · Waitara · Georges

13 Military Reserve · Holsworthy Barracks · Heathcote Rd · 61 · Pleasure Point · Sandy Point · Picnic Point · 25 · Georges River Parklands · 45 · Nallada Rd · Alfords Pt. · Alfords Pt · Lugarno · Lime Kiln · Jew Fish Bay · Gungah Bay · Mimosa · Neville · Connells Pt. · Connells Pt · Oatley · River · Oatley · Oatley Pt. · 101

A B C D 101 E F G H I

Sydney Map

0 1 2 3 4 5 6 km

J K L M N O P Q R

99

PACIFIC HWY · Cammeray · Crows Nest · St Leonards · Wollstonecraft · Mosman · Georges Heights · Middle Head · Inner South Head · SYDNEY HARBOUR NATIONAL PARK

Riverview · Longueville · Greenwich · Neutral Bay · Cremorne · Clifton Gardens · Chowder Bay · Watsons Bay · The Gap

Hunters Hill · Woolwich · North Sydney · Kirribilli · Bradleys Head · Outer South Head

Chiswick · Drummoyne · Balmain · Pyrmont · SYDNEY · Potts Point · Darling Point · Point Piper · Rose Bay · Dover Heights · Vaucluse

Russell Lea · Rozelle · Lilyfield · Glebe · Ultimo · Kings Cross · Rushcutters Bay · Elizabeth Bay · Double Bay · Bellevue Hill · North Bondi

Haberfield · Leichhardt · Annandale · Darlington · Surry Hills · Darlinghurst · Paddington · Edgecliff · Woollahra · Bondi · Bondi Junction · Bronte · Waverley

Petersham · Camperdown · Stanmore · Newtown · Redfern · Waterloo · Moore Park · Centennial Park · Clovelly

Lewisham · Enmore · Erskineville · Alexandria · Zetland · Rosebery · Kensington · Randwick · Coogee

Dulwich Hill · Marrickville · Sydenham · St Peters · Beaconsfield · Kingsford · South Coogee

Earlwood · Turrella · Undercliffe · Tempe · Mascot · Eastlakes · Daceyville · Pagewood · Maroubra Junction · Maroubra

Arncliffe · SYDNEY AIRPORT · Botany · Botany East · Hillsdale · Matraville · Malabar

Rockdale · Banksia · Kyeemagh · Chifley · Anzac Rifle Range

Kogarah · Brighton-le-Sands · BOTANY · Phillip Bay · Little Bay · Prince Henry Hospital

Beverley Park · Ramsgate · La Perouse · NSW Golf Course

FOR MORE DETAIL SEE MAPS OF CENTRAL SYDNEY AND NORTH SYDNEY

N

Kurnell · **101**

PACIFIC OCEAN · SOUTH · BOTANY BAY · PORT JACKSON

101

96

A B C D E F G H I

1 2 3 4 5 6 7 8 9 10 11 12 13

Mt.Kuring-gai
Visitors Centre
Kalkari Wildlife Centre
Koala Reserve

PARK
O'Hares Ck
CRANSTON RD
PITT TOWN RD

Middle Dural
MID DURAL
ARCADIA RD
BAYFIELD RD
CROSSLANDS RD
Res.
Ck

Galston
Galston Pool Reserve
Cabbage Tree Hollow
GALSTON RD
Galston Gorge
Berowra Ck
SOMMERVILLE RD
China Ck
KU-RING-GAI CHASE
Cockle Ck

Kenthurst
KENTHURST RD
ANNANGROVE RD
SAGARS RD

Hornsby Heights
Mt.Colah
NEWCASTLE HWY
PACIFIC HWY
SYDNEY - NEWCASTLE

Dural
OLD NORTHERN RD
GALSTON RD
CARTERS RD
URALLA RD
SAN REMO DR
QUARRY RD

Hookhams Corner
Asquith
JERSEY ST
ROYSTON PDE
HORNSBY
Curagul HEAD G.C.
BOBBIN HEAD RD

Round Corner
Elouera Bushland Reserve
Rifle Range Res.
Reserve
Trunk RD
Fish Ponds
BRIDGE RD
GEORGE ST
SHERBROOK RD
PALMERSTON RD

Hornsby
Waitara
Wahroonga East
Wahroonga
BOUNDARY JUNCTION
GROSVENOR RD

Glenhaven
GLENHAVEN RD
NORTHERN RD
Cumberland S.F. Extension
Georges Ck
Castlehill Ck
Normanhurst
Westleigh
Warrawee
Turramurra
NORMAN RD
KOORINGAL AV
SEFTON RD
MILSON PDE
THE ESPLANADE
PRETORIA PDE
CLARKE RD
PACIFIC HWY
BURNS RD
EASTERN RD
THE CHASE RD

Cherrybrook
Englefield Sports Stadium
NEW LINE RD
JENNER RD
PURCHASE RD
GUMNUT RD
HASTINGS RD

Rogans Hill
Thornleigh
Pennant Hills
Pymble
Kissing Point
West Pymble
Fox Valley
BOUNDARY RD
YARRARA RD
PENNANT HILLS RD
CUMBERLAND RD
COMENARRA PKWY
COMENARRA PARKWAY
BEECHWORTH RD
AVON RD
RYDE RD

Castle Hill
SHOWGROUND RD
CASTLE HILL RD
CRANE RD
CHURCH ST
DARLEY RD
HIGHS RD
TAYLOR ST
VICTORIA AV
CARDINAL RD

Pennant Hills West
State Forest Koala Park
ORATAVA AV
ALBERT RD
HANNAH ST
COPELAND RD
Beecroft
Cheltenham
MALTON RD
KETTEL RD
DEVLIN RD
NORFOLK RD
WATERLOO RD
LANE COVE
Macquarie University
LANE COVE NATIONAL PARK

Baulkham Hills
WINSTON HILLS
PARSONAGE RD
COOLONG RD
EXCELSIOR AV
EDWARD ST
CROSS ST
Rifle Range
State Forest
Royal Deaf & Blind Institute
North Rocks
AIKEN RD
EATON RD
OAKES RD
MAHERS RD
MURRAY FARM RD
Pennant Hills G.C.
Devlins Ck
PLYMPTON RD
ALAMEIN AV
DUNROSSIEL AV
DENT ST
RAY RD
MIDSON RD
KENT ST
Epping
Marsfield
BLAXLAND RD
EPPING RD
KHARTOUM RD
VIMIERA RD
TALAVERA RD
WATERLOO RD
BALACLAVA RD
ABUKLEA RD
HERRING RD

Winston Hills
ROXBOROUGH PK
WINDSOR RD
HILDA RD
KEENE ST
SEVEN HILLS RD
CHARLES ST
Muirfield G.C.
BARCLAY RD
NTH ROCKS RD
JENKINS RD
HILLS RD
ROCKS RD
MOSELEY ST
CARLINGFORD RD
WILLOUGHBY ST
DUNLOP ST
BORONIA AV
BRIDGE ST
EASTWOOD AV
Eastwood
North Ryde
EPPING
COXS RD
East Ryde
Denistone
BRIDGE RD
NTH RYDE WCOS
Psychiatric Centre
Drive-in Th.

Northmead
Lake Parramatta Reserve
WINDERMERE AV
JUNCTION RD
LANHAMS RD
LOMOND CK
BARNETTS RD
CAPRERA RD
CUMBERLAND HWY
ADDERTON RD
Telopea
Dundas Valley
ALEXANDER AV
YATES AV
KING RD
Brush Farm
TERRY RD
DARVALL RD
RUTLEDGE RD
SHAFTSBURY RD
RYEDALE RD
LOVELL RD
KINGS RD
NORTH RD
West Ryde
MELVILLE RD
ANZAC AV
BENNETT RD
ADELAIDE RD
Ryde
VICTORIA RD
PARKES RD
GOULDING RD

Wentworthville
Westmead Hospital
Tramway Museum
Westmead
Parramatta Park
HAMMERS RD
GLEN AV
BOURKE ST
BELLEVUE RD
GLADSTONE ST
ISABELLA ST
JAMES RUSE
BETTINGTON RD
GANNAN ST
Oatlands G.C.
VINEYARD CK
KISSING POINT
Drive-in Res.
SPURWAY RD
Melrose Park
G.C.
CONSTITUTION RD
BOWDEN
Putney
WATERVIEW ST
CHARLES ST
Ryde Bridge

North Parramatta
Psychiatric Centre
CHURCH ST
JAMES RUSE
PENNANT ST
CUMBERLAND HWY
Dundas
Bishop Ck
VICTORIA RD
Rydalmere
Ermington
SILVERWATER RD
Meadowbank
WHARF RD
ANDREW ST
Tennyson

Parramatta
GEORGE ST
MACQUARIE ST
HASSALL ST
GRAND AV
WESTON ST
Camellia
Rosehill Racecourse
SOUTH ST
ANTOINE AV
Parramatta River
Silverwater Bridge

COPYRIGHT, UBD AUSTRALIA LTD

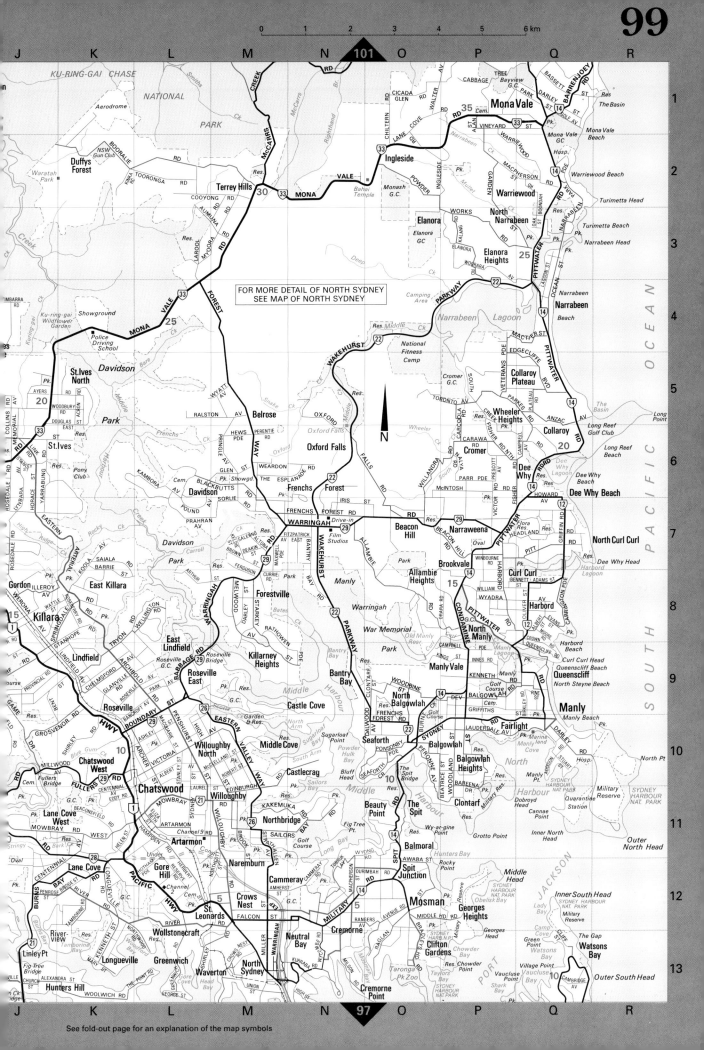

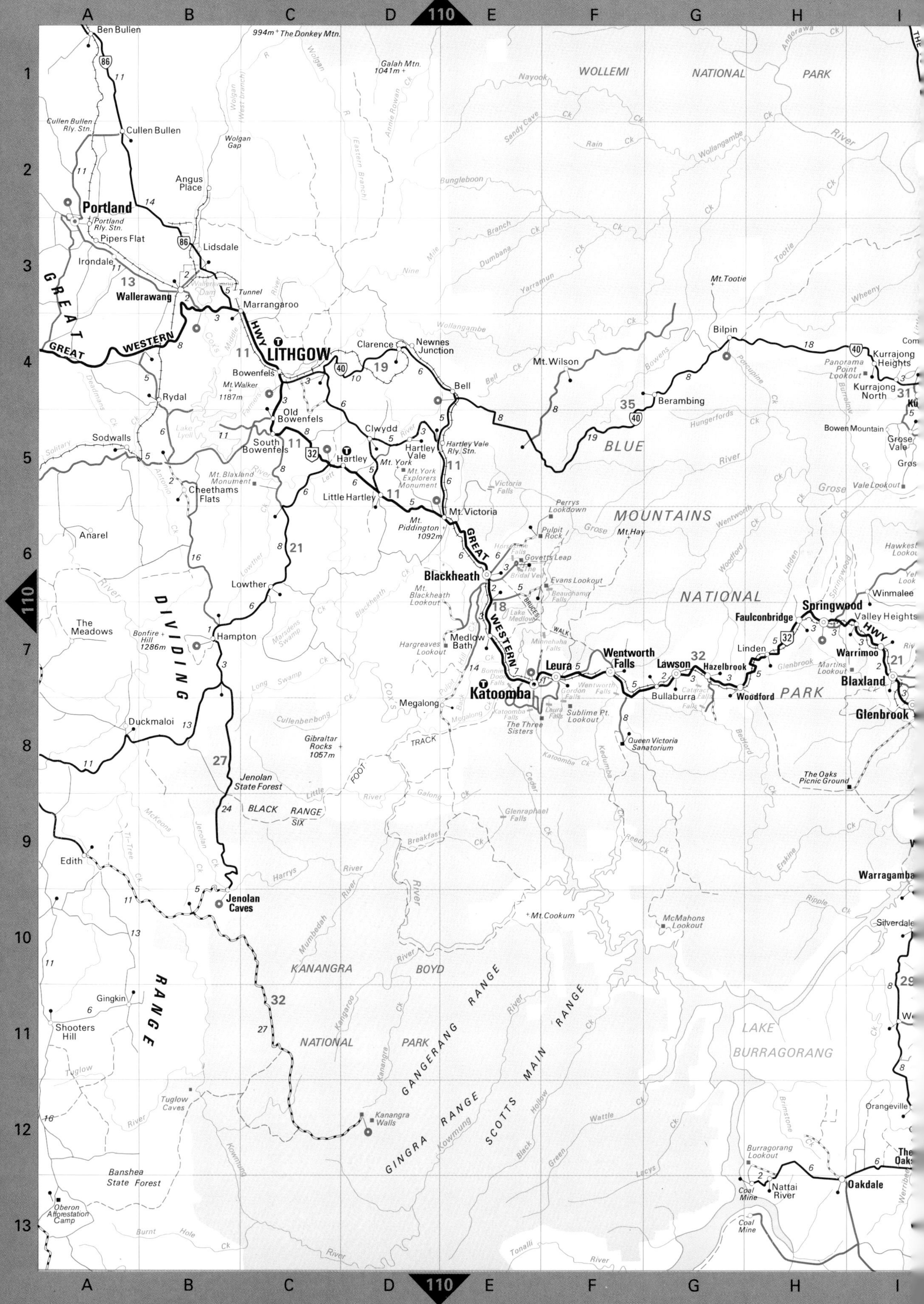

A B C D **110** E F G H I

Ben Bullen
86
11
994m⁺ The Donkey Mtn.
Galah Mtn.
1041m⁺
WOLLEMI NATIONAL PARK
Nayook Ck.
Angorawa Ck.
1
Cullen Bullen
Rly. Stn.
Cullen Bullen
Wolgan
Gap
West branch
Wolgan River
Sandy Cave
Rain Ck.
Wollangambe Ck.
River
2
11
Angus
Place
Annie Rowan
Eastern Branch
Bungleboon Ck.
Wollangambe
Wheeny Ck.
Portland
14
86
Lidsdale
Branch Ck.
Dumbana Ck.
Mt.Tootie
Tootie Ck.
3
Portland Rly. Stn.
Pipers Flat
Irondale
11
13
Marrangaroo
Tunnel
5
Nine Mile
Yarramun
Mt. Wilson
Bilpin
18
40
Com
Kurrajong
Heights
4
GREAT
Wallerawang
Wallerawang Dam
2
2
3
LITHGOW
40
19
Clarence
Newnes Junction
6
Bell
Bell Ck.
8
Bowens River
8
Porcupine
Panorama
Point Lookout
40
Kurrajong
North
31
Ku
Bowenfels
Mt. Walker
1187m
3
Old Bowenfels
11
10
Clwydd
Hartley Vale
35
Berambing
Hungerfords Ck.
Bowen Mountain
Grose
Vale
5
GREAT
WESTERN
8
5
Rydal
6
11
South Bowenfels
11
32
8
Hartley
Mt. York
5
Hartley Vale Rly. Stn.
Mt. York
Explorers
Monument
11
BLUE
40
Grose River
Bowen Mountain
Grose Vale Lookout
Gros
5
Sodwalls
13
5
Deadmans Ck.
Lake Lyell
Cheethams Flats
2
Mt. Blaxland
Monument
Little Hartley
6
11
Mt. Victoria
Mt. Piddington
1092m
Victoria Falls
MOUNTAINS
Mt. Hay
Wentworth Ck.
Hawkesl
Lookout
6
Anarel
16
Lowther River
8
21
GREAT
Perrys Lookdown
Grose
Pulpit Rock
Govetts Leap
The Bridal Veil
Evans Lookout
NATIONAL
Winmalee
Yel Look
Springwood
Valley Heights
The Meadows
Bonfire Hill
1286m⁺
Lowther
6
Hampton
Blackheath
Mt. Blackheath Lookout
2
3
Beauchamp Falls
Woodford Ck.
Springwood Ck.
Faulconbridge
3
32
Warrimoo
21
7
DIVIDING
1
3
Marsdens Swamp
18
WESTERN
Medlow Bath
Minnehaha Falls
Leura
5
Wentworth Falls
Lawson
32
Hazelbrook
Linden
Martins Lookout
Blaxland
Duckmaloi
13
Long Swamp
14
7
Katoomba
Hargreaves Lookout
Megalong
WALK
Wentworth Falls
5
2
Bullaburra
3
Glenbrook
3
Erskine River
Glenbrook
8
Jenolan
State Forest
27
Gibraltar Rocks
1057m⁺
Cullenbenbong
Cox's River
Bonnie Doon Falls
Gordon Falls
Sublime Pt. Lookout
Queen Victoria Sanatorium
The Oaks
Picnic Ground
11
24
BLACK RANGE SIX
FOOT
Little River
Galong Ck.
Megalong Ck.
Katoomba Falls
The Three Sisters
Leura Falls
Cedar Ck.
Kedumba River
Bedford Ck.
9
Edith
11
13
McKeons Ck.
TRACK
Breakfast Ck.
Reedy Ck.
Warragamba
Mt.Cookum⁺
Jenolan Caves
5
Harrys River
McMahons Lookout
Silverdale
10
11
Tuglow River
13
Jenolan Ck.
KANANGRA BOYD
Kanangra River
RANGE
LAKE BURRAGORANG
29
We
Gingkin
6
32
NATIONAL
PARK
GANGERANG RANGE
Kowmung River
SCOTTS MAIN RANGE
Ripple Ck.
Shooters Hill
27
Orangeville
Tuglow Ck.
16
Tuglow Caves
Kanangra Walls
GINGRA RANGE
Black Ck.
Wattle Ck.
Green Ck.
Brimstone Ck.
Burragorang Lookout
The Oaks
12
Banshea State Forest
Kowmung River
Lecys Ck.
2
Coal Mine
Nattai River
Oakdale
6
Oberon
Afforestation Camp
Burnt Hole Ck.
River
Tonalli River
River
Coal Mine
13

A B C D **110** E F G H I

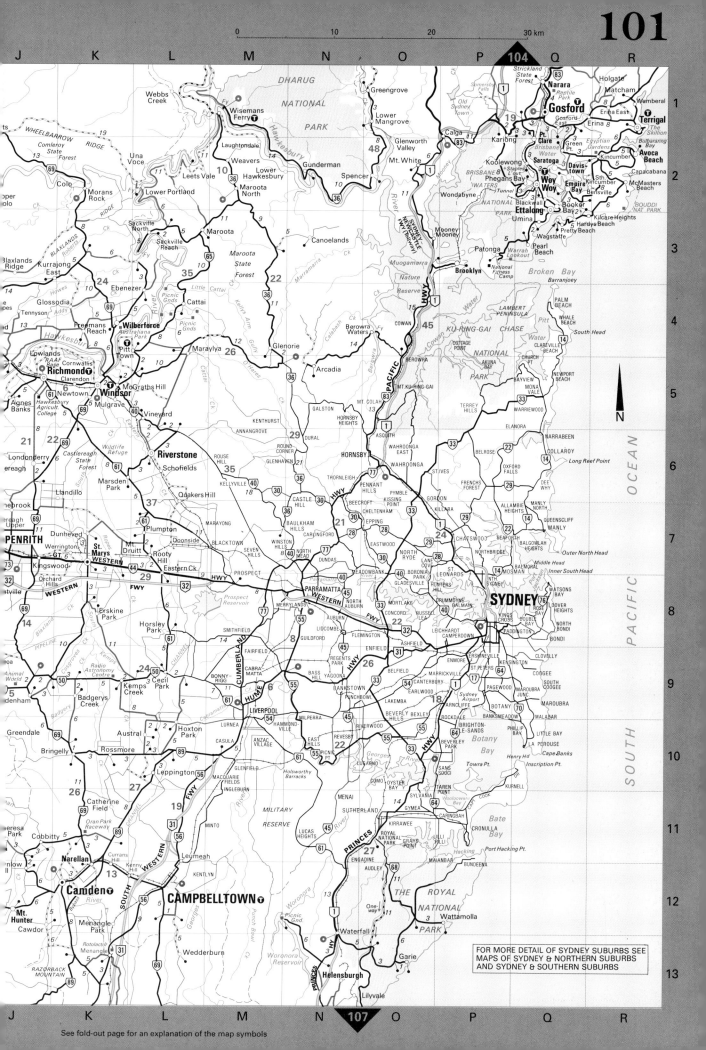

FOR MORE DETAIL OF SYDNEY SUBURBS SEE
MAPS OF SYDNEY & NORTHERN SUBURBS
AND SYDNEY & SOUTHERN SUBURBS

SYDNEY Approach & Bypass Routes

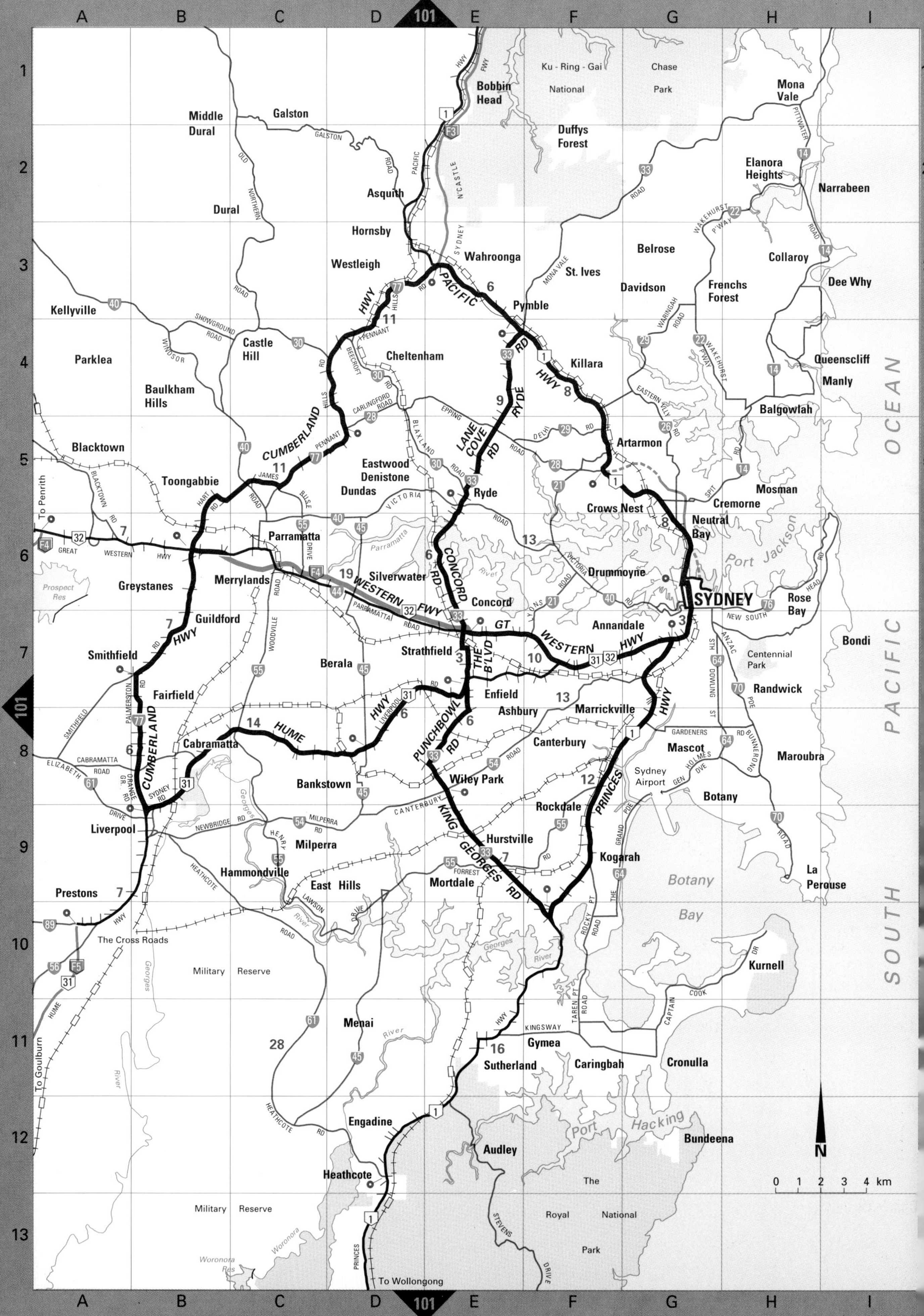

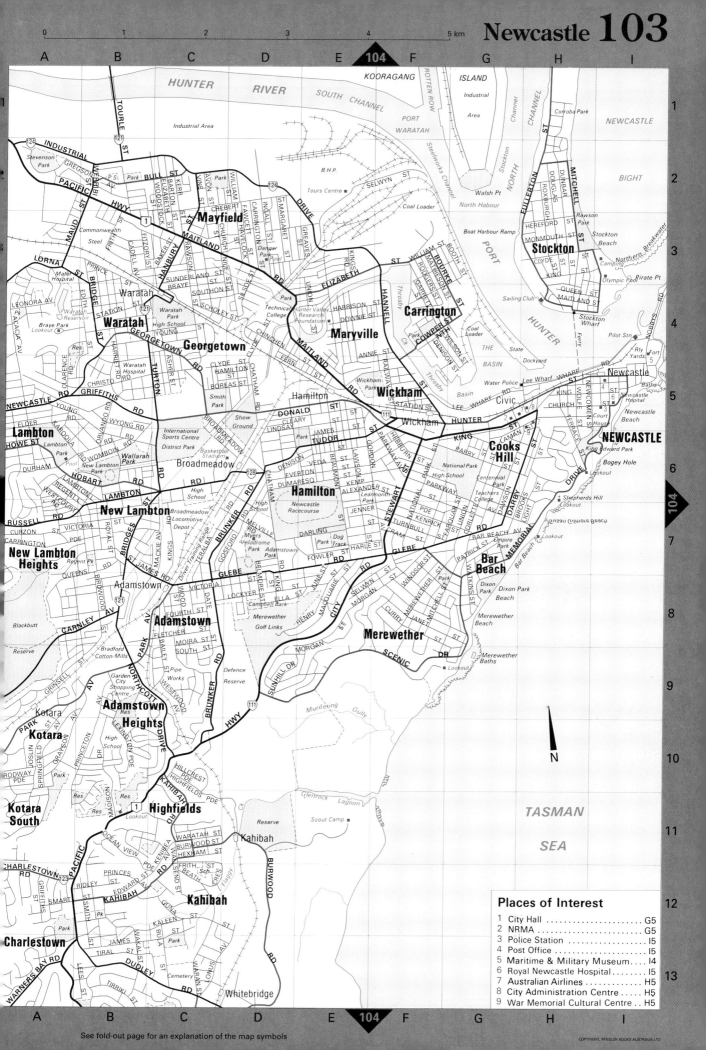

Places of Interest

1 City Hall G5
2 NRMA G5
3 Police Station I5
4 Post Office I5
5 Maritime & Military Museum I4
6 Royal Newcastle Hospital I5
7 Australian Airlines H5
8 City Administration Centre H5
9 War Memorial Cultural Centre . . H5

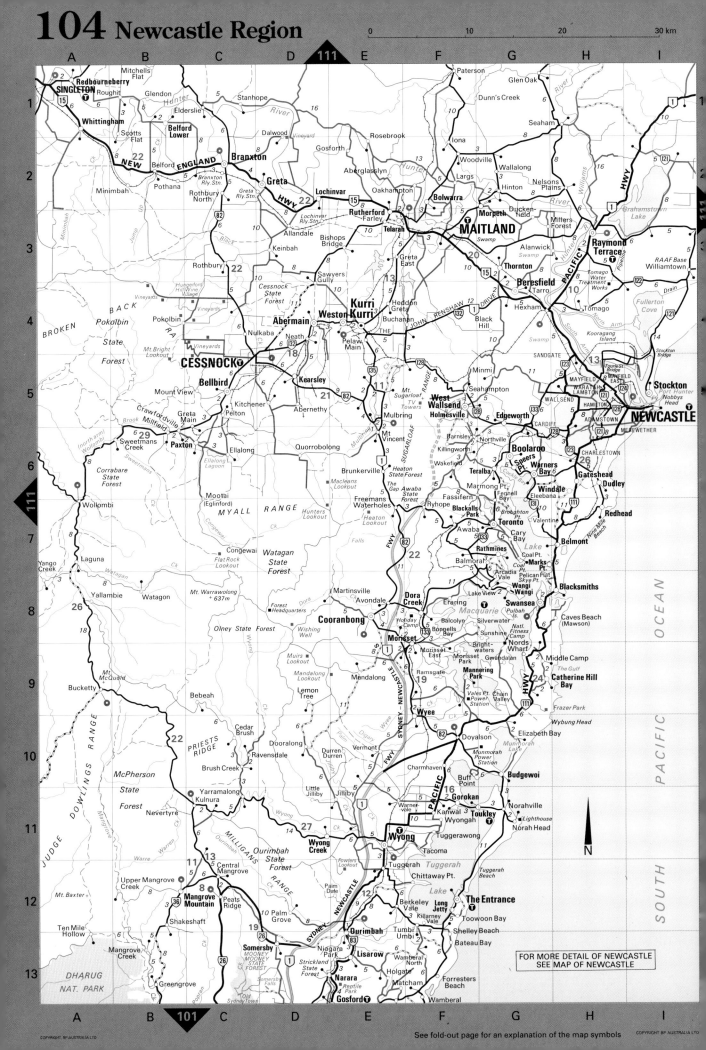

104 Newcastle Region

See fold-out page for an explanation of the map symbols

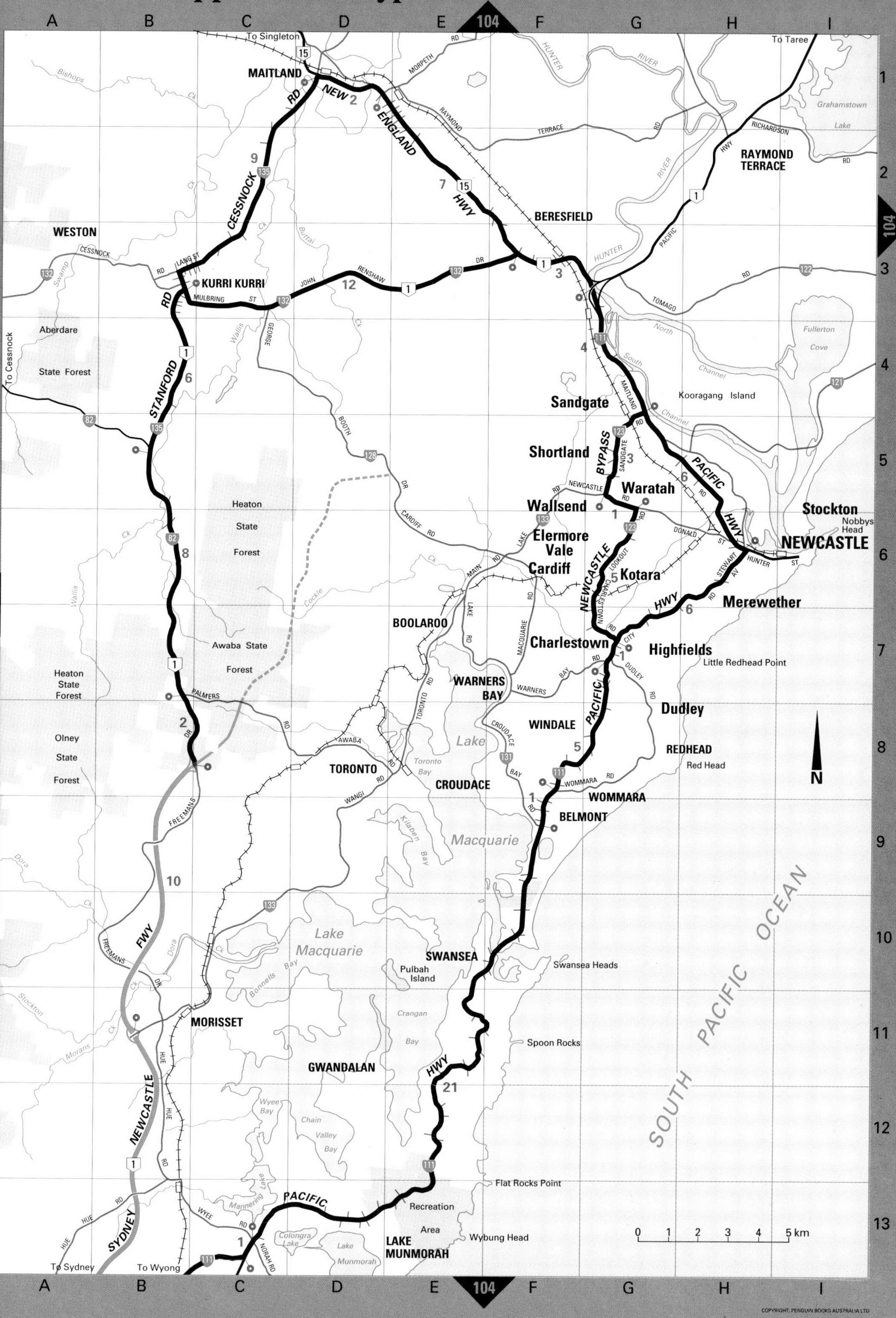

104

To Singleton

To Taree

MAITLAND

15

RD

NEW 2

CESSNOCK

135

9

ENGLAND

MORPETH

RAYMOND

HUNTER

RIVER

RIVER

TERRACE

7 15

HWY

BERESFIELD

RICHARDSON
HWY

RAYMOND
TERRACE

104

WESTON

CESSNOCK

RD

LANG ST

KURRI KURRI

JOHN ST

RENSHAW

1

132

DR

3

RD

HUNTER

122

132

MULBRING

RD

12

132

1

TOMAGO

RD

Aberdare

STANFORD RD

GEORGE

4 11

Fullerton
Cove

To Cessnock

State Forest

1

6

135

82

BOOTH

Kooragang Island

North

Channel

Sandgate

RD

Channel

South

121

Heaton
State
Forest

128

BYPASS

123

3

Shortland

SANDGATE

PACIFIC

5

82

NEWCASTLE

RD

6

8

CARDIFF RD

RD

Waratah

1

RD

Wallsend

133

123

DONALD

HWY

Stockton
Nobbys
Head
NEWCASTLE

Awaba State
Forest

1

LAKE

RD

Elermore
Vale
Cardiff

NEWCASTLE

123

CHISHOLM

LOOKOUT

Kotara

5

STEWART

AV

HUNTER ST

Heaton
State
Forest

MAIN

RD

HWY

6

Merewether

Cockle

BOOLAROO

RD

Charlestown

RD

CITY

1

PACIFIC

Highfields

Little Redhead Point

PALMERS

2

DR

MACQUARIE RD

WARNERS
BAY

WARNERS

BAY

DUDLEY

RD

Dudley

Olney
State
Forest

Lake

Windale

PACIFIC

REDHEAD

Red Head

FREEMANS

1

AWABA

TORONTO RD

Toronto
Bay

CROUDACE

131

BAY

5

111

WOMMARA

RD

FWY

10

TORONTO

WANGI

RD

RD

CROUDACE

1

RD

WOMMARA

BELMONT

133

Lake
Macquarie

Kilaben

Bay

Macquarie

MORISSET

HUE

RD

SWANSEA

Pulbah Island

Swansea Heads

10

NEWCASTLE

HUE

RD

Crangan
Bay

Spoon Rocks

HWY

11

GWANDALAN

Wyee
Bay

Chain
Valley
Bay

21

Flat Rocks Point

111

SOUTH PACIFIC OCEAN

1

PACIFIC

Recreation
Area

Wybung Head

To Sydney

To Wyong

111

1

WYEE

RD

NORAH RD

Colongra
Lake

Lake
Munmorah

LAKE
MUNMORAH

0 1 2 3 4 5 km

N

104

106 Wollongong

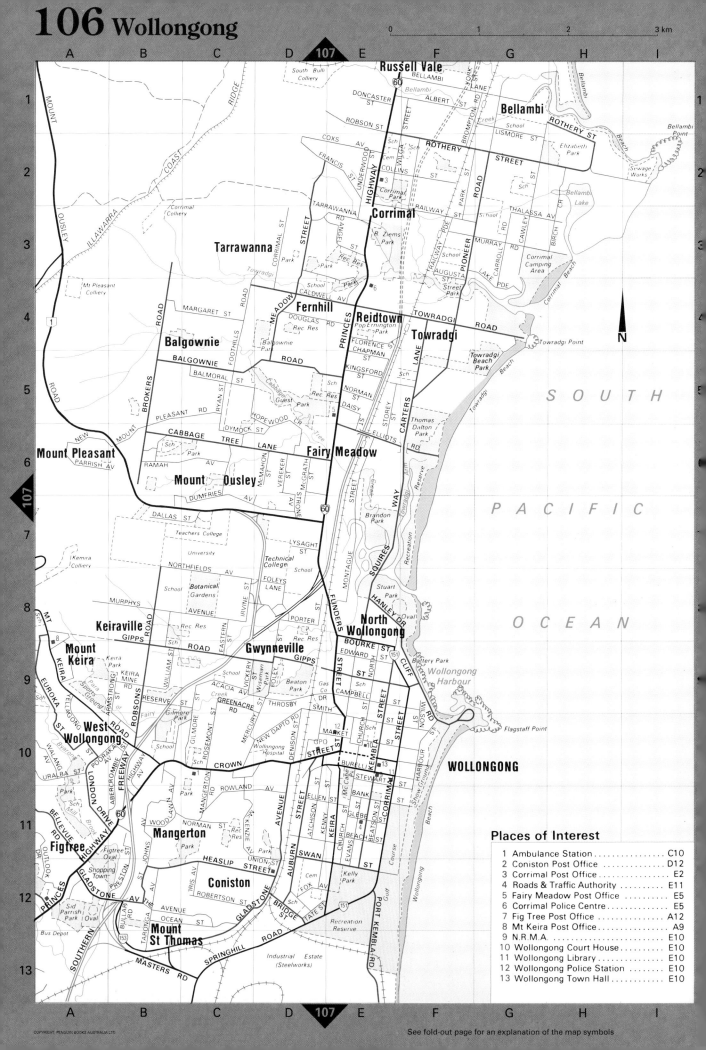

Places of Interest

See fold-out page for an explanation of the map symbols

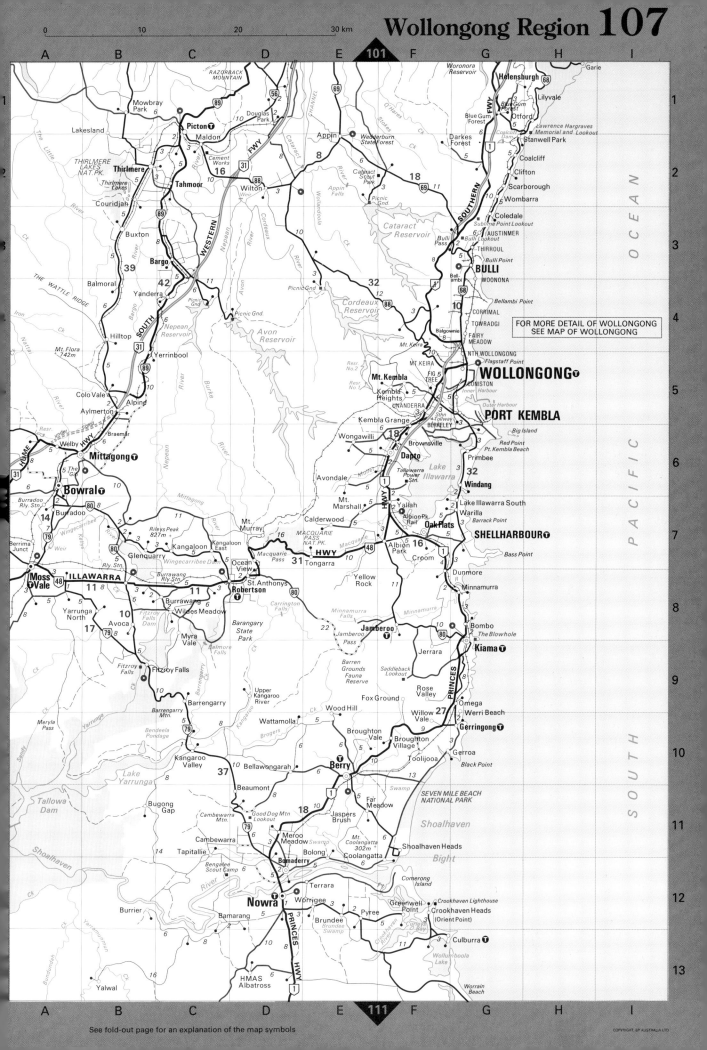

0   10   20   30 km

101

RAZORBACK MOUNTAIN

Woronora Reservoir

Garie

Helensburgh 68

Mowbray Park 6

Lakesland

Blue Gum Forest

Lilyvale

WESTERN FWY

89

Douglas Park

Maldon

Picton T

56

Appin

Wedderburn State Forest

Darkes Forest

Lawrence Hargraves Memorial and Lookout

Otford

6

Stanwell Park

Coalcliff

THIRLMERE LAKES NAT. PK.

Thirlmere

16

Tahmoor

88

Cement Works

31

Wilton

Weir

Appin Falls

Cataract Scout Park

18

69

Clifton

Scarborough

Wombarra

Thirlmere Lakes

Couridjah

Wollondoola

Picnic Gnd.

Coledale

SOUTHERN

Buxton

89

Bargo

39

Balmoral

42

Yanderra

Picnic Gnd.

Cordeaux River

Cataract Reservoir

Picnic Gnd.

Bulli Pass

Sublime Point Lookout

AUSTINMER

Bulli Lookout

THIRROUL

Bulli Point

BULLI

WOONONA

THE WATTLE RIDGE

Hilltop

SOUTH

Nepean Reservoir

Avon Reservoir

Cordeaux Reservoir

32

88

Bell-ambi

68

Bellambi Point

Iron Ck

Mt. Flora 742m

Yerrinbool

89

Burke River

Resr No.2

Mt Keira

CORRIMAL

TOWRADGI

Balgownie

10

Colo Vale

Alpine

Aylmerton

Resr No.1

MT KEIRA

FAIRY MEADOW

NTH WOLLONGONG

FOR MORE DETAIL OF WOLLONGONG
SEE MAP OF WOLLONGONG

HUME HWY

Welby

Braemar

Mt. Kembla

Kembla Heights

FIG TREE

Flagstaff Point

WOLLONGONG T

CONISTON

31

Mittagong T

UNANDERRA

Inner Harbour

Kembla Grange

Stn Tollway

Outer Harbour

PORT KEMBLA

Bowral T

80

Burradoo

Wongawilli

18

BERKELEY

Big Island

Red Point

Pt. Kembla Beach

Burradoo Rly. Stn.

14

Mittagong River

Rileys Peak 827m +

Dapto

Brownsville

Primbee

Berrima Junct.

79

Weir

Kangaloon

Kangaloon East

Mt. Murray

Avondale

Mullet

Tallawarra Power Stn.

Lake Illawarra

32

Windang

Glenquarry

80

Wingecarribee Dam

MACQUARIE PASS NAT. PK.

Mt. Marshall

HWY

Yallah

Albion Pk. Rail

Lake Illawarra South

Warilla

Barrack Point

Ocean View

Calderwood

Oak Flats

ILLAWARRA

Burrawang Rly. Stn.

Robertson

Macquarie Pass

31

HWY

Tongarra

48

Albion Park

16

Croom

1

SHELLHARBOUR T

Bass Point

Moss Vale T

48

11

11

St. Anthonys

80

Carrington Falls

Yellow Rock

Dunmore R

Minnamurra

Yarrunga North

10

Burrawang

Wildes Meadow

Barangary State Park

Minnamurra Falls

11

Minnamurra

17

79

Avoca

Myra Vale

Belmore Falls

22

Jamberoo Pass

Jamberoo T

80

Bombo

The Blowhole

Fitzroy Falls

Fitzroy Falls Dam

Jerrara

Saddleback Lookout

Kiama T

Meryla Pass

10

Barrengarry

Upper Kangaroo River

Wood Hill

Barren Grounds Fauna Reserve

Fox Ground

Rose Valley

PRINCES

Barrengarry Mtn.

Wattamolla

Brogers

Willow Vale

27

Omega

Werri Beach

Lake Yarrunga

79

Bendeela Pondage

Kangaroo Valley

37

Bellawongarah

Broughton Vale

Broughton Village

Gerringong T

Gerroa

Tallowa Dam

Beaumont

Berry T

Toolijooa

Black Point

SEVEN MILE BEACH NATIONAL PARK

Bugong Gap

Cambewarra Mtn.

Good Dog Mtn Lookout

18

Jaspers Brush

1

Far Meadow

Swamp

Shoalhaven

Tapitallie

79

Cambewarra

Meroo Meadow

Swamp

Mt. Coolangatta 302m +

Shoalhaven Heads

Bight

Bengalee Scout Camp

Bolong

Coolangatta

Bomaderry

Comerong Island

Burrier

Terrara

Greenwell Point

Crookhaven Lighthouse

Nowra T

Worrigee

Crookhaven Heads (Orient Point)

Bamarang

PRINCES HWY

Brundee

Pyree

Brundee Swamp

Yalwal

HMAS Albatross

1

Wullamboola Lake

Worrain Beach

OCEAN

PACIFIC

SOUTH

Shoalhaven

111

See fold-out page for an explanation of the map symbols

COPYRIGHT, BP AUSTRALIA LTD

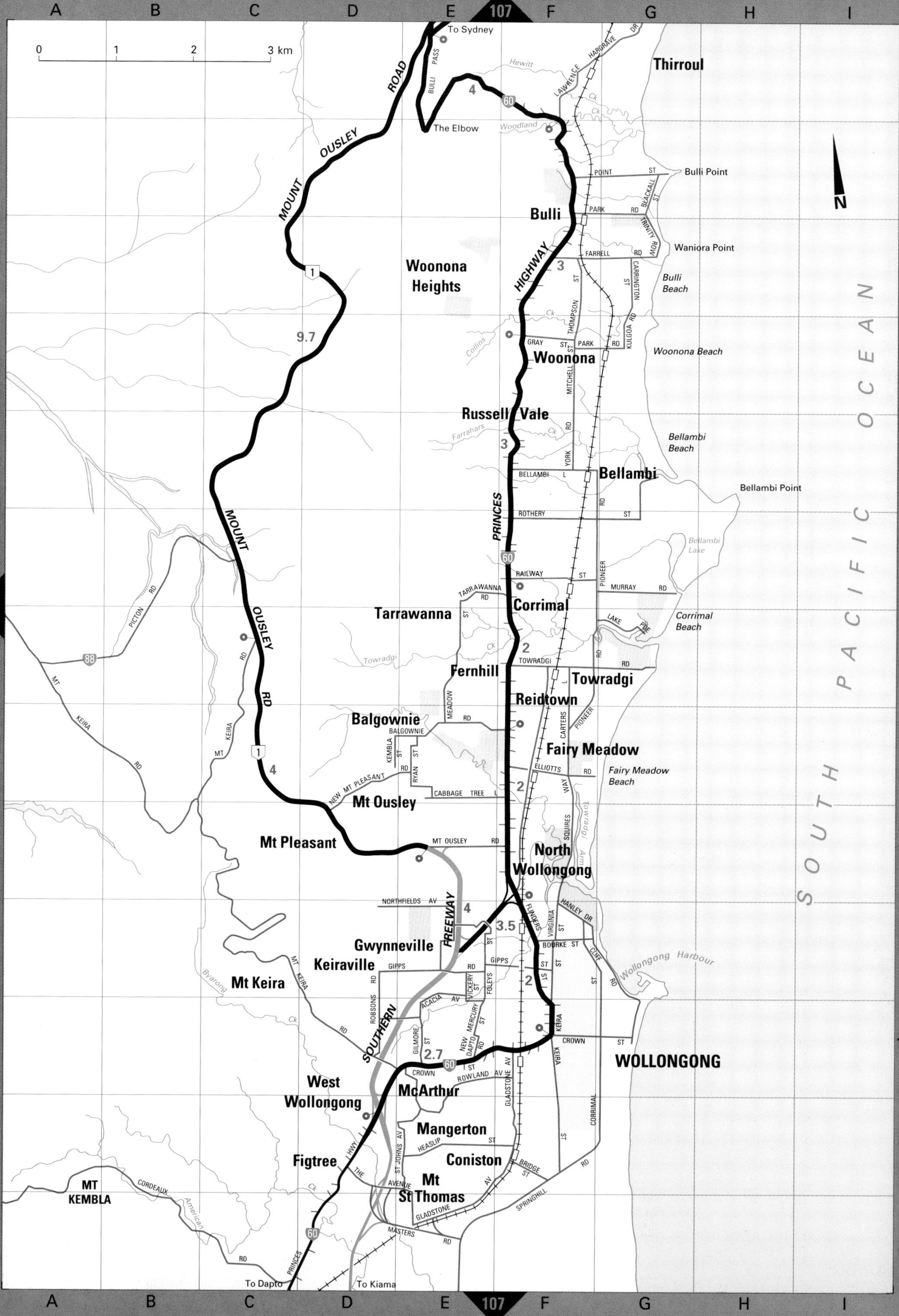

A B C D E F G H I

107

1 1

Thirroul

To Sydney

Hewitt

MOUNT OUSLEY ROAD

BULLI PASS

4

60

2 2

The Elbow

Woodland

POINT ST

Bulli Point

Bulli

PARK RD

BLACKALL ST

TRINITY ROW

3 **Woonona** 3

Heights

HIGHWAY

3

FARRELL ST

CARRINGTON RD

Waniora Point

Bulli Beach

1

9.7

THOMPSON ST

Ck

GRAY ST

PARK RD

4 *Collins* **Woonona** 4

MITCHELL RD

KILGOA RD

Woonona Beach

MOUNT

Russell Vale

Farrahars

PRINCES

3

YORK RD

Bellambi Beach

5 5

BELLAMBI L

Bellambi

RD

Bellambi Point

OUSLEY RD

ROTHERY

ST

6 6

60

Bellambi Lake

107

RAILWAY ST

PIONEER

107

Tarrawanna

TARRAWANNA RD

Corrimal

MURRAY RD

Corrimal Beach

7 *Towradgi Ck* 2 7

PICTON RD

ST

TOWRADGI

LAKE PDE

88

Towradgi

Fernhill

MEADOW RD

RD

RD

Towradgi

MT KEIRA RD

Balgownie

BALGOWNIE RD

CARTERS

PIONEER

8 KEMBLA ST RYAN ST 2 **Fairy Meadow** 8

MT

RYAN ST

ELLIOTTS

WAY

RD

Fairy Meadow Beach

1 4

NEW MT PLEASANT

CABBAGE TREE

Mt Ousley

2

SQUARES

Towradgi Arm

9 **Mt Pleasant** MT OUSLEY RD **North** 9

MT KEIRA RD

Wollongong

HANLEY DR

FREEWAY

4

NORTHFIELDS AV

FLINDERS

VIRGINIA

10 3.5 10

Gwynneville

GIPPS

BOURKE ST

CLIFF RD

Wollongong Harbour

Keiraville

GIPPS ST

2

Byarong

ROBSONS RD

VICKERY ST

FOLEYS ST

Mt Keira

ACACIA AV

KERA ST

Ck

GILMORE ST

NEW DAPTO RD

MERCURY ST

CORRIMAL

11 2.7 CROWN ST **WOLLONGONG** 11

SOUTHERN

60

ROWLAND AV

KEIRA

CROWN ST

West

CROWN

GLADSTONE AV

Wollongong **McArthur**

ST JOHNS AV

12 **Mangerton** 12

HWY

HEASLIP ST

Figtree THE AVENUE

Coniston

BRIDGE

MT CORDEAUX

GLADSTONE

Mt

SPRINGHILL

AV

KEMBLA *American*

AVENUE

St Thomas

RD

13 60 13

Ck MASTERS RD

RD

PRINCES

To Dapto To Kiama

A B C D E 107 F G H I

SOUTH PACIFIC OCEAN

N

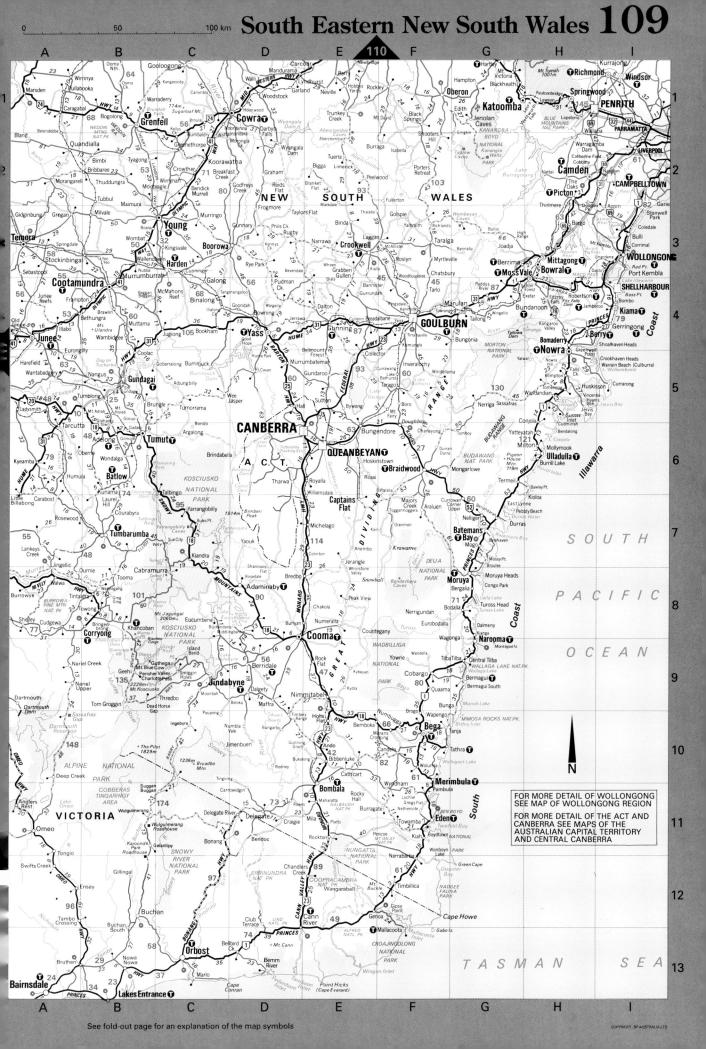

FOR MORE DETAIL OF WOLLONGONG
SEE MAP OF WOLLONGONG REGION

FOR MORE DETAIL OF THE ACT AND
CANBERRA SEE MAPS OF THE
AUSTRALIAN CAPITAL TERRITORY
AND CENTRAL CANBERRA

0   50   100   150 km

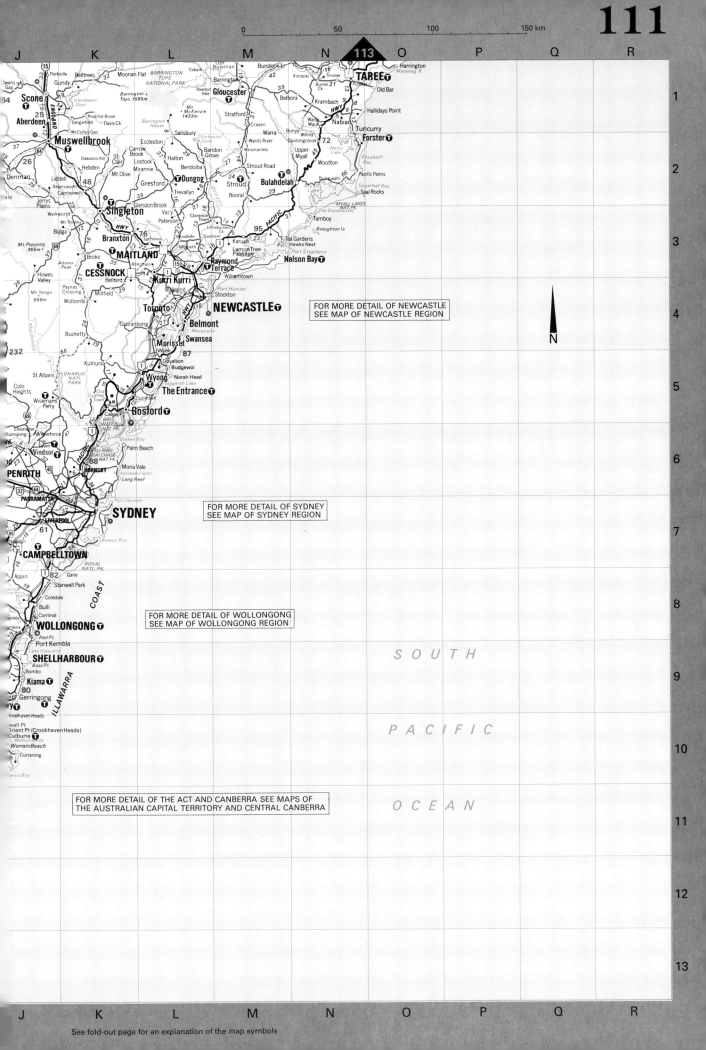

FOR MORE DETAIL OF NEWCASTLE
SEE MAP OF NEWCASTLE REGION

N

FOR MORE DETAIL OF SYDNEY
SEE MAP OF SYDNEY REGION

FOR MORE DETAIL OF WOLLONGONG
SEE MAP OF WOLLONGONG REGION

S O U T H

P A C I F I C

FOR MORE DETAIL OF THE ACT AND CANBERRA SEE MAPS OF
THE AUSTRALIAN CAPITAL TERRITORY AND CENTRAL CANBERRA

O C E A N

See fold-out page for an explanation of the map symbols

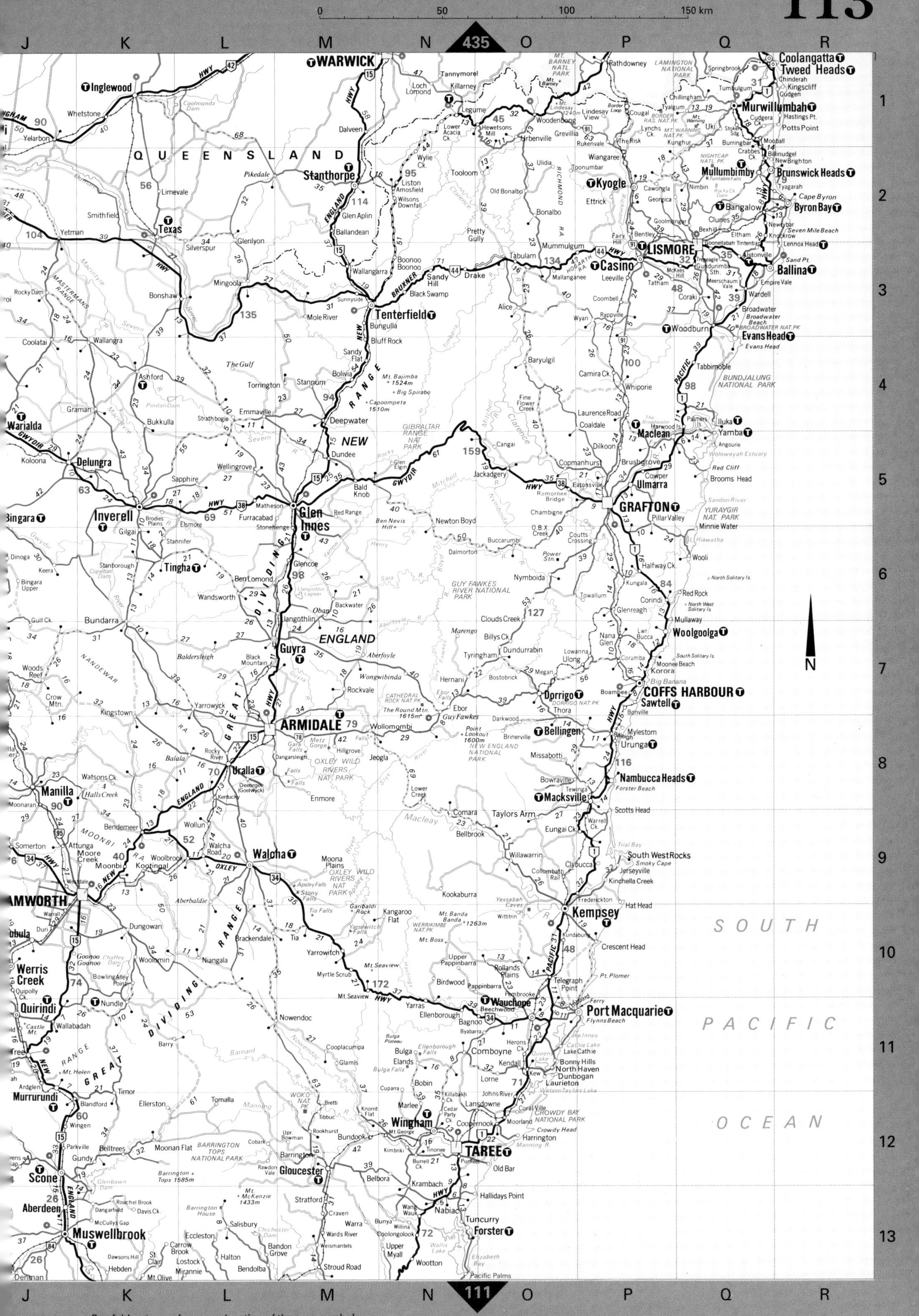

0 50 100 150 km

J K L M N O P Q R

435

1

WARWICK
Inglewood
Whetstone
Yelarbon
Coolangatta
Tweed Heads
Chinderah
Kingscliff
Gudgen
Murwillumbah
Cudgera
Hastings Pt.
Potts Point
Mooball

QUEENSLAND

2

Stanthorpe
Texas
Kyogle
Mullumbimby
Brunswick Heads
Cape Byron
Byron Bay
Bangalow
Clunes
Lennox Head

3

Tenterfield
Casino
LISMORE
Ballina
Woodburn
Evans Head
Broadwater

4

Deepwater
NEW
ENGLAND
RANGE
Maclean
Yamba
Iluka
BUNDJALUNG
NATIONAL PARK

5

Glen Innes
Inverell
GRAFTON
Ulmarra
Red Rock
YURAYGIR NAT. PARK

6

Tingha
Woolgoolga
Mullaway

7

Guyra
ENGLAND
Dorrigo
COFFS HARBOUR
Sawtell
Bellingen
Urunga

8

ARMIDALE
Uralla
Nambucca Heads
Macksville
Forster Beach

9

Manilla
Walcha
Kempsey
South West Rocks
Smoky Cape

10

TAMWORTH
Werris Creek
Port Macquarie
SOUTH

11

Quirindi
Wauchope
Beechwood
PACIFIC

12

Murrurundi
Wingham
TAREE
OCEAN
Harrington

13

Scone
Aberdeen
Gloucester
Forster
Tuncurry
MUSWELLBROOK

J K L M N O P Q R

111

N

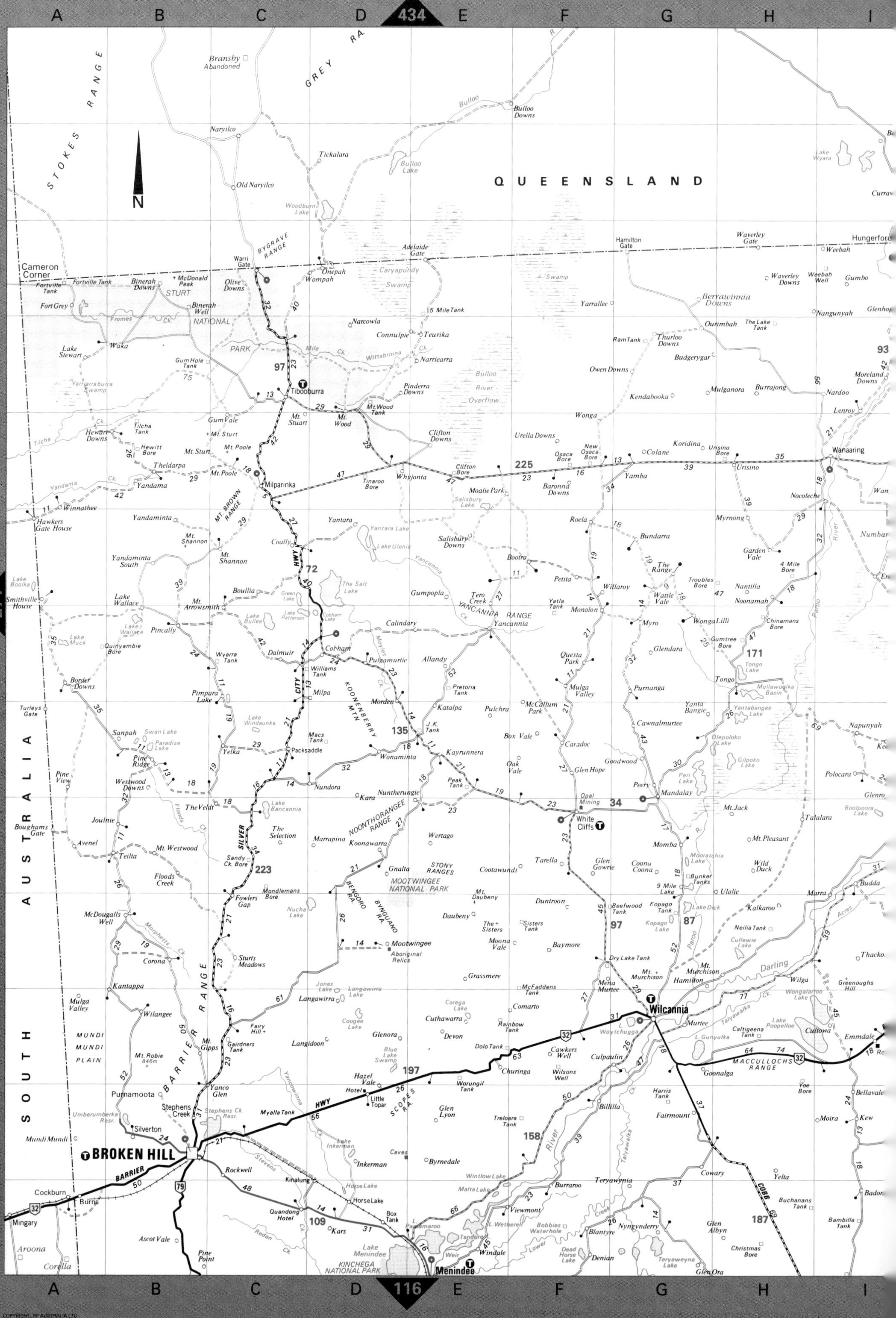
A B C D E F G H I
434
1 2 3 4 5 6 7 8 9 10 11 12 13
271
116
QUEENSLAND
SOUTH AUSTRALIA
N
STOKES RANGE
GREY RA.
Bransby
Abandoned
Naryilco
Old Naryilco
Tickalara
Bulloo Lake
Bulloo Downs
Woodburn Lake
BYGRAVE RANGE
Warri Gate
Cameron Corner
Fortville Tank
Fort Grey
Binerah Downs
McDonald Peak
Binerah Well
STURT NATIONAL PARK
Olive Downs
Onepah
Wompah
Adelaide Gate
Caryapundy Swamp
Hamilton Gate
Waverley Gate
Hungerford
Weebah
Waverley Downs
Weebah Well
Gumbo
Berrawinnia Downs
Yarrallee
Nangunyah
5 Mile Tank
Narcowla
Connulpie
Teurika
Narriearra
Lake Stewart
Waka
Gum Hole Tank
Tibooburra
Pinderra Downs
Bulloo River Overflow
Mt. Wood Tank
Mt. Stuart
Mt. Wood
Ram Tank
Thurloo Downs
Ourimbah
The Lake Tank
Budgerygar
Owen Downs
Kendabooka
Mulganora
Burrajong
Moreland Downs
Nardoo
Lenroy
Tilcha Tank
Hewart Downs
Gum Vale
Mt. Sturt
Mt. Poole
Hewitt Bore
Theldarpa
Yandama
Milparinka
Tinaroo Bore
Whyjonta
Clifton Downs
Clifton Bore
Urella Downs
Wonga
Osaca Bore
New Osaca Bore
Yamba
Colane
Koridina
Urisino Bore
Urisino
Wanaaring
Moalie Park
Salisbury Lake
Baronna Downs
Winnathee
Hawkers Gate House
MT. BROWN RANGE
Yandaminta
Mt. Shannon
Yantara
Yantara Lake
Lake Ulenia
Salisbury Downs
Roela
Bundarra
Myrnong
Nocoleche
Garden Vale
Numbarr
Yandaminta South
Coally
HWY
Bootra
Petita
The Range
Troubles Bore
4 Mile Bore
Nantilla
Noonamah
Lake Bookla
Smithville House
Lake Wallace
Mt. Arrowsmith
Boullia
Green Lake
Lake Patterson
The Salt Lake
Gumpopla
Tero Creek
YANCANNIA RANGE
Yancannia
Willaroy
Yatla Tank
Monolon
Wattle Vale
Myro
Wonga Lilli
Chinamans Bore
Lake Bullea
Pincally
Cobham Lake
Calindary
Lake Muck
Quinyambie Bore
Wyarra Tank
Dalmuir
Cobham
Pulgamurtie
Allandy
Questa Park
Glendara
Gumtree Bore
Tongo Lake
Tongo
Border Downs
Williams Tank
Milpa
CITY
KOONENBERRY MTN
Pretoria Tank
Mulga Valley
Purnanga
Mullawoolka Basin
Turleys Gate
Pimpara Lake
Morden
Katalpa
Pulchra
McCallum Park
Yanta Bangie
Yantabangee Lake
Sanpah
Swan Lake
Paradise Lake
Lake Windaunka
J.K. Tank
Cawnalmurtee
Napunyah
Pine Ridge
Yelka
Macs Tank
Packsaddle
Wonaminta
Kayrunnera
Box Vale
Caradoc
Olepoloko Lake
Gilpoko Lake
Pine View
Westwood Downs
Nundora
Peak Tank
Oak Vale
Glen Hope
Goodwood
Peery
Mandalay
Peri Lake
Polocara
Boughams Gate
The Veldt
Lake Bancannia
Kara
Nuntherungie
Opal Mining
White Cliffs
Mt. Jack
Talalara
Boolpoora Lake
Joulnie
SILVER
The Selection
NOONTHORANGEE RANGE
Wertago
Momba
Mt. Pleasant
Avenel
Teilta
Mt. Westwood
Sandy Ck. Bore
Marrapina
Koonawarra
Gnalta
STONY RANGES
MOOTWINGEE NATIONAL PARK
Cootawundi
Tarella
Glen Gowrie
Coona Coona
Mooratchia Lake
Wild Duck
Bunker Tanks
Ulalie
Marra
Budda
Floods Creek
Mondlemans Bore
BENGORO RA.
BYNGUANO RA.
Mt. Daubeny
Duntroon
Beefwood Tank
9 Mile Lake
Kopago Tank
Lake Dick
Kalkaroo
McDougalls Well
Fowlers Gap
Nucha Lake
Daubeny
The Sisters
Sisters Tank
Kopago Lake
Neilia Tank
Morphetts Ck.
Corona
Mootwingee
Aboriginal Relics
Moona Vale
Baymore
Cullewie Lake
Thackor
Sturts Meadows
Dry Lake Tank
Darling
Mt. Murchison
Murchison
Hamilton
Wilga
Greenoughs Hill
Kantappa
Jones Lake
Langawirra Lake
Langawirra
Grassmere
McFaddens Tank
Mena Murtee
Wilcannia
Wongalarroo Lake
Mulga Valley
Wilangee
BARRIER RANGE
Coogee Lake
Corega Lake
Cuthawarra
Comarto
Rainbow Tank
L. Woytchugga
Murtee
Talyawalka
Lake Poopelloe
Caltigeena Tank
Cultowa
Emmdale
MUNDI MUNDI PLAIN
Mt. Robie 846m
Fairy Hill
Mt. Gipps
Gairdners Tank
Langidoon
Glenora
Devon
Dolo Tank
Blue Lake Swamp
Churinga
Cawkers Well
Culpaulin
L. Gunyulka
MACCULLOCHS RANGE
Goonalga
Yoe Bore
Bellavale
Purnamoota
Yanco Glen
Hazel Vale
Hotel
Little Topar
SCOPES RA.
Worungil Tank
Wilsons Well
Harris Tank
Stephens Creek
Stephens Ck. Resr.
Umberumberka Resr.
Myalla Tank
Glen Lyon
Treloara Tank
Billilla
Fairmount
Moira
Kew
Silverton
Mundi Mundi
BROKEN HILL
BARRIER
Rockwell
Stevens Ck.
Inkerman Lake
Inkerman
Caves
Byrnedale
Wintlow Lake
Cowary
Yelta
Cockburn
Burns
Mingary
Kinalung
Horse Lake
Quandong Hotel
Malta Lake
Burraroo
Teryawynia
COBB
Buchanans Tank
Bador
Ascot Vale
Pine Point
Kars
Box Tank
Pamamaroo
L. Wetherell
Viewmont
Bobbies Waterhole
Nyngynderry
Blantyre
Glen Albyn
Bambilla Tank
Aroona
Corella
Redan Ck.
Lake Menindee
KINCHEGA NATIONAL PARK
Tandure
Weir
Windale
Menindee
Dead Horse Lake
Denian
Teryaweyna Lake
Glen Ora
Christmas Bore
Lower
River
Yancannia
Bulloo
Tilcha
Frome Ck.
Mile Ck.
Wittabrinna Ck.
Yarrarraburra Swamp
Moyles Ck.
Paroo
Acres
Yancowinna
97 72 135 223 225 34 97 87 171 93 158 109 187 197
32 79 69

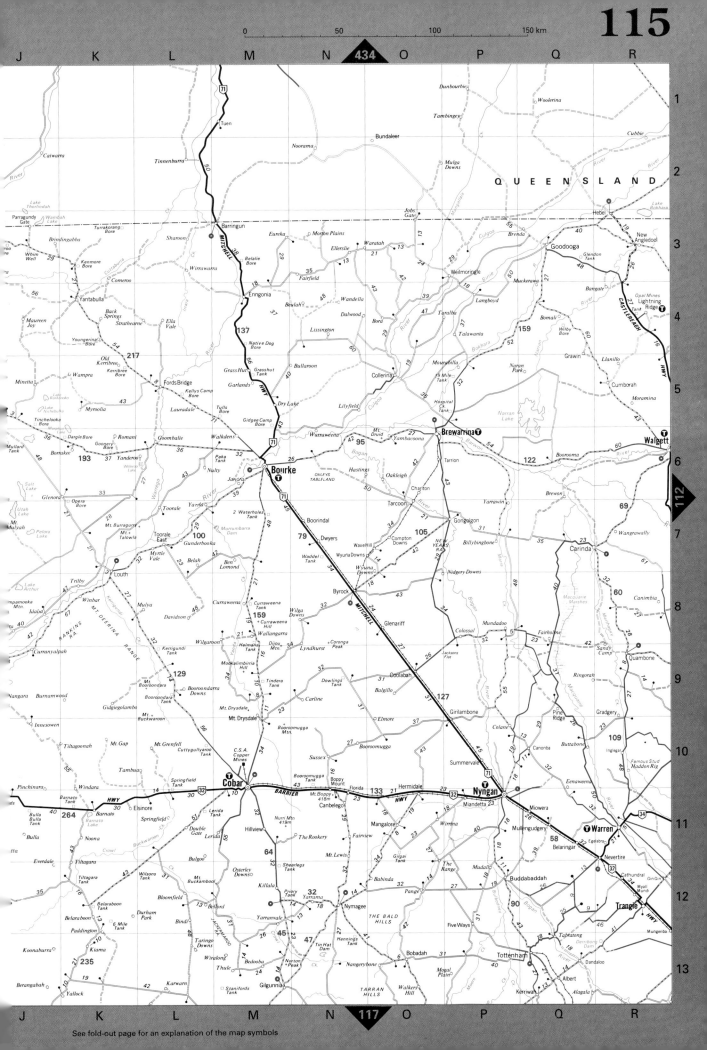

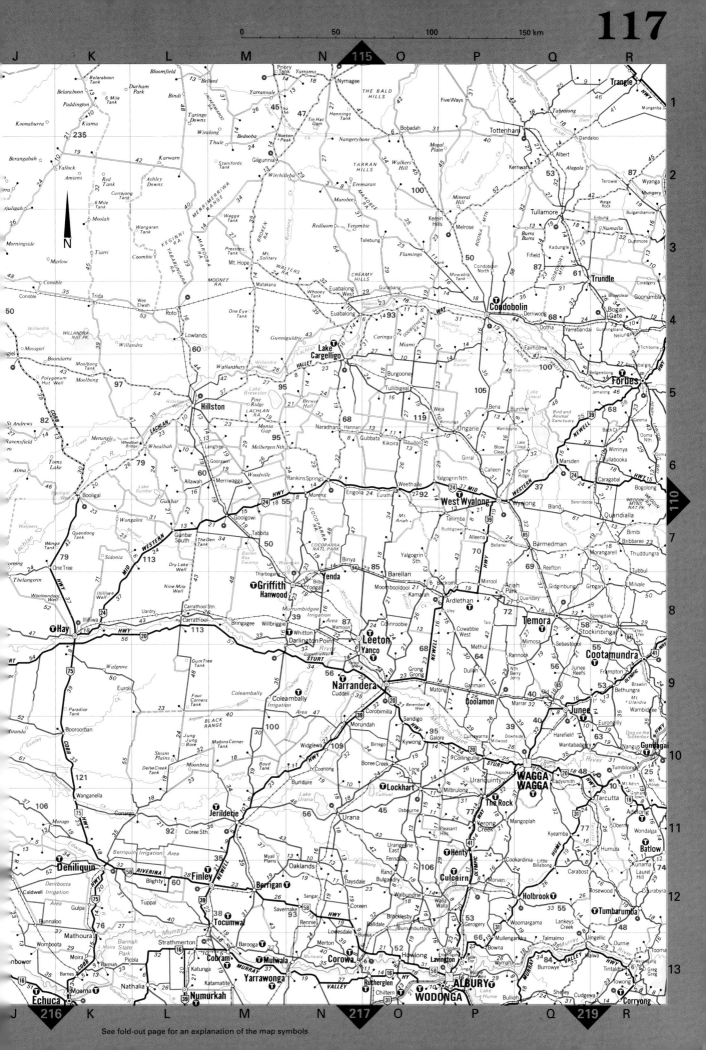

AUSTRALIAN CAPITAL TERRITORY

The Capital State

The ACT is a 250 000-hectare area which has an air of spaciousness and grace enhanced by the beautiful valley of the Molonglo River and the surrounding hills, mountains and pastureland, typical of eastern rural Australia. It is surrounded by New South Wales and lies roughly halfway between Sydney and Melbourne. The ACT was created by the Commonwealth Constitution Act of 1901 when the Commonwealth of Australia was inaugurated: a nation was formed from the six colonies. One of the provisions of the Act was that the seat of government should be on land vested in the Commonwealth. Nine years of prolonged wrangling followed, as two Royal Commissions and parliamentary committees considered the various claims of established towns and cities to be the federal capital, before the location of the new territory and the site for the new city was decided. In addition the area of Jervis Bay was ceded to the Commonwealth to provide a seaport for the nation's capital. Melbourne was the provisional seat of government until 1927 when a temporary building was erected in Canberra. This building was used until 1988 when the new House of Parliament was completed.

Canberra, Australia's modern capital city, was built on an undulating plain in an amphitheatre of the Australian Alps. The Molonglo River, a tributary of the Murrumbidgee, runs through the city and was dammed in 1964 to create Lake Burley Griffin, around which Canberra has been developed.

It is one of the world's best-known fully-planned cities and over the last sixty years has become an increasing source of pride and interest for Australians and for overseas visitors. Its impressive public buildings, its areas of parkland and bush reserves, its leafy suburbs and broad tree-lined streets have resulted from brilliant planning by its architect, Walter Burley Griffin, and from care and pride taken in its development over the years. Its architecture and its atmosphere are unique and stimulating in that there is so little that is more than fifty years old. Because of this the city exudes an air of being contrived and self-conscious, but it contains so much that will educate, absorb and stimulate the visitor that this somewhat sterile quality is soon forgotten.

The land on which the city is sited was first discovered in 1820 by a party of explorers led by Charles Throsby Smith. The area became known as Limestone Plains and was destined for settlement as grazing property. The first white settler, Joshua Moore, took up a thousand acres of land on the Murrumbidgee River in 1824 and named his property Canberry, an Aboriginal word meaning 'meeting place'. A year later Robert Campbell, a wealthy Sydney merchant, took up 4000 acres of land which formed the first part of the Duntroon estate.

When the land on which the city is now built was acquired by the Commonwealth Government in 1911, it contained only two small villages.

Construction of the first public buildings started in 1913, and in 1914 a rail service was opened between Sydney and the new capital. The Depression and World War II slowed building construction, but the rate of development has been spectacular since the mid-1950s and the population is now over 285 000.

There are four distinct seasons: a warm spring, a hot dry summer, a brilliant cool autumn, and a cold winter with occasional snow. Perhaps the best time to visit the ACT is in the autumn, when there is a magnificent display of golden foliage. Over two million Australian and overseas visitors come to the ACT each year.

The High Court

The Telecommunications Tower reflected in Lake Burley Griffin

CANBERRA

The Nation's Capital

As well as being Australia's capital, Canberra is a model city. Its unique concentric circular streets, planted with more than ten million trees and shrubs, are set graciously on the shores of the man-made Lake Burley Griffin. Driving in Canberra can be confusing; it is wise to study a map before beginning to tour.

The old Parliament House, completed in 1927, a number of government department buildings and hostels for public servants were among the first buildings in the national capital. They are now dwarfed by the grand buildings of later development which have turned Canberra into a gleaming showplace.

There are a number of lookouts on the surrounding hills which give superb views of the city. The 195-metre **Telecom Tower** on Black Mountain is the highest. **Mount Ainslie** offers fine views of central Canberra and Lake Burley Griffin. **Red Hill** overlooks Parliament House, South Canberra and the Woden Valley. **Mount Pleasant** has memorials to the Royal Regiment of Australian Artillery and the Royal Australian Armoured Corps at its summit.

The city took on a new character in 1964 when Lake Burley Griffin was created. The shoreline totals 35 kilometres and the lake has become popular for rowing, sailing and fishing.

In recent years Canberra has spread outwards into the plains, with satellite towns at Belconnen, Woden, Tuggeranong, Weston Creek and Gungahlin, but the focus still remains on the city centre and the modern architectural development around Lake Burley Griffin.

Black Mountain, close to the city centre and the shore of the lake, is topped by a telecommunications tower, which has public viewing galleries and a revolving restaurant. On the lower slopes of Black Mountain are Canberra's **Botanic Gardens**. They follow Walter Burley Griffin's original plan for a garden devoted to plants and trees native to Australia. The superbly laid-out gardens have arrowed walks, which allow for varying degrees of

The imposing Anzac Parade

stamina, and take visitors through areas of foliage indigenous to various Australian regions. A highlight is the rainforest area, where a misting system has been installed to create simulated rainforest conditions. The **Australian Institute of Sport** is on the edge of Black Mountain Reserve in **Bruce**. Tours of the institute's network of indoor and outdoor training facilities and stadiums are conducted daily.

Most of Canberra's major buildings lie within a triangle formed by **Constitution**, **Commonwealth** and **Kings Avenues**, with Capital Hill at the apex and the central business district on the northern corner. Standing aloft on Capital Hill is the new **Parliament House**, topped by its massive flagpole. A grassed walkway forms the roof of Parliament House and provides visitors with splendid views of Canberra. In front is the **old Parliament House**; open to the public.

A new attraction in Constitution Avenue is the **Canberra Casino** at the Na-

tional Convention Centre, which opened in late 1992.

On the southern foreshore of **Lake Burley Griffin** is the **Australian National Gallery**, which houses an outstanding collection of modern and post-modern art, including a wide representation of Australian painters. In the grounds surrounding the gallery, works by Australian and international sculptors are placed in a landscape setting of native trees and plants. The gallery has a restaurant which overlooks the lake. A footbridge connects the National Gallery and the **High Court of Australia**, the nation's final court of appeal. The court's lofty public gallery is encircled by open ramps that lead off to the courts and it features murals by Jan Senbergs that reflect the history, functions and operations of the High Court.

Further along the foreshore is the **National Library**, which contains over five million books, as well as newspapers, periodicals, films, documents and photographs. The foyer features three magnificent tapestries woven with Australian wool in Aubusson, France, and superb stained-glass windows, the work of the Australian artist Leonard French.

Also on the foreshore of the lake between the National Library and the High Court is the **National Science and Technology Centre** in King Edward Terrace. The Centre features an excellent interactive 'hands-on' science display where simple do-it-yourself experiments and explanations make the understanding of everyday scientific principles easy. Adults and children alike are enthralled for hours by the hundreds of exhibits in the five galleries ('0011-OTC', Microcosm, Forces, Visions and Waves). Further south of the lake is the **Canberra Railway Museum**, which has Australia's oldest working steam locomotive (built in 1878), as well as four other engines and forty carriages.

Lake Burley Griffin is the centrepiece of Canberra. On the lake are the **Carillon**, a three-column belltower which

Hotels
Capital Parkroyal
1 Binara St, Canberra City
(06) 247 8999
The Hyatt
Commonwealth Ave, Yarralumla
(06) 270 1234
Lakeside Hotel
London Circuit, Acton
(06) 247 6244
The Pavilion
Cnr Canberra Ave and National Circuit, Forrest
(06) 295 3144

Family and Budget
Canberra City Motor Inn
74 Northbourne Ave, Braddon
(06) 249 6911
Eagle Hawk Hill Resort
Federal Hwy, Sutton
(06) 241 6033
Heritage Motor Inn
203 Goyder St, Narrabundah
(06) 295 2944
Macquarie Private Hotel
18 National Circuit, Barton
(06) 273 2325

Motel Groups: Bookings
Flag (008) 01 1177
Best Western (008) 22 2166
Travelodge (008) 22 2446

This list is for information only; inclusion is not necessarily a recommendation.

cruises of the lake are available, and also occasional inspections of the Murray paddlesteamer *Enterprise*. Paddle-boats, wind-surfers and sailing boats also can be hired. Hot-air ballooning is popular throughout the year, and during the **Canberra Festival** in March and the **Floriade**, Canberra's Spring Festival, a fleet of balloons take flight each morning. Although the **National Museum of Australia** is still in the planning stage, its Yarramundi Visitor Centre off Lady Denman Drive on the shores of the lake features a model and plans of the project, objects from the museum's extensive collections, a viewing platform and a theatrette. The **National Aquarium**, further along Lady Denman Drive near Scrivener Dam, has over sixty display tanks containing marine life from giant sharks to tiny reef fish.

Imposing **Anzac Parade** stretches from the northern side of the lake to the outstanding **Australian War Memorial,** one of Australia's most frequently visited attractions. The War Memorial houses a huge collection of relics, models and paintings from all theatres of war. Its cloisters, pool of reflection, hall of memory and many galleries of war relics provide an unforgettable experience. An interesting walk to the summit of **Mount Ainslie** starts from the picnic grounds behind the War Memorial.

Another distinctive landmark in Canberra is the **Academy of Science**, situated in Gordon Street, **Acton**. Its copper-covered dome rests on arches set in a circular pool. Nearby, the **National Film and Sound Archive** in McCoy Circuit displays movie memorabilia and has public screenings from its collection of historic films, radio and television programs. Also at Acton is the **Australian National University**, set in 145 hectares of landscaped gardens.

Diplomatic missions bring an interesting international flavour to the city's architecture. It is well worth driving around the suburb of Yarralumla to view the many embassy buildings. The official residence of Australia's Governor-General is on Dunrossil Drive at Yarralumla. In **Deakin**, on the corner of Adelaide Avenue and National Circuit, is the **Prime Minister's Lodge**, the official residence of the Australian Prime Minister. The **Royal Australian Mint** in Denison Street, Deakin, has plate-glass windows in its visitors' gallery, allowing excellent views of the money-making process.

Despite the gleaming modern style of the city of Canberra, there are still interesting vestiges of the old Limestone Plains settlement which existed before the city was developed. In Campbell the sandstone homestead of the **Duntroon estate**, now the Officer's Mess at Duntroon Royal Military College, is the finest old house in the ACT. The single-storey part of the house was built in 1833 and the two-storey extension was completed in 1856. Tours of the **Australian Defence Force Academy** and the **Royal Military College** are available.

The **Church of St John the Baptist** off Anzac Park dates back to 1841 and its tombstones and other memorials provide

was a gift from the British Government to mark Canberra's Jubilee; the Captain Cook Memorial, a towering 150-metre water jet and terrestrial globe on the foreshore; and the Canberra Planning Exhibition at Regatta Point, which has a pavilion with exhibits showing Canberra's development. Overlooking the lake is the striking Australian–American Memorial, which celebrates America's contribution to Australia's defence during World War II.

The lake is surrounded by parklands, most with picnic facilities. One of the largest is **Commonwealth Park** on the northern foreshore, with its wading pools and cherry-tree grove. Another lakeside park is **Weston Park**, which features superb conifer trees, a miniature train, a maze and a playground for able and disabled children. Cycling is extremely popular in Canberra; there are more than 200 kilometres of cycle paths. It is possible to cycle around the complete perimeter of the lake. Bikes can be hired near the ferry terminal. Sightseeing

Autumn colours, Brisbane Avenue

Canberra cityscape from Mount Ainslie

opposite top: View over Lake Burley Griffin
opposite below left: Blundell's farmhouse
opposite below right: Australian War Memorial

a record of much of the area's early history. The adjacent schoolhouse containing relics of this history is regularly open to visitors. Many of the stained-glass windows of St John's Church commemorate members of the pioneer families, including Robert Campbell, the founder of Duntroon estate. **Blundell's farmhouse** on the northern shore of the lake was built in 1858 by Campbell for his ploughman and has been furnished by the Canberra and District Historical Society with pieces contemporary to the district's early history.

The **Central Business District** for Canberra is situated around London Circuit at the end of Commonwealth Avenue. **Civic Centre** is the major retail area. At the head of the **Civic Square** is the **Canberra Theatre Centre** and nearby in **Petrie Plaza** is the old St Kilda merry-go-round, a favourite with children. The **General Post Office** in Alinga Street displays Australia's largest and most valuable collection of stamps. To see as many of the above attractions as possible, the **Canberra Explorer** bus service runs every hour, seven days a week, around a 25-km route with 19 stops. Leave the bus anytime and reboard or take the full hour tour.

Around Canberra too there are many attractions. **Cockington Green** on the Barton Highway, 9 kilometres north of the city, is a quaint miniature English village (named after Cockington in Devon, UK). Adjacent is the historic village of **Ginninderra**, featuring craft studios, an art gallery, shops and a restaurant. Directly opposite is Australia's finest collection of opals in the **Australian Opal and Gemstone Museum**, on the Barton Highway between Gold Creek Road and Northbourne Avenue. Further north off the Federal Highway is **Rehwinkel's Animal Park**, popular for its Australian fauna collection displayed in a natural bushland setting.

At the **Tidbinbilla Nature Reserve**, 40 kilometres south-west of the city, an area of more than 5000 hectares has been developed to enable visitors to see Australian flora and fauna in natural surroundings. Nearby is the **Corin Forest Recreation Area**, with a one-kilometre alpine slide, bushwalking, and skiing in winter. Another favourite spot is the **Cotter Dam** and Reserve, 22 kilometres west of the city, where there are pleasant picnic and camping areas, a restaurant, river swimming and a children's playground. Nearby is the **Mount Stromlo Observatory**, its large silver domes and buildings housing the huge

telescope of the Department of Astronomy of the Australian National University. Further south at Tidbinbilla, **Canberra Space Centre**, a deep-space tracking station, features spacecraft models and audio-visual presentations. It is operated by the Department of Science for the US National Aeronautics and Space Administration.

The historic homestead **Lanyon**, 30 kilometres south of the city, enjoys the National Trust's highest classification. Set in landscaped gardens and parklands on the banks of the Murrumbidgee River, Lanyon serves as a reminder of nineteenth-century rural living. As well there is a gallery housing a collection of Sidney Nolan paintings. Further south and also on the Murrumbidgee River is the historic **Cuppacumbalong** homestead with its cottages, outbuildings and private cemetery. A craft centre, restaurant, picnic areas and river swimming are features.

For further information on Canberra and the ACT, contact the **ACT Tourism Commission**, Visitors Information Centre, Northbourne Ave, Dickson; (06) 205 0044.

TOURS FROM CANBERRA

Although Canberra is primarily urban, the Australian bush is only minutes away from the city centre. A leisurely drive takes the visitor to the heart of the Snowy Mountains in the south or to the picturesque coastal resorts in the east.

Bungendore and Braidwood, 35 km and 90 km from Canberra via the Kings Highway

This is a popular drive with the locals, particularly on Sundays. The route passes Lake George, which mysteriously empties periodically. At Bungendore, the Village Square features a historic re-creation from the 1850s telling the story of a local bushranger. The entire town of Braidwood is classified by the National Trust. Antique and art and craft shops, museums and restaurants are found in many of the town's lovely old sandstone buildings.

Batemans Bay, 150 km from Canberra via the Kings Highway

This popular resort is at the mouth of the Clyde River. Of particular interest are the penguins and other birds at Tollgate Island Wildlife Reserve. In the area are many picturesque coastal resorts and the old gold-mining towns of Mogo and Araluen.

Snowy Mountains region

The Snowy Mountains, 228 km from Canberra via the Monaro and Snowy Mountains Highways

The Snowy Mountains, centre of the world-famous hydro-electric scheme, is an all-year-round resort and tourist area. Thredbo is the centre of activity during the ski season. Lake Eucumbene is popular for water sports and trout fishing.

Jervis Bay, 285 km from Canberra via the Kings and Princes Highways

This fine natural port has never been developed commercially. It was the site of the Royal Australian Navy Training College, established in 1915. In that year its jurisdiction was transferred from New South Wales to the ACT, to give the federal capital sea access. Fifteen years later the Naval College was transferred to Flinders in Victoria; in 1958 the Navy returned to Jervis Bay. Of particular interest in the area are several pleasant holiday resorts, ideal for swimming, fishing, boating and bushwalking.

Namadgi National Park, 30 km from Canberra via the Tuggeranong Parkway and Tharwa Drive to Tharwa

This park, the most northerly alpine environment in Australia, covers some 40 per cent of the ACT. The special qualities of remoteness and rugged beauty that make up a wilderness are evident in the area surrounding Bimberi Peak (1911 m), the park's highest point.

Public access roads within the park pass through majestic mountain scenery. Picnic areas, some with toilets and barbecues, are located along most roads. The pleasant bushland settings at Mt Clear and Orroral are ideal for low-key camping. Much of Namadgi's attractions lie beyond its main roads and picnic areas. Over 150 km of marked walking tracks allow further exploration. Bushwalkers who venture into Namadgi's more remote parts reap some of the park's greatest rewards. Namadgi streams attract trout fishermen, horseriding is permitted in certain areas and cross-country skiing is possible when snow conditions permit.

Maps of Australian Capital Territory

Location Map

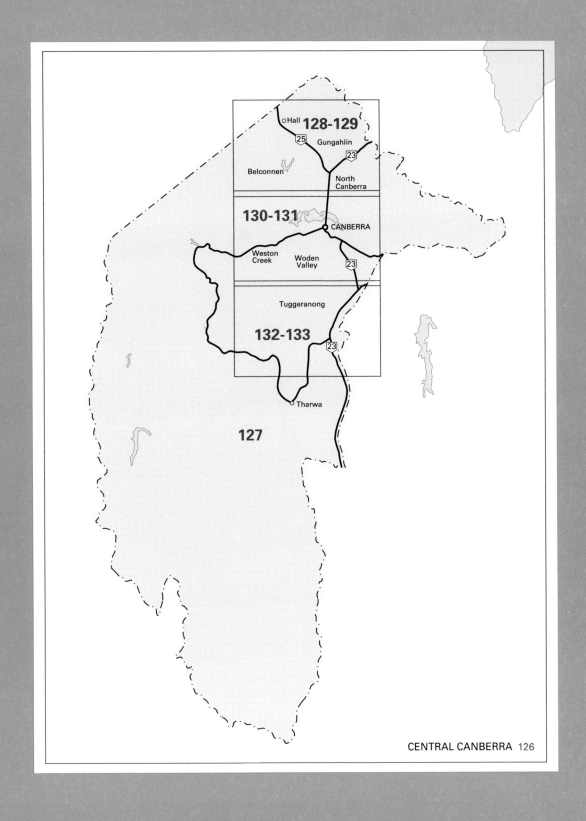

Hall

128-129

25 Gungahlin

23

Belconnen

North
Canberra

130-131

CANBERRA

Weston
Creek

Woden
Valley

23

Tuggeranong

132-133

23

Tharwa

127

CENTRAL CANBERRA 126

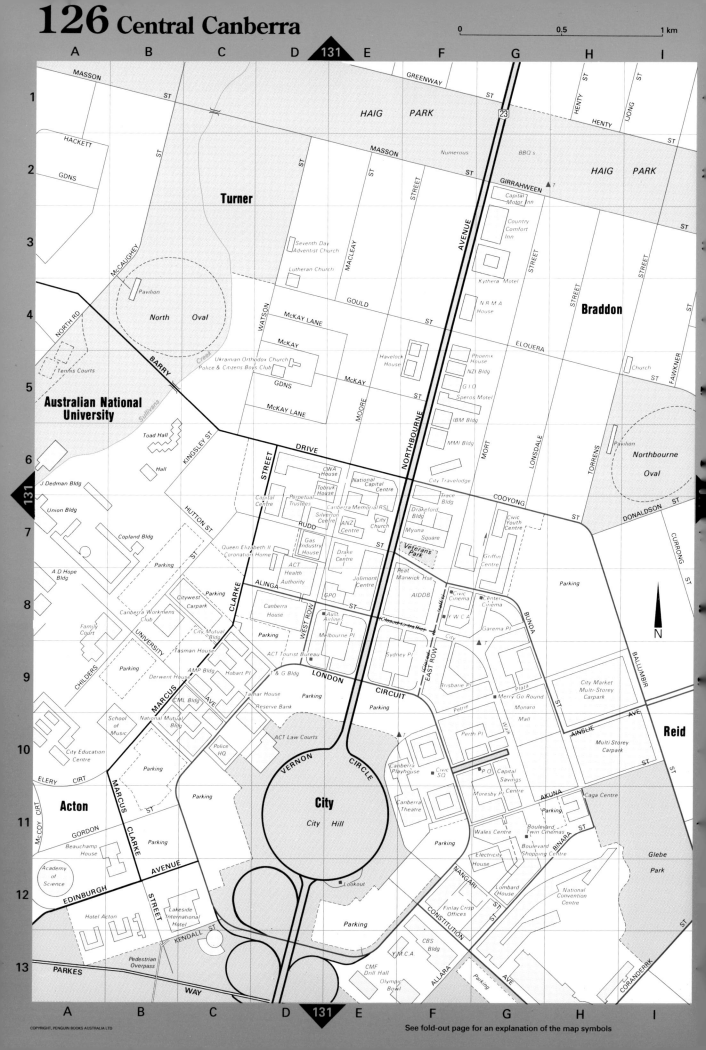

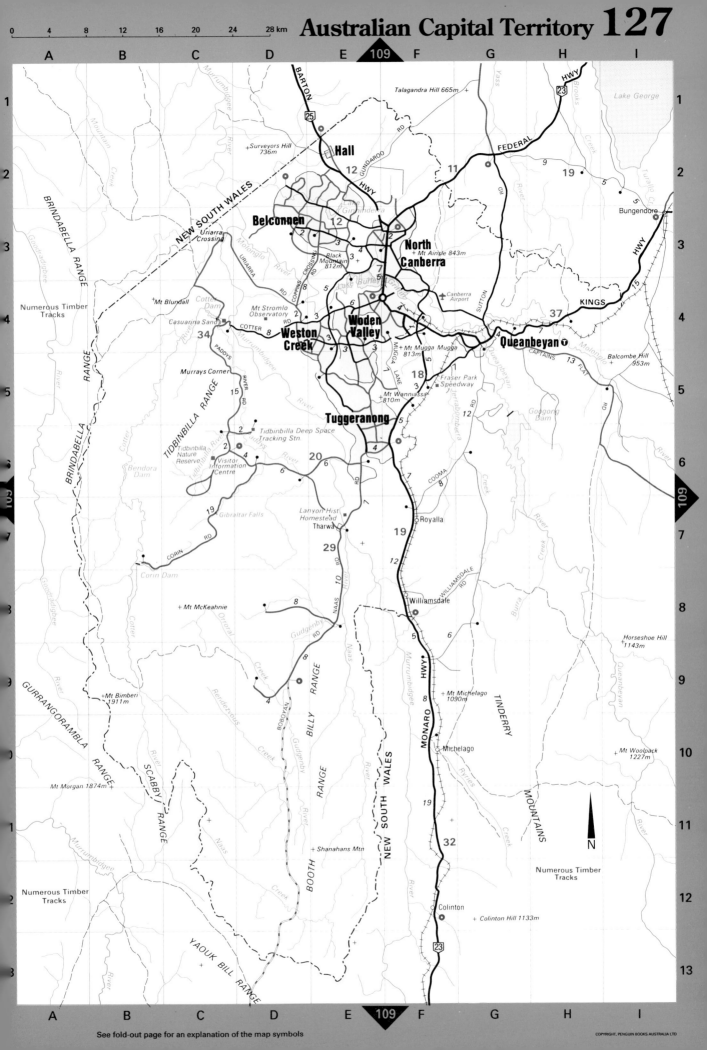

0   4   8   12   16   20   24   28 km

A   B   C   D   E   **109**   F   G   H   I

109

Lake George

BARTON HWY

25

Talagandra Hill 665m

HWY

23

Brooks

Yass

FEDERAL

RD

Surveyors Hill
736m

□ **Hall**

12   11   9   19   5   5

GUNDAROO HWY

Belconnen

Lake
Ginninderra

12

NEW SOUTH WALES

Uriarra
Crossing

2   3   4

Bungendore

HWY

15

URIARRA

Molonglo River

COPPINS CROSSING RD

Black
Mountain
812m

3   4   +Mt Ainslie 843m

**North
Canberra**

KINGS

5

Lake Burley Griffin

7

Canberra
Airport

SUTTON

37

Mt Blundall

Cotter
Dam

Mt Stromlo
Observatory

2   3   5   6

5   4

Queanbeyan

13   Balcombe Hill
953m

Numerous Timber
Tracks

Casuarina Sands

COTTER

34   8

**Weston
Creek**

3   3

**Woden
Valley**

3

4   +Mt Mugga Mugga
813m

CAPTAINS FLAT

Molonglo River

BRINDABELLA RANGE

PADDYS

Murrays Corner

RIVER RD

15

MUGGA LANE

7   18

Jerrabombera

Fraser Park
Speedway

12

Googong
Dam

RD

Tidbinbilla Deep Space
Tracking Stn.

2

Tuggeranong

Mt Wanniassa
810m

5

RD

TIDBINBILLA RANGE

2

Tidbinbilla
Nature
Reserve

Visitor
Information
Centre

4

20   6

6

4

7

COOMA

8

RIVER RD

Paddys River

Bendora
Dam

19   Gibraltar Falls

Lanyon Hist
Homestead
Tharwa

7

29

Royalla

19

Creek

CORIN RD

Corin Dam

Mt McKeahnie

8

NAAS RD

10

12

WILLIAMSDALE RD

Butts Creek

Horseshoe Hill
1143m

GURRANGORAMBLA RANGE

Mt Bimberi
1911m

8

Gudgenby RD

4

Williamsdale

5   6

MONARO HWY

Mt Michelago
1090m

TINDERRY

Mt Woolpack
1227m

Mt Morgan 1874m

SCABBY RANGE

Murrumbidgee River

Naas Creek

BOOYAN

Gudgenby River

BILLY RANGE

SEEN

8

8

Michelago

19

MOUNTAINS

N

Numerous Timber
Tracks

Shanahans Mtn

NEW SOUTH WALES

32

Colinton

Colinton Hill 1133m

YAOUK BILL RANGE

23

A   B   C   D   E   **109**   F   G   H   I

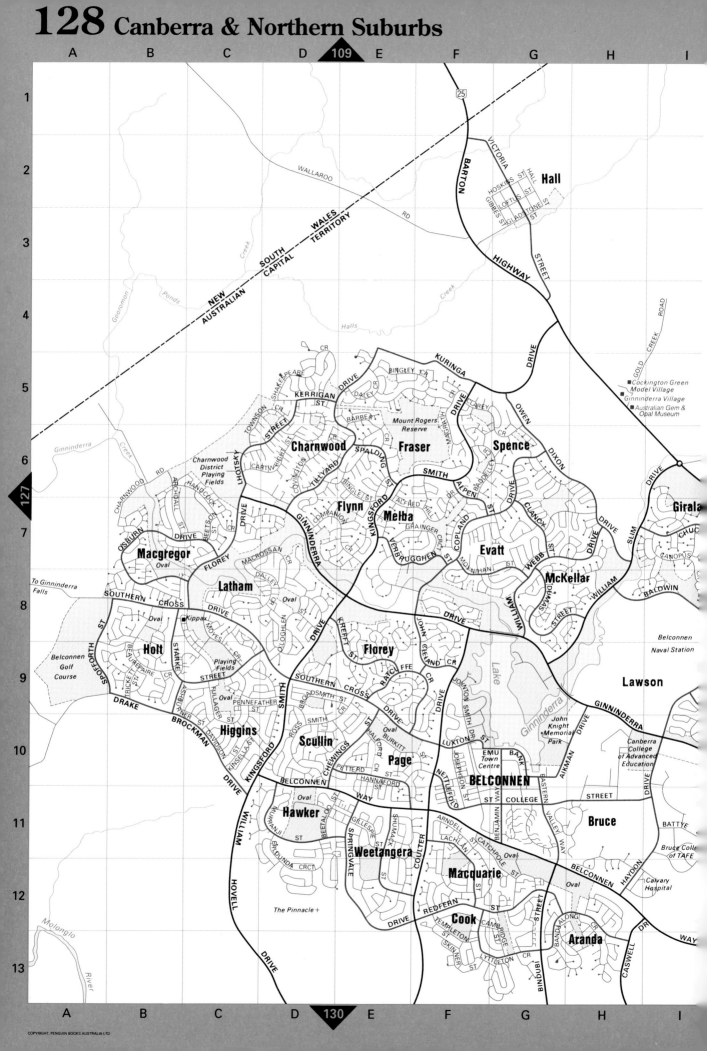

A B C D ▼ 109 E F G H I

1
2
3
4
5
6
7
8
9
10
11
12
13

▶ 127

WALLAROO

Creek

NEW SOUTH WALES
AUSTRALIAN CAPITAL TERRITORY

Gooromon Ponds

Creek

Ginninderra Creek

Halls

Creek

To Ginninderra Falls

Molonglo River

BARTON HIGHWAY

VICTORIA ST
HOSKINS ST
GIBBES ST
LOFTUS ST
HALL ST
GLADSTONE ST

Hall

STREET

RD

25

DRIVE

GOLD CREEK ROAD

■ Cockington Green
Model Village
■ Ginninderra Village
■ Australian Gem &
Opal Museum

KURINGA
BINGLEY
SHAKESPEARE
KERRIGAN ST
DALEY
BARBER
Mount Rogers
Reserve
TOWNSON
CARTWRIGHT
COVINGTON
TILLYARD
SPALDING ST
CLAREY
HALSWORTH
OWEN
DIXON
DRIVE

Charnwood **Fraser** **Spence**

CR
LHOTSKY
STREET
CR
ARCHDALL
HANDCOCK
BEETSON ST
DRIVE
SMITH
BINGLE ST
ALFRED
HILL
ALPEN
BADDELEY
CLANCY ST
WEBB ST
DRIVE

Flynn **Melba** **Evatt** **McKellar**

GIRALA
CHUC
CANOPUS
SLIM DRIVE
BALDWIN

OSBURN
FLOREY
COMPANION
KINGSFORD
VERBRUGGHEN
GRAINGER
CRCT
COPLAND
MOLNIHAN
DUMAS STREET

Macgregor Oval

MACROSSAN CR

Latham

DALLEY
OLOGHLEN ST
Oval
KRERT
DRIVE

JOHN CLELAND CR
WILLIAM
WILLIAM

SOUTHERN CROSS DRIVE
Kippax

SPOFFORTH ST
Belconnen
Golf
Course

Holt
BEAUREPAIRE
TRICKETT
STARKE
ASHBURNER ST
DAVIDSON ST
KINSELLA ST
Playing
Fields
STREET
FULLAGER
Oval
PENNEFATHER ST

DRAKE
BROCKMAN
KINGSFORD

Higgins

ROSS
SMITH
BROADSMITH ST

SOUTHERN CROSS DRIVE

Florey

RATCLIFFE
CR

DRIVE

Scullin

CHEWINGS
PETTERD
HALFORD CR
BURKITT
Oval
HANNAFORD ST

Page

BELCONNEN WAY

JOHN CLELAND CR
JOINTON SMITH DR
LUXTON DR
JOSEPHSON ST
NETTLEFOLD ST
EMU
Town
Centre
BANK

BELCONNEN

COLLEGE

Lake
Ginninderra

John
Knight
Memorial
Park

GINNINDERRA DRIVE

Belconnen
Naval Station

Lawson

AIKMAN DRIVE
EASTERN
VALLEY WAY

Canberra
College
of Advanced
Education

STREET

Bruce

BATTYE
Bruce College
of TAFE

BELCONNEN

Calvary
Hospital

HOVELL DRIVE
WILLIAM

Hawker
MURRANJI ST
BEETALOO
ERLDUNDA CRCT
GILLESPIE ST
SHUMACK ST
SPRINGVALE DRIVE

Weetangera

COULTER
ARNDELL
LACHLAN ST
CATCHPOLE
BENJAMIN WAY
Oval

Macquarie

CAMBRIDGE ST
REDFERN ST

Cook

TEMPLETON
SKINNER ST
LYTTLETON ST
BINDUBI ST

BANDJALONG CR

Aranda

CASWELL DR
HAYDON
WAY

The Pinnacle +

A B C D ▼ 130 E F G H I

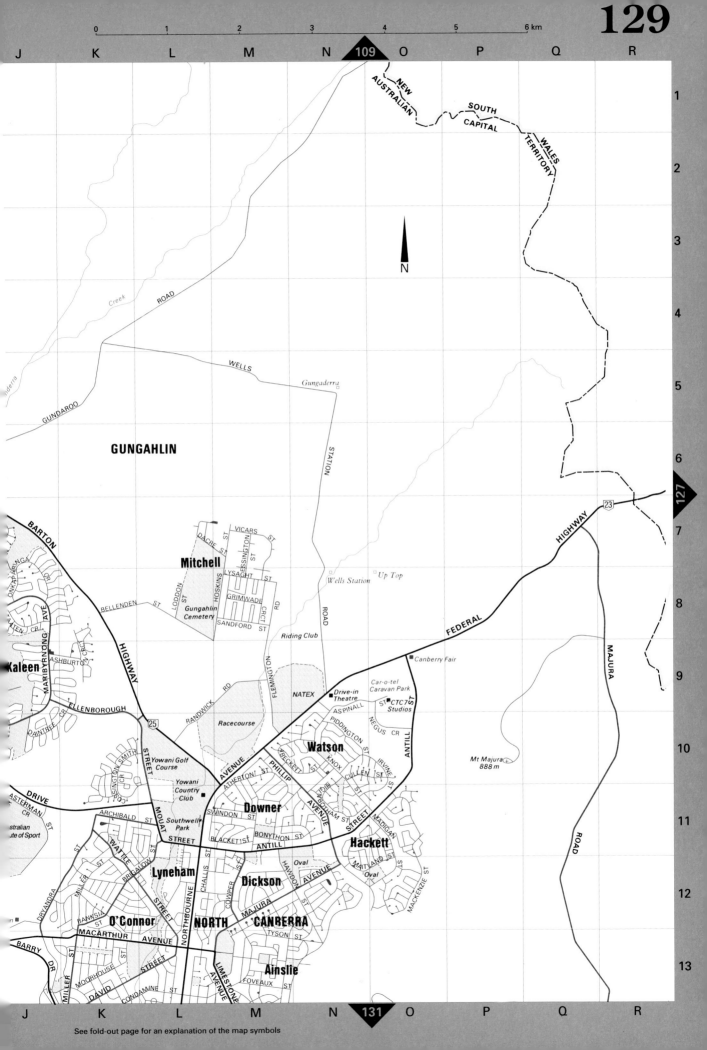

0 1 2 3 4 5 6 km

1

NEW
AUSTRALIAN
SOUTH
CAPITAL
WALES
TERRITORY

2

3

N

Creek ROAD

4

WELLS

Gungaderra

5

GUNDAROO

GUNGAHLIN

STATION

6

127

23

Ideira

BARTON

VICARS ST

DACRE ST

LYSAGHT ST

ESSINGTON ST

Mitchell

HIGHWAY

7

HOSKINS ST

LODDON ST

GRIMWADE CRCT

Gungahlin
Cemetery

SANDFORD ST

FEDERAL

HIGHWAY

MAJURA

8

ONKAPARINGA CR

ALLEN CR.

MARIBYRNONG AVE

BELLENDEN ST

RD

FLEMINGTON

Riding Club

Wells Station

Up Top

Kaleen

ASHBURTON CRCT

ELLENBOROUGH

25

RANDWICK

RD

NATEX

Drive-in
Theatre

Car-o-tel
Caravan Park

Canberry Fair

9

DAINTREE CR

Racecourse

CTC7
Studios

ANTILL ST

NEGUS CR

ASPINALL

PIDDINGTON ST

Mt Majura
888 m

10

DRIVE

MASTERMAN CR

ST

Yowani Golf
Course

AVENUE

ATHERTON ST

BECKETT ST

PHILLIP

Watson

KNOX ST

CULLEN ST

IRVINE ST

MADIGAN

ROAD

australian
ute of Sport

ARCHIBALD ST

SMITH ST

COLLISON ST

STREET

MOUAT

Yowani
Country
Club

Southwell
Park

SWINDON

Downer

AVENUE

OTHAM ST

STREET

11

WATTLE ST

BRIGALOW ST

STREET

MILLER ST

BANKSIA ST

DRYANDRA ST

O'Connor

BARRY DR

MILLER ST

MACARTHUR

MOORHOUSE ST

DAVID ST

CONDAMINE ST

Lyneham

CHALLIS ST

NORTHBOURNE

ARCHIBALD ST

BLACKET ST

BONYTHON ST

ANTILL

Dickson

COWPER ST

MAJURA

AVENUE

NORTH CANBERRA

AVENUE

TYSON ST

Ainslie

LIMESTONE AVENUE

FOVEAUX ST

HAWDON ST

Oval
Oval

Hackett

MAITLAND ST

MACKENZIE ST

12

13

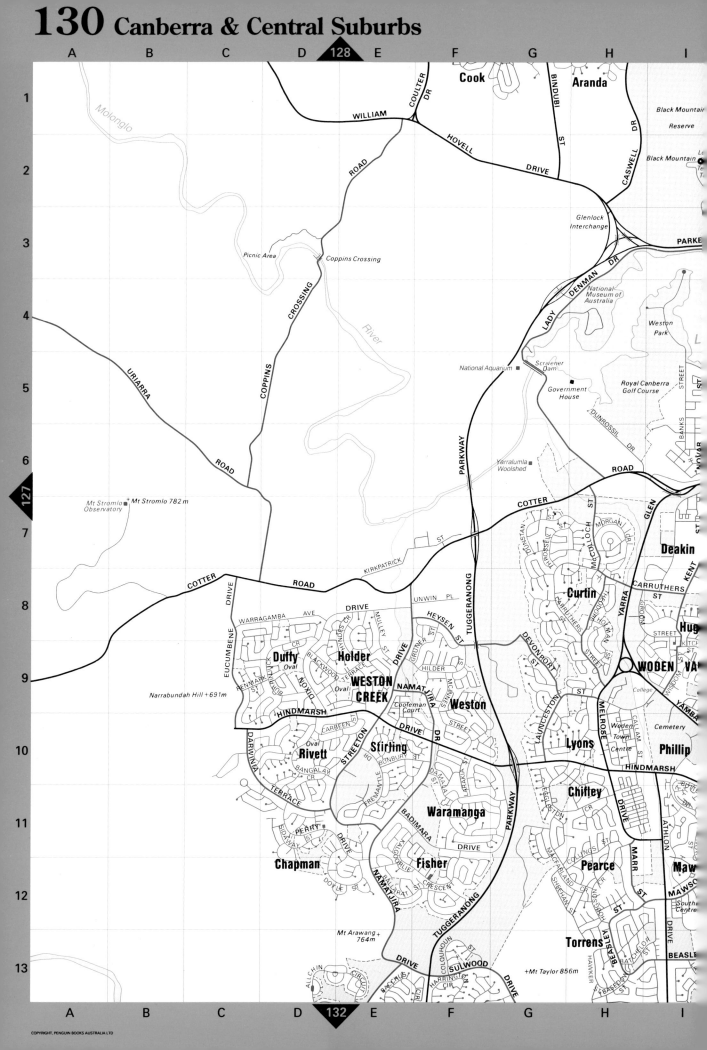

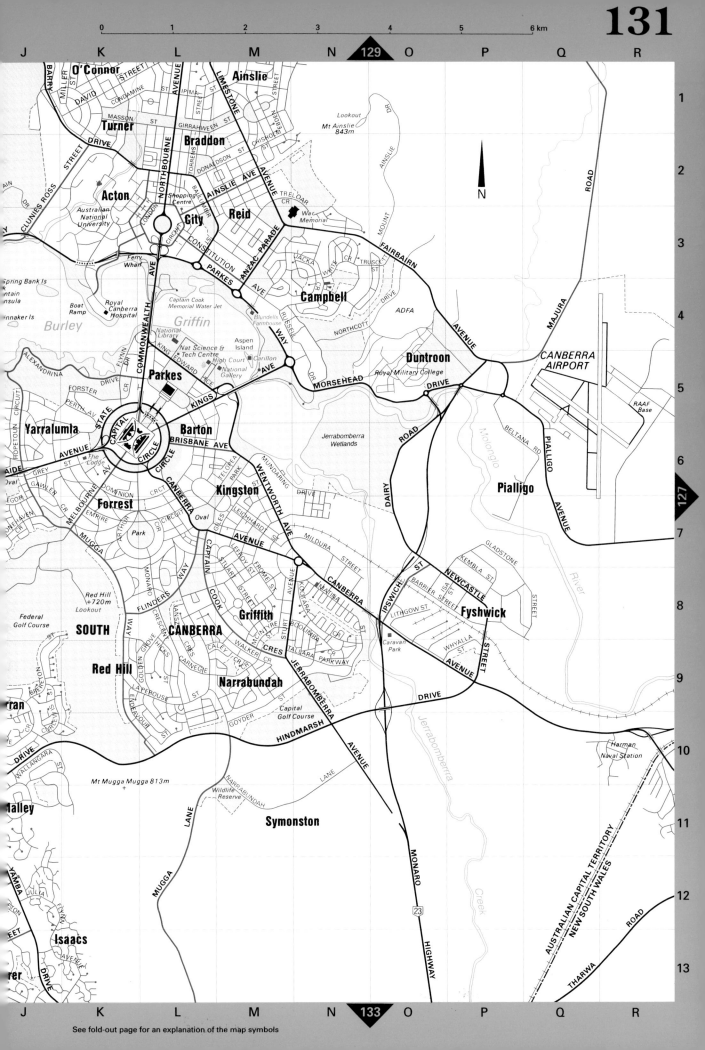

0   1   2   3   4   5   6 km

J   K   L   M   N   O   P   Q   R

1

O'Connor
BARRY
MILLER STREET
DAVID
CONDAMINE
ST
Turner
MASSON
ST
DRIVE

Ainslie
Braddon
IPIMA ST
GIRRAHWEEN
CHISHOLM ST
TORRENS
DONALDSON
BULL MAIN
BOOTH
Lookout
Mt Ainslie
843m

2

Acton
Shopping
Centre
Australian
National
University
City
Reid
NORTHBOURNE AVENUE
AINSLIE AVE
AINSLIE
AVENUE
LIMESTONE
AVENUE
TRELOAR
CR
War
Memorial
MOUNT
AINSLIE
DR

N

3

Ferry
Wharf
CONSTITUTION
PARKES
ANZAC PARADE
AVE
JACKA
CR
WHITE CR
TRUSCOTT
Campbell
ST
FAIRBAIRN
ROAD
MAJURA

4

Burley
Spring Bank Is
Capt Cook
Memorial Water Jet
Captain Cook
Memorial Water Jet
Royal
Canberra
Hospital
Boat
Ramp
Griffin
National
Library
Blundells
Farmhouse
Aspen Island
Nat Science &
Tech Centre
RUSSELL DRIVE
NORTHCOTT
ADFA
AVENUE
CANBERRA
AIRPORT

5

Alexandrina
DRIVE
COMMONWEALTH
FLYNN
KING EDWARD
High Court
National Gallery
Carillon
Parkes
KINGS
AVE
MORSEHEAD
DRIVE
Duntroon
Royal Military College
DRIVE
RAAF
Base

6

Yarralumla
STATE CIRCLE
CAPITAL CIRCLE
The Lodge
Barton
BRISBANE AVE
WENTWORTH
MUNDARING DRIVE
Jerrabomberra
Wetlands
DAIRY ROAD
Molonglo
BELTANA RD
PIALLIGO
Pialligo
PIALLIGO AVENUE

127

7

ADE
Oval
GREY ST
GAWLER
CR
MELBOURNE AVE
DOMINION
EMPIRE
CIR
ARTHUR
MUGGA
CANBERRA
CIRCUIT
Park
Forrest
Kingston
Oval
TELOPEA
PARK
GILES ST
LEICHHARDT ST
FROME ST
AVENUE
MILDURA
STREET
CANBERRA
River
GLADSTONE
KEMBLA ST

8

Red Hill
+720m
Lookout
Federal
Golf Course
SOUTH
CANBERRA
FLINDERS
WAY
COOK
CAPTAIN WAY
MONARO
CRES
ANZAC PARK
Griffith
McINTYRE
STURT
BOOLIMBA CR
MATINA ST
KOOTARA CR
Caravan
Park
IPSWICH
ST
LITHGOW ST
BARRIER STREET
NEWCASTLE STREET
Fyshwick
WHYALLA ST

9

fran
Red Hill
GOLDEN GROVE
HICKS
CARNEGIE
CALEY CR
WALKER CR
CRES
LAPEROUSE
ENDEAVOUR
Narrabundah
GOYDER
JERRABOMBERRA
AVENUE
DRIVE

10

DRIVE
NYALLANGARA ST
Mt Mugga Mugga 813m
NARRABUNDAH
LANE
Capital
Golf Course
HINDMARSH
LANE
Jerrabomberra
Harman
Naval Station

11

Malley
YAMBA
MUGGA
LANE
Wildlife
Reserve
Symonston
Creek
AUSTRALIAN CAPITAL TERRITORY
NEW SOUTH WALES

12

JULIA
FINN
Isaacs
MONARO
HIGHWAY
23
THARWA ROAD

13

J   K   L   M   N   O   P   Q   R

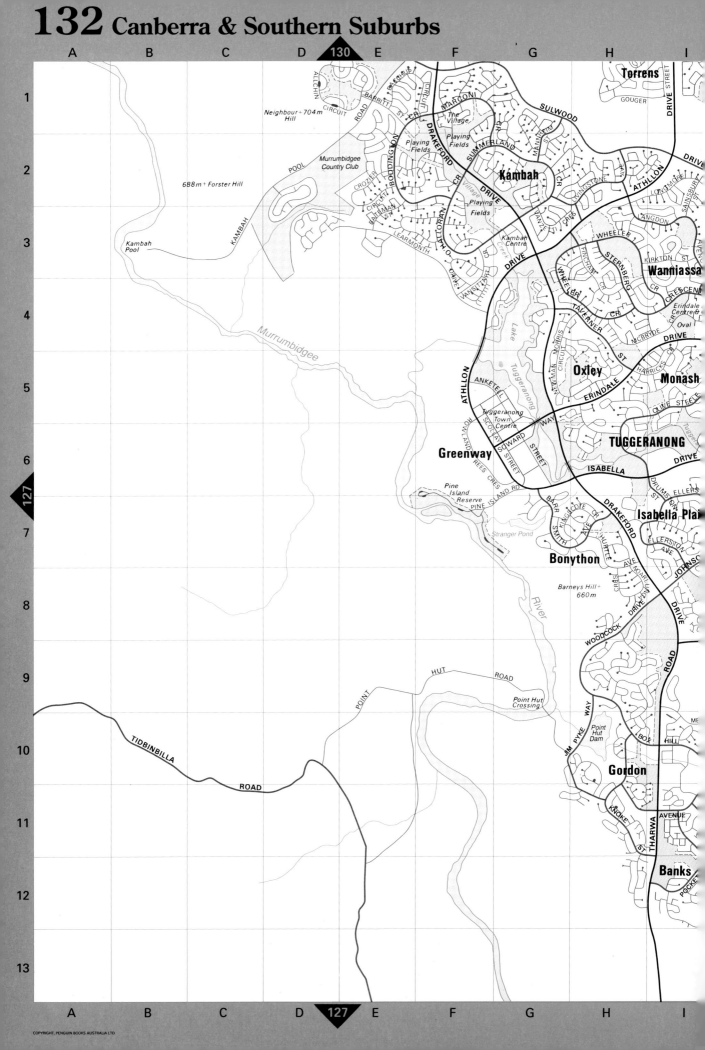

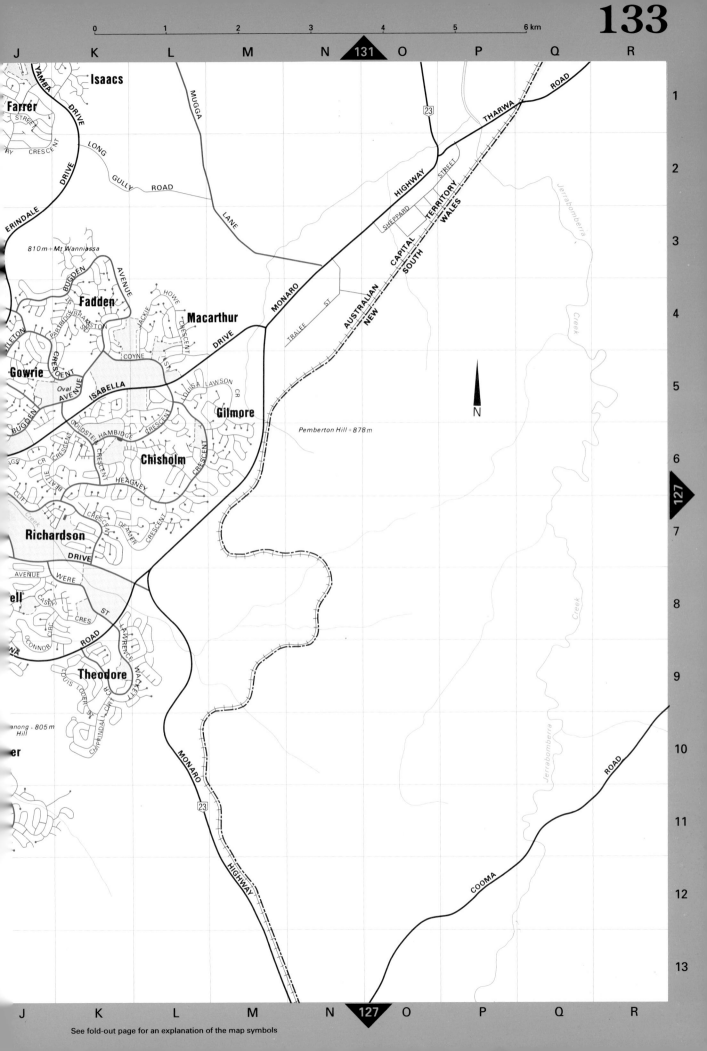

Isaacs

Farrer

YAMBA DRIVE

ERINDALE DRIVE

LONG GULLY ROAD

MUGGA LANE

810 m + Mt Wanniassa

BUGDEN AVENUE

Fadden

Macarthur

BRAMSTON ST

PATRIDGE ST

JACKIE ST

HOWE CRESCENT

COYNE ST

CRESCENT

ISABELLA DRIVE

MONARO DRIVE

TRALEE ST

HIGHWAY

SHEPPARD

STREET

TERRITORY

CAPITAL

SOUTH

WALES

AUSTRALIAN

NEW

23

THARWA ROAD

Jerrabomberra

Creek

Gowrie

Oval

ISABELLA AVENUE

BUGDEN

LOUISA LAWSON CR

Gilmore

GOLDSTEIN

HAMBIDGE CRESCENT

CRESCENT

CRESCENT

Chisholm

HEAGNEY CRESCENT

BLATTLE CR

CLIFF

Creek

Pemberton Hill + 878 m

N

▲127

Richardson

DRIVE

WERE ST

CRESCENT

DEAMER CRESCENT

CRESCENT

AVENUE

CASEY CRES

CIRC

OCONNOR

ROAD

LAWRENCE WACKETT

ell

NA

Theodore

LOUIS LODER ST

CHIRNDALL CIR

anong + 805 m Hill

er

MONARO

23

MONARO

HIGHWAY

Jerrabomberra

Creek

COOMA ROAD

VICTORIA

Garden State

Rose garden, Numurkah

Victoria is an ideal state for the motoring tourist. It is easy, during one day's drive, to explore mountain country, pastoral landscape and spectacular coastline, yet still arrive at your destination in time to watch the sunset.

Victoria's earliest explorers, of course, were from a pre-motor age. What they saw did little to arouse their enthusiasm. After an unsuccessful attempt at settlement in the Port Phillip area in 1803, it was not until 1834 that parties from Van Diemen's Land, searching for more arable land, settled along the south-west coast of Victoria. Their glowing reports prompted John Batman and John Fawkner to investigate the Port Phillip area. They liked what they saw and purchased land on opposite sides of the Yarra from Aboriginal tribes. The Colonial Office in London expressed disapproval of these transactions, but in those times possession was nine points of the law. A squatting colony grew up rapidly in the district and the new town was named Melbourne after the British prime minister of the day.

Nervous of inheriting the penal system of settlement, Victoria sought separation from New South Wales; it was granted in 1851. At about that time, gold was discovered near Ballarat and the state's population more than doubled within a year. Apart from a serious, but short-lived, setback caused by land speculation in the early 1890s, Victoria has gone from strength to strength ever since.

Today Victoria is the most closely settled and industrialised part of the nation, responsible for about one-third of the gross national product. Melbourne has been traditionally regarded as the 'financial capital' of the country.

Melbourne's inner areas are graced by spacious parks and street upon street of elegant and well-preserved Victorian and Edwardian architecture, contrasting strongly with modern tower blocks. Other attractions include the city's parks and gardens and its renowned retail shopping, theatres, restaurants and unusual theatre restaurants.

Beyond the city, the Dandenong Ranges, fifty kilometres to the east, are noted for their forests of eucalypts and graceful tree-ferns, their many established European-style gardens and an increasing number of good restaurants and galleries. Phillip Island, less than two hours' drive away, is famed for its unique fairy penguin parade as well as for its good surfing. To the south-east and south-west, the Mornington and Bellarine Peninsulas provide Melbourne with its seaside playgrounds, extremely popular during the summer months.

The weather can be unpredictable in Victoria, particularly along the coastal regions. Despite its rather volatile weather, however, the state enjoys a generally temperate climate. Spring, late summer and autumn provide the most settled and pleasant touring weather. The state's road system is good and penetrates to all but a few remote areas; much of the state can be reached easily in a day's driving.

Each of Victoria's five main geographical regions has its own special attraction. The central and western districts, due north and west of Melbourne, offer touring highlights such as the historic gold-rush areas, with well-preserved, attractive towns such as Bendigo, Castlemaine and Ballarat—which is always popular during its March Begonia Festival—and the Grampians, Victoria's most beautiful natural garden, particularly with its spring wildflowers. Travelling south from these impressive ranges brings you into the Western District, where rich grazing land is dotted with splendid old properties. No exploration of this region would be complete without a drive along the Great Ocean Road, which runs for 320 kilometres along the dramatic south-west coast. The spectacular rock formations in the Port Campbell National Park are without doubt its most imposing sights, but along its length there are excellent beaches and pleasant small resort towns.

The north-east high-country region has equally magnificent scenery and is dotted with well-patronised winter ski resorts. Although popular in spring and summer, this unspoiled region would hardly ever be described as crowded and the wildflowers, sweeping views and clear air can be enjoyed with a fair degree of solitude. Fishing, bushwalking and climbing are well provided for and, down in the foothills, the Eildon Reservoir and Fraser National Park area are popular for water sports.

Gippsland stretches to the south-east; it contains some of the state's most beautiful and varied country. Rolling pastures lead to densely wooded hill country, still relatively unpopulated and peaceful. National parks such as the Tarra-Bulga and the famous Wilsons Promontory Park, with its lush growth and secluded beaches, are all well worth visiting. The coastal region of Gippsland includes the Ninety Mile Beach bordering the Gippsland Lakes system, Australia's largest inland waterway network, and Croajingolong National Park, a wilderness area.

Following the Murray can be an interesting way of exploring Victoria's north. The river begins as a narrow, rapidly flowing alpine stream, and changes to a broad expanse near the aquatic playgrounds of Lakes Hume and Mulwala; it has water-bird and wildlife reserves and sandy river beaches and offers fascinating glimpses of life in the riverboat era at towns such as Echuca and Swan Hill. Perhaps the Murray best sums up the contrasting landscape which is Victoria, the Garden State.

The Jaws of Death, one of the attractions of the Grampians

MELBOURNE

World's Most Livable City

Australian Rules Grand Final, Melbourne Cricket Ground

At first glance Melbourne may look like any other modern city with its skyline chock-a-block with concrete and glass. However, if you look a little closer you'll find the real Melbourne: clanging trams, swanky boutiques, friendly taxi drivers, Australian Rules football, fickle weather, and 'BYOs' (restaurants to which you bring your own liquor) by the hundred. Add to this Melbourne's traditional virtues of tree-lined boulevards, glorious parks, elegant buildings and imposing Victorian churches and banks — and the Melbourne Cricket Ground — and you'll have some idea of the city.

In recent years it has become a polyglot society with its huge influx of migrants from many countries, particularly Greece. The city has one of the largest Greek-speaking populations in the world. This cosmopolitan influence is reflected in Melbourne's bustling markets, delicatessens and restaurants. Eating out has become one of the great Melbourne pastimes and the city and suburban restaurants give an opportunity to literally eat your way around the world; the food of almost every nation imaginable is available.

At the head of Port Phillip Bay and centred on the north bank of the Yarra River, Melbourne's population of over three million lives in the flat surrounding suburbs which stretch in all directions, particularly round the east coast of the bay right out to the blue hills of the Dandenongs.

Both John Batman and John Pascoe Fawkner were associated in the founding of Melbourne in 1835, and Melbourne soon entered a boom period with the discovery of gold in the state in 1851. The goldfields of Bendigo, Ballarat and Castlemaine attracted fortune-hunters from all over the world, and by 1861 Melbourne had become Australia's largest city. By the end of the century it was firmly established as the business and cultural centre of the colony.

Today Melbourne's traditional position as the financial and cultural centre of the nation has been challenged by Sydney, but it still has an unruffled elegance and style all its own. Melbourne was the only Australian capital to retain its network of pollution-free electric trams, and the clang of the old green thunderers adds a special flavour to the city. Many of these have been given a new lease of life after being decorated by leading artists, while others have been replaced by new trams and the light rail. The World Health Organisation has rated Melbourne as one of the least polluted cities of its size; Melbourne has also been acclaimed the world's most livable city.

Melbourne has a huge range of retail stores, and shopping in the city and in suburbs such as fashionable **South Yarra** is one of the joys of the city. Several other suburbs such as **Carlton**, **Prahran**, **Armadale**, **Toorak** and **Camberwell** rival the city centre with their retail stores and restaurants.

Melburnians are also great sports lovers and this is reflected in the huge crowds that attend cricket and Australian Rules football matches. A peculiarly Melbourne phenomenon is the 'football fever' which grips the city each year, with enthusiasm building up to mass hysteria on Grand Final day in September.

The **Melbourne Cricket Ground** is the venue for many international Test matches. Just outside the Members' entrance, the **Australian Gallery of Sport** celebrates Australian sporting history. The **Olympic Museum**, located in the

Melbourne skyline and parks

Gallery of Sport, houses memorabilia dating back to the first modern Olympics, held in Olympia in 1896.

Horse-racing is another popular Melbourne spectator sport and the **Melbourne Cup** at Flemington Racecourse brings Australia to a halt for three minutes each first Tuesday in November.

Melbourne's other main racecourses are at Caulfield, Moonee Valley and Sandown Park; the **Victorian Racing Museum** is at Caulfield Racecourse. The city's 3 1/2-week spring racing carnival runs from mid-October to early November. The annual **Moomba and Comedy Festival** in March and the annual **Melbourne International Festival of the Arts** in September are other outstanding events on the Melbourne calendar.

The **National Tennis Centre** at Flinders Park hosts the first leg of the international grand slam in January each year. The Centre Court with its unique retractable roof seats 16 000 people and is used also as a venue for entertainment extravaganzas. Tours of the city's top sporting venues are available through the Melbourne Sports Network.

For cyclists, there is a comprehensive network of trails throughout the city and suburbs. Skiers can practise all year round on a dry ski slope conveniently located at Ski Haus in the north-eastern suburb of **Ivanhoe**.

The **World Congress Centre** is on the corner of Flinders and Spencer Streets. Next door are the **Centra Melbourne**

Hotels
Como
630 Chapel St, South Yarra
(03) 824 0400
Grand Hyatt
123 Collins St, Melbourne
(03) 657 1234
Le Meridien Melbourne
495 Collins St, Melbourne
(03) 620 9111
Regent
25 Collins St, Melbourne
(03) 653 0000
Rockman's Regency
Cnr Exhibition and Lonsdale Sts,
Melbourne
(03) 662 3900
Windsor
103 Spring St, Melbourne
(03) 653 0653

Family and Budget
Lygon Lodge
220 Lygon St, Carlton
(03) 663 6633
City Limits
20 Little Bourke St, Melbourne
(03) 662 2544
Victoria
215 Little Collins St, Melbourne
(03) 653 0441
YWCA
489 Elizabeth St, Melbourne
(03) 329 5188
Motel Groups: Bookings
Flag (008) 01 1177
Best Western (008) 22 2166
Travelodge (008) 22 2446

This list is for information only; inclusion is not necessarily a recommendation.

on the Yarra hotel and the **World Trade Centre** which hosts international trade displays. Further along Flinders Street past the Banana Alley Vaults is the **Flinders Street Station** complex with its restaurants and shops. It is the main terminus for the suburban rail system. Melbourne's **Underground Rail Loop** has three stations located on the edge of the central business district. Above ground, the **City Explorer** tourist bus departs Flinders Street Station hourly, stopping at some major attractions. On the opposite banks of the river is the new Southgate development, which includes the **Sheraton Towers Southgate** hotel, shops and entertainment venues. To get a different view of Melbourne, take a river cruise on the Yarra, departing from the **Princes Walk Terminal**.

The city centre is compact, its wide streets laid out in an orderly grid system. Take a tram to the top of **Collins Street** and wander down — the street somehow epitomises Melbourne. At night, hundreds of small bud lights in the trees lining the street create a spectacular effect.

Looking down on Collins street, in Spring Street, is the elegant **Old Treasury Building**, which was built in 1853, and just down from Spring Street is the august **Melbourne Club**, mecca of Melbourne's Establishment. On the opposite side of the street on the Exhibition Street corner is **Collins Place**, a multi-storey complex which houses the **Regent Melbourne** in one of its high towers. Called 'the City within a City', many of the shops and boutiques in this complex are open all weekend. Another tall building, **Nauru House**, is diagonally opposite.

Continuing down the hill you will see fashionable boutiques and two old churches, the **Uniting Church** and **Scots Church**. Across the road the **Grand Hyatt** hotel complex has an interesting food hall and shopping plaza. Between Russell and Swanston Streets there are pavement tables shaded by colourful sunshades. Opposite these is a unique Melbourne institution—**Georges**, Australia's most elegant department store. Just down the hill is the graceful porticoed **Baptist Church**, built in 1845. Melbourne's imposing **Town Hall** and soaring **St Paul's Cathedral** in Swanston Street provide an attractive contrast to the modern **City Square** on the corner of Collins and Swanston Streets with its huge glass canopy, shady trees and fountains; this is an ideal place for browsing or meeting a friend. Other popular meeting places are the stylish Australia-on-Collins complex and the Centreway Arcade nearby.

Further down Collins Street is the elegant old **Block Arcade** with its mosaic floor, glass and iron-lace roof and stylish shops. The small lane at the back of this arcade (Block Place) leads through to Little Collins Street and to another gracious old arcade. This is the **Royal Arcade** where, every hour, the huge statues of mythical figures, Gog and Magog, strike the hour. This arcade leads through to the **Bourke Street Mall**, between Elizabeth and Swanston Streets. Several department stores and fashion chains including **Myer**, Australia's largest department store, and **David Jones** front on to the mall. David Jones has another store on the opposite side and its food hall is worth a visit to see the beautifully presented displays. Nearby the shopping complex **Centre Point** is a handy place to browse under shelter, or to stop for a snack in one of its many coffee bars. You can sit and watch city buskers from the seats provided in the mall, but beware of the trams—the only traffic, apart from delivery and emergency vehicles, allowed in this block. The **Half-Tix** booth in the mall offers the opportunity to purchase theatre tickets for the day's performances at reduced prices.

Swanston Street Walk, a recently developed and innovative pedestrian mall, encourages a stroll between Flinders and Latrobe Streets. Window-shop at your leisure or take time for coffee at one of the many sidewalk cafes. An appealing combination of bookshops and bistros has sprung up in the uppermost block of **Bourke Street**. The front coffee bar at Pellegrini's, a bustling Italian restaurant, is a great favourite, and the BYO restaurant at the rear is an Italian-style cafeteria where you make your selection from mouth-watering hot and cold dishes. On the Spring Street corner is one of the last of Melbourne' grand old hotels, the elegant twin-towered **Windsor** (1883), which looks over the peaceful **Treasury Gardens**. Proudly surveying the city from Spring Street is the impressive classical-style **State Parliament House**. The plush Corinthian style of the Legislative Council Chamber is legacy of Melbourne's golden era. The spires of massive bluestone **St Patrick's Cathedral** can be seen beyond. Melbourne's elegant and beautifully restored theatre, the **Princess**, is also in Spring Street.

At the top of Little Bourke Street is **Gordon Place**, a unique old building designed by the colonial architect William Pitt in 1883. The building is now an attractive apartment complex.

If you like Chinese food don't miss Melbourne's **Chinatown** in Little Bourke Street, between Exhibition and Swanston Streets. This fascinating conglomeration

Parliament House

of dozens of oriental restaurants, quaint grocery shops and mixed stores dates back to Melbourne's post-gold-rush days, when it became the city's Chinese quarter. The standard of the restaurants is good and prices vary from fairly cheap to very expensive. Among the outstanding restaurants are the Bamboo House, the Flower Drum and the Mask of China. Located in the heart of Chinatown at Cohen Place, the **Museum of Chinese Australian History** is worth a visit.

Further down Little Bourke Street is the **Information Victoria Centre**, which provides the public with access to Victorian Government information resources, including public record research facilities.

Just half a block away in Lonsdale Street, is Melbourne's newest department store **Daimaru** and the retail complex **Melbourne Central**, which together occupy most of the block bounded by Lonsdale, Swanston, Latrobe and Elizabeth Streets. Further east along Lonsdale Street, Greek music cafes, and flaky pastry shops make Melbourne a mini-Athens for a couple of blocks.

The **Science Museum** in Swanston Street has many interesting exhibits, including Australia's first plane and car. This imposing old building also houses the **Planetarium** (where slides are projected on the ceiling of the dome); the magnificent domed **State Library**; the **La Trobe Library**; and the **National Museum**, which includes a large collection of Australiana, natural history exhibits—including the legendary racehorse Phar Lap—and the **Children's Museum**, a first in Australia.

A block away, opposite the Russell Street Police Station, is the grim **Old Melbourne Gaol** and **Penal Museum** with its chillingly macabre exhibits, including the gallows where folk-hero and bushranger Ned Kelly swung.

More cheerful sights such as cheeses, sausages and decoratively arrayed vegetables can be seen at Melbourne's bustling **Victoria Market**, at the corner of Peel and Victoria Streets, held on Tuesdays, Thursdays, Fridays, Saturdays and Sundays. Opposite the market on the corner of Queen and Franklin Streets is the fascinating **Queen Victoria Arts and Craft Centre**, open daily. From here it's only a short stroll to the beautiful **Flagstaff Gardens**, once used as a pioneer graveyard and later a signalling station. Today this is a pleasant place to relax, with shady old trees and a children's playground. Facing the park in King Street you can see **St James' Old Cathedral**, which was built in 1839.

The lower part of the city is the sedate legal and financial sector. Back towards the city centre along William Street are the former **Royal Mint** and the **Supreme Court** and **Law Courts**, which were built between 1877 and 1884. At the bottom end of Collins Street is the luxury hotel **Le Meridien Melbourne**. The elaborate Rialto building and its neighbours, erected between 1889 and 1893, have been retained as a facade to this towering hotel and office complex.

In complete contrast, two of Melbourne's finest city parks, the quiet old **Treasury Gardens** and the beautiful **Fitzroy Gardens**, lie to the eastern boundary of the central city 'grid'. The John F. Kennedy Memorial is located beside the lake in the Treasury Gardens. The Fitzroy Gardens have superb avenues of huge English elms planted along gently contoured lawns, giving them a serene beauty all year round. Attractions within the gardens include **Cook's Cottage**, the '**Fairy Tree**', a model Tudor village, a restaurant and kiosk, and a children's playground. In summer the Fitzroy Gardens and other city parks have a programme of entertainment called Fantastic Entertainment in Public Places (FEIPP), including the Melbourne Symphony Orchestra's Prom Concerts, art shows, children's plays, jazz and ballet.

The **Carlton Gardens**, north-east of the city, flank the **Exhibition Buildings** — a grandiose domed hall originally built for the Great Exhibition in 1880 and still used for trade fairs. The southern side of the gardens has an ornamental pond and ornate fountain and the northern section an adventure playground and mini-traffic circuit popular with junior cyclists.

The **Victorian Arts Centre** is just over Princes Bridge on St Kilda Road, south of the central business area, and comprises the **National Gallery of Victoria**, the **Melbourne Concert Hall**, the **Theatres**, a variety of restaurants and bars, and the imposing Spire. The National Gallery features a fine collection of Australian and overseas masterpieces. The intricate stained-glass ceiling of the Great Hall was designed by Australian artist Leonard French. The Concert Hall is used for symphony music and concerts. It also contains the **Performing Arts Museum**, which offers a programme of regularly changing exhibitions covering the whole spectrum of the performing arts. The theatres include the State Theatre for opera, ballet and large musicals, the Playhouse for drama and the Studio for experimental theatre; not far away at the Malthouse, 117 Sturt Street, South Melbourne, the Playbox Theatre Company has two theatres.

Victorian Arts Centre spire

Rippon Lea

The **Kings Domain**, across St Kilda Road, is a huge stretch of shady parkland where you will see the **Myer Music Bowl**, used in the summer months as the venue for outdoor concerts and in the winter months as an ice-skating rink; the tower of **Government House** (tours operate at set times); the majestic, pyramid-style **Shrine of Remembrance,** which dominates St Kilda Road and is open to the public; the **Old Observatory** in Birdwood Avenue and, just past this, **La Trobe's Cottage**, Victoria's first Government House. This quaint cottage with many original furnishings—a reminder of Melbourne's humble beginnings — was brought out from England by the first Governor (La Trobe) in pre-fabricated sections. It is now a National Trust property, furnished in the original style with many of La Trobe's personal belongings and open daily. The main entrance to the **Royal Botanic Gardens** is nearby. These lush, beautifully landscaped gardens with gently sloping lawns, attractively grouped trees and shrubs, shady ferneries and ornamental lakes, are a peaceful retreat for city-dwellers. Many of the majestic old oaks in the western end of the garden are more than 100 years old. The kiosk, open daily, serves morning and afternoon teas and lunch.

If you walk through the gardens you will come to shady **Alexandra Avenue**, which runs beside the Yarra River. Barbecues are dotted along the Yarra's grassy banks. At weekends, hire bicycles and ride the scenic **Yarra River Cycle Path**, or take a ferry trip from Princes Bridge downriver to Morrell Bridge, or past historic **Como House**.

Nearby **Albert Park**, just south of St Kilda Road, is another good place for families—and sports enthusiasts. There are barbecues on the edge of the huge Albert Park Lake and boats are for hire at the Jolly Roger boat-shed. You can jog or cycle around the lake, or play golf on the adjoining public golf course. The Carousel restaurant overlooks the lake and there is a Keg restaurant on the opposite side.

Albert Park and its neighbouring suburbs, **South Melbourne** and **Port Melbourne**, are popular places with their trendy restaurants, bookshops, pubs and markets leading down to Melbourne's bayside beaches. **Albert Park Beach** has a brightly equipped playground with a tunnel slide on to the sand. In summer you can hire windsurfers on the beach near Fraser Street, West St Kilda.

Cosmopolitan **St Kilda** is a combination of London's 'Soho' and an old-fashioned fun resort. **Luna Park** and the enormous **Palais Theatre** are relics of the days when St Kilda was Melbourne's leading seaside playground. St Kilda is worth a visit, particularly on Sundays, when a collection of art and craft stalls appears on the **Esplanade** and **Acland Street** offers bookshops, restaurants and luscious continental cakes. For a delightful fish meal, visit Jean Jacques restaurant or take-away on the Lower Esplanade.

Just outside St Kilda at 192 Hotham Street, Elsternwick, is **Rippon Lea**, a National Trust property open daily. This huge Romanesque mansion is famed for its beautiful English-style landscaped gardens, which contain ornamental ponds and bridges, sweeping lawns, herbaceous borders, a superb fernery and strutting peacocks.

Two of Melbourne's wealthiest suburbs are **South Yarra** and **Toorak**. **Como**, another magnificent National Trust mansion, is in Como Avenue, off Toorak Road. Set in pleasant gardens, which once spread right down to the river, charmingly balconied Como is a perfectly preserved example of nineteenth-century colonial grandeur.

Although many of Toorak's and South Yarra's grand old estates have been subdivided, there is no shortage of imposing gates and high walls screening huge mansions. You could easily spend the best part of a day strolling down **Toorak Road**. This is a place to see and be seen—where there are probably more boutiques, expensive restaurants and gourmet food shops per metre than in any other part of Melbourne. The **Jewish Museum** is on the corner of Toorak Road and Arnold Street in South Yarra.

Another of Melbourne's great shopping streets, **Chapel Street**, crosses Toorak Road in South Yarra. Here yet more fashion boutiques and antique and jewellery shops abound, but the air is not quite so rarefied, nor are the price tags quite as high. The **Jam Factory** is a huge redbrick building, which still looks like a factory from the outside but inside there is an arcade of shops, an attractive glass-topped courtyard and a restaurant. Further on towards Malvern Road, Chapel Street becomes more cosmopolitan and the emphasis shifts from fashion to food. The **Prahran Market** is just around the corner in Commercial Road. This market springs to life on Tuesdays, Thursdays, Fridays and Saturdays. Catch a tram down nearby **High Street** to Armadale and you will come upon Melbourne's antique area. Art and craft galleries, antique shops and designer-clothes shops stretch along High Street for several blocks.

As Melbourne's city centre has become more impersonal her once-depressed inner suburbs north of the Yarra have been recharged with life. Theatres, theatre restaurants, antique shops, fashion boutiques and dozens of BYOs have bloomed in the suburbs of **Carlton**, **North Fitzroy** and **Richmond**. Most of the elegant iron-lace terrace houses in the more fashionable inner suburbs have been lovingly restored, but these areas still have a lively mixture of migrants and Australian old-timers. **Carlton**, the site of **Melbourne University**, also has one of the largest concentrations of beautiful Victorian houses in Melbourne. Its shady wide streets and squares of restored terraces can make you forget you are within walking distance of a modern city.

Lygon Street, known locally as 'little Italy', has three blocks of Italian restaurants, delicatessens, bookshops, boutiques and 'arty' shops. Have lunch and take in the Carlton scene at Jimmy Watson's, Melbourne's oldest wine bar, at 333 Lygon Street. The wine is good but cheap, the food self-service and the atmosphere frenetic, with everyone talking at once. If the weather is good the clientele spills out into the rear courtyard.

Walk through the Melbourne University grounds—a mixture of original ivy-clad buildings and modern blocks — and you come to **Parkville**, another little pocket of gracious Victorian terraces and shady streets. And at the **Melbourne Zoo**, just across nearby **Royal Park**, you can see a magnificent collection of butterflies in the unique walk-through Butterfly House, and families of lions at play from the safety of a 'people cage', an enclosed bridge which takes you right through the lions' large, natural-looking enclosure. This innovation is typical of the zoo's policy of providing enclosures for animals which are as large and as natural as possible, with a minimum of bars. There is also an amusement park and kiosk.

Melbourne's old metropolitan meat market at 42 Courtney Street, North Melbourne has been converted to a large craft gallery and workshop complex. The **Meat Market Craft Centre** features changing exhibitions, demonstrations and sales of high-quality crafts. For more information on craft shops and galleries, contact Craft Victoria on (03) 417 3111.

Another old inner suburb worth exploring is **Fitzroy**, which is similar in character to Carlton. Raffish Brunswick Street, Fitzroy, has an interesting mixture of antique shops, bookshops, clothes boutiques, pubs and first-class BYOs. In the suburb of **Fairfield**, a few kilometres east of Fitzroy, are the Fairfield Park Boathouse and Tea Gardens, with rowing skiffs and canoes for hire.

East Melbourne, another extremely well-preserved area of beautiful terrace houses, has such 'grand old ladies' as **Clarendon Terrace** (in Clarendon Street) with its graceful, colonnaded central portico and **Tasma Terrace** in Parliament Place, which now houses the National Trust Preservation Bookshop. The **Melbourne Fire Museum** is at 48 Gisborne Street, East Melbourne.

Swan Street, **Richmond** has one of the best selections of Greek restaurants in Melbourne. There is no need to book: if one is full, you try the next. Most are cheap and unpretentious with excellent food enhanced by a lively atmosphere. **Victoria Street** is the Vietnamese heartland of the city. Restored Victorian shops in **Bridge Road** house both boutiques and bargain 'seconds' outlets.

It is possible in Melbourne to dine and see the sights at the same time. The Colonial Tramcar Company runs a restaurant aboard a 1927 tram, thus allowing patrons to enjoy a meal in elegant style while travelling through Melbourne and some of its suburbs. Another novel way to dine is aboard Lighters on the Yarra, where you can wine and dine while anchored on the Yarra River, opposite the World Trade Centre. A water taxi from Princes Bridge will take passengers to

Cafe Alma in **Abbotsford**. Or try a Bar-B-Boat, a novel way to enjoy a barbecue while cruising on the Yarra past parks, gardens and the busy port area.

South-west of the city is Melbourne's oldest suburb, **Williamstown**, founded in the 1830s. This fascinating former maritime village has many quaint old seafront pubs, historic churches, fishermen's cottages and relics of its days as an important seaport. Because it was shielded from modern development until the completion of the **West Gate Bridge** to the city centre, much of Williamstown has changed little and retains a strong seafaring character. At weekends you can see over HMAS *Castlemaine* — a World War II minesweeper restored by the Maritime Trust—and picnic along the grassy foreshore. You can also see model ships, early costumes and relics at the Williamstown **Historical Museum** in Electra Street and look over a superb exhibition of old steam locomotives at the **Railway Museum** in Champion Road, North Williamstown. Williamstown Bay and river cruises are available.

A new science and technology museum, **Scienceworks**, has opened in a former pumping station in the suburb of **Spotswood**, close to Williamstown and only a ten-minute drive from the city. Closer to the city is the **Living Museum of the West** at Pipemakers Park, Van Ness Avenue, in the suburb of **Maribyrnong**; Australia's first ecomuseum, it presents the environment and heritage of the total community, the focus being upon the people of the region. Cruises on the Maribyrnong River visit some of the attractions to the west and north-west of

Melbourne. Further north, in the suburb of **Broadmeadows**, near Melbourne (Tullamarine) Airport, are the Australian Film Studios, the largest film studios in the southern hemisphere; the centre was used for the interior scenes in the film *Evil Angels*; tours are available. At the **Craigieburn** note-printing branch of the Reserve Bank of Australia, visitors can observe the printing of Australian currency notes.

The *Polly Woodside*, a square-rigged commercial sailing ship built in 1885, is moored at the old Duke and Orr's Dry Dock at the corner of Phayer Street and Normanby Road (near Spencer Street Bridge), **South Melbourne**, and is the focal point of the **Melbourne Maritime Museum**. In Coventry Street, South Melbourne are three portable houses, assembled in the 1850s, of the kind popular in Victoria during the gold-rush era.

For detailed information on Melbourne there are a number of guidebooks available. **Victorian Information Centre**, 230 Collins Street, (03) 790 3333, and the **Royal Automobile Club of Victoria (RACV)**, 422 Little Collins Street (03) 790 3333, provide maps, brochures and other information. The **Melbourne Tourism Authority**, Level 5, 114 Flinders Street, (03) 654 2288, has an excellent information service. **The Met**, Melbourne's public transport system, offers a tourism package, the Met Pass, which includes an all-day ticket for all Met services, a map and a 92-page booklet of tourist attractions in and around Melbourne and suggested day-trips on public transport. Contact (03) 617 0900 or visit the Met shop at 103 Elizabeth Street.

Melbourne's restaurant tram

PARKS AND GARDENS

Melbourne is a city which has grown to become a place of dignity and beauty, designed as it was with wide, tree-shaded streets and magnificent public gardens. The feeling for greenery and open space has been maintained by individual residents, many of whom take great pride in their gardens, whether they be planted with European species or with the increasingly popular native trees and shrubs.

The jewel of Victoria is the **Royal Botanic Gardens**, situated beside the Yarra River, only two kilometres from the city. Here there are thirty-six hectares of plantations, flower-beds, lawns and ornamental lakes, so superbly laid out and cared for that they are considered to be among the best in the world.

The site for the gardens was selected in 1845 but the main work of their development was carried out by Baron Sir Ferdinand von Mueller, who was appointed Government Botanist in 1852. He was succeeded by W. R. Guilfoyle, a landscape artist, who further remodelled and expanded the gardens. The gardens and the riverside are now a favourite place for Melburnians on Sundays. Families flock to picnic, feed the swans and waterbirds on the lakes or simply take a pleasant stroll.

Adjoining the gardens and flanking St Kilda Road is another large area of parkland, the **Kings Domain**, which comprises forty-three hectares of tree-shaded lawns and contains the Shrine of Remembrance, La Trobe's Cottage, which was the first Government House, and the Sidney Myer Music Bowl, an unconventional aluminium and steel structure which creates a perfect amphitheatre for outdoor concerts in the summer months. During winter, the Bowl is converted into an ice-skating rink. This vast garden area is completed by the adjoining **Alexandra and Queen Victoria Gardens**, a further fifty-two hectares of parkland.

The city's first public gardens were the **Flagstaff Gardens** at William Street, West Melbourne. A monument in the gardens bears a plaque describing how the site was used as a signalling station to inform settlers of the arrival and departure of ships at Williamstown. On the other side of the

Royal Botanical Gardens

city, not far from the centre, in East Melbourne are the **Treasury and Fitzroy Gardens** close by the State Government offices. In the Fitzroy Gardens is Captain Cook's cottage, which was transported in 1934 from the village of Great Ayton, Yorkshire, where Cook was born, and which was re-erected to commemorate Melbourne's centenary. Also in these gardens is a model Tudor village, laid out near an ancient tree trunk, a fairy tree carved with tiny figures by the late Ola Cohn. Another garden close to the city is the **Carlton Gardens**, in which the domed Exhibition Buildings are situated. They were erected for the Great Exhibition of 1880. The building was for twenty-seven years the meeting-place of the Victorian Parliament, while Federal Parliament met in the State Parliament buildings awaiting the building of Canberra.

Apart from these formal gardens — Melbourne's suburbs are endowed with large municipal garden areas — Melbourne also has large recreational areas around the city and throughout the urban regions, and these are always expanding to meet the demands of a sport-loving populace. The most notable is Albert Park, where there are golf courses, indoor

sports centres, two major cricket and football grounds and many other ovals, and a lake for sailing and rowing. Another large sporting area in East Melbourne contains the famous **Melbourne Cricket Ground**, which has been established for more than 100 years as a venue for test cricket and football and which now has stands that can accommodate 110 000 people. Nearby is the architecturally award-winning **National Tennis Centre**, the venue for international tennis tournaments. Courts are available for public hire. The Melbourne metropolitan area has eighty golf courses, many of which are accessible to the public. The **Royal Melbourne Golf Club** ranks sixth in world ratings, and hosts many world-class tournaments.

The man-made beauty of Melbourne is surpassed by nature in the Dandenong Ranges, about forty-nine kilometres from the city. The heavily forested ranges have trees such as mountain ash, grey gums, messmate, peppermint and box eucalypts interrupted by spectacular fern gullies. A network of good roads connects the many small towns in the Dandenongs, most of which blend into their bushland surroundings. The private gardens in the district are beautifully maintained and a drive through the hills is delightful at any time of the year, but particularly so in spring when fruit trees and ornamentals are in blossom, or in autumn when the European trees are at their most colourful.

There are a number of natural forests in the Dandenongs with tracks for bushwalkers. The best known is **Sherbrooke Forest**, which seems beautifully unspoiled despite the fact that it is visited by tens of thousands of people every year. It is a bird sanctuary and a home of the famous, but shy, lyrebird. A rare delight is to see the elaborate mating dance and display of these birds and to hear their brilliant mimicking calls.

A fascinating way to see the Dandenongs is to take a trip on the Puffing Billy, a delightful narrow-gauge steam railway maintained by a preservation society. It runs from Belgrave to Emerald Lake through bushland and flower farms. Visits to art galleries, antique shops, restaurants, sanctuaries or plant nurseries can add to the pleasure of a visit to the Dandenongs.

There are many other spectacular natural areas throughout Victoria and over the years the Government has been active in preserving many of these for the people—places such as the **Wilsons Promontory National Park** with its secluded beaches and superb coastal scenery; the **Tarra-Bulga National Park** in the Strzelecki Ranges, with its mountain ash trees and rainforest vegetation; the **Wyperfeld National Park** in the north-west, with its spring wildflowers and dry-country birdlife; the **Alpine National Park** which stretches across 6460 square kilometres of the state's high country; and many others.

The quality of Victoria's public and private gardens is exceptional wherever you go. Each year, Victoria's Garden Scheme, publishes a guidebook to numerous private gardens open throughout spring, summer and autumn, right across the State and into southern NSW. Most major towns have large, meticulously maintained garden areas, each with its own special quality. The **Ararat** Botanical Gardens are noted for their orchid glasshouse displays. The gardens at **Ballarat** are the centre of the famous annual Begonia Festival held in March. **Benalla** conducts a rose festival every year. In autumn, visitors are attracted to the colours of autumn foliage on the trees in and around the small town of Bright.

Details of various garden festivals and displays may be obtained from the Victorian Information Centre, 230 Collins St, Melbourne; (03) 790 3333.

Albert Park Lake

Cook's Cottage, Fitzroy Gardens

Botanic Gardens, Ballarat

TOURS FROM MELBOURNE

Some of Australia's most beautiful and interesting tours emanate from Melbourne and include historic towns and stunning scenery. Many require an overnight stop to do them justice and in such cases booking ahead is recommended.

Ballarat and Sovereign Hill, 110 km from Melbourne via the Western Freeway

A must for the tourist if only to visit Sovereign Hill, arguably the most authentic reconstruction of a nineteenth-century gold-mining township in the world. Ballarat is one of Victoria's most attractive old cities with many splendid colonial buildings, parks and gardens. Other attractions in Ballarat include the Eureka Stockade and the Begonia Festival held in March. Allow plenty of time for your Sovereign Hill visit. At Sovereign Hill you can stay overnight in the re-creation of Government Camp. **See also:** The Golden Age and Ballarat entry in A - Z listing.

Geelong, Queenscliff and Point Lonsdale, 107 km from Melbourne via the Princes Highway and Bellarine Highway

Allow two days for this tour. Spend some time in Geelong, especially around the historic waterfront, before continuing to Queenscliff, Melbourne's favourite summer resort of the late nineteenth century and still a favourite. Look for Benito Bonito's buried treasure and visit Fort Queenscliff, Melbourne's first defence establishment, before continuing on to William Buckley's cave at Point Lonsdale. Stay overnight at a classic nineteenth-century hotel; try the Ozone or the Queenscliff, both located in Queenscliff. **See also:** Individual entries in A–Z listing.

Werribee Park, 35 km from Melbourne via the Princes Highway

Just outside the township of Werribee, now almost a suburb of Melbourne, Werribee Park is a large estate with a magnificent Italianate mansion of some sixty rooms, built in the 1870s for the Chirnside brothers, who had established a pastoral 'empire' in the Western District. Now owned by the Victorian Government, Werribee Park is open daily. There are extensive formal gardens, including the Victorian State Rose Garden, a wildlife reserve, a friendship farm, restaurant, kiosk, picnic facilities, electric barbecues, a golf course and tennis courts. Nearby Point Cook RAAF Museum (open Sun. to Fri.) has adjacent picnic and barbecue facilities. There is nude bathing at Campbell's Cove.

The Great Ocean Road and the Otway Range, 200 km from Melbourne along the south-west coast

See: The Great Ocean Road.

Port Phillip Bay Cruises from 11 North Wharf

The steam tug *Wattle*, a beautifully restored 1933 tugboat, makes daytrips to Portarlington on the Bellarine Peninsula on Saturdays, and fascinating two-hour trips around the Port of Melbourne on Sundays and public holidays. In January the *Wattle* runs daily seal-colony cruises from Rye. The *Wattle* does not operate during July and August. Bookings are essential; contact (03) 328 2739.

Healesville Sanctuary, 60 km from Melbourne via the Maroondah Highway

To see all of Australia's distinctive fauna in one huge natural enclosure, take a one-day tour to Healesville Sanctuary. Many of the animals roam freely; there are 'walk-through' aviaries, excellent nocturnal displays and viewing of the extraordinary platypus. However, the highlight is the new 'Where Eagles Fly' exhibit, where rangers and birds of prey combine in an awe-inspiring display. Open daily, with kiosk, picnic and barbecue facilities.

Sovereign Hill, Ballarat

Werribee Park

Mt Saint Leonard north of Healesville offers a fine 360-degree view, but requires a one-kilometre uphill walk. **See also:** Healesville entry in A–Z listing.

The Dandenong Ranges, 49 km from Melbourne via the Burwood Highway
See: The Dandenongs.

Phillip Island, 140 km from Melbourne via the Mulgrave Freeway and the South Gippsland and Bass Highways
Famous for the nightly parade at dusk of little fairy penguins up to their burrows at Summerland Beach, Phillip Island attracts thousands of visitors annually. Other wildlife attractions include fur seals all year, but especially in November – December and mutton birds in spring and summer. The island is situated in Western Port and also offers excellent surfing and fishing. There is usually some activity at the Phillip Island Motor Racing Circuit, venue for the first 500 cc motorcycle Australian Grand Prix. **See also:** Phillip Island; and Cowes entry in A–Z listing.

Mornington Peninsula, 100 km from Melbourne via the Nepean Highway
See: The Mornington Peninsula.

South Gippsland and Wilsons Promontory, 180 km from Melbourne via the South Gippsland Highway
Leaving Melbourne behind, this tour takes you through the townships of Cranbourne, Korumburra and Leongatha and through the lush, rolling hills and the spectacular countryside of South Gippsland to Foster, where you turn right for the southernmost point on the Australian mainland at Wilsons Promontory National Park. See kangaroos and koalas and take some short (or long) bushwalks to tiny coves and sandy beaches. This tour deserves at least two days. Return along the coast road through Inverloch and Wonthaggi. **See also:** Individual entries in A – Z listing.

Warburton and the Upper Yarra Dam, 120 km via the Maroondah and Warburton Highways
On the way to some of Victoria's high country, visit wineries in the Yarra Valley region and sample some superb vintage reds and whites. Some of this region is snow-covered in mid-winter. If you visit during the warmer months, picnic by the Upper Yarra Dam and go trout fishing at

Tommy Finn's Trout Farm. Hot-air balloon flights are available at Yarra Glen. Warburton has giant waterslides and an art gallery; the Lala Falls are just outside of town. You can cross the range to Noojee (but take care as the road is unsealed), and return via Warragul and the Princes Highway. The Gippsland region produces some of the world's great cheeses. **See also:** Warburton entry in A –Z listing.

Yarra Valley wineries, 40–60 km from Melbourne via the Maroondah and Melba Highways, or via Heidleberg, Greensborough and the Diamond Valley
Throughout the Yarra Valley, centred on Coldstream/Yarra Glen, 37 wineries and 82 vineyards produce premium and quality wines that are acclaimed worldwide. Of these, 20 have cellar-door facilities, mostly open on weekends and public holidays; several—such as Fergusson's, De Bortoli, Kellybrook and Yarra Burn—include restaurants on the premises. Further information and a listing of cellar-door details from the Yarra Valley Wine Growers Association, (059) 64 9388.

Fairy Penguins, Phillip Island

Wilsons Promontory National Park

THE MORNINGTON PENINSULA

This boot-shaped promontory separates Port Phillip Bay and Western Port and provides Melburnians with a beachside playground. It is a mixture of resort towns, varying in size and tourist development, and inland rural countryside. As well as safe bayside beaches, there are excellent surf beaches, particularly along the stretch of rugged coast between Portsea and Cape Schanck at the end of the Peninsula. The Point Nepean National Park includes the key beaches in this area — **Portsea**, **Sorrento**, **Diamond Bay**, **Koonya** and **Gunnamatta**. A number of walking-tracks have been established. Swimming is considered safe only in those areas controlled by the Surf Lifesaving Association.

The Western Port side of the Peninsula is less developed, much of its foreshore having remained relatively unspoiled and being still devoted to farming and grazing land. **French Island**, which is set in the centre of this bay, was a Victorian penal settlement for forty years and is now administered by the Victorian government as a holiday and sports centre. The island is notable for its fauna.

Port Phillip Bay is linked for vehicle access by the Peninsula Searoad Transport ferry which operates between Sorrento and Queenscliff. Quaint passenger ferries link Sorrento, Portsea and Queenscliff in the summer season as well.

Frankston, now mainly a residential area for Melbourne commuters, could also be considered the gateway to the Peninsula. It is a thriving town within easy reach of good beaches on Port Phillip Bay at Daveys Bay, Canadian Bay and Mount Eliza. McClelland Art Gallery is open daily. Sage's Cottage (1850), at nearby Baxter, is now a colonial-style restaurant.

The Peninsula itself is well developed for tourists, with good sporting facilities and many art galleries, craft shops, restaurants and take-away food shops. Because of its popularity, it is advisable to book accommodation, whatever your choice, well ahead during the summer and Easter seasons. The Port Phillip Bay foreshore from **Dromana** to **Blairgowrie** is almost entirely devoted to campers and caravans during these peak seasons.

Mornington was established in 1864. The deep safe harbour at Point Schnapper first attracted settlers to this area and it has been a popular resort town ever since. Today it is a pleasant commercial, farming and recreational centre. Between the town and nearby Mount Martha stretches a fine coastline with sheltered sandy bays separated by rocky bluffs and backed by steep wooded slopes. A self-guided walk introduces the town's historic buildings, including the gaol and court-house on the Esplanade, and the old post office on the Esplanade corner, which is now a historic museum. The Australian Museum of Modern Media, 1140 Nepean Highway, has film, television, radio and pop music memorabilia. The new Mornington Peninsula Arts Centre is in the Civic Reserve, Duns Road. Fossil Beach, between Mount Martha and Mornington, is one of only two exposed fossil plains in the world. Parasailing is available at Mount Martha Beach. Located at Mount Martha, 'The Briars', an old homestead (1866) and property, incorporates wetland areas, bird hides, a Woodland Walk and the Briars Peninsula Wine Centre.

Dromana rests at the foot of Arthurs Seat, the 305-metre-high mountain that provides the Peninsula with panoramic views over both bays. Safety Beach has boat-launching ramps and trailer facilities. A good road leads to the summit and a chair-lift operates at weekends and school and public holidays May to mid September, but daily from

Beach at Mount Martha

Cape Schanck

Beach cricket, Mornington

then until to the end of April. At the summit there are a lookout tower, picnic reserve and licensed restaurant. Also nearby is Seawinds, a section of the Arthurs Seat State Park, which has beautiful gardens complete with sculptures, picnic facilities and great views.

Main Ridge and **Red Hill**, in the hinterland behind Arthurs Seat, are known for wineries. At Main Ridge attractions include Kings Waterfall, also in Arthurs Seat State Park, the Drum Drum wildflower farm,Seaview Nursery and tearooms, Sunny Ridge Strawberry Farm, a riding school and the Pine Ridge Car Museum. Red Hill is particularly well known for its Community Market, held on the first Saturday of the months September to May.

McCrae is a small resort centre, noted for the McCrae Homestead, built in 1844, now a National Trust property, open daily. It was the first homestead on the Peninsula.

Rosebud is a busy commercial centre with wide foreshore camping areas. Just outside the town is the Peninsula Gardens Sanctuary, set back from the Nepean Highway.

Rye has extensive camping, picnicking and recreational foreshore areas, and boat-launching facilities.

Sorrento was the site of Victoria's first settlement in 1803, when Colonel Collins landed in this area. The early settlers' graves and a memorial to Collins can be found in the cliff-top cemetery overlooking Sullivans Bay. Sorrento was energetically developed as a 'watering place' by George Coppin in the 1870s; the Sorrento, Koonya and Continental Hotels have been restored

as fine examples of early Victorian architecture. At nearby Point King, the Union Jack was raised for the first time in Australia. South Channel Fort, a man-made island that is now a bird habitat, lies six kilometres off Sorrento and is open to visitors.

Portsea, situated at the end of the Nepean Highway, is an attractive resort with excellent deepwater bayside beaches and first-class surfing at its Back Beach. Victoria's first Quarantine Station (now an Army training camp) was built here in 1856 after eighty-two deaths from smallpox on the vessel *Ticonderoga* anchored in Weroona Bay. Off-limits to the public until recently, this area is now incorporated into the Point Nepean National Park; open daily. Panoramic views of the impressive rocky coastline abound and near Back Beach is London Bridge, a spectacular rock formation created by sea erosion.

Flinders is the most southerly Peninsula township, on Western Port. It is a fishing and holiday resort, with good surfing, swimming and fishing. Cape Schanck lighthouse (1859) with its museum, the Blowhole and Elephant Rock are worth visiting.

Hastings, also fronting Western Port, is an attractive fishing port and holiday centre with a sea-water swimming pool, yacht-club, marina and boat-launching ramps south of the pier. There is a fauna park next to the high school in High St, and over 50 000 ha of designated wetlands north of town.

Other towns in Western Port include **Shoreham**, a sprawling holiday settlement on Stony Creek, close to

the sea. On Red Hill Road is Ashcombe Maze, which features hedge mazes surrounded by gardens. Five kilometres from Shoreham is **Point Leo**, which has one of the safest surf beaches on the Peninsula. Between Point Leo and **Balnarring**, short access roads from the main Flinders–Frankston road lead to very pleasant beaches at Merricks, Coles, Point Sumner and Balnarring.

Somers, a quiet village with many holiday homes, has good beaches, excellent fishing, tennis and yacht-clubs. Coolart mansion, a National Trust classified homestead dating from the 1890s, is set on eighty-seven hectares, with landscaped gardens, a lagoon and walking-trails. Between Somers and Crib Point is HMAS *Cerberus*, a Royal Australian Navy training establishment.

The Mornington Peninsula is a rapidly growing wine-producing area. From the hinterland of Mount Martha to the shores of Western Port, seventeen vineyards open regularly for cellar-door tastings and sales; thirteen more open by appointment. For further detailed information, contact the Mornington Peninsula Vignerons Association; PO Box 400, Mornington 3931; (059) 74 4200.

For further information on the area contact the Dromana Information Centre, Nepean Hwy, Dromana, (059) 87 3078; the Frankston Information Centre, 54 Playne St, Frankston, (03) 781 5244; or the Mornington Information Centre, cnr Main and Elizabeth Sts, Mornington, (059) 75 1644.

THE DANDENONGS

These ranges, fifty kilometres from the centre of Melbourne, are a renowned beauty area and tourist attraction. Heavy rainfall and rich volcanic soil have created a lush vegetation with spectacular hills and gullies crowded with creepers, tree-ferns and soaring mountain ash. The area is fairly closely settled and there are a number of pretty townships dotted about the hills.

It has long been a traditional summer retreat for people from Melbourne and many of the gracious old homes have now been converted into guesthouses and restaurants.

The entire area is famous for its beautiful gardens and for its great variety of European trees, particularly attractive in spring and autumn. Many excellent restaurants, art and craft galleries, antique shops and well-stocked plant nurseries add to the charm of these hills, ideally placed for a relaxed day's outing from Melbourne. At 633 metres, Mount Dandenong is the highest point of the ranges, and at its summit there are excellent views, picnic facilities and the 'Skyhigh' restaurant from which a magnificent night-time view of Melbourne can be seen.

Ferntree Gully National Park, Doongalla and Sherbrooke Forest are now the 1900-hectare **Dandenong Ranges National Park**, where you can see lush trees and ferns and a wide variety of flora and fauna. The lyrebird and eastern whipbird can be heard here. Sherbrooke Forest, on the road from **Belgrave** to **Kallista**, is unspoiled bushland with many lyrebirds. A tourist road runs through the park area from **Ferntree Gully** to **Montrose**. At Montrose, visit Gumnut Village in the Australflora plant nursery, Belfast Road. William Ricketts Sanctuary

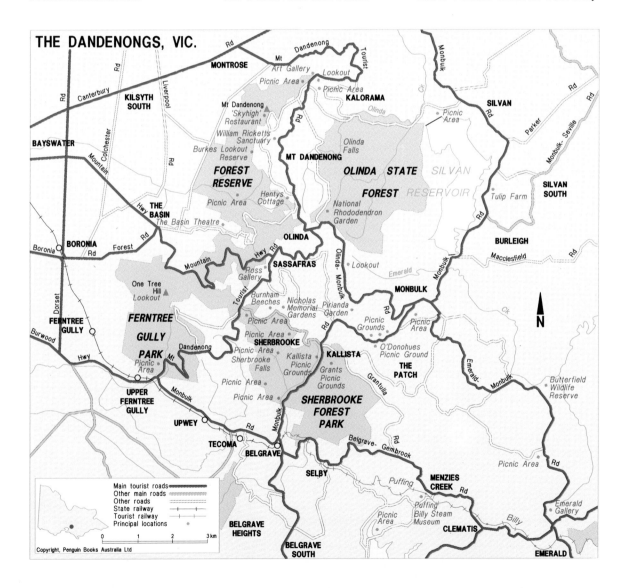

THE DANDENONGS, VIC.

Main tourist roads
Other main roads
Other roads
State railway
Tourist railway
Principal locations

0   1   2   3 km

Copyright, Penguin Books Australia Ltd

(open daily), on Mount Dandenong Tourist Road, is a natural forest area in which Ricketts, a musician and naturalist, has sculpted in clay a number of Aboriginal figures and symbolic scenes. Near **Sherbrooke**, the Nicholas Memorial Gardens, thirteen hectares of a formerly private garden, are open daily.

'Puffing Billy', one of the Dandenongs' most famous attractions, leaves from **Belgrave** and travels 13.5 kilometres to **Emerald Lake**. The Puffing Billy Steam Museum at **Menzies Creek**, open Saturday, Sunday and public holidays, displays some restored locomotives and rolling-stock. Puffing Billy runs daily throughout the year, except on Christmas Day and fire-ban days. A timetable is available from the Victorian Information Centre, 230 Collins St, Melbourne, (03) 790 3333; or telephone (03) 870 8411 for recorded information. Each April, the Great Train Race is held: runners attempt to race Puffing Billy from Belgrave to Emerald Lake Park.

Emerald was the first settlement in the area and is situated on a high ridge. It has a number of interesting galleries and in the surrounding countryside there are lavender farms and attractive picnic spots. **Olinda** is a pretty township with some good restaurants. The home of one of Victoria's first settlers, Edward Henty, is now sited here on Ridge Road. Constructed from prefabricated sections brought from England, inside there are a number of historic domestic items and original furnishings; open daily except Friday. Also of interest is the National Rhododendron Garden, especially in spring, when the annual show is held. Another spring flower festival is held at **Silvan**, where tulip bulbs are cultivated. **Ferntree Gully**, at the foot of the ranges, is now virtually an outer suburb of Melbourne.

For further information on the Dandenongs, contact the Victorian Information Centre, 230 Collins St, Melbourne; (03) 790 3333.

top: Puffing Billy
centre: Sherbrooke Forest
bottom: Tulip Gardens, Silvan

VICTORIA from A to Z

Alexandra   Population 1790

Alexandra is a farming and holiday centre, 24 km west of Lake Eildon. **Of interest:** Timber and Tramway Museum housed in former railway station, Station St. Historic buildings include National Trust classified Post Office and adjacent Law Courts, Downey St (Goulburn Valley Hwy). Community Market, usually held on last Sat. of every month. Annual Easter Art Show. **In the area:** Fraser National Park, 12 km east; excellent walks. Southern edge of town, McKenzie Nature Reserve; virgin bushland with an abundance of orchids in winter and spring. Stonelea Country Retreat at Acheron, 8 km south. Taggerty, 18 km south in the Acheron Valley; offers good trout-fishing. Taggerty Pioneer Settlement. Cathedral Range State Park, 3km further south from Taggerty, for camping, bushwalking, rock-climbing and fishing. Bonnie Doon, 37 km north-east, on Lake Eildon; base for trail-riding, bushwalking, water sports and scenic drives. Starglen Lodge, Bonnie Doon, offers comfortable accommodation with horse-riding, 4WD tours or relaxing. **Tourist information:** Redgate Nursery/Craft Cottage, 47 Grant St; (057) 72 2169. **Accommodation:** 4 hotels, 2 motels, 2 caravan/camping parks. MAP REF. 209 K1, 217 K12, 218 F4

Anglesea   Population 1652

This attractive seaside town on the Great Ocean Road has excellent swimming and surfing, and an interesting golf-course, noted for its tame kangaroos. Behind the town, in Coalmine Rd, there is an open-cut brown coal mine and power-station; viewing platform and information. **Of interest:** Melaleuca Gallery, Gt Ocean Rd. Coogoorah Park; bushland reserve, picnics and bushwalking. Annual Angair Festival in September. **In the area:** J.E. Loveridge Lookout, 1 km west. Point Roadknight beach, 2 km west. Angahook - Lorne State Park, an attractive reserve with many walking-tracks; access from either behind Anglesea or from Airey's Inlet, 10 km south-west, on Gt Ocean Rd; features include Ironbark Basin, Currawong Falls, Treefern Grove and Melaleuca Swamp. **Tourist information:** Christmas – Easter from caravan, College Pl, west bank Anglesea River; other months from Shire Offices, Grossmans Rd, Torquay; (052) 61 4202. **Accommodation**: 3 motels, 4 caravan/camping

parks. **See also:** The Great Ocean Road; The Western District. MAP REF. 205 D11, 208 C9

Apollo Bay   Population 888

The Great Ocean Road leads to this attractive coastal town, the centre of a rich dairying and fishing area and the base for a huge fish-freezing plant. The wooded mountainous hinterland offers memorable scenery and there is excellent sea and river fishing in the area. The rugged and beautiful coastline has been the scene of many shipwrecks in the past. **Of interest:** Bass Strait Shell Museum, Noel St. Old Cable Station Museum, Gt Ocean Rd. **In the area:** Guided walks available from Tourist Information Centre. Grey River Scenic Reserve, 24 km north-east. Elliot River, 6 km south-west, and adjacent Shelly Beach Viewpoint. Otway National Park, 13 km south-west; excellent for bushwalking: through park to sea or through forest to waterfalls. Cape Otway Lighthouse, 36 km south-west; grounds open weekdays. Turton's Track, 25 km north and Wild Dog Road, 3 km east, are scenic touring roads. Follow signs to Barham Paradise Scenic Reserve, 10 km north-west, in beautiful Barham River Valley. Lavers Hill, 53 km west; tiny now in comparison with the booming timber centre of its heyday. Enchanting Melba Gully State Park, 3 km west of Lavers Hill; covers 49 ha with self-guided rainforest walk; a glow-worm habitat. **Tourist information:** 155 Great Ocean Rd; (052) 37 6529. **Accommodation:** 3 hotels, 10 motels, 6 caravan/camping parks. **See also:** The Great Ocean Road. MAP REF. 211 Q12

Ararat   Population 8015

The Ararat area gold boom came in 1857. It was short-lived, however, and sheep farming became the basis of the town's economy. Today the town is the commercial centre of a prosperous farming and wine-growing region. The area also produces fine merino wool. The first vines in the district were planted by Frenchmen in 1863 and the little town of Great Western, 16 km north-west of Ararat, gave its name to some of Australia's most famous champagnes and wines. **Of interest:** Beautiful bluestone buildings in Barkly St: Post Office, the splendid Town Hall, Civic Square and War Memorial. Chinese Gold Discovery Memorial, Lambert St. Langi Morgala Folk Museum, Queen St;

includes collection of Aboriginal weapons and artefacts. Ararat Art Gallery, a regional gallery specialising in wool and fibre pieces by leading artists. Alexandra Park and Botanical Gardens, noted for their orchid glasshouse display. Water sports at Green Hill Lake, a man-made lake, close to Western Hwy. Golden Gateway 10-day festival held annually in October. **In the area:** Langi Ghiran State Park, 13.5 km east off Western Hwy; scenic walks to nearby reservoir, picnic and barbecue facilities, and children's playground. Buangor, 5 km on, with century-old Buangor Hotel, Buangor Store and, opposite, old Cobb & Co. changing station, (c.1860). Mt Buangor State Park and Fern Tree Waterfalls, with picnic facilities, 18 km further on. Wynette Villa (1865), Vincent St; lavender and herb gardens. Lavender Green store at Great Western features crafts and lavender products. Several wineries in the area: Seppelt's Great Western Vineyards, 17 km north-west, specialises in dry red wines and champagnes. Vineyard established in 1865; underground cellars classified by National Trust. Best's Wines, 2 km on through Great Western; open for inspection, tastings and sales. Mt Langi Ghiran Wines, 20 km east on Western Hwy. Montara Winery, 3 km south of Ararat, on Chalambar Rd. Cathcart Ridge Winery at Cathcart, 6 km west. Cathcart and, 20 km further west, Mafeking, are historic gold areas. Mafeking, once a bustling settlement with 10 000 people, has picnic facilities. Care must be taken when walking in these areas: many deep mine shafts. **Tourist information:** Barkly St; (053) 52 2096. **Accommodation:** 5 hotels, 6 motels, 2 caravan/camping parks. MAP REF. 211 M1, 213 L13

Avoca   Population 1032

In the Central Highlands region, Avoca was established with the discovery of gold in the area in 1852. Located at the junction of the Sunraysia and Pyrenees Hwys, the surrounding Pyrenees Range foothills offer attractive bushwalking and are the home of numbers of kangaroos, wallabies and koalas. **Of interest:** Early bluestone buildings classified by National Trust include the old gaol and powder magazine in Camp St, the court-house and one of the state's earliest pharmacies, Lalor's, in High St. Rock and Gem Museum in High St. Annual Wool and Wine Festival in October. **In the area:** Avoca and Wimmera Rivers, through town and 42 km west respectively, and Bet Bet Creek, 11 km east, are popular for fishing. Several wineries within easy driving distance of town include: Mt Avoca vineyard, 7 km west; Chateau Remy Vineyards, 8 km west on Vinoca Rd; Redbank Winery at Redbank, 20 km north-west; Summerfield Winery in Moonambel Village, 20 km north; Warrenmang Vineyard, 1 km east; Taltarni and Dalwhinnie wines, each another 2 km further east. **Tourist information:** 199 High St; (054) 65 3017. **Accommodation:** 1 caravan/camping park. **See also:** Victoria's Wine Regions. MAP REF. 213 O12

Bacchus Marsh   Population 7640

The trees of the Avenue of Honour provide an impressive entrance to Bacchus Marsh, 49 km from Melbourne on the Western Hwy. This old-established town is situated in a fertile valley, once marshland, between the Werribee and Lerderderg Rivers. **Of interest:** Manor House, home of town's founder, Captain Bacchus, in Manor St; privately owned. In Main St, original blacksmith's shop and cottage, court-house, lock-up and National Bank, all classified by National Trust. Border Inn, opened in 1850, also in Main St; thought to have been first coaching service stop in Victoria; Bacchus Marsh was staging-post for Cobb & Co. coaches travelling to goldfields. Holy Trinity Anglican Church (1877), Gisborne Rd. Gallery 22, Maddingley Blvd; Express Building Art Gallery, Gisborne Rd; Ra Ceramics and Crafts, Station St; Fragrant Butterfly, Main St; gifts and tourist information. Big Apple Tourist Orchard, Avenue of Honour. **In the area:** Werribee and Lerderderg Gorges, 10 km west and 5 km north respectively; picnics, bushwalking and swimming. Merrimu Reservoir and Wombat State Forest, both about 10 km north; Brisbane Ranges National Park, 16 km south-west, and Anakie Gorge, 26 km south-west; Long Forest Fauna Reserve, 2 km north-east, with its bull mallee, some specimens centuries old, and rare orchids; all popular with anglers and bushwalkers. On the Western Fwy, 6 km west, St Anne's Vineyard; old bluestone cellar, built from remains of old Ballarat gaol; open daily. Willows Historical Homestead at Melton, 14 km east. Craiglee Winery and Goonawarra Vineyard at Sunbury, 47 km north-east and Wildwood Vineyard, 9 km south-east at Bulla. Mineral Springs Reserve and Garden of St Erth at Blackwood, 26 km north-west. Maddingley open-cut coal mine, 3 km south. **Tourist information:** Shire Offices, Main Street; (053) 67 2111 and Fragrant Butterfly, 154

Main St; (053) 67 5019. **Accommodation:** 4 hotels, 2 motels, 1 caravan/camping park. **See also:** The Golden Age. MAP REF. 200 G11, 208 D4

Bairnsdale   Population 10 328

This Gippsland trade centre and holiday town is at the junction of the Princes Hwy, the Omeo Hwy and the road east to Lakes Entrance, which makes it an excellent touring base. It is a pleasant town with good sporting facilities and attractive gardens. **Of interest:** St Mary's Church, Main St; wall and ceiling murals by an Italian artist. Bairnsdale Recreation Centre, McKeen St; includes sports hall. Annual Riviera Festival in March. **In the area:** Lindenow, 19 km west, close to Mitchell River National Park. Park has good bushwalking tracks and, in a gorge on the Mitchell River, the Den of Nargun, an Aboriginal cultural site. River empties into Lake King at Eagle Point Bluff, where world's second longest silt jetties can be seen. Metung, 30 km east, a picturesque fishing village on shores of Lake King; some solid pioneer holiday homes still standing. About 2 km south, a boardwalk leads across part of McLeod's Morass, a bird wetland habitat; main access is about 10 km south. Boardwalk closed during duck season. Scenic drive north along Omeo Hwy through Tambo River valley; stunning in spring when wattles are in bloom. Nicholson River Winery, 10 km east, and Golvinda winery, 5 km north. **Tourist information:** 240 Main Street; (051) 52 3444. **Accommodation:** 8 ho-

tels, 8 motels, 3 caravan/camping parks. **See also:** Gippsland Lakes. MAP REF. 220 E8

Ballan   Population 846

A small township on the Werribee River, noted for its mineral springs. **Of interest:** Caledonian Park, eastern edge of town; picnic areas and swimming. **In the area:** Pikes Creek Reservoir, 12 km east, with good trout fishing. **Tourist information:** Shire Offices, cnr Stead and Steiglitz Sts; (053) 68 1001. **Accommodation:** 3 hotels, 2 caravan parks. MAP REF. 200 E10, 208 C4

Ballarat   Population 63 802

Ballarat is Victoria's largest inland city, situated in the Central Highlands. Its inner areas retain much of the charm of its gold-boom era, with many splendid original buildings still standing and parks and gardens adding to its attractive appearance. The begonia is the city's floral emblem and the annual Begonia Festival in March attracts many enthusiasts. Ballarat was just a small rural township in 1851, when its enormously rich alluvial goldfields were discovered. Within two years it had a population of nearly 40 000. Australia's only civil battle occurred here in 1854, when miners refused to pay Government licence fees and fought with police and troops at the Eureka Stockade. Today Ballarat is a bustling city with the added attraction of many galleries, museums, antique and craft

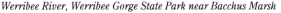

Werribee River, Werribee Gorge State Park near Bacchus Marsh

shops. It has excellent recreational facilities and beautiful garden areas, making it most attractive to visitors. The Royal South Street Eisteddfod, which focuses on music and the dramatic arts, is held each September/October. Bridge Street Mall in the centre of the city has many shops in a relaxed atmosphere. **Of interest:** Man-made Lake Wendouree, accessed from Hamilton Ave, is popular for all kinds of water sports. Paddle-steamer tours available with a commentary on the history of the city. Adjoining the lake area are the peaceful Botanic Gardens (40 ha), containing splendid begonia conservatories. Located here is Prime Ministers' Avenue, displaying busts of Australian prime ministers. An elegant statuary pavilion is nearby. The Tourist Tramway, access in Wendouree Pde, takes visitors for rides around the gardens at weekends, and on public and school holidays. Hymettus Cottage in Cardigan St has a formal French-style garden. Old steam locomotive on display at railway workshops in Creswick Rd. Ballarat's most notable gallery, the Fine Art Gallery in Lydiard St Nth, has a comprehensive collection of Australian art, including works by the Lindsay family. Montrose Cottage (1856), Eureka St, was the first masonry cottage built on the goldfields and is classified by the National Trust; winner of the 1990 State Heritage and Cultural Tourism Award of Social History. Beside it is the Eureka Museum, displaying a large collection of gold-era relics. Golda's World of Dolls, Eureka St, features antique and modern dolls. Orpheus Radio Museum in Ring Rd. The Old Curiosity Shop, Queen St, has a fascinating collection of pioneer relics. In Stawell St Sth is the Eureka Stockade Park, which has a life-size replica of the famous battle. Self-guided Eureka Trail for visitors. Sovereign Hill, a major tourist attraction 2 km south, is a reconstruction of a gold-mining settlement with an orientation centre and working displays. During the annual Begonia Festival in March, there are guided lamplight tours of Sovereign Hill. Excellent barbecue facilities, kiosk, restaurant and a licensed hotel offer refreshment. The Government Camp provides comfortable family-type accommodation. Adjoining Sovereign Hill is the Gold Museum, which contains exhibits of gold history; there is a large collection of gold coins and a display of the uses of gold 'today and tomorrow'. Ballarat Wildlife and Reptile Park, cnr of York and Fussell Sts. Craig's Royal Hotel, George Hotel, and Ballarat Terrace (1889) all in Lydiard St, offer dining and/or accommodation in gracious old-world surroundings. Annual Antique Fair in March. Annual Super Southern Swap Meet at Ballarat Airport

in March. Opera Festival at Easter. **In the area:** Kryal Castle, 8 km east on Western Hwy; an amazing reconstruction of a medieval castle, offers entertainment for all the family. On the western edge of the city are the Avenue of Honour (22 km) and the Arch of Victory, honouring those who fought in World War I. Lake Burrumbeet, 22 km north-west, offers a variety of water sports, picnic spots and excellent trout-fishing. Ercildoune Homestead, 8 km north of Burrumbeet. Lal Lal Falls (30 m) on Moorabool River, 25 km south-east of city. White Swan Reservoir, 8 km north of Ballarat off Daylesford Rd; another attractive picnic spot with lawns, water views, picnic and barbecue facilities. Mooramong Homestead, National Trust property at Skipton, 53 km west; open for inspection by appointment. Mt Widderin Caves, 6 km south of Skipton. Yellowglen Winery, 24 km south-west, at Smythesdale. Berringa Mines Historic Reserve, 8 km from Smythesdale. Wallace Cheesery, 8 km east of Ballarat. Ballarat Aviation Museum, 4 km north-west on Learmonth Rd. Enfield State Park, near Enfield, 16 km south of Ballarat. **Tourist information:** Cnr Sturt and Albert Sts; (053) 32 2694. **Accommodation:** 5 hotels, 21 motels, 5 caravan/camping parks. **See also:** The Golden Age.
MAP REF. 200 A9, 207, 208 A3, 211 Q3

Beaufort   Population 1199
This small town on the Western Hwy, midway between Ballarat and Ararat, has a gold-rush history, like so many of the other towns in this area. The discovery of gold at Fiery Creek swelled its population in the late 1850s to nearly 100 000. Today Beaufort is primarily a centre for the surrounding pastoral and agricultural district. **Of interest:** Historic court-house. Band rotunda dating back to turn of century. **In the area:** Mt Cole State Forest, part of Great Dividing Range, 16 km north-west, via Raglan; peaceful natural area with camping grounds, ideal for bushwalks, picnics and observation of native flora and fauna. Lake Goldsmith, 14 km south of Beaufort. Steam Rally held 2 km east of lake in April and November. **Tourist information:** Map opposite band rotunda. **Accommodation:** 3 hotels, 1 motel, 1 caravan/camping park.
MAP REF. 211 O3

Beechworth   Population 3252
Once the centre of the great Ovens gold-mining region, Beechworth lies 24 km off the Ovens Hwy, between Wangaratta and Wodonga on 'The Kelly Way' (Old Sydney Rd). This is one of Victoria's best-preserved and most beautiful gold towns,

magnificently sited in the foothills of the Alps. Its public buildings are of architectural merit and the whole town has been classified historically important by the National Trust. The fabulously rich alluvial goldfield at Woolshed Creek was discovered by a local shepherd during the 1850s. A total 1 121 918 ounces of gold was mined in 14 years. A story is told of Daniel Cameron, campaigning to represent the Ovens Valley community: he rode through the town at the head of a procession of miners from Woolshed, on a horse shod with golden shoes. Sceptics claim they were merely gilded, but the tale is an indication of what Beechworth was like during the 'boom era', when its population was 42 000 and it boasted 61 hotels and a theatre at which international celebrities performed. **Of interest:** Fine government buildings built of local honey-coloured granite in the 1850s, all still in use. Particularly interesting are Camp and Ford Sts. Daily historic town tour from Tourist Information Centre; bookings essential. In Camp St, Harness and Carriage Museum, run by National Trust; Tanswell's Hotel, privately restored gracious lacework building; under Shire Offices, cell in which Ned Kelly was held; and Beechworth Gaol (built 1859), still used as a prison. On corner of Camp and Ford Sts, Bank of Victoria building housing the Rock Cavern with a gemstone collection. The historic former Bank of Australasia, in Ford St, offers fine dining in elegant surroundings. Country Rustica and Buckland Gallery, Ford St. Beechworth Galleries in Camp St. **In the area:** Robert O'Hara Burke Memorial Museum, Loch St, with relics of gold-rush and group of 16 mini-shops depicting town's main street as it was more than 100 years ago. Golden Hills Trout Farm, 2 km south. Fletcher Dam, on Beechworth Forest Drive, only 2.5 km south towards Stanley, has picnic facilities. The historic village of Stanley, 4 km south, sits among apple orchards, berry farms, nut plantations and tall forests high in the hills above Beechworth. Woolshed Creek, about 4 km north, is Kelly's Lookout. Waterfalls at Reid's Creek, Woolshed and Clear Creek. Black Springs Bakery, National Trust property 5 km west, an early goldfields bakery (no interior inspection). On road north to Chiltern, at Beechworth Cemetery, Chinese burning towers and Chinese cemetery. At Chiltern, 26 km north, 'Lake View', home of Henry Handel Richardson, restored and landscaped by National Trust and open daily. Beechworth Historic Park with Woolshed Falls historic walk, Gorge Scenic Drive (5 km), and gold-fossicking in limited areas. Lake Sambell for fishing, swimming, sailing, boating and canoeing. **Tourist information:** The

Rock Cavern, cnr Ford and Camp Sts; (057) 28 1374. **Accommodation:** 2 hotels, 5 motels, 2 caravan/camping parks. MAP REF. 217 P6

Benalla   Population 8490

This small city on the Hume Hwy is 40 km south of Wangaratta. Lake Benalla was created in the Broken River, which runs through the city, and there are recreation and picnic facilities there, with a protected sanctuary area for birdlife. During the late 1870s, Benalla was a focal-point of the activities of the notorious Kelly Gang, who were eventually captured at nearby Glenrowan in 1880. **Of interest:** Some splendid rose gardens; Benalla's popular Rose Festival is held in November. Botanical Gardens, Bridge St. Benalla Art Gallery, Bridge St, on shores of lake, contains important Ledger Collection of Australian paintings. Pots 'n' More in Mair St; paintings, pottery and craftwork. Benalla's Costume and Pioneer Museum, also in Mair St; Ned Kelly's cummerbund on display. Further items in Kelly Museum, Bridge St. Gliding Club of Victoria, on outskirts of town, at aerodrome. Also at aerodrome, hot-air ballooning. **In the area:** Lake Mokoan, 11 km to north-east; offers swimming, boating and picnic facilities. West of Midland Hwy about 4 km, Reef Hills State Park, 2030 ha of forest and wide variety of native flora and fauna. Pleasant day-trips to King Valley and spectacular Paradise Falls. Winton Motor Raceway, 6 km north-east. **Tourist information:** Pots 'n' More, 14 Mair St; (057) 62 1749. **Accommodation:** 1 hotel, 8 motels, 2 caravan/camping parks. MAP REF. 217 M8

Bendigo   Population 53 944

This is one of Victoria's most famous gold-mining towns. Sited at the junction of five highways, it is centrally located for trips to many of the other gold towns in the surrounding areas. Bendigo's history is indeed golden: the rush began here in 1851 and gold production continued for 100 years. The affluence of the period can still be seen today in many splendid public and commercial buildings. Built in 1897, the historic Shamrock Hotel has been restored to its original charm. **Of interest:** A drive around the city's streets, particularly Gladstone, Barkly and Rowan Sts, reveals many attractive lacework-verandahed buildings; the Sacred Heart Cathedral, Wattle St, the largest outside Melbourne, with a splendid 92-m-high spire; the Alexandra Fountain at Charing Cross; and the elaborate Renaissance-style Post Office (1887) and Law Courts (1896) in Pall

Mall. Self-guided Heritage Walk available. Bendigo Art Gallery (1890), View St. Central Deborah Mine, Violet St; a vivid reminder of Bendigo's history, which has been restored to working order; open daily. The famous Bendigo Vintage 'Talking Trams' run from mine on an 8 km city trip, which includes a stop at the Tram Barn Museum, Arnold St; 30 vintage trams on display. Trams run daily and a taped commentary gives information about the many points of interest seen. Golden Dragon Museum, Bridge St; features Chinese history on the goldfields, as well as largest display of Chinese processional regalia in the world, including world's oldest imperial dragon 'Loong' and largest imperial dragon, 'Sun Loong', more than 300 m long. Bendigo's Easter Fair (first held in 1871) features the ceremonial Chinese dragon. Dudley House (1859), View St, classified by National Trust; gracious old home in lovely gardens, now houses historical display. Lookout tower in Rosalind Park, town centre. Australia's largest National Swap Meet for vintage car and bike enthusiasts held annually in November. Annual Go-Cart Grand Prix held in February. **In the area:** Fortuna Villa mansion (1871), Chum St, 2 km south; open Sunday.

Chinese Joss House at Emu Point, 1 km north; built by Chinese miners who worked diggings here; classified by National Trust and open daily. At Myers Flat, 12 km north-west, Sandhurst Town, a recreation of a colonial town, complete with gold diggings, eucalyptus distillery, display of antique vehicles and working 2-ft-gauge railway. At Epsom, 6 km north-east, Epsom Market held every Sun. Hartland's Eucalyptus Factory and Historic Farm, Whipstick Forest, off Neilborough Rd, 12 km north; built in 1890 to process eucalyptus oil obtained from surrounding scrub. Bendigo Mohair Farm at Lockwood, 15 km south-west of town; open daily with guided tours. All in Mandurang Valley, 8 km south: Cherry Berry Farm and Water Fun Park for picking fresh berries, water sports, trout-fishing, Thunder Cave rapid-river ride and picnicking; historic Chateau Dore winery; Orchid Nursery and Tannery Lane Pottery. The vineyards and wineries around Bendigo produce some fine wines; many are open for sales and tastings. Chateau Le Amon winery, 10 km south of Bendigo. Balgownie Vineyard, 10 km west of Bendigo at Maiden Gully. Cannie Ridge Pottery, 29 km south, in Harcourt Valley, surrounded by apple and pear orchards.

Interior of Joss House, Emu Point, Bendigo

THE GOLDEN AGE

The cities and towns of the goldfields region of Victoria came to a peak of style and affluence in the 1880s, an affluence built on the first gold discoveries in the 1850s. The towns display all the frivolity and grandeur of Victorian architecture, having grown up in an age when it was believed that gold and wealth were going to be a permanent benefit in Victoria.

The two major cities of the region are Ballarat and Bendigo, but there are many other towns, large and small, dotted around. They all have beautiful old houses and public buildings, and many have other trappings of the past—statues, public gardens (sometimes with lakes), ornamental bandstands and grand avenues of English trees. Spring and autumn are the best seasons to visit this region, because then there are not the extremes of summer and winter temperatures and the flowers and foliage are at their best.

It is a quiet region now. The remaining small towns serve the rich pastoral district and secondary industries and services centre on the two cities.

It was once, however, an area of frantic activity. Gold was discovered at Clunes in 1851 and within three months 8000 people were on the diggings in the area between Buninyong and Ballarat. Nine months later there were 30 000 men on the goldfields and four years later 100 000. The population of the city of Melbourne dwindled alarmingly and immigrants rushed to the diggings from Great Britain, America and many other countries. Ships' crews, and sometimes even their captains, abandoned their vessels and trekked to the diggings to try their luck. Tent cities sprang up on the plains as men dug and panned for gold. There were remarkable finds of huge nuggets in the early days but, finally, the amount of gold obtained by panning in the rivers and by digging grew less and less. They were remarkable communities: 'shanty' towns, the streets crowded day and night with hawkers and traders; there were pubs and dancing-rooms and continuous sounds of music and revelry.

As time went on, the surface gold was worked out and it was followed by expensive company-backed operations, mining in deep shafts, stamping and crushing the ore in steam-powered plants on the surface.

The success of these methods heralded a new era, that of the company mines, outside investors and stock exchange speculation. It led to a more stable workforce and to the well-established communities which slowly evolved into towns of the region today. As the pastoral potential began to be fully exploited, it was the perfect scene for expansion and optimism.

The years between 1870 and 1890 saw the towns embellished with fine civic buildings, mansions, solid town houses, churches, hotels and all the trappings of affluence. Thus Ballarat, Bendigo, Castlemaine and, to a lesser extent, Clunes, Creswick, Daylesford and Maldon became extraordinary *nouveau riche* visions of the current British taste.

The Western Highway between Melbourne and Ballarat is at its most scenic as it rises into the Pentland Hills. Rounded volcanic hills encircle **Bacchus Marsh**, which is approached by a magnificent avenue of North American elms commemorating those who died in the Great War. Bacchus Marsh is adjacent to the Lerderderg and Werribee Rivers, which enter

Sovereign Hill, Ballarat

dramatic gorges close to the town. Just off the highway are the small rural towns of Myrniong and Ballan, Gordon and Bungaree. South of the highway near Bungaree is Dunnstown, dominated by its bluestone distillery and the bulk of Mount Warrenheip, where an excellent view of the district can be had from the summit.

A turn-off to the south near Ballarat leads to **Buninyong**, the scene of one of the first gold strikes in Victoria. This impressive township with a grand tree-lined main street has a number of striking buildings—the Crown Hotel and white-walled Uniting Church are of the 1860s, while the combined council chambers and court-house of 1886 are in rich Italianate design, unified by a central clock-tower.

The city of **Ballarat** was laid out to the west of the diggings within twelve months of the first discovery of gold. The design included a magnificent chief thoroughfare, Sturt Street, wide enough for future plantations and monuments. The primitive buildings of early settlement were gradually replaced by boom-style architecture in the 1880s. Italianate, Romanesque, Gothic and French Renaissance styles mingle together; porticoes, colonnades and ornamental stone facades vie with verandahs of lavish cast-iron decoration. There are many superb buildings, the most notable being the post office, the railway station, the town hall, the stock exchange, the former Ballarat gaol, the Wesley Church, the George Hotel, Reids Coffee Palace, the Bailey Mansion, the Roman Catholic bishop's residence, Loreto Abbey and the art gallery. It is a city of many beautiful gardens, particularly the Botanical Gardens adjacent to Lake Wendouree, famous for the annual begonia display in March.

Without doubt Ballarat's major attraction is **Sovereign Hill**. This re-created gold-mining township is a fascinating place for a day's outing to interest all the family. Commence your outing by visiting the excellent 'Voyage to Discovery' orientation centre, near the main entrance.

Gold was discovered in Ballarat in 1851, and a visit to the Red Hill Gully Diggings at Sovereign Hill will show you something of the life of those early days. Your visit will not be complete without the chance to pan for 'colour'. A friendly digger will give you a lesson, but you must be sure to purchase your licence first or you may find yourself being arrested by the watchful trooper!

Main Street is lined with faithfully re-created shops and businesses of the 1851–1861 period. These are based on actual shops and businesses that were operating in Ballarat at that time. Perhaps you will be tempted by the aroma of freshly-baked bread from the wood-fire brick oven of the Hope Bakery. Next door you may dress in topcoat or crinoline and be photographed in true Victorian pose. Across the road, mid-nineteenth-century printing-presses in the Ballarat *Times* office can be used to print your name on a WANTED poster, similar to that issued for Lalor and Black after the uprising at the Eureka Stockade in 1854.

Few can even pass the well-stocked grocery without a surge of nostalgia for days gone by. The tiny sweet-shop nearby sells all manner of sweets made to Victorian recipes at Brown's confectionery factory, further up the street.

Those with larger appetites may wine and dine at the United States Hotel or enjoy a digger's lunch of soup, roast meat and apple pie at the New York Bakery. For some energetic relaxation, try your hand at ninepin bowling on the 40-metre-long alley in the Empire Bowling Saloon. The accommodation complex, Government Camp, provides comfortable and inexpensive lodging ranging from tents to self-contained units.

During school terms you will be enchanted to watch a 'class of 1856' at the Red Hill National School. Here children dress in period costume, learn from actual 1850s texts, and are totally involved in living the life of a mid-nineteenth-century goldfields child.

The towering poppet-head, the hiss of steam and the thunder of the stamper battery will draw you to the Sovereign Quartz Mine. Take a guided tour of the underground area; here you will see examples of early mining techniques and even some original workings of the 1880s period.

As you wander through the streets you will meet costumed diggers and businessfolk, and ladies in bell-shaped

crinolines and bonnets. Stop and talk to them and you will learn more about life in the days of the 'rush'.

Sovereign Hill is open daily, except Christmas Day. There are admission charges, and ample parking is available. Enquiries to the Marketing Department, Sovereign Hill Post Office, Ballarat 3350.

The Gold Museum, opposite Sovereign Hill, has a collection of nuggets, alluvial gold and coins, as well as a Eureka Exhibition outlining the Eureka rebellion.

Beyond Ballarat, on the Midland Highway is **Creswick**, a picturesque valley town with a wonderfully ornate town hall. The bluestone tower of St John's Church dominates the town's western hill and on the hilltop across the valley is a Tudor-style hospital building which is now a school of forestry.

To make a turn off the highway to **Clunes** is well worth while. Gold was first discovered here in July 1851, but it proved difficult to get supplies to this remote township, so the rush was limited and the later discoveries at Buninyong and Ballarat quickly diverted attention from the area. Of

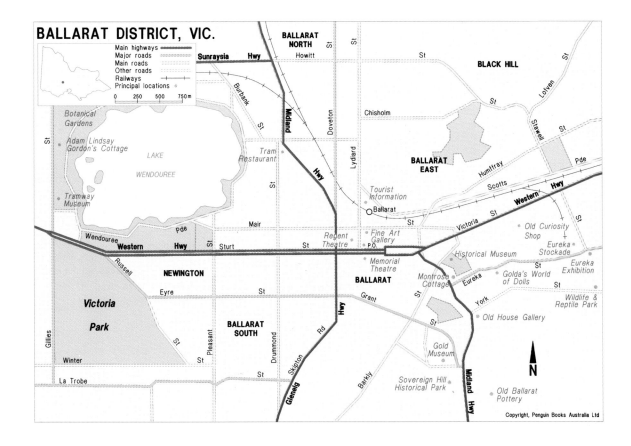

particular interest in Clunes are the rich verandahed facades in the shopping area of Fraser Street and the elegant architectural style of the banks, hotels, post office and town hall.

On the Western Highway, 133 kilometres north-west of Ballarat, past **Ararat** (where a gold-rush began in 1857), is **Stawell**. Gold was discovered at the present site of Stawell in 1853; by 1857 there was a population of 30 000, and the township was proclaimed the following year. Gold-mining continued in the area until 1920. Today visitors can recapture some of the atmosphere of the gold-rush era at the Mount Pleasant Diggings and Alluvial Gold Memorial.

North-east of Ballarat up the Midland Highway is **Daylesford**, another former gold-mining town set in picturesque wooded hills around Wombat Hill Gardens and Lake Daylesford. The town has a number of churches in the 'Gothic revival' style and an imposing town hall, post office and school. On the hill are groves of rhododendrons, exotic trees and a lookout tower which provides a view of Mount Franklin (a perfectly preserved volcanic crater) and Mount Tarrengower. Several kilometres north of Daylesford are natural springs containing lime, iron, magnesia and other minerals. This is the famed Hepburn Spa, which attracted visitors in the nineteenth century for its medicinal properties. Bottling mineral water is still the town's main industry.

Further north on the road to Bendigo is **Castlemaine**, a larger town and one of the most picturesque in the region. The streetscape in the centre of the town has remained virtually unaltered since the early days, for the prosperity of the 1860s diminished and the town settled down to a quieter rural life. One of the most notable buildings is the Castlemaine Market, an unusual Palladian-inspired building which was restored in 1974 and which now contains a museum portraying the history of the town and the Mount Alexander goldfields. The town boasts some other fine buildings, including the great post office in Italianate style with a central clock-tower, the former telegraph office, the mechanics' institute, the Imperial Hotel and the Commercial Banking Company building. High on a hill above the town are the stone and redbrick gaol and the obelisk built in 1862 to commemorate the ill-fated Burke and Wills expedition.

Central Deborah Goldmine, Bendigo

Nearby **Maldon** was declared a notable town by the National Trust in 1962. The winding streets are flanked by low buildings, with deep verandahs shading the bluestone pavements which were laid in 1866.

The city of **Bendigo** is the jewel of the region and is Victoria's most outstanding example of a boom town. Gothic- and classical-styled buildings have been designed in vast proportions, richly ornamented and combined with the materials of the age, cast iron and cast cement.

The post office and law courts are among the most impressive high-Victorian public buildings in Australia. Opposite the post office is the Shamrock Hotel—a massive, verandahed structure which once boasted an electric bell to ring for service in each of its 100 rooms. Many of Bendigo's important buildings were designed by the German architect William Charles Vahland. His work included the Benevolent Asylum and Hospital, the school of mines, the mechanics' institute, the town hall, the Masonic hall, the Capital Theatre, four banks and the handsome Alexandra fountain at Charing Cross, the centre of Bendigo.

Bendigo Art Gallery houses a large collection of 19th-century British and European artworks and decorative arts, which complements its outstanding collection of Australian paintings.

Central Deborah Goldmine was the last deep-reef goldmine in Bendigo. Sunk in 1909 and closed in 1954, it has been restored and is open for inspection. The mine is 411 metres deep with seventeen levels, and the visitor level at sixty-one metres has a 350-metre

circuit illustrating the geological features of the Bendigo region and the machinery used in the gold-retrieval process. At ground-level are the 21-metre poppet head, engine room, installations and other exhibits, all of which can be inspected. The mine is also the point of departure for the eight-kilometre (one-hour) tour through Bendigo by the city's famous vintage talking trams, with their taped commentary on attractions and historic points of interest.

Sandhurst Town, off the Loddon Valley Highway, 12 kilometres from Bendigo, represents a typical country town of 1929 with all the glamour of the gold-rush days. Its attractions include the Fair Dinkum Eucalyptus Distillery, the Honey Pavilion and various fascinating shops. The Red Rattler train leaves the town regularly to travel through the Whipstick Forest to the Goldrush Gully diggings with its entertaining street theatre involving colourful characters. During the last weekend in August, in odd years, Sandhurst Town stages a re-enactment of Bendigo's gold-digger uprising of 1854, in which more than eighty actors replay the struggle against the injustice of the Gold Licence.

Australian Designer Travel, Bendigo, organise personal itineraries to include accommodation in homes, farms, retreats and cottages throughout the goldfields area. Bendigo Goldseeker Tours organise gold-fossicking excursions and include instruction in the use of metal detectors.

The goldfields region can be enjoyed in three days or three weeks according to time and taste. Reasonably priced accommodation is available throughout the region. An excellent way to see the region is via the **Goldfields Tourist Route**, a 450-kilometre triangle road route linking Ballarat, Ararat, Stawell, Bendigo and Castlemaine. Free maps marking the route are available at the Victorian Information Centre, RACV offices and various tourist information centres throughout the goldfields.

More detailed information can be obtained also from the Bendigo Tourist Information Centre, Charing Cross, Bendigo, (054) 41 5244; and at 26 High St, Kangaroo Flat.

Lake Eppalock, 26 km south-east of town, for camping, fishing, water sports, picnics and barbecues. Horsedrawn caravans can be hired at Bridgewater, 37 km north-west. **Tourist information:** Charing Cross, (054) 41 5244; 26 High St, Kangaroo Flat. **Accommodation:** 10 hotels, 25 motels, 9 caravan/camping parks. **See also:** The Golden Age; Victoria's Wine Regions.
MAP REF. 216 C9

Birchip   Population 845
On the main rail link between Melbourne and Mildura, Birchip gets its water supply from the Wimmera - Mallee stock and domestic channel system. **Of interest:** Junction of two major irrigation channels constructed in early 1900s, 1 km north of town. Sections of original Dog Fence, 20 km north, vermin-proof barrier constructed in 1883 between the Murray River near Swan Hill and South Australian border. Tchum Lake, 8 km east, with facilities for motor boats; caravan park at lake has excellent facilities. Sites of historic interest within Shire are indicated by a series of markers; descriptive brochure of sites available from Shire Offices, Main St. **Tourist information** Birchip Motel, Sunraysia Hwy; (054) 92 2566. **Accommodation:** 2 hotels, 1 motel, 1 caravan/camping park.
MAP REF. 116 F13, 213 L4

Boort   Population 801
A pleasant rural and holiday town on the shores of Lake Boort with excellent sporting facilities. The lake is popular for water sports, has good picnic facilities and beaches, and offers trout and redfin fishing. There is prolific native birdlife in the area. **Tourist information:** Lake Boort Motel, opposite lake; (054) 55 2106. **Accommodation:** 1 motel, 2 hotels, 1 caravan/camping park.
MAP REF. 213 P5, 216 A4

Bright   Population 1673
In the heart of the beautiful Ovens Valley and at the foothills of the Victorian Alps, Bright is an attractive tourist centre and a base for winter sports enthusiasts. The town offers easy access to the resorts at Mt Hotham, Mt Buffalo and Falls Creek, and a number of ski-hire shops in the town stay open late during the winter season. The area is excellent for bushwalking and trout-fishing, and is very photogenic, particularly in autumn. The discovery of gold was responsible for the town's beginnings. Tensions between white and Chinese miners led to the notorious Buckland Valley riots of 1857 in which the Chinese were driven from their claims with some brutality. The remains

of the alluvial goldfields can still be seen about the area. There is a good variety of restaurants, counter meals, cafes and take-away food shops. **Of interest:** The many English and European trees in Bright display spectacular autumnal colours and Bright holds Spring and Autumn Festivals in October and May respectively. In Main St, Gallery 90 and Country Collectables. Bright Art Gallery and Cultural Centre, Mountbatten Ave. Historical Museum, located in old railway station, in Station Ave. Lotsafun Amusement Park adjacent, entrance in Mill Rd. Ovens River runs through town; areas along its banks are popular picnic and camping spots; walk to Riverside Canyon. Excellent summer swimming in deep weir next to Memorial Park in Main St; coin-operated barbecues, children's playground and shallow pool. **In the area:** Pleasant walking-tracks lead to Clearspot Lookout, from Bakers Gully Rd, and Huggins Lookout, from Deacon Ave. The Alpine Road south-east to Mt Hotham gives superb views of Mt Feathertop, the Razor Back and Mt Bogong. Wandiligong, a National Trust classified hamlet in a scenic valley, 6 km south, is linked to Bright by

a walking and cycle track. At Harrietville, a tiny and tranquil township 25 km south of Bright, Pioneer Park open-air museum; 4 km north of town, two trout farms. Porepunkah, 6 km north-west of Bright, at junction of Ovens and Buckland Rivers with convenient access to Mt Buffalo, has district's newest attraction, Boynton's of Bright Winery and Restaurant; open daily. Horse-riding available. **Tourist information:** Delany Ave, opposite Centennial Park; (057) 55 2275, Sports Centre, Gavan St; (057) 55 1339. **Accommodation:** 2 hotel/motels, 9 motels, 7 caravan/camping parks.
MAP REF. 217 R9, 219 B9

Broadford   Population 1893
A small town off the Hume Hwy near Mt Disappointment, the State Forest and Murchison Falls. Picnic facilities at Anderson's Gardens, at the entrance to the State Forest. **Of interest:** Display of old printing equipment in *Broadford Courier* building, High St. Barbecues and picnic facilities in park in town centre; also replica of drop-slab pioneer cottage. **In the area:** Turn-off 20 km east to Strath Creek for scenic drive through Valley of a

Autumn trees at Bright

VICTORIA'S NATIONAL PARKS

Twelve Apostles, Port Campbell National Park

Although it is Australia's smallest mainland state, Victoria houses over one hundred national, state, wilderness and regional parks; there will be something for everyone in every season among them.

Victoria's parks protect the wide range of her land and vegetation types: from alps, open grasslands and desert mallee, to rainforests, tall forests, coasts, volcanic plains and heathlands. Spring and summer are the best seasons to visit, when wildflowers bloom in natural surroundings and sun-lovers can head for parks along the coast to swim, surf, canoe, boat or fish. Autumn, with its mild weather, beckons the bushwalker, and winter means skiing at alpine parks.

The 646 000 hectare **Alpine National Park**, created in December 1989, is the state's largest national park. Stretching along the Great Dividing Range, the park links with the Kosciusko National Park in New South Wales and its neighbour Namadgi National Park in the Australian Capital Territory. The park protects the habitats of a variety of flora and fauna, including the rare mountain pygmy possum (the world's only exclusively alpine marsupial). The Alps are renowned for their sublime landscapes, features characterised by Mount Bogong and Mount Feathertop (Victoria's two highest mountains) and the unique Bogong High Plains. During spring and summer the high plains are carpeted with wildflowers; more than 1100 native plant species are found in the park, including twelve found nowhere else in the world. The park is ideal for

bushwalking, horseriding and cross-country skiing. In the summer months most roads provide easy access for two-wheel-drive vehicles, allowing a range of scenic drives with short walks to lookouts and other points of interest.

Yanga-nyawi (Murray Sunset) National Park in the north-west, is the State's most recent, and, at 633 000 hectares, the second largest national park. It contains a diversity of semi-arid environments from riverine floodplains to heathlands, salt lakes and woodlands, which support a tremendous variety of wildlife, particularly birdlife. This park is best avoided in the heat of summer. **Wyperfeld National Park** nearby, also contains hundreds of species of plants and birdlife and is also best avoided in the high heat of summer. It's a great park to visit in the winter and spring in good rainfall years for wildflower displays and also in autumn for crisp, clear days—perfect for bushwalking and birdwatching.

Another park in the north west of the state is the smaller **Hattah-Kulkyne National Park**. Typically, summers here are long, hot and dry: rainfall is usually under 300 mm per year. Both plants and animals of this area have evolved strategies for avoiding or tolerating heat and dryness. Some animals burrow and others just rest during the heat of the day and feed and drink early and late; while some birds catch thermals to cooler air. After rainfall and flooding from the Murray River, the serenely beautiful Hattah Lakes sytem transforms the park into a bird haven and a wonderful wildflower landscape.

The **Gariwerd (Grampians) National Park** is the state's third largest. Its 167 000 hectares comprise marvellous scenery, wildlife and tourist facilities. The park is famous for its rugged sandstone ranges, waterfalls, wildflowers, wide variety of birds and mammals, as well as its Aboriginal rock art sites. The peaks rise to heights of over 1000 metres and form the western edge of the Great Dividing Range. Gariwerd is no doubt best seen by foot and there are many interesting walking tracks, such as the easy graded, well marked Wonderland Track, through to the more challenging walks across the Major Mitchell Plateau. Also those with limited time or who don't want to walk are not left out of the feeling of spaciousness and grandeur, with many scene drives available on good roads.

The main thing most visitors to the **Little Desert National Park** discover is that it is neither little nor a desert. It is, in fact, best know for its amazing displays of wildflowers in the spring; more than 600 species of flowering plants are found here, including more than 40 ground orchids. Another special thing about the Little Desert is that it is the home of the mallee fowl. These birds build mounds for eggs that can be as much as five metres in diameter and 1.5 metres high.

Several parks contain rock formations of great geological interest. At **Mount Eccles**, an extinct volcano in south-west Victoria. A lava canal, lava cave and the formation called the Stony Rises are exceptional features here, while the crater contains the tranquil Lake Surprise.

More well-known and unusual rock structures are found at **Port Campbell National Park**: 'The Twelve Apostles', 'The Arch' and 'Loch Ard Gorge' are majestic formations sculpted out of soft limestone cliffs by the restless sea.

Obviously, it is the spectacular coastal scenery which makes this park so popular, however this is an interesting linear park for birds, with around 100 species being recorded. It was a popular place with Aboriginal people too if the number of shell middens along the coast is a gauge. And, it is especially notorious for being part of the shipwreck coast.

Closer to Melbourne are the beautiful lush tree fern gullies and towering mountain ash forests of the **Otway National Park**, plus the special **Melba Gully State Park** to the north-west of the national park near Lavers Hill. Because of the treacherous nature of the waters, a lighthouse was the first piece of 'civilisation', being opened in 1848 after two years in the building. Activities to be enjoyed include sightseeing all year (even in winter storms), camping, surfing, fishing and walking are most enjoyed in spring and summer. There are guided walks in summer to see the glow worms at Melba Gully.

Eastern Victoria's mild and fairly wet climate, combined with rich soils, has produced vast areas of dense forest, particularly in the uplands. These are especially attractive to bushwalkers and campers, who will find here a wide range of trees—mainly eucalypts, but also native pines, banksias and paperbarks. In summer, many bushwalkers prefer to explore a coastal park; **Wilsons Promontory National Park** is the best known and one of the most popular in Gippsland. The Prom, as it is known, really does have something for everyone. There is the concentration of amenities and accommodation, including camping and caravan sites, at Tidal River, plus the visitor information centre and park office. Leaflets for around 80 km of walking tracks are available here. Other natural attractions include secluded bays and magnificent stretches of beaches, granite outcrops, wildflowers which begin blooming in late winter and keep spring colourful, while in summer there is the highest usage of everything with campsites only available by ballot!

At **Organ Pipes National Park**, only 20 km north-west of Melbourne, more interesting rock formations; a series of hexagonal basalt columns rising more than twenty metres above Jacksons Creek. These 'organ pipes' were formed when lava cooled in an ancient river-bed. While this is the best known feature of the small, 85 ha park, it is also excellent for picnics, walks and bird observing. Another favourite haunt of bushwalkers 50 km north-east of Melbourne is **Kinglake National Park** where wooded valleys, fern gullies and timbered ridges provide a perfect setting for two breathtakingly beautiful waterfalls, Masons and Wombelano Falls. From a lookout point, visitors can take in a panoramic view of the Yarra Valley, Port Phillip Bay and the You Yangs Range.

Just thirty-five kilometres east of Melbourne is the green wonderland of the 1900-hectare **Dandenong Ranges National Park**. This park includes pockets of rainforest in which huge fronds of ferns form a canopy overhead, screening the sun and creating a cool, moist environment in which mosses, delicate ferns and flowers, including over thirty species of orchids, all thrive. There are more than twenty species of native animals, including echidnas, platypuses, ring-tailed possums and sugar gliders, in the park; kookaburras, rosellas and cockatoos often visit picnic areas. The spectacular rufous fantail can be seen in the summer months. There are over 100 species of birds, but make sure you identify them by sight and not only by sound, because the lyrebird can mimic their calls.

Point Nepean National Park is probably the most interesting park close to Melbourne mainly because for more than 100 years it has been out of bounds to most people. It has associations with early settlement, shipping, quarantine and defence which give it a special air. As one of Victoria's major bicentennial projects, an information centre, walking tracks, displays and other facilities were provided during 1988/89 and today the total area of the park, including former Cape Schanck Coastal Park, is 2200 hectares.

To prevent overcrowding and damage to the environment, no more than 600 people are permitted in the Point Nepean area at one time. So bookings for day visits with a park-use fee are required, especially during summer. Vehicles are not permitted beyond the orientation centre, so walking or taking the transporter are the only ways to get around. Highlights of the park are Fort Nepean itself, the cemetery with burials dating from the 1850s and Cheviot Hill walk.

Canoeists will find excitement shooting the rapids or exploring the gorge of **Snowy River National Park** or **Mitchell River National Park**, while bushwalkers can hike through forests of native pine, alpine ash, messmate and shining gum.

Some of the most attractive coastal scenery close to any major regional centre can be found in and around **The Lakes National Park**. The park is surrounded by the waters of the Gippsland Lakes, ideal for sailing and boating. The 2390 hectares is based on Sperm Whale Head and harbours a large population of kangaroos and more than 140 bird species. Camping, picnicking and an excellent network of walking tracks provide the distractions for those who are land based.

Croajingolong National Park has 87 500 hectares of coastline and hinterland stretching from Sydenham Inlet to the New South Wales border. The area contains remote rainforest, woodland, ocean beaches, rocky promontories, inlets and coves. Several rare species of wildlife can be found here, such as the smoky mouse and the ground parrot, and an array of spring wildflowers. There is a wide range of activities for visitors at Croajingolong, with a resort centre at Mallacoota and other towns along the Princes Highway offering comfortable accommodation and fine food.

For more information, contact the Department of Conservation and Environment at 240 Victoria Pde, East Melbourne; (03) 412 4011.

Thousand Hills. At Kilmore, 14 km south-west, some fine old buildings, including Whitburgh Cottage (1857). Cable tram rides in Hudson Park. **Tourist information:** Shire Offices, 113 High St; (057) 84 1204. **Accommodation:** 2 hotels, 1 motel.
MAP REF. 201 M4, 208 H1, 216 G12

Buchan   Population 220

This small township, set in the heart of Gippsland mountain country north-east of Bairnsdale, is famous for its remarkable series of limestone caves. The two main caves, Royal and Fairy, have been opened up and tours are conducted daily. A park and a spring-fed swimming pool are located in the hills behind the caves. **In the area:** Spectacular views from lookout over Little River Gorge, 70 km north of Buchan on road to McKillops Bridge. Suggan Buggan schoolhouse (1865), 64 km north of Buchan. Cobberas-Tingaringy National Park, 10 km north-west of Suggan Buggan; spectacular mountain scenery. Stonehenge Rockhounds Museum at Buchan South, 7 km south-west. **Tourist information:** General Store, Main St; (051) 55 9202. **Accommodation:** 1 motel, 1 hotel, 2 caravan/camping parks.
MAP REF. 220 H6

Camperdown   Population 3458

This south-western town on the Princes Hwy has an English-style charm due to its many gracious buildings and avenues of elms. Over fifty buildings are of historical significance and can be viewed by following the Heritage Trail; brochure available from Tourist Information Centre. The centre for a rich pastoral district, Camperdown is also noted for the fishing in the numerous volcanic crater lakes in the area. **Of interest:** Clock Tower (1896), cnr Manifold and Pike Sts. Historical Society Museum in Manifold St. Buggy Museum, Ower St. Court-house and Post Office, both in Manifold St. Elm Avenue Tea-rooms. **In the area:** The lookout at Mt Leura, 1 km west, an extinct volcano next to the perfect cone shape of Mt Sugarloaf, gives many superb views over the numerous crater lakes and volcanoes looking north across the plains to the Grampians. Lake Corangamite, a salt lake 13 km east, is Victoria's largest. Excellent fishing lakes include Bullen Merri, 3 km east, and Purrumbete, 4 km south-east, which is well stocked with Quinnat salmon. It also has excellent water sports facilities, picnic spots and a caravan park. Cobden, 13 km south, is a peaceful dairying town. Timboon, 27 km further south, is a pretty timbered township also

centred on dairying. Timboon Farmhouse Cheese, just south of the township, has tastings and door sales. The 10-km Old Timboon Railway Line Walk takes about 3 1/2 hours and requires a 14-km car shuttle. A picturesque road leads 18 km south from Timboon to the tiny seaside village of Port Campbell, which has good rock fishing and is close to a spectacular stretch of scenery along the Great Ocean Road. This is the area of the Port Campbell National Park, which has camping and caravan facilities. Otway Ranges Deer and Wildlife Park, 20 km east of Port Campbell. Mt Noorat has the Alan Marshall Memorial Walking Track off Glenormiston Rd, Noorat, 20 km north-west, options are a 3 km summit and return (1 hr) and a crater-rim 1.5 km circuit (1/2 hr); this perfect volcanic cone provides excellent views over the Western District. Farm holidays at Pilgrims Way dairy farm near Cobden. **Tourist information:** 188 Manifold St; (055) 93 1025. **Accommodation:** 3 hotels, 3 motels, 1 caravan/camping park. **See also:** The Western District.
MAP REF. 211 N8

Cann River   Population 318

A popular stop for Sydney - Melbourne motorists using the Princes Hwy. Excellent fishing and bushwalking in the rugged hinterland. **Of interest:** Croajingolong National Park, main access 15 - 20 km south; stretches from Sydenham Inlet to the NSW border, incorporating the Captain James Cook Lighthouse Reserve at Point Hicks, Wingan, Timboon and Mallacoota Inlets. **Tourist information:** Conservation and Environment Information Centre, Princes Hwy; (051) 58 6351. **Accommodation:** 1 hotel, 3 motels, 2 caravan/ camping parks.
MAP REF. 109 D13, 221 L6

Casterton   Population 1842

Given the Roman name meaning 'walled city' because of lush hills surrounding the valley, Casterton is on the Glenelg Hwy, 42 km east of the South Australian border. The Glenelg River runs through the town and as well as providing excellent fishing and mineral and gem fossicking along its banks near to the town, it also offers water-skiing at Nelson, some 70 km south. Launch trips can be taken at Nelson to the river's mouth on the coast at Discovery Bay. **Of interest:** Casterton Historical Museum in old Railway Buildings, cnr Jackson and Clarke Sts. Bryan Park, the Soldiers Memorial Park, Henty St, has a children's playground. David Geschke Fine Porcelain Gallery, Casterton Racecourse Rd. Alma and Judith

Zaadstra Fine Art Gallery, Henty St. Excellent sporting facilities, swimming pool and trail-bike riding facilities at Long Lead Swamp, Penola Rd. Tourist Information Centre has displays of locally made art and craft, and picnic and barbecue facilities. **In the area:** Angling Club Reserve at Roseneath, 24 km north-west; picnic and camping facilities. Warrock Homestead (1843), classified by National Trust, 26 km north-east; a unique collection of buildings and open for inspection. The area surrounding Casterton is mainly grazing land with rolling hills and areas of natural forest with excellent bush walks and a variety of fauna and flora. Baileys Rocks, 50 km north; a collection of giant granite boulders of a unique green colour. Other interesting geological formations to be found at the Hummocks, 12 km north-east, and Bahgalah Bluff, 20 km south-west. **Tourist information:** Shiels Tce; (055) 81 2070. **Accommodation:** 2 hotel/motels, 1 motel, 1 caravan/camping park. **See also:** The Western District.
MAP REF. 210 D4

Castlemaine   Population 7656

Along with Kyneton and Maldon, Castlemaine epitomises the gold-mining towns of north-western Victoria. A very attractive and interesting town, it is built on low hills at the foot of Mt Alexander, on the Calder Hwy, 119 km from Melbourne. During the 1850s and 1860s enormous quantities of gold were found in its surface fields. This gold boom saw Castlemaine grow rapidly and many of the fine old buildings which remain today were built during this period. **Of interest:** The Town Market, Mostyn St, built in 1862 and based on classical Roman design, is an impressive building unusual in its Victorian environment; operated by the National Trust, it houses audio-visual displays, a photographic collection and relics of the town and district in its heyday. Other splendid buildings are the Midland and Imperial hotels, Templeton and Lyttleton Sts respectively, both with verandahs decorated with iron lacework. The court-house, town hall and library, the art gallery and museum are all in Lyttleton St. Buda, Urquhart St, the home from the late 1850s of silversmith/jeweller Ernest Leviny and his family, has beautifully preserved gardens of the era and the home is a delight. Botanic Gardens, Parker St. Every even year the Castlemaine State Festival incorporates theatre, opera, children's shows, art, craft and music for all early in November; in the other years a Spring Garden Festival is held. **In the area:** The Wattle Gully gold-mine and Badger's Keep Nursery at Chewton, 4 km south-east; trees, roses,

THE WESTERN DISTRICT

Some famous Australians have been born and bred in this south-western part of Victoria, including a prime minister or two. Many have been members of the wealthy land-owning families whose gracious homesteads are dotted about this beautiful pastoral area. The Western District supports one-third of Victoria's best sheep and cattle, and the region's merino wool is acknowledged to be the finest in the land.

Many of the Western District towns boast some splendid pioneer buildings. Of special interest are **Hamilton** — recognised as the 'Wool Capital of the World' — and the attractive little towns of **Coleraine** and **Casterton**. Several of the district's historic homesteads are open for inspection, including 'Warrock' (near Casterton), which has thirty-three original farm buildings still in operation. Of particular interest to nature-lovers are the remaining colonies of the eastern

Surf fishing at Warrnambool

barred bandicoot. **Warrnambool**, situated on the south coast, is the commercial capital of the Western District and gateway to the Great Ocean Road,

15 kilometres east of the city. The winter visits of southern right whales are a popular attraction.

The heart of the district is fairly flat grazing land. To the east, the volcanic lake area around **Camperdown** offers great fishing and is well developed for water sports. To the south, a rugged coastline stretches from **Anglesea** to the tiny hamlet of **Nelson**, at the mouth of the Glenelg River. To the north, the high rocky ranges of the Grampians break through the gently rolling countryside. An excellent scenic route to Halls Gap is along the Mt Abrupt Road from **Dunkeld**.

Further information can be obtained from local tourist information centres, especially the Hamilton and District Tourist Information Centre, Lonsdale St, Hamilton; (055) 72 3746; and the Warrnambool Tourist Information Centre, 600 Raglan Pde, Warrnambool; (055) 64 7837.

---

herbs and other plants, including a large collection of apple varieties on show at the nursery. Pottery at Newstead, 16 km north-west, and the Burnett Gallery and Garden on the Burnett Road in North Castlemaine; open weekends. Harcourt, 10 km north, has good fishing and picnic spots; the Harcourt Valley Estate and the Mt Alexander wineries. Nearby on Mt Alexander there is a koala reserve. Vaughan, 12 km south-east, Fryerstown, 10 km south-east, and Guildford, 11 km south-west villages; Chinese cemetery and mineral springs at Vaughan, the Duke of Cornwall mine buildings at Fryerstown and the Big Tree at Guildford. **Tourist information:** Duke St; (054) 72 2480. **Accommodation:** 5 hotels, 3 motels, 2 caravan/camping parks. **See also:** The Golden Age.
MAP REF. 200 E2, 216 C11

Charlton   Population 1341
A supply centre for a rich wheat district, Charlton is set on the banks of the Avoca River, at the intersection of the Calder and Borung Hwys in north-central Victoria. **Of interest:** Fishing in Avoca River. Walking-track along river, about 2 km one way, from town to weir. **In the area:** Wooroonook Lake, 12 km west, for

swimming and boating. Bish Deer Farm, further 18 km west. Wychitella State Forest, 27 km east, for interesting native flora and fauna, including the lowan, or mallee fowl. **Tourist information:** Shire Offices, High St; (054) 91 1755. **Accommodation:** 2 hotels, 2 motels, 1 caravan/camping park.
MAP REF 213 N6

Chiltern   Population 935
Halfway between Wangaratta and Wodonga, Chiltern is 1 km off the Hume Hwy. It was once a gold-mining boom town with 14 suburbs. Many of its attractive buildings have been classified by the National Trust; Historic Walk leaflet available. **Of interest:** Athenaeum Museum, Conness St (1866); contains Goldfields Library collection. Cats Whisker Wireless Museum, Gaunt St. The Pharmacy, Conness St, (1868); chemist shop with all original features. Stephen's Motor Museum, Conness St; collection of motoring memorabilia. *Federal Standard* newspaper office, Main St; dating from gold-mining era (1860-61) and classified by National Trust; open by appointment for groups. Grape Vine Gallery, formerly Grape Vine Hotel, cnr Conness and Main Sts; boasts a vast grape vine. Picnic spots

with barbecues at Lake Anderson, access Main St. Walking-track from lakeshore over a bridge to 'Lake View', Victoria St, home of well-known author Henry Handel Richardson, classified by National Trust; open weekends, public and school holidays. **In the area:** Chiltern State Park surrounds the town and is popular for its historic drive and for bushwalking, nature observation and picnicking. Magenta open-cut mine, 2 km east. Black Dog Creek Pottery, 3 km north-west on Chiltern Valley Rd. Pioneer Cemetery, 2 km south-west. **Tourist information:** Shire Offices, Main St; (057) 26 1206. **Accommodation:** 1 motel, 1 caravan/camping park. **See also:** Victoria's Wine Regions.
MAP REF. 117 O13, 217 P5

Clunes   Population 817
The first reported gold find in the state was made at Clunes on 7 July 1851 when James Esmond announced his discovery of 'pay dirt'. The town, some 40 km north of Ballarat, has several sandstone buildings classified by the National Trust and the verandahed elegance of Fraser St is worth noting. Surrounding the town are a number of rounded hills (extinct volcanoes) and a good view of them can be

obtained about 3 km south, on the road to Ballarat. **Of interest:** Town hall and court-house (1870), Baily St. William Barkell Memorial Arts and Historical Centre, Fraser St. Bottle Museum, Baily St, housed in former Clunes State School. Queens Park, maintained as garden was established over 100 years ago on banks of Creswick Creek; picnics, barbecues, playground. Butter Factory Gallery, Cameron St; sculpture and art gallery. Jindalee Arts and Crafts Centre, Talbot Rd; handmade pottery. The Weavery, Fraser St; handwoven fabrics. **In the area:** Mt Beckworth, 8 km west; scenic reserve, variety of birds and native flora and fauna, picnic and barbecue facilities. Clunes Homestead Furniture, 1 km north on Talbot Rd. Talbot, 18 km north-west; historic town featuring many buildings from 1860s–1870s, particularly in Camp St and Scandinavian Cres. Talbot Arts and Historical Museum, Camp St, housed in former Primitive Methodist Church (1870). Bull and Mouth restaurant; bluestone building (1860s) that housed former hotel of same name. Keebles of Clunes guesthouse, Baily St. **Tourist Information:** (053) 45 3085. **Accommodation:** 1 hotel, 1 motel, 1 caravan/camping park. **See also:** The Golden Age.
MAP REF. 208 A1, 211 Q1, 213 Q13, 216 A13

Stegosaurus, World of Dinosaurs, near Creswick

Cobram   Population 3651

Magnificent wide sandy beaches are a feature of the stretch of the Murray River at Cobram, so picnicking and water sports can be enjoyed. This is fruit-growing country and Cobram is well known for its 'Peaches and Cream' Festival held Australia Day weekend every odd year. **Of interest:** Houseboats for hire. Australian Yabby Farm with Australia's largest yabby hatchery, Karook St. **In the area:** Tyrrell's Heritage Farm Winery, on Murray Valley Hwy, 5 km south; 116-m-long wood carving depicting scenes of early River Murray life. Binghi Boomerang Factory and Kramner Cellars at Barooga, 4 km north-east. Spikes and Blooms cactus farm and Coonanga Homestead at Strathmerton, 16 km west. Monichino Wineries 15 km south towards Numurkah. Matata Deer Farm on Tocumwal road, 5 km north-west of Cobram. Sportavia Soaring Centre, at Tocumwal airport, 20 km north-west. **Tourist information:** The Old Grain Shed, cnr Station St and Punt Rd; (058) 72 2132. **Accommodation:** 5 motels, 4 caravan/camping parks. **See also:** The Mighty Murray.
MAP REF. 117 M13, 217 K3

Cohuna   Population 2103

Between Kerang and Echuca on the Murray Valley Hwy, Cohuna is beside Gunbower Island, formed by the Murray on the far side and Gunbower Creek just across the highway from the town. This island is covered in red gum and box forest which provides a home for abundant water-fowl and other birdlife, as well as kangaroos and emus. The central zone of the forest is a sanctuary. The forest is subject to flooding and a large part of the island has breeding rookeries during the flood periods. Picnic and barbecue facilities can be found on the island, and forest tracks give access for driving and riding. Maps are available from the Forests Officer or from stores in Cohuna. **Of interest:** Cohuna swimming pool with 45-m waterslide; open daily from November to Easter. **In the area:** Box Bridge, at Kow Swamp, 23 km south; also a sanctuary, has picnic spots and good fishing. Mount Hope (110 m), about 28 km south, is popular for easy rock-climbing, with good views from its summit and beautiful wildflowers in spring; picnic facilities. Torrumbarry Lock, 40 km south-east; during winter, entire weir structure is removed from the river; in summer, water-skiing above the weir. **Tourist information:** Rotunda, Main St. **Accommodation:** 1 hotel, 2 motels, 2 caravan/camping parks.
MAP REF. 116 I12, 216 C2

Colac   Population 10 545

Colac is situated on the eastern edge of the volcanic plain which covers much of the Western District of Victoria. It is the centre of a prosperous, closely settled agricultural area and is sited on the shores of Lake Colac, which has good fishing and a variety of water sports. **Of interest:** Historic homes, not open to the public; Balnagowan in Balnagowan Ave, The Parsonage, 81 Wallace St and The Elms, 16 Gellibrand St. Self-guided walk and car tour available. Botanic Gardens (18 ha), Queen St; picnic and barbecue facilities. Barongarook Creek; walking track to sculpture park, also birdwatcher's haven. Annual Kana Festival in March. **In the area:** Alvie Red Rock Lookout, 22 km north, from which 30 of the surrounding volcanic lakes can be seen, including Lake Corangamite, Victoria's largest salt-water lake. Barongarook Winery, 15 km south. The beautiful Otway Ranges lie about 50 km to the south. Winding roads pass through them, revealing lush mountain scenery, and lead down to the coast. Floating Island Reserve, 28 km west of Colac, is a lagoon with islands that change position. Birregurra, about 20 km east of Colac, has some interesting old buildings. **Tourist information:** cnr Murray and Queen Sts; (052) 31 3730. **Accommodation:** 1 hotel, 5 motels, 4 caravan/camping parks.
MAP REF. 211 P9

Coleraine
Population 1153

Situated in the attractive Wannon River valley, 35 km west of Hamilton, this area was first settled by the Henty and Whyte brothers in 1838 for pastoral grazing. The primary products of the area are fine-wool sheep and beef cattle. **In the area:** The Wannon Falls, 14 km south-east, and Nigretta Falls, 24 km south-east. Point's Reserve, lookout on western edge of town; unique planting of over 700 species of native trees and shrubs. Historic homesteads include Warrock Homestead (1843), classified by National Trust, with some 30 buildings to explore, 20 km north-west towards Casterton; Glendinning Homestead, near Balmoral, 50 km north, with a wildlife sanctuary and farm holiday accommodation. Rocklands Reservoir, 12 km east of Balmoral, for excellent fishing and boating; caravan park nearby. Black Range State Park, northern shores of reservoir, has walking-tracks and picnic areas. The gardens of 'Nareen', the property of Malcolm and Tamie Fraser, 31 km north-west, are open weekdays by appointment, (055) 79 0244, and through Victoria's Open Garden Scheme (closed Christmas, Easter and May–Aug). **Tourist information:** Cobb & Co. Cafe, 75 Whyte St; (055) 75 2386. **Accommodation:** 2 hotels, 1 caravan/camping park. **See also:** The Western District.
MAP REF. 210 F4

Corryong
Population 1274

Situated in alpine country, Corryong is at the gateway to the Snowy Mountains. The district offers superb mountain scenery and excellent trout-fishing. The Murray near Corryong is still a brisk and gurgling stream running through forested hills. **Of interest:** Jack Riley, reputedly 'The Man from Snowy River', came from these parts and his grave is in Corryong cemetery. 'The Man from Snowy River' Folk Museum, Hanson St, has an antique ski collection and a replica of Riley's original shack. Annual Corryong High Country Festival in March. Annual Nariel Creek Folk Music Festival in late December. **In the area:** Playles Hill Lookout, 1 km south-east of town. Cudgewa Bluff Falls area, 27 km north-west of Corryong in Burrowa–Pine Mountain National Park; excellent scenery and bushwalking tracks. At Upper Nariel, 43 km south, Upper Murray Fish Farm and Upper Murray Historical Society. Trout-fishing at Tintaldra, 23 km north. Canoeing and mountain bike excursions from Walwa, 47 km north-west. Khancoban, 27 km east; horse trekking and whitewater rafting. Scenic drive west from Corryong. Towong, 12 km north-east; lookout with views over Kosciusko National Park. Mt Mittamite and Emberys Lookout, 10 km north, and Sassafras Gap, 66 km south; scenic views. **Tourist information:** Corryong Newsagency, 43–49 Hanson St, (060) 76 1381; or Mt Mittamite Caravan Park, Tallangatta Rd, (060) 76 1152. **Accommodation:** 2 hotel/motels, 2 motels, 2 caravan/camping parks.
MAP REF. 109 B8, 110 C13, 117 R13, 219 G5

Cowes
Population 2251

This is the main town on Phillip Island, a popular resort area in Western Port linked to the mainland by a bridge at San Remo. Cowes is on the northern side of the island and is the centre for hotel and motel accommodation. It has pleasant beaches, safe for children, and the jetty is popular for fishing and swimming. The town has a number of art and craft shops, an amusement centre and a variety of restaurants. **Of interest:** Down Under Clock Display, Findlay St. **In the area:** Summerland Beach, on southern shore, about 13 km south-west; famous for its nightly penguin parade. Colonies of fur seals can be seen all year round on Seal Rocks off southern shores, and mutton-birds during Oct.–Apr. Mini Europe, Ventnor Rd; display of 200 miniature European buildings. Australian Dairy Centre at Newhaven, 16 km south-east; museum and cheese factory. Phillip Island Wildlife Park, Phillip Island Rd; 32 ha of bushland with native animals and birds. Churchill Island, 2 km from Newhaven; historic homestead and walking tracks. **Tourist Information:** Phillip Island Rd, Newhaven; (059) 56 7447. (Bookings for island tours and cruises.) **Accommodation:** 13 motels, 10 caravan/camping parks. **See also:** Phillip Island.
MAP REF. 199 O11, 208 I10

Creswick
Population 2266

This picturesque township, 18 km north of Ballarat, nestles at the foot of the State Forest. One of the richest alluvial goldfields in the world was discovered here. **Of interest:** Mullock heaps on Lawrence Rd. Gold panning. Surrounding volcanic bushland and forest areas attract field naturalists and bushwalking enthusiasts. Creswick Historical Museum, Albert St; collection of early history of area. Gold Battery, Battery Cres. Local cemetery, Clunes Rd; early miners' graves and a Chinese section. Koala Park, Creswick Rd, and St Georges Lake, Melbourne Rd; picnic facilities. Olympic pool at Calambeen Park, Cushing St. **In the area:** World of Dinosaurs, 1.5 km east off Midland Hwy; life-size models in bushland setting. Creswick Forest Nursery, 1 km east. Tumblers Green Nursery, 1 km west. At Smeaton, 16 km north: Smeaton House (1850s). Anderson's Mill (1860s) and Tuki Trout Farm. **Tourist information:** Rotunda, cnr Raglan and Cambridge Sts; (053) 45 2000. **Accommodation:** 1 motel, 1 caravan/camping park. **See also:** The Golden Age.
MAP REF. 200 A7, 208 B2, 211 R2

Daylesford
Population 3111

Daylesford and nearby Hepburn Springs, 5 km north, are popular holiday centres, set in attractive hill country. They are both 'spa' towns, with 65 documented mineral springs, many with hand pumps. Hepburn Springs Spa Complex within the Mineral Springs Reserve, Main Rd, offers public and private baths, massage and a sauna; open daily. Daylesford rambles up the side of Wombat Hill, at the top of which are the Botanical Gardens, Central Springs Rd, with a lookout tower from which there are commanding views in all directions. **Of interest:** Jubilee Lake, Lake Rd; Daylesford Lake, Leggatt Rd; and Central Springs Spa Reserve, Central Springs Rd, for picnicking. Historical museum in former School of Mines, Vincent St. Market near railway station on Sundays. During the market, Central Highlands Tourist Railway runs rail-motor services between Daylesford and Musk on 1st and 3rd Sundays and ganger's trolleys operate to Wombat Forest on alternate Sundays. **In the area:** Breakneck Gorge, 5 km north, Sailors Falls, 10 km south, Trentham Falls, 15 km north, and 13 km north, Mt Franklin, an extinct volcano. Bin Billa Winery and Restaurant, 6 km south; open daily. Farm holidays available at Truro dairy farm, Franklinford, 15 km north, Oldeborg Family Farm and Holcombe Homestead near Glenlyon, 12 km north-east. Yandoit, a town of Swiss/Italian heritage, 18 km north-west of Daylesford; Jajarawong Holiday Park offers bushwalking, water sports and wildlife. Horse-riding at Boomerang Holiday Ranch, 2 km south-west. **Tourist information:** Spa Centre Variety Store, 49 Vincent St; (053) 48 3707. **Accommodation:** 8 hotels, 5 motels, 3 caravan/camping parks. **See also:** The Golden Age.
MAP REF. 200 D6, 208 C2, 216 C13

Derrinallum
Population 300

Small rural town servicing the local pastoral farming community and surrounded by volcanic plains typical of the Western District of Victoria. **In the area:** Mt Elephant, 2 km south-west; scoria cone of volcanic origin rising high above surrounding plains. Deep Lake, 5 km north-west; fishing and water sports. Significant dry-stone walls, immediately west of

town. Elephant Bridge Hotel, at Darlington, 15 km west; two-storey bluestone building classified by National Trust. Lake Tooliorook, 6 km south-east; fishing and swimming. **Accommodation:** 1 hotel/motel.
MAP REF. 211 N6

Dimboola   Population 1514
This is a peaceful town on the tree-lined Wimmera River, 35 km north-west of Horsham. **Of interest:** Annual rowing regatta in November. **In the area:** Little Desert National Park, 6 km north; self-guided walks include Pomponderoo Hill Nature Walk (1 km) from Horseshoe Bend picnic and camping area at river's edge. Ebenezer Mission Station (founded 1858), on Jeparit Rd, 15 km north; restored by National Trust. At Kiata, 26 km west, mallee fowl can be seen in Lowan Sanctuary throughout year. Pink Lake, a coloured salt lake, 9 km north-west. Wail, 11 km south, has well-stocked forest nursery run by Department of Conservation and Environment. **Tourist information:** Horsham Information Centre, 20 O'Callaghan's Pde, Horsham; (053) 82 1832. **Accommodation:** 2 hotels, 1 motel, 1 caravan/camping park. **See also:** The Wimmera.
MAP REF. 212 G7

Donald   Population 1465
At the junction of the Sunraysia and Borung Hwys, Donald is situated on the Richardson River and in a Wimmera district renowned for its fine wheat, sheep and fat lambs. **Of interest:** Historic police station (1874), Wood St. Steam Loco Park, cnr Hammill and Walker Sts. Agricultural museum, railway steam-engine and historic water pump by lake in Wood St. Bullocks Head Lookout, Byrne St; large, unusual growth on box tree beside Richardson River. **In the area:** Lake Buloke, 10 km north; duck- and quail-shooting in season. **Tourist information:** Shire Offices, McCulloch St; (054) 97 1300. **Accommodation:** 2 hotels, 1 motel, 1 caravan/camping park.
MAP REF. 213 L6

Drouin   Population 3974
Drouin is on the Princes Hwy not far from Warragul and the Latrobe Valley. A large milk products factory and a plastics factory are two of the major industries. **Of interest:** Old brick police station in Main St; exhibits organised by Buln Buln Historical Society. **In the area:** Attractive camping and picnic spots on Tarago River at Glen Cromie, 8 km north, and Picnic Point on the Princes Hwy, 10 km west of town. At Nayook, 38 km north: Nayook Fruit and Berry Farm, and Country Farm Perrenials Nursery and

Gardens. At Drouin West, 3 km west: Fruit and Berry Farm and Hilston Lodge Deer Farm. At Neerim South, 31 km north: Gippsland Blue Cheese farm factory, and picnic and barbecue area at Tarago Reservoir; Woodlyn Park offers horse-riding safaris into adjacent state forest. Alpine Trout Farm at Noojee, 40 km north. Jindivick Smokehouse (hand-made smallgoods) and Hirschberg Deer Farm at Jindivick, 19 km north. Gumbuya Park, 25 km west on Princes Hwy; wildlife and family fun park. The Farm Shed, Princes Hwy, Tynong, 22 km west; farm animal and agricultural displays, including shearing, sheep-dog workouts and milking; open daily. Many of the above 'food' attractions are featured on the Gourmet Deli Trail; brochure available locally and at the Victorian Information Centre, 230 Collins St, Melbourne; (03) 790 3333. **Accommodation:** 2 hotels, 2 motels, 3 caravan/camping parks.
MAP REF. 209 L8

Drysdale   Population 1166
This is primarily a service centre for the local farming community on the Bellarine Peninsula. **Of interest:** Old Court-house museum and Drysdale Community Crafts, both in High St. Community Market, Recreation Reserve, Duke St; every 3rd Sunday, Sept.–Apr. **In the area:** Lake Lorne picnic area, 1 km south-west; nearby Bellarine Peninsula Railway offers steam-train rides between Drysdale and Queenscliff; locomotives and carriages dating back to the 1870s on display. Adjoining township of Clifton Springs had a brief burst of fame in the 1870s when the therapeutic value of its mineral-spring water was discovered; today it offers sporting facilities and a restaurant. **Tourist information:** A Maze'N Things, cnr Bellarine Hwy and Grubb Rd, Wallington; (052) 50 2669. **Accommodation:** 1 hotel.
MAP REF. 205 H7, 208 E8

Dunkeld   Population 412
On the Glenelg Hwy, 31 km from Hamilton, Dunkeld is the southern gateway to the Grampians and is conveniently located for trips to the Victoria Valley (world famous fine-wool growing district), the Chimney Pots and Billywing Plantation within Gariwerd (Grampians) National Park, 25 km north. **Of interest:** Historical museum, Templeton St; exhibits portray history of area's Aboriginal tribes and also explorer Major Mitchell's journeys. Detailed map available of historic sites and buildings. Skin Inn (sheepskin products and crafts) and The Chimney Pot (handcrafts and light refreshments), both in Parker St. **In the area:** Walking-tracks to top of

Mt Sturgeon and Mt Abrupt; both climbs are steep but the fine views are rewarding. Picnic spots at Freshwater Lake Reserve, 8 km north of town. **Tourist information:** Dunkeld Cafe, Parker St; (055) 77 2256. **Accommodation:** 1 hotel/motel, 2 caravan/camping parks. **See also:** The Western District.
MAP REF. 210 I4

Dunolly   Population 649
A small township in north-central Victoria, in the heart of the gold country and on the Goldfields Tourist Route. The 'Welcome Stranger', claimed to be the largest nugget ever discovered, was found 15 km north-west at Moliagul. The district has produced more nuggets than any other goldfield in Australia; 126 were unearthed in the town itself. A Goldrush Festival is held each October. **Of interest:** Some handsome original buildings in Broadway, the main street. Goldfields Historical and Arts Museum, Broadway; replicas of some of town's most spectacular nuggets; open weekends. Restored Dunolly Court-house, Market St; acts as information centre and has display relating to historic gold discoveries in area. **In the area:** Melville Caves, 30 km north; haunt of bushranger Captain Melville. Laanecoorie Reservoir, 16 km east; pleasant picnic spot. The countryside around Dunolly abounds with wildflowers in spring and many native birds and animals can be seen. Enthusiasts can pan for gold in the local creeks. Gold'n'Rocks Museum at Tarnagulla, 15 km north-east. Monuments at Moliagul mark the spot where the Welcome Stranger nugget was found in 1869 and the birthplace of Rev. John Flynn, the founder of the Royal Flying Doctor Service. **Tourist information:** Market St; (054) 68 1205. **Accommodation:** 1 motel, 1 caravan/camping park.
MAP REF. 213 P10, 216 A10

Echuca–Moama   Population 8409
This town is at the junction of the Murray, Campaspe and Goulburn Rivers and was once Australia's largest inland port. Echuca is an Aboriginal word for 'meeting of the waters' while Moama means 'place of the dead'. An iron bridge joins the city of Echuca to the NSW town of Moama, which is on the other side of the Murray River. **Of interest:** Along the Murray Esplanade, the Port of Echuca: a massive red-gum wharf restored to the period of its heyday; includes paddle-steamer *Pevensey* (renamed *Philadelphia* for TV mini-series *All the Rivers Run*), which cruises during peak periods, D26 logging barge, PS *Alexander Arbuthnot* (being restored) and PS *Adelaide*; Star Hotel,

with underground bar and escape tunnel; and Bridge Hotel, built by Henry Hopwood, founder of Echuca, who ran original punt service across river. Also part of the Port's attractions are the Red Gum Works, Sharp's Magic Movie House and Penny Arcade, Echuca Wharf Pottery, Tisdall Wines Cellar Door and Restaurant, Wistaria Tearooms, and the Coach House Collection, all in Murray Esplanade. Echuca Historical Society Museum (1867) in former police station, classified by National Trust, High St. Gumnutland and World in Wax Museum, both in High St. Njernda Aboriginal Cultural Centre in former Law Courts, Law Pl. One-hour cruises can be taken on paddlewheelers *Canberra* and *Pride of the Murray*, while paddle-steamer *Emmylou* features accommodation cruises as well as one-hour cruises. MV *Mary Ann* is a cruising restaurant. Houseboat hire available. Annual Southern 80 ski-race from Torrumbarry to Echuca, held in February. Annual Rich River Festival in October. Annual Steam, Horse and Vintage Car Rally in June. Barmah Muster in April. **In the area:** Camping, fishing, kayaking, canoeing, swimming, bushwalking and water-skiing available. Joalah Fauna Park, Rich River Yabbie Farm and Aeroscenic Joy Flights, all on Cornelia Creek Rd, 4 km south. Rich River Deer Farm, 5 km north of Moama. Barmah Red Gum Forest, 41 km north-east, covers an area of 50 000 ha and has a Murray River frontage of 192 km; wildlife includes 230 species of birds; river tours via flat-bottomed boat. Dharnya Centre, 36 km from Echuca within Barmah Forest; illustrates traditions and lifestyle of area's Aboriginal inhabitants. Kyabram Fauna Park, 35 km south-east; one of the best in Victoria. **Tourist information:** 2 Leslie St, Echuca, (054) 82 4525; or Cobb Hwy, Moama, (054) 82 6001. **Accommodation:** 33 motels, hotels, homesteads, 11 caravan parks. **See also:** The Mighty Murray; Victoria's Wine Regions. MAP REF. 117 K13, 216 F5

Edenhope   Population 819

On the Wimmera Hwy, just 30 km from the border, Edenhope is situated on the shores of Lake Wallace, a haven for waterbirds. When full, the lake is popular for water sports and has a boat-ramp; golf-course and tennis courts nearby. **Of interest:** Cairn beside the lake in Lake St, commemorating visit of first all-Aboriginal cricket team to England. The team was coached by T.W. Willis, who was also the founder of Australian Rules football. **In the area:** Harrow, 32 km south-east; one of Victoria's oldest inland towns, with many interesting buildings,

ALPINE COUNTRY

To the east and north-east of Melbourne, the gently rounded peaks of the Victorian Alps stretch, seemingly endlessly, under clear skies. They are much lower than alpine ranges in other parts of the world, lacking sheer escarpments and jagged peaks, but they still stand majestic, especially when covered in snow. These blue ranges are not high enough to have a permanent cover of snow, but the expanses of the rolling mountains are ideal for cross-country skiing as well as for the more popular downhill variety.

The skiing season officially opens on the Queen's Birthday long weekend each June and closes in October, but it often actually extends beyond these dates. Each year, thousands of people flock to the snow: for the enjoyment of downhill skiing, for leisurely cross-country skiing, for snowboarding or just to enjoy the beauty of nature. Children can have a great time throwing snowballs and building snowmen.

There is bountiful fishing in the lakes and trout streams. Tennis, rock-climbing, sailing, swimming, canoeing and water-skiing are popular sports in the summer months. Many riding schools in the valleys provide a leisurely pastime for those who want to explore the countryside on horseback. For the more energetic, bushwalking in this beautiful rugged country is a must. Despite their summer beauty, however, the Alps can still claim the life

Skiers, Falls Creek

of an ill-prepared bushwalker. Make sure you have the necessary equipment and knowledge to tackle this recreational activity, and always tell someone where you are going and when you expect to be back.

Victoria has nine ski resorts, all within easy reach of Melbourne.

Falls Creek, 356 km from Melbourne, via the Snow Road through Oxley. Protected ski-runs for novices, intermediate and advanced skiers; good cross-country skiing. Ski hire and instruction.

Lake Mountain, 109 km from Melbourne, via Healesville. Sightseeing and novice skiing.

Mount Baw Baw, 177 km from Melbourne, via Drouin. Beginners, novices and cross-country skiing.

Mount Buffalo, 331 km from Melbourne, via Myrtleford. Includes Dingo Dell and Cresta. Beginners, families and cross-country skiing. Ski hire and instruction.

Mount Buller, 241 km from Melbourne, via Mansfield. For beginners to advanced skiers. Ski hire and instruction.

Mount Stirling, 250 km from Melbourne, near Mount Buller. Cross-country skiing. Most trails start at Telephone Box Junction, which has a visitor centre with public shelter, ski hire and trail maps.

Mount Donna Buang, 95 km from Melbourne, via Warburton. Sightseeing and novice skiing.

Mount Hotham, 367 km from Melbourne, via Wangaratta. The 'powder snow capital' of Australia. For experienced downhill skiers; unlimited cross-country skiing. Ski hire and instruction.

Dinner Plain, is a ten-minute ski-shuttle ride from Mount Hotham.

For further information on all resorts, contact the Alpine Resorts Commission, Amev House, Whitehorse Road, Box Hill; (03) 895 6900, or at the Falls Creek Information Centre, Bogong High Plains Tourist Rd, Falls Creek; (057) 58 3224.

See also: Safe Skiing.

including Hermitage Hotel (1851) and log gaol (1862). About 50 km west, over SA border, Naracoorte Caves Conservation Park. Rocklands Reservoir, 65 km east of Edenhope, part of Wimmera - Mallee irrigation system; popular for fishing and boating. **Tourist information:** Shire Offices, Main St; (055) 85 1011. **Accommodation:** 1 hotel, 1 motel, 1 caravan/ camping park.
MAP REF. 212 C12

Eildon   Population 740
Built to irrigate a vast stretch of northern Victoria and to provide hydro-electric power, Lake Eildon is the state's largest man-made lake and is a very popular resort area, surrounded by the beautiful foothills of the Alps within Eildon State Park. There are excellent recreational facilities around the foreshores, two major boat harbours, launching ramps, picnic grounds and many lookout points. The towns of Eildon and Bonnie Doon, 42 km north, are popular holiday centres. Power-boats and houseboats can be hired at the boat harbours. **In the area:** Signposted Lake Eildon Wall lookout. Mt Pinninger (503 m), 3 km east; panoramic views of Mt Buller, the Alps and lake. Snobs Creek Fish Hatchery, 6 km south-west, where millions of trout are bred and used to stock lakes and rivers; visitors welcome. Eildon Deer Park nearby, on Goulburn Valley Hwy; open weekends and public holidays. Just past the hatchery, Snobs Creek Falls, Rubicon Falls, 18 km south-west, via Thornton. Jamieson, 57 km south-east; old mining town at junction of Goulburn and Jamieson Rivers, surrounded by dense, bush-clad mountain countryside. Mt Skene, 48 km south-east of Jamieson; usually covered with wildflowers Dec. – Feb. (road closed in winter). Eildon Pondage and Goulburn River offer excellent fishing. Fishing competition June long weekend. There is no closed season for trout in Eildon Lake, which is also stocked with Murray cod; redfin abound naturally. Inland fishing licence required for anglers over age of 16. Scenic flights. Sailing, water-skiing. Fraser National Park, 13 km north-west, and Eildon State Park which surrounds the town; bushwalking, camping, boating and fishing. Candlebark Gully Nature Walk, popular walk within Fraser National Park. **Tourist information:** Redgate Nursery Craft Cottage, 47 Grant St, Alexandra; (057) 72 2169. **Accommodation:** 4 motels, 6 caravan/ camping parks.
MAP REF. 209 L1, 217 L13, 218 H4

Emerald   Population 3608
The Puffing Billy steam railway runs between this pretty township, which was the first settlement in the Dandenong Ranges and Belgrave. **Of interest:** Number of galleries and craft shops; restaurants include Choo Choos, Monbulk Rd, a restored Victorian red 'rattler' train with gallery and model railway. Emerald Lake Park, Emerald Lake Rd, once part of famous Nobelius Nursery; walking-tracks; self-guiding pamphlets available at kiosk. Emerald Lake, one of hills' most attractive and best-equipped picnic and swimming sites; waterslides, paddle-boats and model railway. Lake sited on Dandenongs Walk Track, 40-km trail stretching from Cockatoo and Gembrook to Sassafras. **In the area:** At Menzies Creek, 5 km west: Cotswold House fine food and views; Lake Aura Vale for sailing and picnics. Monbulk Animal Kingdom in Swales Rd, Monbulk, 11 km north. Tulip farms at Silvan, 14 km north. Bimbimbie Wildlife Park in Paternoster Rd, Mount Burnett, 12 km south-east. Sherbrooke Art Gallery, 8 Monbulk Rd, Belgrave, 11 km west. Olinda, 18 km north, a picturesque town with antique gallery, National Rhododendron Garden and nursery, and good restaurants; home of settler Edward Henty on Ridge Rd. Australian Rainbow Trout Farm at Macclesfield, 8 km north of Emerald. **Tourist information:** Emerald Lake Kiosk; (059) 68 4109. **Accommodation:** 1 resort. **See also:** The Dandenongs.
MAP REF. 202 H12, 209 J6

Euroa   Population 2730
A small town 151 km north-east of Melbourne, recently bypassed by the Hume Hwy, Euroa is a good base from which to explore the Strathbogie Ranges and tablelands. It was at Euroa that the Kelly gang pulled off a daring robbery, rounding up some 50 hostages at the nearby Faithfull Creek station and then making off with £2200. **Of interest:** Farmers Arms historical museum, Kirkland Ave. **In the area:** Seven Creeks Run Woolshed complex, 1 km north; sheepdog and shearing demonstrations, also bush market, pottery and souvenirs. Faithfull Creek homestead, 9 km north-east near Balmattum; burnt out in 1939 bushfires, but ruins remain. Nearby, Faithfull Creek Waterfall, with picnic facilities. Euroa Soaring Club offers glider flights; also balloon flights, 10 km south of town. At Violet Town, 20 km north-east: parachuting centre and Dorset Hill Wildlife Park. Forlonge Memorial, off Euroa–Strathbogie road, 10 km south-east, commemorates Eliza Forlonge, who with her sister imported first merino sheep into Victoria. Scenic drive to Gooram Falls and around Strathbogie Ranges to south-east recommended. **Tourist**

information: Jumping Jumbuck, Hume Hwy; (057) 95 3381. **Accommodation:** 3 motels, 1 caravan/ camping park.
MAP REF. 217 J9

Foster   Population 1007
A picturesque small township within easy reach of Corner Inlet, Waratah Bay and Wilsons Promontory on the south-east coast of Victoria, about 170 km from Melbourne. **Of interest:** Historical Museum, housed in old post office, Main St. Stockyard Gallery, Main St. **In the area:** Scenic drive to Fish Creek, 11 km south-west; Fish Creek Potters. Waratah Bay, 34 km south-west, Walkerville, 36 km south-west and Port Franklin, 12 km south-east, all pleasant beach resorts. Cape Liptrap, 46 km south-west; excellent views of rugged coastline and Bass Strait. Toora, 12 km east; home of Bonlac milk products. Good surf beach at Sandy Point, 22 km south; surrounding protected waters of Shallow Inlet popular for fishing and swimming. Foster North Lookout, 6 km north-west. Turtons Creek, 18 km north; old gold-rich village where lyrebirds can sometimes be seen in tree-fern gullies nearby. Horse-drawn wagons operate near Turtons Creek. **Tourist information:** Stockyard Gallery/Dept. of Conservation and Environment, Main St; (056) 82 2133/82 2466. **Accommodation:** 2 motels, 1 caravan/camping park.
MAP REF. 209 N11

Geelong   Population 125 833
Geelong, located on Corio Bay, is the largest provincial city in Victoria. A major manufacturing and processing centre, Geelong also has a large petroleum refinery. It is also a traditional wool-selling centre. The Corio Bay area was first settled in the 1830s and, apart from a rush to the diggings during the gold boom, Geelong has grown and prospered steadily. It is a pleasant and well-laid-out city with more than 14% of its area reserved for parks and sports grounds. **Of interest:** National Wool Centre and Museum, cnr Moorabool and Brougham Sts; museum has 3 galleries. Geelong Otway Convention and Visitors Bureau in foyer. Swimming at Eastern Beach and Park. Geelong Beachfront Scenic Drive. Botanic Gardens in Eastern Park, Garden St, overlooking Corio Bay. Johnstone Park, cnr Mercer and Gheringhap Sts; art gallery, war memorial, library and city hall, and Geelong Historical Records Centre. Queens Park, Queens Park Rd, Newtown; golf-course, sports oval, and walks to Buckley's Falls. Geelong boasts many interesting buildings, more than 100 with National Trust classifications. They include: Merchiston Hall, Garden St, East

Geelong, an eight-roomed stone house built in 1856 for an early settler, James Cowie. In North Geelong, Osborne House in Swinburne St, a bluestone mansion built in 1858. At Eastern Beach, the beautiful Corio Villa, a prefabricated cast-iron house built in 1856. The Heights, Aphrasia St, Newtown, a 14-roomed pre-fabricated timber mansion built in 1855 for Charles Ibbotson; open to public. Also open is Barwon Grange (1855), Fernleigh St, Newtown. The oldest Anglican church in Victoria still in continuous use, Christ Church in Moorabool St. Also of interest, the Customs House and Maritime Museum in Brougham St. Performing Arts Centre in Little Malop St. Pegasus Antiques, 560a Latrobe Tce. Wintergarden Gallery, 51 McKillop St. Pottage Crafts, 189 Moorabool St. Deb's Cottage Collections Crafts, 178 Swanston St, South Geelong. Great Galah Australiana and Gifts, 91 Little Malop St. Balyang Bird Sanctuary in Shannon Ave, Newtown. Annual Show, Geelong Cup Carnival and Spring Festival in October/November. There are boat-ramps on the Corio Bay beaches and the area offers good river and bay fishing. **In the area:** Norlane Water World, 7 km north. Deakin University's Institute of the Arts, 13 km south-west at Waurn Ponds. Fyansford, 5 km west, on outskirts of city, one of oldest settlements in region; Monash Bridge across Moorabool River thought to be one of first reinforced-concrete bridges in Victoria. Also at Fyansford, historic buildings include the Swan Inn, the Balmoral Hotel (1854), now an art gallery, and the Fyansford Hotel. Brownhill Observation Tower at Ceres, 10 km south-west, for an excellent view of surrounding areas. Batesford, 10 km north-west of Geelong; now a picturesque market-garden township, with a history of wine-making. Idyll vineyard, 11 km north-west on Ballan road; open Tues. – Sun. for tastings and sales. The sandstone Travellers Rest Inn was built in 1849 and is across the Moorabool River from the present hotel. Lara (population 4231), 19 km north of Geelong, was swept by bushfires in 1969, but some historic buildings remain. It is located at the foot of the You Yangs, a range of granite hills, which feature the You Yangs Forest Park. Between the township and the You Yangs is the Serendip Sanctuary, once purely a wildlife research station but now open to the public with a visitor centre, walking tracks, bird hides and a picnic area. Some 46 km north-west, along the Midland Hwy, is the Happy Hens Egg World at Meredith, one of the oldest towns in Victoria, and once an important stopping-place for diggers on their way to the goldfields. The shire hall, railway station and bluestone state school are of interest. Anakie, 31 km

north, and the Anakie Gorge, 36 km north (with a picnic area). Accessed via Batesford, the township is located at the foot of the Brisbane Ranges, a national park area. Many species of ferns and flowering plants in the park; walking-tracks lead to the gorge and adjoining wildlife sanctuary. Nearby Fairy Park displays quaint miniature houses and scenes from fairy-tales, for enjoyment of children. Mt Anakie Winemakers, 4 km north of Anakie on Staughton Vale Rd, produces local wines; open Sat. Steiglitz, 10 km north-west of Anakie; popular camping ground and court-house dating back to 1875. The Bellarine Peninsula begins about 16 km east and includes the towns of Queenscliff, Portarlington, Ocean Grove and Barwon Heads (see separate town entries). Horseriding at Koombahla Park in Wallington, 16 km east of Geelong. Also at Wallington, A Maze'N Things. Lake Connewarre Wildlife Reserve, 2 km south of Leopold. Bellarine Peninsula Railway runs both steam and diesel trains on 16-km track between Drysdale (see separate town entry) and Queenscliff. Venturing further afield, Great Ocean Rd to Torquay and Lorne provides spectacular coastal scenery. At Moriac, 20 km south-west, horsedrawn caravans for hire. Vineyards in area include Rebenberg and Tarcoola. Alden Lodge Museum and Coral Gardens at Grovedale, 6 km south of Geelong; shell and coral displays, and flower

gardens. **Tourist information:** GO Tourism, National Wool Centre, Bay end of Moorabool St; (052) 22 2900. **Accommodation:** 2 hotels, 24 motels, 9 caravan/camping parks. **See also:** The Great Ocean Road; Victoria's Wine Regions. MAP REF. 204, 205 E7, 208 D8

Gisborne   Population 1966
Once a stopping-place for coaches and foot travellers on their way to the Castlemaine and Bendigo goldfields, Gisborne is now an attractive township on the road to Woodend and Kyneton. **In the area:** Barringo Wildlife Reserve, 4 km north at New Gisborne; area of natural bushland with herds of deer, many wallabies and kangaroos, and lake stocked with trout. Mount Macedon, 20 km north, with its memorial cross at summit. Mt Aitken Estates Winery, 6 km south of Gisborne. Craiglee and Goonawarra wineries at Sunbury, 18 km south-east of Gisborne. **Accommodation:** 1 motel, 1 caravan/camping park. **See also:** Victoria's Wine Regions. MAP REF. 200 I8, 208 E3

Glenrowan   Population 216
Glenrowan is the famous site of the defeat of Ned Kelly and his gang by the police in 1880. Today the village, set in picturesque country, has craft and souvenir shops, nurseries and tea and coffee shops. **Of interest:** All along Old Hume Hwy: Ned

Big Wool Bales Centre, Hamilton

Kelly Memorial Museum and Homestead, with Kate's Cottage gifts in front and huge statue of Ned Kelly; Glenrowan Pottery; Tourist Centre, with engrossing computer-animated show of capture of Ned Kelly. **In the area:** Warby Ranges and State Park, 12 km north; historic villages, scenic drives, walking tracks and picnic spots. Lake Mokoan, 5 km west; boating, fishing and water-skiing. Glenrowan wineries include Booth's Winery, Auldstones Cellars, H.J.T. Vineyards and Bailey's Bundarra Vineyards. Milawa-Oxley wineries, 16 km east. **Tourist information:** Wangaratta and Region Visitors Information Centre, Hume Hwy, Wangaratta; (057) 21 5711. **Accommodation:** 1 motel, 1 caravan park. **See also:** Victoria's Wine Regions.
MAP REF. 217 N7

Halls Gap — Population 234

Beautifully sited in the heart of the Grampians (Gariwerd), one of Victoria's largest national parks, this little township is adjacent to the Wonderlands Forest Park and Lake Bellfield and is the focus of a network of scenic roads. **Of interest:** Tearooms, restaurants, an art gallery and potteries; also good sporting facilities. The area is famous for its wildflowers and Halls Gap holds an annual spring wildflower exhibition in Sept.–Oct. **In the area:** Trail riding, rock climbing, abseiling and bushwalking in the national park. Brambuk Aboriginal Living Cultural Centre, 2 km south. Reids Lookout and The Balconies, 12 km north-west. McKenzie Falls, 17 km north-west. Lake Fyans, 17 km east, for swimming, fishing, yachting and water-skiing. Wallaroo Wildlife Park, 5 km south-east, open daily. Roses Gap Recreation Centre, 21 km north. Boroka Vineyards, 2 km east; open daily. Wartook Pottery and Restaurant, 20 km north-west. **Tourist information:** Gariwerd (Grampians) National Park Visitors Centre, Grampians Rd; (053) 56 4381 or Halls Gap Newsagency, Grampians Rd; (053) 56 4247. **Accommodation:** 8 motels, 4 caravan/camping parks. **See also:** The Grampians; Victoria's National Parks.
MAP REF. 213 J12

Hamilton — Population 9969

Known as the 'Wool Capital of the World', Hamilton is a prosperous and pleasant city less than an hour's drive from the resort towns of Portland, Port Fairy and Warrnambool on the south coast and the Grampian Ranges to the north. **Of interest:** Big Woolbales Centre, Henty Hwy, recreates the story of wool production and processing; shearing demonstrations, woolshed memorabilia, animal nursery, craft centre and cafeteria. HIRL (Hamilton Institute of Rural Learning), North Boundary Rd; community, craft and educational centre surrounded by gardens, nature trail and breeding area for eastern barred bandicoots. HEAL (Hamilton Environmental Awareness and Learning) conducts tours in area to discover how to care for the land; bookings essential (055) 78 6223. Hamilton Art Gallery, Brown St; varied collections, including decorative arts. Trout fishing in Lake Hamilton, Ballarat Rd; sandy beach, water sports and picnic facilities. On banks of lake, within original hangar, Sir Reginald Ansett Transport Museum; houses history and memorabilia of Sir Reginald's life and transport industry begun in Hamilton in 1931. Small zoo at Botanical Gardens, French St (established 1870); free-flight aviary, duck-pond and children's playground. Hamilton Pastoral Museum, Glenelg Hwy, housed in former St Luke's Lutheran Church; open by appointment. Hamilton History Centre and Aboriginal Keeping Place, Gray St; displays on aspects of local Aboriginal culture. **In the area:** Summit Park, Nigretta Rd, 15 km north-west; specialises in raising Saxon-Merino sheep for superfine wool production; open daily. Wannon and Nigretta Falls, 15 km north-west. Mt Eccles National Park, near Macarthur, 35 km south. Mt Eccles, with its crater Lake Surprise, one of three extinct volcanoes nearby. For a pleasant day-trip from Hamilton, the Grampians Tour (about 250 km north), to Dunkeld, Halls Gap, Ararat and back via Glenthompson. Farm holidays at Baloo sheep and cattle property near Macarthur, 35 km south. **Tourist information:** Lonsdale St; (055) 72 3746 and (008) 807 056. **Accommodation:** 6 hotels, 8 motels, 2 caravan/camping parks. See also: The Western District.
MAP REF. 210 H5

Harrietville — Population 100

Tucked high into the foothills of Mt Hotham and Mt Feathertop, Harrietville is a convenient accommodation centre for those who want to ski at Mt Hotham and/or sightsee in north-east Victoria. Gold was discovered here in 1862, and the gold-rush village was proclaimed a township in 1879. **Of interest:** Bicycles, fishing-rods and gold-panning dishes for hire. Horse-trail riding. Pioneer Park and open-air museum and picnic area, Alpine Rd. **In the area:** Walking-tracks to Mt Feathertop (1922 m), 20 km return, and Mt Hotham (1859 m), about 32 km one-way. Bushwalking in high mountain country of Bogong National Park, which surrounds town (weather conditions can vary and must be considered). Stony Creek Trout Farm and adjacent Mountain Fresh Trout Farm, 4 km north; fishing and educational facilities. **Tourist information:** Old General Store, Alpine Rd; (057) 59 2553. **Accommodation:** 1 hotel/motel, 1 resort, 1 lodge.
MAP REF. 217 R10, 219 B10, 220 B1

Healesville — Population 5759

Surrounded by mountain forest country, Healesville is about an hour's drive from Melbourne along the Maroondah Hwy. It has been a popular resort town since the turn of the century, as the climate is cool and pleasant in summer and the area offers excellent bushwalks and scenic drives. **In the area:** Famous Healesville Sanctuary, 4 km south, on Badger Creek Rd; open daily. This 32-ha reserve houses a variety of native animals and birds in a largely natural bushland setting. Key attractions are the Platypus Research Station, the subterranean display of nocturnal animals, the new 'Where Eagles Fly' exhibit and dense fern glades which have been constructed to simulate a natural habitat for lyrebirds. Nature trail, barbecue and picnic facilities and a restaurant. Corranderrk Aboriginal Cemetery, 5 km south. Pottery, lapidary and art gallery at Nigel Court, off Badger Creek Rd, 2 km south; open daily. Drives from Healesville include a tour of the Toolangi State Forest, criss-crossed with logging roads, 14 km north; or a trip through the forests to Donnelly's Weir Reserve and Falls, 45 km north at Murrindindi. The drive 37 km north-east to Marysville, via the Black Spur, passes the Maroondah Reservoir, where there are picnic and barbecue areas, and on through towering stands of mountain ash and lush tree-fern glades; Steavensons Falls is an attraction, 4 km south-east of Marysville. With nearly 40 wineries, the Yarra Valley is a wine-buff's delight; many are open for sales and tastings, including Yarra Yering, Prigorje and Warramate wineries at Gruyere, 8 km south-west of Healesville, and others in the surrounding areas, such as Bianchet, Yarinya Estate, Coldstream Hills, Domaine Chandon, De Bortoli, Fergusson's, Kellybrook, Lilydale, Long Gully, Shantell, St Hubert's, Yarra Vale, Yarra Burn, Lovey's Estate, Miller's Chateau Yarrinya, Diamond Valley and Lovegrove of Cottles Bridge. Gulf Station Homestead (1854), 2 km north of Yarra Glen, itself 14 km west of Healesville. Yarra Valley Tourist Railway runs mechanised trolleys from Healesville to Tarrawarra each Sunday from railway station on Healesville–Kinglake Rd. The 5000-km Bicentennial National Trail for walkers and horse-riders runs from Healesville to Cooktown in Queensland. **Tourist information:**

Piquant Palate, 278 Maroondah Hwy; (059) 62 3625. **Accommodation:** 2 hotels, 5 motels, 3 caravan/camping parks. MAP REF. 201 R10, 209 J4, 218 D10

Heathcote   Population 1364
In attractive countryside on the McIvor Hwy, Heathcote is set along the McIvor Creek, 47 km south of Bendigo. **In the area:** Lake Eppalock, 10 km west, one of the state's largest lakes; popular for motor-boat racing. Excellent views from Mount Ida Lookout, 4 km north. Scenic attraction: the Pink Cliffs, created by eroded spoil from gold sluices, with their brilliant mineral staining. McIvor Range Reserve; historic powder magazine. Old Heathcote Hospital (1859) and listed for preservation by National Trust. Wineries include Heathcote Winery and Zuber Estate within town; Jasper Hill and Huntleigh Vineyards, 6 km north, McIvor Creek Wines and Eppalock Ridge vineyards, 10 km and 22 km south-west respectively. **Tourist information:** Shire Offices, 125 High St; (054) 33 2000. **Accommodation:** 1 caravan/camping park.
MAP REF. 216 F10

Hopetoun   Population 750
This small Mallee town, just south of the Wyperfeld National Park, was named after the seventh Earl of Hopetoun, who was the first Governor-General of Australia. Hopetoun was a frequent visitor to the home of Edward Lascelles, who was largely responsible for opening up the Mallee area. **Of interest:** Hopetoun House, built for Lascelles; classified by National Trust. Lake Lascelles for boating, swimming and picnics. **In the area:** Wyperfeld National Park, 50 km north. Swamp Tank Museum at Turriff, 45 km north-east of Hopetoun. **Accommodation:** 1 hotel, 1 motel, 1 caravan/camping park.
MAP REF. 212 I2, 214 I13

Horsham   Population 12 174
At the junction of the Western, Wimmera and Henty Hwys, Horsham is generally regarded as the capital of the Wimmera region. Its location makes it a good base for tours of the region, particularly to the Little Desert National Park, 40 km west, and to the Grampians, some 50 km southeast. **Of interest:** Botanic Gardens, cnr Baker and Firebrace Sts. Wool Factory, Golf Course Rd, 3 km south-west, produces top-quality, extra-fine wool from Saxon-Merino sheep; tours daily. Horsham Art Gallery, Wilson St; collection of photography and Mack Jost collection of Australian art. Slip-rail Art Gallery,

Lake at Tower Hill State Game Reserve, near Koroit

Dimboola Rd. Olde Horsham Village, 3 km south-east; collection of historic buildings, art, craft and antique market, also fauna park; open daily. The Wimmera River runs through town and provides attractive picnic spots and good fishing for trout, redfin and Murray cod. Annual Apex Fishing Contest held in March. Victorian Institute of Dry Land Agriculture, Natimuk Rd, and Victorian College of Agriculture and Horticulture cereal research centre, 13 km north-east at Longerenong; inspections by prior arrangement. Cottage Delights, Dooen Rd, has plants and crafts. **In the area:** Black Range Cashmere and Thryptomene Farm, 40 km south, 4WD tours and inspection; bookings essential through Tourist Information Centre. Rocklands Reservoir, 90 km south on Glenelg River, built to supplement Wimmera–Mallee irrigation scheme; popular for water sports, picnics and caravan and camping at lake's western edge, 14 km from Balmoral. Green Lake, 13 km south-east of city, and Lake Natimuk, 24 km northwest; picnic and barbecue facilities. Toolondo Reservoir, 44 km south, home of the fighting brown trout; excellent fishing; caravan park. **Tourist information:** 20 O'Callaghan's Pde; (053) 82 3778. **Accommodation:** 7 hotels, 15 motels, 2 caravan/camping parks. **See also:** The Wimmera.
MAP REF. 212 H9

Inglewood   Population 712
North along the Calder Hwy from Bendigo are the 'Golden Triangle' towns of Inglewood and Bridgewater. Sizeable gold nuggets have been found in this area, the largest being the 'Welcome Stranger', which weighed 65 kg. **Of interest:** Old eucalyptus oil distillery. **In the area:** Kooyoora State Park, 16 km west of Inglewood; within park the Melville Caves, once haunt of notorious bushranger, Captain Melville. Loddon River, at Bridgewater, 8 km south-east, popular spot for fishing and water-skiing, barbecue and picnic facilities. Horsedrawn caravans for hire at Bridgewater. **Tourist information:** Brook St; (054) 38 3405. **Accommodation:** 1 motel, 1 camping/caravan park.
MAP REF. 213 Q8, 216 A8

Inverleigh   Population 227
On the Leigh River, this little town 29 km west of Geelong has a number of historic buildings. **Of interest:** Former Horseshoe Inn and two-storey hotel opposite; Church of England, Presbyterian Church, State School and Wilma's Cottage Art Gallery, all on Hamilton Hwy. **In the area:** Barunah Plains homestead, 17 km west; not open to public. **Accommodation:** Limited.
MAP REF. 205 B7, 208 B7

Inverloch   Population 1838
This is a small seaside resort on Anderson Inlet, east of Wonthaggi. It has good surf and long stretches of excellent beach, and is very popular in summer. **Of interest:** South Gippsland Conservation Society, Environment Centre and Shell Museum, in Information Centre building,

PHILLIP ISLAND

Situated at the entrance to Western Port, 140 kilometres south-east of Melbourne, Phillip Island (10 300 hectares) is a year-round destination for those who want to 'get away from it all'.

Once over the bridge between **San Remo** and **Newhaven**, the visitor is greeted by wide open spaces of farming land with panoramic views of ocean and bay. Most of the native bush has been cleared, although there are remnant pockets of native vegetation.

The greatest attraction for visitors is the fascinating fairy penguins on Summerland Beach. The penguins spend the day out at sea, catching whitebait for their young. Each evening at sunset they return in small groups and waddle up the beach to their sand-dune burrows. Visitors watch the parade under subdued floodlights from elevated stands and walkways. No flashlight photography is permitted. The Phillip Island Penguin Reserve is open daily. Enquiries (059) 56 8300; bookings for parade (059) 56 8691.

Seal Rocks at the south-west tip of the island, is the home of colonies of fur seals. The best time to observe them is during the breeding season in November and December. A ferry service from Cowes allows close-up views of the seals sunbathing on the rocks. Tours operate daily, weather permitting. Coin operated telescopes give landlubbers a view of the seals from The Nobbies kiosk.

Take the road down to the surf beach at Cape Woolamai, a rugged granite headland. A two-hour walk leads to the highest point on the island, from where there are breathtaking views of the coastline. The sand-dunes all along the Cape are the home of many mutton birds. Arriving from Siberia on their annual migration, the birds nest in the rookeries here in spring and summer. Koalas also make their home on this island and can be viewed in their natural habitat in the Oswin Roberts Reserve as well as at the koala conservation centre at Five Ways Reserve.

Visit nearby historic Churchill Island, reached by bridge near Newhaven. A pamphlet available at the island shop outlines the Homestead Walk and there are several walking-trails.

Everyone will enjoy hand-feeding the tame kangaroos and wallabies as well as observing other wildlife at the Phillip Island Wildlife Park, which is set in 32 hectares of bushland. Nearly seven hectares is wetlands: ponds and waterways which are breeding-grounds for rare and endangered birds.

Some unusual species of birds make their homes in The Nits at **Rhyll**, a fishing resort on the northern side of the island. Pelicans, ibis, royal spoonbills, swans and gulls inhabit the swamplands there.

Also on the north coast is **Cowes**, the most popular summer resort on Phillip Island. Its unspoilt beaches are sheltered for safe swimming, yachting and other water sports. A peak season ferry service runs from Cowes to Stony Point (via French Island) across Western Port.

For further information, ticket sales for penguins, free map and visitors guide as well as interesting displays, contact the Phillip Island Tourist Information Centre, Phillip Island Rd, Newhaven; (059) 56 7447.

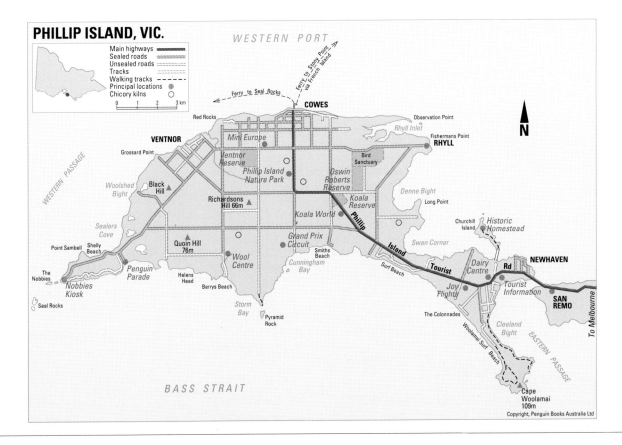

The Esplanade. **In the area:** Inverloch to Cape Paterson Scenic Road, through the Bunurong Cliff Coastal Reserve, 15 km south-west, has views as fine as those on the Great Ocean Rd. Spear-fishing and surfing at Cape Paterson. Adjacent to the town, Anderson's Inlet, the most southerly habitat of mangroves. Townsend Bluff and Maher's Landing for birdwatching. **Tourist information:** Cnr Ramsay Blvd and The Esplanade; (056) 74 2706. **Accommodation:** 1 hotel, 1 motel, 4 caravan/camping parks. MAP REF. 209 K11

Jeparit   Population 479
This little town in the Wimmera, 37 km north of Dimboola, is on the shores of Lake Hindmarsh, which is the largest natural freshwater lake in Victoria and has many kilometres of safe, sandy beaches, good fishing and a variety of birdlife. **Of interest:** A thistle-bedecked spire commemorates the fact that the town is the birthplace of Sir Robert Menzies; illuminated at night. Wimmera–Mallee Pioneer Museum, 4-ha complex of colonial buildings at southern entrance to town; furnished in period, with displays of restored farm machinery. **In the area:** Near Antwerp, 20 km south, Ebenezer Mission, founded in 1859 by Moravian missionaries and restored by National Trust. Wyperfeld National Park, 44 km north. **Tourist information:** Shire Offices, Roy St; (053) 97 2070. **Accommodation:** 1 hotel, 1 caravan/camping park. MAP REF. 212 G5

Kaniva   Population 821
Kaniva in the west Wimmera, 43 km from Bordertown, SA, is just north of the Little Desert, which is famous for its wildflowers in spring. **Of interest:** Historical museum with large collection of items of local history. **In the area:** Billy-Ho Bush Walk begins some 10 km south of town; a 3-km self-guiding walk in the Little Desert National Park, numbered pegs allow identification of various species of desert flora. Safaris to the Big and Little Deserts from Kaniva, Nhill and Dimboola. Mooree Reserve, 20 km south-west of town, a pleasant picnic spot. Farm holidays at Parlawidgee cropping and grazing farm. Railway station (1889) at Serviceton, 23 km west, classified by National Trust. Tourist information: Shire Offices, 25 Baker St; (053) 92 2260. **Accommodation:** 2 hotels, 1 motel, 1 caravan/camping park. MAP REF. 212 C7

Kerang   Population 4031
Some 30 km from the Murray and 60 km from Swan Hill, Kerang is the centre of a productive rural area and lies at the southern end of a chain of lakes and marshes. Some of the largest breeding-grounds in the world for ibis and other water-fowl are found in these marshes. The ibis is closely protected because of its value in controlling locusts and other pests. **Of interest:** The old water tower on the corner of Murray Valley Hwy and Stadford St houses the Gem Club and provides tourist information. The Apex Park recreation area is sited by the first of the three Reedy Lakes; the second has a large ibis rookery and the third is popular for water sports. All the lakes in the Kerang area are popular for sailing and boating and have picnic facilities. **In the area:** Lake Boga, 44 km north-west; good sandy beaches. Murrabit, 29 km north, on the Murray and surrounded by picturesque river forests; country market on first Sat. of each month. Australian Tractor Pull Championships at Quambatook, 42 km south-west, on Easter Sunday. Shannkist Cashmere Stud Farm, Koondrook Cottage and Riverside Crafts at Koondrook-Barham, 24 km north-east. **Tourist information:** 25 Murray St, Barham; (054) 53 3100. **Accommodation:** 4 hotels, 2 motels, 2 caravan/camping parks. **See also:** The Mighty Murray. MAP REF. 116 I12, 213 Q2, 215 Q13, 216 A2

Koo-wee-rup   Population 1081
Well known for its annual Potato Festival every March, this town is in the middle of

Coal Creek Historical Park, Korumburra

a rich market-garden area, near Western Port. **In the area:** Bayles Flora and Fauna Park, 8 km north-east. Royal Botanic Gardens Cranbourne Garden, 28 km north-west. Berwick–Pakenham Historical Society Museum in John St, Pakenham, 21 km north. Military Vehicle Museum in Army Rd, Pakenham. Tooradin, 10 km west, situated on Sawtell's Inlet; popular with fishing and boating enthusiasts. Victoria's Farm Shed displays at Tynong, 20 km north-east. Also at Tynong, Gumbuya Fun Park, set in landscaped native bushland. **Accommodation:** 1 motel. MAP REF. 209 J8

Koroit   Population 958
Koroit is 18 km west of the coastal resort of Warrnambool in the south-west of Victoria. It is a quiet agricultural town with historic botanic gardens and where the commercial and church precincts of the town, both containing many historic buildings, have been classified by the National Trust. **In the area:** Tower Hill State Game Reserve, a volcanic area 3 km south; walking tracks, Natural History Centre, bird hides. The nearby coast between Port Fairy and Warrnambool offers some delightful scenery. **Tourist information:** City of Warrnambool Tourist Information Centre, 600 Raglan St, Warrnambool; (055) 64 7837. **Accommodation:** 1 hotel, 1 caravan/camping park. MAP REF. 211 J9

Korumburra   Population 2774
The giant Gippsland earthworm, sought by fishermen and geologists alike, is found in the area. Situated on the South Gippsland Hwy, 116 km south-east of Melbourne, the area surrounding the town is given to dairying and agriculture, and the countryside is hilly. **Of interest:** Coal Creek Historical Park, cnr Sth Gippsland Hwy and Silkstone Rd, recreation of 19th-century coal-mining village; located on original site of Coal Creek mine, begun in 1890s; orientation centre in Mechanics' Institute inside park near entrance, open daily. Ten-day Karmai (giant worm) Festival held annually in March. **In the area:** Leongatha, 14 km south-east, for excellent fishing, and beaches at Waratah Bay (66 km) and Corner Inlet (58 km). Top Paddock Cheeses at Bena, 4 km south-west, encourage tastings and sales of their traditional, curd and soft cheeses. Loch, 16 km west, for antiques and arts and crafts. At Poowong, 18 km north-west: Poowong Pioneer Chapel, fine example of German architecture, and Mudlark Pottery. **Tourist information:** Coal Creek Historical

Park, South Gippsland Hwy; (056) 55 2233. **Accommodation:** 2 hotels, 1 motel, 1 caravan/camping park. MAP REF. 209 L10

Kyabram — Population 5342

A prosperous town in the Murray - Goulburn area, just 40 km north-west of Shepparton, Kyabram is in a rich dairying and fruit-growing district. **Of interest:** Community-owned waterfowl and fauna park on Lake Rd has five lakes with varieties of duck, ibis, swans and pelicans, a 16-ha enclosure for emus and kangaroos and a huge flight aviary; open daily. The Stables, adjacent to fauna park, for pottery and crafts. Mr Ilzyn's Cottages, Breen Ave; mansions, pubs, farm houses, from around the world, all in miniature. Annual Antique Aeroplane Fly-in at Easter. Annual Rodeo on March Labour Day holiday. **Tourist information:** Fauna park, 75 Lake Rd; (058) 52 2883. **Accommodation:** 3 hotels, 2 motels, 2 caravan/camping parks. **See also:** The Mighty Murray. MAP REF. 216 H6

Kyneton — Population 4010

Little more than an hour's drive from Melbourne, along the Calder Hwy, Kyneton is an attractive and well-preserved town with several interesting bluestone buildings. Farms around the town prospered during the gold-rushes, supplying large quantities of fresh food to the diggings at Ballarat and Bendigo. **Of interest:** Kyneton Museum, Piper St, housed in what was a two-storey bank (c.1865); drop-log cottage in grounds. Botanic Gardens, Clowes St, area of 8 ha above the river, contains 500 specimen trees. Historic buildings include the town's churches, mechanics' institute and the old police depot. Willis flour mill in Piper St has been restored to operational condition; open for inspection at weekends. Also in Piper St, Meskills Woolstore, wool spinning mill with yarn and garments for sale. Magnolia Cottage Nursery in Fiddlers Green Rd. Kyneton Food and Wine Festival held annually in February. Antique fair each Easter and Daffodil Festival in September. **In the area:** Two-storey bluestone mills on either side of town. Upper Coliban, Lauriston and Malmsbury Reservoirs, all 8 km west. At Malmsbury, 10 km north-west: historic bluestone railway viaduct, Bleak House (1850s) with its rose garden, and Etherlings of Malmsbury crafts. Both Carlsruhe Gallery and Campaspe Art Gallery at Carlsruhe, 5 km south-east, are worth a visit. At Trentham: 22 km south-west: Trentham Falls and Minifie's Berry Farm; pick-your-own in season. At Blackwood, further 14 km south, the Garden of St Erth. **Tourist information:** Kyneton Florist, 6 High St; (054) 22 1007. **Accommodation:** 5 hotels, 2 motels, 1 caravan/camping park. MAP REF. 200 G5, 208 D1, 216 D13

Lake Bolac — Population 211

In the Western District plains area, this small town on the Glenelg Hwy is by a 1460-ha freshwater lake which has good sandy beaches around its 20-km shoreline and is very popular for fishing (eels, trout, perch and yellow-belly), boating and swimming. There are several boat-launching ramps and an aquatic club. A sporting complex is located between town and lake. A four-day yachting regatta is held each Easter. **Tourist information:** Lake Bolac Motel, Glenelg Hwy; (053) 50 2218. **Accommodation:** 1 motel, 1 caravan/camping park. MAP REF. 211 L5

Lakes Entrance — Population 4104

This extremely popular holiday town is at the eastern end of the Gippsland Lakes, which form the largest inland network of waterways in Australia. They cover an area of more than 400 sq km and are separated from the ocean by a thin sliver of sand dunes which form a large part of the Ninety Mile Beach, which stretches south to Seaspray. A bridge across the Cunningham Arm gives access to the surf beach from Lakes Entrance. The town is well developed for the holiday-maker, catering for both seaside recreation and exploration of the mountain country to the north. It is the home port for a very large fishing fleet and also for many pleasure-craft. Large cruise-vessels conduct regular sightseeing tours of the lakes throughout the year. Boats can also be hired. Fishing, both ocean and beach, is popular, as are swimming and surfing on a variety of good beaches. **Of interest:** Fisherman's Co-operative, Bullock Island; viewing platform and fish for sale. Shell Museum, the Esplanade. Growing number of potteries and galleries. **In the area:** Ramsdell's sawmill and gardens, Buchan Rd, 23 km north-east. Kinkuna Country fauna park and family entertainment centre, Princes Hwy, 3.5 km east. Good views from Jemmy's Point, 3 km west, and Nyerimilang Park, 10 km north-west. Within the park is the original homestead, the north wing built in 1892; open for inspection. The sheltered waters of Lake Tyers (6 – 23 km east, depending on access point) are popular for fishing, swimming and boating; cruises depart from Fishermans Landing. Braeburne Park Orchards and tearooms; 6 km east. The Buchan Caves, 55 km north, are well worth a visit. Day-trips can be made to the old mining areas around Omeo, 126 km north. Boats for hire at Metung, 15 km west by road. Metung Hot Pools; open daily. Lake Bunga, 3 km east; nature trail. Wyanga Park Vineyard and Winery, 10 km north; reached by boat trips from town. Nicholson River, 24 km west, and Golvinda wineries, 50 km north-west, via Bairnsdale. Nowa Nowa, 23 km north; fun park, go-kart track, and timber mill with

Angahook-Lorne State Park

visitor facilities. **Tourist information:** Cnr Esplanade and Marine Pde; (051) 55 1966. **Accommodation:** 3 hotels, 16 motels, 22 caravan/camping parks. **See also:** Gippsland Lakes; Victoria's Wine Regions.
MAP REF. 109 B13, 220 G8

Lancefield
Population 2000

This historic township with its wide streets and Victorian buildings is located 67 km north-west of Melbourne. **Of interest:** Mechanics Hall (1868), old Macedonia Hotel (1889) and Clevelands, fine private property. **In the area:** Lancefield Estate, 4 km west, and Granite Hills Winery, 18 km north-west. Burke and Wills Camel Farm, 12 km north, on Burke & Wills Track; 'hands-on' workshops and education days; camel safaris and one-day camel trek (12 km) to Knight's Winery. **Accommodation:** 1 hotel, 1 motel.
MAP REF. 201 J5, 208 F1, 216 F13

Leongatha
Population 3957

Near the foothills of the Strzelecki Ranges, Leongatha, the centre of a dairying area, is a good base from which to make trips to Wilsons Promontory National Park and the seaside and fishing resorts on the coast. **Of interest:** Murray Goulburn Co-operative, one of Australia's largest dairy factories. Historic Society Museum, McCartin St. Magic Mushroom Pottery, Roughend St. **In the area:** Along the coast road there are impressive plantations of English trees, areas of natural bushland, picnic and camping facilities. About 21 km north, the Grand Ridge Rd offers excellent scenic driving and can be followed into the Tarra-Bulga National Park. Firelight Museum, 9 km north, displays antique lamps and firearms. Moss Vale Park, 16 km north-east, has picnic and barbecue facilities. At Mirboo North, 23 km north-east of Leongatha: Grand Ridge Brewing Company for inspection of beer-brewing process; also Erimae Lavender Farm and Colonial Bank Antiqu es. Korumburra, with its Coal Creek Historical Park, 14 km west along South Gippsland Hwy. **Tourist information:** Shire Offices, Woorayl; (056) 62 2111. **Accommodation:** 2 motels, 1 caravan/camping park.
MAP REF. 209 L10

Lorne
Population 935

The approaches to Lorne along the Great Ocean Road, whether from east or west, are quite spectacular. The town is one of Victoria's most attractive coastal resorts, with the superb mountain scenery of the Otways behind, and a year-round mild

THE WIMMERA

Travelling through the Wimmera on a hot summer's day is an unforgettable experience. The Wimmera is the granary of the state; the wheatfields stretch as far as the eye can see, an endless golden plain broken only occasionally by a gentle ripple in the terrain. In the south-east corner, however, are the Grampians, surrounded by a network of lakes, understandably popular with anglers and water-sports lovers.

The region takes its name from the Aboriginal word for throwing stick. Evidence of occupation by the original inhabitants, the Wotjobaluk and Jardwa tribes, can still be seen: canoe trees are common and there are many cave paintings in the Grampians area. The Ebenezer Mission Station at Antwerp, near Dimboola, founded by Moravian missionaries to Christianise the Aboriginal population, has been restored by the National Trust and local inhabitants.

Horsham, with its delightful private, public and Botanical gardens, intriguing Olde Horsham Village and an excellent regional art gallery, makes a good base from which to explore the whole region. If you are visiting in March, do not miss the famous annual Wimmera Machinery Field Days, held at the Victorian College of Agriculture and Horticulture, Dooen, and the Labour Day weekend annual fishing competition on the Wimmera River. Natimuk, 34 km west of Horsham, is the centre for visitors drawn to climb Mt Arapiles, a 356 metre sandstone monolith.

The agricultural life of the last century has been remembered at **Warracknabeal**, the largest wheat-receiving centre in the state, where an agricultural machinery museum houses huge steam-powered chaff-cutters, headers and tractors and depicts the history of the wheat industry. Near Dimboola, set along the banks of the Wimmera River, is one entrance to the Little Desert National Park. 'Little Desert' is something of a misnomer because the park is not 'little', and it does not look like a 'desert'. There is a proliferation of plant and animal life, particularly in spring when the scrub and heathlands come into bloom.

For further information, contact Wimmera Tourism, 20 O'Callaghan's Pde, Horsham; (053) 82 3778.

climate. Captain Loutit gave the district the name of Loutit Bay. The village of Lorne was established in 1871, became popular with pastoralists from inland areas, and developed rather in the style of an English seaside resort. When the Great Ocean Road opened in 1932 Lorne grew more popular, however, the town

Main street, Maldon

itself has remained relatively unspoiled, with good beaches, surfing, and excellent bushwalking in the hills behind adding to its charm. **Of interest:** Teddy's Lookout, at the edge of George St behind the town, offers good bay views. Lorne's foreshore reserve has a children's playground, pool, amusement centre, trampolines and picnic ground. Shipwreck Walk along beach. Pedal-boats can be hired. Qdos Contemporary Art Gallery, Mountjoy Pde. Lorne Fisheries on the pier has daily supplies from the local fleet. Also on pier, the Pier Gallery Restaurant. Shell Shop and Museum, William St. The Cumberland Resort, Mountjoy Pde. **In the area:** Angahook–Lorne State Park which surrounds the town has many walking tracks, including one to Kalimna and Phantom waterfalls from the Sheoak Picnic area; about 4 km from town. Erskine falls and rapids are 8 km north. Gentle Annie Berry Gardens, 26 km north-west, via Deans Marsh. Mt Defiance, 10 km south-west. The Cumberland River Valley, 4 km south, has walking tracks and a camping ground. Allenvale, 2 km west, is also an attractive area for walking and has barbecue and picnic facilities. At Wye River, 17 km south-west, fishing and surfing, but limited accommodation. Scenic drives west in the Otway Ranges and south-west along Great Ocean Rd. **Tourist information:** 144 Mountjoy Pde; (052) 89 1036. **Accommodation:** 2 hotels, 4 motels, 6 caravan/camping parks. **See also:** The Great Ocean Road.
MAP REF. 205 A13, 208 B10, 211 R10

Macedon Population 1137
Situated on the Calder Hwy, an hour from Melbourne, large sections of the Macedon area were destroyed by terrible bushfires in 1983. Today it is difficult to imagine this devastation as the residents have restored or rebuilt homes and re-established the beautiful gardens for which the area is renowned. Mount Macedon is an extinct volcano, 1013 m high. At its summit, there is a memorial cross, erected in honour of those who died in World War I. **Of interest:** Lavender Place at Mount Macedon township for art and craft. **In the area:** Wineries include Hanging Rock at Hanging Rock, 8 km north-east, Romsey Vineyards at Romsey, 21 km east, and Lancefield Estate near Lancefield, 26 km north-east. Scenic tours to Trentham Falls, 32 km west, and Blackwood mining hamlet, 46 km south-west. Woodend, 10 km north, is an attractive old township and hill resort. The Hanging Rock made famous by Joan Lindsay's story, 8 km north-east of Woodend, is a massive volcanic rock formation, ideal for climbing; picnic reserve

at base. Annual picnic horserace meetings at Hanging Rock on New Year's Day and Australia Day. Barringo Wildlife Reserve, 8 km south-east. **Tourist information:** Black Forest Motel, 573 Calder Hwy; (054) 26 1600. **Accommodation:** 1 motel.
MAP REF. 200 H7, 208 E2

Maffra–Heyfield
Pop. 3973, 1635
The Shire of Maffra includes both these towns and extends from the fertile farming lands of the Macalister Irrigation Area north to the magnificent mountain scenery of the Great Dividing Range. **Of interest:** Maffra Sugar Beet Museum, River St. All Seasons Herb Gardens, Foster St. **In the area:** Lake Glenmaggie, 11 km north of Heyfield; popular watersports venue with camping facilities. The forest road north (closed in winter) that follows the Macalister Valley to Licola (49 km from Heyfield), or to Jamieson, (147 km), passes through some spectacular scenery. This road leads to Mt Tamboritha (20 km north from Licola) and Mt Howitt (50 km) and gives access to alpine country and the snowfields. The road north from Maffra, via Briagalong (14 km), leads over the Dargo High Plains and follows Freestone Creek; the Blue Pool and Quarries for swimming. Lake Tarli Karng, within the Alpine National Park, 60 km north-east of Licola, is a major focus for bushwalking in the park. Trail-riding and horseback tours of area start from Valencia Creek, 17 km north of Maffra, and Licola. Historic hotel and Avonlea Gardens at Briagalong. **Tourist information:** Central Gippsland Tourism Assocn Inc., Princes Hwy, Sale; (051) 44 1108. **Accommodation:** Maffra, 3 hotels, 1 motel, 1 caravan/camping park. Heyfield, 2 hotels, 1 motel.
MAP REF. 209 R6, 220 B9

Maldon Population 1116
The National Trust has declared Maldon the 'First Notable Town' in Victoria, on the basis that no other town has such an interesting collection of 19th-century buildings, nor such a collection of European trees. Situated 20 km north-west of Castlemaine in central Victoria, Maldon is very popular with tourists, especially during the annual Maldon Easter Fair, and in spring when the wildflowers are in bloom. The deep reef gold-mines were among Victoria's richest and at one stage 20 000 men worked on the nearby Tarrangower diggings. Enthusiasts still search for gold in the area. **Of interest:** Anzac Hill, at southern end of High St, affords a good view of the town. Many of the town's buildings, mostly constructed of local

stone, are notable: in particular, Maldon Hospital (1860), cnr Adair and Chapel Sts; the Post Office (1870), High St; the old council offices, High St (now converted into a folk-museum); and Dabb's General Store in Main St, where the old storefront has been faithfully restored. Former Denominational (Penny) School and Welsh Congregational Church, cnr Camp and Church Sts, are National Trust properties. In High St, Cumquat Tea Rooms. The Beehive Chimney (1862) stands out at the southern end of Church St. Castlemaine and Maldon Preservation Society runs steam trains from railway station, Hornsby St, on Sundays. Town walking tour brochure available. **In the area:** Delightful bushwalks and intriguing rock formations. Panoramic Views from Mt Tarrangower Lookout Tower, 2 km west. Cairn Curran Reservoir, 10 km north-west; popular for water sports, fishing and picnics. Nuggetty Ranges and Mt Marvel, 2 km north. Carmen's Tunnel, 2 km south-west, a vivid reminder of the hardships of gold-mining days; open for inspection. Gold mining dredge beside road to Bendigo. To the north-west, Tarnagulla (38 km), Dunolly (37 km) and Bealiba (58 km), all former gold settlements. **Tourist information:** High St; (054) 75 2569. **Accommodation:** 2 caravan/camping parks. **See also:** The Golden Age.
MAP REF. 200 C1, 213 R11, 216 B11

Mallacoota Population 826
On the Gippsland coast, at the mouth of a deep inlet of the same name, Mallacoota is a seaside and fishing township growing in popularity as a holiday centre. It offers the remote and beautiful Croajingolong National Park, which surrounds the town, to explore, as well as good beaches and excellent fishing. (Mallacoota's specialties are oysters and abalone.)Bushwalking and birdwatching also popular. **In the area:** Scenic lake and river cruises. Gipsy Point, 16 km north, is set in attractive countryside. Genoa, 24 km north, on Princes Hwy, is the last township before entering NSW and nearby Genoa Peak has some magnificent coastal views. Karbeethong Lodge, on inlet 4 km from Mallacoota. Bastion Point and Betka surfing beaches. **Tourist information:** 57 Maurice Ave; (051) 58 0788. **Accommodation:** Mallacoota, 3 motels, 5 caravan/camping parks. Genoa, 1 motel, 1 caravan/camping park. **See also:** Victoria's National Parks.
MAP REF. 109 F3, 221 O6

Mansfield Population 2039
A popular inland resort at the junction of the Midland and Maroondah Hwys, Mansfield is 3 km east of the northern arm of Eildon Weir. It is the nearest

sizeable town to the Mt Buller Alpine Village. **Of interest:** In High St, a marble obelisk erected to the memory of three police officers shot by Ned Kelly at Stringybark Creek, near Tolmie, in 1878. Their graves are in the Mansfield cemetery. Highton Manor (1896), Highton Lane. Apart from its role as a resort, Mansfield is also a timber town and boasts six sawmills, some open for inspection. Annual Mountain Country Festival held in November. **In the area:** Horse and trail-bike riding. The road north-east over the mountains to Whitfield in the King River Valley (62 km) passes through spectacular scenery. To the south are the Goulburn and Jamieson Rivers, both offering trout-fishing and gold-fossicking. Delatite Winery on Pollards Rd, 7 km south. Mt Samaria State Park, 14 km north, for scenic drives, picnics, camping and bushwalking. Nearby Lake Nillahcootie for boating, fishing, canoeing and sailing. Children's Adventure Camps; Nillahcootie camps. Howqua Dale Gourmet Retreat, at Howqua, 29 km south, has food weekends and sporting facilities. Historic buildings at old gold-mining town of Jamieson, 37 km south, on Jamieson River. Lake William Hovell, 85 km north-east, has picnic and barbecue facilities and a children's playground, and offers boating, canoeing and fishing. *The Man from Snowy River* and its sequel were filmed at Merrijig, 18 km south-east of Mansfield. Hot-air balloon flights available. The Alpine National Park, 60 km east, is less accessible than other Victorian national parks but offers bushwalks through remote terrain. Kratlund Park, Mansfield, for farm holidays. Houseboats for hire on Lake Eildon. **Tourist information:** Visitors Centre, 11 High St; (057) 75 1464. **Accommodation:** 3 hotels, 9 motels, 2 caravan/camping parks. **See also:** Victoria's Wine Regions. MAP REF. 217 M11

Maryborough   Population 7705

First sheep-farming, then the gold-rush, contributed to the development of this small city on the northern slopes of the Great Dividing Range, 70 km north of Ballarat. Modern Maryborough is in the centre of an agricultural and forest area and is highly industrialised. **Of interest:** Pioneer Memorial Tower, Bristol Hill. Worsley Cottage (1894), Palmerston St, a historical museum. The splendid Maryborough railway station, Victoria St, and the imposing Civic Square buildings, Clarendon St. Princes Park, Park Rd, with good sports facilities. Maryborough Highland Gathering on New Year's Day and annual Golden Wattle Festival in September. **In the area:** Aboriginal

Shearing-shed, Mildura

wells, 4 km south. To the north, the once thriving gold towns of Bowenvale-Timor (6 km), Dunolly (23 km) and Tarnagulla (37 km). **Tourist information:** Tuaggra St; (054) 61 1566. **Accommodation:** 7 motels, 2 caravan/ camping parks. MAP REF. 213 P11, 216 A11

Marysville   Population 519

The peaceful and attractive sub-alpine town of Marysville, which owes its existence first to gold as it was on the route to the Woods Point goldfields, and to timber milling, is 37 km north of Healesville, off the Maroondah Hwy. The town is surrounded by attractive forest-clad mountain country and is a popular resort all year. **Of interest:** Marysville Crafts, Murchison St; Arbour Green Gallery, Falls Rd. Goulds Sawmill, Racecourse Rd; open for inspection. Nicholl's Lookout, Cumberland Rd; excellent views. Burrengeer Park, Murchison St; historic display within grounds of park. **In the area:** Numerous bushwalking tracks lead to beauty spots in the area, including 4 km loop walk in Cumberland Scenic Reserve, 16 km east, 1 hr walk to Keppel's Lookout, 1 1/2 hour walk to Mt Gordon and 2 hr walk to Steavenson Falls (illuminated at night); after dark, visitors can hand-feed the local possums. Lake Eildon, 46 km north-east, and Fraser National Park, 59 km north-east, are within easy driving distance. Lake Mountain, 19 km east; often has sufficient snow for tobogganing and sightseeing in winter. Buxton Camel Farm, Buxton Trout Farm and Australian Bush Pioneer's Farm, at foot of Mt Cathedral, 10 km north. Marysville Trout Farm, Marysville Rd, 2 km south-west. Big River State Forest, 30 km east, for camping, fishing, hunting, trail-bike riding and gold-fossicking. **Tourist information:** Falls Rd; (059) 63 3333. **Accommodation:** 1 hotel, 4 motels, 1 caravan/camping park. MAP REF. 209 K3, 218 G8

Milawa–Oxley

Population under 200

On what is known as the Snow Road, Milawa, 16 km south-east of Wangaratta, is the home of Brown Brothers vineyard. John Gehrig's and Read's wineries are to be found at Oxley, 4 km west, and the Markwood Estate vineyard is 6 km east of Milawa. Bogong Jack Adventures runs a range of bicycle tours from Oxley. The Snow Road links Oxley, Milawa and Markwood with Wangaratta to the west and the Ovens Hwy to the east. **Of interest:** Milawa Royal general store, which provides supplies and light meals. Old Emu Restaurant. Earthly Goods craft shop. Milawa Cheese Company. Milawa Mustards. **Tourist information:** Wangaratta and Region Visitors Information Centre, Hume Hwy, (057) 21 5711; Fingers and Thrumbs, Whorouly South, (057) 27 1290. **Accommodation:** 1 motel, 1 caravan/ camping park. **See also:** Victoria's Wine Regions. MAP REF. 217 O7

Mildura   Population 20 512

Sunny mild winters and picturesque locations on the banks of the Murray make Mildura and neighbouring towns popular tourist areas. Mildura, on the Sunraysia Hwy, 557 km north of Melbourne, is a small and pleasant city which developed along with the irrigation of the area. Alfred Deakin, statesman and advocate of irrigation, persuaded the Chaffey brothers, Canadian-born irrigation experts, to visit this region. They recognised its potential and selected Mildura as the first site for development. The early days of the project were fraught with setbacks, but by the turn of the century the citrus-growing industry was well established and with the locking of the Murray completed in 1928, Mildura soon afterwards became a city. **Of interest:** W.B. Chaffey became Mildura's first mayor; his statue is in Deakin Ave. The Mildura Arts Centre, Chaffey Ave, includes Rio Vista, the original Chaffey home and now a museum with a collection of colonial household items, and the first irrigation pump. Paddle-steamers leave from Mildura Wharf, end of Madden Ave, for trips on the Murray and Darling Rivers. The PS *Melbourne* does 2 hr round trips. PS *Avoca* has luncheon and dinner cruises. The *Murray River Explorer* is a luxury cruiser able to carry over 100 passengers. PS *Coonawarra* offers 5- and 6-day cruises. The Humpty Dumpty Tourist Farm, Cureton Ave, and the Sultana Sam Vineyard, Benetook Ave, are popular with children. The Mildura Lock Island and Weir can be inspected. The longest bar in the world is housed in the Mildura

Working-man's Club, Sturt Hwy. Other attractions include: Aquacoaster water-slide, cnr Seventh St and Orange Ave; Dolls on the Avenue, Benetook Ave; Pioneer Cottage, Hunter St; Marina's Fuchsia and Herb Gardens, Benetook Ave. The Citrus Shop, Pine Ave; educational aids and sales. Annual Great Mildura Paddleboat Race usually held in March. **In the area:** River Road Pottery, 10 km west. Woodsie's Gem Shop, 6 km south-west. Many vineyards, including Lindemans (largest winery in southern hemisphere), Mildura Vineyards, Stanley, Trentham Estate and Mildara Blass, are open weekdays for tastings and sales. Capogreco Wines, Riverside Ave, Mildura, are open Mon.–Sat. Orange World, 6 km north, and in NSW, offers tours of citrus-growing areas. Golden River Zoo, 3 km north-west; large collection of native and exotic species in natural surroundings. Murray River Boatshare has houseboats as timeshare units. PS *Rothbury* offers day-cruises. Yabbies at Gol Gol Fisheries, 2 km north in NSW; open daily. Hattah–Kulkyne National Park, 70 km south, for bushwalking. At Irymple, 6 km south, Sunbeam Dried Fruits; tours available. Red Cliffs, 15 km south, is in an important area for the citrus and dried fruit industries. Reptile Park and Zoo, and 'Big Lizzie' steam traction engine at Red Cliffs. **Tourist information:** Langtree Mall; (050) 23 3619. **Accommodation:** 3 hotels, 43 motels, 25 caravan/camping parks. **See also:** The Mighty Murray; Victoria's Wine Regions.
MAP REF. 116 D8, 214 H2

Moe–Yallourn   Population 18 376
Situated on the Princes Hwy, 135 km south-east of Melbourne, Moe is a rapidly growing residential city in the Latrobe Valley. Nearby, what was the State Electricity Commission town of Yallourn has been demolished to make way for an extension to the enormous brown coal open-cut mine, and most of Yallourn's residents have been moved to other towns in the area. **Of interest:** The 'Old Gippstown' Pioneer Township, Lloyd St, is a re-creation of a 19th-century community, with over 30 restored buildings brought from surrounding areas; barbecues, picnic facilities and adventure playground; open daily. The nearby power-station is open for guided inspections. **In the area:** Mair's Coalville Vineyard at Moe South. A scenic road leads north-east 46 km to the old mining township of Walhalla, and through the mountains to Jamieson, 147 km further north. The Baw Baw plateau and the Mt Baw Baw ski village are accessed 47 km north via Willow Grove. The plateau is the

highest alpine point in central Gippsland and in the summer has abundant wildflowers and is excellent for bushwalking. Blue Rock Dam, 20 km north of Moe, has fishing, swimming and sailboating, as well as picnic facilities. **Tourist information:** Old Gippstown Pioneer Township, cnr Princes Hwy and Lloyd St; (051) 27 3082. **Accommodation:** 1 hotel, 3 motels, 1 caravan/camping park.
MAP REF. 209 N8

Morwell   Population 16 387
Morwell, 150 km south-east of Melbourne, has grown to become one of the main cities of the Latrobe Valley. This valley contains one of the world's largest deposits of brown coal. Electricity generated by the State Electricity Commission's power-stations on the coalfields at Morwell, Hazelwood, Churchill and Yallourn accounts for more than 85% of Victoria's power needs. Morwell is an industrial town with a number of secondary industries. **Of interest:** The city's immense open-cut mining projects, power-houses and briquette-making plants are open daily for free guided inspections. La Trobe Valley Arts Centre, Commercial Rd. **In the area:** Many scenic day-tours can be made from the three main cities in the Latrobe Valley, Morwell, Moe, 20 km west, and Traralgon, 12 km east. Lake Narracan and the Hazelwood pondage, 5 km south of Morwell, are ideal for water sports and picnics. There are views of Moe, Yallourn North and the valley between the Strzelecki Ranges and the Baw Baw mountains at Narracan Falls, about 27 km west. Tarra-Bulga National Park, 47 km south-east, is renowned for its fern glades, waterfalls, rosellas, lyrebirds and koalas. To the north, for 66 km, through dense mountain country, the road leads to the old mining township of Walhalla, and further on, to the Moondarra Reservoir and the beautiful Tanjil and Thomson River valleys. **Tourist information:** SEC Visitors Centre, off Commercial Rd (051) 35 3170. **Accommodation:** 3 hotels, 7 motels, 3 caravan/camping parks.
MAP REF. 209 O8

Mount Beauty   Population 1564
Situated in the Upper Kiewa Valley, 344 km north-east of Melbourne, Mount Beauty was originally an accommodation township for workers on the Kiewa Hydro-electric Scheme in the 1940s. An ideal holiday centre, the town lies at the foot of Mount Bogong, Victoria's highest mountain (1986 m). **Of interest:** Leaflets outlining walks, excursions and other

activities are available from the Tourist Information Centre and the National Parks Office. The Conquestathon, a race to the summit of Mt Bogong, is held annually on the Labour Day weekend in March. **In the area:** Scenic road, 32 km south-east to Falls Creek and the Bogong High Plains; bicycle hire and horseriding tours available. Mount Beauty Pondage offers all water sports and fishing. Bogong village, 16 km south-east, with walks around Lake Guy. Tours of the Kiewa and other power stations; advance bookings through SEC recommended. Skiing holidays to suit both cross-country and downhill skiers available at Mount Beauty and Falls Creek. **Tourist information:** Pyles Coach Service, (057) 57 2024; or SEC Information Centre, Kiewa Valley Hwy, (057) 57 2307. **Accommodation:** 6 motels, 2 caravan/camping parks.
MAP REF. 219 C9

Murtoa   Population 863
Murtoa is situated on the edge of picturesque Lake Marma, 30 km north-east of Horsham on the Wimmera Hwy. It is in the centre of Victoria's wheat belt and with two other old wheat towns, Minyip and Rupanyup, makes up the Shire of Dunmunkle. **Of interest:** A huge wheat-storage silo, and a four-storey railway water-tower, built in 1886, now a museum which houses the district's past, including James Hill's taxidermy collection of some 500 birds, prepared between 1885 and 1930. Lake Marma has trout and redfin fishing, water sports and caravan park on its eastern side. Rupanyup, 16 km east, is an attractive old township and the administrative centre of the Shire. Barrabool Forest Reserve, 7 km south of Murtoa, has an attractive spring display of wildflowers. **Accommodation:** 2 hotels, 1 caravan/camping park.
MAP REF. 213 J8

Myrtleford   Population 2853
On the Ovens Hwy, 45 km south-east of Wangaratta, the town of Myrtleford is surrounded by a rich hops- and tobacco-growing area. It also has some of the largest walnut groves in the southern hemisphere. The Ovens Valley was opened up by miners flocking to the area and creeks there are still popular for gold-panning and gem-fossicking. **Of interest:** The Phoenix Tree, the sculptured butt of a red gum crafted by Hans Knorr, on highway at town entrance. Reform Hill Lookout, end of Halls Rd. Jaycees Historic Park and Swing Bridge, Standish St. The town has many other delightful picnic spots and rest areas. Annual Tobacco Hops and Timber Festival held

THE PROM

Wilsons Promontory, at the southernmost tip of the Australian mainland, is one of Victoria's largest and most spectacular national parks. 'The Prom', as it is affectionately known to Victorians, has an impressive range of landscapes, including tall forested ranges, luxuriant tree-fern valleys, open heaths, salt marshes and long drifts of sand dunes. Its wide, white sandy beaches are magnificent, some dominated by spectacular granite tors and washed by spectacular rolling surf. There are also very safe swimming beaches, particularly at Norman Bay near the main camping area at Tidal River and also the aptly named Squeaky Beach, where the sands squeak underfoot.

Birds and other wildlife abound on the Prom; flocks of lorikeets, rosellas and flame robins, kookaburras and blue wrens are in evidence, even in the main general store area at Tidal River village, and for the more dedicated and patient bird-watcher, sightings of tree-creepers, herons and lyrebirds can be the reward.

Emus 'graze' unperturbed on the open heath by the side of the main road at the park entry area at Yanakie Isthmus, and kangaroos and wallabies seem unimpressed by their human observers. At night wombat-spotting by torchlight is a favourite pastime with children staying in the Tidal River area.

There are more than eighty kilometres of walking-tracks in the Wilsons Promontory National Park. Some cover short walks, such as the nature trail in Lilly Pilly Gully, where the vegetation varies from bushland, inhabited by many koalas, to rainforest, with ancient tree-ferns and trickling streams; other longer walks can be taken to places such as Sealers Cove or to the tip of the Prom, where there is a lighthouse dating from 1859. Hikers should consider tide times to make creek crossing easier.

At the visitor information centre and park office at **Tidal River**, leaflets are available detailing walking-tracks and the flora and fauna of the park. During summer and Easter, information officers give talks and spotlight tours as well as leading children's nature activities. Permits are required for all overnight hikes.

For further information, contact the Department of Conservation and Environment, 240 Victoria Pde, East Melbourne; (03) 412 4011.

above top: Aerial view of lighthouse
above: Norman Point

---

over Labour Day weekend in March. **In the area:** Lake Buffalo, 25 km south, the Ovens River and the Buffalo River, 31 km south, all offer good fishing. The Mt Buffalo National Park is within easy driving distance, as are the historic towns of Beechworth, Yackandandah and Bright. (4WD vehicles for hire in Myrtleford.) Swinburne Reserve, 5 km south of Myrtleford on road to Bright, is starting-point for self-guided forest walks and a fitness track; picnic facilities. Historic Merriang Homestead and sculpture studio of Hans Knorr, 6 km south-west. Guided tours to hop and tobacco farms. **Tourist information:** Ponderosa Cabin, 29 - 31 Clyde St; (057) 52 1727. **Accommodation:** 1 hotel, 1 hotel/motel, 2 motels, 2 caravan/camping parks.
MAP REF. 217 Q8

Nagambie
Population 1099

Between Seymour and Shepparton on the Goulburn Valley Hwy, Nagambie is on the shores of Lake Nagambie, which was created by the construction of the Goulburn Weir in 1891. Rowing and yachting regattas, speedboat and water-ski tournaments are held here throughout the year. There is a 65-m water slide at one of the swimming areas. **Of interest:** Several buildings classified by National Trust. Historical Society display of colonial Victoriana and early horsedrawn vehicles. Annual Boxing Day rowing regatta. Pottery, art and craft shops. House in Miniature in Information Centre, High St. **In the area:** Two of Victoria's best-known wineries, Chateau Tahbilk and Mitchelton. The buildings at Chateau Tahbilk, 6 km south-west, have been classified by the National Trust and the cellars are open for tastings, inspections and sales. Mitchelton Winery, 10 km south-west, off Goulburn Valley Hwy, has cellar-door sales and tastings, and tours are available; open daily. The winery features a 60-m observation tower, and one of the three licensed restaurants is open daily. Scenic river cruises on the Goulburn River from Mitchelton Winery operate frequently in the summer months, and weekends and public holidays throughout the year. At Graytown, 24 km west, are Walkershire Wines and Osicka's Vineyard. Belvedere Cellars on Goulburn Valley Hwy at northern end of town. Italian War Memorial and chapel at Murchison, 23 km north. Longleat Winery, 2 km south of Murchison. Days Mill, flour-mill with buildings dating from 1865, 5 km south of Murchison. **Tourist information:** 243 High St; (057) 94 2647. **Accommodation:** 5 motels, 2 caravan/camping parks. **See also:** Victoria's Wine Regions.
MAP REF. 216 H9

Natimuk
Population 462

This Wimmera town, 27 km west of Horsham, is close to the striking Mt Arapiles, a 356-m sandstone monolith which has been described as 'Victoria's Ayers Rock', within the Mount Arapiles - Tooan State

Park. A drive to the summit reveals a scenic lookout and a telecommunications relay station. The mountain was first climbed by Major Mitchell in 1836 and is popular with rock-climbing enthusiasts. **Of interest:** Arapiles Historical Society museum in old court-house. **In the area:** Lake Natimuk, 2 km north of town; popular for water sports. Mount Arapiles–Tooan State Park, 12 km south-west. Duffholme Cabins and Museum, 21 km west. **Tourist information:** Natimuk Hotel, Main St; (053) 87 1300. **Accommodation:** 1 caravan/ camping park. MAP REF. 212 G9

Nhill Population 2028
The name of this town is possibly derived from the Aboriginal word 'nyell', meaning 'white mist on water'. A small wheat town on the Western Hwy, exactly half-way between Melbourne and Adelaide, it claims to have the largest single-bin silo in the southern hemisphere. **Of interest:** Cottage of John Shaw Neilson, lyric poet, in Shaw Neilson Park, Western Hwy. Draught Horse Memorial in Goldsworthy Park, built to the memory of the famous Clydesdales, which were indispensable in opening up the Wimmera region. Nhill's Post Office, built in 1888, classified by National Trust. **In the area:** Access to Little Desert National Park and Little Desert Lodge via Kiata, 23 km east. Little Desert Wildflower Exhibition each spring. Lake Hindmarsh, largest freshwater lake in Victoria, 45 km north. Access to the Big Desert Wilderness via Yanac, 32 km north-west, on track north to Murrayville; exploration of this remote area by walking tracks only. **Tourist information:** Centre in park off Main St. **Accommodation:** 3 hotels, 5 motels, 2 caravan/camping parks. MAP REF. 212 E6

Numurkah Population 2840
Numurkah, 35 km north of Shepparton on the Goulburn Valley Hwy, is only a half-hour drive from some excellent beaches and fishing spots on the Murray River. The town is in an irrigation area which concentrates on fruit-growing and dairying, and which was originally developed through the Murray Valley Soldier Settlement Scheme. **Of interest:** Steam and Vintage Machinery Display. Rose Festival each Easter. **In the area:** Barmah Red Gum Forest, 40 km north-west. Morgan's Beach Caravan Park, at edge of forest on bank of Murray, offers bushwalking, horseriding and resident koalas and kangaroos. Monichino's Winery at Katunga, 11 km north. Ulupna Island flora and fauna reserve, near Strathmerton, 21 km north. Kraft cheese

factory, and Spikes and Blooms cactus garden (1 ha), both at Strathmerton. Brookfield Historic Holiday Farm and Museum, 6 km south-east. Historic buildings set on banks of Broken Creek, at Nathalia, 12 km west. **Tourist information:** Log Cabin, cnr Melville and Saxton Sts; (058) 62 1481. **Accommodation:** 2 motels, 2 caravan/camping parks. MAP REF. 117 L13, 217 J4

Ocean Grove–Barwon Heads
Population 8680
At the mouth of the Barwon River, the resort of Ocean Grove offers fishing and surfing, while nearby Barwon Heads offers safe family relaxation along the shores of its protected river. Both resorts are very popular in the summer months as they are the closest ocean beaches to Geelong, 22 km to the north-west. **Of interest:** Ocean Grove Nature Reserve, Grubb Rd. **In the area:** Jirrahlinga Koala and Wildlife Sanctuary, Taits Rd, Barwon Heads; open daily. At Wallington, 8 km north: A Maze'N Things, Moorfield Wildlife Park, Koombahla Park Equestrian Centre and the Fruit Bowl. At Lake Connewarre, 7 km north, mangrove swamps and Lake Connewarre State Game Reserve. **Tourist information:** A Maze'N Things, cnr Bellarine Hwy and Grubb Rd, Wallington; (052) 50 2669. **Accommodation:** Ocean Grove, 2 motels, 5 caravan/camping parks. Barwon Heads, 1 hotel, 1 motel, 2 caravan/camping parks. MAP REF. 205 G9, 208 E8

Omeo Population 285
The high plains around Omeo were opened up in 1835 when overlanders from the Monaro region moved their stock south to these lush summer pastures. Its name is an Aboriginal word meaning mountains, and the township is set in the heart of the Victorian Alps at an altitude of 643 m. It is used as a base for winter traffic approaching Mt Hotham from Bairnsdale, 120 km to its south, and for bushwalking and fishing expeditions to the Bogong High Plains in summer and autumn. **Of interest:** Omeo has suffered several natural disasters: it was devastated by earthquakes in 1885 and 1892 and was destroyed by the 'Black Friday' bushfires of 1939. Nevertheless, several old buildings remaining in the area are of historic interest, some seen in the A.M. Pearson Historical Park, in the main street; including the old court-house (1892), at the rear of the present court-house. Also in the grounds are the log gaol (1858), stables and blacksmith's shop. **In the area:** Scenic road leads to

Corryong, 148 km north-east, past the Dartmouth Reservoir; difficult to negotiate in bad weather; motorists should be alert for timber trucks and wandering cattle. The Tambo River valley to the south is especially beautiful in autumn. Omeo has a gold-rush history and the high cliffs left after sluicing for gold can be seen at the Oriental Diggings. Gold-panning is still popular along Livingstone Creek and pans can be hired from the Shire Offices. Blue Duck Inn (1890s) is a base for fishing at Anglers Rest, 29 km north-west. High country horseback tours operate from Benambra, 22 km north-east of Omeo. **Tourist information:** Octagon Bookshop, Day Ave; (051) 59 1411. **Accommodation:** 2 hotels, 1 motel, 1 caravan/camping park. MAP REF. 219 E12, 220 E3

Orbost Population 2502
Situated on the banks of the Snowy River, this Gippsland timber town is on the Princes Hwy, surrounded by spectacular coastal and mountain territory. **Of interest:** Historical Museum, Nicholson St. Old Pump House, behind Slab Hut Information Centre (1872); hut relocated from its original site, 40 km from Orbost. Rainforest Interpretation Centre, Lockiel St; audio-visual display explaining complex nature of rainforest ecology. **In the area:** The beautiful Bonang Hwy, unsealed in parts, leads north through the mountains to Delegate in NSW, as does the road to Buchan and on to the Little River Falls and McKillop's Bridge on the Snowy River. At the village of Bonang, 97 km north-east; the Aurora Mine, a working gold mine, open daily. Fishing; walking in the surrounding national parks, including a rainforest boardwalk at Errinundra, 30 km south-east. Tranquil Valley Tavern on the banks of the Delegate River near the NSW border has log cabin accommodation and a licensed restaurant. For a coastal drive, the Cape Conran Rd, just west of Orbost, leading to Marlo. The road on to Cape Conran, 18 km east, offers coastal views. Cape Conran Reserve has accommodation in holiday cabins. Bemm River, on the Sydenham Inlet, 57 km from Orbost, is a very popular centre for bream fishermen. Baldwin Spencer Trail, 262 km circuit driving tour. Cabbage Tree Palms Flora Reserve, 27 km east of Orbost. Coopracambra National Park, 136 km north-east of Orbost, near NSW border. Errinundra National Park, 83 km north-west of Orbost. **Tourist information:** The Slab Hut, cnr Nicholson and Clarke Sts; (051) 54 2424. **Accommodation:** 2 hotels, 3 motels, 2 caravan/camping parks. MAP REF. 109 C13, 220 I7

GIPPSLAND LAKES

Many people regard the area of the Gippsland Lakes as Victoria's most outstanding holiday area. Dominated as it is by Australia's largest system of inland waterways, it certainly does live up to all the superlatives accorded it. With the foothills of the high country just to the north and the amazing stretch of the Ninety Mile Beach separating the lakes from the ocean, the region offers an incredible variety of natural beauty and recreation activities. Here the choice really is yours — lake, river or ocean fishing, boating, cruising, surfing, bird-watching or just lazy sunning.

Within easy reach of the Lakes area the high country begins, so it is possible to vary a waterside trip with days exploring the alpine reaches and some of the fascinating little old townships such as **Walhalla**, **Omeo, Briagolong** and **Dargo**. The road across the Dargo High Plains and the Omeo Highway leading to Hotham Heights pass through some stunning country. Check your car thoroughly before you set off—service stations are scarce along the way.

Wellington, King, Victoria, Tyers, Reeve and Coleman — these six lakes cover more than 400 square kilometres and stretch parallel to the Ninety Mile Beach for almost its entire length. **Sale**, at the western edge of the region, is the local base for the development of the Bass Strait oil and gas fields. Both Sale and **Bairnsdale**, further east on the banks of the Mitchell River, make excellent bases for holidays on the Lakes or alpine trips. The main resort towns are **Lakes Entrance**, at the mouth of the Lakes, **Paynesville**, a mecca for boating and fishing enthusiasts, and **Metung**, where a cruising holiday on the Lakes can be commenced and **Loch Sport**, nestled between Ninety Mile Beach, Lake Victoria and the national park.

The **Lakes National Park**, the **Mitchell River National Park** and the hills and valleys of the alpine foothills to the north all provide plenty of opportunities for bushwalking or for simply enjoying the peace.

For further information on the Gippsland Lakes, contact the local Tourist Information Centres: cnr Esplanade and Marine Pde, Lakes Entrance; (051) 55 1966, Main St, Bairnsdale; (051) 52 6444 and Princes Hwy, Sale; (051) 44 1108.

Lakes Entrance, Gippsland

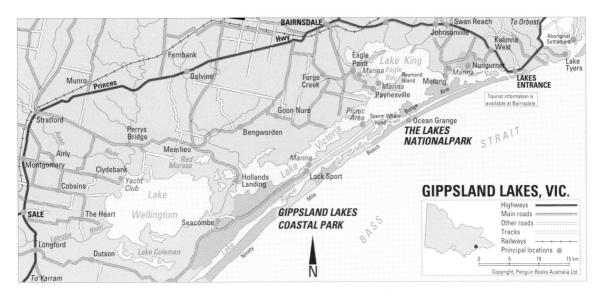

THE GREAT OCEAN ROAD

Very few roads in Australia can offer a continuous stretch of more than 300 kilometres of breathtaking scenery, but the Great Ocean Road, along Victoria's south-west coast, does exactly that. This area suffered devastation on Ash Wednesday 1983 as bushfires burned from Lorne through to Airey's Inlet and Anglesea.

Built to honour the servicemen of World War I, and completed in 1932, it has dramatic stretches of precipitous cliffs, idyllic coves and wide beaches.

The Great Ocean Road begins at **Torquay**, not far from Geelong. This is a popular surfing spot and the Road leads past a collection of famous surfing and safe swimming beaches and resorts. **Lorne** is one of the most charming of these. Despite offering modern holiday amenities and plenty of seaside entertainment for families, its gracious old hotels and guesthouses remain as a reminder of days gone by. Behind the town, the **Otway Ranges**, which stretch from **Anglesea** to **Cape Otway**, offer beautiful hills, waterfalls, excellent walking-tracks and lovely picnic spots. At **Apollo Bay**, the Road leaves the coast and winds through the ferny slopes of Cape

Great Ocean Road

Otway. This is rainforest country, silent and untouched, and well worth exploring. Many of the roads are unsealed but quite adequate for standard cars. Do try to visit the Melba Gully State Park to the west of the tiny township of **Lavers Hill**. Shipwreck trail signs begin on the eastern side of Lavers Hill which marks the beginning of the 'Shipwreck Coast', which stretches through **Port Campbell** and **Warrnambool** to **Port Fairy**. Photographers can be seen risking life

and limb to take advantage of the dramatic coastal scenery. It is advisable, however, for drivers to keep their eyes firmly on the road. The coastline takes on tortured, twisted shapes, with amazing rock formations like 'The Twelve Apostles' — huge stone pillars looming out of the surf, carved over time by the incessantly boiling sea. A one-and-a-half-hour nature trail runs between Port Campbell and Two Mile Bay to the west; guiding leaflets are available from the Port Campbell and Warrnambool information centres.

At **Princetown**, the Great Ocean Road returns to hug the coastline along the entire length of the **Port Campbell National Park** and it follows the coast to the Bay of Islands, eight kilometres east of the small seaside township of **Peterborough** where four shipwrecks are located. Here the Curdies River enters the sea in a wide, sandy inlet beloved of fishermen.

For further information, contact the Great Ocean Road Tourism Association, 55 Great Ocean Road, Apollo Bay; (052) 37 6258.

Ouyen   Population 1503
On the Sunraysia Hwy, Ouyen is about 100 km south of Mildura, north-east of the Big Desert area. **In the area:** Hattah-Kulkyne National Park, 34 km north, provides habitats for abundant wildlife; bird-watching, bushwalking, canoeing, and wildflowers in spring. Pink Lakes State Park, 60 km west of Ouyen; lakes are outstanding subjects for photography. **Tourist information:** Resource Centre, Oke St; (050) 92 1047. **Accommodation:** 1 hotel, 2 motels, 1 caravan/camping park. **See also:** The Mallee. MAP REF. 116 E10, 214 I9

Paynesville   Population 2209
A popular tourist resort 18 km from Bairnsdale on the McMillan Straits, Paynesville is a mecca for the boating enthusiast, and is famous for yachting and speedboat racing as well as water-skiing. It is the headquarters of the Gippsland Lakes Yacht Club, and speedboat

championships are held each Christmas and Easter. **Of interest:** St Peter-by-the-Lake (1961); incorporates seafaring symbols. Community Craft Centre. **In the area:** The Ninety Mile Beach 10 km south by boat, and a punt crosses the Straits to Raymond Island. The Lakes National Park, 5 km by boat to Sperm Whale Head; otherwise accessed via Loch Sport. Rotomah Island Bird Observatory, 8 km south of Paynesville by boat. Cruises on MV *Lakes Odyssey*. **Accommodation:** 2 hotels, 1 motel, 3 caravan/camping parks. **See also:** Gippsland Lakes. MAP REF. 220 E8

Port Albert   Population 280
This tiny and historic township on the south-east coast, 120 km from Morwell, was the first established port in Victoria. Sailing-boats from Europe and America once docked at the large timber jetty here. Boats from China brought thousands of Chinese to the

Gippsland goldfields. Originally established for trade with Tasmania, Port Albert was the supply port for Gippsland pioneers for many years until the railway line from Melbourne to Sale was completed in 1878. The timber jetty is still crowded with boats as it is a commercial fishing port and its sheltered waters are very popular with fishermen and boat owners. Some of the original stone buildings are still in use and are classified by the National Trust. **Of interest:** Historic buildings in Tarraville Rd include original government offices and stores, and the Bank of Victoria (1861), housing the Maritime Museum, with photographs and relics of the area. Port Albert Hotel, Wharf St, first licensed in 1842, possibly the oldest hotel still operating in the state. Wildlife sanctuary on St Margaret Island, 12 km east. Annual Seabank fishing competition on Sun. of March Labour Day long weekend. **In the area:** Christ Church at Tarraville (1856), 5 km north-east, the first church

in Gippsland. Also to north-east, Alberton, (8 km), once the administrative capital of Gippsland and Yarram (14 km). Swimming at Mann's Beach, 10 km east. Tarra-Bulga National Park, 41 km north-west. Surfing at Woodside on Ninety Mile Beach, 34 km north-east. **Accommodation:** 1 hotel/motel, 2 caravan/ camping parks.
MAP REF. 209 P11

Port Campbell   Population 224
This small crayfishing village and seaside resort is situated in the centre of the Port Campbell National Park and on a spectacular stretch of the Great Ocean Road. **Of interest:** Historical Museum, Lord St; open school holidays. Self-guided Discovery Walk. Good fishing from rocks and pier. **In the area:** Otway Deer and Wildlife Park, 20 km east. Port Campbell National Park, which surrounds the town, includes the world-famous Twelve Apostles and Loch Ard Gorge, 5–10 km east, and London Bridge, 5 km west. Walking-tracks and historic shipwreck sites; Historic Shipwreck Trail links sites along the 'Shipwreck Coast', from Princetown to Port Fairy. **Tourist information:** National Parks Office, Tregea St; (055) 98 6382. **Accommodation:** 1 hotel, 4 motels, 1 caravan/camping park. **See also:** The Great Ocean Road.
MAP REF. 211 M11

Port Fairy   Population 2504
The home port for a large fishing fleet and an attractive, rambling holiday resort, Port Fairy is 29 km west of Warrnambool with both ocean and river as its borders. The town's history goes back to whaling days and at one time it was one of the largest ports in Australia. Many of its small cottages and bluestone buildings have been classified by the National Trust—over fifty in all. This charming old-world fishing village is popular with heritage-lovers and holiday-makers. **Of interest:** Historical Society Museum, Bank St. Society booklet and map for Town Walk and Port Fairy Shipwreck Walk available. Battery Hill, end Griffith St; old fort and signal station at mouth of river. Both the splendid timber home of Captain Mills, a whaling skipper, in Gipps St, and Mott's Cottage, 5 Sackville St, have National Trust classifications. Other attractive buildings include the Old Caledonian Inn, Bank St, Seacombe House, Cox St, the stone court-house, Gipps St, and ANZ Bank building, Cox St. St John's Church of England (1856), Regent St. The *Gazette* Office (1849), Sackville St. Main annual events include New Year's

Eve procession, Moyneyana Festival in January, Port Fairy Folk Festival in March (Labour Day weekend) and Heritage Discovery Weekend in November. **In the area:** Griffiths Island, connected to east of town by causeway, has lighthouse and muttonbird rookeries; spectacular nightly return of the muttonbirds to island during Sept.–Apr. Other rookeries at Pea Soup Beach and South Beach, on southern edge of town, Australia's only mainland colony of muttonbirds. Lady Julia Percy Island, 10 km off coast, a home for fur seals; only accessible by experienced fishermen in calm weather. Waters off coast also attract big-game fishing for the white pointer shark. Tower Hill, a fascinating area with an extinct volcano, crater lake and islands, 15 km east. Mt Eccles National Park, 56 km north-west. Yambuk and Lake Yambuk, 17 km north-west. **Tourist information:** Borough Chambers, Bank St; (055) 68 2682. **Accommodation:** 5 motels, 6 caravan/ camping parks. **See also:** The Great Ocean Road.
MAP REF. 210 I10

Portarlington   Population 2271
Named after an Irish village and with a history of Irish settlement in the area, Portarlington is a popular seaside resort on the Bellarine Peninsula, 31 km east of Geelong. It has a safe bay for children to swim, good fishing and a variety of water sports. **Of interest:** Historic flour mill (1857), Turner Crt; restored by National Trust, houses historical and educational display. Isadora's Coffee and Collectables, Geelong Rd. Lavender Cottage Gallery, Fenwick St. Public Reserve, Sprout St; picnic facilities. **Tourist information:** A Maze'N Things, cnr Bellarine Hwy and Grubb Rd, Wallington; (052) 50 2669. **Accommodation:** 1 motel, 3 caravan/ camping parks.
MAP REF. 205 I7, 208 F7

Portland   Population 10 934
Portland, situated about 75 km east of the South Australian border, is the most western of Victoria's major coastal towns and is the only deep-water port between Melbourne and Adelaide. It was the first permanent settlement in Victoria, founded by the Henty brothers in 1834, and today it is an important industrial and commercial centre and also a popular summer resort with good beaches, surfing, fishing and outstanding coastal and forest scenery. There are a number of short walks in and around Portland; self-guiding brochures are available at the Tourist Information Centre. For the more energetic, the 250 km Great South West Walk, a circular track that begins and ends at the Centre and travels through national parks

and state forests to Discovery Bay and Cape Nelson and return, can be covered in easy stages. **Of interest:** Botanical Gardens, Cliff St, established in 1857. The town has many early and attractive buildings, some classified by the National Trust; among them are the Customs House and court-house in Cliff St, and several old inns, including the Steam Packet Hotel (1842) and Mac's Hotel in Bentinck St. Portland's historic museum, History House, is in the old town hall (1864). Fawthrop Lagoon, Glenelg St, has around 140 bird species. Nearby Powerhouse Museum in Percy St. Good views and picnic facilities at Portland Battery on Battery Hill. Kurtze's Museum in Wellington Rd. Guided tours of Portland Aluminium Smelter on Tues. afternoons; bookings (008) 035567 and (055) 23 2671. **In the area:** Historic homesteads, including Maretimo, 3 km north, and Burswood, Cape Nelson Rd. Cape Nelson State Park, 11 km south-west, with spectacular coastal scenery and lighthouse classified by National Trust. At Cape Bridgewater, 16 km south-west, petrified forest and blowholes, freshwater springs and the Watering Place, as well as walks to Discovery Bay and Cape Duquesne, both further west. Good swimming and surfing. Mt Richmond National Park, 45 km to north-west; displays of spring wildflowers. Narrawong State Forest, 18 km north-east of Portland. Cave Hill Gardens at Heywood, 27 km north of Portland, with picnic facilities. Bower Birds Nest Museum at Heywood. Caledonian Inn Museum, 8 km north of Portland. The Princes Hwy swings inland at Portland, but 70 km west along the coastal road is the tiny, charming hamlet of Nelson. This is a popular resort, particularly favoured by people from Mt Gambier, over the border. The nearby Princess Margaret Rose Caves are worth a visit and there are pleasant guided river tours up the Glenelg River. The Lower Glenelg National Park, 44 km north-west via Kentbruck and 73 km via Nelson, is notable for its spectacular gorges, colourful wildflowers and native birds. Known for its excellent fishing, the area however offers only limited accommodation. Farm holidays available at Quamby Park property near Tyrendarra, 25 km north-east, and at Nioka, near Mt Richmond National Park. **Tourist information:** Cliff St; (055) 23 2671. **Accommodation:** 11 motels, 7 caravan/camping parks.
MAP REF. 210 F9

Pyramid Hill   Population 542
A small country town some 40 km south-west of Cohuna and 100 km north of Bendigo, Pyramid Hill was named for its unusually shaped hill, 187 m high. **Of interest:** Historical museum. A climb to

THE MIGHTY MURRAY

As a modern-day explorer, a trip following the course of the Murray gives you a chance to discover a rich cross-section of Australian country and history, as well as the infinite variety of natural beauty and wildlife the river itself supports.

The Source

The Murray has its source on the slopes of Mount Pilot, high in the Alps. Here it is just a gurgling mountain stream, rushing through some breathtaking mountain scenery. This is the area of the Snowy Mountains Scheme and the great Australian snowfields.

The Upper Murray

The river flows through the scenic area around **Jingellic** and **Walwa** and on to the beautiful Lake Hume near **Albury** and **Wodonga** before continuing past **Corowa**, the birthplace of Federation, and into Lake Mulwala.

Lakes, Beaches and Red Gums

As it flows from the aquatic playgrounds of Lakes Hume and Mulwala, the Murray becomes a wide and splendid river. Lined with magnificent red gums, in the region around **Cobram**, banks are transformed into wide sandy beaches. This is ideal holiday country, with pleasant resort towns to be found at **Yarrawonga–Mulwala**, **Barooga** and **Tocumwal**.

Wine Country

Victoria's main wine-growing area is centred around **Rutherglen** and extends to the wineries of Cobram and the Ovens and Goulburn Valleys. The wineries welcome visitors and many offer conducted tours.

The Heyday of the Riverboats

Famous river towns like **Echuca**, **Swan Hill** and **Wentworth** have carefully preserved much of the history of this colourful era. The Port of Echuca, the Swan Hill Pioneer Settlement and the historic Murray Downs homestead are a must if you are in the area. Children especially will delight in the 'living museum', where original buildings, paddle-steamers and old wharves have been restored.

Wildlife

The Murray's abundant bird and animal life is protected in a number of sanctuaries and reserves surrounding the banks of the river. Spoonbills, herons, eagles, harriers and kites are plentiful. Near Picnic Point in the Moira State Forest, which is near **Mathoura**, waterbirds and wildlife abound and can be seen from the observatory in this beautiful red gum forest. At **Kerang**, which lies at the beginning of a chain of lakes and marshes, you can see huge breeding-grounds for the splendid ibis. **Kyabram** has a famous community-owned fauna and water-fowl park which is open daily, and almost all of Gunbower Island is a protected sanctuary for wildlife.

Sunraysia

Proud residents of **Mildura** may mention to you that their city enjoys 400 more hours of sunshine a year than does Surfers Paradise! This beautiful climate supports flourishing citrus and wine-growing industries as well as attracting countless holiday-makers to the Mildura area during both the summer and winter seasons. Upstream is **Red Cliffs**, a town which was founded after World War I by returned soldiers, who turned it into a model irrigation town, and the surrounding areas into prosperous winelands. At the junction of the Murray and the Darling lies **Wentworth**, one of the oldest of the river towns, with a historic gaol and a beautifully preserved paddle-steamer called *Ruby*.

Riverland

The Murray crosses into South Australia and at **Renmark** begins its splendid flow down to its mouth at Lake Alexandrina. The banks are lined with historic river towns such as **Renmark**, **Morgan**, **Murray Bridge**, and **Goolwa** at its mouth, which has a strong tradition of shipbuilding, originating from the busy riverboat days. Renmark, like Mildura, is famous for its year-round sunshine and all these towns make attractive and interesting places for a holiday. This South Australian stretch of the Murray offers splendid river scenery and birdlife, excellent fishing and water sports and the chance to enjoy the many wineries in the area. The Riverland winelands produce more than forty per cent of the entire national vintage in an average year.

Further information is available from the tourist information centres in the various towns along the river, including Swan Hill (050) 32 3033; Mildura (050) 23 3619; Cobram (058) 72 2132; Echuca–Moama (054) 82 4525 and Yarrawonga–Mulwala (057) 44 1989.

PS Melbourne, near Mildura

the top of Pyramid Hill itself (also Braille walking trail) allows scenic views of the surrounding irrigation and wheat district. **In the area:** Mt Hope, 10 km north-east, named by Major Mitchell. To the south, 2833-ha Murray Pine forest reserve with numerous granite outcrops. Southernmost outcrop, Mitiamo Rock, has adjacent picnic ground; walks through reserve reveal variety of birdlife and other fauna. **Tourist information:** Newsagency; (054) 55 7036. **Accommodation:** 1 caravan/camping park.
MAP REF. 116 I13, 213 R4, 216 C4

Queenscliff–Point Lonsdale
Population 3739
Queenscliff, 31 km east of Geelong on the Bellarine Peninsula, was established as a commercial fishing centre in the 1850s and still has a large fishing fleet based in its harbour. The town looks out across the famous and treacherous Rip at the entrance to Port Phillip Bay. **Of interest:** Queenscliff Maritime Centre, Weeroona Pde; explores the town's long association with the sea and the days of sailing-ships. Adjacent Marine Studies Centre operates summer holiday programme for visitors. Queenscliff Fine Arts Gallery in old Wesleyan Church, Hesse St. Hobson's Choice Gallery, Hobson St. Seaview Gallery in Seaview House, Hesse St. Many old buildings, including Fort Queenscliff (1882), built during the Crimean War, and the Black Lighthouse (1861), King St; some grand old hotels including the Vue Grand in Hesse St, the Ozone and the Queenscliff in Gellibrand St. Queenscliff Historical Tours leave from Queenscliff Pier. Steam train operates between Queenscliff (station in Symonds St) and Drysdale on weekends and daily in summer holidays. Regular passenger ferry service operates in summer and school holidays between Queenscliff and Portsea across the bay. Car and passenger ferry service between Queenscliff and Sorrento (about 35 min.) operates daily all year. 'Snorkelling with the seals' can be arranged through the Tourist Information Centre. Point Lonsdale has been extensively developed as a holiday and tourist resort and offers good swimming and surfing. Queenscliff Market, Symonds St; last Sun. of months Aug.–April. Pt Lonsdale Sunday Market, Bowen Rd; 2nd Sun. every month. **In the area:** Marine life viewing at Harold Holt Marine Reserve, which includes Mud Island and coastal reserves. Lake Victoria, 1 km west of Point Lonsdale. **Tourist information:** A Maze'N Things, cnr Bellarine Hwy and Grubb Rd, Wallington; (052) 50 2669. **Accommodation:** Queenscliff, 3 hotels, 4 caravan/camping

parks. Point Lonsdale, 1 motel, 2 caravan/camping parks.
MAP REF. 198 A5, 205 I9, 208 F8

Rainbow
Population 655
This Wimmera township, 70 km north of Dimboola, is near Lake Hindmarsh, popular for fishing, boating and water-skiing. **Of interest:** Yurunga homestead, on northern edge of town, classified by National Trust; large selection of antiques and retaining original fittings. **In the area:** Old Lutheran church (1901) at Pella, 10 km west. Lake Albacutya Park, 12 km north; camping facilities. Wyperfeld National Park, 40 km north; access via sealed road north from Yaapeet. **Accommodation:** 2 hotels, 1 motel, 1 caravan/camping park.
MAP REF. 212 G3

Robinvale
Population 884
This small, well-laid-out town on the NSW border, 80 km from Mildura, is almost entirely surrounded by bends in the Murray River, and the surrounding area is ideal for the production of citrus, dried fruit and wine grapes. It is a picturesque town, and water sports and fishing are popular along the river. **Of interest:** McWilliams Wines and the Lexia Room, with historical exhibits, in Moore St. **In the area:** Euston weir and lock on Murray, 2.5 km downstream. Robinvale Wines, Greek-style winery, 5 km south on Sea Lake road. Kyndalyn Park almond farm, 23 km south-east of Robinvale. Hattah-Kulkyne National Park, 66 km southwest. **Tourist information:** Swan Hill Regional Information Centre, 306 Campbell St, Swan Hill; (050) 32 3033. **Accommodation:** 1 hotel, 3 motels, 2 caravan/camping parks. **See also:** Victoria's Wine Regions.
MAP REF. 116 F9, 215 K5

Rochester
Population 2395
On the Campaspe River, 28 km south of Echuca, Rochester is the centre for a rich dairying and tomato-growing area. A small, busy town, it has some attractive older buildings and boasts the largest dairy factory in Australia. **Of interest:** Historical Plaque Trail. **In the area:** An engineering achievement, the Campaspe Siphon, 3 km north, where the Waranga–Mallee irrigation channel runs under the Campaspe River. These district channels are popular with anglers, and cod and bream are plentiful. Random House homestead, amid 4 ha of gardens beside the river in Bridge Rd, on eastern edge of town. Pleasant lakes in the district, popular for fishing and water sports, include Greens Lake and the Corop Lakes, 14 km

south-east. Scenic Mt Camel Range attracts gem-fossickers. Field's Cactus Farm and Lochlomand Gardens and Tearooms near Tennyson, 18 km north-west. **Tourist information:** Shire Offices; (054) 84 1700. **Accommodation:** 1 motel, 1 caravan/camping park.
MAP REF. 216 F6

Romsey
Population 2600
Romsey, 7 km south of Lancefield, was settled in the mid 1850s and possesses some excellent Victorian architecture. **In the area:** Award-winning Romsey Vineyard. Mintara, at nearby Monegeetta, built by Captain Gardiner in 1882, (it is a smaller replica of Melbourne's Government House). Huntingdon just north of Romsey township. The Chase at Monegeetta North and historic Glenfern Stud. **Accommodation:** 1 hotel.
MAP REF. 201 J5, 208 F1, 216 F13

Rushworth
Population 948
Rushworth is 20 km off the Goulburn Valley Hwy, 46 km north of Seymour via Murchison, and still shows traces of its gold-rush days. **Of interest:** Many of the town's attractive original buildings still stand, witnesses to the days when Rushworth was the commercial centre for the surrounding mining district. Nearly all the buildings in High St are classified by the National Trust: St Pauls Church of England, the band rotunda, the former Imperial Hotel (now a private residence), the Glasgow Buildings and the Whistle Stop. Rushworth's local history museum in the Mechanics Institute (1913), High St, is open weekend afternoons. **In the area:** Rushworth State Forest, 3 km south, comprises 24 300 ha of ironbark forest with a variety of plant and animal life. Whroo Historic Area, 7 km south, features Balaclava Hill Open Cut, Whroo Cemetery and Aboriginal Waterhole, all with visitor access. Further south, the remnants of gold-mining towns Bailieston, Angustown and Graytown remain, although like Whroo they are now deserted. Waranga Basin, 6 km north, for water sports, fishing and camping; excellent picnic facilities. Longleat Winery and Campbell's Bend picnic reserve, 20 km east. **Tourist information:** Guided Tours of Victoria, 31 High St; (058) 56 1612. **Accommodation:** 1 hotel, 1 hotel/motel, 2 caravan/camping parks.
MAP REF. 216 G8

Rutherglen
Population 1586
Rutherglen is the centre of the most important wine-growing area in Victoria. There is a cluster of vineyards surrounding the town, with wine-growing country

stretching south to the Milawa area. Most wineries reflect their history, however; of particular interest is the winery building at All Saints, 10 km north-west, which has a National Trust classification. Other wineries include Bullers, Campbells, Chambers, Cofield-Anderson, Fairfield, Gehrig Brothers, Jones, Morris's, Mount Prior, Pfeiffers, Stanton and Killeen, and St Leonards. Rutherglen sponsors three major events: The Tastes of Rutherglen, held over the March Labour Day weekend, the annual Winery Walkabout Weekend on the Queen's Birthday long weekend in June and the Rutherglen Wine Show in September. Most wineries are open daily for tastings and sales. **Of interest:** The House (1882) at Mount Prior vineyard, 14 km north-east, now a guest-house. In the area: Lake Moodemere, 8 km west, is popular for water sports and there is a pleasant fauna sanctuary nearby. The old Customs House at Wahgunyah, 10 km north-west, is a relic of the days when duty was payable on goods coming from NSW. A history walk at Wahgunyah traces the area's beginnings. Rutherglen is well situated for day trips to Albury–Wodonga, Yarrawonga, Lake Mulwala, Corowa, Beechworth, Bright and Mt Buffalo. **Tourist information**: Jasper Bros Service Station, Main St; (060) 32 9404. **Accommodation:** 2 hotels, 5 motels, 1 caravan/ camping park. **See also:** The Mighty Murray; Victoria's Wine Regions. MAP REF. 117 O13, 217 O4

St Arnaud
Population 2692

This old gold-mining town is on the Sunraysia Hwy between Donald and Avoca and is surrounded by forest and hill country. Many of the town's historic iron-lacework-decorated buildings have been classified by the National Trust. **Of interest:** Josephine Coppens Gallery, Napier St. Squash, basketball, badminton, table tennis and indoor tennis facilities at local sports stadium. Queen Mary Gardens, a pleasant site for picnics. In the area: Good fishing in Avoca River and at Teddington Reservoir, 28 km south. At Lake Batyo Catyo, 35 km northwest, fishing and water sports. Melville Caves, 38 km east, between St Arnaud and Inglewood, famous as haunt of bushranger Captain Melville; picnic facilities nearby. St Peter's Church (1869) at Carapooee, 11 km south-east. **Tourist information:** Josephine Coppens Gallery, 2 Napier St; (054) 95 2313. **Accommodation:** 2 hotels, 2 motels, 1 caravan/camping park. MAP REF. 213 N8

St Leonards
Population 1170

A small beach resort, 11 km south-east of Portarlington on the Bellarine Peninsula, St Leonards has excellent coastal fishing, and calm waters for boating and yachting and is popular for family summer holidays. **Of interest:** Edwards Point Wildlife Reserve, Beach Rd; varied birdlife and picnic facilities. Memorial on The Esplanade commemorating landing by Matthew Flinders in 1802 and John Batman and his party in 1835. **Tourist information:** A Maze'N Things, cnr Bellarine Hwy and Grubb Rd, Wallington; (052) 50 2669. **Accommodation:** 1 hotel, 2 caravan/camping parks. MAP REF. 198 B2, 205 I7, 208 F8

Sale
Population 13 559

Sale is the main administrative city in Gippsland. In nearby Bass Strait, there is a concentration of off-shore oil development. Just over 200 km east of Melbourne on the Princes Hwy, it is conveniently located for exploration of the whole Gippsland Lakes area, from Wilsons Promontory to Lakes Entrance, bordered to the north by the foothills and mountains of the Great Divide and most of the way along the coast by the famous Ninety Mile Beach. **Of interest:** Oil and Gas Display at Tourist Information Centre on Princes Hwy at western approach to city; depicts development of offshore oil reserves. The Port of Sale, thriving during the days of the paddle-steamers; picnic facilities and boat-launching ramps. Cruises from here through 400 sq km lakes system. Lake Guthridge, on Foster St in city centre; popular picnic spot, also fauna park and adventure playground. Historical Museum, located in Foster St nearby. The city has many attractive buildings, including Our Lady of Sion Convent, the clocktower, Victoria Hall and the Criterion Hotel with its beautiful lacework verandahs. Tours of the RAAF base, home of the famous Roulettes aerobatic team. Sale Regional Arts Centre, Macalister St. Pedestrian Mall, cnr Cunningham and Raymond Sts, for local artworks. Sale Common and State Game Refuge, on southern edge of town, provide a protected wetlands area. **In the area:** To the north, the towns of Maffra and Heyfield (18 km), in intensively cultivated country, and Lake Glenmaggie, 6 km north of Heyfield. The road from Stratford, 18 km north, leads across the Dargo High Plains to Mt Hotham, and offers a scenic drive through the high country. Carawah Gallery, 15 km west of Stratford, has stone sculptures of wildlife; further on is the Black Cockatoo Pottery. To the south, Seaspray, on the Ninety Mile Beach, 32 km from Sale, has excellent surfing and fishing, as do Golden/Paradise Beaches, 35 km from Sale, and Loch Sport, another 30 km further away. Nearby are The Lakes National Park and Rotamah Island Bird Observatory, 15 km from Loch Sport. Marlay Point, on shores of Lake Wellington, 25 km from Sale, has extensive launching facilities. The yacht club here sponsors the annual overnight yacht race to Paynesville each March. Popular fishing rivers include the Avon, close to Marlay Point, and the Macalister, Thomson and Latrobe, especially at Swing Bridge (1883), 5 km south of Sale. Holey Plains State Park, 14 km south-west, for wildlife and wildflowers. **Tourist information:** Central Gippsland Tourism Assocn Inc, Princes Hwy; (051) 44 1108. **Accommodation:** 9 motels, 2 caravan/ camping parks. **See also:** Gippsland Lakes. MAP REF. 209 R7, 220 B10

Seymour
Population 6510

On the Goulburn River, at the junction of the Goulburn Valley Hwy and Hume Fwy, Seymour is a busy commercial, industrial and agricultural town, serving the local rural community. The area was recommended by Lord Kitchener during his visit in 1909 as being particularly suitable for a military base. Nearby Puckapunyal, 18 km west, was an important training base for troops during World War II and is still operating as a major army base. **Of interest:** Royal Hotel, Emily St, featured in Russell Drysdale's famous painting of 1941, Moody's Pub. Somerset Crossing Vineyard and restaurant, Emily St. Goulburn Park, cnr Progress and Guild Sts; picnic and swimming areas, and adjoining caravan park. Old Goulburn Bridge, at end of Emily St; built in 1891 and preserved as a historic relic. **In the area:** Mitchelton and Chateau Tahbilk Vineyards, near Nagambie, 23 km north. Other wineries include Seymour Vineyards, 2 km south, Hankin's Wines, 5 km north-west on Northwood Rd, and Hayward's Winery, 12 km south-east near Trawool. Army Tank/Transport Museum at Puckapunyal, 10 km west. Trawool Valley Angora Stud and tearooms, 11 km south-east. Capalba Park 'Alpacas', on Coobybone Rd, 11 km east. **Tourist information:** Old Court House Craft Shop, Emily St; or Goulburn Tourism Association, 243 High St, Nagambie; (057) 94 2647. **Accommodation:** 5 motels, 3 caravan/ camping parks. **See also:** Victoria's Wine Regions. MAP REF. 201 N1, 216 H11

Shepparton–Mooroopna
Population 30 238

The 'capital' of the rich Goulburn Valley,

this thriving, well-developed city, now known as The Solar City, 175 km north of Melbourne, has 4000 ha of orchards within a 10-km radius and 4000 ha of market gardens along the river valley nearby. The area is irrigated by the Goulburn Irrigation Scheme and is on the junction of the Goulburn and Broken Rivers. The central shopping area of Shepparton is surrounded by 68 ha of parkland, including an open-air music bowl and a Civic Centre housing an art gallery, town hall, theatre and municipal centre. **Of interest:** Solar display at Tourist Information Centre, Wyndham St. Art gallery at Civic Centre, Marungi St; traditional Australian paintings and collection of Australian ceramics. On Parkside Dr, the International Village and Aboriginal Keeping Place; tourist, educational and cultural centre. Gem display and Tourist Inspection Centre, Nixon St; open afternoons. Historical Museum, within the Historical Precinct, High St; open Sun. afternoons. Redbyrne Pottery, on Old Dookie Rd; wide variety of locally made pottery and ceramics. Victoria Park Lake, Tom Collins Dr; yachting, water sports and a caravan park. Shepparton Preserving Company, Andrew Fairley Ave, largest cannery in southern hemisphere; guided inspections during canning period Jan. – Apr. Driver Education Centre of Australia, on Wanganui Rd. Reedy Swamp Walk, at end of Wanganui Rd; wetland area abundant with birdlife. **In the area:** Mud Factory Pottery, 6 km south on Goulburn Valley Hwy. Boxwood Pottery, Elm Vale Nursery and Le-Bella Ostrich Farm at Kialla, 5 km south-east. Vineyards, including Gravina Winery, Old Dookie Rd, and Broken River Wines at Lemnos, 10 km east. South down Goulburn Valley Hwy for 36 km, 1860-built Chateau Tahbilk, near Nagambie, recorded by National Trust. Historic Brookfield Homestead, 20 km north along Goulburn Valley Hwy, with old farm machinery and shearing-sheds; open for inspection by appointment. Victoria's Irrigation Research Institute, east of Tatura, 16 km west of Shepparton. **Tourist information:** Wyndham St, Shepparton, (058) 32 9870. **Accommodation:** Shepparton, 3 hotels, 19 motels, 6 caravan/camping parks. Mooroopna, 4 motels, 5 caravan/camping parks. **See also:** Victoria's Wine Regions.
MAP REF. 217 J6

Skipton   Population 510

This township on the Glenelg Hwy, southwest of Ballarat, lies in an important pastoral and agricultural district. The town was an important centre for merino sheep sales in the 1850s. **Of interest:** Eel

THE GRAMPIANS

The massive sandstone ranges of the Grampians in Western Victoria provide some of the state's most spectacular scenery. Rising in peaks to heights of over 1000 metres, they form the western extremity of the Great Dividing Range. Major Mitchell climbed and named the highest peak, Mt William, in July 1836 and gave the name 'The Grampians' to the ranges because they reminded him of the Grampians in his native Scotland.

On 1 July 1984 these rugged mountain ranges, famous for their spectacular wildflowers, became a national park. It is a superb area for scenic drives on good roads, bushwalking and rock-climbing being some of the most popular activities; Lake Bellfield provides for sailing and rowing, and there is excellent trout-fishing in the lake and in Fyans Creek. The Western Grampians have Aboriginal cave paintings. In October, 1991, the National Park became known as Gariwerd National Park.

There is plenty of wildlife to be seen; koalas, kangaroos and deer are numerous, and echidnas, possums and duck-billed platypuses can be found,

while more than 100 species of birds have been identified.

Apart from their scenic grandeur, the Grampians are best known for the beauty and variety of their wildflowers. There are more than 1000 species of ferns and flowering plants native to the region and they are at their most colourful from August to November, the most popular time for a visit to the Grampians. The Halls Gap Wildflower Exhibition is held annually in the Grampians National Park in September/October.

Halls Gap, which takes its name from a pioneer pastoralist who settled in the eastern Grampians in the early 1840s, is the focal point of the area; its wide variety of accommodation includes motels, guest-houses and B&B options, holiday flats, cottages and cabins, a youth hostel and caravan and camping parks.

For further information, contact the Halls Gap Newsagency, Grampians Rd, Halls Gap, (053) 56 4247; the Stawell and Grampians Information Centre, 54 Western Hwy, West Stawell, (053) 58 2314; or the Gariwerd (Grampians) National Park Visitors Centre, Grampians Rd, Halls Gap, (053) 56 4381.

factory; eels netted in region, snap-frozen and exported mainly to Germany. Bluestone Presbyterian Church, classified by National Trust. **In the area:** Mooromong, 11 km north-west, a notable historic homestead; property donated in its entirety to National Trust by D.J.S. and C. Mackinnon (formerly Claire Adams, silent movie star); open by appointment and on National Trust open days; accommodation available in converted shearer's quarters. Mt Widderin Cave, 6 km south; volcanic cave with large underground chamber; tours by appointment. Kaolin Mine, 10 km east. **Accommodation:** 1 hotel.
MAP REF. 211 O4

Stawell   Population 6252

North-east of Halls Gap, and 123 km north-west of Ballarat on the Western Hwy, Stawell is well sited for tours to the northern Grampians. It is the home of the Stawell Easter Gift, Australia's most famous professional foot-race, held annually. **Of interest:** Stawell Gift Hall of Fame Museum, within Athletic Club,

Central Park, cnr Seaby and Napier Sts; history of the footrace. Big Hill, local landmark and place where gold was first discovered; Pioneers Lookout at summit with indication of locations of famous mines. Casper's World in Miniature Tourist Park, London Rd; re-creation in miniature of scenes of life in Australia and Pacific countries, using indoor and outdoor scale working models with dioramas and commentaries; open daily. Pleasant Creek Court-house Museum. **In the area:** Gold-mining at Stawell Joint Venture; public viewing areas off Reefs Rd and Jubilee Rd. Bunjil's Cave, with Aboriginal rock paintings in ochre, off Pomonal Rd, 11 km south. The Sisters Rocks, collection of huge granite tors beside Western Hwy, 3 km south-east; saved from destruction in 1867 by a local resident, who bought and fenced off the land on which they rest. Grampians scenic flights available. Bellellen Rise merino sheep station for farm holidays. White Gums Gardens and Nursery, 13 km north-west of Stawell at Deep Lead. Also Deep Lead Flora and Fauna Reserve. Tottington Woolshed, a

National Trust property and a rare example of a 19th-century woolshed, 55 km north-east on road to St Arnaud. Boating on Lake Fyans, 15 km south-west of Stawell, near Halls Gap; picnic and camping facilities. Wineries include Stawell, Great Western, Garden Gully, Saint Gregory's, Ararat and Halls Gap. Great Western, 14 km south-east, a picturesque wine village; hotel, tea-rooms, craft and antique shops. Overdale Station, Landsborough Rd, 10 km east; guided tours during school holidays; farm holidays available. Old Coongee host farm. Roses Gap Recreation Centre, holiday centre within Gariwerd (Grampians) National Park, 34 km west of Stawell, off Western Hwy. **Tourist information:** 54 Western Hwy; (053) 58 2314. **Accommodation:** 8 motels, 2 caravan/camping parks, holiday cottages. **See also:** The Grampians; The Golden Age; Victoria's Wine Regions.
MAP REF. 213 K11

Swan Hill   Population 8831

When the explorer Thomas Mitchell camped on the banks of the Murray, he named the spot Swan Hill because of the black swans which had kept him awake all night. The township became a busy 19th-century river port and today it is a pleasant city and major holiday centre on the Murray Valley Hwy, 338 km north-west of Melbourne. The climate is mild and sunny and the river offers good fishing, boating and water-sports relaxation. Swan Hill is a well-laid-out city with a unique garden-like main street. The design is similar to that in Grand Junction, Colorado. **Of interest:** Swan Hill won

Pioneer Settlement, Swan Hill

recognition by establishing Australia's first Folk Museum, the Pioneer Settlement, at end of Gray St on Little Murray River, which depicts, in a natural environment, life in the last century and local Aboriginal culture; staff wear period costume and old-fashioned forms of transport are used. The Settlement features the 'Sound and Light' tour, a nightly theatrical performance of music, lighting and dialogue — an exciting journey back into the pioneering past (bookings essential). Swan Hill Regional Gallery of Contemporary Art and Dowling House Art and Craft Centre, both in Gray St. Llanvair Gallery, Beveridge St. Military Museum, Campbell St. River boats: PS Pyap offers Murray cruises; stationary PS Gem has a restaurant. Annual Italian Festa held in mid-July. Heritage Walk; brochure available from Tourist Information Centre. **In the area:** Lake Boga, 16 km south, popular for water sports and picnicking. Historic Tyntyndyer Homestead (c. 1846), classified by National Trust, 17 km north on Murray Valley Hwy. Murray Downs Homestead, 2 km northwest over bridge into NSW on Moulamein Rd; historic sheep, cattle and irrigation property, with animal park and children's playground. Murray Downs Golf and Country Club, 5 km north-west over bridge into NSW. Ceramics and china-painting studio at Pental Island, 5 km east. Amboc Mohair Farm at Mystic Park, 29 km south. Pheasant farm and aviaries at Nowie North, 32 km north-west. Buller's winery at Beverford, 11 km north, Best's St Andrew's Vineyard near Lake Boga, 16 km south. Piambie State Forest, 70 km north. Tooleybuc, 45 km north,

pleasant spot for fishing, bird-watching and picnics. **Tourist information:** 306 Campbell St; (050) 32 3033. **Accommodation:** 4 hotels, 15 motels, 5 caravan/camping parks. **See also:** The Mighty Murray; Victoria's Wine Regions.
MAP REF. 116 H11, 215 O11

Tallangatta   Population 963

When the old town of Tallangatta was submerged due to the construction of the Hume Weir, many of its buildings were moved to a new location above the shoreline. Today, situated 42 km from Wodonga on the Murray Valley Hwy, the town has the benefit of this large lake and boasts an attractive inland beach. It is the most eastern of the main Murray River towns and is directly north of the beautiful alpine region of Victoria. The centre of a productive dairying area since early settlement, Tallangatta is the home of the Australian Red Breed Society, established to recognise red dairy cattle breeds throughout the world as a single breeding population. **Of interest:** The Hub, Tallangatta's Community Centre, in Towong St, sells art and craft. An Arts Festival is held each October. **In the area:** A number of forest drives are recommended by the Forests Commission. They extend from Mitta Mitta south down the Omeo Hwy, and include trips to Cravensville, Mt Benambra, Tawonga and Omeo via the Snowy Creek Rd. Alpine Walking Track passes over Mt Wills, 48 km south of Mitta Mitta. Lake Dartmouth, 58 km from Tallangatta, has good trout-fishing, boating, picnic and barbecue facilities. **Tourist information:** The Hub, Towong St; (060) 71 2695. **Accommodation:** 2 hotels, 1 motel, 1 caravan/camping park. **See also:** The Mighty Murray.
MAP REF. 219 C5

Terang   Population 2040

Terang, located on the Princes Hwy in a predominantly dairy farming area, is a well laid out town with grand avenues of deciduous trees: recognised by the National Trust. The town has excellent sporting facilities with a particular emphasis on horse sports. **Of interest:** Early 20th century commercial architecture and a classic Gothic sandstone Presbyterian church. Cottage crafts shop in a century-old cottage, originally the police station. **In the area:** Noorat, 6 km north, birthplace of Alan Marshall, author of *I Can Jump Puddles* and many other stories. Here, the Alan Marshall Walking Track makes a gentle climb to the summit of an extinct volcano with excellent views of the crater, surrounding district

and across to the Grampians. Farm accommodation available. Glenormiston Agricultural College, 4 km further north, tastefully developed around an historic homestead mansion. **Accommodation**: 4 hotels, 2 motels, 1 caravan/camping park.
MAP REF. 211 M8

Torquay   Population 3522
The popularity of this resort, 22 km south of Geelong, is well known. Close to the town, the excellent surfing beaches, Bells and Jan Juc, attract surfers from all over the world. Bells Beach Surfing Championships are held at Easter. The Torquay Surf Lifesaving Club is the largest in the state. Torquay also marks the eastern end of the Great Ocean Road, offering spectacular drives west to Anglesea and beyond. **Of interest**: Surfing products at Surf Coast Plaza, Geelong Rd. Mary Elliott Pottery, Geelong Rd. Craft Cottage, Park Lane. Barbara Peake's Studio, Sarabande Cr. Redwood Gallery, Geelong Rd. **In the area**: Southern Rose, 1 km south, with rose gardens, tea-rooms and restaurant. Museum of early Australian horse-drawn carriages near Bellbrae, 6 km west. Rebenberg Winery (open weekends) and Downunda Weaving Studio at Mt Duneed, 11 km north. Experimental wind-power generator at Breamlea, 10 km north-east. **Tourist information**: Shire Offices, Grossmans Rd; (052) 61 4202, and Mary Elliott Pottery, Geelong Rd; (052) 61 3310. **Accommodation**: 2 motels, 4 caravan/camping parks. **See also**: The Great Ocean Road.
MAP REF. 205 E10, 208 D9

Traralgon   Population 19 233
Situated on the Princes Hwy, 160 km south-east from Melbourne, Traralgon is one of the Latrobe Valley's main cities, the others being Moe and Morwell. It is a residential area based on an industrial core. **In the area**: Tambo Cheese Factory, 3 km east of town; cheese and tourist information. The dense forests of the mountain country to the north have made Traralgon the centre of the paper-making industry in Victoria. Loy Yang power-station, 5 km south. **Tourist information**: Mobil Service Station, Princes Hwy. **Accommodation**: 2 hotels, 5 motels, 4 caravan/camping parks.
MAP REF. 209 O8

Walhalla   Population under 200
The tiny gold-mining town of Walhalla is tucked away in dense mountain country in south-east Gippsland. The 46-km drive north from Moe passes through some spectacular scenery. Walhalla is set in a narrow, steep valley, with sides so sheer that its cemetery has graves that have been dug lengthways into the hillside. **Of interest**: Historic buildings and relics of the gold-boom days have been preserved. Visit the Long Tunnel Extended Goldmine, named after the most successful in the state; the mine is open at weekends and holidays and there are guided tours to inspect its underground workings. The old fire station still houses a hand-operated fire-engine and fire memorabilia. Spett's Cottage, built in 1871, is furnished in the period and is open at weekends and on public holidays. There is a museum opposite the Rotunda, at the end of the Gold Era shops. The Post Office also houses crafts. The old bakery, the oldest surviving building in the town, was built in 1865 and stands near the rebuilt hotel. The Museum, Spett's Cottage, the Band Rotunda and the two-storey Windsor House (1890) have all been classified by the National Trust. **In the area**: Alpine Walking Track and Baw Baw National Park, which edges western side of town. Moondarra State Park, 30 km south. Thomson River, 2 km south, has fishing, picnicking and is a canoe trail. Scenic road between Walhalla and Jamieson, 140 km north. **Tourist information**: Old Gippstown, Princes Hwy, Moe; (051) 27 3082. **See also**: Gippsland Lakes.
MAP REF. 209 O6

Wangaratta   Population 16 598
The Ovens Hwy to Bright and the Victorian Alps, through the Ovens Valley, branches off the Hume Fwy at Wangaratta, 66 km south-west of Wodonga. The surrounding fertile area produces wool, wheat, tobacco, hops and table wine grapes. The city is well planned with good areas of parkland. **Of interest**: In the local cemetery, the grave of Daniel 'Mad Dog' Morgan, the bushranger, can be seen. His headless body was buried here, the head having been sent to Melbourne for examination. Kooringa Native Plants. Wangaratta Woollen Mills. The IBM plant, opened in 1984, supplies all IBM personal computer requirements for Australia, New Zealand and South-east Asia. Annual Festival of Jazz in November. **In the area**: Airworld Aviation Museum, 7 km south, houses the world's largest collection of flying antique civil aircraft, as well as a large collection of antique bicycles, cars, motor cycles and trucks. Glenrowan, 16 km south-west, is famed for its Kelly history. Ned was captured here after a bloody gunfight at the local hotel and was subsequently condemned and hanged in Melbourne. The tourist centre in the town focuses on the history of the Kelly Gang. Eldorado, 20 km east of Wangaratta, is an interesting old gold-township with the largest gold-dredge in the southern hemisphere, built in 1936. There is a historical museum, a general store with tourist information and a pottery open at weekends. Nearby Reedy Creek is popular with gold-panners and gem-fossickers. The road 27 km south to Moyhu leads to the beautiful King Valley and Paradise Falls. This area includes the tiny townships of Whitfield, 54 km south, Cheshunt and Carboor; a network of minor roads allows exploration of an area which is still unspoiled and well worth visiting in all seasons. King Valley Scenic Drive beside the river to Whitfield and Powers Lookout. There are many vineyards in the area. These include John Gehrig Winery; Brown Brothers Milawa Vineyards, 16 km south-east, a family winery since 1889; Baileys Bundarra Vineyards (established 1870), 7 km north of Glenrowan, which offers tastings and has a collection of vineyard antiques; Auldstones Winery; Booth Brothers, 4 km north of Baileys. Warby Range State Park, 12 km west, has good vantage points, picnic spots and a large variety of bird and plant life. Newton's Prickle Berry Farm at Whitfield. Brookfield Pottery at Everton, 22 km south-east. 'Carinya' Ladson Store at Tarrawingee, 11 km south-east. Byrne House and Gallery at Byrne, 25 km south. Fingers and Thrums craft workshop, and Wombi Toys, at Whorouly, 25 km south-east. **Tourist information**: Hume Hwy, Wangaratta South; (057) 21 5711. **Accommodation**: 2 hotels, 1 hotel/motel, 11 motels, 3 caravan/camping parks. **See also**: Victoria's Wine Regions.
MAP REF. 217 N6

Warburton   Population 2304
Warburton was established with the gold finds of the 1880s; however, by the turn of the century, it had found its niche as a popular tourist town with fine guesthouses. It is surrounded by the foothills of the Great Dividing Range and only about an hour's drive from Melbourne. **Of interest**: Swingbridge Gallery and Crafts. **In the area**: The Acheron Way begins 2 km east of Warburton, giving access to views of Mt Donna Buang, Mt Victoria and Ben Cairn, on the scenic 37 km drive to St Fillans. Mt Donna Buang, 7 km north-west, is a popular day-trip destination from Melbourne and is sometimes snow-covered in winter. The Upper Yarra Dam, 23 km north-east, has picnic facilities. To the south of the town along the Warburton Hwy is an attractive area of vineyards: Yarra Burn, Lilydale and Oak Ridge Estate. The countryside around Warburton is ideal for bushwalking, riding and bird-watching. Tommy

VICTORIA'S WINE REGIONS

Viticulture developed in Victoria following the 1850s gold-rush. Unsuccessful diggers began planting vines as a source of income. Later, Edward Henty and William Rye brought cuttings to the new colony and by 1868 more than 1200 hectares of vines had been established.

The light, dry wines produced in these vineyards won wide acclaim, but the event of phylloxera saw a promising industry decline until the early 1960s, when it started to re-emerge and develop into what it is today. One of the oldest regions is in the north-east of the state, 270 kilometres from Melbourne. **Rutherglen** and the other nearby winemaking towns of **Wahgunyah**, **Glenrowan** and **Milawa** produce distinct wine unique to each of the region's environmental sub-cultures. Many of the wineries are still managed by the descendants of the founders. The wines of the region are famed for their rich flavoursome red, and the exotic range of fortified wines such as Rutherglen Muscat, Rutherglen Tokay and their famous Port-style wine. On the Queen's Birthday long weekend each June, a winery walkabout is organised so that winelovers can visit the vineyards and sample some of the fine wines of the north-east. It is advisable to book your accommo-

dation in advance if you plan to visit the area at this time.

West along the Murray, the towns of **Echuca**, **Swan Hill** and **Mildura** are part of the Murray Valley and northwest region known for the production of everyday drinking wines.

About 200 kilometres west of Melbourne, between Stawell and Ararat, is the little town of **Great Western**, where the Seppelt and Best wineries developed in the 1860s. Since then they have consistently produced fine wines, including the renowned champagne-style Great Western Special Reserve from the Seppelt winery. The vineyards of Great Western are also noted for their rich red and full-flavoured white table wines.

At **Ararat**, Trevor Mast's Mt Langi Ghiran vineyard and the McCrae's Montara vineyard both produce excellent wine with their own individual character.

To the north-east of Great Western is the region of the Pyrenees with the townships of **Avoca**, **Redbank** and **Moonambel**. Here are the Taltarni, Mt Avoca, Redbank, Chateau Remy, Summerfield, Dalwhinnie and Warrenmang wineries.

Stretching from **Shepparton** along to **Nagambie**, **Seymour** and **Mansfield** is

the picturesque region of the Goulburn Valley with a contrast in wineries from the historic, classified buildings of Chateau Tahbilk to the modern wineries of Delatite and Mitchelton. One grape variety from the region that has won acclaim is the Marsanne, a white wine that is distinct and rather unusual.

One of the two oldest regions nearest to Melbourne is the Yarra Valley region, which is centred round the towns of **Cottles Bridge**, **Yarra Glen**, **Lilydale**, **Coldstream** and **Seville**. This region's premium wine has had a rebirth after starting in the early 1850s and petering out as late as the 1920s. There is a wide range of wines produced in the area from sparkling wine to quality reds and white table wines. In the Yarra Valley, wineries of particular interest include Domaine Chandon for its sparkling wines, and as each has a restaurant, Fergusson's, Kellybrook, Yarra Burn and De Bortoli for an enjoyable lunch in the Valley, especially near to vintage. There are many other wineries worth visiting, including Bianchet for the merlot and verduzzo wines and St Huberts, for it was one of the first wineries in the re-birth of the district.

Another wine-producing area close to Melbourne is the burgeoning

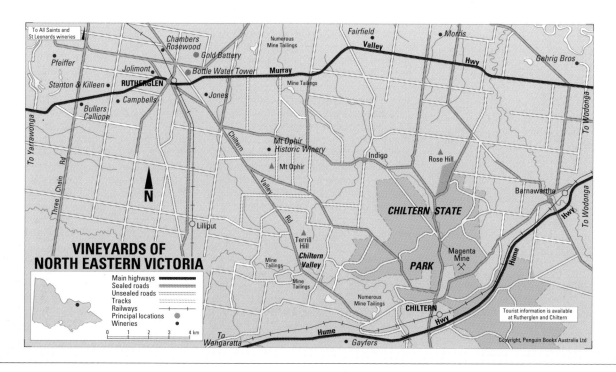

Mornington Peninsula area. A cool-climate wine-growing district, its 83 vineyards nestle in between farming and coastal hamlets. The main spread covers the area from **Dromana**, through **Red Hill** and across the Peninsula to **Merricks** and **Balnarring**, with **Mornington, Main Ridge** and **Mt Martha** offering isolated vineyards. Of these, 17 vineyards are open, usually on weekends and public holidays, for cellar-door tastings and sales. Another 13 cellar doors are open for sales and visits by appointment.

North of Melbourne's Tullamarine Airport, wineries dot the landscape with little pockets of vines stretching into the Macedon Ranges; some were established in the 1860s, others more recently. They include Knight's Granite Hills, Wildwood, Hanging Rock, Virgin Hills, Craiglee, Goonawarra, Cleveland, Cope Williams, Flyn and Williams—each with its own disinct quality and character.

The Heathcote–Bendigo region is, like so many of Victoria's wine regions, gold-mining country that gave up much of its hidden wealth in the 1850s to 1900s. Today there are many wineries scattered throughout the region, round the townships of **Heathcote, Kingower, Bendigo** and **Bridgewater-on-Loddon**. Wineries include Passing Clouds, Blanche Barkly, Jasper Hill, Osicka's, Zuber Estate, Water Wheel, Le Amon and Mildara's Balgownie.

In the last 20 years Victoria's wine industry has changed from an industry in decline with about 25 commercial vineyards, to a flourishing state with the number of commercial vineyards hovering round the 300 with another 100 in the wings.

Most larger wineries are open daily for wine-tasting and sales; some of the small wineries have restricted opening times, so it is worth checking before visiting.

For more information contact: the Victorian Wine Centre, (03) 699 6082; Mornington Peninsula Vignernons Association, (059) 74 4200; Yarra Valley Wine Growers Association, (059) 64 9388. For tourist information, contact the Victorian Information Centre (03) 790 3333.

Finn's Trout Farm at Millgrove, 3 km west of town. Yellingbo State Fauna Reserve, 25 km south-west. Yarra Junction Historical Museum, 10 km west. A Department of Conservation and Environment leaflet giving details of a walk from Powelltown, 27 km south, to East Warburton can be obtained from the tourist information outlet; this is one branch of the Centenary Trail (the other branch leads from Warburton to Baw Baw National Park). **Tourist information:** Cabaret Restaurant, Main St; (059) 66 2071. **Accommodation:** 1 hotel, 3 motels, 1 caravan/camping park.
MAP REF. 209 K5, 218 F12

Warracknabeal   Population 2689
On the Henty Hwy, 350 km north-west of Melbourne, Warracknabeal is in the centre of a rich wheat-growing area. The name is Aboriginal, meaning 'the place of the big red gums shading the water course'. **Of interest:** The Historical Centre, 81 Scott St, contains many items and displays of the history of the area. Self-guiding leaflets are available suggesting a tour of the historic buildings in the town. Some of these have been classified by the National Trust, including the attractive old Warracknabeal Hotel (1872) with iron lacework and the original log lock-up (1872), built when Warracknabeal acquired its first permanent policeman. The Wheatlands Agricultural Machinery Museum has a unique collection of farm machinery used over the past century; there are picnic and barbecue facilities in the grounds. At the Lions Park, situated in a bend of the Yarriambiack Creek, are picnic spots and a fauna park. Vintage Machinery and Vehicle Rally during annual Wheatlands Easter Carnival. **In the area:** Sections of the dog-fence remain, some 30 km north; this was a vermin-proof barrier erected in 1883 from the Murray near Swan Hill to the border. Jeparit, 45 km west, has the Wimmera–Mallee Pioneer Museum. Lake Hindmarsh is 74 km north; Lake Buloke, 56 km east, provides duck-shooting in season. **Tourist information:** 119 Scott St; (053) 98 1632. **Accommodation:** 3 motels, 1 caravan/camping park. **See also:** The Wimmera.
MAP REF. 212 I6

Warragul   Population 8170
Most of Melbourne's milk comes from this prosperous dairy-farming area 103 km from Melbourne. **Of interest:** West Gippsland Arts Centre. Warragul Vintage Craft Park. **In the area:** Darnum Musical Village, 8 km east. Wildflower sanctuary at Labertouche, 16 km west; nature reserves and picnic spots at Glen

Cromie, Glen Nayook and Toorongo Falls. Mountain country and trout-fishing near Neerim South, 19 km north. Gippsland cheeses can be sampled at Neerim South (Gippsland Blue, Jindi Brie), at Yarragon, 13 km east (Dairy Delicacies), Trafalgar, 21 km east, and Traralgon, 60 km east (Tambo Cheese Factory). Gourmet Deli Trail (brochure available locally), for a further food fantasy trip. **Accommodation:** 4 hotels, 2 motels, 1 caravan/camping park.
MAP REF. 209 L8

Warrnambool   Population 22 706
A beautiful seaside city located 263 km south-west of Melbourne, where the Princes Hwy meets the Great Ocean Road, Warrnambool combines history and thriving progress on the shores of Lady Bay. First-class sporting, cultural and entertainment facilities and beautifully developed and maintained parks and gardens have resulted in Warrnambool being awarded Victoria's prestigious Premier Town title a record three times. **Of interest:** Major attractions include Flagstaff Hill, Merri St, a unique 19th-century Maritime Village, used as a location in the filming of *Quigley Down Under*. The Entrance Gallery orientation centre introduces visitors to the Maritime Village experience, and includes the Flagstaff Hill tapestry, the themes of which include Aboriginal history, sealing, whaling, exploration, immigration and settlement. Over 100 ships were wrecked on the coast near Warrnambool; the famous earthenware Loch Ard Peacock, recovered from the wreck of the *Loch Ard* in 1878, is on permanent display at Flagstaff Hill Maritime Village. The Mahogany Ship Restaurant specialises in seafood and overlooks Warrnambool's picturesque Lady Bay and the Village. The annual visit of rare southern right whales usually occurs between May and October (viewing platform east of town, at Logans Beach). The Kid's Country Treasure Map (available at Tourist Information Centre) provides a fun and informative way for the whole family to enjoy Warnambool. Performing Arts Centre, Art Gallery, Timor St; Botanic Gardens, Botanic Rd (designed by Guilfoyle in 1879); Fletcher Jones Gardens, Raglan Pde; and Lake Pertobe Adventure Playground, Pertobe Rd, a children's paradise. The Potter's Wheel, Liebig St. Time and Tide Museum, Stanley St, features shells, musical instruments and memorabilia. Annual Wunta Fiesta in February; 3-day May Racing Carnival and Melbourne to Warrnambool Cycling Classic in October. A Heritage Trail walk and an arrow tour of the city start at the Tourist Information

Centre (self-guiding leaflets available). Thunder Point Reserve, end of Macdonald St. Middle Island, off Pickering Point, has a colony of fairy penguins. Wollaston Bridge, over 100 years old and of unusual design, on northern outskirts of town. **In the area:** Historic Shipwreck Trail, highlighting wrecks along the coast from Moonlight Head (112 km east) to Port Fairy (29 km west), allows visitors to explore Victoria's 'Shipwreck Coast'. Tower Hill State Game Reserve, 14 km west, is one of Victoria's largest and most recently active volcanoes; a nature walk starts at the National History Centre. Robert Ulmann Studio, 4 km east of Warrnambool, for paintings of Australian flora and fauna. Allansford Cheese World, 10 km east, a dairy promotion store featuring cheese tasting and sales, has a video of cheeses, butter and honey production. Ralph Illidge Sanctuary, 32 km east, has wildlife, picnic area and nature walks. Timboon Farmhouse, Cheese and Berry World, both at Timboon, 53 km east of Warrnambool. Port Campbell National Park, 54 km south-east, a 32 km stretch of scenic and historic coastline, incorporates a magnificent series of sheer cliffs, deep caverns, great archways, grottos, island gorges, blowholes and spectacular off-shore rock stacks. The world-famous Twelve Apostles lie 77 km south-east of Warrnambool. Helicopter flights along the coast are available. **Tourist information:** 600 Raglan Pde; (055) 64 7837. **Accommodation:** 10 hotels, 23 motels, 8 caravan/camping parks. **See also:** The Great Ocean Road.
MAP REF. 211 J9

Wedderburn   Population 878
Once one of Victoria's richest gold-mining towns in the 'Golden Triangle', Wedderburn is on the Calder Hwy, 74 km north-west of Bendigo. Gold can still be found in and around the town — nuggets worth over $20 000 were discovered in a local backyard in the 1950s. **Of interest:** Government Battery on northern edge of town. Hard Hill area, former gold diggings and Christmas Reef Mine. Museum and General Store (1910), a restored building furnished and stocked as it was at the turn of the century. Coach-building factory, and an old bakery converted into a kiln for a group of potters, using local clay. **In the area:** Wychitella Forest Reserve, a wildlife sanctuary, 16 km north. Mount Korong, 16 km south-east, for picnics and some rock scrambling, as well as bushwalking. **Tourist information:** Shire Offices, High St; (054) 94 3200. **Accommodation:** 1 hotel, 1 motel, 1 caravan/camping park.
MAP REF. 213 P7

Welshpool–Port Welshpool
Population 514
Welshpool is a small dairying town and Port Welshpool is a deep-sea port servicing fishing and oil industries and now the Sea Cat car ferry to Tasmania. Barry Beach Marine Terminal, 8 km south of the South Gippsland Hwy, services the offshore oil rigs in Bass Strait. **In the area:** Excellent fishing and boating. Agnes Falls, 19 km north-west, the state's highest. Panoramic views from Mt Fatigue, 10 km north, off South Gippsland Hwy at Toora, 11 km west. Scenic drive from Toora; accommodation at historic Ambleside guesthouse. At Port Welshpool, a Maritime Museum. Tarra-Bulga National Park, 56 km north. **Accommodation:** 1 motel, 2 caravan/camping parks.
MAP REF. 209 O11

Winchelsea   Population 890
This township is in the centre of a farming area, on the Barwon River, 37 km west of Geelong. It originated as a watering-place and shelter for travellers on the road to Colac from Geelong. **Of interest:** Barwon Bridge, with its graceful stone arches, was opened in 1867 to handle increasing westward traffic. The Barwon Hotel, built in 1842, houses a museum of Australiana. Barwon Park homestead, a National Trust property, 3 km north on Inverleigh Rd, is open on the first Sun. of each month. B-Winched Crafts. Alexandra's Antiques and Art Gallery. Lake Modewarre, 14 km east, offers good fishing and water sports. **Tourist information:** Shire Offices; (052) 67 2104. **Accommodation:** 1 motel, 1 caravan/camping park.
MAP REF. 205 B9, 208 B8, 211 R8

Wodonga   Population 22 000
Wodonga is the Victorian city in a twin city complex astride the Murray in north-east Victoria. Albury–Wodonga is a fast-growing city being developed as a decentralised region by the Federal, Victorian and NSW State Governments and, with the attractions of the Murray and nearby Lake Hume, makes a good base for a holiday. **Of interest:** Wodonga has a number of historic buildings still in use. The city has about 30 km of bicycle paths. The Linc Inn, Lincoln Hwy, offers teas. Miniature steam railway runs on 3rd Sun. each month at Diamond Park, off Lincoln Causeway. Sumsion Gardens, Batt Ave, a beautiful lakeside park. **In the area:** The Hume Weir, 19 km east, is a good place for a picnic; inspections of Hume Weir Trout Farm. Military Museum at

Bandiana, 4 km south-east. Wodonga is close to four areas of interest: Upper Murray, mountain valleys of north-east Victoria, Murray Valley, and the Riverina district. A short drive 36 km south leads to the picturesque historic township of Yackandandah. The towns of Beechworth (47 km), Wangaratta (68 km), both south-east, and Rutherglen, 42 km west, are all well worth visiting. **Tourist information:** Information Centre, Lincoln Causeway; (060) 41 3875. **Accommodation:** Albury–Wodonga, 3 hotels, 55 motels, 13 caravan/camping parks. **See also:** The Mighty Murray.
MAP REF. 117 P13, 217 Q5, 219 A5

Wonthaggi   Population 5346
Once the main supplier of black coal to the Victorian Railways, Wonthaggi, situated 8 km from Cape Paterson in south Gippsland, is the regional centre and now primarily a pastoral and dairying centre. Wonthaggi began as a 'tent town' in 1909 when the coal-mines were opened up by the State Government following industrial unrest in the coalfields in NSW. The mines operated until 1968. **In the area:** State Coal Mine, 1.5 km south on Cape Patterson Rd; tours of re-opened Eastern Area Mine and Museum on mining activities, with experienced ex-coalminer as guide; picnic shelter and facilities. Scenic drives to beaches at Inverloch, 13 km south-east, and Tarwin Lower, 35 km south-east. Self-drive tour of 25 km links places of interest in area. Cape Paterson, 8 km south, within Bunurong Marine Park, has surfing, swimming and fishing. **Accommodation:** 2 hotels, 2 motels, 2 caravan/ camping parks.
MAP REF. 209 J11

Wycheproof   Population 854
A railway line runs down the middle of the main street of this little township on the edge of the Mallee, 140 km from Bendigo. **Of interest:** Boomerang factory in town; check opening times. 'Mt Wycheproof', a mere 43 m high and the smallest mountain in the world; site of a tough footrace each year where contestants carry a bag of wheat to the summit. **Tourist information:** Shire Offices, 367 Broadway; (054) 93 7400. **Accommodation:** 1 motel, 1 caravan/camping park.
MAP REF. 116 G13, 213 N4

Yackandandah   Population 473
About 27 km south of Wodonga, this exceptionally attractive township, with avenues of English trees and traditional verandahed buildings, has been classified by the National Trust. Yackandandah

is in the heart of the north-east gold-fields country (gold was discovered here in 1852), but today it is more famous for its historic buildings. **Of interest:** Number of original buildings in High St, including Post Office, several banks and general stores; also Bank of Victoria (1865), now a historical museum. Self-guided walking tour brochure available. Art and craft from Yackandandah Workshop, cnr Kars and Hammond Sts, and Haldane Artist Studio in High St. Wildon Thyme, High St, herb nursery with tea-rooms and restaurant. Ray Riddington's Premier Store and Gallery, High St. Country Music Festival held annually on New Year's Day. **In the area:** At Allans Flat, 10 km north-east, Mr Red's Farm, with nursery and animal farm, and Schmidt's Strawberry Winery. Picturesque Indigo Valley, 6 km west; classified by National Trust. Road leads through rolling hills along valley floor to Barnawatha. Creeks and old diggings in Yackandandah area still yield specimens of alluvial gold to amateur prospectors. At Dederang, 25 km south-east, art, craft and plants for sale; Devonshire teas at Clifton Cottages. At Leneva, 16 km north-east, Wombat Valley Tramways small-gauge railway operates on last Sun. of each month. **Tourist information:** Court-house, William St; (060) 27 1222. **Accommodation:** 2 hotels, 1 caravan/camping park.
MAP REF. 217 Q6

Yarram   Population 2004
This old-established south Gippsland town, 225 km by road from Melbourne, has some interesting original buildings and a pleasant golf-course, inhabited by relatively tame kangaroos. It is situated between the Strzelecki Ranges and Bass Strait. **In the area:** To the south, the historic towns of Alberton (6 km), Tarraville (11 km) and Port Albert (14 km); Christ Church (1856) in Tarraville is the oldest church in Gippsland. The Ninety Mile Beach, very popular with surfers and anglers, begins just north of Port Albert. Woodside (29 km east) and Seaspray (68 km north-east) beaches are patrolled during the summer season. For fishing, Mann's (16 km east), or McLoughlin's (29 km east) beaches. To the north is the Australian Omega Navigation Facility with its 427-m-high steel tower. In the Strzelecki Ranges, 27 km north-west, is the Tarra-Bulga National Park. This is very hilly country, densely forested with mountain ash, myrtle and sassafras, with spectacular fern glades and splendid river and

mountain views. Rosellas and lyrebirds can be seen, as can the occasional koala. There are walking-tracks in both parks and two caravan parks at Tarra Valley; horseriding nearby. At Hiawatha, a short drive from Yarram (circuit 46 km), are the appropriately named Minnie Ha Ha Falls on the Albert River, with picnic facilities. Horses for hire at Hiawatha. At Wron Wron Forest, on the Hyland Hwy, 16 km north, wildflowers can be seen in spring. Yarram holds Tarra Valley Festival every Easter. **Tourist information:** Ooly Dooly Motors, Commercial Rd; (051) 82 5119. **Accommodation:** 2 hotels, 3 motels, 3 caravan/camping parks.
MAP REF. 209 P11

Yarragon   Population 650
This small highway town in the Latrobe Valley is situated 120 km east of Melbourne in an agricultural and dairying district. It is convenient to explore the Upper Latrobe and Tanjil River valleys in the mountainous area to the north and for scenic drives along the beautiful Grand Ridge Road to the south. **Of interest:** Dairy Delicacies, Princes Hwy; sample Gippsland and Australian cheeses; craft shop and gallery in complex. **In the area:** Mt Worth State Park, 10 km south. Childers, 16 km south-east; Sunny Creek Berry Farm and Windrush Cottage for teas. Trafalgar Lookout, Narracan Falls and Henderson's Gully near Trafalgar, 8 km east. Thorpdale, 22 km south-east, known for its potatoes; potato bread from bakery. Potato Festival held March Labour Day weekend. **Tourist information:** Dairy Delicacies, Princes Hwy; (056) 34 2451. **Accommodation:** 1 motel.
MAP REF. 209 M8

Yarrawonga–Mulwala
Population 3388
A pleasant stretch of the Murray and the attractive Lake Mulwala have made these border towns an extremely popular holiday resort. The 6000-ha lake was created in 1939 during the building of the Yarrawonga Weir, which controls the irrigation waters in the Murray Valley. **Of interest:** Around the lake and along the river, sandy beaches and still waters provide an ideal environment for all kinds of water sports, picnicking and general relaxation. The towns have excellent sports facilities, including a 45-hole golf course. The islands and backwaters of the lake contain abundant birdlife. Cruises can be taken on the lake. The Yarrawonga and Mulwala foreshore areas have well-tended green lawns and shady willows, and facilities

include children's playgrounds, giant waterslides, kiosk, barbecues and boat-ramps. Old Yarra Mine Shaft houses a large collection of gems, minerals and fossils. Carinya Pottery, off Burley Rd. Hallworth House Gallery, Woods Rd. Tudor House Clock Museum, Lynch St. Daily cruises on the Paradise Queen and the Lady Murray. Ski club conducts exhibitions and lessons. Tunzafun amusement park. Clip Clop Tours offers horsedrawn coach rides. **In the area:** Byramine Homestead and Country Gardens, 15 km west. Matata Deer Farm at Cobram, 42 km west. Match Tree Plantation, 600 ha of poplars on Spring Drive, between Mulwala and Corowa. Historical Museum at Katamatite, 35 km south-west of Yarrawonga. Fishing in Murray River (no licence required). **Tourist information:** Irvine Pde, Yarrawonga; (057) 44 1989. **Accommodation:** 4 hotels, 2 hotel/motels, 16 motels, 10 caravan/camping parks. **See also:** The Mighty Murray.
MAP REF. 117 N13, 217 M4

Yea   Population 1017
The town, 58 km north of Yarra Glen, stands beside the Yea River, a tributary of the Goulburn. Set in attractive pastoral and dairy-farming land, it is well situated for touring to Mansfield, Eildon and the mountains, and to the gorge country between Yea and Tallarook, as well as south-east to Marysville. There are some beautiful gorges and fern gullies close to the Yea – Tallarook road and easy access to the mountain country south of Eildon Weir. **Of interest:** Yea Dairy Co. trading as Ballantyne's Cheeses; specialty cheese-makers. Helen's Cafe, Station St; open for skier's breakfasts. **In the area:** Kinglake National Park, 30 km south-west; beautiful waterfalls, tall eucalypts, fern gullies and impressive views. Visitors can pick their own fruit at Berry King Farm, Two Hills Rd, Glenburn, 30 km south. Farm holidays available Glenwaters, Glenburn. Spectacular Wilhelmina Falls, 32 km south via Melba Hwy. Murrindindi Cascades 11 km away in Murrindindi Reserve; wildlife includes wombats, platypuses and lyrebirds. Mineral springs at Dropmore, 47 km north of town, off back road to Euroa. Grotto at Caveat, 27 km north; ibis rookery at Kerrisdale, 17 km west; several good campsites along Goulburn River. Flowerdale Winery. **Tourist information:** Shire Offices; (057) 97 2209; Goulburn Tourism, 243 High St, Nagambie; (057) 94 2647. **Accommodation:** 2 motels, 1 caravan/camping park.
MAP REF. 201 Q4, 216 I12, 218 C4

Maps of Victoria

Location Map

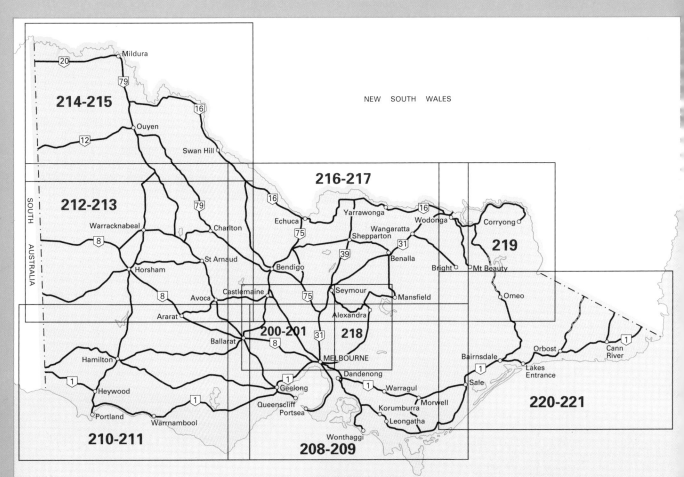

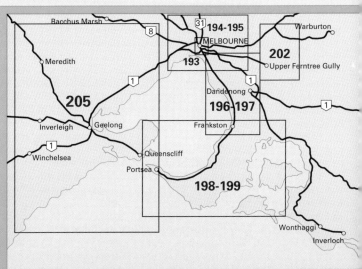

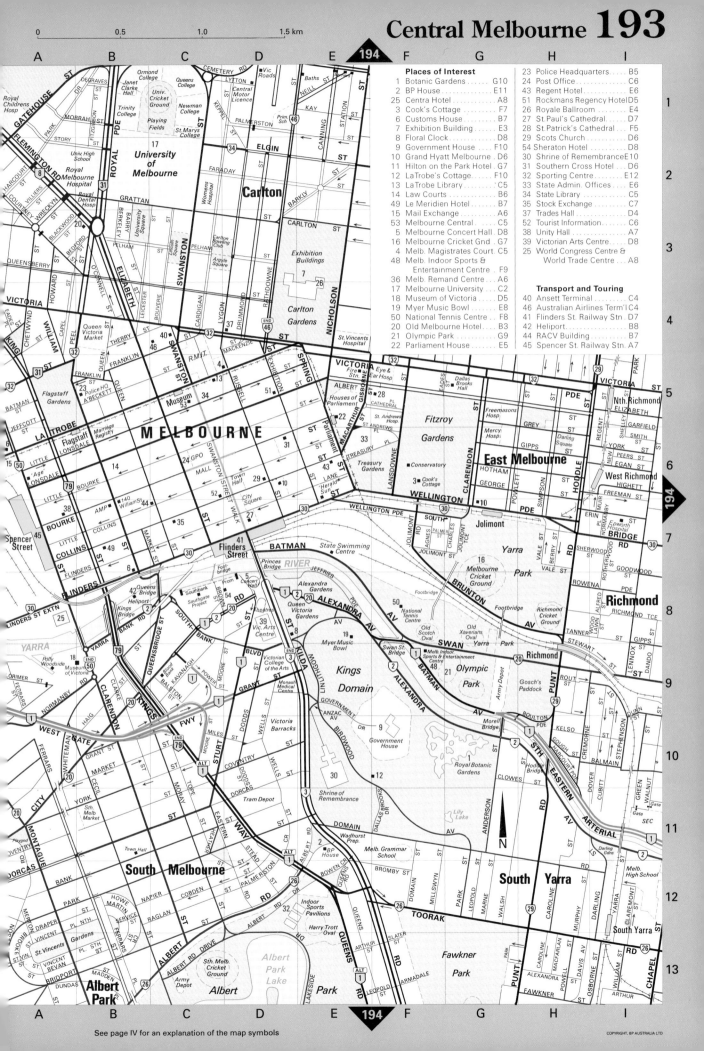

0   0.5   1.0   1.5 km

Places of Interest

1	Botanic Gardens	G10	
2	BP House	E11	
25	Centra Hotel	A8	
3	Cook's Cottage	F7	
6	Customs House	B7	
7	Exhibition Building	E3	
8	Floral Clock	D8	
9	Government House	F10	
10	Grand Hyatt Melbourne	D6	
11	Hilton on the Park Hotel	G7	
12	LaTrobe's Cottage	F10	
13	LaTrobe Library	C5	
14	Law Courts	B6	
49	Le Meridien Hotel	B7	
15	Mail Exchange	A6	
53	Melbourne Central	C5	
5	Melbourne Concert Hall	D8	
16	Melbourne Cricket Gnd	G7	
4	Melb. Magistrates Court	C5	
48	Melb. Indoor Sports & Entertainment Centre	F9	
36	Melb. Remand Centre	A6	
17	Melbourne University	C2	
18	Museum of Victoria	D5	
19	Myer Music Bowl	E8	
50	National Tennis Centre	F8	
20	Old Melbourne Hotel	B3	
21	Olympic Park	G9	
22	Parliament House	E5	

23	Police Headquarters	B5	
24	Post Office	C6	
43	Regent Hotel	E6	
26	Royale Ballroom	E4	
51	Rockmans Regency Hotel	D5	
27	St.Paul's Cathedral	D7	
28	St.Patrick's Cathedral	F5	
29	Scots Church	D6	
54	Sheraton Hotel	D8	
30	Shrine of Remembrance	E10	
31	Southern Cross Hotel	D6	
32	Sporting Centre	E12	
33	State Admin. Offices	E6	
34	State Library	C5	
35	Stock Exchange	C7	
37	Trades Hall	D4	
52	Tourist Information	C6	
38	Unity Hall	A7	
39	Victorian Arts Centre	D8	
25	World Congress Centre & World Trade Centre	A8	

Transport and Touring

40	Ansett Terminal	C4	
46	Australian Airlines Term'l	C4	
41	Flinders St. Railway Stn.	D7	
42	Heliport	B8	
44	RACV Building	B7	
45	Spencer St. Railway Stn.	A7	

See page IV for an explanation of the map symbols

COPYRIGHT, BP AUSTRALIA LTD

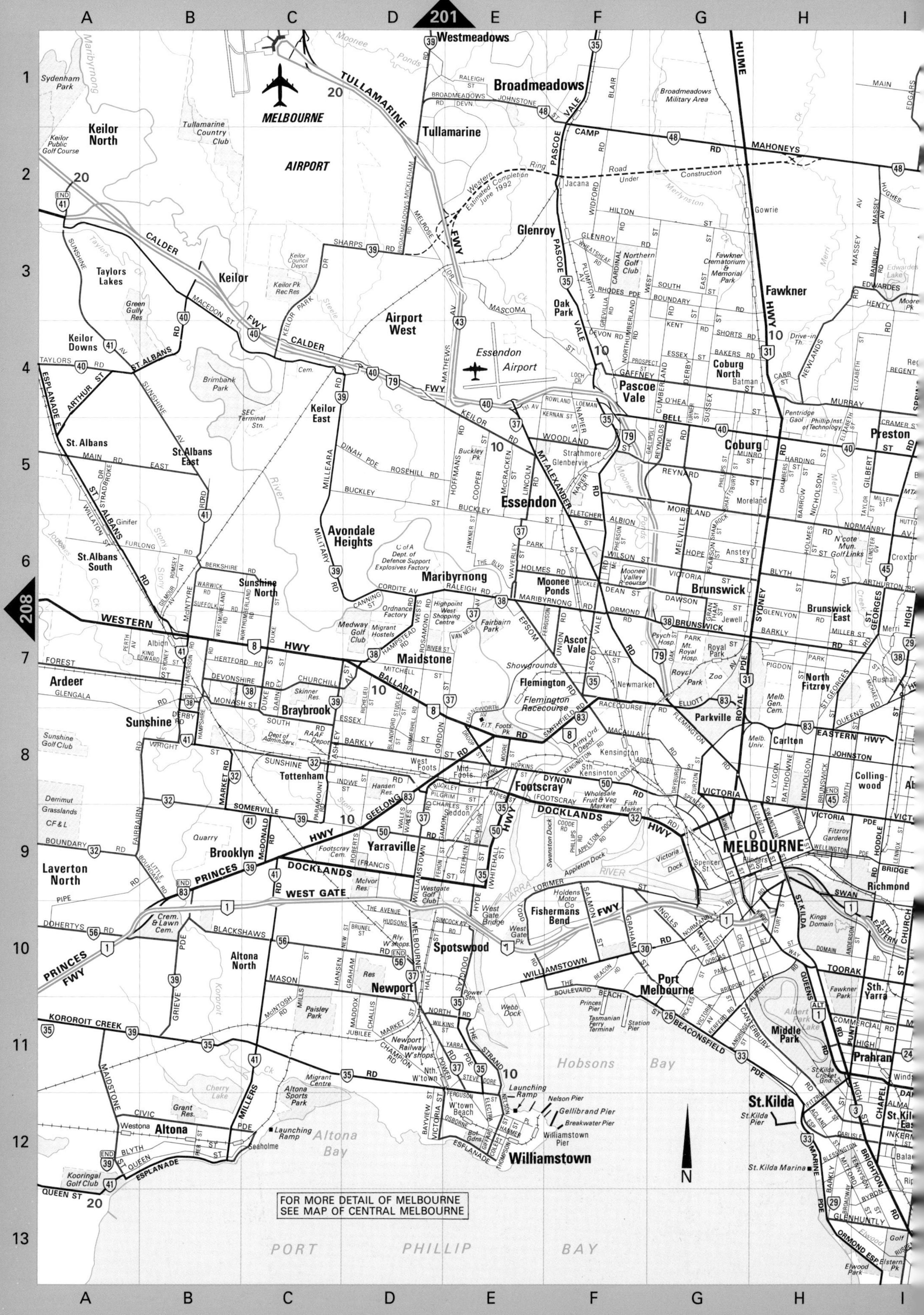

201
208
A
B
C
D
E
F
G
H
I
1
2
3
4
5
6
7
8
9
10
11
12
13
Westmeadows
Broadmeadows
Tullamarine
MELBOURNE
AIRPORT
Tullamarine Country Club
Sydenham Park
Keilor North
Keilor Public Golf Course
Broadmeadows Military Area
Western Ring Road Under Construction
Estimated Completion June 1992
Jacana
Gowrie
Glenroy
Keilor
Taylors Lakes
Green Gully Res
Keilor Council Depot
Keilor Pk Rec Res
Airport West
Oak Park
Northern Golf Club
Fawkner Crematorium & Memorial Park
Fawkner
Keilor Downs
Brimbank Park
SEC Terminal Stn.
Keilor East
Essendon Airport
Pascoe Vale
Coburg North
Coburg
Preston
Pentridge Gaol
Phillip Inst of Technology
St. Albans
St. Albans East
Strathmore
Glenbervie
Essendon
Moreland
Ginifer
Avondale Heights
St. Albans South
C of A Dept. of Defence Support Explosives Factory
Maribyrnong
Moonee Ponds
Moonee Valley R'course
Brunswick
Brunswick East
North Fitzroy
Sunshine North
Ordnance Factory
Highpoint West Shopping Centre
Fairbairn Park
Medway Golf Club
Migrant Hostels
Ascot Vale
Albion
Ardeer
Maidstone
Showgrounds
Flemington
Flemington Racecourse
Royal Park
Zoo
Psych Hosp.
Mt. Royal Hosp.
Parkville
Melb. Gen. Cem.
Melb. Univ.
Carlton
Skinner Res.
Braybrook
Sunshine
Sunshine Golf Club
F.I.T. Foots. Pk
Newmarket
Army Ord. Depot
Kensington
Dept of Admin.Serv.
RAAF Depot
Tottenham
West Foots
Mid Foots
Footscray
Wholesale Fruit & Veg Market
Fish Market
Collingwood
Hansen Res.
Seddon
Derrimut Grasslands CF & L
Quarry
Brooklyn
Footscray Cem.
Yarraville
Swanston Dock
Appleton Dock
Victoria Dock
Spencer St.
Flinders St.
MELBOURNE
Fitzroy Gardens
Richmond
Laverton North
McIvor Res.
Westgate Golf Club
Holdens Motor Co
Fishermans Bend
West Gate Bridge
West Gate Pk
Kings Domain
Crem. & Lawn Cem.
Altona North
Rly. W'shops.
Spotswood
Res
Newport
Port Melbourne
South Yarra
Sth. Yarra
Fawkner Park
Paisley Park
Power Stn.
Webb Dock
Princes Pier
Tasmanian Ferry Terminal
Station Pier
Albert Park Lake
Middle Park
Prahran
Newport Railway W'shops
Nth. W'town
Hobsons Bay
Migrant Centre
Altona Sports Park
Cherry Lake
Grant Res.
Launching Ramp
Nelson Pier
Gellibrand Pier
Breakwater Pier
Williamstown Pier
W'town Beach
Bot Gdns
Williamstown
St.Kilda
St.Kilda Pier
St.Kilda Cricket Gnd.
St. Kilda Marina
Altona
Seaholme
Altona Bay
Kooringal Golf Club
N
FOR MORE DETAIL OF MELBOURNE SEE MAP OF CENTRAL MELBOURNE
PORT PHILLIP BAY
Elwood Park
Elstern. Pk
TULLAMARINE FWY
CALDER FWY
WESTERN HWY
PRINCES FWY
PRINCES HWY
WEST GATE FWY
HUME HWY
SYDNEY RD
BALLARAT RD
GEELONG RD
DOCKLANDS HWY
BEACONSFIELD PDE
MARINE PDE
ROYAL PDE
MT. ALEXANDER RD
PASCOE VALE RD
KEILOR RD
SUNSHINE RD
MILLERS RD
KOROROIT CREEK RD
QUEEN ST
ESPLANADE
DYNON RD
FLEMINGTON RD
VICTORIA ST
BRUNSWICK RD
BELL ST
MURRAY RD
CAMP RD
MAHONEYS RD
ST. KILDA RD
QUEENS RD
PUNT RD
HIGH ST
BRIGHTON RD
GLENHUNTLY RD
ORMOND ESP
TOORAK RD
SWAN ST
CHURCH ST
HODDLE ST
ST. GEORGES RD
NICHOLSON ST
CANTERBURY RD
WILLIAMSTOWN RD
THE STRAND
BLACKSHAWS RD
MARIBYRNONG RD
RACECOURSE RD
MILLEARA RD
MILITARY RD

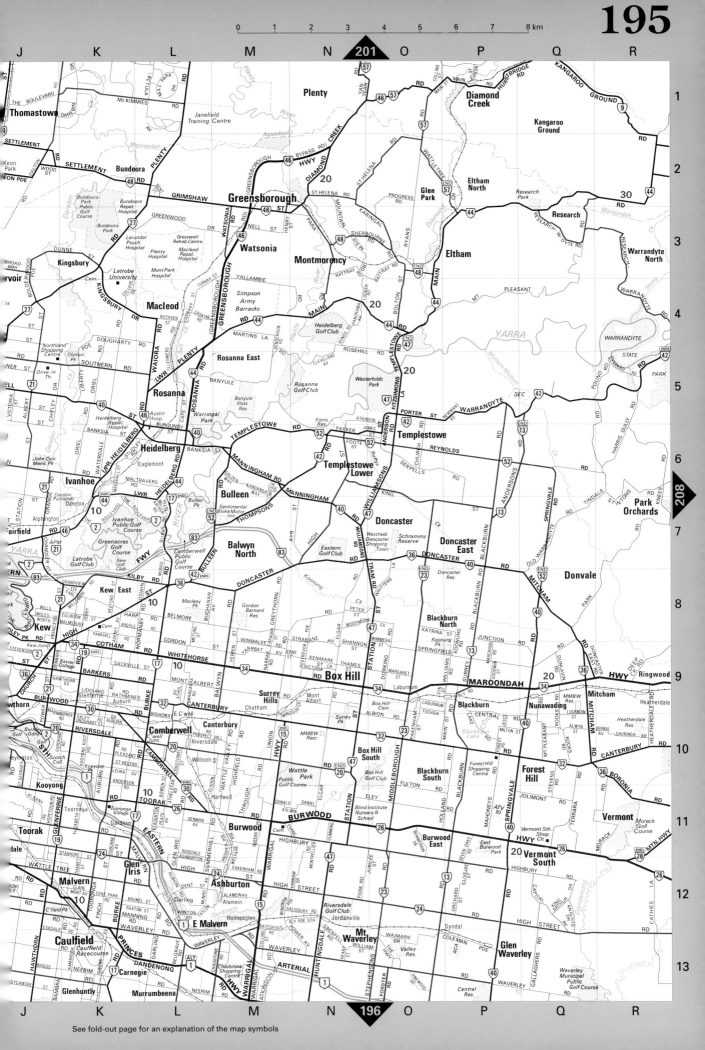

0 1 2 3 4 5 6 7 8 km

J K L M N O P Q R

Thomastown

Plenty

Diamond
Creek

Kangaroo
Ground

1

Keon
Park

SETTLEMENT   Bundoora

Janefield
Training Centre

Glen
Park

Eltham
North

Research
Park

30   44

2

Greensborough

St Helena

Research

Kingsbury

Watsonia

Montmorency

Eltham

Warrandyte
North

3

Macleod

Latrobe
University

Simpson
Army
Barracks

Yallambie

PLEASANT

4

"Northland"
Shopping
Centre

Rosanna East

YARRA

Rosanna

Warringal
Park

Rosanna
Golf Club

Westerfolds
Park

WARRANDYTE

STATE

5

Ivanhoe

Heidelberg

Templestowe

Templestowe

Templestowe
Lower

Park
Orchards

6

208

Fairfield

Ivanhoe
Public Golf
Course

Bulleen

Doncaster

Donvale

7

Kew

Kew East

Balwyn
North

Eastern
Golf Club

Doncaster
East

8

Box Hill

Blackburn
North

MAROONDAH   HWY   Ringwood

9

Surrey Hills

Camberwell

Canterbury

Blackburn

Nunawading

Mitcham

Forest
Hill

10

Kooyong

Toorak

Wattle
Park

Box Hill
South

Blackburn
South

Forest Hill
Shopping
Centre

Vermont

11

Burwood

Burwood
East

Vermont
South

Toorak

Glen
Iris

Malvern

Ashburton

Mt
Waverley

Glen
Waverley

12

Caulfield

E Malvern

Waverley
Municipal
Public
Golf Course

13

Carnegie

Glenhuntly

Murrumbeena

ARTERIAL

1

J K L M N O P Q R

See fold-out page for an explanation of the map symbols

208

195

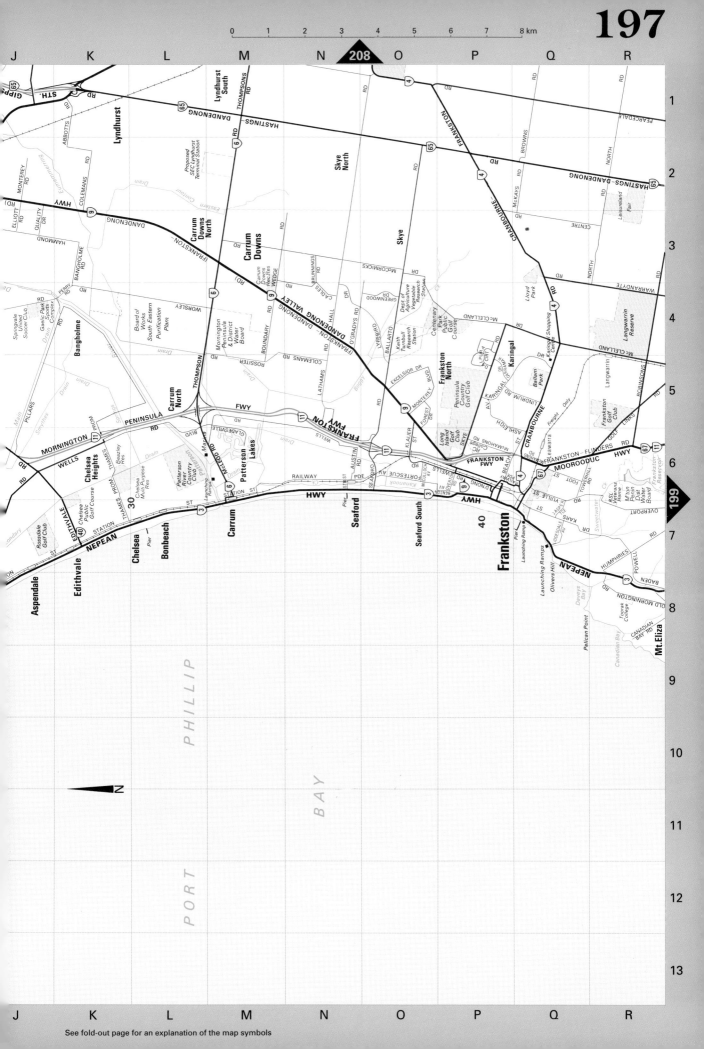

0 1 2 3 4 5 6 7 8 km

BELLARINE

PENINSULA

Indented Head

St.Leonards
South Red Bluff

PORT

PHILLIP

Mo

M

BAY

Swan
Bay

Edwards Pt.

Swan
Island

Golf
Bridge
Rabbit Island
Bridge
Pier

Mud
Island

Mt.Mart
Balcombe Pt.

Queenscliff

Lighthouse

Scout
Cam

MARINE

Martha Pt.

Mt. Martha
Public Pk.

THE RIP

Point
Nepean

Nepean
Bay

Ticonderoga
Bay

Dromana

Safety Beach

Cheviot
Beach

Weeroor
Bay

Lord Mayors
Pier
Camp

Collins
Bay

POINT
NEPEAN
NATIONAL
PARK

205

Portsea
Golf
Links

3

Sorrento
Golf
Club

Aquarium
Pier

CAPEL

SOUND

Dromana

"The Rocks"

NEPEAN
FWY

London
Bridge

LONDON
BRIDGE
RD

Portsea
Surf Beach

HOTHAM

RD

Sorrento

Sullivan Bay
"The Sisters"
Settlers Monument

Cameron
Bay

McCrae
Lighthouse

6

Chairlift
Arthurs Seat
Lookout

BOUNDARY

ARTHURS
SEAT
STATE
PARK

Sorrento
Ocean Beach

ST PAULS
RD

Sorrento
Down
Golf Club

20

Rosebud

MORNINGTON PENINSULA

11

Arthurs Seat
305m

R

Jubilee Pt.
Diamond
Bay

Blairgowrie

"Canterbury"

White
Cliffs

Rosebud
West

HWY

ARTHURS
SEAT
STATE
PARK

ARTHURS SEAT

Higgins
Corner

71

Koonya Beach
Pelleys Pt.
Spray Pt.

MELBOURNE

BULLDOG RD

NEPEAN

Rye

Tootgarook

3

1

Golf
Links

Kings
Waterfalls
Reserve

PURVES

MAIN CREEK

MORNINGTON

TUCKS

Koreen Pt.
Pearses Beach
Glenn Pt.

CANTERBURY

JETTY
RD

DUNDAS
RD

Observation
Hill

4

Rosebud
Country
Club

6

Drum

Drum

Falls

RD

Splitters

RD

4

MORN
Ridge

71

The Divide

RD

BROWNS

TRUEMANS
RD

BROWNS
3

RD

4

SHANDS

FLINDERS

Main
Ridge

BASS

Rye
Ocean
Beach

SANDY

67

Boneo

2

LIMESTONE
RD

RD

BALDRYS

BARKERS

RD

School Hill
184m

Meakin
Junction

PENINS

Capri
Beach

NATIONAL

TRUEMANS
RD

67

OLD CAPE SCHANCK RD

PATTERSON
RD

Lightwood

Point
Nepean
Nat Pk

GREENS
RD

Main
Ck

6

11

MORNINGTON-FLINDERS RD

Cotton

Hyldberry

Tree

Boags Rocks

Gunnamatta
Surf Beach

PARK

National
Golf
Club

Cape
Schanck
Golf
Club

ROGERS

LONG PT RD

22

ROSEBUD-

BONEO
RD

MEAKIN

Stockyard

Tea Tree Ck

South

Double

67

71

The Pinnacle
77m

Rowley
Rocks

4

Burrabong

4

FLINDERS

RD

The
Blowhole

STRAIT

N

Lighthouse
Angel Cave

Cape Schanck

Pulpit
Rock

Bushranger Bay

Picnic
Pt.

The Arch

Simmons
Bay

The Arch

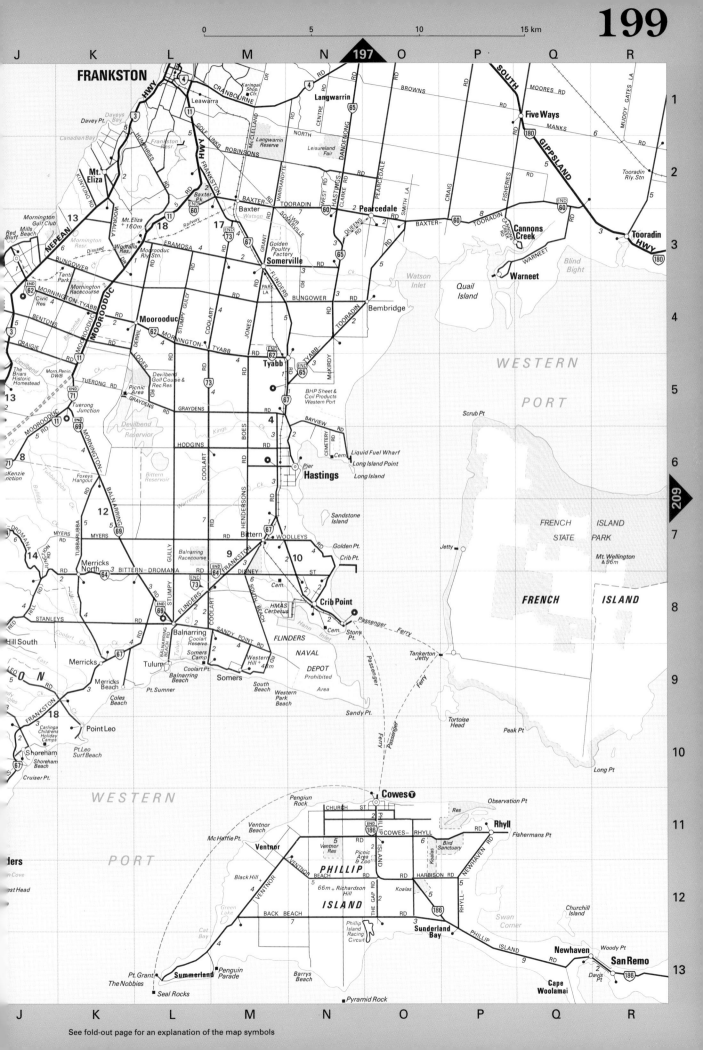

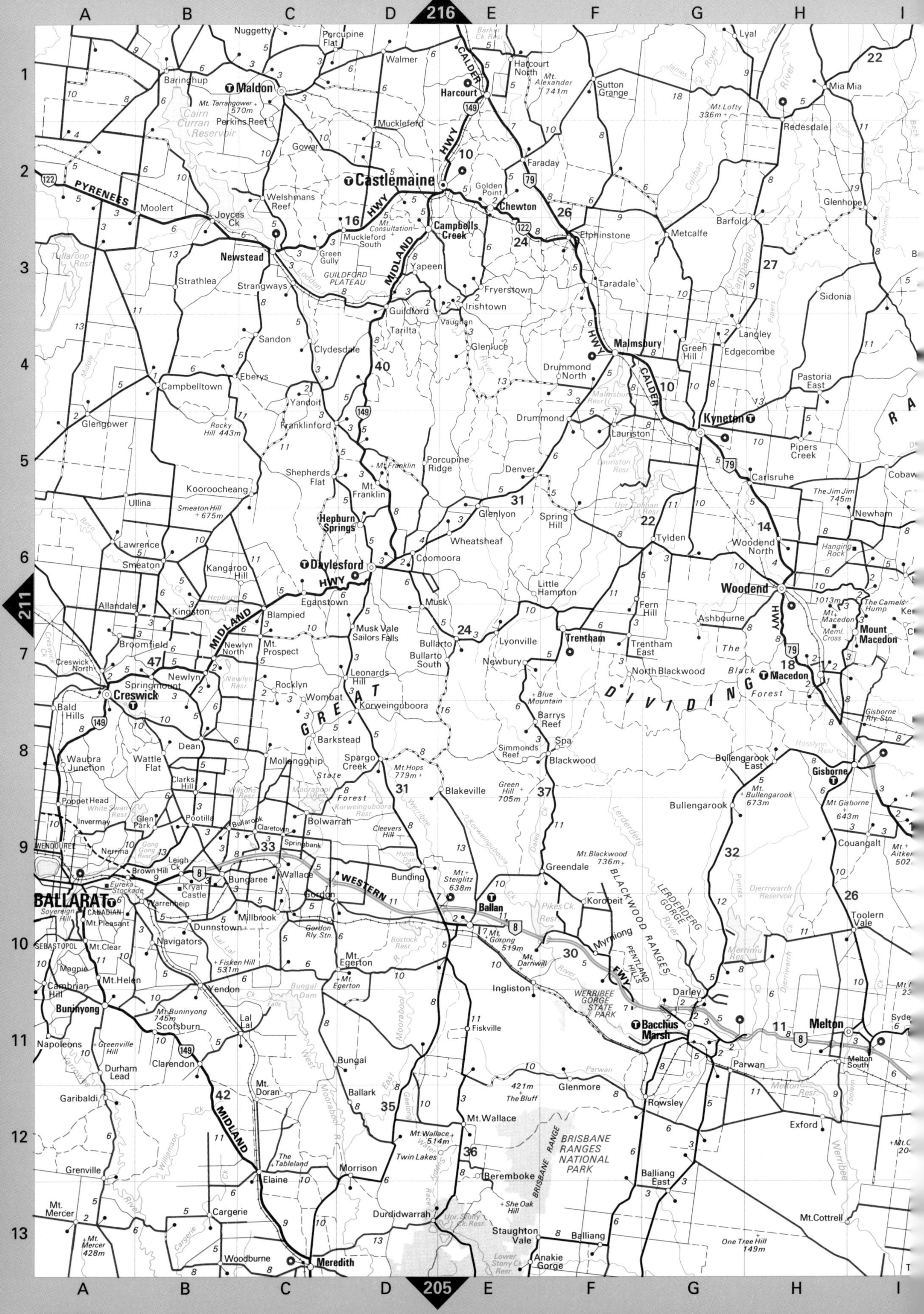

A B C D 216 E F G H I

1

Nuggetty
Porcupine Flat
Baringhup
Walmer
Harcourt North
Mt. Alexander 741m
Sutton Grange
Lyal
Mia Mia
22
Maldon
Mt. Tarrangower 570m
Harcourt
CALDER HWY
149
Mt. Lofty 336m
Redesdale

2
122
PYRENEES
Muckleford
10
Castlemaine
79
Faraday
Barfold
Glenhope
19
Cairn Curran Reservoir
Perkins Reef
Gower
Welshmans Reef
Joyces Ck
16
Mt. Consultation
Campbells Creek
Chewton
26
122
24
Elphinstone
Metcalfe

3
Moolort
Newstead
MIDLAND HWY
Yapeen
Golden Point
Taradale
27
Sidonia
Strathlea
Strangways
GUILDFORD PLATEAU
Green Gully
Muckleford South
Fryerstown
Irishtown
HWY

4
Sandon
Guildford
Vaughan
Tarilta
Drummond North
Malmsbury
Greeh Hill
Langley
Edgecombe
Pastoria East
Campbelltown
Clydesdale
40
Glenluce
CALDER
10
RA

5
Glengower
Ebery s
Yandoit
149
Franklinford
Rocky Hill 443m
Porcupine Ridge
Drummond
Denver
Lauriston
Kyneton
79
Pipers Creek
Carlsruhe
Cobaw
Ullina
Kooroocheang
Shepherds Flat
Mt. Franklin
Glenlyon
Spring Hill
22
The Jim Jim 745m
Newham

6
211
Lawrence
Smeaton
Smeaton Hill 675m
Kangaroo Hill
Hepburn Springs
Daylesford
Wheatsheaf
Coomoora
Little Hampton
Tylden
Woodend North
Hanging Rock
14
Woodend
Mt. Macedon
Meml. Cross
Mount Macedon
Allandale
Kingston
HWY
Eganstown
Musk
Lyonville
Fern Hill
Ashbourne
HWY

7
Creswick North
Broomfield
47
Newlyn North
MIDLAND
Mt. Prospect
Blampied
Musk Vale
Sailors Falls
24
Bullarto
Bullarto South
Newbury
Trentham
Trentham East
North Blackwood
The
Black
79
Macedon
18
Newlyn
Rocklyn
Leonards Hill
Korweinguboora
16
+ Blue Mountain
DIVIDING
Forest
Creswick
Springmount
Wombat
Barrys Reef
Spa

8
Bald Hills
149
Dean
Barkstead
Mt. Hops 779m
Blakeville
Green Hill 705m
Simmonds Reef
Blackwood
Bullengarook East
Gisborne
Waubra Junction
Wattle Flat
Clarks Hill
Mollongghip
Spargo Creek
31
37
Mt. Blackwood 736m
Bullengarook
Mt. Gisborne 643m

9
WENDOUREE
Invermay
Glen Park
Pootilla
Bullarook
Claretown
Bolwarrah
Cleevers Hill
Greendale
32
Couangalt
26
Nerrina
Leigh Ck
33
Springbank
Bunding
Mt. Steiglitz 638m
Koroobit
Mt. Aitken 502
BALLARAT
Brown Hill
8
Bungaree
Wallace
WESTERN
Ballan
8
BLACKWOOD RANGES
Toolern Vale

10
SEBASTOPOL
Mt. Clear
Navigators
Millbrook
Gordon
Gordon Rly. Stn.
Mt. Gorong 519m
30
Myrniong
FWY
Darley
11
Melton
Magpie
Cambrian Hill
Mt. Helen
Yendon
Mt. Egerton
Ingliston
Darriwill
PENTLAND HILLS
8
Melton South

11
Buninyong
Scotsburn
Lal Lal
Fiskville
Bacchus Marsh
Parwan
Napoleons
Greenville Hill
149
Clarendon
Bungal
Glenmore
Rowsley
Exford

12
Durham Lead
42
Mt. Doran
MIDLAND
35
Ballark
Mt. Wallace
36
Mt. Wallace
BRISBANE RANGES NATIONAL PARK
Balliang East
Garibaldi
Grenville
The Tableland
Elaine
Morrison
Twin Lakes
BRISBANE RANGE
Mt. Cottrell

13
Mt. Mercer
Mt. Mercer 428m
Cargerie
Woodburne
Meredith
Durdidwarrah
She Oak Hill
Staughton Vale
Anakie Gorge
Balliang
One Tree Hill 149m

A B C D 205 E F G H I

0   10   20   30   40 km

J K L M N O P Q R

216
39
31

1

Dellars Hill +281m
MILITARY TRAINING AREA
Mt.Puckapunyal 413m+
Scrub Hill 295m+
Army Camp
Puckapunyal
Mt. Rose +
Tarombe
The Peak +431m
Ruffy

75
Tooborac
Mt.Koala +574m
Mt.Lookout +487m
296m+ Stony Creek Hill
Heywoods Hill 320m
Greenshields Hill 336m
Seymour
Whiteheads Creek
WAGGS RANGE
Mt Helen 576m+
Mt.Tickatory 604m+
Dropmore

2

Emu Flat
Pyalong
Glenaroua
Tallarook
53
29
Meadows Hill 611m
Breech Peak 490m
Trawool
Granite
168
GOULBURN
Mt.Stewart
Kobyboyne
60
Wattle Hill 681m
Highlands
Caveat

29
34
High Camp
Moranding
BROWN RANGE
806m+ Mt.Tallarook
43
Kerrisdale
VALLEY
Goulburn
Ghin Ghin
Homewood
168
Yea
SWITZERLAND RANGES
Mt.Broughton 877m
Mt.Eaglehawk +532m
Killingworth
Cottons Pinch
153
14

3

ulla Vale
Mt.William 804m+
Broadford
Mt.Piper 442m+
Tyaak
One Tree Hill 486m
Strath Creek
HWY
Mt.Marianne 486m
THE YEA SPUR
Mt.Charlotte +
HWY
Cheviot
Limestone

4

Lancefield
17
Willowmavin
BALD HILLS
Sunday Creek
Reedy Creek
Murchison Gap 365m
473m+ Lades Hill
MINTOS HILLS
Mt.Bullamalite +523m
Spion Kopje 486m+
Murrindindi River

5

22
Kilmore
Kilmore East
75
HWY
32
Clonbinane
Monument Hill 490m+
Flowerdale
Hazeldene
557m+ Flagpole Hill
Break O'Day
Junction Hill 513m
Mt.Caroline 515m
42
218

6

Romsey
Springfield
Bylands
Pretty Sally
Wandong
Heathcote Junction
GREAT
HUME
Mt.Disappointment 795m+
RANGE
22
Devlins Bridge
153
MELBA
Glenburn
Mt.Klondyke
YEA RIVER PK
Wests Bridge
KINGLAKE NATIONAL PARK

7

Monegeetta North
Chintin
Darraweit Guim
Wallan
21
37
Bolinda
32
Wallan East
35
Merriang
Glenvale
Eden Park
Toorourrong Reservoir
Humevale
SHERWIN RANGES
Kinglake West
Masons Falls
Pheasant Creek
39
Kinglake Central
Gordons Bridge
Castella
Toolangi

8

Beveridge
Kalkallo
Bald Hill 358m
FWY
Whittlesea
Yan Yean Reservoir
Howatts Lookout 515m
Strathewen
Kinglake East
Kinglake
DIVIDING
KINGLAKE NATIONAL PARK
Mt.Jerusalem +
Mt.Slide

9

Sunbury
Konagaderra
Mickleham
Donnybrook
Woodstock
Yan Yean
Arthurs Creek
Mt.Everard +472m
34
Steels Creek
Dixons Creek
PAULS RANGE
25
26
Healesville West

10

Diggers Rest
Bulla
Yuroke
Mt.Aitken 266m
Craigieburn
Wollert
Mernda
Doreen
Nutfield
St.Andrews
One Tree Hill 372m+
Rob Roy
153
Tarrawarra
Healesville

Oaklands Junction
Somerton
Epping
40
South Morang
Yarrambat
Hurstbridge
Cottles Bridge
Panton Hill
Christmas Hills
Yarra Glen
Yering
34
22
HWY
Coldstream
Gruyere

11

32
39
40
Calder Raceway
Organ Pipes National Park
Melbourne Airport
TULLAMARINE
Greenvale Resr.
LALOR
MORANG SOUTH
WATTLE GLEN
DIAMOND CREEK
WATSONS CREEK
KANGAROO GROUND
WARRANDYTE STATE PK
Sugarloaf Reservoir
WARRANDYTE
WONGA PARK
CROYDON NORTH
LILYDALE
174
PIRIANDA GARDENS
WANDIN
WARBURTON
18
Woori Yallock

12

HWY 40
SYDENHAM
KEILOR
CALDER FWY
ST.ALBANS
KEILOR EAST
NIDDRIE
AIRPORT WEST
BROADMEADOWS
GLENROY
PASCOE VALE
FAWKNER
PRESTON
RESERVOIR
THOMASTOWN
BUNDOORA
GREENSBOROUGH
RESEARCH
ELTHAM
LOWER PLENTY
MONTMORENCY
MACLEOD
HEIDELBERG WEST
WARRANDYTE SOUTH
PARK ORCHARDS
RINGWOOD NORTH
CROYDON
MOOROOLBARK
MOUNT EVELYN
SILVAN
Yellingbo

13

37
Calder Park
radio Mast
Bottom Homestead
Pentons Hill
ESSENDON
MOONEE PONDS
COBURG
BRUNSWICK
THORNBURY
NORTHCOTE
FAIRFIELD
IVANHOE
ROSANNA
HEIDELBERG
TEMPLESTOWE LOWER
TEMPLESTOWE
DONCASTER EAST
DONCASTER
MITCHAM
40
MAROONDAH
RINGWOOD
BAYSWATER
THE BASIN
MONTROSE
Silvan Resr.
MT DANDENONG
OLINDA

DEER PARK
BRAYBROOK
MAIDSTONE
FOOTSCRAY
ASCOT VALE
PARKVILLE
CLIFTON HILL
KEW
BALWYN NORTH
SURREY HILLS
BOX HILL
BLACKBURN
NUNAWADING
FOREST HILL
VERMONT
BORONIA
WANTIRNA

SUNSHINE
ARDEER
BRAYBROOK
HWY
SOUTH YARRA
RICHMOND
HAWTHORN
CAMBERWELL
BURWOOD
BLACKBURN SOUTH
VERMONT SOUTH

8
Truganina
DERRIMUT
TOTTENHAM
BROOKLYN
YARRAVILLE
MELBOURNE
PRAHRAN
TOORAK
ARMADALE
MALVERN
ASHBURTON
BURWOOD HWY

WEST GATE
ALTONA NORTH
NEWPORT
Hobsons Bay
ST.KILDA

SPRING FWY
1
EASTERN FWY

196

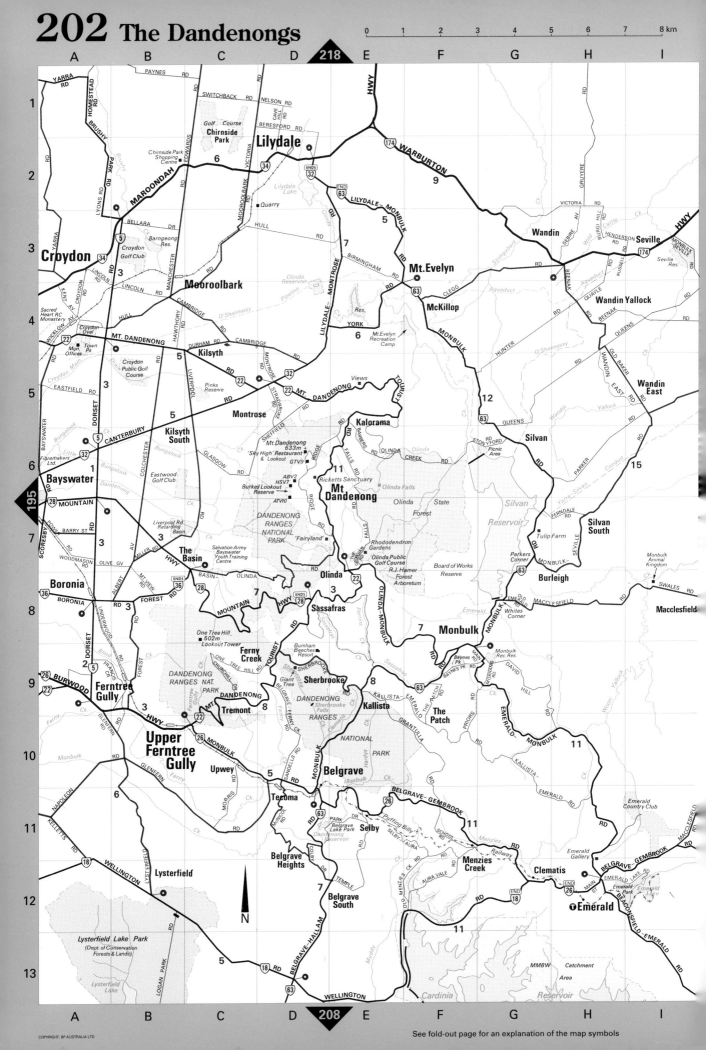

202 The Dandenongs

See fold-out page for an explanation of the map symbols

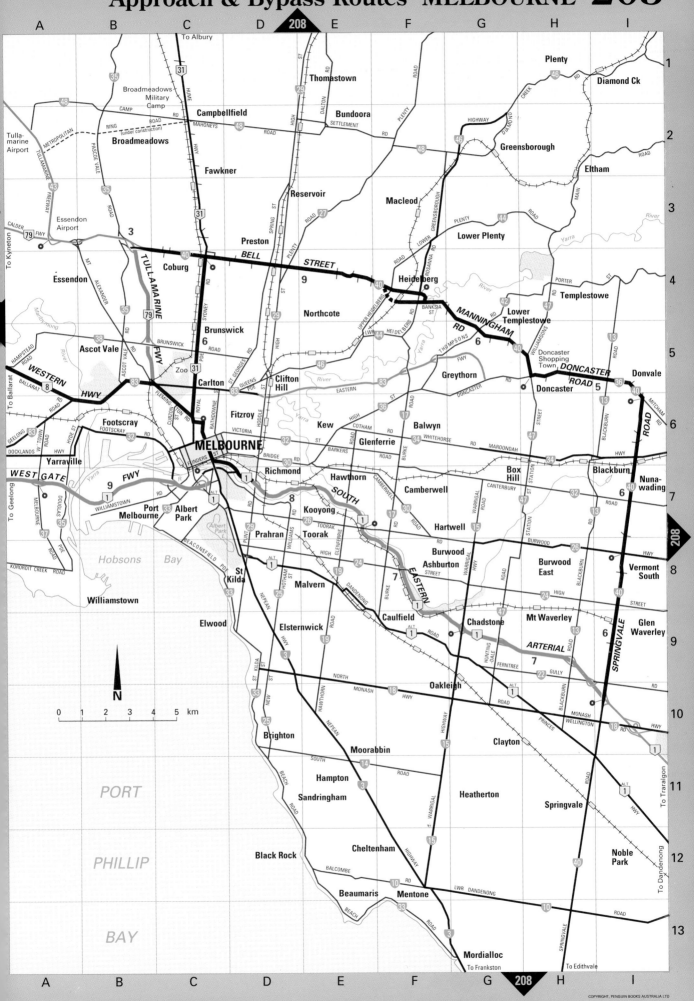

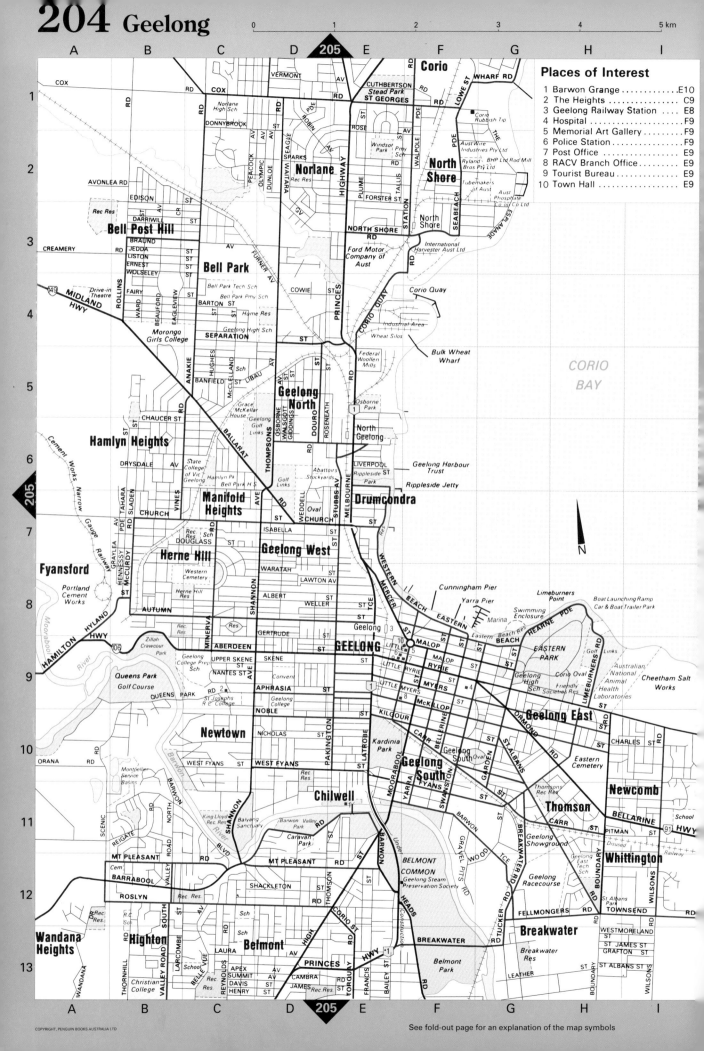

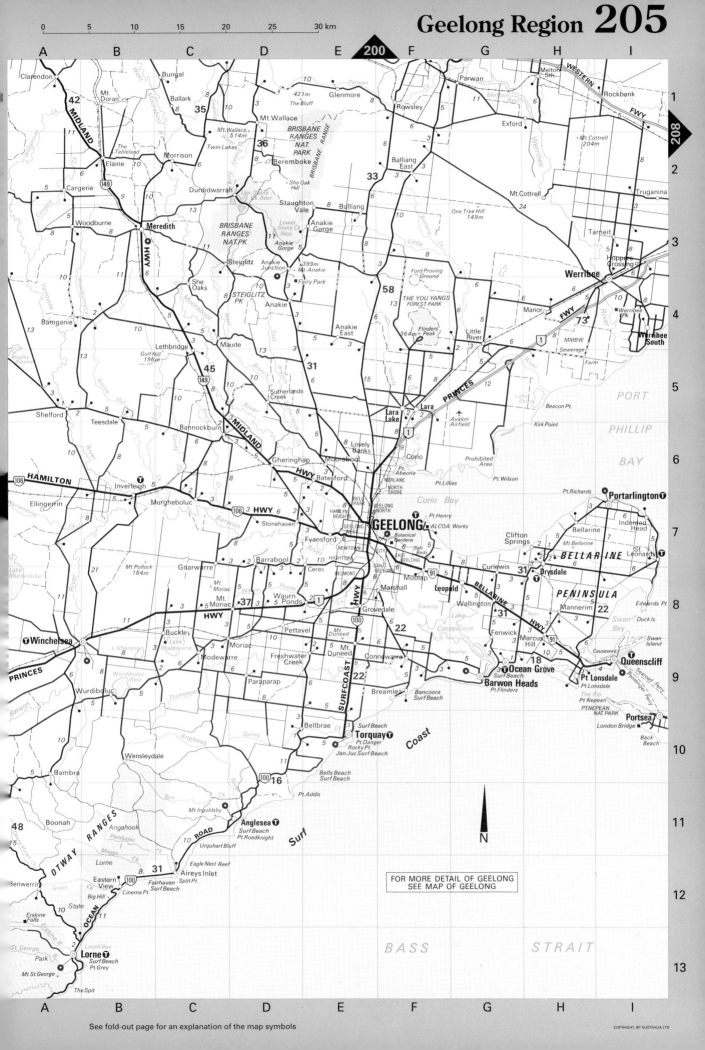

COPYRIGHT, BP AUSTRALIA LTD

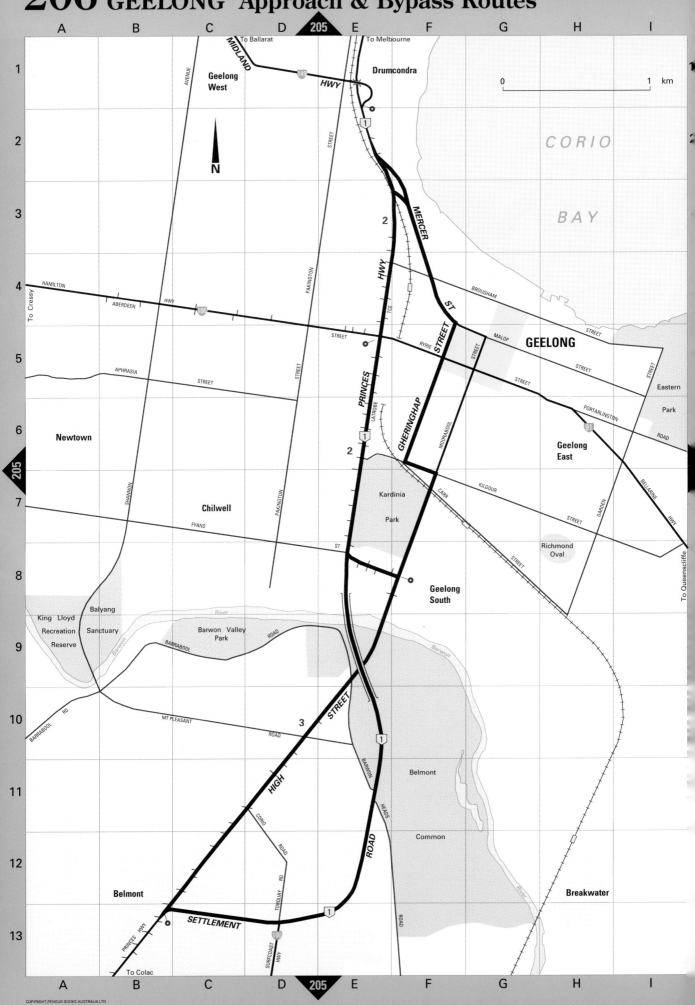

To Ballarat

To Melbourne

MIDLAND

HWY

149

Geelong
West

AVENUE

Drumcondra

N

0   1 km

CORIO

BAY

2

MERCER

HWY

STREET

PAKINGTON

HAMILTON

ABERDEEN   HWY   106

BROUGHAM

STREET

TCE

RYRIE   STREET   MALOP   STREET   GEELONG

PRINCES

STREET

LATROBE

STREET   STREET

Eastern
Park

APHRASIA   STREET

GHERINGHAP

MOORABOOL

PORTARLINGTON

91

Newtown

STREET

ROAD

BELLARINE

Geelong
East

2

SHANNON

PAKINGTON

Kardinia

Park

CARR   KILGOUR

STREET

GARDEN

HWY

Chilwell

FYANS

ST

Richmond
Oval

205

To Queenscliffe

Balyang

River

STREET

King Lloyd
Recreation
Reserve

Sanctuary

Barwon Valley
Park

BARRABOOL

ROAD

Barwon

Barwon

Geelong
South

River

Breakwater

BARRABOOL   RD

MT PLEASANT

ROAD

3

STREET

1

HIGH

BARWON

Belmont

CORIO

ROAD

HEADS

Common

Belmont

TORQUAY   RD

ROAD

SETTLEMENT

1

River

PRINCES HWY

SURFCOAST HWY

100

To Colac

205

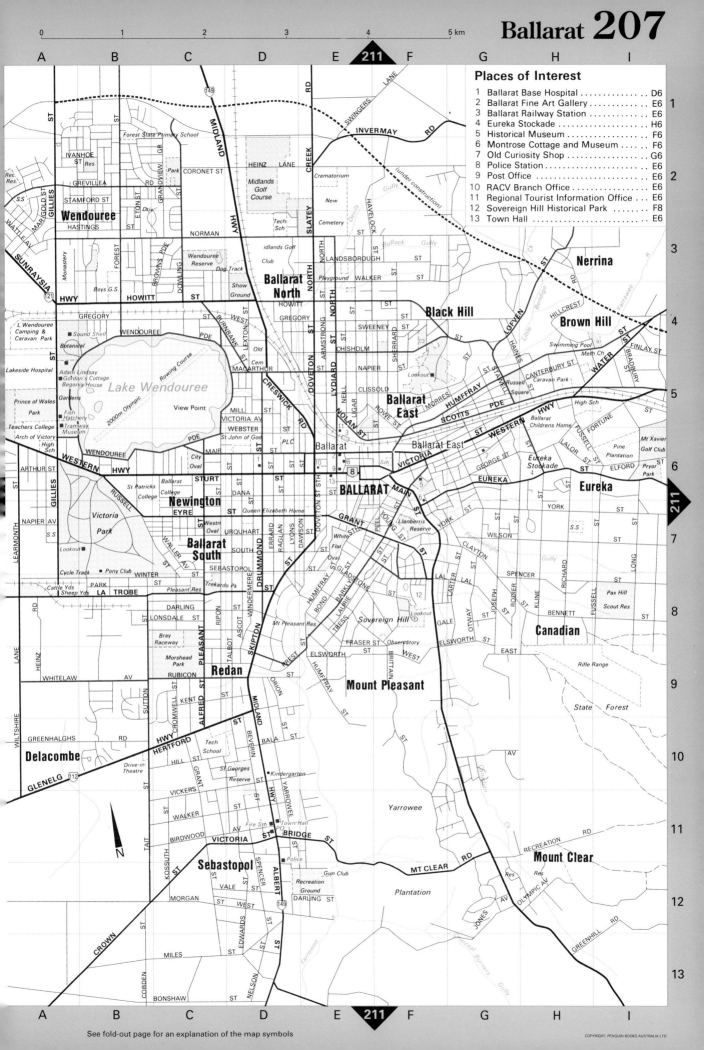

0 1 2 3 4 5 km

A B C D E **211** F G H I

Places of Interest

1 Ballarat Base Hospital D6
2 Ballarat Fine Art Gallery E6
3 Ballarat Railway Station E6
4 Eureka Stockade H6
5 Historical Museum F6
6 Montrose Cottage and Museum F6
7 Old Curiosity Shop G6
8 Police Station E6
9 Post Office E6
10 RACV Branch Office E6
11 Regional Tourist Information Office . . . E6
12 Sovereign Hill Historical Park F8
13 Town Hall E6

Nerrina

Wendouree

Ballarat North

Black Hill

Brown Hill

HILLCREST

Lake Wendouree

Ballarat East

Ballarat East

Newington

Ballarat South

BALLARAT

Eureka Stockade

Eureka

Sovereign Hill

Mount Pleasant

Canadian

State Forest

Redan

Delacombe

Rifle Range

Yarrowee

Mount Clear

Sebastopol

Plantation

See fold-out page for an explanation of the map symbols

COPYRIGHT, PENGUIN BOOKS AUSTRALIA LTD

216

211

FOR MORE DETAIL OF BALLARAT SEE MAP OF BALLARAT
FOR MORE DETAIL OF GEELONG SEE MAP OF GEELONG REGION
FOR MORE DETAIL OF MELBOURNE SEE MAP OF MELBOURNE AND SUBURBS

MELBOURNE

BALLARAT

GEELONG

Werribee

Sunbury

Kyneton

Woodend

Daylesford

Creswick

Bacchus Marsh

Melton

Broadford

Kilmore

Lancefield

Frankston

Mornington

Hastings

Dandenong

Queenscliff

Ocean Grove

Barwon Heads

Torquay

Anglesea

Lorne

Winchelsea

Sorrento

Rosebud

Rye

Cowes

Portarlington

Drysdale

Port Phillip Bay

Bass Strait

WILSONS PROMONTORY NATIONAL PARK

Wilsons Promontory

Tidal River

Mt.Vereker 637m

N

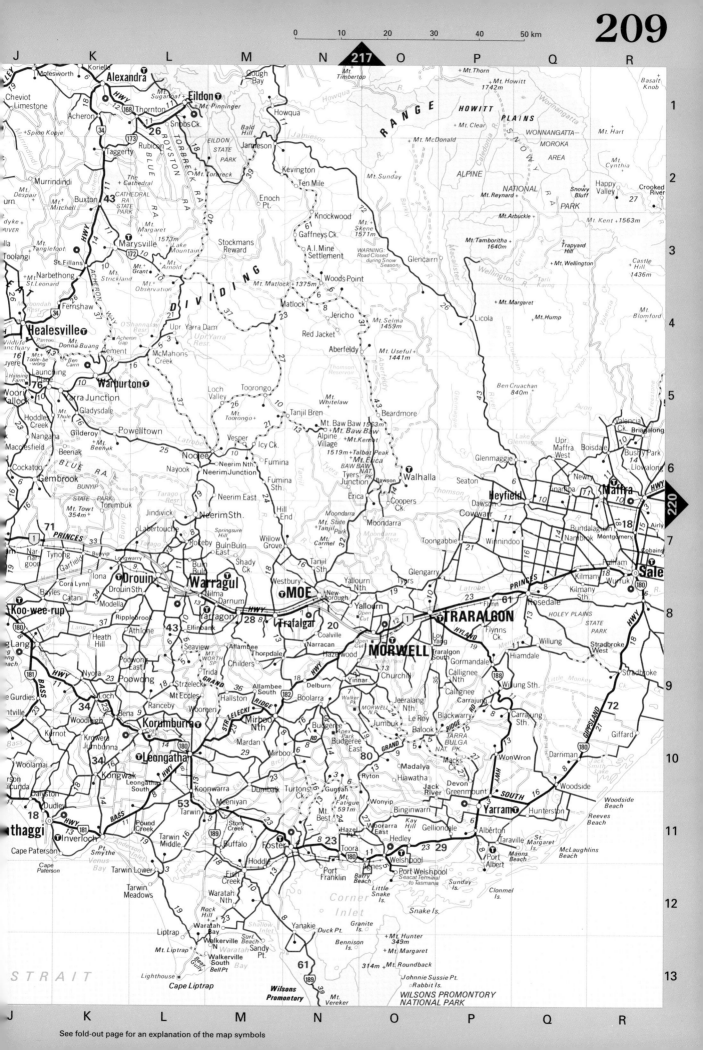

212

273

SOUTH AUSTRALIA

WESTERN DISTRICT

Discovery Bay

Portland Bay

SOUTHERN

N

Struan, Joanna, Langkoop, Kadnook, Harrow, Glenelg, THE BLACK RANGE, BLACK RANGE STATE PARK, Mt Becha, Cave of Fishes
Wrattonbully, Powers Creek, Connewirricoo, Moree, Culla, Balmoral, Rocklands Reservoir, Glenisla, Cave of Hands, GRAMPIANS NATIONAL, Woohlpooer
Glenroy, Poolaijelo, Chetwynd, Tarrayoukyan, Pigeon Ponds, Glendinning, Caddens Flat, The Chimney Pots, VICTORIA
Comaum, DERGHOLM STATE PARK, Brimboal, Nareen, Coojar, Englefield, Vasey, Gatum, Mooralla
Coonawarra, Dorodong, Dergholm, Konong Wootong North, Brit Brit, Mt Dundas 468m, Mt Machersay, Mona Park
Penola, Roseneath, Wando Bridge, Wando Vale, Konong Wootong, Wootong Vale, Melville Forest, Gringegalgona, Cavendish, Victoria Pt, Victoria Point
Krongart, Lake Mundi, Dunrobin, Carapook, Gritjurk, Bulart, Kyup, Mt Cavendish, Karabeal, Vic Vall
Nangwarry, Heathfield, Casterton, Sandford, Hilgay, Coleraine, Parkwood, Wannon, Strathkellar, Moutajup, Dun
Kalangadoo, Lindsay, Strathdownie, Henty, Paschendale, Tarrenlea, Hensley Park, Kanawalla, Bochara, Tarrington, Warrayure
Tarpeena, Ardno, Myaring, Menno, Tahara Bridge, Tahara, Hamilton, Yulecart, Yatchaw, Croxton East, Tabor
Mt Gambier, Glenburnie, Puralka, Marp, Digby, Grassdale, Branxholme, Buckleys Swamp, Mt Napier 412m, Penshurst
O.B. Flat, Yahl, Caroline, Dartmoor, Winnap, Hotspur, Wallacedale, Byaduk North, Gazette
Mt Schank, Mumbannar, Greenwald, Myamyn, Condah, Byaduk, Warrabrook, Macarthur, Mt Eccles
Allendale East, Wanwin, Drik Drik, Lyons, Milltown, Lake Condah, Knebsworth, Hawkesdale
Ewens Ponds, Nelson, Mt Vandyke, Drumborg, Homerton, Mt Eccles Nat Pk, Broadwater, Dunmore
Port Macdonnell, LOWER GLENELG NATIONAL PARK, Kentbruck, Heywood, Tyrendarra, Bessiebelle, Orford, Widatook
Mt Kincaid, Mt Richmond, Heathmere, Mt Clay, Tyrendarra East, St Helens, Tooloo
Gorae West, Gorae, Narrawong, Codrington, Yambuk, Rosebro
Cashmore, Bolwarra, PRINCES HWY, Aringa, Port Fairy
Tarragal, Portland, Cape Reamur
Cape Duquesne, Cape Bridgewater, Trewalla, Mt Chaucer, Pt Danger, Lawrence Rocks, Cape Sir William Grant, Lady Julia Percy Is.
Cape Nelson, CAPE NELSON STATE PK

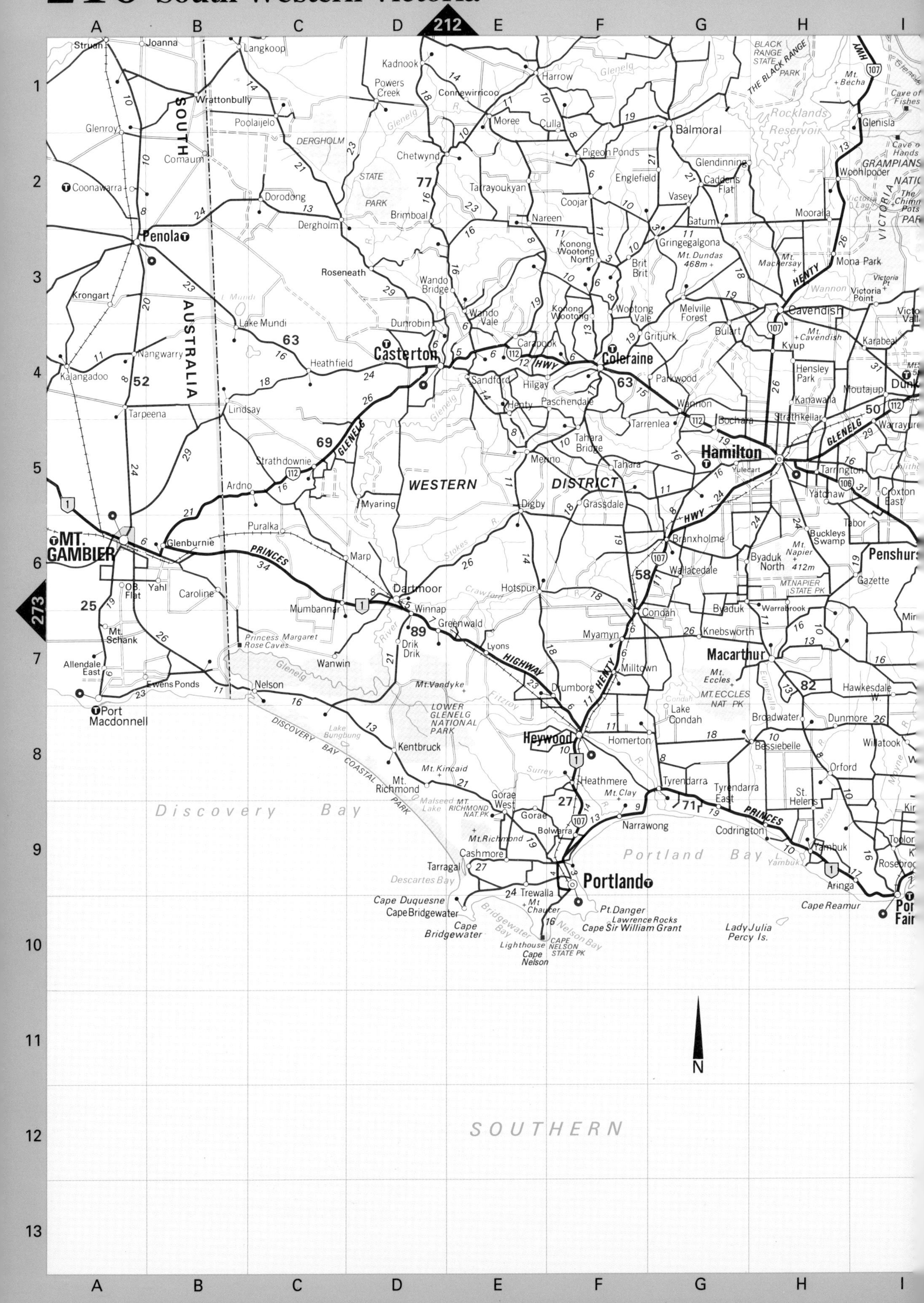

COPYRIGHT, BP AUSTRALIA LTD

FOR MORE DETAIL OF BALLARAT
SEE MAP OF BALLARAT

A B C D ▼214 E F G H I

1

WYPERFELD

BIG   DESERT   NATIONAL

Dattuck
Burroin
L. Brambruk
Hopetoun
West
Nypo
Goyura

PARK

2

LAKE
ALBACUTYA
PARK

SOUTH

BIG DESERT
WILDERNESS

Moonlight
Tank

Lake
Albacutya

Hopetoun

Yaapeet
Albacutya
16

3

VICTORIA

Mt.Little Doughboy

N

Kurnbrunin

Pella

21
Hopevale
48
Roseber
Beula
25

Rainbow
16 Kenmare
Beulah
West

4

Mt.Shaugh
Mt.Shaugh
Conservation
Park
Red Bluff

Broken Bucket
Tank

WIMMERA

Lake
Hindmarsh

Perenna

Werrap
Pullut

Brentwood
Dalmalee

32

Ellam

68
Galaqui
61
Br

Willenabrina

5

AUSTRALIA

Yanac

Baker

Netherby

Lorquon
West

Lorquon

8
10

Detpa
22
Allanby

Jeparit
Peppers
Plain
45
27
Angip
Batchica
Crymillan
Yellangip

Aubrey
18
Warracknabeal

Telopea
Downs

Broughton

Yanac
South

8

Woorak
West

23

Tarranyurk
10

6

Sandsmere
Bleak
House

Boyeo

Propodollah
Balrpotan
North

Ni Ni
45

Glenlee

Woorak

Antwerp
37

Cannum

20
BORUNG

Yearinga
Yarrock

Diapur

Katyll
Wallup
Ailsa
Kellala

7

273
Bordertown

Dinyarrak
Lillimur

Miram

Tarranginnie
18

Nhill
13
13

Salisbury
39
Gerang
Gerung

Arkona
17

138
42

Murra
Warra
Blackheath
60

12
5
13
8
43
Serviceton
Kaniva
10
WESTERN
Mt.Elgin
40
21
HWY
Kiata
10
16
11
Dart
Dart
Byrneville

Lawloit
6
13
Wolseley

Lillimur
South
Miram
South
Kinimakatka
Winiam
Winiam
East

Dimboola
11
Wail
9
Kalkee

8

Poognagoric
Custon

Yanipy

LITTLE   DESERT   NATIONAL   PARK

35

8
Pimpinio

Jung
16

Bangham
45
35
Dahlen
19
Dooen
107

9

Wallabrook
13

Lemon
Springs

Grass Flat

Polkemmet
15

130
Horsham

Minimay
Peronne
Goroke
13
Duffholme
Mitre
Quantong
Vectis
Haven

Frances
13

Mortat
10

Gymbowen
18
Mt.
Arapiles
TOOAN
Natimuk
27

Green
Lake
Drung
Sth.

10

Binnum
Neuarpurr
Morea
(Carpolac)
Dopewarra
23
Kangawall
MT.ARAPILES
STATE
PARK
Tooan
Tooan
East
10
Lwr
Norton

McKenzie
Creek
Wonwondah
East

Booroopki
18
Karnak
16
98
Noradjuha
Wonwondah
North
21
124

Tallageira
Bringalbert
14
Ozenkadnook
15
130
Clear
Lake
Jallumba
6
Nurrabiel
Mockinya

Kybybolite
24
Patyah
Awonga
Ullswater
Miga Lake
14
Clear
Lake

11

Hynam
Jessie
53
130
Apsley
Charam
Wombelano
13
23
Toolondo
Connangorach
21
AMH
Brimpaen

Naracoorte
11
11
10
WIMMERA
21
Douglas
107
77

Naracoorte Caves
Conservation Park
Koppamurra
21
Edenhope
11
Scrubby
Lake
Charam
21
Mt.
Evins
Jeffries
21
Telangatuk
East
RANGE

12

Joanna
Meereek
Langkoop
19
Kadnook
5
18
Harrow
18
Telangatuk
Kanagulk
BLACK
RANGE
STATE
PARK
Cherrypool
Zumst
McKenzie

Struan
8
14
Powers
Creek
14
Connewirricoo
10
19
Balmoral
Mt.
Becha

13

Glenroy
Poolaijelo
DERGHOLM
STATE PARK
Moree
Culla
Pigeon Ponds
Glendinning
Rocklands
Reservoir
Glenisla
Cave of NA
Fishes

Comaum
Chetwynd
Cave of
Hands
GRAM

A B C D ▼210 E F G H I

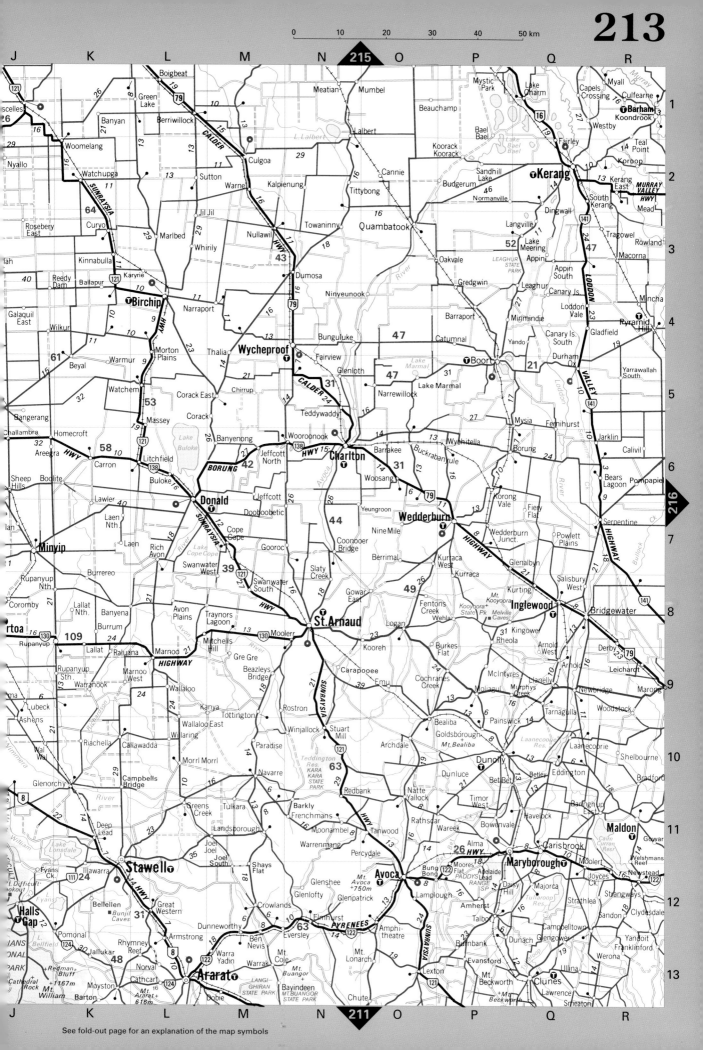

0   10   20   30   40   50 km

J   K   L   M   N ▼215 O   P   Q   R

Myall
Murray
Capels
Crossing 76   Culfearne
♦Barham
Koondrook
Westby
Teal
Point
Koroop

Boigbeat
Meatian   Mumbel
Beauchamp
Mystic
Park
Lake
Charm

79
19
Green
Lake
Berriwillock
CALDER
Lalbert

Woomelang
Banyan
Watchupga
L. Lalbert
Culgoa

Bael
Bael
Lake
Bael
Bael
Fairley
16

Koorack
Koorack
♦Kerang
Kerang
East
MURRAY
VALLEY
HWY

Nyallo
Sutton
Warnel
Kalpienung
Tittybong
Cannie
Quambatook

Sandhill
Lake
Budgerum
Normanville
46
Langville
South
Kerang
141
Mead

SUNRAYSIA
64
Curyo
Jil Jil
Nullawil
Towaninny
18

Dingwall
Appin
52
Lake
Meering
Appini
Langville
24
47
Tragowel
Rowland
Macorna

Rosebery
East
Marlbed
Whirily
43

Oakvale
River
Gredgwin
Appin
South
Leaghur
LEAGHUR
STATE
PARK
Canary Is.
Loddon
Vale
23
Durham
Ox
Mincha

Kinnabulla
Karyrie
121
Ballapur
Reedy
Dam
40
10
Dumosa
Ninyeunook
79
Barraport
Catumnal
47
Minmindie
Canary Is.
South
Yando
Gladfield
Yarrawallah
South

Galaquil
East
Wilkur
♦Birchip
Narraport
MH
16
Buluguke
Fairview
♦Boort
Mysia
Femihurst
Pyramid
Hill
19

61
Beyal
Warmur
Morton
Plains
Thalia
WYCHEPROOF
47
CALDER
Glenloth
31
Narrewillock
Lake
Marmal
21
141
Bears
Lagoon
Pompapie

Challambra
Watchem
53
Corack East
Chirrup
Corack
Teddywaddy
Lake
Marmal
Borung
24
Calivil

Bangerang
Homecroft
58
Massey
Litchfield
Banyenong
Wooroonook
Barrakee
Wychitella
Jarklin

Sheep
Hills
Bodlite
Carron
BORUNG
42
Jeffcott
North
HWY
CHARLTON
Woosang
31
13
Buckrabanyule
79
Korong
Vale
Fiery
Flat
Serpentine

Lawler
Donald
Jeffcott
26
Yeungroon
Nine Mile
♦Wedderburn
Wedderburn
Junct.
Powlett
Plains
HIGHWAY

Minyip
Laen
Nth.
SUNRAYSIA
Dooboobetic
44
Coonooer
Bridge
Berrimal
Kurraca
West
Kurraca
Glenalbyn
21

Rupanyup
Nth.
Laen
Rich
Avon
Cope
Cope
Gooroc
Slaty
Creek
49
Kurting
Salisbury
West
Inglewood
Bridgewater
141

Coromby
Burrereo
Swanwater
West
39
121
Swanwater
South
Gowar
East
Fentons
Creek
Wehla
Mt.
Kooyoora
Kooyoora
State Pk
Melville
Caves
Rheola
Arnold
West
Arnold
Derby
79
Leichardt
Marong

Lubeck
Ashens
Banyena
Burrum
Avon
Plains
Traynors
Lagoon
Mooler
130
St.Arnaud
Logan
Kooreh
Burkes
Flat
McIntyres
Llanelly
Murphys
Creek
Newbridge
Woodstock

Wal
Wal
Riachella
Callawadda
Kanya
Tottington
Rostron
13
HIGHWAY
Carapooee
Emu
Cochranes
Creek
Bealiba
Goldsborough
Mt.Bealiba
Moliagul
Painswick
Tarnagulla
Laanecoorie
Res.
Laanecoorie
Shelburne

Glenorchy
Campbells
Bridge
Morrl Morrl
Paradise
Winjallock
Stuart
Mill
63
Archdale
Dunolly
Betley
Eddington
Bradford
Maldon

Deep
Lead
Greens
Creek
Tulkara
Navarre
Redbank
121
KARA
KARA
STATE
PARK
Natte
Yallock
Dunluce
Bet Bet
Betley
Barnghup
East

Stawell
Joel
Joel
Joel
South
Barkly
Frenchmans
Moonambel
Tanwood
Rathscar
Timor
West
Wareek
Bowenvale
Havelock
Carisbrook
Cairn
Curran
Res.
Gowar
Welshmans
Reef
Newstead

Halls
Gap
Illawarra
111
24
Bellellen
Great
Western
Shays
Flat
Warrenmang
Percydale
Alma
26
HWY
Moores
Flat
Adelaide
Lead
Amherst
Daisy
Hill
Majorca
Joyces
Ck
122

Pomonal
Rhymney
Reef
Dunneworthy
Armstrong
Crowlands
Glenshee
Glenlofty
Avoca
Bung
Bong
122
PADDYS
RANGE
SP
Maryborough
Moolert
Strathlea
Strangways

124
Jallukar
48
Norval
Ben
Nevis
Eversley
63
Elmhurst
Glenpatrick
Amphi-
theatre
Lamplough
PYRENEES
122
Talbot
Dunach
Campbelltown
Glengower
Yandoit
Franklinford

Cathcart
Ararat
Warra
Yadin
Warrak
Mt.
Cole
Mt.
Lonarch
Chute
Lexton
Burnbank
Mt.
Beckworth
Clunes
Ullina
Lawrence
Smeaton

Halls
Gap
Moyston
Dobie
LANGI
GHIRAN
STATE PARK
BAYINDEEN
MT.BUANGOR
STATE PARK

J   K   L   M   N ▼211 O   P   Q   R

214 North Western Victoria

116

Lake Victoria

SILVER CITY HWY 79

Cal Lal
Rufus River
16
Lock 7
Lindsay
Lindsay Island
43
Murray River
Darling R.
Curlwaa
18
Wentworth
Lock 10
8
16
Yelta
32
29
19
Merbein
Buronga
Gol Gol
Lindsay Point
Neds Corner
Lock 8
Wallpolla Island
Ck.
14
Merbein West
Birdwoodton
Merbein Sth
MILDURA
Lake Wallawalla
Lock 9
Kulnine E.
15
Irymple
Billabong
Sunny Cliffs
Monak
Yamba
13
20
18 STURT
16
Meringur North
24 HWY
Kulnine
Lake Cullulleraine
19
Merrinee North
24
Koorlong
16
6
8
Red Cliffs
Karadoc
117
Lake Cullulleraine
Cardross
Thurla
CALDER
Yatpool
20

Taldra
11
13
13
11
Benetook
18
Iraak
Ingatta
Morkalla
Karween
Meringur
19
Werrimull
Karawinna
Merrinee
19
Pirlta
Ginquam
Carwarp
Nangiloc
23
16
Yarrara
26
Bambill
Tarrango
10
68
Colignan
Noora
Tunart
Kurnwill
Bambill South
Boonoonar
8
Pungonda
Nowingi
Nangri
10
79
20
HATTAH–KULKYNE NATIONAL PARK
Taplan
Rocket Lake
Meribah
267
SUNSET
YANGA – NYAWI
Hattah
14
COUNTRY
(MURRAY – SUNSET)
NATIONAL PARK
HWY
12
N
Mt. Crozier
Mt. Cowra
Trinita
Bernook
PINK LAKES
Wymlet
34
14
Peebinga
STATE - PARK
Kiamal
8
Mt. Gnarr
Mt. Jess
Paignie
Galah
Ouyen
AUSTRALIA
Pink Lakes
Kattyong
30
Tiega
10
Koonda
Mt. Grey
Walpeup
Timberoo
Boulka
Nun
Boltons Bore
"Goongee"
Pallarang
HWY
14
Torrita
8
35
Bronzewing
Sunset
Linga
19
Underbool
24
12
Manya
Tyalla
Boinka
Timberoo Sth.
Gypsum
Mulcra
Duddo
Tutye
24
12
Gunner
66
Panitya
18 Carina
137
13
Temp
MALLEE
Cowangie
Dering
Pinnaroo
Murrayville
18 Danyo
Kelley Lookout
Mt. Observatory
Patchewollock
27
Sp
Ngallo
6
O'Sullivan Lookout
Mt. Jenkins
Baring
Willa
Tur We
Lake Agnes
Yarto
Scorpion Springs Conservation Park
WYPERFELD
Wonga L.
52
BIG DESERT
NATIONAL
Dattuck
WILDERNESS
PARK
L. Brambruk
BIG   DESERT
LAKE ALBACUTYA PARK
Burroin
Hopetoun West
Mt. Little Doughboy
Nypo
Hopetoun

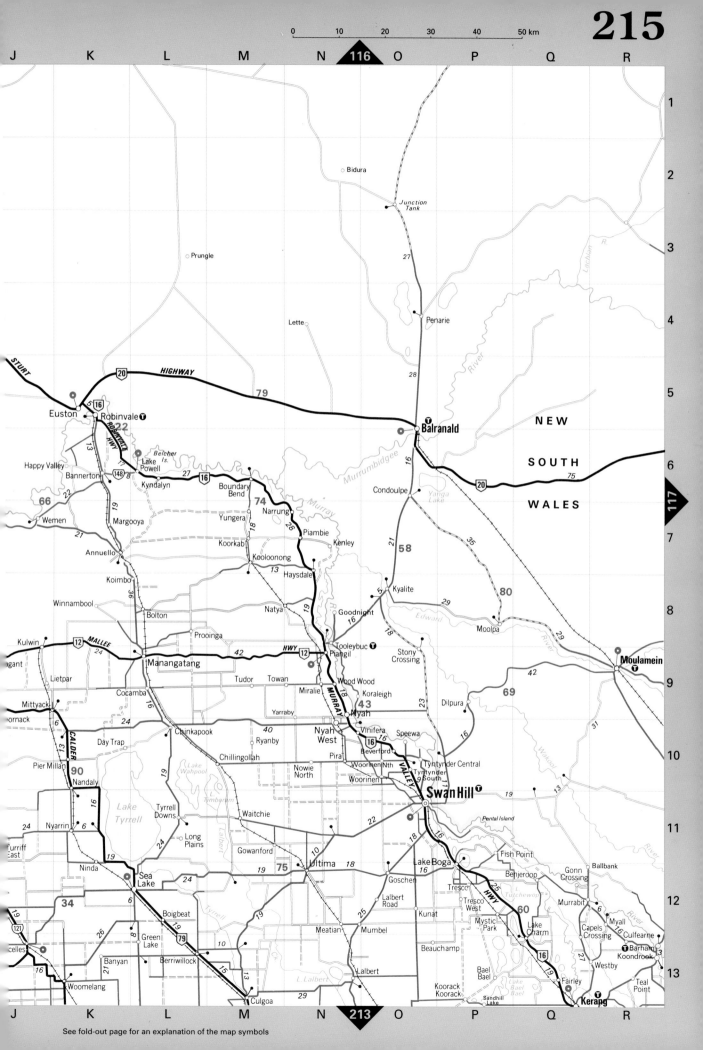

A B C D 116 E F G H I

RIVERINA

1   Lake Charm   Myall   Capels Crossing   Culfearne   Caldwell   Barham   Koondrook   Murray Valley Hwy   16   Fairley   Westby

2   Kerang   Kerang East   Teal Point   Koroop   Gannawarra   Cohuna   Bunnaloo   Mathoura   76   Highway   South Kerang   Mead   McMillans   Wee-Wee-Rup   82   75

3   Normanville   Dingwall   Langville   Lake Meering   Appin   52   Leaghur State Pk   47   Tragowel   Rowland   Macorna   Leitchville   Torrumbarry Weir   Womboota   Barmah State Park   Top Is.   Barmah   Picola North   Yalca North   16

4   Minmindie   Appin South   Canary Is.   Loddon Vale   Mincha   Mt. Hope   Bald Rock   Gunbower   Patho   97   Torrumbarry   Barnes   Murray   Barmah Is.   Barmah   Picola   Barwo   Narioka   Nathalia

5   Yando   Boort   21   Canary Is. South   Gladfield   Durham Ox   Pyramid Hill   Terrick Terrick State Park   Terrick Terrick   Sylvaterre   Roslynmead   Wharparilla Nth   Wharparilla   Moama   Echuca   Echuca Village   McCoys Bridge   Kanyapella   Yambuna   Kotupna   Wyuna   Undera Nth   57   Kaarimba

6   Mysia   Ferrihurst   Yarrawalla South   Mologa   Mt. Terrick Terrick   Mitiamo   Kotta   Bamawm Extension   Lockington   Barnawm   47   Strathallan   Koyuga   Simmie   Tongala   Kyvalley   Kyabram   St. Germains   Undera

7   Borung   213   Fiery Flat   Jarklin   Calivil   Prairie   Bears Lagoon   Pompapiel   Milloo   Tennyson   Warragamba   Ballendella   Rochester   Diggora   TarryDell   Nanneella   Timmering   Girgarre   Stanhope   Merrigum   Gillieston   Cooma   Tatura   149

8   Serpentine   82   Highway   Summerfield   Tandarra   Dingee   Drummartin   Hunter   Elmore   149   Mt. Burrumboot   Runnymede   Corop   60   Midland   Highway   Harston   Toolamba   Dhurringile   Arcadia

9   Glenalbyn   Powlett Plains   Salisbury West   Inglewood   Kurting   Bridgewater   Raywood   Kamarooka State Park   Neilborough East   Neilborough   Goornong   Wellsford   Avonmore   May Reef   Avonmore   Creek View   Colbinabbin   Colbinabbin West   Burrumboot   Rushworth   Wanalta   Mathiesons   Waranga Res.   Waranga   Murchison   Murchison East

10   Kingower   Arnold West   Derby   79   Leichardt   Myers Flat   Eaglehawk   Epsom   Fosterville   Ragshot   Barnadown   Myola   Muskerry West   52   Toolleen   Mt. Camel   Cornella   Angustown   Goulburn Weir   Whroo   Wahring   79

11   Murphys Creek   Arnold   Newbridge   Marong   Maiden Gully   BENDIGO   Kangaroo Flat   Junortoun   Longlea   Axedale   McIvor   47   141   Knowsley   Ladys Pass   Mt Camel   Redcastle   Moormbool   Mt Black +318m   Bailieston   Graytown   Wattle Vale   Reedy Lake   Nagambie   Locksley

12   Tarnagulla   Woodstock   Painswick   Laanecoorie Res.   Lockwood   Lockwood South   Shelbourne   Sedgwick   79   149   Mandurang   Strathfieldsaye   Axe Creek   Eppalock   Lake Eppalock   Knowsley   Mt Ida +450m   Costerfield   Graytown   Mitchellstown   Tabilk   Monea   39   Avenel   Mt. Bernard   HUME

13   Llanelly   Dunolly   Betley   Eddington   Bradford   Ravenswood   Ravenswood South   29   Pilchers Bridge   Myrtle Bridge   Sutton Grange   Lyal   Derrinal   Heathcote   Mt. Puckapunyal 413m   Puckapunyal   Army Camp   Northwood   Seymour   31   Whiteheads Creek

Havelock   Baringhup East   Maldon   Gowar   Barkers Ck   Mt Alexander 741m   Harcourt   10   Mia Mia   Redesdale   Argyle   Majors Line   Tooborac   50   Range   Trawool   Mt. Eaglehawk

Maryborough   122   Carisbrook   Moolort   Castlemaine   Welshmans Reef   Chewton   14   Faraday   Metcalfe   Barfold   Glenhope   Emu Flat   Pyalong   Glenaroua   Tallarook   Granite   29   Kerrisdale

Daisy Hill   Majorca   Joyces Ck   48   Newstead   Elphinstone   Taradale   122   Langley   Sidonia   Baynton   Nulla Vale   High Camp   Glenaroua   Broadford   Mt. Tallarook   Homewood   Strath Ck

Strathlea   Strangways   Yapeen   Guildford   Vaughan   Malmsbury   22   Edgecombe   Pastoria   Dividing   Range   Tyaak

Campbelltown   Glengower   Sandon   Clydesdale   Glenluce   Drummond   Franklinford   Werona   Yandoit   Mt Franklin   Denver   Laurison Res.   Kyneton   Pipers Ck   Carlsruhe   Langley   Great   Lancefield   Reedy Ck   Lades Hill   Flowerdale

Dunach   Ullina   Clunes   Lawrence   Smeaton   Hepburn Springs   Daylesford   Glenlyon   Tylden   Newham   Cobaw   Rochford   Romsey   Kilmore   31   Springfield   Wandong   Clonbinane   Hazeldene

A B C D 208 E F G H I

0 10 20 30 40 50 km

J K L M N O P Q R

1

HWY Finley ⊤ 23
NEWELL Berrigan 21 31
22 RIVERINA 27 Rand
Savernake Daysdale 24 18
Tocumwal ⊤ 31 35 11 Coreen HIGHWAY Walbundrie 32 ⊤ Culcairn
39 15 Koonoomoo Rennie 16 WallaWalla 2
Mywee 10 Barooga 24 16 19 Balldale Brocklesby OLYMPIC Gerogery
Yarroweyah 5 5 Cobram ⊤ 48 NEW SOUTH WALES Burrumbuttock 53 22 HUME HWY 3
10 Katunga 42 16 Murray Lake Mulwala 21 RIVERINA Jindera 16 23 31
Muckatah 37 Burramine 5 Mulwala ⊤ 37 Howlong 3 56 Ettamogah
Boosey MURRAY Yarrawonga Bundalong 6 8 Lavington 10 ALBURY 4
Katamatite 32 Bathumi 20 Brimin 11 Wahgunyan 14 Browns Plains Barnawartha North 42
Burramine Sth. 18 47 VALLEY 27 16 Rutherglen Barnawartha Interchange WODONGA 5
Telford Esmond Bundalong South Indigo 18 Mt.Lady Franklin Huon Hill Bonegilla
Youarah Boomahnoomoonah Norong Chiltern 9 Middle Indigo Ebden HUME

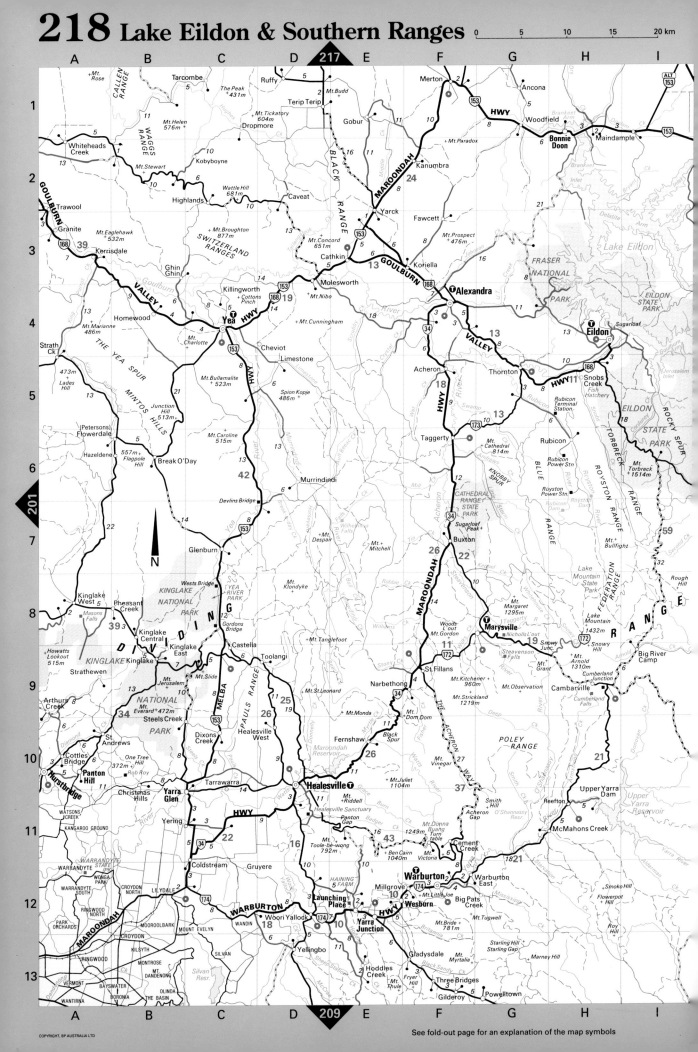

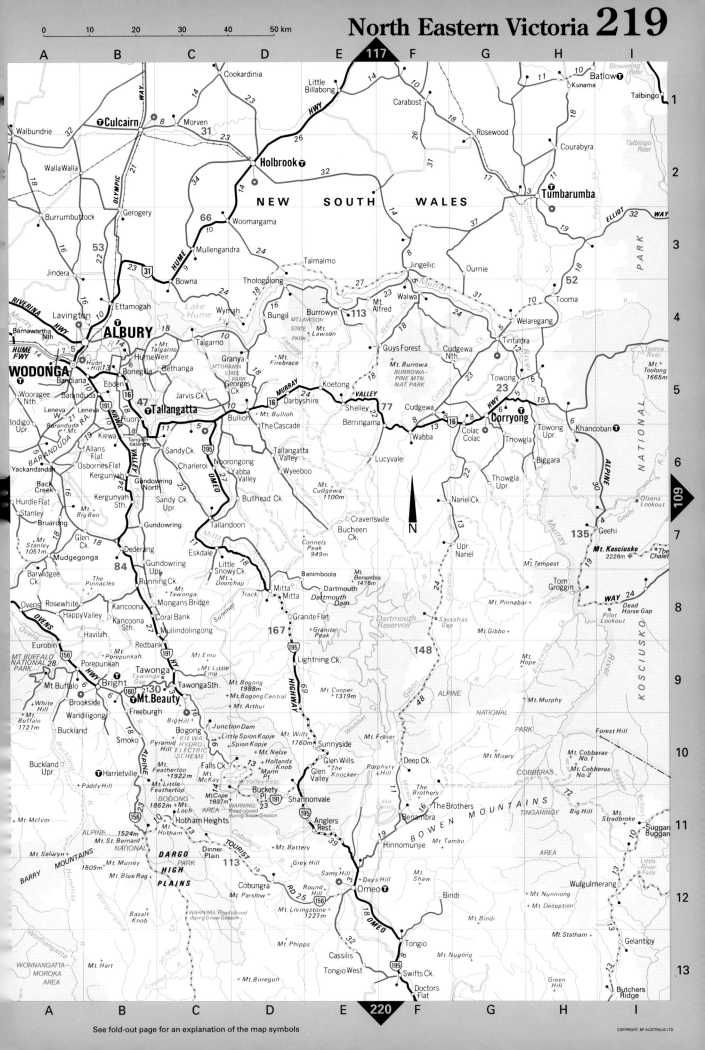

0   10   20   30   40   50 km

117

A   B   C   D   E   F   G   H   I

Walbundrie
Culcairn
Cookardinia
Little Billabong
Batlow
Talbingo
Blowering Resr
Kunama
1

32
8
Morven
31
23
14
23
26
Carabost
14
10
11
10
18

Walla Walla
Gerogery
Holbrook
Rosewood
Courabyra
Talbingo Resr
2
18
21
34
14
32
18
26
17
11
3
Tumbarumba

NEW   SOUTH   WALES

Burrumbuttock
66
Woomargama
31
37
52
PARK
3
16
53
22
10
Mullengandra
24
14
8
19
ELLIOT 32 WAY
Jindera
23
31
Bowna
Thologolong
Talmalmo
Jingellic
Ournie
18

OLYMPIC WAY
HUME
24
Talmalmo
16
27
23
Walwa
31
10
Tooma
R.
Lavington
Ettamogah
Lake Hume
Wymah Fy.
Bungil
Burrowye
113
Mt. Alfred
24
Welaregang
4
RIVERINA
16
10
9
16
Mt. LAWSON STATE PARK
+Mt. Lawson
18
Guys Forest
Cudgewa Nth.
Tintaldra
12
Tooma Resr.
Murray
ALBURY
Talgarno
Mt. Talgarno
10
Koetong
Mt. Burrowa
BURROWA-PINE MTN. NAT. PARK
23
Towong
Mt. Toolong 1665m
5
HUME WEIR
14
HumeWeir
Granya
Georges Ck
18
18
5
23
WODONGA
Huon Hill 13
Bethanga
MT.GRANYA STATE PARK
MURRAY
24
Darbyshire
VALLEY
Shelley
Cudgewa
8
Corryong
15
NATIONAL
Bandiana
Ebden
Bonegilla
Jarvis Ck.
16
Bullioh
77
22
Berringama
13
8
Colac Colac
Towong Upr.
Khancoban
Wooragee Nth.
Baranduda
47
Tallangatta
10
Mt. Bullioh
The Cascade
22
Wabba
8
16
8
Thowgla
6
5

Leneva W.
Huon
5
Tallangatta Valley
Lucyvale
Biggara
ALPINE
609
6
Indigo Upr.
Leneva
21
Sandy Ck.
Charleroi
Noorongong
Yabba Valley
Wyeeboo
22
Thowgla Upr.
30
Olsens Lookout
Yackandandah
Allans Flat
Kergunyah
Gundowring North
23
27
Bullhead Ck.
Mt. Cudgewa 1100m
Nariel Ck.
13
135
Geehi
Mt. Kosciusko 2228m
The Chalet
7
Back Creek
Osbornes Flat
Kergunyah Sth.
Sandy Ck. Upr.
Tallandoon
Cravensville
Bucheen Ck.
Upr. Nariel
19
Mt. Tempest
Hurdle Flat
Stanley
Mt. Big Ben
Gundowring
Connels Peak 949m
Tom Groggin
Bruarong
Mitta
Eskdale
11
Banimboola
Mt. Benambra 1476m
24
Mt. Pinnabar
WAY 24
Dead Horse Gap
8
Glen Ck.
18
Mudgegonga
84
Gundowring Upr.
Little Snowy Ck.
Mitta Mitta
Dartmouth
Dartmouth Dam
Dartmouth Reservoir
Sassafras Gap
Mt. Gibbo
Pilot Lookout
Barwidgee Ck.
The Pinnacles
Running Ck.
Mt. Doorchap
Track
Granite Flat
167
Granite Peak
148
Mt. Hope
Ovens
Rosewhite
Happy Valley
Kancoona
Mt. Tawonga
Mongans Bridge
27
Summer
Lightning Ck.
195
69
ALPINE
Mt. Murphy
9
OVENS
Eurobin
156
Redbank
191
Mt. Emu
Mt. Little Emu
Mt. Bogong 1988m
Mt. Bogong Central
Mt. Cooper 1319m
HIGHWAY
NATIONAL
Porepunkah
Mt. Porepunkah
21 30
Tawonga Sth.
Mt. Arthur
Mt. Wills 1760m
Sunnyside
Mt. Fraser
PARK
Mt. Buffalo
Bright
160
Mt. Beauty
Tawonga Gap
Big Hill
Junction Dam
Bogong
Little Spion Kopje
Spion Kopje
Mt. Nelse
Glen Wills
The Knocker
Porphyry Hill
Deep Ck.
Mt. Misery
Forest Hill
10
MT. BUFFALO NATIONAL PARK 28
White Hill
Brookside
Wandiligong
Freeburgh
KIEWA HYDRO-ELECTRIC SCHEME
Hollands Knob
Marm
Glen Valley
11
The Brothers
Mt. Cobberas No.1
Mt. Buffalo 1721m
Buckland
18
Smoko
Pyramid Hill
Falls Ck.
13
Rocky Valley Resr.
Buckety Pl.
191
Shannonvale
Mt. Cobberas No.2
COBBERAS
Suggan
Harrietville
Mt. Feathertop 1922m
Mt. McKay
195
Benambra
BOWEN MOUNTAINS
72
Buckland Upr.
Mt. Little Feathertop
Cope 1837m
WARNING: Road closed during Snow Season 23
Anglers Rest
39
TINGARINGY
Big Hill
Mt. Stradbroke
Suggan Buggan
11
Mt. McIvor
156
BOGONG 1862m
Loch
AREA
Hotham Heights
Mt. Hotham 1524m
Mt. St. Bernard
Dinner Plain
TOURIST
Hinnomunjie
Mt. Tambo
Mt. Nunniong
Little River Falls
Mt. Selwyn
ALPINE
NATIONAL
DARGO HIGH PLAINS
113
18
Grey Hill
Sams Hill
Days Hill
Mt. Shaw
AREA
Mt. Deception
12
Mt. Murray 1609m
Mt. Blue Rag
Cobungra
Mt. Parslow
RD 25
Round Hill
Omeo
Bindi
Mt. Bindi
Wulgulmerang
Gelantipy
BARRY MOUNTAINS
Basalt Knob
WARNING: Road closed during Snow Season
Mt. Livingstone 1227m
156
18 OMEO
Tongio
Mt. Nugong
Mt. Statham
13
WONNANGATTA-MOROKA AREA
Mt. Hart
Mt. Phipps
32
Cassilis
Tongio West
195
Swifts Ck.
Green Hill
Butchers Ridge
Doctors Flat

A   B   C   D   E   F   G   H   I

220

COPYRIGHT, BP AUSTRALIA LTD

A B C D E F G H I

219

1

Buckland Upr.
Smoko
Pyramid Hill
KIEWA HYDRO-ELECTRIC SCHEME
Little Spion Kopje
Spion Kopje
Mt. Nelse
1760m
Sunnyside
Mt. Fraser
Deep Ck.
Mt. Misery
Mt. Cobberas No. 1
Mt. Cobberas No. 2
KOSCIUSKO
Harrietville
Mt. Feathertop +1922m
Falls Ck.
13
Hollands Knob
Mt. McKay
Glen Wills
The Knocker
Porphyry Hill
The Brothers
COBBERAS
TINGARINGY
Big Hill AREA
Mt. Stradbroke
Paddy Hill
156
Mt. Little Feathertop
Buckety
Shannonvale
Glen Valley
Lake Omeo
The Brothers
ALPINE
21
Suggan Buggan

2
Mt. Sefwyn
ALPINE
1524m Mt. St. Bernard
Mt. Hotham
Hotham Heights
BOGONG 1862m Mt. Loch
Mt. Cope 1837m
WARNING: Road Closed during Snow Season
Anglers Rest
Mt. Battery
Hinnomunjie
Mt. Tambo
NATIONAL
PARK
174
Little River Falls
McK Br
Dinner Plain
DARGO HIGH PLAINS
Cobungra
Grey Hill
Sams Hill
Days Hill
Omeo
Mt. Shaw
Bindi
Mt. Nunniong
Mt. Deception
Wulgulmerang
Wulgulmerang Roadhouse

3
Mt. Murray 1609m
Mt. Blue Rag
Basalt Knob
WARNING: Road Closed during Snow Season
Mt. Parslow
Round Hill
156
Mt. Livingstone 1227m
Mt. Bindi
Tongio
Mt. Nugong
Mt. Statham
Gelantipy
Karoonda Park Roadhouse
SNC
RIV

4
WONNANGATTA MOROKA AREA
Mt. Hart
Mt. Cynthia
Mt. Grant
155
Mt. Birregun
Cassilis
Tongio West
Swifts Ck.
195
Doctors Flat
Mt. Delusion
Brookville
Ensay
Timbarra
Green Hill
Gillingal
NAT

5
Snowy Bluff
Happy Valley
Mt. Kent +1563m
27
Crooked River
Dargo
Mt. Steve
Notch Hill
Mt. Baldhead
Stirling
Ensay Sth.
Reedy Flat
96

6
Mt. Hump
Trapyard Hill
Mt. Wellington
Castle Hill 1436m
Waterford
9
Tabberabbera
19
Cobbannah
Mt. Blomford
Mt. Hood
Mt. Welcome
Deptford
Little Sugarloaf
Tambo Crossing
HWY 32
Spanker Knob
Flukes Knob
50
32
Buchan Caves
Buchan
Mt. Tara 608m
Mt. Pinnak
Stringer Knob
58
Mt. Buc 507

7
209
MITCHELL RIVER NATIONAL PARK
Davey Knob
Yellowman Knob
Mt. Difficulty
42
12
Iguana Ck.
Mt. Alfred
Bulumwaal
Mt. Taylor
Waterholes
24
11
195
Mossiface
Bruthen
23
Nowa Nowa
29
Mt. Nowa Nowa
6
16
11
Wairewa
37
35
Tostaree
Bete Bolong
Waygara
Corringle
Newn

8
Upr. Maffra West
Boisdale
Valencia Ck.
Briagolong
Bushy Park
Glenaladale
Stockdale
56
58
Walpa
Coongulmerang
Lindenow
Wy Yung
Sarsfield
Nicholson
Tambo Upr.
Johnsonville
Swan Reach
Colquhoun
LAKE TYERS NAT PK
Aboriginal Settlement
Lake Tyers
Bairnsdale
20
34
Kalimna West
23
Metung
Lakes Entrance

9
Newry
Maffra
Tinamba
10
Llowalong
Munro
HWY
Fernbank
51
Delvine
Bengworden
Forge Ck.
Goon Nure
Eagle Pt.
Paynesville
Pt. Wilson
Sperm Whale Head
Ocean Grange
THE LAKES NATIONAL PARK
BEACH

Heyfield
Bundalaguah
Nambrok
14
Airly
Montgomery
Clydebank
29
Meerlieu
Perry Bridge
Red Morass
Hollands Landing
Loch Sport
Causeway Stockyard Hill (Good Fishing)
Gippsland Lakes Coastal Park

10
Rosedale
Kilmany
Kilmany Sth.
PRINCES
Fulham
Wurruk
Sale
Longford
The Heart
Lake Wellington
Seacombe
Lake Coleman
NINETY
Reeve

11
Willung
Stradbroke West
Dutson
29
Gas Processing Plant
Letts Beach (Paradise Beach)
Golden Beach
THE
MILE

180
Stradbroke

12
72
GIPPSLAND
Giffard
Seaspray
Lake Denison
N

13
Darriman
8
Woodside
Hunterston
Woodside Beach
Reeves Beach

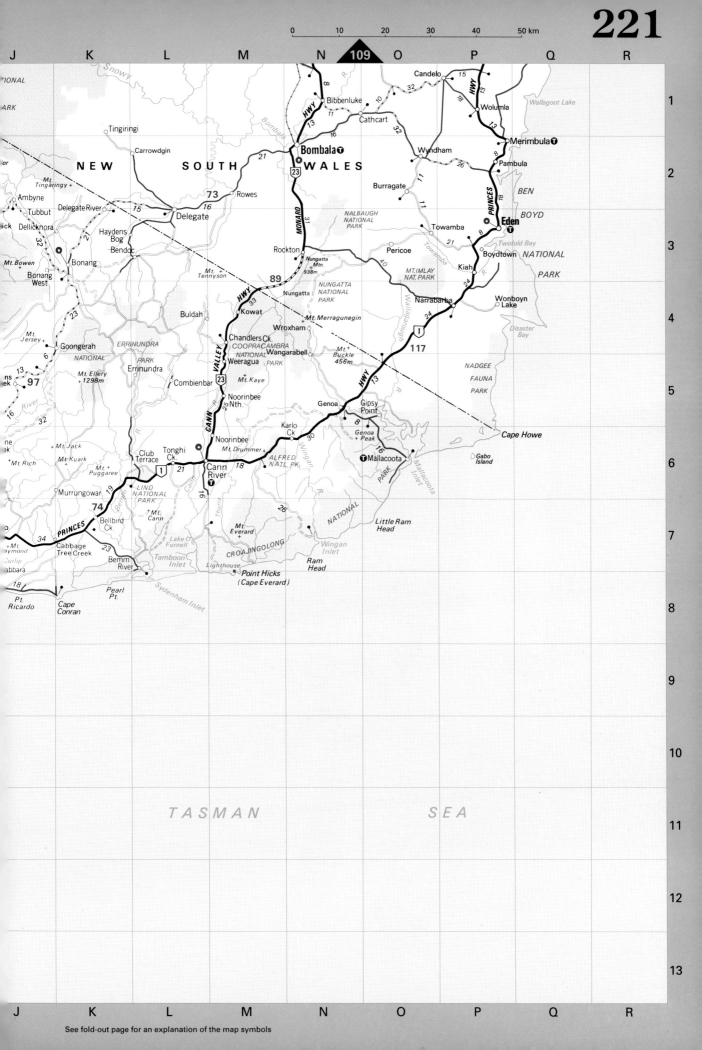

0   10   20   30   40   50 km

J   K   L   M   N   109   O   P   Q   R

NEW   SOUTH   WALES

Snowy R.

Tingiringi

Carrowdgin

Bibbenluke

Candelo

15

HWY

13

*Mt.
Tingaringy*

Ambyne

Tubbut

Delegate River

15

73

Rowes

16

Cathcart

32

Wolumla

Wallagoot Lake

13

Dellicknora

32

Haydens
Bog

Delegate

21

Bombala T

23

Wyndham

26

Merimbula T

8

Pambula

Mt. Bowen

Bonang

Bendoc

MONARO

31

Burragate

11

PRINCES

BEN

BOYD

Bonang
West

*Mt.
Tennyson*

Rockton

Nalbaugh
National
Park

11

Towamba

8

Eden T

NATIONAL

*Mt.
Jersey*

Goongerah

ERRINUNDRA

89

Nungatta
Mtn.
938m

Pericoe

21

Kiah

Boydtown

PARK

6

NATIONAL

PARK

HWY

33

Kowat

Nungatta

NUNGATTA
NATIONAL
PARK

40

Mt.Imlay
Nat. Park

24

Twofold Bay

13

97

*Mt. Ellery
+1298m*

Errinundra

Buldah

Wroxham

Mt. Merragunegin

117

Narrabarba

Wonboyn
Lake

Chandlers Ck.

COOPRACAMBRA

Wangarabell

*Mt.
Buckle
456m*

24

Disaster
Bay

16

River

32

Combienbar

VALLEY

23

Weeragua

PARK

Mt. Kaye

NADGEE

Mt. Jack

Mt. Kuark

*Mt.
Puggaree*

CANN

Noorinbee
Nth.

25

Genoa

Gipsy
Point

8

FAUNA

PARK

Mt. Rich

Club
Terrace

Tonghi
Ck.

Noorinbee

Mt. Drummer

Karlo
Ck.

30

Genoa
+ Peak

Cape Howe

Murrungowar

19

1

21

**Cann
River** T

18

ALFRED
NATL. PK.

Wingan

16

Mallacoota T

74

LIND
NATIONAL
PARK

*Mt.
Cann*

Thurra

Mallacoota
Inlet

Gabo
Island

PRINCES

Bellbird
Ck.

26

NATIONAL

34

Cabbage
Tree Creek

23

Lake O
Furnell

*Mt.
Everard*

Little Ram
Head

Curlip

Bemm
River

Tamboon
Inlet

CROAJINGOLONG

Wingan
Inlet

18

Pearl
Pt.

Lighthouse

Ram
Head

*Pt.
Ricardo*

Cape
Conran

Sydenham Inlet

Point Hicks
(Cape Everard)

T A S M A N   S E A

J   K   L   M   N   O   P   Q   R

SOUTH AUSTRALIA

Festival State

The Adelaide biennial Arts Festival, the Barossa Valley Vintage, Schuetzenfest, Australian Formula One Grand Prix, the Greek Glendi Festival, the Cornish Kernewek Lowender — from the number and variety of festivities held every year, it seems clear that South Australians enjoy making the most of life. For the visitor, these festivals provide an excellent chance to discover a community at its liveliest.

This energetic spirit also seems to indicate that South Australians have triumphed over what might seem to be rather depressing statistics: it is the driest state in the driest continent, two-thirds is near-desert and eighty-three per cent receives an annual rainfall of less than 250 millimetres. But these facts are easily forgotten when you visit the lush green Barossa Valley or explore the beauty of the Flinders Ranges.

As a result of innovative social changes in the 1960s, today South Australia's conservative image has virtually disappeared. It seems apt that its initial settlement began as the result of one man's ideas of how to create a model colony. Edward Gibbon Wakefield believed that the difficulties of other Australian colonies were caused by the ease with which anyone could obtain land. He claimed that if land were sold at two pounds an acre, only men of capital could buy; those who could not would provide a supply of labour, and the finance generated would encourage investment and the development of resources. In 1834 he tested his ideas in the Gulf St Vincent area. Lieutenant-Colonel Light was dispatched as Surveyor-General to select a site.

Today, although South Australia's economy remains traditionally agrarian, secondary industry provides nine out of ten jobs. Olympic Dam is one of the world's biggest copper-mines and probably the biggest uranium-mine. The Leigh Creek coalfields meet most of the state's power needs.

South Australia also boasts most of the world's opals. Coober Pedy, the main opal-mining town, produces ninety per cent of Australia's opals.

Glendi Festival

The gulf lands of South Australia enjoy a Mediterranean climate. The further north you go, the hotter and more inhospitable the temperatures become. Adelaide, with its average annual rainfall of 585 millimetres, enjoys a midsummer average maximum temperature of about 28.3°C and a midwinter average maximum of 15°C. Seventy-two per cent of the population lives here, making South Australia the most urbanised of all the states. Adelaide inherited its orderly and pleasant layout from its first Surveyor-General, Colonel Light, and many of its attractive original stone buildings have survived. Once known as the 'city of churches', it is today more talked about in terms of its Festival Centre, excellent galleries and museums and splendid restaurants. The Mount Lofty Ranges make a picturesque backdrop. With the Stuart Highway now completely sealed, it is possible to drive from Port Augusta to central Australia on an all-weather road. Certain precautions should be taken before negotiating other roads in the north and west desert regions. (See: Outback Motoring.) If you feel intrepid, the opal towns of Coober Pedy and Andamooka are fascinating. Temperatures climb to over 50°C in Coober Pedy during summer (much of the town is built underground), so choose a cool period for your trip.

The spectacular Flinders Ranges have passable roads, although some are unsealed.

The best way to explore this colourful region of peaks and gorges, carpeted in spring with wildflowers, is by four-wheel drive, on horseback or on foot. Wilpena Pound and Arkaroola are the main resort bases. The Heysen Trail (commemorating South Australian painter Sir Hans Heysen) is a well-defined hiking trail that reaches from Cape Jervis almost to Quorn, with extensions into the Flinders Ranges.

Both the Yorke and Eyre Peninsulas have attractive, unspoiled coastlines. Port Lincoln, on the Eyre Peninsula, is a popular base for big-game fishing and on the Yorke Peninsula the three little towns of Wallaroo, Moonta and Kadina, collectively known as Little Cornwall, with their history of copper mining, are well worth a visit.

South of Adelaide is Victor Harbor, the south coast's largest resort. A little further on is the Coorong National Park, near the mouth of the Murray at Lake Alexandrina. Here the river completes its 2600-kilometre course. A trip along the Riverland section of the Murray reveals historic river towns, bountiful citrus orchards and extensive vegetable crops, all maintained by irrigation from the Murray. The lakes and lagoons at the river's mouth abound with birdlife and offer excellent fishing and seasonal duck-shooting. On the southern Victorian border is Mount Gambier, the commercial centre of the south-east, which has Australia's largest pine forest and the beautiful Blue Lake.

The fame of South Australia's wine regions now extends well beyond Australian shores. McLaren Vale on the Fleurieu Peninsula produces excellent wines, and the Riverland region is responsible for much of the national vintage. In the famed Barossa Valley region, there are more than fifty wineries. The valley was originally settled by German Lutherans who planted orchards, olive groves and vineyards and built charming towns and wineries very much in their native European style. To explore this area, particularly during the Vintage Festival every odd-numbered year, is to discover a region and lifestyle unique in Australia.

ADELAIDE

An Elegant City

Adelaide is a gracious, well-planned city set on a narrow coastal plain between the rolling hills of the Mount Lofty Ranges and the blue waters of Gulf St Vincent. Surrounded by parkland, Adelaide combines the vitality of a large modern city (population nearly one million) with an easy-going Australian lifestyle.

Thanks to Colonel Light's excellent planning and foresight, Adelaide is well endowed with greenery. The city centre is completely surrounded by parklands, known as the Green Belt, with children's playgrounds and sports fields, barbecues, and tables and chairs under shady trees. At **Rymill Park** there is a children's boating lake with canoes and dinghies for hire. Flanagan's Riverfront Restaurant is set in parkland overlooking the waters of **Torrens Lake** near the Weir, north of North Terrace. At **Veale Gardens** to the south of the city there are fountains, rockeries and the Pavilion on the Park restaurant. Further east along South Terrace is the **Adelaide-Himeji Garden**, a blend of traditional Japanese lake, mountain and dry gardens. The gate is modelled on that of a temple, and a water bowl is provided for visitors to purify themselves by washing their hands and mouths. The beautiful, formal **Botanic Gardens** have sixteen hectares of Australian and imported plants and man-made lakes where children can feed ducks and swans; guided tours are available. While there, try not to miss the Palm House, an extensive glasshouse brought out from Germany in 1871. In the northeast corner of the gardens is the **Bicentennial Conservatory**, said to be the largest conservatory in the southern hemisphere, housing exotic tropical plants from all over the world. Two serpentine viewing paths on upper and lower levels have wheelchair access.

Near the tree-lined boulevard of **North Terrace** on the edge of the city centre there are some fine colonial buildings: **Holy Trinity Church** is the oldest church in South Australia; the foundation stone was laid by Governor Hindmarsh in 1838, and the clock was made by Vulliamy, clockmaker to King William IV.

St Peter's Cathedral

Near this western end of North Terrace is the **Adelaide Gaol**, last used in 1988 and now open for inspection on the first and third Sunday of each month. Also in North Terrace are the grand **Newmarket Hotel**, built in 1884, and the **Living Arts Centre**, home of the exciting biennial Fringe Festival.

Further along is the **Old Parliament House**, which today houses Australia's only museum of political history and has an excellent audiovisual display and delightful restaurant. On the corner of King William Road is the present **Parliament House**. Nearby is **Government House**, the oldest building in Adelaide, in a beautiful garden setting.

The **State Library**, on the corner of Kintore Avenue, houses over 200 000 volumes. Behind the State Library is the **Migration and Settlement Museum**, the first museum to tell the story of the Australia's migrants. Also in this complex is the **Natural History Museum** with the largest display of Aboriginal artefacts in the world. Opposite at 237 North Terrace, is **Scots Church**, built in 1851 and

now a National Heritage building. The **Art Gallery of South Australia** has an important collection of Australian and overseas paintings, sculpture and artworks. The **Royal South Australian Society of Arts** building runs an extensive programme of exhibitions of fine and applied arts. **The South Australian Police Museum** and adjacent **Police Armoury** have displays on policing history.

The **University of Adelaide** is also on North Terrace. Walk through the landscaped grounds to see the blend of classic and contemporary architecture, and visit the **Museum of Classical Archaeology** in the grounds to view some 500 objects, many dating back to the third millennium BC. **Elder Hall**, with its spectacular pipe organ, is a fine concert venue.

The historic Adelaide Railway building, also in North Terrace, has been restored magnificently for the **Adelaide Casino**. The casino is part of the Adelaide Plaza Complex, which includes the **Adelaide Convention Centre**, **Exhibition Hall** and the luxurious **Hyatt Regency Hotel**. A special Australian National Railways train (the 'Pokie Express', with an entertainment lounge carriage fitted with poker machines) runs approximately once a fortnight, taking gamblers for a weekend at the Barrier Social Democratic Club in Broken Hill, New South Wales.

Opposite the Royal Adelaide Hospital is **Ayers House**, headquarters for the National Trust of South Australia. Sir Henry Ayers bought the property in 1855; the house was extended and became one of the major venues for social functions during Ayers' seven terms as Premier of the state. A charming nineteenth-century residence with slate roof and shuttered bay windows, Ayers House has an elegant formal restaurant and a more relaxed bistro extending into the courtyard, enabling visitors to enjoy the historic surroundings whilst dining. The Aboriginal Cultural Institute **Tandanya** is on the corner of Grenfell Street and East Terrace.

In King William Street, only a block from North Terrace, is another important reminder of Adelaide's heritage, **Edmund**

The modern face of Adelaide

Hotels
Hilton International
233 Victoria Sq., Adelaide
(08) 217 0711
Hindley Parkroyal
65 Hindley St, Adelaide
(08) 231 5552
Hyatt Regency
North Tce, Adelaide
(08) 231 1234
The Terrace Adelaide
150 North Tce, Adelaide
(08) 217 7552

Family and Budget
Adelaide Paringa
15 Hindley St, Adelaide
(08) 231 1000
Austral
205 Rundle St, Adelaide
(08) 223 4660
YMCA
76 Flinders St, Adelaide
(08) 223 1611

Motel Groups: Bookings
Flag (008) 01 1177
Best Western (008) 22 2166
Travelodge (008) 22 2446

This list is for information only;
inclusion is not necessarily a
recommendation.

Wright House. Built in 1878, the building with its elaborate Renaissance facade is used for civil weddings. Other historic buildings in the city include the **Town Hall** in King William Street, with formal portico entrance and graceful tower, the **General Post Office**, and the **Treasury Buildings** on the corner of Victoria Square.

In North Adelaide there are fine old colonial buildings, from delightful stone cottages to stately homes and grand old hotels with lacework balconies and verandahs. **St Peter's Cathedral** in King William Road is one of Australia's finest cathedrals and is a fitting backdrop to the beautiful **Pennington Gardens**. There is a particularly fine view from **Light's Vision** on Montefiore Hill. A bronze statue of Colonel Light overlooks the city with its broad streets and spacious parks.

The **River Torrens** flows through many of Adelaide's parks. The banks are landscaped, lined with gums and willows, and perfect for a lazy picnic lunch. A fleet of *Popeye* motor launches cruises the river, providing a delightfully different way of travelling to the **Adelaide Zoological Gardens**. The zoo has an enormous collection of animals and reptiles and is noted for its variety of Australian birdlife. There is a walk-through aviary sheltering many types of unusual land and water birds, and a nocturnal house designed to display those animals and birds that are most active at night. The zoo grounds are in a perfect setting with magnificent trees (including exotic species), rock beds and rose gardens.

Also situated on the curving banks of the Torrens is the famous **Festival Centre**, hub of Adelaide's biennial festival, held in even-numbered years. This streamlined, modern building contains a 2000-seat lyric theatre, drama and experimental theatres and an imposing amphitheatre for outdoor entertainment. The building has been acclaimed by international critics as one of the finest performing venues in the world. The Southern Plaza incorporates a spectacular environmental sculpture by West German artist O. H. Hajek. There are also some fine contemporary tapestries and paintings hung inside the building. Guided tours are conducted, and restaurant and bar facilities are available. The Centre has walkways linking it to King William Road, Parliament House, Adelaide Railway Station and the Casino. Nearby is an attractive old band rotunda in **Elder Park**.

Adelaide has a bustling shopping complex centred around **Rundle Mall**. The paved mall has trees and a fountain, modern sculpture, colourful fruit- and flower-stalls and seats where you can sit and watch the passing parade. Buskers and outdoor cafes give the area a European

Adelaide Casino

Town Hall, Glenelg

atmosphere. Surrounding arcades and streets have everything from major department stores to tiny specialist boutiques. King William Street is lined with bank and insurance buildings, and in Hindley Street there are clusters of restaurants and continental food shops. A bonus for shoppers is the free Bee-line bus service which operates in the inner-city area.

Make a trip to **Melbourne Street** in North Adelaide for some of the city's most exclusive shops; **Unley Road** for exclusive boutiques; **Magill Road** if you are hunting for antiques; and **Norwood Parade** for secondhand treasures. **King William Road** at Hyde Park has a number of stylish specialty shops and boutiques. The **Jam Factory and Craft Centre**, close to the city at 169 Payneham Road, St Peters, features high-quality contemporary South Australian crafts.

A real shopping experience is a visit to the **Central Market** behind the Hilton Hotel, with its stalls packed high with fresh produce (open Tuesday, Thursday, Friday and Saturday). Nearby arcades sell clothing, wine and spirits. Close to Rundle Mall in Rundle Street is the **East End Market** (open Friday, Saturday and Sunday and public holidays). The **Brickworks Market** at Thebarton (Friday, Saturday and public holiday Mondays) sells produce and bric-a-brac, and is part of a

six-hectare complex featuring an amusement park and international restaurants. Other markets featuring fresh foodstuffs and a variety of other goods are the **Junction Market** in Prospect Road, Kilburn (Saturday, Sunday and public holiday Mondays), and the **Reynella Markets** at 255 Old South Road, Reynella (Friday, Saturday, Sunday and public holiday Mondays).

One of Adelaide's main attractions is its restaurants. Indian, Spanish, Italian, Mexican, Lebanese—the choice seems endless. Some restaurants are tiny and crowded, with fast service and super-cheap prices. Others are set in historic buildings, serving international-class cuisine in gracious surroundings. **Hindley Street** in the city has some of Adelaide's most colourful restaurants: bright red lacquer ducks hang in the windows and giant pizzas are tossed in the air. Fish is a specialty, of course, fresh from South Australian waters. **Windy Point Starlight Room**, Belair Road, Belair, has one of the finest views of Adelaide and surrounding suburbs. At **Montezuma's** in Melbourne Street, North Adelaide, you can enjoy a delicious variety of Mexican food at reasonable prices. There are also Japanese, Indian and French restaurants in **Melbourne Street**; and this being Australia's premier wine-producing state, the capital's restaurants serve first-class wines.

Adelaide also has some fine old pubs. Some are friendly 'locals', others incorporate restaurants, wine bars and dancefloors. The **Old Lion Hotel** in North Adelaide is a handsome 1880s bluestone building with a first-class restaurant, a sheltered courtyard and popular disco. It is typical of the new boutique-style hotel where beer is brewed on the premises; there are a number of these hotels within the inner-city area.

Not to be missed in Adelaide are the marvellous beaches, stretching right along the coastline with wide sandy shores and clear blue waters. Most are only a short drive from the city centre and perhaps the most famous is **Glenelg**. The best way to see it is by taking the famous **Bay Tram** from Victoria Square to the top of Jetty Road in Glenelg. Spoil yourself by dining at the **Ramada Grand Hotel**, or stroll down Jetty Road to the shopping centre. The **Magic Mountain Waterslide and Amusement Centre** provides entertainment. Restaurants abound, and Greek food here is a specialty. Grand old homes and guest-houses along the foreshore are a reminder of Glenelg's days as a seaside resort for the wealthy. The first settlers came ashore here in 1836 and proclaimed the colony of South Australia under a gum tree. The **Old Gum Tree** remains, with a commemorative plaque.

HMS *Buffalo* played a significant part in South Australia's early settlement and a replica of the vessel at Glenelg is an appropriate setting for a maritime museum and restaurant.

Other beaches include **Marino**, **Brighton**, **West Beach**, **Henley**, **Grange** and **Semaphore**. At Semaphore, **Fort Glanville** is the oldest fortress in South Australia. A restaurant in the restored Customs House (1850) overlooks the esplanade and the ocean. South, near Hallett Cove, is the **Hallett Cove Conservation Park**, established to preserve the remnants of glacial features that probably occurred 270 million years ago. Many beaches have sailboards and catamarans for hire, while the jetties are used for promenading, swimming and fishing.

Adelaide's suburbs have much to offer the visitor. A short drive west towards the beachside suburb of **Grange** is **Sturt's Cottage** (built in 1840), home of Captain Charles Sturt, the famous pioneer and explorer. Managed by the Charles Sturt Memorial Museum Trust, its period furniture and many of Sturt's belongings recall the early days of South Australia.

In **Wayville**, just south-west of the city, is **The Investigator, Science and Technology Centre** with hands-on 'gizmos' and fun for all the family; located in the International Pavilion, Wayville Showgrounds (enter from Rose Tce). Also at the showgrounds in early September, the **Royal Adelaide Show** brings the country to the city.

Port Adelaide has many imposing buildings, a reminder of the port's heyday in the 1880s. The police station and courthouse, town hall, shipping and transport building and Ferguson's bond store are noteworthy. The historic **Port Dock Station Railway Museum** in Lipson Street contains the Mile End Railway Museum with its large collection of locomotives and rollingstock, platform displays, a theatrette and an operating HO-gauge model railway; visitors can ride miniature steam trains. The nearby **Maritime Museum**, complete with lighthouses and ships, is also in Lipson St. A few blocks away is the **South Australian Historical Aviation Museum** in Mundy St. Cruises and fishing trips are available from Port Adelaide and Outer Harbour.

At **St Kilda**, further north, there is an **Electric Transport Museum** where you can take trips on restored trams. A guided walk along the 1.7km boardwalk of the **Mangrove Walking Trail** is an experience not to be missed.

Near the suburb of **Rostrevor**, east of the city, the **Morialta Conservation Park** has a ruggedly beautiful gorge and many walking-tracks. Further east, past the townships of Norton Summit and Ash-

Bay Tram, Glenelg

ton, are the remains of **Marble Hill** (1879), an old home preserved by the National Trust as a historic ruin; the 32-hectare property has a large picnic ground, tea-rooms and walking-trails. **Brownhill Creek Recreation Park** has giant pine and gum trees in a quiet valley setting. There are barbecue facilities and pretty picnic spots. **Belair Recreation Park** has picnic grounds, bushland, a children's playground and the former summer residence of the Governor. **Cleland Conservation Park** shows kangaroos, koalas, wombats and other native fauna in their natural surroundings.

The longest guided busway system in the world, **The O-Bahn**, runs north-east from the city centre. It travels beside the River Torrens in its own landscaped park from Adelaide to a major shopping centre at **Tea Tree Plaza**, and has a station at **Paradise**, a suburb named by early settlers. Walking-paths follow the busway track to Tea Tree Plaza, with views over reservoirs, foothills and the city.

Cowell Jade, at **Unley**, sells jewellery and carvings made from South Australian jade. The **South Australian Society of Model and Experimental Engineers** headquarters, in the nearby suburb of **Millswood**, has field days (open to visitors) twice a month. For magnificent views of Adelaide, take a trip to **Windy**

Point Lookout or to the summit of **Mount Lofty**. At night, the lights of the city look particularly impressive. Adelaide is the **Formula One Grand Prix** city of Australia. This exciting race is through city streets, open parklands and the racecourse in November; the course is regarded by many as the best street circuit in the world. As well, Adelaide offers sports enthusiasts horse-racing at **Victoria Park**, **Morphettville** and **Cheltenham**; greyhound-racing at **Angle Park**; tennis, squash, swimming and golf. The **Adelaide Aquatic Centre** in **North Adelaide** features pools, waterslides, fountains, river rapids and waterfalls. The **Municipal Golf Course** in North Adelaide commands splendid views of the city. The **Adelaide Oval**, on King William Road, is a venue for interstate and international cricket matches, while the **Memorial Drive Tennis Courts** have played host to international players since 1929. Memorial Drive also is used for outdoor concerts and performances by visiting entertainers. The **Ice Arena** at 23 East Terrace in the suburb of **Thebarton** has skating and the world's first indoor artificial ski-slope.

For further information on Adelaide and South Australia, contact Tourism South Australia Travel Centre, 1 King William St, Adelaide; (08) 212 1505.

TOURS FROM ADELAIDE

One of Adelaide's greatest assets is its close proximity to a number of fascinating regions. Vineyards and wineries, rolling hills and quaint villages, seaside resorts and beautiful wildlife reserves are all within an easy drive of South Australia's capital.

The Barossa Valley, 50 km from Adelaide via the Sturt Highway

A must for visitors to Adelaide is the Barossa Valley, Australia's premier wine-producing region. In this area to the north-east of Adelaide there are more than forty wineries and a multitude of historic buildings and galleries, with restaurants and cafes serving top-class cuisine. Visit Gawler, Lyndoch, Tanunda, Nuriootpa and Angaston, detouring at will to the smaller villages and visiting the tasting facilities at the wineries; make sure the driver is happy to forgo this pleasure! Alternatively, extend your visit and stay overnight at the many and varied accommodation outlets in the area. **(See also:** Vineyards and Wineries; individual entries in A–Z listing.)

The Clare Valley, 135 km from Adelaide via the Sturt Highway and Highway 32 (Highway 83 optional north of Tarlee)

The Clare Valley produces superb wines and the region is known nationally for its riesling. Driving north through Kapunda, Australia's first mining-town, you will pass some of the state's richest pastoral country, noted for its stud sheep. The wine towns begin at Auburn and continue to Watervale and Sevenhill to Clare. The area is noted for its prize-winning red and white table wines. Sevenhill Cellars winery was started by two Jesuit priests in 1848 and still operates today. Slightly further afield, there are some fine colonial buildings, such as the magnificent Martindale Hall at Mintaro (open daily), which was used in the film *Picnic at Hanging Rock*. The area also has many charming parks and picturesque picnic spots. **(See also:** Vineyards and Wineries; individual entries in A–Z listing.)

The Wine Coast, 42 km from Adelaide via the South Road

Another trip for wine-lovers is to the vineyards of the Fleurieu Peninsula. There are over fifty wineries in the area, often in picturesque bush settings. Most are well signposted and have wine tastings and cellar-door sales. Hardy's, D'Arenberg, Seaview and Coriole are some of the names to recognise. Stop for lunch in McLaren Vale at The Barn, a gallery - restaurant complex in a historic old coach-station, or enjoy a light snack at Pipkins. Your return trip could include a visit to the nearby beaches — Moana, Port Noarlunga and Christies Beach. At Hackham there is a fascinating Pioneer Village, re-creating an 1870s Australian settlement, with thatched-roof cottage, blacksmith, general store, Cobb & Co. office and horse-drawn vehicles. **(See also:** Vineyards and Wineries; The Fleurieu Peninsula; individual entries in A–Z listing.)

The Adelaide Hills and Hahndorf, 25 km from Adelaide via the South Eastern Freeway

The Adelaide Hills are only half an hour's drive from the city. Stop on the way at Cleland Wildlife Park in the Cleland Conservation Park, to see native birds and animals in a natural bush setting. The Gorge Wildlife Park at Cudlee Creek is open every day. The hills themselves are a blend of gently rolling mountains, market gardens and orchards with farm buildings nestled in valleys off winding roads. Go off the main highway to visit Stirling (the nearby Mount Lofty Botanic Gardens offer magnificent views of Piccadilly Valley) and Aldgate, then Bridgewater with its historic water-wheel (1860), now part of the restored mill which houses the wine-making and maturation plant for Petaluma's premium sparkling wines; wine tasting and tours available. Mount Lofty (725 m) offers panoramic views of Adelaide.

Hahndorf is probably the best-known and most interesting town in the area. A unique German-style village, its main street is lined with magnificent old elms and chestnut trees. Most of the buildings have been carefully restored and the town has a leisurely, old-world feel about it. The Hahndorf Academy and Art Gallery has a permanent exhibition of paintings

Martindale Hall, Clare Valley

German Arms Hotel, Hahndorf

Port Noarlunga on the Fleurieu Peninsula

by Sir Hans Heysen, who lived in the town for many years and depicted the area's beauty so well. A German folk-museum is next door, and both are open daily. The bakeries here sell delicious *apfelstrudel*, cheesecake and Black Forest cake, and small shops offer interesting local handicrafts and home-made preserves. Other attractions include a model train village, a clock museum and a strawberry farm. A German beer festival, *Schutzenfest*, is held each year. Settlers Hill Pioneer Village at Hochstens, Hahndorf, is a recreation of a turn-of-the-century town. Two of South Australia's oldest townships, Nairne and Mount Barker, lie to the east and southeast of Hahndorf.

In the little town of Oakbank, the Great Eastern Steeplechase, Australia's biggest picnic race meeting, is held with great fanfare every Easter. North of Oakbank are Apple World at Forest Range and an archive and historical museum at Lobethal. Spennithorne Herb and Flower Farm is open for pick-your-own herbs, near Lobethal. At Woodside, Melba's Chocolates offer daily tours and tastings. From Hahndorf you can take the back road through winding hills and farmland to the old gold-mining town of Echunga, and return to Adelaide via the sleepy township of Mylor, where Warrawong Sanctuary, a leader in the preservation of rare and endangered animals, offers guided tours. Stop at the Belair Recreation Park on your return trip to Adelaide. There are some beautiful walks, fireplaces for picnics and a wildlife park.

Stay in one of the many home-style accommodation houses dotted through-

out the Adelaide Hills and experience inexpensive, quality bed-and-breakfast accommodation or rent a self-contained, historic cottage. For further information, contact the Adelaide Hills Tourist Information Centre, 64 Main St, Hahndorf; (08) 388 1185. (**See also:** Vineyards and Wineries; Festival Fun; individual entries in A–Z listing.)

The Fleurieu Peninsula, 112 km from Adelaide to its furthest point via the South Road

The Fleurieu Peninsula extends south of Adelaide and has much to offer. Down the length of the west coast there are idyllic sandy beaches, such as Maslin (Australia's first official nudist beach), Sellicks and Christies Beach, right to the tip at wild but beautiful Cape Jervis. Some beaches have sheltered coves, some have excellent surf, still others are ideal for fishing. Inland there are historic buildings, particularly at Willunga, where public buildings vie with small cottages for the visitor's attention. The almond orchards around here are a marvellous sight, especially when they bloom in early spring. There are a number of conservation parks, ideal for keen walkers as well as those looking for a quiet picnic spot. There is a pleasant scenic drive around Myponga Conservation Park. Only 84 km from Adelaide is Victor Harbor, one of the state's most popular seaside resorts. The sandy beach is perfect for swimming. Across the causeway is rugged Granite Island and The Bluff (Rosetta Head) has a whaling museum and a licensed restaurant. Further around is Port Elliot on splen-

did Horseshoe Bay. Further east is Goolwa, the historic river port at the mouth of the Murray River; here one of the focal points is the Signal Point River Murray Interpretive Centre. A ferry will take you across to Hindmarsh Island for panoramic views of the area. Driving back to Adelaide, do not miss Strathalbyn on the banks of the Angas. Milang, 20 km to the south-east, is on the shores of Lake Alexandrina. Take your camera — the birdlife is fascinating. (**See also:** The Fleurieu Peninsula; individual entries in A–Z listing.)

Birdwood Mill Museum, 46 km from Adelaide via the North-East Road

The Birdwood Mill Pioneer Museum (open daily) houses what is believed to be the most important motor vehicle display in Australia. Veteran, vintage and classic cars and motor cycles number over 300. Tearooms serve light refreshments. At Gumeracha, on Torrens Gorge Ring Route en route from Adelaide, is the 'Toy Factory', which has the largest wooden rocking-horse in the world. Drive back to Adelaide through Mount Torrens to the small town of Lobethal, which was founded in the 1840s. The Archives and Historical Museum houses a most remarkable exhibit: the old Lobethal College, complete with shingled roof, which was built in 1845; open Sunday afternoons. Fairyland Village at Lobethal has fourteen chalets, each depicting a fairytale or a nursery rhyme. There is an enjoyable scenic route through Basket Range and Norton Summit back to Adelaide.

FESTIVAL FUN

Because good food and wine go hand-in-hand with festivities, it seems appropriate that South Australia is both the nation's wine capital and the Festival State. During the year, a wide variety of festivals is held throughout South Australia — from the cultural extravaganza of the Adelaide Festival to the country-town carnivals. In November each year the city is galvanised by the roar of engines as the world's top car-racing drivers compete in the **Australian Formula One Grand Prix.**

For three weeks in March of each even-numbered year, Adelaide becomes the cultural centre of Australia, as it stages its **Festival of Arts**. During this time the city is like a giant magnet, drawing to it throngs of people from interstate and overseas. Hotels are often booked months ahead; restaurants, taxi services and retailers do a roaring trade.

Since it started in 1960, the Adelaide Festival has grown from a modest 51 performances to over 300, with as many as 30 competing for attention in one day, including many concerts, carnivals and street theatre escapades for free. The cosmopolitan atmosphere and the world-renowned guest artists have ranked this festival as an outstanding international event.

Although the Festival emphasises performances in theatre, dance, musical recitals, opera and ballet, it is not confined solely to the performing arts. There are exhibitions, lectures, a writers' week, artists' week to celebrate the visual arts, poetry readings and plenty of outdoor activities to coincide with this three-week-long cultural feast.

The focal point is the Adelaide Festival Centre, which stands on 1.5 hectares on the banks of the River Torrens, just two minutes' walk from the commercial heart of the city.

This 21-million-dollar performing arts complex contains the Festival Theatre, a multi-purpose concert hall and lyric theatre which seats 2000. The hall, with its special acoustic properties, is capable of accommodating 100 orchestral players and a choir of 200, making it the largest stage in the country. The drama theatre, the Playhouse, seats 600 and is the permanent home

Adelaide Formula One Grand Prix

Folk concert at Adelaide Festival Centre

of the South Australia Theatre Company, which presents at least ten major productions annually. The Festival Centre also contains the Space, an experimental theatre with seating for 380 and flexible performance areas. The most frequently used area is probably the Amphitheatre, the open-spaced venue which seats 800 and which is used mainly for free concerts, puppet shows and story-telling for children during the summer months.

Even when the Festival is not on, Adelaide visitors and residents still make good use of the parks and gardens surrounding the centre, as well as the two restaurants and a terrace-style cafe, which are open six days a week.

Each odd-numbered year, in May, the Festival Centre organises a youth festival, 'Come Out', which focuses its attention on the arts for children and young people.

The **Barossa Valley Vintage Festival**, in Australia's premier wine-producing district, just one hour's drive from Adelaide, is also held in odd-numbered years. The mellow autumn weather and picturesque towns of the Barossa Valley draw large crowds to this event, which is traditionally a thanksgiving celebration for a successful harvest. The seven-day festival, held during the week after Easter, is strictly *gemuütlichkeit* — a gathering of happy people. There is music and dancing, good food, wine tasting, grape-picking and grape-treading competitions, a vintage fair, float processions and a *weingarten* — a big feast featuring German folk-songs. The grand finale takes the form of a spectacular fair held in the oval of Tanunda Park, where dancers in colourful national costumes dance around an 18-metre-high maypole, while food and wine are served in the marquees surrounding the oval. The **Barossa Classic Gourmet Weekend** in August combines the pleasures of wine, food and good music over two days.

During the long weekend in May the Clare Valley wineries host the **Gourmet Weekend**, which includes tastings and a progressive luncheon on the Sunday around the wineries.

McLaren Vale is the venue for the **Sip'N Savour** festival, held in June, when wineries and restaurants offer opportunities to sample the vintages of the Wine Coast. Another vineyard festival is the **McLaren Vale Bushing Festival** held annually in October. It is

Christmas Pageant

a time of fun and festivity, with craft exhibitions, parades, picnic days and formal balls to celebrate the new vintage.

The **Riverland Wine Festival** is held in November each odd-numbered year. The region's wineries combine with local restaurants to provide good food and wine, jazz music and other entertainment.

South Australia is a state of many cultures, which accounts for the many ethnic festivals held throughout the year. The largest of these is the *Schutzenfest* held at Hahndorf, a historic German-settled town in the lovely Adelaide Hills. Traditionally a shooting festival to raise funds for the Hahndorf Academy, it has grown into the biggest German-style beer festival held outside Germany. Located just 35 kilometres from Adelaide, the tranquil countryside is transformed into a bustling carnival with 'oompah' music, imported German beer, German folk-dancers in colourful national costume and restaurants serving platters of *sauerbraten* and *apfelstrudel*. The hot, thirsty month of January is ideal for drinking steins of ice-cold beer while listening to brass bands and waiting for a variety of *wü*ste (cold sausage meats) to be served at your table.

In March, the Greek community organises the **Glendi Festival** to coincide with the Greek National Day. In odd-numbered years in May, the colourful **Kernewek Lowender** (Cornish family festival) is held, centred around Kadina, Moonta and Wallaroo on the scenic Yorke Peninsula. Quaint

old miners' cottages, abandoned mining installations and numerous museums remind visitors of the heyday of copper mining. There is music and Cornish dancing, a pasty-making competition and a hilarious wheelbarrow race.

In October in even-numbered years, the Italian community launches a festival in the city and in country areas to promote its culture and lifestyle. In the Riverland region, the **Multicultural Festival** brings all cultural groups of the region together in a shared celebration of their heritage each even-numbered year in November.

During the June long weekend Barmera becomes the country music capital of the state, when visitors from all over Australia attend the **Country Music Festival**. **Citrus Week** promotes the Riverland citrus industry, with various events being held in all the towns in the region.

South Australia boasts many other festivals, among them the **Tunarama Festival** at the major fishing-port and resort of Port Lincoln, held every Australia Day long weekend. Australia's only festival dedicated to a fish, it includes a street procession, sports, competitions, displays, a fireworks spectacular and the famous tuna-tossing event; there is fun for the whole family in a gala atmosphere on the beautiful Tasman Terrace foreshore. In April the people of Laura, a small town in the lower Flinders Ranges, organise a **Folk Fair** which attracts thousands of visitors.

In September, Renmark stages a **Spring Family Festival** for family fun. Each Easter Monday, the **Great Eastern Steeplechase** is raced at Oakbank racecourse. This event is billed as the largest picnic meeting in the southern hemisphere and is a carnival which leads up to the running of the Adelaide Cup in May at Morphettville racecourse.

One event which is looked forward to by children and adults is the **Christmas Pageant** in the city streets of Adelaide. Floats depicting nursery rhymes and fairytale characters thrill all those who line the streets to welcome Father Christmas to South Australia.

Information on all the SA festivals can be obtained from Tourism South Australia Travel Centre, 1 King William St, Adelaide; (08) 212 1505.

SOUTH AUSTRALIA from A to Z

Aldinga   Population 3041

This small coastal town 45 km from Adelaide is on the west coast of the Fleurieu Peninsula. **Of interest:** St Ann's Church of England (1866) and Uniting Church (1863). **In the area:** Aldinga Beach, 4 km south-west; good swimming, surfing, diving and fishing. Maslin, Australia's first nude bathing beach, 6 km north. McLaren Vale, 12 km north-east, centre of wine-growing region with over 40 wineries. **Tourist information:** The Cottage, Main Rd, McLaren Vale; (08) 323 8537. **Accommodation:** Limited. **See also:** The Fleurieu Peninsula. MAP REF. 264 F5, 266 I8

Andamooka   Population 402

Andamooka is a lonely outback opal field around 600 km from Adelaide, to the west of the saltpan Lake Torrens. It is off the beaten track, where conditions are harsh, weather is severe and water precious. There are rough shacks along the dirt road, with many people living in dugouts to protect themselves from the extreme heat. Visitors who have obtained a precious-stone prospecting permit from the Mines Department in Adelaide can stake out a claim and try their luck. Looking for opal on mullock dumps left by miners requires permission from the owners of a claim. There are tours of the area and showrooms with opals for sale. The road to Andamooka is fair, but quickly affected by rain. **Of interest:** Duke's Bottle Home, made entirely of empty beer bottles.

Opal Festival held in October. **In the area:** Roxby Downs, 30 km west, service town for nearby Olympic Dam mining operations for copper, gold, silver and uranium; tours of mining operations available. At Woomera, 120 km south, Heritage Centre and Missile Park with displays of rockets and aircraft. **Accommodation:** 1 hotel/motel, 1 motel, 1 caravan/camping park. MAP REF. 271 M9, 272 H1

Angaston   Population 1823

Angaston is situated in the highest part of the Barossa Valley: within 79 km of the coast, it is 361 m above sea-level. The town is named after prominent 1830s Barossa Valley settler, George Fife Angas. **Of interest:** Angas Park Fruit Co., Murray St, produces dried fruit and nuts; open daily. Gawler Park Fruits, Valley Rd, for glace fruits; open weekdays. Angaston Galleria, Murray St, for home-made goods, art and craft. **In the area:** Collingrove Homestead (1850), 7 km south-east; National Trust owned property, once belonging to Angas pioneering family, now open for viewing, accommodation and meals. Springton Gallery, Herbig Tree and Robert Hamilton & Son Winery at Springton, 27 km south-east. Wineries: Saltram Wine Estates and Yalumba Winery, 2 km west and south of Angaston respectively, and Henschke's Wines near Keyneton 10 km south-east: all open for tastings and sales. Magnificent view of Barossa Val-

ley from Mengler's Hill Lookout, 8 km south-west. **Tourist information:** Angaston Galleria, 18 Murray St; (085) 64 2648. **Accommodation:** 2 hotels, 1 motel. **See also:** Vineyards and Wineries. MAP REF. 263 M4, 267 K4, 269 K13

Ardrossan   Population 963

Ardrossan, 148 km north-west of Adelaide, is the largest port on the east coast of the Yorke Peninsula. An important outlet for wheat and barley, it is an attractive town with excellent crabbing and fishing from the jetty. **Of interest:** Ardrossan and District Historical Museum, Fifth St. The stump jump plough was invented here in the late 1800s; restored plough on display on cliffs at end of First St in East Tce. **In the area:** BHP Lookout, 2 km south. For keen divers, Zanoni wreck off coast, 20 km south-east; permission required to dive. Clinton Conservation Park, 40 km north. **Tourist information:** Ardrossan Independent Store, First St; (088) 37 3209. **Accommodation:** 2 hotel/motels, 2 caravan/camping parks. MAP REF. 266 F4, 268 F13

Arkaroola   Population under 200

Founded in 1968, Arkaroola is a remote village settlement in the rugged northern Flinders Ranges, about 660 km north of Adelaide. This privately owned property of 61 000 ha has been opened as a flora and fauna sanctuary. The rugged outback country is crossed by incredible quartzite ridges, deep gorges and rich mineral deposits, and is a haven for birdlife and rare marsupials. **Of interest:** Mineral and Fossil Museum, Outdoor Pastoral Museum, Astronomical Observatory (check viewing times), art gallery and pioneer cottage. **In the area:** Marked walking-trails; self-guiding pamphlets from Information Centre. Old Cornish-style smelters (1861) and scenic waterholes, 12 km north-west at Bolla Bollana. About 18 km further west, old log cabin (1856) at Yankaninna Homestead. Famous Mt Painter, 10 km north; further 20 km north, breathtaking views from Freeling Heights overlooking Yudnamutana Gorge and Siller's Lookout over Lake Frome (a salt lake). The radioactive Paralana Hot Springs, 27 km north, originate deep within the earth's crust, along a great earth fracture. Gammon Ranges National Park, 20 km south-west, has extensive wilderness areas; recommended

Arkaroola settlement, Flinders Ranges

THE YORKE PENINSULA

Settled primarily as agricultural country, Yorke Peninsula was put on the map by the discovery of rich copper-ore deposits in 1861 and the influx of thousands of miners, including so many from Cornwall that the **Wallaroo–Moonta–Kadina** area became known as Little Cornwall.

The beautiful drive down the highway on the east coast is mainly within sight of the sea. Many of the east-coast towns have excellent fishing from long jetties once used for loading grain ships. Also beach, surf and rock fishing are excellent, as is crabbing.

The west coast of Yorke Peninsula is lined with safe swimming beaches and spectacular coastal scenery. **Port**

Old copper-mine buildings, Moonta

Victoria, the last of the windjammer ports, was once the main port of call for sailing-ships transporting grain.

Further north, Moonta's old stone buildings give it a sense of history and the Moonta mines tell of its mining heyday.

The southern tip of the Peninsula is for the more adventurous and includes Innes National Park with its desolate countryside and impressive coastal scenery. Visit the historic site of a once-flourishing township, Inneston. Pondalowie Bay is a must for surfers. Rocky cliff-tops and windswept headlands offer spectacular views across Investigator Strait.

For further information, contact the Yorke Peninsula Tourist Information Centre, Victoria Sq., Kadina; (088) 21 2093. **See also:** Individual entries in A–Z listing.

---

for experienced bushwalkers only. Balcanoona Homestead, Big Moro Gorge (with rock pools) and Chambers Gorge (with Aboriginal rock carvings) 20 km south of Arkaroola. Ridgetop Tour, a spectacular 4WD trip across Australia's most rugged mountains. Scenic flights. **Tourist information:** Visitors Information Centre. **Accommodation:** 3 motels, 1 caravan/camping park. **See also:** The Flinders Ranges; South Australia's National Parks.
MAP REF. 271 P9

Balaklava
Population 1365

Balaklava has a picturesque setting on the banks of the River Wakefield, 91 km from Adelaide. The town was named after a famous battle in the Crimean War. **Of interest:** National Trust Museum, May Tce, has relics of district's early days; open Sun. Courthouse Gallery and Shop, Edith Tce; community art gallery. Urlwin Park Agricultural Museum, Short Tce. Lions Club Walking Trail, along Wakefield River and through town; brochure available at Council offices. Agricultural Show in September. Festival of Gardens and Galleries in October. **In the area:** Devils Gardens, 7 km north-east on Auburn Rd, and The Rocks Reserve, 10 km east, both with picnic facilities. Beachside town of Port Wakefield, 26 km west at head of Gulf St Vincent. **Tourist information:** (088) 62 1811. **Accommodation:** 1 caravan/camping park.
MAP REF. 266 H3, 268 H12

Barmera
Population 1912

The sloping shores of Lake Bonney make a delightful setting for the Riverland town of Barmera, 214 km north-east of Adelaide. Lake Bonney is ideal for swimming, water-skiing, sailing, boating and fishing. The irrigated land is given over mainly to vineyards, but there are also apricot and peach orchards and citrus groves. Soldier settlement after World War I marked the beginning of today's community-oriented town. **Of interest:** Donald Campbell Obelisk, Queen Elizabeth Dr, Lake Bonney; commemorates Campbell's attempt on world water speed record in 1964. Pioneer Park, Scott Ave, opposite police station; collection of early farming implements. Bonneyview Wines, Sturt Hwy, eastern edge of town; tastings, sales, gallery, restaurant and picnic facilities; open daily. Barmera hosts SA Country Music Festival in June. **In the area:** Take the road to Overland Corner, and at North Lake, 10 km north-west visit Napper's Old Accommodation House (1850), built on the overland stock route from NSW; ruins preserved by National Trust. At Overland Corner, 19 km north-west on Morgan Rd: hotel (1859), now also National Trust museum; fascinating self-guided historical walking trail. Rocky's Country Hall of Fame for country music fans, 5 km north-east on Renmark Bypass; open daily. At Cobdogla, 5 km west, Irrigation Museum has world's only working Humphrey Pump, as well as steam rides, historic displays and picnic areas; check operating days. South-

west 16 km, near Moorook, Moorook Loch Luna Game Reserve includes Wachtels Lagoon with birdlife and walking trail around foreshore; nearby, Yatco Lagoon abounds with birdlife. At Monash, 8 km north-east: Wein Valley Estates; tastings and sales, Mon. – Sat; Grant's Super Playground, over 180 items of equipment; free entrance; open daily. **Tourist information:** Barwell Ave; (085) 88 2289. **Accommodation:** 2 motels, 1 hotel/motel, 3 caravan/camping parks. **See also:** Festival Fun.
MAP REF. 267 P3, 269 P12

Beachport
Population 413

The site of the South-east's first whaling station, in the 1830s, Beachport is a quiet little town 51 km south of Robe. Rivoli Bay nearby provides safe swimming beaches as well as shelter for lobster-fishing boats. **Of interest:** Old Wool and Grain Store, Railway Tce; National Trust Museum with whaling, shipping and local history exhibits. Military Museum, Foreshore Rd; open daily. Artifacts museum, McCourt St; Aboriginal heritage. Jubilee Lagoon Park in centre of town; barbecues, tennis, playgrounds, canoeing and skateboard track. **In the area:** Lake George, 4 km north, is a haven for waterbirds and popular for windsurfing and fishing. Beachport Conservation Park, between Lake George and the Southern Ocean, has Aboriginal shell middens. The winding Bowman Scenic Drive off McArthur Pl, offers spectacular views of the Southern Ocean. Swimming in Pool of

SOUTH AUSTRALIA'S NATIONAL PARKS

Nowhere else in Australia can wildlife be seen in such close proximity and in such profusion as in the parks of South Australia. To protect its valuable native animals and plants and to conserve the natural features of the landscape, this state has set aside 17 per cent of its total area as national, conservation and recreation parks, and regional and game reserves.

In addition to 14 national parks, the SA National Parks and Wildlife Service also manages 200 conservation parks, 14 recreation parks, 9 game reserves and 4 regional reserves. The main criteria for each category, as stated in the National Parks and Wildlife Act of 1972, were as follows:

- **National parks** Areas with wildlife or natural features of significance.
- **Conservation parks** Areas for the preservation and conservation of native flora and fauna representative of South Australia's natural heritage, although historical features may also be included in these parks.
- **Recreation parks** Areas for outdoor recreation in a natural setting.
- **Game reserves** Areas suitable for the management and conservation of native game species, usually duck and quail. Hunting of some species during restricted open seasons.
- **Regional reserves** A new category established in 1988 which protects, at present, four large areas within

South Australia considered to contain important wildlife and natural features, but where natural resources, such as minerals, may be needed in the future.

The range of climatic zones in South Australia enables visitors to enjoy the attractions of these parks throughout the year; coastal parks are cool in summer and autumn, while mountain areas are ideal to visit in winter and spring.

The Flinders Ranges, which extend for 430 kilometres, contain the **Flinders Ranges National Park**, which, with its total area of 94 908 hectares, is one of the major national parks in Australia. The Wilpena section, located in the south of the park, comprises the famed Wilpena Pound and the Wilpena Pound Range, covering an area of 10 000 hectares. The Pound is one of the most extraordinary geological formations in Australia. Developed in the Cambrian period, it is a vast oval rock bowl, ringed with sheer cliffs and jagged rocks and with a flat floor covered with trees and grass. An old homestead dating back to 1889 still stands. At Arkaroo Rock, native rock paintings indicate that this was a significant area in Aboriginal mythology.

Twenty-five kilometres north of Wilpena is the Oraparinna section of the park. The 68 500 hectares of this section were a sheep-station last century, at one time maintaining more than 20 000 sheep. Further north, near the

Gammon Ranges National Park, Arkaroola offers both motel accommodation and a serviced camping-ground. The park, an arid, isolated region of rugged ranges and deep gorges, offers visitors the opportunity to experience an extensive wilderness area. The mountains sparkle with exposed formations of quartz, fluorspar, hematites and ochres, making the region a gemhunter's paradise. The Gammon Ranges are a sanctuary for many native birds and animals, including the western grey kangaroo, the big red kangaroo, the grey euro or hill kangaroo and the yellow-footed rock wallaby.

Further north, in the state's arid lands, over 8 million hectares have been set aside to protect the unique desert environment. These desert parks include the **Lake Eyre National Park, Witjira National Park, Innamincka Regional Reserve** and the **Simpson Desert Conservation Park**. Lake Eyre, the central feature of the park of the same name, is one of the world's greatest salinas or salt lakes, found 16 metres below sea level. Contrarily, it is both the hub of a huge internal drainage system while being located in the driest part of the Australian continent. Vegetation is sparse but after heavy rains when the area floods, the ground is covered with colourful wildflowers and the animal and bird populations, attracted by the plant

Flinders Ranges

rejuvenation, rise accordingly. Care needs to be taken when visiting; only 4WD vehicles can access the park and campers must be fully self-sufficient.

Witjira National Park, located 120 km north of Oodnadatta, is an area of vast desert landscapes; gibber plains, sand dunes, salt pans and mound springs, upwellings of the Great Artesian Basin. Visitors may explore this extremely arid environment from the park's oasis, Dalhousie Springs.

The Innamincka Regional Reserve covers much of the flood-out country of the Cooper and Strzlecki Creeks from the Queensland border. These arid wetlands, which comprise a series of semi-permanent overflow lakes, hold many surprises for bird-watchers.

The Simpson Desert Conservation Park, for the more adventurous park visitor, consists of spectacular red sand dunes which in places can run parallel for hundreds of kilometres, salt lakes, flood-out plains, hummock grasslands, gibber desert, gidgee woodland, tablelands and mesas.

Visitors who wish to enjoy the attractions of the parks and reserves in this vast desert area must obtain a Desert Parks Pass (included in the **Desert Parks South Australia Handbook** and maps kit), from the SA National Parks and Wildlife Service (SA NPWS), P.O. Box 102, Hawker, SA 5434; telephone (086) 48 4244. The pass is valid from the date of purchase; and allows twelve months bush camping in Lake Eyre National Park, Witjira National Park, Innamincka Regional Reserve and the Simpson Desert Conservation Park and Regional Reserve, and also Flinders Ranges and Gammon Ranges National Parks. Maps and information on each park and reserve are included along with a vehicle identification sticker and three renewal forms.

One of the finest national parks in South Australia is **The Coorong**, 185 km from Adelaide, south of the mouth of the mighty Murray River. The Coorong — a corruption of the Aboriginal word *karangh*, meaning 'narrow neck' — is a series of saltwater lagoons fed by the Murray and separated from the sea by the Younghusband Peninsula.

In the park are six island bird sanctuaries, prohibited to the public, but which can be viewed through binoculars. These islands house rookeries of pelicans, crested terns and silver gulls. The ocean beach of the Coorong is a favourite haunt of fishermen, but you can take the pleasant drive along the coast road beside the waterway, stopping to camp or picnic. There are more than 160 species of birds in the ti-tree and wattle thickets along this road. At dusk, big grey kangaroos and red-necked wallabies come out to feed on the grassed open areas.

On the southern flat plains of South Australia, near Naracoorte, is **Bool Lagoon Game Reserve**. The lagoon's natural cycle of flooding and drying out is perfect for the breeding of waterbirds. In spring, when the water is deepest, thousands of black swans crowd the lagoon, creating a wildlife spectacle. In summer and autumn, when the water is shallow, waterfowl and waders flock to feed on the rich plant life. Bool Lagoon is also the largest permanent ibis rookery in Australia. Dense thickets of paperbark and banks of reeds in its central reaches provide safe places for breeding. A boardwalk network provides access to wildlife without disturbing the natural environment.

A conservation park in the southeast of the state, preserves the **Naracoorte Caves**. These limestone caves enclose a wonderland of stalagmites, stalactites, shawls, straws and other calcite formations. Four caves, including Blanche Cave, the first to be discovered, in 1845, are open for inspection by guided or adventure tours. A museum is set up within Victoria Fossil Cave, where a tour shows visitors skeletons of such extinct animals as giant browsing kangaroos, a hippopotamus-sized wombat, the marsupial lion and the Tasmanian tiger.

Flinders Chase National Park, situated at the western end of Kangaroo Island, is in wild and rugged country, which enjoys mild summers. It is popular with bushwalkers, who enjoy hiking through trackless forests of gum and mallee scrub.

Seal Bay Conservation Park, also on Kangaroo Island, allows visitors the unique opportunity to view breeding colonies of Australia sea-lions. The adjoining **Cape Cantheaume Conservation Park** is a wilderness area attracting experienced bushwalkers.

A twelve-month Kangaroo Island Pass, available from the NPWS office at Kingscote (PO Box 39, Kingscote 5223; telephone (0848) 22 381) gives access to all parks on the island where an entrance fee is charged.

On the Yorke Peninsula is **Innes National Park**, where birdwatching is a favourite pastime; there is good fishing at the beaches; and walking trails lead to the coastal beach and to the historic site of Inneston. This small settlement, now in ruins, once housed miners who dug for gypsum, used for plaster and chalk; for many years nearly every schoolchild in Australia was taught with the aid of blackboard chalk mined here and shipped from Stenhouse Bay.

The Eyre Peninsula, 'bordered' to the north by the Eyre Highway, contains several parks. At **Coffin Bay National Park** and **Lincoln National Park** the main feature is the coastal scenery. As well, the opportunities for bush camping, bird-watching and bush-walking in delightful natural surroundings attract visitors.

Coffin Bay is only 50 kilometres west of Port Lincoln and the park takes in all of the Coffin Bay Peninsula; the western coast of which faces the Great Australian Bight while the southern side has the calming influence of sandy beaches and several offshore islands.

A 25 km drive south of Port Lincoln finds **Lincoln National Park** which occupies much of the Jussieu Peninsula, surrounded by small islands. At its northern tip, on Stamford Hill, the Flinders Monument commemorates a visit by Matthew Flinders in 1802. Beach fishing is popular, but rip tides and sharks prevent swimming.

The salt lakes of **Lake Gilles Conservation Park**, also on Eyre Peninsula, are bird-watching country.

A unique and successful experiment of familiarising people with native fauna is evidenced at the Cleland Wildlife Park in the centre of the larger **Cleland Conservation Park**, located on the slopes of Mount Lofty overlooking Adelaide. Here visitors are able to walk freely among the animals, which are housed in conditions similar to their native habitat.

Located within Adelaide's southern suburbs in **Belair Recreation Park**, the most popular park in the state. The park's bushland setting, together with its resident birds and animals, attract family groups.

Camping and entrance fees are charged at many of South Australia's national parks. For further information on camping restrictions, entry permits and fees, and general advice on visiting national parks, contact SA NPWS Information Centre, 55 Grenfell St, Adelaide 5000 (GPO Box 1782, Adelaide 5001); (08) 207 2000.

THE COORONG

The Coorong National Park curves along the southern coast of South Australia for 145 kilometres, extending from Lake Alexandrina in the north almost to the small township of Kingston S.E. in the south. A unique area, it has an eerie desolation, a silence broken only by the sounds of any of the 400 species of native birds wheeling low over the scrub and dunes and the thunder of the Southern Ocean.

The Coorong proper is a shallow lagoon, a complex of low-lying saltpans and claypans. Never more than three kilometres wide, the lagoon is divided from the sea by the towering white sandhills of Younghusband Peninsula, known locally as the Hummocks.

One of the last natural bird sanctuaries in Australia, giant pelicans, shags, ibises, swans and terns are at home here. During the summer, access is gained by turning off at **Salt Creek**, leaving the Princes Highway, and following the old road along the shore. The coastal scenery is magnificent. Explore the unspoiled stretches of beach where the rolling surf washes up gnarled driftwood and beautiful shells. Year-round access is from a point further south known as the '42 mile'.

For those who wish to explore in comfort, **Meningie** in the north and the fishing port of **Kingston S.E.** have a range of accommodation and can be used as touring bases. Camping is permitted in the Coorong National Park; however, in the Younghusband Peninsula section, it is allowed in designated areas only. Permits must be obtained from the NPWS (see below).

The area is rich in history as well as being a naturalists' haven; pick up the Coorong Tourist Brochure for details. Fishing, boating and walking are popular.

A game reserve within the Coorong National Park extends between Policemans Point and Salt Creek.

For further information, contact the National Parks and Wildlife Service Office, Salt Creek; (085) 75 7014. **See also:** Entries for Kingston S.E. and Meningie in A–Z listing.

Siloam, on Scenic Drive; lake with high salt content and reputed therapeutic benefits. Woakwine Cutting, 10 km north off Robe Rd; extraordinary drainage project, with observation platform and machinery exhibit. Canunda National Park, 20 km south, 40-km stretch of spectacular wind-swept sand dunes and virgin bushland, with fascinating flora and fauna. Day-trips to see penguins on Penguin Island, a conservation park, in summer. **Tourist information:** Southern Ocean Caravan Park, Somerville St; (087) 35 8153. **Accommodation:** 1 hotel, 1 motel, 2 caravan/camping parks. MAP REF. 273 E10

Berri   Population 3502
The commercial centre of the Riverland region, Berri is 227 km north-east of Adelaide. Originally a wood-refuelling stop for the paddle-steamers and barges which plied the Murray, the town was first proclaimed in 1911. This is fruit- and vine-growing country, dotted with peaceful picnic and fishing areas. **Of interest:** Lookout tower (17 m), Fiedler St; panoramic views of river and town. River tours on Riverland's only twin ferries crossing Murray River. Houseboats for hire. Easter Festival and rodeo held annually; Multicultural Festival held every October. **In the area:** Large range of dried fruit and confectionery from Berri Fruit Tree Kiosk, 3 km west on Sturt Hwy. Berri Estates winery and distillery, largest in Australia, 13 km west on Sturt Hwy, near town of Glossop; tastings and sales Mon. – Sat. Berrivale Orchards, 4 km north on Sturt Hwy; tastings and sales of Berri fruit juices; also educational audiovisual on Riverland's history and various stages in processing of fruit; open Mon.–Fri., Sat. morning. Wilabalangaloo flora and fauna reserve, 5 km north off Sturt Hwy; walking trails, spectacular scenery, museum and paddlewheeler; check opening times. On the Sturt Hwy, opposite access to Wilabalangaloo reserve, the Big Orange, the largest orange in the world; open daily. Impressive vintage car collection at adjacent Riverland Display Centre. On Morgan Rd, art and craft exhibits at the Parlour Australiana Gallery, also accessed from the Big Orange. Martin's Bend, 2 km east; popular for water-skiing and picnicking. Township of Monash,12 km north-west on Morgan Rd; features famous Grant's Super Playground for young and old with over 180 weird and wonderful contraptions. Wine tastings and sales (Mon.– Sat.) at Wein Valley Estate, off Morgan Rd. Banyula Aboretum, 8km south-west at Winkie, features displays and nursery of native plants. Katarapko Game Reserve, 10 km south-west, features Kia Kia Nature Trail for bushwalkers; canoes for hire. **Tourist information:** 24 Vaughan Tce; (085) 82 1655. **Accommodation:** 1 hotel/motel, 3 motels, 1 caravan/camping park. MAP REF. 116 A8, 267 P3, 269 P12

Blinman   Population under 200
Blinman, 478 km north of Adelaide near the northern boundary of the Flinders Ranges National Park, was a thriving copper-mining centre from 1860 to 1890. The countryside is magnificent, particularly when the wild hops bloom. **Of interest:** Several historic buildings, including hotel (1869), post office (1862) and police station (1874), all in main street. **In the area:** Great Wall of China, impressive ironstone-capped ridge, 10 km south on Wilpena Rd. Further south, beautiful Aroona Valley, with ruins of old Aroona Homestead; nearby Mt Hayward and Brachina Gorge. 'Almost ghost' town of Beltana, 60 km north, declared a historic reserve. Midway between Blinman and Parachilna is Angorichina, located 15 km west in scenic Parachilna Gorge; nearby, the Blinman Pools, fed by a permanent spring. Scenic drive east through Eregunda Valley to Chambers Gorge with rock pools and Aboriginal carvings; then north, spectacular Big Moro Gorge on Arkaroola Rd. **Accommodation:** 1 hotel/motel, 1 caravan/camping park. MAP REF. 271 O10

Bordertown   Population 2318
Bordertown is a quiet town on the Dukes Hwy, 274 km south-east of Adelaide. The town's growth was stimulated after 1852 when it became an important supply centre for the goldfields of western Victoria. Today the area is noted for wool, cereals, meat and vegetable production. **Of interest:** Robert J.L. Hawke, Australian Prime Minister, was born here and his childhood home, in Farquhar St, has been

renovated and includes a memorabilia display; open Mon.–Fri. Town parks offer picnic facilities. Bordertown Wildlife Park, Dukes Hwy; native birds and animals, including pure white kangaroos. **In the area:** Historic Clayton Farm, 3 km south; vintage farm machinery and thatched buildings; open Sun.–Fri. Clayton Farm Vintage Field Day held October long weekend. At Mundalla, 10 km southwest: Mundalla Hotel (1884), now National Trust Museum, and Wirrega Council Chambers. At Padthaway, 42 km south-west, 1882 homestead houses Padthaway Estate winery; accommodation and meals available. Picnic areas among magnificent red gums and stringybarks at Padthaway Conservation Park. Bangham Conservation Park, 30 km south-east, near Frances. **Tourist information:** Council Chambers, 43 Woolshed St; (087) 52 1044. **Accommodation:** 2 hotels, 3 motels, 1 caravan/camping park.
MAP REF. 212 A7, 267 Q13, 273 H4

Burra

Population 1187

Nestled in Bald Hills Range, 154 km north of Adelaide, Burra is a former copper-mining centre. The district of Burra Burra (the name is Hindustani for 'great great') is now famous for stud merino sheep, and Burra serves as the market town for the surrounding farmland. *Breaker Morant* was filmed here. Copper was discovered in 1845 and copper to the value of almost $10 million was extracted before the mine closed in 1877. **Of interest:** A passport system (details from Tourist Information Office) gives visitors access to walk or drive around 11 km of heritage buildings, museums, mine-shafts and look-out points. Daily 2-hr bus tours of town and its fascinating mining history from Tourist Information Office; bookings essential. Burra Creek Miners' Dugouts, alongside Blyth St, where more than 1500 people lived during the boom period. Burra cemetery, off Spring St. Burra Mine Open Air Museum, off Market St, includes ore dressing tower, powder magazine; spectacular views of open-cut mine and town. Nearby Enginehouse Museum, built in 1858 and reconstructed in 1986; alongside archaeological excavation of 30-m entry tunnel to Morphett's Shaft. Market Square Museum, across from Tourist Information Office. Malowen Lowarth Museum, Kingston St, in original miner's cottage.Underground cellars of old Unicorn Brewery, Bridge Tce. Also in Bridge Tce, Paxton Square Cottages (1850), 33 two-, three- and four-roomed cottages built for Cornish miners, now restored as accommodation for visitors. In Burra North: police lock-up and stables (1849), Tregony St; Redruth

Underground library, Coober Pedy

Gaol (1857), off Tregony St; and Bon Accord Mine buildings (1846), Railway Tce, now a museum complex. Picturesque spots alongside creek for swimming, canoeing and picnicking. **In the area:** Chatswood Farm Gallery, 14 km south at Hanson. Wineries in the Clare Valley, about 30 km south-west. Picturesque Burra Gorge, 27 km east. Scenic 90 km drive, Dares Hill Drive, begins 30 km north on Broken Hill Rd. **Tourist information:** 2 Market Sq.; (088) 92 2154. **Accommodation:** 4 hotels, 1 caravan/ camping park.
MAP REF. 269 J9

Ceduna

Population 2877

Near the junction of the Flinders and Eyre Hwys, 786 km from Adelaide, Ceduna is the last major town you go through before crossing the Nullarbor from east to west. It is the ideal place to check over your car and stock up with food and water before the long drive. The port at Thevenard, 3 km east, handles bulk grain, gypsum and salt. The fishing-fleet is noted for its large whiting hauls. Snapper, salmon, tommy ruff and crab are other catches. Ceduna is set on Murat Bay and the sand coves, sheltered bays and offshore islands of this bay make it an ideal base for a beach holiday. There was a whaling-station on St Peter Island back in the 1850s. According to map references in Swift's *Gulliver's Travels*, the tiny people of Lilliput might well have lived on one of the islands visible from Thevenard — St Peter and St Francis. The beaches are ideal for swimming, fishing, water-skiing, windsurfing and boating. **Of interest:** Old Schoolhouse National Trust Museum, Park Tce; pioneering items, artefacts from atomic testing at Maralinga and historic medical room; open daily. **In the area:** Oestmann's Fish Factory at Thevenard Boat Haven; open daily. At Denial Bay, 13 km west: McKenzie Ruins, site of original settlement; also oyster farm. Denial Bay and Davenport Creek, west, and Decres Bay, Laura Bay and Smoky Bay, all south-east, for picnicking and safe fishing (boat charter available at Ceduna); all within day-tripping distance from town. Amazing sand dunes and excellent surf at Cactus Beach, near Penong, 54 km west. Southern right whales can be seen during June – Oct. along coast west of Ceduna. Overseas Telecommunications Earth Station, 37 km north, links Australia with countries in Asia, Africa and Europe; open for inspection weekdays, tours available. Spectacular coastline includes prominent headland at Point Brown, 56 km south. **Tourist information:** 58 Poynton St; (086) 25 2780. **Accommodation:** 1 hotel/motel, 3 motels, 4 caravan/camping parks. **See also:** The Eyre Peninsula.
MAP REF. 270 H12, 272 A6

Clare

Population 2591

Set in the midst of rich agricultural and pastoral country, the charming town of Clare was first settled in 1842; it was named after County Clare in Ireland. The area is renowned for its prize-winning table wines. Wheat, barley, fruit, honey, stud sheep and wool are other important regional industries. The first vines were planted by a group of Jesuit priests at Sevenhill in 1848. The priests are still producing table and sacramental wines from the Sevenhill Cellars. The Clare Valley wineries host a Gourmet Weekend on the May long weekend. Horse-racing adds to carnival atmosphere of Clare Valley Easter Festival. **Of interest:** National

Trust museum housed in old police station (1850), cnr Victoria Rd and West Tce; open Sat., Sun. and holidays. Inchiquin Lake, White Hut Rd. Lookouts at Billy Goat Hill, from Wright Place, and Neagles Rock, Neagles Rock Rd. Pioneer Memorial Park, Pioneer Ave; walking-tracks and picnic facilities. Plaque commemorates arrival of Burke and Wills in 1862. Historic town walk self-guiding leaflets available. **In the area:** Stately Wolta Wolta Homestead, West Tce, on western edge of town, built by pioneer pastoralist John Hope in 1846 and still owned by Hope family; open for inspection weekends. Over 20 wineries (most open for inspection and cellar-door sales; check opening times): around Clare — Jim Barry Wines, Hutt River Estate, Tim Knappstein Wines, Stanley Wine Co. Wendouree Cellars, Tim Adams' Wines, Duncan Estate; around Sevenhill (7 km south) — Sevenhill Cellars (established 1851, with monastery buildings, including St Aloysius Church (1864), Paulett Wines, Pike's Polish Hill River Estate, Wilson's Polish Hill River Winery; around Penwortham (10 km south) — Skillogalee Vineyards, Mitchell's Cellars; around Mintaro (15 km south-east) — Mintaro Cellars; around Watervale (12 km south) — Watervale Cellars, Eaglehawk Estate (also wine museum), Rosenberg Cellars, Mount Horrocks Winery, Fareham Estate; around Auburn (26 km south) — Taylors Wines, Grosset Wines. Also at Mintaro, fascinating Heritage town, 15 km south-east: historic Martindale Hall (featured in the film *Picnic at Hanging Rock*); accommodation, dining and tours in afternoons daily; Robinson's Cottage, 1851 settler's cottage now housing historic fire engine collection; Reilly's Cottage Gallery (1870s); slate quarry, operational since 1856. Also at Auburn, town of historical and cultural interest, many historical buildings maintained by National Trust and open for inspection; self-guided walking tour leaflets available. Birthplace of poet C.J. Dennis in 1876, Stonehurst Gallery and Library (1866) contain original Dennis handworks. Scenic drive to Blyth, 13 km west; native flora and fauna in Padnaindi Reserve; Medika Gallery, originally a Lutheran church (1886), specialising in Australian bird and flower paintings, open daily, not Thurs. Scenic drive 12 km south to Spring Gully Conservation Park, which has a stand of rare red stringybarks. Bungaree Station Homestead (1841),12 km north, historic merino sheep-station; tours and accommodation; knitting yarns, original patterns and hand-knitted Bungaree jumpers available from Station Store. Geralka Rural Farm, 25 km north of Clare. **Tourist information:** Main North Rd; (088) 42 2131.

Accommodation: 2 hotels, 1 hotel/motel, 2 motels, 2 caravan/camping parks. **See also:** Festival Fun.
MAP REF. 266 I1, 268 I10

Cleve   Population 809
An inland town on the Eyre Peninsula, settled in 1853 by Europeans, Cleve is surrounded by rich farming country. **Of interest:** Cleve Fauna Park. Old Council Chambers Museum. Eyre Peninsula Field Days (agricultural shows) held around August every even year. **In the area:** Scenic drive along escarpment of Cleve – Cowell Hills. Cowell, 43 km east, and Arno Bay, 26 km south-east, both have good swimming beaches and fishing jetties. Hincks (35 km west) and Bascombe Well (90 km west) Conservation Parks. **Tourist information:** Whyalla Tourist Centre, Lincoln Hwy, Whyalla; (086) 45 7900. **Accommodation:** 1 hotel/motel, 1 caravan park.
MAP REF. 268 A10, 272 G10

Coffin Bay   Population 341
A picturesque holiday town and fishing-village in a sheltered bay, 51 km northwest of Port Lincoln; sailing, water-skiing and swimming are popular here. The coastal scenery in this area is magnificent and fishing is excellent. Oysters cultivated in Coffin Bay are amongst the best in Australia. The bay's unusual name was bestowed by Matthew Flinders in 1802 to honour his friend Sir Isaac Coffin. **Of interest:** Oyster Farm, The Esplanade; also renowned for its lobster. Oyster Walk, a delightful 2.5 km foreshore walkway between caravan park and Crinolin Point. **In the area:** Coffin Bay National Park and Kellidie Bay Conservation Park surround township; wildflowers in spring. Camping in national park areas; permit required. Farm Beach and nearby 'Anzac Cove', location for film *Gallipoli*. Yangie Trail drive, 10 km south, through bush to Point Avoid and Yangie Lookout for coastal views and surf beaches. Old stone buildings in Wangary, 29 km north. Further north 50 km, scenic stretch of Flinders Hwy between Mount Hope and Sheringa. Blacksmith's museum at Koppio, 45 km north-west. **Tourist information:** Beachcomber Agencies, The Esplanade; (086) 85 4057. **Accommodation:** 1 motel, 1 caravan/ camping park. **See also:** The Eyre Peninsula.
MAP REF. 272 E12

Coober Pedy   Population 2103
In the heart of South Australia's outback, 848 km north of Adelaide on the Stuart Hwy, is the opal-mining town of Coober Pedy. This is the last stop for petrol

between Cadney Homestead (155 km north) and Glendambo (253 km south) on the Stuart Hwy. The name is Aboriginal for 'white fellow's hole in the ground' — very appropriate, since most of the population live in dugouts as protection from the severe summer temperatures, often reaching 45°C, and the cold winter nights. There is also a complete lack of timber for building. The countryside is desolate and harsh, and the town has reticulated water provided. Opals were discovered here in 1911 and today there are hundreds of mines. Anyone can try their luck after obtaining a precious-stones prospecting permit from the Mines Department in Adelaide. Trespassers on claims can be fined. **Of interest:** Guided tours of mines and tours and demonstrations of opals being cut and polished. Jewellery and polished stones available for purchase. Big Winch Lookout and Old Timers Mine, a mine museum and interpretive centre with self-guided walks, on eastern edge of town. Umoona underground mine behind Hutchison St; museum and motel. Underground churches, Hutchison St, including St Peter and St Pauls, and the Catacomb Church, east of town. Desert Cave, Hutchison St; underground pictorial mining display. Underground Pottery, west of town, features locally made pottery. Opal Festival, combined with Outback Festival, held annually at Easter. **In the area:** Opal fields are pocked with diggings; beware of unprotected mine shafts. Avoid entering any field area unless escorted by someone who knows the area. The Breakaways, 30 km north, colourful 40 sq.km reserve containing unique landscape, flora and fauna. **Tourist information:** Council Offices, Hutchison St; (086) 72 5298. **Accommodation:** 3 hotels, 1 hotel/motel, 4 motels, 3 caravan/camping parks. **See also:** The Outback of South Australia.
MAP REF. 270 I6

Coonalpyn   Population 312
This tiny town on the Dukes Hwy, 180 km south-east of Adelaide, makes a good base to explore the Mt Boothby (30 km south-west) and Carcuma (20 km north-east) Conservation Parks, and see grey kangaroos, echidnas, emus and mallee fowl in their natural environment. **Tourist information:** Bakery and Craft Shop, Dukes Hwy; (085) 71 1200. **Accommodation:** 1 hotel, 1 caravan/camping park.
MAP REF. 267 N10, 273 E1

Coonawarra   Population under 200
The history of Coonawarra goes back to 1890, when John Riddoch subdivided 2000 acres of his own vast land holding for the development of orchards and vineyards.

KANGAROO ISLAND

Only 120 kilometres south-west of Adelaide, Kangaroo Island, the largest island off South Australia's coast, and third largest Australian island, shows nature at its wildest and purest form in a magical combination of sun and sea, native flora and fauna. A walk through bush or along coastal cliffs may provide glimpses of koalas, echidnas or, of course, kangaroos; there are also many species of birds and wildflowers.

To reach the island, visitors may fly from Adelaide (Air Kangaroo Island and Lloyds Aviation) or go by ferry. The vehicular ferry *Island Seaway* journeys from Port Adelaide to Kingscote. The *Philanderer III* operates from Cape Jervis to Penneshaw.

There is no public transport on the island, but land and sea tours are available and hire vehicles include cars, scooters, mopeds and bicycles. Kangaroo Island's waters — freshwater, surf, rocks and ocean — offer excellent fishing; big-game-fishing charters available and fishing equipment can be hired.

At the three main towns, **Kingscote**, **American River** and **Penneshaw**, there is a range of accommodation from hotels and motels, through self-contained flats and cottages to camping and cabins.

American River is a small resort nestled in a protected pine-fringed bay, ideal for fishing (charter boats available), scuba-diving and canoeing. Pelican Lagoon is a sanctuary for birds and fish. Penneshaw overlooks the passage separating the island from the mainland. Fairy penguins promenade on the rocks here at night.

The coastline of the island varies from the several kilometres of safe swimming beach at **Emu Bay** on the north, to the rugged cliffs and roaring surf of the south. However, in the south, **D'Estrees Bay**'s wide deserted beach is ideal for fishing, shell collecting and exploring — there is an old whaling station at Port Tinline. **Cape Gantheaume** and **Seal Bay Conservation Parks** are located on this exposed southern coast. Seal Bay is the home of a permanent colony of sea-lions, with fur seals and leopard seals frequent residents. Also on the south coast are fascinating limestone formations in the caves at **Kelly Hill Conservation Park**. At **Cape Borda**, on the north-west tip of the island, is one of the most picturesque of Australia's old lighthouses; inspections arranged through National Parks and Wildlife Service at Kingscote. Other attractive spots along the northern coast include the rugged rocks at **Harveys Return**; **Western River Cove** with its idyllic white beach; a superb protected bay at **Snelling Beach**; and **Stokes Bay**, where a secret tunnel leads to the beach. On the west coast, which is dominated by the soaring eucalypt forests of the Flinders Chase National Park, are two of the island's natural wonders: **Admirals Arch**, a huge arch where on sunny afternoons stalactites can be seen in silhouette, and the **Remarkable Rocks**, huge unusually-shaped granite boulders.

For further information, contact the Kangaroo Island Tourist Information Centre, National Parks and Wildlife Services, 37 Dauncey St, Kingscote, (0848) 2 2381; or the Kangaroo Island Tourist Association, 1 Ryberg Rd, American River, (008) 08 8206. Island camping passes can be purchased from National Parks and Wildlife Service. **See also:** Entry for Kingscote in A–Z listing.

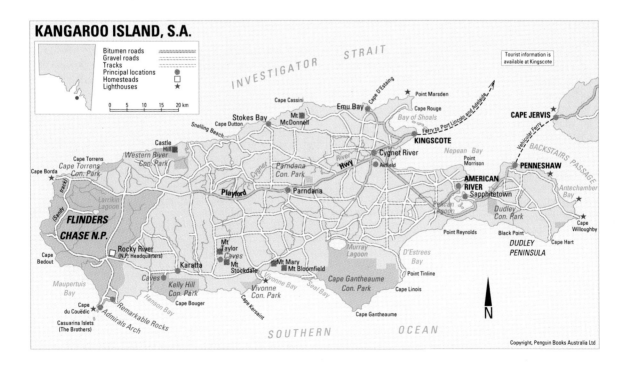

KANGAROO ISLAND, S.A.

Although the vines flourished and excellent wines were made, demand was not high until a resurgence of interest in the 1950s and 1960s, when the region became recognised as an important wine-growing area. The rich terra rossa soil and dedicated viticulturalists and winemakers now combine to produce award-winning white and red table wines. **Of interest:** Chardonnay Lodge, Penola Rd, has a motel, restaurant, art gallery and wine information centre. **In the area:** Wineries: Bowen Estate, Brands Laira, Hollick Wines, Hungerford Hill, James Haselgrove, Katnook Estate, Ladbroke Grove Wines, Leconfield Coonawarra, Mildara Wines, Penowarra Wines, Redman Winery, Rouge Homme, The Ridge Wines, Wynns Coonawarra Estate, Zema Estate. **Tourist information:** Arthur St, Penola; (087) 37 2855. **Accommodation:** 1 motel. **See also:** Vineyards and Wineries.
MAP REF. 210 A2, 273 H9

Cowell   Population 692

A small, pleasant township 108 km south of Whyalla, Cowell is on the almost landlocked Franklin Harbour. One of the world's major jade deposits is in the district, and Cowell is the processing centre for Australia's only commercial jade-mining operation. The sandy beach is safe for swimming and the fishing is excellent. Oyster farming is a new local industry and in season, fresh oysters can be purchased from various outlets. **Of interest:** Old post office and attached residence, (1888), Main St; now Franklin Harbour National Trust Historical Museum. Open-air Agricultural Museum, Lincoln Hwy. Jade Workshop, Lincoln Hwy, for viewing the cutting and processing of the stone; opposite, at the Cowell Jade Motel, displays of jewellery and sales (open daily). Lionel Deer's Camels, Kimba Rd. Smithy's Shell House, Warnes St. **In the area:** Franklin Harbour Conservation Park, south of Cowell, has good fishing spots. Swimming and fishing locations abound, including Port Gibbon, 15 km south, and Point Price Sandhills, 5 km further on. Cowell Jade Safaris offers jade-fossicking safaris into the picturesque Minbrie Ranges. Arno Bay, 48 km south, is a popular holiday resort with sandy beaches and a jetty for fishing. Entrance Island, accessible only by boat. **Tourist information:** Council Offices, Main St; (086) 29 2019. **Accommodation:** 1 hotel, 1 motel, 2 caravan /camping parks. **See also:** The Eyre Peninsula.
MAP REF. 266 C1, 268 C10, 272 H9

Crystal Brook   Population 1294

Originally part of a vast sheep-station, this town, 25 km south-east of Port Pirie, is now a thriving centre for the sheep, dairy and beef industries of the region. **Of interest:** National Trust Museum, Brandis St; local history collection in first two-storey building in town, which was original butcher's shop and bakery. Underground bakehouse to view. Picnicking and swimming in creekside parks. **In the area:** Bowman Park, 5 km east, surrounds ruins of Bowman family property, Crystal Brook Run (1847); excellent Native Fauna Zone, including reptile collection, regular feeding of animals and demonstrations of snake venom extraction (open afternoons daily). For walkers, the Heysen Trail runs through Bowman Park. Guided walking tours through southern Flinders Ranges available. In small town of Gladstone, 21 km north-east, set in rich rural country in Rocky River Valley, once an important railway centre: railway yards contain one of world's few junction points of 3 different gauges — narrow, standard and broad — interlaid together in one siding; tours of Gladstone gaol (1881); Trend Drinks Factory, home of 'Old Style Ginger Beer' (tours available). Laura, 11 km further north; boyhood town of C.J. Dennis, author of *The Songs of a Sentimental Bloke*, also renowned for its Folk Fair (held in April) and its cottage craft industry and art galleries; many historic buildings, (self-guided walking tour leaflet available). Picturesque Beetaloo Valley and Reservoir, nearby. Further 18 km north, near Wirrabara, scenic walks through pine forests. Salt lakes around Snowtown, 50 km south; Lochiel-Ninnes Road lookout for superb view of inland lakes and countryside. **Tourist information:** Bowman St; (086) 36 2699. **Accommodation:** Crystal Brook, 2 hotels, 1 caravan/camping park. Gladstone, 1 caravan/camping park. Laura, 1 caravan/camping park.
MAP REF. 268 G8

Edithburgh   Population 446

Located on the cliff-top of the southern tip of the Yorke Peninsula, Edithburgh overlooks Gulf St Vincent and Troubridge Shoals, a chain of tiny islands. **Of interest:** Edithburgh Museum, Edith St; historical maritime collection. Native Flora Park (17.5 ha), Ansley Tce. Town jetty, end of Edith St, built in 1873. Rock-pool at cliff-base is excellent for swimming. Offshore skindiving is popular and nearby Sultana Bay is good for boating, fishing, swimming and sailboarding. State Sailboarding Championships held in October. **In the area:** Coobowie, 5 km north, popular coastal resort with caravan park and fuchsia nursery. Tours to Troubridge Island Conservation Park; half-hour by boat. Scenic drive along coast passes wreck of *Clan Ranald*. **Tourist information:** Edithburgh Caravan Park, O'Halloran Pde; (088) 52 6056. **Accommodation:** 1 hotel, 1 motel, 1 caravan/camping park.
MAP REF. 266 F7, 272 I13

Elliston   Population 209

Nestled in a small range of hills on the shore of Waterloo Bay, Elliston is a pleasant coastal town and the centre for a cereal-growing, mixed-farming and fishing community. Widely known for its rugged and scenic coastline, excellent fishing and safe swimming beaches, Elliston is a popular holiday destination. **Of interest:** Town hall mural, Main St; an art history of town and district. **In the area:** Clifftop walk at Waterloo Bay; fossilised cocoons of species of weevil, believed to be over 100 000 years old, can be found. Talia Caves, 40 km north. Good surfing just north of town near Anxious Bay. Lock's Well and Sheringa Beach to south, for surf fishing. Scenic drives north and south of town offer outstanding views of magnificent coastline; spectacular views also from Cummings Monument Lookout, just off hwy near Kiana, 52 km south. Day-trip to summit of Mt Wedge and return via Bramfield. Flinders Island, 35 km offshore; limited accommodation. **Tourist information:** Rally's Roadhouse, Beach Tce; (086) 87 9170. **Accommodation:** 1 hotel/motel, 2 caravan parks. **See also:** The Eyre Peninsula.
MAP REF. 272 D9

Gawler   Population 11 354

Settled in 1839, Gawler, 40 km north-east of Adelaide, is a prosperous town in a thriving agricultural district and also the gateway to the wineries of the Barossa Valley. **Of interest:** Historical buildings, including Gawler Mill, telegraph station (now a Folk Museum) and old post office, west of Murray St. Walking tour of Church Hill district, a State Heritage Area. Brochures detailing self-guided walking, driving and cycling tours from Tourist Office. Para Para (1862), Penrith Ave; historic residence open Sat. and Sun. prior to renovation. Dead Man's Pass Reserve, end Murray St; picnic facilities and walking trails. **In the area:** Astronomical Society of SA's observatory at Stockport, 30 km north; public viewing nights; enquire at Tourist Office. Scholz Park Museum at Riverton, 54 km north. Wellington Hotel at Waterloo, 76 km north, near Manoora, once Cobb & Co. staging-point. **Tourist information:** 61 Murray St; (085) 22 6814. **Accommodation:** 1 hotel, 1 motel, 2 caravan parks.
MAP REF. 262 I6, 267 J5

THE OUTBACK OF SOUTH AUSTRALIA

Motorists contemplating travel in the outback should prepare their vehicles well and familiarise themselves with expected conditions before setting out.

The outback of South Australia covers almost sixty million hectares and is one of the most remote areas of the world; conditions are harsh, the climate extreme and distances are daunting.

The countryside is usually dry, barren and dusty, but freak rains and heavy floods can transform the land. Dry creek-beds and water-holes fill, wildflowers bloom and birdlife flocks to the area. The enormous salt **Lake Eyre** has been filled rarely since Europeans first saw the desert.

The main road to the Northern Territory, the Stuart Highway, is a sealed all-weather road. From **Port Augusta** to **Alice Springs** the road covers a distance of 1243 kilometres. Turn off the highway to visit **Woomera**, the new mining town of **Roxby Downs**, the opal-mining town of **Andamooka** and **Tarcoola**.

Petrol, food and supplies are available at Port Augusta, **Pimba**, **Glendambo, Coober Pedy, Cadney Park** Roadhouse, Marla and **Kulgera**, which is just over the Northern Territory border.

The notorious Birdsville Track starts at **Marree**, once a supply outpost for Afghan camel traders, and follows the route originally used to drove cattle from south-west Queensland to the railhead at Marree. The track skirts the fringes of the Simpson Desert, with its giant sand dunes, and the desolate Sturt's Stony Desert. Artesian bores line the route, pouring out sixty-four million litres of salty boiling water every day. The road is fair; however, sometimes it is washed out by torrential rains and travellers can be left stranded for weeks. Sandstorms are another problem. Petrol and supplies are available at Marree and **Munger-**

anie, and at **Birdsville** over the Queensland border.

The Strzelecki Track begins at **Lyndhurst;** a harsh, dusty road, it stretches 494 kilometres to the almost deserted outpost of **Innamincka** with no stops for petrol or supplies.

Only experienced and well equipped outback motorists should consider driving along the Birdsville and Strzelecki Tracks.

For further information on the area, contact Flinders Ranges and Outback of South Australia Regional Tourism, PO Box 41, Port Augusta 5700; (086) 42 2469. **See also:** Individual entries in A–Z listing.

Break Aways, Coober Pedy

Goolwa

Goolwa   Population 2359
Goolwa is a rapidly growing holiday town 12 km from the mouth of the Murray near Lake Alexandrina. Once a key port in the golden days of the riverboats, the area has a strong tradition of shipbuilding, trade and fishing; today, the lakes area is ideal for boating, fishing and aquatic sports and popular with bird-watchers and photographers. **Of interest:** Many historic buildings, including distinctive railway superintendent's house (1852), known as 'the round-roofed house', and RSL Club, in former stables of Goolwa Railway (1853), both in B.F. Laurie Lane, off Cadell St. First railway carriage used in South Australia, horse-drawn and between Goolwa and Port Elliott in the 1850s, displayed in Cadell St. Steam train

rides between Goolwa and Victor Harbor; enquire at Tourist Office. National Trust Museum, Porter St; housed in former blacksmith's shop dating from 1870s. Next door, in original but rebuilt cottage, Goolwa Print Room. Both Goolwa hotels, the Goolwa in Cadell St and the Corio in Railway Pl, date from 1850s. Signal Point River Murray Interpretive Centre, The Wharf, has a computerised display of the river and district before European settlement, and the impact of development. Wooden Boat Festival in February. **In the area:** Fishing is excellent and catches include yabbies. Bird sanctuary east of Goolwa has swans, pelicans and other waterfowl; also bird hide. Nearby, the Barrages, desalination points that prevent salt water from reaching the Murray.

MV *Aroona* and PS *Mundoo* cruise to mouth of the Murray, the Barrages, Lake Alexandrina and the Lower Murray. Hindmarsh Island, via ferry, for different view of Murray mouth. Malleebaa Woolshed, 2 km north; wool displays, shearing videos, art and craft (open by appointment). Scenic flights available; airport 5 km north. At Currency Creek, 8 km north: Canoe tree, Tonkin's Currency Creek Winery (with restaurant and fauna park) and creekside park and walking trail. Tooperang Trout Farm, 20 km northwest. **Tourist information:** Old Library Bldg, cnr Cadell St and Goolwa Tce; (085) 55 1144. **Accommodation:** 4 motels, 2 caravan/camping parks. **See also:** The Fleurieu Peninsula.
MAP REF. 265 J9, 267 J9

Lighthouse at Kingscote, Kangaroo Island

Hawker
Population 302

This outback town in the centre of the northern Flinders Ranges is 400 km from Adelaide. Once a railway town, it is now the centre of a unique and world-renowned area that attracts visitors from both Australia and overseas who marvel at the colouring and grandeur of the many ranges that together make up the Flinders. **Of interest:** Museum at Hawker Motors, cnr Wilpena and Cradock Rds. Historic buildings: old railway station complex (1885), Hawker Hotel (1882), post office (1882). Self-guided Historic Walk brochure available. **In the area:** Moralana Scenic Drive, 42 km north, joins roads to Wilpena and Leigh Creek. Further north, Arkaroo Rock, with paintings by Adnajamathana tribe; nearby Rawnsley Bluff, majestic southern rampart of Wilpena Pound. Scenic flights and 4WD tours available. Rock paintings at Yourambulla Caves, 11 km south. Walking trail and scenic lookout at Jarvis Hill, 5 km south-west. Scenic drive west through Yappala, past Middle and Buckaringa Gorges to Gordon (check road conditions before departure). Historic Kanyaka ruins, south off main road to Quorn. From Hawker, ruins also at Wilson, Hookina, Wonoka and Willow Waters (check directions before departure). **Tourist information:** Hawker Motors, cnr Wilpena and Cradock Rds; (086) 48 4014. **Accommodation:** 1 hotel/motel, 1 motel, 2 caravan/camping parks. **See also:** The Flinders Ranges.
MAP REF. 268 H1, 271 N11

Innamincka
Population under 200

This tiny settlement, 1027 km north-east of Adelaide, is built around a hotel and trading-post on the Strzelecki Track, and 'sometimes' on the banks of Cooper Creek. Motorists intending to travel along the Track should read the section on Outback Motoring before attempting the journey. There are no supplies or petrol between Lyndhurst and Innamincka. **Of interest:** Ruins of Australian Inland Mission hostel. Cullyamurra Waterhole on Cooper Creek; picturesque spot, excellent fishing and Aboriginal carvings. **In the area:** Graves of explorers Burke and Wills near Innamincka; famous 'Dig Tree' 40 km over border in Qld. Coongie Lakes, 112 km north-west (road conditions can vary considerably; 4WD recommended); freshwater lakes are a haven for wildlife. **Accommodation:** 1 hotel/motel. **See also:** The Outback of South Australia.
MAP REF. 271 R4, 441 F10

Jamestown
Population 1372

Jamestown is an attractive, well-planned country town 205 km north of Adelaide. The surrounding rural country produces stud sheep and cattle, cereals, dairy produce and timber. The importance of agriculture in the area means Jamestown's Agricultural Show in October is regarded as one of the best in the state. **Of interest:** Railway Station Museum; open Sun. afternoons. Parks ideal for picnicking along banks of Belalie Ck. **In the area:** Scenic drive through Bundaleer Forest Reserve, 9 km south, up towards New Campbell Hill for panoramic view of plains stretching towards Mt Remarkable and The Bluff. Around Spalding, 34 km south, series of open waterways with picnic areas and trout fishing opportunities; Geralka Rural Farm, 15 km further south, a working commercial farm with tourist facilities. At Gladstone, 29 km south-west: railway yards for train enthusiasts; tours of gaol (1881), and tours of Trend Drinks

Factory, home of 'Old Style Ginger Beer'. Appila Springs, scenic picnic spot 8 km from Appila, 24 km north-west. **Accommodation:** 3 hotel/motels, 1 caravan/camping park.
MAP REF. 268 I7

Kadina
Population 3263

The largest town on the Yorke Peninsula, Kadina is the chief commercial and shopping centre of the region. The town's history is related to the boom copper-mining era during the 1800s and early 1900s, when thousands of Cornish miners flocked to the area; the community is still proud of its ancestry. A Cornish festival, the 'Kernewek Lowender', is held in conjunction with the towns of Wallaroo and Moonta in May every odd-numbered year. **Of interest:** Historic hotels, including the Wombat, Taylor St, and Royal Exchange, Digby St, with iron-lacework balconies and shady verandahs. National Trust Kadina Museum complex includes Matta House, (1863) home of manager of Matta Matta Copper Mine; agricultural machinery, printing museum, blacksmith's shop and old Matta mine. Banking and Currency Museum, unique private museum, Graves St; open daily except Thurs. Booklet detailing self-guided walking tours of town available from Tourist Office. **In the area:** Towns of Moonta (18 km south-west) and Wallaroo (10 km west), both of interest. Yorke Peninsula Field Days (agricultural shows) held at Paskeville (19 km south-east) in September every even year. **Tourist information:** Victoria Sq.; (088) 21 2093. **Accommodation:** 2 hotels, 2 motels, 1 caravan/camping park. **See also:** Festival Fun; The Yorke Peninsula.
MAP REF. 266 F2, 268 F11, 272 I10

Kapunda
Population 1622

Situated 80 km north of Adelaide on the edge of the Barossa Valley, Kapunda is a market town for the surrounding farm country. Copper was discovered here in 1842 and Kapunda became Australia's first mining-town. At one stage the population rose to 5000 and there were 16 hotels in the town. A million pounds' worth ($2m) of copper was dug out before the mines closed in 1878. **Of interest:** Many historic buildings; Heritage Trail and Historic Mine Walking Trail (maps available from Tourist Information Office). 'Map Kernow' (Son of Cornwall), 8-m-tall bronze statue at southern entrance to town, end of Main St. Historical Museum (1870s), Hill St. High School's main building, off Clare Rd; formerly residence of famous cattle king Sir Sidney Kidman. **In the area:** At Marrabel, 25 km

THE EYRE PENINSULA

The Eyre Peninsula is a vast region stretching from Whyalla in the east to the Western Australian border in the west, and, in a north-south direction, from the Gawler Ranges to Port Lincoln.

Spencer Gulf borders the eastern edge of the Peninsula, along which are located a number of small coastal towns featuring sheltered waters, safe swimming, white sandy beaches and excellent fishing from either shore or boat. The charm and tranquillity of the peaceful resort towns of **Cowell**, **Arno Bay** and **Port Neill** has a natural appeal. Cowell has the added appeal of being one of the world's major sources of jade.

Whyalla is the second largest city in South Australia and acts as an important gateway to Eyre Peninsula. Located near the top of Spencer Gulf, this bustling, industrially-based city also offers a wide range of attractions for the visitor.

The southern Eyre Peninsula encompasses the tourist resort towns of **Tumby Bay**, famous for fishing and beautiful offshore islands; **Coffin Bay**, with magnificent sheltered waters; and the jewel in the crown, the city of **Port Lincoln**, nestled on blue Boston Bay.

In stark contrast to the sheltered waters of Spencer Gulf, the west coast is exposed to the full force of the Southern Ocean, offering some of the most spectacular coastal scenery to be found anywhere in Australia. This rugged coast is punctuated by a number of bays and inlets and, not surprisingly,

resort towns have flourished where shelter can be found from precipitous cliffs and pounding surf. **Elliston**, **Venus Bay**, **Streaky Bay**, **Smoky Bay** and **Ceduna** all offer the visitor a diverse range of coastal scenery, good fishing and water-related activities.

Ceduna provides a vital service and accommodation facility for east-west traffic across Australia, and acts as a gateway information centre for visitors approaching the region from the west.

The hinterland of the Eyre Peninsula encompasses the picturesque Koppio Hills in the south, the vast grain-growing tracts of the central region and the timeless beauty of the Gawler Ranges in the far north.

The Nullarbor, the western corridor into the region, is a vast treeless plain, bordered in the south by towering limestone cliffs that drop sheer to the pounding Southern Ocean. Here schools of southern right whales can be seen along the coastline, which leads to the Great Australian Bight, between June and October on their annual breeding migration. Sightings of these beautiful creatures are on the increase and occur regularly.

For further information on the area, contact the Whyalla Tourist Centre, Lincoln Hwy, Whyalla; (086) 45 7900. **See also:** Individual entries in A–Z listing.

Fishing fleet, Port Lincoln

north, South Australia's biggest rodeo, held every October. Scenic drive 26 km north-east through rich sheep, wheat and dairy country to Eudunda; walks and scenic lookouts in area. Just north of Eudunda, Old Immanuel College at Point Pass, Australia's first Lutheran seminary, now providing a variety of accommodation. Scholz Park Museum at Riverton, 14 km north. Historic local stone buildings at Tarlee, 16 km west. **Tourist information:** 5 Hill St, (085) 66 2902. **Accommodation:** 1 hotel, 1 caravan/camping park.

MAP REF. 263 K2, 267 J4, 269 J13

Keith   Population 1189
Keith is a farming town on the Dukes Hwy, 241 km from Adelaide. In the centre of the former Ninety Mile Desert, now called Coonalpyn Downs, the area has been transformed from infertile scrubby pasture to productive farming by the use of plant nutrition and modern farming methods. **Of interest:** Recently renamed, the main road is now Heritage St in recognition of the town's past. Pride of place is the former Congregational Church (1910) with its four locally made leadlight windows depicting the town's pioneering history. The Mechanics In-

stitute, old post office and Penny Farthing Coffee and Crafts add to the streetscape. Old Settlers Cottage (1894), Emu Flat Rd. **In the area:** Mount Rescue Conservation Park, 16 km north, vast expanse of sandplain with heath, pink gums and native wildlife. Ngarkat Conservation Park, 25 km north-east. Mt Monster Conservation Park, 10 km south, with panoramic views and diverse wildlife. **Tourist information:** Old Congregational Church building, Heritage St; (087) 55 1125. **Accommodation:** 1 hotel/motel, 1 motel, 1 caravan/camping park.

MAP REF. 267 P12, 273 F3

THE FLINDERS RANGES

The Flinders Ranges are part of a mountain chain which extend for 430 kilometres from its southern end (between Crystal Brook and Peterborough) to a point about 160 kilometres east of Marree. The most spectacular peaks and valleys are in two areas — the first north-east of Port Augusta and the second north of Hawker. Although the Flinders are similar in scale to many of Australia's mountain ranges, they are totally different in both colouration and atmosphere.

There is something unique in the contrast of the dry, stony land and richly lined rock-faces — the characteristics of a desert range — with the rich vegetation of the river red gums, casuarinas, native pines and wattles which clothe the valleys and cling to hillsides and rock-crevices. In spring, after rain, the display of wildflowers is breathtaking, carpeting the whole region with masses of reds, pinks, yellows, purples and white. The wildflowers, together with the natural beauty of the rock shapes, pools and

Road through Bunyeroo Valley

caves and twisted trees which abound in the Flinders Ranges, make them a favourite haunt of photographers and artists. Many paintings by Sir Hans Heysen embody the shape and spirit of the ranges.

The Flinders is served by reasonably good roads. A pleasant trip which will take in the best of the scenery is the drive north-east from Port Augusta over Pichi Richi Pass to **Hawker** and

from there on the loop road to **Parachilna**, circling the Wilpena Pound area.

But it is better to stay and explore, preferably on foot or by four-wheel drive. There are kilometres of signposted tracks in the ranges, but as it is still only too easy to lose your way, it is important to be equipped with a good map and to follow a planned route. Drivers should avoid using the secondary roads after rain, which can be treacherous when wet.

The best-known feature of the Flinders is the **Wilpena Pound**, an immense, elevated basin covering about fifty square kilometres and encircled by sheer cliffs which are set in a foundation of purple shale and rise through red stone to white-topped peaks. The only entrance is a narrow gorge, through which a creek sometimes flows. The external cliffs rise to over 1000 metres, but inside is a gentle slope to the floor of the plain. The highest point in the Pound is **St Mary's Peak**, at 1188 metres, which dominates

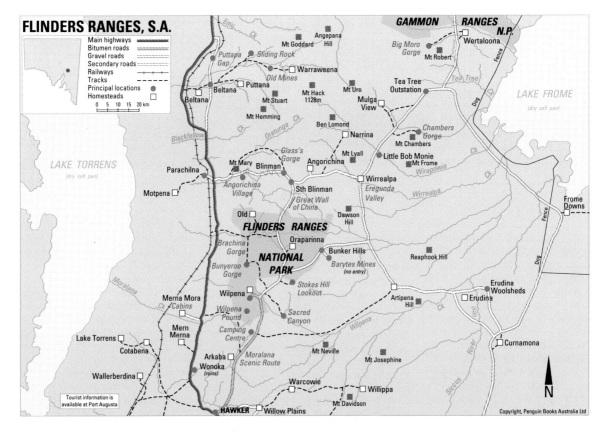

FLINDERS RANGES, S.A.

Main highways
Bitumen roads
Gravel roads
Secondary roads
Railways
Tracks
Principal locations
Homesteads

0   5   10   15   20 km

Tourist information is available at Port Augusta

Copyright, Penguin Books Australia Ltd

the northern wall and provides a magnificent view over the surrounding mountains. Within the Pound are low, rounded hills and folded ridges, grasslands and pine-clad slopes which run down to the gums along Wilpena Creek. It is a wonderland of birdlife — rosellas, galahs, red-capped robins, budgerigars and wedge-tailed eagles are common here. Bushland possums and rare yellow-footed wallabies also can be seen.

There is a well-organised resort at **Wilpena**, catering for levels of accommodation from camping to modern motel. Near the Pound in this central section of the ranges are **Warren Gorge, Buckaringa Gorge, Yourambulla Cave** with its Aboriginal drawings, the **Hills of Arkaba**, considered the most beautiful spur in this region, **Bunyeroo** and **Aroona Valleys** and the **Flinders Ranges National Park**.

Some features in the northern section of the Flinders — **Willow Springs Lookout**, the **Great Wall of China**, a long rocky escarpment, and **Mount Chambers** and **Chambers Gorge**, which can be reached by vehicle or on foot — are among the most beautiful of all the attractions that can be seen in the Flinders.

Another region of the Flinders, **Arkaroola** in the far north of the ranges, also invites exploration. The 61 000-hectare **Arkaroola – Mt Painter Sanctuary** is situated in rugged outback country featuring quartzite razorback ridges over elongated valleys, once the sea-bed of a great continental shelf which has left a legacy of rippled rock with embedded marine fossils. There is a profusion of wildlife: emus, ducks, parrots, cockatoos and galahs, possums, marsupial mice and yellow-footed rock wallabies all abound here.

From the heavily timbered slopes in the southern ranges, through picturesque gorges and gently rolling plains to the harsh, arid ranges of the north, the Flinders offers a variety of experiences. In addition to its unique flora and fauna, its rugged beauty and panoramic vistas, the region contains an important Aboriginal heritage and traces of early pioneering days.

For further information on the area, contact Flinders Ranges and Outback of South Australia Regional Tourism, PO Box 41, Port Augusta 5700; (086) 42 2469. **See also:** South Australia's National Parks; and individual entries in A–Z listing.

Kimba   Population 795
A small township on the Eyre Hwy, Kimba is at the edge of SA's outback. This is sheep and wheat-growing country. **Of interest:** Historical museum, Eyre Hwy, featuring Pioneer House (1908), school and blacksmith's shop. **In the area:** Walking trail from the edge of town, 3 km through bushland to White's Knob lookout. Gawler Ranges, north-west, a vast wilderness area; check road conditions. Lake Gilles Conservation Park, 20 km north-east; Caralue Bluff, 20 km west; rock-climbing and diverse flora and fauna. Pinkawillinie Conservation Park, 45 km west. **Tourist information:** Kimba Halfway Across Australia Gem Shop, Eyre Hwy; (086) 27 2112. **Accommodation:** 1 hotel/motel, 1 caravan/camping park.
MAP REF. 268 A7, 272 G8

Kingscote   Population 1403
Kingscote is the largest town and principal port of Kangaroo Island, 120 km south-west of Adelaide. Kingscote was the first officially settled part of SA, in 1836. A vehicular ferry arrives here from Port Adelaide and there is an airfield nearby (travelling time, about 7 hr or 30 min., respectively). **Of interest:** Cairn on foreshore marks State's first post office. Hope Cottage, National Trust Folk Museum, Centenary Ave. Town's cemetery is oldest in State. Rock-pool and Brownlow Beach for swimming. Fishing from jetty for tommy ruffs, trevally, garfish and snook. Chriso's Wagon Rides, from The Esplanade; Clydesdale-drawn wagon rides in summer. **In the area:** Jumbuk Shearing demonstrations, Birchmore Rd, 17 km south. Eucalyptus oil distillery, Wilsons Rd, 20 km south off South Coast Rd. The small resort town of American River, a fishing village, about 50 km east, and, on the north-east coast of Dudley Peninsula, the Cornish village of Penneshaw, where the vehicular ferry arrives from Cape Jervis, about an hour away. Folk Museum in former Old Penneshaw School. Dudley, Cape Hart and Pelican Lagoon Conservation Parks on peninsula. Antechamber Bay, about 20 km south-east of Penneshaw, for swimming, fishing and bushwalking. On western end of island, Flinders Chase National Park, one of SA's most important parks and sanctuary for some of Australia's rarest wildlife. Cape Borda Lighhouse. Remarkable Rocks and Admiralty Arch, southwest. **Tourist information:** National Parks and Wildlife Services, 37 Dauncey St; (0848) 22 381. **Accommodation:** 2 hotels, 4 motels, 2 caravan/camping parks. **See also:** Kangaroo Island.
MAP REF. 266 F10

Kingston S.E.   Population 1367
At the southern end of the Coorong National Park in Lacepede Bay, Kingston S.E. is a farming town and seaside resort. It was first named Maria Creek after a ship wrecked in the bay. The multitude of shallow lakes and lagoons in the area are a haven for birdlife and a delight for naturalists and photographers. **Of interest:** Unusual analemmatic sundial, located adjacent to Apex Park, in East Tce. Post office (1867), Hanson St, one of seven selected nationally for a special Commonwealth Stamp Issue in 1982. National Trust Pioneer Museum (1872), Cooke St. Cape Jaffa Lighthouse (1860s; dismantled and re-erected in 1970s), Marine Pde. Maria Memorial, a granite cairn, commemorates massacre of 27 shipwrecked Europeans by Aborigines in 1840. Giant 'Larry Lobster' at entrance to town, East Tce (Hwy). **In the area:** Mt Scott Conservation Park, 20 km east. Jip Jip Conservation Park, 50 km north-east. **Tourist information:** The Big Lobster, Princes Hwy; (087) 67 2555. **Accommodation:** 3 motels, 1 caravan/camping park. **See also:** The Coorong.
MAP REF. 273 E6

Lameroo   Population 569
A quiet little settlement 212 km east of Adelaide on the Ouyen Hwy. **In the area:** Baan Hill Reserve, 20 km south-west, a natural soakage area surrounded by sandhills and scrub; picnic facilities. Ngarkat Conservation Park, 25 km south. Byrne Homestead (1898), built of pug and pine, 3 km along old Yappara road. Billiat Conservation Park, 37 km north. **Tourist information:** Council Offices; (085) 76 3002. **Accommodation:** 1 hotel/motel.
MAP REF. 267 P8

Leigh Creek   Population 1967
Leigh Creek, in the Flinders Ranges, is the largest town north of Port Augusta. The economy is based on the large opencut coalfield. The open-cut eventually consumed the original Leigh Creek township, and in 1982 residents moved to the new township about 13 km south. An extensive development and tree-planting scheme has transformed the new site into an attractive oasis. **In the area:** Visitors' viewing area for coal workings, 3 km from turnoff to coalfields, on Hawker to Marree Hwy; free tours of coalfields on Sat. (Mar. – Oct.) and school holidays. Aroona Dam, 4 km west, in steep-sided valley with richly coloured walls; scenic picnic area near gorge. Rugged Gammon Ranges National Park, 64 km east; wilderness area, recommended for experienced bushwalkers only. Lakes Eyre, Frome and Torrens, all dry salt pans, which occasionally fill with water. Lyndhust

and Marree, 38 km and 119 km north, respective endpoints of Strzelecki and Birdsville Tracks. At Lyndhurst, unique gallery of sculptures by noted talc-stone artist 'Talc Alf'; open to visitors. **Accommodation:** 1 motel, 1 caravan/camping park. MAP REF. 271 N9

Loxton   Population 3372

Affectionately known as the Garden City of the Riverland region, Loxton is situated 251 km north-east of Adelaide. The surrounding irrigated land supports thriving citrus, wine, dried-fruit, wool and wheat industries. The area was first named Loxtons Hut, after a boundary rider from the Bookpurnong Station built a primitive pine and pug hut here. Like all towns in the region, Loxton has a strong sense of community and civic pride. There are many landscaped parks and gardens, a modern shopping centre and extensive sporting facilities. The largest war-service settlement scheme in SA was carried out here. **Of interest:** Fascinating Historical Village on riverfront with 25 re-created buildings, including bank, bakery, sheds and railway station, as well as machinery and implements from pioneer days of late 1880s to mid-1900s; open daily. Nearby, pepper tree planted by Loxton almost 100 years ago. River cruises available. Art galleries and craft shops selling local paintings and handcrafts. Fisherama held in January, Mardi Gras in February and Historical Village Fair in September. **In the area:** Sample excellent wines at Penfolds Winery, Bookpurnong Road (to Berri) in Loxton North; tastings and sales Mon.–Sat. Nearby, Medea Cottage Garden for herbs and unusual perennials; open daily. Kia Kia Nature Trail, for bushwalkers, in Katarapko Game Reserve, 10 km north-west; canoes for hire. Picnics at Habels Bend, 3 km north-west, on sandy shores of river. Lock 4 and Moore's Woodlot (600 000 trees watered and fertilised by factory waste), 14 km north of town. Unique wood sculpture display, southeast on Paruna Rd; open daily. **Tourist information:** East Tce; (085) 84 7919. **Accommodation:** 1 hotel/motel, 1 motel, 1 caravan/camping park. MAP REF. 116 A9, 267 P4, 269 P13

Lyndoch   Population 706

At the southern end of the Barossa and only a 40-minute drive from Adelaide, Lyndoch is one of the oldest towns in SA. Early industry was farm-oriented, and four flour-mills were known to operate in the area. The nearby Para River was used to operate a water-mill in 1853. Vineyards were established early, but the first winery was not set up until 1896. Some ten wineries in the area are all family-owned businesses, ranging from very small to one of the largest in the Barossa. **Of interest:** SA Museum of Mechanical Music, Barossa Valley Hwy; open daily. **In the area:** Wineries: Wards Gateway Cellar, Chateau Yaldara Winery, Charles Cimicky Wines, Burge Family Winemakers, Grant Burge Wines, Orlando Wines, Kies Estate Cellars, Kellermeister Wines, Barossa Settlers. Chateau Collection (antique Dresden china, porcelain and glassware) at Chateau Yaldara Winery. Barossa Reservoir and Whispering Wall, north-west of Williamstown, 8 km south. Kersbrook, 22 km south; historic buildings and trout farm. **Tourist information:** Kies Estate Cellars, Barossa Valley Hwy; (085) 24 4511. **Accommodation:** 1 motel, 1 caravan/camping park. MAP REF. 263 K6, 267 J5

McLaren Vale   Population 1196

Centre of the Wine Coast or McLaren Vale wine-growing region in which around fifty wineries flourish, McLaren Vale is only 24 km south of Adelaide. Winemaking really began in 1876 when Thomas Hardy bought Tintara Vineyards; Hardy's Tintara today is the largest winery in the area. **Of interest:** Annual Wine Bushing Festival in late October celebrates release of new vintage, and includes wine tastings and vineyard tours. Historic buildings include Hotel McLaren, Willunga Rd, Congregational Church and Salopian Inn, Willunga Rd. Almond Train, Main Rd; selection of almond products from local production housed in restored railway carriage. **In the area:** Many historic buildings have now been put to use as tea-rooms, restaurants, wineries and galleries. The wineries are often in bushland settings; most are open for inspection, tastings and cellar-door sales; information and maps at information centres. **Tourist information:** The Cottage, Main Rd; (08) 323 8537. **Accommodation:** 2 motels, 1 caravan/camping park. **See also:** Festival Fun; Vineyards and Wineries. MAP REF. 264 G4, 266 I8

Maitland   Population 1103

Maitland is a modern, well-planned town in the centre of the Yorke Peninsula. It serves as the supply centre for the surrounding rich farmland. Wheat, barley, wool and beef cattle are the main primary industries here. Parks surround the town centre. **Of interest:** Self-guided nature and history trail; information from local District Council, Elizabeth St. St John's Anglican Church (1876), cnr Alice and Caroline Sts; stained-glass windows depicting Biblical stories in Australian settings. Lions Bicycle Adventure Park, off Elizabeth St. Maitland National Trust Museum, in former school, cnr Gardiner and Kilkerran Tces. **In the area:** Paradean Gardens and teas, 10 km south-east; check opening times. **Tourist information:** Yorke Peninsula Tourist Information Centre, Victoria Sq., Kadina; (088) 21 2093. **Accommodation:** 2 hotels. MAP REF. 266 F4, 268 F13, 272 I11

Mannum   Population 2056

Mannum, 82 km east of Adelaide, is one of the oldest towns on the Murray, with an historic and lively past. Picturesque terraced banks overlook the curving river. Wool, beef and cereals are produced in the region and the town is the starting-point for the Adelaide water-supply pipeline. The first paddle-steamer on the Murray, the *Mary Ann*, left Mannum in 1853 and the first steam-car was built here in 1900 by David Shearer. **Of interest:** Recreation Reserve, on banks of Murray; picnic spots, barbecue facilities and lookout tower. 'Leonaville' (1883), River Lane, built by town's first private developer, Gottlieb Schuetze. At Arnold Park, Randell St, PS *Marion*, built 1898, now National Trust Museum. Twin ferries to eastern side of river and scenic upriver drive alongside river. Mannum River Festival in October. Lookout tower off Purnong Rd to east offers sweeping views of area. **In the area:** Award-winning Choni Leather, 10 km north-west on Palmer Rd. Scenic drive along Purnong Rd runs parallel to bird sanctuary for 15 km. Excellent scenic drive from Wongulla to Cambrai, begins some 20 km north. Mannum Waterfalls Reserve, 10 km south, for picnics, swimming and scenic walks. Boats and houseboats for hire and river cruises available at weekends during summer. Pleasure cruises, weekends in summer. Water-sports at Walker Flat. **Tourist information:** PS *Marion* Museum, Arnold Park, Randell St; (085) 69 1303. **Accommodation:** 2 hotels, 1 motel, 2 caravan/camping parks. MAP REF. 263 P11, 267 L6

Marree   Population 334

Marree is a tiny outback town 645 km north of Adelaide at the junction of the infamous Birdsville Track and the rugged road to Oodnadatta, which leads to the Kingoony – Alice Springs road. There are remnants of the old date-palms planted by the Afghan traders who drove their camel

The magnificent Blue Lake, Mount Gambier

trains into the outback with supplies in the 1800s. Desolate saltbush country surrounds the town, which is now a small service centre for the vast properties of the north-east of the state, and far northbound travellers. **In the area:** The Frome, 6 km north, a sandy watercourse which floods after heavy rains, surging across the Birdsville Track, often leaving travellers stranded for weeks. Lake Eyre, 90 km north, accessible via Marree and Muloorina Station. Mungeranie Roadhouse, 204 km north of Marree on the Birdsville Track, has fuel, food, accommodation, emergency repairs and a camping area. Oodnadatta Track, southern section (check track conditions with Marree police before departing; read section on Outback Motoring; fuel available only at Marree and William Creek, 210 km north-west). Ruins of railway sidings from original Ghan line to Alice Springs at Curdimurka Siding and Bore, about 90 km west; annual Outback Ball held here in Sept. Bubbler Mound Springs and Blanchecup Mound Springs, 6 km south of track, near Coward Springs, 136 km west; at Coward Springs: extensive pond formed by warm water bubbling to the surface; old date palms, remnants of an old plantation. **Accommodation:** 1 hotel. **See also:** The Outback of South Australia. MAP REF. 271 N7

Melrose
Population under 200

Melrose is the oldest town in the Flinders Ranges, a quiet settlement at the foot of Mt Remarkable, 268 km north of Adelaide. **Of interest:** Historical buildings:

old police station and court-house (1862), Stuart St, now a National Trust Museum; ruins of Jacka's Brewery (former flour mill, 1877), Lambert St; North Star Hotel (1881), Nott St; Mt Remarkable Hotel (1857), Stuart St. Melrose Inn, Nott St; now National Trust property but privately owned. Heritage Walk available. Serendipity Gallery, Stuart St. Pleasant walks and picnic-spots along creek. Panoramic views from War Memorial and Lookout Hill, Joe's Rd. Further on, Cathedral Rock. **In the area:** Walking trail (allow 5 hr return) from town to top of Mt Remarkable (956m); superb views. Mt Remarkable National Park, 2 km west. Booleroo Steam and Traction Preservation Society's Museum, Booleroo Centre, 15 km east; open by appointment. Near Murray Town, 14 km south: scenic lookouts at Box Hill, Magnus Hill and Baroota Nob; scenic drive west through Germein Gorge. Murratana sheep property, 3 km south-west; visitors welcome. **Tourist information:** Council Offices, Stuart St; (086) 66 2014. **Accommodation:** 2 hotels, 1 caravan/camping park. MAP REF. 268 G5, 271 N13

Meningie
Population 803

Meningie is set on the edge of the freshwater Lake Albert and at the northern tip of the vast saltpans of the Coorong National Park, 159 km from Adelaide. Apart from rural pursuits, over 40 professional fishermen are employed on the lakes and Coorong; fishing is a significant industry in the town. The area abounds with bir-

dlife such as ibises, pelicans, cormorants, ducks and swans. Sailing, boating, water-skiing and swimming are popular. **In the area:** The Coorong, stretching south and west, with its inland water, islands, ocean beach and wildlife. Scenic drive west following Lake Albert, adjacent to Lake Alexandrina, the largest permanent freshwater lake in Australia (50 000 ha). The channel between Lakes Alexandrina and Albert is crossed by a free ferry service at Narrung, 39 km north-west. Poltalloch Homestead (1876) at Narrung. **Tourist information:** Melaleuca Centre, 76 Princes Hwy; (085) 75 1259. **Accommodation:** 1 hotel, 2 motels, 1 caravan/camping park. **See also:** The Coorong. MAP REF. 267 L10, 273 C1

Millicent
Population 5075

A thriving commercial and industrial town, Millicent is situated 50 km from Mt Gambier in the middle of a huge tract of land reclaimed in the 1870s. Today rural and fishing industries contribute to the area's prosperity, with extensive pine forests supporting two paper-mills and a sawmill. **Of interest:** On northern edge of town, gum trees surround a fine swimming lake and pleasant picnic area. Award-winning National Trust Museum and Admella Gallery, Mt Gambier Rd; housed in original primary school (1873) with several theme rooms, plus farming equipment, 16 horse-drawn carriages and T-Class locomotive. Shell Garden, Williams Rd; unusual display surrounded by fuchsias, ferns and begonias. Radiata Festival Week held in March. **In the area:** Tantanoola, 21 km south-east, home of famous Tantanoola Tiger, shot by Tom Donovan in 1890s. The 'tiger' (in reality a Syrian wolf), stuffed and now displayed in a glass cage in the Tantanoola Tiger Hotel. Underground caves within Tantanoola Caves Conservation Park featuring fascinating limestone formations; open daily and wheelchair accessible. Scenic drive to Mount Burr, 10 km north-east through magnificent pine forests; sawmill opens for inspection. National Trust Woolshed (1863) at Glencoe, 29 km south-east; tours available. Massive sand dune system within Canunda National Park; accessed at Southend, 27 km west. **Tourist information:** Admella Gallery, 1 Mt Gambier Rd; (087) 33 3205. **Accommodation:** 1 hotel/motel, 2 motels, 2 caravan/camping parks. MAP REF. 273 G10

Minlaton
Population 813

Minlaton is a prosperous town serving the nearby coastal resorts of Yorke Peninsula. The town, 209 km west of Adelaide, was originally called Gum Flat because of the giant eucalypts in the area. Pioneer aviator Harry Butler, pilot of the *Red Devil*, a 1916 Bristol monoplane, was born here. The plane is displayed at the Harry Butler Museum in Main St. **Of interest:** Fauna park, Main St; adjacent to Harry Butler Memorial. National Trust Museum, Main St. Jolly's Vintage Tractor and Engine Collection, Main St, open daily. **In the area:** Gum Flat Homestead Gallery, 1 km east; pioneer homestead with local artists' work. At Port Vincent, 25 km east: swimming, yachting and water-skiing; annual yacht-race in January; Grainstore Galleries and Doll Museum. Short drive, 16 km north-west, to Port Rickaby and Bluff Beach, a unique bay with abundant birdlife. Farm holidays and horsedrawn wagon holidays at Brentwood, 14 km south-west. **Tourist information:** Council Offices, Main St; (088) 53 2102. **Accommodation:** 1 hotel/motel, 1 caravan/ camping park. MAP REF. 266 E6, 272 I12

Mintaro   Population 80
The township nestles among rolling hills and rich pastoral land, 15 km east of Clare. Classified as a Heritage Town, Mintaro is a fascinating timepiece of early colonial architecture. Many of the buildings display the fine slate for which the district is world-renowned; the quarry opened in 1854. **Of interest:** Early colonial buildings; walking guide available. Robinson's Cottage, Hill St, first settler's cottage in town (1851), and historic fire-engine collection; open daily. Reilly's Cottage Gallery (1870s), Burra St, one of SA's best; check opening times. **In the area:** Magnificent classic architecture of Martindale Hall (1880), 3 km south-east; location for film *Picnic at Hanging Rock*; tours, afternoons daily; overnight accommodation and dining available. Self-contained accommodation at a number of historic cottages. Mintaro Cellars winery, 2 km south-west. **Tourist information:** Robinson's Cottage; (088) 43 9029. **Accommodation:** 1 hotel
MAP REF. 266 I1, 268 I11

Moonta   Population 2199
The towns of Moonta, Kadina and Wallaroo form the corners of the area known as the 'Copper Triangle' or 'Little Cornwall'. Moonta is a popular seaside resort 163 km north-west of Adelaide, with pleasant beaches and good fishing at Moonta Bay. A rich copper-ore deposit was discovered here in 1861 and soon thousands of miners, including many from Cornwall, flocked to the area. The mines were abandoned in the 1920s with the slump in copper prices and rising labour costs. Recently the new Poona mine began operations at Moonta, bringing life back to the mines area. **Of interest:** The town has many solid-stone buildings, a charming city square (Queen Square) and a picturesque town hall, opposite the Square in George St. All Saints Church (1873), cnr Blanche and Milne Tces. Galleries include The Peppers Gallery and the Pug 'n' Dabble, Robert St. The 'Kernewek Lowender', a Cornish festival, is held, in conjunction with Kadina and Wallaroo, in May every odd-numbered year. **In the area:** Moonta Mines State Heritage Area, Arthurton Rd, about 2 km south-east; historical guide available. Highlights include Moonta Mines National Trust Museum (old primary school); typical Cornish miner's cottage (1870) furnished in period style; and pump house, various shafts and tailings heaps and mines offices. On weekends Moonta Mines Railway takes visitors from old railway station, Blanche Tce, through mines area. **Tourist information:** Town Hall, George St; (088) 25 2622. **Accommodation:** 1 hotel, 1 motel, 1 caravan/camping park. **See also:** Festival Fun; The Yorke Peninsula.
MAP REF. 266 E2, 268 E11, 272 I10

Morgan   Population 430
Once one of the busiest river ports in SA, Morgan today is a quiet little township 164 km north-east of Adelaide. **Of interest:** Self-guided Heritage Trail leaflets cover all historical sites, including the impressive wharves (1877), standing 12.2 m high, constructed for the riverboat industry. Customs house and court-house near railway station, reminders of town's thriving past. Port of Morgan Historic Museum in old railway buildings on riverfront, off High St. PS *Mayflower* (1884), still operating; enquiries to Museum's caretaker. Nor-West Bend private museum, Renmark Rd; open by appointment. Houseboats for hire. **In the area:** Fossicking for fossils near township. Morgan Conservation Park, across river. White Dam Conservation Park, 9 km north-west. **Tourist information:** Morgan Roadhouse, Fourth St; (085) 40 2205, and Council Offices Fourth St; (085) 40 2013. **Accommodation:** 1 hotel, 1 hotel/motel, 1 motel, 1 caravan/camping park.
MAP REF. 267 M2, 269 M11

Mount Gambier   Population 20 813
Lieutenant James Grant, in 1800, sighted and named Mount Gambier, an extinct volcano. Mount Gambier township is built on its slopes in the centre of the largest pine plantations in Australia surrounded by rich farming and dairy country 460 km from Adelaide on the Princes Hwy. The Hentys built the first dwelling in the area in 1841 and by 1850 a weekly postal service to Adelaide was operating. The local white Mount Gambier stone used in most of the buildings, together with many fine parks and gardens, make it an attractive city. **Of interest:** Historic buildings include town hall (1862) and post office (1865), in Bay St, and many old hotels; Heritage Walk leaflet from Tourist Information Centre. Open caves at Cave Gardens, Bay Rd, adjacent to town hall, and Umpherston Cave, Jubilee Hwy East. Engelbrecht Cave, Jubilee Hwy, water-filled cave or sink-hole. Old Court-house Law and Heritage Centre, Bay Rd, National Trust museum; open daily. Lewis' Museum, Pick Ave; open daily. Lady Nelson Tourist and Interpretive Centre, Jubilee Hwy East; full scale replica of *Lady Nelson* forms part of Centre's structure. Riddoch Art Gallery, Commercial St East; housed within complex of 19th century buildings. Yoey's Cheese and Gourmet Shop, Commercial St West; local and imported cheeses. Blue Lake Festival, held 10 days in November. **In the area:** Mount Gambier's four crater lakes, particularly Blue Lake (197 m at its deepest), which changes from dull grey to brilliant blue each November and then reverts at end of summer; scenic 5 km drive offers several lookouts. Pumping Station, providing town's water-supply; inspections daily. Tours of CSR Softwoods; inspection of treatment process, including pines being felled, trimmed and cut ready for loading; contact Tourist Centre for details. Haig's Vineyard, 4 km south. Animal and Reptile Park, 10 km north, off Penola Rd, animal nursery, native gardens, train carriage. Glencoe Woolshed (1863), National Trust building, 23 km north-west; open Sun. afternoons. Tarpeena Fairy Tale Park, 22 km north on Penola Rd. Chant's Place flora and fauna park at Kongorong, 25 km south-west. Mount Schank, 12 km south; views of surrounding district. Glenelg River cruises from Victorian town of Nelson, 36 km south-east; tours of spectacular Princess Margaret Rose Caves. **Tourist information:** Jubilee Hwy East; (087) 24 1730. **Accommodation:** 3 hotels, 1 hotel/motel, 18 motels, 6 caravan/camping parks.
MAP REF. 210 A6, 273 H11

Murray Bridge   Population 11 893
Murray Bridge is SA's largest river town. Only 80 km from Adelaide, a modern freeway links the two cities. First settled in the 1850s, the town overlooks a broad sweep of the Murray and still retains some of the feeling of the time when it was a centre for the bustling riverboat traders. Water sports, river cruises and excellent accommodation make Murray Bridge a perfect holiday spot. **Of interest:** Cap-

THE FLEURIEU PENINSULA

Starting twenty-two kilometres south of Adelaide, the Fleurieu Peninsula region stretches from O'Halloran Hill for about 90 km to Cape Jervis on the west coast, and east around the vast fresh waters of Lake Alexandrina, where the Murray River meets the sea.

The ocean scenery varies from magnificent cliff-faces and roaring surf to wide, sandy beaches and sheltered bays and coves. Maslin Beach is renowned as Australia's first nude bathing beach. Cape Jervis, at the tip of the Peninsula, commands a spectacular view across Backstairs Passage to Kangaroo Island.

McLaren Vale is the centre of the Southern Vales or Wine Coast wine-producing district. With over 50 wineries, many in historic buildings and with attached restaurants, this is certainly an area in which to linger.

Horse-drawn tram, Victor Harbor

Victor Harbor is one of South Australia's most popular beach resorts. Either walk or take the old horse tram to Granite Island, joined to the mainland by a long causeway, with its colony of wallabies and fairy penguins. On the way to Goolwa, spend time in Port Elliot to take in its history and perhaps take 'The Cockle Train' to Goolwa, a steam train which has been restored from the original line opened in 1854.

There is superb fishing at Goolwa, once a busy port but now the starting-point for leisurely paddlewheeler cruises up the Murray and cruises to Hindmarsh Island and the Barrages.

For further information on the area, contact the Victor Harbor Tourist Information Centre, Torrens St, Victor Harbor; (085) 52 4255. **See also:** Individual entries in A–Z listing.

---

tain's Cottage Museum, Thomas St. Butterfly House, Jervois Rd. Puzzle Park, also in Jervois Rd, a fun park for adults as well as children. Mary the Blacksmith, SA's only female blacksmith, Doyle Rd; open weekends, daily in school holidays. Cottage Box chocolate factory, Rocky Gully Rd; open daily. Sturt Desert Pea Gardens on Pilmore Rd; daily tours of glasshouses. Sturt Reserve, on banks of the river; fishing and swimming, and excellent picnic and playground facilities. Big River Challenge Festival each November incorporates speedboat racing, water-skiing events and land-based sporting challenges. **In the area:** Charter and regular cruises on MV *Kookaburra* and MV *Zane Grey*; houseboats for hire. Cruises lasting 2, 3 or 5 days on PS *Proud Mary*. Avoca Dell, 5 km upstream, for boating, water-skiing and mini-golf; picnic facilities. Thiele Reserve, east of river, popular for water-skiing. Other riverside reserves include Hume, Long Island, Swanport and White Sands. Mypolonga, 14 km north, centre of beautiful citrus and stone-fruit orchards and rich dairying country. Lowan Conservation Park, 40 km northeast. Earthworks Pottery, 9 km northeast, on Karoonda Rd. Willow Glen Wines, 10 km south on Jervois Rd. Kooringal Park wildlife reserve, 11 km south. Several lookouts, including White Hill, west on Princes Hwy, and east at new Swanport Bridge. **Tourist information:** Community Information and Tourist Centre, South Tce; (085) 32 6660. **Accommodation:** 2 hotels, 4 motels, 5 caravan/camping parks.
MAP REF. 265 P3, 267 L7

Naracoorte   Population 4636

Situated 390 km south-east of Adelaide, Naracoorte was first settled in the 1840s. The area is world-renowned for its intriguing limestone caves. Beef cattle, sheep and wheat are the local primary industries. **Of interest:** Sheep's Back Wool Museum, housed in former four mill (1860), MacDonnell St; incorporates National Trust Museum, Art Gallery and Tourist Information Centre. Naracoorte Museum, Jenkins Tce, houses 100 'collections', including coins, candles, gemstones and antiques. Regional Art Gallery, Smith St. Mini Jumbuk Factory, Smith St; woollen products. Restored locomotive on display in Pioneer Park. Jubilee Park and Swimming Lake, off Park Tce; 28 ha shaded by gums and surrounded by lawns. For anglers, trout and redfin abound in local streams and creeks. **In the area:** Tiny Train Park, 3 km south; trains, mini-golf. Naracoorte Caves, 12 km south-east, in Conservation Park; Victoria Fossil Cave is of world significance, containing unique fossilised specimens of ice-age animals, while Blanche Cave and Alexandra Cave have spectacular stalagmites and stalactites; guided tours daily. Bool Lagoon Game Reserve 17 km south, sanctuary for ibises, brolgas and Cape Barren geese; guided boardwalks and bird hide. Coonawarra wine region, 40 km south, and Padthaway and Keppoch wine districts, about same distance north-west. St Aubins host farm, 40 km north; Wongary host farm, 25 km south. **Tourist information:** MacDonnell St; (087) 62 1518. **Accommodation:** 2 hotels, 1 hotel/motel, 4 motels, 2 caravan/camping parks. **See also:** South Australia's National Parks.
MAP REF. 212 A11, 273 H7

Nuriootpa   Population 3209

The Para River runs through the town of Nuriootpa, its ourse marked by beautiful parks and picnic spots, including Coulthard Reserve off Penrice Rd. The town is the commercial centre of the Barossa Valley. **Of interest:** Coulthard House, pioneer settler's home, now Barossa Information Centre. St Petri Church, First St. The Pheasant Farm, award-winning restaurant, Samuel St. **In the area:** Wineries, including Elderton, Kaesler, Penfolds, Stockwell Wines and Wolf Blass; sales and tastings, and vineyard tours. Also Tarac Distillers. **Tourist in-**

formation: 66 Murray St; (085) 62 1866. **Accommodation:** 1 hotel/motel, 1 motel, 1 caravan/camping park. **See also:** Vineyards and Wineries.
MAP REF. 263 L4, 267 K4, 269 K13

Old Noarlunga   Population 669

A small village on the Wine Coast, situated 32 km south of Adelaide on the Fleurieu Peninsula. **Of interest:** The Horseshoe Mill (1844); Church of St Philip and St James (1850), Church Hill Rd; Uniting Church, Malpas St; old Jolly Miller Hotel (1850), now Noarlunga Hotel, Patapinda Rd; and Market Square, where first public market was held in 1841. **In the area:** Port Noarlunga and Christies Beach, 10 km north-west, and Moana and Maslin Beaches, 3 km and 6 km south, all offer good swimming and fishing. About 8 km further north of Port Noarlunga, Hallett Cove has tracks left by glaciers hundreds of millions of years ago. Pioneer Village Museum at Hackham, 4 km north, re-creates 1860s settlement with cottage, smithy, barn, general store and inn. Lakeside Leisure Park at Hackham. At McLaren Vale, 5 km south, some 50 vineyards and wineries. At Myponga, 27 km south, Myponga Reservoir, for barbecues or picnics; several historic buildings. **Tourist information:** The Cottage, Main Rd, McLaren Vale; (08) 323 8537. **Accommodation:** 1 hotel, 1 motel, 1 caravan/camping park.
MAP REF. 264 F4

Oodnadatta   Population 229

A tiny, but famous, outback town around 1050 km north-west of Adelaide, Oodnadatta is an old railway town with a well-preserved sandstone station (1890), now a museum. It is thought the name Oodnadatta originated from an Aboriginal term meaning 'yellow blossom of the Mulga'. Petrol and supplies available. **In the area:** Witjira National Park, 120 km north; free tepid thermal baths in Dalhousie Mound Springs. Camping and accommodation at Mt Dare Homestead, within park. The Oodnadatta Track runs from Maree to Oodnadatta and continues to join Stuart Hwy at Marla, 200 km west. **Accommodation:** 1 hotel, 1 caravan/camping park.
MAP REF. 271 J4

Paringa   Population 507

One of the fastest-growing towns in SA, Paringa, only 4 km from Renmark, is the eastern gateway to the Riverland region. **Of interest:** Paringa Suspension Bridge (1927). Bert Dix Memorial Park, adjacent to Paringa Bridge. Houseboat marina, Lock 5 Rd; houseboats for hire.

Billy Boiling Championships and Bush Picnic held in August. **In the area:** Headings Cliff lookout tower, 12 km north on Murtho Rd; fine views of surrounding irrigated farmland and river cliffs. Murtho Forest Park; picnic and camping facilities. E & WS Lock 5 and Weir, Lock 5 Rd. Also on Lock 5 Rd, Margaret Dowling National Trust Park, area of natural bushland. The Black Stump, root system of river red gum estimated to be 500–600 years old; found on Murtho Rd. Dunlop Big Tyre (14 m high, 26 m wide) spans Sturt Hwy at Yamba, 12 km south-east; also fruit fly depot. Scenic drive, 36 km east into Victoria, to see delicate blossoms at Lindsay Point Almond Park in early spring. **Tourist information:** Council Offices, Murtho Rd; (085) 85 5102. **Accommodation:** 1 hotel/motel, 1 caravan/camping park.
MAP REF. 267 Q3, 269 Q12

Penola   Population 1222

Penola, 52 km north of Mount Gambier, is the oldest town in the south-east of SA, and contains fine examples of slab and hewn-timber cottages, erected in the 1850s, which have been maintained and restored. Many famous names are associated with Penola. Poets Adam Lindsay Gordon, John Shaw Neilson and Will Ogilvie all spent time here. The first school in Australia which catered for all children regardless of income or social class was established here in 1866 by Mother Mary McKillop, who may be Australia's first Saint. The stone classroom in which she taught is on the corner of Portland St and Petticoat Lane. **Of interest:** John Riddoch Interpretive Centre, Arthur St, housed in former Mechanics Institute; audio-visual, poetry recitals. In Petticoat Lane, heritage buildings and arts and crafts. Self-guided Heritage walk; details from Tourist Information Centre. **In the area:** Yallum Park Homestead (1880), 8 km west, historic two-storeyed Victorian homestead built by John Riddoch, founder of Coonawarra wine industry. Penola Conservation Park, 10 km west; picnic areas and signposted interpretive walk. The Coonawarra vineyards, 10 km north, produce magnificent red table wines from 15 wineries; most open for tastings and cellar-door sales. **Tourist information:** Arthur St; (087) 37 2855. **Accommodation:** 1 hotel, 1 hotel/motel, 1 motel.
MAP REF. 210 A3, 273 H9

Peterborough   Population 2239

Peterborough is a railway town 250 km north of Adelaide, surrounded by grain-growing and pastoral country. Three different rail systems meet here and there are locomotive sheds and marshalling

yards. It is the principal town on the important Port Pirie to Broken Hill railway line. **Of interest:** The Steamtown Peterborough Railway Preservation Society runs limited historic narrow-gauge steam train journeys from town to Orroroo or Eurelia on holiday weekends. Rann's Museum, Queen St; exhibits of historic railway equipment. The RoundHouse Exchange, housing unique railway turntable and other railway equipment; open by appointment. The Gold Battery, end Tripney Ave, an ore-crushing machine; open by appointment. Saint Cecilia, Callary St, a gracious home (with some splendid stained-glass windows) built originally as a bishop's residence; accommodation, dining and guided tours available. Art gallery, Main St, adjacent to Tourist Information Centre. Victoria Park, Grove St; picnic facilities and children's playground. **In the area:** Terowie, 24 km south-east; old railway town with many historic buildings. At Orroroo, 37 km north-west: historic buildings and Yesteryear Costume Gallery with display of fashion from 1850; nearby, scenic walk among Aboriginal carvings along Pekina Ck; panoramic views from Black Rock Peak, east. At Magnetic Hill, 8 km west of Black Rock, a vehicle, with the engine turned off, rolls uphill! **Tourist information:** Main St; (086) 51 2708. **Accommodation:** 3 hotels, 1 hotel/motel, 1 motel, 1 caravan/camping park.
MAP REF. 269 J6, 271 O13

Pinnaroo   Population 746

This little township on the Ouyen Hwy is only 10 km from the Victorian border. **Of interest:** Australia's largest cereal collection (1300 varieties), Pinnaroo Institute, Railway Tce Sth. Historical Museum in railway station, Railway Tce Sth. Working printing museum, South Tce; animal park and aviary with parrots and other native birds. Farm-machinery museum at showgrounds, Homburg Tce. **In the area:** Walking Trail in Karte Conservation Park, 21 km north-west, on Karte Rd. Peebinga Conservation Park, 42 km north, on Loxton Rd. Scorpion Springs Conservation Park, 28 km south. Ngarkat Conservation Park, 48 km south. Pertendi Walking Trail, 49 km south. **Tourist information:** Council Offices; (085) 77 8002. **Accommodation:** 1 hotel, 1 motel, 1 caravan/ camping park.
MAP REF. 116 B11, 214 A10, 267 R8

Port Augusta   Population 15 291

Port Augusta, a thriving industrial city at the head of Spencer Gulf and in the shadow of the Flinders Ranges, is the most northerly port in SA. It is 317 km from Adelaide and is a vital supply centre for

the outback areas of the state and the large sheep-stations of the district. Port Augusta is an important link on the east-west Indian-Pacific railway and the famous *Ghan* train to Alice Springs, which departs from Adelaide. The city has played an intrinsic role in SA's development since the State Electricity Trust built a series of major power-stations here. Fuelled by coal from the huge open-cut mines at Leigh Creek, the stations generate more than one-third of the state's electricity. **Of interest:** Wadlata Outback Centre, Flinders Tce, for introduction to the sights and sounds of the outback. Homestead Park Pioneer Museum, Elsie St has a large photographic collection, pleasant picnic areas, blacksmith's shop, old steam train and crane, as well as rebuilt 130-year-old pine-log Yudnappinna Homestead. Royal Flying Doctor Service Base, Vincent St; open weekdays. School of the Air, southern end of Commercial Rd; tours available during term time. Curdnatta Art and Pottery Gallery in town's first railway station, Commercial Rd. Self-guided Heritage Walks (2 hr) include town hall (1887), Commercial Rd, court-house (1884) cnr Jervios St and Beauchamp's Lane, with cells built of Kapunda marble, and St Augustine's Church (1882), Church St, with magnificent stained-glass windows. McLellan Lookout, Whiting Pde, site of Matthew Flinders landing in 1802; panoramic views, picnic facilities in adjacent park. Red Cliffs lookout, end of McSporran Cres.; excellent view of Gulf and Flinders Ranges; adjacent area is site for Australian Arid Lands Botanic Gardens. Australian National Railway Workshops, Carlton Pde; guided tours on Tues. **In the area:** Conducted tours of Northern power-station, 4 km east, weekdays. Scenic drive 23 km north-east to splendid Pichi Richi Pass, where Railways Preservation Society runs old steam-engines during school holidays and to the historic town of Quorn, 39 km north-east, and Warren and Buckaringa Gorges, 21 km and 37 km further north, respectively. Winninowie Conservation Park, 30 km south-east. Hancocks Lookout, 38 km south-east towards Wilmington, offers views of surrounding country, Port Augusta and Whyalla; turn-off road dangerous when wet. Mt Remarkable National Park 63 km southeast, has rugged mountain terrain, magnificent gorges and abundant wildlife. Historic Melrose, 65 km south-east is the oldest town in Flinders Ranges. **Tourist information:** Wadlata Outback Centre, Flinders Tce; (086) 41 0793. **Accommodation:** 6 hotels, 9 motels, 3 caravan/camping parks.
MAP REF. 268 F4, 271 M12, 272 I7

Port Broughton   Population 657

A small port on the extreme north-west coast of the Yorke Peninsula, Port Broughton is 169 km from Adelaide. On a protected inlet of the sea, the town is a major port for fishing-boats and is renowned for its deep-sea prawns. **Of interest:** Safe swimming beach along foreshore. Historical Museum, Bay St (previously old council chambers) and Cottage Museum, Kadina Rd, contain much of town's history. Shandelé porcelain dolls made and displayed, Harvey St. **In the area:** Fisherman's Bay, 10 km north; popular fishing, boating and holiday spot. Heritage copper-mining towns of Moonta, Wallaroo and Kadina, 47 km south. Clare Valley and surrounding wine districts 100 km east. **Tourist information:** Yorke Peninsula Tourist Information Centre, Victoria Sq., Kadina; (088) 21 2093. **Accommodation:** 1 hotel, 1 hotel/motel, 2 caravan/ camping parks.
MAP REF. 268 F9

Port Elliot   Population 1050

Only 5 km north-east of Victor Harbor, Port Elliot is a charming, historical coastal town with the main focus these days being on scenic Horseshoe Bay, the town's beach. The town was established in 1854, the same year Australia's first public iron railway operated between Goolwa and Port Elliot. **Of interest:** Along The Strand: National Trust historical display, within Port Elliot railway station (1911), council chamber (1879), police station (1853) and St Jude's Church (1854); guided walks available Sun. afternoons. Spectacular views from Freeman's Knob, end of The Strand. Port Elliot Art Pottery, Main Rd. **In the area:** Middleton Winery, 11 km north-east via Middleton. **Tourist information:** Old Library Bldg, cnr Cadell St and Goolwa Tce, Goolwa; (085) 55 1144. **Accommodation:** 2 hotels, 1 motel, 1 caravan/camping park.
MAP REF. 264 H9, 266 I9

Port Lincoln   Population 11 552

Port Lincoln is attractively sited on the clear waters of Boston Bay, which is three times the size of Sydney Harbour. The port, 250 km due west of Adelaide across St Vincent and Spencer Gulfs, was discovered by Matthew Flinders in 1802 and settled in 1839. It was originally chosen as the state's capital. With its sheltered waters, Mediterranean climate, scenic coastal roads and attractive farming hinterland, Port Lincoln is becoming an increasingly popular tourist resort. It is the base for Australia's largest tuna fleet and is also an important export centre for wheat, wool, fat lambs and live sheep, frozen fish, lobster, prawns and abalone. The coastline is deeply indented, offering magnificent scenery: sheltered coves, steep cliff-faces and impressive surf beaches. Nearby offshore islands can be rented for exclusive family holidays. The Tunarama Festival, held every Australia Day weekend, celebrates the opening of the tuna season. **Of interest:** Boston Bay for swimming, water-skiing, yachting and excellent fishing. Mill Cottage Museum (1867) and Settler's Cottage Museum, both in picturesque Flinders Park. 'Old Mill' lookout, Dorset Place, for views of town and bay. Lincoln Hotel (1840), Tasman Tce, oldest hotel on Eyre Peninsula. Axel Stenross Maritime Museum, north end of town; First Landing site nearby. Rose-Wal Memorial Shell Museum in grounds of Eyre Peninsula Old Folk's Home. The Silk Factory, Angas St, for local art. Arteyrea Gallery, Washington St; community art centre, Sunday workshops open to the public. Barbed Wire and Fencing Equipment Museum; open by appointment only, (086) 82 1162. M.B. Kotz Collection of Stationary Engines, Baltimore St. Lincoln Cove, off St Andrews Tce, with marina. Dangerous Reef - Marine Life Viewing Platform; *Dangerous Reef Explorer* ferries visitors to reef, home for large sea-lion colony, and a commercial tuna farm. Apex Wheelhouse, original wheelhouse from tuna-boat *Boston Bay*, adjacent to Kirton Point Caravan Park, Hindmarsh St. **In the area:** Skippered boat charter available for game fishing, diving, day fishing and island cruises. Yacht charters available. Regular launch cruises of Boston Bay and Boston Island. Several pleasant parks close to town and vast natural reserves abounding in wildlife, no more than a day's outing away. Winter Hill Lookout, 5 km north-west on Flinders Hwy. Port Lincoln Fauna Park, 9 km north-west on Flinders Hwy at Little Swamp. At Koppio, 38 km northwest, Koppio Smith Museum; Tod Reservoir; museum with heritage display and picnic area. Coffin Bay, 49 km north-west, with lookout and Coffin Bay Oyster Farm for fresh oysters and other seafood, and nearby Coffin Bay National Park. Boston Bay Wines, 6 km north on Lincoln Hwy; cellar-door sales on weekends. Tiny Tots Gnome Village, Lincoln Hwy. Karlinda Collection, adjacent to post office at North Shields, 16 km north; shells, marine life and Deepwater Trawl Fish Exhibit. At Poonindie, 20 km north, an intriguing church (1850) with two chimneys. Tumby Bay, 48 km north, a small beach resort. Lincoln National Park, 20 km south, offers wildlife and cliff-top walk to view impressive coastal scenery. Southernmost tip of Eyre Peninsula, known as Whalers Way, offers stunning coastal

VINEYARDS AND WINERIES

South Australia provides about sixty-five per cent of the wines and eighty-three per cent of the brandy made in Australia. In the equable dry climate of the southern and eastern regions of the state, kilometres of vineyards stretch over valleys, plains and hillsides. The state has eight distinct grape-growing regions: the Barossa Valley, the Wine Coast region of the Fleurieu Peninsula, the Clare Valley, Murraylands, Riverland, the Adelaide Hills, the Coonawarra area of the south-east, and Boston Bay on Eyre Peninsula.

The **Barossa Valley**, Australia's most famous wine-producing area, is located about fifty-five kilometres north-east of Adelaide. It is a warm and intimate place of charming old towns, with vineyards spreading across undulating hills in well-tended, precise rows. Visitors can view the valley from a hot-air balloon and afterwards enjoy a champagne breakfast.

The Barossa Valley was named in 1837 by Colonel Light in memory of Barrosa in Spain, where he had fought a decisive battle in 1811. The recorded spelling 'Barossa' was an error that was never rectified. The district was settled in 1839 by English and German settlers. Today the Barossa has a distinctive culture and atmosphere which derives from this German concentration in the mid-nineteenth century and is evidenced in the vineyards, the stone buildings, the restaurants, the bakeries and the Lutheran churches which dot the valley.

The Barossa produces brandy, dry and sweet table wines, and fortified styles of wine. Some of the most famous wineries of the Barossa are Yalumba, Orlando, Penfolds and Seppelts. Some of these wineries are still run by members of the same families that established them over one hundred years ago. Others have been taken over by big international companies, but the distinctive qualities of the wine remain. There are many medium-sized wineries making excellent wines, such as Wolf Blass, Basedows and Krondorf, and many boutique wineries specialising in producing a small number of quality wines, including Barossa Settlers, Henschke, Grant Burge and Elderton.

Tanunda, Barossa Valley

The **Wine Coast** region is on the Fleurieu Peninsula, just south of Adelaide. Nestled in the gentle folds of the Mount Lofty Ranges with a westerly view to the sea lies McLaren Vale, the centre of this wine-growing area, which is particularly well suited to red wines. There are over fifty wineries in the region, among them Chapel Hill, Hardy's Reynella, James Haselgrove, Seaview, and Wirra Wirra, and they range from very large to very small. In most of the wineries, the person at the cellar door is the person who makes the wine, so — meet your maker at McLaren Vale!

The vineyards of the **Clare Valley** are about 130 kilometres north of Adelaide and produce fine light table wines, hock, riesling, chablis and some reds. Two of the better-known of the twenty-odd wineries in this district are Eaglehawk Estate and Stanley Leasingham.

The **Murraylands** region extends from Middleton Estate Wines at Middleton, north-east to Willowglen Wines near Murray Bridge. Another wine region that includes a stretch of the Murray River near the Victorian border is **Riverland**. Famous for a wide range of products from top-quality table wines to ouzo and brandy, the region is represented by such wineries as Kingston Estate at Kingston on Murray eastwards to Angove's near Renmark.

There are vineyards scattered throughout the **Adelaide Hills**. Wineries to the north (south-east of the Barossa Valley) include Hamiltons,

Craneford and Grand Cru Estate; this area is noted especialy for its riesling. Closer to Adelaide are Petaluma and Stonyfell Wineries.

Many vineyards at **Coonawarra** in the far south-east produce magnificent red wines from a small area of unique rich, volcanic soil, such as Ladbroke Grove, Mildara and Rouge Homme. Further vineyards have been established in the south-east at Keppoch and Padthaway.

Boston Bay, perched on the southern tip of the spectacular Eyre Peninsula, is one of Australia's newest wine regions. Its reputation as the 'home of the great white shark' is fast changing to an area for 'great white wines', with national award recognition for the region's first major vintage. There are two wineries in the area.

Most of the South Australian wineries are open for inspection, tastings and cellar-door sales.

For further information about hours of inspection and winery tours, contact the Tourism South Australia Travel Centre, 1 King William Street, Adelaide; (08) 212 1505.

scenery; permit required, available from tourism outlets. On road to Whalers Way: Constantia Designer Craftsmen, world-class furniture factory and showroom (guided tours available); historic Mikkira sheep station, open during winter. Off-shore islands for boating enthusiasts: Boston Island offers homestead accommodation for 'getaway' holidays; Thistle and Wedge Islands (both privately owned), popular with bluewater sailors and fishermen. Greenpatch Farm, 25 km north, opportunity to take part in farm working day; native fauna, walk-through aviary and fishing for trout in four well-stocked dams. **Tourist information:** Eyre Travel, Civic Centre, Tasman Tce; (086) 82 4577. **Accommodation:** 5 hotels, 7 motels, 2 caravan/camping parks. **See also:** Festival Fun; The Eyre Peninsula.
MAP REF. 272 F12

Port MacDonnell   Population 651
Port MacDonnell was once a thriving port. Today it is a quiet, well-planned fishing-town, 28 km south of Mount Gambier. The rock-lobster fishing fleet here is the largest in SA. **Of interest:** Old Customs House (1860) with National Trust classification. Maritime Museum, Meylin St; salvaged artefacts from shipwrecks, plus photographic history of town. **In the area:** 'Dingley Dell' (1862, but restored), home of poet Adam Lindsay Gordon, now a museum, 2 km west. Cape Northumberland Lighthouse, on dramatically beautiful coastline west of town. Devonshire teas at quaint Ye Olde Post Office Tea Rooms at Allendale East, 6 km north. For keen walkers, track to summit of Mt Schank, 10 km north; crater of extinct volcano, with picnic facilities. Mt Schank Fish Farm, for fresh fish, yabbies. Heading east, surf fishing at Orwell Rocks. Sinkholes for experienced cave-divers at Ewens Ponds and Picaninnie Ponds Conservation Parks, 7 km and 20 km east. **Tourist information:** Council Offices, Meylin St; (087) 38 2437 or 38 2207. **Accommodation:** 1 hotel, 1 motel, 2 caravan/camping parks.
MAP REF. 210 A7, 273 H12

Port Pirie   Population 13 960
Huge grain silos and smelters' chimneys dominate the skyline of Port Pirie, 227 km north of Adelaide on Spencer Gulf. Situated on a curve of the tidal Port Pirie River, the city is a major industrial and commercial centre. The first settlers came in 1845; wheat farms and market gardens were established around the sheep industry in the region. The company Broken Hill Associated Smelters began smelting lead in 1889 and today the largest lead-smelters in the world treat thousands of tonnes of concentrates annually from the rich silver, lead and zinc deposits at Broken Hill, NSW. Wheat and barley from the mid-north are exported and there is a thriving fishing industry. Port Pirie is also a vital link in the road and rail routes to Alice Springs, Darwin, Port Augusta and Perth. Wheat farms, rolling hills and the ocean are all close by. Swimming, water-skiing, fishing and yachting are popular summer sports on the river. **Of interest:** National Trust Museum Buildings, Ellen St, include old Victorian pavilion-style railway station; open daily. Historic residence 'Carn Brae', Florence St, antique exhibits and a collection of over 2500 dolls on display; open daily. The waterfront, where loading and discharging of Australian and overseas vessels takes place. Tours of Pasminco Metals BHAS smelting works; details from tourist office. Northern Festival Centre in Memorial Park, Gertrude St, cultural heart of the north and venue for local and national performances. Port Pirie Festival of Country Music held in October. Blessing of the Fleet and associated festivals, early Sept.; reminder of role of Italians at turn of century in establishing fishing industry. **In the area:** Weeroona Island, 13 km north. Port Germein, beach resort 24 km north; wooden jetty said to be longest in southern hemisphere. Southern reaches of beautiful Flinders Ranges are within 50 km; further east, ruggedly beautiful Telowie Gorge, lined with giant red river gums. **Tourist information:** Jubilee Place; (086) 33 0439. **Accommodation:** 2 hotels, 1 hotel/motel, 4 motels, 3 caravan/camping parks.
MAP REF. 268 G7

Port Victoria   Population 243
A tiny township on the west coast of the Yorke Peninsula, Port Victoria was once the main port for sailing-ships carrying grain from the area; the last windjammer sailed from here in 1949. **Of interest:** Swimming and jetty fishing, from original 1888 jetty, end of Main St. National Trust Maritime Museum at beginning of jetty; check opening times. Wardang Island, Aboriginal reserve, 10 km off coast, can be visited with permission from Point Pearce Community Council. **In the area:** Conservation Islands are breeding grounds for several bird species. New underwater Heritage Trail in waters around Wardang Island, for scuba-divers visits 8 wrecks; self-guiding leaflet available. **Tourist information:** Yorke Peninsula Tourist Information Centre, Victoria Sq., Kadina; (088) 21 2093. **Accommodation:** 1 hotel/motel, 2 caravan parks. **See also:** The Yorke Peninsula.
MAP REF. 266 E4, 272 I12

Quorn   Population 1079
Nestled in a valley in the Flinders Ranges, 331 km north of Adelaide, Quorn was established as a railway town in 1878. Part of the Great Northern Railway, the line was built by Chinese coolies and British stonemasons. Closed in 1957 for economic reasons, part of the line through Pichi Richi has been restored; a steam locomotive operates Mar.–Nov., taking passengers on the 33-km round trip. **Of interest:** Many historic buildings; Historic Walk leaflet available. Quorn Mill (1878), Railway Tce; once a flour mill, now art gallery, museum, motel and restaurant. Quornucopia Galley, Railway Tce. Nairana Craft Centre, First St. **In the area:** Colourful rocky outcrops of Dutchman's Stern, 6 km north. Arden Vale Ceramics, 15 km north on Arden Vale Rd. Junction Gallery, 16 km north on Yarrah Vale Rd. Warren Gorge, 22 km north, popular with climbing enthusiasts; Buckaringa Gorge, 10 km further north, scenic picnic areas. Kanyaka Homestead 42 km north, ruins of sheep-station that supported 70 families from the 1850s to the 1870s; some buildings restored. Kanyaka Death Rock, also 42 km north, overlooking a permanent waterhole, once an Aboriginal ceremonial ground. Scenic drive 50 km south to Devil's Peak, Pichi Richi Pass, Mt Brown, Mt Brown Conservation Park and picturesque Waukarie Falls, 16 km away; walking trails. Towns of Bruce and Hammond, 22 km and 38 km south-east; 1870s architecture. Hammond has unusual museum in town's original bank building. **Tourist information:** Council Offices, Seventh St; (086) 48 6031. **Accommodation:** 1 hotel, 2 hotel/motels, 1 motel, 1 caravan/camping park.
MAP REF. 268 G3, 271 N12

Renmark   Population 3489
Renmark is at the heart of the oldest irrigation area in Australia, 260 km north-east of Adelaide on the Sturt Hwy. In 1887 the Chaffey brothers from Canada were granted 250 000 acres to test their irrigation scheme. Today lush orchards and vineyards thrive with the water piped from the Murray. There are canneries, wineries and fruit-juice factories. Wheat, sheep and dairy cattle are other local industries. The first community-run hotel in the British Commonwealth, the Renmark Hotel, is an impressive three-storeyed building overlooking a sweeping bend of the river. **Of interest:** National Trust Museum 'Olivewood', cnr Renmark Ave (Sturt Hwy) and 21st St; former Chaffey homestead. Old hand-operated winepress, on display in Renmark Ave, and one of the Chaffeys' original wood-

burning irrigation pumps, on display outside Renmark Irrigation Trust Office, Murray St, original Chaffey Bros. office. *PS Industry*, built in 1911, now floating museum moored adjacent to Tourist Centre, Murray Ave. Rivergrowers Ark packing shed, Renmark Ave, near 19th St; sales of local products; group tours available. Frank Harding's Folklore Gallery and Zenith Art Gallery, Murtho St; Ozone Art Gallery, Murray Ave. Luxury 5-day cruises on *PS Murray Princess* or day cruises aboard *MV Barrangul*. Houseboats for hire. **In the area:** Renmano Winery, 5 km south-west on Sturt Hwy; tastings and sales Mon.–Sat. Unique collection of fauna, particularly reptiles, at Bredl's Wonder World of Wildlife, 7 km south-west on Sturt Hwy; open daily. Ruston's Roses, 3000 varieties, 7 km south-west off Sturt Hwy; open Oct. – end May. Angove's winery and distillery, Bookmark Ave, 5 km south-west; tastings and sales Mon. – Fri. Cooltong Winery, 11 km north-west, specialises in retsina, ouzo and kokkinelli wines and spirits; open by appointment through Tourist Centre. Danggali Conservation Park, 60 km north, vast area of mallee scrub with bluebush and black oak woodland and abundance of bird and animal life. **Tourist information:** Murray Ave; (085) 86 6703. **Accommodation:** 1 hotel/motel, 4 motels, 3 caravan/camping parks. **See also:** Festival Fun.
MAP REF. 116 A8, 267 Q3, 269 Q12

Robe   Population 742
A small, historic town on Guichen Bay, 336 km south of Adelaide, Robe is a fishing-port and holiday centre. The rugged, windswept coast has many beautiful and secluded beaches, including the 17 km of Long Beach, north of town. Lagoons and salt lakes are all round the area and wildlife abounds. Fairy penguins appear on the beach in the evening. In addition to these natural attractions, there are interesting historic sites; many of the town's original buildings still remain and have been restored. In the 1850s it was a major wool-shipping port. From 1857, 16 500 Chinese disembarked at Robe and travelled overland to the goldfields to avoid the Victorian Poll Tax. **Of interest:** National Trust buildings and small art and craft galleries; especially Smillie and Victoria Sts. Robe Historic Interpretation Centre in Library building, Victoria St, has displays and tourist information; leaflets on self-guided Heritage Walks and drives available. Old Customs House Museum, (1863), Royal Circus. Karatta House, off Christine Dr, summer residence of Governor Sir James Fergusson in 1860s. Caledonian Inn (1858), Victoria St; accommodation and meals. **In**

the area: Lakeside (1884), Main Rd, 2km south-east; historic home with b & b accommodation, also caravan park. Water-skiing on adjacent Lake Fellmongery. Narraburra Woolshed, 14 km south-east; sheep and wool activities. Beacon Hill, 2 km south, provides panoramic town and area views. Little Dip Conservation Park, 13 km south; complex moving sand dune system, salt lakes and freshwater lakes, where wildlife abound. The Obelisk at Cape Dombey, 3 km west; northern vantage point for views of area. Telegraph Yabbie Farm, 12 km north; trout and barramundi fishing as well as yabbies, Nov–end Mar. Crayfish fleet anchors in Lake Butler in town; fresh crays and fish are available Oct. – end Apr. Boat charters available for fishing, sightseeing or diving trips. **Tourist information:** Robe Library, Victoria St; (087) 68 2465. **Accommodation:** 2 hotels, 6 motels, 4 caravan/camping parks.
MAP REF. 273 D8

Roxby Downs   Population 2000 (est.)
A modern, newly established township built to accommodate the employees of the Olympic Dam Mining Project, Roxby Downs is 85 km north of Pimba, which is just off the Stuart Hwy, 555 km north of Adelaide. A road from Roxby Downs joins the Oodnadatta track just south of Lake

Eyre South, 125 km north of Roxby. **In the area:** Olympic Dam, 15 km north; tours of mining operations available. Heritage Centre and Missile Park, 90 km south at Woomera. **Tourist information:** Council Offices, Richardson Place. **Accommodation:** 1 motel, 1 caravan/camping park.
MAP REF. 272 H2

Stansbury   Population 547
Situated on the lower east coast of Yorke Peninsula, Stansbury was originally known as Oyster Bay because it was once one of the best oyster-beds in South Australian waters. In days gone by, ketches shipped grain across the gulf from Stansbury to Port Adelaide. A popular holiday resort, the town has scenic views of the Gulf St Vincent. The bay is ideal fo rwater sports, including diving and water-skiing. **Of interest:** Museum, North Tce; within first Stansbury School (1878) and residence. Jetty fishing. **In the area:** Lake Sundown, 15 km north-west, one of many salt lakes in area ; photographer's deligh t at sunset. **Tourist information:** Yorke Peninsula Tourist Information Centre, Victoria Sq., Kadina; (088) 21 2093. **Accommodation:** 1 hotel, 2 motels, 2 caravan parks.
MAP REF. 266 F6, 272 I13

ALTERNATIVE ACCOMMODATION

The South Australian Host Farms Association is a group of farming families who welcome guests on their properties. There are over fifty of these farms, varying from outback station properties to sheep and wool farms, horse studs and dairy farms, vineyards and orchards.

The range of host farm accommodation includes self-contained cottages, shearers' quarters and accommodation in the homestead as a member of the family; many host farms offer bed and breakfast or welcome guests to dine with the family. Guests also have the opportunity to observe, or become involved in, seasonal activities on the property.

Bed and Breakfast Town and Country is an association of hosts willing to share their establishments with visitors. The accommodation ranges from modest to luxury in a wide variety of settings, including historic self-contained cottages,

homestay and small guest houses.

Houseboats. With a meandering section of the Murray River flowing through the south-east section of the state, beautiful scenery, temperate weather and good shore facilities, houseboating is a viable and enjoyable holiday alternative.

From Murray Bridge to Renmark and Paringa, with several towns in between, houseboats ranging from 'monsters' sleeping ten to twelve to those sleeping four to six can be hired. Some are equipped with dinghys, sundecks, air-conditioning, microwaves, colour TV and videos; while others have the bare essentials for comfort such as refrigerators, barbecues and heating.

Pre-booking is recommended in December and January. For further information, contact the nearest Tourism South Australia Travel Centre.

Strathalbyn   Population 1924
An inland town with a Scottish heritage, on the Angas River, Strathalbyn is 58 km south of Adelaide and a designated heritage township. Picturesque Soldiers Memorial Gardens follow the river through town, offering shaded picnic-grounds. **Of interest:** National Trust Museum, Rankine St; housed in old police station and courthouse. St Andrew's Church (1848), Alfred Pl. Old Provincial Gas Company (1868), South Tce; now Gasworks Gallery. Over 10 antique and craft shops. International Penny Farthing Cycle Challenge Cup and Colonial Street Fair held in March. **In the area:** Lakeside resort of Milang, 20 km south-east; museum. Langhorne Creek, 15 km east; wine-growing district. Pottery at Paris Creek, near Meadows, 15 km north-west; iris gardens open Oct. – Mar. **Tourist information:** Old Railway Station, South Tce; (085) 36 3212. **Accommodation:** 3 hotels, 1 caravan park.
MAP REF. 265 K5, 267 J8

Streaky Bay   Population 992
Streaky Bay, 727 km from Adelaide, is a holiday resort, fishing port and agricultural centre for the cereal-growing hinterland. The explorer Matthew Flinders named the bay because of the streaking effect caused by seaweed in its waters. The town is almost surrounded by small bays and coves, pleasant sandy beaches and spectacular towering cliffs. Crayfish and many species of fish abound in Streaky Bay waters and fishing from boat or the jetty is good. **Of interest:** Old School House Museum, Montgomery Tce. Hospital Cottage (1864), the first building in Streaky Bay. **In the area:** Magnificent coastal scenery and rugged cliffs. Point Labatt Conservation Park, 55 km south, has only permanent colony of sea-lions on Australian mainland. Murphy's Haystacks, 40 km south-east off Flinders Hwy, a sculptural group of ancient pink granite rocks. Port Kenny, 62 km south on Venus Bay; excellent fishing. Further 12 km south, fishing village of Venus Bay; nearby, breathtaking views from Needle Eye Lookout. Spectacular limestone caves at Talia, 88 km south. **Tourist information:** Council Offices, Alfred Tce; (086) 26 1001. **Accommodation:** 1 hotel/motel, 1 motel, 1 caravan/camping park. **See also:** The Eyre Peninsula.
MAP REF. 270 I13, 272 B7

Swan Reach   Population 226
Swan Reach is a quiet little township on the Murray River about 100 km east of Gawler. Picturesque river scenery and good fishing are making it an increasingly popular holiday resort. **In the area:** Sandleton Museum; 23 historic buildings depicting life of early settlers.

Houseboats for hire. Punyelroo, 7 km south; fishing, boating and water-skiing. Swan Reach, 11 km west, and Ridley Conservation Parks, 5km south. Water sports at Walker Flat, 26 km south. Yookamurra Sanctuary, 21 km north-west; conservation project, including eradication of feral animals and restocking with native animals. Guided tours only, on Sun.; booking essential, (08) 388 5380. **Accommodation:** 1 hotel, 1 caravan/camping park.
MAP REF. 267 M5

Tailem Bend   Population 1542
A railway-workshop town at the junction of the Dukes and Princes Hwys, 107 km from Adelaide, Tailem Bend has some excellent views across the Murray as the river bends sharply towards Wellington. **Of interest:** Gumi Racing Festival held each February. **In the area:** Scenic drive via vehicular ferry across river to Jervois; cheese factory here (tours by appointment); then 11 km south to Wellington, where river meets lake. At Wellington, old restored court-house complex (1864); includes cells, stables, post and telegraph office, courtyard and kiosk. Historic buildings, south-east on Dukes Hwy: old woolshed on left, approaching Cooke Plains; Braeside Homestead on left, after town. Old Tailem Town Pioneer Village, 5 km north of Tailem Bend; open daily. **Tourist information:** 15 Railway Tce; (085) 72 3537. **Accommodation:** 1 motel, 1 caravan/camping park.
MAP REF. 265 R5, 267 L8

Tanunda   Population 2856
The town of Tanunda is the heart of the Barossa Valley. It was the focal point for early German settlement, growing out of the village of Langmeil, established in 1843, part of which can be seen in the western areas of town. The National Trust has classified Goat Square, site of the old market square, surrounded by century-old cottages. **Of interest:** Fine Lutheran churches. Historical museum, Murray St; former 1865 post and telegraph office houses collections specialising in German heritage. Old Siegersdorf Winery, Barossa Valley Way; Kev Rohlach Collection, from local heritage to technology. Barossa Kiddypark, Magnolia St; funpark with rides and wildlife. **In the area:** Local wineries include St Hallett Wines, Rockford Wines, Charles Melton Wines, Bethany Wines, High Wycombe Wines, Basedow Wines, Veritas Winery, Hardy's Siegersdorf, Chateau Dorrien, Peter Lehmann Wines and Krondorf Wines. Story Book Cottage and Whacky Wood, Oak St, for children. Norm's Coolie Sheep Dogs, south off Barossa Valley Way; 3 performances weekly. The Keg Factory, St Hallett Rd;

makers of kegs, barrel furniture and wine racks. Bethany, 4 km south, first German settlement in the Barossa; pretty village with creekside picnic area, art and craft galleries, pioneer cemetery, attractive streetscapes and two wineries. **Tourist information:** Tanunda Caravan and Tourist Park, Murray St, (085) 63 2784. **Accommodation:** 1 hotel, 1 hotel/ motel, 5 motels, 1 caravan/camping park. **See also:** Festival Fun; Vineyards and Wineries.
MAP REF. 263 L5, 267 J4

Tintinara   Population 363
A quiet little town 206 km south-east of Adelaide in the Coonalpyn Downs. **Of interest:** Post office (1865), Becker Tce. Lake Indawarra, end Northcott Tce, for water sports. **In the area:** Historic Tintinara Homestead, 9 km west; historic buildings and host farm accommodation. Access to Mt Rescue Conservation Park, 15 km east; sandplains with heath, native fauna, Aboriginal campsites and burial-grounds. Mt Boothby Conservation Park, 20 km west. **Tourist information:** Council Offices; (087) 57 2100. **Accommodation:** 1 hotel, 1 motel, 1 caravan/camping park.
MAP REF. 267 O11, 273 E2

Tumby Bay   Population 996
Tumby Bay is a pretty coastal resort 49 km north of Port Lincoln on the east coast of the Eyre Peninsula. The town is noted for its long crescent beach and white sand, and the well-kept lawns along the foreshore are always popular for picnics and barbecues. **Of interest:** C. L. Alexander National Trust Museum, housed in old wooden schoolroom; open Fri. and Sat. afternoons. Police station (1871). Two jetties, one more than 100 years old. **In the area:** Rock and surf fishing. Island Lookout for panoramic views. Rugged but beautiful scenery at Poonta and Cowley's Beaches; catches include snapper, whiting and bream. Koppio, about 40 km west, through attractive fertile countryside, with National Trust classified Smithy Museum. Tod Reservoir Museum in Koppio hills. At Port Neill, 42 km north, grassed foreshore for picnics and safe swimming beach. Vic and Jill Fauser's Museum (open daily) and 1 km north, Port Neill Lookout for spectacular views. At Wanilla, wildflowers in spring. At Thuruna, excellent fishing. Lipson Cove, where visitors can walk across to Lipson Island at low tide. Fishing, sea-lions, dolphins and birdlife at Sir Joseph Banks Group of islands; charter tours available. Trinity Haven Scenic Drive. **Tourist information:** Hales Minimart, 1 Bratten Way; (086) 88 2584. **Accommodation:** Tumby Bay, 2 hotels, 1 motel, 1 caravan/camping

park; Port Neill, 1 hotel, 2 caravan/camping parks. **See also:** The Eyre Peninsula. MAP REF. 272 F11

Victor Harbor
Population 5318

A popular coastal resort town and unofficial capital of the Fleurieu Peninsula, Victor Harbor is 84 km south of Adelaide. Established in the early days of whaling and sealing in the 1830s, 'Victor', overlooks historic Encounter Bay, protected by Granite Island. **Of interest:** Historical buildings: Adare (1860s), The Drive, Mount Breckan (1879), Renown Ave, Newland Memorial Congregational Church (1869), Victoria St, and St Augustine's Church of England (1869), Burke St. Telegraph Station Art Gallery, Coral St; housed in former telegraph station (1866). **In the area:** Granite Island, joined to mainland by 1 km causeway; walk or take horse-drawn tram across. Chair-lift (operates SA school holidays and weekends) offers magnificent views of land and sea. Penguin rookeries and seals to be seen also. The Bluff, or Rosetta Head, 5 km south, worth 100 metre climb for views. Greenhills Adventure Park, 3.5 km north on banks of Hindmarsh River. Native animals and birds at Urimbirra Wildlife Park, 5 km north. Opposite, Nangawooka Flora Reserve with over 1000 named trees and plants. At Mt Compass, 24 km north: pottery, strawberry and blueberry farms, begonia farm, nursery and Tooperang Trout Farm. The Steam-Ranger, a railway service, operates between Victor Harbor and Goolwa, via Port Elliot. North, both Hindmarsh and Inman Rivers provide good fishing and peaceful picnic spots. Spring Mount Conservation Park, 14 km north-west. Glacier Rock at Inman Valley, 19 km north-west, shows effect of glacial erosion. Hindmarsh Valley Falls, 15 km north-east; pleasant walks and spectacular waterfalls. Waitpinga Beach, 17 km south-west. Deep Creek Conservation Park, 50 km south-west, has Heysen Trail for walking, and spectacular flora and fauna; park is famous for its rugged cliffs and orchids and ferns in its gullies. Talisker Conservation Park (adjacent to Deep Creek Conservation Park) is site of historic silver-lead mine; old mine buildings and diggings. At tip of Fleurieu Peninsula is Cape Jervis, 70 km south-west, with splendid views. **Tourist information:** Torrens St; (085) 52 4255. **Accommodation:** 3 hotels, 8 motels, 3 caravan/camping parks. **See also:** The Fleurieu Peninsula. MAP REF. 264 H10, 266 I9

Waikerie
Population 1593

Waikerie, the citrus centre of Australia, is surrounded by an oasis of irrigated vegetables, orchards and vineyards in mallee-scrub country in the Riverland. Situated 170 km north-east of Adelaide, the town has beautiful views of the river gums and magnificent sandstone cliffs along the Murray. The name means 'anything that flies' and the river and lagoons teem with birdlife; the mallee scrub is a haven for parrots and other native birds. **Of interest:** Co-op Fruit-packing House, Sturt Hwy, largest in Australia; tours Mon. – Fri. afternoons in season. Harts Lagoon, Ramco Rd; bird wetlands. Houseboats for hire. **In the area:** Orange Tree kiosk, Sturt Hwy, 2 km east; fruit products and river-viewing platform. Internationally acclaimed as a glider's paradise, joy rides and courses available from Gliding Club, off Sturt Hwy, 4 km east. Terrigal Fauna Park, Baldock Rd, 4 km east. On northern side of river near Lock 2, close to Taylorville, spectacular fossil deposit area, one of few in Australia where crystallised gypsum fossils are found in abundance. Pooginook Conservation Park, 12 km north-east, sanctuary for mallee fowl, echidnas and hairy-nosed wombats. Holder Bend Reserve and Maize Island Conservation Park, 6 km north-east. At Blanchetown, 42 km west, first of Murray's six SA locks; lookout at Blanchetown Bridge; floating restaurant. Brookfield Conservation Park, 11 km west, home of southern hairy-nosed wombat. **Tourist information:** Waikerie Travel Centre, 20 McCoy St; (085) 41 2295. **Accommodation:** 1 motel, 1 hotel/motel, 1 caravan/camping park. MAP REF. 267 N3, 269 N12

Wallaroo
Population 2224

Situated 154 km north-west of Adelaide, Wallaroo is a key shipping port for the Yorke Peninsula, exporting barley and wheat. Processing of rock phosphate is another major industry here. The safe beaches and good fishing in this historical area make it a popular tourist resort. In 1859 vast copper-ore deposits were discovered. A smelter was built, thousands of Cornish miners arrived and Wallaroo and surrounding areas boomed until the 1920s, when copper prices dropped and the industry gradually died out. The nearby towns of Moonta and Kadina form part of the trio known as 'Little Cornwall', and the area still has many reminders of its colourful past. The 'Kernewek Lowender', a Cornish festival, is held in conjunction with Moonta and Kadina in May every odd-numbered year. **Of interest:** Cemetery, Moonta Rd, holds grave of Caroline Carleton, author of 'Song of Australia'. Number of charming old Cornish-style cottages in district. National Trust Wallaroo Heritage and Nautical Museum, in town's first post office (1865) in Jetty Rd; collection of maritime exhibits. Wallaroo Historical Walks brochure available at museum or town hall, Irwine St; guided tours on Sun. Historic buildings include old railway station, Owen Tce, customs-house (1862) and Hughes chimney stack (1865), Jetty Rd, which contains over 300 000 bricks and is more than 7 m square at its base. **In the area:** Wallaroo Mines site; open for signposted self-guided walking tour.Towns of Moonta and Kadina. Bird Island, 10 km south for crabbing. **Tourist information:** Yorke Peninsula Tourist Information Centre, Victoria Sq, Kadina; (088) 21 2093. **Accommodation:** 2 hotels, 2 motels, 1 caravan/camping park. **See also:** Festival Fun; The Yorke Peninsula. MAP REF. 266 E2, 268 E11, 272 I10

Whyalla
Population 26 900

In 90 years Whyalla, northern gateway to the Eyre Peninsula, has grown from a small settlement known as Hummock Hill to the largest provincial city in the state and an important industrial centre based on steel. It is famous for its heavy industry, particularly the enormous BHP iron and steel works and ore mining at Iron Knob and Iron Monarch in the Middleback Ranges. A shipyard operated from 1939 to 1978 and the largest ship ever built in Australia was launched from here in 1972. Whyalla is a modern, well-planned city with a good shopping centre, safe beaches, fishing, boating and excellent recreational facilities. The area enjoys a sunny, Mediterranean-type climate. **Of interest:** Whyalla Maritime Museum, Lincoln Hwy; features now land-locked 650 tonne corvette *Whyalla*; and Tanderra Building, housing collection of models, including what is believed to be largest OO gauge model railway in Australia. Mount Laura Homestead Museum (National Trust), Ekblom St; check opening times. Whyalla Art Gallery, Darling Tce; open daily. Foreshore re-development includes attractive beach, jetty, landscaped area very popular for picnics and marina. Hummock Hill lookout from Queen Elizabeth Dr; spectacular views. Flinders Lookout, Farrel St; Ada Ryan Gardens, Cudmore Tce; mini-zoo and picnic facilities under shady trees. Guided tours of BHP steel-works; bookings at Tourist Centre (for safety reasons, visitors must wear closed footwear). Fauna and reptile park, south-east on Lincoln Hwy, near airport, offers Nocturnal Walk Guided Tour; bookings essential. Whyalla Tourist Drive; brochure from Tourist Centre. Whyalla Show held in August. **In the area:** Port Bonython (20 km east) and Point Lowly (14 km further on); Point Lowly Lighthouse (1882), oldest building in area (not open

for inspection); and scenic coastal drive through Fitzgerald Bay to Point Douglas. Whyalla Conservation Park, 10 km north off Lincoln Hwy, near Port Bonython turnoff. At Iron Knob, 50 km north: iron-ore quarries (tours available); BHP Mining Museum and Iron Knob Mineral and Shell Display. Lake Gilles Recreation Park, 72 km west; varied birdlife, kangaroos, western pigmy possums and reptiles. **Tourist information:** Lincoln Hwy; (086) 45 7900. **Accommodation:** 5 hotels, 2 hotel/ motels, 3 motels, 1 caravan/camping park. **See also:** The Eyre Peninsula.
MAP REF. 268 E6, 271 M13, 272 I8

Willunga
Population 826
An historic township first surveyed in 1839, Willunga is located just south of the famous Southern Vales wine-growing regions and is Australia's major almond-growing centre. **Of interest:** Historic pug cottages and fine examples of colonial architecture. National Trust police station and court-house (1855), Main St. Church of England, St Andrews Tce, has Elizabethan bronze bell. Bush Inn (1889) and 'Vanessa's' restaurant, both Main Rd. Almond Blossom Festival held annually in late July. **In the area:** Cowshed Gallery at Yundi, 9 km east. Mt Magnificent Conservation Park, 12 km east; western grey kangaroos in bushland, scenic walks and picnic areas. Strawberry farm, 4 km north. Kyeema Conservation Park, 14 km north-east. **Tourist information:** The Cottage, Main Rd, McLaren Vale; (08) 323 8537. **Accommodation:** Limited.
MAP REF. 264 G5, 266 I8

Wilmington
Population 233
A tiny settlement formerly known as Beautiful Valley, Wilmington is 290 km north of Adelaide in the Flinders Ranges. **Of interest:** Police station (1880) and old coaching stables (1880) at rear of Wilmington Hotel, both Main St. Beautiful Valley Aussie Relics Museum, Melrose Rd; open Sun. **In the area:** Mount Remarkable National Park, 13 km south, with crystal-clear mountain pools, dense vegetation and abundant wildlife; Mambray Creek and spectacular Alligator Gorge in park. Historic Melrose, 21 km south, oldest town in the Flinders. Hancock's Lookout, 7 km west, at top of Horrocks Pass off road to Port Augusta, for views of Spencer Gulf. Booleroo Steam and Traction Preservation Society's Museum (open by appointment), Booleroo Centre, 48 km south-east. At Carrieton, 56 km north-east: historic buildings; Aboriginal carvings, 5 km along Belton Rd; scenic drive to deserted Johnberg. **Tourist information:** General Store, Main St; (086)

67 5155. **Accommodation:** 1 hotel, 2 caravan/camping parks.
MAP REF. 268 G4, 271 N13

Wilpena
Population under 200
Wilpena, 429 km north of Adelaide, is the small settlement outside Wilpena Pound. The Pound, part of the Flinders Ranges National Park, is a vast natural amphitheatre surrounded by colossal peaks which change colour as the light falls on them through the day. The only entrance is through a narrow gorge and across Sliding Rock. In 1900 a wheat farmer built a homestead within the Pound, but a flood destroyed the log road and the farm was abandoned. **In the area:** Bushwalking and mountain climbing in surrounding countryside. Numerous walking trails into Wilpena Pound, including one to St Mary's Peak, the highest point (1188 m). Aboriginal rock carvings and paintings at Arkaroo Rock on slopes of Rawnsley Bluff, south, and at Sacred Canyon, southeast. Rawnsley Park Station, 20 km south on Hawker Rd; demonstrations of sheep-drafting and shearing Sept.–Oct. Appealinna Homestead (1851), 16 km north off Blinman Rd; ruins of house built of flat rock from creek-bed. Scenic drives—most of area within confines of Flinders Ranges National Park (headquarters at Oraparinna Station)—to Stokes Hill Lookout, 2 km north-east; Bunyeroo and Brachina Gorges, Aroona Valley, 5 km north-west; Moralana Scenic Drive, 25 km south. Organised tours and scenic flights of area available. **Tourist information:** Wilpena Pound Motel; (086) 48 0004. **Accommodation:** 1 motel, 2 caravan/camping parks. **See also:** The Flinders Ranges.
MAP REF. 271 O11

Woomera
Population 1805
Established in 1947 as a site for launching British experimental rockets, Woomera was, until 1982, a prohibited area to visitors. The town, 490 km north-west of Adelaide, is still administered by the Defence Department. **Of interest:** Missile Park and Heritage Centre; displays of rockets, aircraft and weapons. Breen Park picnic area. **In the area:** Roxby Downs, 78 km north, service centre for Olympic Dam mining operations; tours of mining operations available. Andamooka opal field, 107 km east; tours available. **Accommodation:** 1 hotel, 1 caravan/camping park.
MAP REF. 271 L10, 272 G3

Wudinna
Population 618
Wudinna is a small settlement on the Eyre Hwy, 571 km north-west of Adelaide. The township has become an important service point for the central Eyre Peninsula. **In the**

area: Wudinna is the gateway to the timeless Gawler Ranges; Wilderness Safaris available. Mt Wudinna, 10 km north-east, second largest granite outcrop in Australia; summit (261 m) offers panoramic views of countryside; recreation area at base. Turtle Rock, another nearby ancient granite rock looking surprisingly like its namesake. Signposted tourist drives to all major rock formations. Prolific wildlife and wildflowers in spring throughout area. At Minnipa, 37 km north-west: Grain Research Centre; Yarwondutta Rock; recreation areas at Minnipa Hill and Tcharkulda Hill. **Tourist information:** Ramsey Bros, Eyre Hwy; (086) 80 2200. **Accommodation:** 1 hotel/motel, 1 motel, 1 caravan park.
MAP REF. 272 E8

Yankalilla
Population 384
A small, quiet settlement just inland from the west coast of the Fleurieu Peninsula, 35 km west of Victor Harbor. **Of interest:** In Main St: Uniting Church (1878); Bungala House, gifts and pottery; leatherwork, woodwork and gumnut creations at the Hobbit House; Yankalilla Hotel for good country-style counter meals; historical museum; tearooms. **In the area:** Tiny seaside town of Normanville, 4 km west. Bay Tree Farm, Cape Jarvis Rd, Second Valley, 14 km west; herbs, flowers, afternoon teas. Steep hillsides and gullies of Myponga Conservation Park, 16 km east; home of western grey kangaroo. Myponga, 14 km north-east; cheese factory, begonia farm and Myponga Reservoir for barbecues or picnics. **Tourist information:** Council Offices, Main St; (085) 58 2048. **Accommodation:** Yankalilla, 1 hotel. Normanville, 1 motel, 2 caravan/camping parks.
MAP REF. 264 D8, 266 H9

Yorketown
Population 723
Principal town at the southern end of the Yorke Peninsula, Yorketown's shopping centre services the surrounding cereal-growing district. Yorketown is surrounded by extensive inland salt lakes (some are pink) which are still worked. **In the area:** Toy Factory, 5 km north-east; locally crafted wooden toys. Rugged coastal scenery and desolate country at tip of Peninsula, including Innes National Park, 77 km south-west. Inneston, historic mining town within park, managed as historic site by NPWS. Surfing at Daly Head, 50 km west. Corny Point, at north-western tip of Peninsula, 55 km away, has lighthouse and lookout; camping and fishing. **Tourist information:** Yorke Peninsula Tourist Information Centre, Victoria Sq., Kadina; (088) 21 2093. **Accommodation:** 1 hotel, 1 hotel/motel, 1 caravan/camping park. **See also:** Yorke Peninsula.
MAP REF. 266 E7, 272 I13

Maps of South Australia

Location Map

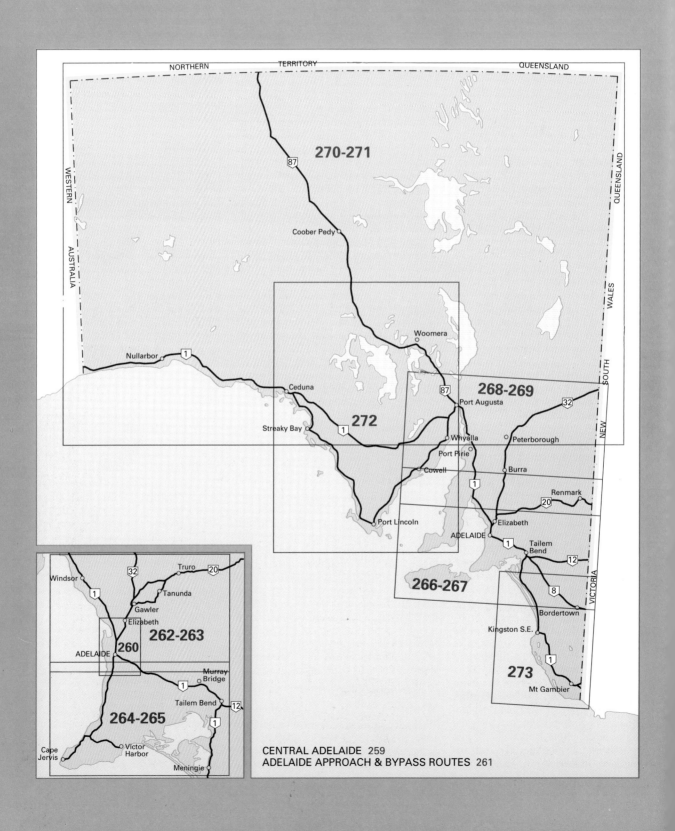

NORTHERN TERRITORY QUEENSLAND

WESTERN AUSTRALIA

SOUTH

QUEENSLAND

NEW WALES

VICTORIA

270-271

87

Coober Pedy

Woomera

Nullarbor 1

Ceduna

87

268-269

32

Port Augusta

272

Streaky Bay

Whyalla

Peterborough

1

Cowell

Port Pirie

Burra

Renmark

20

1

Port Lincoln

Elizabeth

ADELAIDE

Tailem
Bend

12

266-267

8

Bordertown

Kingston S.E.

273

Mt Gambier

Windsor

32

Truro

20

1

Tanunda

Gawler

Elizabeth

262-263

ADELAIDE

260

Murray
Bridge

1

Tailem Bend

12

264-265

1

Cape
Jervis

Victor
Harbor

Meningie

CENTRAL ADELAIDE 259
ADELAIDE APPROACH & BYPASS ROUTES 261

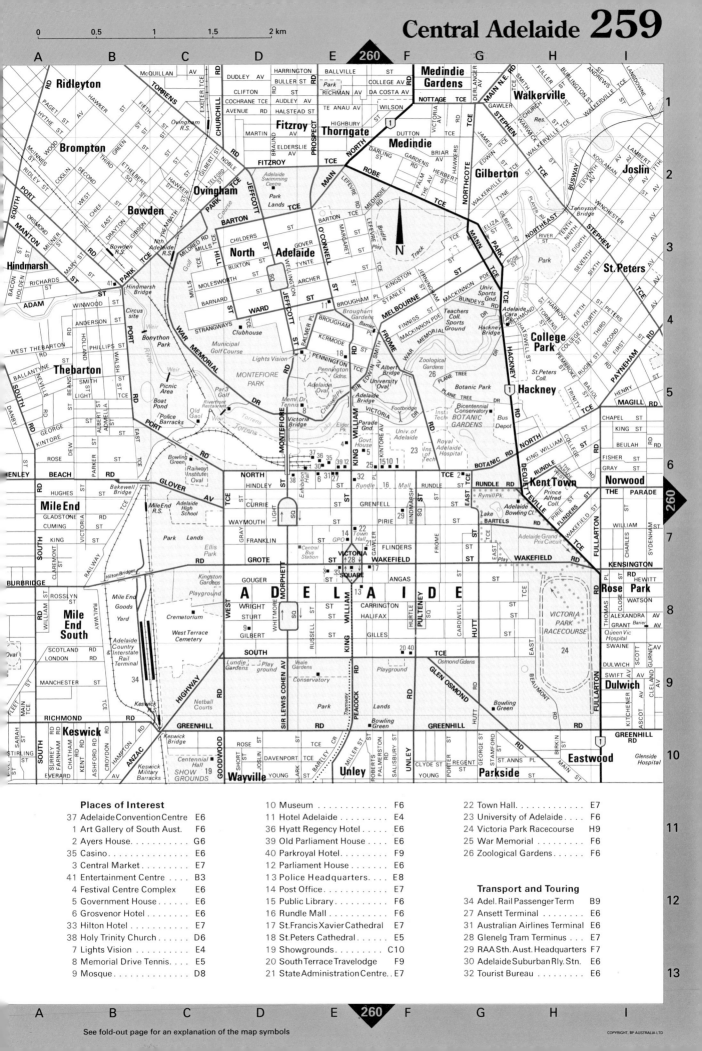

Places of Interest
- 37 Adelaide Convention Centre E6
- 1 Art Gallery of South Aust. F6
- 2 Ayers House G6
- 35 Casino E6
- 3 Central Market E7
- 41 Entertainment Centre B3
- 4 Festival Centre Complex E6
- 5 Government House E6
- 6 Grosvenor Hotel E6
- 33 Hilton Hotel E7
- 38 Holy Trinity Church D6
- 7 Lights Vision E4
- 8 Memorial Drive Tennis E5
- 9 Mosque D8

- 10 Museum F6
- 11 Hotel Adelaide E4
- 36 Hyatt Regency Hotel E6
- 39 Old Parliament House E6
- 40 Parkroyal Hotel F9
- 12 Parliament House E6
- 13 Police Headquarters E8
- 14 Post Office E7
- 15 Public Library F6
- 16 Rundle Mall F6
- 17 St. Francis Xavier Cathedral . E7
- 18 St. Peters Cathedral E5
- 19 Showgrounds C10
- 20 South Terrace Travelodge . F9
- 21 State Administration Centre .. E7

- 22 Town Hall E7
- 23 University of Adelaide F6
- 24 Victoria Park Racecourse . H9
- 25 War Memorial F6
- 26 Zoological Gardens F6

Transport and Touring
- 34 Adel. Rail Passenger Term . B9
- 27 Ansett Terminal E6
- 31 Australian Airlines Terminal . E6
- 28 Glenelg Tram Terminus ... E7
- 29 RAA Sth. Aust. Headquarters F7
- 30 Adelaide Suburban Rly. Stn. . E6
- 32 Tourist Bureau E6

See fold-out page for an explanation of the map symbols

COPYRIGHT, BP AUSTRALIA LTD

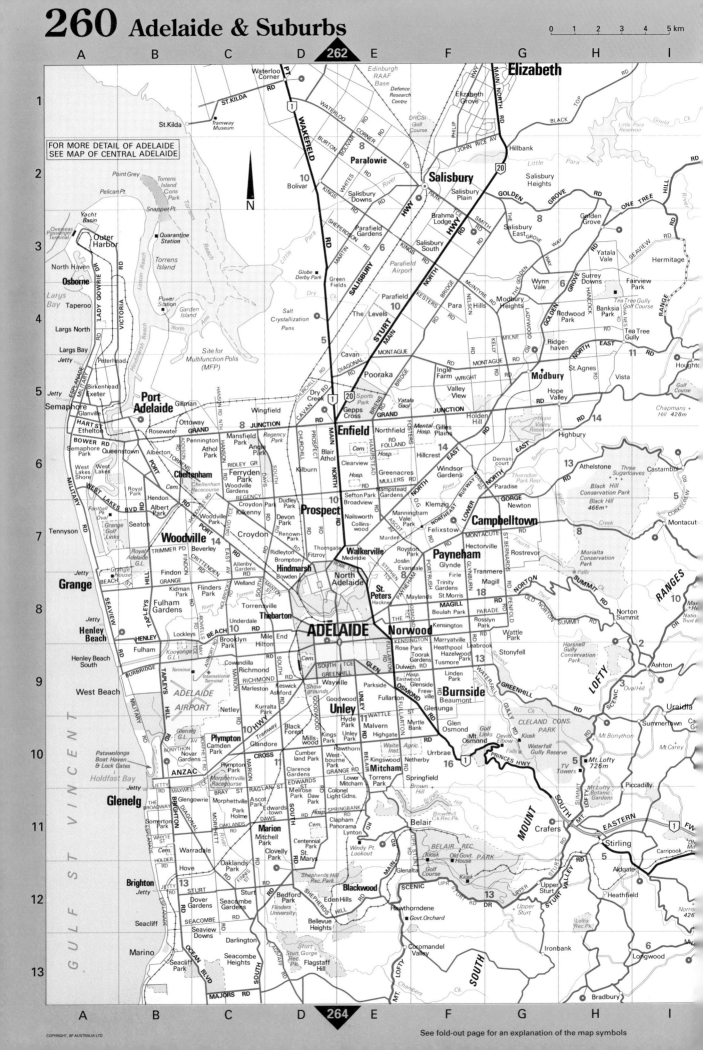

0 1 2 3 4 5 km

A B C D ▼262 E F G H I

Elizabeth

FOR MORE DETAIL OF ADELAIDE
SEE MAP OF CENTRAL ADELAIDE

Waterloo
Corner

St. Kilda

Tramway
Museum

Point Grey

Pelican Pt.

Snapper Pt.

Torrens
Island Cons.
Park

Edinburgh
RAAF Base

Defence
Research
Centre

DRCSI
Golf
Course

Elizabeth
Grove

N

Bolivar

Paralowie

Salisbury

Hillbank

Yacht
Basin

Outer
Harbor

Quarantine
Station

Torrens
Island

Salisbury
Downs

Salisbury
Plain

Salisbury
Heights

North Haven

Osborne

Larys
Bay

Taperoo

Power
Station

Garden
Island

Globe
Derby Park

Green
Fields

Dry
Ck.

Parafield
Gardens

Salisbury
South

Brahma
Lodge

Salisbury
East

Golden
Grove

Overseas
Passenger
Terminal

Largs North

Largs Bay

Jetty

North
Arm

Site for
Multifunction Polis
(MFP)

Salt
Crystallization
Pans

Parafield
Airport

Parafield

Para
Hills

Modbury
Heights

Wynn
Vale

Surrey
Downs

Redwood
Park

Banksia
Park

Fairview
Park

Yatala
Vale

Hermitage

Tea Tree
Gully Golf Course

Semaphore

Peterhead

The Levels

Cavan

Ingle
Farm

Ridge-
haven

Tea Tree
Gully

Birkenhead

Exeter

Gillman

Wingfield

Montague

Pooraka

Valley
View

Modbury

St. Agnes

Vista

Houghton

Port
Adelaide

Rosewater

Dry Creek

Gepps
Cross

Yatala
Gaol

Holden
Hill

Hope
Valley

Hope
Valley
Reservoir

Golf
Course

Chapmans
Hill 428m

Etholton

Queenstown

Ottoway

Junction

Enfield

Northfield

Gilles
Plains

Highbury

Semaphore
Park

Pennington

Athol
Park

Mansfield
Park

Angle
Park

Regency
Park

Blair Athol

Clearview

Mental
Hosp.

Windsor
Gardens

Dernan
court

Paradise

Athelstone

Three
Sugarloaves

Castambul

West
Lakes
Shore

West
Lakes

Cheltenham

Ferryden
Park

Kilburn

Hosp.

Greenacres

Klemzig

Newton

Black Hill
Conservation Park

Black Hill
466m

Montacut

Royal
Park

Hendon

Albert
Park

Cheltenham
Racecourse

Woodville
Gardens

Croydon

Dudley
Park

Sefton Park

Broadview

Hampstead
Gardens

Manningham

Campbelltown

Morialta
Conservation
Park

Tennyson

Seaton

Findon

Kilkenny

Devon
Park

Nailsworth

Collins-
wood

Vale
Park

Felixstow

Hectorville

Rostrevor

Woodville

Beverley

Woodville
Park

Renown
Park

Prospect

Marden

Payneham

Grange
Golf
Links

Welland

Ridleyton

Brompton

Thorngate

Fitzroy

Royston
Park

Joslin

Glynde

Firle

Tranmere

Magill

Grange

Royal
Adelaide
G.L.

Kidman
Park

Flinders
Park

Allenby
Gardens

Bowden

Walkerville

Medindie

Evandale

Trinity
Gardens

Grange
House

Fulham
Gardens

Torrensville

Underdale

North Adelaide

St. Peters

Hackney

St.Morris

Maylands

Beulah Park

Rosslyn
Park

Wattle
Park

Norton
Summit

Henley
Beach

Lockleys

Brooklyn
Park

Mile
End

Hilton

Magill

Kensington

Stonyfell

Horsnell
Gully
Conservation
Park

Ashton

Henley Beach
South

Fulham

Kooyonga
G.L.

Cowandilla

Richmond

ADELAIDE

Norwood

Kensington

Marryatville

Rose Park

Heathpool

Hazelwood

Leabrook

West Beach

Adelaide
Airport

Netley

Marleston

Keswick

Ashford

Show
grounds

Wayville

Parkside

Goodwood

Fullarton

Dulwich

Tusmore

Toorak
Gardens

Eastwood

Glenside

Frew-
ville

Linden
Park

Burnside

Beaumont

Uraidla

Summertown

Mt. Carey

Kurralta
Park

Unley

Hyde
Park

Malvern

Highgate

Glen
Osmond

Glenunga

Mt.
Osmond

Golf
Links

Cleland Cons.
Park

Mt. Bonython

Plympton

Glenelg
G.L.

Camden
Park

Glandore

Black
Forest

Mills-
wood

Kings
Park

Unley
Park

Wattle

Myrtle
Bank

Devils
Elbow

Kiosk

Waterfall
Gully Reserve

Mt. Lofty
726m

TV
Towers

Novar
Gardens

Plympton
Park

Cross

Cumber-
land Park

Hawthorn

West-
bourne
Park

Netherby

Urrbrae

Waite
Inst.

Agric.

Patawalonga
Boat Haven
& Lock Gates

Holdfast Bay

Morphettville
Racecourse

Clarence
Gardens

Melrose
Park

Daw
Park

Lower
Mitcham

Mitcham

Springfield

Brown
Hill

Piccadilly

Glenelg

Glengowrie

Park
Holme

Ascot
Park

Edwards-
town

Colonel
Light Gdns.

Torrens
Park

Kingswood

Brownhill
Ck.Rec.Pk.

Mt.Lofty
Botanic
Gardens

Somerton
Park

Warradale

Marion

Mitchell
Park

Clovelly
Park

St.
Marys

Springbank

Clapham

Panorama

Lynton

Belair

Crafers

Stirling

Carripook

Hove

Oaklands
Park

Centennial
Park

Windy Pt.
Lookout

Belair Rec.
Park

Kiosk

Old Govt.
House

Aldgate

Brighton

Jetty

Dover
Gardens

Seacombe
Gardens

Bedford
Park

Eden Hills

Blackwood

Golf
Course

Glenalta

Kiosk

Upper Sturt

Heathfield

Seacliff

Seacombe

Darlington

Flinders
University

Bellevue
Heights

Shepherds Hill
Rec. Park

Hawthorndene

Upper Sturt

Govt.Orchard

Norris
426

Marino

Seacliff
Park

Seacombe
Heights

Sturt Gorge
Rec. Pk.

Flagstaff
Hill

Coromandel
Valley

Ironbank

Longwood

Bradbury

MAJORS RD

A B C D ▼264 E F G H I

See fold-out page for an explanation of the map symbols

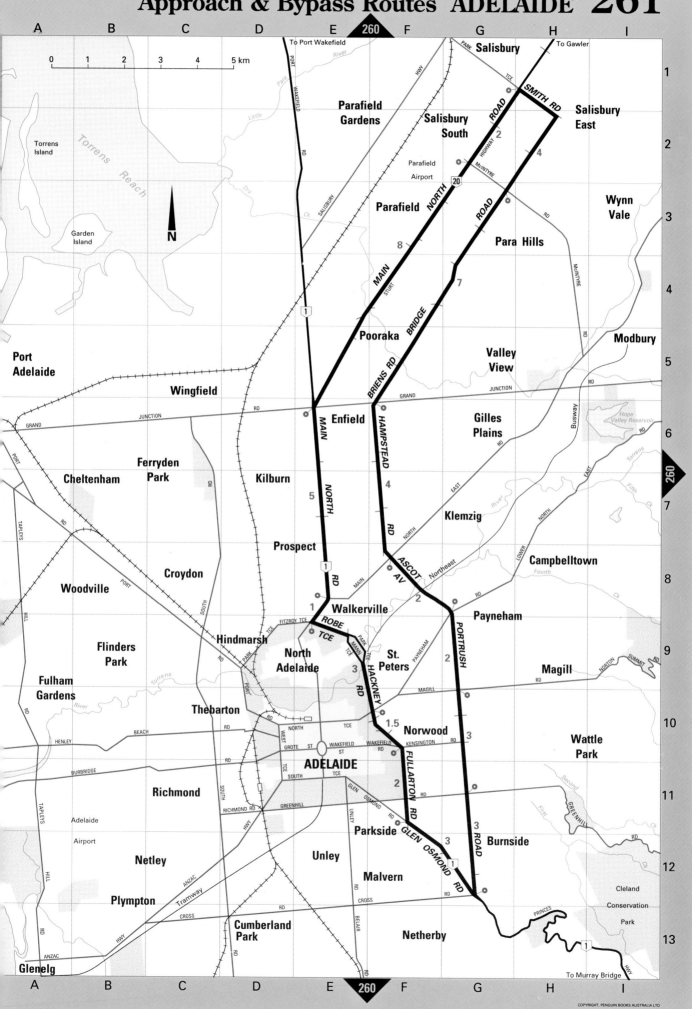

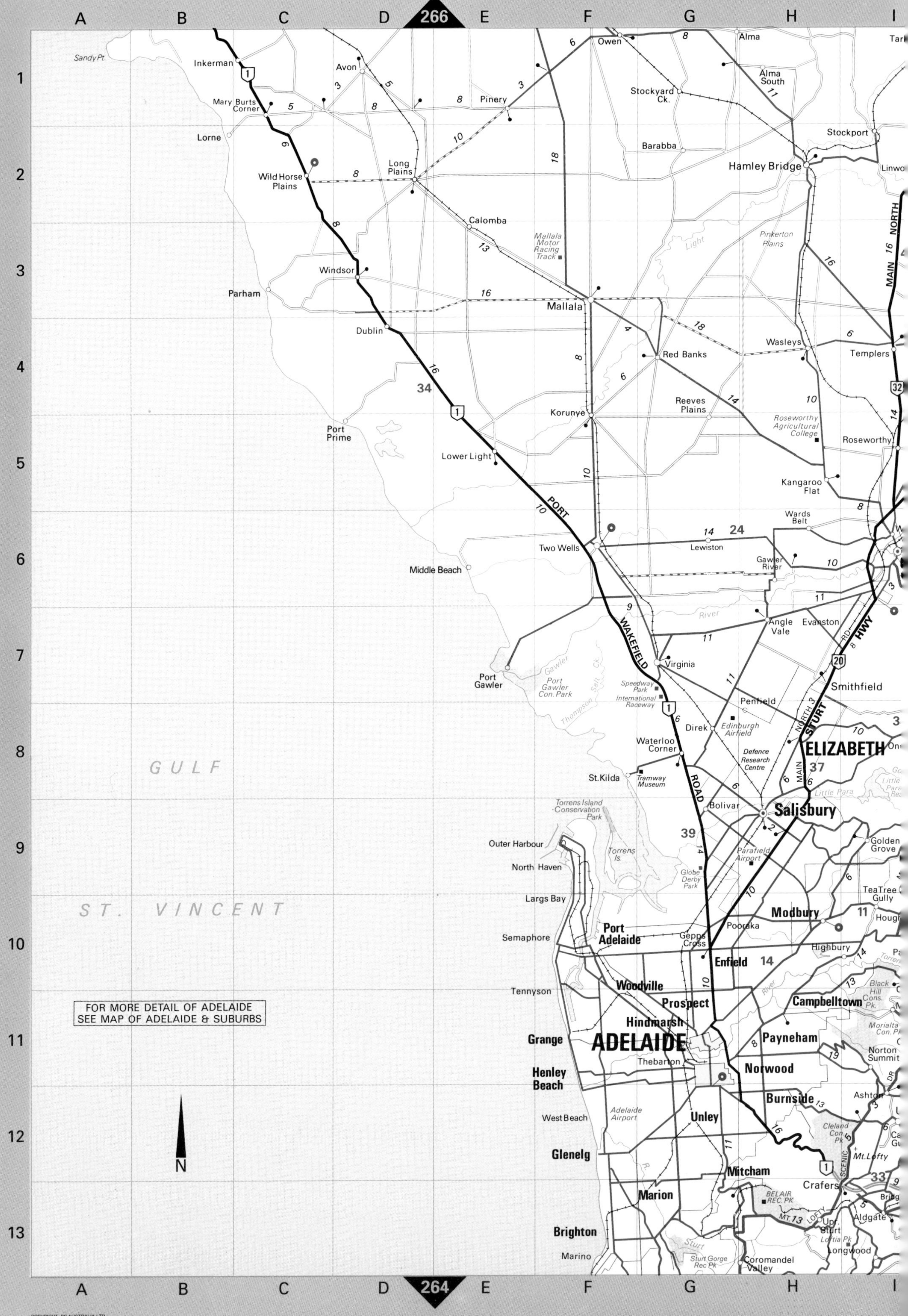

A B C D **266** E F G H I

1
Sandy Pt.
Inkerman
Owen
Alma
Alma South
Stockyard Ck.
Avon
3
5
8
Pinery
3
6
8
11
Tar
Mary Burts Corner
5
Lorne
8
Barabba
Stockport
Hamley Bridge
Linwo

2
6
Wild Horse Plains
8
Long Plains
10
18
Light
Pinkerton Plains
16
MAIN NORTH
16

3
8
Windsor
Calomba
13
Mallala Motor Racing Track
Mallala
Wasleys
6
Templers
Parham
16
18
4
Red Banks
32

4
Dublin
16
8
6
Reeves Plains
14
Roseworthy Agricultural College
10
14
Port Prime
34
1
Korunye
Roseworthy

5
Lower Light
10
Kangaroo Flat
Wards Belt
8
PORT
10

6
Two Wells
14
24
Lewiston
Gawler River
10
Middle Beach
9
WAKEFIELD
River

7
Port Gawler
Gawler
Port Gawler Con. Park
Salt Ck.
Virginia
11
11
Angle Vale
Evanston
ROAD
HWY
20
Smithfield

8
GULF
Thompson
1
6
Direk
Speedway Park International Raceway
Penfield
Edinburgh Airfield
NORTH
STURT
MAIN
10
3
ELIZABETH
37
Go
Waterloo Corner
Defence Research Centre
Little Para

9
St. Kilda
Tramway Museum
Bolivar
Salisbury
39
2
Parafield Airport
Golden Grove
Outer Harbour
Torrens Island Conservation Park
Torrens Is.
TeaTree Gully
Hough
North Haven
Globe Derby Park
10
6

10
ST. VINCENT
Largs Bay
Gepps Cross
Pooraka
Highbury
Torren
Semaphore
Port Adelaide
Enfield
14
Modbury
11
Tennyson
Woodville
River
Campbelltown
3
Black Hill Cons. Pk.
Pa

11
FOR MORE DETAIL OF ADELAIDE SEE MAP OF ADELAIDE & SUBURBS
Prospect
Morialta Con. Pk.
Grange
Hindmarsh
ADELAIDE
Payneham
Norton Summit
8
19
Thebarton
Norwood
Ashton
Henley Beach
Burnside
13

12
N
West Beach
Adelaide Airport
Unley
11
16
Cleland Con. Pk.
Mt.Lofty
Glenelg
Mitcham
1
SCENIC
33
Marion
Crafers
Ca

13
Brighton
BELAIR REC. PK.
MT 13 LOFTY
Up. Sturt Lottia Pk
Aldgate
Bridg
Marino
Sturt
Sturt Gorge Rec Pk
Coromandel Valley
Longwood

A B C D **264** E F G

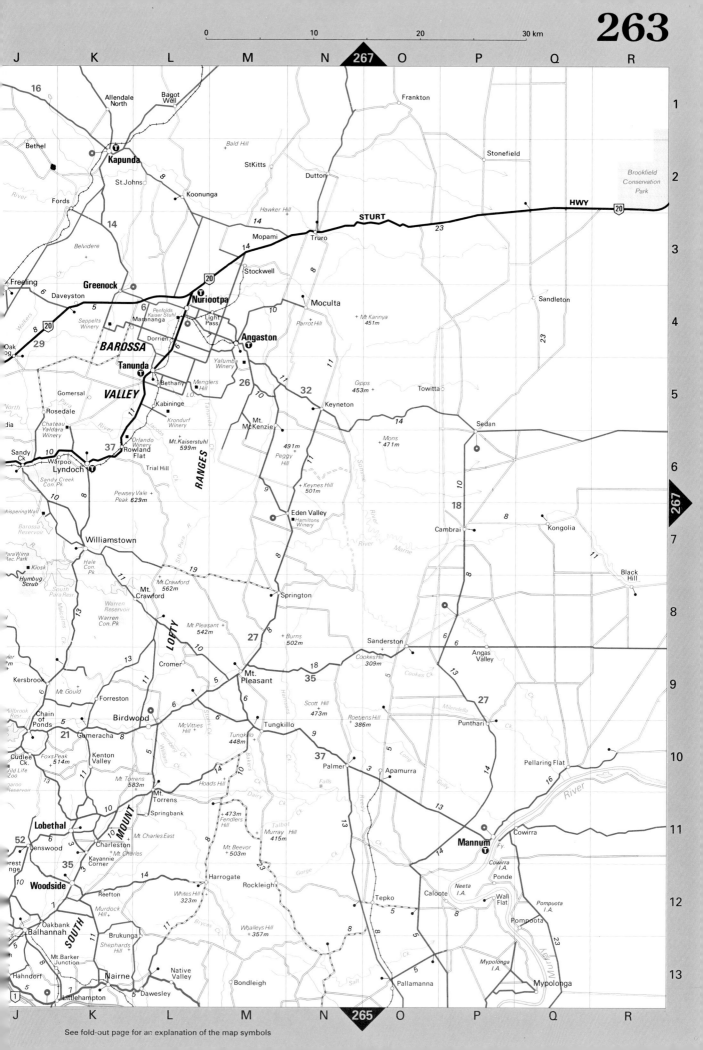

0   10   20   30 km

J   K   L   M   N   267   O   P   Q   R

16   Allendale North   Bagot Well
Bethel   Kapunda   St Kitts   Frankton   1
St.Johns   Dutton   Stonefield
Fords   8   Koonunga   Hawker Hill   STURT   HWY   20   Brookfield Conservation Park   2
14   Mopami   14   Truro   23
Freeling   14   Stockwell   Sandleton
Greenock   Daveyston   Nuriootpa   Moculta   23   3
5   6   Penfolds Kaiser Stuhl   Light Pass   +Mt.Karinya 451m   4
Seppelts Winery   Marananga   10   Parrot Hill
8   20   Dorrien   Angaston
Oak   29   BAROSSA   Tanunda   Yalumba Winery   11   Gipps 453m+   Towitta
dia   VALLEY   Bethany   Menglers Hill   26   32   Keyneton   Sedan   5
Gomersal   Kabininge   10   Mt. McKenzie   14
Rosedale   Kronдорf Winery   11   491m   Mons +471m
Chateau Yaldara Winery   Mt.Kaiserstuhl 599m   Peggy Hill   11
Sandy   10   Orlando Winery   RANGES   9   +Keynes Hill 501m   10   18   Cambrai   Kongolia
Ck   37   Rowland Flat   Trial Hill   Eden Valley   8   Black Hill   7
Warpoo   Lyndoch   Hamiltons Winery   11
8   Pewsey Vale Peak 629m   27   Sanderston   Angas Valley
Williamstown   Hale Con. Pk   19   Mt.Crawford 562m   Springton   Cookes Hill 309m   13
Humbug Scrub   11   Mt. Crawford   5   6   6   8
13   Warren Reservoir   Mt.Pleasant 542m   27   +Burns 502m   18   Scott Hill +473m   27   9
Kersbrook   13   Cromer   Mt. Pleasant   35   Roetjens Hill 386m   Punthari
Mt Gould   11   6   9   Milendella
Chain of Ponds   Forreston   McVitties Hill   Tungkillo   Tungkillo 448m   37   Palmer   3   Apamurra   14   Pellaring Flat   10
21   Gumeracha   Birdwood   5   Hoads Hill   Falls   13
Cudlee Ck   Kenton Valley   14   13   Mannum   11
FoxsPeak +514m   Mt Torrens   +473m Fendlers Hill   Talbot Murray Hill 415m   Cowirra
52   Lobethal   Mt Torrens 583m   Springbank   Charleston   Mt Charles East   Harrogate   Rockleigh   Caloote   Ponde   Pompoota
35   10   Mt Charles   14   Whites Hill 323m   Tepko   Neeta I.A.   Wall Flat   12
Woodside   Reefton   Murdock Hill   Whalleys Hill +357m   Bondleigh   Pallamanna   Mypolonga
Balhannah   Brukunga   Shephards Hill   Native Valley   Mypolonga I.A.   13
Hahndorf   Nairne   Dawesley
1   Littlehampton

J   K   L   M   N   265   O   P   Q   R

See fold-out page for an explanation of the map symbols

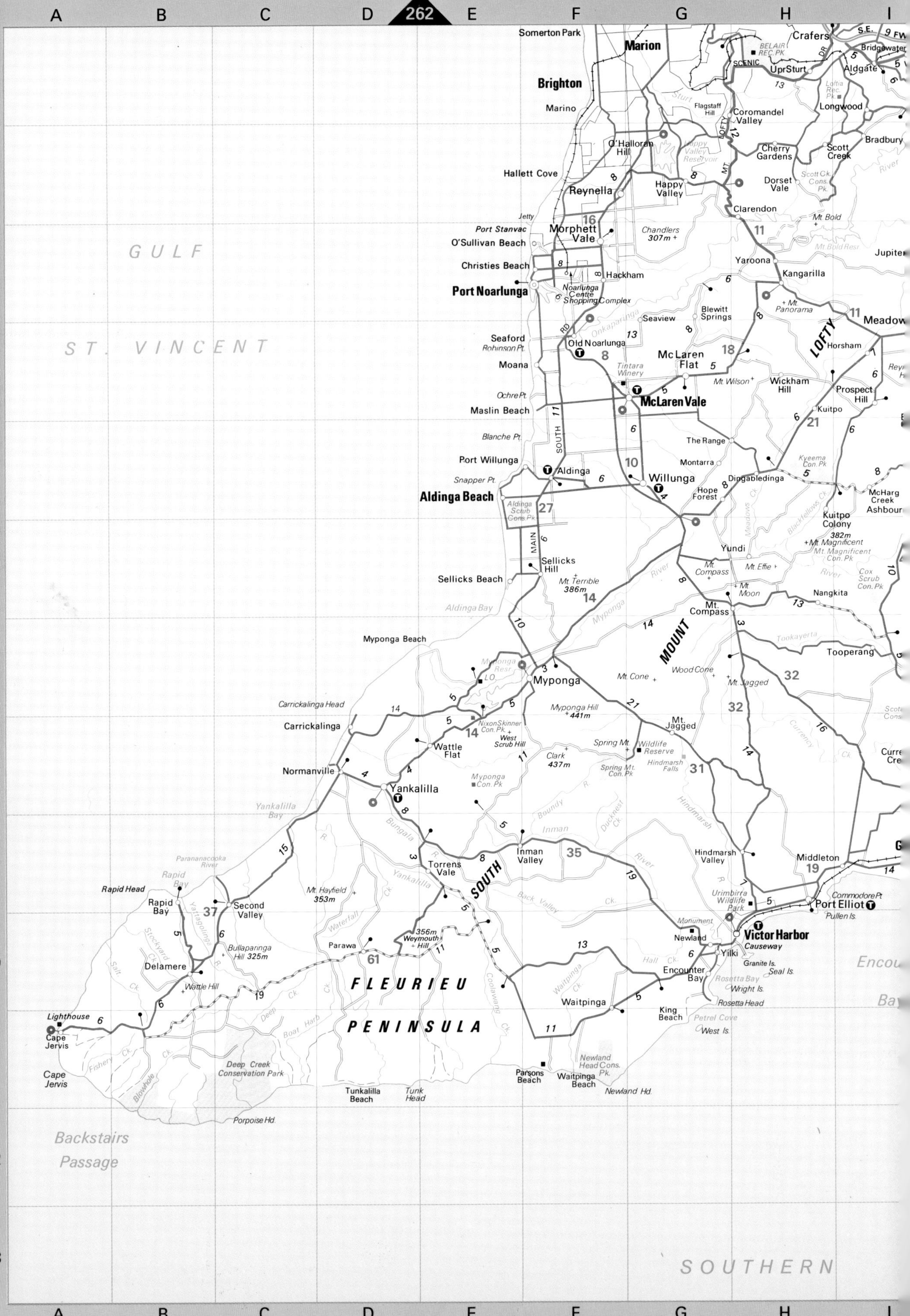

A B C D 262 E F G H I

1 2 3 4 5 6 7 8 9 10 11 12 13

Somerton Park
Marion
Brighton
Marino
Crafers
S.E.
9 FW
Bridgewater
Aldgate
BELAIR REC. PK.
SCENIC
UprSturt
13
Flagstaff Hill
Coromandel Valley
Longwood
Loftus Rec. Res.
Hallett Cove
O'Halloran Hill
Happy Valley Reservoir
Cherry Gardens
Scott Creek
Bradbury
Reynella
Happy Valley
Dorset Vale
Mt Bold
Clarendon
Mt Bold Res.
Jupiter
Jetty
Port Stanvac
O'Sullivan Beach
Morphett Vale
16
Chandlers 307m +
11
Yaroona
Kangarilla
Christies Beach
Hackham
8
8
Mt Panorama
11
Meadow
Port Noarlunga
Noarlunga Centre Shopping Complex
Blewitt Springs
Seaview
LOFTY
Seaford
Robinson Pt.
Old Noarlunga
13
McLaren Flat
18
Horsham
Moana
8
Tintara Winery
5
Mt Wilson +
Wickham Hill
Prospect Hill
Ochre Pt.
McLaren Vale
Mt Wilson
Kuitpo
21
Reyn
Maslin Beach
SOUTH
11
6
The Range
Blanche Pt.
Port Willunga
Aldinga
6
Willunga
Montarra
Dingabledinga
5
McHarg Creek
Ashbour
Snapper Pt.
Aldinga Beach
Aldinga Scrub Cons. Pk.
27
Hope Forest
Kuitpo Colony 382m + Mt Magnificent
8
Sellicks Hill
MAIN
6
Yundi
Mt Magnificent Con. Pk.
Sellicks Beach
Mt Terrible 386m
14
Mt Compass
Mt Effie +
Cox Scrub Con. Pk.
Nangkita
10
Aldinga Bay
River
14
MOUNT
Mt Moon
13
Myponga Beach
Myponga Res.
3
Myponga
Mt Compass
3
Tooperang
Carrickalinga Head
14
5
Myponga Hill + 441m
21
Mt Jagged
32
16
Carrickalinga
5
14
Nixon Skinner Con. Pk. + West Scrub Hill
Mt Jagged
32
Curre Cre
Wattle Flat
11
Clark 437m
Spring Mt.
Wildlife Reserve
Hindmarsh Falls
31
14
Normanville
4
4
Myponga Con. Pk.
Spring Mt. Con. Pk.
Yankalilla
Yankalilla Bay
Boundy
Inman
Duckworth
Hindmarsh Valley
Middleton
19
Paranacooka River
Rapid Bay
15
Bungala
3
Torrens Vale
8
SOUTH
Inman Valley
35
19
River
Urimbirra Wildlife Park
Commodore Pt.
Port Elliot
Rapid Head
Rapid Bay
37
Second Valley
Mt Hayfield 353m
Waterfall
Back Valley
5
Monument
Newland
Hindmarsh Valley
5
Pullen Is.
Yattagolinga
5
6
Bullaparinga Hill 325m
356m Weymouth + Hill
11
13
Victor Harbor Causeway
Delamere
Parawa
61
Yilki
Granite Is.
Seal Is.
Encou
+ Wattle Hill
19
FLEURIEU
5
Encounter Bay
Rosetta Bay
Wright Is.
Bay
Lighthouse
6
6
Boat Harb
PENINSULA
Waitpinga
King Beach
Rosetta Head
Cape Jervis
Deep Creek Conservation Park
Petrel Cove
West Is.
Cape Jervis
Fishery
Blowhole
Tunkalilla Beach
Tunk Head
Parsons Beach
Waitpinga Beach
Newland Head Cons. Pk.
Newland Hd.
Porpoise Hd.
Backstairs Passage
SOUTHERN

GULF
ST. VINCENT

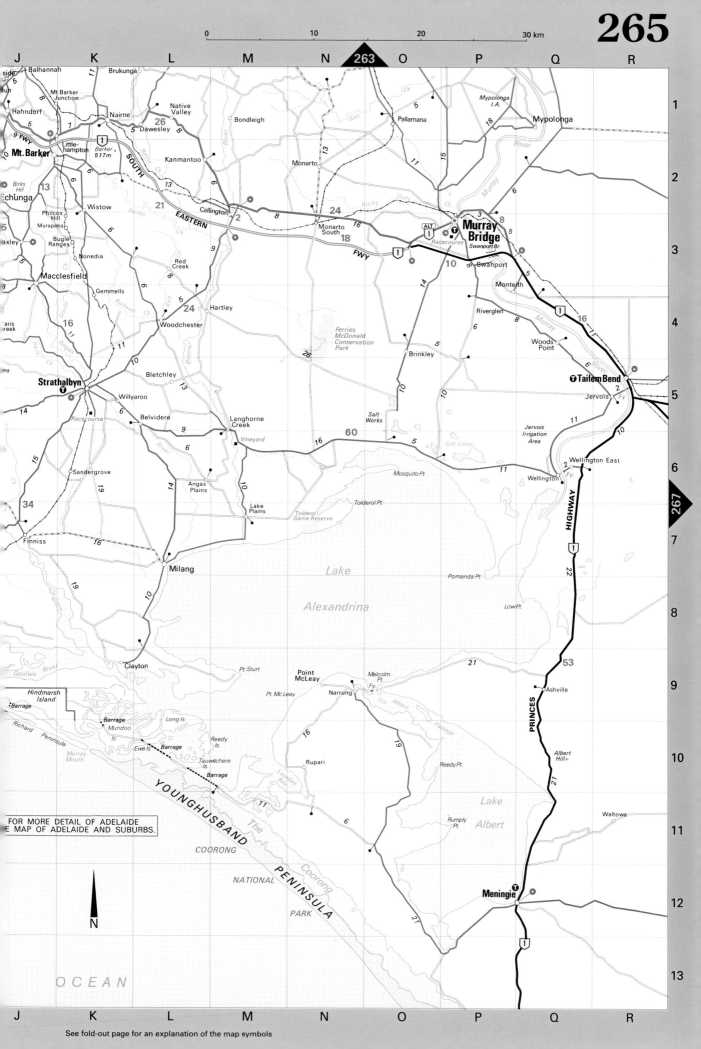

0   10   20   30 km

J K L M N O P Q R

Balhannah
Brukunga
Mt. Barker
Junction
Nairne
Native Valley
Bondleigh
Hahndorf
26
Dawesley
Mypolonga
I.A.
Mypolonga
Littlehampton
Kanmantoo
Mt. Barker
Barker
517m
1
Pallamana
SOUTH
Birks Hill
13
Wistow
Callington
EASTERN
24
Monarto
chunga
21
2
Philcox Hill
Murapena
Bugle Ranges
Macclesfield
Nonedia
Red Creek
Monarto South
16
18
ALT
1
Murray Bridge
Swanport Br.
FWY
1
Racecourse
Swanport
Hartley
24
Woodchester
14
Monteith
Ferries McDonald Conservation Park
Brinkley
6
Riverglen
16
Strathalbyn
Bletchley
26
Woods Point
Willyaroo
13
10
Belvidere
Langhorne Creek
Salt Works
5
Salt Lakes
Jervois Irrigation Area
Tailem Bend
Jervois
Fy.
Sandergrove
9
Vineyard
16
60
11
Angas Plains
Mosquito Pt.
Wellington East
Fy.
Wellington
34
Lake Plains
HIGHWAY
Finniss
16
Milang
10
Pomanda Pt.
Low Pt.
22
Clayton
Lake
Alexandrina
21
53
Pt. Sturt
Point McLeay
Malcolm Pt.
Fy.
Ashville
Hindmarsh Island
Barrage
Narrung
PRINCES
Albert Hill
Barrage
Mundoo Is
Long Is
Reedy Is.
Richard Peninsula
Ewe Is
Barrage
Tauwitchere Is
Barrage
Rupari
Reedy Pt.
Lake Albert
Waltowa
Murray Mouth
FOR MORE DETAIL OF ADELAIDE
E MAP OF ADELAIDE AND SUBURBS.
Rumply Pt.
11
YOUNGHUSBAND
6
COORONG
NATIONAL
PENINSULA
PARK
Meningie
N
21
1
OCEAN
J K L M N O P Q R

268

272

EYRE PENINSULA

YORKE PENINSULA

KANGAROO ISLAND

SPENCER GULF

GULF ST. VINCENT

Investigator Strait

SOUTHERN OCEAN

ADELAIDE

Cleve, Yabmana, Boothby, Carpa, Elbow Hill, Mt Priscilla, Arno Bay, Cape Driver, Karinya, Port Neill, Cape Burr, Dutton Bay

Cowell, Lucky Bay, Victoria Pt, Germein Pt, Franklin Harbor Cons. Park, Port Gibbon, Pt Gibbon, LINCOLN HWY, ALT 1

Tickera Bay, Tickera, Brucefield, Lincolnfields, Alford, Bute, Mona, Willamulka, Thomas Plains, Myponie Pt, Pt Riley, Wallaroo Bay, Wallaroo, Pt Hughes, Kadina, Boors Plain, Thrington, Paskeville, Ninnes, Sth. Hummocks, Myphree, Kulpara

Illawarra Hill, Snowtown, Barunga Gap, Lochiel, Bumbunga, Everard Cent., Nantawarra, Condowie, Hart, Blyth, Spring Gully Con. Park, Kybunga, Boowilla, Watervale, Leasingham, Hoyleton, Stow, Wanappe, Watchman, Halbury, Undaly

Warburto Pt, Tiparra Bay, Moonta, Moonta Bay, Moonta Nth, Yelta, Port Hughes, Cunliffe, Sunnyvale, Melton, Kainton, Clinton Cons. Pk, Beaufort, Whitwarta, Saints, Mary Burts Corner, Wild Horse Plains, Long Plains, Windsor, Dublin

Cape Elizabeth, Agery, Clinton Centre, Port Wakefield, Port Clinton, Sandy Pt, Mangrove, Price, Dowlingville, Inkerman, Kallora, Avon, Owen, Stockyard Ck., Pinery, Hamle Bridge, Mallala, Wasle

Weetulta, Kilkerran, Balgowan, Reef Pt, Pt Pearce Mission, Island Pt, Pt Pearce, South Kilkerran, Maitland, Cunningham, Petersville, Yorke Valley, Sandilands, Pine Point, Port Alfred, Black Pt, Two Wells, Ardrossan, Port Julia, Ga, Virginia, Gawler River

Port Victoria, Urania, Wauraltee, Mt Rat, Koolywurtie, Curramulka, Dowcer Bluff, Port Vincent, Salisbury, Port Adelaide, Outer Harbour, Torrens

Port Rickaby, Bluff Beach, Minlaton, Port Minlacowie, Brentwood, Hardwicke Bay, Roger Corner, Stansbury, Wool Bay, Reynella, Morphett Vale, Port Noarlunga, Old Noarlunga, McLaren Vale, Aldinga

Greig Lookout, Souttar Pt, Corny Pt, Berry Bay, Corny Pt., Daly Head, White Hut, Warooka, Yorketown, Coobowie, Edithburgh, Giles Pt, Salt Creek Bay, Honiton, Sultana Pt, Troubridge Is, Pt Turton, Oaklands, Moorowie, Sturt Bay, Pt Gilbert, Pt Devonport, Waterloo Bay, Troubridge Bay, Mt Compass, Myponga, Formby Bay, Pt Margaret, Carribie, Warrenben Cons. Park, Happy Valley, Foul Bay, Pt Yorke, Hillock Point, Marion Bay, INNES NATIONAL PARK, Royston Head, Pondalowie Bay, West Cape, Stenhouse Bay, Cape Spencer

Aldinga Bay, Normanville, Yankalilla, Yankalilla Bay, Rapid Bay, Second Valley, FLEURIEU PENINSULA, Cape Jervis, Vehicular Ferry to Port Lincoln & Adelaide

Athorpe Islands, North Islet, Gambier Islands, Wedge Is, Revesby Is., Hareby Is., Roxby Is., Joseph Banks Group, Spilsby Is.

Cape D'Estaing, Smith Bay, Emu Bay, Mt Marsden 182m, Pt Marsden, Cape Rouge, Bay of Shoals, Kingscote, Beatrice Pt, Nepean Bay, Pt Morrison, Kangaroo Head, American River, Penneshaw, Muston, Backstairs Passage, Antechamber Bay, Dudley Con. Pk, Newland Head Cons. Pk

Cape Cassini, Cape Dutton, Stokes Bay, Mt McDonnell, Wisanger, ROAD, Cygnet River, Cygnet Park, Western River Con. Pk, Middle River, Woodlana, Buiong, Pioneer Bend, Western Cove, McGillivray, Sapphiretown, Cape Willoughby, Cape Hart Con. Park, Cape Hart, DUDLEY PENINSULA, Pennington Bay, D'Estrees Bay, Pt Tinline

Cape Forbin, Cape Torrens Con. Pk, Cape Borda, FLINDERS CHASE NATIONAL PARK, WEST END HWY, PLAYFORD HWY, Gosse, Gremlin Lodge, Parndana, Corr Amar, Pembram, Wirtilda, Warrawee, Moreview, Vivonne Heights, Karatta, Kelly Hill Caves, Kelly Hill Con. Pk, Vivonne Bay Cons. Pk, Hawks Nest, Cape Gantheaume Cons. Park, Cape Linois, Cape Gantheaume

Vennachar Pt, West Bay, Breakneck R., Rocky River, Cape Bedout, Cape du Couedic, Maupertuis Bay, Sanderson Bay, C Younghusband, Kirkpatrick, Hanson Bay, Karatta, Mt Bloomfield, Seal Bay, Cape Bouguer, Seal Bay Cons. Park, Cape Kersaint

FOR MORE DETAIL OF ADELAIDE
SEE MAP OF ADELAIDE & SUBURBS

FOR MORE DETAIL OF ADELAIDE REGIONS
SEE MAPS OF ADELAIDE NORTHERN REGION
AND ADELAIDE SOUTHERN REGION

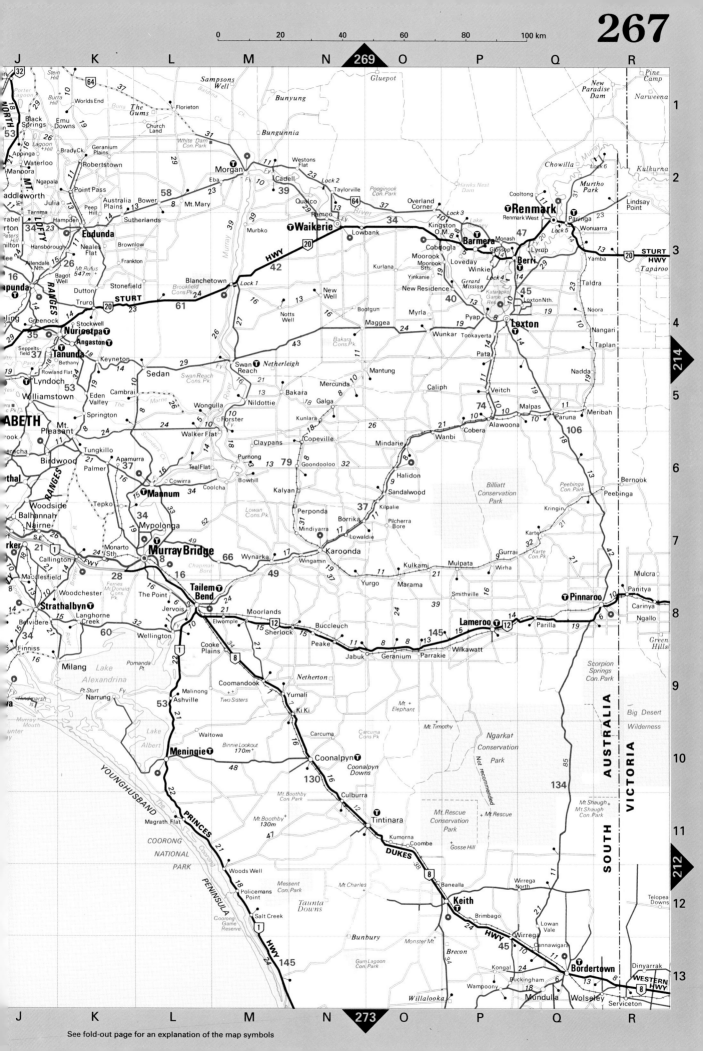

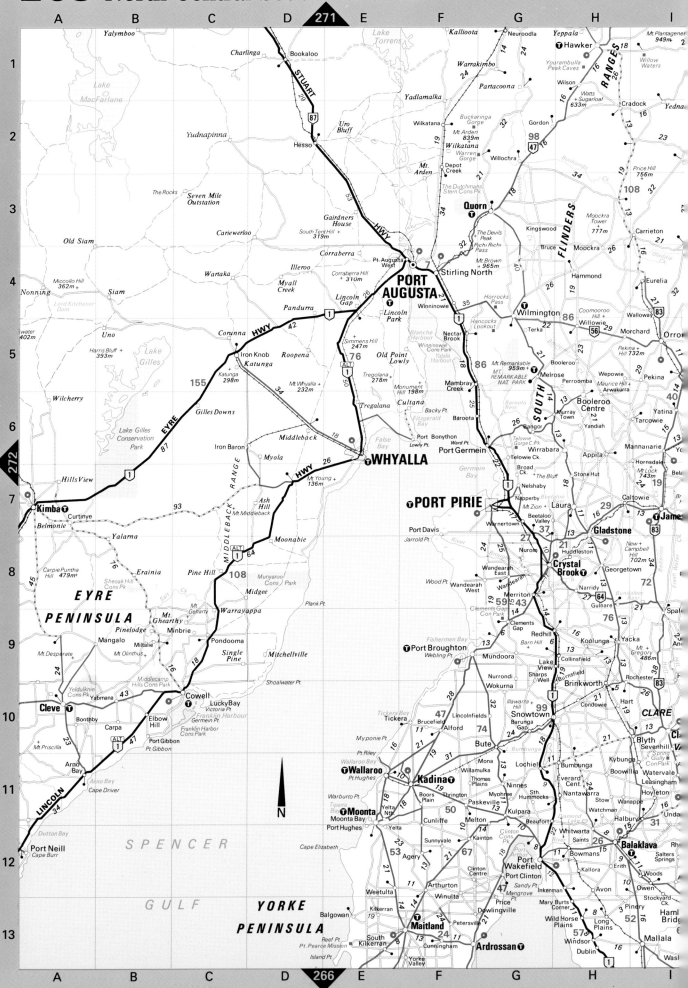

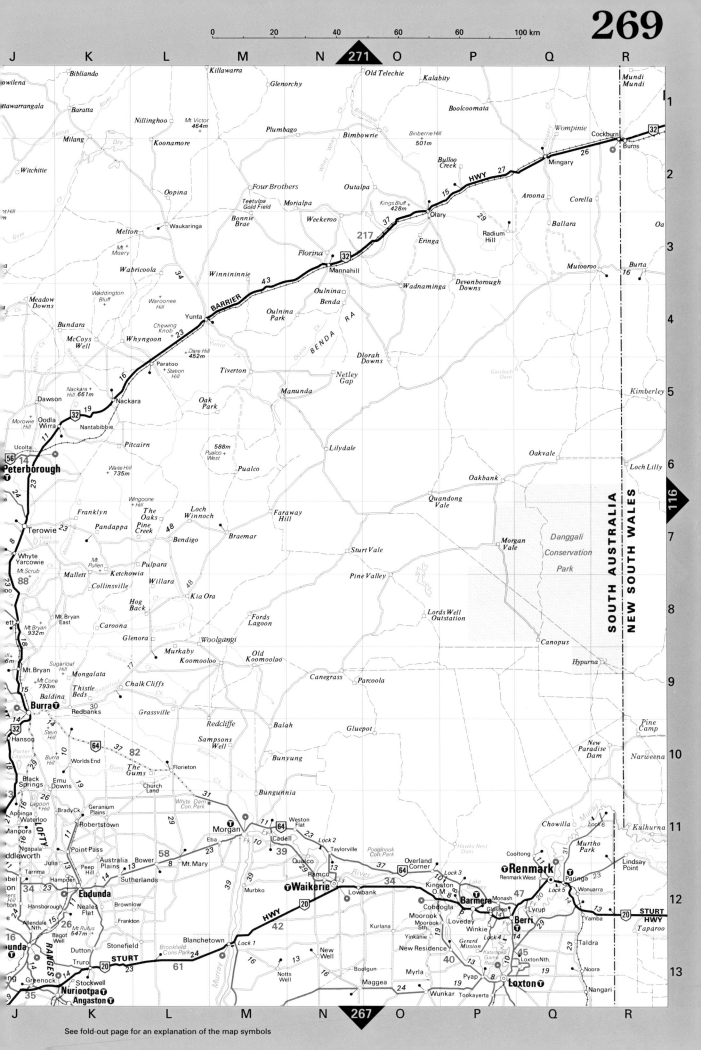

270 Northern South Australia

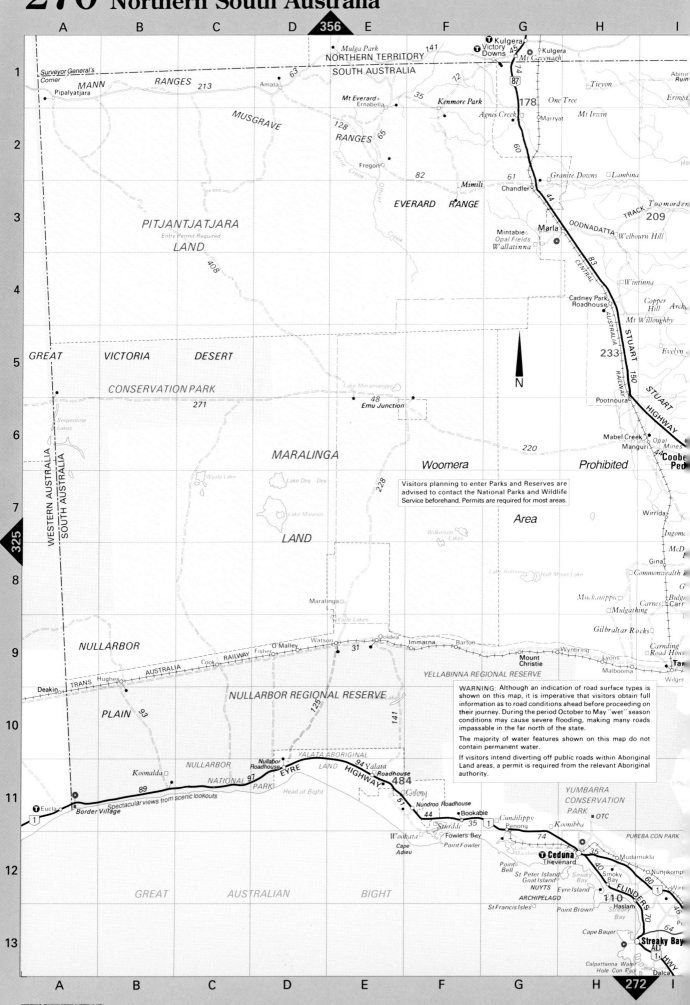

A B C D E F G H I

1
2
3
4
5
6
7
8
9
10
11
12
13

Surveyor General's Corner
Pipalyatjara
MANN RANGES 213
MUSGRAVE RANGES
Amata 63
Mt Everard
Ernabella 35
Kenmore Park
Mulga Park
NORTHERN TERRITORY
SOUTH AUSTRALIA 141
Kulgera Victory Downs 45
Mt Cavenagh
Kulgera
72
87
178
One Tree
Tieyon
Agnes Creek
Marryat
Mt Irwin
60

PITJANTJATJARA
Entry Permit Required
LAND
128
65
Curtie Creek
Fregon
82
Olifier Creek
408
Mimili
EVERARD RANGE
61
Granite Downs
Lambina
Chandler
44
Marla
OODNADATTA TRACK 209
Mintabie Opal Fields
Wallatinna
Welbourn Hill
CENTRAL 83
Wintinna
Cadney Park Roadhouse
Copper Hill
Mt Willoughby
Evelyn

GREAT VICTORIA DESERT
CONSERVATION PARK
271
Serpentine Lakes
Lake Meramangye
48
Emu Junction
N
AUSTRALIA 233 150
STUART RAILWAY
Pootnoura
STUART HIGHWAY
Mabel Creek
Opal Mines
Manguri
Coober Pedy
220

MARALINGA
Wyola Lake
Lake Dey-Dey
Lake Maurice
228
Woomera
Prohibited
Wilkinson Lakes
Lake Anthony
Half Moon Lake
Wirrida
Ingoma
McD
Gina
Commonwealth

LAND
Maralinga
Yarle Lakes
Mackanippie
Mulgathing
Carnes
Bulge
Carr
Gilbraltar Rocks
Carnding Road Hous

Visitors planning to enter Parks and Reserves are advised to contact the National Parks and Wildlife Service beforehand. Permits are required for most areas.

Area

NULLARBOR
TRANS
Deakin
Hughes
Cook
AUSTRALIA RAILWAY
Fisher
O'Malley
Watson
31
Ooldea
Immarna
Barton
Wynbring
Lyons
Malbooma
Mount Christie
YELLABINNA REGIONAL RESERVE
Tar
Wilger

PLAIN 93
NULLARBOR REGIONAL RESERVE
125
141

WARNING: Although an indication of road surface types is shown on this map, it is imperative that visitors obtain full information as to road conditions ahead before proceeding on their journey. During the period October to May "wet" season conditions may cause severe flooding, making many roads impassable in the far north of the state.

The majority of water features shown on this map do not contain permanent water.

If visitors intend diverting off public roads within Aboriginal Land areas, a permit is required from the relevant Aboriginal authority.

NULLARBOR
Koonalda
NATIONAL PARK
97
89
EYRE
YALATA ABORIGINAL
Nullarbor Roadhouse
94 Yalata Roadhouse
LAND HIGHWAY
484
Head of Bight
Colona
51
Nundroo Roadhouse
44
Sturde
35
Penong
Cundilippy
Koonibba
YUMBARRA CONSERVATION PARK
OTC
PUREBA CON PARK

Eucla
Border Village
Spectacular views from scenic lookouts
1
Bookabie
74
Wookata
Fowlers Bay
Point Fowler
Cape Adieu
Point Bell
St Peter Island
Goat Island
NUYTS ARCHIPELAGO
St Francis Isles
Point Brown
Lake Macdonnell
Ceduna
Thevenard
Smoky Bay
35
40
FLINDERS 60
110 70
Haslam
Mudamukla
Nunjikompita
Wirt
Streaky Bay
64

GREAT AUSTRALIAN BIGHT
Cape Bauer
Calpattanna Water Hole Con Park
Dalca
HWY

0   30   60   90   120   150   180   210   240   270   300   330   360 km

J   K   L   M   N   441   O   P   Q   R

NORTHERN TERRITORY

SOUTH AUSTRALIA

Poeppel Corner

Birdsville   QUEENSLAND

Roseberth

Dare
Perri Creek

WITJIRA NATIONAL PARK

Purni Bore

SIMPSON DESERT CONSERVATION PARK

Pandie Pandie

Cadelga Outstation (uninhabited)

Haddon Corner

Mokari Airstrip

Dalhousie Thermal Ponds

Macumba Well (abandoned)

Poolowanna No. 1 Well

Lake Etamunbanie

STURT

Alton Downs

194

STONY

Mt Sarah

SIMPSON DESERT REGIONAL RESERVE

SIMPSON   DESERT   DESERT

Cordillo Downs   117

107

Macumba

Macumba River

EPHEMERAL LAKES

Goyder Lagoon

Clifton Hills

Coongie Lakes

Arrabury

73   Barka Ruin

Warburton River

120

Coongie (abandoned)

INNAMINCKA

144

Oodnadatta

46

New Kalamurina

Lake Howitt

Kanowana

Kudriemitchie (abandoned)

REGIONAL RESERVE

Nappa Merrie

Mt Dutton Ruin

Cowarie

Cooper Creek

Innamincka   90   Aboriginal Rock Carvings

QUEENSLAND

441

65   Warrina Ruin

203   Peake

520

Mungeranie Roadhouse

Moomba Gas Field

Edwards Creek Ruin

Nilpinna

92

LAKE EYRE

Lake Kittakittaooloo

Ruin   84   Mulka

Lake Warrakatanna   Lake Walpayayperunna

STRZELECKI   DESERT   98   157

Box Creek Ruin

Anna Creek

160   William Creek

74

(NORTH)

NATIONAL   PARK   Cooper Creek

Lake Killamperpunna

Etadunna

Lake Kopperekoppinna

Lake Gregory

Merty Merty

ELLIOT PRICE CONSERVATION PARK

Lake Florence

38   Dulkaninna

Strzelecki Crossing   Bollards Lagoon

Cameron Corner

Strangways Bore

Beresford Bore

LAKE EYRE (SOUTH)

Muloorina

84   Clayton   Clayton

Lake Blanche

The Woomera Prohibited Area is by permit except state corridors of the Stuart Highway and the road near Pedy to William Creek. Camping is not permitted in the area. Note the overlap with Aboriginal Lands which need additional separate permits.

Coward Springs Bore

Curdimurka Bore

210   136   Wangianna

Finniss Springs   Ruin   Marree

Murnpeowie   200

RANGES

Winnathee

Hawker Gate

The Twins

54   Billa Kalina

Millers Creek

Stuart Creek

Callanna   Mundowdna

54   Witchelina   Wilpoorinna

Mt Freeling   87   Moolawatana

Tilcha

Cuttacuddy

Mt Eba

Bamboo Swamp

Farina   Avondale   Mt Lyndhurst   Freeling Heights   Paralana Hot Springs   Smithville House

219   Umberatana

North Mulga

Lyndhurst   Mt Lyndhurst   Arkaroola

South Vivian   Orwell Well

Parakylia

Lagoon

119   Copley   Leigh Creek   Angepena   GAMMON RANGES NATIONAL PARK

Moorab

Roxby Downs   Andamooka   Myrtle Springs   Yankaninna   Woolnana   Balcanoona

Opal Fields   38   Aroona Valley   Old Warraweena   LAKE

Mt Vivian   Locks Well   Andamooka   Leigh Creek   83   Warraweena   Old Arrowie

Broughams Gate

Kingoonya   Glendambo   Purple Downs   Beltana   Beltana   Old Warraweena   Narrina   FROME   Avenel

53   Young-husband

Knoll   18   Bosworth   Arcoona   Blinman   Wircalpa   Eurilla   114

Glendambo   Lake Hanson   East Well   Beltana   NORTH   Great

Wirramina   Parachilna   Wall   Frome Downs

Kokatha   Woomera   Pimba   LAKE   FLINDERS   Oraparinna   China   Kantappa

114 HWY   27   Witrappa   TORRENS   156   RANGES   Martins Well   Benagerie

Lake Johnston   35   Mt Gunson   NATIONAL   PARK   Erudina

Pernatty   92   Wilpena   Curnamona   Mulyungarie

Lake Gairdner   STUART   South Gap   Moralana   Rawnsley Park   Mooleulooloo

Island Lagoon   Woocalla   Lake Torrens   Holowilena   Bibliando   Old Telechie

Mahanewo   29   Cotabena   Baratta

Yalymboo   Kalliota   Hawker   FLINDERS   Killawarra

Kumburra   Charlinga   173   66   Warrakimbo   Koonamore   Plumbago   Old Lake Dismal   Silverton

Moonaree   Bookaloo   Cradock   26   Baggalowie   Cockburn   76   32

29   Wilkatana   Langiwarren   Morialpa   Burns

Willana   47   RANGES   Belton   Mingary   Aroona

Hesso   Arden Vale   East Boolcunda   Melton   Mt Victor   Mannahill   267   Olary   Cutana   Ballard

87   Tent Hill   83   Wirra Downs   Waukaringa   42   Eringa   Coultra Hut

Quorn   108   Carrieton   BARRIER   Oulnina   Wadnaminga   Burta

Port Augusta   40   40   Ivy Glen   Meadow Downs   HIGHWAY   42   Devonborough Downs

HIGHWAY   Wilmington   Yalpara   Teetulpa   Yunta   Mannahill   Oak   Netley Gap   Mutooroo

26   56   Willowie   Orroroo   Black Rock   Dawson   32   69   Tiverton   Netley Gap

Iron Knob   PRINCES   51   Pekina   Paratoo   Park   Maminda   Mazar

42   LINCOLN   Melrose   Booleroo Centre   14   Pitcairn   Lilydale

74   Iron Baron   HWY   Murray Town   Port Germein

Pinkawillinie Con Park   EYRE   1   SOUTH   Peterborough

Lake Gilles Con Park   Whyalla   Spencer Gulf

Buckleboo

J   K   L   272   M   N   268   O   P   267   Q   R

1   2   3   4   5   6   7   8   9   10   11   12   13

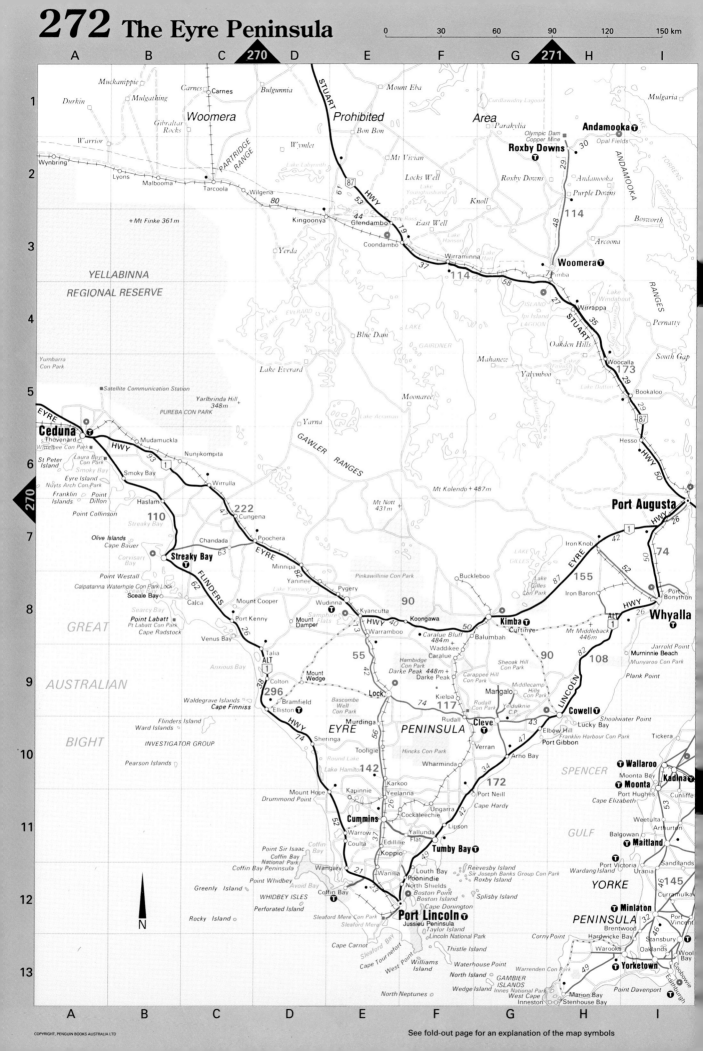

See fold-out page for an explanation of the map symbols

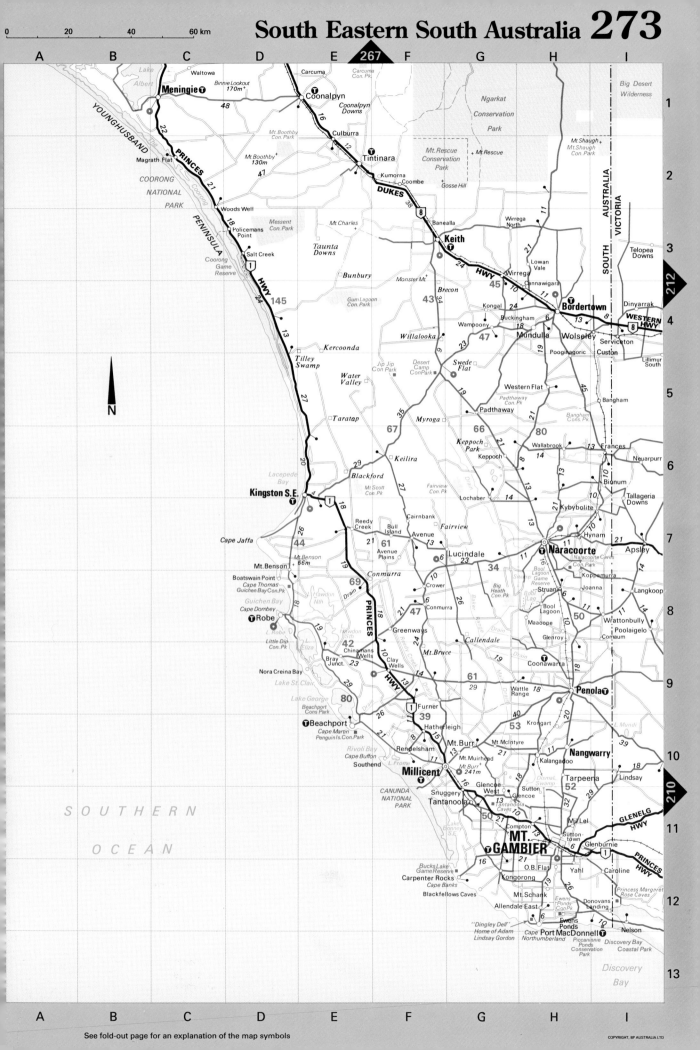

COPYRIGHT, BP AUSTRALIA LTD

WESTERN AUSTRALIA

The Golden West

Gwalia, an old gold-mining town

Even a casual glance at a map of Australia will quickly reveal that a motor touring holiday in Western Australia requires a great deal of thought and advance planning. For one thing, just getting there from the eastern states involves travelling huge distances, so fly/drive or MotoRail facilities are well worth investigation; and, given that it is almost one-third the size of the whole of Australia, unless you have unlimited time and energy, touring by road is only going to get you to certain sections. The south-west region is relatively easily and pleasantly covered by car, but to travel the unique north and north-east requires more time and careful planning.

Although the state has some 175 000 kilometres of roads, the vast distances to be covered are such that it is worth considering some touring by air when planning your itinerary and budget. Ansett WA operates tours, varying in length, to all the spectacular remote regions. There is a network of almost 100 heritage trails across the state, each designed by the local community.

Once you have settled your method of travel, you will find you have a really amazing state waiting to be explored. Despite the fact that the Dutch had mapped the western coastline of Australia as early as the sixteenth century, it was not until 1826 that a British party from Sydney landed at King George Sound (Albany) and then only for fear of possible French colonisation. Three years later Perth, the first non-convict settlement in the country, was founded by Captain James Stirling. Due mainly to the ruggedness and sheer size of the land, the West remained pretty much as it had always been until 1892. In that year gold was discovered at Coolgardie and the first economic boom for the region began. Today, of course, it is an immensely rich mineral state, its thriving economy still growing in leaps and bounds.

The beautiful city of Perth has the best climate of any Australian capital. It is a true Mediterranean climate, with a mid-winter average maximum temperature of 18°C, a year-round average of 23°C and an average of almost eight hours of sunshine a day. The climate in the north of the state is tropical, and as you travel south it becomes subtropical and then temperate.

It is easy to assume from the map that Perth is a coastal city, though actually it is nineteen kilometres inland, up the broad and beautiful Swan River, home of the black swan. A city of over one million people, Perth is large enough to offer excitement and variety, yet compact enough to be seen quite easily. King's Park, 404 hectares of natural bushland, is only a short drive from the city centre, and nearby ocean beaches provide year-round swimming and surfing.

Once you start touring, the Swan Valley is a must, whether or not you are interested in wine. Up in the Darling Range the valley is lush, fertile and beautiful. The vineyards flourish on the rich loam that is perfect for grape-growing, and at the end of a day's drive you can sample some notable results of these conditions.

Nearby Rottnest Island is low, small, sandy and only twenty kilometres off the coast from Fremantle. Regular air and ferry services from Perth will take you to this popular holiday island, where even the surrounding sea has been declared a sanctuary. Conditions for skin-diving could not be better.

Although Victoria has claimed the title of Australia's 'Garden State', the southern corner of the state is still the 'garden of Western Australia', ablaze every spring with wildflowers. Hardwood forests of massive karri and jarrah trees soar above the hundreds of different species of wildflowers that bloom from September to November. Great surfing beaches and coastal panoramas add to the attractions of the south-west region, with such popular locations as Margaret River, Busselton and Yallingup.

North-east of this well-vegetated corner, and 596 kilometres from Perth, is the one-time gold-boom area around Kalgoorlie–Boulder, surrounded by ghost towns such as Coolgardie (where it all began) and Broad Arrow. South of Kalgoorlie–Boulder the modern town of Kambalda owes its prosperity to nickel. Further east you reach the Nullarbor Plain; further north are the Great Victoria and Gibson Deserts.

Along the Brand Highway, 424 kilometres north of Perth, is Geraldton, ideally situated between Western Australia's agricultural heartland and the beautiful coastline. Here you can sample freshly caught crays, and a little farther north you can see an excellent range of flora and fauna in the Kalbarri National Park and explore the spectacular coastal gorges and cliffs

The Pilbara region has some of the country's most spectacular gorges in Karijini (Hamersley Range) National Park. This is where Western Australia's second economic boom began, with the exploitation of the dramatic Hamersley Range, which is literally a mountain of iron. Despite the fact that the Range stretches for 320 kilometres, from the air it seems dwarfed by endless stretches of red sand.

At the state's very top is the Kimberley region, with the spectacular King Leopold Range in the west and Bungle Bungle National Park in the east. The region's economy is based on diamond mining, as well as the more traditional cattle industry, supported by the Ord River irrigation scheme. A visit to this remote, dramatic region with its gorges and rivers is a unique experience — in keeping with many areas of Australia's largest state.

PERTH

A Friendly City

Perth's easy-going pace and its picturesque location combine to win the hearts of most visitors.

The city itself appears to sit on the edge of a lake; in fact it is the wide expanse of the Swan River. Within easy reach of the city lie clean surf beaches, rolling hills, tranquil forests and well-kept parklands. Blessed with a Mediterranean-type climate and a river setting, Perth is a city made for an outdoor lifestyle. The **Swan River** winds through Perth and its suburbs, widening to the size of a lake at Perth and Melville Waters; and the Canning River provides another attractive waterway through the southern suburbs.

The city centre, nineteen kilometres upstream from the port of Fremantle, is on the Swan River and is ringed by a series of gardens, parks and reserves, including the magnificent 404-hectare **Kings Park**. The green bushland slopes of Mount Eliza in Kings Park contrast dramatically with Perth's impressive skyline, and the serene blue hills of the Darling Range can be seen in the distance.

Perth was founded by Captain James Stirling in 1829, but the progress of the isolated Swan River Settlement, made up entirely of free settlers, was slow at first and it was not until the first shipment of convicts arrived in 1850 that the colony found its feet. The convicts were soon set to work building roads, bridges and several fine public buildings, and in 1856 Perth was proclaimed a city. Gold discoveries in the state in the 1880s gave Perth another boost and the recent diamond finds in the Kimberley and the reopening of gold-mines in the Kalgoorlie - Boulder region have stimulated new growth.

Perth's citizens live mainly in pleasant suburbs that stretch north and south of the city, bounded by the Indian Ocean on the west and the Darling Range on the east. There are quite large Greek and Italian communities and smaller groups from the Netherlands, Germany, Poland and Yugoslavia, although most of the population these days is Australian-born.

Perth's city centre is compact, making

Kangaroo paws, Kings Park

it easy to find your way around. Also you can travel by bus or train within the city's **Free Transit Zone** (FTZ) without paying a fare, day or night, seven days a week. A free bus service, the City Clipper, circles the city every ten minutes during the day; other **Clipper** services connect the city with East and West Perth, and Northbridge.

Most of Perth's shops and arcades are in the blocks bounded by St Georges Terrace and William, Wellington and Barrack Streets, centring around **Hay Street Mall**, **Raine Square Shopping Plaza**, and **Murray Street Mall** and **Forrest Chase**. Perth's shopping area and business district is linked by pedestrian malls, overpasses and underground walkways enabling access unhampered by motor vehicles. Perth's unique **London Court**, an Elizabethan-style arcade, runs from Hay Street Mall to St Georges Terrace. At the Hay Street entrance, four knights on horseback 'joust' above a replica of Big Ben every fifteen minutes, while St George and the Dragon do battle above the clock over the St Georges Terrace entrance. Perth's decorative **Town Hall**

on the corner of Hay and Barrack Streets was built by convicts between 1869 and 1879.

Stately **St Georges Terrace**, Perth's financial and professional heart, is worth strolling down for its wealth of historic buildings, cheek by jowl with towering modern glass giants. Start at the western end, where you will see the mellow brickwork of **Barracks Arch** (all that remains of the Tudor-style Pensioner Barracks built in 1863) in front of Parliament House. When Parliament is not sitting, there are guided tours Monday to Friday.

Continuing along St Georges Terrace you reach the charming **Cloisters**, a former boys' school dating back to 1858, which has been integrated into the modern complex behind, and nearby is an ecclesiastical-looking building, another former boys' school and now the headquarters of the **National Trust**. The **Palace Hotel**, a grand old Victorian iron-lace balconied hotel, has been modified as a banking chamber and forms an impressive exterior facade for Perth's largest building, the **R & I Bank Tower**. Further along the terrace is an ornate Victorian church—Trinity Church Chapel—and the arched entrance to London Court. The handsome **Treasury Building** on the corner of Barrack Street overlooks **Stirling Gardens**, part of the **Supreme Court Gardens** and a popular picnic spot for shoppers and city workers. **St George's Cathedral** and the **Deanery** are another two interesting old buildings at this end of St Georges Terrace. Tucked behind the imposing modern **Council House** on the opposite side is one of Perth's oldest buildings, the **Old Court-house**, built in 1836, and the turrets of the Gothic-style **Government House** in its lush private gardens.

Further along is the modern **Perth Concert Hall**, which seats 1900 and is used for everything from hard rock to opera. Inside, a restaurant, a tavern and a cocktail bar cater for music-lovers.

Just north of the city centre in Northbridge is the attractive **Perth Cultural Centre** complex. Here the **Art Gallery of Western Australia** displays nationally

Perth skyline

Hotels
Burswood Resort Hotel
Great Eastern Hwy, Victoria Park
(09) 362 7777
Hilton International (Parmelia)
Mill St, Perth
(09) 322 3622
Hyatt Regency
99 Adelaide Tce, Perth
(09) 225 1234
Sheraton
207 Adelaide Tce, Perth
(09) 325 0501

Family and Budget
Freeway
55 Mill Point Rd, South Perth
(09) 367 7811

Jewell House Private Hotel (YMCA)
180 Goderich St, Perth
(09) 325 8488
YMCA
119 Murray St, Perth
(09) 325 2744

Motel Groups: Bookings
Flag (008) 01 1177
Best Western (008) 22 2166
Travelodge (008) 22 2446

This list is for information only; inclusion is not necessarily a recommendation.

and internationally renowned artworks. Nearby is the **Alexander Library**, and the original Perth Gaol, built in 1856 and within the modern complex of the **Western Australian Museum**. A blue whale skeleton, Aboriginal artefacts and veteran and vintage cars are among the exhibits.

A visit to the Cultural Centre could be combined with a meal at one of the many reasonably priced restaurants in this area, as **Northbridge** is also the centre of Perth's nightlife. Numerous hotels, nightclubs and piano bars offer live entertainment and dancing until dawn.

At the City West shopping complex in **West Perth** are the **Omni Theatre** and the **Scitech Discovery Centre**; the specially constructed theatre presents visitors with real adventure experiences, and the centre has a hands-on science and technology display.

Kings Park, just west of the city centre, is one of Perth's major attractions. Within this huge natural bushland reserve there are landscaped gardens and walkways, lakes, children's playgrounds, lookouts and the **Botanic Gardens** on Mount Eliza Bluff, where a blaze of Western Australian wildflowers is to be seen in spring. You can drive by car through the park or hire a bicycle, stopping at the many scenic lookouts over the city and river; or you can wander on foot along the many walking-trails right to the top of Mount Eliza.

Other city parks include **Hyde Park**, with its waterbirds, ornamental lake and English trees, and the beautiful **Queens Gardens**, with a replica of London's Peter Pan statue. Just outside the city centre is **Lake Monger**, a favourite picnic spot which is also the home of black swans, ducks and other varieties of birds. **Matilda Bay** offers grassed areas and ample shade, with stunning views of the Swan River and Perth city skyline. The **Swan River Estuary Marine Park** includes three areas at Alfred Cove, Pelican Point and Milyu, about halfway between the Narrows and Canning Bridges.

A pleasant way to visit **Perth's Zoo**, with its magnificent garden environment and nocturnal house, is to catch a ferry from the Barrack Street Jetty. The trip can be combined with a visit to the **Old Mill**, on the South Perth foreshore. This picturesque whitewashed windmill, built in 1838, now houses an interesting collection of early colonial relics.

Further north along the coast at **Sorrento** is the **Hillarys Boat Harbour**. A day can easily be spent here, enjoying the atmosphere and variety of Sorrento Quay or experiencing the thrill of Underwater World, where you are transported through a submerged acrylic tunnel on moving walkways to see the enormous variety of underwater life. From September to November, charter boats offer visits to view whales basking between Perth and Rottnest Island. **Carnac Island**, a nature reserve fifteen kilometres off the coast near Perth, has a colony of sea-lions and its main beach is accessible in daylight hours by private boat.

Swimming and surfing are part of the joy of Perth and several beautiful Indian Ocean beaches—including **Cottesloe**, **Swanbourne** (a nude bathing beach), Port, City, Scarborough and Trigg Island—are within easy reach of the city, and the sheltered Swan River beaches dotted along Perth's riverside suburbs are even closer.

There are many other places of interest around Perth, including the historic port of **Fremantle**, which underwent a complete facelift in preparation for the America's Cup challenge. In Fremantle you can relive the past by strolling along the streets of terraced houses, or visiting the city's magnificent historic buildings and the many galleries, museums and craft workshops. Cottesloe Civic Centre, in Broome Street, **Cottesloe**, is one of Perth's showplaces and the magnificent grounds of this beautiful Spanish-style mansion are open during office hours. The **University of Western Australia**, with its Mediterranean-style buildings and landscaped gardens in the riverside suburb of **Crawley**, is also worth seeing. The university's new **Fortune Theatre** has been built as a replica of Shakespeare's Fortune Theatre in Elizabethan London. Adventure World in the suburb of **Bibra Lake** includes rides, a wildlife park, animal circus and Australia's largest swimming-pool among its attractions.

Perth's sporting facilities are excellent, with two racecourses, **Ascot** and **Belmont Park**; night pacing at **Gloucester Park** (the famous WACA cricket ground is near here); greyhound racing at **Cannington** and speedcar and motor-cycle racing at the **Claremont Showgrounds**. Major athletics meetings, rugby and soccer matches are held at **Perry Lakes Stadium** (built for the 1962 British Empire and Commonwealth Games), and Australian Rules football finals at **Subiaco Oval**. Hockey is played at the **Commonwealth Hockey Stadium**, the first Astroturf stadium in Australia. The **Superdrome** hosts many international sporting events.

By night, Perth offers a wide range of entertainment: the modern **Perth Entertainment Centre** (home of the Perth Wildcats basketball team), in Wellington Street, seats 8000. At the **Burswood Casino**, across the river at **Rivervale**, you can try your luck at the tables, or enjoy the five-star splendour of the hotel. Another resort complex is **Observation City Resort Hotel** on the coast at **Scarborough**. Perth offers an excellent range of accommodation to suit all requirements—from the many five-star hotels to convenient self-contained family accommodation and dozens of quality hotels and motels.

During February and March, the Festival of Perth combines the visual arts, theatre, music and film.

For further information on Perth and Western Australia, contact the Western Australian Tourist Centre, Albert Facey House, cnr Forrest Place and Wellington St, Perth; (09) 483 1111.

Pioneer Women's Memorial, Kings Park

Hillarys Boat Harbour, Sorrento

TOURS FROM PERTH

With the sparkling Indian Ocean surf beaches beckoning from the west, the peaceful Darling Range on the east and the Swan River meandering through Perth's attractive suburbs from Fremantle to the Swan Valley vineyards, there are many enjoyable trips within easy reach of Perth.

A delightful way to visit the vineyards is by river. Cruisers operate wine-tasting tours; the *Lady Houghton* and the *Miss Sandalford* leave Barrack Street Jetty. Coffee, wine, cheese and biscuits are served on board, and lunch is served at Mulberry Farm. At Houghtons Winery, you can tour the vineyard and sample a variety of wines.

Other cruises will take you to the historic riverside home Woodbridge. From Wednesday to Saturday nights, in season, you can have dinner aboard a vessel that leaves the Barrack Street Jetty in the early evening and returns at midnight.

There is a daily ferry service from the Barrack Street Jetty to Rottnest Island—Perth's popular hideaway, once the site of the infamous Rottnest Native Prison. (**See:** Rottnest Island.)

Travel to Adventure World on Transperth—Route 600; buses depart Perth central bus station daily. Adventure World is open most weekends, and daily in peak season and school holidays. If you have any enquiries regarding tours, information is available from the Western Australian Tourist Centre, Albert Facey House, cnr Forrest Place and Wellington St, Perth; (09) 483 1111.

Fremantle, 19 km from Perth via the Stirling or Canning Highways
A visit to this fascinating old port can make an interesting round trip by car if you return via the opposite side of the river. With the old-world charm of colonial buildings contrasting with the development that occurred in preparation for the America's Cup, it is worth setting aside a day for this tour. Fremantle is also easily accessible by bus, train and boat. **See also:** Entry in A - Z listing.

Historic Guildford in the Swan Valley, 18 km from Perth via Guildford Road or the Great Eastern Highway
This pleasant tour takes you near the vineyards of the Swan Valley, noted for their high-quality wines, to Guildford, one of the earliest settlements in the state. Many reminders of the colony's early days remain, including Woodbridge, a gracious, towered, two-storey mansion overlooking the river, beautifully restored and furnished by the National Trust. The Mechanics Hall in Meadow Street houses a folk-museum, and a rail museum in the nearby suburb of Bassendean is also of interest. The Vines Resort, 15 km north of Guildford, has a world-class golf course and many different sporting and fitness facilities for guests. Whiteman Park, 7 km north of Guildford, has train and tram rides, a picnic area and the Trade Village, where tradesmen ply traditional crafts.

Walyunga National Park, 35 km from Perth via Guildford Road and the Great Northern Highway
The Avon River flows swiftly through a narrow gorge of the Darling Range in this beautiful bushland park.

John Forrest National Park, 28 km from Perth on the Great Eastern Highway
This huge unspoiled bushland park in the Darling Range is very popular with tourists. Walking-trails, streams, waterfalls and a safe swimming-pool for children are among its many attractions. At weekends you could round off the outing with a Devonshire tea at the old Mahogany Inn, built in 1837 and now the oldest licensed inn in Western Australia.

Mundaring Weir, 42 km from Perth via the Great Eastern Highway
This impressive water catchment area which provides water for the goldfields, more than 500 kilometres away, is surrounded by pleasant picnic areas. A visit to the O'Connor Museum will help you to understand the construction and operation of this complex water scheme. Kalamunda History Village is a short drive away.

Serpentine Dam, 54 km from Perth via the South Western Highway
The picnic grounds here overlook the Serpentine Dam, which is set among peaceful hills and beautiful landscaped gardens of wildflowers.

Pioneer World, Armadale, 29 km from Perth via the Albany Highway
Pioneer World is a reconstruction of the days of the gold-rush when every town boasted a blacksmith and a coach-house. Elizabethan Village has sixteenth-century-style buildings and a superb collection of early English oak furniture dating from 1300 to 1690. Close to Armadale, Mundijong's Agridome features sheep parades, shearing demonstrations and working sheepdogs. At nearby Gosnells, the Cohuna Wildlife Park has an abundance of Australian fauna, including a koala sanctuary.

Pinjarra, 84 km from Perth on the South Western Highway
This picturesque old town on the Murray River, only 19 km east of Mandurah, is becoming a popular base for exploring the area. Several historic buildings in the township include the National Trust's Old Blythewood, a former coaching-house built in the 1830s. Later used as a family homestead, it is now open to the public daily (closed Friday). A novel way of seeing the surrounding country is on board a steam train that occasionally runs from Pinjarra to Dwellingup, a quiet little timber-town in the foothills of the Darling Range. **See also:** Entry in A - Z listing.

Yanchep National Park and Caves, 51 km from Perth via Wanneroo Road
The Yanchep National Park is one of Perth's most popular recreation areas, where you can see native bush, kangaroos and, in springtime, a stunning array of wildflowers. The park is perfect for family outings and lakeside picnics. Yanchep Beach, 6 km west, is a safe ocean beach protected by reefs. **See also:** Yanchep entry in A - Z listing.

Rockingham, 46 km from Perth via the Canning Highway and Cockburn Road
Sheltered swimming and shady lawns along the foreshore make this seaside resort south of Perth a pleasant place for a daytrip. At Rockingham Museum you can see documents and memorabilia which give an idea of the town's early days as a busy seaport (open daily, except Mondays and Fridays). Nearby Safety Bay Beach, south of Point Peron, is another attractive swimming area. You can visit Penguin Island by ferry to see the fairy penguins. **See also:** Entry in A - Z listing

WESTERN AUSTRALIA from A to Z

Albany   Population 16 316

Albany is WA's oldest town and one of its most picturesque. On the edge of King George Sound and the magnificent Princess Royal Harbour, and known as the 'heart of the Great Southern', the town overlooks both the coast and inland towards the spectacular Stirling and Porongurup Ranges. Situated 406 km south of Perth, Albany has a surprisingly English feel about it. As WA's most important holiday centre, it offers visitors a wealth of history with its impressive stone colonial buildings and a rich variety of coastal, rural and mountain scenery. Its harbours, weirs and estuaries provide excellent fishing. The town dates back to 1826, when a military post was established to give the English a foothold in the West. Whaling was important in the 1840s and in the 1850s Albany became a coaling station for steamers bound from England. **Of interest:** Colonial Buildings Historic Walk; self-guiding brochure from Tourist Information Centre. Old Post Office-Intercolonial Communications Museum, opposite cnr Stirling Tce and Spencer St. Some Victorian shopfronts in Stirling Tce, at base of York St. Historical and environmental exhibits in Albany Residency Museum (1850s), Residency Rd, originally home of Resident Magistrates; open daily. Old Gaol and Museum (1851), Residency Rd; actually two gaols in one. Vancouver Arts Centre, Vancouver St. House of Gems, Frenchman Bay Rd. Old Farm (1836), Middleton Rd, Strawberry Hill; site of Government Farm for Albany, begun in 1872. Patrick Taylor Cottage (1832), Duke St; faithfully restored and containing extensive collection of period costume and household goods. Extravaganza Gallery, next to Esplanade Hotel, Middleton Beach; vintage and veteran cars, and variety of art and craft. Two restored 'forts'—Princess Royal Fortress (commissioned 1893), Forts Rd; Green Hill Fort on Thursday Island, Albany's first federal fortress; open for inspection. The Amity, Princess Royal Dr, full-scale replica of brig that brought Major Lockyer and party of convicts to establish settlement of Albany in 1826. On Princess Royal Dr, Amity Crafts (local art and craft) and Renewable Resources (wildflower shop). Anzac Light Horse Memorial statue, near top of Mt Clarence, off Marine Dr. Spectacular view from here and from John Barnesby Memorial Lookout at Mt Melville. 'Genevieve 500', international classic car race, and Skywest Albany Ocean Yacht Race held in November. **In the area:** Jolly Barnyard family farm, 3 km north; deer farm, 6 km north. 'Locomotion' tourist railway, 15 km east; train rides, historic trams, art and craft, tearooms, holiday accommodation. Jimmy Newhill's Harbour (20 km south), Frenchman Bay (25 km south), Emu Point, (8 km north-east), and Oyster Harbour (15 km north-east) have good beaches for swimming and fishing. Cheyne's Beach Whaling Station (25 km north), which ceased operation in 1978, now houses Albany Whaleworld. In its heyday, Station's chasers took up to 850 whales per season. Drives through some spectacular coastal scenery. To the south are The Gap and Natural Bridge (18 km), massive granite formations, the Blow Holes and The Gorge (19 km), with a sheer drop to the sea. To the east, Nanarup (20 km) and Little Beach (40 km) have sheltered waters. Towards Denmark, west of Albany, are Cosy Corner (20 km) and West Cape Howe National Park (30 km), one of the south coast's most popular parks; walking-trails, fishing, swimming, hang-gliding and one of the best lookouts on coast. Torbay Head in park is southernmost point in WA. Care should be taken when exploring along the coast; king waves can be dangerous and have been known to rush in unexpectedly, causing loss of life. To the north, Porongurup National Park (37 km), with its huge granite peaks, and Stirling Range National Park (80 km), offer mountain climbing, memorable bushwalks and breathtaking scenery. Many brilliantly coloured wildflowers in spring, some unique to area. Torndirrup National Park, 17 km south, for fine coastal views. Willowie Game Park, 30 km east. Two Peoples Bay Nature Reserve, 40 km east. **Tourist information:** Cnr Peels Pl and York St; (098) 41 1088. **Accommodation:** 5 hotels, 11 motels, 12 caravan/ camping parks. **See also:** The Great Southern.
MAP REF. 321 N13, 324 G13

Augusta   Population 933

Set on the slopes of the Hardy Inlet, the town of Augusta overlooks the mouth of the Blackwood River, the waters of Flinders Bay and rolling, heavily wooded countryside. Augusta is one of the oldest settlements in WA and a popular holiday resort. Jarrah, karri and pine forests supply the district's hundred-year-old timber industry. **Of interest:** Historical Museum and Lumen Christi Catholic Church, both in Blackwood Ave. Crafters Croft, Ellis St; art and craft. Dragon Boat racing in March. Augusta Spring Flower Show held in Sept.–Oct. **In the area:** Jewel Cave, 8 km north, world-famous for its magnificent and colourful limestone formations. Moondyne Cave, 8 km north; guided 'adventure' tours. Miniature railway, 18 km north of Bussell Hwy. Alexandra Bridge, 10 km north; charming picnic spot with towering jarrah trees and beautiful wildflowers. Lake Cave and Mammoth Cave, both 30 km north. Cape Leeuwin, 8 km south-west, most south-westerly point of Australia, where Indian and Southern Oceans meet; lighthouse and fascinating old water-wheel, both built in 1895. Hillview Lookout, 6 km west. Picturesque coastline near Augusta offers fine swimming and surfing. Good fishing in both river and ocean. Marron (freshwater lobster) can be caught in season. Amateur and Inland Fishing Licences required and obtainable from Leeuwin Souvenirs. **Tourist information:** Leeuwin Souvenirs, Blackwood Ave; (097) 58 1695; Augusta–Margaret River Tourist Bureau, cnr Tunbridge Rd and Bussell Hwy, Margaret River; (097) 57 2147. **Accommodation:** 1 hotel/motel, 4 caravan/ camping parks.
MAP REF. 320 C9, 324 E12

Australind   Population 2864

The popular holiday resort of Australind is located 11 km north of Bunbury on the Leschenault Estuary. Fishing, crabbing, swimming and boating on the estuary and the Collie River are the main attractions. **Of interest:** Henton Cottage (1841), Paris Rd; displays of local art and craft. Restored Church of St Nicholas (1842), Paris Rd; said to be smallest church in WA. Gem and Rock Museum, Old Coast Rd. Boats for hire. **In the area:** To north, pleasant beach towns of Binningup (26 km) and Myalup (30 km). Kemerton Industrial Park (SCM Chemicals), 15 km north; guided tours. **Tourist information:** Harvey Tourist and Interpretative Centre, South West Hwy, Harvey; (097) 29 1122. **Accommodation:** 3 caravan/camping parks.
MAP REF. 320 E3

Balladonia   Population 12

Balladonia is on the Eyre Hwy, 191 km east of Norseman. At this point, the road crosses gently undulating dry-land forest surrounding the Fraser Range. Claypans typical of the region and old stone fences built by pioneer farmers in the 1800s can be seen. In July 1979, debris from the US

ROTTNEST ISLAND

Commodore Willem de Vlamingh referred to Rottnest Island as a 'terrestrial paradise' when he landed there in 1696, and holiday-makers still flock to the island to enjoy its peace, beauty and unique holiday atmosphere. A low, sandy island, just twenty kilometres north-west of Fremantle, Rottnest is a public reserve. Only eleven kilometres long and about five kilometres wide, the island has an attractive coastline, with many small private bays and coves, sparkling white beaches and turquoise waters. Vlamingh named it Rottnest, or Rat's Nest, for the island's quaint marsupial resident, the quokka, which he believed to be a type of rat.

The Rottnest Hotel, completed in 1864, was originally the summer residence of the governors of Western Australia. Now commonly known as the Quokka Arms, it is a good place to stay, or just to enjoy a relaxing drink in the beer garden. Rottnest Lodge Resort has modern convention facilities in an informal setting.

There is no lack of things to do on Rottnest. Cars are not permitted (which contributes to the wonderful sense of peace), but you can hire a bicycle

Quokkas

and explore the island. You may even catch a glimpse of peacocks and pheasants, which were introduced at the turn of the century. Special coach tours of the island are conducted during the summer months (from the end of September to the end of April). There are tennis courts, a nine-hole golf course and bowling facilities. You can hire a boat, dinghy or canoe, play mini-golf or go trampolining; or you can just laze on the beach in the sunshine.

The *Underwater Explorer*, a glass-bottomed pleasure cruiser, leaves regularly from the Main Jetty, giving glimpses of shipwrecks, reefs and a startling array of fish. Ferries operate daily services to Rottnest from Barrack Street Jetty in Perth and also from Fremantle and Hillarys Boat Harbour. There are daily flights from Perth. As all wildlife on Rottnest is protected, no pets and no guns of any description, including spear guns, are allowed on the island.

For further information, contact the Rottnest Island Authority, (09) 372 9729; or the Information Kiosk, Main Jetty.

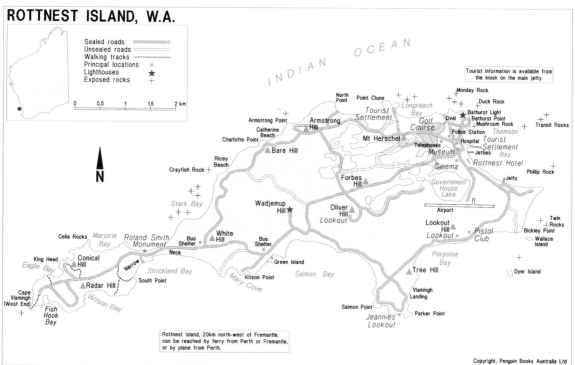

ROTTNEST ISLAND, W.A.

Sealed roads
Unsealed roads
Walking tracks
Principal locations
Lighthouses
Exposed rocks

0   0.5   1   1.5   2 km

Rottnest Island, 20km north-west of Fremantle, can be reached by ferry from Perth or Fremantle, or by plane from Perth.

Skylab fell to earth near the town. **In the area:** Balladonia Station Homestead, (1882), off north side of highway, behind old telegraph station, 28 km east of Balladonia Hotel complex; gallery of paintings depicting history of Balladonia and Eyre Hwy. **Tourist information:** Roadhouse; (090) 39 3453. **Accommodation:** 1 hotel/motel, 1 caravan/camping park (with limited facilities). **See also:** Crossing the Nullarbor.
MAP REF. 325 L10

Beverley   Population 725

On the Avon River, 130 km east of Perth, is the town of Beverley. **Of interest:** Aeronautical exhibition, Vincent St; showing development of aviation in WA; included is a bi-plane built in 1929 by local aircraft designer Selby Ford. Dead Finish, Hunt Rd; oldest building in town. Constructed in 1872 in the then centre of Beverley, it was first used as a hotel, but with the coming of the railway in 1886 the town centre moved nearer the station, leaving Dead Finish out of the mainstream. Old Railway Station Bazaar, off Vincent St; memorabilia, antiques and tearooms. Cross-country Regatta, held by gliding club in January. Agricultural Show in August. **In the area:** Restored St Paul's Church (consecrated 1862), opposite original town-site, 5 km north-west. Magnificent view from top of nearby Seaton Ross Hill. Yenyening Lakes, 36 km south-east; popular recreation area for skiing, motor boating, yachting, swimming and duck-shooting. County Peak (362 m), 35 km south-east; popular hiking and picnic area. Restored St John's in the Wilderness (consecrated 1895), 27 km south-west. Avondale Discovery Farm, 6 km west. **Tourist information:** Shire Offices, 138 Vincent St; (096) 46 1200. **Accommodation:** 2 hotels, 1 caravan/camping park.
MAP REF. 319 J9, 324 F10

Boyup Brook   Population 503

A small township near the junction of Boyup Creek and the Blackwood River, Boyup Brook is a market centre for the district's sheep, dairy-farming and timber industries. Shaded pools, charming cottages and farms are scenic features. Blackboys and huge granite boulders line the river valley. **Of interest:** Old Railway Museum, Railway Pde; pioneering memorabilia. Sandy Chambers Art Studio, Gibbs St; artworks, aviaries and camels. Flax Mill, on Blackwood River, off Barron St. Haddleton Flora Reserve, Arthur River Rd. Pioneer Garden, Kojonup Rd; picnic ground with barbecues. Carnaby Collection of beetles and butterflies at tourist centre. Bicentennial Walk Trail;

details from tourist centre. Country Music Awards held in Feb. Autumn Art Affair in May. Upper Blackwood Agricultural Show in Nov. **In the area:** Glacial rock formations at Glacier Hill, 18 km south. Vintage engines and old timbermill at Wilga, 22 km north. Harvey Dickson Country Music Centre, 5 km north-east. To north-east (24 km), Old Rose Cottage and Condinup Farm. School and teacher's house (1900), at Dinninup, 21 km north-east. Blackwood Crest Winery at Kulikup, 40 km north-east. Visits to local farms (wheat, sheep, pig, goat, deer, angora) can be arranged through tourist centre. Boyup Brook Flora Drive; details from tourist centre. **Tourist information:** Cnr Bridge and Able Sts; (097) 65 1444. **Accommodation:** 1 hotel, 1 caravan/camping park. **See also:** The Great Southern.
MAP REF. 320 H6, 324 F12

Bremer Bay   Population under 200

Bremer Bay, a popular holiday destination 181 km north-east of Albany, was named in 1849 by Surveyor-General John Septimus Roe in honour of the captain of HMS *Tamar*, Sir Gordon Bremer. The township was built around the Old Telegraph Station at the mouth of Wellstead Estuary (named after John Wellstead, who first settled in the area in the 1850s). **Of interest:** Fishing, boating, scuba-diving, water-skiing. Tavern, in Franton Way, and rammed-earth church, in John St, overlooking estuary. **In the area:** Fitzgerald River National Park, 17 km east. Military museum at Jerramungup, 60 km north. **Tourist information:** Roadhouse, Gnombup Tce; (098) 37 4093. **Accommodation:** 1 hotel, 1 caravan/camping park. **See also:** The Great Southern.
MAP REF. 324 H12

Bridgetown   Population 1478

Bridgetown is a quiet spot set in undulating country in the south-west corner of WA. Here the Blackwood River, well stocked with marron and trout, curves through some of the prettiest country in the state. Bridgetown was first settled in 1857 and the first apple trees were planted soon after. **Of interest:** Bridgetown Pottery, Brierley Jigsaw Gallery (in Tourist Centre), Country Classic Crafts and Gentle Era craft shop, all in Hampton St. Geegelup Pottery, Mount St. Orchard Studio, Allnutt St. Elizabeth Endisch Studio, Steere St. Bridgedale (1862), on South West Hwy, near bridge and overlooking river; constructed of local clay and timber by John Blechynden, first settler in area, and restored by National Trust. St Paul's Church (1911), Hampton St; paintings by local artist. Memorial Park, Hampton St; peaceful picnic location. October heralds the wildflower season, apple blossom time with orchards laden with blossoms (the orchards' packing-sheds are worth a visit), the town's annual art exhibition and flower

St Werburgh's Chapel and cemetery, Mount Barker, near Albany

show, and two major sporting events: the Blackwood Classic, a 3-day power-boat event over a 250 km course, and the Blackwood Marathon Relay, which attracts international and local competitors to participate in segments of running, canoeing, swimming, horseriding and cycling over a 58.3 km course. **In the area:** Sutton's Lookout, off Phillip St, and Hester's Hill, 5 km north, offer fine views. Greenbushes Historical Park, 18 km north; historical displays on tin-mining industry. Donnelly Whippole Well, 15 km south. Bridgetown Jarrah Park, 20 km south-west, for picnics and bushwalking. Geegelup Heritage Trail (52 km), retracing early history of agriculture, mining and timber industries; details from Tourist Centre. Scenic drives through rolling green hills, orchards and valleys and into karri and jarrah timber country for which south-west is famed. **Tourist information:** Hampton St; (097) 61 1740. **Accommodation:** 2 hotels, 3 hotel/motels, 1 caravan/ camping park. **See also:** The South-west. MAP REF. 320 G7, 324 F12

Brookton   Population 592

An attractive town 137 km south-east of Perth, near the Avon River in the heart of fertile farming country, Brookton was founded in 1884 when the Great Southern Railway line was opened. **Of interest:** In Robinson Rd, Old Police Station Museum, St Mark's Anglican Church (1895) and eye-catching Old Railway Station, which houses Tourist Centre and art and craft shop. Lions Picnic Park, off Corrigin Rd, at eastern entrance to town. Old Time Motor Show held in March every even year. **In the area:** Nine Acre Rock on Aldersyde Rd, 12 km east, one of largest of natural granite outcrops commonly found in area. Reserve and picnic ground at Boyagin Rock, 18 km south-west. Yenyening Lakes nature reserve, 35 km north-east; picnic and barbecue facilities. Brookton Pioneer Heritage Trail; details from tourist centre. **Tourist information:** Old Railway Station, Robinson Rd; (096) 42 1316. **Accommodation:** 2 hotels, 1 caravan/ camping park. MAP REF. 319 K11, 324 F10

Broome   Population 5778

Broome is situated on the coast at the southern tip of the Kimberley region. It is bounded by wide beaches and turquoise water and enjoys a warm climate with plenty of sunshine. The discovery of pearling grounds off the coast in the 1880s led to the foundation of Broome township in 1883. By 1910 Broome was the world's leading pearling centre. However, the industry began to suffer when world markets collapsed in 1914. Today with increasing tourism, Broome is again rapidly expanding into the most populous town in the Kimberley. **Of interest:** Many fascinating old buildings; self-guided Broome Heritage Trail (2 km) introduces buildings and places of historic interest. Chinatown, a reminder of Broome's early multi-cultural mix. Historical Society Museum, in Old Customs House, Saville St. Library, Haas St. Captain Gregory's House, Carnarvon St; not open to public. Kimberley Kreations Gallery in Matso's Store, Hamersley St; specialises in Kimberley art. Bedford Park, Hamersley St, contains relics of Broome's history. Court-house (former Cable House), Hamersley St; gardens and markets open Sat. Pearl Coast Zoological Gardens, Lullfitz Dr; home of world's largest collection of Australian parrots. Broome Crocodile Park, Cable Beach Rd. Shell House, Guy St; one of largest shell collections in Australia. Sun Pictures, Carnarvon St; opened 1916 and believed to be oldest operating picture garden in world. On Port Dr, Chinese Cemetery and Japanese Cemetery (graves of many early Japanese pearl-divers). Pioneer Cemetery in Apex Park. Each Aug.–Sept. Shinju Matsuri, or Festival of the Pearl, recalls Broome's heyday. Fringe Arts Festival held May–June. Sailfish Premiere and Kimberley Aboriginal Culture and Arts Festival in July. Mango Festival in Nov. **In the area:** Broome's beaches are ideal swimming spots and prized by collectors for their beautiful shells. Cable Beach (3 km from town centre), which stretches for 22 km, was named after the underwater cable that links Broome to Java. At Gantheaume Point, when the tide is out, giant dinosaur tracks, believed to be 130 million years old, can be seen. A natural phenomenon, visible at most full moons during the dry season (Apr.–Oct.), is the Staircase to the Moon, caused by the moonlight reflecting off the exposed mudflats at extreme low tides; best seen from southern end of Dampier Tce (dates and times from tourist centre). Hovercraft Spirit of Broome visits remote beaches. Broome area has good fishing all year round. Cable Beach Club, Auski and Roebuck Bay resorts. Broome Bird Observatory at Roebuck Bay, 18 km east. Safaris, cruises, scenic flights and short tours. Charter boats offer 6- to 10-day Kimberley expeditions with excursions to such attractions as coral reefs, Lacepede Islands, Coppermine Creek and waterfalls at Kings Cascades. Willie Creek Pearl Farm, 35 km north; tours include history of pearling industry. Day tours north to Lombardina Mission (190 km) and Cape Leveque (320 km). **Tourist information:** Cnr Bagot Rd and Great Northern Hwy; (091) 92 2222. **Accommodation:** 7 motels, 5 caravan/ camping parks. **See also:** The Kimberley. MAP REF. 327 K5

Bunbury   Population 23 031

Bunbury, 'Harbour City', is the second largest urban area in WA and serves as the major port and commercial centre for the south-west region. Situated 180 km south of Perth on the Leschenault Estuary, at the junction of the Preston and Collie Rivers, it is one of the state's most popular tourist resorts, with a warm-temperate climate, beautiful beaches along the coast, and the foothills of the Darling Range in the distance. Bunbury, originally called Port Leschenault, was first settled in 1838, and the whalers who anchored in Koombana Bay provided a market for the pioneer farmers. Today the port is the main outlet for the thriving timber industry, mineral sands and the produce of the fertile hinterland. **Of interest:** Visitors can drive along the breakwater, which extends into Koombana Bay, to view the modern harbour facilities. King Cottage (1880), Forrest Ave; fascinating historical museum (open weekends. Shell Museum, Mangles St; collection of shells from around the world, Aboriginal artefacts and minerals. Tree-lined pathways lead to Boulter's Lookout, Haig Cres; a vantage-point for views of the city and suburbs, surrounding hills and farmland. Bunbury Lighthouse, Ocean Dr; notable landmark, painted in bold black and white checks with lookout at base. Marlston Hill Lookout, Apex Dr; Art Gallery, Wittenoom St. Centenary Gardens, cnr Wittenoom and Prinsep Sts, in city centre; peaceful picnic spot with kiosk. Grassed foreshore of estuary also popular for picnics and family outings; barbecue facilities, children's playground and boat-ramp. Bunbury has some excellent beaches and a surf club at Ocean Beach. Koombana Bay is ideal for waterskiing and yachting; dolphins inhabit the bay. There is good fishing for bream, flounder, tailor and whiting in the bay, also deep-sea fishing. Succulent blue manna crabs can be caught in season in the estuary. There is a great variety of birdlife in the bush near the waters of the inlet. Big Swamp Bird Park, Prince Phillip Dr. Historic old wooden jetty in outer harbour; popular for fishing and crabbing. Miniature railway in Forrest Park, Blair St. Bunbury Show and Peters Aqua Spectacular, both held in March. Discover Bunbury–The Good Life in Nov. **In the area:** Gelorup Museum, 12 km south. Wirrawee Adventure Playground, at Stratham, 17 km south. St Mark's, Picton, 5 km south-east, oldest church in WA, erected in 1842. Although restored, church still retains some of its original timber structure. Boyanup Transport Museum, 20 km south-east. At Australind, 11 km north, Church of St Nicholas (1860), thought to be smallest church in WA. Spring Hill Homestead (1855), 26 km north, off Old Coast Road; not open to public. Pleasant scenic drive off Old Coast

Road with good crabbing and picnicking spots. Bunbury Heritage Trails; details from tourist centre. **Tourist information:** Old Railway Station, Carmody St.; (097) 21 7922. **Accommodation:** 6 hotels, 9 motels, 5 caravan/camping parks. **See also:** The South-west.
MAP REF. 320 E4, 324 E11

Busselton   Population 7784

First settled in the 1830s, Busselton is one of the oldest-established areas in WA. Nowadays it is a pleasant seaside town at the centre of a large rural district. Situated 228 km south of Perth, on the sweeping shores of Geographe Bay and the picturesque Vasse River, the town is a very popular holiday resort. Inland there are jarrah forests which supply the local timber industry, and agricultural land carrying dairy and beef cattle and vineyards. Fishing is also important, with crayfish and salmon in season. **Of interest:** Prospect Villa (1855), Pries Ave; two-storey colonial building (now motel) with antiques. Opposite, first steam locomotive used in WA. St Mary's (1844), Peel Tce; oldest stone church in state. Villa Carlotta (1897), Adelaide St; boarding school for 50 years, now guesthouse. Oceanarium and Nautical Lady outdoor family fun centre, both near jetty on beachfront. Old Court-house Arts Centre, Queen St. Allan Jones Cinema Museum, Albert St; historic collection of cinema equipment. Old Butter Factory Museum, Peel Tce; on banks of river has exhibits including antiquated butter- and cheesemaking equipment. Wonnerup House (1859), Layman Rd, National Trust Museum; fine example of colonial Australian architecture and furnished in period style. Old school and teacher's house, Layman Rd; restored buildings of local undressed timber. Busselton Jetty, (2 km long), on beachfront near Queen St; longest timber jetty in Australia. Partially destroyed by Cyclone Alby in 1978, but still very popular with fishermen. Vasse River Parkland, Peel Tce; barbecue and picnic facilities. Archery Park and Minigolf, Bussell Hwy. The bay has good sheltered beaches for swimming and the western coast is ideal for surfing. Festival of Busselton held on Jan. long weekend. Down South Dive Classic in Nov. **In the area:** Several protea nurseries near Busselton open to visitors. Bunyip Craft Centre, 7 km east. Orchid farm at Vasse, 9 km west. Wildwood Pottery, 16 km west. Bannamah Wildlife Park, 26 km west. Yallingup, 32 km south-west, for surfing enthusiasts; also sheltered rock-pool. Yallingup Caves open daily. Over 20 wineries in Woodlands–Metricup district, 30 km south-west, and around town of Margaret River, 47 km south-west. Many scenic drives in area. To west, Eagle Bay (30 km),

Sugar Loaf Rock, (35 km) and Cape Naturaliste (39 km), all offer excellent views of rugged coast. Wildflower, scenic and 4WD tours available. Farm holidays at Kerriley Park, 24 km south-west. Augusta–Busselton Heritage Trails; details from tourist centre. **Tourist information:** Civic Centre, Southern Drive; (097) 52 1091. **Accommodation:** 3 hotels, 8 motels, 13 caravan/camping parks. **See also:** The South-west.
MAP REF. 320 D5, 324 E12

Caiguna   Population 10

This is the first stop for petrol and food after the long drive from Balladonia, 181 km to the west along the Eyre Hwy, one of the longest straight stretches of sealed road in the world, a total of 145 km west of Caiguna to Balladonia. **In the area:** Afghan Rocks, 14 km east; natural freshwater dams, used as resting-place by camel drivers in 1890s. **Tourist information:** Roadhouse; (090) 39 3459. **Accommodation:** 1 motel, 1 caravan/camping park. **See also:** Crossing the Nullarbor.
MAP REF. 325 N10

Carnamah   Population 398

Carnamah is a small, typically Australian country town, 290 km north of Perth. Wheat and sheep-farming are the local industries. **In the area:** MacPherson Homestead (1880), 1 km east. Several old gold-mining and ghost towns 40–50 km east; area rich in minerals and popular with gemstone enthusiasts. Yarra Yarra Lakes, 2 km west, where waters range in colour from red to green to blue; lakes attract many varieties of migratory birds and are surrounded by wildflowers in season. Perenjori, 58 km north-east. Tathra National Park, 50 km south-west; variety of wildflowers in spring. Lake Indoon, 61 km south-west, for waterskiing. **Accommodation:** 1 motel, 1 caravan/camping park.
MAP REF. 322 F9, 324 E7

Carnarvon   Population 6847

Carnarvon, at the mouth of the Gascoyne River, 904 km north of Perth, is the commercial centre of the highly productive Gascoyne region. The district was sighted as long ago as 1616 by Dirk Hartog. Another explorer, Willem de Vlamingh, landed at Shark Bay in 1697. The first pioneers arrived in 1876 and by the 1880s there were a number of settlers in the region. Today most of the land is used for pastoral activities, with sheep and beef cattle. The Gascoyne River often flows beneath its bed, and its resources have been tapped for irrigation. The Overseas Telecommunications Commission (OTC) earth station (no longer operating) and Radio Australia base

are both located at nearby Browns Range. The USA National Aeronautics and Space Administration (NASA) operated here between 1964 and 1974. Carnarvon has warm winters and hot summers and takes on a tropical appearance when the bougainvilleas and hibiscus bloom. The main street, built in the 1880s, is a gracious 40 m wide, to enable camel trains to turn. **Of interest:** Museum, Correia St. Jubilee Hall (1887), Francis St. D and B Banana Plantation, Robinson St. Pioneer Park, Olivia Tce. Rotary Park, North West Coastal Hwy. Fishing for snapper or groper, or game fishing for marlin or sailfish; charter boats available. Yachting Regatta held in March. Mirari Tropical Festival in May. Dry River Regatta held between July and Sept. **In the area:** On Babbage Island, 5 km off Carnarvon: Museum at lighthouse keeper's cottage. Prawning factory; tours organised by tourist centre during season, usually mid-April to late Oct. One Mile Jetty, almost 1500 m long. Pelican Point, good spot for picnics and swimming. Dwyer's Leap, popular with water-skiers. OTC earth station with its mammoth 157-m diameter reflector (known as the 'Big Dish') at Browns Range, 8 km east; open to visitors; scenic views of area from platform of disc. Six km along highway from centre of Carnarvon, is turn-off at South River Rd to Munro's Banana Plantation (5 km from turn-off). In season, fresh-picked bananas, melons and other fruit and vegetables for sale. At Department of Agriculture Research Station, 3 km from South River Rd turn-off, inspections of experimental farmings. Miaboolya Beach, 22 km north, has good fishing, crabbing and swimming. The hot water from Bibbawarra artesian bore, 16 km north, surfaces at 70°C. There are blowholes 70 km north where the water is dramatically forced some 20 m into the air. About 1 km south of the blowholes is a superb sheltered beach; search for oysters on the rocks, but beware of king waves and tides. Excellent fishing at Cape Cuvier, 30 km north of blowholes. Drive 55 km east inland from Carnarvon, along Gascoyne Rd, leads to Rocky Pool, deep freshwater billabong ideal for swimming and picnics. **Tourist information:** Robinson St; (099) 41 1146. **Accommodation:** 5 hotel/motels, 7 caravan/camping parks.
MAP REF. 324 C2

Cocklebiddy   Population 12

The ruins of an Aboriginal mission station can be seen at this tiny settlement on the Eyre Hwy, between Madura and Caiguna, about 280 km from the SA border. **In the area:** Cocklebiddy Cave, for experienced speleologists only (directions available at Roadhouse). Bird observatory and Post Office Historical Society Museum at Eyre on coast, 47 km south (4WD only).

WESTERN WILDFLOWERS

The sandplains, swamps, flats, scrub and woodlands of south-western Australia light up with colour in spring as the 'wildflower state' puts on its brilliant display. The plains can become carpeted, almost overnight, with the gold of everlastings or feather flowers or the red and pinks of boronia and leschenaultia. The banksia bushes throw up their red and yellow cylinders along the coast and in the woodlands, grevilleas spill their flowers down to the ground and orchids proliferate. Flowering gums become a mass of red and the felty kangaroo paws invade the plains. Lilies, banksias, parrot bush, flame peas, feather flowers and native foxgloves, all are displayed in a magnificent abundance.

There are over 8000 different named species and 2000 unnamed species of wildflowers in Western Australia, givng the state one of the richest floras known to man. Around seventy-five per cent of them are unique to the region, although they may have family connections with other plants of northern or eastern Australia. Isolation by the barrier of plain and desert that separates the west from the eastern states and has caused plants on both sides to pursue their own evolution; some families of plants are unique to the west.

On even a short trip to Perth, visitors can see a wide variety of Western Australian wildflowers. At **King's Park** close to the city, wildflower species abound and give a brilliant display in the August to October period. Visitors in any part of the south-west at that time will see wildflowers all around them. Often, however, it is in the state's national parks that the full beauty of massed wildflower displays is best seen. Only twenty-five kilometres east of Perth on the Great Eastern Highway is the **John Forrest National Park**, on the edge of the Darling Range escarpment. On these undulating hills and valleys the undergrowth of the jarrah forest is rich in flowering plants — red and green kangaroo paw, swamp river myrtle, blue leschenaultia and pink calytrix are the most common. Fifty kilometres north of Perth is the

Cowslip orchids,
Stirling Range National Park

Yanchep National Park, a place of coastal limestone and sandy plains, covered with wildflowers.There are many places farther north that are worth visiting, if only for the unique quality of their scenery. One such is the **Kalbarri National Park**, 670 kilometres north of Perth, at the mouth of the Murchison River. It contains magnificent flowering trees and shrubs of banksia, grevillea and melaleuca while the ground beneath is covered with many species, such as leschenaultia, twine rushes and sedges. Prolific displays of wildflowers also can be found throughout the wheat-belt, forests and sandplains of the south west.

The **Dryandra State Forest**, a few kilometres from Narrogin in the southwest, has magnificent woodlands of wandoo and powderbark with brown mallet and bush thickets. An important sanctuary for mallee fowl and numbat, this forest contains a number of species of dryandra.

Another fascinating area of Western Australia is the **Stirling Range National Park**, 400 kilometres south of Perth and near the Porongurup Range. The Stirlings are very jagged peaks which rise above flat farmlands. The scenery is magnificent and wildflowers abound, many unique to the region. There are banksias here, as well as dryandra, cone bushes, cats paws and a number of mountain bells which have red or pink flower heads. The bare granite domes and the boulders of the Porongurup Range tower over slopes of flowering trees and creepers such as the *Banksia grandis* and clematis.

There are many coastal parks around Albany. The **Torndirrup National Park** is an area of coastal hills and cliffs and such fascinating scenic features as the Gap, the Blowhole and the Natural Bridge. In the stunted, windswept coastal vegetation there are many wildflowers, including the endemic giant-coned Banksia praemorsa and the Western Australian Christmas tree with its brilliant orange flowers.

Twenty-five kilometres east of Albany is the peaceful and beautiful **Two Peoples Bay** flora and fauna reserve, which has thickets of mallee, banksia and peppermint, together with many flowering shrubs and plants. Along the coast west of Albany is the **Walpole-Nornalup National Park**, where dense karri forest mingles with red tingle, jarrah, marri, casuarina and banksia, and many wildflowers including the tree kangaroo paw, the babe-in-cradle orchid and the potato orchid.

Although most wildflowers occur in the south-west of the state, northern areas also have displays peculiar to times of rainfall and climatic changes. While enjoying Western Australia's brilliant flora displays, visitors should remember that wildflowers are protected under the State's *Native Flower Protection Act.*

For further information on national parks and wildflower display areas, contact the Western Australian Tourist Centre or the Department of Conservation and Land Management, 50 Hayman Rd, Como WA 6152; (09) 367 0333.

Tourist information: Roadhouse; (090) 39 3462. **Accommodation:** 1 motel, 1 caravan/camping park (limited facilities). **See also:** Crossing the Nullarbor.
MAP REF. 325 O10

Collie   Population 7829
Collie, the centre of WA's only coal-producing region, plays an integral part in the state's development. The town is set in dense jarrah forest, 202 km south of Perth, near the winding Collie River, and has an abundance of attractive parks and gardens. The drive into Collie from the South West Hwy, climbing the Darling Scarp, offers some of the finest views in WA. **Of interest:** Historical museum, Throssell St, in old Roads Board buildings, traces history of area and of coal industry. Opposite, steam locomotive museum with some fine restored trains. Impressive All Saints' Anglican Church, Venn St, built in Norman style. Art gallery, Throssell St; collection of Australian paintings. Soldiers Park, Steer St, on banks of Collie River; shady trees and lawns, ideal for picnics. Minninup Pool off Mungalup Rd, also popular spot, surrounded by bushland and, in season, beautiful wildflowers. **In the area:** Harris River Dam, 10 km north. Wellington Dam, 27 km west, in heart of Collie River Irrigation Scheme; major tourist attraction with fishing, pleasant bushwalking tracks and recreation areas with grassy picnic-spots. Delicious marron, or freshwater crayfish, abounds in dam Dec.–Apr. (Inland Fishing Licence required.) Scenic drive to Collie River, 5 km west, takes visitor through some magnificent scenery. Muja open-cut mines and Muja power-station, 15 km east. 'Muja' is Aboriginal word used to describe bright yellow Christmas tree that grows in area. **Tourist information:** Throssell St; (097) 34 2051. **Accommodation:** 4 hotels, 4 motels, 1 caravan/camping park.
MAP REF. 320 G4, 324 F11

Coolgardie   Population 989
The old gold-mining town of Coolgardie is one of the best-known 'ghost towns' in Australia. Alluvial gold was discovered here in 1892 and Coolgardie grew from nothing to a boom town of 15 000 people, 23 hotels, six banks and two stock exchanges in just ten years. The main street was wide enough for camel trains to turn, splendid public buildings were erected and ambitious plans were made for the future. Sadly, the gold soon petered out. By 1985 there were only 700 people in the town; however, at the beginning of the 1990s, with an increase in tourism, there is a wave of confidence emerging and the population is increasing. **Of interest:** Historic buildings in Bayley St include: Goldfields Exhibition building (1898), most comprehensive prospecting museum in WA; Post Office (1898); Old Gaol; Denver City Hotel (1898), with handsome verandahs; Ben Prior's Open-air Museum, with covered wagons, horse- and camel-driven vehicles; and Railway Lodge, wonderfully preserved building entering into 'ghost town' atmosphere. Railway station (1896), Woodward St; transport exhibition and display of famous Varischetti mine rescue. Warden Finnerty's house (1895), McKenzie St; striking example of early Australian architecture and furnishings. St Anthony's Convent, Lindsay St; now boarding-school for Aboriginal Self Help Group–Concerned Parents Society (CAPS). Goal Tree, Hunt St. Lions Bicentennial Lookout, near southern end of Hunt St. Lindsay's Pit Mine Lookout, Ford St. Coolgardie Day and Camel Races, both held in Sept. **In the area:** Camel farm, 4 km west. Kurrawang Emu Farm, 20 km east. Cemetery, 1 km west, evokes harsh early days of gold-rush. Eastern Goldfields Heritage Trail; details from tourist centre. **Tourist information:** Bayley St; (090) 26 6090. **Accommodation:** 1 hotel, 3 motels, 2 caravan/camping parks. **See also:** The Goldfields.
MAP REF. 325 J8

Coral Bay   Population under 200
The Ningaloo Coral Reef system approaches the shore at Coral Bay, 150 km south of Exmouth. Unspoilt expanses of white beaches offer good swimming, snorkelling, boating and fishing. **In the area:** Ningaloo Marine Park, just off beach; underwater viewing platform. Views of reef from glass-bottomed boats. Diving equipment for hire. Numerous shipwreck sites at Pt Cloates, 10 km north, and ruins of Norwegian Bay whaling station (1915), 30 km south. **Tourist information:** Coral Reef Cafe; (099) 42 5900. **Accommodation:** 1 motel, 2 caravan/camping parks.
MAP REF. 326 C12

Corrigin   Population 694
Rich farming country surrounds Corrigin, 230 km south-east of Perth. **Of interest:** In Kunjin St, folk museum with historical exhibits, including photographs; also miniature railway and steam train. Art and craft shop, Walton St. Agricultural Show in Sept. Creative Arts Exhibition in Nov. **In the area:** Dog Cemetery, 5 km west. Observation tower, 8 km west, affords good views; on Wildflower Scenic Drive, Trott Dr (well signposted). Gorge Rock, 20 km south-east; swimming, picnics. **Tourist information:** Shire Offices, Lynch St; (090) 63 2203. **Accommodation:** 1 hotel, 1 motel, 1 caravan/camping park.
MAP REF. 319 N11, 324 G10

Cossack   Population nominal
Cossack, once called Tien Tsin, has had a chequered history. It was the first port in the north-west, and has been a thriving pearling centre, the focus of a gold-rush and the location for a factory producing turtle products. Today it is a ghost town. **Of interest:** Historic buildings: in Pearl St, court-house (now museum), bond store, post and telegraph office; in Perseverance St, police quarters. Cemetery, off Perseverance St; headstones reflect town's colourful past. Located at mouth of Harding River, Cossack is ideal area for picnics, fishing, crabbing or swimming. Boats for hire. Cossack Fair and Regatta in June. **In the area:** To north-west, Wickham (8 km), a modern company town, and Point Samson (18 km), a popular seaside resort. **Tourist information:** Roebourne Tourist Bureau, 173 Roe St, Roebourne; (091) 82 1060. **Accommodation:** Backpackers hotel. **See also:** The Pilbara.
MAP REF. 326 F9

Cranbrook   Population 351
In the 1800s sandalwood was exported from Cranbrook to China, where it was used as incense. Today this attractive town, near the foothills of the Stirling Range, 320 km south-east of Perth, is a sheep and wheat farming centre. **Of interest:** Annual Wildflower Display, Sept.–Oct. **In the area:** Gateway to the Stirling Arch, Salt River Rd; picnic area, native garden and tourist information. Stirling Range National Park, 40 km south-east. Lake Poorarrecup, 55 km south-west; popular spot in summer. Sukey Hill Lookout, 5 km east, off Saltwater Rd. High-quality table wines produced at Frankland district vineyards, 50 km west. Frankland Heritage Trail; details from tourist centre. **Tourist information:** Shire Offices, Gathorne St; (098) 26 1008. **Accommodation:** 1 hotel, 1 caravan/camping park.
MAP REF. 321 M9, 324 G12

Cue   Population 399
Cue, 640 km north-east of Perth on the Great Northern Hwy, grew up as a boom town, an important centre for the Murchison goldfields. Today its well-kept stone buildings are a silent testimony to those frenzied days. **Of interest:** Buildings in National Trust-classified Austin St, including bandstand built over a well, water from which was said to have started a typhoid epidemic, and impressive government offices. Masonic Hall (1899), Dowley St, built largely of corrugated iron. **In the area:** Ghost towns left from mining boom: Austin Island, Austin Mainland (20 km south), Cuddingwarra (originally called 'Dead Finish', 10 km west),

Pinnacles (24 km east), Reedys (60 km north-east), Tuckanarra (40 km north). Day Dawn, 5 km west, where town was established on site of gold reef; town disappeared when reef died out in 1930s. Ghost town of Big Bell, 30 km west, another crumbling reminder of gold boom; current open-pit mine opened in 1989 (access restricted). Walga Rock, monolith 50 km west; Aboriginal rock paintings. Wilgie Mia Red Ochre Mine, 64 km north-west; gemstone fossicking. Aga Khan Emerald Mine, Poona, 75 km north-west; gem and rock hunting. Cue Heritage Trail; details from tourist centre. **Tourist information:** Dorsett's Guesthouse, Austin St; (099) 63 1291. **Accommodation:** 1 hotel, 1 guest-house, 1 caravan/camping park.
MAP REF. 324 G4

Dampier   Population 2201

A model town with all modern conveniences, Dampier lies on King Bay, facing the unique islands of the Dampier Archipelago. Hamersley Iron Pty Ltd established the town as a port outlet for ore mined from two of the world's richest iron-ore deposits, Tom Price and Paraburdoo. The town's deepwater port with its export facilities sees over 400 million tonnes of ore loaded each year. Salt is harvested from ponds near the port. **Of interest:** Jurat Park, Haig Close; picnic area with barbecues and children's playground. Tours of the Hamersley Iron port facility, Mon.–Fri.; bookings (091) 43 5364. Boating, sailing, fishing, diving,

windsurfing and swimming. Gamefishing; charter boats for hire. In the first weekend of August, Dampier and Karratha hold their FeNaCLNG festival (Fe: iron; NaCl: salt; LNG: liquefied natural gas). A major feature of the festival is the Dampier Classic, a sailfish competition for which almost 100 fish are caught, tagged and released. **In the area:** North West Shelf Gas Project on Burrup Peninsula 8 km north-west; Visitors Centre open weekdays, except public holidays. Nearby Hearsons Cove, popular tidal swimming beach and picnic area. Aboriginal rock carvings on Burrup Peninsula; details from tourist centre. Pilbara Railway Historical Society Museum, 10 km west, home of 'Pendennis Castle' steam locomotive. **Tourist information:** King Bay Holiday Village, The Esplanade; (091) 83 1440. **Accommodation:** 2 motels, 1 caravan/camping park. **See also:** The Hamersley Range; The Pilbara.
MAP REF. 326 F9

Denham–Shark Bay

Population 1118
Two peninsulas form the geographical feature of Shark Bay, 833 km from Perth. Denham is the most westerly town in Australia and the main centre of the Shark Bay region. Dirk Hartog, the Dutch navigator, landed on an island at the entrance to Shark Bay in 1616. Pearling developed as the main industry and the population was a mixture of Malays, Chinese and Europeans. Until recently Shark Bay was known only for its

excellent fishing, but today its most spectacular tourist attraction is the wild dolphins of Monkey Mia, who after years of love and understanding come of their own accord to be fed. **In the area:** Francis Peron National Park, 7 km north. Eagle Bluff, 20 km south, habitat of sea eagle and good fishing spot. Catamaran MV Explorer offers a variety of cruises. Nanga Station, 50 km south; this half-million-acre sheep-station also has motel units, restaurant, tourist facilities, sailboards and dinghies for hire on beach, and charter fishing. Zuytdorp Cliffs, 160 km west and extending south to Kalbarri, offer striking scenery. Shell Beach, 40 km south; 110 km stretch of unique Australian coastline comprising countless tiny shells. Hamelin Pool, 100 km south-east; historic displays in Flint Cliff Telegraph Station and Post Office Museum (1894), and stromatolites ('living rocks' communities) in nature reserve. Tourist information: Shark Bay Visitor and Trav**el Centre, 83 Knight** Tce, Denham; (099) 48 1253. **Accommodation:** 1 motel, 4 caravan/camping parks..
MAP REF. 324 C3

Denmark   Population 1217

The attractive coastal town of Denmark, 55 km west of Albany, is at the foot of Mt Shadforth, overlooking the tranquil Denmark River. The town is known for its good fishing, sandy white beaches and scenic drives through farming country and karri forests. The dense hardwood forests supply timber for the mills in the area. **Of interest:** Historical Museum, Mitchell St. Denmark Gallery, Strickland St. Cottage Industries Shop, Price St. Alpaca stud and tourist farm, Scotsdale Rd. Jassi Skincraft, Glenrowan Rd off Mt Shadforth Scenic Drive; local handcrafts, wines and sheepskin products. Esplanade Parkland, along the river-bank, with shaded picnic areas, recreation and sports facilities. Winery and Craft Centre in Old Butter Factory, North St. Mt Shadforth Lookout, top of Isley Dr, for magnificent views of countryside. Winter Festival held in Aug. Art and Craft Market Days in Dec. and Jan. and on Easter Sat. **In the area:** Knoll Drive, 3 km east. Wynella Museum, 15 km west. William Bay, 18 km west; sheltered swimming beach. Greens Pool–William Bay National Park, 23 km west. Parry's Beach, 25 km west, for fishing, with salmon in season, and Ocean Beach, 8 km south, for surfing. Picturesque town of Albany, 50 km east, with its rich history and beautiful beaches is a short drive away. Another pleasant drive through the Valley of the Giants, 45 km west, reveals the massive karri and tingle trees. Boating, fishing, bushwalking and scenic drives in area of Nornalup, 50 km west, and Walpole, 66 km west, adjacent to Walpole–Nornalup National Park. Some dozen wineries in

The Residency, Warden Finnerty's house, Coolgardie

WESTERN AUSTRALIA'S NATIONAL PARKS

The national parks of Western Australia are tourist attractions in themselves: their spectacular displays of wildflowers create a paradise for photographers and a colourful wonderland for bushwalkers and campers.

Western Australia has more than 800 named species and 2000 unnamed species of wildflowers, growing undisturbed in their natural surroundings. One quarter of these species cannot be found anywhere else in the world and they lure admirers from interstate and overseas. The best months to see them are from August to October. This is also the best time for camping trips and bushwalking.

Within a 100 kilometre radius of Perth there are ten National Parks well worth a visit. **Yanchep National Park**, about 50 kilometres north on a belt of coastal limestone, has forests of massive tuart trees. Islands on Loch Ness within the park are waterfowl sanctuaries. Yanchep is also famed for its underground limestone caves and displays of spring wildflowers.

Some 80 kilometres north-east of Perth is the **Avon Valley National Park;** its most popular attractions are upland forests and river valleys, as well as the beautiful wildflowers that abound in season. The highest point in the park is Bald Hill, which gives panoramic views of the Avon River. After winter rains, a tributary of the Avon, Emu Spring Brook, spills 30 metres in a spectacular waterfall.

A cluster of national parks to the east of Perth includes **John Forrest National Park**, which was Western Australia's first proclaimed national park. With the Darling Escarpment within its boundaries, the park features granite outcrops, dams and waterfalls, creeks and rockpools.

Other nearby national parks are **Kalamunda, Greenmount, Gooseberry Hill** and **Lesmurdie Falls**. All are within 20 to 25 kilometres from Perth. Lookouts at various vantage points offer panoramic views over the suburbs and cities of Perth. The Bibbulmun Track, once an Aboriginal walk trail, begins its 500 kilometre route in Kalamanda National Park.

Nature's Window, Murchison Gorge, Kalbarri National Park

Proclaimed as the state's first flora and fauna reserve in 1894, **Serpentine National Park** is about 60 kilometres south from Perth and a firm favourite of day picnickers to the falls area within the park. Jarrah and marri forests, and wildflowers in spring are some of the park's attractions.

Stirling Range National Park, 450 kilometres south-east of Perth, is one of Australia's outstanding reserves. Surrounded by a flat, sandy plain, the Stirling Range rises abruptly to over 1000 metres, its jagged peaks veiled in swirling mists. The cool, humid environment created by these low clouds contribute to the survival of more than 1000 species of flowering plants, some of which, like the mountain bell, are found nowhere else in the world.

Brilliant displays of wildflowers are also a feature of the nearby **Porongurup National Park**, where the granite domes of the Porongurup Ranges are clothed in a luxuriant forest of karri trees. The South Western Highway bisects the **Shannon National Park,** 358 kilometres south of Perth. A base

from which to explore the park is located at the former timber-milling townsite of Shannon. The remainder of the park consists of towering karri and jarrah forests, surrounding the Shannon River, which empties into the sea at Broke Inlet to the south.

Spectacular coastal scenery is the main attraction of the **Torndirrup National Park** on the Flinders Peninsula, 460 kilometres south of Perth. Also on the south coast are outstanding parks, including **Cape Le Grand National Park,** with its wide beaches and magnificent bays, protected by imposing granite headlands, located 40 kilometres east of Esperance.

Other parks near to Esperance, both to the west of the township, are **Peak Charles National Park** and **Stokes National Park**. Stokes hugs the coastline around Stokes Inlet and features long sandy beaches and rocky headlands backed by sand dunes and low hills. Stokes Inlet and its associated lakes support a rich variety of wildlife. Inland from Stokes, about 100 kilometres, lies Peak Charles National

Park. A walk to the ridge of this ancient granite peak allows sweeping views of its companion, Peak Eleanora, and over the dry sandplain heaths and salt-lake systems of the surrounding country.

One of the loveliest sections of the south coast of Western Australia is **Fitzgerald River National Park,** through which the rugged Barren Range (named by Matthew Flinders) stretches from west to east. The park's 330 000 hectares comprise gently un-dulating sandplains, river valleys, pre-cipitous cliff-edges, narrow gorges and beaches for swimming and rock fish-ing. The park contains many rare species of flora and fauna, including unique species of flowering plants; one, the exotic royal hakea, resembles a flame shooting from the earth.

Along the lower south-west coast is **Walpole-Nornalup National Park,** 18 166 hectares of wilderness where creeks gurgle under tall eucalypts, rivers meander between forested hills and inlets rich in fish create a haven for anglers and boating enthusiasts. An intricate network of roads and walk-ing-tracks, through forests of karri and tingle, attracts bushwalkers and bird-watchers, who enjoy the diverse var-iety of animal and bird life.

About 100 kilometres east is **West Cape Howe National Park**, the spec-tacular coastline of which includes the gabbro cliffs of West Cape Howe and the granite of Torbay Heads, fronting the cold waters of the Southern Ocean. Extensive coastal heath, swamps, lakes and karri forest cover the inland area and the park is popular with anglers, naturalists, bushwalkers, rock-climbers, and hang-gliding enthusiasts.

Keeping to the coast but travelling north of Perth, the visitor will discover the wild beauty of ancient landscapes, unsurpassed at **Kalbarri National Park.** Its 186 076 hectares encom-passes the lower reaches of the Mur-chison River, which winds its way through spectacular gorges to the In-dian Ocean. Sea cliffs in layers of multi-coloured sandstone loom over the crashing white foam at Red Bluff.

Unusual rock formations are to be found at **Nambung National Park**, 230 kilometres north of Perth on the coast. Here a moonscape of coloured quartz is studded with fantastic lime-stone pillars ranging in size from stony 'twigs' to columns more than 2 metres tall. This is the unique Pinnacle Desert,

a favourite subject for photographers.

In the Pilbara, 1400 kilometres north of Perth, is **Karijini (Hamer-sley Range) National Park,** part of a massive block of weathered rock over 450 kilometres long. Within this huge, spectacular park are many well-known gorges, including Dales Gorge, its strata, in horizontal stripes of blue, mauve, red and brown, dating back almost 2000 million years. Further north, still in the Pilbara, **Millstream-Chichester National Park** contains almost 20 000 hectares of clay table-lands and sediment-capped basalt ranges. At Millstream, on the Forte-scue River, natural freshwater springs have created an oasis in arid country. In contrast, there are the **Chichester Ranges:** rolling hills, hummocks of spinifex, white-barked snappy gums on the uplands, and pale coolibahs along the usually dry water-courses.

In the far north of Western Australia are the national parks of the Kimberley region—mountain ranges formed mil-lions of years ago. The largest of these parks, **Geikie Gorge**, has an area of 3136 hectares and is 20 kilometres north-east of Fitzroy Crossing. The multi-coloured cliffs are reflected in the placid waters of the Fitzroy River, which flows through the gorge. The area is too rugged for walking, but organised boat trips go up the river through the gorge, enabling visitors to view one of Austra-lia's most beautiful waterways.

Other nearby national parks are **Windjana Gorge** and **Tunnel Creek,** both north-west of Geike Gorge. Tun-nel Creek, a permanent watercourse, flows underground for 750 metres. The tunnel is high and wide enough to walk through.

South of Lake Argyle is **Purnululu (Bungle Bungle) National Park**, with its tiger-striped, beehive-shaped domes.

Hidden Valley National Park, only 2.5 kilometres east of Kununurra, has features typical of the Kimberley: banded sandstone outcrops similar to those of the Bungle Bungle massif, boab trees, red soil dotted with eucal-pyts and black kites circling overhead. Aboriginal rock paintings are also a feature of the park.

For further information on Western Aus-tralia's national parks, contact the Depart-ment of Conservation and Land Management, 50 Hayman Rd (GPO Box 104), Como, WA 6152; (09) 367 0333.

Denmark–Mount Barker–Albany region, 15 km east. Farm holidays at Rannock West, 32 km west, cattle and sheep property. Scotsdale Rd–McLeod Rd Tour-ist Drive (details from tourist centre), pro-vides excellent views of coast and attractions along way. Denmark Timber, Mokare and Wilson Inlet Heritage Trail; details from tourist centre. **Tourist infor-mation:** Strickland St; (098) 48 1265. **Ac-commodation:** 2 hotels, 2 motels, 3 caravan/camping parks. **See also:** The Great Southern.
MAP REF. 321 L12, 324 G13

Derby   Population 3258

Derby operates as an administrative centre for a hinterland rich in pastoral and mineral wealth. The town is located on King Sound, 220 km north-east of Broome, and is an ideal base for expeditions into the outback re-gions of the Kimberley. Roads have been greatly improved in recent years, including the Gibb River road, spanning the 645 km from Derby to the junction of the Great Northern Hwy between Wyndham and Ku-nunurra. However, as 'wet season' rain usually closes the road between Nov. and Mar., it is always advisable to check local conditions before setting out. **Of interest:** In Loch St: Botanic Gardens; Old Derby Gaol; museum containing collection of Abo-riginal artefacts and photographic display at Wharfinger House; and Raintree Craft Shop. In Clarendon St: Art Gallery; Royal Flying Doctor Service; and Ngunga Craft Shop. Country Music Festival held in July. Boab Festival, also held in July, features rodeo, mardi gras and Derby's famous mud football. **In the area:** Prison Tree, 7 km south, boab (or baobab) tree reputedly used as prison in early days. Close by, My-all's Bore, an enormous cattle-trough, 120 m long and 4.2 m wide; also Pigeon's Cave, hideout of Aboriginal outlaw. Mowanjum Aboriginal Mission, 10 km south. Fitzroy River empties into King Sound, 13 km south. Spectacular Windjana Gorge and re-markable Tunnel Creek, with its colonies of flying foxes, 145 km and 184 km east re-spectively. Mitchell Plateau, 580 km north-east, via Gibb River Rd and Kalumburu Rd; includes spectacular Mitchell Falls, King Edward River and Surveyor's Pool; in this remote region, visitors must be entirely self-sufficient. Motor yacht charter to Prince Regent River available. Charter flights over Kimberley coast and Cockatoo and Koolan Islands. Pigeon Heritage Trail, from Derby to Windjana Gorge and Tunnel Creek Na-tional Park, following adventures of Pigeon, Aboriginal outlaw active in 1890s; details from tourist centre. **Tourist information:** 1 Clarendon St; (091) 91 1426. **Accommo-dation:** 3 hotels, 1 caravan/camping park. **See also:** The Kimberley.
MAP REF. 327 M5

Dongara–Port Denison
Population 1496
These quiet towns are on the coast 359 km north of Perth. Dongara has beaches, reef-enclosed bays and an abundance of delicious rock-lobster. There is good fishing in the waters around Port Denison, which also has swimming and golf. **Of interest:** Fisherman's Lookout, near Leander Point, Port Denison, gives panoramic views of harbour. Historic buildings include Anglican rectory and church, and old police station in Waldeck St; Royal Steam Flour Mill (1894)), the 'Old Mill', on Brand Hwy; and Russ Cottage (1870), St Dominicks Rd. Restaurant, blacksmith's shop and bed and breakfast accommodation in historic cottages on Brand Hwy. Dongara's main street, Moreton Tce, shaded by huge 85-year-old Moreton Bay fig trees.Dongara Cemetery, Dodd St; headstones date back to 1874. heritage Trail from Old Mill to Russ Cottage; details from tourist centre. Blessing of the Fleet held in Nov. **In the area:** Eneabba, 81 km south of Dongara; mineral sand mining, with large concentrations of rutile. South-west of Eneabba, holiday towns of Leeman (38 km) and Green Head (50 km). Historic hamlet of Greenough, 40 km north; deer and emu park in Georgina Rd. **Tourist information:** Old Police Station Building, 5 Waldeck St; (099) 27 1404. **Accommodation:** 2 hotels, 1 motel, 3 caravan/camping parks.
MAP REF. 322 B7, 324 D7

Donnybrook
Population 1352
The township of Donnybrook, the home of the Granny Smith apple, is at the heart of the oldest apple-growing area in WA, 210 km south of Perth. Gold was discovered here in 1897, but it was mined for only four years. Donnybrook stone has been used in construction state-wide. The town's biennial Apple Festival is held at Easter. **Of interest:** On South West Hwy, Anchor and Hope Inn (1865), once staging-post for mail-coaches, and Big Apple Deer Park; open daily. Rotary Lookout, Trigg St. Arboretum, junction Irishtown Rd and South West Hwy. Trigwell Place, near river at southern end of town; picnic area with barbecues and children's playground. **In the area:** Glen Merryn Dam, 30 km north-east; picnic area with barbecues. At Balingup, 20 km south: Old Cheese Factory, now art and craft centre; Tinderbox, for herbs and herbal remedies; Bailiwick woodwork; and, 2 km from town, Golden Valley Tree Park. Scenic drives; details from tourist centre. **Tourist information:** 'Old' Railway Station; (097) 31 1720. **Accommodation:** 2 hotels, 1 motel, 1 caravan/camping park. **See also:** The South-west.
MAP REF. 320 F5, 324 E12

Dumbleyung
Population 284
Dumbleyung lies in the central south of WA, 217 km east of Bunbury and 224 km north of Albany. **In the area:** Lake Dumbleyung, 10 km west, where Donald Campbell established a new world water-speed record in 1964; area ideal for swimming, boating, birdwatching and picnicking.Wheatbelt Wildflower Drive, beginning at Kukerin, 39 km east; includes Tarin Rock Nature Reserve. Kukerin Tracmach Vintage Fair held in Sept.–Oct. Historic Schools Heritage Trails, 4 scenic drives; details from tourist centre. **Tourist information:** Shire Offices, Harvey St; (098) 63 4012. **Accommodation:** 1 hotel, 1 caravan/camping park.
MAP REF. 321 N4, 324 G11

Dunsborough
Population 817
Dunsborough is a quiet town on Geographe Bay, west of Busselton, popular because of its fine beaches. **Of interest:** Greenacres, shell museum, off Naturaliste Tce. Bush Cottage Markets, Commonage Rd. Hutchings Museum, Gifford Rd. Moonshine Brewery and Rivendell Gardens, both in Wildwood Rd. **In the area:** Bannamah Wildlife Park, 2 km west. Yallingup Caves and surfing beach, 8 km west. Gunyulgup Galleries, 4 km south of Yallingup. Cape Naturaliste Lighthouse, 13 km north; several walking tracks in area. Torpedo Rock, 10 km west; Sugarloaf Rock, 12 km north; Canal Rocks, 15 km south-west. Good beaches at Meelup, 5 km north; Eagle Bay, 8 km north; and Bunker Bay, 12 km north. Scuba-diving, snorkelling, canoeing; 4WD day tours, wildflower tours, winery and craft tours, and day trips to Pemberton; details from tourist centre. **Tourist information:** Naturaliste Tce; (097) 55 3517. **Accommodation**: 1 hotel, 1 motel, 1 caravan/camping park.
MAP REF. 320 C5

Dwellingup
Population 344
This quiet little town is 24 km south-east of Pinjarra and 109 km from Perth. The road into Dwellingup offers panoramic views of the Indian Ocean and Peel Inlet. The impressive jarrah forests nearby supply the local timber-mill and bauxite is mined in the area. **Of interest:** Real country-style meals in friendly Dwellingup Community Hotel, Marrinup St. Hotham Valley Tourist Railway runs old-style steam train between Pinjarra and Dwellingup (Sun., May–Oct.). **Tourist information:** Murray Tourist Centre, George St, Pinjarra; (09) 531 1438. **Accommodation:** 1 hotel.
MAP REF. 318 G12, 324 F11

Esperance
Population 6440
Wide sandy beaches, scenic coastline and the offshore islands of the Recherche Archipelago are all attractions of Esperance, on the south coast of WA. The town, 720 km from Perth, via Wagin, is both the port and service centre for the highly productive agricultural and pastoral hinterland. The first permanent settlers came in 1863. The town boomed during the 1890s as port for the goldfields, but it was not until the 1950s, when scientists realised that the heath plains could be transformed into fertile pasture and farming country, that the town's development began in earnest. **Of interest:** Municipal Museum, Dempster St; collection of machinery, furniture and farm equipment from yesteryear, also display of Skylab, which fell to earth over Esperance in 1979. Public Library, Windich St; collection of books on history of Esperance. Art and craft centre on the Esplanade. Fishing and seal watching from Tanker Jetty. **In the area:** Rotary Lookout, or Wireless Hill, 2 km west, offers excellent panoramas of bay, township and farmlands. Pink Lake, 5 km west; dense saltwater lake that really is pink. Twilight Bay, 12 km west, on tourist loop, for swimming and fishing, and nearby Picnic Cove, with sheltered swimming-beach. Views of bay and islands from Observatory Point and Lookout, 17 km west. The Recherche Archipelago, or Bay of Isles, consists of almost 100 small unspoiled islands off Esperance which are a haven for native fauna. Launch cruises to Gull, Button, Charlie and other islands. Regular cruises during summer and other holiday periods to Woody Island, south-east of Esperance (50 min. by boat), which has been developed as a tourist attraction and has overnight camping facilities. Parrot Farm, 15 km east, on Fisheries Rd. Cape Le Grand National Park, 56 km east, with spectacular coastline and many attractive beaches; scenic walks and beautiful wildflowers for which the region is famous. Magnificent view from Frenchmans Peak, in park. Cape Arid National Park, 140 km east, popular with fishermen, campers and four-wheel-drivers. **Tourist information:** Museum Village, Dempster St; (090) 71 2330. **Accommodation:** 3 hotels, 4 motels, 7 caravan/camping parks. **See also:** Crossing the Nullarbor.
MAP REF. 325 K12

Eucla
Population 30
Eucla is just 12 km from the WA/SA border, on the Eyre Hwy. **Of interest:** Guided fishing trips available. **In the area:** A cross on an escarpment overlooking the ocean and the sand-covered ruins of the old telegraph station and former town site, 5 km south of present town, is dedicated to all Eyre Hwy travellers and

is illuminated at night. The highway westward from Eucla descends to the coastal plain via Eucla Pass. Midway down the Pass (about 200 m) a track to the left leads to the old town site and ruins amongst the sand dunes. **Tourist information:** Roadhouse; (090) 39 3468. **Accommodation:** 1 motel, 1 caravan/camping park. **See also:** Crossing the Nullarbor.
MAP REF. 270 A11, 325 Q9

Exmouth   Population 3514

Exmouth is one of the newest towns in Australia and was founded in 1967 as a support town for the US Naval Communications station. The station, a joint USN/RAN facility run by a civilian contractor, is the main source of employment for people living in Exmouth. The American and Australian communities are fully integrated and the town has many modern sporting and community facilities. Excellent year-round fishing and its beaches has made Exmouth a main tourist destination. The town is situated on the north-eastern side of North West Cape, which juts out north from the mainland. The Cape is the nearest point in Australia to the continental shelf, so there is an abundance of fish and other marine life in the surrounding waters. **Of interest:** Exmouth House of Dolls, Craft St. Ocean Exhibits Museum, Pellew St. **In the area:** Beaches for swimming, snorkelling, fishing. Shothole Canyon Rd provides easy access into one of many spectacular gorges in Cape Range National Park; park's Milyering Visitor Centre, 52 km south-west. Charles Knife Canyon Rd has picnic spots, scenic lookouts and walking-trail. Prawn fishery, 23 km south; inspections during season early May–late Oct. Learmonth RAAF base, 34 km south. Charter fishing available at Bundegi Beach jetty, 14 km north. Panoramic views from Vlaming Head Lighthouse, 19 km north; guided tours. Wreck of SS Mildura nearby. Ningaloo Marine Park, 14 km west of Cape, largest coral reef in WA; 500 species of fish and 220 species of reef-building corals. Daily coral-viewing trips from both Exmouth and Coral Bay. Safari tours of Cape. Lightfoot Heritage Trail; details from tourist centre. **Tourist information:** Thew St; (099) 49 1176. **Accommodation:** 2 motels, 4 caravan/camping parks.
MAP REF. 326 C10

Fitzroy Crossing   Population 1028

In the Kimberley, where the road north crosses the Fitzroy River, is the settlement of Fitzroy Crossing, 260 km inland from Derby. Once a sleepy little hamlet, the last few years have seen unprecedented growth of the town due to Aboriginal settlement, mining by BHP at Cadjebut, 50 km east, and an increase in the number of visitors attracted by the nearby Geikie Gorge National Park. **In the area:** Picturesque waterholes, which support abundance of fish and other wildlife. Magnificent Geikie Gorge, 20 km north-east; sharks, sawfish and stingrays, which have adapted themselves to fresh water, abound, as do barramundi and freshwater crocodiles. Regular boat-trips available during tourist season. Fitzroy River Lodge tourist complex on Great Northern Hwy. **Tourist information:** Fitzroy River Lodge; (091) 91 5141. **Accommodation:** 1 hotel, 1 motel, 3 caravan/camping parks.
MAP REF. 327 O6

Fremantle   Population 24 000

The largest port in the state, and known as the 'Western Gateway to Australia', Fremantle is a bustling city 19 km south of Perth. It is a city of contrasts, with galleries and museums, beautiful sandy white beaches and many historic buildings as a reminder of the city's heritage. Captain Charles Fremantle arrived in May 1829 to take possession of 'the whole of the west coast of New Holland', and was followed one month later by Captain James Stirling, who arrived with a small group of settlers to found the first colony in Australia made up entirely of free settlers. The engineer C. Y. O'Connor, who instigated the Goldfields Water Scheme, was also responsible for building the artificial harbour which turned Fremantle into an important port. The city was the first stop for many migrants arriving in Australia and as a result has a large European population. With its old-world charm and colourful cosmopolitan culture, Fremantle is one of the most fascinating port cities in the world. **Of interest:** Many coffee shops and restaurants in South Terrace–Cappucino Strip. Maritime Museum, Cliff St, built in 1860s and fine example of colonial Gothic architecture. Fremantle Museum and Arts Centre, Finnerty St; during summer, courtyard used for musical performances. Sails of the Century boat museum on Victoria Quay, not far from Maritime Museum. Energy Museum, Parry St. Film and Television Institute, Adelaide St. Birukmarri Aboriginal Art Gallery, High St. Round House (1830), end of High St, oldest building in WA; twelve-sided structure, constructed as gaol. Joan Campbell's Pottery Workshop, near The Round House, in converted boat-shed. Magnificent Samson House (1900), cnr Ellen and Ord Sts; guided tours. Shell Museum, Beach St. Spare Parts Puppet Theatre, Short St; permanent puppet display and regular performances. Endeavour Replica, Mews Rd. Fremantle Gaol (1851–59), forbidding building of local stone; no longer in use as prison and open to visitors. Fremantle Prison Museum, with displays recording penal system in WA, adjacent to prison. Warders' Quarters, Henderson St; Georgian terrace still used by prison. Old Customs House (1853), Cliff St, also in Georgian style. St John's Church and Square (1882). Gracious Town Hall in Kings Square, cnr William and Adelaide Sts; opened in 1887. Quaint old building at 5 Mouat St, which originally housed German Consulate and shipping offices. Port Authority Building, Cliff St; Fremantle's tallest building, with panoramic views from roof viewing area. Impressive Fremantle Markets, Henderson St; range of food, including delicious seafoods, handcrafts, antiques, clothing and souvenirs. Adjacent to Marine Tce and the Esplanade, modern Success Yacht Harbour marina facilities developed for first Australian defence of the America's Cup, yachting's most prestigious trophy. Fremantle's large fishing fleet, which works Australia's most valuable fishing grounds (mainly lobster), and its considerable Italian community give the city a Mediterranean flavour, with sidewalk cafes and excellent restaurants. Sail & Anchor hotel on South Tce, Australia's first pub brewery, serves specialty beers. Fremantle Crocodile Park at Fishing Boat Harbour, off Mews Rd; both saltwater and smaller freshwater species. Swimming at Port, Leighton and South Beaches. Ferries to Rottnest Island, 20 km west, leave from wharf daily; charter boats to Rottnest also available. Daily 'tram' tours; details from tourist centre. **Tourist information:** Town Hall Shop, St John's Sq., High St; (09) 430 2346. **Accommodation:** 7 hotels, 2 hotel/motels, 2 motels, 1 caravan park.
MAP REF. 316 C8, 318 F9, 324 E10

Gascoyne Junction   Population 45

Located 178 km east of Carnarvon, at the junction of the Gascoyne and Lyons Rivers, the town is the administration centre for the Shire of Upper Gascoyne. The old-fashioned pub is a good-rest stop before enjoying the many scenic attractions of the Kennedy Ranges, 60 km north. **Tourist information:** Carnarvon District Tourist Bureau, Robinson St, Carnarvon; (099) 41 1146. **Accommodation:** 1 hotel.
MAP REF. 324 D2

Geraldton   Population 21 726

The key port and administration centre for the Midwest region, Geraldton is 424 km north of Perth on Champion Bay. A year-round sunny climate, combined with a mild winter, makes it one of the state's most popular holiday resorts. The city itself is flourishing, with a modern shopping centre, interesting museums and excellent accommodation. The beaches are sandy and white and the fishing is good.

THE GOLDFIELDS

The land that boasted the first gold-mining boom in Western Australia is almost as forbidding as that of the far north-west. This is the vast region to the east of Perth that contains the famous towns of Kalgoorlie–Boulder, Coolgardie, Norseman, Kambalda, Leonora, Gwalia and Laverton. Although some towns, like Gwalia, are colourful but nearly deserted reminders of the great rush days, all are once again active gold-mining areas, with Kalgoorlie–Boulder the main centre.

The western gold-rush began in 1892 with strikes around **Coolgardie**. The town sprang up from nowhere and enjoyed a boisterous but short life. With great optimism diggers flocked to the area. In 1900 there were 15 000 people, twenty-three hotels and six banks. The main street was wide enough for camel trains to turn. Today Coolgardie has a population of close to 1000 and is a popular tourist destination. The grand old court-house, built at the height of the boom, is used as a museum and has a fascinating record of life on the fields as it once was.

In 1893 the Irishman Paddy Hannan made an even bigger strike of gold at **Kalgoorlie**. The area became known as the Golden Mile, reputedly the richest square mile in the world. Kalgoorlie, and its twin town Boulder boasted a population of 30 000 in 1902. Magnificent wide streets and impressive, stately stone buildings were erected.

Bayley Street, Coolgardie

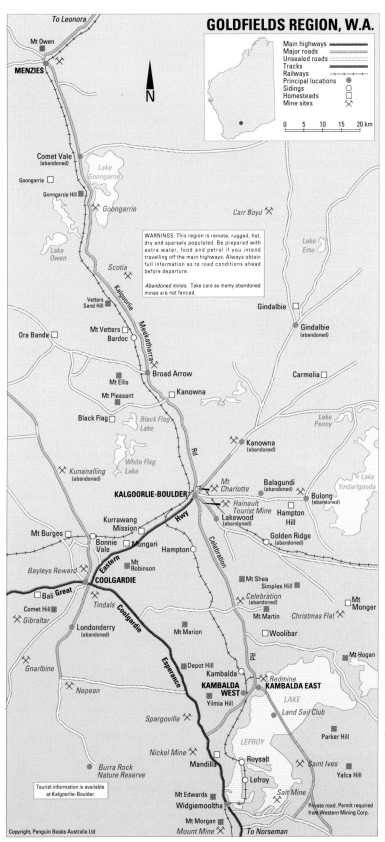

GOLDFIELDS REGION, W.A.

Main highways
Major roads
Unsealed roads
Tracks
Railways
Principal locations
Sidings
Homesteads
Mine sites

0   5   10   15   20 km

WARNINGS: This region is remote, rugged, hot, dry and sparsely populated. Be prepared with extra water, food and petrol if you intend travelling off the main highways. Always obtain full information as to road conditions ahead before departure.

Abandoned mines. Take care as many abandoned mines are not fenced.

Tourist information is available at Kalgoorlie-Boulder

Kalgoorlie–Boulder, is a prosperous gold-mining centre, producing seventy per cent of the gold mined in Australia. At Hannans North Historical Mining Complex visitors can don a hard hat and cap lamp and go below the surface, where experienced miner guides explain in graphic detail the hardships endured by the miners in their search for gold. To the south is **Kambalda**, a new boom town, founded on rich nickel deposits, and noted for its modern facilities and tree-lined streets.

Most of the towns north of Kalgoorlie are alive again due to the current gold-mining operations. Deep underground mines are being replaced by massive open-cuts, which in turn create their own adjacent table-top mountains of overburden. The little town of **Menzies** continues as a pastoral and mining town, a shadow of its former self. The superbly renovated, stately old Gwalia Hotel just outside **Leonora** is one of the few buildings left in what was once one of the state's most prosperous gold-mining centres. Herbert Hoover, later President of the United States, was manager of the Sons of Gwalia mine in 1897.

Kanowna once boasted a population of 12 000. Now all that remains is old and new mine-workings, and historic markers describing what used to be. Siberia, Broad Arrow, Niagara and Bulong are the exotic names of some of the towns that flourished and died in a few short years. Nevertheless, mining is once again active in most of these areas, although the workers live in nearby towns.

Kalgoorlie goldmines

Rich agricultural land surrounds Geraldton and the district is noted for its beautiful spring wildflowers and picturesque countryside. The Houtman Abrolhos Islands, which were first sighted and named in the sixteenth century, lie 64 km off the coast and are used mainly as a base for rock-lobster fishermen. **Of interest:** St Francis Xavier Cathedral, Cathedral Ave, designed by Mons. John C. Hawes, architect responsible for some fine buildings in and around Geraldton. Sir John Forrest Memorial, Marine Tce. Geraldton Museum (includes Maritime Display building and Old Railway building), Marine Tce; collection of earthenware pots and wine-vessels, bronze cannon, coins and other relics from shipwrecks off coast. Queens Park Theatre (1922), Cathedral Ave, surrounded by gardens. Art Gallery, cnr Durlacher St and Chapman Rd. Old Gaol Craft Centre, Bill Sewell Complex, Chapman Rd. Tourist Lookout and Wishing Well on Waverley Heights, Brede St, for panoramic views. Point Moore Lighthouse (1878), Willcock Dr. Fishing is popular and many varieties can be caught; town's breakwater is good location. At Fisherman's Wharf, during season (from mid-Nov. to end of June), watch huge hauls of lobster being unloaded. Geraldton–Midwest Sunshine Festival held in spring. **In the area:** Good fishing at Sunset Beach, 6 km north; fishing and surfing at Drummond Cove, 10 km north; and mouth of Greenough River, 10 km south. Greenough River also favourite place for picnics and has safe swimming for children. Greenough hamlet, 24 km south; National Trust-restored village preserved to look as it did in 1880s; guided tours. Ellendale Bluffs and Pool, 45 km south-east; permanent waterhole at base of steep rock-face. Chapman Valley, 35 km north-east; farming district with brilliant wildflower displays in spring. From Mill's Park Lookout, on Waggrakine Cutting, 15 km north-east; views over Moresby Range and coastal plain towards Geraldton. Kalbarri National Park, 170 km north. The sheer coastal rock-faces and deep gorges of the Murchison River, at Kalbarri, 164 km north, are stunningly beautiful. Farm holidays available near Badgingarra, 250 km south, halfway between Geraldton and Perth. Geraldton Heritage Trail; details from tourist centre. **Tourist information:** Bill Sewell Community Recreation Complex, cnr Bayley St and Chapman Rd; (099) 21 3999. **Accommodation:** 9 hotels, 5 motels, 5 caravan/camping parks.
MAP REF. 322 A5, 324 D6

Gingin   Population 420
Situated 83 km north of Perth and 30 km from the coast, Gingin is a mainly sheep, wheat and cattle farming centre. As an interesting day-trip from Perth, it offers alternative return trips touring coastal centres or inland via the scenic Chittering Valley. The town is built around a loop of Gingin Brook, which rises from springs not far from town and flows strongly all year round. **Of interest:** Gingin has the charm and appeal of an English village and offers some fine examples of traditional Australian architecture, including St Luke's Anglican Church (1860s), Granville (1871), Uniting Church (1868) and Dewar's House (1886), all in Weld St; and Philbey's Cottage (1906), Brockman St. **In the area:** At Bullsbrook, 30 km south: the Maze and Bullsbrook Antiques and Cottage Crafts. At Bindoon, 24 km east: Neroni Wines and Chittering Valley Estate, Rosecliff Gardens and Kay Road Art and Craft Gallery. At Lower Chittering, 30 km south-east: Golden Grove Citrus Orchard and Aussie Yarns. **Tourist information:** Shire Offices, 7 Brockman St; (09) 575 2211. **Accommodation:** 1 hotel, 1 caravan/camping park.
MAP REF. 318 F6, 324 E9

Guilderton   Population 385
Guilderton is at the mouth of the Moore River, 94 km from Perth, and is a popular day-trip and holiday destination. There is excellent fishing in both the river and the sea and safe swimming for children. Many Dutch relics have been found here, possibly from the wreck of the Gilt Dragon in 1656. **In the area:** Seabird, 20 km north, small but growing fishing village offering 'away from it all' tranquillity with safe beach and ample recreational options. Ledge Point, 28 km north, centre built around fishing industry, providing activities for all age groups; sporting facilities, safe swimming and boating, and picnic facilities complement relaxed lifestyle and friendly atmosphere of this holiday spot. World-famous Ledge Point to Lancelin windsurfing classic held in Jan. **Tourist information:** Shire Offices, 7 Brockman St, Gingin; (09) 575 2211. **Accommodation:** 1 caravan/camping park.
MAP REF. 318 E5

Halls Creek   Population 1182
In the heart of the Kimberley, 2832 km from Perth, at the edge of the Great Sandy Desert, is Halls Creek, site of WA's first gold discovery in 1885. In the years from 1885 to 1887, 10 000 men came to the Kimberley fields in search of gold, then gradually drifted away, leaving 2000 on the diggings. Today the future of Halls Creek looks bright, as mineral exploration is still being carried out and the pastoral industry is being supported by steady beef prices. **Of interest:** Russian Jack Memorial, Thomas St, honours courage and endurance of

Kimberley pioneers. **In the area:** China Wall, natural quartz formation, 6 km north; picnic spot above creek. Prospecting at Old Halls Creek, 16 km east; mud-brick ruins of original settlement. Caroline Pool, off Duncan Rd, near old town site; picnic spot with swimming in wet season. Ruby Queen Mine, and Sawpit Gorge for fishing, swimming and picnicking, both 40 km south-east. Town also offers a relaxing staging-point for travellers who wish to visit such wonders as the Wolfe Creek Meteorite Crater, 148 km south (almost 1 km wide, 49 m deep and second largest meteorite crater in world), and Purnululu (Bungle Bungle) National Park, 165 km south-east. Aerial tours and 4WD safaris available. **Tourist information:** Great Northern Hwy; (091) 68 6262. **Accommodation:** 1 hotel, 1 motel, 1 caravan/ camping park. **See also:** The Kimberley.
MAP REF. 327 Q6

Harvey — Population 2498

The thriving town of Harvey is set amidst some of the finest agricultural country in Australia, 139 km south of Perth. Bordered by the Darling Range and the Indian Ocean, the fertile coastal plains make perfect dairying country. The town's irrigation storage dams, with their recreation areas, have become a popular tourist attraction. **Of interest:** J. Knowles' House and Store (1890), Harvey St, first business in Harvey; now museum. Next door, Harvey Historical Society Museum, housed in old Harvey railway station (1914). Harvey Fruit Bowl, site of town's famous 'Big Orange' Tourist Complex; train rides, wildlife park, restaurant and craft shop. Harvey Tourist and Interpretative Centre, South West Hwy; industry displays, including dairy industry in 'Moo Shoppe', and crafts. Harvey Internment Camp Memorial Shrine, South Coast Hwy, built by prisoners-of-war in 1940s; open for inspection. Harvey Show held in Oct. **In the area:** Harvey Weir, 3 km east, off Weir Rd. Jardup, restored home of Clarke family, early pioneers in district, 9 km east on road to Stirling Dam; art gallery, open Sun. Scenic drive (7 km) around north-west side of dam leads to Harvey Falls and Trout Ladder; popular fishing spot. Myalup and Binningup beaches, 25 km west, off Old Coast Rd, are wide and sandy, ideal for swimming, fishing and boating. Emu Tech Farm, Old Coast Rd, Myalup; restaurant and picnic area. Logue Brook Dam, 10 km north; popular venue for bushwalkers, swimmers, water-skiers and trout fishermen. Timbermill Workshop at Yarloop, 15 km north; proposed working exhibit, open for inspection. Yarloop Heritage Trail; details from Tourist Centre. Yalgorup National Park, 35 km north-west. Deer and Tourist Park at Wokalup, 4 km south, on South West Hwy; deer and native animals, restaurant, indoor barbecue and fresh fruit at fruit barn. Kemberton Industrial Park (SCM Chemicals), 18 km south; guided tours. **Tourist information:** South West Hwy; (097) 29 1122. **Accommodation:** 1 hotel, 2 caravan/camping parks. **See also:** The South-west.
MAP REF. 320 F2

Hopetoun — Population 271

Hopetoun is a peaceful holiday resort overlooking the Southern Ocean. The town is 59 km south of Ravensthorpe and offers some rugged but beautiful coastal scenery and wildflowers all year round. The town was once called Mary Anne Harbour and has a colourful history. **Of interest:** The beaches with their white sand, the sheltered bays and the excellent fishing are the main attractions. **In the area:** Dunn's Swamp, 5 km north, for picnics, bushwalking and bird-watching. Fitzgerald River National Park, 10 km west, features the Barrens, a series of rugged mountains, undulating sandplains and steep narrow gorges; Hamersley Inlet, within the park, is a scenic picnic spot. Take care fishing from rocks—king waves can roll in unexpectedly. **Tourist information:** Hardware and Tackle Store, Veal St; (098) 38 3088. **Accommodation:** 1 hotel, 1 caravan/camping park.
MAP REF. 324 I12

Hyden — Population under 200

Hyden is in the Shire of Kondinin, 351 km from Perth, in the eastern wheat-growing area of WA. **In the area:** The country is semi-arid, but has some fascinating rock formations nearby, the most famous of which is Wave Rock, 4 km east of Hyden, an incredible granite outcrop that rises 15 m high, like a giant wave about to break. Not a separate rock but an overhanging wall more than 100 m long, it is streaked with bands of colour from deep grey and ochres to rusty reds and a sandy grey, simulating the rolling movement of the sea. Studies have shown the rock to be 2700 million years old. Wildlife park, coffee shop and caravan park with chalets at Wave Rock. Pioneer Town, collection of Australiana, at base of rock. Lace collection (from 1600 to present) from many parts of world at Wave Rock Wildflower Shop. Other rock formations within walking distance of Wave Rock include Hippo's Yawn, The Falls and The Breakers. Aboriginal rock paintings at Mulka's Cave, 18 km north of Wave Rock; nearby is The Humps, another unusual granite formation. Signposted 72 km scenic tour introduces natural attractions of region. **Tourist information:** Wave Rock Wildflower Shop, Lynch St; (098) 80 5182. **Accommodation:** 1 hotel, 1 motel, 1 caravan/camping park.
MAP REF. 319 R11, 324 H10

Jurien — Population 730

On the shores of an attractive, sheltered bay between Perth and Geraldton, Jurien is important as a lobster-fishing centre. The town is also a growing holiday centre because of its magnificent safe swimming beaches, excellent climate and reputation as a fisherman's paradise. Jurien boat

St Catherine's Church, Greenough

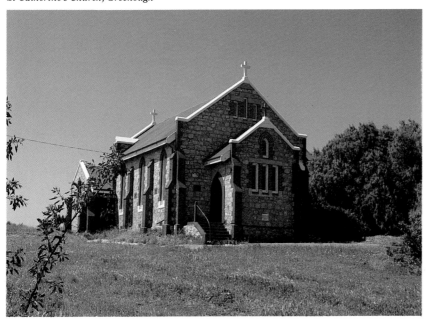

harbour, a 17.5 ha inland marina, offers excellent facilities for the boating enthusiast. **Of interest:** Tours of rock-lobster processing factory during fishing season. **In the area:** Cockleshell Gully, 31 km north, has great diversity of flora and fauna. Stockyard Gully National Park, 50 km north (4WD only); walk through Stockyard Gully Tunnel (300 m long), along winding underground creek; flashlight necessary. Spectacular sand dunes along coast. Nambung National Park, boundary 55 km south; check road conditions before leaving Jurien if taking coastal track; main, signposted route further inland recommended. The Pinnacles, further 17 km within park, thousands of spectacular calcified spires, around 30 000 years old, scattered over some 400 ha of multi-coloured sand; guided tours by coach daily. Waddi Farms, Koonah Rd, Badgingarra, 60 km south-east; displays of wildflowers, emu farm, native gardens, shop and restaurant; complex sited off Brand Hwy. **Tourist information:** Lot 124, Bashford St; (096) 52 1020. **Accommodation:** 1 hotel, 1 motel, 1 caravan/ camping park. MAP REF. 322 C12, 324 D8

Kalbarri   Population 2898

This popular holiday resort is ideally located between Geraldton and Carnarvon, 661 km north of Perth. The town's picturesque setting on the estuary of the Murchison River, its year-round sunny climate and the spectacular gorges of the river running through the Kalbarri National Park attract a growing number of tourists each year. Kalbarri is also renowned for its excellent fishing and the brilliance and beauty of more than 500 species of wildflowers which grow in the district. **Of interest:** Kalflora, off Ajana Rd, with wide range of Kalbarri wildflowers. In Grey St: Doll and Marine Museum, Fantasy Land and Gemstone Mine. Echoes Restaurant, Porter St, overlooking river; fully licensed and serves fresh seafood. Kalbarri Entertainment Centre, Porter St; bicycles for hire. **In the area:** Kalbarri National Park, large area of magnificent virgin bushland surrounding town; picnic and barbecue facilities, but camping not permitted. Horse-riding at Kalbarri Big River Ranch, 3 km east, within park. Also within park, 11 km east, spectacular Murchison River gorges with abundance of wildlife and native flora; canoe safaris and abseiling adventure tours available. Coach tours of park and joy flights over gorges available. Red Bluff, 4 km south of town, ideal for swimming, fishing and rock-climbing. Rainbow Jungle and Tropical Bird Park, 4 km south. Cairn at Wittecarra Creek, 4 km south, marks what is believed to be site of first permanent landing of white men in Australia: two Dutch-

men sent ashore for their part in *Batavia* mutiny in 1629. Meanarra Lookout, 7 km south-east. Z Bend and The Loop lookouts, 30 km north-east. Coastal gorges, with precipitous red cliffs dropping to the Indian Ocean below, are a majestic sight throughout the area; coach tours and joy flights available. **Tourist information:** Allen Community Centre, Grey St; (099) 37 1104. **Accommodation:** 1 hotel, 3 motels, 5 caravan/camping parks. MAP REF. 324 C5

Kalgoorlie–Boulder

Population 22 232

At the heart of WA's largest gold-mining area is the city of Kalgoorlie–Boulder, centred on the famous Golden Mile, reputed to be the richest square mile in the world. Over 1300 tonnes of gold have been mined from this small area. Paddy Hannan discovered gold in 1893 and the rush began. By 1902 the population was 30 000 and there were 93 hotels operating. Men made fortunes overnight and the impressive stone buildings and magnificent wide streets recall the town's fabulous boom past. Rather than walk daily to the Great Boulder Mine, the miners set up their tents on the Golden Mile, which soon grew into the town of Boulder. Kalgoorlie is 597 km east of Perth. One of the greatest difficulties facing the miners in this semi-desert area was lack of water. Determination and the brilliant scheme initiated by the engineer C. Y. O'Connor saved the day. A pipeline was established, carrying water an incredible 563 km from a reservoir near Perth. The water began flowing in 1903. Gold-mining continues, with renewed vigour now that the price of gold has risen. The Kalgoorlie–Boulder region is also an important pastoral district, with high-quality wool being produced. **Of interest:** Some fine examples of early Australian architecture to be seen. Buildings worthy of note in Hannan St include: Exchange and Palace Hotels, Australia House, Government Buildings and Kalgoorlie Post Office. Distinctive Kalgoorlie Town Hall, (1908) has impressive staircase and display of paintings by local artists. Museum of the Goldfields in former British Arms Hotel (1899), with fascinating display recalling heyday of gold-rush boom. Goldfields Aboriginal Art Gallery next to museum. Close to museum is Paddy Hannan's Tree, Outreach Tce, marking spot where gold was first found in Kalgoorlie. Also in Hannan St, bronze statue of Paddy Hannan. School of Mines Museum, Egan St; world-class display, including most of minerals found in WA. Big Pit Lookout at Finiston, on

Boulder Block Rd. Hannans North Historical mining Complex, Broad Arrow Dr; underground and surface tours, and gold pouring demonstrations. Take care in area: many dangerous open shafts, Super Pit Lookout, Lyne St; open daily. Boulder Town Hall (1908), Burt St, with permanent art exhibit. Goldfields War Museum, Burt St. Eastern Goldfields Historical Museum, Burt St, in Boulder railway station. Picturesque Cornwall Hotel (1898), Chesapeake St. Royal Flying Doctor Base, Killarney St, serves one of largest areas in Australia, tours weekdays. Hammond Park, Lyall St; wildlife sanctuary with small lake and scale model of Bavarian castle. Mt Charlotte Reservoir and Lookout, off Sutherland St; storage for Kalgoorlie's vital fresh-water supply. The Loop Line, tourist railway line around the Golden Mile. **In the area:** Kalgoorlie–Boulder is an ideal base from which to visit old gold-mining towns, some now ghost towns, in the district. Coolgardie (37 km south-west), Broad Arrow (38 km north), Ora Banda (54 km north), Kookynie (200 km north) and Leonora–Gwalia (235 km north) are all within a day's drive and all are active again. WA's only two-up school, 7 km north of Kalgoorlie, on eastern side of road to Menzies. Eastern Goldfields Heritage Trail; details from tourist centre. **Tourist information:** 250 Hannan St, Kalgoorlie; (090) 21 1966. **Accommodation:** Kalgoorlie; 13 hotels, 9 motels, 4 caravan/camping parks. Boulder, 8 hotels, 2 motels, 6 caravan/ camping parks. **See also:** Crossing the Nullarbor; The Goldfields. MAP REF. 325 J8

Kambalda   Population 3519

Kambalda's gold-mining history lasted from 1897 to 1906, during which time 30 000 ounces of gold were produced. When the gold petered out, so did the town. In 1966, however, rich nickel deposits were discovered and the town has since boomed. Today Kambalda, 634 km east of Perth, consists of two well-planned centres (Kambalda East and Kambalda West), several kilometres apart, and is noted for its environmental protection policy. **Of interest:** Several pleasant picnic areas in centre of town. Red Hill Lookout, off Gordon Adams Rd; excellent views of area, including vast Lake Lefroy. **In the area:** Land-yachting on salt bed of lake. Defiance Open Cut Gold Mine Lookout, 20 km south; entry permit necessary. Eastern Goldfields Heritage Trail; details from tourist centre. **Tourist information:** Irish Mulga Dr, Kambalda West; (090) 27 1446. **Accommodation:** 1 hotel, 1 caravan/camping park. **See also:** The Goldfields. MAP REF. 325 J9

Karratha
Population 9533

Karratha was established on Nickel Bay in 1968 as a result of the continuing development of the Hamersley Iron Project, when there was a lack of suitable land for expansion at Dampier and a need for a regional centre was emerging. The town's growth gained even greater momentum with the development by Woodside Petroleum of the immense off-shore gas reserve on the North West Shelf and Karratha now has the best service facilities in the North-west. Karratha's near to perfect warm winter temperatures make it just the place for visitors to escape the southern cold and soak up the sun in a clean, modern town. **Of interest:** Largest shopping centre outside Perth. Swimming, boating; golf, bowls. Views from TV Hill Lookout, Millstream Rd. Safari tours of Pilbara outback available. Jaburara Heritage Trail (3.5 km) includes sites of Aboriginal rock carvings; details from tourist centre. Also Chichester Range Camel Trail. **Tourist information:** Caravan Park, Rosemary Rd; (091) 44 4600. **Accommodation:** 2 motels, 3 caravan/camping parks. **See also:** The Hamersley Range; The Pilbara.
MAP REF. 326 F9

Katanning
Population 3771

A thriving township 186 km north of Albany, Katanning's well-planned streets have some impressive Victorian buildings. The countryside is given over to grain-growing and pastoral activities, and is noted for its fine merino sheep. **Of interest:** Old Mill Museum (1889), cnr Clive St and Austral Tce; outstanding display of vintage roller flour-milling process. Majestic Kobeelya mansion (1902), Brownie St. All Ages Playground, Clive St; miniature steam railway with 600 m of track. Old Winery, Andrews Rd. Largest country-based sheep-selling facility in WA, Dore St; regular sales throughout year. Meatworks on Wagin Rd; guided tours. Katanning Show held in Oct. **In the area:** Lakes surrounding town offer swimming, boating and water-skiing. Stirling Range National Park, 80 km south. Katanning–Piesse Heritage Trail; details from tourist centre. **Tourist information:** Cnr Austral Tce and Clive St; (098) 21 2634. **Accommodation:** 3 hotels, 2 motels, 2 caravan/ camping parks. **See also:** The Great Southern.
MAP REF. 321 M6, 324 G12

Kojonup
Population 986

Situated on the Albany Hwy, 154 km north of Albany, Kojonup takes its name from the Aboriginal word 'Kodja', meaning 'stone axe'. In 1837, when surveying the road from Albany to the newly established Swan River settlement, Alfred Hillman was guided to the Kojonup Spring by local Aborigines. Later a military outpost was set up on the site, and this marked the beginning of the town. **Of interest:** Kojonup Spring and picnic area. Military Barracks Museum (1845), Barracks Pl. Elverd's Cottage (1850s), Soldier Rd; display of tools and implements of early years. Sundial in Hillman Park, on Albany Hwy. Walsh's Cattle Complex, Broomehill Rd. **In the area:** Wide variety of flora (including more than 60 species of orchids) and fauna (especially birds). Yeedabirrup Rock, 10 km east, one of many granite monoliths in area. **Tourist information:** Benn Pde; (098) 31 1686. **Accommodation:** 1 hotel, 1 hotel/motel, 1 motel, 1 caravan/camping park.
MAP REF. 321 K6, 324 G12

Kondinin
Population 329

The small settlement of Kondinin is 278 km east of Perth. There are sheep stud-farms nearby. **In the area:** Kondinin Lake, 8 km west, popular with water-skiing and yachting enthusiasts. **Accommodation:** 1 hotel, 1 motel, 1 caravan/camping park.
MAP REF. 319 P11, 324 G10

Kulin
Population 296

A centre for the sheep and grain-growing farms of the district, Kulin lies 283 km south-east of Perth. **Of interest:** The silvery Macrocarpa flowering gums are a spectacular feature of the local flora. **In the area:** Several species of native orchids in the bush. Jilakin Rock and Lake, 18 km east. Buckley's Breakaway (pit caused by granite decomposing to kaolin), 58 km east, has unusual coloured rock formations. Dragon Rocks Nature Reserve, 75 km east. **Tourist information:** Shire Offices, Johnston St; (098) 80 1204. **Accommodation:** 1 hotel, 1 caravan/camping park.
MAP REF. 319 O12

Kununurra
Population 3137

Kununurra is situated along Lake Kununurra on the Ord River, and holds the magnificent Hidden Valley National Park within its boundaries. The town supports several industries, including agriculture and mining. It is the major centre for the Argyle Diamond Mine (the largest diamond mine in the world) and the Ord River Irrigation area. **Of interest:** Ord River Festival, held in Aug.; includes float parade, rodeo, mardi gras, art and craft exhibitions and famous Ord Tiki Race and water-ski display. **In the area:** Warringarri Aboriginal Arts, 2 km north. Kelly's Knob Lookout, 3 km north; good vantage-point for viewing surrounding irrigated land. Hidden Valley National Park, 3 km east. Top Rockz Gallery, 10 km north. Ivanhoe Crossing, 13 km north, popular fishing spot. Kimberley Research Station, 16 km north. Cruises on Lake Kununurra and upstream past the Everglades and spectacular rugged gorges teeming with birdlife; beginning at Pump Station, 6 km west. Fishing is good, with barramundi a prized catch. Kununurra is a major starting-point for flights over and ground tours of the remarkably coloured and shaped Bungle Bungles, the Mitchell Plateau, Kalumburu and the untouched wilderness of the lower Ord River. At Lake Argyle, 72 km south in Carr Boyd Range, tourist village with hotel, caravan park and camping area. The lake, created by the Ord River Dam, contains nine times the volume of water in Sydney Harbour, transforming mountain peaks into rugged islands; it is one of the largest man-made lakes in the southern hemisphere. Middle Springs, 30 km north, and Black Rock Falls, 32 km north, are wet-season attractions. Durack Homestead, 70 km south, Argyle Downs, reconstructed homestead of Durack family, now pioneer museum and memorial to settlers of district. Sleeping Buddha/Elephant Rock, 10 km south. Pandanus Wildlife Park, Nimberlee Art Gallery and Zebra Rock Gallery, all 16 km south. Visits to Argyle Diamond Mine through Belray Diamond Tours. Charter flights and bush camping holidays available. **Tourist information:** Coolibah Dr; (091) 68 1177. **Accommodation:** Kununurra, 1 hotel, 2 motels, 5 caravan/camping parks. Lake Argyle, 1 private hotel, 1 caravan/camping park. **See also:** The Kimberley.
MAP REF. 327 R3

Kwinana
Population 11 798

Kwinana, 20 km south of the port of Fremantle, is a symbol of WA's rapidly developing industrial strength. Containing the BP Oil Refinery and Alcoa's Alumina Works, it is one of the nation's major industrial centres. Construction of the Kwinana complex, built on Cockburn Sound, one of the world's finest natural harbours, was begun in 1951. **Of interest:** Escorted group tours of local industries. Hull of the wrecked SS *Kwinana*, at Kwinana Beach, filled with cement and used as diving-platform for swimmers. **In the area:** Seaside resort city of Rockingham, 10 km south; cruises to offshore islands, Cape Peron (7 km west) and Penguin Island (10 km south-west). **Tourist information:** Rockingham and Districts Tourist Centre, 43 Kent St, Rockingham; (09) 592 3464. Accommodation: 1 motel.
MAP REF. 318 F10, 324 E10

Lake Grace
Population 625

A pleasant country town with first-class service facilities, situated 252 km north of

Albany in the peaceful rural countryside of the central south wheat-belt, Lake Grace derives its name from the shallow lake just west of the settlement. **Of interest:** Wildlife sanctuary, South Rd. Restored Inland Mission hospital, Stubbs St, last in WA. **In the area:** Lookout, 5 km west. Roe Heritage Trail; details from tourist centre. **Tourist information:** Lake Grace Newsagency; (098) 65 1029. **Accommodation:** 1 hotel, 3 motels, 1 caravan/camping park.
MAP REF. 321 Q2, 324 H11

Lake King   Population 10
A crossroads centre with a tavern and store, Lake King is a stopping-point for visitors travelling across arid country and through Frank Hann National Park to Norseman. **Of interest:** Interdenominational community church. **In the area:** Frank Hann National Park, 35 km east, with cross-section of heath flora of inland sandplain east of wheat-belt; park is traversed by Lake King–Norseman Rd, a formed gravel all-weather road. (No visitor facilities or supplies available between Lake King and Norseman.) Wildflowers in season. Hollands Track, early goldfields access route. Lakes in area include Lake King, 5 km west, and Lake Pallarup, 15 km south. Mt Madden cairn and lookout, 25 km south-east; picnic area. Pioneer well at Pallarup, 18 km south. **Tourist information:** Morgane St, Ravensthorpe; (098) 38 1163. **Accommodation:** 1 motel, 1 caravan park.
MAP REF. 324 I11

Lancelin   Population 724
This quiet little fishing town on the shores of Lancelin Bay is 127 km north of Perth. A natural breakwater extends from Edward Island to Lancelin Island, providing a safe harbour and a perfect breeding-ground for fish. There are rock-lobsters to be caught on the offshore reefs outside the bay. Lancelin is fast becoming known as the sailboard mecca of WA and affords a colourful spectacle each January with large numbers of international and interstate windsurfers taking part in the annual Ledge Pt ocean race. Long stretches of white sandy beaches provide an ideal swimming area for children. **Of interest:** Large off-road area for dune-buggies. WA dune-buggy championships held each Easter. **In the area:** Track (4WD only) leads 55 km north to Nambung National Park; check road conditions before setting out. **Tourist information:** The Centre Store, Gingin Rd; (096) 55 1054. **Accommodation:** 1 hotel, 1 hotel/motel, 2 caravan/camping parks.
MAP REF. 318 D4, 324 E9

THE HAMERSLEY RANGE

Stretching more than 300 kilometres through the heart of the mineral-rich Pilbara, the Hamersley Range forms a wild and magnificent panorama. The mountains slope gently up from the south to the flat-topped outcrops and Western Australia's highest peak, Mt Meharry. In the north they rise majestically from golden spinifex plains.

Although today the main activity in the area is centred on mining towns like **Tom Price**, **Paraburdoo** and **Newman**, visitors will find many other areas of interest.

Spectacular gorges have been carved by the waters of the Fortescue and other rivers. Precipitous walls of rock are layered in colours from reddish-brown to green and blue to pink in the changing light. The gorges are up to 100 metres deep, with waterflow at their base sometimes only one metre wide. Others have wide, crystal-clear pools reflecting the colour of the sky. Lush green vegetation thrives and the gorges are cool oases in the harsh climate.

Tom Price is a good base from which to explore the beauty of the Hamersley Ranges. The Wittenoom Gorge is a popular spot because it is so easily accessible. At Yampire Gorge is a watering-well once used by Afghani camel-drivers in the 1800s. The breathtaking Dales Gorge, approached through Yampire Gorge, is forty-five kilometres long. Here are found crystal-clear pools and the splendid Fort-escue Falls. The small but intriguing Rio Tinto Gorge and Hamersley Gorge with its folded bands of coloured rock are also quite beautiful.

One particularly enchanting oasis in the Hamersley Range area is the tropical paradise of Millstream-Chichester National Park, on the Fortescue River, inland from Roebourne. Thousands of birds flock to this delightful spot, where ferns, lilies, palms and rushes grow in abundance. There are two long, deep, natural pools. The springs produce over thirty-six million litres of water a day from an underground basin, which is piped to Roebourne, Dampier, Karr-atha, Wickham and Cape Lambert to supply much-needed water. In contrast to the Karajini (Hamersley Range) National Park, the scenery in the Millstream-Chichester National Park varies from magnificent views over the coastal plain to the deep permanent river-pools of tropical Millstream. This attractive spot offers excellent swimming conditions and pleasant camping areas.

The Hamersley Range is rugged, exciting country, and is enticing and often beautiful. Keep in mind, however, you are travelling in remote areas. Old roads are being improved and new ones constructed in an effort to open up one of the oldest areas in the world.

Kalamina Gorge and pool, Karijini (Hamersley Range) National Park

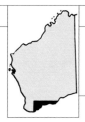

THE GREAT SOUTHERN

The Great Southern, also known as the Rainbow Coast, is bounded by a dramatically rugged coastline and the roaring Southern Ocean. During the winter months spectacular rainbows regularly occur. The coast gives way to an amazingly beautiful hinterland with rivers winding through forests, ancient mountain ranges and gentle valleys.

The district has an important historical heritage. **Albany** was the first town in Western Australia, established two and a half years before the Swan River colony. Major Edmund Lockyer landed here in 1826, to claim the western half of the continent as British territory.

Albany is the unofficial capital of the area, and it retains a charming English atmosphere from the colonial days. The town looks out over the magnificent blue waters of Princess Royal Harbour in King George Sound. Albany has a number of fine old homesteads, museums and galleries. There are numerous scenic drives around the coast, to the Gap, the Natural Bridge, and the Blowholes. There are also stretches of golden sand and secluded bays. The fishing is superb. Denmark,

Bluff Knoll, Stirling Range National Park

a holiday resort, lies on the banks of the tranquil Denmark River and the little village of Nornalup nestles near the Frankland River. Near Nornalup is the awe-inspiring Valley of the Giants, with tingle and karri trees towering over the tangled undergrowth and vivid splashes of wildflowers.

The Great Southern has a new industry — viticulture. The vineyards around **Mt Barker** have already produced award-winning wines. Mt Barker itself is the gateway to the Stirling and Porongurup mountain ranges, both within the con-

fines of national parks. The Porongurup Range has granite peaks dominating giant hardwood trees and a maze of wildflowers and creepers. There are many easy climbs, rewarded by panoramic views: Castle Rock, Howard's Peak and Devil's Slide are three of the most popular.

The high jagged peaks of the Stirling Range (the highest is Bluff Knoll at 1037 metres) tower over virgin bushland. From a distance, with the changing light, the vegetation varies from heathery shades to blues and reds. The peaks can sometimes be seen mysteriously shrouded in mist, and on occasions even tipped with snow.

There are more than 100 species of birds in the park and a great deal of native wildlife. Look for the beautiful wild orchids, Stirling banksia and mountain bells.

The inland area of the Great Southern is dotted with small, friendly towns including **Tambellup** with its fine colonial buildings and the thriving towns of Katanning, **Kojonup**, **Gnowangerup** and **Jerramungup**, are all surrounded by peaceful rural farmland.

Laverton   Population 1140

Laverton, situated 360 km north-east of Kalgoorlie, is a modern satellite town sustained by the nickel mine at Windarra, 28 km west, and gold-mining operations in the district. With an annual rainfall of only around 200 mm, summers are hot and dry; April to October are recommended times to travel. From Laverton to Ayers Rock (1200 km), all roads are unsealed, and the following points should be noted:

- Permit required to travel the Laverton–Yulara Road. Obtained from Aboriginal Planning Authority in Perth or Alice Springs.
- Water is scarce.
- Supplies are available at Laverton. Fuel and accommodation at Warburton and Giles.
- Check on road conditions at the Laverton Police Station: roads can be hazardous when wet.

Tourist Information: Shire Offices; (090) 31 1202. **Accommodation:** 1 hotel, 1 caravan/camping park. **See also:** The Goldfields.
MAP REF. 325 K6

Leonora   Population 1004

A busy mining-centre 240 km north of Kalgoorlie, Leonora has a typical Australian country-town appearance, with its wide streets and verandahed shop-fronts. The town is the centre-point of and railhead for the north-eastern goldfields, with nickel, copper and gold-mines to the north and east (at Laverton, 120 km north-east, and Leinster, 134 km north-west). **In the area:** Small gold-mining town of Menzies, 110 km south. Most of the country is flat mulga scrub, but after good rains there are brilliant wildflowers to be seen in August and early September. Leonora has three major gold-producers on its doorstep, including the famous Sons of Gwalia. The township of Gwalia, 2 km south, has an impressive museum that captures the miners' lifestyle; walk the 1 km Heritage Trail. Malcolm, 20 km north-east, good picnic spot, and Malcolm Dam. Old mine workings and ghost town of Kookynie, 92 km south-east; the Grand Hotel still offers a warm welcome. **Tourist information:** Shire Offices; (090) 37 6044. **Accommodation:** 2 hotels, 1

motel, 1 caravan/ camping park. **See also:** The Goldfields.
MAP REF. 325 J6

Madura   Population under 20

The Hampton Tablelands form a backdrop to Madura, 195 km from the WA/SA border, on the Eyre Hwy. The settlement dates back to 1876 when horses for the Indian Army were bred here. **Tourist information:** Roadhouse; (090) 39 3464. **Accommodation:** 1 motel, 1 caravan/ camping park. **See also:** Crossing the Nullarbor.
MAP REF. 325 O10

Mandurah   Population 18 016

The popular holiday resort of Mandurah is located on the coast only 72 km south of Perth. The Murray, Serpentine and Harvey Rivers meet here, forming the vast inland waterway of Peel Inlet and the Harvey Estuary. The river waters and the Indian Ocean offer excellent conditions for yachting, boating, swimming, water-skiing and fishing, and the town becomes

a mecca for tourists in holiday periods. **Of interest:** Hall's Cottage, Leighton Rd; small whitewashed cottage, built in 1845 by two of the colony's earliest settlers. Christ Church (1870), cnr Pinjarra Rd and Sholl St, has hand-carved wood furnishings. Mandurah Farm World, Fremantle Rd; group bookings only. Kerryelle's Collectors Museum, Gordon Rd. Boats for hire and cruises on inlet and river. Watch for dolphins, which sometimes can be seen in estuary. Waters also attract abundance of birdlife. Mandurah Estuary Bridge is particularly good fishing spot. King Carnival Amusement Park. Beaches at Halls Head, just over old traffic bridge; also Peel Pottery. **In the area:** Pleasant picnic areas near numerous storage dams in nearby Darling Range. Boating and swimming at Waroona and Logue Brook Dams. Bavarian Castle Fun Park, Old Coast Rd, 2 km south. Threlfall Galleries, 10 km south. House of Dunnies Studio, Henry Rd, Melros, 15 km south. Lakes Clifton and Preston, 20 km south, two long, narrow lakes running parallel to coast; Cape Bouvard Wines, Mt John Rd, 22 km south (weekends only). Hamel Forestry Department Nursery, 42 km south-east; open for inspection. Durago Gallery, Amarillo Dr, Karnup, 14 km north. Peel Estate Winery, Fletcher Rd, Baldivis, 20 km north. Western Rosella Bird Park, 5 km east. Houseboats for hire. **Tourist information:** 5 Pinjarra Rd; (09) 535 1155. **Accommodation:** 2 hotels, 5 motels, 11 caravan/camping parks.
MAP REF. 318 E12, 324 E10

Manjimup   Population 3960

Fertile agricultural country and magnificent karri forests surround Manjimup, 307 km south of Perth. This is the commercial centre of the south-west corner of WA, and the state's largest apple-growing area. Dairying, beef, sheep and vegetable farming are other pastoral activities. The wood-chip mill represents a flourishing industry contributing to the town's more recent growth. The first settlers arrived here in 1856 and Manjimup's history has been closely tied to the timber industry since then. **Of interest:** Manjimup Regional Timber Park, Rose St; attractions include: Timber Museum with excellent display on development of timber industry in WA, Age of Steam Museum, art and craft gallery, historical hamlet and fire tower lookout. WA Chip and Pulp (Paper Wood Co.) mill, Eastbourne Rd; guided tours. Yallambee Gem Museum, Chopping St. **In the area:** Diamond Woodchip Mill, 12 km south; guided tours. Diamond Tree Fire Tower, 9 km south, in use 1941–74; may not be climbed, but

surrounded by picnic area. Warren National Park, 40 km south; ideal for bushwalkers and peaceful picnic location. One Tree Bridge, 21 km west. Pleasant walk along river-edge, near bridge, to Four Aces: four magnificent karri trees, standing in line, believed to be 300–400 years old. King Jarrah, 4 km east; 47-m-high tree estimated to be 600 years old. Fonty's Pool, 10 km south-west; popular swimming pool and picnic area with spacious lawns and gardens. The 19-km round trip to Dingup, north-east of Manjimup, takes you through farmland and forest. Dingup Church (1896) and historic Dingup House (1870). Southern Wildflowers farm at Quininup, 33 km south-east. Abundant bird and other wildlife at Donnelly River Holiday Village 28 km west; also horseriding. Timber tours depart from Timber Park in Manjimup. King Jarrah Heritage Trail; details from tourist centre. **Tourist information:** Cnr Rose and Edward Sts; (097) 71 1831. **Accommodation:** 1 hotel, 1 hotel/motel, 2 motels, 3 caravan/camping parks. **See also:** The South-west.
MAP REF. 320 G8, 324 F12

Marble Bar   Population 332

Widely known as the 'hottest town in Australia' because of its consistently high temperatures, Marble Bar lies 203 km south-east of Port Hedland. The town takes its name from the unique bar of red-coloured jasper which crosses the Coongan River, 6 km from town. Alluvial gold was discovered in 1891, and in 1931 at the Comet Mine. Today the major industries are primarily tin-, copper- and gold-mining and pastoral activities. Marble Bar is a very typical WA outback town. **Of interest:** Government buildings, cnr Francis and Contest Sts, built of locally quarried stone in 1895, and still used by police and mining registrar. Marble Bar State Battery, Newman–Tabba Rd; not open to public. **In the area:** Jasper deposit at Marble Bar Pool, from which town takes its name, 6 km west; and nearby Chinaman's Pool, ideal picnic spot. The scenery in the area is beautiful, especially in winter and after rainfall, when the spinifex is transformed into a multitude of flowering plants. Rugged ranges, rolling plains, steep gorges, deep rock-pools and many natural scenic spots abound. Town of Nullagine, 120 km south, in mineral-rich area, dotted with old gold-mines. Scenic gorges, picnic spot and swimming at Coppin's Gap, 68 km north-east, and Kitty's Gap, further 6 km. Annual Marble Bar Cup and Ball held in June–July, over long weekend. **Tourist information:** BP Garage; (091) 76 1041. **Accommodation:**

1 hotel/motel, 1 motel, 1 caravan/camping park. **See also:** The Pilbara.
MAP REF. 326 I9

Margaret River   Population 1276

Margaret River is a pretty township nestled on the side of the Margaret River near the coast 280 km from Perth. The town is noted for its world-class wines, magnificent coastal scenery, surfing beaches, wineries and spectacular cave formations in the district. **Of interest:** Rotary Park, Bussell Hwy; heritage walk trails start from park (details from tourist centre). Old Settlement Craft Village; entrance from Wallcliffe House (1865), Wallcliffe Rd; not open to public. Greek Chapel, Wallcliffe Rd. Margaret River Gallery and Margaret River Pottery, both on Bussell Hwy. Melting Pot Glass Studio, Boodjidup Rd. Eagles Heritage, Boodjidup Rd; large collection of birds of prey. Inn and restaurant, Farrelly St; formerly 1885 homestead. **In the area:** Among over 20 wineries of Cowaramup (10 km north) Willyabrup (20 km north) and Margaret River areas is Leeuwin Estate Winery, 8 km south, featuring especially welcoming tasting-room, splendid function room with Australian paintings, and picnic and barbecue facilities. Bellview Shell Museum, and timber mill, both at Witchcliffe, 6 km south. Marron Farm, 11 km south. Vardos Clydesdale Museum and Village, 20 km south. Boranup Gallery, Caves Rd, Boranup, 20 km south. Berry Farm, 13 km south-east. Mammoth Cave, 21 km south-west, with fossil remains of prehistoric animals; 4 km on is Lake Cave. At Cowraramup, 10 km north, Cowraramup Pottery, Antique-a-Brac, Quinda Crafts and Silverpot Silversmith. Gunyulgup Gallery, Caves Rd, Yallingup, 45 km north. Ellensbrook Homestead (1853–55), National Trust property, 15 km north-west. Prevelly, 8 km west; Gracetown, 15 km north-west; Coastal areas of Redgate, 10 km south; and Hamlin Bay, 34 km south. Augusta–Busselton, Margaret River and Hamelin Bay Heritage Trails; details from tourist centre. **Tourist information:** Cnr Tunbridge Rd and Bussell Hwy; (097) 57 2911. **Accommodation:** 1 hotel, 4 motels, 4 caravan/camping parks.
MAP REF. 320 C7, 324 E12

Meekatharra   Population 1018

Meekatharra lies 768 km north-east of Perth on the Great Northern Hwy. Gold, copper and other minerals are mined, and there are huge sheep and cattle stations in the area. Meekatharra was once important as the railhead for cattle which had travelled overland from the Northern Territory or the East Kimberley. **Of**

THE KIMBERLEY

Until relatively recently the Kimberley region in the far north of Western Australia was a place only for hardened pioneers and prospectors. Now, with the National Highway completed, it is on Australia's travel map and it can offer both excitement and adventure. In addition, the 40-tonne, 18-metre ketch-rigged motor yacht *Opal Shell* cruises along the Kimberley coast out of Derby.

There are two seasons throughout the Kimberley. The northern towns generally have higher maximum temperatures and the southern coastline towns experience a higher humidity and average minimum temperature. The long dry period in winter brings delightful weather, while the green season brings higher temperatures, with monsoonal rains falling usually between December and March.

Geikie Gorge, near Fitzroy Crossing

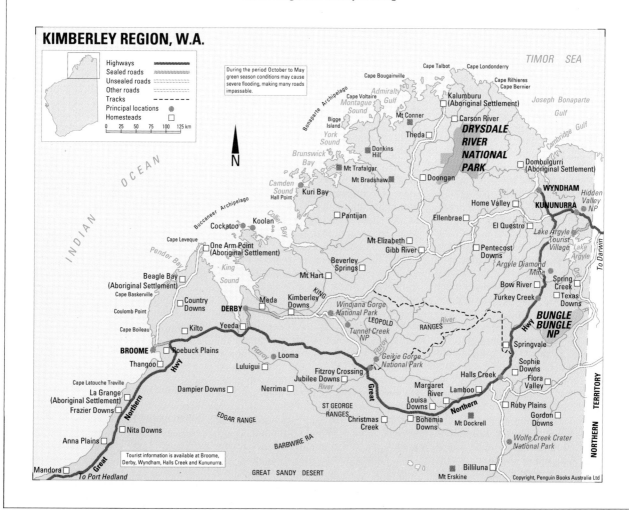

The gateway to the Kimberley is the old pearling town of **Broome**. In the boisterous days of the early 1900s the pearling fleet numbered some 400 luggers with 3000 crewmen. Today Broome is rapidly expanding into one of Western Australia's most popular tourist destinations. There are many points of interest, including a set of dinosaur tracks believed to have been embedded in limestone 130 million years ago and Buccaneer Rock, reputed to be the place where Dampier was wrecked in the *Roebuck* in 1699.

Further north-east is **Derby**, on King Sound near the mouth of the Fitzroy River, a centre for the beef-cattle industry of the Fitzroy Valley and the King Leopold Ranges. Just seven kilometres south of the town is a centuries-old boab tree. Shaped like an inverted wineglass and fourteen metres in diameter, it is hollow and is reputed to have been used as a cell for prisoners.

Derby is an ideal base for excursions to Windjana Gorge and Tunnel Creek in the Napier Range, and Geikie Gorge near the town of Fitzroy Crossing. These are among the most colourful and spectacular of all the river gorges of northern Australia.

The old gold settlement of Halls Creek was the scene of the first goldrush in Western Australia in 1885. Scores of diggers perished of hunger and thirst and very little gold was found. Nearby is the meteorite crater at Wolfe Creek, the second largest in the world, with an average depth of fifty metres. The meteorite is believed to have struck the earth about one million years ago. Also near Halls Creek is the China Wall, a natural white stone wall above a placid creek.

The most northerly town and safe port harbour in Western Australia is Wyndham, the terminus of the Great Northern Highway and now also the port for the Ord River irrigation area as well as for the east Kimberley cattle-stations. A 100-kilometre road from Wyndham to **Kununurra** winds through spectacular ancient gorge country. Kununurra is the base for nearby attractions such as Lake Argyle, Hidden Valley National Park and the Bungle Bungle National Park. South of Lake Argyle is the Argyle diamond mine, the world's largest. Kununurra is then linked to **Darwin** by the National Highway, which is being used more and more by travellers making a 'round trip' of Australia.

interest: Royal Flying Doctor Service base, Main St. Old Court-house, Darlot St. **In the area:** Old gold-mining towns, relics of mining equipment and mine shafts can be seen. Since the upturn in gold prices several mines, such as Peak Hill, Gabanintha, Nannine and Quinns, have reopened. State Battery remains, 4 km east. Peace Gorge (The Granites), 5 km west. Mt Gould, 15 km west. Mt Yagahong, 40 km south-east. Bilyuin Pool, 88 km north-west. **Tourist information:** Shire Offices, Main St; (099) 81 1101. **Accommodation:** Meekatharra, 2 hotels, 2 motels, 1 caravan/camping park. Sandstone (to south-east), 1 hotel, 1 caravan park.
MAP REF. 324 H3

Merredin　　　　Population 3001
A main junction on the important Kalgoorlie–Perth railway line, Merredin is situated 259 km east from Perth. During the late 1800s, Merredin grew up as a shanty town as miners stopped on their way to the goldfields. The town has excellent parks and recreation facilities. **Of interest:** Harling Memorial Library, Barrack St, and Old Railway Station Museum, Gt Eastern Hwy. CHM wheat storage and transfer depot, Gamenya Ave, built in 1966 with additions in 1978; largest horizontal storage in southern hemisphere, with a capacity of 220 000 tonnes. **In the area:** Pumping Station No. 4, 3 km west; designed by C. Y. O'Connor in 1902, and fine example of early industrial architecture, station closed in 1960 to make way for electrically driven stations. Hunts Dam, 5 km north, for picnics and bushwalking. Lake Chandler, 45 km north. Mangowine Homestead, 56 km north at Nungarin; National trust property. Museum at Koorda, 140 km north-west; number of wildlife reserves in vicinity. Totadjin Dam Reserve, 16 km south-west; Totadjin Rock has wave formation similar to that at Wave Rock. Bruce Rock, 50 km south-east, with museum, craft centre and Australia's smallest bank. Folk Museum at Kellerberrin, 55 km west. Durakoppin Wildlife Sanctuary, 27 km north of Kellerberrin, and Gardner Flora Reserve, 35 km south-west. Merredin Peak Heritage Trail; details from tourist centre. **Tourist information:** Barrack St; (090) 41 1668. **Accommodation:** 2 hotels, 4 motels, 2 caravan/camping parks. **See also: Crossing the Nullarbor.**
MAP REF. 319 P6, 324 G9

Mingenew　　　　Population 353
The little township of Mingenew is in the wheat-growing district of the mid-west, 378 km north of Perth. **Of interest:** Mingenew Museum, Victoria St, in small,

original Roads Board office, pioneer relics. Mingenew Hill Lookout and Pioneer Memorial, off Mingenew–Mullewa Rd, for views. Mingenew Rural Expo and Wildflower Display, both held in Sept. **In the area:** Picnic at Depot Hill, 15 km west. Superb beaches and excellent fishing at Dongara, 53 km west. WA's first coal shafts can be seen in Irwin Gorge at Coalseam Park, 32 km north-east; rock-hunting in river-bed, wildflowers in spring. **Tourist information:** Post Office building; (099) 28 1060. **Accommodation:** 1 hotel, 1 caravan/camping park.
MAP REF. 322 D7, 324 E7

Morawa　　　　Population 595
Renowned for its plentiful grain harvests, Morawa is situated in the mid-west, 394 km north of Perth. Spring is the perfect time to visit, when the wildflowers are in brilliant bloom. **Of interest:** Historical Museum, Prater St. St David's Anglican Church, Prater St. Holy Cross Catholic Church, Davis St. **In the area:** Koolanooka Springs reserve and Koolanooka Hills mine site, 24 km east; ideal for picnics. Bilya Rock Reserve, 4 km west. **Tourist information:** Shire Offices; (099) 71 1004. **Accommodation:** 1 hotel/motel, 1 caravan/camping park.
MAP REF. 322 G7, 324 E7

Mount Barker　　　　Population 1390
Mount Barker is a quiet, friendly town in the Great Southern district of WA. It is 360 km from Perth, with the Stirling Ranges to its north, and the Porongurups to the east. Mt Barker was discovered in 1829, and the first settlers arrived in the 1830s. Vineyards in the area, though relatively new, have produced some top-quality wines. **Of interest:** Old police station and gaol (1868), Albany Hwy; now museum. Wilson's Wildflowers, Marion St. Handcrafted works by Timber Trend available at tourist centre. **In the area:** Lookout on summit of Mt Barker, easily pinpointed by its 168-m-high television tower, provides splendid panoramic views of area and well worth 5 km drive. Privately owned St Werburgh's Chapel (1872), 12 km west; small mud-walled chapel overlooking Hay River Valley. Historic town of Kendenup, 16 km north; WA's first gold discovery made here. Narrikup Country Store and Kalangadoo Krafts, 16 km south; large collection of art and craft. Porongurup National Park, 24 km east; granite peaks and brilliant seasonal wildflowers. Farm holidays at Warrawing sheep farm, 42 km east. Stirling Range National Park, 80 km north-east; tall peaks, picturesque plains, native flora and fauna. Lake Poorrarecup, 50 km north-west. Area also noted for orchids and

THE SOUTH-WEST

The south-west corner of Western Australia is a lush green land. Its gently rolling hills are crossed by rivers winding through deep-sided valleys. The soils are fertile and the farms prosperous. Along the coast there are beautiful bays, and inland, majestic towering karri and jarrah forests. The countryside is dotted with picturesque orchards and in any season the vibrant colours of many wildflowers can be seen; Western Australia is one of the richest areas of flora in the world. The Mediterranean climate ensures warm, dry summers and mild, wet winters.

Pinjarra, eighty-four kilometres south of Perth, is one of the state's oldest districts.

Near **Harvey** there is fine agricultural land and the undulating farms stretch to the foothills of the Darling Range. To the north-west is **Yalgorup National Park** (one of only three sites in Western Australia with stromatolites), where the lakes attract a wide variety of birdlife. The Old Coast Road,

which edges down the coast to Bunbury, is a perfect choice if you want to go 'off the beaten track'.

The coast of the south-west is fascinating: an unusual mixture of craggy outcrops and promontories, sheltered bays with calm waters and beaches pounded by rolling surf. From **Cape Leeuwin** it is possible to see the sun rising over one ocean and setting over another. The length of the coast, together with the many rivers and estuaries, makes the south-west an angler's paradise. The Murray, Harvey and Brunswick and their tributaries are only some of the streams annually stocked with trout.

The main port for the south-west, **Bunbury** rests on Geographe Bay looking out over the Indian Ocean. It is a perfect holiday town, flanked by golden beaches and peaceful rural farmland. One of the oldest towns in the state, **Busselton**, sited on the Vasse River, has a wealth of pioneer homes, many restored and open to the public.

Leeuwin–Naturaliste National Park combines a scenic coast with magnificent wildflowers and the tall timbers of karri and jarrah forests.

Yallingup is known for its excellent surf and spectacular limestone caves. Dripping water has created strange shapes in the limestone, with magic colours reflected in the glittering underground water.

Bridgetown, Donnybrook and **Greenbushes** are small townships tucked away in green hilly country and pretty apple orchards. Gold-mining flourished briefly here at the turn of the century. **Manjimup** and **Pemberton** are world-famous for the source of their timber, the giant karri and jarrah trees. Here some of the world's tallest trees reach straight up, often eighty and ninety metres, to the sky. The Pemberton, Scott, Warren and Brockman National Parks are all nearby, introduced to protect the unique environment.

---

brown and red boronia, which bloom Sept.–Nov. Mt Barker Heritage Trail; details from tourist centre. **Tourist information:** 57 Lowood Rd; (098) 51 1163. **Accommodation:** 1 hotel, 2 motels, 1 caravan/camping park, self-contained chalets, 1 lodge.
MAP REF. 321 M11, 324 G13

Mount Magnet   Population 1000
The former gold-mining town of Mount Magnet, 562 km from Perth on the Great Northern Hwy, is now a popular stopping-place for motorists driving north to Port Hedland. The surrounding land is used for pastoral farming. **In the area:** The Granites, 7 km north, picnic spot with some Aboriginal rock art. Fossick for gemstones, but take care as there are dangerous old mine shafts. Ghost town, Lennonville, 11 km north. **Tourist information:** Shire Offices; (099) 63 4001. **Accommodation:** 2 hotels, 1 motel, 1 caravan park.
MAP REF. 323 N1, 324 G5

Mullewa   Population 758
Gateway to the Murchison goldfields, Mullewa is 99 km from Geraldton. **Of interest:** Kemble Zoo, Stock Rd. Our Lady of

Mount Carmel Church and Mons. John C. Hawes Priesthouse Museum, both in Maitland Rd. Water Supply Reserve, Lovers Lane; native plants. Annual Wildflower Show held in Aug.–Sept. Agricultural Show in Sept. **In the area:** Waterfalls (after heavy rain), 5 km north, near airport. Wildflowers at Tallering Peak and Gorge, 58 km north. St Mary's Agricultural School and Pallatine Mission, both near Tardun, 40 km south-east. Tenindewa Pioneer Well, 18 km west. Mons. Hawes Heritage Trail; details from tourist centre. **Tourist information:** Shire Offices; (099) 61 1007. **Accommodation:** 2 hotels, 1 caravan park.
MAP REF. 322 E3, 324 E6

Mundaring   Population 951
Mundaring is situated on the Great Eastern Hwy, 34 km east of Perth. The picturesque Mundaring Weir, 8 km south of the town, set in wooded hilly country, is the source of water for the eastern goldfields. The original dam was opened in 1903, and the pumping station was used until 1955. The attractive bush setting makes the weir a popular picnic spot in summer. **In the area:** The C. Y. O'Connor Museum, 8 km south; intriguing collection

of models of Eastern Goldfields water supply. Old Mahogany Inn (1837), 7 km west, served as military outpost to offer protection to travellers from hostile Aborigines. John Forrest National Park, on high point of Darling Range, 26 km east. **Tourist information:** Shire Offices, 7000 Great Eastern Hwy; (09) 295 1400. **Accommodation:** 2 hotels, 1 caravan/camping park.
MAP REF. 318 G8, 324 F10

Mundrabilla   Population 12
A tiny settlement on the Eyre Hwy where you can break the journey across the continent. There is a bird and animal sanctuary behind the motel. **Tourist information:** Roadhouse; (090) 39 3465. **Accommodation:** 1 motel, 1 caravan/camping park.
MAP REF. 325 P10

Nannup   Population 505
Nannup is a quiet, friendly town in the Blackwood Valley, 290 km south of Perth. The surrounding countryside is lush, gently rolling pasture alongside jarrah and pine forests. **Of interest:** Old police station (1922), Brockman St. Arboretum, Brockman St. Art and craft centre, Warren Rd.

Bunnings Timber Mill, Warren Rd; largest jarrah sawmill in state; open for inspection. Crafty Creations, Warren Rd; local art and craft, especially jarrah goods. Gemstone Museum, Warren Rd. Apatches Gallery, cnr Warren and Grange Rds. **In the area:** Scenic drives around area's jarrah forest. Canoeing on Blackwood River. Barrabup Pool, 10 km west. Hillside Tourist Farm, 8 km east; offers hands-on experience. Tathra Wines, 14 km north-east. Nannup Heritage Trail; details from tourist centre. **Tourist information:** 4 Brockman St; (097) 56 1211. **Accommodation:** 2 caravan/camping parks.
MAP REF. 320 F7, 324 E12

Narrogin   Population 4266
Narrogin is important as the centre of prosperous agricultural country and as a major railway junction. Sheep, pigs and cereal farms are the main primary industries. The town is 189 km south-east of Perth on the Great Southern Hwy, and its name is derived from an Aboriginal word meaning 'waterhole'. The annual Three Day Horse Competition, held in Sept., attracts entrants from all over Australia. **Of interest:** Court-house Museum (1894), Egerton St; originally school and later district court-house. Foxes Lair, Williams Rd; 5 ha of natural bushland. Lions Lookout, Kipling St; panoramic views of Narrogin. Restoration Group Museum, Federal St; fully restored cars, stationary engines and other machinery. Narrogin Agrolympics held in Mar. Narrogin Speed Classic (vintage car racing) in Mar.–Apr. **In the area:** Unusual rock formations, 11 km east, at Yilliminning and Birdwhistle Rocks. South Central Wheatbelt Heritage Trail; details from tourist centre. **Tourist information:** 23 Egerton St; (098) 81 2064. **Accommodation:** 2 hotels, 2 motels, 1 caravan/camping park.
MAP REF. 321 K2, 324 G11

New Norcia   Population under 200
Spanish Benedictine monks established a mission at New Norcia in 1846 to help the Australian Aborigines. Today Salvado College is a secondary school catering for nearly 200 boarders from all over WA. The handsome Spanish-inspired buildings come as a surprise, surrounded by dusty Australian paddocks and distant bushland. The settlement is in the secluded Moore Valley, and wheat, wool and other farm products are grown. **Of interest:** Museum and art gallery, Great Northern Hwy; priceless collection, including gifts sent by Queen Isabella of Spain, fine paintings and Roman, Egyptian and Spanish artefacts; gallery's shop also sells locally made products and

souvenirs. Heritage Trail (2 km) includes inspection of oldest operating flour-mill in WA (built 1879); also 19th-century blacksmith's forge and historic olive press; details from tourist centre. **Tourist information:** Museum and art gallery, Great Northern Hwy; (096) 54 8056. **Accommodation:** 1 hotel, 1 guest-house.
MAP REF. 318 G4, 324 F9

Newman   Population 4899
This town was built by Mt Newman Mining Co. to house its employees involved in the extraction of iron ore. Mt Newman ships its ore from Port Hedland, and the two towns are connected by a 426 km railroad. In 1981 responsibility for the town was handed over to the local shire. With the sealing of the National Hwy and improved tourist facilities in the town, Newman has become a popular stopover. **Of interest:** Tours of Mt Whaleback mine, Newman Dr, largest open-cut mine in world. Mining and pastoral museum, behind tourist centre. Radio Hill Lookout, off Newman Dr. **In the area:** Ophthalmia Dam, 15 km north, for swimming and barbecues. Good views from Mt Newman, 20 km north. Aboriginal rock carvings, rockpools and waterholes at Wanna Munna, 70 km west, and Punda, 75 km north-west. **Tourist information:** Cnr Fortescue Ave and Newman Dr; (091) 75 2888. **Accommodation:** 1 motel, 1 backpackers budget hotel, 3 caravan/camping parks. **See also:** The Pilbara.
MAP REF. 326 I12

Norseman   Population 1775
Norseman, 200 km south of Kalgoorlie, is the last large town on the Eyre Hwy for travellers heading east towards SA. Gold put Norseman on the map back in the early 1890s, and the richest quartz reef in Australia is still being mined today. The town is steeped in gold-mining history, with the colossal tailings dumps a reminder of the area's wealth. The area is popular with amateur prospectors and gemstone collectors; gemstone fossicking permits are available from Norseman Tourist Bureau. There is a quarantine checkpoint for westbound travellers at Norseman, so visitors should make sure they are not carrying fruit, vegetables, honey, used fruit and produce containers, plants or seeds. **Of interest:** Historical Collection of mining tools and household items, Battery Rd. Post Office (1896), cnr Prinsep and Ra Sts. Heritage Trail (33 km), following original Cobb & Co. route, includes descent into a 'decline'; details from tourist centre. Statue in Roberts St commemorating horse called Norseman who allegedly pawed at ground and unearthed a nugget of gold, thus starting a gold-

rush in area. Mine tours of massive open-cut mine conducted weekdays. Norseman Tourist Reception Centre, Roberts St, has complete visitor facilities, day parking and barbeques. **In the area:** Dundas Rocks, 22 km south, are 550 million years old; excellent picnic area and old Dundas town site nearby. Easy climb of Beacon Hill (otherwise known as Mararoa or Lookout Hill), 2 km east, yields good views of surrounding salt lakes (spectacular when seen at sunrise and sunset), old mines and Jimberlana Dyke, reputedly one of oldest geological areas in world. Mt Jimberlana, 7 km east; easy walking trail to summit for good views. Peak Charles, 50 km south, then 40 km off hwy; magnificent views, but only for energetic climbers. Gemstone leases on Eyre Hwy and off Kalgoorlie Hwy; details from tourist centre. Frank Hahn National Park, 50 km east of Lake King township, tranversed by Lake King–Norseman Rd. Twice-daily bus tours of town, the 'decline', Beacon Hill and part of Heritage Trail. **Tourist information:** 68 Roberts St; (090) 39 1071. **Accommodation:** 2 hotels, 2 motels, 2 caravan/camping parks. **See also:** Crossing the Nullarbor; The Goldfields.
MAP REF. 325 K10

Northam   Population 6377
The regional centre of the fertile Avon Valley at the junction of the Avon and Mortlock Rivers, Northam is an attractive rural town. On the Great Eastern Hwy, 100 km east of Perth, it is an important supply-point for the farms of the eastern wheat-belt. Northam is also a major railway centre and the main depot for the Goldfields Water Scheme, which takes water as far east as Kalgoorlie. WA's largest military training camp is on the outskirts of town. **Of interest:** Old Railway Station Museum, Fitzgerald St. Avon Valley Arts Society art and craft shop, Wellington St. Weir across Avon River, near Peel Tce bridge, forms lake that attracts both black and white swans and many other species of native birdlife. Byfield House, Gordon St; elegant, stately late-Victorian home built by James Byfield, now restored to its original grandeur and operating as restaurant. Shamrock Hotel (1886), Fitzgerald St; 'local pub'. Morby Cottage, Old York Rd, built in 1836 by one of Northam's first families, the Morrells, stands as tribute to spirit of district's early pioneers. Annual scenic cycling tour of wheat-belt begins at Northam in May. **In the area:** Restored Buckland Homestead (1874), 8 km north; stately home set in landscaped gardens; contains valuable collection of antique furniture, silver and paintings. At Dowerin, 58 km north-east: museum,

craft centre and Hagbooms Lake. Muresk Agricultural College, former early farming property, 10 km south. Blue Gum Camel Farm, located near Spencer Brook Rd, at Clackline, 19 km south-west; camel- and trail-riding in picturesque bushland surroundings. In area: hot-air ballooning, horseriding, gliding, canoeing. In spring, wildflowers abound near Wubin, 190 km north. Northam–Katrine Heritage Trail and Farming Heritage Trail; details from tourist centre. **Tourist information:** Beavis Pl.; (096) 22 2100. **Accommodation:** 4 hotels, 1 motel, 1 caravan/camping park.
MAP REF. 318 I7, 324 F9

Northampton   Population 827
Northampton nestles amidst gentle hills in the valley of Nokarena Brook, 48 km north of Geraldton. Inland there is picturesque country with vivid wildflowers in spring. The drive west leads to the coast, with beaches for swimming and fishing. **Of interest:** Chiverton House Folk Museum, Hampton Rd. Gwalla church-site and cemetery, Gwalla St. St Mary's Convent and Church, Main St, designed by Mons. Hawes. Miners' cottages (1860s), Brook St. **In the area:** Alma Schoolhouse and disused Ghurka lead mine, 12 km north. At Horrocks Beach, 20 km west, pleasant bays, sandy beaches and good fishing. Near coast at Port Gregory, 47 km north-west, labour-hiring depot for convicts dating from 1800s; this squat building with slits for windows was probably erected as protection from Aborigines. Hutt Lagoon, near Port Gregory, turns pink in light of midday sun. **Tourist information:** Shire Offices; (099) 34 1008. **Accommodation:** 2 motels, 1 caravan/camping park.
MAP REF. 322 A2, 324 D6

Northcliffe   Population 208
Magnificent virgin karri forests surround the little township of Northcliffe, 32 km south of Pemberton in the extreme southwest corner of the state. **Of interest:** In Wheatley Coast Rd: Pioneer Museum, with historical relics and photographs; and at Tourist Centre, rock and mineral collection, Aboriginal Interpretation Room and photographic folio of native flora. Forest Park, off Wheatley Coast Rd; features Hollow Butt Karri, Twin Karri walking trails and picnic areas. Warren River, for fishing. **In the area:** Mt Chudalup, 20 km south; giant granite outcrop with walking trail to summit for panoramic views. Sandy beaches of Windy Harbour and Salmon Beach, 29 km south, ideal for fishing and swimming. Cliffs at Point D'Entrecasteaux, 27 km south, popular with climbers. D'Entrecasteaux

(5 km south), Warren (20 km north-west) and Shannon (30 km east) National Parks, with Bibbulmun Track linking all three. Boorara Tree (once used as fire lookout) and Lane–Poole Falls, 24 km south-east. **Tourist information:** Adjacent to Pioneer Museum, Wheatley Coast Rd, in town centre; (097) 76 7203. **Accommodation:** 1 hotel, 1 caravan/camping park.
MAP REF. 320 G11, 324 F13

Onslow   Population 750
Onslow, on the north-west coast of the state, is important as the base for the oilfields off the coast at Barrow Island. The town was originally located at the mouth of the Ashburton River, but was moved to its site on Beadon Bay after constant cyclones. The remains of the old town-site can still be seen. Onslow was a bustling pearling centre and in the 1890s gold was discovered. US submarines refuelled here during World War II, and the town was bombed by the Japanese. In 1952 it was the mainland base for Britain's nuclear experiments at Monte Bello Islands. **In the area:** Excellent fishing. Native fauna includes emus, red kangaroos, sand goannas, bustards and a wide variety of birdlife. In spring, after rain, the wildflowers bloom, including the Sturt Desert Pea and wild hibiscus. **Tourist information:** Shire Offices; (091) 84 6001. **Accommodation:** 1 hotel, 1 holiday units, 1 caravan/camping park.
MAP REF. 326 D10

Pemberton   Population 802
The town of Pemberton, 335 km south of Perth, is nestled in a quiet valley, surrounded by towering karri forests. This lush forest area has some of the tallest hardwood trees in the world, and, in spring, brilliant flowering bush plants. **Of interest:** Pemberton is known as a centre for high-quality woodcraft, and there are a number of craft outlets. Pemberton Arts and Craft, Broadway Ave. Wooddawn Woodcrafts, Ellis St. Warren River Arts and Craft, Jamieson St. Woodcraftsman's Studio, Jamieson St. Fine Woodcraft, Dickinson St, in restored squatter's cottage. In Brockman St: Museum, with collection of historic photographs and authentic forestry equipment; tourist centre includes historical museum. Trout and Marron Hatchery supplies fish for WA rivers and dams; daily tours. Fishing in local rivers; Inland Fishing Licence required for trout and marron. Wineries with cellar-door sales and/or tastings include Warren Vineyard, Dickinson St; Gloucester Ridge, off Brockman St; and Mountford Wines, Bamess St. Pemberton

Sawmill, Brockman St; open for inspection. **In the area:** Gloucester Tree, signposted off Brockman St, tallest fire lookout in world; over 60 m high with 150 rungs spiralling upwards; open for climbing during daylight hours. Further south are picturesque Lane Poole Falls and at Northcliffe, pioneer museum. The Cascades, 8 km south; popular for picnics, bushwalking and fishing. King Trout Farm, 9 km south. Brockman Sawpit, 13 km south; restored to show how timber was sawn in 1860s. Moon's Crossing, 18 km south, for picnics. Marron and dairy farm, 1 km north. Big Brook Dam and Arboretum, 7 km north-west. Donnelly River Wines, 35 km north-west. Piano Gully Vineyard, 24 km north-east, off South West Hwy. Eagle Springs marron farm, 18 km west. Sandy beaches line rugged coast at Windy Harbour, where fishing is good. Warren (9 km south), Brockman (13 km south) and Beedelup (18 km west) National Parks all close by. Some of best accessible virgin karri forest in Warren National Park, where tallest of karri trees (89 m) can be found. Swamp Willow Craft on Hawke Rd near park, 12 km south. Tram cars based on 1907 Fremantle trams operate daily through tall-timber country between Pemberton and Northcliffe; details from tourist centre. **Tourist information:** Brockman St; (097) 76 1133. **Accommodation:** 2 hotels, 2 motels, 1 caravan/camping park. **See also:** The South-west.
MAP REF. 320 G9, 324 F13

Perenjori   Population 241
On the Northam–Mullewa Hwy (known as the 'Wildflower Way'), 352 km north-east of Perth, Perenjori lies on the fringes of the Murchison goldfields and the great sheep-stations of the west. **Of interest:** Historical Museum behind tourist centre, Fowler St. Arts and Crafts Centre, Russell St. **In the area:** Fossickers will find many gemstones in this mineral-rich region. The wildflower season lasts from July to September and there are many scenic drives. The salt lakes attract a variety of waterbirds. Old gold-mining and ghost towns include Rothsay, 67 km east (working mine not open for inspection); Warriedar, 107 km east; and Nows Nest, 176 km east. Care should be taken as unfenced pits make the area dangerous. Mongers Lake Lookout, 35 km east. Camel Soak, picnic spot, 47 km east. Aboriginal Stones at Damperwah Soak, 40 km north-east. Perenjori-Rothsay Heritage Trail (180 km), recalls district's early goldmining days; details from tourist centre. **Tourist information:** Fowler Street; (099)73 1105. **Accommodation:** 1 hotel, 1 caravan/camping park.
MAP REF. 322 H8, 324 F7

Pingelly Population 794

On the Great Southern Hwy, 154 km south-east of Perth, Pingelly is part of the central southern farming district. The cutting of sandalwood was once a local industry, but today the land is given over to sheep and wheat-growing. **Of interest:** Art and Crafts Cottage, Park St. Courthouse Museum, Parade St. Apex Lookout, Stone St, for fine views of town and country. **In the area:** Lange Wildlife Sanctuary, 2 km east. Historic St Patrick's Church (1873) at Mourambine, 10 km east. Tuttanning Flora and Fauna Reserve, 21 km east. Yealering Lake and picnic ground, 58 km east. Dryandra Reserve, 40 km south-west, with unique examples of flora; fauna includes the numbat, WA's fauna emblem. Timber also produced in reserve, which has been called an ecological oasis. Boyagin Rock Picnic Ground and Reserve, 26 km north-west. Moorumbine Heritage Trail; details from tourist centre. **Tourist information:** Shire Offices, 17 Queen St; (098) 87 1066. **Accommodation:** 2 hotels, 1 motel.
MAP REF. 319 K12, 324 F10

Pinjarra Population 1589

Pinjarra is a pleasant drive 84 km south of Perth, along the shaded South Western Hwy or the scenic Old Coast Road. The town has a picturesque setting on the banks of the Murray River in one of the oldest-established districts in WA. The Alcoa Refinery, 4 km north-east of town on South West Hwy is the largest alumina refinery in Australia. Pinjarra is becoming increasingly popular with tourists as a base from which to explore the area. Bus tours are available from the Tour Reception Centre at the Pinjarra Refinery. **Of interest:** St John's Church (1845), Henry St. Heritage Rose Garden, Henry St. Edenvale and Liveringa (1880), George St. **In the area:** Marrinup Falls, 3 km walk from Scarp Rd. Alcoa Scarp Lookout, 14 km east. Athlone Angora Stud and Goat Farm, 16 km east. Scarp Pool, 20 km south-east, popular for picnics and swimming. Fairbridge Village, 5 km north. Whittakers Mill, for bushwalking, camping and barbecues, and Dandalup Studio (art and craft), both at North Dandalup, 10 km north. Old Blythewood (1840s), 4 km south, has served as post office, coach stop and family home. Hotham Valley Tourist Railway runs old-style steam train between Pinjarra and Dwellingup (Sun., May–Oct.). Farm holidays available at Nanga Dell Farm near Waroona, 24 km south. Yalgorup National Park on coast, 48 km south-west of Waroona. Pinjarra Heritage Trail; details from tourist centre. **Tourist infor-** **mation:** Murray Tourist Centre, George St; (09) 531 1438. **Accommodation:** 1 hotel, 1 motel, 1 caravan/camping park. **See also:** The South-west.
MAP REF. 318 F12, 324 E11

Point Samson

Population under 200

Point Samson was named in honour of Michael Samson, who accompanied the district's first settler, Walter Padbury, on his 1863 journey. The town was established in 1910 as the major port for the Roebourne district, replacing Cossack, where the harbour had silted up following a cyclone. The port was very active for many years, but today Point Samson supports a small fishing industry and its extremely attractive setting has made it a popular beach resort. **Of interest:** Point Samson's sandy beach is protected by a coral reef, making it perfect for swimming, fishing and skin-diving. The tidal rivers contain an immense variety of marine life, from barramundi to mud crabs. Offshore waters have some of the best game fishing along the entire coast. Swimming and picnicking at Honeymoon Cove on Johns Creek Rd; boat-ramp and jetty at nearby John's Harbour. Trawlers Tavern for local seafood. **In the area:** Fishing boat harbour at Sam's Creek, 1 km north. Samson Reef can be explored at low tide. Emma Withnell Heritage Trail; details from tourist centre. **Tourist information:** Point Samson Fisheries, Point Samson Rd; (091) 87 1414. **Accommodation:** 1 motel, 1 caravan park.
MAP REF. 326 F9

Port Hedland Population 13 069

Port Hedland's remarkable growth has been due to the iron-ore boom, which started in the early 1960s. The town was named after Captain Peter Hedland, who discovered the harbour in 1829. Today Port Hedland handles the largest tonnage of any Australian port. Iron ore from some of the world's biggest mines is loaded on to the world's biggest ore-carriers. Gathering of salt is another major industry, with about 2 million tonnes exported per annum. The Spinifex Spree, held each August, is ten days of sport, social and cultural activities. **Of interest:** Observation Tower at tourist centre, Wedge St. Drysdales Shell Collection, Richardson St. Lions Park, Hunt St, has pioneer relics. Royal Flying Doctor Base, Richardson St. Visitors are welcome at wharf, where ore is loaded on to giant ships. Mt Newman Mining (BHP) mine tours can be booked through tourist centre. Don Rhodes Mining Museum, Wilson St. Opposite the fire brigade in Wilson St on limestone ridge are some impressive Aboriginal carvings (no public access). Olympic pool in McGregor St, next to Civic Centre. The long trains (usually around 2 km) operated by Mt Newman Mining come into town about 6 times daily. Port development display, Wharf Rd, opposite Port Control Tower, open to visitors. **In the area:** Swim, picnic and fish at Pretty Pool, next to Cooke Point caravan park. Giant cone-shaped mounds of salt, piled high awaiting export, 8 km south. Good fishing near Port Hedland. Charter boats for hire. Birdlife is abundant in district: watch for bustards, eagles, cockatoos, galahs, ibises, pelicans and parrots. Stone carvings at Woodstock, 300 km south-east. Whale-watching, June–Sept. Port Hedland Heritage Trail; details from tourist centre. **Tourist information:** 13 Wedge St; (091) 73 1650. **Accommodation:** 3 hotels, 2 backpackers budget, 4 motels, 3 caravan/camping parks. **See also:** The Pilbara.
MAP REF. 326 G8

Ravensthorpe Population 299

Ravensthorpe, situated 533 km south-east of Perth, is the centre of the old Phillips River goldfield. Copper mining was also important here, reaching a peak in the late 1960s. Many old mine shafts can be seen around the district. Wheat and sheep are the local industries. **Of interest:** Historical Society Museum, Morgan St. Several historic buildings: Anglican Church, Dunn St; old mine manager's house, Carlisle St; Dance Cottage (museum), Commercial Hotel and Palace Hotel, all in Morgan St. **In the area:** Ravensthorpe Range, 3 km north, and Mt Desmond, 10 km south-east, for panoramic views. WA Time Meridian at first restbay west of town. Fitzgerald River National Park, 46 km south. Old copper smelter, 2 km east. Annual wildflower display in Sept. features over 600 species from Fitzgerald River National Park. Rock-hunting; check locally to avoid trespass. Catlin Creek Heritage Trail; details from tourist centre. **Tourist information:** Morgane St; (098) 38 1163. **Accommodation:** 1 hotel, 1 motel, 1 caravan/camping park.
MAP REF. 324 I11

Rockingham Population 30 635

At the southern end of Cockburn Sound, 45 km south of Perth, Rockingham is a coastal city and seaside resort. Begun in 1872 as a port, the harbour fell into disuse with the opening of the Fremantle inner harbour in 1897. Today its magnificent golden beaches and protected waters are Rockingham's main attraction. **Of interest:** Museum, Kent St. Lookout at Point Peron, Peron Rd. WA Waterski Park, St Albans Rd. Sunday markets, Flinders

CROSSING THE NULLARBOR VIA THE EYRE HIGHWAY

The trip from Adelaide to Perth along the Eyre Highway is one of Australia's great touring experiences. It is far from monotonous, with breathtaking views of the Great Australian Bight only a few hundred metres from the road in many places. There is nothing quite like a long straight road stretching as far as the eye can see ahead and in the rear-vision mirror.

If planning a return journey, it is well worth considering driving one way and placing the car on the train for the return. As there is a limited amount of space for cars, train bookings need to be made well in advance, even at off-peak times. (**See:** Planning Ahead.)

The Eyre Highway is bitumen for its entire length. The highway is extremely well signposted, with indications of the distance to the next town with petrol and other services.

If the journey is undertaken at a sensible pace, it can be surprisingly relaxing, especially during the quieter times of year. The standard of accommodation is good and reasonably priced, with a friendly atmosphere in the bars and dining-rooms of the large motel/roadhouses that are strategically situated along the highway. Many friendships have been made during the trip across the Eyre Highway as the same carloads of travellers meet at stopping-places each night.

Although the highway is bitumen, there are certain hazards to avoid. The road can have breakaways on the shoulders in places, requiring caution when overtaking. And it can be difficult to overtake the big semi-trailers as they thunder along the highway, particularly when they 'tailgate' to save fuel. Overtaking also can be hazardous in damp conditions when the spray from the vehicle in front completely cuts visibility ahead. On the other hand, the semi-trailer drivers are usually courteous and signal when it is safe to overtake. Kangaroos also can be a problem, especially at dusk or after rain.

When travelling in a westerly direction, the setting sun can make driving somewhat unpleasant. Also, do not

Koonalda Cliffs, Great Australian Bight, SA

forget the time changes that you will encounter on the way! (**See also:** Time Zones.)

Above all, it is most important to have a safe, reliable car. The settlements along the highway are mainly motels with garage and roadhouse. You could have a long wait for mechanical or medical help.

The trip begins properly at **Port Augusta**, 330 kilometres north-east of Adelaide at the head of Spencer Gulf, a provincial city that services a vast area of semi-arid grazing and wheat-growing country to the north and west. As you head out of Port Augusta on the Eyre Highway, you see behind it the last hills of any size for 2500 kilometres, the red peaks of the Flinders Ranges soaring above the sombre blue bushplains. Through the little towns of **Kimba** and **Kyancutta** the scenery can vary from mallee scrub to wide paddocks of wheat. This area was once called Heartbreak Plains, a reminder of the time when farmers walked off their land in despair, leaving behind them the crumbling stone homesteads that today dot the plains.

The highway meets the sea at **Ceduna**, a small town of white stone buildings and limestone streets against a background of blue-green sea. The waters of the Great Australian Bight here are shallow and unpredictable, but they yield Australia's best catches of its most commercially prized fish, whiting. On the outskirts of Ceduna is a warning sign about the last reliable water. This marks the end of cultivated country and the beginning of the deserted, almost treeless land that creeps towards the Nullarbor Plain. The highway stays close to the coast and there is always a little scrub and other vegetation on the plains or on the sand dunes that lie between the highway and the ocean.

Further north the Nullarbor Plain covers an area greater than the state of Victoria. The name 'Nullarbor' is a corruption from Latin for 'no trees' and the name is more than apt. Geologists believe that the completely flat plain was once the bed of a prehistoric sea, which was raised to dry land by a great upheaval of the earth.

West of Ceduna are **Penong**, a town of 100 windmills, and the breathtaking coastal beauty around Point Sinclair and Cactus Beach. Then on to **Nundroo** and south to the abandoned settlement of **Fowlers Bay**, once an exploration depot for Edward John

Eyre and now a charming ghost town best known for its fishing. At the **Yalata Roadhouse**, run by the Yalata Aboriginal Community, there are genuine artefacts for sale at reasonable prices. Between **Nullarbor** and **Border Village** are five of the most spectacular coastal lookouts anywhere on the Australian coastline, where giant ocean-swells pound the towering limestone cliffs that make up this part of the Great Australian Bight. From June to October, an added bonus is the chance of spotting the majestic southern right whale on its annual migration along the southern part of the continent. Fuel, refreshments and accommodation are all available at Penong, Nundroo, Nullarbor and Border Village.

The stone ruins of an Aboriginal mission remain at **Cocklebiddy**. The road continues until it reaches the first real town in more than 1200 kilometres, **Norseman**. The town is an ideal stopping-place on the road to Perth.

From here you turn north to **Kalgoorlie** or south to **Esperance** on the coast. At **Kalgoorlie–Boulder** you will see one of the longest-lived and most prosperous gold-mining centres in Western Australia. After a working life of more than ninety years, the mines around Kalgoorlie still produce more than seventy per cent of Australia's gold. Set in vast dryland eucalypt forest, the town is picturesque in its frontier style.

Esperance, on the other hand, offers coastal scenery, long, empty beaches and nearby, wildflowers spread across the countryside in spring.

The undulating forest and wildflower scrub continues for a further 250 kilometres until the road reaches the wheat and wool-growing lands around the towns of **Southern Cross** and **Merredin**. The farmland becomes increasingly rich as it rises into the Darling Range, the beautiful, wooded mountain country that overlooks Perth. At the end of this long journey Perth glitters like a jewel on the Indian Ocean—a place of civilisation and style, of beaches, waterways and greenery.

For further information on the Eyre Highway, see South Australian entries on **Ceduna**, **Kimba**, **Penong** and **Wudinna** and Western Australian entries on **Balladonia, Caiguna, Cocklebiddy**, **Eucla**, Mundrabilla and **Madura**.

Lake. Cockburn Yacht Regatta held in Jan. **In the area:** Nearby Penguin Island, with a colony of fairy penguins. Garden Island, home to HMAS *Stirling*, naval base; normally closed to public, but accessed by bus tour from Perth weekly; causeway link to mainland not open to public. Kwinana Industrial Complex, 10 km north. Scenic drive 48 km inland to Serpentine Dam, WA's major water conservation area. Brilliant wildflowers, gardens and bushland surround dam and Serpentine Falls are close by. Shoalwater Bay Islands Marine Park, 6 km north-west, extends from just south of Garden Island to Becher Point in Warnbro; cruises, including dolphin cruises, available. Marapana Deer Park, 16 km south. Baldivis Estate Winery, 15 km south-east. Peel Estate Winery, 17 km south-east. Old Rockingham Heritage Trail and Rockingham–Jarrahdale Heritage Trail; details from tourist centre. **Tourist information:** 43 Kent St; (09) 592 3464. **Accommodation:** 2 hotels, 1 motel, 3 caravan/camping parks.
MAP REF. 318 E10, 324 E10

Roebourne   Population 1269
Named after John Septimus Roe, the state's first surveyor-general, Roebourne was established in 1864 and is the oldest town on the north-west coast. It was developed as the capital of the North West and at one time was the administrative centre for the whole area north of the Murchison River. The town was the centre for the early mining and pastoral industries in the Pilbara; it was connected to the port of Cossack, and later to Point Samson, by tramway for the transport of passengers and goods. Although now overshadowed by the iron-ore and other industries, Roebourne has retained its own special character. **Of interest:** Old stone buildings (some classified by National Trust) include police station, Queen St; Post Office (1887), Shell St; in Hampton St: hospital (1887) and court-house; Holy Trinity Church (1894), Withnell St; and in Roe St: Union Bank (1889; now Shire library) and Victoria Hotel, last of town's five original pubs. Old Roebourne Gaol (1886), Queen St, with art and craft centre; open daily for inspection. Good views from top of Mt Welcome, Fisher Dr. Wirraway Art Gallery, Hampton St. **In the area:** Emma Withnell Heritage Trail, 52 km drive north, taking in towns of Wickham (15 km) and Cossack (17 km) and terminating at Point Samson. Fishing at Cleaverville; 25 km north. **Tourist information:** 173 Roe St; (091) 82 1060. **Accommodation:** 1 hotel, 1 caravan/camping park. **See also**: The Pilbara.
MAP REF. 326 F9

Southern Cross   Population 898
A small but flourishing town on the Great Eastern Hwy, 368 km east of Perth, Southern Cross is a unique town, being the centre of a prosperous agricultural and pastoral area and a significant gold-producing area. **Of interest:** First court-house in eastern goldfields (1893), Antares St; now history museum, open daily. Other historic buildings include Post Office (1891), Antares St, and Railway Tavern (1890s), Spica St. The town and its wide streets, originally designed to allow camel trains to turn around, are named after stars and constellations. Gold-mining activities around Southern Cross, Marvel Loch (35 km south) and Bullfinch (36 km north). **In the area:** Wildflowers bloom on sandplains in spring. Koolyanobbing, 56 km north; built for miners extracting iron ore and now ghost town since closure in 1983. Several interesting rock formations; areas around ideal for picnicking. Hunt's Soak, 7 km north Southern Cross, also has picnic area. Old State Battery, 34 km south. **Tourist information:** Shire Offices, Great Eastern Hwy; (090) 49 1001. **Accommodation:** 1 hotel, 1 motel, 1 caravan/camping park. **See also:** Crossing the Nullarbor.
MAP REF. 324 H9

Three Springs   Population 572
Sir John Forrest named Three Springs, 170 km south-east of Geraldton. WA's finest talc, exported for use in the ceramics industry, is mined here from an open-cut mine 13 km east. **Of interest:** At town entrance, information bay and path through living display of wildflowers. Heritage Walk, including wildflowers; details from tourist centre. **In the area:** Yarra Yarra Lake system, 5 km west, attracts many migratory birds. Eneabba, major mineral sands mining centre, 56 km west. Blue Waters, near Arrino, 18 km north; picnic area amid river gums. Pink Lakes, 6 km east, Cockatoo Canyon, 6 km west, and old copper-mine ruins, 7 km north-west. Wildflower Drives (best between Aug. and Nov.); details from tourist centre. **Tourist information:** Thomas Street; (099) 54 1041. **Accommodation:** 1 hotel/motel.
MAP REF. 322 F8, 324 E7

Tom Price   Population 3435
The huge iron-ore deposit now known as Mt Tom Price was discovered in 1962, after which the Hamersley Iron Project was established. The construction of a mine, two towns (Tom Price and Dampier) and a railway between the mine followed, all of which was achieved in a remarkably short period of time. **Of**

interest: Nameless Festival held in Aug. In the area: Proximity of Tom Price to spectacular Karijini (Hamersley Range) National Park, 38 km north, and chance to tour open-cut mining operation make town a popular stopping-point. Views of remarkable scenery around Tom Price from Mt Nameless lookout, 6 km west, via walking trail. Tourist information: Central Ave; (091) 89 2375. Accommodation: 1 hotel, 1 motel, 1 caravan/camping park. See also: The Hamersley Range; The Pilbara.
MAP REF. 326 G11

Toodyay   Population 557
The historic town of Toodyay, nestled in the Avon Valley, has many charming old buildings recalling its pioneering past. Situated 85 km north-east of Perth, Toodyay is surrounded by picturesque farming country and, to the west, virgin bushland. Of interest: Classified by the National Trust as a historic town, Toodyay has many buildings of historic significance in or near Stirling Tce. Connor's flour-mill, built in the 1870s, is an imposing structure, now housing the local tourist centre, displays and a fascinating steam-engine, still in working order. Old Newcastle Gaol Museum (1865), Clinton St, and police stables (1870), opposite, were built by convicts with random rubble stone. In the area: Hoddywell Archery Park, 8 km south. On Perth road, 4 km south-west, Coorinja Winery, begun in 1870. White Gum Company, 9 km south-west, just off road to Perth, flower farm with a difference; native and exotic flowers under cultivation. Avon Valley National Park, 25 km south-west, with spectacular scenery and seasonal wildflowers. Northam, 27 km south-east, and, nearby, Avon River Weir, sanctuary for swans. Grassy river-bank is a delightful picnic spot. Tourist information: Connor's Mill, Stirling Tce; (09) 574 2435. Accommodation: 2 hotels, 2 caravan/camping parks.
MAP REF. 318 H6, 324 F9

Wagin   Population 1372
The prosperous rural countryside surrounding Wagin supports grain crops and pastures for livestock, especially sheep. Wagin's development has been tied to its important location as a railway-junction town, 177 km east of Bunbury. The annual 'Woolorama' held in Wagin over two days in March is attended by sheep-farmers from all over Australia and attracts crowds of over 25 000. Of interest: Wagin Historical Village, Ballagin Rd; collection of early pioneer artefacts, set in 16 authentic old buildings. Town has some fine Victorian buildings and shop-fronts in Tudhoe and Tudor Sts. Giant Ram (7 m

high), Arthur Rd, and adjacent park with ponds and waterfalls. Great Southern Gamebirds, Ware St; many varieties of native birds. In the area: Corralyn Emu Farm, 4 km north. Granite Mt Latham, 6 km west, affords scenic views and opportunities for bushwalkers. Puntapin, another rock formation, 6 km south-east, used as a water-catchment area. Wildflowers abound in spring. Lakes Norring, 13 km south-east, for picnics, swimming, sailing and water-skiing; and Dumbleyung, 30 km east, for sightseeing. Rockleigh Farm, 18 km south-west, for farm holidays. Wagin Heritage Trail; details from tourist centre. Tourist information: Shire Offices, Arthur Rd; (098) 61 1177; Wagin Historical Village, Ballagin Rd. Accommodation: 3 hotels, 1 motel, 1 caravan/camping park. See also: The Great Southern.
MAP REF. 321 L4, 324 G11

Walpole   Population 1000
Walpole is literally where the forest meets the sea. Surrounded by the Walpole–Nornalup National Park where a variety of trees, including karri, jarrah and the tingle species, unique to the area, all grow. The area is known for its wildflowers in season as well as its wildlife. Of interest: Pioneer Cottage, Pioneer Park; opened in 1989 to commemorate district pioneers, cottage follows basic design of early pioneer homes, but is not intended as a replica. Bibbulmun Track (530 km), leading south from Kalamunda, 30 km east of Perth, ends at Walpole. In the area: Knoll Drive, 3 km east. For bushwalkers, Nuyts Wilderness area, 7 km west, and other walking trails, whilst anglers have choice of ocean, river and inlet. Valley of the Giants, 16 km east; Fernhook Falls, 32 km north-west; Mt Frankland, 29 km north; Circular Pool, on Frankland River, 11 km north-east; and Peaceful Bay, 28 km south-east. Coalmine Beach Heritage Trail; details from tourist centre. Tourst information: Pioneer Cottage, Pioneer Park; (098) 40 1111. Accommodation: 1 hotel/motel, 1 motel, 2 caravan/camping parks.
MAP REF. 320 I12 324 F13

Wanneroo   Population 6745
Just a short drive from Perth, the district around Wanneroo stretches along 50 km of constantly changing coastline. Of interest: Botanic Golf, Burns Beach Rd. Dizzy Lamb Park, cnr Karoborup Rd and Wanneroo Rd. Hillarys Boat Harbour, Sorrento Quay and Underwater World, all at junction of Whitfords Ave, Hepburn Ave and West Coast Dr. Mindarie Keys Resort, Ocean Falls Bvd. Gumnut Factory and Wanneroo Weekend Markets, both

in Prindiville Dr, Wangara. Conti Estate Wine Cellars and Restaurant, and Magic Wildflowers, both in Wanneroo Rd. International competitors are attracted to regular meetings at Wanneroo Motor Racing Circuit. In the area: Lakes Joondalup, 1 km west, Jandabup, 4 km east, and Gnangara, 7 km south-east, are close by. Vineyards in area open for inspection and cellar-door sales: Faranda Wines, 2 km south; Conti Estate Wines, 4 km south; and Hartridge Wines, 10 km north-west. Wildflower Cottage, 10 km north. Yanchep National Park, 27 km north-west; Gloucester Lodge Museum in park. Tourist information: 935 Wanneroo Rd; (09) 405 4678. Accommodation: 3 caravan/ camping parks.
MAP REF. 318 F7

Wickepin   Population 239
Wickepin dates back to the 1890s, when the first settlers came to the district. The town is 214 km south-east of Perth in farming country. Of interest: Good examples of Edwardian architecture in Wogolin Rd. In the area: The town has become well known following the publication of Albert Facey's autobiography A Fortunate Life and his recollections of the time he spent living and working in the area; the house he built still stands 15 km south of Wickepin. Toolibin Lake reserve, 20 km south, attracts wide variety of waterfowl. Tiny town of Yealering and Yealering Lake, 30 km north. Sewell's Rock Nature Reserve, 14 km east of Yealering, ideal for picnics and nature walks. Albert Facey Heritage Trail; details from tourist centre. Tourist information: Wickepin Newsagency and Milkbar, 56 Wogolin Rd; (098) 88 1070. Accommodation: 1 hotel, 1 caravan/camping park.
MAP REF. 319 M13, 321 M1, 324 G11

Wickham   Population 2445
Construction of Wickham, 40 km north of Karratha, was commenced in 1970 by the Cliff's Robe River Iron Associates. Today the town is still company-owned and operated, now by Robe River Iron Associates. Wickham is the sister town to Pannawonica, and it is here that iron ore mined out of Pannawonica is processed before being exported from nearby Cape Lambert. Of interest: Daily tours of processing plant and port operations commence at Robe River Visitors Centre, Wickham Dr. Boat Beach off Walcott Dr Lookout at Tank Hill for views of town. Annual Cossack to Wickham Fun Run held July–Aug. In the area: Wharf at Cape Lambert, 10 km north-west, is tallest and longest open-ocean wharf in Australia. Point Samson, 9 km west, popular beach resort with game

fishing. Partly restored town of Cossack, 8 km south-east, once pearling port. Roebourne, 10 km south, oldest town in north-west; old gaol and government buildings. **Tourist information:** Roebourne Tourist Bureau, 173 Roe St, Roebourne; (091) 82 1060. **Accommodation:** 1 hotel/motel. **See also:** The Hamersley Range; The Pilbara.
MAP REF. 326 F9

Williams   Population 343
Williams enjoys a picturesque setting on the banks of the Williams River, 161 km south-east of Perth. **In the area:** Dryandra State Forest, 25 km north. **Accommodation:** 1 hotel, 1 motel, 1 caravan/camping park.
MAP REF. 321 J2, 324 F11

Wittenoom   Population 50
Wittenoom is situated at the north of Wittenoom Gorge on the northern face of the magnificent Karijini (Hamersley Range) National Park. The town lies 289 km from Roebourne and 322 km from Port Hedland. Wittenoom grew up as a service centre for the workers of the blue asbestos mining industry, but world demand had declined by 1966 and mining ceased. **In the area:** Karijini (Hamersley Range) National Park, 9 km east, renowned for its spectacular mountains and gorges. Wittenoom Gorge, 13 km south. Oxer's Lookout, 30 km south, at junction of Red, Weano and Hancock Gorges, has a breathtaking view. Yampire Gorge, 52 km south-east, used a watering-spot by camel-drivers. Less than 2 km of 45 km gorge is accessible, but at its mouth are the beautiful Fortescue Falls and enticing crystal-clear pools. Dales Gorge, 60 km south-east. Mt Bruce (1235 m), WA's highest peak, 45 km south-west. Hamersley Gorge, 65 km west. Warning: Although the asbestos mine at Wittenoom was closed in 1966, there is still a significant health risk from microscopic asbestos fibres created by the milling process; these fibres are present in tailing dumps near the Wittenoom mine site and in landfill used in and around the town site. While the risk from airborne asbestos fibres to short-term visitors in the town is considered to be significantly low, **warning is given that inhaling asbestos fibres may cause cancer.** Any activity that disturbs asbestos tailings and generates airborne fibres should be avoided. Visitors travelling through Wittenoom are advised to take the following precautions:
• Keep to main roads in the town and gorge areas.
• When driving in windy or dusty conditions, keep car windows closed.

THE PILBARA

In the far north-west of their state, the Western Australians are moving mountains with giant earth-movers that chew their way through the red iron ore. The discovery of vast mineral wealth has created a major economic breakthrough for the state. The arid Pilbara region, one of the most heavily mineralised areas in the world, also contains some of the oldest rock formations in the world—perhaps 2000 million years old. The iron-ore boom has created employment opportunities in this desolate land of sand spinifex, mulga scrub and massive red mountains, and model towns have sprung up. Gardens, swimming pools, golf courses and communal activities help compensate for the isolation and harsh climate.

The largest towns of the Pilbara are company towns, residential and administrative centres for the iron-ore mines, or ports for the export of ore. **Dampier**, on King Bay, is a modern iron-ore company town, with a major salt industry nearby. Offshore is the Woodside North West Shelf Gas Project. The project is the largest single resource development ever undertaken in Australia and includes a 1500-kilometre pipeline for the domestic market. Another side to the town can be found within the attractions of the Dampier Archipelago, comprising 42 islands of which 25 are incorporated into reserves for flora and fauna conservation. The area is a natural playground with fishing, diving, swimming, boating, camping and bushwalking allowed around and on several of these outcrops.

Roebourne, the oldest town in the north-west, has been a centre for the pastoral, copper and pearling industries.

The old pearling port of **Cossack** is a short drive away. Inland on the Fortescue River, lush ferns, palms and lilies grow near the deep pools at **Millstream**, the source of water for many Pilbara towns. The **Millstream–Chichester National Park** is also well worth a visit. To the south, the fishing village of Onslow and its off-shore islands is the perfect holiday retreat.

Karratha is a modern town and regional centre, as is **Wickham**. Wickham's port at Cape Lambert has the longest and tallest jetty in Australia, standing three kilometres long and 18.5 metres above water. **Port Hedland**, streamlined port facilities cope with more tonnage than any other port in the country. Ore mined inland at **Tom Price**, **Newman**, **Paraburdoo** and other centres is railed on giant trains to the ports for export.

The fishing here is good with many world records being set. Swimming can be dangerous: sharks, sea snakes and poisonous fish frequent the waters. **Tom Price** affords easy access to the magnificent gorges in the **Karijini (Hamersley Range) National Park**, with their many-coloured walls, deep cool waters and lush green growth. And, of course, there is **Marble Bar**, living up to its reputation as the hottest place in Australia and keeping alive the tradition of 'the great Australian outback'.

Despite great improvements to the main roads—much is sealed—they are still liable to deteriorate, and can have long stretches of rough and dangerous surface. It is wise to check on local conditions before setting out. **(See also:** Outback Motoring.)

Millstream–Chichester National Park

- Avoid parking on or adjacent to asbestos tailings.
- Prevent children from playing in asbestos tailings in the town or at mine site.
- Camp only in designated camping areas. **Camping is not allowed in the Wittenoom Gorge.**

Tourist information: Wittenoom Souvenir and Tourist Shop, Sixth Ave; (091) 89 7096. **Accommodation:** 1 hotel, 1 caravan/camping park.
MAP REF. 326 G11

Wyndham   Population 1329

Wyndham is the most northerly town and safe port harbour in WA. The town consists of two main areas: the original town site of Wyndham port, situated on Cambridge Gulf, and Wyndham East (or 'Three Mile', as it is known), on the Great Northern Hwy, the residential and shopping area. In October 1985 the meatworks, representing Wyndham's main industry, closed. Today Wyndham is a service town for the pastoral industry, mining exploration, tourism and nearby Aboriginal communities. **Of interest:** Historic buildings in main street (Great Northern Hwy) include Port Post Office, Durack's Store, court-house and Anthon's Landing. Warriu Park Aboriginal Monument in town centre. Port display next to Marine and Harbours Offices, near wharf. Nearby is Crocodile Lookout. Crocodile Farm, Priority Rd; daily feeding. Annual Top of the West Festival held in Aug. **In the area:** Afghan cemetery, 1 km east. Abundant birdlife at Marlgu Billabong, 19 km east. The Grotto, rock-edged waterhole, 30 km east (2 km off road), is a cool, shaded oasis. Huge boab tree in Three Mile Caravan Park. The 93 km sealed road to Kununurra passes through splendid gorge country. To south-east, Aboriginal rock paintings, (25 km) and prison tree (30 km). Five Rivers Lookout, 2 km north, atop Bastion Range, offers spectacular views of Kimberley landscape, mountain ranges, Cambridge Gulf, Wyndham port and rivers. Alligator Airways resort on Drysdale River, 80 km north-west. El Questro Station, 100 km south-west; offers accommodation and touring options on this vast cattle station. **Tourist information:** O'Donnell St, Wyndham Port; (091) 61 1054. **Accommodation:** 2 motels, 1 caravan/camping park. **See also:** The Kimberley.
MAP REF. 327 Q3

Yalgoo   Population 423

Yalgoo lies 216 km east of Geraldton along an excellent road in real Australian outback country. Alluvial gold was discovered in the 1890s and recently the 'Emerald' mine has been reopened. Small traces of gold are still found in the district, which encourages fossicking by locals and visitors. **Of interest:** Court-house Museum, Gibbons St. Restored Dominican Convent Chapel, Henty St. Old railway station (1895), Piesse St. **In the area:** Joker's Tunnel, 10 km south of Paynes Find Rd, carved through solid rock by early prospectors and named after Joker mining syndicate. Area harbours abundant native wildlife and there are prolific wildflowers in season (July–Sept.). Farm holidays at Yuin Station, Yalgoo, and Thundelara Station, 80 km south-east. **Tourist information:** Shire Offices; (099) 62 8042. **Accommodation:** 1 motel, 1 caravan park.
MAP REF. 322 I2, 324 F5

Yallingup   Population nominal

Yallingup is known for its excellent surf, with the Australian Surf Championships held in the area. Its caves were a well-known attraction before the turn of the century. **Of interest:** Caves House Hotel, off Caves Rd, built by government as holiday hotel in 1903. Early visitors arrived from Busselton via horse and buggy along dirt road, a journey of 2 1/2 hours. Hotel was rebuilt in 1938 after a fire, using locally milled timber. **In the area:** Yallingup Caves, 2 km east; open daily. Gunyulgup Gallery, 2 km south. At Rivendell Gardens, 10 km south-east, Devonshire teas and 'pick-your-own' vegetables and strawberries in season. Canal Rocks and Smith's Beach, with good fishing, surfing and swimming, as well as spectacular scenery, 5 km south-west.Only a short drive to top-class wineries of Metricup district (20 km south) and Margaret River area (40 km south). Wineries near to Yallingup include: Hunts Foxhaven Estate (3 km south), open by appointment; Wildwood (5 km south); Cape Clairault Wines (10 km south); Happ's Vineyard and Pottery (8 km south-east); and Moonshine Brewery and Abbey-vale Vineyards (11 km south-east). **Tourist information:** Civic Centre, Southern Dr, Busselton; (097) 52 1091. **Accommodation:** 1 hotel, 1 hotel/motel, 3 caravan/camping parks.
MAP REF. 320 C5 324 E12

Yanchep   Population 775

Within easy driving distance from Perth is the resort of Yanchep, 51 km to the north. **In the area:** Yanchep National Park, 15 km east, covering 2799 ha of natural bushland, has a wildlife sanctuary. In park, Gloucester Lodge Museum; startling limestone formations in Crystal Cave (open to public) and Yonderup Cave; and launch cruises on freshwater Loch McNess. Marina at Two Rocks, 6 km north-west. Wild Kingdom wildlife park and zoo, 3 km north-east, halfway between Yanchep and Two Rocks. Wreck of *Alkimos*, south of Yanchep, is said to be guarded by a ghost. Gnangara Lake, 30 km south-east; picturesque location with picnic facilities. **Tourist information:** Information Office, Yanchep National Park; (09) 561 1004; and 935 Wanneroo Rd, Wanneroo; (09) 405 4678. **Accommodation:** 1 hotel/ motel.
MAP REF. 318 E7

York   Population 1122

Founded in 1830, York is the oldest inland town in WA, set on the banks of the Avon River in the fertile Avon Valley. The town has a wealth of historic buildings, carefully preserved. Many festivals are held annually, including the York Jazz Festival in Sept. **Of interest:** Faversham House, Grey St; a beautifully preserved building over 130 years old. Post Office, court-house and police station, all in Avon Tce, were built of local stone in 1895. Restored two-storey mud-brick building, Settlers' House (1850), also in Avon Tce, offers old-world accommodation. Castle Hotel, fine example of early coaching inn and York's first licensed hotel, and Romanesque-style Town Hall (1911), with impressive dimensions, both in Avon Tce. Old railway station (1886), Railway Rd, now houses railway museum. Old hospital (now recreation camp), Brook St, has its original shingle roof. Residency Museum (1843), Brook St; collection of colonial furniture and early photographs. York's fine churches include Holy Trinity (consecrated 1858), Suburban Rd; St Patrick's (1886), South St; and Uniting Church (1888), Grey St. All in Avon Tce: Art Gallery, York Pottery and Loder Antiques. Also in Avon Tce: Motor Museum, Australia's best collection of veteran, classic and racing cars (and some bicycles and motor-cycles); and Balladong Farm, offering visitors the chance to handfeed many friendly animals. Suspension Bridge across river in Low St, erected originally in 1906. Follow signs from Castle Hotel to Pioneer Drive and then to Mt Brown; lookout and picnic and barbecue facilities. Facilities also at Avon Park, Low St, and Railway Park, Railway Rd. **In the area:** Near Quairading, 64 km east, Toapin Weir and Mt Stirling, offering panoramic views. Self-guided leaflet outlines the Quairading District Heritage Trail. York, York to Goldfields, Guildford to York and Farming Heritage Trails; details from tourist centre. **Tourist information:** 105 Avon Tce; (096) 41 1301. **Accommodation:** 3 hotels, 2 motels, 1 caravan/camping park.
MAP REF. 319 J8, 324 F10

THE ORD RIVER

The introduction of the Ord River Scheme was a progressive and far-sighted move to develop the tropical north of Western Australia. During 'the wet' the rivers of the Kimberley become raging torrents and at times the waters of the Ord River empty more than fifty million litres a second into Cambridge Gulf. With the end of the monsoon rain, the rich seasonal pastures die and the land becomes dry again. The Ord River Dam was built to harness this tremendous wealth of water for agriculture.

The Kimberley Research Station was established in 1945 to investigate the potential of the area and the likelihood of producing crops on the black alluvial soil of the plains. The land was found to be suitable for a variety of tropical crops. By 1963 the Diversion Dam at Kununurra was built to divert water from the river into supply channels. **Lake Argyle**, seventy-two kilometres south of the Carr Boyd Range, is the main storage reservoir. It is the largest man-made lake in Australia, and holds nine times the volume of water of Sydney Harbour, its normal capacity being 5674 million cubic metres. This vast expanse of water is dotted with islands that were once peaks rising above the surrounding valleys. The water of the Ord is now capable of irrigating 72 000 hectares of land. A third of the projected irrigation area will be along the Kreep River Plain in the Northern Territory.

The area is becoming increasingly attractive to tourists. Surrounding Lake Argyle are rugged red slopes, a haven for native animals such as the bungarra lizard, the brush-tailed wallaby and the grey kangaroo. Looking out over the lake is a tourist village, with a modern hotel/motel, caravan and camping facilities and areas of shaded lawns. There are lake cruises and for the more energetic, fishing trips, bushwalks or tennis.

The **Durack Homestead, Argyle Downs** is also to be found here; once the residence of the famous pioneering Durack family, the homestead was moved to its present site to prevent it being covered by the waters of the lake. A fascinating memorial to the pioneers of the district, it re-creates life as it once was in the Kimberley.

The town of **Kununurra** — the name means 'big water' — has been established as the residential and administrative centre of the Ord River Scheme.

Lake Argyle, main storage reservoir for the Ord River Scheme

Maps of Western Australia

Location Map

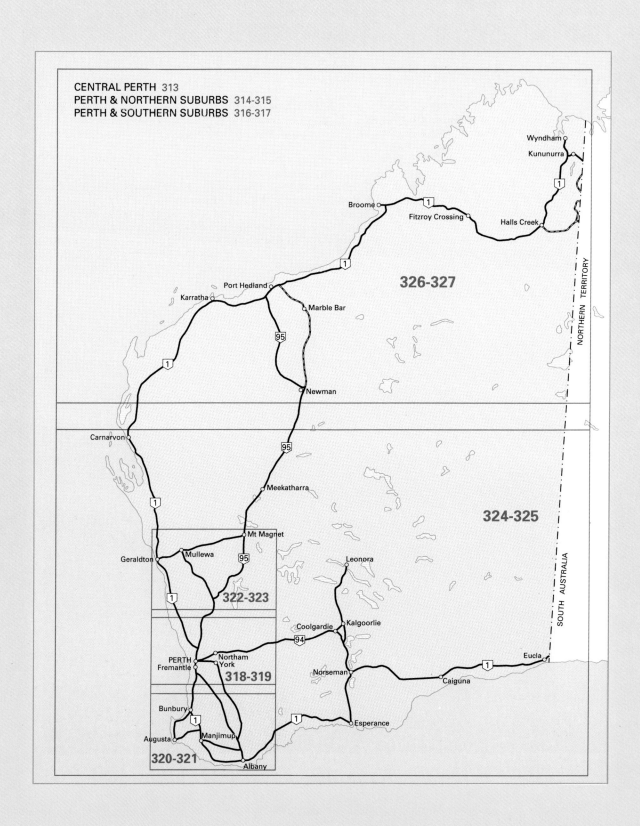

CENTRAL PERTH 313
PERTH & NORTHERN SUBURBS 314-315
PERTH & SOUTHERN SUBURBS 316-317

Wyndham
Kununurra

Broome
Fitzroy Crossing
Halls Creek

Port Hedland
Karratha
Marble Bar

326-327

NORTHERN TERRITORY

Newman

Carnarvon

Meekatharra

324-325

Mt Magnet
Geraldton Mullewa
Leonora

322-323

SOUTH AUSTRALIA

Coolgardie Kalgoorlie

PERTH Northam
Fremantle York

318-319

Norseman
Eucla
Caiguna

Bunbury
Esperance

Augusta Manjimup

320-321 Albany

Central Perth **313**

Places of Interest

1 Art Gallery	D4
2 Cloisters	C4
4 Deanery	D5
5 Entertainment Centre	C4
42 Freeway Hotel	B8
18 General Post Office	D4
7 Government House	D5
8 Hay Street Mall	D4
24 Hyatt Regency Perth Hotel	G6
9 Kings Park	A5
37 Langley Plaza Hotel	F6
3 Legacy Lookout	A4
10 Museum	E4
13 Old Mill	B7
14 Orchestral Shell	D5
15 Parliament House	B4
6 Perth International Hotel	E5
19 Perth Mint	F5
16 Peter Pan Statue	G6
17 Police Headquarters	G6
40 Princess Margaret Childrens Hospital	A3
36 Royal Perth Hospital	E5
38 Sheraton Hotel	F6
20 St.Andrews Church	E5
41 St.Annes Hospital	H1
21 St.Georges Cathedral	D5
22 St.Mary's Cathedral	E5
23 State Library	D4
11 Supreme Court of W.A.	D5
25 The Hilton Intl. Hotel	C5
39 The Metro Inn Hotel	H10
35 The Orchard Perth Hotel	C4
26 Town Hall	D5
27 War Memorial	B6
28 Zoological Gardens	C10

Transport and Touring

29 Ansett Terminal	E5
33 Australian Airlines Term.	D5
30 Bus Station	C4
31 Perth Railway Station	D4
32 Royal Auto Club WA	E5
34 WA Tourist Centre	D4

One way streets shown →

See fold-out page for an explanation of the map symbols

COPYRIGHT, BP AUSTRALIA LTD

314 Perth & Northern Suburbs

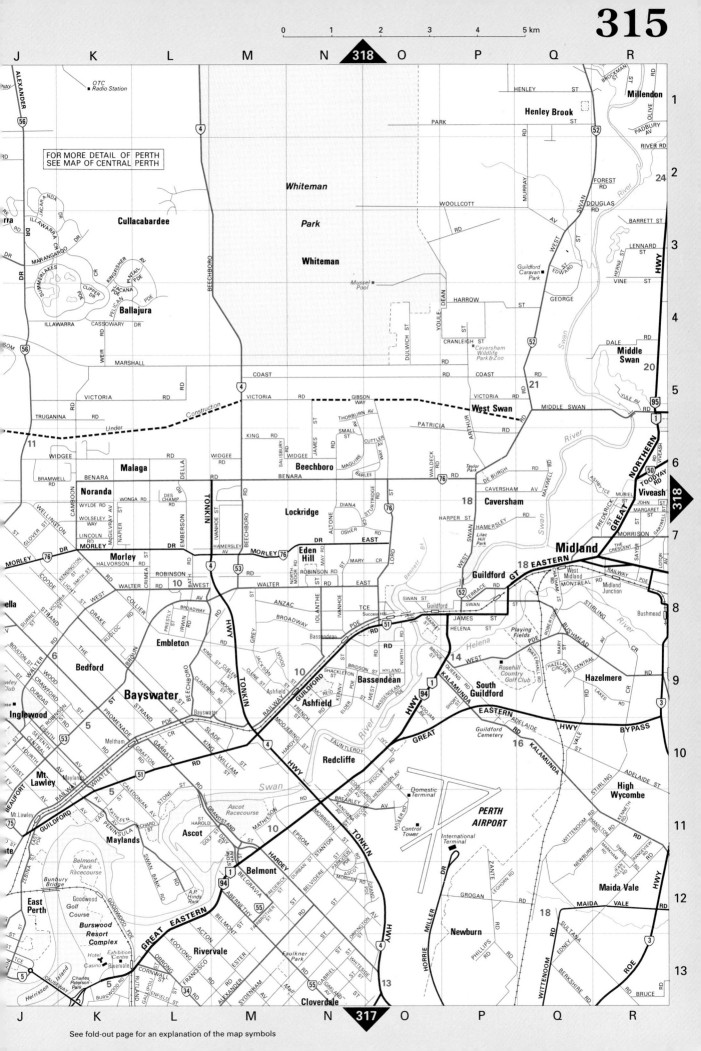

0 1 2 3 4 5 km

318

J K L M N O P Q R

1

OTC
Radio Station

Millendon

HENLEY   ST

Henley Brook

PADBURY AV
OLIVE

FOR MORE DETAIL OF PERTH
SEE MAP OF CENTRAL PERTH

PARK   RD

52

RIVER RD

2

24

FOREST
RD

Cullacabardee

Whiteman

WOOLLCOTT

MURRAY

Douglas
RD

SWAN
River

BARRETT ST

3

rra

illawarra

JACARANDA

ILLAWARRA CR

MARANGAROO

DR

DR

KINGFISHER AV
PINTAIL PDE

CLIPPER DR
PDE

JACANA PDE

Park

Whiteman

Guildford
Caravan
Park

ST

ST
EDWARD

WEST

LENNARD ST

HERNE
ST

VINE   ST

HWY

3

Ballajura

PELICAN

Mussel
Pool

HARROW

ST

GEORGE

52

DALE   RD

Middle
Swan

4

SUMMERLAKES

56

SOM

ILLAWARRA

CASSOWARY DR

WEIR

MARSHALL

Caversham
Wildlife
Park & Zoo

DULWICH ST

YOULE DEAN

CRANLEIGH ST

RD

20

20

VICTORIA   RD

4

COAST

RD

COAST

RD

95

5

TRUGANINA   RD

Under Construction

VICTORIA   RD

GIBSON
WAY

RD

West Swan

MIDDLE SWAN

21

1

11

THORBURN AV

PATRICIA

ARTHUR

River

NORTHERN

VIVEASH

6

WIDGEE

BRAMWELL
RD

BENARA   RD

Malaga

DELLA   RD

WIDGEE   RD

KING   RD

SALISBURY

WIDGEE

SMALL
ST

JAMES   RD

CUTTLER
WAY

MAGUIRE

BARLEE

Beechboro

WALDECK   RD

76

Taylor
Park

DE BURGH

50

TOODYAY RD

FREDERICK

MURIEL
JOHN

318

6

Noranda

CAMBOON

WYLDE RD

DES CHAMP
RD

WONGA RD

NAPIER   ST

TONKIN

IVANHOE   RD

BEECHBORO   RD

Lockridge

DIANA

STIRTRIDGE

ST

76

East

18

Caversham

CAVERSHAM   AV

MAXWELL RD

HARPER ST

Swan

ASHBY TCE

MARGARET ST

GREAT

MORRISON

7

WELLINGTON

GLOVER

MCGILVRAY AV

WOLSELEY
WAY

LINCOLN   RD

EMBERSON

MORLEY   DR

Morley

Eden Hill

MAY RD

OSHER

LORD

HAMERSLEY

HARPER ST

Lilac Hill
Park

Midland

THE
CRESCENT

SAYER

LOTON

7

ST
MORLEY

76

DR

HALVORSON RD

CRIMEA
ST

ROBINSON RD

BATH
WEST   ST

WALTER

ROBINSON RD

NORTH MOOR RD

EAST

ANZAC

IOLANTHE

MARY ST

EAST

Guildford

52

TERRACE

18   EASTERN

West Midland
Montreal

RAILWAY
PDE

Midland
Junction

8

ella

6

BOULTON STTER

WALTER

CRAWFORD
WOOD

DUNDAS

Bedford

THE

KENSINGTON

VICTORIA
LIGHT

SMITH ST

DRAKE
RUDLOC

BROADWAY
PRIESTLY
IRWIN

Embleton

GREY

BROADWAY

Bassendean

SWAN   ST

Success Hill

Guildford

JAMES   ST

Helena

MARKET ST

BRIDGE ST

QUEENS RD

Playing
Fields

Rosehill
Country
Golf Club

MARY

HAZELMERE CIRCUS

ROBERTSON

STIRLING

CENTRAL

Bushmead

River

8

Inglewood

5

ROBINSON

SEVENTH

53

AV

Bayswater

FIFTH

KING   ST
CULLEN   ST

CLAVERING   RD

MOONEY

Ashfield

REID

KENNY

ELDER   ST

ST

BASSENDEAN   PDE

WEST

NORTH

14

KALAMUNDA RD

South
Guildford

WATERHALL RD

HAZELMERE

LAKES   RD

RD

Hazelmere

CR

9

Mt.
Lawley

FOURTH

FIRST   AV

Mt.Lawley

53

GUILDFORD

EAST

Maylands

BEECHBORO   RD

STRAND   ST

Bayswater

PDE

SLADE   ST

KING
WILLIAM   ST

CLUNE

Ashfield

FRENCH   ST

MOOLIEBING   RD

RIVER

FAUNTLEROY   AV

HYLAND

94

1

KOJAN   AV

GREAT

Guildford
Cemetery

EASTERN   ADELAIDE   RD

16

KALAMUNDA

VALE   RD

BYPASS

3

10

5

BEAUFORT

75

GUILDFORD

EAST   AV

51

Meltham

PROMENADE

GARRATT   RD

Swan

River

Redcliffe

RD

HWY

Domestic
Terminal

Control
Tower

PERTH
AIRPORT

STIRLING

ADELAIDE   ST

High
Wycombe

10

East
Perth

Belmont
Park
Racecourse

Bunbury
Bridge

Goodwood
Golf Course

CALEDONIAN   AV

WHATLEY

PENINSULA   RD

KATHLEEN

STONE   ST

GOLF

HAROLD   ST

RICHARD   ST

DALY   ST

Ascot

10

Ascot
Racecourse

STONEHAM

EPSOM   AV

DURBAN

STANTON   ST

ASCO

MORRISON

BREARLEY   AV

SECOND   ST

TONKIN

MILLER   RD

International
Terminal

ZANTE   ST

LEGHORN RD

WITTENOOM

SWAN

JEAN
HILL   RD

RANGEVIEW   RD

NEWBURN   RD

KENNETH   RD

HWY

Maida Vale

11

Maylands

5

SWAN BANK RD

GOODWOOD PDE

STONE   ST

STONEHAM

Belmont

BELGRAVIA

94

ABERNETHY   RD

55

FREDERICK   ST

BELVIDERE   ST

PARKVIEW   PDE

MORGAN   RD

GRAND   RD

HORRIE

GROGAN   RD

Newburn

PHILLIPS   RD

MAIDA

18

SULTANA   RD

VALE   RD

12

ZEBRA   ST

Herrisson

5

A.P. Hinds
Track

AP
HARDEY
RD

A.P. Hinds
Track

Burswood
Resort
Complex

Hotel
Exhibition
Centre

Casino

Charles
Paterson
Park

Rivervale

KOOYONG   RD

OBRONG

Rivervale

FRANCISCO   ST

ESTER   ST

CORNWALL   ST

SYDENHAM   ST

Faulkner
Park

WHITESIDE   ST

MELL   ST

GABRIEL   ST

OAKLAND   AV

55

EDNEY   RD

WITTENOOM   ST

BERKSHIRE   RD

ROE   RD

BRUCE   RD

13

5

GALLIPOLI

RUTLAND   ST

ENFIELD   ST

ALEXANDER   RD

Cloverdale

MEAD   ST

13

HWY

3

J K L M N O P Q R

317

See fold-out page for an explanation of the map symbols

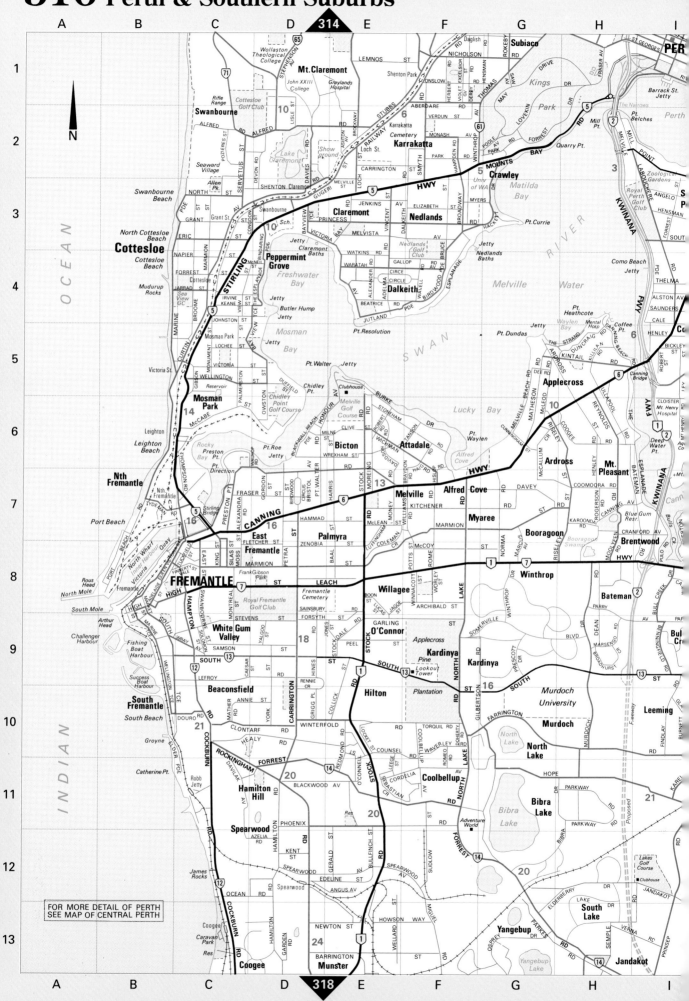

316 Perth & Southern Suburbs

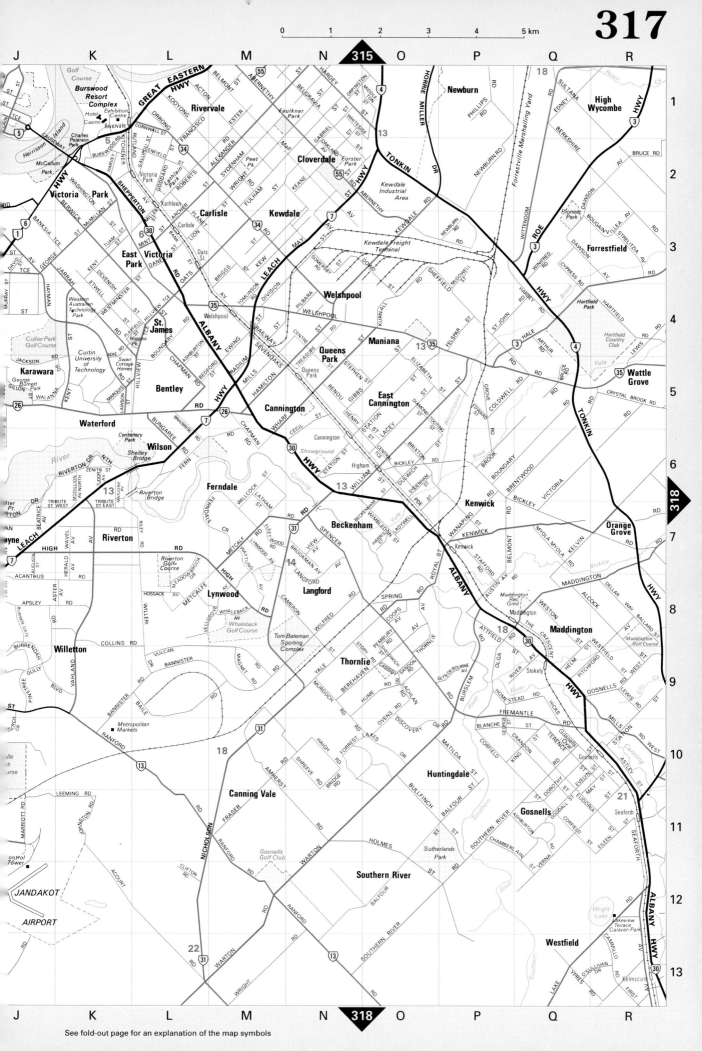

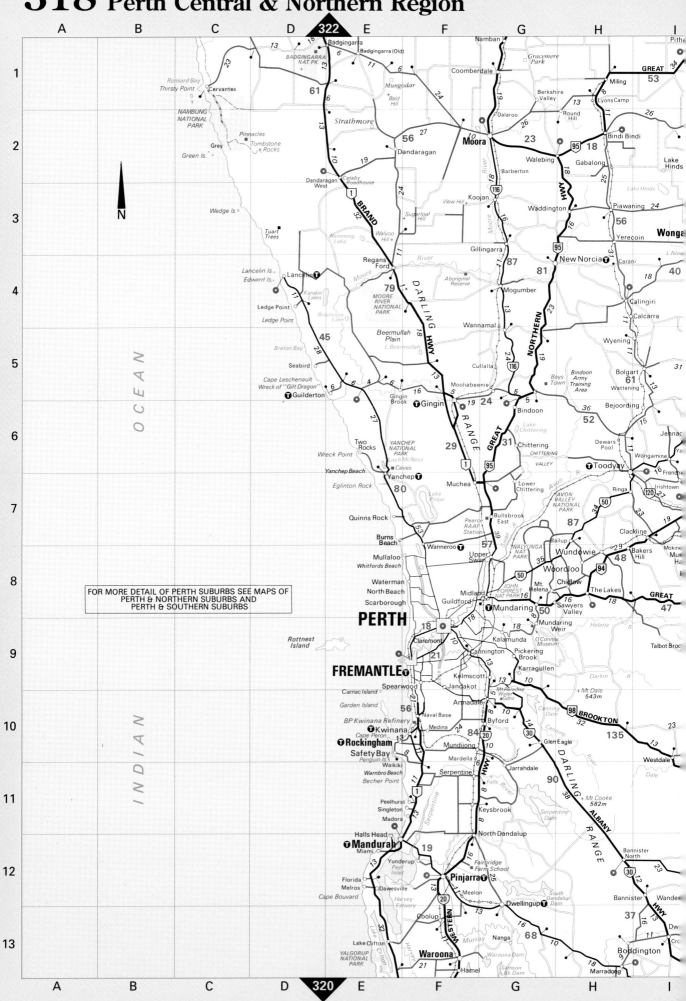

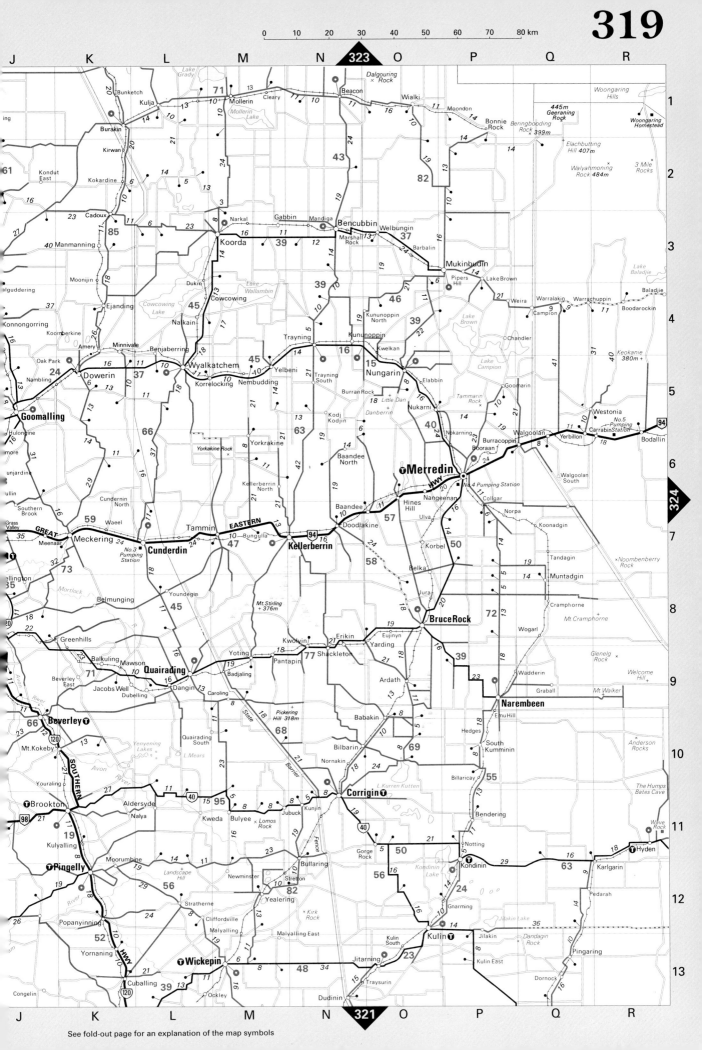

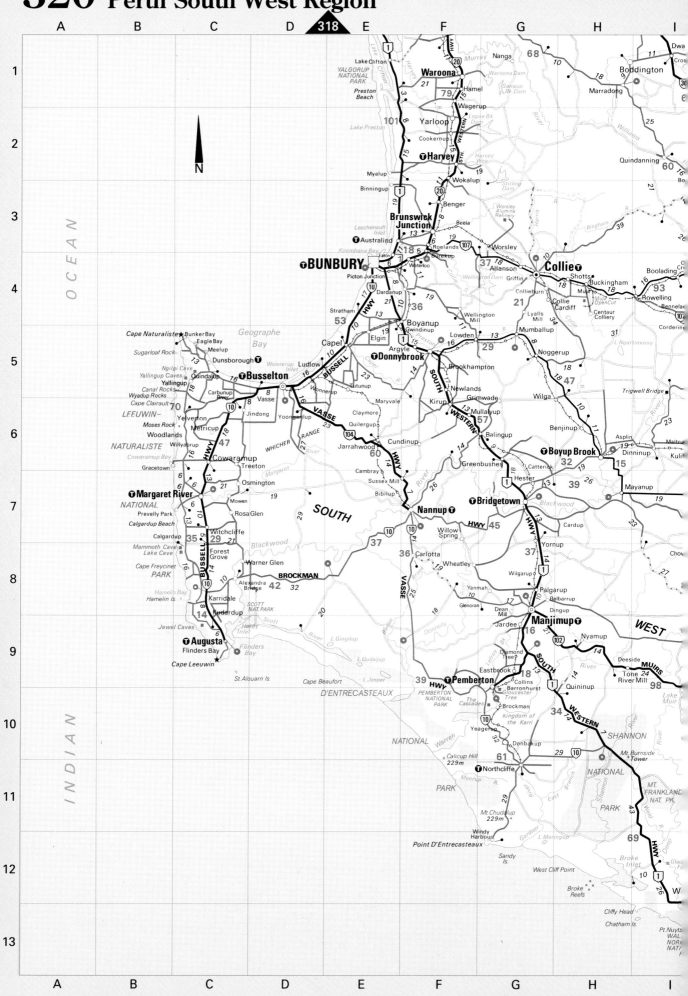

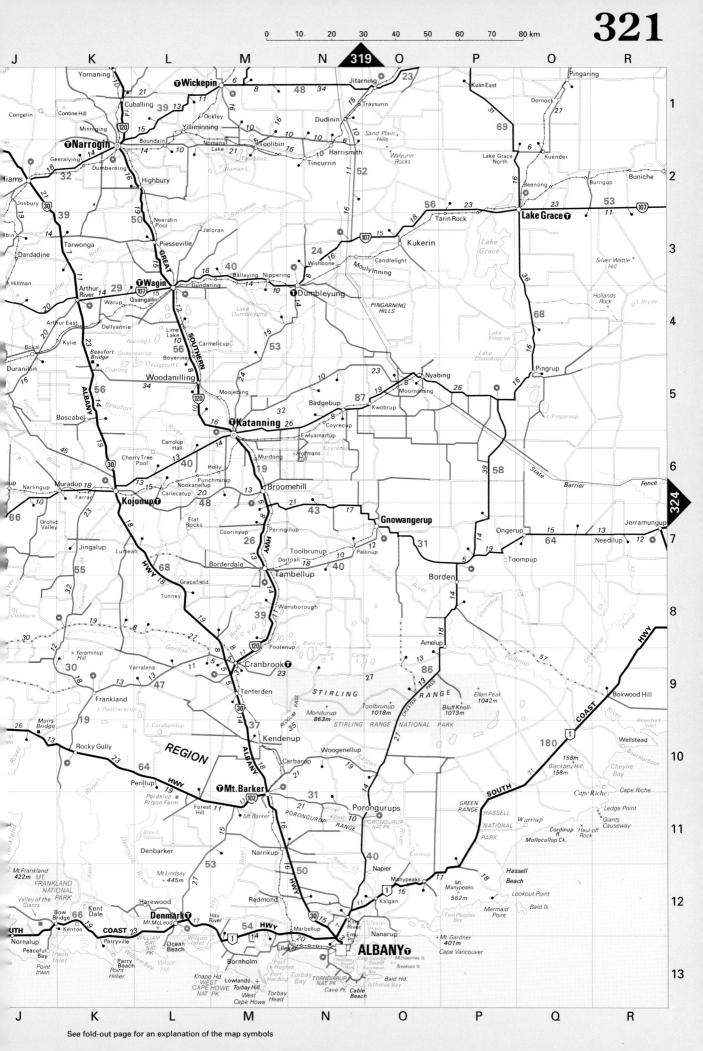

0   10.   20   30   40   50   60   70   80 km

J   K   L   M   N   O   P   Q   R

319

324

See fold-out page for an explanation of the map symbols

322 Geraldton Region

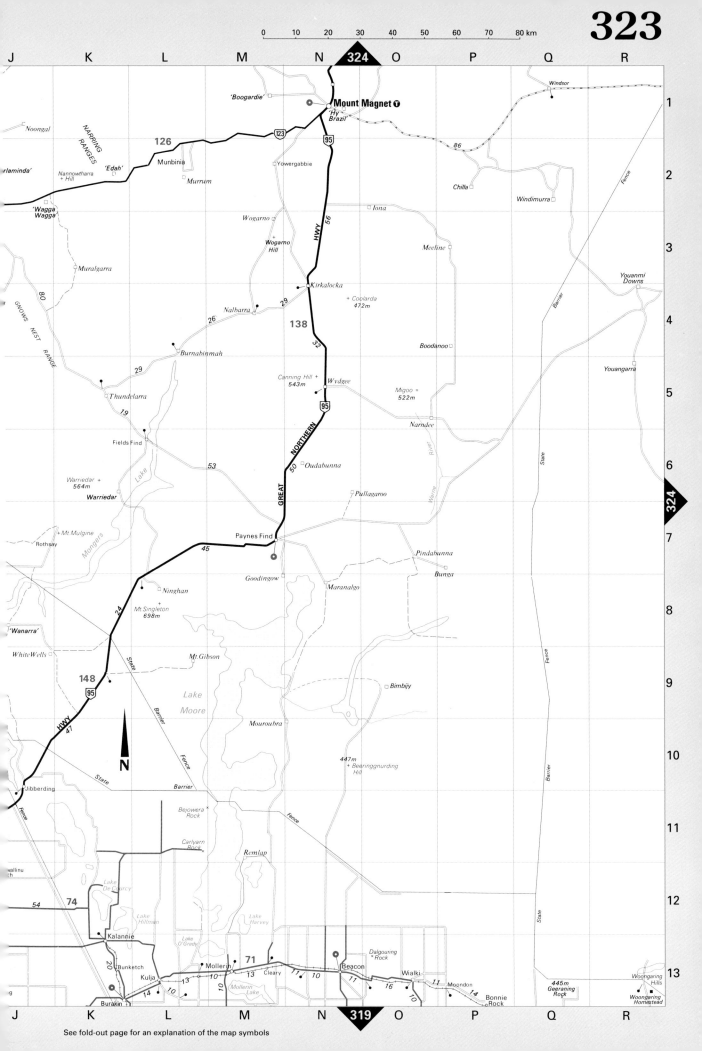

0 10 20 30 40 50 60 70 80 km

J K L M N **324** O P Q R

1

Noongal

NARRING RANGES

'Boogardie' **Mount Magnet** ⊕

126 *'Hy Brazil'*

'Edah' Munbinia

123 Windsor

rlaminda' Nannowtharra + Hill 86

2

Murrum *Yowergabbie* Chilla

'Wagga Wagga' *Windimurra*

Wogarno *Iona*

3

Muralgarra Wogarno Hill 56 *Meeline* Youanmi Downs

80 HWY

Kirkalocka

GNOWS 4

NEST 26 *Nalbarra* 29 + *Coolarda 472m*

RANGE 138

32 *Boodanoo*

Burnabinmah 5

29 Canning Hill + 543m Wvdgee *Migoo + 522m* *Youangarra*

Thundelarra 95

19 Warne River *Narndee*

Fields Find NORTHERN 6

Lake 53 50 *Oudabunna* **324**

Warriedar + 564m **Warriedar** GREAT

State 7

+ Mt.Mulgine *Pullagaroo*

Rothsay Morgers Paynes Find *Pindabunna*

45 *Bunga*

'Wanarra' Goodingow *Maranalgo*

24 *Ninghan* 8

White Wells + Mt.Singleton 698m

State Mt.Gibson *Bimbijy* 9

148 Barrier

95 Lake Moore Fence

HWY 47 *Mouroubra* 10

447m + Beeringgnurding Hill

N Barrier

Jibberding 11

Fence Bejowera Rock

State Carlyarn Rock

Barrier *Remlap* Fence

12

Lake De Courcy

vallinu 54 74 Lake Hillman Lake Harvey State

Kalannie Lake O'Grady Dalgouring Rock

20 Bunketch 71 Beacon *Wialki* 445m Geeraning Rock Woongaring Hills

g Kulja 13 10 13 Cleary 11 10 Moondon Woongaring Homestead

14 10 Mollerin 16 11 Bonnie Rock 14

Burakin 10 Mollerin Lake 10

J K L M N **319** O P Q R

324 Southern Western Australia

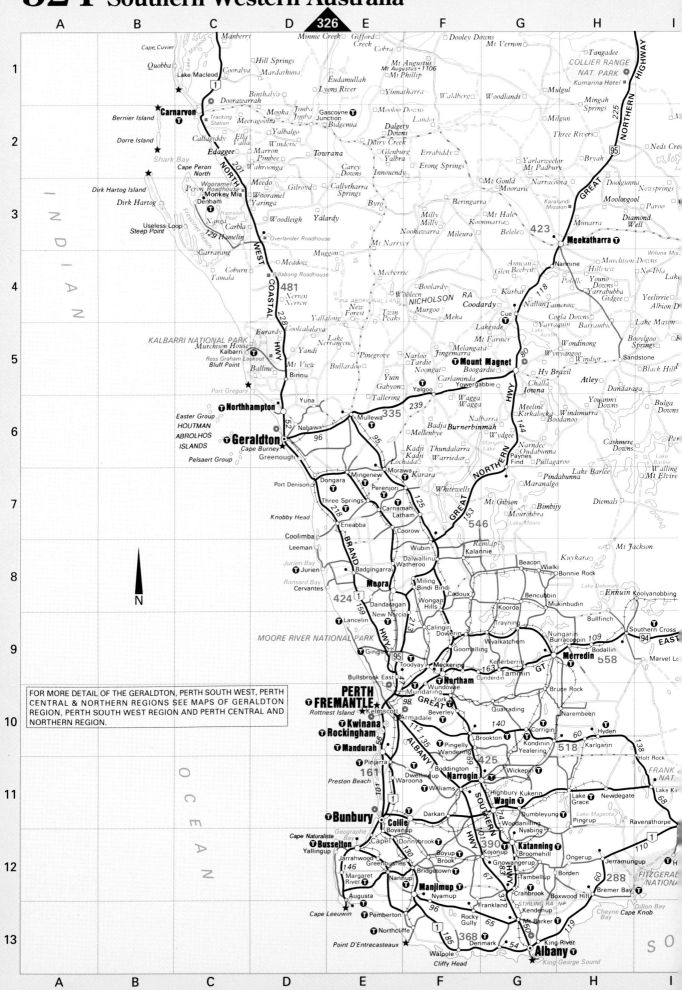

326

FOR MORE DETAIL OF THE GERALDTON, PERTH SOUTH WEST, PERTH CENTRAL & NORTHERN REGIONS SEE MAPS OF GERALDTON REGION, PERTH SOUTH WEST REGION AND PERTH CENTRAL AND NORTHERN REGION.

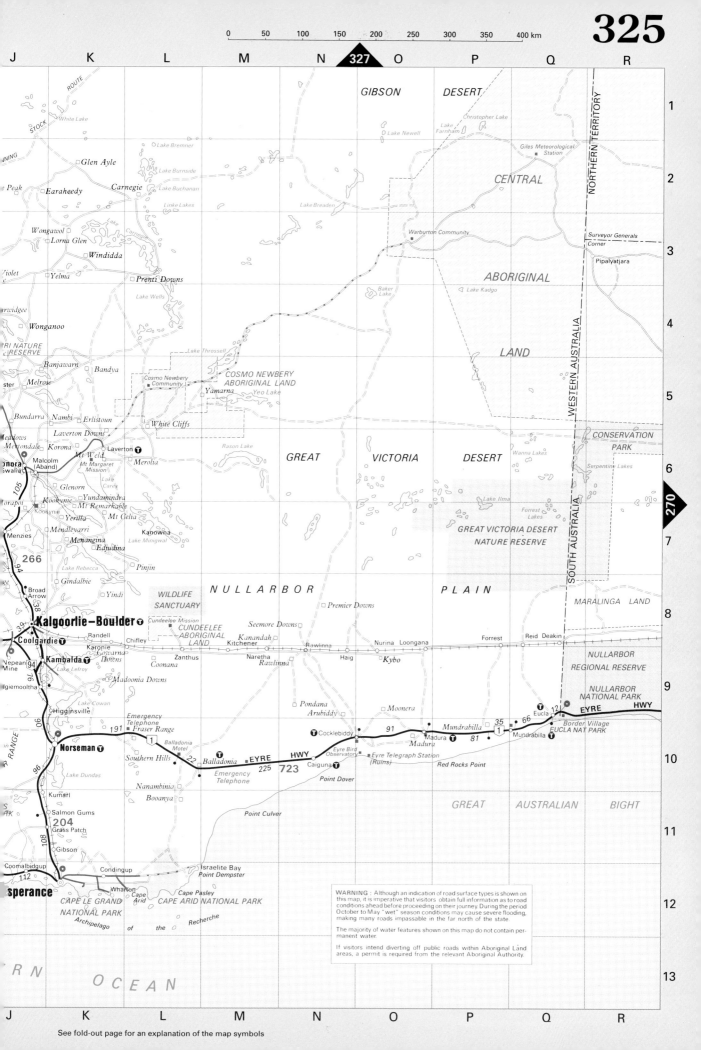

0 50 100 150 200 250 300 350 400 km

327

J K L M N O P Q R

1

GIBSON   DESERT

White Lake
Lake Bremner
Glen Ayle
Lake Burnside
Carnegie *Lake Buchanan*

Lake Newell
Lake Farnham
Christopher Lake
Giles Meteorological Station

CENTRAL

NORTHERN TERRITORY

2

Peak *Earaheedy*
Linke Lakes
Lake Breaden

Warburton Community

Wongawol
Lorna Glen
Windidda

Surveyor Generals Corner

ABORIGINAL

3

Violet *Yelma* *Prenti Downs*
Lake Wells
Baker Lake
Lake Kadgo

Pipalyatjara

LAND

WESTERN AUSTRALIA

4

Wongawol
RI NATURE RESERVE
Lake Throssell

CONSERVATION

5

Banjawarn *Bandya*
Melrose
COSMO NEWBERY ABORIGINAL LAND
Cosmo Newbery Community
Yamarna *Yeo Lake*
White Cliffs

PARK

Bundarra *Nambi* *Erlistoun*
Meadows
Mertondale *Korona*
Laverton Downs
Laverton
Rason Lake

GREAT   VICTORIA   DESERT

Wanna Lakes

Serpentine Lakes

6

onora (Aband)
walia
Malcolm (Aband)
Mt Weld
Mt Margaret Mission
Merolia

Lake Ilma

SOUTH AUSTRALIA

270

orapul *Glenorn*
Kookynie *Yundamindra*
Kookynie *Mt Remarkable*
Yerilla *Mt Celia*
Menzies *Mendlevarri*
Kanowna
Menangina
Edjudina
Lake Minigwal

Lake Carey

Forrest Lakes

GREAT VICTORIA DESERT NATURE RESERVE

7

266
94

Lake Rebecca
Gindalbie
Pinjin
Yindi

N U L L A R B O R   P L A I N

MARALINGA   LAND

8

Broad Arrow
38

WILDLIFE SANCTUARY

Cundeelee Mission
CUNDEELEE ABORIGINAL LAND

Premier Downs

Kalgoorlie–Boulder
39
Coolgardie
Randell
Chifley
Kitchener
Rawlinna
Nurina *Loongana*
Forrest
Reid *Deakin*

Seemore Downs
Kanandah

NULLARBOR REGIONAL RESERVE

Kambalda
94
Nepean Mine
76
Karonie
Gowarna *Downs*
Zanthus
Coonana
Naretha
Rawlinna
Haig
Kybo

NULLARBOR NATIONAL PARK

9

Lake Lefroy
Madoonia Downs

Pondana
Arubiddy
Moonera

Eucla 121

EYRE   HWY

giemooltha
90
Lake Cowan

Higginsville
191
Emergency Telephone
Fraser Range

91
Mundrabilla
35
66
Border Village

Cocklebiddy
Madura
81
Mundrabilla
1
EUCLA NAT PARK

10

RANGE
Norseman
1
Balladonia Motel
22
Balladonia
EYRE   HWY
225 **723**

Southern Hills
Eyre Bird Observatory
Eyre Telegraph Station (Ruins)
Red Rocks Point

96
Lake Dundas
Nanambinia
Emergency Telephone
Caiguna
Point Dover

Booanya

GREAT   AUSTRALIAN   BIGHT

11

Kumarl
Salmon Gums
204
Grass Patch
801
Gibson

Point Culver

S
PARK
112
Coomalbidgup
Condingup
Israelite Bay
Point Dempster

12

sperance
Wharton *Cape Arid*
Cape Pasley
CAPE ARID NATIONAL PARK

CAPE LE GRAND NATIONAL PARK
Archipelago
of *the*
Recherche

WARNING : Although an indication of road surface types is shown on this map, it is imperative that visitors obtain full information as to road conditions ahead before proceeding on their journey. During the period October to May "wet" season conditions may cause severe flooding, making many roads impassable in the far north of the state.

The majority of water features shown on this map do not contain permanent water.

If visitors intend diverting off public roads within Aboriginal Land areas, a permit is required from the relevant Aboriginal Authority.

13

RN   O C E A N

J K L M N O P Q R

See fold-out page for an explanation of the map symbols

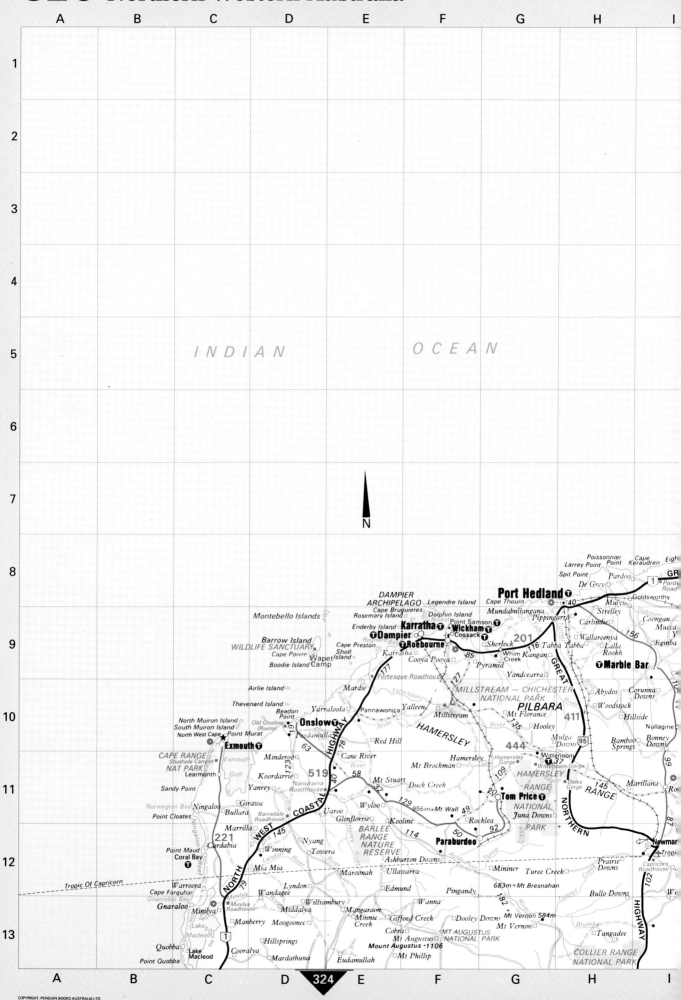

INDIAN   OCEAN

N

DAMPIER
ARCHIPELAGO
Montebello Islands
Cape Bruguieres
Rosemary Island
Legendre Island
Dolphin Island
Cape Thouin
Point Samson
Enderby Island
Karratha
Wickham
Cossack
Port Hedland
Poissonnier Point
Cape Keraudren
Larrey Point
Spit Point
Pardoo
De Grey
Goldsworthy
GR
Pardo
Road
1
Mundabullangana
Pippingarra
40
Mulye
Strelley
Carlindie
Coongan
Mucca
y
Eginba
156
Dampier
Roebourne
Barrow Island
WILDLIFE SANCTUARY
Cape Poivre
Sholl
Island
Boodie Island
Wapet
Camp
Cape Preston
Karratha
Sherlock
Whim
Creek
Kangan
116
Tabba Tabba
201
Wallareenya
Lulla
Rookh
Marble Bar
Regnard Bay
Cooya Pooya
85
85
Pyramid
Yandearra
Abydos
Corunna
Downs
Fortesque Roadhouse
127
MILLSTREAM — CHICHESTER
NATIONAL PARK
Woodstock
Airlie Island
Mardie
Yalleen
Millstream
PILBARA
411
Hillside
Nullagine
Thevenard Island
Yarraloola
Pannawonica
Fortesque River
Mt Florance
Hooley
135
Bamboo
Springs
Beadon
Point
Old Onslow
(Ruins)
Onslow
Red Hill
HAMERSLEY
444
Mulga
Downs
Wittenoom
Marillana
North Muiron Island
South Muiron Island
North West Cape
Point Murat
Exmouth
Shothole Canyon
123
Minderoo
Cane River
Hamersley
Mt Brockman
Hamersley
Gorge
109
HAMERSLEY
145
CAPE RANGE
NAT PARK
Learmonth
Exmouth
Gulf
Koordarrie
519
40
58
Mt Stuart
Duck Creek
956m+Mt Wall
49
Tom Price
20
RANGE
87
Sandy Point
Yanrey
Nanutarra
Roadhouse
32
Wyloo
129
Rocklea
92
NATIONAL
Juna Downs
PARK
Norwegian Bay
Ningaloo
Girawa
Bullara
Glenflorrie
Kooline
50
114
Paraburdoo
Newmar
Point Cloates
Barradale
Roadhouse
Uaroo
145
Ashburton Downs
Tropi
Marrilla
221
Cardabia
Point Maud
Coral Bay
Nyang
Towera
Mininer
Turee Creek
Prairie
Downs
Capricorn
Roadhouse
Tropic Of Capricorn
Warroora
Cape Farquhar
Gnarraloo Bay
79
Minilya
Mia Mia
Winning
Lyndon
Wandagee
Maroonah
Ullawarra
Edmund
Pingandy
683m+Mt Bresnahan
182
Bullo Downs
102
HIGHWAY
Gnaraloo
Minilya
Williambury
Middalya
Moogooree
Mangaroon
Minnie
Creek
Gifford Creek
Wanna
Dooley Downs
Mt Vernon 584m
Mt Vernon
Tangadee
Ck
Manberry
Hillsprings
Cobra
MT AUGUSTUS
NATIONAL PARK
Brumby
Quobba
Cooralya
Mardathuna
Mt Augustus
Mount Augustus +1106
Mt Phillip
COLLIER RANGE
NATIONAL PARK
Lake Macleod
Point Quobba
Eudamullah

Scale: 0 50 100 150 200 250 300 350 400 km

TIMOR SEA

Cape Talbot • Cape Londonderry
Cape Bougainville • Cape Rulhieres
Gibson Point • Cape Bernier
Admiralty Gulf • Cape St Lambert • Buckle Head
Kalumburu Mission
Joseph Bonaparte Gulf

BONAPARTE ARCHIPELAGO
Bigge Island
Cape Pond
Coronation Island
Heywood Island
Champagny Is

ADMIRALTY GULF ABORIGINAL LAND
MITCHELL PLATEAU
Mitchell River
Carson River
Theda
DRYSDALE RIVER NAT PARK
Oombulgurri
Forrest River Mission (Aband)

Doongan

GARDNER PLATEAU

Wyndham
Ivanhoe
Kunumurra
Kimberley Research Stn

Camden Sound
KUNMUNYA Hall Point
Kwinana Mission (Aband)
GEORGE Water
Prince Regent Nature Reserve
Drysdale River
Ellenbrae
Home Valley
El Questro
Lake Argyle
Ord Dam

Cape Leveque
One Arm Point
Mt Elizabeth
482m • Tabletop Mt
Beverley Springs
Gibb River
Pentecost Downs
Dunham River
CARR BOYD RA
Argyle Diamond Mine
Glen Hill
Rosewood
Lissadell
Spring Creek
Texas Downs

KIMBERLEY REGION
374
Mt House 539m
936m • Mt Ord
Glenroy
Mt Broome 935m
Tableland
Bedford Downs
Bow River
Turkey Creek
Warmun Aboriginal Community
Mabel Downs
BUNGLE BUNGLE N.P.

Derby
Kilto 145
Yeeda 42
Blina
Camballin Irrigation Area
WINDJANA GORGE NAT PARK
TUNNEL CREEK NAT PARK 257
LEOPOLD RANGES
Mornington
Lansdowne
VIOLET HILL ABORIGINAL LAND
Springvale
Alice Downs

Broome 222
Waterbank
Roebuck Plains
Mt Anderson
Ellendale
GEIKIE GORGE NAT PARK
323m • Mt Winifred
Fossil Downs
Halls Creek
Saunders Creek
Sophie Downs
Nicholson
Flora Valley

Cable Beach (Village)
Gantheaume Point
Roebuck Bay
Thangoo
Leopold Downs 173
Calwynyardah
Fitzroy Crossing
Quanbun Downs
Noonkanbah
Jubilee Downs
Mt Amhurst
Moola Bulla
Koongie Park
184

Dampier Downs
Myroodah
Nerrima
Kalyeeda
Margaret River
Louisa Downs
Ruby Plains
DENISON PLAINS
Gordon Downs

Frazier Downs
Nita Downs
Mowla Bluff
Cherrabun
Christmas Creek 296
Bohemia Downs
WOLF CREEK CRATER NAT PARK
Carranya
Sturt Creek

NORTHERN HIGHWAY 610
GREAT SANDY DESERT

Billiluna Community
Balgo Community
BALWINA (BALGO) ABORIGINAL LAND
Locked Gate

WARNING: Although an indication of road surface types is shown on this map, it is imperative that visitors obtain full information as to road conditions ahead before proceeding on their journey. During the period October to May, 'wet' season conditions may cause severe flooding, making many roads impassable in the far north of the state.

The majority of water features shown on this map do not contain permanent water.

If visitors intend diverting off public roads within Aboriginal Land areas, a permit is required from the relevant Aboriginal authority.

Beware of man-eating crocodiles in rivers and estuaries.

Telfer Mining Centre
Percival Lakes
Tobin Lake
Lake Willis
Lake White
Lake Hazlett

RUDALL RIVER NATIONAL PARK
Lake Dora
Lake Auld
GIBSON DESERT
Lake Mackay

Lake Disappointment
CENTRAL
Tropic Of Capricorn
Lake MacDonald

CANNING STOCK ROUTE
ABORIGINAL LAND

WESTERN AUSTRALIA / NORTHERN TERRITORY

See fold-out page for an explanation of the map symbols

NORTHERN TERRITORY

Outback Australia

Victoria River Downs cattle station

There are only three main highways that take motorists into the Northern Territory: the Barkly Highway from Mount Isa in Queensland, the Stuart Highway from South Australia and the Victoria Highway from the extreme north-east of Western Australia. Given the enormous distances involved, you may well decide to fly, either to Darwin or to Alice Springs, and then hire a car. Alternatively, airlines, coach companies and tour operators offer day and extended coach tours, coach camping tours, adventure and safari trek tours which allow you to discover this unique, relatively uninhabited and exciting Territory in experienced hands.

Six times the size of Great Britain, with a population similar to that of Newcastle in New South Wales, and boasting the famous 'red centre' and the world's largest monolith, the Northern Territory abounds with staggering statistics.

The first, unsuccessful, attempt to settle this huge, forbidding region was in fact not on the mainland at all, but on Melville Island, in 1825, and it was not until 1869 that a town called Palmerston was established on the coast, the town which was later to become Darwin. Originally the Territory was part of New South Wales, when that state's western boundary extended to the 129th east meridian. Later it was annexed to South Australia and it did not come under Commonwealth control until 1911. In July 1978 the Territory attained self-government.

In terms of monetary value, the Territory's main industry is mining. Gold, bauxite, manganese ore, copper, silver, iron ore and uranium all contribute to this industry. The tourist industry ranks second in importance, but beef cattle farming is by no means unimportant, even though sixteen hectares or more are often required to support one animal. Poor soil, huge distances from markets and winter droughts all combine to render commercial crop-growing virtually impossible.

The 'dry season', between the months of April and October, is the best time to visit the Northern Territory; and 'dry' *means* dry — during the 'wet season' Darwin has an average annual rainfall of 1500 millimetres, while only 25 millimetres falls in the 'dry season'. July is the Territory's coolest month. Temperatures in Darwin range then between 20° and 30°C. In 'the Alice' (as Alice Springs is affectionately known) the average maximum in August is 22.5°C, cooling at night to a low of around zero.

The Northern Territory's two main centres are more than 1500 kilometres apart. Darwin, at the 'Top End', has a population of about 76 000. It suffered extensively from Cyclone Tracy in 1974 and has since been virtually rebuilt. It is renowned for its relaxed lifestyle and beautiful beaches. Darwin makes a perfect jumping-off spot for exploring the Top End region.

If, however, you are 'going it alone' by car, you should research your trip thoroughly before setting out; read the section on Outback Motoring and bear in mind that the dry season is definitely the most pleasant weather for touring. Always be sure to make full enquiries as to conditions before leaving sealed roads. Both the Stuart and Barkly Highways are now all-weather roads, sealed for their entire length. Even so, any driving at night should be undertaken with care.

East of Darwin is the spectacular Kakadu National Park. Further east is Arnhem Land, which can be explored by extended coach tour or adventure tour. Many Aboriginal reserves require entry permission from an Aboriginal Land Council. These reserves belong to the Aborigines; much of the land is sacred to them and should be respected by visitors.

South of Darwin is Katherine with its spectacular gorge, on the southern fringe of Arnhem Land. Freshwater crocodiles are common in the Katherine River, so its dramatic beauty is best viewed from either bank. From Katherine, the Stuart Highway continues south through the Tanami Desert to Alice Springs. The only town of any size along the way is Tennant Creek. South of this desert outpost are the Devil's Marbles, a random pile of granite boulders, some of which are almost perfect spheres. An Aboriginal legend says that they are eggs laid by the mythical Rainbow Serpent.

Many people outside Australia think of Alice Springs as one of the most important towns in Australia. Certainly, it has been immortalised on film and in snapshots countless times. No other town, or even tiny settlement, is nearer to the geographic centre of the country. In 1872 Alice Springs was simply a repeater station for the Overland Telegraph Service. Today it is not only the centre for the outback cattle industry but also a lively tourist centre with a population of over 22 500.

Uluru (Ayers Rock), 450 kilometres to the south-west in Uluru National Park, is the world's biggest monolith: one enormous rock, nine kilometres in circumference and rising 348 metres above the plain on which it stands. The Aborigines made it a part of their sacred rituals, and guides will explain the mythology of the cave paintings at its base.

The magnificent Kata Tjuta (The Olgas) and, closer to the Alice, the prehistoric palms at Palm Valley, the dramatic Kings Canyon, Standley Chasm and Ormiston Gorge, all add their own fascination to the many wonders of the Northern Territory.

DARWIN

A Relaxed City

The first coastal town established in the Northern Territory was Palmerston, in 1864. Located at the mouth of the Adelaide River, it was quickly abandoned after a disastrous wet season in 1865.

Another expedition, led by Surveyor-General George Goyder, established a base at Adam Bay about fifty kilometres east of present-day Darwin. After surveying the area, he recommended that Port Darwin, which had been discovered in 1839 and named after Charles Darwin, would be the best place for a settlement. The town was officially called Palmerston, but the locals referred to it as Port Darwin to distinguish it from the original settlement. The name was officially changed to Darwin in 1911 when the Federal Government took control of the Territory.

In its early days, Darwin's development was hampered by its isolation. During World War II, however, the Stuart Highway was completed, linking Darwin with the railhead at Alice Springs, but after recovering from bomb damage in the war, growth was still slow.

The new Darwin's prosperity is based largely on the mineral wealth of the Northern Territory. It is the exploitation of this resource that has finally led to Darwin's development into the modern city it is today, despite the major setback when Cyclone Tracy struck in 1974.

A new Darwin grew out of the ruins of the cyclone, as befits the city's role as the capital of a self-governing territory. Until recently, Darwin had been largely maintained by the Commonwealth Government because of its strategic location, as much as for its function as a route centre and supply base for a grazing and mining area by no means yet fully developed.

Life for the early citizens was hard and changed very little until World War II. Graziers and agriculturalists could only hope to cope with the violent climatic changes. Development of modern techniques saw the population grow to 45 000 by 1974, when Cyclone Tracy struck. Now the figure has pushed past 76 000, which says something for either the hardiness of its people or the desirability of the city as a place to live, or perhaps a

Beer Can Regatta

bit of both. With Broome, in Western Australia, Darwin is one of Australia's most multicultural settlements, embracing people of forty-seven racial and cultural backgrounds. Chinese people have always formed a major part of the city's population and, in more recent years, Timorese and South-east Asian refugees have been arriving in Darwin and many have stayed. Quite large contingents of armed-forces personnel are also stationed at bases around Darwin.

Temperatures in the city area itself average around 28°C; there is very little or no rain during the 'dry'. In the 'wet', maximum temperatures average close to 34°C with high relative humidity, which can be uncomfortable for people from more equable climes. But always Darwin is good for sailing, swimming, water-skiing or soaking up the sun.

City sightseeing is conveniently done from air-conditioned motor coaches that make regular tours. The main features to see are the splendidly tropical 34-hectare **Botanical Gardens**, the few surviving historic buildings, churches, memorials, the **Reserve Bank**, the **Supreme Court**,

Darwin's busy **harbour** area and the **Beaufort Darwin Centre** (including a world-class hotel and the **Performing Arts Centre**) on the Esplanade overlooking the harbour. A lookout on the Esplanade commemorates the fiftieth anniversary of the bombing of Darwin in 1942. Day and half-day cruises around the harbour are available.

The city's business district is much like any other similar-sized city, but the relaxed and tropical atmosphere has a distinct character of its own. Modern air-conditioned shopping centres now serve Darwin's suburbs, which are in two main sections, divided by the airport.

Christchurch Cathedral was completed and consecrated in March 1977. It incorporates the porch from its predecessor, which was destroyed by Cyclone Tracy. During the war it was a garrison church and came under fire from Japanese bombers. The new cathedral was built at a cost of $800 000 and features a stained-glass window in memory of the trawler-men lost at sea during the cyclone. The altar, weighing 2.5 tonnes, has been hewn from a solid jarrah log believed to be more than 400 years old. Not far from the cathedral is the 'Tree of Knowledge', an ancient, spreading banyan tree.

There are several other interesting places of worship in Darwin, particularly the **Chinese Temple**. Visitors are welcome to inspect the interior.

One of Darwin's most historic hotels, The **Old Victoria** in the Smith Street Mall, has been restored into a modern shopping complex, at the same time retaining its colonial character with 'punkahs' to cool the Balcony Bar.

For those with cultural interests, the city boasts a theatre group which welcomes visitors' participation in its workshops held in **Brown's Mart**, another building that survived Tracy. The **Beaufort Centre** includes a 1000-seat theatre for the performing arts. Cinemas are located in Mitchell Street, at Parap and at Nightcliff.

Several art galleries, including some which feature the art and craft of the Aboriginal people, can be seen in the city area.

The elegant colonial architecture of **Government House** (near the southern end of the Esplanade) and **Old Admiralty House** (on the Esplanade), now an art gallery and garden cafe, is a reminder of the city's past. The **Museum of Arts and Sciences** at Bullocky Point houses important collections of Aboriginal, Balinese and New Guinean artefacts, as well as works by Australia's most famous painters. At the end of the Esplanade, at Doctors Gully off Mitchell Street, **Aquascene** provides the opportunity to hand-feed the ocean fish, which come in to the jetty each evening. Also in Mitchell Street is the **Indo-Pacific Marine** coral-reef ecosystem exhibit.

The **East Point Military Museum** at **Fannie Bay** displays artillery, war planes and other militaria close to the gun turrets that were constructed during World War II. Fannie Bay is also the site where Ross and Keith Smith landed their Vickers Vimy aircraft in 1919, completing the first flight from the UK to Australia. One of the most beautiful spots in the world to build a prison, Fannie Bay has some fine beaches. Darwin boasts of its beautiful sunsets and the nearby **East**

Aerial view of Darwin city centre

Hotels
Beaufort
The Esplanade, Darwin
(089) 82 9911
Diamond Beach Hotel Casino
Gilruth Ave, Mindil Beach
(089) 46 2666
Sheraton
32 Mitchell St, Darwin
(089) 82 0000

Family and Budget
Darwin
10 Herbert St, Darwin
(089) 81 9211
Poinciana Inn
84 Mitchell St, Darwin
(089) 81 8111
Top End Frontier
Cnr Daly and Mitchell Sts, Darwin
(089) 81 6511
YWCA
119 Mitchell St, Darwin
(089) 81 8644

Motel Groups: Bookings
Best Western (008) 22 2166
Travelodge (008) 22 2446

This list is for information only; inclusion is not necessarily a recommendation.

Point Reserve is a popular viewing place.

Darwin's best-known annual event is probably the Beer Can Regatta, held each September. The competing boats and other floating craft are constructed out of beer cans, a commodity of which there never seems to be a shortage in this city!

Darwin's restaurants offer an excellent choice of cuisine, from the fare of simple steak houses to French, Italian and Indonesian menus. There are also some wine bars which offer varied menus and pleasant settings for lunch and dinner.

To the north of the city area, Darwin's suburbs have been virtually rebuilt since 1974. The tropical climate has encouraged a lush regrowth and the gardens are a feast of beautiful bougainvilleas, hibiscus and alamanders. The rebuilt houses have been designed to better withstand any future cyclonic onslaught.

Sporting interests are well served. There is a golf course, a speedway track, a race-course at Fannie Bay, and the usual facilities for tennis, squash, bowls and football (Aussie Rules and Rugby). An

Olympic Pool is located on Ross Smith Avenue. Sea wasps are common in the waters off Darwin, so swimming in the sea for much of the year is not recommended.

Darwin is the natural jumping-off point for touring the Top End. The good hotels and motels are as well-found as their counterparts in other Australian capitals. The pressure on these services is often great and a range of alternative, less luxurious, accommodation has developed which can still be very comfortable. Many of the numerous caravan parks in Darwin are occupied by permanent residents, so it is worth booking ahead.

The **Diamond Beach Casino** in Darwin is a few metres from the shores of **Mindil Beach**. As well as gambling facilities, this thirty-million-dollar complex offers luxury accommodation, restaurants and discos, sporting and convention facilities.

For further information on Darwin, contact the Darwin Regional Tourism Association, 31 Smith St Mall (PO Box 1155, Darwin 0801); (089) 81 6611.

TOURS FROM DARWIN

The eight million hectares of the Arnhem Land Aboriginal Land, one of Australia's most fascinating wilderness areas, lie to the east of Darwin. It is a land that changes from broken mountains to vast plains, irrigated by constantly flowing rivers. An entry permit is required, which tourist agencies arrange through local government authorities. In the 'dry', many tours of places of interest in and around the city are available, by bus or hire car. Safaris by air and four-wheel-drive take sporting enthusiasts to less accessible areas for sightseeing, shooting and fishing.

The best month for the bush is July when, on a clear night, the stars seem to get in your eyes and you would not swap your cutlet of barramundi, grilled in the traditional manner on a shovel over an open fire, for the finest dish in the world. Almost any time from April to September is suitable for getting back to nature. When you do, it is hard to conceive that Darwin, serving all this vastness, has an airport that can take not only jumbo jets but also the supersonic Concorde.

Cruises on the Adelaide River, 64 km from Darwin via the Arnhem Highway
The *Adelaide River Queen* offers 2.5 hour cruises for crocodile-viewing.

Fogg Dam, 70 km from Darwin via the Arnhem Highway
A sunrise or sunset tour of this area offers an excellent opportunity to view animals and birds on the move between their feeding-grounds and where they sleep.

Not only is Fogg Dam a likely spot to see a crocodile, but you will also see many wallabies. The nearby swamps are the haunt of the elegant jabiru stork. Other birds in abundance are the pelican, egret, galah, cockatoo and kitehawk. The tour route then goes on to the Marakai Plains where many species of birds can be seen. Millions of dollars were lost in this area when the rice irrigation scheme at Humpty Doo failed. Stop at Reptile World at Humpty Doo, which has the largest range of snakes in Australia (250 species), as well as many lizards.

Kakadu National Park, 250 km from Darwin via the Arnhem Highway
Apart from abundant wildlife, the scenery here is dramatic and there are many fine examples of ancient Aboriginal art at sites

Saltwater crocodile, Yellow Waters, Kakadu.

throughout the park. The drive is fascinating, and can be topped off by a cruise on the South Alligator River. You would be unlucky not to see crocodiles, as well as wallabies, and the birdlife is prolific; however, sightings of buffalo are becoming rare. The Arnhem Highway is sealed all the way to Jabiru, and you could do the trip in your own car or a hired car.

Approximately 100 kilometres south of Jabiru are the Jim Jim Falls, accessed only by four-wheel-drive. There are many good camping spots on Jim Jim Creek and other billabongs. The deep and clear stretches of water on Nourlangie Creek, west of the Kakadu Highway, afford excellent opportunities for fishing. The safari guides have local knowledge and can show you far more than if you explore on your own. **See also:** Aboriginal Art; Kakadu National Park; The Top End.

Howard Springs, 35 km from Darwin via the Stuart Highway
There is safe swimming here in a spring-fed pool surrounded by monsoon forest. Avid birdwatchers can spot fifty or more species in a few hours; varieties of reptiles abound. Picnic areas and a kiosk are provided. On the way you could visit Nostalgia (one of Darwin's oldest homes) and the Territory Oils Art Centre.

Territory Wildlife Park at Berry Springs, 65 km from Darwin via the Stuart Highway
An exciting tourist development of international standard, located in more than 400 ha of natural bushland at Berry Springs, the Territory Wildlife Park is designed to display only animals native and feral to the Northern Territory. The exhibits are all connected by a 4 km link road and include open-moated enclosures with

kangaroos, wallabies, dingoes, bustards, buffalo and banteng; a naturally occurring lagoon where native birds can be viewed from a hide; an aquarium which features an acrylic walk-through tunnel for underwater viewing of large freshwater fish; a series of aviaries which display birds in natural habitats; a walk-through rainforest aviary; and the second largest nocturnal house in the world, artificially moonlit, where visitors can see about fifty species of mammals, birds and reptiles. The park is a project of the Conservation Commission of the NT.

Crocodile Farm, 40 km from Darwin via the Stuart Highway
Australia's first and largest commercial crocodile farm with over 7000 inmates, ranging in length from a few centimetres to four metres. There are feeding displays and tours daily. Be adventurous and try some farm-raised crocodile delicacies.

Ferry trips to the Cox Peninsula
Daily trips depart from the wharf in Darwin Harbour to either Mandorah Inn or the Golden Sands Holiday Resort, ideal for a relaxed day on the beach, swimming or fishing. From Mandorah, it is possible to arrange a tour of Woods Everglades, where dense tropical growth overhangs a narrow waterway.

Air tours
Several tours by air from Darwin are available, including day or weekend trips to Jim Jim Falls and fishing and shooting trips. A three-day air tour into Western Australia, including a jungle cruise at Lake Kununurra, the Hidden Valley, the Carr Boyd Ranges, Lake Argyle and the Ord River, makes a most enjoyable trip, if you can spare the time.

NORTHERN TERRITORY from A to Z

Adelaide River Population under 200
A small settlement set in pleasant country, 112 km south of Darwin on the Stuart Hwy, Adelaide River is the starting-point for visits to Rum Jungle, an old uranium-mining area (30 km north-west), Litchfield Park with its clear pools and spectacular waterfalls (30 km north), the Daly River district (110 km south-west), and the Batchelor and Tipperary experimental farming areas (40 km north and 90 km south-west). **In the area:** Majestic Orchids, part of Hydro Majestic, 48 ha horticultural and recreational development, 7 km south-west of Berry Springs Nature Park and near Litchfield Park entrance; 16 ha orchid-growing area. Freshwater Lake Bennett, 35 km north, recreation resort for picnicking, camping, swimming, sailing, canoeing, fishing and bushwalking. 4WD tours available. **Accommodation:** 1 hotel/motel, 1 caravan/camping park.
MAP REF. 352 E6

Aileron Population under 200
On the Stuart Hwy, 139 km north of Alice Springs. **Of interest:** Rest-stop; Aboriginal art available. **Accommodation:** 1 hotel/motel.
MAP REF. 356 I5

Alice Springs Population 22 759
Alice Springs is at the heart of the Red Centre of Australia, almost 1500 km from the nearest capital city. It is the gateway to the NT's biggest single tourist attraction, Uluru (Ayers Rock). A modern and well-maintained town, in the heart of the MacDonnell Ranges, some 350 000 visitors a year pass through between May and Sept. In this period, cloudless skies and warm days usher in refreshingly cool nights. The rest of the year is very hot and dust storms are common. Rains, usually brief, can come at any time of year. While there is plenty to see in the town itself, many natural wonders lie within a day's journey. Like any other big town, 'the Alice', as it is affectionately called, offers a variety of restaurants, together with an international casino, sports grounds, a swimming-pool and an 18-hole golf course. There is a wide variety of shops and a number of art galleries, including some that specialise in Aboriginal art. The Todd River, which runs through the town, is dry except after flash floods, but this does not stop the locals holding their annual Henley-on-Todd Regatta in October. The boats are carried, or fitted with wheels, for the occasion. The few areas of land that can be irrigated support small dairy and fruit-growing enterprises, but the main produce of the area is beef cattle from huge runs. The site of the town was discovered by William Whitfield Mills in 1871, who was at the time surveying a route for the Overland Telegraph Line. He named the Todd River after the South Australian Superintendent of Telegraphs, Sir Charles Todd, and a nearby waterhole he named Alice Springs after his boss's wife. The first settlement was at the repeater station, built for transmitting messages across the continent. Most of the thick-walled stone buildings have been restored and can be viewed. About ten years before Mills, John McDouall Stuart recorded in his diary that he passed about 50 km west of the site. Stuart also discovered and named Central Mt Sturt (since renamed Central Mt Stuart) in 1860. He named it after Captain Sturt, who had commanded an earlier expedition in which he (Stuart) had taken

The MacDonnell Ranges form a backdrop to Alice Springs

THE RED CENTRE

An ideal way to see the multitude of tourist attractions in the Red Centre is to base yourself in Alice Springs and to take advantage of the many and varied coach tours which operate from there.

Of course, what you should not miss is **Uluru (Ayers Rock)**. About 450 kilometres south-west of the Alice, the world's greatest monolith rises majestically 348 metres above a wide, sandy floodplain which is covered in spinifex and desert oak. The rock is nine kilometres in circumference and with the movement of the sun during the day, it changes colour through shades of fiery red, delicate mauve, blues, pinks and browns. When rain falls, it veils the rock in a torrent of silver, before running into the waterholes and desert beneath.

Yulara Resort, which has transformed facilities in this area, is about a twenty-minute drive north of Uluru. It offers a range of accommodation: the top-class Sails in the Desert Hotel, the Outback Pioneer Hotel and Lodge, the Four Seasons Desert Gardens four-star resort and Spinifex Lodge, together with a range of budget accommodation and well-equipped camping grounds.

An excellent way to familiarise yourself with the region is to spend an hour or so at the Yulara Visitors Centre. Displays depict the geology, history, flora and fauna of the region and there is a spectacular collection of photographs. Audiovisual shows are held regularly.

Yulara is a self-contained township; it has accommodation for the resort's staff (about 500), a supermarket, and other shops and services. Naturally, as everything has to be freighted in, shopping is not cheap, but a surprisingly wide range of goods and services can be obtained.

Yulara, with its prize-winning design, does not intrude into the land-scape but blends into the ochre colours of the desert around. If you can, allow for a stay of at least three days. This will give you time to see a sunrise and a sunset, to explore Uluru and visit Kata Tjuta (The Olgas).

According to Aboriginal legends, Uluru and Kata Tjuta were created and given their distinctive forms during the Tjukurpa or creation period. At the base of Uluru, there are cave paintings and carvings made thousands of years ago by members of the Loritja and Pitjanjatjara tribes. It is not difficult to appreciate that this is a sacred place of ancient times.

Do not attempt the 1.6 kilometre climb of Uluru unless you are fit and well, and have a good head for heights. As the climb follows a religious track, the Anungu (the traditional owners) would prefer visitors took other discovery walks within the park.

Taking the nine kilometre circuit walk around the base of Uluru, you will

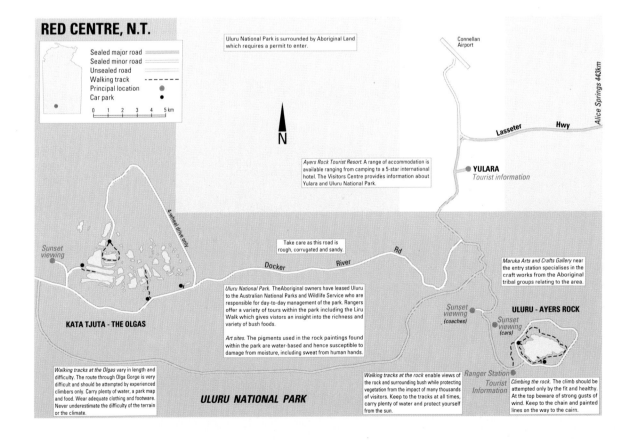

RED CENTRE, N.T.

Sealed major road
Sealed minor road
Unsealed road
Walking track
Principal location
Car park

0 1 2 3 4 5 km

N

Connellan Airport

Alice Springs 443km

Lasseter Hwy

Uluru National Park is surrounded by Aboriginal Land which requires a permit to enter.

Ayers Rock Tourist Resort. A range of accommodation is available ranging from camping to a 5-star international hotel. The Visitors Centre provides information about Yulara and Uluru National Park.

● **YULARA**
Tourist information

4-wheel drive only

Sunset viewing

Take care as this road is rough, corrugated and sandy.

Docker   River   Rd

Maruka Arts and Crafts Gallery near the entry station specialises in the craft works from the Aboriginal tribal groups relating to the area.

Uluru National Park. TheAboriginal owners have leased Uluru to the Australian National Parks and Wildlife Service who are responsible for day-to-day management of the park. Rangers offer a variety of tours within the park including the Liru Walk which gives visitors an insight into the richness and variety of bush foods.

Art sites. The pigments used in the rock paintings found within the park are water-based and hence susceptible to damage from moisture, including sweat from human hands.

KATA TJUTA - THE OLGAS

Sunset viewing (coaches)

ULURU - AYERS ROCK

Sunset viewing (cars)

Walking tracks at the Olgas vary in length and difficulty. The route through Olga Gorge is very difficult and should be attempted by experienced climbers only. Carry plenty of water, a park map and food. Wear adequate clothing and footware. Never underestimate the difficulty of the terrain or the climate.

ULURU NATIONAL PARK

Walking tracks at the rock enable views of the rock and surrounding bush while protecting vegetation from the impact of many thousands of visitors. Keep to the tracks at all times, carry plenty of water and protect yourself from the sun.

Ranger Station ●
Tourist Information

Climbing the rock. The climb should be attempted only by the fit and healthy. At the top beware of strong gusts of wind. Keep to the chain and painted lines on the way to the cairn.

see the Mutitjulu (Sound Shell), a cavity as smooth as if formed by the sea, and the Taputji (Kangaroo Tail), a 160-metre strip of stone hanging at one end of the rock. Tours include the Mala Walk, the Edible Desert Walk (Aboriginal bush tucker) and the Liru Walk, conducted by Aboriginal guides.

Some fifty kilometres to the west are **Kata Tjuta (The Olgas)**, a cluster of rounded, massive rocks which are equally mysterious. They too are dramatic and vividly coloured, lacking only the majesty of Uluru's great bulk. The tallest dome of Kata Tjuta, Mount Olga, is 546 metres above the oasis-like 'Valley of the Winds' that runs through the rock system. Ernest Giles, who first saw Mount Olga and named it after the Queen of Spain, described the rocks as 'minarets, giant cupolas and monstrous domes ... huge memorials of the ancient times to the earth'.

Curtin Springs cattle-station and roadside inn is on the Lasseter Highway, eighty-two kilometres east of Yulara. Accommodation is available; also tours from Yulara to Mount Conner.

Ross River Homestead, eighty-eight kilometres east of Alice Springs, is a delightful place to base yourself for exploration of the East MacDonnells. This ranch-style homestead resort features a range of outback experiences in comfortable surroundings. The historic pub bar has an interesting display of antiques. **Trephina Gorge**, **John Hayes Rockhole**, **N'Dhala Gorge** and **Corroboree Rock** are among the principal attractions in the area.

The **Arltunga Historical Reserve**, 110 kilometres south-east of Alice Springs, has been set aside to preserve memorabilia of the gold-mining era in the region. Little evidence remains of the shanty town that grew up after 1887 when alluvial gold was found here. You can explore the stone ruins, scattered workings, gravestones and go down a mine. The police station and gaol have been restored and a Visitors Centre displays historical exhibits. Camping is available in a private caravan park next to the reserve and there is good fossicking in the area.

If you take advantage of the organised Ross River tour from Alice Springs, you will be able to visit these attractions, and also hear much of the folklore relating to the Eastern Aranda Aborigines, sample billy tea and damper, and learn how to throw a boomerang.

A turning off the Stuart Highway about 140 kilometres south-west of

above top: Yulara and Ayers Rock
above: Camel safari passing the Centre's only winery

Alice Springs leads to the **Henbury meteorite craters** and, a further 200 kilometres west, the spectacular beauty of **Kings Canyon** within Watarrka National Park. The **Kings Canyon Frontier Lodge** and **Kings Creek Campground** are good accommodation bases from which to see these attractions.

The Henbury craters are believed to have been formed several thousand years ago when a falling meteor broke into pieces and hit the earth. The largest of the twelve craters is 180 metres wide and 15 metres deep. The smallest is six metres wide and only a few centimetres deep.

Kings Canyon, 323 kilometres south-west of Alice Springs, is one of the most interesting and scenic areas of the Centre. The climb to the rim of the canyon is fairly arduous, but well worth the effort. Even more spectacular views can be obtained by crossing the tree-trunk bridge—a nerve-racking experience, as there is no handrail—to the north wall. The Lost City and the Garden of Eden are superb sights here.

Within easy reach of Alice Springs for a day-tour is the beautiful **Standley Chasm**. About fifty kilometres west of Alice Springs, this colourful cleft in the West MacDonnells is only five metres wide. At midday when the sunlight reaches the floor of the chasm, turning the walls a blazing red, it is a memorable sight. **Simpsons Gap National Park**, eighteen kilometres west of Alice Springs, can be visited at the same time and has walking access.

Further west, about 133 kilometres from Alice Springs, are **Glen Helen** and **Ormiston Gorges**. Located on the Finke River, their colours were captured by Aboriginal artist Albert Namatjira and today lend themselves to photography, as does the sunrise on Mount Sonder, which can be seen to the west. Glen Helen Lodge is an accommodation base for this area, or a coach tour lasting approximately ten hours is available at Alice Springs.

A twelve-hour tour from Alice Springs will take you to **Palm Valley** and the **Finke River Gorge,** 155 kilometres south-west. The Finke River is one of the oldest watercourses in the world and to walk along its bed is an unforgettable experience, the spectacular red walls towering metres above you.

Palm Valley, with its rock pools, cycad palms and *Livistona* palms unique to the area, is yet another of the incredible sights of the Centre. The valley's plant life has such a 'prehistoric' appearance, to enter the area seems like taking a trip back in time.

These two attractions can also be visited by taking a two-day tour from Alice Springs, staying overnight at Glen Helen. Also worth a visit is the restored **Hermannsburg Mission**, 125 km west of Alice Springs.

Much nearer 'home', the Alice Springs **Telegraph Station Historical Reserve** is only three kilometres north of town. The site of the original settlement in the Alice Springs area, the station and a number of the original stone buildings have been restored by the Conservation Commission of the Northern Territory. These house furnishings and artifacts from early this century and a historic interpretative display. The Reserve occupies 570 hectares and offers opportunities for bushwalking, picnicking and wildlife observation. A small waterhole, the original water source for the settlement, from which Alice Springs obtained its name, is adjacent to the old station buildings.

The telegraph station was originally built to link Port Augusta to Darwin, thence by submarine cable to Java. The line was completed in 1872 and was used from then until 1932, when operations were transferred to the site at the corner of Parsons Street and Railway Terrace in Alice Springs.

For further information about the attractions of the Red Centre, contact the tourist information centre in Hartley St, Alice Springs; (089) 52 5199.

Standley Chasm, West MacDonnell Ranges

Palm Valley, Finke River Gorge National Park

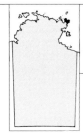

GOVE

The Gove Peninsula, named after W.H.J. Gove, an Australian airman killed in the area during World War II, is situated at the far north-east point of Arnhem Land.

The whole of the peninsula is set aside as Aboriginal Land and the main centres are **Yirrkala** and **Nhulunbuy**. Hideaway Safari Lodge near Nhulunbuy's airport offers visitors long white beaches and good fishing. Nine kilometres west of Nhulunbuy, near Dundas Point, is **Melville Bay**, which the explorer Matthew Flinders described as the best natural harbour on the Gulf of Carpentaria. Accommodation is limited.

The **Yirrkala Mission**, near Mount Dundas, provides a residential base for many of the Aborigines in the area. Its name became familiar during the struggle by its people to win title to their land. The *Aboriginal Land Rights (Northern Territory) Act* was finally assented to on 16 December 1976. It represents to the people of Yirrkala the culmination of years of struggle to win recognition for their claims to land on which their people have lived for many thousands of years. The Yirrkala area is noted for Aboriginal carvings of birds and fish.

The easiest way to visit Nhulunbuy is by air (either commercial or charter). If you plan to explore by four-wheel-drive and without a tour guide, a permit is required from the Northern Land Council.

---

part, but the South Australian Government renamed it in Stuart's honour after he had completed his successful expedition to the northern coast of Australia. John Ross, a pastoralist, was also active in the area, seeking new grazing lands. He also helped look for a route for the telegraph line. The repeater station was for many years the only reason for the existence of a handful of people in this remote area, but in 1888 the South Australian Government became eager to open up the country and sent surveyors north seeking suitable sites for railheads. The township of Stuart, 3.2 km from the telegraph station, was gazetted in the same year; but the railway remained unbuilt and Stuart stagnated. Regular supply was maintained by camel train from Port Augusta, which was both expensive and slow. Even the discovery of gold at Arltunga, 96 km east of the settlement, did little to develop it. The Federal Government took control of the NT from SA in 1911. From that time the township began to develop steadily, if still slowly. The Australian Inland Mission stationed Sister Jane Finlayson there in 1916. She was supposed to stay only one year, but the growing needs of the area led to the establishment of Adelaide House nursing hostel in 1926. The railway was finally completed in 1929 and the first train reached Stuart in August that year. The service became known as 'The Ghan', after the Afghan camel drivers it had replaced. The white population increased from 40 in 1926 to 200 in 1931 as the supply of materials became more reliable and less expensive. As the township grew there came the need for better identification: there was too much confusion between Stuart and the telegraph station Alice Springs, only 3 km apart, so Stuart was dropped and the name of the township changed to Alice Springs. Now it is the jumping-off point for tourists who visit the Red Centre. **Of interest:** Royal Flying Doctor Service base, Stuart Tce; tours daily. School of the Air, Head St; open to visitors weekday afternoons. Araluen Arts Centre, Larapinta Dr; focal point for performing and visual arts. Panorama 'Guth', Hartley St; 360° landscape painting of Central Australia. Aboriginal Art and Culture Centre, Todd St. Flynn Memorial Church, Todd Mall, built in memory of founder of RFDS. Old Stuart Gaol, Parsons St. Lasseter's Casino, Barrett Dr. Technology, Transport and Communications Museum, Memorial Dr. Olive Pink Flora Reserve, cnr Barrett Dr and Causeway; Australia's only arid-zone botanic garden. Annual Bangtail Muster street parade and sports carnival, and Lions Camel Cup held in May; Finke Desert motorcycle endurance race in June; Show Day in July; and Harts Range race meeting, Old Timers Fete and Alice Springs Rodeo in Aug. **In the area:** Views from top of Anzac Hill at north end of town. Old telegraph station, 3 km north, off Stuart Hwy; historic reserve with original buildings and equipment. Old Timers' Museum, 5 km south; exhibits of 1890s pioneering era. Pitchi Richi Sanctuary, 3 km south-west; features clay sculptures by William Ricketts, and open-air pioneer museum. Frontier Camel Farm, 7 km south-east, off Ross Hwy; camel rides and museum with displays highlighting importance of camels and their Afghan masters in early development of central Australia. Nearby, Mecca Date Gardens, Australia's first commercial date farm. The Old Ghan still runs on 23.5 km of private line between MacDonnell Siding and Ewaninga; train is feature of Ghan Preservation Society rail museum at MacDonnell Siding, 10 km south. Chateau Hornsby, NT's only commercial winery, 11 km south. East of town: Emily Gap, Jessie Gap and Ruby Gap Nature Parks (13, 18 and 141 km); Corroboree Rock Conservation Park (48 km); Trephina Gorge and N'Dhala Gorge Nature Parks (80 and 98 km); Ross River Homestead (88 km); and Arltunga Historical Reserve (110 km). To west: Simpsons Gap and Ormiston Gorge and Pound National Parks (18 and 132 km); Standley Chasm (50 km); Ellery Creek Big Hole, Serpentine Gorge, Glen Helen Gorge and Redbank Nature Parks (93, 104, 133 and 170 km); Hermannsburg Mission (125 km); and Gosses Bluff meteor crater (210 km). To north: Ryan Well and Central Mt Stuart Historical Reserves (126 and 216 km); Barrow Creek Telegraph Station (284 km); Wycliffe Well and Bonney Well (392 and 422 km); and Devils Marbles (420 km). To south: Ewaninga Rock Carvings Conservation Reserve (39 km); and Chambers Pillar Historical Reserve (149 km). To south-west: Henbury Meteorites Conservation Reserve (147 km); Palm Valley in Finke Gorge National Park (155 km); Kings Canyon in Watarrka National Park (323 km); and Uluru National Park (450 km). Great variety of tours of varying duration covering scenic attractions, Aboriginal culture and specialist interests, many 'off beaten track'. Experience these by bus or coach, limousine, 4WD safari, camel, horse, aircraft, helicopter or balloon. **Tourist information:** Hartley St; (089) 52 5199. **Accommodation:** 3 hotels, 16 motels, 6 caravan/camping parks. **See also:** Aboriginal Art; The Red Centre.
MAP REF. 357 J8, 359 M5

TOURING THE TERRITORY

Many people will not want to embark on a tour of the Northern Territory's outback areas alone. Fortunately, an enormous variety of accompanied tours leave from all capital cities, enabling even the least intrepid visitor to see Australia's magnificent centre. These tours range from quite basic holidays under canvas, travelling by coach or four-wheel-drive between overnight stops, to air-conditioned coaches (for those who prefer a few 'home comforts'), choosing a route served by motel, hotel or tourist camp accommodation.

The main tourist season operates from approximately April to September, but intending visitors are now exhorted to 'See Alice while she's hot' and excellent reductions on travel and accommodation costs during the 'off season' months between October and March are being offered. This is the 'hot season', and if you do not like intense heat, it may be a better idea to save up until you can afford the higher in-season prices.

On a camping tour, it is usual for campers to help put up the tents, prepare, serve and wash up after meals, and generally clean up, but all this lends itself to making the holiday a truly 'different' experience. It does also mean, however, that adaptability is an advantage, since you cannot choose the people who accompany you.

Another way to tackle the outback is to join a convoy expedition, where you drive your own vehicle, but are guided by experts. Motoring organisations arrange such tours, but departure times are limited and you will not be permitted to join the tour if your vehicle is not in an acceptable condition.

If you do decide to travel alone on roads that are off the beaten track, it is wise to take a few precautions for your own security. It is not advisable to pick up hitchhikers or to camp, other than in a lockable caravan, outside organised sites. **See also:** Outback Motoring.

The 'Ghan' train is another way of avoiding the long, boring stretches of road. To travel one way by train and return by air is a time-saving way of seeing the Centre. There is a great variety of organised tours operating from Alice Springs which will convey you to the main tourist attractions of the region. This is an excellent way of seeing the Centre. Coach operators also combine a one-way rail trip (approximately twenty-two hours) with a return coach journey.

Campers at Ayers Rock camping ground and caravan park

Barkly Homestead
Population under 200
On the Barkly Hwy, 185 km from the junction of the Stuart and Barkly Hwys. **Accommodation:** 1 motel, 1 caravan/camping park.
MAP REF. 355 N10

Barrow Creek   Population under 200
On the Stuart Hwy, 283 km north of Alice Springs. **Of interest:** Old Telegraph Station (1872). **Accommodation:** 1 hotel.
MAP REF. 355 J13, 357 J3

Batchelor   Population 358
Former town for Rum Jungle Uranium Mine, now a major education centre for the training of Aboriginal teachers at Batchelor College. **Of interest:** Mini replica of Karlstein Castle of Bohemia. Swimming at Rum Jungle Lake. Parachuting and gliding. **In the area:** Batchelor is gateway to Litchfield Park, 40 km west, with its spectacular waterfalls (Wangi, Sandy Creek, Florence and Tolmer) and pockets of scenic rainforest. Fishing for barramundi on Daly River, 70 km southwest (4WD). **Tourist information:** Rum Jungle Motor Inn, Rum Jungle Rd; (089) 76 0123. **Accommodation:** 1 motel, 1 caravan/camping park.
MAP REF. 352 E6

Borroloola   Population 659
Small settlement on the McArthur River. Once one of the north's larger and more colourful frontier towns, it is now very popular with fishing enthusiasts. **Of interest:** Museum in old police station (1886), off Robinson Rd. Borroloola Fishing Classic, held every Easter. **Tourist information:** McArthur River Caravan Park, Robinson Rd; (089) 75 8734. **Accommodation:** 1 hotel, 1 caravan/camping park; cabins.
MAP REF. 353 O12, 355 O2

Daly Waters   Population under 200
Situated 4 km north of the junction of the Stuart and Carpentaria Hwys. **Of interest:** Historic pub (1893), Stuart St. **In the area:** Tree (1 km north), reputedly marked with the letter S by explorer John McDouall Stuart. **Tourist information:** Daly Waters Pub, Stuart St; (089) 75 9927. **Accommodation:** 1 motel, 1 caravan/camping park.
MAP REF. 352 I13, 354 I2

Dunmarra   Population under 200
At the junction of the Stuart and Buchanan Hwys, 363 km north of Tennant Creek. **Accommodation:** 1 motel, 1 caravan/camping park.
MAP REF. 352 I13, 354 I3

ABORIGINAL LANDS

Since the declaration of the *Aboriginal Land Rights (Northern Territory) Act* 1976, visitors MUST obtain a permit to enter Aboriginal Land.

It should be noted that as a general rule, Land Councils have been asked by Traditional Owners not to issue entry permits for unaccompanied tourist travel. This does not affect visitors travelling on one of the organised tours on to Aboriginal Land where tour bookings include the necessary permit.

When making application for entry to any Aboriginal Land, applicants must state the reason for entry, dates and duration of intended stay, names of persons travelling, and itinerary and routes to be used while on these lands. Permits can be issued only after consultation and approval of the relevant Aboriginal communities. Processing permit applications can take four to six weeks.

All public roads that cross Aboriginal Lands are exempt from the permit provisions; the exemption covers the immediate road corridor only. If there is a likelihood of a need for fuel stops, travellers should seek transit permits from the relevant Land Councils. For those roads that are not designated as public roads, travellers should seek advice from the Land Councils before departure. Some towns within Aboriginal Land are also exempt from the provisions.

It is the right of Traditional Owners of Aboriginal Land to refuse entry permits. Applications and any enquiries must be directed, in writing, to the relevant Land Council listed below.

By agreement with the Tiwi Land Council, Australian Kakadu Tours runs the Putjamirra tourist camp (with tent accommodation) on Melville Island. Entry permission for visitors is arranged by the tour operator.

Bathurst Island artists and craftspeople have found expanding markets for their paintings, carvings, screen prints, batik, pots and other artefacts. The annual NT Barra Classic fishing tournament is held on Bathurst Island in September.

Alice Springs and Tennant Creek regions:
Central Land Council
33 Stuart Hwy
PO Box 3321
Alice Springs NT 0871
(089) 52 3800

Darwin, Nhulunbuy and Katherine regions:
Northern Land Council
PO Box 42921
Casuarina NT 0811
(089) 20 5100

Melville and Bathurst Islands:
Tiwi Land Council
PO Box 38545
Winnellie NT 0821
(089) 47 1838

Arnhem Land Aboriginal Land

Elliott   Population 422
On the Stuart Hwy, 254 km north of Tennant Creek. **In the area:** Lake Woods, 13 km west, NT's largest lake; water is curious milky-white. **Accommodation:** 1 hotel, 1 motel, 2 caravan/camping parks.
MAP REF. 355 J5

Glen Helen   Population under 200
On Namatjira Drive, 136 km west of Alice Springs, Glen Helen is an excellent base for exploring the superb scenery of Ormiston Gorge, 12 km north-east, the 'jewel of the MacDonnell Ranges'. At Glen Helen Gorge, 300 m east, you can walk along the bed of the Finke River between towering, rugged red cliffs. Glen Helen Lodge has won many awards for its food and accommodation standards and its hospitality, including Cloudy's Restaurant. **In the area:** Finke River Gorge, 37 km south-east, with amazing rock formations: the 'amphitheatre', 'sphinx' and 'battleship'. Red cabbage palms (*Livistona mariae*) in nearby Palm Valley, found nowhere else in the world. Hermannsburg, 25 km south-west; restored Aboriginal mission, birthplace of artist Albert Namatjira. Redbank Gorge, 24 km west. **Tourist information:** Glen Helen Lodge, Namatjira Dr; (089) 56 7489. **Accommodation:** Glen Helen Lodge.
MAP REF. 356 H8, 358 D5

Jabiru   Population 1410
A mining town within the Kakadu National Park, 247 km from Darwin on the Arnhem Hwy, Jabiru has a range of services enhanced to cater for special environmental requirements necessary to limit the effect of the town on the surrounding World Heritage National Park. **Of interest:** Four Seasons Kakadu, Flinders St, hotel built in shape of 250-m-long crocodile; design was approved by the Gagadju people, to whom the crocodile is a totem. Kakadu Frontier Lodge and Caravan Park, Civic Dr, laid out in traditional Aboriginal circular motif. Jabiru Olympic Swimming Pool, Civic Dr, largest in NT; also 9-hole golf course. **In the area:** Inspection of Ranger Uranium Mine, 6 km east; daily tours May–Oct. (information from Kakadu Air Services at Jabiru Air Terminal). Scenic flights over the unique Kakadu territory with its virtually inaccessible sandstone formations standing some 400 m above vast floodplains, seasonal waterfalls, wetland wilderness and remote beaches. Boat, gorge and waterfall, and safari tours available. **Tourist information:** 6 Tasman Plaza; (089) 79 2548. **Accommodation:** 1 hotel, 1 caravan/camping park. **See also:** Kakadu National Park.
MAP REF. 352 H5

THE TOP END

A new **Darwin** arose from the old city which was devastated by Cyclone Tracy on Christmas Eve 1974. Business and industry were re-established and houses and public buildings were rebuilt. Today the gardens are flourishing and the attractive layouts of street plantations, reserves and public gardens give the city an air of colour and well-being. There is a free and friendly spirit and an open community life in this city, which swelters in summer but has the best winter climate in Australia.

With improved roads and the vast increase in tourism in Australia, Darwin has become a major tourist destination. Rebuilding has brought a number of high-quality hotels and motels to the city and there is accommodation to suit either luxury or family means. Darwin itself is a winter haven, with its excellent beaches, abundance of fish and warm weather, but its real attraction is as a base for exploring the wild and fascinating country at the 'Top End'. Here you might see wide billabongs covered with lilies, clouds of geese wheeling above the trees, crocodiles sunning themselves on waterside rocks, plunging waterfalls, rows of pillar-like ant hills, spectacular cliff and rock features, caves and cliffs carrying the Aboriginal cave paintings of the past.

The Northern Territory Government has created a number of reserves to preserve the features of the region and to make them accessible to travellers. The most spectacular of these, in an area fast becoming one of the top natural tourist attractions in Australia, is **Kakadu National Park** in the dense and wild country along the East Alligator River, bordering Arnhem Land.

The park is rich in vegetation, ranging from pockets of rainforest through dwarf shrubland to open forest and swamps. The abundant wildlife includes several animals unique to the area, such as the banded pigeon, the rock possum and a species of rock wallaby. There are emus, a rich variety of pigeons and parrots, many marsupials, freshwater and saltwater crocodiles, waterbirds and rivers teeming with fish. Features within the park include Yellow Waters, a spectacular wetlands area where prolific birdlife can be seen, particularly in the dry season, and Nourlangie Rock, where Aboriginal rock art can be viewed. A most spectacular point in the park is the Jim Jim Falls, 215 metres high and with a sheer drop of 152 metres of water pouring (in the wet season) over the rugged and colourful escarpment which is a feature of the area.

North of the Jim Jim Falls is the East Alligator River, a well-known fishing ground where barramundi can be caught in plenty and where the river reaches wind through spectacularly beautiful country. The park can be accessed via the main Arnhem Highway, east of Darwin.

Two small parks close to Darwin are **Berry Springs**, 65 kilometres south, and **Howard Springs**, 35 kilometres south-east. Berry Springs is noted for its warm water, a continual 20 deg. C for pleasant and safe swimming, and its marvellous birdlife. More than 120 species of birds have been recorded, the most colourful ones including rainbow lorikeets, the northern rosella, red-winged parrots, rainbow birds and blue-faced honeyeaters. At Howard Springs, the pool is surrounded by rainforest, including pandanus palms, milkwood, red ash, white cedar, wild nutmeg and camphorwood trees. Again, the park abounds in birds and other wildlife.

Along the Stuart Highway, known as

Berry Springs, near Darwin

Aboriginal corroboree, Katherine

Ranger uranium mine,
Kakadu National Park

'the track', 354 kilometres south-east of Darwin are the town of **Katherine** and the spectacular **Nitmiluk (Katherine Gorge) National Park**. Here the clear river flows between the brilliantly coloured walls of the gorge, towering sixty metres high. A boat tour through the gorge is guaranteed to be an exciting highlight of any holiday.

A further 110 kilometres south-east of Katherine is the **Mataranka Pool Reserve**, near the Mataranka Homestead, where thermal springs are surrounded by lush tropical forest and the water is permanently at body temperature. Four-wheel-drive wildlife safaris can be arranged in Darwin and they are an ideal way to see the country and to experience something of life in the Top End.

There are major roads to all these Top End attractions. However, if you are contemplating an unguided tour of the region, it is vital that you recognise that should you stray into some unknown areas you may get into difficulties. **See also:** Outback Motoring.

Tourist boats at Katherine Gorge

Katherine   Population 5691

In times of drought—sometimes for years on end—you can travel northern Australia for 2000 km and more before you see the sheen of flowing water in a permanent river. Perhaps it is the instant impact of the incredible contrast between unending arid plain and Katherine Gorge that heightens its dramatic beauty. The town of Katherine is 337 km south of Darwin, by a stretch of bitumen that reaches from horizon to horizon in an almost ruler-straight line. Nowadays Katherine's economic mainstays are tourism and the Tindal RAAF airbase, 27 km south-east, but still this neat township is the centre of scientific agricultural experiments designed to improve the efficiency of the traditional beef cattle industry on which it was founded. Indeed it is sited in some of the NT's most promising agricultural and grazing country. The township is located on the southern side of the Katherine River and has good facilities, including several churches, parks, a golf course and showground. **Of interest:** Katherine Museum, Gorge Rd. Railway Station Museum, Railway Tce. School of the Air, Giles St. O'Keefe House, Riverbank Dr; one of oldest homes in town. **In the area:** The Katherine River was named after a beautiful daughter of one of the sponsors of John McDouall Stuart, who discovered it in 1862. The gorge, named Nitmiluk by the Aboriginal people, towers above the sparkling, slow-moving water in the dry season. The ancient rock walls are dotted with caves. Aboriginal paintings, from miniatures to huge murals, decorate both faces above the floodline. The scene changes in the wet, when the water-level often rises 18 m as the river boils through. The caves are swamped and a bigger flood than average may wash away another piece of an irreplaceable art form that was developed thousands of years ago. The rock is grey, black and ochre, the vegetation bright green. Fifty-eight species of reptiles and amphibians have been identified in the area, including a burrowing frog, the freshwater crocodile, a tortoise with a neck so long it looks like a snake when its body is submerged, three kinds of frog that climb trees, a lizard without legs, pythons that often grow to 2 m, and many poisonous snakes. In the higher reaches of the gorge kangaroos and wallabies in mobs of hundreds at a time crowd in to drink. You may catch a barramundi—if you don't hook a tortoise or crocodile. The only way to see the gorge properly is by flat-bottomed boat. You can hire one yourself or take a guided tour; cruises run daily. There are three easily-reached pools in the gorge; if you hire a boat, organise a party to go with you because the aluminium craft

ABORIGINAL ART

Art is an essential element in Aboriginal culture, often using symbols to communicate ideas which cannot be expressed in any other way. Traditional art serves this purpose throughout the Australian continent, but the actual form of expression varies considerably from region to region.

Much of the artwork at Ayers Rock, for example, is symbolic and may appear to the uninitiated eye to be quite abstract. Aboriginal artists in Central Australia also traditionally used the ground as their 'canvas'; large sand paintings are made with coloured earths, feathers and other natural objects to represent the travels of the 'Dreaming' ancestors, the ancient beings that created the landforms on the vast plains. These sand paintings are intricate patterns made up of varying combinations of circles, lines, dots and tracks.

The designs found in the traditional art of the Top End, particularly at the spectacular art sites in Kakadu National Park, are quite different in style: here the visitor can see examples of 'X-ray' art, so named because great attention is given to internal detail. This style has been practised in other civilisations, but is believed to have reached its highest level of expression in Western Arnhem Land.

Some of the galleries where Aboriginal art can be seen are listed below.

Alice Springs
The **Alice Springs Aboriginal Art and Culture Centre** located at 86–88 Todd Street features works by Central Australian and Western Desert artists and craftspeople. Stock includes paintings on canvas and bark, watercolours, carvings, weavings, weapons, didjeridus, seed necklaces and ornaments, silk fashion batiks, books and cassettes. Worldwide mail-order and delivery services available.

The origin of the **Ewaninga Rock Carvings** (39 kilometres south of Alice Springs) is lost in time. More correctly known as petroglyphs, the carvings are considered to be the work of an extremely old culture, since present-day Aborigines do not understand their meaning. The rock carvings form a part of the Ewaninga Rock Carvings Conservation Reserve.

Uluru region
The **Maruku Arts and Crafts** complex, next to the Ranger Station, at entrance to Uluru National Park, specialises in works of more than 800 artists and craftsmen from the tribal groups in the area—Pitjantjatjara, Yankunytjatjara, Matuntjara and Luritja.

Anangu cave art sites around Uluru and Kata Tjuta (the Olgas), fifty kilometres west of Uluru, are extremely vulnerable. Protection of this art is given a high priority by the Anangu, the traditional owners, and measures are being taken to ensure it is not damaged. Unlike some other cave art in Australia, the pigments used in the paintings are water-based and are very susceptible to damage from moisture, such as sweat from human hands.

Darwin
The **Museum of Arts and Sciences** at Bullocky Point houses a fine permanent collection of Aboriginal art. Each September it also brings together the finest traditional and contemporary Aboriginal art from around Australia for the National Aboriginal Art Award, which coincides with the Danggalaba Festival of Aboriginal Art and Life. The award gives visitors the opportunity to see and purchase some of the best bark and sand paintings, carvings, fabric prints and contemporary art offered in Australia.

The **Raintree Gallery** at 18 Knuckey Street has a wide range of northern Australian Aboriginal paintings and artefacts for both collectors and gift buyers. The stock includes canvas and bark paintings, carvings, weapons, weavings, fashion garments, books, musical instruments and cassettes. A gift shop is open at least six days a week, just off the Smith Street Mall. Worldwide packing and mailing facilities are available.

Kakadu National Park
The rock art in Kakadu National Park is among the finest in the world, and represents a close personal and spiritual relationship between man and the

Aboriginal Artist's Gallery, Alice Springs

Rock art, Nourlangie Rock, Kakadu National Park

environment. The richness of Kakadu's Aboriginal art can be viewed at **Nourlangie Rock** and **Ubirr**, both of which are accessible by road. There are four main periods or art and much can be learned about the early history of the Aborigines—some of the occupation sites have been carbon dated at 23 000 years, and others go back even earlier.

The main subject of the *pre-estuarine* period (which ended with the rise of the sea-level 7000 to 9000 years ago) was man the hunter, with stone axes, simple spears and boomerangs. The *estuarine* period is marked by the introduction of paintings representing the estuarine species of animals, especially the barramundi fish. This was also the era when 'X-ray' art emerged, with its depiction of the internal organs and skeletons of animals. Between 2000 and 4000 years ago freshwater systems began to replace estuarine conditions. This is reflected in the art with the depiction of freshwater species such as the long-necked tortoise and the magpie goose. The *contact* period began when Aboriginal people were subject to intense contact with outsiders. The Europeans' activities and their material possessions, particularly rifles and steel axes, are most graphically portrayed in the main gallery at Ubirr.

Katherine
The township of Katherine has developed historically as the regional centre for a diverse group of Aboriginal communities. The artefacts available at **Mimi Arts and Crafts Gallery** in Lindsay Street reflect this diversity in art, from the desert communities of the west to the coastal communities in the east, and include contemporary music, weavings, canvas and bark paintings. Aboriginal-designed fabrics are also available from the Pearce Street shop.

Tennant Creek
Anyinginyi Art and Crafts, 139 Patterson Street, specialises in the art work of the four groups that share this part of the country: the Warlpiri (renowned for their sand paintings), and the Warumungu, Kaititja and Alyawarre, whose paintings and carvings depict aspects of life from the Tanami and Barkly regions.

Arnhem Land
A group of ancient rock paintings, ranging from simple stick figures and handprints to more intricate and heavily symbolic paintings, was discovered in 1988 in caves deep in escarpment country in an area known as **Umorrduk**, near Mount Borradaile, 225 kilometres east of Darwin. Tours are available from Darwin, travelling through Kakadu National Park and Arnhem Land, to visit these 20 000-year-old rock-art sites in Gummulkbin tribal lands.

need portage over the rock bars. The weather is always hot, but there is little humidity for the nine not-quite-so-hot months of the year. You will need a top covering over cotton clothes in the early morning and at night from about mid-April to mid-July. Historic Springvale Homestead, 8 km west, is the oldest remaining homestead in the NT, having been built by Alfred Giles in 1879. An Aboriginal Corroboree is performed here three times a week. Manyallaluk (formerly Eva Valley Station), 100 km south-east of Katherine, offers visitors the experience of Aboriginal culture combined with the magnificent scenery of a wilderness park. Edith Falls, for picnics, swimming and camping, 62 km north-east. Mataranka Homestead, 115 km south, has a thermal pool believed to have therapeutic powers. The tourist resort here has excellent facilities. Tours are available to view rock art in the Land of the Lightning Brothers, 140 km southwest, and to Muniyung, 170 km southeast. Other tours available include guided tours of Cutta Cutta Caves, 26 km south, 4WD safaris, barramundi fishing tours and horse trail rides. Boat tours on Victoria River at Timber Creek, 285 km west, in Gregory National Park; also fishing and bushwalking. **Tourist information:** Cnr Stuart Hwy and Lindsay St; (089) 72 2650. **Accommodation:** 2 hotel/motels, 7 motels, 7 caravan/camping parks. **See also:** Aboriginal Art. MAP REF. 352 G9

Kulgera   Population under 200
About 20 km from the SA border on the Stuart Hwy. **Of interest:** Town's name is Aboriginal for 'place of weeping eye', named for 45 m-high rocks where water continuously trickles down the sides. **Tourist information:** Kulgera Hotel, Stuart Hwy; (089) 56 0973. **Accommodation:** 1 hotel, 1 caravan park. MAP REF. 270 G1, 356 I12

Larrimah   Population under 200
On the Stuart Hwy, 90 km north of Daly Waters. **Of interest:** Crocodiles and buffalo at Green Park, Stuart Hwy. **Tourist information:** Green Park Tourist Complex, Stuart Hwy; (089) 75 9937. **Accommodation:** 1 hotel, 2 caravan/camping parks. MAP REF. 352 I11, 354 I1

Mataranka   Population under 200
This settlement, 110 km south-east of Katherine, has a well-developed tourist resort with a thermal spring pool

NORTHERN TERRITORY NATIONAL PARKS

There are over fifty parks and reserves in the Northern Territory. The major ones are grouped in two sections, separated by 1500 kilometres of road. One group is at the Top End, close to Darwin, and the other at the southern end, around Alice Springs in central Australia.

Best-known of all the parks in the Centre is **Uluru** (Ayers Rock–Mount Olga) National Park, which contains the monolith Uluru (Ayers Rock) and Kata Tjuta (The Olgas) rising abruptly from the surrounding plains. The area is of vital cultural and religious significance to the Anangu (the traditional owners), whose ancestors have lived in the area for at least 10 000 years.

An easy way to explore Uluru's attractions is either by undertaking the Circuit Walk or joining a guided coach party tour around the nine-kilometre rock base to see significant traditional sites, such as the Mutitjulu Cave containing elaborate Aboriginal paintings, and Kantju Gorge.

The climb to the 348-metre-high summit is strictly for those with a good head for heights. It should not be attempted by anyone who is unfit or unwell, or in hot weather; injuries are common.

Further west, the great domes of Kata Tjuta are separated by deep clefts, many of which hold sweet water and support abundant wildlife. The name Kata Tjuta means 'manyheads'. There are several walks—Lookout, Valley of the Winds, Olga Gorge— which take from one to two hours to complete. Please keep to these marked tracks and consult a ranger before attempting any unmarked walks.

The town of Alice Springs lies in the MacDonnell Ranges, the land of the Aranda people and a paradise for photographers and artists. Cutting through the ranges are spectacular gorges offering some of the finest scenery in Australia—crimson and ochre rock walls bordering deep blue pools and slopes covered with spring wildflowers.

Within the West MacDonnells are

Finke Gorge National Park

five scenic parks. The best-known is **Ormiston Gorge and Pound National Park**, where fish bury themselves in the mud as a string of waterholes shrink to puddles, then wait for the rains to fill them again. The deepest part of Ormiston Creek is a magnificent permanent pool the Aranda believed to be inhabited by a great watersnake. At the far end of the gorge, the walls are curtained by a variety of ferns and plants, including the lovely Sturt's desert rose and the relic macrozamia.

Finke Gorge National Park also lies in this part of the MacDonnells. This scenic wilderness straddles the Finke River and includes the picturesque Palm Valley. This valley is a refuge for cycad palms and the ancient Livistona mariae, estimated to be about 5000 years old. The park is particularly rugged and visitors who do not join tours are advised to use four-wheel-drive.

The closest park to Alice Springs,

Simpsons Gap only 8 km west, is best seen on foot; there are several walking tracks, as well as guided ranger tours daily, through rocky gaps, along steep sided ridges overlooking huge gums and timbered creek flats.

Between the delights of Finke and the spectacular Uluru lies **Watarrka National Park**, its main attraction being the beautiful Kings Canyon. Waterholes, rock formations, and abundant wildlife provide excellent photographic and bushwalking opportunities.

The East MacDonnells contain five parks and reserves, all rich in Aboriginal history and culture. The **Corroboree Rock Conservation Reserve** protects the sacred grounds of the Aranda.

The **Ewaninga Rock Carvings Conservation Reserve** contains a small group of rock outcrops on which prehistoric Aboriginal carvings trace a maze of wavy lines, circles and animal tracks. However, the rock engravings in **N'Dhala Gorge National Park** are so ancient, their meaning is unknown to the present-day Aboriginal people of central Australia.

South-west of Alice Springs, just off the Stuart Highway, are the twelve **Henbury Meteorite Craters**, which were formed several thousand years ago. This is a haunt of the ferocious-looking, but harmless, bearded dragon lizard.

At the Top End of the Territory are several impressive national parks, including the scenic Kakadu. Located 348 kilometres south of Darwin is **Nitmiluk (Katherine Gorge) National Park**. This fascinating river canyon, with its abundant wildlife and Aboriginal rock paintings, is best seen from a flat-bottomed boat, available for hire with or without a guide. When the Katherine River flows peacefully in 'the dry', anglers will boast with delight of the good catches of barramundi and other species of fish that are found in the gorge's deep pools.

Smaller than most parks, **Litchfield National Park**, 100 km south of Darwin, features four spectacular waterfalls that flow throughout the year. The Lost City with its fascinating sandstone formation and Sandy Creek Falls are on four-wheel drive vehicle tracks. Swimming, photography, wildlife observation and bushwalking, ranging from a 20 minute stroll to an extended wilderness walk, are all popular activities.

One of the newest parks in the Territory, **Gregory National Park**, features tropical and semi-arid plant life, together with spectacular range and gorge scenery. Significant Aboriginal sites and evidence of early European settlement and pastoral history are also features. Boat tours are available at Timber Creek on Victoria River Crossing. Vehicle access within the park is by 4WD only.

In **Gurig National Park**, on the Cobourg Peninsula, a wilderness lodge overlooks Coral Bay. Also on Cobourg Peninsula is Seven Spirit Bay (reached from Darwin by air with ground and boat transfers), a rugged complex that offers a true wilderness experience. Fishing, sailing, a trip to historic ruins at Victoria, and exploration of the area's natural environment are the park's other attractions.

Note: In national parks and reserves and other areas, it is wise to heed local advice on the dangers of swimming because of the possibility of lurking crocodiles. The saltwater crocodile (found mainly in river estuaries) is highly dangerous, although the freshwater or Johnstone's crocodile (found in billabongs and rivers) is generally regarded as harmless — it lives on fish and there is no reported case of it ever having attacked a human.

For more information about the Territory's parks and reserves, contact the Conservation Commission of the Northern Territory, PO Box 496, Palmerston NT 0831; telephone (089) 89 4411. For Kakadu and Uluru, contact the Australian National Parks and Wildlife Service, GPO Box 636, Canberra ACT 2601, telephone (06) 250 0200; or PO Box 1260, Darwin NT 0801, telephone (089) 81 5299.

See also: Kakadu National Park; The Top End.

nearby. **Of interest:** Stockyard Museum and P. J. Wildlife Park, both on Stuart Hwy. **In the area:** Camping, horse-trail riding, 4WD safaris and barramundi fishing. Elsey National Park, 5 km east; swimming, fishing, canoeing, pleasant walks and Mataranka thermal pool. Elsey Cemetery, 25 km south, with graves of outback pioneers, who Mrs Aeneas Gunn, who lived at Elsey Station Homestead during 1902–3, immortalised in her classic, *We of the Never-Never*. **Accommodation:** 1 hotel, 2 motels, 2 caravan/camping parks.
MAP REF. 352 I10

Noonamah   Population under 200
On the Stuart Hwy, 38 km south of Darwin. **Accommodation:** 1 motel.
MAP REF. 352 E5

Pine Creek   Population 393
On the Stuart Hwy, 92 km north-west of Katherine, Pine Creek experienced a brief gold-rush in the 1870s; today the town is experiencing a resurgence following the reopening of goldmining operations. **Of interest:** Numerous historic buildings, including restored railway station and track, and open-air goldmining museum in National Trust reserve. **In the area:** Gold fossicking (licence required). Gold-mine tours; scenic drive; hunting safaris. Douglas Hot Springs Nature Park, 64 km north, off Stuart Hwy (52 km west) and Butterfly Gorge Nature Park, 14 km south of Springs (4WD); camping and bushwalking. **Accommodation:** 1 hotel/motel, 1 caravan/camping park.
MAP REF. 352 F7

Renner Springs
Population under 200
On the Stuart Hwy, 161 km north of Tennant Creek. **Accommodation:** 1 hotel/motel.
MAP REF. 355 J6

Ross River   Population under 200
Settlement 85 km east of Alice Springs. **Of interest:** Horse, camel and wagon rides at Ross River Homestead ranch-style outback resort; also whipcracking, boomerang-throwing, and billy tea and damper. **In the area:** Trephina Gorge, 17 km north-west. N'Dhala Gorge, 11 km south-west; Aboriginal rock engravings and ancient fossil deposits. Arltunga Historical Reserve, 25 km east. **Tourist Information:** Ross River Homestead, Ross Hwy; (089) 56 9711. **Accommodation:** Ross River Homestead; 1 camping/caravan park.
MAP REF. 357 K8, 359 R4

KAKADU NATIONAL PARK

Kakadu, one of the most popular national parks in Australia, has World Heritage status and is considered to be of outstanding worth for both its natural features and its cultural significance. Situated 250 kilometres from Darwin, it encompasses an area of 1 307 300 ha (approx. 20 000 square kilometres).

The name Kakadu is derived from Gagudju, one of the several languages of the Aboriginal people who are the park's traditional inhabitants. The park is leased to the Australian National Parks and Wildlife Service (ANPWS) to manage for all visitors to enjoy.

Kakadu is one of the few places in Australia where the original Aboriginal inhabitants maintain personal and spiritual links with their traditional lands. Kakadu contains a wealth of archaeological and rock-art sites that provide insights into Aboriginal culture. The park's traditional owners are willing to share their knowledge and understanding of their land, so visitors will appreciate the importance of Kakadu and share responsibility for its protection.

Kakadu is unique in that it encompasses an entire river catchment, the black-soil floodplains and paperbark lagoons of the South Alligator River system, and within it are found all the major habitat types of the Top End. The wetlands, woodlands and rugged walls of the Arnhem Land escarpment, which is deeply indented with gorges, streams and waterfalls, offer outstanding scenery anddiverse wildlife.

The shallow lagoons and billabongs in the central and northern sections of Kakadu attract hundreds of thousands of migratory and waterbirds. The park's prolific birdlife may be viewed on a boat cruise of the wetlands at Yellow Water. Other popular tourist destinations include Jim Jim, Makuk and Waterfall Creek falls. A variety of self-guided walking tracks provide opportunities to explore a range of habitats. A camping permit is required for overnight bushwalking.Boat cruises on the South Alligator River, scenic flights and commercial tours are also available. During the 'dry' (May–September), there are free guided walks

and talks by Park Rangers.

Visits to some isolated locations within the park are subject to a permit system and limited visitor numbers because of the sensitive nature of those areas.

As crocodiles are present in the park, swimming is not recommended and those who fish from the banks of rivers or from boats should take care.

Accommodation in the park consists of hotels, caravan parks, a youth hostel and private camping-grounds. Facilities are available for disabled persons. Fuel, food and provisions may be obtained at Jabiru township and at Border Store.

Visitors over sixteen years of age pay a park use fee (valid for fourteen days).

For further information, contact Park Manager, Kakadu National Park, PO Box 71, Jabiru NT 0886; (089) 79 9101. *Visitor Guides* to the park are available from the ANPWS: GPO Box 636, Canberra ACT 2601; and GPO Box 1260, Darwin NT 0800; or from Park Headquarters.

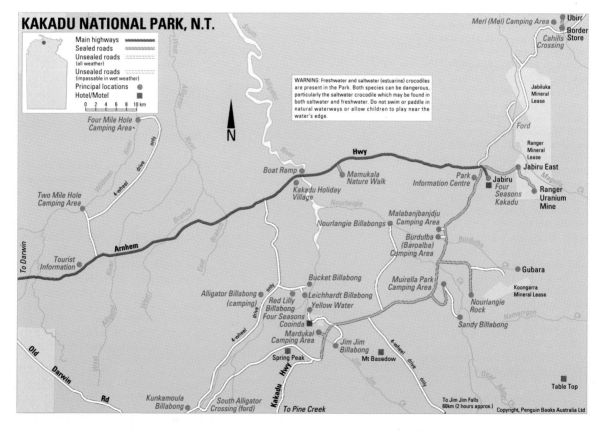

Tennant Creek Population 3503
According to legend, Tennant Creek was founded when a beer wagon carrying building supplies destined for the nearby Overland Telegraph Station broke down at the site of the present town. The township is 507 km north of Alice Springs, on the Stuart Hwy. Gold and copper deposits account for its development today, and the town has grown into a thriving regional centre for the Barkly Tablelands. **Of interest:** Civic Centre, Peko Rd; impressive art, gem and mineral collection. Travellers Rest Area, Purkiss Reserve, Ambrose St; picnic area with full facilities and adjacent swimming pool. **In the area:** Government-owned Stamp Battery and Museum, 1 km east; one of very few batteries still operational. Nobles Nob, 16 km east, once richest open-cut gold-mine of its size in world. Three Ways, junction of Stuart and Barkly Hwys, 25 km north; nearby, John Flynn Historical Reserve. Attack Creek Historical Reserve, 73 km north, site of encounter between John McDouall Stuart and local Aborigines. Mary Ann Dam, 4 km north-east; popular for swimming, canoeing, windsurfing, cycling and bushwalking. The Devil's Marbles, 103 km south; huge 'balancing rocks'. Less well-known but equally impressive, though smaller, the Devils Pebbles, 16 km north-west. **Tourist information:** New Coach Transit Centre, Paterson St; (089) 62 3388. **Accommodation:** 2 hotel/motels, 3 motels, 2 caravan/camping parks. **See also:** Aboriginal Art.
MAP REF. 355 K9

Victoria River Crossing
Population under 200
Located where the Victoria Hwy crosses the Victoria River, between Timber Creek and the junction with Delamere Road. **In the area:** Boat tours and fishing cruises on Victoria River from Timber Creek, 92 km west. **Touristinformation:** Victoria River Wayside Inn, Victoria Hwy; (089) 75 0744. **Accommodation:** 1 hotel/motel, 1 caravan/camping park.
MAP REF. 352 E11, 354 E1

Victory Downs
Population under 200
Situated on the border with SA, just off the Stuart Hwy, 316 km from Alice Springs.
MAP REF. 270 G1, 356 I13

Wauchope Population under 200
On the Stuart Hwy, 115 km south of Tennant Creek. **In the area:** Devil's

SPORTSMAN'S TERRITORY

Even though the Northern Territory has an area of 135 million hectares—six times the size of Great Britain and one-sixth of the Australian continent—there are few places where you can legally shoot game. Even fishing is restricted in some areas.

Every kind of firearm must be registered. The possession of high-powered rifles and pistols is tightly controlled. Visitors with a high-powered weapon properly licensed in their home state or country may be allowed it in the Territory if a valid certificate or licence is produced at a police station. The police must be satisfied that the weapon is safe, that the applicant is over twenty-one years and that there is a 'substantial reason' for carrying the weapon. The term 'substantial reason' does not include sporting purposes. Visitors carrying firearms must report to police within two days of entering the Territory. The booklet *Before You Shoot,* available at any NT police station, outlines licensing requirements for shooters and firearms in the Territory.

Firearms are prohibited in the Territory's main sanctuaries and protected areas. Sanctuaries now in existence include: Cobourg Peninsula, Tanami Desert, Woolwonga Aboriginal Land, Daly River Aboriginal Land, Murgenella River and the Arnhem Land Aboriginal Land. All Aboriginal Lands are protected areas. It is an offence to take firearms or traps into any protected area. Penalties range from fines of up to $400 to imprisonment for up to twelve months. Maps showing existing sanctuaries and protected areas can be seen at police stations. Firearms and shooting are prohibited in NT parks, except for the hunting reserves Howard Swamp, Lambell's Lagoon, Harrison Dam and Marrakai (all in the Top End). Further information about these reserves, and the necessary permits that must be obtained prior to arrival, is available from the Northern Territory Conservation Commission, Gaymark Building, Palmerston; (089) 89 4411.

Property owners rarely give permission for strangers to shoot on their land because of the danger and disturbance caused to stock. Trigger-happy tourists are known to have caused serious stock losses in the Territory and those who shoot on private property without permission from the owner are liable to find themselves under fire. Some fish are protected in some areas, but fishing is otherwise unrestricted both inland and in the sea. Visitors who want to mount a hunting, shooting and fishing expedition in the Territory could well save themselves heavy fines and confiscation of guns and gear by booking into an organised safari through a hometown travel agency.

Marbles, 8 km north. Wycliffe Well, 18 km south; well-known for large selection of international beers. Old Wolfram mines, 10 km east (4WD only). **Tourist information:** Wauchope Well Hotel, Stuart Hwy; (089) 64 1963. **Accommodation:** 1 hotel, 1 caravan/camping park.
MAP REF. 355 K12, 357 K1

Yulara Population 1158
Situated on outskirts of Uluru National Park, this township is the location for a world-class tourist resort offering full visitor facilities and comfortable air-conditioned accommodation in all price brackets. **Of interest:** Visitors Centre provides displays and information on national park. Audiovisual shows daily. Uluru Experience Night Star Talk offers nocturnal sky viewing; also narration of Aboriginal and European legends relating to the night sky. **In the area:** Uluru (Ayers Rock), 20 km southeast; Australia's famous sandstone monolith. Kata Tjuta (The Olgas), 50 km west. Tours can be booked at Visitors Centre or reception in accommodation areas. **Tourist information:** Yulara Visitors Centre; (089) 56 2240. **Accommodation:** 3 hotels, backpackers' units, flats, caravan/camping ground. **See also:** The Red Centre.
MAP REF. 356 E11

Maps of Northern Territory

Location Map

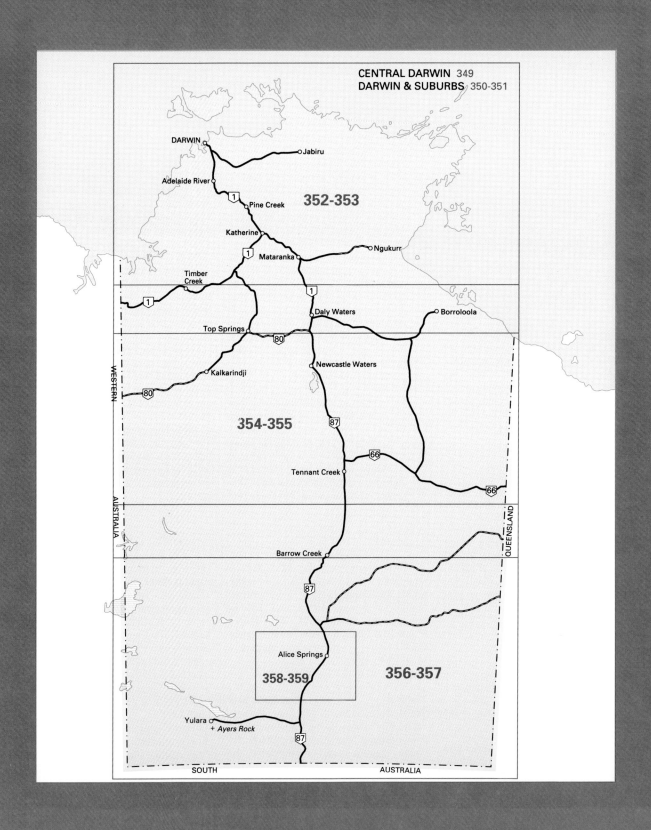

CENTRAL DARWIN 349
DARWIN & SUBURBS 350-351

352-353

354-355

356-357

358-359

DARWIN

○ Jabiru

Adelaide River ○

① Pine Creek

Katherine ○

① Mataranka

○ Ngukurr

Timber
Creek

① Daly Waters

○ Borroloola

Top Springs ○ 80

Kalkarindji ○

80

Newcastle Waters

87

66

Tennant Creek ○

66

WESTERN

AUSTRALIA

QUEENSLAND

Barrow Creek ○

87

Alice Springs ○

Yulara ○
+ Ayers Rock

87

SOUTH   AUSTRALIA

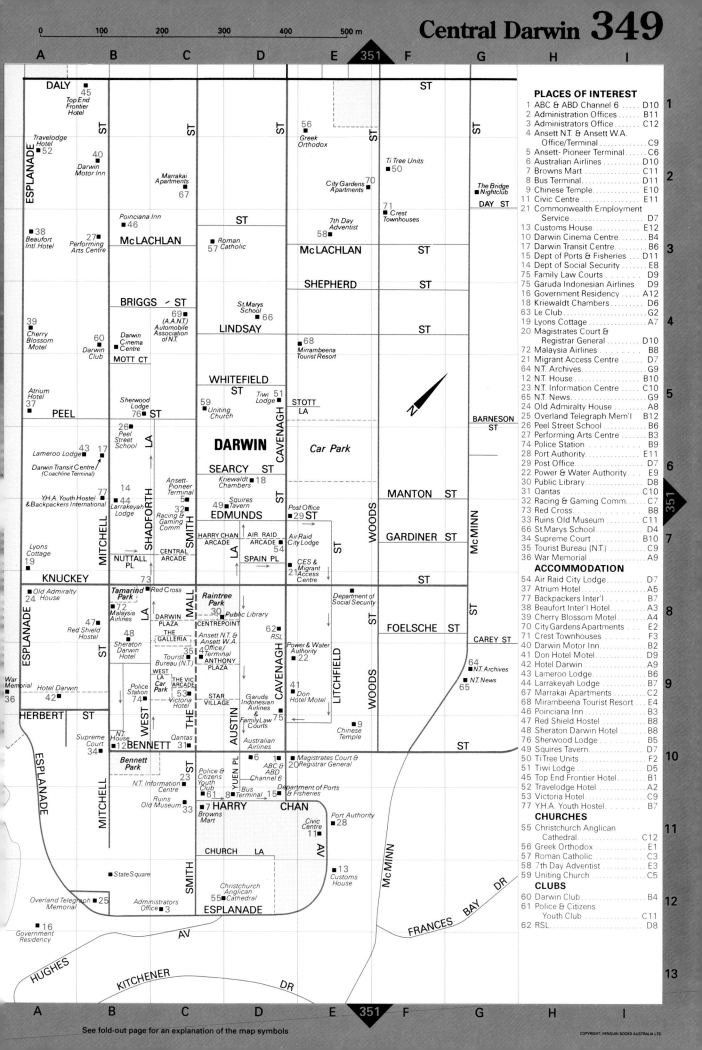

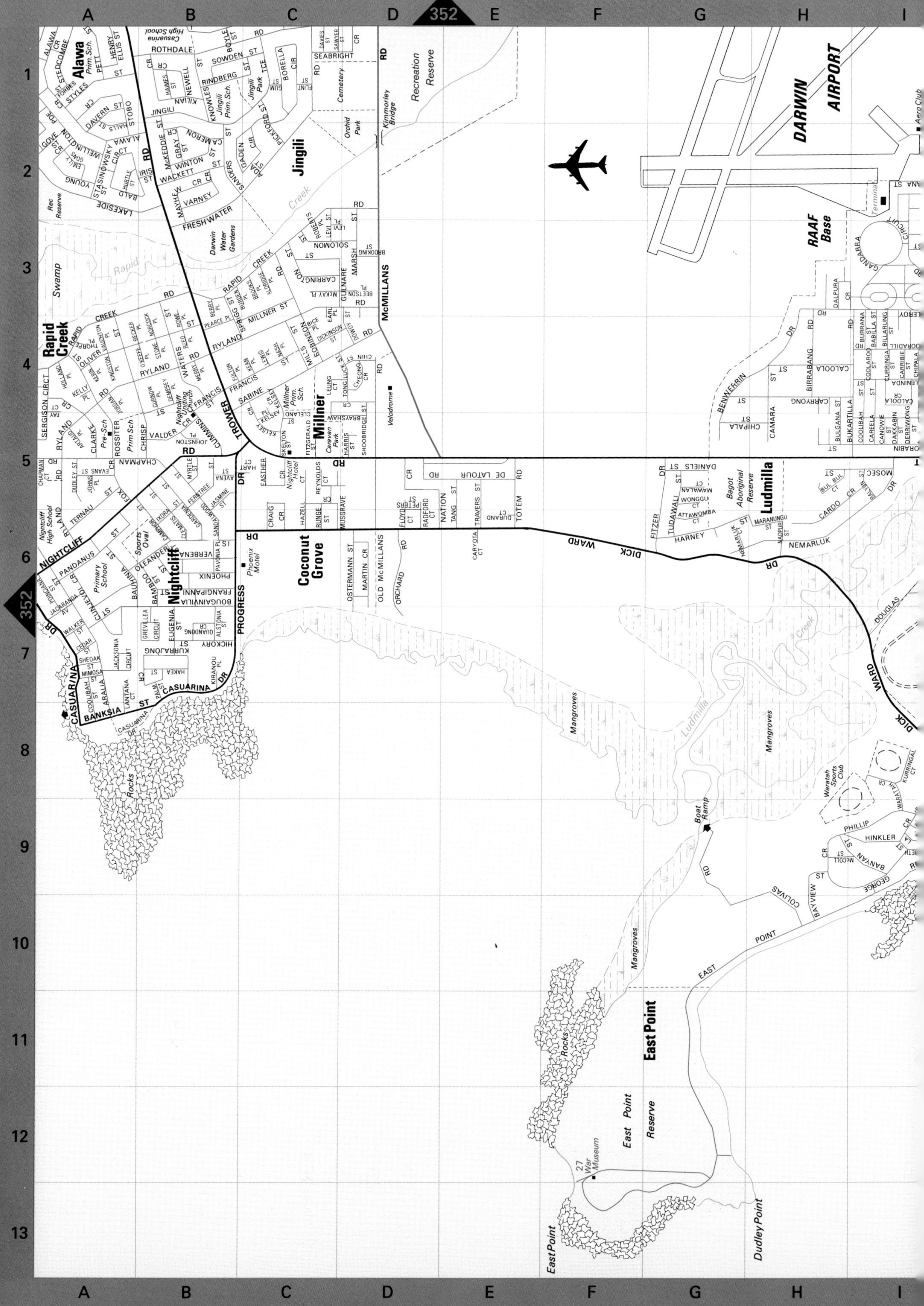

352

DARWIN AIRPORT

RAAF Base

Aero Club

Alawa

Jingili

Rapid Creek

Millner

Ludmilla

Bagot Aboriginal Reserve

Nightcliff

Coconut Grove

Casuarina

Banksia

East Point

East Point Reserve

27 War Museum

East Point

Dudley Point

Boat Ramp

Mangroves

Ludmilla

Rocks

Waratah Sports Club

Recreation Reserve

Kimmorley Bridge

Cemetery

Orchid Park

Rec Reserve

Swamp

Rapid Creek

Darwin Water Gardens

Phoenix Motel

Nightcliff Hotel

Caravan Park

Velodrome

Old McMillans

Rocks

McMILLANS RD

TROWER RD

DICK WARD DR

PROGRESS DR

CASUARINA DR

DE LATOUR RD

0   0.5   1   1.5   2 km

FOR MORE DETAIL OF DARWIN
SEE MAP OF CENTRAL DARWIN

Mangroves

Winnellie

Stuart Park

Frances Bay

Small Ships Facility

Stokes Hill
Old Powerhouse

Stokes Hill Wharf

Darwin Harbour

Fort Hill Wharf

Land Backed Wharf

Iron Ore Wharf

Fort Hill

Chinese Cemetery

Dinah Beach

Dinah Beach Cruising Yacht Association

Small Boat Harbour

under construction

DARWIN

Parap

Public Car Park

Lameroo Beach

Botanical Gardens

Amphitheatre

Radio

Historical Cem

St Johns College

Haase Cottage

Leichhardt Memorial

Esplanade

Performing Arts Centre

Fannie Bay

Darwin Bowling Club

Ski Club

Museum & Art Gallery Complex

Darwin High School

Darwin High Sch

Darwin Trailer Boat Club
Darwin Sailing Club

Vesteys Beach

Bullocky Point

The Gardens

Mindil Beach

Gardens Oval

Palmerston Park

Mun Golf Course

Tennis Courts

Casino

University College of N.T. Myilly Campus

Doctors Gully

Slipway

Shipway

Cullen Beach

Myilly Point

Military Area

Larrakeyah

Patrol Boat Harbour

Fannie Bay

N

Emery Point

Elliott Point

See fold-out page for an explanation of the map symbols

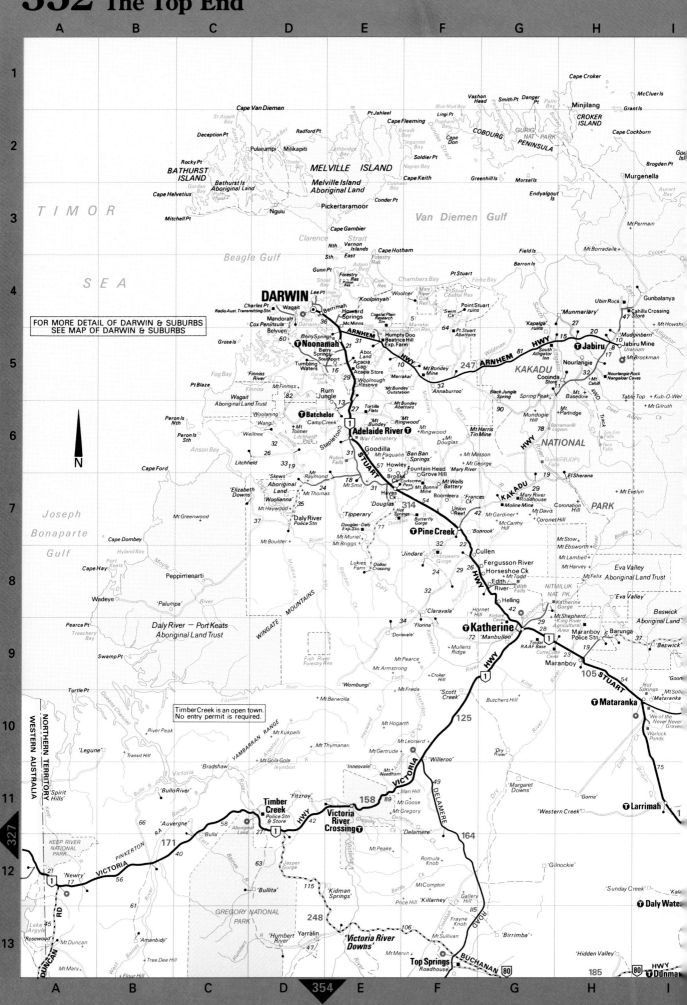

FOR MORE DETAIL OF DARWIN & SUBURBS
SEE MAP OF DARWIN & SUBURBS

N

TimberCreek is an open town.
No entry permit is required.

0 50 100 150 200 250 km

J K L M N O P Q R

1

ARAFURA SEA

WARNING: Although an indication of road surface types is shown on this map, it is imperative that visitors obtain full information as to road conditions ahead before proceeding on their journey. During the period October to May 'wet' season conditions may cause severe flooding, making many roads impassable. The majority of water features shown on this map do not contain permanent water.

If visitors intend diverting off public roads within Aboriginal Land areas, a permit is required from the relevant Aboriginal authority.

Cape Wessel

WESSEL ISLANDS

Marchinbar Island

2

Cumberland Strait

Drysdale Is

Guluwuru Island

Cunningham Islands

Alger Is

Wigram Island

North West Crocodile Island

ELCHO ISLAND

Pt. Napier

Ingis Is

The English Company's Islands

Cape Wilberforce

3

Cuthbert Pt

Braithwaite Pt

Junction Bay

Hawkesbury Pt

Nth East Pt

Cape Stewart

Mooroongga Is

Galiwinku

Flinders Is

Malay Road

Bremer Is

Melville Bay

Nhulunbuy

Rolling Bay

Boucaut Bay

Maningrida

Milingimbi

HOWARD ISLAND

Castlereagh Bay

Buckingham Bay

Arnhem Bay

GOVE PENINSULA

Yirrkala

Gove

4

Nangalala

Ramingining

Gapuwiyak

Lake Evella

Port Bradshaw

Cape Arnhem

FREDERICK HILLS

Camburinga

Pt Alexander

5

ARNHEM LAND

MITCHELL RA

Durabudboi R

Mt Caledon

Caledon Bay

Cape Grey

Koolatong

Trial Bay

Bald Pt

6

Arnhem Land Aboriginal Land Trust

PARSONS RANGE

BATH RA

Mt Fleming

Jalma Bay

Isle Woodah

Cape Shield

Nicol Is

Weker R

Mt Ranken

Morgan Is

Burney Is

GULF OF

7

'Weemol'

'Bulman'

Mt Marumba

Mt Weir

Black Mtn

Mt Stretton

Mt Gatt

Blue Mud Bay

Bennet Bay

Cape Barrow

Bickerton Is

Winchelsea Is

Port Langdon

Umbakumba

8

Mt Bridges

'Mainoru'

Mt Leane

Mt Bray

Lowrie Channel

Warwick Channel

Alyangula

Angurugu

Gemco Mine

Anindilyakwa Aboriginal Land Council

GROOTE EYLANDT

'Mountain Valley'

Mainoru

10

43

Mt Throsby

Three Graces

Rose River

Tasman Pt

South Pt

Cape Beatrice

'Whamelk Bluff'

Mt Furner

9

Mt Karmain

Mt Bagster

Mt Phillip

Mt Favenc

DOWNERS RA

Phelp R

156

Numbulwar

CARPENTARIA

Mt Chapman

COLLERA MTNS

Edward Is

Mt Warrington

31

Ngukurr

Roper

Roper Bar Police Stn

Urapunga

Mt Eclipse

'St Vidgeon'

Mt Roper

Port Roper

Limmen Bight

Maria Is

HWY

65

213

Aboriginal Land

'Roper Valley'

Mt Harriet

'Price'

Mt St Vidgeon

Mt Boxall

Marra Aboriginal Land Trust

10

Mt Forrest

Mt Hughes

Hodgson R

Towns R

Mt Davidson

Mt Kelly

'Hodgson Downs'

11

Alawa Aboriginal Land Trust

The Four Archers

'Nathan River'

Rosie R

SIR EDWARD PELLEW GROUP

North Is

West Is

'Lorella'

'Bing Bong'

S W Is

Centre Is

Vanderlin Is

'Nutwood Downs'

Port McArthur

12

103

Limmen Bight R

Borroloola is an open town. No entry permit is required.

80

'Manangoora'

Borroloola PO

18

Mt Feathertop

74

24

'Greenbank'

CARPENTARIA

171

HWY

'Tanumbirini'

'Broadmere'

'Bauhinia'

'Billengarrah'

'Tawallah'

Narwinbi Aboriginal Land Trust

31

'Seven Emu'

13

21

'OT Downs'

CARPENTARIA HWY

McArthur R

'McArthur River'

'Spring Creek'

Robinson River Aboriginal Land Trust

Robinson R

J K L M N O P Q R

See fold-out page for an explanation of the map symbols

A B C D E F G H I

1

Timber Creek
Police Stn & Store

Victoria River Crossing

HWY

'Cooliban'
Mt Goose
Mt Gregory
'Delamere' Ck
Mt Peake
Romula Knob
'Gilnockie'
'Sunday Creek'
Larrimah
Western Creek

'Auvergne'
'Bulla'
Aboriginal Land
171
1   40
58
Baines
East
27
42
Gregory

KEEP RIVER NAT PK
PINKERTON
RA
VICTORIA
'Newry'
21
17
56
Mt Brookins

2

Timber Creek is an open town. No entry permit is required.

GREGORY
'Bullita'
NATIONAL
61
63
115
Jasper Gorge
'Kidman Springs'
248
GREGORY NATIONAL PARK
Mt Compton
Price Hill
'Killarney'
Gallery Hill
115
'Birrimba'
Daly Wate

Lake Argyle
45
Mt Duncan
'Amanbidji'
Frayne Knob
106
'Hidden Valley'
HWY
Dunma
Roadhe

3

DUNCAN
263
'Rosewood'
94
Mt Mary
'Waterloo'
Tree Dee Hill
Flour Hill
View Hill
'Humbert River'
Yarralin
47
Victoria River Downs
Mt Mervn
'Montejinni'
Top Springs Roadhouse
Stoney Knob
80
BUCHANAN
131
185
80
54

NATIONAL
PARK
108
Mt Hodgson
Mt Stevens
'Pigeon Hole'
Mt Northcote
HWY
127
'Dungowan'
'Murranji'
PMG Memo

4

Mt Elder
46
'Mistake Creek'
Mt Wickham
Warriki Hill
Mt Kimon
'Mt Sanford'
Gregorys Remarkable Pillar
Cusack Rock
'Camfield'
Mt Williams
172
80
'Limbunya'
66
'Daguragu'
'Wave Hill'
29
Newca Wat

DUNCAN
Mt Panton
Mt Copley
Mt Rose
Mt Napie
Blackgin Hill
Kalkarindji
Formerly Wave Hill
Red Hill
16
'Cattle Creek OS'

5

RD
'Kirkimbie'
78
Mt Maivo
50
238
108
Dagaragu Aboriginal Land Trust
Mt Seale
Mt Gordon
Toms Rock
Mt Barton
Gap Hill
105

6

BUCHANAN
80
'Inverway'
Mt Farquharson
'Bunda'
Mt Archie
'Riveren'
Kalkarindji is an open town. No entry permit is required.
SEMI   DESERT

327
'Nicholson'
70
Nongra Lake

7

NORTHERN TERRITORY
WESTERN AUSTRALIA
124
(Abandoned) 'Wallamunga'
'Birrindudu'
Lajamanu
Winnecke Ck

WARNING: Although an indication of road surface types is shown on this map, it is imperative that visitors obtain full information as to road conditions ahead before proceeding on their journey. During the period October to May 'wet' season conditions may cause severe flooding, making many roads impassable. The majority of water features shown on this map do not contain permanent water.

If visitors intend diverting off public roads within Aboriginal Land areas, a permit is required from the relevant Aboriginal authority.

8

238
'Suplejack'
Only
Drive
Wheel
Four
Witton Ck
BUCHANAN HILLS
'Lothari Hill'

9

210
'Mallee Hill'
Mt Frederick
Lake Buck
N   Central   Desert

Aboriginal   Land   Trust

10

82
Mt Tanami
Tanami
40
Lake Surprise
SEMI   DESER

11

Rabbit Flat Roadhouse
60
Mt Davidson
Mt Solitaire
Lanifer

12

'Tanami Downs'
The Granites
Hordern Hills
Lake Lucas
TANAMI
Mt Bennett
River
Mt Windajong

13

260
McDiarmid Hill
'Willowra'
Lake White
Mt Theo
Mt Patricia
Mt Rennie
Ingellar Ck
Sowden Hill

A B C D E F G H I

352

356

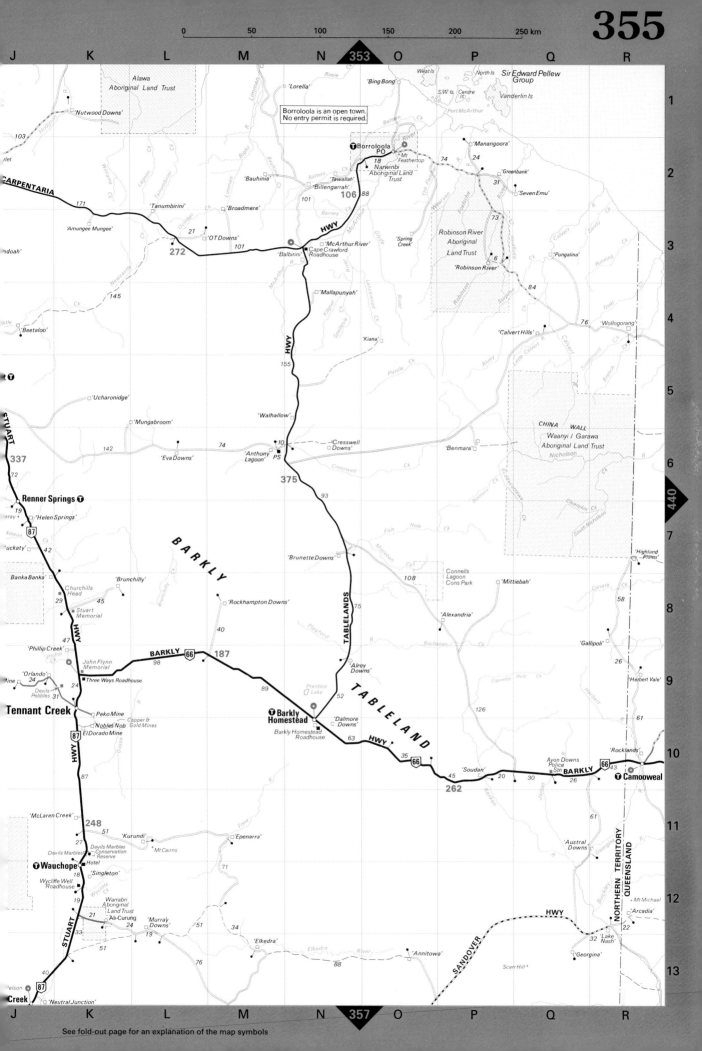

0   50   100   150   200   250 km

J   K   L   M   N   O   P   Q   R

1

'Nutwood Downs'

Alawa
Aboriginal Land Trust

'Lorella'   'Bing Bong'   West Is   North Is
                                                    Sir Edward Pellew
Rosie   Group
                                        S.W. Is. Centre
                              Port McArthur   Is.   Vanderlin Is

Borroloola is an open town.
No entry permit is required.

2

CARPENTARIA

103

171

'Amungee Mungee'

'Tanumbirini'

21

272

'OT Downs'

101

'Broadmere'

'Bauhinia'

'Tawallah'

'Billengarrah'

Borroloola
PO

106   88

18   Mt
Featherton
Narwinbi
Aboriginal Land
Trust

'Manangoora'

74   24

'Greenbank'
31

'Seven Emu'

'McArthur River'
Cape Crawford
Roadhouse

'Balbirini'

'Spring
Creek'

73

Robinson River
Aboriginal
Land Trust

6

'Robinson River'

'Pungalina'

76

'Calvert Hills'

'Wollogorang'

3

145

'Beetaloo'

155

'Mallapunyah'

'Kiana'

84

4

STUART

337

72

'Ucharonidge'

142

'Mungabroom'

'Eva Downs'

74

'Walhallow'

10

'Anthony
Lagoon' PS

375

'Cresswell
Downs'

'Benmara'

CHINA   WALL
Waanyi / Garawa
Aboriginal Land Trust

Nicholson

5

6

Renner Springs

19

'Helen Springs'

87

'uckaty'

42

Banka Banka

Churchills
Head

29   45

Stuart
Memorial

BARKLY

'Brunchilly'

'Rockhampton Downs'

40

93

'Brunette Downs'

75

108

Connells
Lagoon
Cons Park

'Mittiebah'

'Alexandria'

'Highland
Plains'

58

'Gallipoli'

26

'Herbert Vale'

7

8

9

47

HWY

'Phillip Creek'

'Orlando'
24

Devils
Pebbles   31

Tennant Creek

87

Peko Mine

Nobles Nob
El Dorado Mine

BARKLY   66   187

98

John Flynn
Memorial

Three Ways Roadhouse

89

Copper &
Gold Mines

Prentice
Lake

52

TABLELANDS

'Alroy
Downs'

Barkly
Homestead

'Dalmore
Downs'

Barkly Homestead
Roadhouse

63   HWY

35

262

45

TABLELAND

126

'Soudan'

20   30

Avon Downs
Police Stn

'Rocklands'

BARKLY   66   43

Camooweal

61

10

87

'McLaren Creek'

248

27   51

'Kurundi'

Devils Marbles
Conservation
Reserve

Mt Cairns

'Epenarra'

71

'Austral
Downs'

NORTHERN TERRITORY
QUEENSLAND

61

11

Wauchope

Hotel

18

'Singleton'

Wycliffe Well
Roadhouse

19

21

Warrabri
Aboriginal
Land Trust

Ali-Curung

33   24

'Murray
Downs'

19

51

34

'Elkedra'

Elkedra   River

'Annitowa'

88

SANDOVER

Scarr Hill

+ Mt Michael

'Arcadia'

22

HWY

32   'Lake
Nash'

'Georgina'

12

13

STUART

40

87

Creek

'Neutral Junction'

'Nelson'

J   K   L   M   N   O   P   Q   R

See fold-out page for an explanation of the map symbols

440

354

A B C D E F G H I

1
Lake Lucas
'Tanami Downs'
The Granites
Hordern Hills
+ Mt Davidson
+ Mt Solitaire
Central Desert
Aboriginal Land Trust
Lander River

2
Lake White
260
+ Mt Bennett
+ McDiarmid Hill
+ Mt Theo
+ Mt Windajong
'Willowra'
Ingalain

3
Lake Hazlett
Sowden Hill +
Chilla Well
ROAD
+ Mt Patricia
+ Mt Barkly
69.
+ Mt Rennie
+ Mt Peake
'Anningie'

4
+ Mt Singleton
Mt Farewell +
TANAMI
Mt Hardy +
+ Mt Campbell
Mt. Leichhardt
Yuendumu Aboriginal Land Trust
'Mt Denison'
+ Mt Treachery
+ Quartz Hill
'Mt Allan'
+ Mt Stafford
'Coniston'
+ Mt Gardiner
58
+ Mt Finniss
'Pine Hill'
'Ti-Tree'
NancyH
48

5
Lake Mackay
Central Desert
Aboriginal Land Trust
Mt Nicker +
'Vaughan Springs'
Mt Davenport +
Yuendumu
79
TANAMI
Napperby Ck
Mt Boothby +
'Napperby'
PO
'Aileron'

6
Mt Stanley +
Mt Gurner +
+ Mt Cockburn
'Newhaven'
106
Lake Bennett
+ Central Mt Wedge
'Mt Wedge'
+ West Bluff
+ Mt Hammond
72
+ Mt Harris
Ex

7
327
Mt Strickland +
Mt Leisler +
4 Wheel Drive Only
188
TROPIC OF CAPRICORN
85
+ Mt Liebig
Papunya
Haasts Bluff
18
62
'Derwent'
'Narwietooma'
29
+ Mt Chapple
290
'Ambu
'Milton Park'
'Ti-Tree'

8
Lake Macdonald
Mt Mein +
Mt Udor +
87
Haasts Bluff Aboriginal Land Trust
+ Mt Forbes
32
19
'Glen Helen'
+ Mt Ziel
+ Mt Sonder
MACDONNELL
NAMATJIRA
48
RANGES
'Hamilton Downs'
Mt Hay +
Glen Helen
26
Serpentine Chalet
129 DR
56
78 LARAPIN
12

9
+ Mt Winter
+ Laycocks Hill
Mt Solitary +
+ Camels Hump
Undandita
Gosse Bluff
Hermannsburg Aboriginal Land Trust
Pile Hill
21
Hermannsberg Mission
Areyonga
Palm Valley
FINKE GORGE NAT PARK
+ Mt Keartlan

10
Lake Hopkins
+ Mt Murray
Mt Tucker +
Lake Neale
Carmichael Crag
Kings Canyon
Kings Ck
WATARRKA NATIONAL PARK
Kings Creek Campground
+ Mt Olifent
+ Tent Hill
Mt Lewis
Petermann Ck
+ Mt Levi
Yowa Bluff
101
'Tempe Downs'
Pelmer
Henbury Meteorite Craters
97
Finke
'Ora C'
29

11
20
Docker
Mt Skene +
+ Mt Cowle
Mt Harris +
+ Mt Carruthers
Petermann Aboriginal
Land Trust
Kaltukatjara
Mt Deering +
PETERMANN RANGES
+ Mt Curdie
206
+ Mt Currie
Lake Amadeus
122
'Angas Downs'
70
'Wallara'
Tourist Chalet
The Twins +
+ Desert Oak Hill
Pa Va
STUART
69

12
Mt Daisy
+Bates
+ Mt Miller
Mt Bowley +
Mt Phillips +
+ Mt McCulloch
+ Katamala Cone
Stevenson + Peak
+ Butler Dome
Benda Hill
Yulara
Mt Olga
'The Olgas'
43
Ayers Rock
ULURU NATIONAL PARK
12
Uluru National Park owned by the Aboriginals and leased by the Australian Government.
82
LASSETER
Curtin Springs
12
Mt Connor
68
+ Mt Robert
'Mulga Park'
+Mt Ebenezer
51
'Imanpa'
Mt. Ebenezer
38
255
HWY
55
Ippia Hill
Erldunda
Karinga
'Kulgera'
74
93
87

13
Mt Gosse +
Mt Aloysius +
+ Bell Rock
+ Mt Le Hunte
+ Mt Cockburn
+ Mt Mann
MANN RANGES
+ Mt Davies
255
+ Mt Hardy
+ Mt Edwin
Mt Angatja +
North West Aboriginal Land
+ Mt Charles
Mt Woodward +
+ Mt Morris
Musgrave Park Aboriginal Community
+ Mt Davenport
Mt Everard +
Mt Woodroffe +
Ernabella
324
141
26
'Kenmore Park'
Victory Downs
'Sundown'
Mt Reynolds +
Mt Sir Henry +
+ Sentinel Hill
Kulgera
19
C

Surveyor General's Corner

A B C D E F G H I

270

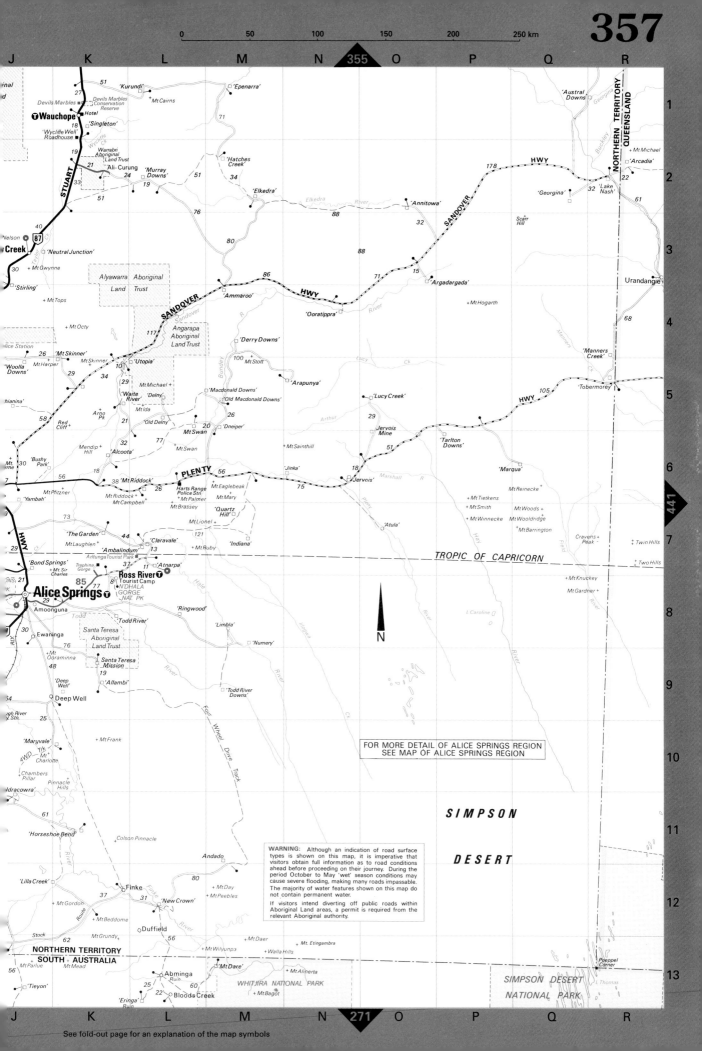

SIMPSON DESERT

WARNING: Although an indication of road surface types is shown on this map, it is imperative that visitors obtain full information as to road conditions ahead before proceeding on their journey. During the period October to May 'wet' season conditions may cause severe flooding, making many roads impassable. The majority of water features shown on this map do not contain permanent water.

If visitors intend diverting off public roads within Aboriginal Land areas, a permit is required from the relevant Aboriginal authority.

FOR MORE DETAIL OF ALICE SPRINGS REGION SEE MAP OF ALICE SPRINGS REGION

TROPIC OF CAPRICORN

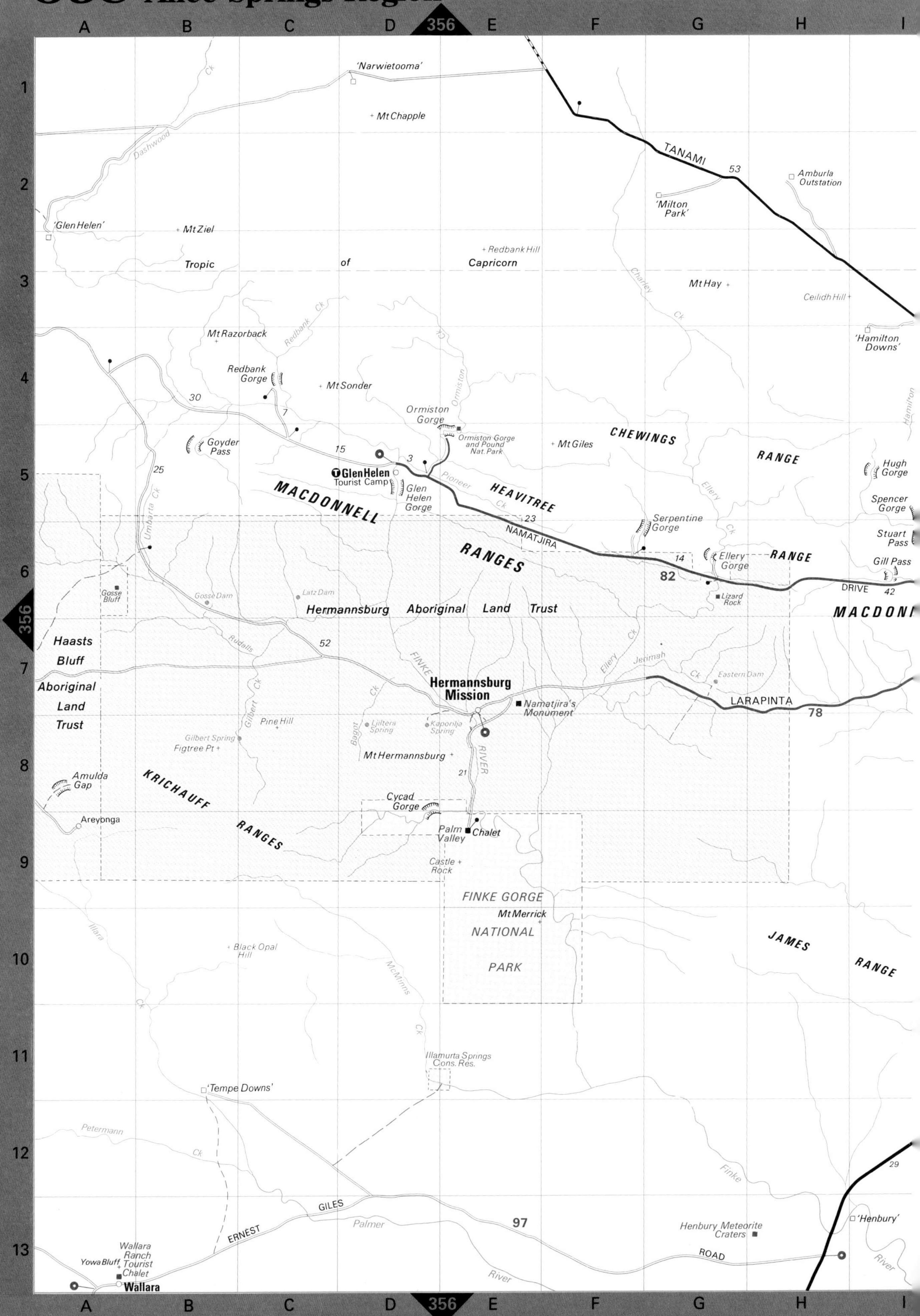

A B C D 356 E F G H I

1

'Narwietooma'

+ Mt Chapple

TANAMI

53

Amburla
Outstation

2

'Milton
Park'

Dashwood Ck

'Glen Helen'

+ Mt Ziel

Tropic   of   Capricorn

+ Redbank Hill

Mt Hay +

Charley Ck

Ceilidh Hill +

3

'Hamilton
Downs'

Mt Razorback +

Redbank Ck

Redbank
Gorge

+ Mt Sonder

Ormiston Ck

CHEWINGS

RANGE

Hugh
Gorge

4

30

7

Goyder
Pass

Ormiston
Gorge

+ Mt Giles

Spencer
Gorge

25

15

3

Ormiston Gorge
and Pound
Nat. Park

Stuart
Pass

5

Umbarta Ck

Glen Helen
Tourist Camp

Glen
Helen
Gorge

Pioneer Ck

HEAVITREE

Ellery Ck

Gill Pass

MACDONNELL

23

Serpentine
Gorge

RANGE

6

Gosse
Bluff

Gosse Dam

Latz Dam

NAMATJIRA

14

82

Ellery
Gorge

Lizard
Rock

DRIVE

42

MACDONI

RANGES

Haasts
Bluff

Hermannsburg   Aboriginal   Land   Trust

Ellery Ck

Jerimah Ck

7

Aboriginal

Rudalls Ck

52

Finke

Namatjira

Eastern Dam

LARAPINTA

78

Land

Trust

Hermannsburg
Mission

Namatjira's
Monument

Gilbert Ck

Bagot Ck

Ljiltera
Spring

Kaporilja
Spring

8

Amulda
Gap

Gilbert Spring
Figtree Pt +

Pine Hill

Mt Hermannsburg +

21

RIVER

Areynga

KRICHAUFF

Cycad
Gorge

Palm
Valley

Chalet

9

RANGES

Castle +
Rock

Iltara Ck

FINKE GORGE

Mt Merrick +

10

Black Opal
Hill

McMinns Ck

NATIONAL

PARK

JAMES

RANGE

11

Illamurta Springs
Cons. Res.

'Tempe Downs'

12

Petermann Ck

Ck

Finke

29

GILES

97

'Henbury'

13

Wallara
Ranch
Tourist
Chalet

ERNEST

Palmer

Henbury Meteorite
Craters

ROAD

River

Yowa Bluff

Wallara

River

A B C D 356 E F G H I

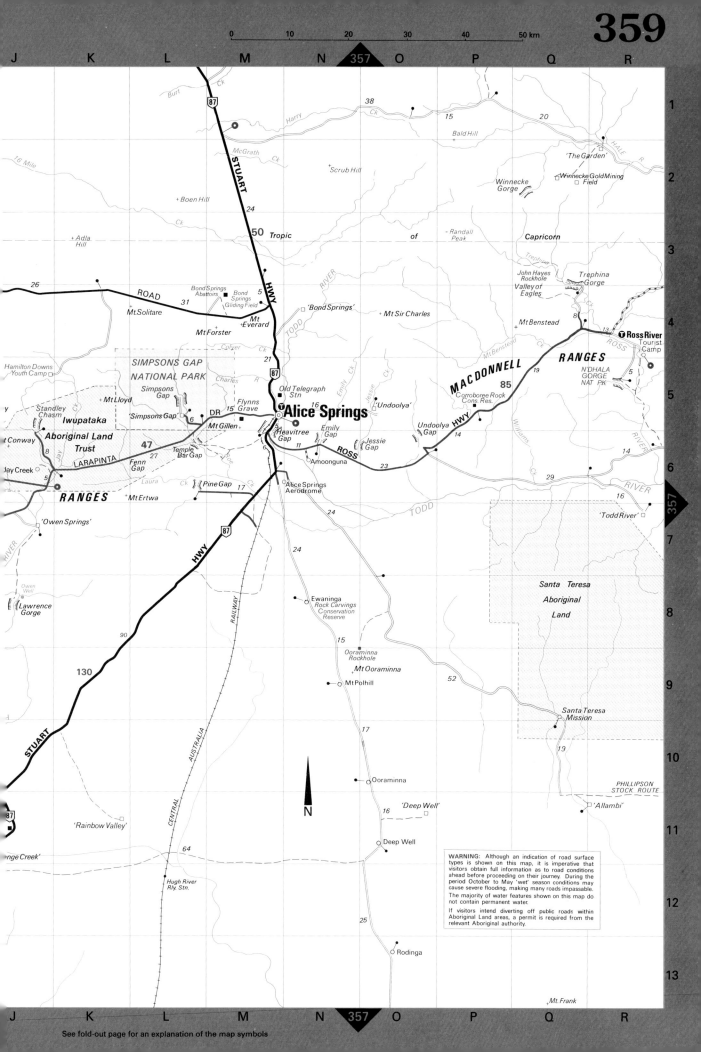

0 10 20 30 40 50 km

J K L M N 357 O P Q R

STUART
87
Burt   Ck
Harry   38
15   20
16 Mile   McGrath   Ck
Bald Hill   'The Garden'
+ Scrub Hill   Winnecke Gold Mining
Winnecke   Field
Gorge
24   Boen Hill
+ Adla   50   Tropic   of   - Randall   Capricorn
Hill   Peak
Ck   Trephina
HWY   John Hayes   Valley of   Trephina
ROAD   Rockhole   Eagles   Gorge
26   31   Bond Springs   RIVER   8
Bond Springs   Abattoirs   5   Bond   'Bond Springs'   Mt Benstead   13
Mt.Solitare   Springs   + Mt Sir Charles   Ross River   Tourist
Gliding Field   Mt   MACDONNELL   RANGES   Camp
Mt Forster   Everard   85   N'DHALA   5
Colyer   Ck   21   TODD   19   GORGE   NAT PK
Hamilton Downs   SIMPSONS GAP   87   RIVER
Youth Camp   NATIONAL PARK   Charles   Corroboree Rock   RANGES   RIVER
+ Mt Lloyd   Old Telegraph   Cons. Res.
Simpsons   Stn   Undoolya'   Undoolya   14
Standley   Iwupataka   Gap   Flynns   16   HWY   Gap
Chasm   'Simpsons Gap'   6   DR   15   Grave   Alice Springs   Emily   29   14
Conway   Aboriginal Land   Mt Gillen   Heavitree   Gap   Jessie   ROSS   16
8   Trust   47   Gap   11   Emily   Jessie   Gap   23   'Todd River'
Jay Creek   LARAPINTA   27   Temple   Amoonguna   Gap
5   Fenn   Bar Gap   6   357
Gap   Laura   5   Pine Gap   17   Alice Springs
RANGES   Ck   + Mt Ertwa   24   Aerodrome   TODD
'Owen Springs'   24
RIVER   Santa   Teresa
Owen   Ewaninga   Aboriginal
Well   Rock Carvings   Land
Lawrence   Conservation
Gorge   Reserve
90   15   Ooraminna
Rockhole
130   Mt Ooraminna   Santa Teresa
Mt Polhill   52   Mission
STUART   19
HWY   PHILLIPSON
87   RAILWAY   Ooraminna   STOCK ROUTE
'Rainbow Valley'   17   'Allambi'
CENTRAL   16   'Deep Well'
nge Creek'   64   Deep Well
Hugh River   25
Rly. Stn.   AUSTRALIA
N
Rodinga
Mt.Frank

J K L M N 357 O P Q R

WARNING: Although an indication of road surface types is shown on this map, it is imperative that visitors obtain full information as to road conditions ahead before proceeding on their journey. During the period October to May 'wet' season conditions may cause severe flooding, making many roads impassable.
The majority of water features shown on this map do not contain permanent water.
If visitors intend diverting off public roads within Aboriginal Land areas, a permit is required from the relevant Aboriginal authority.

QUEENSLAND

Sunshine State

To visitors from other states, as well as to many Queenslanders, the Sunshine State is holiday country, evoking dreams of long, golden days, tropical islands set in jewel-blue seas and the chance to get 'a really good tan'. The first settlers in the tropical north, however, were there for grimly practical reasons.

In 1821, Sir Thomas Brisbane, Governor of New South Wales, sent John Oxley, his Surveyor-General, to explore the almost unknown country north of the Liverpool Plains. Oxley's task was to find a suitable site for a penal settlement and he decided on Moreton Bay. In 1824, troops and convicts arrived at Redcliffe, but a lack of fresh water and the hostility of the Aborigines persuaded them to move south and they settled at the present site of Brisbane. By 1859, the settlement was well established and the free settlers were urging separation from New South Wales; and so, on 10 December, the state of Queensland was proclaimed.

Having gained legislative independence, the population of just 23 000 then set about achieving economic independence. Fortunately, the new state was well endowed with excellent farming land, and wool and beef production were soon established on the western plains and tablelands. It was not long before sugar production, worked by 'kanaka' labour from the Pacific Islands, became much more important, and it has remained so.

As well as being blessed with fertile land which produces grain, sugar, dairy produce, wool, mutton, beef, cotton, peanuts and timber, Queensland is immensely rich in minerals, and the vast Mount Isa mining complex in the west produces copper, lead and zinc in enormous quantities.

Over the years, Queensland has been developing another, very different, form of industry—tourism. Its attraction as a holiday destination is very much due to its climate.

In the west, the climate is very similar to that of the arid Red Centre, with fierce daytime heat, but on the coast the temperature rarely exceeds 38°C and for seven months or so of the year the

Sunshine on the Gold Coast

weather is extremely pleasant. If you are unused to high humidity, however, the period from December to April can be uncomfortably damp.

Four geographic and climatic regions run north to south, neatly dividing the state. In the west is the Great Artesian Basin: flat and hot. Parched and bare during drought, it becomes grassy after rain, thanks to a complex system of boreholes which distribute water through channels and allow grazing. The tablelands to the east are undulating and sparsely timbered, broken up by slow, meandering rivers. The backbone of Queensland is the Great Dividing Range—most spectacular in its extreme north and south, where it comes closest to the coast. Although the coastal region is the area most popular with visitors, Queensland's hinterland is lushly beautiful and its national parks, with many species of bird, animal and plant life unique to the state, total more than a million hectares. The state's highway and road system is good in the south-east and close to the larger northern towns, but elsewhere roads tend to be

narrow and poorly graded and conditions deteriorate during drought or heavy rain.

The two main towns of the tropical northern region are Townsville and Cairns. The more northerly Cairns is fast becoming a fashionable holiday centre and makes an excellent base for deep-sea fishing and for exploring the region, with its lush sugar-lands, mountainous jungle country and the wilds of the Cape York Peninsula. The Atherton Tableland is a rich volcanic area west of Cairns, with superb lakes, waterfalls and fern valleys. Stretching along this coastline are Queensland's famed islands: Lizard, north of Cooktown to Green Island, Dunk, Hinchinbrook, Magnetic, the beautiful Whitsundays, Great Keppel, Heron, Fraser and Lady Musgrave. If you are planning an island holiday, make sure your choice fits in with your idea of a tropical paradise. Many islands are extensively developed for tourism; others are quiet and offer simple accommodation. Beyond, and protecting them from the South Pacific, is the outer Great Barrier Reef, the world's largest and most famous coral formation.

South of the Reef is the Sunshine Coast. Less developed than the Gold Coast, it is renowned for its superb beaches. And Bribie Island, the weird and wonderful shapes of the Glass House Mountains and the beautiful Lakes District are nearby.

Brisbane, Australia's third city, is a far-spread capital, built on both sides of the Brisbane River. An easygoing, friendly city, its parks and gardens lush with subtropical plants, Brisbane has a year-round average of seven and a half hours of sunshine a day. The Gold Coast, seventy-five kilometres to its south, is the heart of holiday country. Luxuriously developed, it offers a wide range of accommodation, glittering nightlife, seemingly endless golden beaches and incessant sun. Inland is rich and rolling wheat and dairy farming country, its peaceful setting a far cry from the tropical north or the mining areas of Mount Isa—which goes to prove, once more, that the Sunshine State is a very diverse place indeed.

BRISBANE

A Subtropical City

The best place from which to see and understand the layout of Brisbane is from the lookout on **Mount Coot-tha**, eight kilometres south-west of the city centre and easily distinguished by its television towers. Brisbane sprawls over the series of small hills below, with the Brisbane River wandering lazily through the suburbs and city and out into **Moreton Bay**, thirty-two kilometres downstream. Surprisingly little use is made of the river for public transport, and most riverside houses back on to rather than face it.

Moreton and Stradbroke Islands look like a protective mountain range against the Pacific Ocean, far to the east. On a good day you can see the rugged mountains behind the Gold Coast to the south, and northward the strange **Glass House Mountains** just south of the Sunshine Coast.

The **City Hall**, Brisbane's best-known building, is now lost among the cluster of high-rise office buildings that dominate the skyline.

Brisbane, although it has developed into an international tourist destination following its hosting of the Commonwealth Games in 1982 and World Expo in 1988, still does not bustle like the larger southern capitals, and the suburban architecture, except for the newer, western areas, is predominantly the traditional galvanised-iron-roofed timber houses on stumps that residents think sensible and visitors find quaint. What is occasionally lacking in paint is more than made up for by colourful subtropical trees and shrubbery.

The city started inauspiciously as a convict settlement as far removed from Britain, and even from Sydney, as possible. In 1799 Matthew Flinders sailed into Moreton Bay on the sloop *Norfolk*. In 1823 John Oxley, then Surveyor-General, on board the cutter *Mermaid* sailed up the river that flowed into the bay and called it the Brisbane, after the Governor of New South Wales, Sir Thomas Brisbane.

The first troops and convicts arrived in 1824 on the brig Amity. The

Old Windmill, Wickham Terrace

original settlement at Redcliffe was soon abandoned, mainly because of a lack of fresh water, and barracks were built on the present site of the city centre, previously investigated by Oxley. The penal settlement was closed in 1839 and the region was opened for free settlement in 1842.

Today Brisbane is a busy city with a modern and extensive public transport system, a wide selection of restaurants, entertainment and night-life, parks and gardens which thrive in the subtropical climate, and a population of over one million.

Among many interesting early buildings is the **Observatory** or **Old Windmill** on Wickham Terrace, overlooking the city. Built in 1828, the mill proved unworkable, so convicts were pressed into service to crush the grain on a treadmill. In 1934 a picture of the mill was the first television image transmitted in Australia, sent to Ipswich, thirty-three kilometres away.

The restored **Commissariat Stores**, at North Quay below the old **State Library** building, were built by convicts in 1829. The nearby **Treasury Building** at the top of Queen Street, an impressive Italian Renaissance structure built of local grey sandstone, was commenced in 1888. (It is to have a new lease of life as Brisbane's first casino, opening in 1994.) **Newstead House**, a charming building overlooking the river at Breakfast Creek, was built in 1846 by Patrick Leslie, the first settler on the Darling Downs. He sold it to his brother-in-law Captain John Wickham, RN, resident of the Moreton Bay Colony, and it was the centre of official and social life in Brisbane until the first **Government House** was built in 1862. It is Brisbane's oldest home and has been restored by a Trust to illustrate a bygone past. Government House, a classic colonial building with additions made between 1882 and 1895, was also the original University. It is now part of the **Queensland University of Technology** complex at the bottom of George Street and is the home of the National Trust of Queensland. Nearby **Parliament House** was designed by Charles Tiffin in a 'tropical Renaissance' style and was opened in 1868. The **Parliament House Annexe** (irreverently called the 'Taj Mahal') is a modern tower block behind Parliament House overlooking the river. The exclusive **Queensland Club** is diagonally opposite Parliament House and was built during the 1880s.

The **General Post Office** in Queen Street was built between 1871 and 1879 on the site of the female convict barracks. The small church behind the Post Office in Elizabeth Street beside **St Stephen's Catholic Cathedral** is the third oldest building in Brisbane, having been dedicated in 1850. The **Customs House** at Petrie Bight at the bottom of Queen Street was built in 1884. The **Deanery**, built in 1849, behind **St John's Anglican Cathedral** in Ann Street, became a temporary residence for the first Governor of Queensland, Sir George Bowen. The pro-

Cityscape, Brisbane

clamation announcing Queensland as a separate colony was read from its balcony in 1859. It became the residence of the Dean of Brisbane in 1910. Further south along Ann Street is **All Saints' Church**, which dates from 1861.

Earlystreet Historical Village is a particularly fine collection of Queensland buildings and architecture at 75 McIlwraith Avenue, Norman Park, east of the city centre. Among the buildings are reconstructions of the ballroom and billiard-room of 'Auchenflower House', and 'Stromness', one of the first houses at Kangaroo Point. The village is open daily and afternoon teas are served on Sundays.

To the north of the city, another building open to the public is 'Miegunyah', a traditional Queensland house with verandahs and ironwork at Jordan Terrace, Bowen Hills. It is the home of the Queensland Women's Historical Society.

There are very few terrace houses in Brisbane, but a row at the **Normanby Junction** has been lovingly restored and incorporates two restaurants. A similar development has occurred on **Coronation Drive**. Brisbane's more impressive houses, including the famous old 'Queenslanders', are scattered throughout the inner-city suburbs. Many small cottages in the **Spring Hill**, **Paddington** and **Red Hill** areas are being restored. The **Regatta Hotel** on the river at Coronation Drive is worth a visit, and the famous **Breakfast Creek Hotel** has a popular beer garden serving excellent steaks.

The main city department stores are located in Queen Street, which, between Edward and George Streets, is now a mall.

A modern plaza containing specialist shops is at the corner of George, Ann and Adelaide Streets. At the top of the Mall is the **Myer Centre**, a vast complex housing specialised shops, restaurants, food halls and an amusement and entertainment area. Two of the city's most popular markets are the kilometre-long stretch of Sunday craft markets at the **Riverside Centre** in Eagle St, and the **South Bank Markets**, held on Friday nights and Sundays.

For the sports enthusiast, Brisbane's famous '**Gabba**' ground at Woolloongabba hosts cricket matches and greyhound racing. There are four horseracing venues at Albion Park, Doomben, Eagle Farm and Bundamba. The **Queen Elizabeth II Jubilee Sports Centre** at Nathan and the Chandler aquatic centre, indoor sports hall and velodrome were all built for the 1982 Commonwealth Games.

The **City Square** facing the **City Hall** is a popular spot for 'watching the world go by'. The **Anzac Memorial and Eternal Flame** is opposite **Central Railway Station** with its towering backdrop, the **Sheraton Brisbane Hotel and Towers**.

Across Victoria Bridge lies **South Bank**, 16 hectares of redeveloped and landscaped parklands with walking and bicycle paths, a man-made beach, a series

Hotels

Chancellor on the Park
Cnr Leichhardt St and Wickham Tce, Spring Hill
(07) 831 4055

The Beaufort Heritage
Cnr Edward and Margaret Sts, Brisbane
(07) 221 1999

Brisbane Hilton
190 Elizabeth St, Brisbane
(07) 231 3131

Sheraton Brisbane Hotel and Towers
249 Turbot St, Brisbane
(07) 835 3535

Family and Budget

Kingsford Hall Private Hotel
114 Kingsford Smith Dr, Hamilton
(07) 862 1317

Queensland Countrywomen's Association Club
89 - 95 Gregory Tce, Spring Hill
(07) 831 8188

Story Bridge Motor Inn
321 Main St, Kangaroo Point
(07) 393 1433

Wickham Terrace Motel
491 Wickham Tce, Spring Hill
(07) 839 9611

Motel Groups: Bookings

Flag (008) 01 1177
Best Western (008) 22 2166
Travelodge (008) 22 2446

This list is for information only; inclusion is not necessarily a recommendation.

MOUNT COOT-THA

Only eight kilometres from Brisbane's city centre, Mt Coot-tha offers city dwellers an attractive 'breathing space'. Here the Brisbane City Council has plans for an ambitious development scheme which will make the best recreational use of the area.

Brisbane's newest Botanic Gardens are in the foothills of Mt Coot-tha. The tropical display house, in the form of a futuristic-looking dome, has a superb display of tropical plants and is open daily. The arid-zone garden and cactus house are nearby. The gardens also include a lagoon and pond, a demonstration garden, ornamental trees and shrubs, areas of Australian and tropical rainforest, and a large collection of Australian native plants.

Situated in the Botanic Gardens is the Sir Thomas Brisbane Planetarium. The largest planetarium in Australia, it accommodates 144 people and was named after the 'founder of organised science in Australia'. When Sir Thomas was Governor of New South Wales, in 1821 he set up an astronomical observatory at Parramatta. His observations resulted in the publication of *The Brisbane Catalog of Stars*.

Various programmes are shown at the Planetarium's Star Theatre. A representation of the night sky is projected on to the interior of the dome and the movements of sun, moon and stars are described as they occur. Special effects can also be obtained by additional projectors to demonstrate more unusual phenomena in the sky.

Programmes are shown in the afternoon and evening, Wednesday to Sunday, with an additional afternoon show at weekends. Children under six are not admitted.

The planetarium complex also contains an observatory which can be used by members of the public, by prior arrangement, to view the day or night sky.

Outside again, there are many picnic areas at Mt Coot-tha, including a particularly attractive spot at the J.C. Slaughter Falls. The Mount Coot-tha Restaurant (BYO) on Sir Samuel Griffith Drive is open daily for lunches and morning and afternoon teas. The view from this vantage-point is superb, across the city and Moreton Bay, and sometimes as far as the Lamington Plateau in the south and the Glass House Mountains in the north.

Perhaps the best view of all from Mt Coot-tha is at night when the lights of the city of Brisbane are spread out before you — a breathtaking sight. Even if you have only one evening in Brisbane, it is worth making the short trip to the lookout to take in this memorable scene.

Tropical display house, Botanic Gardens, Brisbane

of artificial canals where the South Ships cruise and several restaurants. The Gondwana Rainforest Sanctuary, the Butterfly and Insect House and Our World Environment Display are special features attracting visitors to Brisbane's newest open space.

For the art-lover, the **Queensland Art Gallery**, within the **Queensland Cultural Centre**, is on the southside riverbank. This impressive gallery includes significant Australian, British and European collections. The Cultural Centre also houses an auditorium, a three-theatre performing arts complex, the **State Library of Queensland** and the **Queensland Museum**. The **Civic Art Museum** in the City Hall, the **Museum of Contemporary Art** at South Brisbane and the **University of Queensland Art Museum** at St Lucia are excellent. Private galleries include the Philip Bacon Gallery at New Farm, the Ray Hughes Gallery at Red Hill, the Victor Mace Gallery at Bowen Hills, Para Galleries at South Brisbane, which specialises in Queensland artists, and the New Central Galleries, the Town Gallery, the Don McInnes Galleries, Barry's Gallery and two Aboriginal galleries in the city proper. The Potter's Gallery in Fortitude Valley has pottery by local artists for sale. The **Leichhardt Street** area of Spring Hill has developed as a centre for arts and crafts enthusiasts.

Brisbane's annual Warana Festival, a feast of art, craft and cultural activities, occurs in September. Also held annually are the Royal National Exhibition (in August) at Bowen Hills and the Spring Hill Fair (usually on the second weekend in September) in the streets of Spring Hill. The Biennial International Festival of Music begins in late May in odd-numbered years.

Queensland University is built mainly from Helidon freestone on a superb site on the river at St Lucia. A second university, **Griffith**, is in beautiful bush country in the southern suburb of Nathan. **Government House** at Bardon was built in 1865 for Johann Heussler, who brought German farm-workers to the state, and it became the official residence in 1920.

The old **Queensland Museum** is an ornate building on the corner of Bowen Bridge Road and Gregory Terrace. The main **Post Office** in Queen Street has a museum of telegraphic material. The **Queensland Maritime Museum** in Stanley Street, South Brisbane, incorporates the old South Brisbane dry dock. Nearby are the newly developed **Riverside Esplanade** walking and bicycle paths leading to Kangaroo Point, with access to picnic areas.

The old **Botanic Gardens** next to Parliament House are particularly magnificent. In contrast, **New Farm Park**, which is close to the city via the Valley, has 12 000 rose bushes that are at their best between September and November, jacaranda trees that blossom in October and November, and poinciana trees in November and December. The **Mount Coot-tha Botanic Gardens**, five kilometres from the city, feature a Tropical Display Dome and the superb Sir Thomas Brisbane Planetarium. The nearby **J.C. Slaughter Falls Park** is popular for picnics, barbecues and bushwalks.

Self-guiding leaflets outlining **Heritage Trails** within the city and suburbs, and a booklet listing a wide choice of attractions and eating-places are available from the **Brisbane Visitors and Convention Bureau** on the ground floor of the City Hall in King George Square.

Brisbane is famous for its seafood, and several good restaurants allow you the opportunity to come to grips with the awesome Queensland mudcrab, Moreton Bay bugs, tiger prawns and delicious reef fish and barramundi. Popular venues are Pier Nine Oyster Bar and Restaurant at Eagle Street Pier; Michael's Riverside Restaurant at the Riverside Centre in Eagle Street; Rumpoles in Turbot Street; Muddie's in Edward Street; the Milano Italian Restaurant in the Queen Street Mall; Oxley's Wharf Restaurant on the river at Milton; and the exotic Cat's Tango in St Lucia. Chinatown in Fortitude Valley offers oriental shopping and dining.

Because of its vast size (the Brisbane City Council controls an area of 1220

Waterfront Place, Brisbane

square kilometres), the city's public transport network is extensive. Council buses take most of the load, while modern electric air-conditioned trains run to many areas. An excellent pocket map is produced by the Metropolitan Transit Authority. Small ferries operate from the city to Kangaroo Point, East Brisbane and New Farm Park. Golden Mile operates river and bay cruises from North Quay, including popular cruises to Lone Pine Koala Sanctuary. The City Ferry Cruise, operated by the Brisbane City Council, leaves the Edward Street ferry terminal (near the Botanic Gardens), travelling downstream to Breakfast Creek and upstream to Queensland University. The magnificent paddlewheeler *Kookaburra Queen* cruises the river daily and is a good place to dine.

There are plenty of hotels and motels offering accommodation in and near Brisbane, together with a number of caravan parks within easy reach of the central city area. And, of course, the tourist mecca of the Gold Coast is only a relatively short distance away.

Several of Brisbane's attractions lie just outside the main city area. Views from the surrounding hills are good, particularly from Bartley's Hill lookout at Hamilton. There is also the Historical Observation Tower at the Boardwalk in Newstead, a 33-m tower affording outstanding city views. The *Southern Cross*, Sir Charles Kingsford Smith's Fokker tri-motor aircraft, is on display at Brisbane airport in Airport Drive. Just across the river is Fort Lytton, a garrison built in 1880 and opened to visitors in 1989. Brisbane's famous Lone Pine Koala Sanctuary, with its photogenic koalas and other fauna, is eleven km away at Fig Tree Pocket. Samford Alpine Adventureland at Samford, twenty-one km from the city, offers grass-skiing, a 700-m bobsled, and swimming and picnic areas. Amazons Aquatic Adventureland at Jindalee, twelve km from the city, has family waterslide entertainment and picnic areas. Bunya Wildlife Sanctuary Park, fourteen km north at Cash's Crossing, has a wildlife sanctuary, World Koala Research Station and picnic and barbecue facilities. Brisbane Forest Park at The Gap, twelve km from the city, provides 'bushranger' and wildlife tours in its 25 000 ha of bushland. Tours of the Golden Circle tropical fruit cannery at Northgate are available.

The Australian Woolshed, fourteen km north-west of the city, offers a true taste of Australia and features trained rams, sheep-shearing demonstrations and tame koalas and kangaroos.

Tourist information: Brisbane Visitors and Convention Bureau, City Hall, King George Square; (07) 221 8411.

TOURS FROM BRISBANE

There is a variety of things to see and do around Brisbane. Most tours can be done in one day, but some will be better enjoyed if you plan an overnight stop.

The Brisbane forest parks concept is being developed as breathing space for the city, and many new national parks have been declared in the surrounding area, so as well as visiting the famous beaches, take advantage of these park—they are well worth a visit.

Redcliffe, 34 km from Brisbane via Gympie Road

Drive to Redcliffe via Petrie and a detour to the North Pine Dam. The Redcliffe Peninsula is almost completely surrounded by the waters of Moreton Bay. The stretches of sandy beaches are safe for swimming and the fishing is good. High on the volcanic red cliffs—after which the area was named—there are spectacular views far across Moreton Bay to Moreton and Stradbroke Islands, famous worldwide for their natural surroundings and mountainous sand dunes. The Redcliffe jetty is a favourite spot for local anglers and a pleasant place for a stroll. **See also:** Entry in A–Z listing.

Bribie Island, 47 km from Brisbane via Bruce Hwy

Take the Bruce Hwy north towards Caboolture before turning off to Bribie Island, which is linked to the mainland by a 1 km bridge across Pumicestone Passage. Bribie, a wildlife sanctuary, is very popular with day-trippers from Brisbane, offering excellent fishing, still-water swimming, surfing, shady picnic spots and scenic walks.

Wynnum - Manly and Redland Bay, 35 km from Brisbane via Routes 23, 30 and 44

You will not have to drive very far to enjoy the bayside suburbs of Wynnum and Manly, south-east of Brisbane on the shores of Moreton Bay. Manly has five excellent marinas and is the headquarters of the Royal Queensland Yacht Squadron. There is also a very good golf course at Wynnum, and a variety of other sporting facilities. Continue on to Redland Bay, a peaceful tourist resort. The area is famed for its market gardens and the Strawberry Festival (on the first Saturday of each September). Wayside stalls sell fruit and flowers at weekends. Boats can be hired all along this coast, so that you can do your own exploring, or go fishing, or you can visit the islands of Moreton Bay. **See also:** Entry in A–Z listing.

The Gold Coast, 70 km from Brisbane via the Pacific and Gold Coast Highways

About an hour's drive south of Brisbane begins the huge holiday area of the Gold Coast, which comprises a strip along the coast from Southport to Coolangatta and includes the famous Surfers Paradise. Excellent surfing beaches and glorious weather have always been the major attractions of the Gold Coast; a day trip, or several days, can be spent enjoying some of the incredible range of tourist attractions that have developed in this area. **See also:** City of the Gold Coast.

Gold Coast Hinterland, about 100 km from Brisbane via the Pacific Highway and Nerang

If possibly you are bored by the Gold Coast, simply drive west. The nearby McPherson Ranges have some of Australia's finest scenery: rainforest, deep ravines, waterfalls, and a spectacular view of the coast.

Tamborine Mountain, 70 km from Brisbane via the Pacific Highway

Tamborine Mountain, some 30 km from Oxenford, is a wonderful retreat from the bustle of Brisbane. Here extensive walking tracks lead through the rainforest, where palms, staghorns, elkhorns, ferns and orchids grow in profusion, to waterfalls and lookouts. Picnic and barbecue facilities are located in the many reserves in the area and in the nearby Joalah, Knoll and Palm Grove National Parks. **See also:** Queensland's National Parks.

O'Reilly's Guest House, Lamington National Park, 112 km from Brisbane via the Mt Lindesay or Pacific Highways and Canungra

The thickly wooded Lamington National Park is one of the wildest and finest in Queensland. On a plateau at the top is O'Reilly's Guest House, and it is worth making this a full weekend's trip, though an advance booking should be made. A maze of walking tracks and an elevated treetop walkway allow you to see the area's many attractions. But if walking is not for you, you can just sit in the sun, breathe in the refreshing mountain air and admire the superb scenery or feed the birds. The subtropical rainforest here has an abundance of wildlife, which has been protected for many years. Information on the area is available at the tourist information centre in Canungra or from the ranger at O'Reilly's. **See also:** Queensland's National Parks.

Binna Burra, Lamington National Park, 108 km from Brisbane via the Mt Lindesay or Pacific Highways and Canungra

If you chose to walk from O'Reilly's to Binna Burra Lodge it would be a distance of some 22 km. It is a much longer trip by road. Binna Burra Lodge is a good centre from which to enjoy the great variety of walks in the area, but a sensible pair of shoes is a must. Bring a sweater, too—it can get cold even in summer. If you plan to spend a weekend 'wilderness camping' in the mountains, a permit is necessary and can be obtained from the Chief Ranger at Binna Burra. Information is available in Canungra about the many walks and places of interest on the way. Those who prefer a few more comforts can plan to stay overnight at the Binna Burra Lodge, but book accommodation in advance. **See also:** Queensland's National Parks.

Toowoomba, 127 km from Brisbane via the Warrego Highway

A comfortable distance from Brisbane for a day trip, this drive takes you past some pretty, small towns and old farmhouses. Stop at Marburg on the way to admire the old timber pub with its latticed verandah, a fine example of early hotel architecture. Toowoomba's most popular tourist attraction is its parks and gardens, with a touch of England in the magnificent oaks, elms, plane trees and poplars. The gardens are best seen during September when the city has its Carnival of Flowers. The carnival is usually held over the last week of September, and includes a procession, dancing and entertainment in the streets. The Blue Arrow Drive around the city, laid out by the city council, is a must for the visitors. You could return to Brisbane via the New England and Cunningham Highways. **See also:** Entry in A–Z listing.

The Jondaryan Woolshed Historical Museum and Park, 176 km from Brisbane via the Warrego Highway

The Jondaryan Woolshed was built in 1859, with space for eighty-eight blade shearers to handle some 200 000 sheep a season. Now an ideal outing for all the family, it has been developed as a working memorial to the early pastoral pioneers. As well as the Woolshed, see the blacksmith's shop, the one-roomed schoolhouse, and the dairy. There is also a fascinating collection of old agricultural machinery. Open every day except Good Friday and Christmas Day; conducted tours operate on the hour.

The Bunya Mountains, 250 km from Brisbane via the Warrego and Brisbane Valley Highways

This three-hour drive is often spectacular, but hairpin bends make the journey unsuitable for cars towing caravans or trailers. Because there is so much to see along the way, it would be wise to stay overnight either camping or at a hotel. On the way, Savages Crossing is a good place for a picnic, and the Bellevue Homestead at Coominya is worth a detour. A major National Trust project, the homestead has been moved from its original site and rebuilding and restoration is continuing. Further on, stop to see the Koomba Falls and King House at Maidenwell. There are many more places to visit on the way to the mountains and all are fully signposted. Most of the area is set aside as the Bunya Mountains National Park; there are two major camping sites in the park. Bushwalkers will enjoy the excellent graded tracks. If you have time, and do not want to camp, continue on to Kingaroy, the peanut-growing area, where there is plenty of accommodation. **See also:** Queensland's National Parks.

Mt Glorious, 40 km from Brisbane via Waterworks Road

One of the more interesting short drives from Brisbane through mountainous country due west of the city is to Mt Glorious, via Mt Nebo, and then back via Samford. From Mt Glorious it is possible to extend this drive to take in the delights of Lake Wivenhoe, only 15 km further on. There are many spectacular views of the mountainous Brisbane Forest Park. Stop at McPhee's and Jolly's Lookouts before arriving at the pretty town of Mount Nebo. Hear bellbirds and whipbirds in the Manorina National Park. In the Maiala National Park at Mt Glorious there are many well-documented short and long walks through the lush rainforest. At the information centre for the Brisbane Forest Park (60 Mt Nebo Rd,

The Gap; (07) 300 4855), you can view exhibits of Queensland's native freshwater fish at the Walkabout Creek aquatic study centre, and then dine in the restaurant upstairs.

The Sunshine Coast, 100 km from Brisbane to its nearest point via the Bruce Highway

The Sunshine Coast is a 200-km-long series of magnificent beaches, punctuated by rocky headlands and river mouths, that stretch north from Bribie Island to Tin Can Bay, one to two hours' driving from Brisbane. Follow the coastal highway from Caloundra to the main beaches of Currimundi, Mooloolaba, Alexandra Headland, Maroochydore, Mudjimba, Marcoola, Coolum, Peregian, Sunshine Beach and Noosa Heads. Explore the hinterland; there is a superb scenic drive along the Blackall Ranges through the towns of Mapleton, Montville and Maleny. The countryside is breathtakingly pastoral—rolling hills, lush valleys, crystal-clear creeks and waterfalls. Montville offers local craft shops and galleries. **See also:** Sunshine Coast; entries in A–Z listing.

Beerwah and Buderim past the Glass House Mountains, 100 km from Brisbane via the Bruce Highway and the Glass House Mountains Tourist Road

Travelling past the Glass House Mountains, you will see the ten spectacular trachyte peaks named by Captain Cook as he sailed up the coast in 1770. The sun shining on the rock-faces reminded him of glasshouses in his native Yorkshire. Further north from Beerwah is the Queensland Reptile and Fauna Park, reputed to be one of the best such parks in

The Big Pineapple, near Nambour

Australia. Here venomous snakes, including taipans, and lizards of all sizes, can be seen. A recent addition is the two-hectare Crocodile Environment Park, where guided tours allow visitors to view crocodiles and alligators in their natural surroundings. Continue on through Landsborough to Buderim. Visit the art galleries and the Pioneer Cottage, one of Buderim's earliest houses, which retains much of its original furnishings from last century. **See also:** Entries in A–Z listing.

The Big Pineapple and Sunshine Plantation, 115 kilometres from Brisbane via the Bruce Highway

Seven kilometres south of Nambour, the Sunshine Plantation is the largest and most popular tourist attraction on the Sunshine Coast. On the pleasant drive up the Bruce Highway, you will pass colourful roadside stalls offering tropical fruit at prices that amaze the southern visitor.

The Big Pineapple itself is a 16-m-high replica of a pineapple, with a top-floor observation deck which looks out on the plantation of tropical fruit below. Two floors of audiovisual displays tell the story of the pineapple and there is a Polynesian-style restaurant and tropical market.

Ride on a sugarcane train through more than 40 ha of pineapples, mangoes, avocados, sugarcane, and nuts and spices. An attractive animal farm is fun for children. The 'Nutmobile' will take you to the Magic Macadamia, a giant Queensland nut. Here the complete process, from cracking the nut to the final product, will be revealed.

Admission to the Big Pineapple and the industry display is free.

Miva Station, 202 km from Brisbane, and Susan River Homestead, 284 km from Brisbane, both via the Bruce Highway

Here is a weekend with a difference and an opportunity for city people to sample life on a cattle station. At Miva Station via Gympie you can camp in your own tent, although an extra charge will secure one already erected on site. Trail riding and hay rides are popular, or you can go canoeing or fishing. If you are very quiet you may see a lungfish or platypus in the creek. The area is a bird and animal sanctuary. At the Susan River property, 15 km past Maryborough on the Hervey Bay road, if you stay at the homestead, full board is provided. Here you can join in the mustering, swim in the pool, or simply feed the emus and wallabies. For further information about station and farm holidays, contact the Queensland Government Travel Centre; (07) 221 6111.

CITY OF THE GOLD COAST

High-rise apartment blocks, Surfers Paradise

The Gold Coast, Australia's premier holiday destination, boasts 42 kilometres of golden, unpolluted beaches stretching from Southport in the north to Coolangatta in the south, with a lush subtropical backdrop in the Gold Coast hinterland—the 'green behind the gold'.

Situated only one hour's drive south of Brisbane, this international resort city offers a multitude of man-made and natural attractions, and, of course, superb surfing beaches—Main Beach, Southport, Surfers Paradise, Broadbeach, Mermaid Beach, Miami, Burleigh Heads, Tallebudgera, Palm Beach, Currumbin, Tugun, Kirra and Coolangatta.

With almost 300 days of sunshine each year—an average winter maximum of 22°C and average summer maximum of 28°C—it is no wonder the region is the country's holiday playground, attracting three million visitors annually.

Accommodation caters for all budgets, ranging from international five-star-plus hotels and resorts to hotels, motels, apartments, guest-houses, caravan parks, camping grounds and backpackers' hostels. It is estimated there are more than 15 000 rooms with more than 50 000 beds available on the Gold Coast.

Nightlife, entertainment, sporting facilities, shopping and restaurants guarantee to satisfy all tastes. In fact, the Gold Coast is said to have the largest number of restaurants per square kilometre in Australia to tantalise all tastebuds.

Surfers Paradise with its towering skyline, beachfront esplanade, glitz and glamour is the hub of the Gold Coast, while the Gold Coast hinterland is a subtropical hideaway filled with massive trees, spectacular views, cascading waterfalls and bush walks only thirty minutes from the hustle and bustle of the city.

Moving west from the coastline into the hinterland, the terrain climbs steadily to 1000 metres to breathtaking scenery in the Numinbah Valley and at Springbrook. Highlights here include the 190-metre-high Purlingbrook Falls, Winburra Lookout and the Hinze Dam.

In the Numinbah Valley on the southern Queensland border is the Natural Arch, a spectacular waterfall that plummets through a stone archway into a rock-pool below. This is an excellent spot for picnics, barbecues and bush walks.

Mount Tamborine rainforests and Lamington National Park provide the backdrop to Beaudesert Shire. The more adventurous are easily tempted into tackling the rugged ranges and gorges of Lamington National Park, the largest preserved natural subtropical rainforest in Australia, with 160 kilometres of graded walking-tracks.

The 'old-time' flavour of the hinterland has been preserved in the design of the area's buildings, some of which date back to the early 1900s.

At the southern end of the Gold Coast the bustling twin towns of Coolangatta - Tweed Heads sit on opposite headlands at the mouth of the Tweed River. Both towns are thriving holiday centres with a range of top accommodation, shopping resorts, restaurants, entertainment and tourist facilities.

At **Coomera:** Warner Bros Movie World, based on the world-famous Hollywood movie set, is a theme park and part of a fully operational studio. The only one of its kind in the southern hemisphere, it (along with the family fun park Dreamworld, Australia's largest water park Wet 'n' Wild and Koala Town) is only 23 kilometres north of Surfers Paradise. Nearby is the exclusive Sanctuary Cove residential resort, which incorporates the Hyatt Hotel, two golf courses and a marina. Just south is Cable-Ski World at Coombabah.

At **Southport:** Sea World, on The Spit at Main Beach, is the largest marine park in the southern hemisphere. Its world-class attractions include performing dolphins, false killer whales, a monorail, a skyway, water-ski ballet, helicopter rides, an Endeavour replica and an Old Fort. It adjoins the Sea World Nara Resort. Also on The Spit overlooking the Broadwater is Fisherman's Wharf, a complex of specialty shops, outdoor cafes and restaurants. The Gold

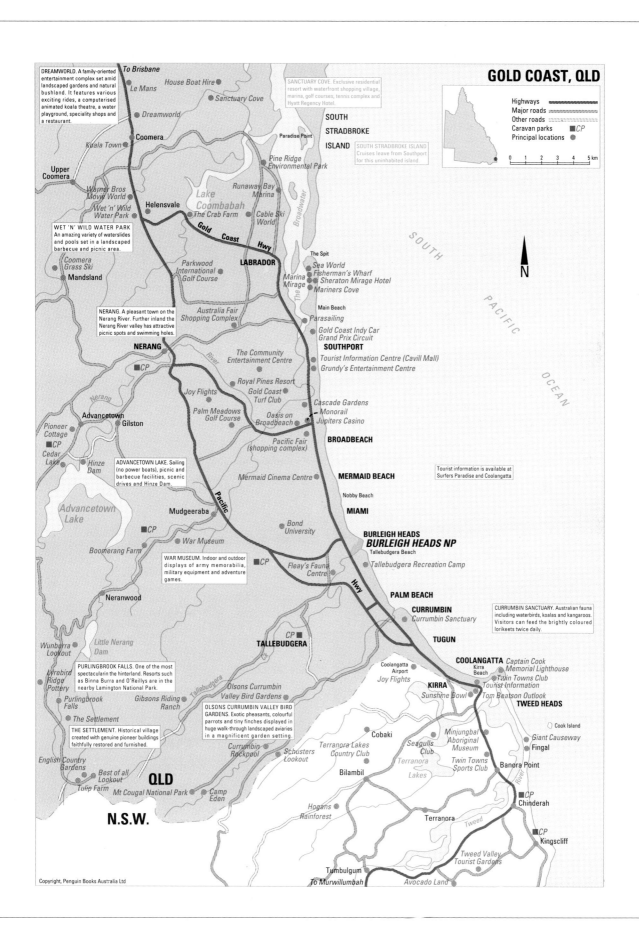

GOLD COAST, QLD

Highways
Major roads
Other roads
Caravan parks ■CP
Principal locations ●

0 1 2 3 4 5 km

DREAMWORLD. A family-oriented entertainment complex set amid landscaped gardens and natural bushland. It features various exciting rides, a computerised animated koala theatre, a water playground, speciality shops and a restaurant.

To Brisbane

Le Mans

House Boat Hire

● Sanctuary Cove

● Dreamworld

SANCTUARY COVE. Exclusive residential resort with waterfront shopping village, marina, golf courses, tennis complex and Hyatt Regency Hotel.

SOUTH
STRADBROKE
ISLAND

Coomera

Koala Town

Upper Coomera

Paradise Point

Pine Ridge Environmental Park

SOUTH STRADBROKE ISLAND Cruises leave from Southport for this uninhabited island.

Warner Bros Movie World

Wet 'n' Wild Water Park

Helensvale

Lake Coombabah

Runaway Bay Marina

The Crab Farm

Cable Ski World

WET 'N' WILD WATER PARK An amazing variety of waterslides and pools set in a landscaped barbecue and picnic area.

Gold Coast Hwy

Broadwater

Coomera Grass Ski

Mandsland

Parkwood International Golf Course

LABRADOR

The Spit

Sea World
Fisherman's Wharf
Sheraton Mirage Hotel
Mariners Cove

Marina Mirage

NERANG. A pleasant town on the Nerang River. Further inland the Nerang River valley has attractive picnic spots and swimming holes.

Australia Fair Shopping Complex

Main Beach

Parasailing

Gold Coast Indy Car Grand Prix Circuit

SOUTHPORT

NERANG

River

The Community Entertainment Centre

Tourist Information Centre (Cavill Mall)
Grundy's Entertainment Centre

■CP

Royal Pines Resort

Joy Flights

Gold Coast Turf Club

Palm Meadows Golf Course

Cascade Gardens
Monorail
Jupiters Casino

Advancetown

Gilston

Oasis on Broadbeach

BROADBEACH

Pioneer Cottage

■CP
Cedar Lake

Hinze Dam

ADVANCETOWN LAKE. Sailing (no power boats), picnic and barbecue facilities, scenic drives and Hinze Dam.

Pacific Fair (shopping complex)

Mermaid Cinema Centre

MERMAID BEACH

Tourist information is available at Surfers Paradise and Coolangatta

Nobby Beach

MIAMI

Advancetown Lake

Mudgeeraba

Pacific

Bond University

BURLEIGH HEADS
BURLEIGH HEADS NP

Boomerang Farm

● War Museum

Tallebudgera Beach

WAR MUSEUM. Indoor and outdoor displays of army memorabilia, military equipment and adventure games.

■CP

Fleay's Fauna Centre

Tallebudgera Recreation Camp

Neranwood

Hwy

PALM BEACH

CURRUMBIN

Currumbin Sanctuary

CURRUMBIN SANCTUARY. Australian fauna including waterbirds, koalas and kangaroos. Visitors can feed the brightly coloured lorikeets twice daily.

Wunburra Lookout

Little Nerang Dam

CP ■
TALLEBUDGERA

TUGUN

PURLINGBROOK FALLS. One of the most spectacular in the hinterland. Resorts such as Binna Burra and O'Reilly's are in the nearby Lamington National Park.

Lyrebird Ridge Pottery

Tallebudgera

Coolangatta Airport

Joy Flights

COOLANGATTA
Kirra Beach

Captain Cook Memorial Lighthouse
Twin Towns Club
Tourist Information

Olsons Currumbin Valley Bird Gardens

KIRRA

Sunshine Bowl

Tom Beatson Outlook

TWEED HEADS

Purlingbrook Falls

Gibsons Riding Ranch

● The Settlement

THE SETTLEMENT. Historical village created with genuine pioneer buildings faithfully restored and furnished.

OLSONS CURRUMBIN VALLEY BIRD GARDENS. Exotic pheasants, colourful parrots and tiny finches displayed in huge walk-through landscaped aviaries in a magnificent garden setting.

Currumbin Rockpool

Schusters Lookout

Cook Island

Minjungbal Aboriginal Museum

Giant Causeway
Fingal

English Country Gardens

Best of all Lookout

Tulip Farm

QLD

Cobaki

Terranora Lakes Country Club

Seagulls Club

Bilambil

Terranora Lakes

Twin Towns Sports Club

Banora Point

Mt Cougal National Park

Camp Eden

■CP
Chinderah

N.S.W.

Hogans Rainforest

Terranora

Tweed

River

■CP
Kingscliff

Tweed Valley Tourist Gardens

Tumbulgum

To Murwillumbah

Avocado Land

Copyright, Penguin Books Australia Ltd

N

Coast's major cruise boats operate from its jetties. Also along the Broadwater is Mariner's Cove with marina, shopping and restaurants and Marina Mirage, an upmarket shopping and boating complex opposite the Sheraton Mirage Hotel. Visitors can enjoy a variety of water sports on the Broadwater, including jet skiing, sailing, windsurfing and parasailing.

At **Surfers Paradise:** Attractions include Grundy's Entertainment Centre, Ripley's Believe It or Not, Hoyts cinema complex, resort shopping, restaurants, many international hotels, numerous nightclubs and the sport of 'people watching'. Near Surfers at Bundall, the Gold Coast Arts Centre has an art gallery, film viewing and a performing arts complex. Five kilometres inland from Surfers is the Gold Coast's newest resort, Royal Pines. The complex includes a 5-star hotel, convention facilities, a 27-hole golf course and a marina.

At **Broadbeach:** Pacific Fair Shopping Centre on the Nerang River, which recently had a $168 million facelift. Hotel Conrad and Jupiters Casino,

Australia's largest casino, is linked by monorail to the Oasis on Broadbeach Shopping Resort and the Pan Pacific Hotel. Cascades Park and Gardens on the Nerang River has man-made waterfalls and still-water pools, ideal for picnicking. One way to view the area is by an open-cockpit flight in a Tiger Moth plane.

At **Mermaid Beach:** A huge cinema complex close to family restaurants, a variety of specialty restaurants and a casino.

At **Miami:** The Festhaus adjoining the Miami Hotel features a traditional German 'oompa' brass band, food and beer; also an Aboriginal ceremonial bora ring.

At **Burleigh Heads:** Burleigh Knoll Environmental Park, Burleigh Heads National Park and Fleays Fauna Reserve are all worth a visit.

Inland at **Mudgeeraba** are the Gold Coast War Museum, Skirmish, Movie Militaria and the Boomerang Farm.

At **Tallebudgera:** Tally Valley art and craft markets, the Camp Eden Fitness Camp and the Playroom rock venue.

At **Currumbin:** Feed the thousands of lorikeets that flock to the Currumbin Bird Sanctuary daily. The Chocolate Expo Factory is opposite. Visit Olson's Bird Gardens, Mount Cougal National Park and the Currumbin Rock Pools. Nearby is the Moran Hospital of Excellence at Tugun.

At **Coolangatta:** Foyster Mall links the main street with the beachfront. The Land of Legend, a fairytale and fable exhibition, delights children. Captain Cook Memorial and Lighthouse at Point Danger.

At **Tweed Heads:** Across the border from Coolangatta, try your luck on the pokies at Twin Towers Services Club and Seagulls Rugby League Club.

For further information on the Gold Coast, contact the Gold Coast Visitors and Convention Bureau, Natwest Building, 5th Floor, 105 Upton St, Bundall; (075) 92 1199. There are information centres at Cavill Mall, Surfers Paradise, (075) 38 4419, and Beach House, Marine Pde, Coolangatta, (075) 36 7765.

See also: Entries in A–Z listing.

Jupiter's Casino, Broadbeach

Mirage Hotel and Marina Mirage, Southport

Sea World, Southport

PS Captain Sturt at Dreamworld, Coomera

QUEENSLAND from A to Z

Airlie Beach   Population 1279

Since 1987 Airlie Beach has been part of the town of Whitsunday. Centre of the thriving Whitsunday coast, Airlie Beach offers many restaurants and eating-places, several major resorts with all facilities, top-grade holiday accommodation and a large range of activities and services for visitors. Twenty km from the Bruce Hwy at Proserpine, Airlie overlooks the Whitsunday Passage and islands, and has its own beach and marina. At Airlie and Shute Harbour, passengers can secure transport to the outer reef and reef-fringed islands. **Of interest:** Annual Fun Race held in Sept. **In the area:** Neighbouring Shute Harbour, islands of Whitsunday Passage, and Conway National Park, renowned for its natural beauty and habitat of many species of butterflies. **Tourist information:** Cnr Mandalay St and Shute Harbour Rd; (079) 46 6673. **Accommo- dation:** 1 hotel, 8 motels, 4 caravan/camping parks, 3 resorts.
MAP REF. 437 K9

Allora   Population 831

North of Warwick on the Toowoomba road, Allora is situated in a prime agricultural area. **Of interest:** Historical museum. Talgai Homestead (c. 1860); accommodation and meals. **In the area:** Goomburra State Forest and Valley, 35 km east. Main Range National Park, 50 km east; camping and picnic areas and extensive walking tracks through dense rainforest. **Tourist information:** 49 Albion St (New England Hwy); (076) 61 3686. **Accommodation:** 1 caravan/camping park.
MAP REF. 435 O11

Aramac   Population 434

This small pastoral township is 67 km north of Barcaldine. Originally called Marathon, it was renamed by explorer William Landsborough as an acronym of Sir Robert Ramsay Mackenzie, Colonial Secretary in 1866 and Premier of Qld from 1867 to 1868. **Of interest:** Tramway Museum housing old engines and rolling stock. **In the area:** The Lake, 68 km north-east; popular for swimming, fishing and birdwatching. **Tourist information:** Shire Offices; (076) 51 3311. **Accommodation:** 1 hotel, 1 caravan park.
MAP REF. 434 F2

Atherton   Population 4639

Atherton is the agricultural hub of the Atherton Tableland, where huge maize silos interrupt the rural and rainforest landscape. This farming hamlet is situated 100 km south-west of Cairns on the Kennedy Hwy and is surrounded by a patchwork of dense rainforest which abounds in exotic varieties of birdlife and tropical vegetation. **Of interest:** Old Post Office Museum, Herberton Rd. Maize Festival held in Sept. and Tablelands Band Festival in Nov. Other festivals on Tableland include Tobacco Festival at Dimbulah (May), Tin Festival at Herberton (Sept.) and Torimba Forest Festival at Ravenshoe (Oct.). Fascinating Facets. Underground tunnels and chambers, and the Crystal Caves, mineral, gemstone and agate museum, both in Main St. **In the area:** Atherton Tableland, one of oldest land masses in Australia, provides picturesque alternative to coastal route; rainforest-fringed volcanic crater lakes, spectacular waterfalls and fertile farmlands. At Tolga, 5 km north: Woodworks and tours of peanut factory. Mareeba, 32 km north, tobacco and rice growing area; annual rodeo held in July. Lake Tinaroo, 15 km north-east; swimming and fishing. Cruises on crater lakes, Lakes Eacham

and Barrine, set in national parks 25 km east, through historic Yungaburra; steeped in Aboriginal legend, lakes are well known for their crystal-clear waters and picturesque beauty. The Curtain Fig Tree, 2.5 km south of Yungaburra; spectacular aerial roots in curtain formation. Mt Hypipamee National Park, 26 km south; sheer-sided explosion crater 124 m deep. At Malanda, 25 km south-east: Malanda Falls Environmental Park with marked rainforest walk at edge of town. McHugh Road Lookout, 20 km south of Malanda, offers panoramic views. At Herberton, 19 km south-west: Foster's Winery and Historical Village with 30 restored buildings. **Tourist information:** 42 Mabel St; (070) 91 3608. **Accommodation:** 3 motels, 3 caravan/camping parks. **See also:** Atherton Tableland; The Far North.
MAP REF. 436 F4, 438 I13, 439 C12

Ayr   Population 8639

This busy sugar town on the north side of the Burdekin delta is surrounded by intensively irrigated sugarcane fields which are the most productive in Australia. Visitors are welcome at the three main sugar mills during the crushing season (June–Dec.). Townsville, 82 km to the north, is

Typical Queensland pub, Malanda

the outlet for the bulk sugar. Rice is also grown. **Of interest:** Ayr Nature Display, Wilmington St; fine collection of butterflies and beetles. Burdekin Cultural Complex, comprising 530-seat theatre, library, art gallery and activities centre. Beautiful Cooktown orchid blooms Mar.–Aug. **In the area:** Home Hill, on opposite side of Burdekin, Ayr's sister town. Alva Beach, 18 km north; beach walks, birdwatching, swimming and fishing. Mt Kelly Orchids, 10 km south-west; orchid displays and sales, also Devonshire teas. **Tourist information:** Community Information Centre, Queen St; (079) 83 2888. **Accommodation:** 6 hotels, 6 motels, 2 caravan parks.
MAP REF. 436 I8

Babinda
Population 1288
A swimming-hole and picnic area known as 'the Boulders' is a feature of interest 10 km west of this small sugar town, which is 57 km south of Cairns in the Bellenden Ker National Park. Qld's two highest mountains, Mt Bartle Frere (1611 m) and Mt Bellenden Ker (1591 m), and the Josephine Falls, are located in the park. Deeral, 14 km north of Babinda, is the departure point for cruises through the rainforest and saltwater crocodile haunts of the Mulgrave and Russell Rivers. **Accommodation:** Limited.
MAP REF. 436 G4, 439 H13

Barcaldine
Population 1427
A pastoral and rail town, Barcaldine is 108 km east of Longreach. All the streets are named after trees, and citrus fruits thrive on local bore water. **Of interest:** Beta Farm Slab Hut, cnr Pine and Bauhinia Sts; restoration of early settler's hut. Folk Museum, cnr Gidyes and Beech Sts. 'Tree of knowledge', ghost gum in main street, meeting-place for 1891 shearers' strike, which resulted in formation of Australian Labor Party. Australian Workers' Heritage Centre, Ash St; opened May 1991 on centenary of shearers' strike. **In the area:** Lake Sanderson, 25 km east, reputedly largest man-made lake in western Qld; native wildlife. Red Mountain scenic drive, 55 km east, on Richmond Hills Station; visits by appointment. Botanical Walk, 9 km south, through variety of bushland. **Tourism information:** Oak St; (076) 51 1724. **Accommodation:** 1 motel, 2 caravan/camping parks.
MAP REF. 434 F3

Bargara
Population 1914
This popular surf beach, 13 km east of Bundaberg, is patrolled by one of Qld's top surf clubs. Nearby beaches include Nielson Park and Kelly's. **In the area:**

Mon Repos Environmental Park, 3 km north, largest and most accessible mainland turtle rookery in Australia; during Nov.–Feb. giant sea turtles come ashore to lay their eggs. In 1912, Bert Hinkler, then an engineering apprentice, flew to height of some 9 m in home-made glider off Mon Repos beach, marking start of his distinguished aviation career. **Tourist information:** Real Estate House, 20 Bauer St; (071) 59 2966. **Accommodation:** 1 hotel, 5 motels, 3 caravan/camping parks, 2 resorts.
MAP REF. 435 P6

Beaudesert
Population 4119
Beaudesert is a major market town on the Mount Lindesay Hwy, 66 km south-west of Brisbane, near the NSW border. A road west leads to the Cunningham Hwy, and the road east leads to the Gold Coast via Tamborine. The district is noted for dairying, agriculture and beef cattle. **Of interest:** Historical Museum, Jane St. Popular Beaudesert race meetings. Australian Rodeo Championships held Nov.–Dec. **In the area:** Woollahra Farmworld, Gleneagle, 5 km north. Lamington National Park, 40 km south. Mt Barney National Park, 55 km south-west. Kooralbyn Valley Resort, 30 km south-east. **Tourist information:** Historical Museum, Jane St; (075) 41 1289. **Accommodation:** 3 hotels, 3 motels, 1 caravan park.
MAP REF. 429 K5, 435 Q11

Beenleigh
Population 10 344
Midway between Brisbane and the Gold Coast, Beenleigh is now almost a satellite town of Brisbane. The Beenleigh Distillery on the Albert River has been producing rum from local sugar since 1884. Rocky Point Sugar Mill, 20 km east, is Australia's only privately owned mill. **In the area:** Coomera, 20 km south; several family attractions include Movie World theme park, Dreamworld family fun park, Wet 'n' Wild Water Park and Koala Town. **Accommodation:** 2 motels, 3 caravan/camping parks.
MAP REF. 429 N1, 435 Q11

Biggenden
Population 669
Set in the shadow of Mt Walsh National Park and The Bluff, 100 km south-east of Bundaberg, this agricultural centre holds a Rose Festival in Sept. every second year. **In the area:** Magnetite mine, 5 km south; inspection tours. Two relatively undeveloped national parks nearby: Coalstoun Lakes (3 km north) protects two volcanic crater lakes, and Mt Walsh (8 km south); wilderness park popular with experienced bushwalkers. **Tourist**

information: Cnr Mulgrave and Bourgong Sts, Bundaberg; (071) 52 2333. **Accommodation:** 1 hotel, 1 hotel/motel, 1 caravan/camping park.
MAP REF. 435 07

Biloela
Population 6174
This modern, thriving town in the fertile Callide Valley is situated at the crossroads of the Burnett and Dawson Hwys, 142 km south-west of Rockhampton. The name is Aboriginal for 'white cockatoo'. Underground water provides irrigation for lucerne, cotton and sunflower crops. **Of interest:** Greycliffe Homestead, Gladstone Rd; open by appointment. Advance Australia Fair, Dawson Hwy; rural-orientated theme park, combines hi-tech of farming life with charms of rural living. **In the area:** Boating and swimming at Callide Dam, 5 km east. Callide open-cut coal mine and power station; viewing platform 15 km east. Cotton Ginnery, 2 km north; tours Mar.–July, video off-season. Lyle Semgreen Gems at Jambin, 32 km north; open by appointment. At Banana, 47 km west: Bindiggin Doll, Bottle and Rock Museum. Mt Scoria, 14 km south; solidified volcano core. **Tourist information:** Callide St; (079) 92 2405. **Accommodation:** 2 hotels, 5 motels, 2 caravan/camping parks. **See also:** Capricorn.
MAP REF. 435 M5

Birdsville
Population under 200
The well-known Birdsville Track starts here on its long path into and across SA. The first settlers arrived in Birdsville, nearly 2000 km by road west of Brisbane, in the 1870s and at the turn of the century it was a thriving settlement, with three hotels, three stores, several offices and a doctor. When the toll on cattle crossing the border near the town was abolished after Federation in 1901, prosperity declined and the population diminished. **Of interest:** Ruins of Royal Hotel, Adelaide St; reminder of Birdsville's boom days. Birdsville Pub, also Adelaide St; comes into its own on first weekend in Sept. when Birdsville Races are held. Population then swells to about 3000 and has been known to consume about 50 000 cans of beer over period of race meeting! Hotel is an important overnight stop for tourists travelling down the Track, west across the Simpson Desert (4WD country), north to Mount Isa or east to Brisbane. **Travel in this area can be hazardous, especially in wet season (approx. Oct.–Mar.). Supplies of food and water should always be carried, as well as petrol, oil and spare parts. Check noticeboard at police station, which details local conditions, before**

setting out. **See also: Outback Motoring.** The famous 'Flynn of the Inland' founded the first Australian Inland Mission at Birdsville and there is still a well-equipped medical outpost in the town. Birdsville's water comes from a 1219-m-deep artesian bore, one of the hottest in Qld. The water comes from the ground almost at boiling-point and four cooling ponds bring it to a safe temperature. Electricity is supplied by two diesel-run generators. **Accommodation:** 1 hotel/motel, 1 caravan/camping park. **See also:** The Channel Country. MAP REF. 271 P1, 441 D7

Blackall   Population 1497

Centre of some of the most productive sheep and cattle country in central Qld, Blackall has many studs in its vicinity. In bygone days the cattle-rustler Captain Starlight roamed the district. In 1892 the legendary Jackie Howe set the almost unbelievable record of shearing 321 sheep with blade shears in less than 8 hours, at Alice Downs station, 25 km north. Blackall sunk the first artesian bore in Qld in 1885, which still pumps up 6.82 million litres of hot water daily. **Of interest:** Jackie Howe statue, junction Short and Shamrock Sts. Millions-of-years-old petrified tree stump. **In the area:** Steam-driven Blackall Wool Scour (1906), 4 km north, on Clematis St; under restoration. Idalia National Park, 100 km south-west; habitat of rare yellow-footed rock wallaby. Farm holidays at Avington Outback Holiday Station. **Tourist information:** Kinsey's Travel, Shamrock St; (076) 57 4616. **Accommodation:** 5 hotels, 2 motels, 1 caravan/camping park. MAP REF. 434 F5

Blackwater   Population 7029

This major mining town is 195 km west of Rockhampton on the Capricorn Hwy. The name comes from the discolouration of the local waterholes caused by ti-trees. Coal mined in the area is railed to Gladstone for use at the power station before export. The town's population is made up of workers of many nationalities and it displays what is claimed to be the most varied collection of national flags this side of the United Nations. Cattle is the traditional industry. **Of interest:** Inspection tours of Utah mine; bookings necessary. **In the area:** Expedition Range (732 m), discovered by Ludwig Leichhardt. Blackdown Tableland National Park, 50 km south-east; picnic/barbecue facilities at Horsehoe Lookout and Mimosa Creek camping area. **Tourist information:** Clermont St, Emerald; (079) 82 4142.

Accommodation: 3 motels, 2 caravan/camping parks. **See also:** Capricorn. MAP REF. 435 K3

Boonah   Population 2040

Eighty-six km south-west of Brisbane between Warwick and Ipswich, Boonah is the main town in the Fassifern district, a highly productive agricultural and pastoral area. Its location was noted as a 'beautiful vale' by the colonial administrator and explorer Captain Logan in 1827, and by explorer Allan Cunningham in 1828. **Of interest:** Potato Festival held first week in Sept. **In the area:** Fassifern Valley National Park, 12 km west. Lake Moogerah, 20 km south-west, for water sports. The Scenic Rim, ring of mountains bordering shire; popular for scenic drives, bushwalking, trail-riding, rock-climbing, skydiving and water sports. Picnic spots and recreation facilities for day-trippers; camping and accommodation for those with more time. Coochin Coochin historic homestead, 14 km south. **Tourist information:** Shire Offices, High St; (075) 63 1599. **Accommodation:** 5 motels, 7 caravan/camping parks. MAP REF. 428 G5, 435 P11

Boulia   Population 287

Situated on the Burke River, 365 km west of Winton, 305 km south of Mt Isa and 200 km east of the NT border, Boulia is the

capital of the Channel Country. **Of interest:** Stone Cottage Museum (1880s), Pituri St; town's oldest house, now contains display of historic relics of region, also Aboriginal artefacts. The Red Stump in main street warns travellers of dangers of Simpson Desert. Artificial 'Min Min' light, Herbert St. Koree Yuppiree Tree, near Boulia State School, thought to be last known corroboree tree of Pitta Pitta tribe. Varied birdlife to be seen around river. Boulia rodeo held in Aug. **In the area:** Mysterious Min Min light, first reportedly sighted near ruins of Min Min Hotel (130 km east), has been seen within 24 km of town. Wills Creek, to north, another reminder in area of ill-fated explorers Burke and Wills. **Travel by road in wet season not possible. See:** Outback Motoring. **Tourist information:** Shire Offices, Herbert St; (077) 46 3188. **Accommodation:** 1 hotel/motel, 1 caravan park. **See also:** The Channel Country. MAP REF. 440 D13, 441 D2

Bowen   Population 7705

A relaxed town exactly half-way between Mackay and Townsville, Bowen was named after Qld's first Governor. The town was established in 1861 on the protected shores of Port Denison and was the first settlement in North Qld. It boasts an excellent climate with an average of eight hours' sunshine daily. Bowen is famous for its tomatoes and, particularly, for its

Tomato growing at Bowen

QUEENSLAND'S NATIONAL PARKS

The diverse regions of Queensland's national parks lure visitors by the million each year. They are drawn not only to the endless stretches of sandy beaches and magnificent Great Barrier Reef cays and islands off the coast, but also to the cooler mountainous regions of the southern ranges, the western desert areas and the wilderness of Cape York.

Most parks and reserves are accessible by private vehicle; their major attraction is the climate—beautiful one day, glorious the next! Certainly, daytime temperatures in the north and west can reach a searing 40°C, and the wet season (November to March) brings the occasional cyclone and rainfall that can be measured in metres, but other than these extremes, the climate makes for pleasant day visits and for extended bushwalking, camping and other recreation-based activities.

Today Cape York Peninsula is like a magnet to tourists, even though the only aim of thousands of visitors may be simply to stand at its tip. The peninsula's vast and monotonous country is interspersed with surprising pockets of forest, broad vegetation-fringed rivers and occasional waterfalls, all the home of a wide variety of wildlife. **Jardine River/Heathlands, Rokeby** and **Iron Range National Parks** are destinations for only the keenest and experienced wilderness explorers. However, a growing number of visitors divert to **Lakefield**, the state's second largest national park, encompassing 537 000 hectares. Its fringing rainforest, paperbark woodland, open grassy plains, swamps and coastal mudflats leading to mangroves along Princess Charlotte Bay, offer a variety of attractions for the most demanding visitor. Basic campsites are located along many watercourses.

Within a several-hundred-kilometre radius of Cairns are scores of national parks catering for all tastes. **Chillagoe-Mungana Caves National Parks**, three hours' drive from Cairns, are dominated by weird limestone outcrops, castle-like pinnacles that house a wonderland of colourful caves. Guided tours are conducted daily. Once Queensland's leading mineral producing area, it is popular with fossickers.

About fifty kilometres from Cairns is the **Atherton Tableland**, within which lie several national parks. Here visitors can follow walking tracks through rainforest at **Mt Hypipamee**, or visit the 65-metre-wide **Millstream Falls**, or the crater lakes of **Eacham** and **Barrine**.

A north Queensland visit would not be complete without a train trip to Kuranda via **Barron Gorge National Park**, or a visit to the **Bellenden Ker**, **Cape Tribulation** and **Daintree National Parks**. This undeveloped mountainous country, with its scenic waterfalls and lush rainforest, should not be missed.

One of the most breathtakingly beautiful scenic reserves in Australia is **Carnarvon National Park**, 720 kilometres by road north-west of Brisbane. The Carnarvon Gorge section of this 223 000-hectare park, a dramatic, twisting chasm of soft sandstone gouged from vertical white cliffs, is a popular destination for campers. Graded tracks lead through forests of eucalypt, she-oaks, tall cabbage palms and relic macrozamia palms. Two major Aboriginal art sites, the Art Gallery and Cathedral Cave, contain rock paintings of great significance. Visitor numbers to the gorge are limited year-round.

The coastal edge of Daintree National Park

Some 300 kilometres east of Carnarvon National Park and north-west of Monto is **Cania Gorge National Park**, featuring prominent sandstone cliffs up to seventy metres high, cave formations, dry rainforest on sheltered slopes and open eucalypt forest. Though not as extensive as Carnarvon Gorge, this park protects a valuable scenic resource and provides an important wildlife habitat. **Auburn River National Park**, south-west of Mundubbera, protects an area of open eucalypt forest and dry scrub. The Auburn River flows through this 389-hectare park over a jumbled mass of pink granitic boulders. Over time, water erosion has sculptured the river's rock-pools and cataracts. Vegetation along the river banks includes stunted figs and bottle trees are common. Rainforest species occur in some areas and small lizards can be seen sunbaking on rocks near the water.

Queensland's coastal islands range from large, steep continental types to coral cays, many of them lying between the mainland and the outer Great Barrier Reef. Several national park islands have been developed for tourism, such as **Hinchinbrook**, the world's largest national park island, an area of wilderness and quiet beaches. More than 90 per cent of the 100 islands in the Whitsunday/Cumberland Group (including **Conway National Park**) are national parks and a number of these islands are resorts. Sail-yourself yachts are a novel way to visit some of the more isolated spots.

Eungella National Park, eighty-three kilometres west of Mackay, is the Aboriginal 'Land of the Clouds'. One of Queensland's wildest and most majestic parks, the cool freshness under the canopy of rainforest makes it a perfect destination for a day trip. Many, however, choose to camp by the Broken River, where the normally shy platypus can be seen swimming casually in the creek waters.

Cape Hillsborough National Park, fifty kilometres north of Mackay, is often referred to as 'the island you can drive to', because it combines the beauty of an island with the accessibility of the mainland. A wide variety of wildlife includes kangaroos, wallabies, possums, echidnas and 100 species of birds.

A launch from Gladstone will take the visitor to Heron Island, rich in coral and marine life, and a paradise for snorkellers and scuba-divers. The Capricorn-Bunker islands are outstanding breeding-places of the loggerhead and green turtles and the nesting-grounds for thousands of muttonbirds returning from their long migratory flights from the northern hemisphere.

Eurimbula National Park is south of Gladstone, near the twin communities of Agnes Water–Town of 1770. Over 200 years ago, Captain Cook and his crew chose this picturesque stretch of coast, with its broad sandy beaches between small rocky headlands, to first set foot on what is now Queensland. Botanically, this is a key coastal area, preserving a complex array of vegetation, including some plants common in southern areas and others found in northern forests.

Lady Musgrave Island is a charming coral cay reached from Bundaberg and Town of 1770. Around the cay's edge, exposed to wind and salt spray, grows a vegetation fringe of casuarina and pandanus, which protects the shady pisonia forest on the inner part of the island. The sheltered lagoon is used by day-trippers for snorkelling and reef viewing in glass-bottomed boats.

Situated only three kilometres east of Bundaberg and covering forty hectares is the Baldwin Wetlands,

Glass House Mountains

Mangrove boardwalk, Cape Tribulation National Park

containing the **Baldwin Swamp Environmental Park**. Walking tracks and a boardwalk allow observation of the park's wildlife. **Mon Repos Environmental Park**, fourteen kilometres east of Bundaberg, is the largest mainland turtle rookery in the southern hemisphere. The turtle season extends from November to March. Visitors will find it of advantage to have some basic knowledge of sea turtles and acceptable human interaction with them, to ensure that a visit to the rookery is an enlightening and enjoyable experience.

Woodgate National Park, south of Bundaberg, is at the mouth of the Burrum River near Woodgate township. This coastal park of 5490 hectares provides an essential habitat for wildlife; plant communities in the park include mangroves lining the Gregory and Burrum Rivers, wallum heathland, eucalypt and angophora forests, ti-tree swamps and small pockets of palm forest. Roads within the park are gravel or sand, and four-wheel-drive vehicles are recommended, although at times conventional vehicle access is possible.

Off Hervey Bay is the world's largest sand island, Fraser Island. The northern third of the island is **Great Sandy National Park**. This and two parks further south, **Moreton Island** and **Cooloola National Parks**, require four-wheel-drive vehicles for access; the latter offers excellent boating opportunities, particularly on the Noosa River.

Noosa National Park, 160 kilometres north of Brisbane, offers the visitor a wide variety of coastal scenery. Walking tracks lead to lookouts from which can be seen such unusual rock formations as 'Hell's Gates', 'Boiling Pot' and 'Fairy Pool'.

Further south towards Brisbane lie the **Glass House Mountains**, eroded volcanic plugs that rise suddenly from the landscape. First sighted by Captain Cook in 1770, four—Mts Coonoorwin, Beerwah, Tibrogargan and Ngungun—are national parks.

Bunya Mountains National Park, 250 kilometres north-west of Brisbane, was established to preserve the last remaining community of bunya pine forest. It was here that Aborigines used to gather every third year to feast on bunyan nuts.

The crescent of national parks, or 'Scenic Rim' around Brisbane includes (among many) **Mount Mistake, Main Range, Mount Barney** and **Springbrook National Parks**. These offer Brisbane residents and visitors panoramic views, extensive walking tracks, picnic facilities and a range of recreational opportunities. **Lamington National Park** attracts visitors by the thousands to its cool rainforest, rich in elkhorn and staghorn ferns and over 700 species of orchids.

Nine small national parks at **Tamborine Mountain** also attract many day visitors to their rainforests, waterfalls and lookouts.

Girraween National Park, 'Place of Flowers', lies south of Stanthorpe and close to the New South Wales border, and offers visitors the best floral displays in the state. This is a photographer's paradise, while the park's massive granite outcrops provide a challenge for the rock-climber.

For more information about Queensland's national parks, including the requirement for camping and driving permits, contact the Queensland National Parks and Wildlife Service, 160 Ann St, Brisbane (PO Box 155, Albert St 4002); (07) 227 8185.

tropical mangoes, in season Nov.–Jan. **Of interest:** Signposted 'Golden Arrow' tourist route starting at Salt Works, Don St. Historical Museum, Gordon St. **In the area:** At Delta, 7 km north, coffee plantation. Collinsville coal mines and power-station, 92 km south-west. Day trips to resort on Stone Island. Charter fishing and diving. **Tourist information:** Court-house, Herbert St. **Accommodation:** 3 hotels, 5 motels, 7 caravan/camping parks.
MAP REF. 437 J9

Buderim   Population 5390
Buderim is a delightful town just inland from the Sunshine Coast, high on the fertile red soil of Buderim Mountain, be-tween the Bruce Hwy and Mooloolaba on the coast. It is a popular residential and retirement area. **Of interest:** Blue Marble and Fine Art Images galleries, Burnett St. Pioneer timber cottage (1876), Ballinger Rd; one of Buderim's earliest houses, faithfully restored and re-taining many of its original furnishings. Buderim Festive Markets, Old Ginger Factory, Burnett St; Sunshine Coast-style paddy's market. **In the area:** Self-guiding Forest Glen–Tenawha Tourist Drive, includes Super Bee honey factory, Forest Glen deer sanctuary and Moonshine Valley Winery with tastings and sales of wines made from locally grown tropical fruits and Italian restaurant. **Tourist information:** Tourism Sunshine Coast Ltd, Alexandra Pde, Alexandra Headland; (008) 07 2041. **Accommodation:** 5 motels, 2 caravan/camping parks.
MAP REF. 427 L10, 435 Q9

Bundaberg   Population 33 368
Bundaberg, 368 km north of Brisbane, is the southernmost access point to the Great Barrier Reef and an important prov-incial city in the centre of the fertile Bur-nett River plains. The district is known for its sugar (the area's main crop), timber, beef production and, in more recent years, tomatoes, avocados and small crops. Bundaberg is a city of parks and botanical gardens; its wide streets lined with poincianas provide a brilliant display in spring. Several famous Australians have called Bundy home: aviator Bert Hinkler, in 1928 the first man to fly solo from England to Australia; singer Gladys Moncrieff; cricketer Don Tallon; and rugby league star Mal Meninga. Sugar has been grown in the area since 1866. Raw sugar is exported from an extensive storage and bulk terminal facility at Port Bundaberg, 16 km north-east. Industry sidelines include the distilling of the fa-mous Bundaberg Rum, refined sugar pro-duction, and the manufacture and export

of advanced Austoft cane-harvester equipment. **Of interest:** Alexandra Park and Zoo, Quay St, on Burnett River; child-ren's playground and cacti garden. Hin-kler House Memorial Museum, Mt Perry Rd, Nth Bundaberg; repository of aviation history within Botanical Gardens. Also Botanical Gardens Railway; steam train rides around lakes; and Bundaberg His-torical Museum. Bundaberg Rum Distill-ery, Avenue St, East Bundaberg; guided tours to see 'Famous Aussie Spirit' being made. Boyd's Antiquatorium, Bourbong St; boasts best Edison Gramophone col-lection in Australia. Schmeider's Cooper-age and Craft Centre, Alexandra St, East Bundaberg; demonstrates ancient art of barrel-making. Bundaberg's unique win-ery for tropical-fruit wine and Sunny Soft Drinks, Mt Perry Rd, Nth Bundaberg. **In the area:** Unexplained mystery, 25 km north: 35 strange craters said to be 25 million years old. Pennyroyal Herb Farm, 6 km south; snacks at 'Culinary Corner'. The Paradise Park, 6 km south; bird and animal sanctuary and nursery. Dream-time Reptile Reserve, 8 km south on Childers Rd; educational tours. Avocado Grove, 10 km south; subtropical gardens. Currajong Gardens and Nursery, 61 km south-west, near Gin-Gin. Bauers Ger-bera Nursery nearby. Hummock Lookout, 7 km east; views over city, 'patchwork quilt' of canefields and coast. Surfing beaches at Bargara–Nielson Park

and Kelly's Beach (15 km east), Moore Park (21 km north) and Elliott Heads (18 km south-east). Turtles can be seen at Mon Repos Environmental Park, 14 km east, Nov.–Feb. Tours to view migrating humpback whales, mid-Aug.–mid-Oct. Fishing at Burnett Heads, 18 km east, at river mouth. House of Rare Bits, The Es-planade, Burnett Heads; locally made handicrafts and Devonshire teas. Cruises to Lady Musgrave Island, uninhabited coral cay, on either MV *Lady Musgrave* (departs Burnett Heads) or MV *1770* (de-parts from Town of 1770). Flights to Lady Elliot Island resort. **Tourist informa-tion:** Cnr Mulgrave and Bourbong Sts; (071) 52 2333. **Accommodation:** Many hotels, 33 motels, 8 caravan/camping parks (most with cabins).
MAP REF. 435 P6

Burketown   Population 232
The centre of rich beef country, Burketown is 230 km west of Normanton and some 25 km from the Gulf of Carpentaria. The Gulf is accessible by boat from Burketown, which sits on the Albert River and on the east–west dividing line between the wet-lands to the north and the beginning of the Gulf Savannah grass plains to the south. **Of interest:** 100-year-old bore, which issues boiling water. Original Gulf meatworks just north of town. Burketown to Normanton telegraph-line, post office and cemetery offer insights into town's historic past. **In**

Sugar cane, near Bundaberg

the area: Nicholson River wetlands, 17 km west, breeding-grounds for crocodiles and variety of fish and birdlife. Escott Lodge, 17 km west, operating cattle station and tourist resort. **Tourist information:** Burke Shire Council; (077) 45 5100. **Accommodation:** 1 hotel/motel, 1 caravan/ camping park. **See also:** Gulf Savannah.
MAP REF. 440 C3

Burrum Heads   Population 614

This pleasant holiday resort on Hervey Bay, 45 km north of Maryborough off the Bruce Hwy, offers excellent fishing. **In the area:** Burrum River and Woodgate National Parks, 5 km north. **Tourist information:** Phillips Travel, 45 Burrum St; (071) 29 5211. **Accommodation:** 1 hotel/motel, 2 caravan/camping parks.
MAP REF. 435 P6

Caboolture   Population 8915

A major dairying centre just off the Bruce Hwy, 46 km north of Brisbane, Caboolture is noted for its butter, yoghurt and cheese. The area is also rich in Aboriginal history and relics. The district was opened up in the 1860s for grazing, sugar and cotton. **Of interest:** Caboolture Historical Village, faithfully restored. **In the area:** Distinctive landmark of Glass House Mountains, 22 km north. Popular fishing resorts of Donnybrook and Toorbul (20 and 22 km north-east), and Beachmere on Deception Bay (13 km south-east). Bribie Island, 23 km east, family day-tripping destination with picnic areas, fishing and safe swimming. Abbey Museum, on road to Bribie Island, traces growth of Western civilisation. **Tourist information:** Shire Offices, Hasking St; (074) 95 3122. **Accommodation:** 3 motels, 2 caravan/camping parks.
MAP REF. 425 K4, 435 Q10

Cairns   Population 54 862

A modern, colourful city and capital of the tropical Far North, where the cosmopolitan esplanade traces the bay foreshore and parks and spectacular gardens abound with colourful blooms and a myriad of other tropical trees and plants. Cairns' location is superb: the Great Barrier Reef to the east, the mountain rainforests and plains of the Atherton Tableland to the west, and palm-fringed beaches to the north and south. Over the past 15 years Cairns has gained worldwide prominence as one of the great black marlin fishing locations and is now further enhanced by easy access to the Great Barrier Reef for snorkelling enthusiasts, scuba-divers and those who simply wish to view the coral from glass-bottomed boats. **Of interest:** Cairns Red Explorer bus from Lake St; links nine stops and attractions in and around city. Cairns Museum, cnr Lake and Sheilds Sts. Big-game fishing boats moor at Marlin Marina, end of Spence St. Trinity Wharf and Pier shopping and entertainment complex, The Wharf. Freshwater Connection historical complex, which is also departure point for 100-ycar old Kuranda Scenic Railway, through Barron Gorge to rainforest village of Kuranda, 34 km north-west. Wetland areas, including the Esplanade, provide opportunities for birdwatching. Flecker Botanic Gardens, Collins St; exotic trees and shrubs, 200 varieties of palms, area devoted to plants used by Aborigines. Walking track links gardens to Centenary Lakes Parkland. Jack Barnes Bicentennial Mangrove Boardwalk, Airport St; two educational walks through mangroves with viewing platforms. Rusty's Bazaar, Grafton and Sheridan Sts; Sun. market with locally produced handicrafts, home-made produce, plants and new and secondhand goods. Royal Flying Doctor Service Visitor Centre, Junction St, Edge Hill. Doll and Bear Museum, Mayers St, Manunda. Fun in the Sun Festival held in Oct. **In the area:** Bulk sugar terminal, Cook St, Portsmith; guided tours during crushing season. Marlin Coast, extending from Machans Beach (10 km north) to Ellis Beach, 26 km of spectacular coastline. Vic Hislop Shark Show, 8 km north. Popular seaside spot of Holloways Beach, 11 km north. Wild World and Outback Opal Mine, 22 km north. Hartley's Creek Crocodile Farm, 40 km north. Reef and islands can be explored by private charters, daily cruises and air (seaplane and helicopter). Longer cruises to resort islands and reef on catamaran *Coral Princess*. Access to nearby Green, Fitzroy and Frankland Islands on cruise vessels. Cairns also offers easy access to wilderness areas of Cape York, Daintree and Atherton Tableland. Sugarworld Gardens, 8 km south at Edmonton. Delightful rural settings of Barron and Freshwater Valleys, north and south of Cairns; attractions include Crystal Cascades, Barron Gorge hydro-electric power-station and Copperlode Dam (Lake Morris); bushwalking, hiking, whitewater rafting and camping. Off-road safaris (4WD) to Cape York and Gulf Savannah. Information from Qld National Parks and Wildlife

Trinity Wharf, Cairns

Service, (070) 51 9811; or Far North Qld Coach and Off Road Association, (070) 31 4565. **Tourist information:** Cnr Sheridan and Aplin Sts; (070) 51 3588. **Accommodation:** 50 hotels, numerous motels from 5-star, international-standard hotels to family and budget; 9 caravan/camping parks. **See also:** The Far North; Sunshine Coast.
MAP REF. 427 M12, 435 Q9

Caloundra Population 16 215

This popular holiday spot on the Sunshine Coast is 96 km north of Brisbane via a turn-off from the Bruce Hwy. The main beaches are Kings, Shelley, Moffatt, Dicky, Golden and Bulcock. The main shipping channel to Brisbane is just offshore. Pumicestone Passage (a state marine park) to the south, between Bribie Island and the mainland, has sheltered waters for fishing, boating, water-skiing and sailboarding. **Of interest:** Queensland Air Museum, at aerodrome, Pathfinder Dr. Teddy Bear World, Bowman Rd; museum, water-slide, mini-golf. **In the area:** Old Lighthouse, Golden Beach, 4 km south. Wreck of SS *Dicky* (1893), Dicky Beach, 4 km north. At Currimundi, 4 km north: Indoor skydiving centre, Nicklin Way; also Lake and Seaside Environment Park. Opals Down Under and House of Herbs, Bruce Hwy, 9 km north. Suncoast Crayfish Farm, off Glenview Rd, 9 km north. Ettamogah Pub, Bruce Hwy, 10 km north; pure *Australasian Post*. Pt Cartwright Lookout, 12 km north. Glass House Mts, 29 km southwest. **Tourist information:** Caloundra Rd; (074) 91 0202. **Accommodation:** 3 hotels, 15 motels, 6 caravan/camping parks. **See also:** Sunshine Coast.
MAP REF. 427 M12, 435 Q9

Camooweal Population 315

On the Barkly Hwy, 188 km north-west of Mount Isa, Camooweal is the last Qld town reached before crossing the NT border, 13 km west. **Of interest:** Shire Hall (1922–23) and Freckleton's Store, both classified by National Trust. Ellen Finlay Park; picnic/barbecue areas. Cemetery; headstones tell local history. **In the area:** Camooweal Caves, within national park, 25 km south; challenge to experienced potholers. **Tourist information:** Inland Qld Tourism and Development Board, Marian St, Mount Isa; (077) 43 7966. **Accommodation:** 1 hotel, 1 motel, 1 caravan park.
MAP REF. 355 R10, 440 A7

Cannonvale Population 1675

Cannonvale is the first of the three seaside resorts along the Shute Harbour

Stock Exchange building, Charters Towers

road from the Proserpine turn-off, and is a suburb of the town of Whitsunday. Located 3 km from Airlie Beach, Cannonvale is fast becoming a vital centre for service and manufacturing businesses in the region. **Of interest:** Wildlife Park, Shute Harbour Rd. **In the area:** Airlie Beach and Shute Harbour, neighbouring resorts to south. Conway National Park, 10 km south. Tours to Whitsunday Islands. **Tourist information:** Cnr Mandalay St and Shute Harbour Rd, Airlie Beach; (079) 46 6673. **Accommodation:** 1 motel, 3 caravan/camping parks, 1 resort.
MAP REF. 437 K9

Cardwell Population 1247

From Cardwell, 58 km north of Ingham, a beautiful view is obtained of Rockingham Bay and many islands, including the well-known Hinchinbrook, all of which may be visited by boat from Cardwell. Local fishing is generally excellent. **In the area:** Scenic drives in Cardwell Forest, with spectacular coastal scenery, and Kirrama Range, 9–10 km north, on Kennedy Rd. Kennedy Falls in Edmund Kennedy National Park, 20 km north. Murray Falls in State Forest Park, 20 km north-west; camping and picnic area. Houseboats and yachts for hire. Cruises

available. **Tourist information:** Cardwell Travel, 91 Victoria St; (070) 66 8539. **Accommodation:** 1 hotel, 6 motels, 5 caravan parks.
MAP REF. 436 G6

Charleville Population 3588

Charleville marks the terminus of the *Westlander* rail service and is at the centre of a rich pastoral district carrying some 800 000 sheep and 100 000 cattle. The town has an interesting history. Charleville's river, the Warrego, was explored by Edmund Bourke in 1847, and in 1862, William Landsborough camped nearby when searching for Burke and Wills. By the 1890s, Charleville was a frontier town with its own brewery, ten pubs and 500 registered bullock teams. Cobb & Co. had a coach-building factory here in 1893. The last coach on Australian roads ran to Surat in 1923. A monument 19 km north of the town marks the spot where Ross and Keith Smith landed with engine trouble on the first flight from London to Sydney in 1919. Amy Johnson also landed here, in 1920. Qantas started flights from Charleville in 1922. Charleville is the heart of the Mulga Country; the mulga provide welcome shade and in drought are cut down and used as sheep fodder. **Of interest:** Historical Museum in restored Qld National Bank building (1880), Albert St; features amazing 5-m-long 'vortex gun' used in unsuccessful rainmaking experiments in 1902. 'Weary Willie' swagman statue in main street. National Parks and Wildlife Service Research Centre, Park St. Cobb & Co. coach can be hired for town tours. Booga Woongaroo Festival held in Oct. **In the area:** Tree blazed by Landsborough in 1862, 16 km south; guide required. **Tourist information:** Shire Offices, Coronation Dr., Blackall; (076) 57 4255. **Accommodation:** 4 hotels, 3 motels, 2 caravan/camping parks.
MAP REF. 434 G8

Charters Towers Population 7208

This peaceful and historic city once had a gold-rush population of some 30 000. Between 1872 and 1916, Charters Towers produced ore worth 25 million pounds ($50m). On 25 December 1871 a young Aboriginal boy named Jupiter made the first 'strike' while looking for horses that had bolted during a thunderstorm. He brought some quartz back to his employer, Hugh Mosman, who rode to Ravenswood to register his claim, and the gold-rush was on. The Government rewarded Mosman and he in turn adopted and educated Jupiter. Charters Towers is 135 km inland from Townsville in hot, dry country on the road and rail line to Mount

THE GREAT BARRIER REEF AND OTHER ISLANDS

The Great Barrier Reef is a living phenomenon. Its coloured coral branches sit upon banks of limestone polyps which have been built up slowly over thousands of years from the seabed. The banks of coral are separated by channels of water, shading from the delicate green of the shallows to the deepest blue. The reef area is over 1200 kilometres long, stretching from near the coast of western Papua to Breaksea Spit, east of Gladstone on the central Queensland coast. It is only between 15 and 20 kilometres wide in the north, but south of Cairns the reef area can extend up to 325 kilometres out to sea. The Great Barrier Reef was proclaimed a marine park in 1979 and a management programme undertaken to balance the interests of scientists, tourists and fishing enthusiasts, and to preserve the reef for future generations. With over 700 islands scattered through the tropical sea, and the banks of reefs darkening the water, this sun-drenched, tropical paradise attracts thousands of visitors each year to its resorts.

The coral presents an incredibly beautiful picture. Visitors can see it through semi-submersible vessels, which allow those in them to go underwater without getting wet, or glass-bottomed boats; or, even better, they can swim around in it using snorkels or diving gear. The colours of purple, pink, yellow, white and red are intermixed and made more startling by the spectacular shapes of the coral. There are more than 340 varieties of identified coral, the most common being the staghorns, brain corals, mushroom corals, organ pipes and blue corals. Spread among these are waving fields of soft coral, colourful anemones, sea urchins and sea slugs. Shellfish of all kinds, ranging from great clams to tiny cowries, cling to the reef while shoals of brightly coloured tropical fish — among them red emperors, coral trout, sweetlip, angel-fish, parrot-fish and demoiselles — glide and dart through the coral gardens. Multitudes of seabirds nest on the islands of the reef through spring and summer.

Brightly coloured clown fish

Three island resorts, Green Island, Heron Island and Lady Elliot Island, are coral cays — actually part of the reef — and at low tide it is possible to walk on the coral ledges which surround them. Other resort islands are continental islands, having once been part of the mainland, and are generally more wooded and mountainous.

The Barrier Reef is Australia's most beautiful tourist attraction, and the best way to see it is by boat. If you do not have your own yacht, and the holiday budget will not stretch to chartering one, there are many excellent cruises available through the reef and its islands. Charter boats, scuba-diving and fishing trips are also available.

The resort islands off the reef and the Queensland coast offer different styles of living to suit various tastes in holidays and entertainment. Their common denominator is their beautiful setting and a consistency of climate, broken only by the sudden and short-lived downfalls of the wet season from December to February.

Southern Reef Islands

The Southern Reef extends offshore from Bundaberg to Rockhampton. One of the uninhabited islands, North West Island, is the largest coral cay in the Great Barrier Reef. It is the major breeding-site for two species of bird — the white-caped noddy and wedge-tailed shearwater — and is also a major nesting-site for the green turtle. A catamaran service to the island operates from Yeppoon.

Great Keppel Island, 48 kilometres north-east of Rockhampton, offers 30 kilometres of white, sandy beaches and unspoiled tropical island scenery. Great Keppel Island is for everyone, from families and couples to young singles. The resort accommodates around 500 people and offers many well-organised activities: tennis, water-skiing, island safari trips, skin-diving, parasailing and coral viewing. During school holidays the Keppel Kids' Klub organises games and activities. **Getting there:** Light plane from Rockhampton, or a launch from Rosslyn Bay near Yeppoon.

Heron Island is a very small, genuine coral island, 72 kilometres offshore from Gladstone. Heron is only about one kilometre across, with a continuous white sand beach and coral reef. It is a true coral cay with part of the reef emerging at low tide. The island has dense palms, pandanus, pisonia, tournefortia and she-oaks, and is world-famous for its birdlife, including sea eagles, noddy terns, muttonbirds and, of course, herons. Over 1150 types of fish have been recorded in the lagoon. The island and reefs are a national park and wildlife sanctuary, and there is a Marine Biological Research Station. It is a mecca for divers and scuba gear may be hired. Turtles come ashore to lay their eggs from October to March, and hatching can be seen from late December to May. The resort overlooks the island's boat harbour and accommodates around 280 people. **Getting there:** Catamaran or helicopter from Gladstone (daily services).

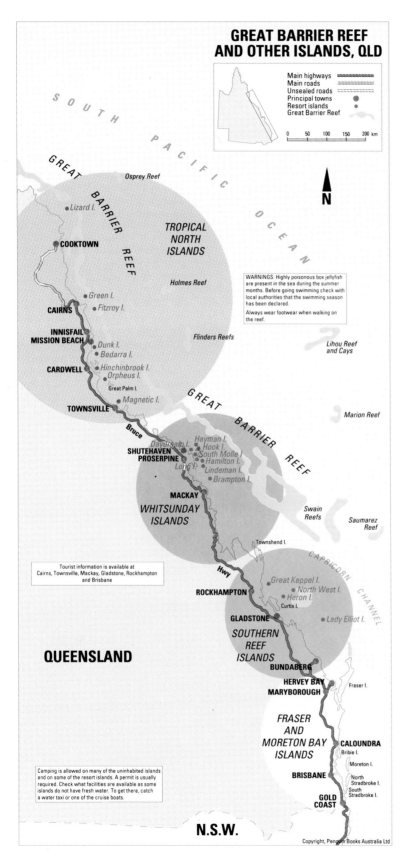

GREAT BARRIER REEF AND OTHER ISLANDS, QLD

Main highways
Main roads
Unsealed roads
Principal towns
Resort islands
Great Barrier Reef

0   50   100   150   200 km

N

WARNINGS: Highly poisonous box jellyfish are present in the sea during the summer months. Before going swimming check with local authorities that the swimming season has been declared.

Always wear footwear when walking on the reef.

Tourist information is available at Cairns, Townsville, Mackay, Gladstone, Rockhampton and Brisbane

Camping is allowed on many of the uninhabited islands and on some of the resort islands. A permit is usually required. Check what facilities are available as some islands do not have fresh water. To get there, catch a water taxi or one of the cruise boats.

Copyright, Penguin Books Australia Ltd

Lady Musgrave Island, 2 hours by catamaran north-north-east of Bundaberg, is a superb coral cay with a navigable lagoon 13 kilometres in circumference. An underwater observatory is available for day trippers to view the coral and prolific sealife at close quarters. The island hosts a myriad of bird life in its gigantic pisonia trees. Turtles nest on the beaches from November through February. The island is uninhabited, but permits are available from the Marine Parks Authorities for camping; numbers are limited to fifty at any one time. **Getting there:** Plane from Brisbane, or by catamaran aboard MV *Lady Musgrave*, from Bundaberg or MV *1770*, from Town of 1770.

Lady Elliot Island, 80 kilometres north-east of Bundaberg at the southern end of the Great Barrier Reef, is a small, sand-covered coral cay. Lady Elliot is extremely popular with snorkellers and divers. Surrounded by 40 metres of deep water and yet right on the reef, the island has ten major dive areas. As it is a coral cay, divers and snorkellers can simply walk into the water and be among the spectacular reefs in a few moments. The island is surrounded by beautiful coral gardens built by hundreds of different varieties of coral. The aquamarine depths are rich with marine life. Sighting exotic fish, giant velvety clams, green turtles, starfish and huge manta rays is normal during an underwater venture. On land, the island is becoming known as one of the most significant bird rookeries off the Australian coast, with up to fifty-six species of birds nesting on the island. In the summer months it is possible to see green turtles laying their eggs. The resort is low-key with simple but comfortable accommodation for a small number of people. **Getting there:** Light plane from Bundaberg.

Whitsunday Islands
The magnificent Whitsunday Islands in the Whitsunday Passage include Lindeman, South Molle, Daydream, Hayman, Hook, Hamilton and Long Island. These are only the resort islands; there are over seventy-three uninhabited islands. Hamilton and Hayman Islands have

marinas and excellent service facilities. All islands have anchorage and their own individual attractions and sporting activities.

Brampton Island is a mountainous island of 8 square kilometres in the Cumberland Group, 32 kilometres from Mackay and south of the major group of the Whitsundays. It is a national park and wildlife sanctuary with lush forests, palm trees and fine white beaches. The island is surrounded by coral reefs, particularly in the passage between Brampton and Carlisle Islands. The resort's world-class facilities include an aquatics centre and a golf course. The island has a beautiful resort beach overlooking neighbouring Carlisle Island. Daily activities vary from cruises to the Great Barrier Reef, to water sports, palm-frond weaving, archery, snorkelling and bushwalking. **Getting there:** Light plane or launch from Mackay.

Lindeman Island, 67 kilometres north of Mackay, is another beautiful national park island. It is some 20 square kilometres in area and seventy-three islands in the Whitsunday Group can be seen from the peak of Mt Oldfield. The island, noted for its birds and butterflies, is covered by extensive walking-tracks and has seven secluded sandy beaches. The island's Club Med resort has all the benefits and services associated with that group. The island will appeal to young professionals, sporty types, nature lovers and young families. The island's golf course is one of the most picturesque in Australia. **Getting there:** From Proserpine, light plane; from Hamilton Island, light plane or water taxi; from Shute Harbour, light plane or launch; from Mackay, light plane or launch.

Hamilton Island is 16 kilometres from Shute Harbour. The island's grazing land was transformed in the early 1980s into one of the most complex island resorts in Australia. Extensive facilities have made Hamilton almost a town on its own, with a school, banks and post office. Its 200-berth marina hosts the nation's most famous yachts, particularly during Hamilton Race Week in May each year. The resort has the largest hotel of any type in Australia, accommodates over 2000 people and features a wide range of activities

and entertainment, including facilities for windsurfing, sailing, scuba diving, parasailing, fishing, tennis and squash. There are also hot spas, a gymnasium, a fauna park and a waterside village. The catamaran *Southern Spirit* offers 7-night cruises around the Whitsundays. **Getting there:** Plane from Melbourne, Sydney, Brisbane, Cairns, Proserpine, Shute Harbour and Mackay, or launch from Shute Harbour.

Long Island is a mountainous, bushy island in the Whitsunday Group, 9 kilometres from Shute Harbour and 43 kilometres from Proserpine. Excellent walking-tracks climb through the rainforest to give 'postcard' views of the other islands. Scrub turkeys are friendly and common. Island oysters are yours for the opening. The island is part of the Conway National Park system, one of the most beautiful waterways in the world. Long Island has three resorts. The Island Resort is a fun-filled location with an exciting range of activities in a beautiful setting. Palm Bay Hideaway Resort, the nature-lover's favourite, is 2 kilometres down the island's coast and offers peaceful, relaxed family and group accommodation, as well as catering to the single visitor. Paradise Bay is ideal for the keen fisherman or families who want to get away from it all. **Getting there:** Launch or helicopter from Shute Harbour or Hamilton Island.

South Molle Island is situated in the heart of the Whitsunday Passage, 8 kilometres from Shute Harbour. The

island is only 4 kilometres by 2.4 kilometres in area, lightly timbered, with numerous inlets, quiet bays, coral gardens and reefs. Walking tracks take hikers to the island's peaks for uninterrupted views of the Whitsunday Passage. The well-known resort accommodates around 500 people and offers a wide range of entertainment and activities, including a golf course and gymnasium, as well as a reef pontoon with a fish observation chamber and a platform for swimmers, snorkellers and scuba-divers. **Getting there:** Launch, helicopter or seaplane from Shute Harbour.

Daydream Island is a small island (1.2 kilometres by half a kilometre) of volcanic rock and coral, 5 kilometres from Shute Harbour. Foliage is dense and tropical, while the beaches end in spectacular coral gardens offshore. The luxurious resort, totally rebuilt in 1990, has a beautifully appointed 303-room hotel at the northern end of the island. Trips to the outer reef and other islands are available. **Getting there:** Launch or helicopter from Shute Harbour or Hamilton Island.

Hook Island is renowned for its breathtaking Underwater Observatory, a must for the visitor, where coral and other reef marine life can be seen in their natural habitat. Accommodation is in twelve bunk-style units, and there is a walking track with great views. The island is 90 minutes by launch from Shute Harbour and most

Viewing the reef, Heron Island

cruises visit Hook Island. It is a perfect retreat from the hustle and bustle of city life. **Getting there:** Launch from Shute Harbour.

Hayman Island is the most northerly of the Whitsunday Group and the closest to the outer reef. There are some 80 varieties of birds in the island's tropical bushland. Hayman is a luxury resort offering culinary delights, enjoyment and relaxation to its pampered guests; its hotel is a member of the leading Hotels of the World group. Fishing, sight-seeing trips, scenic flights or diving adventures can be arranged. **Getting there:** Launch from Abel Point Marina, Airlie Beach or plane from Airlie Beach, Townsville, Mackay or Cairns, but accommodation bookings must be made first with the island.

Tropical North Islands

This group of islands is located off the north coast of Queensland between Townsville and Cooktown. Generally speaking, the Reef in this section is closer to the mainland than it is further south. The resort islands include Magnetic, Orpheus, Hinchinbrook, Bedarra, Dunk, Fitzroy, Green and Lizard.

Magnetic Island is only a 29-minute catamaran ride across Cleveland Bay from Townsville. The island is a seaside 'suburb' of Townsville, with some 2500 permanent residents. Over 2709 hectares of this 5184-hectare mountainous island is a national park and bird sanctuary, with good walking tracks. Trees are mostly pines, with she-oaks, pandanus, poincianas and banyans giving variety. Hotels and accommodation places range from economy to resort. Buses and taxis operate on the island. **Of interest:** The Koala Park Oasis at Horseshoe Bay, Shark World at Nelly Bay, horseriding, snorkelling, beautiful beaches and excellent fishing. **Getting there:** Vehicular ferry, catamaran or water taxi from Townsville.

Orpheus Island, a small, volcanic island surrounded by coral reefs, is 80 kilometres north of Townsville and 16 kilometres off Lucinda Point. The island is a densely wooded national park, and some fifty varieties of birds have been seen. Turtles regularly nest on the

Dunk Island resort

Hamilton Island

beaches and it is the base for a giant-clam farm. There is a five-star exclusive resort on the island. **Getting there:** Plane from Townsville or Cairns.

Hinchinbrook Island is the largest island national park in the world; all of its 642 square kilometres are totally protected, and even insecticides are banned. There are rugged mountain ranges with thick tropical vegetation and waterfalls, which contrast with long sandy beaches and secluded coves on the eastern side. A marine research station has been set up at Cape Ferguson to study the ecology of mangroves. Permits to camp on the island may be obtained from the National Parks and Wildlife Service in Townsville or Cardwell. A small, pleasant resort at Cape Richards accommodating a maximum of thirty people offers natural, unsophisticated holidays. **Getting there:** Resort's launch collects visitors from Cardwell.

Bedarra Island is a very small, heavily wooded island, 6 kilometres from the mouth of the Hull River near Tully. The island is an oasis of untouched tropical beauty. There are two resorts: Bedarra Bay, which accommodates thirty-two people, and the exclusive Bedarra Hideaway, which has sixteen individual units. No day visitors are permitted on the island. **Getting there:** Plane from Townsville or Cairns to Dunk Island and launch from Dunk Island.

Dunk Island, a national park 5 kilometres off the coast near Tully, is one of the most popular of the resort islands. The island's resort is owned by Australian Airlines and can accommodate 200 guests in various degrees of luxury. There are extensive walking tracks through the island's superb rainforest. More than ninety varieties of birds have been identified. Butterflies and wild orchids complete the tropical picture. The writer E.J. Banfield (Beachcomber) lived on the island from 1897 to 1913, and the film Age of Consent was made here. **Getting there:** Plane from Townsville or Cairns, or launch from Clump Point near Mission Beach.

Fitzroy Island, 30 kilometres from Cairns, covers 324 hectares. The island offers magnificent native flora and fauna, secluded sandy beaches and giant clams being bred to restock the Reef. Visitors to the lighthouse are rewarded with breathtaking 360-degree panoramas. The island, once a well-kept secret of divers and boat and fish enthusiasts, now has accommodation ranging from villa-style to bunk-house, with communal amenities. **Getting there:** Catamaran from Cairns.

Green Island, 27 kilometres from Cairns, is a coral cay surrounded by beautiful patches of reef and crested with thick tropical vegetation. It has holiday units and a hotel with dining and recreation facilities, but is better known as the daily host to visitors from Cairns, who can see the reef through glass-bottomed boats and at the underwater observatory. There is a theatrette showing colour films of the reef and a display of coral and other marine and animal life. **Getting there:** Catamaran from Cairns.

Lizard Island, 95 kilometres northeast of Cooktown, caters for a small number of guests in a resort built in homestead style, facing a beautiful lagoon. The reefs around this national park are magnificent, with excellent fishing, including the famous black marlin. Big-game fishing enthusiasts descend on Lizard Island during the marlin season (September to November). The first 'tourist' was Captain James Cook in August 1770. He landed and climbed Cook's Look (359 metres) to spy out a safe passage through the reefs to the open sea. The island takes its name from the large but harmless monitor lizards he found. **Getting there:** Plane from Cairns.

Other Islands
Fraser Island If you like sand, sea, sailing, fishing and plenty of peace and quiet, Fraser Island would be your ideal holiday place. One hundred and twenty-three kilometres long, Fraser is the largest sand island in the world and the largest island on Australia's east coast. It acts as a breakwater, protecting the coast from Bundaberg to well south of Maryborough, and forms the eastern shores of Hervey Bay, a magnificent stretch of sheltered water which is ideal for sailing and which also attracts hundreds of fishermen each year for the annual tailor season.

Lizard Island, the most northerly resort island

Deserted beach, Fraser Island

Fraser's remote and abundant sand dunes are particularly attractive to those with four-wheel-drives and beach buggies, but the island is large enough to accommodate them in certain areas without upsetting the peace and quiet. Apart from its long stretches of beautiful beach, Fraser Island has a unique area of freshwater lakes and tangled rainforests. There are over forty lakes on the island, all of them above sea-level, and the dense forests surrounding them attract a wide range of bird and animal life.

An odd geological feature of the island is its ever-moving creeks, which may run parallel to the ocean for several kilometres, then spill through a dune, carving a new course through the sand to the sea.

The island is accessible by air service from Brisbane, Maroochydore, Maryborough, Hervey Bay or Toowoomba, or by barge from Inskip Point (Rainbow Beach) and Hervey Bay. Visitors to the island are required to have permits.

Kingfisher Bay Resort Village is at North White Cliffs, on the western side of the island opposite Mary River Heads.

There are five areas of accommodation on the ocean side of Fraser Island, at Orchid Beach, Happy Valley, Eurong, Dilli Village and Cathedral Beach Camping Park. Korawinga Lodge at Eurong has time-share units.

The Orchid Beach island village is at the northern end of the island, overlooking the 32-kilometre sweep of Marloo Bay and the main surf beach — a rarity on Queensland islands, as those further north are sheltered from the surf by the Barrier Reef. All these holiday centres offer family accommodation.

Moreton Bay Islands
Bribie Island is a largely undeveloped island, 69 kilometres north of Brisbane, reached via a turn-off on the Bruce Highway and a one-kilometre bridge across Pumicestone Passage. Bribie is about 31 kilometres long, the northern tip being opposite Caloundra on the Sunshine Coast. Matthew Flinders landed on the southern tip in 1799. Apart from the townships of Bongaree on the mainland side and **Woorim** on the surf side, little has changed since those days. Bribie is a wildlife sanctuary, with excellent fishing, boating and crabbing. **Accommodation:** 4 motels, 6 caravan/camping parks.

Moreton Island, predominantly a national park, is a remarkable wilderness island only 35 kilometres east of Brisbane. Apart from rocky headlands, the island is mostly huge sandhills, native scrub, banksias and freshwater lakes, which attract over 125 species of birds. A lighthouse at the northern tip was built in 1857 and still guides shipping into Brisbane. There are no roads on the island, but the occasional four-wheel-drive vehicle uses the tracks and the magnificent 40-kilometre-long beach. Mt Tempest (280 m) is probably the highest permanent sandhill in the world. The pleasant tourist resort of **Tangalooma** is on the leeward side and can accommodate 225 guests; it is a popular base for big-game fishing. There are several camp sites in the park. Transport is by launch or air from Brisbane.

North Stradbroke Island or 'Straddie', as it is affectionately called, is a large and unspoiled island directly east of Brisbane across Moreton Bay. It is a popular spot for fishermen, surfers and weekenders. The small settlements of **Dunwich** and **Amity Point** are on the leeward side, and **Point Lookout** is on the north-east corner. Dunwich started as a quarantine station for the port of Brisbane in 1828, and a typhoid plague in 1850 resulted in some historic local gravestones. Point Lookout has the only hotel on the island, some impressive rocky headlands, and great fishing and surfing. The 500 hectare **Blue Lake National Park** offers walks through coastal woodland and a variety of wildlife. Vehicular ferries sail regularly from Redland Bay and Cleveland to Dunwich. **Accommodation:** 2 resorts, 1 motel, 9 caravan/camping parks.

South Stradbroke Island was separated from North Stradbroke Island by a cyclone in 1896, and the channel between them is called Jumpinpin. South Stradbroke stretches down to Southport on the Gold Coast, the protected Broadwater being a well-used boating playground. The island is almost uninhabited. Day cruises operate from Southport. **Accommodation:** 1 resort.

For further information on the islands of the Great Barrier Reef, contact the Queensland Tourist and Travel Corporation, 36th Floor, Riverside Centre, 123 Eagle Street, Brisbane, (07) 833 5400; or any Queensland Government Travel Centre.

Isa. Cattle-raising is the main industry in the Dalrymple Shire, together with citrus and grapes and another gold boom. **Of interest:** Much classic early Australian architecture with verandahs and lacework still remains, particularly facades in Mosman and Gill Sts. Historic homes: Ay-Ot-Lookout (1890s), Hodgkinson St, and Pffither House (1890s), Paul St. Zara Clark Museum, Mosman St; local history. Tourist centre in restored Stock Exchange, Mosman St. Buckland's Hill lookout, Fraser St. **In the area:** Mount Leyshon goldmine, 24 km south. Old Venus gold treatment battery, 5 km east. Ravenswood, 88 km east; small mining town. Burdekin Wilderness Lodge, 150 km south-east. **Tourist information:** Mosman St; (077) 87 2374. **Accommodation:** 5 hotels, 6 motels, 2 caravan/camping parks. **See also:** The Far North.
MAP REF. 436 G9

Childers Population 1409
Childers is a picturesque sugar town, 53 km south of Bundaberg, much of which was destroyed by fire in 1902. Today it is a National Trust Town. **Of interest:** Historic Childers, self-guiding town walk taking in many historic buildings: Old Butcher's Shop (1896), North St, with many original features; Grand, Royal and Federal Hotels, also North St; Gaydon's Building (1894), Churchill St; now Pharmaceutical Museum, art gallery and tourist centre; and Historic Complex, Taylor St; includes school, cottage and locomotive. **In the area:** Cane Cutters Cottage, Apple Tree Creek, 5 km north; crafts and Devonshire teas. Isis Central Sugar Mill, Cordalba, 10 km north; tours July–Nov. Woodgate National Park, 45 km east. **Tourist information:** Pharmaceutical Museum, Churchill St; (071) 26 1994. **Accommodation:** 4 motels, 2 caravan/camping parks.
MAP REF. 435 P6

Chillagoe Population 202
Chillagoe, once a thriving town where copper, silver, lead, gold and wolfram were mined, is now a small outback town where the recent development of tourism, international-standard marble mines and the Red Dome gold mine have returned to the town some of its former glory. **Of interest:** Local museum gives glimpse of history of town, with relics of old mining days on display. **In the area:** Rugged limestone outcrops in Chillagoe Mungana National Park, 8 km south, contain many magnificent caves; guided tours. **Tourist information:** Far North Qld Promotion Bureau, cnr Sheridan and Aplin Sts, Cairns;

(070) 51 3588. **Accommodation:** 1 hotel, 1 motel, 1 caravan/camping park. MAP REF. 436 E4, 438 G12

Chinchilla   Population 3235
Chinchilla is a prosperous town in the western Darling Downs, 354 km west of Brisbane on the Warrego Hwy. Ludwig Leichhardt named the area in 1847 from 'Jinchilla', the local Aboriginal name for cypress pines. Grain growing is the traditional industry, as well as cattle, sheep, pigs, timber and, more recently, grapes and watermelons. **Of interest:** Chinchilla Historical Museum, Villiers St; working steam engines and 1880s slab cottage. Newan's Collection of Petrified Wood, Boyd St. Fishing on Charley's Creek and Condamine River. Polocrosse Carnival held 3rd weekend in July. **In the area:** Barakula State Forest, 40 km north, Qld's largest commercial forest. Petrified wood, fossils and gemstones fossicking near Eddington, 20 km south-west. Cactoblastis Hall at Boonarga, 8 km east. **Tourist information:** Chinchilla Historical Museum, Villiers St; (076) 62 7014. **Accommodation:** 2 motels. MAP REF. 435 M9

Clermont   Population 2452
Centre of a fertile region which breeds cattle and sheep, and grows wheat, sorghum, safflower and sunflower as well as hardwood timber, Clermont is 350 km south-west of Mackay, just off the Gregory Hwy. Nearby is the Blair Athol open-cut mine, the largest seam of steaming coal in the world. About 170 houses were built in 1982 in Clermont for coal workers. The town takes its name from Clermont in France, and was established over 120 years ago (the first inland settlement in the tropics) after the discovery of gold. Many remnants of the gold-rushes can still be seen. **In the area:** Picnics and bush walks at Theresa Creek Dam, 5 km south-west. Clermont and District Historical Museum, 4 km north-west on Charters Towers Rd. **Tourist information:** Shire Offices, Daintree St; (079) 83 1133. **Accommodation:** 4 hotels, 4 motels, 2 caravan parks. MAP REF. 434 I2, 436 I13

Cleveland   Population 6581
Centre of the Redland Shire, 35 km south-east of Brisbane, Cleveland was nearly the capital for the new colony of Qld. However, when Governor Gipps and his official party arrived for an inspection, the tide was out and the trudge over the mud-flats created a less than favourable impression. **Of interest:** Ye Olde Court House (1853); built by Francis Bigge for timber-getters, later first police station

James Cook Historical Museum, Cooktown

and court-house, now restaurant. Cleveland Lighthouse (1847), Cleveland Point, which guided timber-carrying vessels. Wooden structure, The Old Lighthouse (1864), restored and relocated close by, held Australian record for length of tenancy by one attendant: 50 years by James Froy. Grand View Hotel (1849); built by Francis Bigge, in anticipation of influx of holiday-makers when Cleveland was named the capital of Qld, it became known as Bigge's Folly. Restored: main bar exhibits murals depicting historic events of the day. Bayside Markets, Bloomfield St; held Sun. Cleveland is departure point for barges and water taxis to Nth Stradbroke and other Moreton Bay islands. **In the area:** Ormiston House (1862), overlooking bay at Ormiston, 5 km north; open Sun., Mar.–Nov. Its builder, Captain Louis Hope, pioneered Qld's sugar industry at this location. Whepstead Manor (1874), at Wellington Point, 7 km north; a historic old Queenslander with beautifully landscaped grounds, now restaurant and function centre. **Tourist information:** Shire Offices, Bloomfield St; (07) 286 8586. **Accommodation:** 2 motels. MAP REF. 425 O11

Clifton   Population 765
Located between Toowoomba and Warwick, Clifton is the centre of a rich grain-growing and dairying area. **Of interest:** Historic buildings, including Club Hotel (1889), King St, and Church of St James and St Johns (1890s), cnr Tooth St and Mears Pl. **In the area:** Tours of local peanut factory, 5 km east. Arthur Hoey Davis (Steele Rudd), author of *On Our Selection*, grew up at East Greenmount,

10 km north. Sister Kenny, remembered for her method of treating poliomyelitis, is buried at Nobby, 8 km north. Also at Nobby, Rudd's Pub (1893); museum in part of dining-room. **Tourist information:** Shire Offices, King St; (076) 97 3299. **Accommodation:** Limited. MAP REF. 435 O11

Cloncurry   Population 2297
An important mining town, 124 km east of Mount Isa, Cloncurry has an interesting history. In 1861, John McKinlay of Adelaide, leading an expedition to search for Burke and Wills, reported distinctive traces of copper in the area. Six years later, pioneer pastoralist Ernest Henry discovered the first copper lodes. A rail link to Townsville was built in 1908. During World War I, Cloncurry was the centre of a copper boom and in 1916 it was the largest source of copper in Australia, with four smelters operating. After copper prices slumped following the war, a pastoral industry took its place. In 1920 a new Qantas air service linked Cloncurry to Winton and in 1928 the town became the base for the famous Royal Flying Doctor Service. In 1974 a rare type of exceptionally pure 22-carat gold, resembling crystallised straw, was discovered. It is now used for jewellery-making. The Cloncurry Shire is mainly cattle country, and Cloncurry is a main railhead for transporting stock. **Of interest:** John Flynn Place, Daintree St; incorporates Fred McKay Art Gallery and RFDS Museum, cultural centre, outdoor theatre and Cloncurry Gardens. Cloncurry/Mary Kathleen Memorial Park, McIlwraith St; four buildings from abondoned town of Mary Kathleen, re-erected and used to display items

THE CHANNEL COUNTRY

The remote Channel Country is an endless horizon of sweeping plains in Queensland's far-west and south-west corner. It seldom rains in the Channel Country itself, but after the northern monsoons the Georgina, Hamilton and Diamantina Rivers and Cooper Creek completely take over the country as they flood through hundreds of channels in their valiant efforts to reach Lake Eyre. There is scarcely any gradient. After the 'wet without rain', the enormous quantities of water carried by these rivers usually vanish into waterholes, saltpans and desert sands; lush grass, wildflowers and bird and animal life miraculously appear, and cattle are moved in for fattening.

The region is sparsely populated, except for large pastoral holdings and scattered settlements, linked by very essential beef-roads. The Diamantina Development Road runs south from Mount Isa through Dajarra and Boulia to Bedourie, then swings east across the many channels of the Diamantina River and Cooper Creek through Windorah to the railhead at Quilpie, then on to Charleville, a journey of some 1335 kilometres.

Boulia, proclaimed the capital of the Channel Country, was first settled in 1877. It is 305 kilometres south of Mount Isa and 365 kilometres west of Winton. A friendly, relaxed town on the Burke River, its name comes from the Aboriginal for 'clear water'. Burke and Wills filled their water-bags here. The first mail service was by horse from Cloncurry, and a telegraph station was established in 1884.

Bedourie, 198 kilometres further south, is the administrative centre for the Diamantina Shire, and has a store, school, police station and Flying Doctor medical clinic. It has ample artesian water, without the usual pungent smell, and swimming is popular. The hotel serves petrol as well as beer.

South of Bedourie the Diamantina Road swings east for the partly-sealed drive to **Windorah**, on Cooper Creek. The name means 'place of large fish'. During drought the area is a dustbowl, during the wet a lake. There is a good pub in town and sheep-raising is the only industry.

A good but narrow sealed road leads 237 kilometres east to **Quilpie**, the eastern gateway to the Channel Country. Cattle, sheep and wool are railed to the coast from here. The name derives from the Aboriginal word for the stone curlew, and all but one of the streets have birds' names. Opals have been found here since 1880. Although it is on the Bulloo River, the town's water supply is obtained from a near-boiling artesian bore.

The Kennedy Developmental Road from Winton to Boulia is sealed for most of its 256 kilometres. There are two welcome stops, the Middleton and Hamilton bush pubs. Visitors are sure to be told about the Min Min light, a totally unexplained phenomenon that often appears at night near the old Min Min pub, some 130 kilometres from Boulia. One theory says it is an earth-bound UFO that chases cars and then disappears.

Betoota has one building (a pub) that basks in the centre of a very large, virtually featureless gibber plain. It is the only stop on the lonely 394-kilometre drive from Windorah to Birdsville, and Betoota can be truly welcome. The pub is open every day and sells fuel.

Birdsville, the most isolated settlement in Queensland, is 11 kilometres from the South Australian border, with the Simpson Desert to the west. It is the top end of the Birdsville Track to Marree in South Australia.

Thargomindah is a small settlement on the eastern fringe of the Channel Country, 187 kilometres from Cunnamulla. Around the turn of the century Cobb & Co. was operating regularly to Cunnamulla, Hungerford, Charleville, Noccundra and Eromanga.

Noccundra, 142 kilometres even further west, has a permanent population of three, but they can put you up at the pub and sell you petrol and car parts. Waterholes on the nearby Wilson River are the places for yellow-belly and catfish, brolgas, pelicans, emus and red kangaroos.

Visitors should realise that summer in the Channel Country can become unbearably hot. The best time to go is between April and October, and particularly for the wildflowers, which usually bloom in late August or early September.

For further information on the Channel Country, contact the Outback Qld Tourism Authority, Council Offices, Coronation Dr, Blackall; (076) 57 4255.

See also: Entries in A–Z listing.

Race day, Birdsville

of historic interest. Royal Flying Doctor Service Historical Museum, cnr King and Gregory Sts. Cloister of Plaques (RFDS memorial), Uhr St. Court-house (1884), Shaeffe St. Afghan Cemetery, Henry St. Chinese Cemetery, Flinders Hwy. Agricultural Show held in June; Merry Muster Rodeo in Aug. **In the area:** Rotary Lookout, near Normanton Rd turnoff. Ruins of Great Australia Copper Mine, 2 km south. Alluvial gold workings at Soldiers Cap, 48 km south-west. Kuridala ghost town, 88 km south-east; amethyst fossicking further 8 km and signposted. Walkabout Creek Hotel at McKinlay, 105 km south-east, location for film *Crocodile Dundee*. Burke and Wills cairn on Corella River, 50 km west. Ruins of old goldmining town of Mount Cuthbert, 10 km from Kajabbi (77 km north-west). **Tourist information:** Cloncurry/Mary Kathleen Memorial Park, McIlwraith St; (077) 42 1361. **Accommodation:** 2 hotels, 2 motels, 1 caravan park.
MAP REF. 440 E8

Cooktown   Population 964

Captain James Cook beached the *Endeavour* here in 1770 to repair damage after running aground on a coral reef. Gold was discovered at the Palmer River in 1872 and by 1874 Cooktown was a booming, brawling gold-rush port with 94 busy pubs and a transient population of some 30 000 people (including 2500 Chinese). Cooktown now has only three hotels left and the town's main industry is tourism. Located 240 km north of Cairns, it is the departure point to tour Cape York Peninsula. The surrounding district has good agricultural potential and the town is also supported by prawning, fishing and tin mining. **Of interest:** Cooktown Cemetery, with graves of heroine Mrs Mary Watson, and some 20 000 Chinese who came to work on goldfields. Grassy Hill offers panoramic views across the reef, township and hinterland. James Cook Historical Museum with collection tracing Cooktown's two centuries of history, and Cooktown Sea Museum, featuring maritime history of area; also shell collection. Discovery Festival, featuring re-enactment of Cook's landing, held in June. **In the area:** Bicentennial National Trail (5000 km) for walkers and horseriders runs from Cooktown to Healesville in Vic. Lakefield National Park, 58 km north-west; rivers, lagoons and swamps provide habitat for great variety of wildlife and are crucial area for crocodile conservation. Lizard Island, 90 km north-west, with resort, national park and beautiful secluded beaches. Quinkan Aboriginal Art Galleries near Laura, 145 km west; guided tours of hundreds of

Surfing at Coolangatta

cave paintings. **Tourist information:** Cooktown Sea Museum, cnr Helen and Walker Sts; (070) 69 5209. **Accommodation:** 3 hotels, 6 motels, 3 caravan/camping parks. **See also:** Atherton Tableland.
MAP REF. 436 F1, 438 I9

Coolangatta

Pop. part of Gold Coast

Coolangatta is the most southerly of Qld's coastal towns, with its twin town of Tweed Heads across the border in NSW. All the typical Gold Coast attractions are to be found at both Coolangatta and Tweed Heads. At Point Danger is the Captain Cook Memorial and Lighthouse. **In the area:** Gold Coast Airport at Coolangatta offers joy flights. For those who prefer to keep their feet on the ground, the Tom Beaston Outlook (Razorback Lookout) behind Tweed Heads provides splendid views. **Tourist information:** Beach House, Marine Pde; (075) 36 7765. **Accommodation:** 2 hotels, 2 motels, many holiday units. **See also:** City of the Gold Coast.
MAP REF. 429 R8, 435 Q12

Crows Nest   Population 1097

This small town, 45 km north of Toowoomba, acquired its name from one Jim Crow, an Aboriginal from the Kabi-Kabi tribe who once made his home in a hollow tree near what is now the police station. A life-size memorial in Centenary Park commemorates this legend. **Of interest:** Salts Antiques. John French VC Memorial Library. Carbethon Folk Museum and Pioneer Village. CN Gallery and Tea Rooms. **In the area:** Authentic split-timber and shingle pioneer's hut

north on Crows Nest–Cooyar Rd. Crows Nest Falls National Park, 6 km north (look for sign to 'Valley of Diamonds'); walking tracks to falls and gorge, picnic and camping (above falls) facilities. Ravensbourne National Park, 25 km south. Farm holidays at Listening Ridge host farm. **Tourist information:** 541 Ruthven St, Toowoomba; (076) 32 1988. **Accommodation:** 1 caravan/camping park.
MAP REF. 435 O10

Croydon   Population 229

This Gulf town is 561 km from Cairns. Restoration work within the Croydon Historic Precinct, the remains of the much larger town of the 1800s, is transforming the surviving town into a showpiece. **Of interest:** Old gaol, butcher shop, general store and hospital. Gaslights still stand on footpaths, and old court-house and mining warden's office still have their original furnishings. Outdoor Museum, featuring a display of early mining machinery from age of steam. Self-guided walking tours of town and surrounding areas. Terminus of Normanton to Croydon railway. **Tourist information:** Shire Offices; (077) 45 6185. **Accommodation:** 1 hotel, 1 roadhouse, 1 caravan/camping park. **See also:** Gulf Savannah.
MAP REF. 436 A6, 440 H4

Cunnamulla   Population 1697

A western sheep town renowned for its friendliness and hospitality, Cunnamulla is on the Warrego River, 122 km north of the NSW border. It is the biggest wool-loading station on the Qld railway network, with some 2 million sheep in the area, plus beef cattle and Angora goats. Explorers Sir Thomas Mitchell and Edmund Kennedy were the first white visitors in 1846 and 1847, and by 1879 it had become a town with regular Cobb & Co. services. **Of interest:** In 1880 a daring but disorganised villain called Joseph Wells held up the local bank and tried to escape with the loot, but could not find his horse. Irate locals bailed him up in a nearby tree, demanding justice, and their money back. The tree, in Stockyard St, is still a landmark. Historical Society display in Bicentennial Museum, John St; history of wool-growing district. Cunnamulla–Eulo Opal Festival held in Aug. **In the area:** Wildflowers in spring. Varied birdlife, including black swans, brolgas, pelicans and eagles. Visits to shearing-sheds in season. Farm holidays at Rosevale Station, 20 km north-west of Wyandra. Yowah opal fields, 144 km west via Eulo on Paroo River. **Tourist information:** Cor-dale Enterprises, Jane St; (076) 55 1416. **Accommodation:** 4 hotels, 3 hotel/motels, 1 caravan/camping park. MAP REF. 434 F11

Currumbin   Pop. part of Gold Coast

Situated at the mouth of the Currumbin Creek, this part of the Gold Coast has many attractions for visitors. Of interest: Currumbin Sanctuary, 20 ha reserve, owned by National Trust of Qld; free-ranging animals in open areas, walk-

Feeding rainbow lorikeets, Currumbin Sanctuary

through rainforest aviary with pools and waterfalls, rides through sanctuary on miniature railway. Opposite, Chocolate Expo Factory. **In the area:** The Land of Legend, 3 km south; thousands of dolls displayed in fairytale settings. Olson's Bird Gardens, Currumbin Valley, 9 km west; large landscaped aviaries amid subtropical setting. Mt Cougal National Park, 22 km southwest, at end of Currumbin Creek Rd; rainforest area for bushwalking and picnicking. **Tourist information:** Beach House, Marine Pde, Coolangatta; (075) 36 7765. **Accommodation:** 1 hotel, 8 motels, 2 caravan/camping parks. **See also:** City of the Gold Coast. MAP REF. 429 Q8

Daintree   Population 150

This quaint, unspoilt township lies in the heart of the Daintree River catchment basin surrounded entirely by the McDowall Ranges, 115 km north of Cairns. The area has an abundance of native plant life, birds and exotic tropical butterflies, and Australia's prehistoric reptile, the estuarine crocodile, can be seen lurking in the mangrove-lined creek and tributaries of the Daintree River. **Of interest:** Daintree Timber Museum. Local art and craft shops, restaurants and a truly old-time local store. River cruises operate. **In the area:** Daintree Coffee Plantation, 5 km west. Daintree Butterfly Farm, 2 km south. Wonga-Belle Orchid Garden, 17

km south; 3.5 ha of lush landscaped gardens. Daintree Rainforest Environmental Centre, 11 km north via ferry; boardwalk through rainforest. Cape Tribulation, 35 km north, where rainforest meets reef; bushwalking, crystal-clear creeks and forests festooned with creepers and vines, palm trees, orchids, butterflies and cassowaries. Bloomfield Falls, 85 km north, via Cape Tribulation. **Tourist information:** Macrossan St, Port Douglas; (070) 99 5599. (Also at Marina Mirage, Wharf St, Port Douglas.) **Accommodation:** 1 caravan/camping park. MAP REF. 436 F2, 438 I11

Dalby   Population 8338

Dalby is a pleasant, well-planned country town at the cross-roads of the Warrego, Bunya and Moonie Hwys, 84 km north-west of Toowoomba on the Darling Downs. It is the centre of Australia's richest grain-growing area, and cattle, pigs and sheep further add to the wealth of the district. **Of interest:** Dalby Pioneer Park Museum, Black St; early buildings, household and agricultural items. Obelisk in Edward St marks spot where explorer Henry Dennis camped in 1841. Cactoblastis Memorial Cairn in Myall Creek picnic area pays homage to the voracious Argentinian caterpillar, which eradicated the dreaded prickly pear cactus in 1920s. Dalby Cultural Centre, Drayton St; theatre, cinema, art gallery and restaurant. Harvest Festival held in Oct. **In the area:** Lake Broadwater, 29 km south-west; boating and water-skiing. Bunya Mountains National Park, 60 km north-east. **Tourist information:** Thomas Jack Park, cnr Drayton and Condamine Sts; (076) 62 1066. **Accommodation:** 5 motels, 2 caravan/camping parks. **See also:** Darling Downs. MAP REF. 435 N10

Dirranbandi   Population 523

A small pastoral township and railhead on the Balonne River, Dirranbandi is south-west of St George, close to the NSW border. **Tourist information:** Balonne Shire Council, Victoria St, St George; (076) 25 3222. **Accommodation:** 1 motel, 1 caravan/camping park. MAP REF. 112 D1, 435 J12

Dysart   Population 4039

This new town in the Denham Range, 80 km east of Clermont, has been built near the coal centre of Moranbah to service the Utah open-cut coal mines of Saraji and Norwich Park. The coal is railed to Hay Point, just south of Mackay, for shipment. **Accommodation:** 1 motel/hotel. MAP REF. 435 J2, 437 J13

SUNSHINE COAST

A chain of sun-drenched beaches bathed by the cobalt-blue Pacific stretches from Rainbow Beach southward to Bribie Island to form Queensland's Sunshine Coast. This scenic coastal region, with its average winter temperature of 25°C, its leisurely pace, and its wide variety of natural attractions and sporting facilities, offers an alternative to the more commercialised Gold Coast.

While huge waves thunder in on to white sand beaches to provide year-round surfing, the calmer waters of protected beaches ensure safe swimming, boating and water-skiing. Rivers and streams alive with fish lure the angler, and forest-fringed lakes become perfect picnic spots for the family.

The Sunshine Coast is blessed with many wonders of nature. The coloured sands of Teewah in **Cooloola National Park**, between Tewantin and Rainbow Beach, rise in multicoloured cliffs to over 200 metres. Geologists say that these sandcliffs are over 40 000 years old and claim the main colouring agent is either the result of oxidisation or from the dye of vegetation decay. However, an Aboriginal legend relates that the colours come from a rainbow which was killed by a boomerang when it came to the rescue of a black maiden.

Another marvel of nature is the **Glass House Mountains**, formed by giant cores of long-extinct volcanoes.

Noosaville and **Tewantin**, at the northern end of the region, have facilities for fishing, boating and golf. Poised on the edge of Laguna Bay is the resort town of **Noosa Heads**, with its 430-hectare national park. This coastal park contains a network of walking tracks that wind through rainforests, giving spectacular ocean views of such unusual rock formations as Hell's Gates, Paradise Caves, Lion's Rock, Devil's Kitchen and Witches' Cauldron. The park also houses an animal sanctuary and coastal lakes inhabited by elegant black swans, pelicans, ducks and cranes.

The southernmost town of the Sunshine Coast is **Caloundra**, 'the beautiful place', where Aborigines once came down from the hills to feast on seafood.

The hinterland of the Sunshine Coast is like a huge cultivated garden, covered with pineapples, sugarcane, ginger and citrus, dotted with dairy farms and enclosing within its folds cascading waterfalls, lush rainforests and bubbling streams. Looming majestically behind this garden of plenty is the **Blackall Range**, a world apart with art and craft galleries, Devonshire tea places, comfortable pubs and a feeling of 'olde England'. The scenic drive through the townships of Mapleton, Flaxton, Montville and Maleny is one of the best in south-east Queensland. The **Kondalilla National Park** and **Mapleton Falls National Park** are a must for nature-lovers. Kondalilla, an Aboriginal word meaning 'rushing waters', is aptly named as the 80-metre waterfall drops into a valley of rainforest. The Mapleton Hotel offers authentic country pub hospitality with panoramic views from the traditional Queensland verandah. Visit the miniature English village with its castles, churches, thatched cottages and inns. A number of art and craft cottages surround Montville's Village Green. Take in the view from the picture window at the De'Lisle Gallery while being surrounded by works of art from the Sunshine Coast's best artists. Mary Cairncross Park, at the southern end of the range, gives breathtaking views of the coast and the Glass House Mountains. **Nambour** is conveniently located on the Bruce Highway for trips to the mountains of the Blackall Range or to the beach.

The Sunshine Coast has accommodation to suit all tastes and budgets, from beachfront caravan parks through to luxury five-star international motels. And if you enjoy dining out, there are dozens of fine restaurants where you can titillate your tastebuds.

For more information on the Sunshine Coast, contact Tourism Sunshine Coast Ltd, Alexandra Pde, Alexandra Headland; (008) 07 2041. **See also:** Entries in A–Z listing.

Noosa Heads

Feeding the pelicans, Caloundra

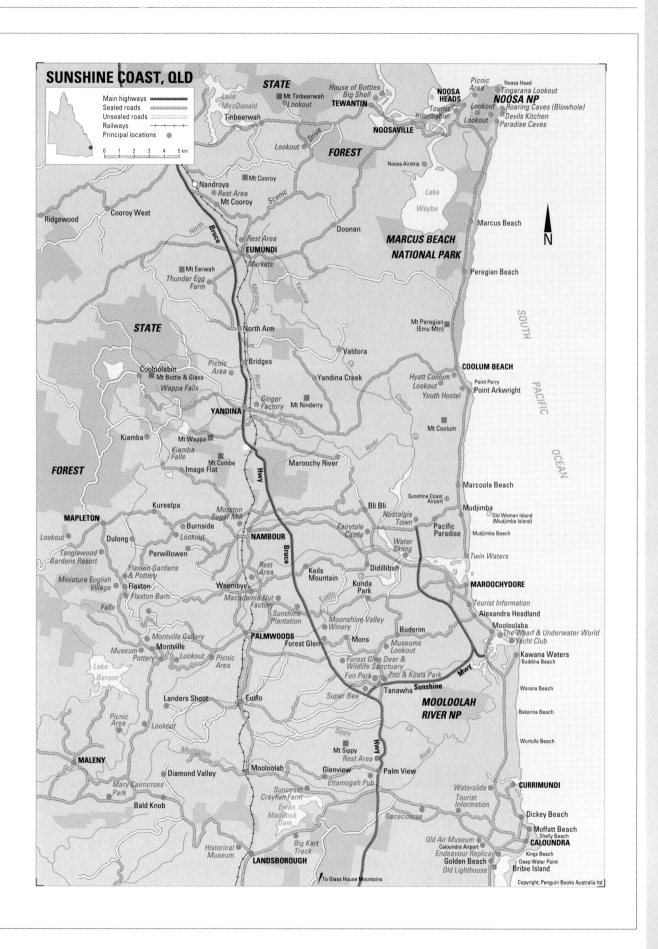

SUNSHINE COAST, QLD

Main highways
Sealed roads
Unsealed roads
Railways
Principal locations

0 1 2 3 4 5 km

STATE

Lake MacDonald

Mt Tinbeerwah
Lookout

House of Bottles
Big Shell

TEWANTIN

Tinbeerwah

NOOSAVILLE

NOOSA HEADS

Picnic Area

Noosa Head
Tingarana Lookout

NOOSA NP

Tourist Information

Lookout

Roaring Caves (Blowhole)
Devils Kitchen
Paradise Caves

Lookout

FOREST

Lookout Drive

Noosa Airstrip

Nandroya

Mt Cooroy

Rest Area
Mt Cooroy

Scenic

Ridgewood

Cooroy West

Doonan

Lake Weyba

Marcus Beach

Marcus Beach

Rest Area

EUMUNDI

Markets

**MARCUS BEACH
NATIONAL PARK**

Peregian Beach

Mt Eerwah
Thunder Egg Farm

North Arm

Valdora

Mt Peregian
(Emu Mtn)

SOUTH

STATE

Cooloolabin
Mt Bottle & Glass
Wappa Falls

Picnic Area

Bridges

Yandina Creek

Hyatt Coolum Lookout
Youth Hostel

COOLUM BEACH

Point Perry
Point Arkwright

Ginger Factory

Mt Ninderry

Mt Coolum

PACIFIC

YANDINA

Kiamba

Mt Wappa

Kiamba Falls
Mt Combe
Image Flat

Maroochy River

OCEAN

FOREST

Kureelpa

MAPLETON

Lookout

Dulong

Burnside

Lookout

Perwillowen

Moreton Sugar Mill

NAMBOUR

Bli Bli

Nostalgia Town

Sunshine Coast Airport

Marcoola Beach

Mudjimba

Old Woman Island
(Mudjimba Island)

Pacific Paradise

Mudjimba Beach

Tanglewood Gardens Resort

Fairytale Castle

Twin Waters

Miniature English Village

Flaxton Gardens & Pottery

Flaxton

Water Skiing

Flaxton Barn

Falls

Woombye

Rest Area

Keils Mountain

Didillibah

MAROOCHYDORE

Kunda Park

Tourist Information
Alexandra Headland

Macadamia Nut Factory

Eudlo

Montville Gallery

Sunshine Plantation

Moonshine Valley Winery

Buderim

Mooloolaba
The Wharf & Underwater World
Yacht Club

Museum

Montville

PALMWOODS

Forest Glen

Mons

Museums Lookout

Kawana Waters
Buddina Beach

Pottery

Lookout

Picnic Area

Forest Glen Deer & Wildlife Sanctuary

Zoo & Koala Park

Warana Beach

Lake Baroon

Fun Park

Sunshine Mwy

Landers Shoot

Eudlo

Super Bee

Tanawha

**MOOLOOLAH
RIVER NP**

Bokarina Beach

Picnic Area

Lookout

Sippy

Wurtulla Beach

MALENY

Diamond Valley

Mooloolah

Mt Sippy
Rest Area

Glenview

Palm View

Waterslide
Tourist Information

CURRIMUNDI

Mary Cairncross Park

Ettamogah Pub

Dickey Beach

Bald Knob

Suncoast Crayfish Farm

Racecourse

Moffatt Beach
Shelly Beach

Ewan Maddock Dam

Qld Air Museum
Caloundra Airport

CALOUNDRA

Historical Museum

Big Kart Track

Endeavour Replica
Golden Beach
Old Lighthouse

Kings Beach

Deep Water Point
Bribie Island

LANDSBOROUGH

To Glass House Mountains

Copyright, Penguin Books Australia ltd

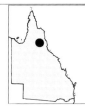

ATHERTON TABLELAND

Few people visiting the peaceful and productive Atherton Tableland realise just what a wild and remote place it was only a hundred years ago. The area was unknown until a colourful and aptly named prospector, James Venture Mulligan, led several expeditions south-west from **Cooktown** between 1874 and 1876, having previously discovered the spectacular Palmer River goldfields in 1873. The northern Aboriginal tribes bitterly resented the miners' intrusion on their land, and during the 1860s and 1870s there were a great many skirmishes between settlers and natives and several massacres.

In 1874 Mulligan, leading a party from Cooktown, named the Hodgkinson and St George Rivers and Mt Mulligan, north of the tobacco town of **Dimbulah**. He returned in 1875 and found a beautiful river flowing north, which he presumed was the Mitchell before it swung west to the Gulf of Carpentaria. He had in fact discovered the Barron River, which eventually flows east to the Pacific coast. Mulligan travelled up the Barron and camped at Granite Creek, where **Mareeba** now stands. He travelled over rich basaltic plains, now the tobacco fields on the Kuranda road, until stopped by dense, impenetrable jungle near what is now **Tolga**. He marvelled at huge cedar and kauri trees, but skirted the jungle westwards and camped three kilometres from the site of **Atherton**. In the

ranges nearby he discovered the Wild River and traces of tin. However, as the nearest ports were Cooktown and Cardwell, some 500 kilometres away, Mulligan considered the area too isolated for tin-mining.

Convinced that there was gold in the Hodgkinson River valley, Mulligan set off again and found extensive strikes as he prospected the valley. The Hodgkinson gold-rush started as soon as he reported his find, most of the diggers coming from Cooktown and the Palmer River. The towns of **Kingsborough** and **Thornborough** quickly sprang up in 1876 between Mt Mulligan and Mareeba. In two years the population was some 10 000, but the field was not as golden as the Palmer.

This caused an unusual situation, the interior being opened up before a direct route to the coast had been discovered and a port founded. During 1876 several difficult tracks were cut down the steep, densely jungled coastal ranges towards Port Douglas and Trinity Bay. Rivalry developed between the two anchorages, with Trinity Bay eventually being dominant and becoming **Cairns**. Some epic hauls up the range were recorded. A double team of bullocks, yoked four abreast, took ten tonnes of mining machinery from Port Douglas to Kingsborough; in 1881, eighty bullocks hauled up the complete battery for the Great Northern tin-mine at **Herberton**. An impressive monument at the foot of

the Cairns–Kuranda road, the Kennedy Highway, commemorates the trailblazers who opened tracks from the Tableland to the coast and the outlet for the Hodgkinson gold.

The railway line from Cairns to **Kuranda**, on the edge of the Tableland, is only thirty-four kilometres long but took four years to build, cost twenty workers their lives, and has fifteen tunnels. It was completed in 1888, and the prosperity of the Atherton Tableland, and Cairns, was assured.

In April 1877, John Atherton settled at the junction of Emerald Creek and the Barron River, and formed Emerald End station. When he found alluvial tin in the headwaters of the creek, he reputedly yelled 'tin-hurroo' to his mate: hence the name of the area, **Tinaroo**. Atherton was interested in cattle, not tin, but he led others to major tin lodes on the Wild River, discovered by Mulligan four years earlier. Mining commenced and the town of Herberton came into existence. The Tate River field was also an important find, and tin proved to be more influential in the development of the area than the short-term excitement of gold.

In 1880, Atherton built a wide-verandahed shanty at Granite Creek, a popular camping ground halfway between Port Douglas and Herberton, used by men flocking to the new field. This became Mareeba. Eventually the railway linked Herberton and Ravenshoe

Malanda Falls

Tin Pannikin museum, Herberton

with Cairns. Today, Herberton is an interesting historic town which holds an annual Tin Festival in August. The local museum, called the Tin Pannikin, is in a classic old (unlicensed) pub, and is a tourist 'must'.

Ravenshoe (pronounced Ravensho, not Raven-shoe) is on the Palmerston Highway, ninety-three kilometres west of Innisfail, and is thirty kilometres south of Atherton on the Kennedy Highway. It is noted for its gemstones and the fine cabinet timbers grown and milled in the area. The Torimba Forest Festival shows off the district's products every October.

Mount Garnet, forty-seven kilometres west of Ravenshoe, is an old copper-mining town where tourists can 'pan the tailings' for alluvial tin.

The rich dairy country around **Malanda**, fourteen kilometres south-east of Atherton, supplies milk for what is known as the longest milk run in the world: to Weipa, Mount Isa, Darwin, and into Western Australia. A Dairy Festival is held every August.

Millaa Millaa, twenty-four kilometres south of Malanda, has a cheese factory, and the Millaa Millaa, Zillie and Elinjaa waterfalls are nearby. McHugh Lookout gives an excellent view of the southern Tableland.

Tinaburra is a popular tourist settlement on Tinaroo Dam. Nearby on the Malanda–Yungaburra road is the amazing and much-photographed Curtain Fig Tree.

For more information on the Atherton Tableland, contact the Far North Qld Promotion Bureau Ltd, 36–38 Aplin St, Cairns; (070) 51 3588.

See also: Entries in A–Z listing.

Railway station, Kuranda

Eidsvold   Population 609
The Eidsvold goldfield was extremely productive for twelve years from 1888 and remains an attractive haunt for fossickers. The district is recognised as the state's best producer of quality beef cattle. **Of interest:** Historical Museum, including Knockbreak Homestead (1850s), and George Schafer and George Schultz Collection of rocks and minerals. **In the area:** Waruma Dam, 48 km north via Burnett Hwy; swimming, sailing and water-skiing. **Tourist information:** Historical Museum, Mt Rose St; (071) 65 1277. **Accommodation:** 1 caravan/camping park.
MAP REF. 435 N7

Emerald   Population 5982
An attractive town, 266 km west of Rockhampton at the junction of the Capricorn and Gregory Hwys, Emerald is rightly called the hub of the Central Qld Highlands. As well as the long-established cattle industry, grain, oilseeds, soybeans and cotton are important. **Of interest:** Shady Moreton Bay fig trees line Clermont and Egerton Sts. Railway station (1901), Clermont St; classified by National Trust. Pioneer Cottage complex, Harris St. Pastoral College, Capricorn Hwy. **In the area:** Gregory coalfields, 54 km north-east. Fairbairn Dam, 19 km south, for picnics and water sports. **Tourist information:** Clermont St; (079) 82 4142. **Accommodation:** 7 motels, 3 caravan/camping parks. **See also:** Capricorn.
MAP REF. 435 J3

Emu Park   Population 1528
On the way to this pleasant seaside resort, 45 km north-east of Rockhampton, is St Christopher's Chapel, built by the US Army in 1942. Emu Park has excellent picnic spots and a safe beach. **Of interest:** Historical Museum. On headland overlooking Keppel Bay, unusual and graceful 'singing ship' memorial to Captain Cook, who discovered bay on voyage up east coast in May 1770. Memorial represents a billowing sail, mast and rigging. Hidden organ pipes create musical sounds with sea breezes. **In the area:** Koorana Crocodile Farm, Emu Park–Rockhampton Rd, 20 km west; boardwalk viewing on guided tours. **Tourist information:** Ross Creek Roundabout, Yeppoon; (079) 39 4888 **Accommodation:** 2 motels, 1 caravan/camping park.
MAP REF. 435 N3

Eromanga   Population 55
A centre for extensive oil exploration, 106 km west of Quilpie, the refinery at Eromanga produces around 1.5 million barrels of oil a year. Named from an

Aboriginal word meaning 'hot, windy plain', Eromanga is reputedly the furthest town from the sea in Australia. **Of interest:** Royal Hotel, once Cobb & Co. staging-post, with some original 19th-century buildings. **Tourist information:** Outback Qld Tourism Authority, Council Offices, Coronation Dr, Blackall; (076) 57 4255. **Accommodation:** 1 hotel, 1 caravan/camping park.
MAP REF. 434 C9

Esk   Population 785
Esk, in the Upper Brisbane Valley, is the largest town within the Esk Shire and known for its lakes and dams. **In the area:** Somerset Dam and Lake Wivenhoe, source of Brisbane's main water supply, and Atkinson Dam — all popular swimming and boating spots. Lake Wivenhoe, 70 km north-west of Brisbane, picnic/barbecue facilities and restaurant; also main centre for championship rowing in state. At Coominya, 22 km south-east of Esk: historic Bellevue Homestead; also camel races held in Sept. Further north in shire, some of finest grazing country in Brisbane Valley; this is 'deer country', where progeny of small herd of deer presented to Qld by Queen Victoria in 1873 still roam. **Tourist information:** Shire Offices, 2 Redbank St; (075) 84 1200. **Accommodation:** 9 hotels, 6 motels, 4 caravan/camping parks.
MAP REF. 424 D6, 435 P10

Eulo   Population 60
Once the main centre for opal-mining in the area, Eulo lies near the Paroo River, 64 km west of Cunnamulla. **Of interest:** Eulo Queen Hotel; owes its name to Isobel Robinson (nee Richardson), who ran hotel and virtually reigned over opal fields at turn of century. Paroo Lizard Race Track, venue for World Lizard Racing Championships, held Aug.–Sept., next to hotel. Destructo Cockroach Monument commemorates death of racing cockroach. Eulo Date Farm, west of town; enquire at caravan park for inspection. **In the area:** Mud Springs, 9 km west on Thargomindah Rd; possible natural safety valves for pressure generated by Great Artesian Basin. Currawinya National Park, 100 km south-west; bird-watching and fishing. **Tourist information:** Outback Qld Tourism Authority, Shire Offices, Coronation Dr, Blackall; (076) 57 4255. **Accommodation:** 1 hotel, 1 caravan/camping park.
MAP REF. 434 F11

Gatton   Population 4597
First settled in the 1840s, this thriving agricultural town in the Lockyer Valley is mid-way between Ipswich and

Toowoomba, and 96 km west of Brisbane on the Warrego Hwy. Small-crop farming, dairy, beef cattle, pig and calf-raising, and sawmilling are the main activities of the area, which also includes the towns of Grantham, Helidon and Wilcott. **In the area:** Qld Agricultural College, now part of Queensland Univ., 5 km east; opened 1897. Helidon, 14 km west, noted for its spa water; also for Helidon freestone, used in many Brisbane buildings. Grantham, 7 km south-west, renowned for its fresh fruit and vegetables; many roadside stalls offer locally grown produce. **Tourist information:** Apex Lake Dr; (074) 62 3430. **Accommodation:** 3 hotels, 2 motels, 3 caravan/camping parks. **See also:** Darling Downs.
MAP REF. 424 B11, 435 P10

Gayndah   Population 1747

Gayndah claims to be Qld's oldest town, having been founded in 1848. It is on the Burnett River and the Burnett Hwy, just over 100 km due west of Maryborough. An Orange Festival is held every odd year, on the Queen's Birthday weekend. **Of interest:** Original school (1863), still in use. Several homesteads in district built in 1850s. Main street location for film *The Mango Tree*. Historical Museum, Simon St; includes Ban Ban Springs homestead. **In the area:** Ban Ban Springs, 26 km south; natural spring and popular picnic area. Claude Warton Weir Recreation Area, 3 km west; fishing and picnics. **Tourist information:** Cnr Mulgrave and Bourbong Sts, Bundaberg; (071) 52 2333. **Accommodation:** 4 motels, 2 caravan/camping parks.
MAP REF. 435 O7

Georgetown   Population 324

A township on the Gulf Developmental Road to Croydon and Normanton, which was once one of many small gold-mining towns on the Etheridge Goldfield. The area is now noted for its gemstones, especially agate and onyx. Georgetown is also a trans-shipping centre for beef road-trains. **In the area:** Gemfields at Agate Creek, 70 km south-west, and O'Briens Creek, 60 km north-east. Tallaroo hot springs, 100 km east. Undara Volcano National Park, 135 km east. **Tourist information:** Etheridge Shire Council; (070) 62 1233. **Accommodation:** 1 hotel, 1 motel, 2 caravan/camping parks. **See also:** Gulf Savannah.
MAP REF. 436 C6

Gin Gin   Population 918

Some of Qld's oldest cattle properties are in the area of this pastoral town on the Bruce Hwy, 52 km west of Bundaberg. **Of interest:** The Residence, Mulgrave St; former police sergeant's home housing district's pioneering memorabilia. **In the area:** Mystery Craters, 17 km north-east; curious formation of 35 craters, estimated to be about 25 million years old. Yellow Windmills Nursery and Goat Farm, 21 km north. Lake Monduran, 24 km north, held back by Fred Haigh Dam, Qld's second largest; boating and picnic facilities. **Tourist information:** Cnr Mulagrave and Bourbong Sts, Bundaberg; (071) 52 2333. **Accommodation:** 2 motels, 1 caravan/camping park.
MAP REF. 435 O6

Gladstone   Population 22 033

Matthew Flinders discovered Port Curtis, Gladstone's impressive deep water harbour, in 1802, but it was not until the 1960s that its potential began to be utilised. As an outlet for Central Qld's mineral and agricultural wealth, Gladstone, 550 km north of Brisbane, is now one of Australia's most prosperous seaboard cities. Its harbour is one of Australia's busiest, handling more shipping tonnage per annum than Sydney. One reason for this growth is the opening-up of the almost inexhaustible coal supplies in the hinterland. Another is that the world's largest single alumina plant is at Parsons Point, operated by the multinational-backed Queensland Alumina Limited. Millions of tonnes of bauxite from Weipa on the Gulf of Carpentaria are processed annually into millions of tonnes of alumina, the 'half-way stage' of aluminium. Comalco has built an aluminium smelter at Boyne Island. A multi-million power station has been built in Gladstone to supply power to the alumina refinery and smelter, as well as feeding into the state's electricity grid. Chemical processing is a new regional industry. Gladstone's most important tourist feature is its proximity to the southern section of the Great Barrier Reef. The city is renowned for its seafood: mud crabs and prawns, and has won the state Tidy Towns Competition six times. **Of interest:** Self-guided Gladstone Visitor Circuit, by car or foot. Historic Kullaroo House (1911) and Grand Hotel (1897), Goondoon St. Gladstone Regional Art Gallery and Museum, cnr Goondoon and Bramston Sts. Potter's Place, art gallery and craft shop, Dawson Hwy. Tondoon Botanic Gardens, end Glenlyon St. Picnic/barbecue facilities at Barney Point Beach and Friend Park, Barney St. Also at Reg Tanna Park, Glenlyon St, with Railway Dam. Waterfall at bottom of Auckland Hill, end Auckland St, floodlit at night; views of harbour and islands from Auckland Hill Lookout. Radar Hill Lookout, Goondoon St, Round Hill Lookout, West Gladstone. Auckland Inlet, anchorage alongside James Cook Park, finishing-line for annual Brisbane to Gladstone yacht race, highlight of 10-day Harbour Festival held every Easter. **In the area:** Tours of Gladstone Power Station, north of town. Curtis Island, Gladstone Harbour; family recreation area. Lake Awoonga, 30 km south; picnic and camping areas, water-based recreation, walking trail and varied wildlife. Port Curtis Historical Village, 26 km south-west at Calliope River. **Tourist information:** 56 Goondoon St; (079) 72 4000. **Accommodation:** 21 motels, 7 hotel/motels, 7 caravan/camping parks. **See also:** Gladstone Region.
MAP REF. 435 N4

Goondiwindi   Population 4103

This attractive and busy country town on the Cunningham Hwy (which continues from the Newell) is on the Qld/NSW border and the Macintyre River, which was discovered by explorer

THURSDAY ISLAND

An unusual place with a magnificent winter climate, Thursday Island is Queensland's most northerly administration centre. Situated 35 kilometres north-west off the tip of Cape York Peninsula in the Torres Strait, it is a colourful outpost. Its population of around 2900 is made up of Europeans, in the minority amongst the native islanders, Malays, Polynesians, Chinese and Japanese. The Harbours and Marine Department's Torres Strait Pilot Service operates from its excellent harbour, once the base for 150 pearling luggers.

For further information on Thursday Island, contact the Far North Qld Promotion Bureau Ltd, 36–38 Aplin St, Cairns; (070) 51 3588.

CAPE YORK

The Cape York Peninsula is a vast triangular area as large as Victoria, with **Cairns** in the lower east corner, **Normanton** in the lower west, and **Thursday Island** as a dot at the northern tip. It is virtually uninhabited except for isolated cattle stations, several Aboriginal communities, and a string of small settlements along the telegraph-line to **Bamaga** at the northern tip. Areas in the north of the peninsula are being considered as a site for the world's first commercial spaceport.

Cape York was first explored during the 1840s and the 1860s by the Jardine brothers, John Bradford, Robert Jack, and the ill-fated Edmund Kennedy and his famous Aboriginal guide Jacky Jacky. Little has changed since then. Vegetation varies from gums and ant-hills in the south to swamps and jungle in the north. Many areas of the Cape are national parks and a sanctuary for much of Australia's unique wildlife, including crocodiles, orchids and insect-eating pitcher plants. Further information and permits may be obtained from National Parks and Wildlife Service, Abbot St, Cairns; (070) 51 9811.

There are two distinct seasons: the wet and the dry. During the wet virtually all road transport stops and the only movement is by regular flights with Australian Airlines into Bamaga. Some fifty kilometres on a dirt track brings the comfortable Pajinka Wilderness Lodge, managed by the Injinoo Aboriginal Community, for those who don't want to 'rough it'. **There are almost no sealed roads or bridges in the area.**

All Aboriginal communities are self-sufficient and may be visited, but it is essential that a permit be obtained in writing beforehand. The main settlements are Lockhart River and Portland Roads on the east coast; Bamaga at the tip; and Edward River, Weipa South, and Aurukun on the Gulf.

For the motorist with an adventurous spirit, the Cape is the ideal place to go exploring. A reliable and well-equipped four-wheel-drive vehicle is essential for this area, preferably with a winch. It is possible to drive north from Cairns or Mareeba to Bamaga through Laura and Coen. The Royal Automobile Club of Queensland provides an excellent map and information sheet and it is essential

reading before an expedition north is planned. **Conditions on the track are unpredictable and the RACQ or police at Cairns should be contacted before heading north.** August to October are the recommended travel months. It should be realised that there are limited facilities and fuel north of Coen. You can drive for days without seeing another car. The Laura, Kennedy, Stewart, Archer, Wenlock, Dulhunty and Jardine Rivers must be forded. During good dry conditions it is possible to take a conventional car, with care, north to Coen and west to Weipa.

Weipa, on the Gulf of Carpentaria, has the world's largest deposits of bauxite, the raw material for aluminium. It is mined and shipped to the huge alumina plant at Gladstone on the central Queensland coast. The red bauxite cliffs were first seen by the Dutch explorer Captain Willem Jansz in 1606. Comalco offers conducted tours of the operation. Direct access to Weipa is by regular Ansett flights from Cairns.

For further information on Cape York, contact the Far North Qld Promotion Bureau Ltd, 36–38 Aplin St, Cairns; (070) 51 3588.

Aerial view of Cape York Peninsula

Allan Cunningham in 1827. The Aboriginal word 'goonawinna' means 'resting place of the birds'. The district's economy is based on cattle and grain-growing industries, supported by irrigation in the area. The Spring Festival in October coincides with the blooming of oleanders, jacarandas and silky oaks. **Of interest:** Botanic Gardens (25 ha); access from Barwon Hwy, 1 km north-west. Sculpture of racehorse Gunsynd, the 'Goondiwindi Grey', in Apex Park, McLean St. Museum in old Customs House, opposite park. Historic Victoria Hotel, Marshall St. Univ. of Qld Pastoral Veterinary College, Leichhardt Hwy (north). Tours of Bulk Grains depot and cotton gin. **In the area:** Boobera Lagoon, 20 km south-west into NSW; wildlife sanctuary. **Tourist information:** McLean St; (076) 71 2653. **Accommodation:** 7 motels, 3 caravan/camping parks.
MAP REF. 112 I1, 435 M12

Gordonvale   Population 2341
This town is only 24 km south of Cairns. **In the area:** Gillies Hwy, with 295 bends, leads west to Atherton. Bellenden Ker National Park, 10 km south; spectacular views from summit of Walsh's Pyramid. The Mulgrave Rambler, 15 km steam train ride along cane railway system through canefields and rainforest; includes visit to spectacular orchid nursery. Hambledon Sugar Mill at Edmonton, 16 km north. **Tourist information:** Cnr Sheridan and Aplin Sts, Cairns; (070) 51 3588. **Accommodation:** 4 hotels, 1 caravan/camping park.
MAP REF. 436 G4, 439 G10

Gympie   Population 10 772
The city of Gympie started with the 'Great Australian Gold-Rush', 1867 version, led by James Nash. The field proved extremely rich, and some four million ounces had been found by the time the gold petered out in the 1920s. By then dairying and agriculture were well established and Gympie continued to prosper. Gympie, on the Mary River, 182 km north of Brisbane by the Bruce Hwy, is the major provincial city servicing the Cooloola region. It is an attractive city, with jacarandas, flowering silky oaks, cassias, poincianas and flame trees very much in evidence. **Of interest:** Woodworks Museum, Frazer Rd. Gympie Gold Rush Festival held mid-Oct. **In the area:** Goldmining Museum at Monkland, 5 km south; nearby, cottage of Andrew Fisher, first Queenslander to become Prime Minister (1908). Part of the Bicentennial National Trail runs through Kilkivan, 51 km north-west. Goomeri, 26 km further west; known as 'clock town' because of unique

memorial clock in town centre. Borumba Dam, for picnics and water sports, 51 km south-west via Imbil and Imbil Forest Drive. Rock-pools and views at Mothar Mountain. Peaceful fishing resort of Tin Can Bay and small resort of Rainbow Beach with its coloured sands, 77 km east through vast pine forests. Ferry to Fraser Island operates from Inskip Point north of Rainbow Beach. Cooloola National Park, 50 km east. Mary Valley Scenic Way runs south between Gympie and Maleny via Kenilworth. **Tourist information:** Bruce Hwy, Lake Alford; (074) 82 5444. **Accommodation:** 14 hotels, 7 motels, 4 caravan/camping parks.
MAP REF. 426 G3, 435 P8

Hervey Bay   Population 14 410
Hervey (pronounced Harvey) Bay is the large area of water between Maryborough and Bundaberg that is protected by Fraser Island. The name is also that of a thriving city which comprises the pleasant strip of seaside resorts along its southern shore, some 34 km north-east of Maryborough, including Gatakers Bay, Pialba, Scarness, Torquay, Urangan, Burrum Heads, Toogoom, Howard and Torbanlea. An ideal climate makes the area popular with residents of nearby Maryborough and Bundaberg, and during the winter months there is a regular influx of visitors from the south. Hervey Bay is actively promoted as 'Australia's family aquatic playground'. As there is no surf, swimming is safe even for children. Fishing is the main recreation and boats may be hired and fresh yabbies caught for bait. **Of interest:** Hervey Bay Historical Society Museum, Zephyr St, Scarness, recalls pioneer days. Cairn at Dayman Point, Urangan, commemorates landing by Matthew Flinders in 1799. Pier 1 km long at Urangan, used by fishermen. Sun. markets at Urangan and Nikenbar. Yachting regatta held at Scarness every Easter. Other attractions include Neptune's Aquarium, Nature World shark show and Vic Hislop's Wildlife Park. Day trips to Fraser Island. Humpback whales visit Hervey Bay from early Aug. to mid-Oct. on their annual migration; viewing cruises available. Humpback Whale Festival held in Aug. **In the area:** Hervey Bay Marine Park. Quiet seaside resorts at Toogoom and Burrum Heads, 15 km north. Historic Brooklyn House at Howard, 25 km north-west. Mining museum at Torbanlea, 20 km west. Susan River Homestead, 15 km east, for farm holidays. **Tourist information:** Polymetric Products, Old Maryborough Rd, Pialba; (071) 28 2603. **Accommodation:** 4 hotel/motels, 18 motels, 24 caravan parks.
MAP REF. 435 Q6

Home Hill   Population 3286
Sister town to Ayr, Home Hill is on the south side of the Burdekin River, 84 km south of Townsville. The towns are joined by a high-level bridge as the river is liable to flood. **Of interest:** Tours of rice and sugar mills. Ashworth's Rock Shop and Museum; also art and craft. **In the area:** Groper Creek, 16 km west, is noted for its fishing and giant mudcrabs; camping and picnic areas. **Tourist information:** Community Information Centre, Queen St, Ayr; (077) 83 2888. **Accommodation:** 3 hotels, 1 motel, 2 caravan/camping parks.
MAP REF. 436 I8

Hughenden   Population 1791
The explorer William Landsborough camped at this spot on the Flinders River in 1862, while unsuccessfully searching for the missing Burke and Wills expedition. A year later a cattle station was established, and Hughenden came into existence. The town is on the Townsville-Mount Isa rail line and the Flinders Hwy, 250 km west of Charters Towers. It is a major centre for wool, cattle and grain produced in the Flinders Shire. **Of interest:** Dinosaur Museum, Gray St; replica of first entire fossil found in Australia. Dinosaur Festival held in Aug. in even years. **In the area:** Views from Mt Walker Lookout, 8 km south. Porcupine Gorge National Park, 65 km north; 'mini-Grand Canyon'. Gemstone fossicking at Cheviot Hills, 200 km north. **Tourist information:** Shire Offices, Gray St; (077) 41 1288. **Accommodation:** 2 hotel/motels, 2 motels, 2 caravan/camping parks.
MAP REF. 436 D10

Ilfracombe   Population 350
This town, 28 km east of Longreach on the Landsborough Hwy, was developed in 1891 as a transport nucleus for Wellshot Station, the largest sheep station in the world (in terms of stock numbers) at that time; the head station was in itself the size of a town. The first Qld motorised mail service departed from Ilfracombe in 1910. **Of interest:** Folk Museum. **Tourist information:** Outback Qld Tourist Authority, Council Offices, Coronation Dr, Blackall; (076) 57 4255. **Accommodation:** 1 hotel.
MAP REF. 434 E3

Ingham   Population 5202
A major sugar and sightseeing town near the waterways of the Hinchinbrook Channel, Ingham is on the Bruce Hwy, 111 km north of Townsville. The town has a strong Italian and Spanish Basque cultural background. **Of interest:** Macknade Mill, oldest sugar mill still operating on original site. Victoria Sugar Mill, largest

in southern hemisphere; guided tours in crushing season, June–Nov. **In the area:** Wallaman Falls National Park, 51 km west; noted for spectacular scenery, excellent camping, swimming and picnic spots, and 300-m-high Wallaman Falls. Jourama Falls National Park, 25 km south. Herbert River Gorge National Park, 100 km north-west. Mt Fox, extinct volcano, 65 km south-west. Forrest Beach, 20 km east, 16 km of sandy beaches overlooking Palm Group of islands; stinger net swimming enclosures installed in summer. Halifax, 20 km northeast on banks of Herbert River, base for fishing holidays; Taylor's Beach, 8 km away, popular family seaside spot. Hinchinbrook and Orpheus resort islands offshore. **Tourist information:** Bruce Hwy; (077) 76 1381. **Accommodation:** 8 hotels, 2 motels, 2 caravan/camping parks. MAP REF. 436 G6

Inglewood
Population 966

An early hostelry called Brown's Inn grew into the town of Inglewood, in the southwestern corner of the Darling Downs, 108 km west of Warwick. Beef cattle and sheep are raised, and lucerne, grain and fodder crops are irrigated from Coolmunda Dam, 20 km east, which attracts boating enthusiasts as well as many pelicans and swans. **Accommodation:** 2 motels, 3 caravan/camping parks. MAP REF. 113 K1, 435 N12

Injune
Population 395

This small cattle and timber town, 89 km north of Roma, is the southern gateway to the Carnarvon National Park. Explorer Ludwig Lechhardt called the region 'ruined Castle Valley'. **In the area:** Carnarvon National Park, 154 km north; spectacular sandstone scenery with gorges and escarpments, and major Aboriginal art sites: Art Gallery and Cathedral Cave. Carnarvon Gorge Oasis Lodge adjacent to park. **Tourist information:** BP Central, Bowen St, Roma; (076) 22 3399. **Accommodation:** 1 motel. MAP REF. 435 J7

Innisfail
Population 8113

Innisfail is a prosperous, colourful town on the banks of the North and South Johnstone Rivers, 92 km south of Cairns. Sugar has been grown here since the early 1880s and its contribution to the area is celebrated with an annual gala Sugar Festival held for nine days from the last Saturday in August. The famous Opera Festival is held in December. Besides sugar, bananas and other tropical fruit are grown, beef cattle are raised, and the town has a prawn and reef fishing fleet. **Of interest:** Local history museum, Edith St. Chinese Joss House, Owen St. **In the area:** Flying Fish Point and Ella Bay, 5 km north, for swimming and camping. Palm-fringed shoreline of Bramston Beach, 23 km north. Johnstone River

Crocodile Farm, 8 km north-east. Canoe tours on North Johnstone River. Mt Bartle Frere (1611 m), 25 km north-west, Qld's highest peak, with track to summit. Johnstone River Gorge, accessed from Palmerston Hwy, 18 km west; walking tracks lead to several waterfalls. Tea plantation at Nerada, 28 km west. Palmerston National Park, 30 km west, from where road leads to Atherton Tableland. Australian Sugar Museum at Mourilyan, 7 km south. Etty Bay, 15 km south, with fine beach and picnic area; also natural history museum. Innisfail is excellent base for exploration of quieter lagoons and islands (including Dunk) of Great Barrier Reef. **Tourist information:** Johnstone Shire Regional Information Centre, Australian Sugar Museum, Bruce Hwy, Mourilyan; (070) 63 2306. **Accommodation:** 7 motels, 4 caravan/camping parks. MAP REF. 436 G4

Ipswich
Population 65 346

In 1827 a convict settlement was established on the Bremer River to work the limestone deposits in the nearby hills. The limestone was ferried down-river to Brisbane in whaleboats. In 1828 explorer Allan Cunningham used Limestone Hills, as the settlement was known, as the starting-point for his exploration of the Darling Downs to the west. In 1842 it was renamed Ipswich after the city in Suffolk,

North Johnstone River, Innisfail

England, and the enormous coal deposits in the area speeded development. The railway from Brisbane arrived in 1876, displacing the busy river trade and Cobb & Co. services. Ipswich is 40 km south-west of Brisbane on the way to both Toowoomba and Warwick. Coal-mining, earthenware works, sawmills, abattoirs and foundries make it a major industrial centre. **Of interest:** Many historic buildings, including Claremont (1858), Gooloowar (1864), Ginn Cottage and grammar school. **In the area:** Northeast: College's Crossing (7 km), Mt Crosby (12 km) and Lake Manchester (22 km), popular swimming and picnic spots. Redbank Railway, 10 km east. Restored historic homestead Wolston House at Wacol, 16 km east. Swanbank Power Station, 12 km south-east; trains run by Qld Pioneer Steam Railway Co-op, first weekend Apr.–Dec. St Brigid's Church, Rosewood, 20 km south-west; largest wooden church in South Pacific. **Tourist information:** Council Offices, South St; (07) 280 9811. **Accommodation:** 4 hotel/motels, 7 motels, 7 caravan/camping parks.
MAP REF. 424 H12, 435 P11

Isisford   Population 150

Established in 1877 by travelling hawkers William and James Whitman, Isisford is 117 km south of Longreach. First called Wittown, the name of the town was changed in 1880 to recall the ford in the nearby Barcoo River and the proximity of Isis Downs Station homestead. **Of interest:** Bicentennial Museum. **In the area:** Huge, semi-circular prefabricated shearing shed, erected in 1913, at Isis Downs Station, 20 km east; largest in Australia. Visits by prior arrangement; (076) 58 8203. Oma Waterhole, 10 km west, popular spot for fishing and water sports. **Tourist information:** Shire Offices; (076) 58 8277. **Accommodation:** 1 hotel.
MAP REF. 434 E4

Julia Creek   Population 624

A small cattle and rail township on the Flinders Hwy, Julia Creek is 134 km east of Cloncurry. A sealed road runs north to Normanton in the Gulf Savannah. The town is an important cattle-trucking centre. **Of interest:** McIntyre Museum, Burke St. Julia Creek Rodeo held in May. **Tourist information:** Shire Offices, Julia St; (077) 46 7166. **Accommodation:** 2 hotels, 1 motel, 1 caravan/camping park.
MAP REF. 436 A10, 440 G8

Jundah   Population 100

Jundah (an Aboriginal word for 'women'), 219 km south-west of Longreach, was

Local market, Kuranda

gazetted as a town in 1880. For about 20 years the area was important for opal-mining, but lack of water eventually caused the mines to close. **Of interest:** Barcoo Historical Museum. **In the area:** Jundah Opal Fields, 27 km north-west. **Tourist information:** Outback Qld Tourism Authority, Shire Offices, Coronation Dr, Blackall; (076) 57 4255. **Accommodation:** 1 hotel, 1 caravan/camping park.
MAP REF. 434 C5, 441 I5

Karumba   Population 535

Karumba, 69 km north from Normanton, is situated at the mouth of the Norman River and is the centre of the prawning industry in the Gulf of Carpentaria. A barramundi fishing industry also operates out of the town. **Of interest:** Slipway once used by Empire Flying Boats Service, which ran from Sydney to England. Old cemetery on road to Karumba Point. **In the area:** Town is surrounded by flat wetlands extending 30 km inland, habitat of saltwater crocodiles and many species of birds, including brolgas and cranes. Karumba is easiest point of access to the Gulf; charter vessels available for fishing and exploration of the Gulf and Norman River. **Tourist information:** Carpentaria Shire Council, Normanton; (077) 45 1166. **Accommodation:** 1 hotel/motel, 1 caravan/camping park. **See also:** Gulf Savannah.
MAP REF. 438 A13, 440 E3

Kenilworth   Population 779

West of the Blackall Range, through the Obi Obi Valley, is Kenilworth, famous for its Kenilworth Country Foods handcrafted cheeses. This enterprise, began

as the Kraft cheese factory closed and six employees mortgaged their homes to start the venture. **Of interest:** Kev Francis Movie Museum and Photo Workshop, on Eumundi Rd; 2 hr shows. **In the area:** Little Yabba Creek, 8 km south; picnic spot with bellbirds. Lake Borumba, 32 km north-west; sailing and water-skiing. Imbil Forest Drive from Lake Borumba, 39 km north, through forests and farmlands to Gympie. **Tourist information:** Alexandra Pde, Alexandra Headland; (008) 07 2041. **Accommodation:** 1 hotel, 1 motel, camping facilities.
MAP REF. 426 H9, 435 P9

Killarney   Population 779

This attractive small town is on the Condamine River, 34 km east of Warwick, and very close to the NSW border. **In the area:** Noteworthy mountain scenery. Dagg's and Brown's waterfalls, 1–2 km south. Cherrabah Homestead Resort, 7 km south; horseriding, golf, sailing and bushwalking. Queen Mary Falls National Park, 7 km east. **Tourist information:** 49 Albion St (New England Hwy), Warwick; (076) 61 3122. **Accommodation:** 1 caravan/camping park, 1 resort.
MAP REF. 428 B10

Kingaroy   Population 6362

This prosperous agricultural town is famous for its peanuts and for its best-known citizen, Sir Johannes (Joh) Bjelke-Petersen, former Premier of Qld. Maize, barley, oats, wheat, soy and navy beans are grown, and specialised agricultural equipment is manufactured. Kingaroy is 233 km north-west of Brisbane and its giant peanut silos are a distinctive landmark. Kingaroy also claims the title 'Baked Bean Capital of Australia', with 75% of Australia's baked, more correctly called navy, beans grown in the district. **Of interest:** Kingaroy Bicentennial Heritage Museum, Haly St; videos on peanut and navy bean industries. **In the area:** Mt Wooroolin scenic lookout, 3 km west. Bunya Mountains National Park, 56 km south. **Tourist information:** Haly St (opp. silos); (071) 62 3199. **Accommodation:** 5 motels, 2 caravan/camping parks. MAP REF. 435 O9

Kuranda   Population 646
This 'village in the rainforest' at the top of the Macalister Range is best known to tourists who have taken the 34 km trip from Cairns on the 100-year-old scenic railway. **Of interest:** Railway station with platforms adorned by lush ferns and orchids. Wildlife Noctarium; rainforest animals normally only active at night. Butterfly Sanctuary, said to be world's largest with over 2000 butterflies in aviary; also static museum display. Tjapukai Aboriginal Dance Theatre; two performances daily. Local markets held Wed.–Fri. and Sun. **In the area:** Guided tours of river and rainforest. Kuranda Rainforestation offers army-duck rides in rainforest, while Paradise in the Rainforest offers scenic rides on 'tractor train'. Barron Falls, spectacular after heavy rain. **Tourist information:** Cnr Sheridan and Aplin Sts, Cairns; (070) 51 3588. **Accommodation:** 2 hotels, 3 motels, 1 caravan/camping park. **See also:** Atherton Tableland; The Far North. MAP REF. 439 E6

Kynuna   Population 22
On the Landsborough Hwy, 161 km north-west of Winton, Kynuna was established in the 1860s and was a staging-point for Cobb & Co. coaches. **Of interest:** Kynuna's only hotel, the famous Blue Heeler. **In the area:** Combo Waterhole, scene of the events described in 'Waltzing Matilda', 14 km south-east on western side of old Winton–Kynuna road. **Tourist information:** Blue Heeler Hotel, Landsborough Hwy; (077) 46 8650. **Accommodation:** 1 hotel/motel, 2 caravan/camping parks. MAP REF. 436 A11, 440 G10

Laidley   Population 2000
Laidley, 75 km from Brisbane, is located between Ipswich and Gatton, in the Lockyer Valley. It is the principal town for the Laidley Shire, a rural area of the Greater Brisbane Region. **Of interest:** Historic home, Das Neumann Haus (1893); tourist centre, arts and craft, art gallery.

Festival Week and Fire in the Valley Duathon held in Sept. **In the area:** Laidley Pioneer Village, 1 km south; original buildings from old township. Lake Dyer, 1 km west, with picnic/barbecue facilities; adjacent, Narda Lagoon, flora and fauna sanctuary. Lake Clarendon, 17 km north-west. **Tourist information:** Cnr William and Patrick Sts; (074) 65 1805. **Accommodation:** Limited. MAP REF. 424 D12

Landsborough   Population 822
Just off the Bruce Hwy, Landsborough is 9 km south of the Caloundra turn-off. **Of interest:** Historical Museum. Bottle, gemstone and shell museum. De Maine Pottery. **In the area:** Queensland Reptile and Fauna Park, 2 km south. **Accommodation:** 1 caravan/camping park. MAP REF. 427 K12

Logan City   Population 132 000
Captain Patrick Logan, one of the founders and first Commandant of the Moreton Bay Penal Settlement, first discovered the area now known as Logan City. On 21 August 1862 he reported the sighting of a 'very considerable river which empties itself into the Moreton Bay … I have named it the Darling'. This river later became the Logan River, an acknowledgment by Governor Darling of Logan's 'zeal and efficient service'. Considering Logan's involvement with its discovery, it seemed natural for the 240 sq. km region to be named after him when it was first declared a shire in 1978, and when it became a city in 1981. Midway between Brisbane and the Gold Coast, Logan is Qld's fastest growing city. Using its close proximity to both Brisbane and the Gold Coast (a little more than half an hour from each), it has a strong and vigorous economic base certainly influenced by its location. **Of interest:** Mayes Cottage (1871), Mawarra St; National Trust Building, once home of early pioneers. Daisy Hill Forest Park (430 ha), Daisy Hill Rd; picnics, bushwalking and horseriding. Kingston Butter Factory Community Art Centre, Milky Way, off Kingston Rd. Logan Hyperdome, off Pacific Hwy; largest shopping complex in Australia. **Tourist information:** 4195 Pacific Hwy, Loganholme; (07) 801 3400. **Accommodation:** 4 motels, 11 caravan/camping parks. MAP REF. 435 Q11

Longreach   Population 3159
Longreach may have a relatively small human population, but if you count the 800 000 sheep and 20 000 beef cattle in the area, it becomes the most important and

prosperous town in the Central-West. It is a friendly modern town of broad streets (and broad hats!) on the Thomson River, some 700 km by road or rail west of Rockhampton. It was here, in 1870, that Harry Redford, better known as Captain Starlight, with four mates rounded up 1000 head of cattle and drove them 2400 km into SA over wild unmapped country that only ten years before had been the downfall of Burke and Wills. There Starlight sold the cattle. Unfortunately, since they did not belong to him, he was arrested in Adelaide and brought back to Qld to be put on trial at Roma. Despite the evidence the jury found him not guilty, probably because of the pioneer philosophy that if you are daring enough to carry out that sort of deed, you deserve to get away with it! The events were the basis for Rolf Boldrewood's novel *Robbery Under Arms*. Although Qantas (**Q**ueensland **A**nd **N**orthern **T**erritory **A**ir **S**ervices) actually started in Winton, it soon moved its base to Longreach and then commenced regular operations. The same hangar used then became Australia's first aircraft factory and the first of six DH-50 biplanes was assembled there in 1926. The world's first Flying Surgeon Service started from Longreach in 1959. **Of interest:** Several historical buildings: Uniting Church (1892), Galah St, built for Grazier's Association; court-house (1892), Eagle St; post office (1902), cnr Duck and Eagle Sts. Stockman's Hall of Fame and Outback Heritage Centre, Capricorn Hwy; exhibition hall, theatre with audio-visuals, library and resource centre. School of Distance Education, Capricorn Hwy; tours during term. Preview Centre for proposed Qantas Founders' Museum in Qantas Park, Eagle St. Longreach Pastoral College, Capricorn Hwy. Jackson's Weapon Museum, Cassowary St. Pamela's Doll Display and Syd's Outback Collection Corner, Quail St. Cruises on Thomson River on *Yellowbelly Express*. **In the area:** Folk Museum at Ilfracombe, 27 km east. Outback station accommodation at Lorraine, Rosedale, Oakley and Toobrack Stations. **Tourist information:** Qantas Park; (076) 58 2133. **Accommodation:** 5 hotels, 3 motels, 2 caravan/camping parks. MAP REF. 434 D3

Lucinda–Dungeness
Population 765
Ingham's sugar terminal port, 29 km away via Halifax, Lucinda's major feature is the world's longest offshore sugar-loading jetty and conveyor-belt (5.76 km), which loads 2000 tonnes of sugar an hour. Charter boats and ferries leave the Dungeness harbour for fishing, cruising

GULF SAVANNAH

Mangrove patterns, Norman River

The Gulf Savannah is a vast, remote, thinly populated region stretching north from **Mount Isa** and **Cloncurry** to the mangrove-covered shores of the Gulf of Carpentaria, and west to the Queensland/Northern Territory border. The unfortunate Burke and Wills were the first white visitors, although the waters of the Gulf itself were first charted by Dutch navigators almost 400 years ago. The country is flat and open and has more rivers than roads. The period April to October is the recommended time to see the Gulf country. During the monsoon period, generally from November to March, rain closes the dirt roads and on rare occasions can flood the sealed roads from Cloncurry and **Julia Creek**. Motorists should realise that this is not 'Sunday-driving' country and should plan accordingly. The safest way to travel during the wet season is by air out of Cairns, Mount Isa or Karumba. It is, however, an ideal corner of Australia if you want to get away from it all, and the people are exceptionally friendly and helpful.

The wide expanses of the Gulf Savannah region divide themselves naturally into three separate areas. The **Eastern Savannah** is easily reached via the Great Top Road (Gulf Development Road), which winds up the east-

ern face of the Dividing Range, passing above Cairns. As an alternative route to Georgetown, or for travellers with limited time to explore the outback, the Undara Loop is a leisurely three-day round trip from Cairns through the Lynd Junction, Einasleigh and Forsayth to Georgetown. **Georgetown**, 411 kilometres from Cairns, is the centre of the Etheridge Goldfield, where nuggets can still be found. Completing the loop back to Cairns takes the traveller to Tallaroo Hot Springs, Mt Surprise and Undara Volcano National Park, where visitors can see the lava tubes, a geological phenomenon.

From Georgetown the traveller can head west 150 kilometres to Croydon, terminus of the railway from Normanton, a historic link established to service Croydon, a rich gold-mining town of the last century.

Normanton is the central town of the whole Gulf Savannah, with a population of 1109, although in the gold days of 1891 it counted some 3000 people. The former gold-mining town of **Croydon** is 152 kilometres to the east. The strangely isolated railway between the two towns is not connected to any other system. It is used once a week by the *Gulflander*, a quaint but practical vintage railmotor, which leaves Normanton every Wednesday

and Croydon every Thursday. Many of Croydon's buildings have been classified by the National Trust and the Australian Heritage Commission.

Karumba, sixty-nine kilometres north of Normanton on the mouth of the Norman River, is the centre of the Gulf prawning industry as well as being home to the barramundi fishing industry. Keen fishermen from all over Australia come to Karumba to test their skill against the fighting barramundi. This famous fish can be caught throughout the Gulf rivers. Experts consider this one of Australia's finest fish, and eaten fresh they are absolutely superb. Prawns are snap-frozen in Karumba and freighted to markets in the south and overseas.

The **Western Savannah** has endless flat grassed plains stretching as far as the eye can see, while the wetlands around Karumba stretch across the top of the Western Savannah above Burketown and beyond to the border. Here rivers which are some eighty kilometres apart overflow their banks during the monsoons and form an unbroken sheet of water.

The town of **Burketown**, close to the Gulf, usually makes the headlines during round-Australia car trials or when it is flooded. It can be isolated for long periods during the wet. Explorers

Leichhardt and Landsborough termed the surrounding area the 'Plains of Promise', and today, like most of the Gulf region, it is cattle country. Barramundi fishing and bird-watching attract adventurers; a well-equipped four-wheel-drive vehicle is advisable.

Lawn Hill National Park, 12 200 hectares of rare vegetation, is to the west of the **Gregory Downs** bush pub, a welcome 'waterhole' for the traveller. Here, sixty-metre sheer sandstone walls form Lawn Hill Gorge with emerald green water at their base. The National Park Service has established 20 km of walking tracks to enable visitors to see safely this rugged and beautiful country.

When travelling on the sealed beef-road from Cloncurry to Normanton, motorists become aware of the curious Bang Bang Jump-up, a change in terrain heights, twenty-nine kilometres north of the Donors Hill station turn-off.

Flight West operate regular flights from both Cairns and Mt Isa, and this is probably the best way to appreciate the vast beauty of the Gulf Savannah and its many sleepy, winding rivers.

Although towns in this area are fully serviced, motorists are advised to carry 'cyclone rations' (basic supplies of food and water) in case of breakdown. Check road conditions before departure and, if possible, notify someone of your destination and expected time of arrival.

The Gulf Savannah is a new frontier in Australia that is opening up to those who are in search of interesting but authentic educational and adventure experiences. To assist visitors to this fascinating region, an organisation of Savannah Guides has been formed. These guides are professional interpreters who each have lived in the Gulf Savannah for many years and are able to offer a wide range of knowledge concerning the wilderness environment. There are guide stations at: Kowanyama Aboriginal Community; Hells Gate near the NT border; the Undara lava fields, 93 kilometres east of Georgetown; the Agate Creek gemfields, 103 kilometres south of Georgetown and Lawn Hill National Park.

For further information on the area and guide bookings, contact Savannah Guide Headquarters, 91 Digger St, Cairns; (070) 51 1420 or (070) 51 4658. **See also:** Entries in A–Z listing.

and trips to the islands, including popular Hinchinbrook. **Accommodation:** 1 hotel/motel, 1 caravan/camping park. MAP REF. 436 G6

Mackay   Population 38 603

Mackay is often called the 'sugar capital' of Australia, producing one-third of the nation's sugar crop. Five mills operate in the area, and the bulk-sugar loading terminal is the world's largest. Sugar was first grown in 1866, a mill was built and in the same year Mackay became a town. It became a major port in 1939 when an ingenious breakwater was built, making it one of Australia's largest artificial harbours. The nearby Hay Point coal-loading terminals handle the massive output from the Central Qld coalfields. Gazetted in 1918, Mackay is now an attractive and progressive tropical city. Besides sugar and coal, the town's economy depends on beef cattle, dairying, timber, grain, seafood, and the growing of tropical fruit. Tourism is a growth industry, with cruises to Brampton, Lindeman, Hamilton, the Great Barrier Reef and the Whitsunday Islands. **Of interest:** Self-guiding Heritage Walk of historic buildings, including Commonwealth and National Banks, town hall, court-house, police station and customs house. Queens Park and Orchid House, Goldsmith St. Mackay Entertainment Centre, Gordon St. Tourism Mackay, Nebo Rd; building is replica of old Richmond sugar mill. Mt Bassett Weather Station and lookout; Mt Pleasant Reservoir and lookout; both just north of town. Numerous beaches: Harbour, Town, Blacks, Bacasia, Illawong, Lamberts and Shoal Point. Illawawong Fauna Park at Illawong Beach. Festival of the Arts held in July; Sugartime Festival in Sept. **In the area:** Cape Hillsborough National Park, 80 km north. Eungella National Park, 84 km north-west. Polstone Sugar Cane Farm and Racecourse Sugar Mill, 20 km west. Greenmount historic homestead, 40 km west, near Mirani. At Mirani, Bicentennial Museum. Kinchant Dam, 12 km further south of Mirani. Orchidways, on Homebush Rd, 25 km south of Mackay; orchid farm. At Homebush, craft and art gallery. Tours of Hay Point coal-loading terminal lookout, 30 km south. Cape Palmerston National Park, 80 km south; 4WD access only. Cruises to Great Barrier Reef and Whitsunday Islands. **Tourist information:** The Mill, Nebo Rd; (079) 52 2677. **Accommodation:** 19 hotels, 29 motels, 10 caravan/camping parks. MAP REF. 437 L11

Maleny   Population 585

A steep road climbs west to Maleny, 50 km south-west of Maroochydore on the Blackall Range. This is excellent dairy country. From Mary Cairncross Park, an area of thick rainforest, there is a fine view of the Glass House Mountains to the south. These ten spectacular trachyte peaks were named by Captain Cook as he sailed up the coast in 1770, for the sun shining on the rock-faces reminded him of glasshouses in his native Yorkshire. **Of interest:** Fig Tree Cottage for pottery and opals. Blue Marlin Handcraft for marine handcraft. **In the area:** Scenic drive from Maleny through Montville and Flaxton to Mapleton, one of best in southeast Qld. Most of Sunshine Coast can be seen: views across to Moreton Island, and closer, pineapple and sugarcane fields. Montville, 17 km north-east, has many excellent potteries and art and craft galleries. Various museums, antique shops, fruit stalls, Devonshire tea places and tourist attractions along the way. Flaxton, 3 km further north; miniature English village and clock museum. Kondalilla and Mapleton Falls National Parks, 7 km west of Montville. **Tourist information:** Montville Tourist Information Centre, Main St, Montville; (071) 42 9214. **Accommodation:** 2 hotels, 2 motels, 2 caravan/camping parks. **See also:** Sunshine Coast. MAP REF. 426 I11, 435 Q9

Mareeba   Population 6614

This town is at the centre of the main tobacco-growing region of Australia. Farms in the Mareeba/Dimbulah area are irrigated from Lake Tinaroo. Another local crop, rice, is processed at the mill at Home Hill. Timber, mining and cattle are also important. **Of interest:** Mareeba Rodeo held in July. **In the area:** Mareeba Coffee Estates, 7 km south-west. Pinevale Ranch, 10 km south-west; day or longer horseriding stays. Granite Gorge, 12 km west. Dirt road via Dimbulah crosses Great Dividing Range to Chillagoe (145 km west), old mining town with some fine limestone caves. **Tourist information:** Shire Offices; (070) 92 1222. **Accommodation:** 4 hotels, 2 motels, 3 caravan/camping parks. **See also:** Atherton Tableland; Cape York. MAP REF. 436 F3, 438 I12, 439 B8

Maroochydore   Population 20 635

A well-established and popular beach resort, Maroochydore is the business centre of the Sunshine Coast, 112 km north of Brisbane. **Of interest:** Famous surfing beaches and Maroochy River, with its pelicans and swans, offers safe swimming. Cotton Tree, at river mouth, popular camping area. **In the area:** Yacht Harbour, beach and Pilot Station at

THE FAR NORTH

Sitting in a tropical garden through dusk and into lush evening, dining superbly on king prawns, Queensland mud crabs and a chilled bottle of white wine, it is hard to believe you are at 'the end of the line' — **Port Douglas**, the most northerly of the easily accessible coastal towns of Queensland.

This is part of the continuing joy of travelling in the north — a region larger than most European countries and considered by many to be the most diversely beautiful and exciting part of Australia.

This Port Douglas scene typifies the beauty of coastal Queensland; the restaurant looks down from a jungle-covered hill which looms over the small town and the seven kilometres of ocean beach. By day the dense tropical forest is revealed in showers of coloured flowers against the intense green of the jungle. The lavish rainforest and the rush of sparkling mountain streams are lasting impressions for the traveller in the north.

Cairns, 1766 kilometres from Brisbane, is the stepping-stone to a variety of sight-seeing excursions. A major city for tourism, Cairns is often known as the 'capital of Far North Queensland'. Nestling beside Trinity Bay, this scenic city is an ideal base for visiting the surrounding tourist attractions. From Cairns, you can relax on a launch cruise which takes you to see the wonders of the Great Barrier Reef or to explore uninhabited islands. Aerial tours from Cairns take you over the Great Plateau, with its lush tablelands and spectacular waterfalls.

The pleasant climate in winter and early spring is one of the main attractions of this city. Visitors can enjoy snorkelling or other water sports, while fishermen flock to Cairns from September to December to catch the big black marlin. Cairns itself is a picturesque city. Delicate ferns, tropical shrubs and fragrant flowers thrive in the Botanical Gardens, where a walking track joins the Centenary Lakes Parkland, created in 1976 to mark the city's hundredth anniversary. Two lakes, one saltwater and the other freshwater, provide a haven for wildlife among native trees and shrubs. You can also see orchids growing to

Millaa Millaa Falls

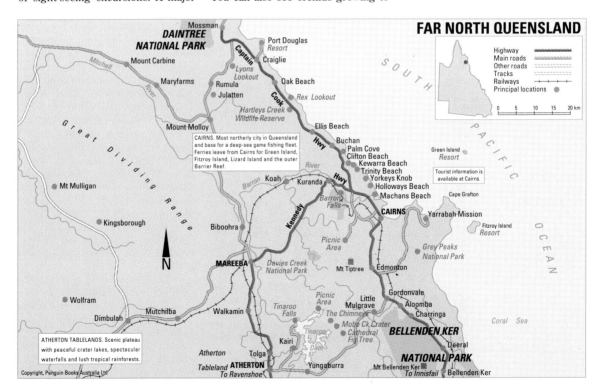

perfection in orchid nurseries, which form the basis of one of Cairns' important export industries.

There are dozens of places around Cairns, all within easy driving distance on good roads, that will claim the traveller's attention. Port Douglas is only one of them. The sixty-kilometre journey from Cairns passes through a magnificent stretch of coastal scenery as the Cook Highway winds past white coral beaches, through archways of tropical forest, and past the islands which dot the azure northern waters. Port Douglas, despite its increasing popularity with tourists, still retains some of its fishing-village atmosphere. The motels and holiday units are all set back from the beachfront. Just out of town is the Sheraton Mirage Resort, with 300 rooms but only three storeys high.

Just inland from Port Douglas (and remember to stop at the cemetery that contains the graves of many pioneer settlers who were lured north by the Palmer River gold-rush) is the sugar town of **Mossman**, where the crushing plant can be inspected from June to December. During these months cane farmers used to create raging fires to prepare the cane for harvesting, however, nowadays cane is more often harvested green. These days the fabled strong man of the north, the cane-cutter, is seldom seen, having exchanged his machete for a seat on an ingenious machine that cuts the cane and throws it, in a shower of short sticks, into the hopper, which trails behind. Sugar-growing is a major industry of the

north and the waving fields of cane wind through the vaulting blue mountains for hundreds of kilometres down the lush coastal plain.

Near Mossman is one of those perfect places that seem so prevalent in the north, the Mossman River Gorge. A short walk under the dense green canopy of the rainforest leads to the boulder-strewn river which rushes in a series of cascades through the jungle-sided gorge. It is a place to picnic, to swim or simply to bask in the rays of the North Queensland sun.

There are many such places, particularly on the edge of the Atherton Tableland where the mountains have thrown up fascinating geological oddities and where waterfalls spill. For example, near Atherton township there are two volcanic lakes, Barrine and Eacham, where walking tracks through the rainforest give beautiful water views and a chance to see the abundant wildlife — parrots, waterfowl, turtles, platypuses, goannas and many marsupials.

South-west of Malanda is Mt Hypipamee National Park where visitors can walk beneath huge rainforest trees, past staghorn ferns and orchids, along Dinner Creek to the falls and up to the crater, a funnel of sheer granite walls which fall away into dark and forbidding water.

Ten kilometres away from the Malanda Falls, where water cascades over a fern-swathed precipice into a delightful swimming pool, is the huge Curtain Fig Tree, which has resulted from a strangling fig taking over its host tree,

climbing higher and higher and throwing down showers of roots to support its massive structure. There are dozens of other delightful waterfalls in this area. Near Millaa Millaa is Falls Circuit, where the Millaa Millaa Falls, Zillie Falls and Elinjaa Falls are sited amid a magnificent panorama of rainforest mountains and plains.

There are four main highways linking the tablelands with the coast. They are all magnificent scenic routes, although the roads are narrow and winding in some parts. Undoubtedly, however, the most novel and popular way of getting up to the tableland is by the scenic railway to **Kuranda**, built to serve the Herberton tin-mine in the 1890s, and now regarded as one of the most difficult feats of engineering achieved in Queensland. The track climbs 300 metres in twenty kilometres to traverse the Barron Gorge and part of it runs over a viaduct along the edge of a 200-metre precipice. The lovely old carriages have rear platforms with decorative iron railings where travellers can stand and take in the superb uninterrupted view. The Kuranda railway station, festooned in tropical plants, ferns and orchids, is a much-photographed stopover before the descent to Cairns.

The Atherton and Evelyn Tablelands are areas of volcanic land at altitudes between 600 and 1000 metres, mild in climate and supporting dairying, maize and tobacco farming. Gradually the tablelands change into dry, rough country, where tin, copper, lead and zinc mining used to take place. Beyond the main tableland settlement of Atherton is the fascinating mining town of **Herberton**, with its Historical Village and old houses proclaiming its boom days of the late nineteenth century.

Southward from Cairns the plain is flanked by the Walter Hill Range on the seaward side and the Bellenden Ker Range, with its superb rainforest. A turn off the highway beyond the town of Innisfail leads into the tropical holiday resort area, where many small towns nestle in the encroaching forest and peep through palms across the sand to the Barrier Reef islands. Further south is the Hinchinbrook Channel, opposite the large continental island of Hinchinbrook.

For further information on the Far North, contact the Far North Qld Promotion Bureau Ltd, 36–38 Aplin St, Cairns; (070) 51 3588.

Road near North Ellis Beach, Port Douglas

Mooloolaba, 5 km south. Fairytale Castle and Ski and Skurf water skiing park at Bli Bli, 10 km north. Nostalgia Town,11 km north via Bli Bli; emphasises humour in history. Mooloolah River National Park, 10 km south (access difficult). Sunshine Coast airport has daily flights to and from Sydney. River cruises up Maroochy River to Dunethin Rock through sugarcane fields. **Tourist information:** Tourism Sunshine Coast Ltd, Alexandra Pde, Alexandra Headland; (008) 07 2041. **Accommodation:** 3 hotels, 9 motels, 7 caravan/camping parks.
MAP REF. 427 L10, 435 Q9

Maryborough   Population 20 177

Maryborough is an attractive provincial city situated on the banks of the Mary River. The area produces sugar, timber, dairy products, grain, fruit and vegetables. Secondary industries include sawmills, engineering works and a sugar mill. The local fish board is the state's largest outside Brisbane, some 260 km to the south. The Mary River was discovered in 1842, and a village and port soon grew to handle wool being grown inland. It was officially proclaimed a port in 1859, and a municipality in 1861. The city itself is well-planned, as are its parks: Queen's Park, with its unusual domed fernery and waterfall; Elizabeth Park, noted for its roses; Anzac Park; and Ululah Lagoon, near the golf links, a scenic waterbird sanctuary where black swans, wild geese, ducks and waterhens may be hand-fed. Maryborough is actively promoted as 'Queensland's Heritage City', and visitors are encouraged to take walks and drives to view the city's heritage precincts. The climate is subtropical with warm moist summers and mild winters, and the seaside resort city of Hervey Bay, 34 km north-east, offers pleasant, unsophisticated holidays and fishing. The city is connected by road to the resorts of Rainbow Beach and Tin Can Bay, some 90 km to the south. **Of interest:** Some fine examples of early Qld colonial architecture, including Baddow House, Queen St, furnished in period style. St Paul's bell tower (1887) has one of first sets of cathedral bells in Qld. Fruit Salad Cottage Heritage Museum, Banana St. Pioneer gravesites and original township site in Alice St, Baddow; historic time gun outside city hall. Midweek markets. Mary River cruises. **In the area:** Hervey Bay seaside resorts. Fraser Island. Teddington Weir, 15 km south. Tuan Forest, 24 km south-east. Pioneer museum at Brooweena, 49 km west on Biggenden Rd. Houseboats for hire. Farm holidays available. **Tourist information:** Cnr Ferry and Queen Sts; (071) 21 4111.

Accommodation: 5 hotel/motels, 8 motels, 6 caravan/camping parks.
MAP REF. 435 P7

Mary Kathleen

Well known to many Australians because of the controversial issue of uranium mining, Mary Kathleen was once a small mining town on the Barkly Hwy between Mount Isa and Cloncurry. The area has now been returned to its natural state, leaving no trace of the former inhabitants. In late 1982 the mine was shut down and by the end of 1983 the houses were sold and removed to new areas. Four buildings have been re-erected in the Mary Kathleen Memorial Park at Cloncurry. **In the area:** Mount Frosty, off Mt Isa Rd; popular swimming-hole and fossicking area for minerals and gemstones. **Note: Not recommended for children; hole is some 9 m deep with no shallow areas.**
MAP REF. 440 D9

Miles   Population 1406

Ludwig Leichhardt passed through the Miles district (340 km west of Brisbane) on three separate expeditions. He named the place Dogwood Creek, after the shrub that grows on the banks of the creek. In 1878 the western railway line reached 'Dogwood Crossing', and Cobb & Co. continued the journey on to Roma. The town was renamed Miles after a local member of parliament. The area has always been good sheep country, but today the emphasis is on cattle, mainly Herefords, and wheat; tall silos dominate the surrounding plains. After the spring rains, the wildflowers are magnificent. **Of interest:** Historical village, Warrego Hwy; 'pioneer settlement' with all types of early buildings and war museum, displays of vehicles and implements. *In the area:* Possum Park, 21 km north; ex-airforce ammunition dump, underground bunkers converted for accommodation. Myall Park Botanical Gardens at Glenmorgan, 100 km south-west. **Tourist information:** Miles and District Historical Village, Warrego Hwy; (076) 27 1402. **Accommodation:** 3 hotels, 2 motels.
MAP REF. 435 M9

Millaa Millaa   Population 343

Located 75 km inland from Innisfail, Millaa Millaa is renowned for the many spectacular waterfalls in the area. The town's main industry is cheese-making. **Of interest:** Eacham Historical Society Museum. **In the area:** Millaa Millaa Falls, Zillie Falls and Elinjaa Falls, all viewed from 15 km gravel road that leaves and rejoins Palmerston Hwy east of town

(impassable in wet weather). Lookout to west of town offers excellent panoramic views of district. **Accommodation:** Limited. **See also:** Atherton Tableland.
MAP REF. 436 F4

Millmerran   Population 1191

This town on the Condamine River produces eggs, cotton, grain, vegetables, cattle and wool. **Of interest:** Historical Society Museum. Bottle and Brick Museum. **Tourist information:** 541 Ruthven St, Toowoomba; (076) 32 1988. **Accommodation:** 1 hotel, 1 motel, 1 caravan/camping park.
MAP REF. 435 N11

Miriam Vale   Population 354

Situated on the Bruce Hwy, 150 km north of Bundaberg, this small township is renowned for its mud crab sandwiches. Watch for the Giant Crab. The twin towns of Town of 1770 and Agnes Water lie 25 km east. Captain Cook, while on his voyage of discovery in Australian waters, made his second landing here. The estuary and beaches provide an ideal spot to get away from it all and the fishing is excellent. **Tourist information:** Gladstone Area Promotion and Development Ltd, 56 Goondoon St, Gladstone; (079) 72 4000. **Accommodation:** 1 hotel, 1 motel, 1 caravan/camping park.
MAP REF. 435 O5

Mission Beach   Population 662

This quiet tropical 8-km-long beach is backed by coconut palms and heavy rainforest, close to Tully. Day trips to Dunk and the surrounding Family Group of islands (excluding Bedarra) can be taken from the jetty at Clump Point. At the southern end of the beach, a cairn at Tam O'Shanter Point commemorates the ill-fated 1848 Cape York expedition of Edmund Kennedy. **In the area:** Riverboat cruises on *River Rat* through mangroves and rainforest include fishing, mudcrabbing and crocodile spotting. Many walks along beach or into rainforest. Whitewater rafting on Tully River, 10 km south. **Tourist information:** Cassowary Dr, Wongaling; (070) 68 8559. **Accommodation:** 1 hotel, 6 motels, 5 caravan/camping parks.
MAP REF. 436 G5

Mitchell   Population 1212

This typical western country town, on the banks of the Maranoa River, lies on the Warrego Hwy between Roma and Charleville and was named after Sir Thomas Mitchell, explorer and Surveyor-General of NSW, who visited the region in 1845. **Of interest:** Working Museum,

Edinburgh St. **In the area:** Neil Turner Weir, 3.5 km north-west. Unsealed tourist road leads north into Great Dividing Range and former stronghold of local turn-of-century bushrangers, the Kenniff brothers. Region behind Carnarvon National Park, 256 km north, is little known; sufficient petrol and supplies must be carried for return trip. Rutland and Arcoona Stations offer accommodation. **Tourist information:** Booringa Shire Council; (076) 23 1133. **Accommodation:** 5 hotels, 1 motel, 1 caravan/camping park. MAP REF. 435 J8

Monto   Population 1475

Monto, on the Burnett Hwy, 250 km inland from Bundaberg, is the centre of a rich dairying, beef cattle and agricultural district. The Monto Dairy Festival is held on the Queen's Birthday long weekend every even year. **In the area:** Cania Gorge National Park, 25 km north, with spectacular sandstone formations. **Tourist information:** Cnr Mulgrave and Bourbong Sts, Bundaberg; (071) 52 2333. **Accommodation:** 2 motels, 1 caravan/camping park. MAP REF. 435 N6

Mooloolaba – Alexandra Headland

Pop. part of Maroochydore
Mooloolaba, due to its excellent clean, sandy beach and variety of restaurants and nightlife, is equally in demand for family and young people's holidays. The Mooloolaba Esplanade, offering beachside resort shopping, rises to the bluff at Alexandra Headland. Alexandra Headland beach is a popular board-riding location. Few visitors forget the panoramic sweeping views up the beach to the Maroochy River and Mudjimba Island, with Mt Coolum creating an impressive backdrop. One of the safest anchorages on the eastern coast is at Mooloolaba Harbour. It is the finishing point for the annual Sydney to Mooloolaba Yacht Race and the starting point for the Mooloolaba to Gladstone Race. **Of interest:** Wharf complex, The Spit, Mooloolaba; dozens of specialty shops. Underwater World oceanarium, cnr River Esplanade and Parkyn Pde; 80 m transparent tunnel for viewing 3 separate marine environments, also freshwater section and seal pool. Harbour is also base for Sunshine Coast's main prawning and fishing fleet, for game and sport fishing trips to near offshore reefs, and for pilot vessels that guide ships into Port of Brisbane. Paraflying off Mooloolaba Beach. **Tourist information:** Alexandra Pde, Alexandra Headland; (008) 07 2041. **Accommodation:** 2 hotels, 8 motels, 3 caravan/camping parks. MAP REF. 427 M10

Moranbah   Population 6883

Just off the Peak Downs Hwy, 200 km south-west of Mackay, this town services the huge open-cut coal mines of Goonyella/Riverside and Peak Downs operated by BHP Utah Coal Ltd. Coking coal is railed to the Hay Point export terminal just south of Mackay. **Of interest:** Inspections of Goonyella/Riverside Mine and Peak Downs Mine. **Tourist information:** Shire Offices, Goonyella Rd; (079) 41 7254. **Accommodation:** 1 hotel/motel, 1 motel, 1 caravan/camping park. MAP REF. 435 J1, 437 J12

Mossman   Population 1637

Mossman, the sugar town of the north, situated 78 km north of Cairns on the Cook Hwy, is surrounded by towering green mountains and fields of green sugarcane. **Of interest:** Mt Demi (1159 m) towers over town. Tours of Mossman Central Mill during cane-crushing season (June–Dec.). Bally Hooley Steam Express, genuine steam train, transports tourists from Port Douglas (20 km southeast) through canefields and on to tour of mill. Bavarian Festival held in June. **In the area:** Popular beaches Cooya, Newell and Wonga; latter two provide public facilities. Mossman Gorge, 9 km south; short walk through rainforest to picturesque cascades. Silky Oaks Wilderness Lodge, backing on to Daintree National Park, 10 km west. Karnak Playhouse Theatre, 12 km north. High Falls Farm at Miallo, 15 km north. Wonga Belle Orchid Garden, 20 km north. Cape Tribulation National Park, 64 km north; largest

Mooloolaba Beach; Point Cartwright in background

tract of tropical rainforest in Australia. **Tourist information:** Far North Qld Promotion Bureau Ltd, 36–38 Aplin St, Cairns; (070) 51 3588. **Accommodation:** 2 hotels, 2 motels, 1 caravan/camping park. **See also:** The Far North.
MAP REF. 436 F2, 438 I11, 439 A1

Mount Isa
Population 23 348

In 1923, John Campbell Miles discovered a rich silver-lead deposit on the western edge of the Cloncurry field. Today the progressive city of Mount Isa is the most important industrial, commercial and administrative centre in north-west Qld. The 'Isa' is a company town, with Mount Isa Mines operating one of the largest silver-lead mines in the world. Copper and zinc are also mined and processed. Ore trains run 900 km east to Townsville for shipment. The 'Isa' is an oasis of civilisation with excellent amenities and facilities in the otherwise hot and monotonous spinifex and cattle country surrounding it. The famous Rotary Rodeo, held every August, attracts roughriders from all over Qld and almost doubles the population of Mount Isa for the period of the festivities. **Of interest:** Surface and underground mine tours; advance bookings essential. Silver smelter stack, Australia's tallest free-standing

structure (265 m). Middlin Mining Display and Visitors Centre, Church St. National Trust Tent House, Fourth Ave. Kalkadoon Tribal Centre and Cultural Keeping Place, Marian St. Riversleigh Fossil Display, Civic Centre, West St. Mt Isa Potters Gallery, Alma St. Flying Doctor Service base, Barkly Hwy. School of Distance Education, Kalkadoon High School. City Lookout, Hilary St. Donaldson Memorial Lookout and Walking Track. Country Music Festival held in Apr.; Agricultural Show in June; Art Society Exhibition in Aug. **In the area:** Man-made Lake Moondarra, 15 km north; swimming, water sports, picnic/barbecue facilities. Lake Julius, 100 km north, offers fishing, water-skiing, nature trails, abandoned gold-mine and Aboriginal cave paintings. Air charter companies provide flights to excellent barramundi fishing grounds near Birri Fishing Lodge at Birri Beach on Mornington Island and Sweers Island, in Gulf of Carpentaria. Mount Frosty, old limestone mine and swimming-hole; popular area for fossickers. Lake Corella, 90 km east; Burke and Wills memorial cairn. Camooweal, 188 km west on Barkly Hwy, last Qld town before crossing NT border. Gunpowder Resort, 140 km north-west, where activities range from bull-catching to water-skiing. Tours of Riversleigh

Fossil Site, 200 km north-west, and Lawn Hill National Park, 500 km north-west. Dreamtime Track bush tours and outback tours. Savannah Safari tours include trips to Gunpowder Resort and Lake Julius. **Tourist information:** Marian St; (077) 43 7966. **Accommodation:** 4 hotels, 13 motels, 8 caravan parks.
MAP REF. 440 C8

Mount Morgan
Population 2866

Found only 32 km south-west of Rockhampton, the crater of the Mount Morgan open-cut gold, silver and copper mine is one of the world's largest man-made holes, measuring some 800 m across and 274 m deep. The mine still produces, but not as profitably as in its golden heyday, when the town had 15 000 people. **Of interest:** Museum, East St. Court-house, gold-bullion store and other historic buildings have National Trust classifications. **In the area:** The Big Dam for swimming, boating and picnics. **Accommodation:** 1 motel, 1 caravan/camping park. **See also:** Capricorn.
MAP REF. 435 M3

Mourilyan
Population 431

Located 7 km south of Innisfail, Mourilyan is the bulk-sugar outlet for sugar

Mount Morgan open-cut mine

produced in the Innisfail area. **Of interest:** Australian Sugar Museum, Bruce Hwy. **In the area:** On Old Bruce Hwy, south-west: tours of South Johnstone Sugar Mill (8 km) in season, July–Oct.; Mena Park Environment Park (9 km), with suspension bridge, waterfall and picnic and camping areas; National Trust classified Paronella Park (15 km), ruins of Spanish castle set in rainforest. Etty Bay, 13 km south; quiet tropical beach. **Tourist information:** Australian Sugar Museum, Bruce Hwy; (070) 63 2306. **Accommodation:** Limited.
MAP REF. 436 G4

Mundubbera   Population 1114
Centre of an important citrus-growing area, Mundubbera is on the Burnett Hwy, 410 km north-west of Brisbane. **Of interest:** 'Enormous Ellendale' or 'Big Mandarin' Information Centre features displays on citrus-growing industry. **In the area:** Golden Mile Orchard, 13 km west; open weekdays for inspection. Rare Neoceratodus, or lungfish, is found in Burnett River nearby (exhibit on display at Information Centre). Jones Weir, Auburn River National Park, 40 km south-west. Gurgeena and Binjour Plateaux; peanut-, maize- and bean-growing areas to north-east. **Tourist information:** 'Enormous Ellendale' Information Centre; (071) 65 4549. **Accommodation:** 2 motels, 2 caravan/camping parks.
MAP REF. 435 N7

Murgon   Population 2249
Murgon, known as the 'Beef Capital of the Burnett', is one of the most attractive inland towns in southern Qld. Settlement dates back to 1843 and the name comes from the Aboriginal word for 'lily pond'. Beef, dairying and mixed crops are the main industries. The town is 101 km inland from Gympie and 46 km north of Kingaroy. **Of interest:** Vic Rewald's Lapiady Display, Nutt St; semi-precious polished gemstones collection. Queensland Dairy Museum, Gayndah Rd; adjacent, relocated Trinity Homestead, one of district's original buildings. Murgon Cheese Factory, Macalister St. Goschnick's Farm Machinery Museum, Bunya Hwy. **In the area:** Cherbourg Emu Farm at Cherbourg Aboriginal Community, 5 km south-west; walk-through enclosures, educational displays and sales of emu products and Aboriginal artefacts. Bjelke-Petersen Dam, 15 km south-east; popular water-sports and recreation area. Jack Smith's Scrub Environment Park, 15 km north-east; nature

walk, scenic views. Adjacent, Boat Mountain Environment Park. **Tourist information:** 12 Lamb St; (071) 68 1984. **Accommodation:** 1 hotel/motel, 1 motel, 2 caravan parks.
MAP REF. 435 O8

Muttaburra   Population 195
Muttaburra, 114 km north of Longreach, was developed as a town in the late 1870s, the name being derived from an Aboriginal word meaning 'meeting of the waters'. **In the area:** Formerly part of an inland sea, the area has many fossil remains. The name 'Muttaburrasaurus' was given to a previously unknown dinosaur (6 m tall and 14 m long) the fossilised bones of which were discovered here. Full-sized replica of dinosaur in Edkins St. Magnificent colonial homestead at Mount Cornish, station property just north of town, built of locally quarried stone. **Tourist information:** Muttaburra Motors and Cafe, Edkins St; (076) 58 7140. **Accommodation:** 1 hotel, 1 caravan/camping park.
MAP REF. 434 E2, 436 E13

Nambour   Population 9579
Nambour is a busy provincial town, 106 km north of Brisbane on the Bruce Hwy. The district was settled in the 1860s, mainly by disappointed miners from the Gympie goldfields, and sugar has been the main crop since the 1890s. Small locomotives pulling trucks of sugarcane regularly trundle across the main street to Moreton Central Mill during the crushing season. Pineapples and tropical fruit are grown extensively. Nambour is the Aboriginal name for the red-flowering ti-tree that grows locally. **In the area:** Spectacular Glass House Mountains to south, and scenic Blackall Ranges to west. Major tourist attractions, the Sunshine Plantation, home of the Big Pineapple, and CSR Macadamia Nut Factory, 7 km south. Moonshine Valley Winery, Forest Glen deer sanctuary and Super Bee honey factory, 10 km further south on Forest Glen–Tanawha Tourist Drive. Beach resorts of Maroochydore and Mooloolaba, 20 km east at mouth of Maroochy and Mooloolah Rivers. **Tourist information:** Sunshine Plantation, Bruce Hwy, Woombye; (071) 42 1333. **Accommodation:** 3 hotels, 5 motels, 1 caravan/camping park. **See also:** Sunshine Coast.
MAP REF. 427 K9, 435 Q9

Nanango   Population 2213
Gold was mined here from 1850 to 1900, but the area, 24 km south-east of Kingaroy, now relies on beef cattle, beans and

grain. The 1400-megawatt Tarong Power Station and Meandu Coal Mine, 18 km south-west, also are of economic importance to the area. **Of interest:** Astronomical Observatory, Faulkners Rd; day and night viewings. **In the area:** Yarraman and Benarkin Forest Drives, including Coomba Falls. Bunya Mountains National Park, 84 km west. **Tourist information:** Shire Offices, Drayton St; (071) 63 1307. **Accommodation:** 3 hotels, 3 motels, 3 caravan/camping parks.
MAP REF. 435 O9

Nebo   Population 650
Nebo is situated 100 km south-west of Mackay on the Peak Downs Hwy. Beef cattle and grain farming are the major industries. **Of interest:** Nebo Museum. **Tourist information:** Shire Offices, Reynolds St; (079) 50 5133. **Accommodation:** 1 hotel, 1 motel.
MAP REF. 437 K11

Nerang   Population 7333
This small township in the Gold Coast hinterland is 10 km from Southport. **In the area:** At Carrara, 5 km south, weekend Hinterland Country Market. Hinze Dam on Advancetown Lake, 8 km south; swimming and sailing, picnic/barbecue facilities. Spectacular scenery in Numinbah Valley area. Natural Arch National Park, 38 km south; popular picnic spot with walking tracks through rainforest and lookout nearby. Glow-worms in cave under arch. Towards Springbrook, 42 km south: Wunburra Lookout on Springbrook Plateau; Best of All View, off Repeater Station Rd; Purlingbrook Falls in Springbrook National Park. **Tourist information:** Albert Shire Council, Nerang–Southport Rd; (075) 78 0211. **Accommodation:** 2 hotels, 3 motels, 1 caravan/camping park.
MAP REF. 429 O5

Noosa – Tewantin Population 11 296
Noosa Heads is the most northerly of the Sunshine Coast resorts and is renowned for its natural scenery. A combination of the Noosa National Park, a protected main beach facing north, the Noosa River and lakes system, and Qld sunshine has resulted in a fashionable resort with a relaxed atmosphere, excellent accommodation and restaurants, but without Gold Coast-style high-rise development. Tewantin is a quiet country town 6 km up the river, first settled in the 1870s as a base for timber-cutters. Noosaville is a relaxed family-style resort on the river between the two centres. **Of interest:** Noosa Regional Gallery. Selina Antiques and Top Spot Gallery at Noosa Junction. Walking

CAPRICORN

This rich and diverse slice of Queensland stretches inland from Rockhampton and the Capricorn Coast out to Emerald, and straddles the Tropic of Capricorn. The area includes the Central Queensland Highlands, and is drained by the Fitzroy, Mackenzie, Comet, Nogoa and Dawson Rivers. The district was first opened up by gold and copper mining around **Emerald** in the 1860s, and the discovery of sapphires around **Anakie**. The original owners of the land have left their heritage in superb and mysterious rock paintings on the silent stone walls of the Carnarvon Ranges to the south. Cattle have been the economic mainstay since European settlement, but vast tracts of brigalow scrub were cleared after World War II to grow wheat, maize, sorghum and safflower. These days coal has become king, with mainly American companies gouging out enormous deposits for local and Japanese markets. On a smaller scale, professional and amateur fossickers are still finding gems, and with a great deal of enjoyment.

For a pleasurable tour of Capricorn, drive west from **Rockhampton**, the commercial and manufacturing capital, along the Capricorn Highway. Detour to Blackdown Tableland National Park where there are waterfalls, rockpools and camping areas; the turn-off is between **Blackwater** and **Dingo**. (You will need a permit from the Queensland National Parks office in Rockhampton to enter the park.) At Emerald turn south to **Springsure**, then east to **Biloela** on the Dawson Highway. Continue north on the Burnett Highway via **Mount Morgan** back to Rockhampton.

Mount Hay Gemstone Tourist Park, forty-one kilometres from Rockhampton, allows visitors to fossick for thunder eggs and rhyolite, which may be cut and polished at the factory in the park. Utah's Blackwater coalmine produces four million tonnes of coking coal and almost three million tonnes of steaming coal annually. Tours can be arranged.

Emerald is the main town in the western Central Highlands region, with the central-western railway continuing much further west to Longreach and the Channel Country. Clermont and the Blair Athol coalfields are 106 kilometres to the north-west. The gemfields of **Anakie**, **Rubyvale**, **Sapphire**, **Willows** and **Tomahawk Creek** are west of Emerald, and are popular with tourists seeking a different holiday. (A fossicker's licence is necessary.) An informative map/ brochure on the area is produced by the Royal Automobile Club of Queensland.

Springsure, sixty-three kilometres south of Emerald, is one of Queensland's oldest towns, having been surveyed in 1854. It produces beef and grain. Nearby is the Old Rainworth Fort at **Burnside**, a fascinating piece of Australiana, where early farm equipment, wool presses and the like are on display. It was built in 1853 from local stone.

Rolleston, seventy kilometres to the south-east, is the turn-off to the magnificent Carnarvon National Park, 103 kilometres further south. The park is some 28 000 hectares of rugged mountains, forests, caves and deep gorges, some of which are Australia's earliest 'art galleries' with countless

Gem mine, Rubyvale

Central Highlands region

Aboriginal paintings and engravings, which in places extend in a colourful frieze for more than fifty metres.

The Callide open-cut mine is situated near **Biloela**, the principal town in the Callide Valley. The nearby Callide Power Station supplies the Rockhampton, Moura and Blackwater districts as well as Biloela.

Mount Larcom, between Gladstone and Rockhampton, is a rich area for dairying and fruit and tomato crops. **Yarwun** is noted for its delicious pawpaws.

What are known as 'Snowy Mounts' are actually huge piles of salt in the Fitzroy River delta between **Bajool** and **Port Alma**. Underground salty water is pumped to the surface into pools called crystallisers, and the salt is 'harvested' during October – November after solar evaporation.

For further information on Capricorn, contact the Capricorn Information Centre, Curtis Park, Gladstone Rd, Rockhampton; (079) 27 2055.

See also: Entries in A–Z listing.

and surfing in Noosa National Park, between Noosa Heads and Sunshine Beach, with its rocky headlands, sandy coves and patches of rainforest. Views of river and lakes from Laguna Lookout. At Tewantin: Big Shell, Coloured Sands Art Gallery and House of Bottles. **In the area:** Camel rides on Noosa's north shore beach. All 20–40 km north: Teewah coloured sandhills, stranded freighter *Cherry Venture*, Noosa River Everglades and Cooloola National Park; may be accessed by 4WD vehicles, and boat tours depart from Noosaville. Noosa Lakes system is ideal for boating, sailing and wind-surfing, being navigable for 50 km into Cooloola National Park. Houseboat holidays are popular. Boreen Point, quiet holiday and sailing centre on Lake Cootharaba, 21 km north of Tewantin. Sat. markets at Eumundi, 16 km south-west. **Tourist information:** Hastings St Information Centre, Noosa Heads; (074) 47 5506. **Accommodation:** 3 hotels, 14 motels, 2 caravan/ camping parks. **See also:** Sunshine Coast.
MAP REF. 427 L6, 435 Q8

Normanton   Population 1109

Normanton, 151 km from Croydon, is the central town of the Gulf Savannah and is situated on a high gravel ridge on the edge of the savannah grasslands that extend to the west and the wetlands that extend to the north. The town is also the terminus of the historic Normanton to Croydon railway, and the Normanton railway station is the home of the *Gulflander*. **Of interest:** Penitentiary, Haig St. Restored Bank of NSW building, Little Brown St. Town well, Landsborough St; no longer in use. **In the area:** Fishing and camping along Flinders River, Archer's Bend and Norman River at Glenore, 23 km south. Lakes on outskirts of Normanton abound with jabirus, brolgas, herons and other birds. Dorunda Station, 170 km north-east; working cattle station, offering accommodation, and barramundi and saratoga fishing in lake and rivers. Karumba, 69 km north-west; prawn-fishing centre for Gulf region. **Tourist information:** Shire Offices; (077) 45 1166. **Accommodation:** 3 hotel/motels, 1 hotel, 1 motel, 1 caravan/camping park. **See also:** Cape York; Gulf Savannah.
MAP REF. 440 F3

Oakey   Population 3279

On the Warrego Hwy, 29 km from Toowoomba, this town is the base for Australian Army Aviation. **Of interest:** Horse-drawn vehicles and memorabilia, and bronze statue of racehorse Bernborough, Tourist Centre, Campbell St.

Oakey Historical Museum, Warrego Hwy. Flypast, Museum of Australian Army Flying, at army base; large collection of original and replica aircraft (most in flying condition) and aviation memorabilia. **In the area:** Acland Coal Mine Museum, 18 km north. Jondaryan Woolshed (1859), on Warrego Hwy, 22 km north-west, with space for 88 blade shearers; shearing demonstrations, billy tea and damper, sales of goods at wool store. Australian Heritage Festival held at Woolshed in Aug. Horse-drawn caravan holidays. **Tourist information:** Bernborough Tourist Centre, Campbell St; (076) 91 1773. **Accommodation:** 4 hotels, 2 motels.
MAP REF. 435 O10

Palm Cove   Population 2800

Part of the Marlin Coast, serene Palm Cove, 27 km north of Cairns, offers visitors an inviting selection of world-class accommodation with an equally splendid range of boutiques, art galleries and souvenir shops — all set on a tropical beach. Dive and tour bookings to the Barrier Reef are available, as are pick-up services for a host of day tours to the Atherton Tableland and surrounding areas. There is also convenient access to Mossman and Port Douglas. **In the area:** Wild World, Australian Wildlife Showpark, 5 km south; exotic range of flora and fauna. Outback Opal Mine at Clifton Beach, 7 km north; simulated mine with displays of Australia's most famous stone. **Tourist information:** Far North Qld Promotion Bureau Ltd, 36–38 Aplin St, Cairns; (070) 51 3588. **Accommodation:** 12 motels, 3 resorts, 2 caravan/ camping parks.
MAP REF. 436 F3, 439 E5

Pittsworth   Population 1992

Pittsworth is a typical Darling Downs town, situated 40 km south-west of Toowoomba on the road to Millmerran. It is the centre of a rich grain and dairying district which produces excellent cheeses. Cotton is grown with the help of irrigation. **Of interest:** Some buildings, especially in Hume St, listed by National Trust. Folk Museum, Pioneer Way; pioneer cottage, blacksmith's shop and early school. Great Australian Team Truck Pull held in Dec. **Tourist information:** Sunkist Cafe, Yandilla St; (076) 93 1246. **Accommodation:** 1 motel, 1 caravan/ camping park.
MAP REF. 435 O11

Pomona   Population 800

This small farming centre is in the northern hinterland of the Sunshine Coast, 33 km south of Gympie. Mt Cooroora

(439 m) dominates the town and in July each year tests the skill of worldwide mountain runners with the 'King of the Mountain' race and festival. **Of interest:** Majestic Theatre; cinema museum and annual film festival. **In the area:** Lake Cootharaba, 18 km north-east; large, shallow saltwater lake on Noosa River where Mrs Eliza Fraser spent her time with Aborigines after wreck of *Stirling Castle* on Fraser Island in 1836. **Tourist information:** Tourism Sunshine Coast Ltd, Alexandra Pde, Alexandra Headland; (008) 07 2041. **Accommodation:** 1 hotel.
MAP REF. 427 J5, 435 Q8

Port Douglas   Population 1333

Just 60 km north of Cairns, along one of the most scenic coastal drives in Australia, Port Douglas offers the contrast of quaint cosmopolitanism in a tropical, tree-covered mountain setting. Once a small, sleepy village, Port Douglas has become an international tourist destination, particularly since the opening of the Sheraton Mirage Hotel, a resort complex with a golf course and marina, just out of town. The township, hidden off the main highway, is surrounded with lush vegetation and pristine rainforests. This setting, along with its proximity to the Great Barrier Reef, makes it an ideal holiday destination. **Of interest:** Ben Cropp's Shipwreck Museum, end of Macrossan St, in Anzac Park. Sun. market in park. Rainforest Habitat, Port Douglas Rd; flora and fauna in natural surroundings. Tours from town include: horse trail-riding, rainforest hiking, 4WD safaris, coach tours, reef tours, outer Barrier Reef tours to Agincourt Reef, tours on famous steam train Balley Hooley, the Lady Douglas paddlewheel cruise, and tours to Wetherby cattle station. **In the area:** Flagstaff Hill, end Murphy St; commands breathtaking views of Four Mile Beach and Low Isles; daily cruises to Isles and lighthouse. Sugar town of Mossman and picturesque Mossman Gorge, 15 km north; Daintree River rainforest cruises begin further 40 km north. **Tourist information:** 23 Macrossan St and Shop 18, Marina Mirage, Wharf St; (070) 99 5599. **Accommodation:** 3 resorts, 47 motels, 4 caravan/ camping parks. **See also:** The Far North.
MAP REF. 436 F3, 438 I11, 439 B1

Proserpine   Population 2762

A sugar town, Proserpine is close to Airlie Beach, Shute Harbour and the islands of the Whitsunday Passage. **Of interest:** Bulk sugar mill, Hinschen St; tours during crushing season. **In the area:** Conway National Park, 10 km south-east; spectacular views across islands of Whitsunday Passage. **Tourist information:** Cnr Mandalay St and Shute Harbour Rd, Airlie Beach; (079) 46 6673. **Accommodation:** 4 motels, 2 caravan/ camping parks.
MAP REF. 437 K9

Quilpie   Population 780

Quilpie, 180 km west of Charleville, was established as a centre for the large sheep and cattle properties in the area, but is better known as an opal town. It takes its name from the Aboriginal world 'quilpeta', meaning 'stone curlew'. **Of interest:** Opal sales in town and opal workings outside town. Altar, font and lectern of St Finbarr's Catholic Church, Buln Buln St, made from opal-bearing rock. **In the area:** Lake Houdrahan, 6 km north on river road to Adavale; water sports and popular recreation area. Duck Creek Opal Mine at Cheepie, 75 km east. **Tourist information:** Shire Offices; (076) 56 1133. **Accommodation:** 1 hotel, 1 hotel/motel, 1 motel, 1 caravan/camping park. **See also:** The Channel Country.
MAP REF. 434 D8

Ravenswood   Population under 200

Ravenswood is a friendly, 'not quite a ghost town', 88 km east of Charters Towers via Mingela. One hundred years ago it was the classic gold-rush town. Visitors will find interesting old workings and, perhaps, a little gold along with the

Old gold-mining equipment, Ravenswood

nostalgia. **Of interest:** Several restored old buildings in town, including courthouse, shops and present ambulance centre. **In the area:** Burdekin Dam, 70 km south-east; popular recreational area with wilderness lodge. **Accommodation:** 2 hotels, 1 motel/camping park, free camping in showgrounds.
MAP REF. 436 H9

Redcliffe   Population 39 073

Redcliffe was actually the first settlement in Qld. Matthew Flinders landed here in 1799 while exploring Moreton Bay and the spot was simply named for what he found: red cliffs. In 1824, John Oxley and Commandant Miller arrived with the first convicts and troops to set up the new Moreton Bay penal colony, which was abandoned the following year in favour of Brisbane. The Aborigines, one of the reasons for the move, called the place Humpybong, meaning 'dead houses', and the name is still used for the Redcliffe Peninsula, which comprises the towns of Woody Point, Margate, Clontarf, Scarborough and Redcliffe. The City of Redcliffe was proclaimed in 1959 and is a fast-growing separate-but-satellite area of Brisbane, 35 km south via the 2.6-km-long bridge known as the Houghton Hwy, which in 1979 replaced the old Hornibrook Hwy. Fishing and boating are popular pastimes. **Of interest:** Historical museum and self-guiding Heritage Walk. **In the area:** Redcliffe is departure point for vehicular ferry to Moreton Island, where sand dunes are reputed to be highest in world. Popular Tangalooma resort on western side of island. **Tourist information:** Jetty Building, Redcliffe Pde; (07) 284 5595. **Accommodation:** 6 hotels, 3 motels, 11 caravan/camping parks. **See also:** Tours from Brisbane.
MAP REF. 425 M6, 435 Q10

Redland Bay

Population 1718
Some 30 km south-east of Brisbane on the shores of Moreton Bay, the famous red soil of this area grows excellent vegetables and strawberries, mainly for the Brisbane market. It is a popular Sunday afternoon drive from the city. Nearby Cleveland is the main centre of the Redland area and beaches at Wellington Point, Victoria Point and Redland Bay offer safe swimming and boating. **Of interest:** Strawberry Festival held in Sept. **In the area:** Roseworld, 2 km south; exhibition gardens showing most varieties of roses. Venman Environmental Park, Mt Cotton, 12 km south-west; fauna sanctuary with walking tracks and

picnic/barbecue area. King Country Nursery at Thornlands, 10 km north; rainforest setting with picnic facilities. At Cleveland, 15 km north: Bayside Markets on Sun. Cleveland is departure point for boats to Stradbroke Island, while Redland Bay is departure point for Russell, Lamb, Macleay and Karragarra Islands. Off Victoria Point, 6 km north: Coochiemudlo Island, quiet but popular. Islands are all excellent places to picnic, swim and explore; full range of facilities and services. **Tourist information:** Cnr Waterloo and Russell Sts, Cleveland; (07) 821 0057. **Accommodation:** 4 motels, 5 caravan/camping parks. **See also:** Tours from Brisbane.
MAP REF. 425 O12

Richmond   Population 704

This small town on the Flinders Hwy, 500 km from Townsville, serves the surrounding sheep and cattle properties. **Of interest:** Restored Cobb & Co. coach. Richmond Rodeo held in May. **In the area:** The area is rich in fossils. **Tourist information:** Shire Offices, Goldring St; (077) 41 3277. **Accommodation:** 1 hotel/motel, 2 motels, 1 caravan park.
MAP REF. 436 C10, 440 I8

Rockhampton   Population 54 362

Rockhampton is often called the beef capital of Australia, with some 2.5 million cattle in the region. Gold was discovered at Canoona, 60 km north-west of Rockhampton, in 1858; however, cattle became the major industry, with Herefords the main breed, since successfully crossbred with more exotic breeds to produce disease-resistant herds. Rockhampton is sited on the Tropic of Capricorn. It is a prosperous provincial city on the Fitzroy River and has considerable architectural charm. Many of the original stone buildings and churches remain, set off by yellow flowering peltophorum, bauhinia and brilliant bougainvilleas. The Capricana Springtime Festival is held each September; Camp Draft and Rough Riding Championships also are an annual feature. The city has several well-established secondary industries, including two of Australia's largest meat processing and exporting factories. **Of interest:** Quay St, alongside river, classified by National Trust; buildings include ANZ Bank (1864) and customs house (1901). Botanic Gardens on Athelstane Range, accessed via Spencer St; fine tropical display, also Japanese-style garden, koala park and walk-in aviary. Cliff Kershaw Gardens, Bruce Hwy; feature Braille Trail. Fitzroy River Barrage, Savage St, provides 63 700 million litres of water and separates tidal salt water from upstream

fresh water. Capricorn Spire (14 m) at Curtis Park, Gladstone Rd, marks exact line of Tropic of Capricorn. St Aubin's Village, Canoona St, has historic 1870 homestead. **In the area:** Dreamtime Cultural Centre, Bruce Hwy, North Rockhampton; largest Aboriginal cultural centre in Australia. Glenmore historic homestead, 5 km north. Gemland, 9 km north. Gangalook Hall of Clocks and Museum, 20 km north; slab cottage, wagons, steam engine and clocks. St Christopher's Chapel, Emu Park Rd, 20 km north; built by American servicemen. Limestone caves, Olsen's and Cammoo systems, 32 km north; conducted tours. Pleasant drive to top of Mt Archer. Cattle Country Craft Shop at Marlborough, 102 km north; town has only chrysoprase mine operating in Qld. Yeppoon and Emu Park beaches, 25–30 km north-east. Mt Morgan Mine and Museum, 38 km south-west. Thunder eggs fossicking at Mt Hay Gemstone Tourist Park, 41 km west on Capricorn Hwy. Great Keppel Island tourist resort, 13 km off Capricorn Coast. Underwater Observatory off Middle Island. **Tourist information:** Curtis Park, Gladstone Rd; (079) 27 2055.

Accommodation: 18 hotels, 28 motels, 7 caravan/camping parks. **See also:** Capricorn.
MAP REF. 435 M3

Roma   Population 6069

Roma is on the Warrego Hwy, 261 km west of Dalby, with the Carnarvon Hwy going south to St George, and north to Injune and the Carnarvon Gorges. It was named after the wife of Sir George Bowen, Qld's first Governor. In 1859 it became the first gazetted settlement after the separation from NSW. The Mt Abundance cattle station was established in 1857 and sheep and cattle have been the area's economic mainstay ever since. The famous trial of Harry Redford, alias Captain Starlight, was held in Roma in 1872. In 1863, the SS *Bassett* brought vine cuttings to Roma and Qld's first wine-making enterprise got under way. Australia's first natural gas strike was made at Hospital Hill in 1900, and the gas from this source was used, briefly, to light the town. Further deposits were found periodically, and 'oil' (actually gas and condensate) caused excitement in the area in the early 1960s.

Plains near Roma

DARLING DOWNS

The 72 500 square kilometres of black volcanic soil on the Darling Downs produce 90 per cent of the state's wheat, 50 per cent of its maize, 90 per cent of its oilseeds, two-thirds of its fruit and one-third of its tobacco, as well as oats, sorghum, millet, cotton, soybeans and navy beans. It is a major sheep, cattle and dairying area and the home of several famous bloodstock studs.

Allan Cunningham was the first white man to ride across these fertile plains in 1827. The Darling Downs is rural Australia at its best, with a touch of England in the magnificent oaks, elms, plane trees and poplars of **Toowoomba's** parks, and the colourful rose gardens of **Warwick** in the south. The climate is cooler and more bracing than in the rest of the state.

Driving across the Downs with its neat strips of grainfields, lush pastures, patches of forest and national parks, and well-established homesteads, gives the visitor an impression of beauty and quiet prosperity.

The Warrego Highway leads northwest from Toowoomba to the wheatfields and silos of **Dalby**, the 'hub of the Downs'. Gowrie Mountain is a popular lookout. At **Jimbour**, twenty-seven kilometres north-west of Dalby, stands the stately two-storey Jimbour House. On an elevated site with panoramic views of the Jimbour Plains, this historic home in landscaped gardens was constructed between 1874 and 1876, mainly from local materials, including cedar from the Bunya Mountains. Part of an earlier (1870) bluestone building still stands at the rear of the house.

The New England Highway, the main Sydney to Brisbane route, turns into the Cunningham Highway at Warwick, and descends from the Downs towards the coast through Cunninghams Gap, discovered in 1827. Main Range National Park has lovely rainforest, palms and native wildlife. An alternative inland route between Brisbane and Melbourne is the Newell Highway, which runs west from Warwick to **Goondiwindi** and then south through **Moree** and **Narrabri**. A less-used, but scenic route is the Heifer Creek Way through the Lockyer Valley from near **Greenmount East** to **Gatton**.

For further information on the Darling Downs, contact the Southern Downs Tourist Association, 49 Albion St (New England Hwy), Warwick; (076) 61 3122.

See also: Entries in A–Z listing.

Farmlands, Darling Downs

Roma now supplies Brisbane with gas via a 450 km pipeline. **Of interest:** Oil rig, named 'Big Rig' by locals; erected as landmark at eastern entrance to town on Warrego Hwy. Romavilla Winery, Injune Rd; tastings and sales. Campbell Park; picnics and walks. Cultural Centre, cnr Bungil and Injune Rds; mural by local artists. **In the area:** Meadowbank Museum, 15 km west on Warrego Hwy. **Tourist information:** BP Central, Bowen St; (076) 22 3399. **Accommodation:** 10 hotels, 8 motels, 4 caravan/camping parks.
MAP REF. 435 K8

St George   Population 2323
Situated at a major road junction, St George is in the centre of a rich cotton-growing district. It is on the Balonne River, 118 km north of Mungindi by the Carnarvon Hwy, and 292 km south-west of Dalby by the Moonie Hwy. As St George has a rainfall of only 500 mm a year, an extensive irrigation programme is carried out by means of a new dam and three weirs. Cotton growing and harvesting is completely mechanised; planting is from October to November, and harvesting is from April to June. The cotton ginnery may be inspected by appointment during the harvesting months. Wheat, barley, oats and sunflowers are also irrigated, and sheep and cattle are raised. **In the area:** Rosehill Aviaries, 64 km west; one of Australia's largest private collections of Australian parrots. Fishing for Murray cod, yellow-belly and freshwater jew on Balonne River. **Tourist information:** Shire Offices, Victoria St, (076) 25 3222; or Merino Motor Inn, (076) 25 3333. **Accommodation:** 4 hotels, 2 motels.
MAP REF. 435 J11

Sarina   Population 3158
In the sugar-belt, Sarina lies 37 km south of Mackay on the Bruce Hwy. The area has many fine beaches, including Sarina, Armstrongs, Campwin, Grasstree, Half-tide and Salonika. Sarina produces molasses and ethyl alcohol as byproducts of the sugar industry. **Of interest:** Plane Creek Central Sugar Mill. CSR Distillery. **In the area:** To north: Tours of Campwin Beach Prawn Farm (8.5 km) and The Big Prawn, Grasstree Beach (13 km). Viewing gallery at Hay Point and Dalrymple Bay coal terminal complex, 12 km north. **Tourist information:** Broad St; (079) 43 1501. **Accommodation:** 4 hotels, 3 motels, 3 caravan/camping parks.
MAP REF. 437 L11

Shute Harbour   Pop. under 200
Shute Harbour (or as it is known to older residents, Shute Haven) is a suburb of the town of Whitsunday. It is also the second largest marine passenger terminal in Australia, second only to Sydney's Circular Quay. Shute Harbour's first marina is a 400-berth project. The jetty at Shute Harbour, 36 km north-east of Proserpine, is the best place to start exploring the 80 or so tropical islands that bask in the beautiful Whitsunday waters. Hayman, Daydream, South Molle and Lindeman Islands are the best known. Every morning big and small launches, yachts and glass-bottomed boats take tourists on board for a memorable, picturesque day out. Booking offices, souvenir and food outlets are on the main jetty, with fuel available nearby. Try boom-net riding on one of the three-island tours available daily. You can even fly by seaplane to Hardy's Lagoon on the outer Barrier Reef for a few hours' snorkelling amongst the coral. An extensive fleet of sail and power vessels of varying sizes and classes is available for charter. Ex-America's Cup challenger Gretel takes visitors on day trips through the Whitsunday Islands. There are also day trips to the pontoon at Hardy Reef for swimming, snorkelling and scuba-diving. The brigantine Romance offers 5-night cruises off the islands and the Reef. **Of interest:** Spectacular views from Lions Lookout. Heritage Doll Museum, Shute Harbour Rd, adjacent to Whitsunday airport. **In the area:** Airlie Beach (5 km north), Conway National Park (15 km south), the Great Barrier Reef (30 min. by air, 90 min. by boat) and Whitsunday Islands. **Tourist information:** Cnr Mandalay St and Shute Harbour Rd, Airlie Beach; (079) 46 6673. **Accommodation:** 2 motels.
MAP REF. 437 K9

Southport
Pop. part of Gold Coast
At the northern end of the Gold Coast strip, Southport is packed with attractions to suit the holidaymaker. It also serves as the commercial and administrative centre for the Gold Coast. **Of interest:** Sea World at The Spit is a marine park where a full day can happily be spent and dolphins delight visitors. Other attractions include a replica of the *Endeavour*, a water-ski ballet, a monorail and a paddlewheel steamer. Also on The Spit are Marina Mirage, Mariner's Cove and Fisherman's Wharf (tourist complexes with speciality shops, restaurants, outdoor cafes and weekend entertainment), and the Southport Yacht Club, the finishing-line of the famous Jupiters Yacht classics. **In the area:** Attractions of the Gold Coast and its hinterland. **Tourist information:** Cavill Mall, Surfers Paradise; (075) 38 4419. **Accommodation:** 2 hotels, 7 motels, 3 caravan/camping parks. **See also:** City of the Gold Coast.
MAP REF. 429 P5, 435 Q11

Stanthorpe   Population 4138
The main town in the Granite Belt, 225 km south-west of Brisbane, in the mountain ranges along the border between Qld and NSW, Stanthorpe came into being after the discovery of tin at Quartpot

Marina Mirage Resort, Southport

Creek in 1872. Silver and lead were discovered in 1880, but the minerals boom did not last. The area has produced excellent wool for more than a century, but is best known for large-scale growing of apples, pears, plums, peaches and grapes. Stanthorpe is 915 m above sea-level and is often the coolest part of the state. Spring is particularly beautiful with fruit trees and wattles in bloom. There are 90 varieties of wild orchids found in the area. **Of interest:** Museum, High St. Art Gallery and Library Complex, Weeroona Park, Marsh St. Apple and Grape Harvest Festival held in Mar. (even years); Brass Monkey Month in July; Spring Wine Festival in Oct. **In the area:** Granite Belt wineries: Mt Magnus at Pozieres (14 km north-west); Heritage at Cottonvale (12 km north-west); Old Caves, just north of Stanthorpe; Stone Ridge, Felsberg, Mountview and Kominos, near Glen Alpin (10 km south); Rumbalara at Fletcher (14 km south); Sundown Valley, Winewood, Bungawarna and Robinson's Family Winery, near Ballandean (19 km south); Bald Mountain at Wallangarra (30 km south). Sunworld Park at Eukey, 13 km south-east; displays of sun- and wind- powered instruments. Storm King Dam, 26 km south-east; popular for canoeing and water-skiing. Mt Marlay for excellent views. Sundown National Park; wilderness area with camping on Severn River in south-west of park. Girraween National Park, 32 km south; camping, bushwalking, rock-climbing and spectacular wildflower displays. **Tourist information:** 61 Marsh St; (076) 81 2057. **Accommodation:** 5 hotels, 6 motels, 3 caravan/camping parks.
MAP REF. 113 M2, 435 O12

Strathpine   Population 10 108

Immediately behind Brisbane and to the north is the Pine Rivers Shire, a peaceful rural district that includes the closest forested areas and national parks to Brisbane. Taking advantage of this rural setting so close to the city are a number of art and craft industries. Here Brisbane's oldest and largest country market is held at Albany Creek, 6 km south of Strathpine, every Sunday, where locally produced artworks, food and produce are sold while buskers entertain and craft demonstrations are given. **In the area:** Alma Park Zoo at Kallangur, 11 km north; Australian native animals, also grizzly bears, camels and many other animals and birds. Friendship Farm for children features baby animals. Bunya Park Wildlife Sanctuary at Eatons Hill, 8 km south-west; Australian native animals in typical bush setting. Samford Grass

Ski, 15 km south-west. Australian Woolshed at Ferny Hills, 16 km south-west; sheep-shearing, spinning, trained rams, working sheepdogs, woolshed dancing and traditional Australian food. Bush dances with bush band. Number of national parks and Brisbane Forest Park just minutes from Brisbane. **Tourist information:** Shire Offices, 220 Gympie Rd; (07) 205 0555. **Accommodation:** Limited.
MAP REF. 420 F3, 425 K7

Tambo   Population 399

Tambo, 101 km south-east of Blackall on the Matilda Hwy, was established in the mid-1860s. From a point where the town now stands, explorer Thomas Mitchell first saw the Barcoo River. **Of interest:** Old Post Office Museum. **In the area:** Salvator Rosa section of Carnarvon National Park, 120 km east; area named by Major Mitchell, who was reminded of landscapes painted by 17th-century artist. Access to park via Dawson Development Rd and Cungelella Station; 4WD recommended. Permission to camp in park must be obtained from Qld NPWS. **Tourist information:** Universal Stores, Arthur St (Matilda Hwy); (076) 54 6288. **Accommodation:** 1 hotel, 1 hotel/motel, 1 motel, 1 caravan/camping park.
MAP REF. 434 G5

Taroom   Population 749

Taroom is almost 300 km due west of Maryborough, on the Dawson River and Leichhardt Hwy. Cattle-raising is the main industry. **Of interest:** Coolibah tree in main street marked 'L.L.' by Ludwig Leichhardt on his 1844 trip from Jimbour House near Dalby to Port Essington (Darwin). **In the area:** Rare Livistona palms near hwy 15 km north. Reedy Creek Homestead, 115 km north-west; outback holidays on working cattle station. Isla Gorge National Park, 55 km north. Robinson Gorge, 108 km north-west. **Tourist information:** Shire Offices, Yaldwyn St; (076) 27 3211. **Accommodation:** 1 caravan/camping park.
MAP REF. 435 L7

Texas   Population 817

Quite the opposite in size to its United States namesake, Texas lies on the Dumaresque River and the NSW border, 55 km south of Inglewood. **Of interest:** Historical Museum in old police station (1893). Agricultural show held in July. **In the area:** Glenlyon Dam, 51 km south-east; good fishing. **Tourist information:** 40 High St. **Accommodation:** 1 motel, 1 caravan/ camping park.
MAP REF. 113 K2, 435 N12

Theodore   Population 576

Grain and cotton are the main crops around this town on the Leichhardt Hwy, 220 km north of Miles. It was named after Edward Theodore, a Premier of Qld. **Of interest:** Dawson Folk Museum. Fishing on Glebe Weir. **In the area:** Isla Gorge National Park, 35 km south. Cracow, 50 km south-east, where gold was produced from famous Golden Plateau mine 1932–76. **Tourist information:** Callide St, Biloela; (079) 92 2405. **Accommodation:** 1 hotel, 1 caravan/camping park.
MAP REF. 435 M6

Thuringowa   Population 36 000

Thuringowa is a growing city, surrounding the city of Townsville, that depends not only on its established grazing and sugar industries but on such diversification as tropical fruit growing plantations, including mango and pineapple, extensive mixed vegetable farming, the Qld Nickel Refinery at Yabulu and, increasingly, tourism. Some of north Qld's best beaches, stretching along more than 120 km of coastline, provide visitors with surfing and fishing. **In the area:** Australian farm display at Alligator Creek, 18 km south-east; also wildlife park at Billabong Sanctuary. Haughton River Company's Invicta Sugar Mill at Giru, 27 km south-east. Tropical Agriculture Research Station at Lansdowne Station, Woodstock, 33 km south. Internationally recognised Australian Institute of Marine Science at Turtle Bay on Cape Bowling Green, 97 km south-east. **Tourist information:** Bruce Hwy, Townsville; (077) 78 3555. **Accommodation:** 3 hotels, 2 hotel/motels, 1 motel, 5 caravan/camping parks.
MAP REF. 436 I8

Tin Can Bay – Rainbow Beach

Population 913

Just half an hour's drive north-east of Gympie takes travellers to Tin Can Bay and Rainbow Beach. These two hamlets are popular fishing, prawning and crabbing areas; the quiet waters of Tin Can Bay are ideal for boating and fishing, while Rainbow Beach has good surfing. **Of interest:** In Aug., Amamoor Creek State Forest Park in Mary Valley becomes 'home among the gum trees' when annual Country Music Muster is held. **In the area:** Road south from Rainbow Beach (4WD) leads to coloured sands and beaches of Cooloola National Park. North, at Inskip Point, ferry to Fraser Island. Fully equipped boats for hire at Tin Can Bay marina for cruising, fishing, swimming. **Tourist information:** 8 Rainbow Beach Rd, Rainbow Beach; (074)

86 3227. **Accommodation:** 2 hotels, 4 motels, 6 caravan/camping parks. MAP REF. 435 Q8

Toowoomba   Population 71 362

The garden city of Toowoomba has a distinctive charm and graciousness, due to its wide, tree-lined streets, colonial architecture and many fine parks and gardens. It is at its best every September for the Carnival of Flowers. Toowoomba is 138 km west of Brisbane, on the rim of the Great Dividing Range. It began in 1849 as a village near an important staging-post for teamsters and travellers, and was known as 'The Swamp'. Aborigines pronounced this as T'wamp-bah, or Toowoomba. Today it is the commercial centre for the fertile Darling Downs, with butter and cheese factories, sawmills, flour-mills, tanneries, engineering and railway workshops, a modern iron foundry, clothing and shoe factories. It has an active cultural and artistic life. **Of interest:** Self-guiding Russell St Heritage Walk. Cobb and Co. Museum, Lindsay St; traces history of horsedrawn vehicles. St Patrick's Cathedral (1880s). St Luke's Anglican Church (1897). Parks include Lake Annand, McKenzie St, for bird-lovers; Laurel Bank, scented gardens; Botanic Gardens and adjacent Queens Park, Lindsay St; and Waterbird Habitat, McKenzie St. Ascot House (1870s), Newmarket St; teas, lunches. Royal Bull's Head Inn (1847), Brisbane St; fully restored by National Trust. Toowoomba Art Gallery, Linton Gallery and Gould Gallery, Ruthven St; Downs Gallery, Margaret St. Willow Springs Adventure Park, Spring St. **In the area:** Several self-guiding scenic drives: many picnic spots on 48 km circuit to Spring Bluff and Murphy's Creek; railway station at Spring Bluff, although closed, has superb gardens; 100 km circuit to Heifer Creek, known as Valley of the Sun, provides some spectacular scenery; 255 km circuit takes in Bernborough Centre, Jondaryan Woolshed, Cecil Plains Cotton Ginnery, Millmerran Museum and Pittsworth Folk Museum. Picnic Point, 5 km east; mountain views and Carnival Falls. Balyarta Fragrant Gardens, Highfields, 15 km north. Acland Coal Mine Museum, near Oakey, 25 km north-west. **Tourist information:** 541 Ruthven St; (076) 32 1988. **Accommodation:** 28 motels, 4 caravan/camping parks. **See also:** Tours from Brisbane; Darling Downs. MAP REF. 432, 435 O10

Townsville   Population 96 230

In 1864, a sea captain named Robert Towns commissioned James Melton Black to build a wharf and establish a settlement on Cleveland Bay to service the new cattle industry inland. Townsville was gazetted in 1865 and declared a city in 1903. Today Australia's largest tropical city, Townsville has an international airport and its rapid expansion is evidenced by the Sheraton Breakwater Island Casino-Hotel and the Great Barrier Reef Wonderland, as well as the Victoria Bridge Complex and the Lakes Project. There are, however, many handsome historic buildings, particularly in the waterfront park area around Cleveland Bay. The city's busy port handles minerals from Mount Isa and Cloncurry; beef and wool from the western plains; sugar and timber from the rich coastal region; and its own manufacturing and processing industries. Townsville is the administrative, commercial and manufacturing capital of northern Qld. Among its impressive new public buildings is the James Cook University, which offers Australia's first tourism degree. Next door to the University is the Institute of Education. A pleasant 20-minute catamaran trip across the bay takes you to Magnetic Island National Park and resort, or you may walk the length of the Strand with its tropical parks, waterfall and overhanging bougainvillea gardens. At the end of the Strand is the Rockpool development, which allows for swimming all year round. Another pedestrian feature is the Flinders Mall in the heart of the city where Cotters Market is held every Sunday morning. Townsville is becoming a renowned centre for research into marine life and is the headquarters for the Great Barrier Reef Marine Park Authority. A major annual attraction is the ten-day Pacific Festival, held Sept.–Oct. **Of interest:** Sheraton Breakwater Casino, Western Breakwater, end Flinders St. Great Barrier Reef Wonderland, Flinders St East; aquarium with touch-tank and walk-through transparent underwater viewing-tunnel, also Omnimax theatre. Museum of Tropical Queensland, Flinders St, adjacent to Wonderland. Perc Tucker Regional Art Gallery, Flinders Mall. Jezzine Military Museum, end The Strand. Copper refinery at Stuart; conducted tours. Queen's Gardens, cnr Paxton and Gregory Sts. Botanic Gardens, Kings Rd. Historic Flinders Street East. Castle Hill Lookout, off Burke St. Town Common Environment Park, Pallarenda Rd; coastline park. Maritime Museum, Palmer St, South Townsville. **In the area:** Four-day cruises to Cairns via resort islands and Reef on catamaran *Coral Princess*. Reef day trips and dive cruises. Day sailing around Magnetic Island. Daily connections to resort islands: Magnetic, Orpheus, Hinchinbrook, Dunk and Bedarra. Day outback tours, rainforest and whitewater rafting tours. Mt Spec, Crystal Creek National Park, Hidden Valley and Paluma, all 80–100 km north-west. Mt Elliott National Park (25 km south), on Bruce Hwy, and Pangola Park (32 km south) at Spring Creek, Giru; waterfalls, bush walks, swimming, picnic and camping facilities. Australian Institute of Marine Science at Cape Ferguson, 46 km south. **Tourist information:** Bruce Hwy; (077) 78 3555. **Accommodation:** 74 hotel/motels, 15 caravan/camping parks. **See also:** The Far North. MAP REF. 433, 436 H7

Tully   Population 2575

Situated at the foot of Mt Tyson, Tully receives the highest annual rainfall in Australia, averaging around 4200 mm. Major industries are sugarcane, tropical fruits, cattle, bananas and timber. **In the area:** Fishing, whitewater rafting, canoeing and reef and island cruising. Popular picnic spot on Tully River near Cardstone, 80 km west. Spectacular rainforests at Mission Beach and Clump Point (9 km north), Bingil Bay (10 km north), and Kareeya Gorge and Murray Falls (26 km south). **Tourist information:** Bruce Hwy; (070) 68 2288. **Accommodation:** 2 hotels, 1 motel, 1 caravan/camping park. MAP REF. 436 G5

Warwick   Population 9435

An attractive city on the Darling Downs, Warwick is 162 km south-west of Brisbane on the Cunningham Hwy, and 82 km south of Toowoomba on the New England Hwy. The area was first explored by Allan Cunningham in 1827; in 1840 the Leslie brothers arrived from the south and established a sheep station at Canning Downs, and other pastoralists followed. The NSW Government asked Patrick Leslie to select a site for a township, and in 1849 Warwick was surveyed and established. It was the first town, after Brisbane, in what became Qld. The railway line from Ipswich was opened in 1871, and Warwick became a city in 1936. In what seemed to be a minor incident in 1917, Prime Minister Billy Hughes was hit by an egg while addressing a crowd on the controversial conscription issue of the day. He asked a local policeman to arrest the man and the policeman refused. The result was the formation of the Commonwealth Police Force. Warwick is on the willow-shaded Condamine River, 453 m above sea-level, and calls itself the 'Rose and Rodeo City'. The surrounding rich pastures support many famous horse and cattle studs, and produce some of Australia's finest wool and grain. Fruit, vegetables and timber grow well, and its dairy products and bacon are famous.

Of interest: Pringle Cottage (1870), Dragon St; museum housing large photo collection, vehicles and machinery. Leslie Park in Palmerin St. Jubilee Gardens, cnr Alice and Helene Sts, for superb displays of roses. Enchanted Garden and Herb Nursery, New England Hwy. Warwick Regional Art Gallery, Albion St. Celebrated Warwick Rodeo held in Oct. Rock Swap at Easter. **In the area:** Leslie Dam, 15 km west, for water sports and picnics. Queen Mary Falls National Park, 45 km east via Killarney, and Carr's Lookout, further 14 km. Main Range National Park, 50 km north-east. Cherrabah Mountain Resort, 35 km east near Killarney. Richmond Homestead (c. 1898) and Talgai Homestead (c. 1860), both via Allora, 26 km north; accommodation and meals. **Tourist information:** 49 Albion St (New England Hwy); (076) 61 3122. **Accommodation:** 13 hotels, 10 motels, 3 caravan/camping parks. **See also:** Darling Downs.
MAP REF. 113 N1, 435 O11

Weipa   Population 2406
Located on the west coast of Cape York, Weipa is home of the world's largest bauxite mine, operated by Comalco. This small mining town provides a surprisingly comprehensive range of services and facilities for those travellers just wishing to visit or those calling in for urgently needed repairs or reprovisioning. **Of interest:** Guided tours of bauxite mine provide comprehensive coverage of whole mining process at Weipa. **In the area:** Tours of local areas such as Rocky Point, Trunding, Nanum and Evans Landing also give insight into town's development and lifestyle. Number of fishing and camping areas near Weipa developed for

well-equipped tourist. **Tourist information:** Far North Qld Promotion Bureau Ltd, 36–38 Aplin St, Cairns; (070) 51 3588. **Accommodation:** Limited. **See also:** Cape York.
MAP REF. 438 C4

Whitsunday   Population 6093
Named by Captain Cook in 1770, Whitsunday Island (uninhabited) is the largest in the group. The mainland town of Whitsunday is one of Australia's fastest-growing tourist destinations. Whitsunday (including the suburbs of Airlie Beach, Cannonvale and Shute Harbour) depends on the tourism industry, and offers a large range of activities for the 500 000 visitors who come each year. Stretching along roughly 15 km of the coastline, Whitsunday town was gazetted in 1987. **Of interest:** Scenic and bush walks through areas behind town in Conway National Park. Whitsunday Festival of Sail held in June and Dec. Whitsunday Gamefishing Championships on Queen's Birthday long weekend. Mardi Gras in Sept. Annual game-fishing tournament in Nov. **In the area:** Coral viewing and tours of Great Barrier Reef and Whitsunday Islands. Extensive half- and full-day mainland tours, taking in Cedar Creek Falls, rainforests and other major attractions. **Tourist information:** Cnr Mandalay St and Shute Harbour Rd, Airlie Beach; (079) 46 6673. **Accommodation:** 2 hotels, 20 motels, 7 caravan parks, 4 resorts.
MAP REF. 437 K9

Winton   Population 1281
Banjo Paterson wrote Australia's most famous song, 'Waltzing Matilda', on

Dagworth Station near Winton in 1895. Combo Waterhole was then part of Dagworth, and the ballad had its first public airing in Winton. The town is 173 km north-west of Longreach on the Matilda Hwy, and at the headwaters of the Diamantina River. A major sheep area, Winton is also a large trucking centre for the giant road-trains bringing cattle from the Channel Country to the railhead. In 1920 the first office of a company called Qantas was registered in Winton. The town's water supply comes out of deep artesian bores at a temperature of 83°C. **Of interest:** Swagman statue near swimming-pool. Qantilda Pioneer Place, Elderslie St, complex of 4 buildings; includes relocated Dagworth Station lounge room, Qantas Room, old telephone exchange, Aboriginal artefacts, steam locomotive, vintage vehicles and bottle (8000) collection. Outback Festival held in Sept. in odd years. **In the area:** Aboriginal paintings and bora ceremonial grounds at Skull Hole, 40 km south. Opalton, 115 km south; ghost town and gemfields. Lark Quarry Environmental Park, 110 km south-west; preserves tracks of dinosaur 'stampede'. Combo Waterhole, 141 km south-east via Matilda Hwy. Outback tours. Farm holidays at Lorraine Station, 60 km south-east. **Tourist information:** Qantilda Pioneer Place, Elderslie St; (076) 57 1618. **Accommodation:** 4 hotels, 2 motels, 1 caravan/camping park.
MAP REF. 434 B1, 436 C13, 440 I11

Wondai   Population 1213
This typical small country town in the South Burnett is 23 km south of Murgon and 31 km north of Kingaroy. The surrounding area produces peanuts and a variety of grains; other industries include dairying, beef and pork production, timber milling and dolomite mining. **Of interest:** Museum, Mackenzie St. **In the area:** Gem-fossicking areas surround district. Boondooma Dam, 50 km north-west near Proston; recreation area and water sports. **Tourist information:** Shire Offices, Scott St; (071) 68 5155. **Accommodation:** 1 hotel/motel, 1 motel, 1 caravan/camping park.
MAP REF. 435 O8

Yandina   Population 600
Yandina lies 10 km north of Nambour on the Bruce Hwy and is the home of the world-famous Ginger Factory and Gingertown, where visitors may partake of ginger 'goodies'. The processing of the crop can be observed from the tower platform at the factory and the Ginger Bell paddlesteamer offers river cruises from the factory to a working ginger

Shute Harbour, departure point for the Whitsunday Islands

GLADSTONE REGION

Gladstone, only six hours' drive north of Brisbane, offers the closest major southern access to the Great Barrier Reef. Reef trips depart daily from Gladstone's marina and regularly from the Town of 1770.

With its gracious palm-studded city centre, Gladstone faces the harbour and offers accommodation ranging from international hotels to caravan parks, as well as restaurants serving the region's famous mud crabs. Gladstone, the outlet for Central Queensland's mineral and agricultural wealth, is a world-class port and one of Australia's busiest.

The hinterland west of Gladstone features national parks, rainforests and an historical village, and is ideal for trailriding, camping, walking and fishing.

South of the city, nestled in the delta of the picturesque Boyne River, **Boyne Island** is linked by a bridge to its twin beachside community, **Tannum Sands**. In an easy blend of scenery and industry, a major smelter on the island produces a quarter of Australia's aluminium output.

Further south, the **Agnes Water–Town of 1770** area is renowned for its unspoiled parkland with natural springs, palm groves, pockets of wilderness and rare birds, animals and plants. The secluded white beaches with their crystal-clear waters are virtually unaltered since Captain Cook

Heron Island

landed here in 1770.

Heron Island, a world-famous coral cay resort, is on the Barrier Reef just off Gladstone. **Wilson Island**, another beautiful coral cay, offers camping holidays in comfortable seclusion. Locally-based helicopters, as well as a host of vessels moored in the Gladstone marina, enable visitors to explore this tropical paradise. A large charter-boat fleet departs regularly for fishing and diving trips or to take campers to the reef islands.

For further information contact Gladstone Area Promotion and Development Ltd, 56 Goondoon St, Gladstone; (079) 72 4000.

See also: A–Z listing.

---

farm. **Of interest:** Carinya, historic homestead on Bruce Hwy on northern edge of town. The Queenslander, for antiques and fascinating bric-a-brac. **In the area:** At Eumundi, 8 km north, Sat. morning country markets; goods range from locally grown fruit and vegetables to art and craft. Eumundi Lager brewed at Imperial Hotel, near markets. **Tourist information:** Hastings St Information Centre, Noosa Heads; (074) 47 5506. **Accommodation:** Limited.
MAP REF. 427 K8

Yeppoon   Population 6452
This popular coastal resort, 40 km northeast of Rockhampton, lies on the shores of Keppel Bay. Yeppoon and the strip of beaches to its south — Cooee Bay, Rosslyn Bay, Causeway Lake, Emu Park and Keppel Sands — are known as the Capricorn Coast. Great Keppel Island tourist resort is 13 km offshore. **Of interest:** Yeppoon Pineapple Festival held in Sept. **In the area:** Capricorn International Resort, 85 000 ha Japanese development, 8 km north. Cooberrie Park, 15 km north; noted flora and fauna reserve with picnic facilities. Byfield National Park, 17 km further north; home of extremely rare Byfield fern. State Forest Parks nearby include Waterpark Creek, Upper Stony and Red Rock. Catamaran service to North West Island, largest coral cay on Great Barrier Reef, off Capricorn Coast. Coral Life Marineland, Kinka Beach, 13 km south. **Tourist information:** Ross Creek Roundabout; (079) 39 4888. **Accommodation**: 8 motels, 6 caravan/camping parks.
MAP REF. 435 N3

Yungaburra   Population 769
On the edge of the Atherton Tableland, 13 km from Atherton and inland from Cairns, the town is known for its National Trust 'Historic Precinct' listing. **Of interest:** Self-guiding Historic Precinct Buildings walk. Rockhounds Shop, Cedar St; mineral display and gem-fossicking information. Artists Gallery, Mulgrave Rd. Produce and craft markets held 4th Sat. of each month, Mulgrave Rd. **In the area:** Curtain Fig Tree, 2.5 km southwest; spectacular example of strangler fig. Lakes Eacham (5 km east) and Barrine (10 km east), volcanic crater lakes. **Tourist information:** Far North Qld Promotion Bureau Ltd, 36–38 Aplin St, Cairns; (070) 51 3588. **Accommodation:** 1 hotel, 3 motels.
MAP REF. 439 D12

Maps of Queensland

Location Map

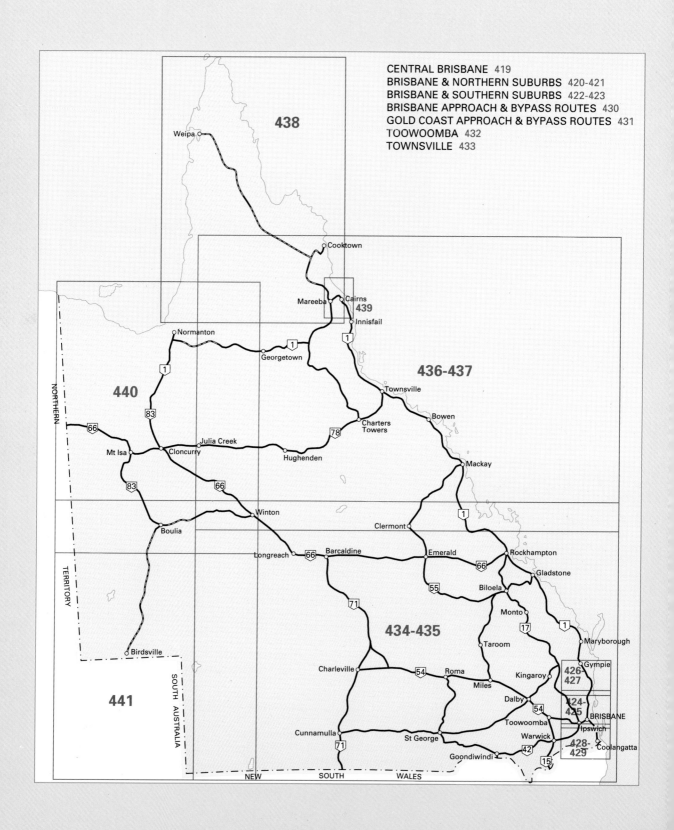

Central Brisbane 419

0   0.5   1 km

Places of Interest

1	Albert St. Uniting Church	D4
2	Anzac Memorial	E4
3	Aust. Government Centre	E4
49	Beaufort Hotel	F6
4	Bellevue Hotel	D6
5	City Administration Bldg.	D5
6	City Hall	D5
7	City Plaza	D5
8	Club 1 Hotel	B4
9	Cultural Centre	B6
10	Festival Hall	E6
11	Gateway Inn	C5
12	Gazebo Terrace Hotel	C3
13	Hilton Hotel	E5
14	Holy Spirit Hospital	C3
15	Lennons Plaza Hotel	D5
16	Main Roads Department	D2
17	Mater Hospital	E11
18	Mayfair Crest Int. Hotel	D4
19	Observatory (Tower Mill)	D4
20	Old Customs House	F4
21	Old School of Arts	D4
22	Parkroyal Motel	E6
23	Parliament House	E7
24	Police Department	B4
25	Post Office (GPO)	E4
26	Public Library	B6
27	Queensland Art Gallery	B6
28	Qld. Country Womens Ass.	C1
29	Queensland Museum	B6
30	Ridge Hotel	E2
31	Riverside Centre	F4
32	St.James School	F2
33	St.Johns Cathedral	F3
34	St Stephens Cathedral	E5
35	Sheraton Hotel	D4
36	Stock Exchange	F4
37	Supreme Court	C5
38	Synagogue	E6
39	Treasury Building	D6
40	Youth Hostel	A3

Transport and Touring

41	Australian Airlines	E4
42	Brisbane Transit Centre	B4
43	Central Railway Station	D4
44	RACQ	E5,E1
45	Railway Centre	D4
46	Roma St. Stn (Suburban)	C3
47	Sunmap Centre	E4,G11
48	Tourist Bureau	E4

See fold-out page for an explanation of the map symbols

COPYRIGHT, BP AUSTRALIA LTD

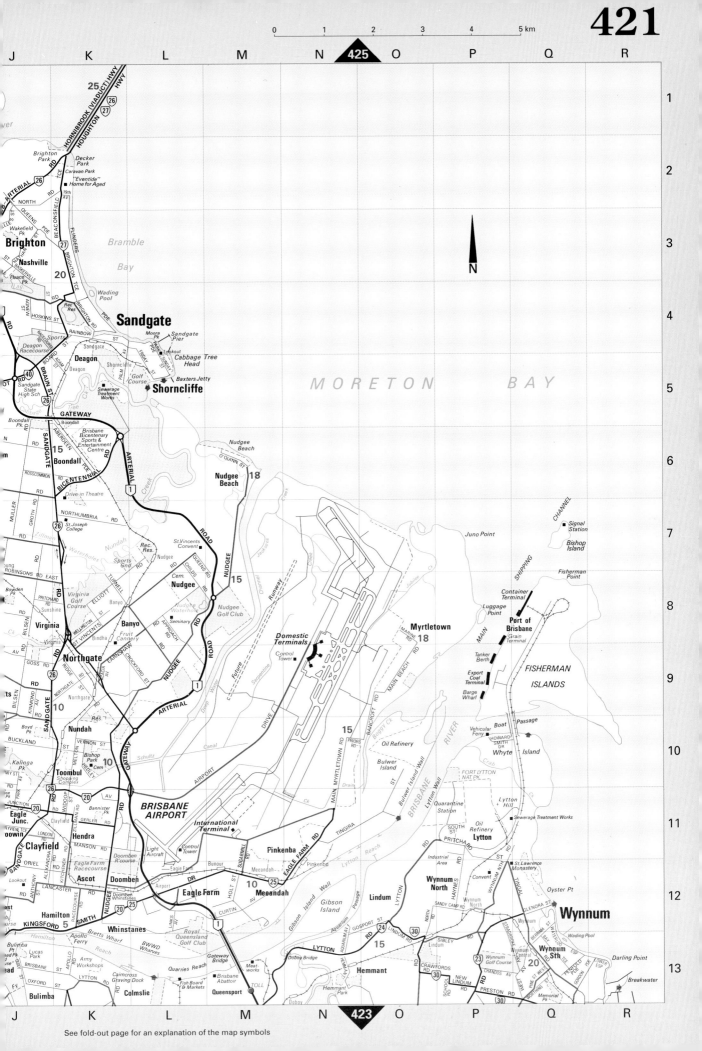

0 1 2 3 4 5 km

J K L M N **425** O P Q R

1

2

HORNIBROOK (VIADUCT) HWY
HOUGHTON HWY
25
26
27

Brighton
Park
Decker
Park
Caravan Park
"Eventide"
Home for Aged
19th
AV
NORTH
ST
QUEENS
PDE
FLINDERS
BRIGHTON
TCE
26
27
BEACONSFIELD
TCE

3

BAYSIDE ARTERIAL
Wakefield
Pk
Peace
Pk
Bramble
Bay
Brighton
Nashville
20

N

4

Sandgate
Sports
Deagon
Racecourse
Sandgate
Deagon
Deagon
Shorncliffe
Golf
Course
Rainbow
ST
BRIGHTON RD
Moora
Pk
Sandgate
Pier
Cabbage Tree
Head
Lookout
Baxters Jetty
Shorncliffe
M O R E T O N   B A Y

5

GATEWAY
Sandgate State
High Sch
40
26
HOSKINS ST
BRAUN ST
BOARD ST
ADAM ST
PALM
PDE
Sewerage
Treatment
Works

6

Boondall Pk P.O
Boondall
Pk
Brisbane
Bicentenary
Sports &
Entertainment
Centre
Boondall
Boondall
15
ABERDEEN
SANDGATE
ROSSCOMMON
RD
BICENTENNIAL
RD
ARTERIAL
Creek
Nudgee
Beach
O'QUINN ST
Nudgee
Beach
18
Nudgee
Beach

7

1
Drive-in Theatre
NORTHUMBRIA
RD
St Joseph
College
26
MULLER
RD
GROTH
RD
Zillman
Waterholes
St Vincents
Convent
ROAD
QUEENS
Juno Point

8

RD EAST
ROBINSONS RD
Bowden
RD
PRITCHARD
RD
Sunshine
Nundah
Sports
Grnd
Rec.
Res.
Virginia
Golf
Course
TUNNELL
ELLIOTT
Cem.
CHILDS
Nudgee
Nudgee
Nudgee
Waterhole
ROAD
Seminary
NUDGEE
15
Nudgee Golf Club
Jacksons
Creek
Jubilee Ck.
Container
Terminal
Luggage
Point
Port of
Brisbane
Grain
Terminal
SHIPPING
Bishop
Island
Fisherman
Point
CHANNEL
Signal
Station

9

Virginia
Virginia
MELLINGTON
ST VINCENTS
Banyo
Bindha
Fruit
Cannery
Banyo
EARNSTAW
CROCKFORD ST
APPROACH
RD
ROAD
Future
Domestic
Terminals
Control
Tower
Myrtletown
18
MARINE
RD
MAIN BEACH
BANCROFT
RD
MAIN
Tanker
Berth
Export
Coal
Terminal
Barge
Wharf
FISHERMAN
ISLANDS

10

Northgate
26
GOSS
RD
BILSEN
RD
KINMOND
Northgate
SANDGATE RD
NORTHGATE
RD
RIDGE
Rec.
Res.
10
1
ARTERIAL
Serpentine
Deep
Water
DRIVE
Canal
Schultz
Boggy Ck
PRIORS
RD
MAIN MYRTLETOWN RD
Oil Refinery
Bulwer
Island
BRISBANE
Bulwer Island Wall
Crab Ck.
Vehicular
Ferry
Boat
HOWARD
SMITH DR
Whyte
Passage
Island

11

Kalinga
Pk
Nundah
VERNON ST
Bishop
Park
Cem.
HEDLEY
Toombul
Shopping
Complex
GATEWAY
NUDGEE RD
Brisbane
Airport
AIRPORT
Light
Aircraft
Control
Tower
International
Terminal
SUGARMILL
HOLT ST
TINGIRA
EAGLE FARM RD
Pinkenba
Lytton Wall
FORT LYTTON
NAT PK.
RIVER
Quarantine
Station
SOUTH
ST
Lytton
Hill
Oil
Refinery
Sewerage Treatment Works

12

Eagle
Junc.
Clayfield
oowin
JUNCTION
RD
20
26
London
ST
Hendra
MANSON
RD
Clayfield
Eagle Farm
Racecourse
ALEXANDRA
KITCHENER
LANCASTER
ANTHONY
Ascot
ORIEL
AV
Bannister
Pk
GERLER
ST
Doomben
R'course
Doomben
Airport
Bunour
DR
Eagle Farm
Doomben
Meeandah
10
Meeandah
Pinkenba
AV
Pinkenba
MAIN
Gibson Island Wall
Gibson
Island
Pinkenba
Lindum
SANDY CAMP RD
HAYNES
Convent
St Lawrence
Monastery
WYNNUM NTH
Industrial
Area
PRITCHARD
Lytton
Control
Tower
Wynnum
North
Wynnum
North
Wynnum
Oyster Pt

13

5
Hamilton
KINGSFORD
SMITH
NUDGEE RACECOURSE RD
25
20
Lucas
Park
OXFORD ST
Hamilton
Whinstanes
Bretts Wharf
LINKS ST
BWIWD Wharves
CURTIN
1
Apollo
Park
Apollo Ferry
Army Workshops
BRISBANE
LYTTON
Cairncross Graving Dock
Bulimba
Quarries Reach
Fish Board
& Markets
Gateway
Bridge
Colmslie
Meatworks
Brisbane
Abattoir
Queensport
TOLL
Doboy Bridge
AQUARIUM AV
Aquarium
Passage
Lytton
Reach
GOSPORT ST
LYTTON
RD
24
30
15
Doboy
Doboy
Hemmant
Hemmant Rd
CRAWFORDS
RD
30
SCHOOL
RD
NEW
LINDUM
PRESTON
RD
30
Wynnum Golf Course
23
WYNNUM
Wynnum
STRAUGHTON
CHANDOS AV
ELENORA ST
GLENORA ST
SIBLEY
LINDUM
RD
Wading Pool
Wynnum
Sth
20
Memorial
Pk
Darling Point
TINGAL
Breakwater

J K L M N **423** O P Q R

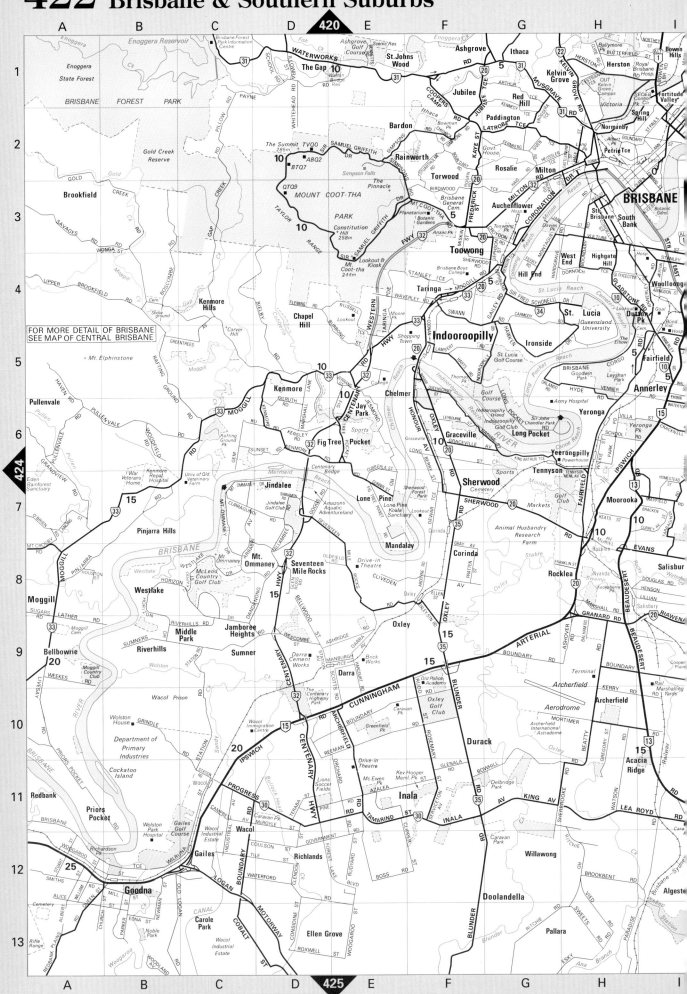

422 Brisbane & Southern Suburbs

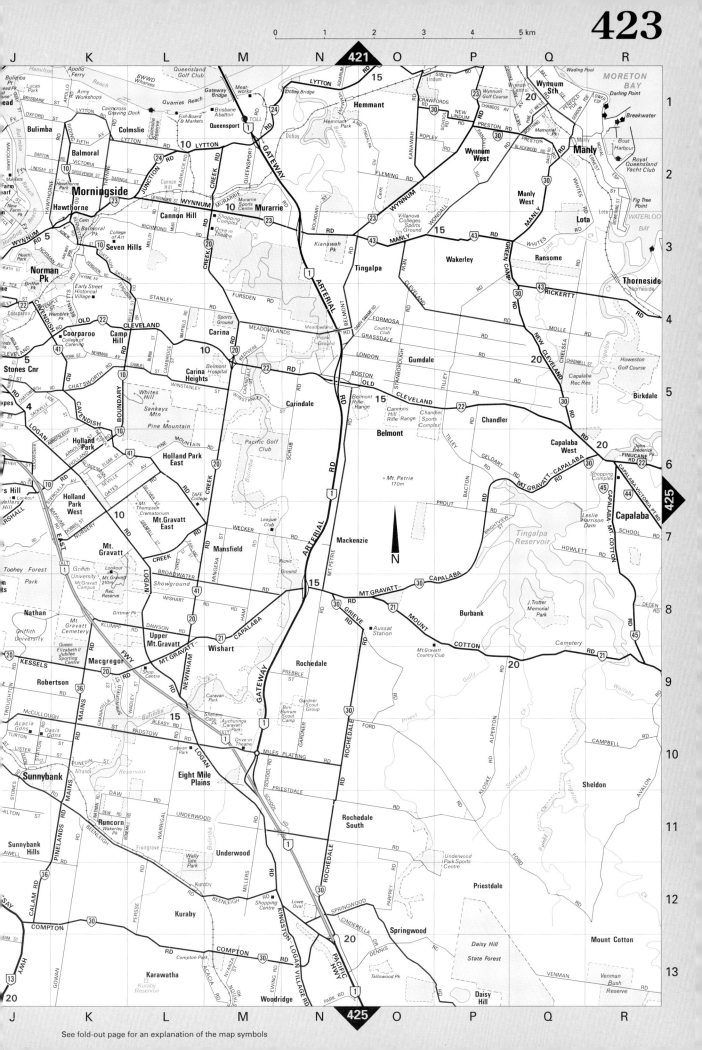

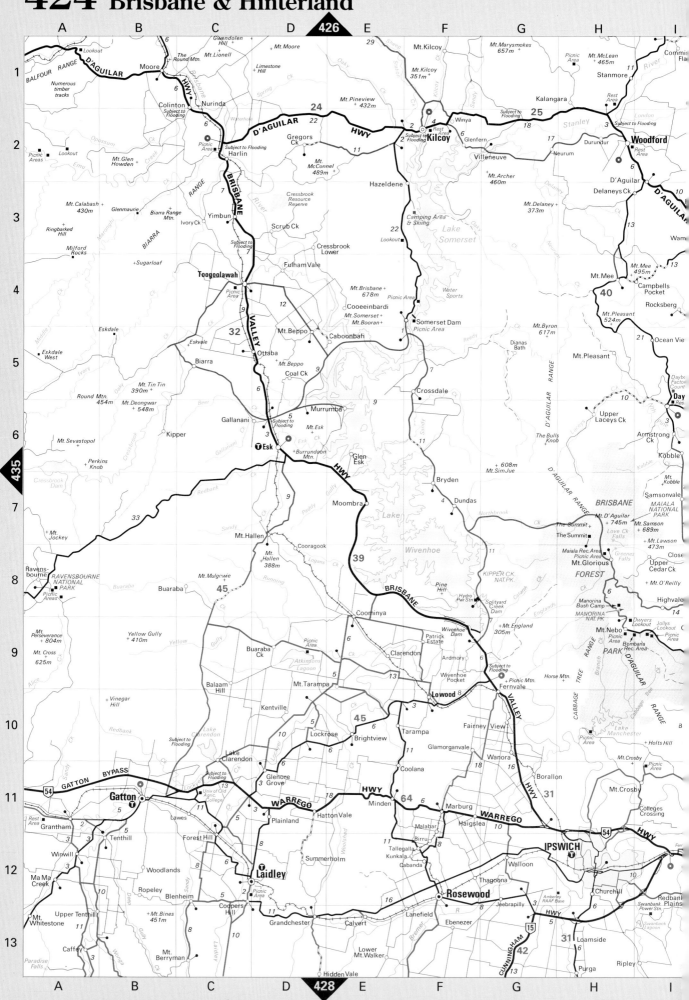

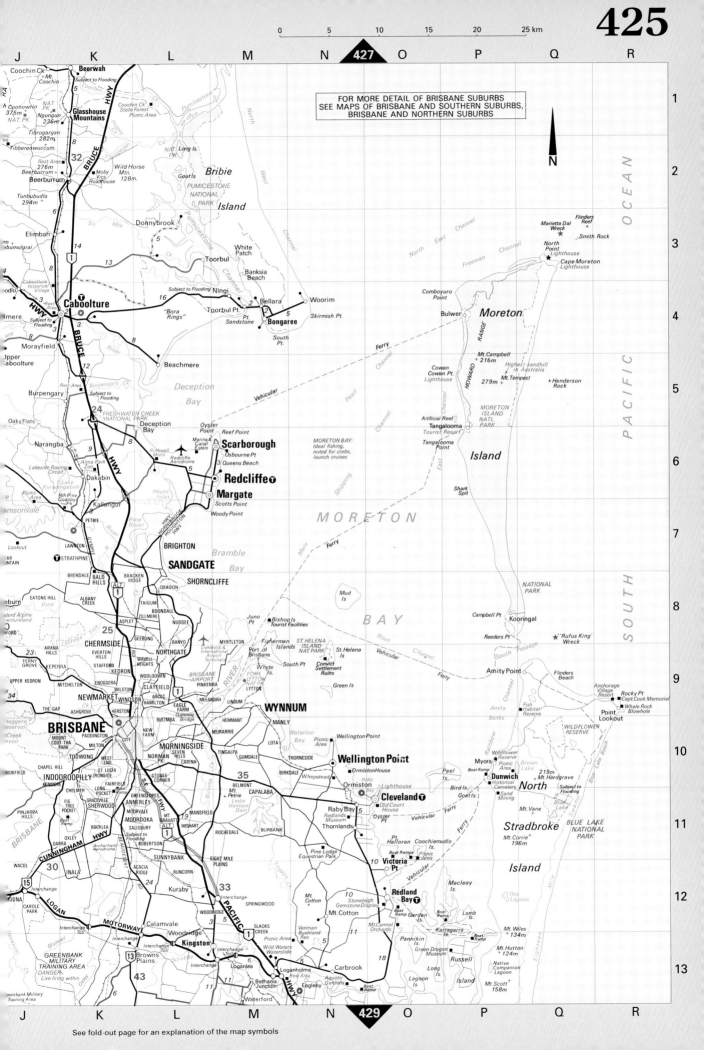

A B C D **435** E F G H I

1 COAST RANGE · Neurum Mt · Mouingba · Nondiga · Woolooga · Curra · BRUCE · Downsfield · Butlers Knob · Mt. South Goomboorian · Goombooloi
Wide Bay HWY · Kilkivan · Oakview · 39 · Wonga Lower · WIDE BAY HWY · 16 · 6 · North Deep Ck · Mt. Corella 336m · Harveys Siding · Rossmount · TAGIGAN

2 Cinnabar · Rossmore · Coppermine Ck · 18 · Gibraltar Rock · Wonga Upper · 8 · Lookouts · Picnic Area · Fishermans Pocket · 1 · Chatsworth · Corella · Enterprise · Wilsons Pocket · BEENAAM · 11 · Ormesby
WIDE BAY · 26 · 18 · Mt. Chucki · Mt. Ghrooman Bille · Greendale · Highbury Hill · Woodworks Forestry & Timber Museum · 12 · Tamaree

3 The Breezer 457m · Mt. Clara 488m · Mt. Coora 594m · Mt. Misery · Widgee Upper · 8 · Glastonbury · Scrubby Ck · 6 · Mary Ck · Stratigos · Nashville · GYMPIE · Monkland · Cedar Pocket · Beena Rang · Mt. Mothar 427m · Mt. Bour 495m
Kinbombi Falls · Picnic Area

4 COAST RANGE · Mt. Mia 610m · Widgee Mtn 688m · Mt. Glastonbury 575m · Mt. Mooroo reerai 610m · Warrawee · Mt. Warrawee 549m · Eel Creek · Mooloo · Calico Ck · Gildora · Long Flats · 14 · Dawn · Lagoon Pocket · Kybong · BRUCE · 24 · Tandur · Woondum · Mothar Mtn · 16 · 18

5 16 · Gobongo · Gobongo North · Mt. Mittarula · Langshaw · Mt. Gentle & Annie · Mt. Wilwarrel · Mt. Teewoo 625m · Amamoor Lookout · The Pocket · Amamoor · Dagun · Greenridge · Traveston · Cooran · Mt. Cooran · HWY · 19
10 · Toomcul · Mt. Amamoor Forest Station · Mt. Coorooi 439 · Federal

6 Manumbar · 10 · 7 · Gallangowan · Mt. Tavinghi 685m · Manumbar Mill · AMAMOOR RANGE · Kandanga Ck · 11 · Kandanga · Nobby Glen · Melawondi · Goomong · Mt. Tuchekoi 292m · Bergins Pocket · 10
Kandanga Upper · Heigh Ridge · Yabba Vale · 8

7 435 · Elgin Vale · BRISBANE RANGE · KANDANGA RANGE · Mt. Kandanga 576m · Bella · Picnic Area · Derriers Flat · Imbil · Brooloo · Carters Ridge · 18 · Ridge · Belli Park · 5

8 Mt. Gibbarnee 396m · 105 · 34 · YABBA RANGE · Yabba · Yabba Falls · Kingaham Creek · Lake Borumba · Borumba 623m · Borumba Mtn · Water Sports · Picnic Area · Kenilworth Bluff 529m · 14 · Gheerulla · 13 · Rest Area · 14

9 Diaper Mtn · JIMNA RANGE · Kenilworth · ROAD · Little Yabba Camping Area & Picnic Res. · Mt. Walli · Connors Knob · ObiObi · MAP
Mt. Stanley 536m · Picnic Area · Kidaman Ck · Coolabine · 21

10 Mt. Stanley · Mt. Monsildale · Jimna · Summer Mtn 789m · Picnic Area · LITTLE YABBA SUNDAY CREEK · Booloumba · CONONDALE NAT PK · 21 · Donovans Knob 662m · Witta
Lookout · Picnic Area

11 Avoca Vale · Monsildale · Lookout · 16 · Mt. Cabinet 732m · CONONDALE NAT PK · Mt. Langley 867m · Mt. Gerald · Mt. Ramsden 792m · Mt. Adelaide 739m · Lookout · CONONDALE RANGE · Conondale · 59 · 19 · Reesville · Subject to Flooding · 9
Hellhole · Mt. Pascoe · Jinker Hill · Mt. Denmark 732m

12 13 · Mt. Spencer 489m · Yednia · Lookout · Lookout · Bellthorpe Forest Station · Booroobin · 13
Monsildale · Lawler · Sheep Stn · Sandy

13 BALFOUR · 48 · D'AGUILAR HWY · Linville · Moore · The Round Mtn · Marion Hill · Gwendolen Hill · Mt. Lionell · Mt. Miner · Mt. Moore · Limestone Hill · 29 · North West Mt 599m · Mt. Kilcoy · Mt. Marysmokes 657m · Bellthorpe · Cedarton · Comm
19 · 6 · Mt. Kilcoy 351m · Picnic Area · Mt. McLean 465m · Stanmore · 11

A B C D **424** E F G H I

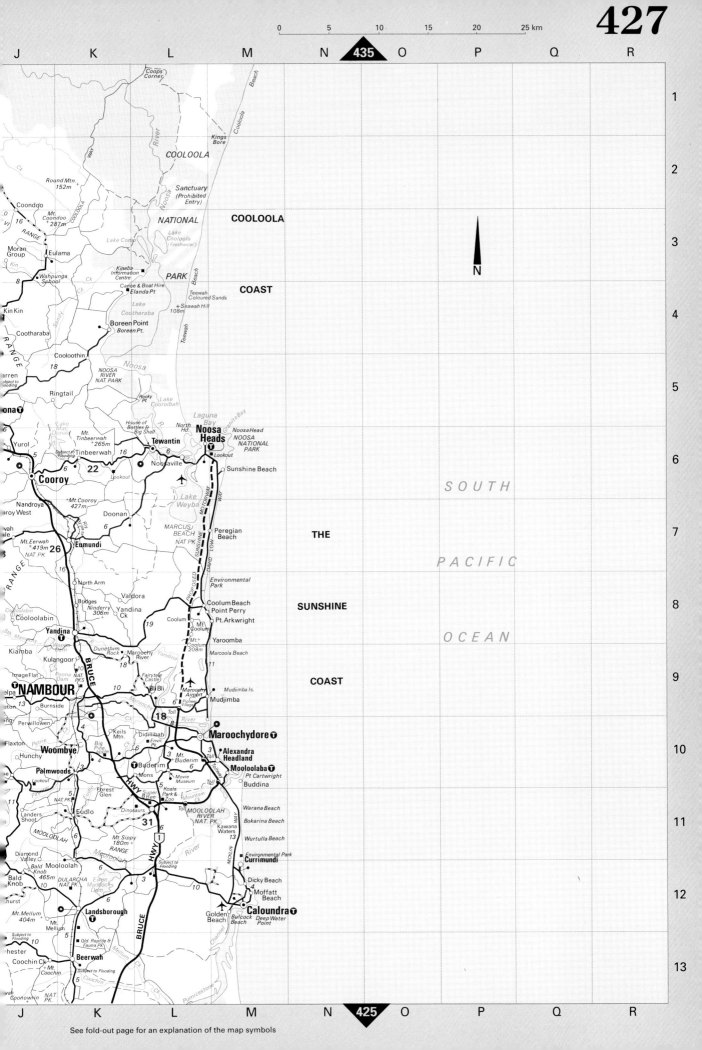

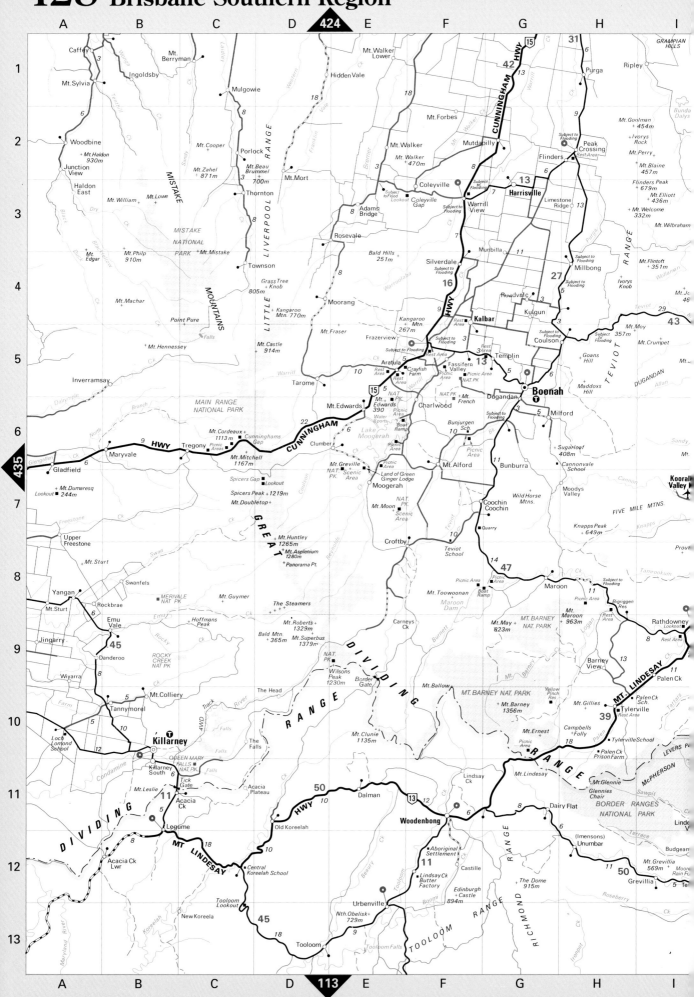

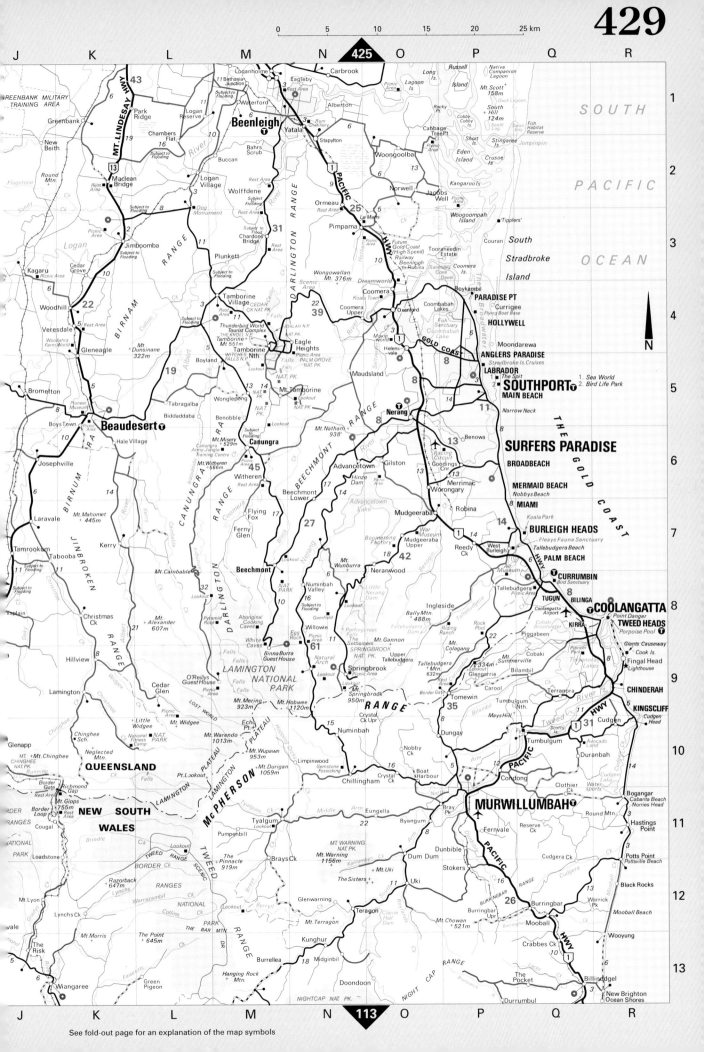

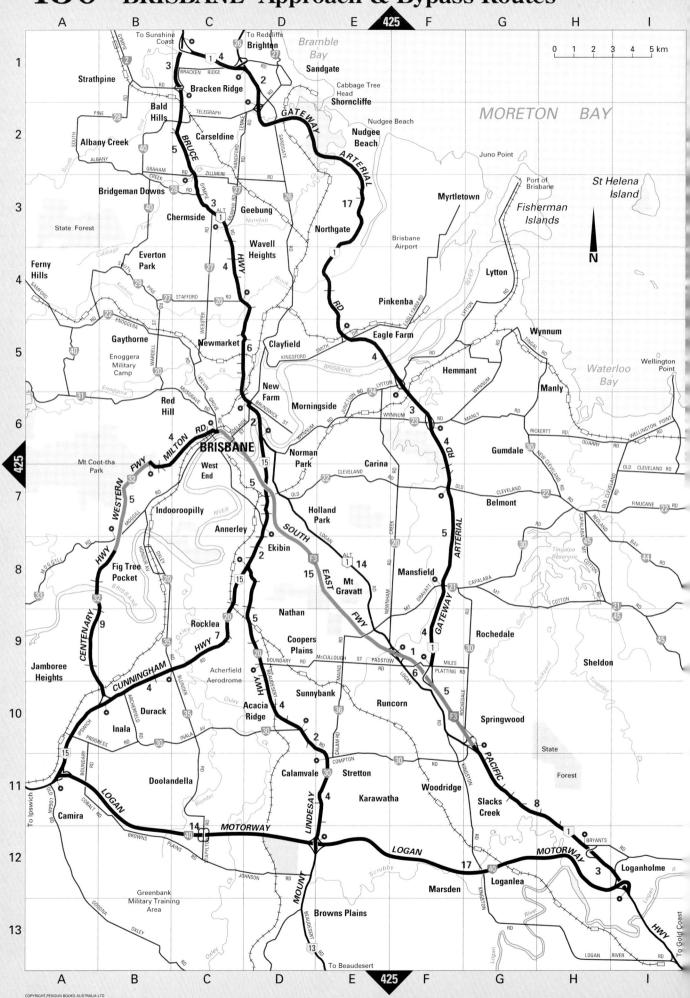

430 BRISBANE Approach & Bypass Routes

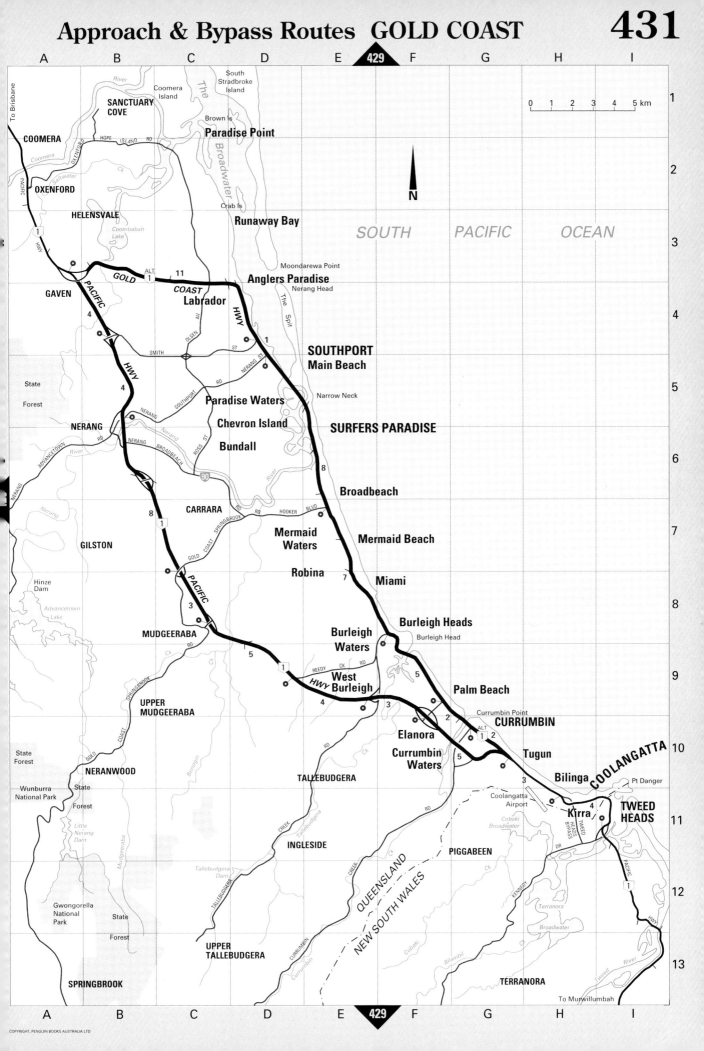

432 Toowoomba

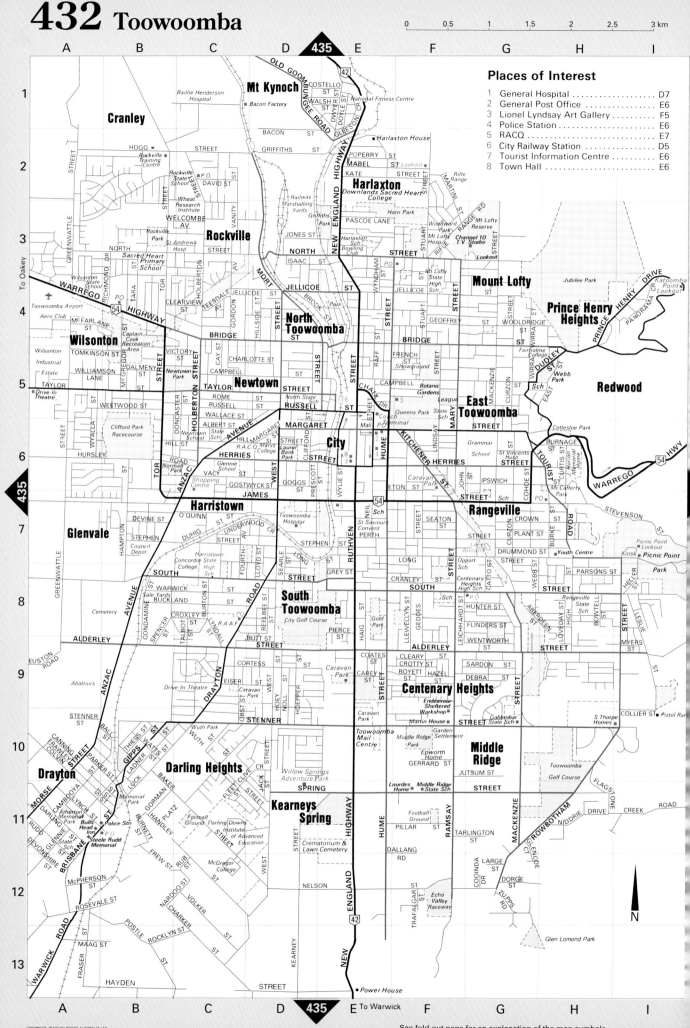

COPYRIGHT, PENGUIN BOOKS AUSTRALIA LTD

0   0.5   1   1.5   2   2.5   3 km

Places of Interest

1 General Hospital	D7
2 General Post Office	E6
3 Lionel Lyndsay Art Gallery	F5
4 Police Station	E6
5 RACQ	E7
6 City Railway Station	D5
7 Tourist Information Centre	E6
8 Town Hall	E6

See fold-out page for an explanation of the map symbols

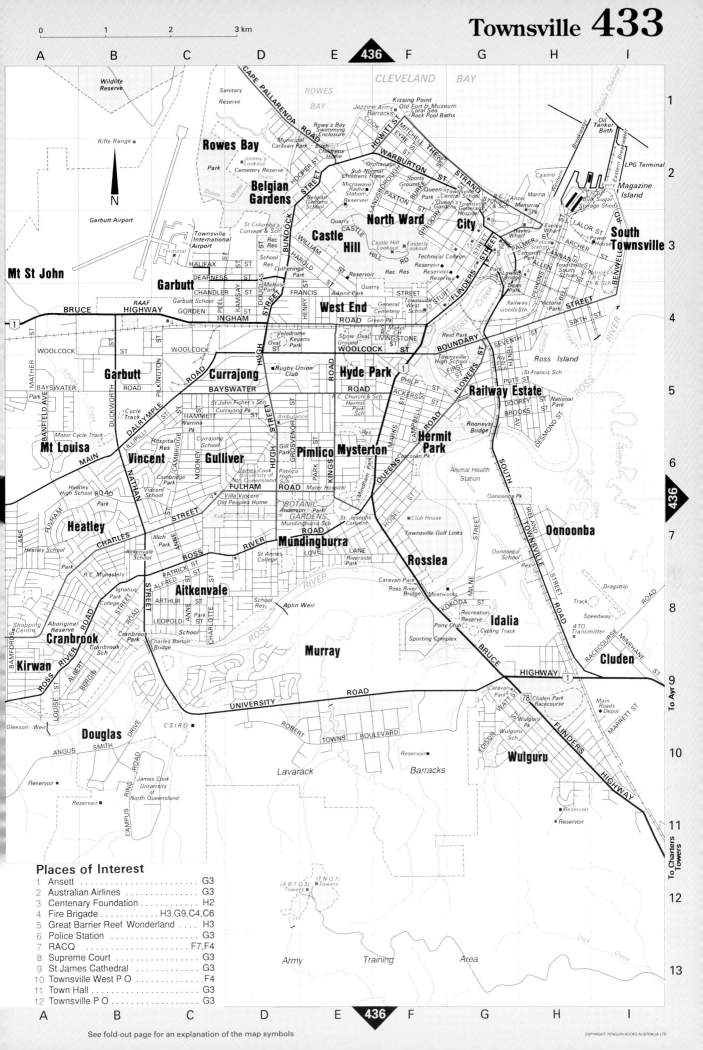

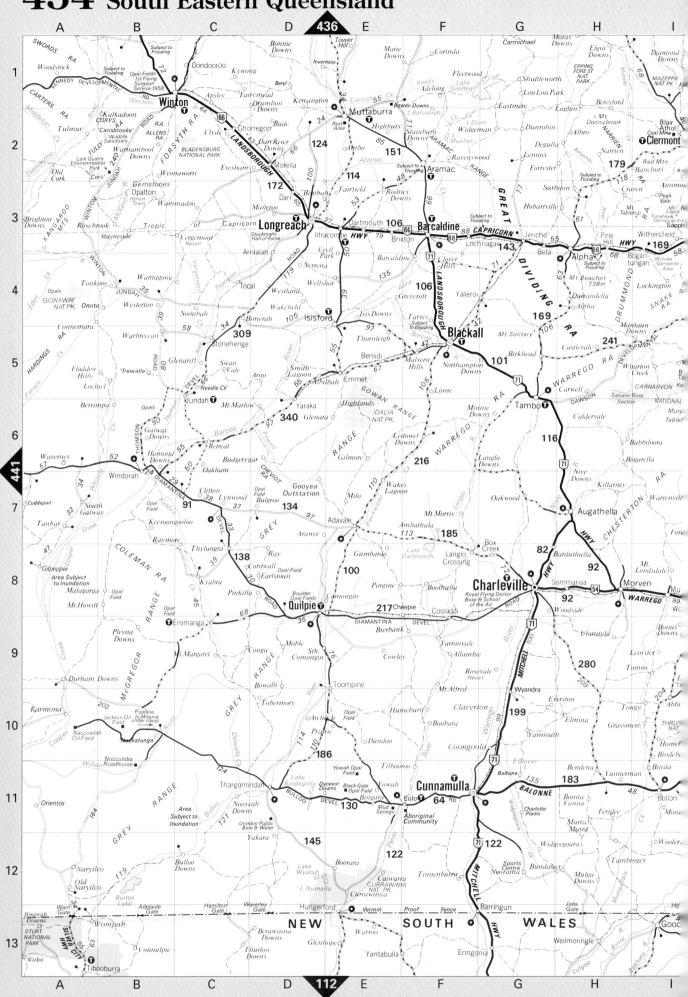

0   100   200   300 km

437

FOR MORE DETAIL OF TOOWOOMBA
SEE MAP OF TOOWOOMBA AND SUBURBS.

FOR MORE DETAIL OF BRISBANE REGION
SEE MAPS OF BRISBANE & HINTERLAND,
BRISBANE & SOUTHERN REGION,
BRISBANE & NORTHERN REGION

GREAT BARRIER REEF
MARINE PARK –
CAPRICORN SECTION

SOUTH

PACIFIC

OCEAN

Tropic of Capricorn

GREAT BARRIER REEF MARINE PARK –
CAPRICORNIA SECTION

GREAT BARRIER REEF REGION BOUNDARY

ROCKHAMPTON
Yeppoon
Emerald
Gladstone
Mt. Morgan
Biloela
Springsure
Theodore
Monto
BUNDABERG
HERVEY BAY
MARYBOROUGH
Taroom
Mundubbera
Gayndah
GYMPIE
Gympie
Nambour
Maroochydore
Caloundra
Wandoan
Roma
Miles
Chinchilla
Kingaroy
THE SUNSHINE COAST
Surat
Dalby
Nanango
Caboolture
Redcliffe
Sandgate
BRISBANE
Ipswich
TOOWOOMBA
Gatton
St.George
Millmerran
WARWICK
SOUTHPORT
Surfers Paradise
Coolangatta
Tweed Heads
THE GOLD COAST
Beaudesert
Dirranbandi
Goondiwindi
Inglewood
Stanthorpe
Murwillumbah
Boggabilla
Texas
Kyogle
LISMORE
Tenterfield
Casino
Ballina

113

See fold-out page for an explanation of the map symbols

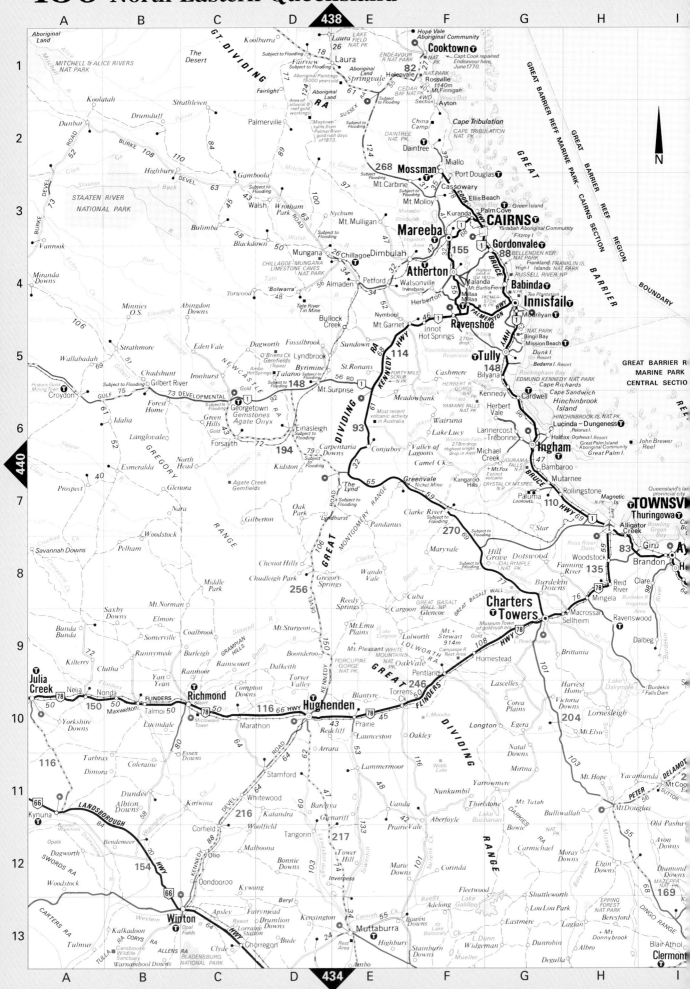

0   100   200   300 km

J K L M N O P Q R

1
2

SOUTH

3

PACIFIC

4

OCEAN

5

FOR MORE DETAIL OF CAIRNS
SEE MAP OF CAIRNS REGION
FOR MORE DETAIL OF TOWNSVILLE
SEE MAP OF TOWNSVILLE

GREAT BARRIER REEF
MARINE PARK
CENTRAL SECTION

6

GREAT

7

BARRIER

CORAL   SEA

REEF

8

GREAT

REGION   BOUNDARY

bbot Pt
PSTART
PARK

Bowen⊤

BARRIER

9

Port of
Bowen
Coal Port
Longford

BRUCE

63
Cannonvale⊤
Airlie
Beach
Petrie
Faust
Dam

HWY

Hayman I.
Hook I.N.PK.
THE
WHITSUNDAYS
Whitsunday I
Daydream I
Shute Harbour⊤
South Molle I.

REEF

Proserpine⊤
insville

1
Whitsunday⊤
Conway
Beach

Hamilton I.
N.PK.   Lindeman I.
Shaw I.

Cape Conway

Noorlah
Bloomsbury
Elaroo
Yalboroo

Midgeton

Cumberland
Islands
Brampton I.
Carlisle I

10

Emu
Plains
BROKEN
RIVER RA

180
Calen

Mt Ossa

CAPE
HILLSBOROUGH &
WEDGE IS   N.P.

HIBISCUS

EUNGELLA
NAT.PK.
Tiverton
Mt.Charlton

53
Kattabul

Farleigh

COAST

Eungella
Eungella
Resr.

82
Finch
Hatton

Miran
Eton⊤

MACKAY⊤

GREAT BARRIER REEF
MARINE PARK-
CAPRICORN SECTION

11

156

MtHillalong
Homevale
Hail Ck

HWY
14

CONNORS

Hay Point Coal Shipping Terminal
Sarina Beach

Sarina⊤
Koumala

SUTTOR DEVEL RD
RD   Lake
Elphinstone

Nebo⊤

RA

Ibilbie

65

CAPE PALMERSTON NAT PARK

Middle I.
PERCY
ISLES

onyella
Coal Mine

-14
29
Floodgate

Carmila

WEST HILL IS.
NAT.PARK

South I.
NAT PARK

Northumberland
Islands

Broadmeadow

DIPPERU
NAT.PK.

MARLBOROUGH

CONNORS RA
57

12

DOWNS
55
286

Saltbush
Park
Subject to
Flooding

SATINA   192

235
Collaroy
Flood gate
Clairview

Broad
Sound

Broad Sound Channel

Couti
Utii

MILITARY TRAINING AREA-
SEAWARD BDY

Subject to
Flooding

FITZROY

Peak Downs
Coal Mine
Saraji
Coal Mine

Bombandy

Subject to
Flooding
Croydon

BROADSOUND

1
St Lawrence
Flood gate

Shoalwater Bay

Pearl Bay

Port Clinton

13

gan
wns

RD
N.P.

Phillips
Dysart⊤

May
Downs

RD

85
Ogmore

HWY
Floodgate⊤

Banksid
N.P.
Marlborough

MILITARY
TRAINING
AREA

Prohibited
Area

CAPRICORNIA
SECTION

J K L M N O P Q R

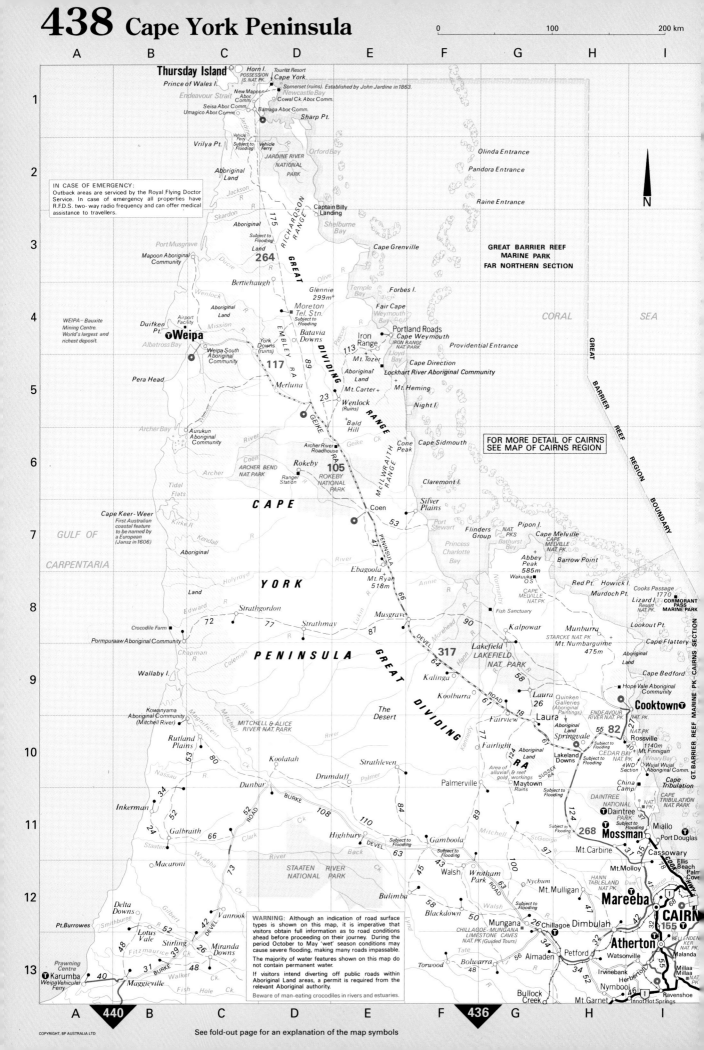

0   100   200 km

A   B   C   D   E   F   G   H   I

Thursday Island
Horn I.
POSSESSION
IS. NAT. PK.
Prince of Wales I.
Tourist Resort
Cape York
Somerset (ruins). Established by John Jardine in 1863.
New Mappon Abor. Comm.
Cowal Ck. Abor. Comm.
Newcastle Bay
Endeavour Strait
Seisa Abor Comm.
Bamaga Abor. Comm.
Umagico Abot Comm.
Sharp Pt.

IN CASE OF EMERGENCY:
Outback areas are serviced by the Royal Flying Doctor Service. In case of emergency all properties have R.F.D.S. two-way radio frequency and can offer medical assistance to travellers.

Vrilya Pt.
Vehicle Ferry Subject to Flooding
Vehicle Ferry
JARDINE RIVER NATIONAL PARK
Orford Bay

Olinda Entrance
Pandora Entrance

Aboriginal Land

Captain Billy Landing
Raine Entrance

Skardon
Subject to Flooding
Land **264**
Shelburne Bay

GREAT BARRIER REEF MARINE PARK FAR NORTHERN SECTION

Port Musgrave
Mapoon Aboriginal Community
Aboriginal
Bertiehaugh
Ducie
Olive
Cape Grenville

Glennie 299m+
Temple Bay
Forbes I.
Fair Cape

WEIPA – Bauxite Mining Centre. World's largest and richest deposit.

Duifken Pt.
oWeipa
Airport Facility
Aboriginal Land
Moreton Tel. Stn.
Subject to Flooding
Batavia Downs
York Downs (ruins)
Weymouth Bay
Portland Roads
Cape Weymouth
IRON RANGE NAT. PARK
CORAL   SEA

Albatross Bay
Weipa South Aboriginal Community
117
Iron Range
Mt. Tozer
113
Lloyd Bay
Cape Direction
Providential Entrance

Pera Head
Merluna
Aboriginal Land
Mt. Carter+
Mt. Heming
Lockhart River Aboriginal Community

23
Wenlock (Ruins)
Night I.

Archer Bay
Aurukun Aboriginal Community
Bald Hill
Cape Sidmouth
Cone Peak

Tidal Flats
Archer
Coen
ARCHER BEND NAT. PARK
Rokeby
105
ROKEBY NATIONAL PARK
Ranger Station
Archer River Roadhouse
Geike Ck.
McILWRAITH RANGE
Claremont I.

Cape Keer-Weer First Australian coastal feature to be named by a European (Jansz in 1606)
Kirke R.
Coen
53
Silver Plains
Port Stewart
Flinders Group
NAT. PKS
Pipon I.
Cape Melville
CAPE MELVILLE NAT. PK.

GULF OF CARPENTARIA
Kendall R.
Aboriginal
Holyroyd
River
47
PENINSULA
Princess Charlotte Bay
Bathurst Bay
Abbey Peak 585m
Barrow Point

C A P E
Land
Edward R.
Strathgordon
Y O R K
Ebagoola
Mt. Ryan 518m
66
Annie
Wakuuka OS
CAPE MELVILLE NAT. PK.
Red Pt.
Howick I.
Murdoch Pt.
Cooks Passage 1770
Lizard I. Resort NAT. PK.
CORMORANT PASS MARINE PARK

Crocodile Farm
72
77
Strathmay
Musgrave
87
Lakin
Fish Sanctuary
90
Kalpowar
Munburra
STARCKE NAT. PK
Mt. Numbargirnie 475m
Lookout Pt.
Cape Flattery

Pormpuraaw Aboriginal Community
Chapman
PENINSULA
The Desert
317
Lakefield
LAKEFIELD NAT. PARK
64
58
Aboriginal Land
Cape Bedford

Wallaby I.
Coleman
GREAT
Kalinga
Koolburra
Laura 26
Quinken Galleries (Aboriginal Paintings)
ENDEAVOUR RIVER NAT. PK.
Hope Vale Aboriginal Community
Cooktown

Kowanyama Aboriginal Community (Mitchell River)
Rutland Plains
53
80
Alice
MITCHELL & ALICE RIVER NAT. PARK
Koolatah
18
Fairview
Laura
Aboriginal Land
Springvale
55
1140m Mt. Finnigan
40
82
Rossville
CEDAR BAY NAT. PK.
4WD Section
Weary Bay
Wujal Wujal Aboriginal Comm.

34
Dunbar
Drumduff
Palmer
Strathleven
124
Lakeland Downs
Subject to Flooding
China Camp!
Cape Tribulation

Inkerman
52
52
BURKE ROAD
108
84
Palmerville
Maytown Ruins
Subject to Flooding
DAINTREE NATIONAL PARK
CAPE TRIBULATION NAT. PK.

Galbraith
24
66
Clark R.
110
Highbury
DEVEL.
Subject to Flooding
Gamboola
89
Mitchell
St.George
268 Mossman
124
Subject to Flooding
Miallo
Port Douglas

Macaroni
73
Back Ck.
63
Mt. Carbine
97
Cassowary

Staaten R.
STAATEN RIVER NATIONAL PARK
45
43
Walsh
Wrotham Park
63
WROTHAM PARK ROAD
Mt. Mulligan
100
HANN TABLELAND NAT. PK
47
Ellis Beach Palm Cove
Mt. Molloy
31
35
Mareeba

Delta Downs
Pt. Burrowes
Gilbert
42
DEVEL.
Vanrook
Bulimba
58
Blackdown
50
Mungana
26
Chillagoe
Dimbulah
42
32
CAIRN
155

Prawning Centre
Karumba
Weipa Vehicular Ferry
48
Lotus Vale
Stirling
52
39
26
Miranda Downs
Nychum
CHILLAGOE-MUNGANA LIMESTONE CAVES NAT. PK. (Guided Tours)
34
Petford
Watsonville
55
Malanda
Atherton

Maggieville
31
BURKE
Walker R.
48
Fish Hole Ck.
Torwood
Bolwarra 48
56
Almaden
34
52
Irvinebank
Herberton
Nymboo
46
Millaa Millaa

Bullock Creek
Mt. Garnet
Innot Hot Springs

FOR MORE DETAIL OF CAIRNS SEE MAP OF CAIRNS REGION

WARNING: Although an indication of road surface types is shown on this map, it is imperative that visitors obtain full information as to road conditions ahead before proceeding on their journey. During the period October to May 'wet' season conditions may cause severe flooding, making many roads impassable.
The majority of water features shown on this map do not contain permanent water.
If visitors intend diverting off public roads within Aboriginal Land areas, a permit is required from the relevant Aboriginal authority.
Beware of man-eating crocodiles in rivers and estuaries.

A   440   **F   436**

See fold-out page for an explanation of the map symbols

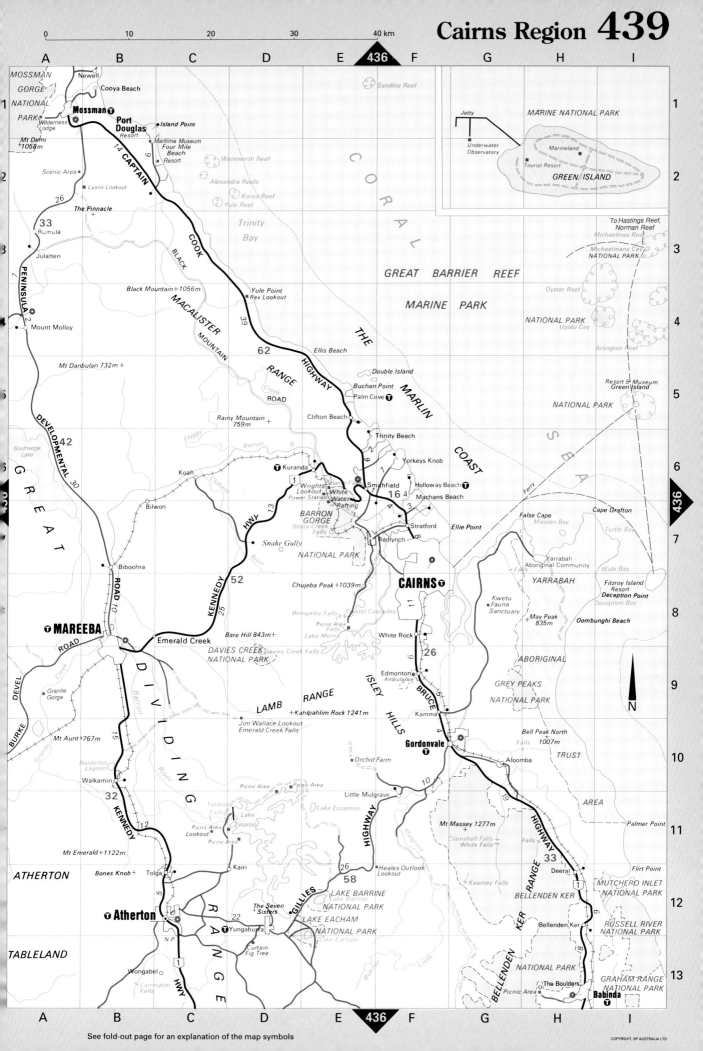

0   10   20   30   40 km

436

A B C D E **436** F G H I

MOSSMAN
GORGE
NATIONAL
PARK
Newell
Cooya Beach

Mossman
Wilderness
Lodge
**Port
Douglas**
Resort
Island Point
Mt Demi
+1058m
Maritime Museum
Four Mile
Beach
Resort

Scenic Area
Lyons Lookout
The Pinnacle

CAPTAIN
14
9

26

33
Rumula
Julatten

PENINSULA

Mount Molloy

Mt Danbulan 732m +

DEVELOPMENTAL
42
30

GREAT

BLACK
MACALISTER
MOUNTAIN
RANGE
ROAD
COOK
HIGHWAY

Black Mountain +1056m

Yule Point
Rex Lookout

Trinity
Bay

39
62

Creek
Flaggy
Barron
R

Ellis Beach

Double Island
Buchan Point
Palm Cove
Clifton Beach
Trinity Beach
Yorkeys Knob

Satellite Reef

Wentworth Reef

Alexandra Reefs

Korea Reef
Yule Reef

CORAL

GREAT   BARRIER   REEF

MARINE   PARK

THE
MARLIN
COAST

SEA

MARINE NATIONAL PARK
Jetty
Underwater
Observatory
Marineland
Tourist Resort
GREEN ISLAND

To Hastings Reef,
Norman Reef
Michaelmas Reef

Michaelmans Cay
NATIONAL PARK

Oyster Reef
Upolu Cay
NATIONAL PARK

Arlington Reef

Resort & Museum
Green Island

NATIONAL PARK

Southedge
Lake

Koah

Rainy Mountain +
759m

Kuranda
Wrights
Lookout
White
Water
Rafting
Power Station
BARRON
GORGE
Stony Creek
Falls
NATIONAL
PARK

Bilwon

Biboohra

HWY
13

KENNEDY
52
25

ROAD 10

MAREEBA
Emerald Creek

Snake Gully

Chujeba Peak +1039m

Wongalee Falls
Picnic Area
Falls
Lake Morris
Crystal Cascades

Smithfield
16 4
Machans Beach
Holloway Beach
Stratford
Redlynch
Ellie Point

CAIRNS

White Rock

ISLEY
HILLS

BRUCE

11

9

26

Edmonton
Ambulance

Kamma

False Cape
Mission Bay
Cape Grafton
Turtle Bay

Yarrabah
Aboriginal Community
Falls
YARRAH
Wide Bay

Fitzroy Island
Resort
Deception Point
Deception Bay

Kwetu
Fauna
Sanctuary
May Peak
835m

Oombunghi Beach

Ferry

ABORIGINAL

GREY PEAKS
NATIONAL PARK

TRUST

N

DEVEL
BURKE
ROAD

Granite
Gorge

Mt Aunt +767m

DIVIDING

Granite

Barron
River

Nardellos
Lagoon

Walkamin
32

KENNEDY
15
12

Mt Emerald +1122m

Bare Hill 843m +
DAVIES CREEK
NATIONAL PARK
Davies Creek Falls

LAMB   RANGE
+ Kahlpahlim Rock 1241m
Jim Wallace Lookout
Emerald Creek Falls

Tinaroo
Falls
Picnic Area
Lookout
Picnic Area
Lake
Tinaroo
Picnic Area
Picnic Area
Lake Euramoo

Orchid Farm

Little Mulgrave

HIGHWAY

Mulgrave

Gordonvale
Aloomba

10

Mt Massey 1277m
Clamshell Falls
White Falls
Falls

Bell Peak North
1007m
Falls

AREA

Palmer Point

RANGE

BELLENDEN KER

HIGHWAY
33

Kearney Falls

Deeral

Flirt Point
MUTCHERO INLET
NATIONAL PARK

ATHERTON

Bones Knob +
Tolga

Kairi

26
58

GILLIES

Heales Outlook
Lookout

LAKE BARRINE
Lake Barrine
NATIONAL PARK
LAKE EACHAM
NATIONAL PARK
Lake Eacham

Bellenden Ker

RUSSELL RIVER
NATIONAL PARK

Atherton
5
22
Yungaburra
The Seven
Sisters

RANGE
N.P.

Curtain
Fig Tree

BELLENDEN   KER

Butcher

GRAHAM RANGE
NATIONAL PARK

TABLELAND

Wongabel

1
HWY

Carrington
Falls

NATIONAL PARK
Picnic Area
The Boulders

Babinda

A B C D E **436** F G H I

1
2
3
4
5
436
6
7
8
9
10
11
12
13

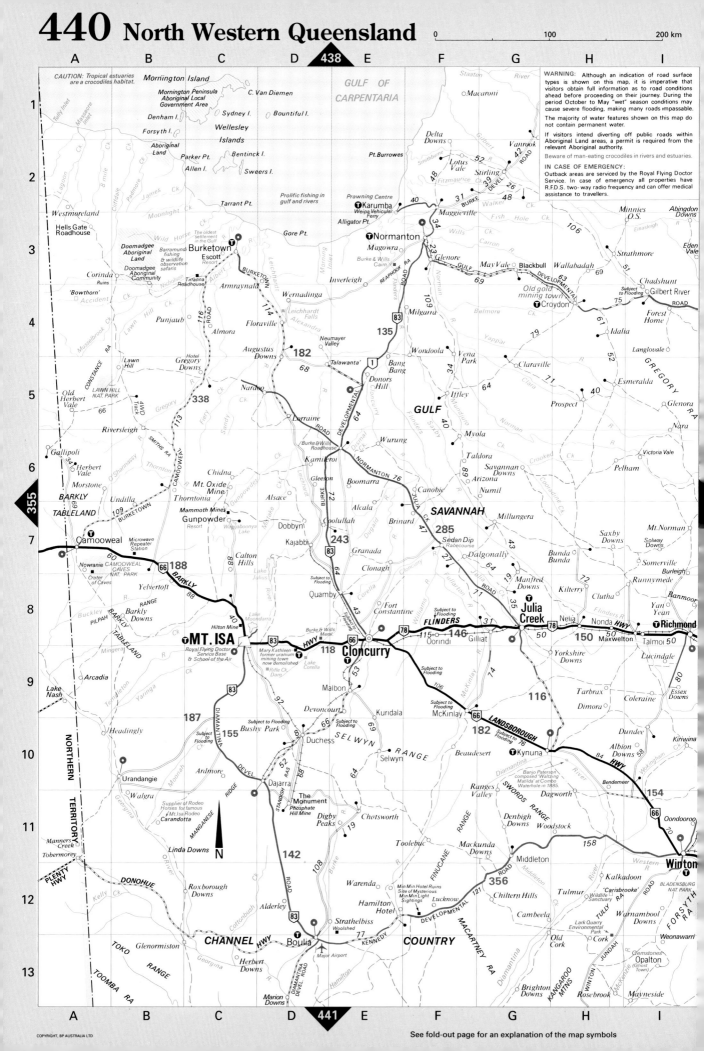

440 North Western Queensland

0   100   200 km

A   B   C   D   ▼438   E   F   G   H   I

GULF OF CARPENTARIA

WARNING: Although an indication of road surface types is shown on this map, it is imperative that visitors obtain full information as to road conditions ahead before proceeding on their journey. During the period October to May "wet" season conditions may cause severe flooding, making many roads impassable.

The majority of water features shown on this map do not contain permanent water.

If visitors intend diverting off public roads within Aboriginal Land areas, a permit is required from the relevant Aboriginal authority.

Beware of man-eating crocodiles in rivers and estuaries.

IN CASE OF EMERGENCY:
Outback areas are serviced by the Royal Flying Doctor Service. In case of emergency all properties have R.F.D.S. two-way radio frequency and can offer medical assistance to travellers.

Mornington Island
Mornington Peninsula
Aboriginal Local Government Area
C. Van Diemen
Sydney I.
Denham I.
Bountiful I.
Forsyth I.
Wellesley Islands
Aboriginal Land
Parker Pt.
Bentinck I.
Allen I.
Sweers I.

Macaroni

Delta Downs
Lotus Vale
Stirling   52
Vanrook   42
ROAD
48   DEVEL   26
BURKE   31   Walker   48

Minnies O.S.
Abingdon Downs
Einasleigh
Strathmore
Eden Vale

Westmoreland
Hells Gate Roadhouse

Tarrant Pt.
Prolific fishing in gulf and rivers
Prawning Centre
Karumba
Weipa Vehicular Ferry
Alligator Pt.
Maggieville   34
Normanton

Corinda Ruins
'Bowthorn'
Accident
Doomadgee Aboriginal Land
Barramundi fishing & wildlife observation safaris
Doomadgee Aboriginal Community
Burketown
Escott Resort
Tirranna Roadhouse
Armraynald

Mugowra
Burke & Wills Cairn
Inverleigh
REAPHOOK RA
Glenore   23
MayVale   Blackbull   Wallabadah   69
GULF   69   DEVELOPMENTAL   63
Old gold mining town   Croydon   75   Gilbert River
Chadshunt   51
Subject to Flooding   ROAD
Forest Home

Punjaub
Almora
Floraville
Wernadinga
Leichhardt Falls
Milgarra   109
83   135   Wondoola   Vena Park
Claraville   79   Idalia   61
Langlovale   52   GREGORY   RA

Lawn Hill
Hotel Gregory Downs
Augustus Downs
182
68   Neumayer Valley   'Talawanta'
1   Bang Bang   Donors Hill
Iffley   64   Myola
Prospect   40   Esmeralda
71   Nara   Glenora   RA

Old Herbert Vale
LAWN HILL NAT. PARK   66
338
Nardoo
Lorraine   DEVELOPMENTAL   64   GULF
Wurung   Taldora
Savannan Downs   89   Victoria Vale
Pelham

Gallipoli   34
Herbert Vale
Riversleigh
SMITHS RA   113
Burke & Wills Roadhouse
Kamileroi
Gleeson
Boomarra
76   NORMANTON   Arizona   Numil   Crooked
Canobie   Millungera   Saxby Downs   Mt. Norman
Solway Downs

BARKLY   Morstone
Undilla   109
Chidna
Mt. Oxide Mine
Thorntonia
Mammoth Mines
Gunpowder Resort
Alsace
Dobbyn
Coolullah   72   Alcala
Brinard   47   SAVANNAH   285
Sedan Dip Racecourse   43   Bunda Bunda   Runnymede   Burleigh

355
TABLELAND
Camooweal
Microwave Repeater Station
Nowranie
CAMOOWEAL CAVES NAT. PARK
66   Yelvertoft   88
Calton Hills
Kajabbi   243   Granada   Clonagh
Quamby   64   Fort Constantine   Dalgonally   72   Kilterry   Clutha   Yan Yean   Ranmoor

PILBAH
BARKLY   RANGE   Barkly Downs
Hilton Mine
Lake Moondarra
Burke & Wills Mem'l   43
118   66   78   FLINDERS   146   31   Julia Creek   78   Nonda   Richmond
Gilliat   50   150   Maxwelton   Talmoi   50

Arcadia
MT. ISA
Royal Flying Doctor Service Base & School of the Air
Mary Kathleen former uranium mining town now demolished
Rifle Ck Dam
83   HWY   118   Cloncurry   53   Oorindi   115   74   Yorkshire Downs   Lucindale
Subject to Flooding   116   Tarbrax   Coleraine   Essex Downs

Lake Nash
187
Diamantina   155
Bushy Park
Duchess   66   Kuridala
Devoncourt   Malbon   Subject to Flooding   McKinlay   66   182   Kynuna   LANDSBOROUGH   HWY
Dundee   Albion Downs   Kiriwina

Headingly
Subject to Flooding
DEVEL   Ardmore
Dajarra   68   SELWYN   RANGE   Selwyn   Beaudesert   Ranges Valley   Banjo Paterson composed 'Waltzing Matilda' at Combo Waterhole in 1885.   Dagworth   SWORDS RANGE   154

NORTHERN
Urandangie
Walgra
Supplier of Rodeo Horses for famous Mt. Isa Rodeo
Carandotta
The Monument
Phosphate Hill Mine
Digby Peaks   19   Chatsworth   Toolebuc   Mackunda Downs   Woodstock   Middleton   158   Oondooroo
Winton

TERRITORY
Manners Creek
Tobermorey
PLENTY HWY
Linda Downs
142
DONOHUE
Roxborough Downs
Alderley   108
Warenda   Hamilton Hotel   Min Min Hotel Ruins Site of Mysterious Min Min Light Sightings   Lucknow   121   356   Chiltern Hills   Tulmur   'Carisbrooke'   WARRNAMBOOL Downs   FORSYTH

TOKO RANGE
Glenormiston
83
Strathelbiss   Woolshed   77   Cambeela   Lark Quarry Environmental Park   Cork   Old Cork   WINTON   Weonawarri

TOOMBA RA
CHANNEL   HWY   Boulia   KENNEDY   COUNTRY   MACARTNEY RA   Brighton Downs   Rosebrook   Mayneside

Herbert Downs
Marion Downs
Major Airport
Diamantina DEVEL ROAD
Hamilton   KANGAROO MTNS   Opalton (Ghost town)

N

A   B   C   D   ▼441   E   F   G   H   I

See fold-out page for an explanation of the map symbols

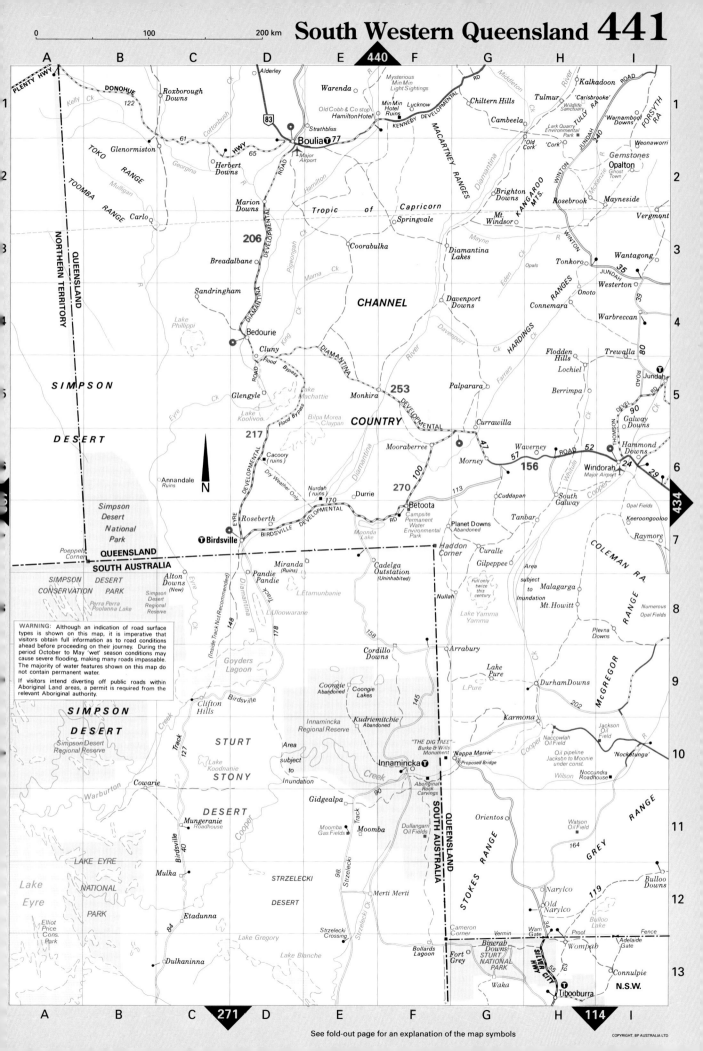

COPYRIGHT, BP AUSTRALIA LTD

TASMANIA

Heritage Island

Tasmania has certainly won many more hearts than it can claim square kilometres. It has only 68 000 of the latter, but it crams into them its rugged west, a central plateau broken by steep mountains and narrow river valleys, and an eastern coastal region offering a soft 'English' pastoral beauty. Its diverse charms have made it a popular tourist attraction for Australians from 'the mainland' for many years.

This pretty island, however, has a far from pretty early history. First sighted by Abel Tasman in 1624, it was later claimed by Captain Cook for the English and was first settled in 1803. For the next fifty years it was maintained primarily as a penal colony, although prosperous settlements developed around Hobart and New Norfolk. The convicts did the hard labour and lived in brutal conditions at Port Arthur. The only people treated more harshly than the convicts were the Aborigines, who naturally resisted the takeover of their tribal lands. Political separation from New South Wales was granted in 1825 and transportation of convicts ceased in 1853. Today the ruins of Port Arthur have taken on a mellow charm and Tasmania is an infinitely more hospitable place.

Tasmania was first called Van Diemen's Land; these days it is known as the 'heritage island', 'treasure island' or the 'apple isle'. Its economy is basically agricultural, but secondary industries such as tourism and mining are gradually taking over. It produces half of Australia's tin, and the largest zinc refinery in the world is at Hobart. The Tasmanian hydro-electric system has a greater output than that of the Snowy Mountains Scheme. Tasmania's high rainfall helps in this area. The climate offers mild summers and cool winters, with much of the mountain regions receiving heavy winter snowfall. Mid-December to late January is very popular with tourists, but it is worth considering a visit in late spring or autumn, when the weather is just as pleasant and the countryside is picturesque with blossom or autumn colours. Even the winter months, with crisp, clear days, offer good touring.

Another consideration when planning a trip to Tasmania is the heavy booking for the Abel Tasman ferry service between

The foothills of Mount Roland

Melbourne and Devonport from December to March. Either book well in advance or consider a fly/drive holiday, which can be a relaxing and economic alternative. Another option is the *Starship Seacat Tasmania* fast catamaran service from Port Welshpool in Victoria to George Town, on Tasmania's northern shoreline.

Tasmania's roads are well suited to relaxed meandering, many of them being winding and narrow. In a fortnight, however, you can happily complete what is virtually a round tour of the island, taking in some interesting detours on the way.

Built on either side of the Derwent River, Hobart, the capital of Tasmania, is dominated by Mount Wellington. The Wrest Point Hotel-Casino, Australia's first casino, with its lavish entertainment and International Convention Centre, is now competing for first place as the city's best-known landmark, towering over Hobart's many colonial buildings, which reflect its early days. Port Arthur, Richmond with its beautiful bridge (the oldest in Australia) and the early settlements of Bothwell and New Norfolk are all within easy reach.

The Derwent Valley with its hop-fields and apple orchards, lovely in blossom-time and in autumn, lies to the west. Further west is Lake Pedder; the flooding of this spectacular country was a source of great controversy when it was made part of the Tasmanian hydro-electric scheme. The surrounding country makes up the Southwest National Park, Tasmania's largest and one which has been given World Heritage status. The Lyell Highway then

leads to the Cradle Mountain–Lake St Clair National Park, with its alpine scenery and deep, still lakes. Queenstown, surrounded by eerie white mountains, is the largest settlement in this wild, forested region. Nearby coastal Strahan was once a mining boom-town and is the starting-point of the Gordon River cruises. North of Queenstown, the town of Zeehan is currently enjoying a mining revival with the reopening of the Renison Bell Tin Mine.

The north coast is yet another contrasting area. Burnie is one of the larger towns and Stanley is a classified historic town situated beneath 'the Nut', an unusual peninsula. East of Burnie, the Bass Highway hugs the coast as far as Devonport, the terminal of the Bass Strait passenger/vehicle ferry Abel Tasman and the centre of a productive apple-growing area. Inland from here is Launceston, Tasmania's second largest city. Situated on the River Tamar, Launceston has many well-preserved old buildings. Only minutes from the city centre is the beautiful Cataract Gorge, and the nearby colonial villages of Evandale, Hagley, Westbury, Carrick, Perth, Longford and Hadspen are well worth a visit.

A mild climate, good surfing beaches and sheltered seaside resorts add to the attraction of the east-coast region. St Helens, 160 kilometres east of Launceston, is the principal resort town. Try not to miss Bicheno, a picturesque old port and one-time whaling-town. Further south, 'the Hazards', a red granite mountain range, tower up behind Coles Bay, at the entrance to the Freycinet National Park, with its beautiful beaches. Nearby Swansea offers top-class ocean and freshwater fishing.

An enriched sense of Tasmania's history can be gained from studying graveyard headstones: in St David's Park in the centre of Hobart; on Maria Island, the Isle of the Dead off Port Arthur and Sarah Island in Macquarie Harbour; at National Trust properties; and in towns like Stanley, Richmond, Ross, Evandale and Corinna.

Whether you complete a round trip or only explore parts of this island state, it is very likely that, by the time you come to leave, Tasmania will have won yet another heart.

HOBART

A Historic City

Hobart is an enchanting city built around a beautiful harbour and under the spell of nearby majestic Mount Wellington. A strong seafaring flavour and sense of the past give Hobart an almost European air. This feeling is heightened in winter when Mount Wellington is snow-capped and temperatures drop to a crisp 5°C. The rest of the year Hobart has plenty of days with sparkling blue skies, but temperatures rarely exceed 25°C.

Many of Hobart's beautiful early colonial sandstone buildings were erected by the unfortunate convicts who formed the majority of the first settlers in 1803.

Hobart's deepwater harbour on the broad estuary of the Derwent River soon became a thriving seaport and by 1842 Hobart was proclaimed a city. The harbour is still Hobart's lifeblood and the port is always busy, especially in autumn when the state's annual apple crop is loaded for export around the world. The suburbs nestle right up to the lower slopes of **Mount Wellington** and the city's population of 172 500 spreads both sides of the graceful **Tasman Bridge**, which made tragic world headlines in January 1975, when it was rammed by the bulk-carrier *Lake Illawarra*.

From the bridge you will see **Government House** and the **Royal Tasmanian Botanical Gardens** set in the Queen's Domain, a large parkland with sporting facilities and an adventure playground. Within the lovely old Botanical Gardens are a children's playground, a Japanese garden and a restaurant which serves lunch and teas.

In a matter of minutes from here you are in the heart of Hobart, which has been bypassed by the usual pressures of modern city life. Parking is no problem, but most of the city streets are one-way.

Hobart's waterfront retains much of its early character and it is not hard to imagine it in the early whaling days when Hobart Town was a lusty, brawling seaport known to sailors all round the world. Foreign ships tie up almost in the centre of town, battered whalers now replaced by Australian fishing-trawlers. Wander around to **Constitution Dock**, the haven

Salamanca Place markets

for the yachts in the famous annual Sydney to Hobart Yacht Race; you can buy live seafood from the local fishermen.

Just around the corner, in Argyle Street, is the **Tasmanian Museum and Art Gallery**, which has a fine collection of early prints and paintings, Aboriginal artefacts and convict relics. From here it is only a short stroll to the **Theatre Royal**, which was built in 1837 and is the oldest theatre in Australia. It is worth going inside to glimpse its charming dolls'-house-scale Georgian interior. Dame Sybil Thorndike rated it as the finest theatre she had played in outside of London. Not far from the Theatre Royal are the **Criminal Courts** and **Penitentiary Chapel**, operated by the National Trust; guided tours are conducted daily.

Heading back towards the centre of the city, you will see Hobart's imposing sandstone old **Town Hall**, built on the site of the original **Government House**, on the corner of Macquarie and Elizabeth Streets.

Australia's second oldest capital, Hobart has a wealth of beautiful Georgian buildings, mostly concentrated in **Macquarie**

and Davey Streets. More than ninety of them have a National Trust classification and the **Anglesea Barracks**, in Davey Street, is the oldest military establishment in Australia still used by the army. The Cascade Brewery in **South Hobart**, over a century and a half old, offers conducted tours.

Several modern complexes blend in with the older buildings without destroying the overall scale and atmosphere. The largest landmark is the tower of Australia's first hotel-casino, **Wrest Point**, built on a promontory in the elite suburb of **Sandy Bay**, just out of town. Back towards the waterfront is the famous **Salamanca Place**, which displays the finest row of early merchant warehouses in Australia. Dating back to the whaling days of the 1830s, the whole area has been sympathetically restored and the warehouses are now used as art and craft galleries, restaurants and a puppet theatre. A colourful open-air craft market, where almost anything is sold for almost any price, is held here each Saturday. Children will particularly enjoy the nearby **Post Office Museum**, in Castray Esplanade, where they can see old telephones, letter-boxes and a small post office.

The steep **Kelly's Steps**, wedged between two old warehouses in Salamanca Place, lead to the heart of Hobart's unique **Battery Point**, a former mariners' village, which has miraculously retained its nineteenth-century character. Battery Point has many excellent restaurants offering a variety of cuisines, and several quaint cottage tearooms.

The area is also Hobart's mecca for antique-hunters. Just round the corner is the **Van Diemen Folk Museum**, with its interesting collection of colonial relics housed in Narryna, a gracious old town house, complete with a shady garden and an ornamental fountain. A short walk from here is the graceful old **St George's Anglican Church**, which was built between 1836 and 1847 and designed by two of Tasmania's most prominent colonial architects, John Lee Archer and James Blackburn. The **Tasmanian Maritime Museum** has a

BATTERY POINT

A most delightful part of Hobart is the former maritime village **Battery Point**, perched between the city docks and Sandy Bay. Battery Point dates back to the early days of Hobart Town, when it soon became a lively mariners' village with fishermen's cottages, shops, churches, a village green and a riot of pubs with such evocative names as the Whalers' Return and the Neptune Inn. Miraculously, it has hardly changed since those days. To anyone strolling through its narrow, hilly streets — with enchanting glimpses of the harbour, yachts and mountains at every turn — it looks almost like a Cornish fishing-village.

Quaint **Arthurs Circus** is built around the former village green, now a children's playground. A profusion of old-fashioned flowers – sweet-william, honeysuckle, daisies and geraniums — grow in pocket-sized gardens.

Pubs such as the Knopwood's Retreat and the Shipwright's Arms add to the feeling that time has stood still. Knopwood Street and Kelly's Steps are

reminders of two pioneer settlers: the Reverend Bobby Knopwood, Battery Point's first landowner, and the adventurer James Kelly, who owned a whaling-fleet and undertook a daring voyage around Van Diemen's Land.

Battery Point gets its name from a battery of guns set up on the promontory in front of a small guard-house in 1818. This soon became a signalling-station and is now the oldest building in Battery Point.

Today the Point has many inviting restaurants and tearooms, and several antique shops to explore, but it is still mainly a residential area. Most of the houses are tiny dormer-windowed fishermen's cottages, with a few grander houses such as Secheron, Stowell, Narryna and Lenna. An attractive leaflet with a detailed map, *Let's Talk About Battery Point*, is available from the Tasmanian Travel Centre, and the National Trust organises walking tours of the area, departing from the Wishing Well, Franklin Square, each Saturday morning.

Arthurs Circus, Battery Point

Hotels
Lenna of Hobart
20 Runnymede St, Battery Point
(002) 23 2911
Sheraton Hobart
1 Davey St, Hobart
(002) 35 4535
Wrest Point Hotel-Casino
410 Sandy Bay Rd, Sandy Bay
(002) 25 0112

Family and Budget
Hobart Pacific Motor Inn
Kirby Crt, West Hobart
(002) 34 6733
Hobart Tower Motel
300 Park St, New Town
(002) 28 0166
Taroona
178 Channel Hwy, Taroona
(002) 27 8748

Motel Groups: Bookings
Best Western (008) 22 2166
Innkeepers (008) 03 0111
Flag 13 2400

This list is for information only; inclusion is not necessarily a recommendation.

collection of old seafaring relics and documents.

Back towards the city, **St David's Park**, with its beautiful old trees, is an ideal place for a rest. One side of this park was Hobart Town's first burial-ground and the pioneer gravestones, which date from 1804, make fascinating reading. Across the road, in Murray Street, is **Parliament House**, one of the oldest buildings in Hobart. Originally used as the Customs House, it was built by convicts between 1835 and 1841. Visitors may ask to see the tiny **Legislative Council Chamber**, which is exactly as it was when it was inaugurated. The ceiling has been painstakingly repainted in its original ornate pastel patterns and the benches have been refurbished in plush red velvet. The building was designed by John Lee Archer.

The **Allport Library and Museum of Fine Arts**, a library of rare books and a collection of antique furniture, china and silver, is also in Murray Street, within the **State Library**.

The main shopping area of Hobart is centred round the **Elizabeth Street Mall**, between Collins and Liverpool Streets. The **Cat and Fiddle Arcade and Square** is located between the Mall and Murray Street. Shoppers can relax in the modern square with its fountain and an animated mural which 'performs' on the hour. In the Mall, added to the hourly antics of the Cat and Fiddle Clock, there is entertainment provided by strolling buskers. Further along Elizabeth Street, in **Franklin Square**, you can play 'giant' chess.

Hobart offers a sophisticated night-life with the Wrest Point Hotel-Casino, cabaret and revolving restaurant, and a wide range of licensed restaurants – from Japanese and Mexican to colonial-style. For a touch of 'olde-worlde' class you can sip cocktails in the drawing-room of **Lenna**, an Italianate former mansion (now a distinctive hotel-motel) in Battery Point, before dining in the lavishly decorated restaurant. Fresh seafood is a specialty of many of the city's restaurants. **Mures Fish Centre**, at Victoria Dock, offers a range from takeaway to the fisherman's basket (brimming with such delicacies as crayfish, mussels, squid and scallops). Hobart also has several interesting old pubs with a nautical flavour, such as the **Customs House Hotel** on the corner of Murray and Morrison Streets.

The suburbs of Hobart have much to offer the visitor. Nearby **Sandy Bay** is the site of both the **University of Tasmania** and a **Model Tudor Village**. Beyond this, just out of **Taroona**, is the convict-built **Shot Tower**, from the top of which you can get a superb view of the Derwent Estuary. Also part of the Shot Tower complex are a small museum and tearooms, both housed in an old (1855) building, as well as the original owner's house, built in 1835. **North Hobart**, only a few minutes from the centre of the city, is the 'gourmet' food suburb, where a concentration of excellent restaurants and delicatessens have proliferated, to the delight of residents and visitors alike. Slightly further north, in the suburb of **New Town** is **Runnymede**, a National Trust homestead. Beautifully restored, it commands an attractive view over New Town Bay and **Risdon,** where Hobart's first settlement was pioneered. Further north, in the suburb of **Goodwood**, the **Derwent Entertainment Centre** stands beside the river and **Elwick Racecourse**. **Bellerive**, the ruins of an old fort at **Kangaroo Bluff**, was built to guard Hobart against a feared Russian invasion late last century. Some of Hobart's best beaches, including **Lauderdale**, **Cremorne** and **Seven Mile Beach**, are in this area. For surfers there is a wild ocean beach at **Clifton**, where the Australian surfing championships have been held.

There are dozens of scenic drives and lookouts around Hobart, with spectacular views from the pinnacle of **Mount Wellington** and from the old **Signal Station** on top of **Mount Nelson**. The **Waterworks Reserve** is an attractive picnic area only a few minutes' drive from town.

The hundreds of yachts moored near the prestigious **Royal Yacht Club** in Sandy Bay are evidence of one of Hobart's most popular sports. Other sports are well catered for with a public golf-course at **Rosny Park**, racing and trotting at **Glenorchy**, and public squash courts at **Sandy Bay**, **New Town** and **Bellerive**. The Southern Tasmanian Tennis Association Courts and an Olympic swimming-pool are in **Queen's Domain**. Tasmania's cricket headquarters is at Bellerive.

Hobart offers a complete range of accommodation, from the modern Sheraton Hobart Hotel and Wrest Point Hotel-Casino, with superb views from its 21-storey tower, to tiny Georgian cottage guesthouses at Battery Point. Between these two extremes there are many modern hotels and motels and numerous guesthouses, as well as caravan parks and holiday flats and cottages. 'Campercraft', small houseboats like floating caravans, can be hired throughout the state.

For further information, contact the **Tasmanian Travel Centre**, 80 Elizabeth St; (002) 30 0250.

Cityscape sunset, Hobart

TOURS FROM HOBART

Hobart is within easy reach of a marvellous range of tourist attractions. To appreciate its superb natural setting, it is worth going on a scenic flight over the city and its surroundings, taking in the beautiful Derwent estuary, the patchwork fields of the Midlands, the Tasman Peninsula and the spectacular lakes and mountains of central and south-western Tasmania. Flight bookings can be made at the Tasmanian Travel Centre, Hobart, which also can arrange half-day and full-day coach tours.

Mt Wellington, 22 km from Hobart via the Huon Road

The most popular short trip from Hobart is to the pinnacle of Mt Wellington, 1271 metres above the city, which commands panoramic views of the Derwent Valley to the north and the D'Entrecasteaux Channel to the south. A novel way to see the glorious views is the half-day tour 'Mt Wellington Downhill': transport to the summit and a gentle bike-ride back down.

Cadbury's Factory, Claremont, 14 km from Hobart on the Lyell Highway

A visit to this beautifully sited model factory, the biggest chocolate and cocoa factory in Australia, is another popular short trip. Privately-run coach tours leave daily and self-drive tours may be made Tuesday–Thursday. Information and bookings at Travel Centre. The factory is usually closed for two weeks in September and from the end of December to mid-January.

Richmond, 26 km from Hobart via the Eastern Outlet Road

Tasmania's oldest and most famous historic village, Richmond has the oldest bridge in Australia, and a wealth of mellow old colonial buildings, including Tasmania's oldest gaol and two historic churches. Prospect House, built in 1830, another historic building, is now a licensed restaurant and colonial accommodation property. **See also:** Entry in A–Z listing.

New Norfolk, 32 km from Hobart on the Lyell Highway

This historic town, in the centre of Tasmania's beautiful hop-growing country, is particularly delightful in autumn when the leaves on the many English trees planted here last century turn to beautiful

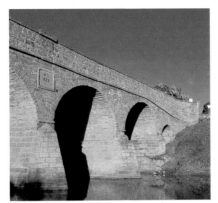

Historic bridge, Richmond

golden tones. Quaint old oast-houses are a feature of the landscape and the town's attractions include the historic Old Colony Inn, now a museum and tearooms set in charming grounds, and the famous Salmon Ponds, 11 km north-west at Plenty, the first successful trout hatchery in Australia. **See also:** Entry in A–Z listing.

Mt Field National Park and Russell Falls, 72 km from Hobart via the Lyell Highway and Gordon River Road

The road from New Norfolk to Mt Field passes through some of the loveliest parts of the Derwent Valley. A nature walk leads to the magnificent Russell Falls, cascades that drop 32 metres into a gorge of rainforest and tree-ferns, from near the park entrance. This large scenic wildlife reserve shelters many native birds and animals, including the elusive Tasmanian devil. **See also:** Tasmania's National Parks.

Lake Pedder and Lake Gordon, 170 km from Hobart via the Lyell Highway and Gordon River Road

In clear weather, the road from Mt Field National Park to the township of Strathgordon is probably the most spectacular stretch of mountain highway in Australia. Unfortunately (from the visitor's point of view), there is a very high rainfall in the area, which of course results in its unique natural topography. Motorists are advised to cancel trips on overcast days. Man-made Lakes Pedder and Gordon, part of the Hydro-Electric Commission's giant Gordon River power development, are liberally stocked with trout. The underground power-station at the Gordon Dam can be inspected on regular tours. You can hire boats and fishing

tackle, and charter scenic cruises from Strathgordon, where a chalet is available for overnight accommodation. Enquiries should be directed to the Tasmanian Travel Centre in Hobart. **See also:** Tasmania's National Parks; Dams for Power.

The Tasman Peninsula and Port Arthur, 151 km from Hobart via the Arthur Highway

There is so much to see on this fascinating trip that it would be well worth staying overnight at the narrow isthmus of Eaglehawk Neck or at Port Arthur. Once guarded by a line of tethered hounds to prevent convicts escaping, Eaglehawk Neck is now a base for game-fishing charter boats. There are four unique coastal formations in the area: the spectacular Devil's Kitchen, the Blowhole, Tasman's Arch and the Tessellated Pavement. The old penal settlement of Port Arthur is Tasmania's number one tourist attraction. Other attractions in the area include Bush Hill, Remarkable Cave and Safety Cove, while a seaplane service from Hobart provides flights around the peninsula. **See also:** Entries in A–Z listing; Tasmania's Convict Past.

Huonville, 37 km from Hobart via Huon Road and the Huon Highway

You can make a scenic trip to Huonville, the centre of Tasmania's picturesque apple-growing district, via the shoulder of Mt Wellington on the Huon Highway, returning via the coastal town of Cygnet and along the Channel Highway, which commands spectacular vistas of the coastline and rugged Bruny Island. **See also:** Entry in A–Z listing.

Hastings Caves, 110 km from Hobart via the Huon Road and Huon Highway

These caves, 13 km from the small township of Hastings, are another popular attraction. There are regular guided tours of the only illuminated cave, Newdegate Cave, regarded as one of the most beautiful limestone caves in Australia. A natural thermal swimming-pool with an average temperature of 27°C is nearby. Motorists are warned that Dover is the last place to buy petrol en route to Recherche Bay. The Ida Bay Scenic Railway is another popular tourist attraction near Hastings. **See also:** Entry in A–Z listing.

TASMANIA from A to Z

Avoca   Population 207

This small town with a mining background, on the Esk Main Road, also serves the small communities of Rossarden and Storys Creek, in the foothills of Ben Lomond, the highest mountain in north-east Tasmania. **Of interest:** Historic buildings include St Thomas's Church and parish hall. **In the area:** Bona Vista (1848), 1 km north-west on Storys Creek Rd, once one of Tasmania's most attractive historic houses, now in disrepair; private property but inspection possible. **Accommodation:** Limited.
MAP REF. 479 O10

Beaconsfield   Population 1064

The ruins of impressive brick buildings with Romanesque arches dominate this quiet town on the West Tamar Hwy, 46 km north-west of Launceston. Formerly a thriving gold township (called Cabbage Tree Hill), the ruins are the remains of buildings erected at the pithead of the Tasmanian Gold Mine in 1904. When the mine closed ten years later due to water seepage, more than six million dollars' worth of ore had been won from the reef. In 1804 a party of officers established a settlement north of the town, called York Town. **Of interest:** Grubb Shaft Museum in one of old mine buildings; restored miner's cottage and original Flowery Gully School alongside museum. **In the area:** York Town monument, on Kelso–Greens Beach Rd. Batman Bridge, 7 km south-east, near Sidmouth; A-frame reaches 100 m above River Tamar. Auld Kirk (1843) at Sidmouth, 9 km south-east. **Tourist information:** Tamar Visitors Centre, Main Rd, Exeter; (003) 94 4454. **Accommodation:** Limited.
MAP REF. 479 K6, 480 B5

Beauty Point   Population 1064

This popular fishing and yachting centre on the West Tamar Hwy, 48 km north-east of Launceston, is the oldest deep-water port in the area and was constructed to serve the Beaconsfield gold-mine. Today cargo is loaded at Bell Bay on the eastern shore of the Tamar River. **Of interest:** Nearby Sandy Beach for safe swimming. **In the area:** Two northern resorts: Kelso, 15 km north, which dates back to early York Town settlement, and Greens Beach, 20 km north, at mouth of River Tamar. Marion's Vineyard at Deviot, 12 km south. **Tourist information:** Tamar Visitors Centre,

Main Rd, Exeter; (003) 94 4454. **Accommodation:** 1 hotel.
MAP REF. 479 K5, 480 B5

Bicheno   Population 661

A fishing port and holiday resort on the east coast, 195 km from Hobart, Bicheno offers surf, rock, sea and estuary fishing. The town's mild climate, outstanding fishing, nearby fine sandy beaches and its picturesque setting make it one of Tasmania's most popular holiday resorts. Licensed seafood restaurants and a range of accommodation add to its appeal. Originally a sealing and whaling town from about 1803, it later became a coal-mining port in 1854. Today crayfishing is the main local industry. **Of interest:** On Tasman Hwy: Sea Life Centre, with aquarium and seafood restaurant; and Bicheno Dive Centre, diving school and charters. Picturesque foreshore walkway from Redhill Point north of town to Blowhole in south. Lookouts at top of town's twin hills. Fairy Penguin Rookery; access Gordon St. Grave of Aboriginal heroine Waubedebar in Lions Park, Burgess St. **In the area:** East Coast Bird Life and Animal Park, 7 km north; Tasmanian devils and other native fauna. Douglas-Apsley National Park, 10 km north-west. Freyinect National Park, 10 km south. Freyinect Vineyard, 18 km south-east; tastings and sales. **Tourist information:** Bicheno Penguin Adventure Tours, Foster St; (003) 75 1333. **Accommodation:** 2 hotels, 2 motels, 2 caravan/camping parks.
MAP REF. 479 R10

Boat Harbour   Population 280

The clear water and rocky points of this attractive resort make it an ideal spot for skin-diving and spear-fishing. Situated on the north-west coast, 31 km west of Burnie, it adjoins one of the richest agricultural areas in the state. **Of interest:** Shannondoah Cottage, Bass Hwy; local crafts, lunches, Devonshire teas. **In the area:** Boat Harbour Beach, 3 km north; safe swimming, marine life in pools at low tide, fishing, water-skiing and bushwalking. Rocky Cape National Park, 19 km north-west. Good fishing and swimming at Sisters Beach, 5 km north-west. Birdland Native Gardens nearby within park. **Tourist information:** 48 Cattley St, Burnie; (004) 34 6111. **Accommodation:** 2 motels, 1 caravan/camping park.
MAP REF. 478 E4

Bothwell   Population 369

This peaceful old country town in the beautiful Clyde River valley, 74 km north of Hobart, has been proclaimed a historic village. It has 53 buildings either classified or recorded as 'worthy of preservation' by the National Trust. Surveyed in 1824 and named by Lieut.-Governor Arthur after the Scottish town of the same name, it is now the centre of quality sheep and cattle country. It is possible that the first golf in Australia was played on the links at the nearby homestead of Ratho during the 1830s. This course still exists and is open to visitors with golf-club membership elsewhere. **Of interest:** Bothwell Grange (c. 1836), Alexander St; guest-house, tearooms and art gallery. St Luke's Uniting Church (1830), Dennistoun St. Georgian brick Slate Cottage (1836), High St; restored and furnished in style of day. **In the area:** Restored and operational Thorpe Water Mill, 2 km north on Interlaken Rd; tours by arrangement. Excellent fishing at Arthurs Lake, Penstock Lagoon, Great Lake and Lake Echo. **Tourist information:** Council Offices, Alexander St; (002) 59 5503. **Accommodation:** 1 camping/caravan park. MAP REF. 477 L3

Branxholm   Population 264

This small, former tin-mining town on the Tasman Hwy, 90 km north-east of Launceston, now serves the surrounding rich vegetable-growing and dairying district. **Of interest:** Pine plantations and Firth Memorial Grove, Mt Horror Rd, Mt Horror. Old tin-mine workings and lapidary. **Accommodation:** 1 caravan/camping ground. MAP REF. 479 O6

Bridgewater   Population 8654

This town, only 19 km north of Hobart, is situated on the bank of the main northern crossing of the Derwent River. The causeway was built in the early 1830s by 200 convicts, who barrowed two million tonnes of stone and clay from the site. The original bridge was opened in 1849; the present one dates from 1946. **In the area:** At Granton, 1 km across bridge: Old Watch House (now petrol station), built by convicts in 1838 to guard causeway, has smallest cell used in Australia (50 cm sq. and 2 m high); and Black Snake Inn (1833), another convict-built building. **Accommodation:** Limited. MAP REF. 474 H5, 477 M6

Bridport   Population 980

Bridport is a popular holiday resort and fishing town on the north-east coast, 85 km from Launceston. **Of interest:** Fine beaches and excellent river, sea and lake fishing. **In the area:** Bowood (1839), historic homestead near town; not open to public. Views from Waterhouse Point and Ranson's Beach. Wine-growing at Piper's Brook, 18 km west. **Accommodation:** 1 hotel, 1 hotel/motel, 1 caravan/ camping park. MAP REF. 479 N4, 480 I2

Brighton   Population 650

This town, near Hobart on the Midland Hwy, has always been an important military post. It was first established in 1826 and today the Brighton Army Camp is the main military base in Tasmania. The town was named after the English resort by Governor Macquarie in 1821. **Of interest:** Bonorong Park Wildlife Sanctuary, 2 km south-east. **In the area:** Historic village of Pontville, 2 km north. **Tourist information:** Council Offices, Tivoli Rd, Gagebrook; (002) 63 0333. **Accommodation:** 1 hotel/motel. **See also:** Rural Landscapes. MAP REF. 474 I4, 477 M6

Bruny Island   Population 340

Almost two islands, separated by a narrow isthmus, Bruny was named after the French Admiral Bruni D'Entrecasteaux, who surveyed the channel between the island and the mainland of Tasmania in 1792. Abel Tasman discovered the island in 1642 but did not land. Other early visitors included Furneaux (1773), James Cook (1777) and William Bligh (1788 and 1792). The first apple trees in Tasmania are said to have been planted here by a botanist with the Bligh expedition. Bruny Island ferry departs from Kettering, on the mainland, several times daily. **Of interest:** Fishing. Camel tours. On South Bruny: Bligh Museum, at Adventure Bay, exhibits island's recorded history. Lookouts at Adventure and Cloudy Bays. Lighthouse (1836) at Cape Bruny, second oldest in Australia. Walking tracks to Mt Mangana and Mt Bruny. Morella Cottage Garden and Farm Shop at Simpsons Bay.

RURAL LANDSCAPES

Tasmania's homesick early settlers were amazingly successful in their attempts to tame their strange new antipodean home. They set about systematically clearing the more accessible lowlands of all traces of native bush, replacing it with neatly tilled fields fringed by hedge-rows and shaded English trees. Georgian farmhouses set in gardens with flowerbeds and borders completed the picture.

Tasmania's main pastoral district is the beautiful Midlands area between **Brighton** and **Perth**, noted for stock-raising and high-quality merino wool. This was one of the first farming areas established in Tasmania and its gently undulating plains are offset by mellow farmhouses, historic villages and a wealth of huge old English trees. The historic township of **New Norfolk** is the centre of Tasmania's

Near New Norfolk

long-established hop-growing district, which is a main supplier of hops for Australian beer. This enchanting countryside is enhanced by quaint old oast-houses, or hop-drying kilns. Apples and dairy products are produced in the **Derwent Valley**, which is also an important beef-raising and wool-growing district.

The **Huon Valley**, south of Hobart, is the centre of Tasmania's famous apple-growing industry, which dates back to the early nineteenth century when Lady Franklin, wife of Governor Sir John Franklin, established a farm at **Franklin.**

Tasmania's richest and most highly productive farmland lies on the north-west coast, where the main industries are potato-growing and the raising of prime beef and dairy cattle.

See also: Individual entries in A–Z listing.

TASMANIA'S NATIONAL PARKS

Tasmanians recognised early that their state had some of the most splendid scenery in Australia, and legislation was introduced in 1863 to preserve certain districts for their scenic value. Today the Department of Parks, Wildlife and Heritage of Tasmania manages not only the state's dozen or so national parks but also many state reserves with their caves, gorges, waterfalls and rivers, Aboriginal areas and historic sites that date back as far as 1803, when settlers first landed on the island.

All parks are accessible year round, but some believe the highland parks are best seen in summer and autumn, when the climate is more reliable, and when wildflowers bloom in profusion and flowering trees and shrubs are alive with birdlife.

The two areas to be declared the first national parks of Tasmania were Mount Field, just eighty kilometres north-west of Hobart, and Freycinet, on the central east coast. **Mount Field** is a popular tourist venue, offering such activities as climbing and bushwalking. It also provides the only developed skiing area in southern Tasmania. There are several delightful waterfalls within the park, the best-known being Russell Falls, which was discovered in 1856. Here the cascading water plunges in two stages into deep gorges shaded by tree-ferns which

filter sunlight and create a mosaic effect. There are two levels of forest, including the ancient Huon pine, 250-year-old gum trees, sassafras, giant tree-ferns, the unique horizontal scrub and a variety of mosses, ferns, lichens and fungi. There is a wide range of walks, from leisurely to strenuous, including the famed Lyrebird Walk, where you may see the black currawong, native to Tasmania, and hear the noisy yellow wattlebird or perhaps the endless repertoire of the lyrebird's mimicry.

Freycinet National Park offers the nature-lover wide stretches of white sands, rocky headlands, granite peaks, quiet beaches and small caves, with windswept eucalypt forests on its slopes and excellent short or long walking tracks. Just north of the park is Moulting Lagoon, the breeding ground of the lovely black swan and a refuge for other waterfowl. Freycinet National Park also includes Schouten Island, separated from the Freycinet Peninsula by a one-kilometre-wide passage, and reached only by boat. Near the park is **Coles Bay**, a fishing and swimming resort with delightful coastal scenery.

A short distance north-west of Freycinet National Park is Tasmania's newest national park, **Douglas-Apsley** (16 080 ha). Proclaimed in 1990, this park contains the state's

last large dry sclerophyll forest and can be traversed along a two-day north to south walking track. Here forest-clad ridges contrast with patches of rainforest and river gorges. Waterfalls and spectacular coastal views add to the grandeur of the area. Facilities are basic.

Many of Tasmania's national parks are important wildlife reserves. One such park, the 13 899 hectare **Mount William** in north-east Tasmania, is a sanctuary for an abundance of native animals, including the Forester kangaroo (Tasmania's only kangaroo), echidna, wombat, pademelon, Bennetts wallaby and Tasmanian devil. Spring brings a carpet of wildflowers to this park: the red and white heaths provide a background for the contrasting colours of the golden wattle and the guinea flower. At Lookout Point, thousands of rock orchids creep over and cover the granite rocks.

Fifty kilometres south-east of Launceston is **Ben Lomond National Park**, one of Tasmania's two main skifields, with an alpine village, ski tows, ski hire, a tavern with accommodation and a public shelter.

Steep, jagged mountains create a natural amphitheatre at the **Walls of Jerusalem National Park** (51 800 ha) in the state's north central zone. Ancient forests of pencil pines ring tiny glacially-formed lakes, making the

The Hazards from Coles Bay

park very popular with bushwalkers.

The central north coastal strip of **Asbestos Range National Park** is an important refuge for the rare ground parrot and the rufous wallaby. Its islands off Port Sorell provide an important breeding area for fairy penguins and the tidal and mud flats are ideal feeding-grounds for a variety of migratory seabirds. On the unspoiled beaches of this park, white sands come to life with thousands of platoons of soldier crabs.

Further west along the coast, **Rocky Cape National Park** (3064 ha) encompasses rugged coastline with small sheltered beaches backed by heath-covered hills. It is known for its rock shelters once used by Aborigines.

Covering some of Tasmania's highest country is **Cradle Mountain–Lake St Clair National Park**. There is a visitors centre near the entrance to the park at Cradle Mountain, and a nature walk into the nearby rainforest incorporates a suspended walkway. Cradle Mountain has a variety of fine bushwalks, including one of Australia's best-known walking routes, the 80 kilometre Overland Track. Here walkers can hike through forests of deciduous beech, Tasmanian 'myrtle', pandani, King Billy pine and a wealth of wildflowers. At the other end of the park, the tranquil Lake St Clair, with a depth of over 200 metres, occupies a basin gouged out by two glaciers more than 20 000 years ago; cruises operate daily, and 6-day treks take in Mt Ossa (Tasmania's highest mountain) and the Pine Valley region. Lake St Clair was discovered as early as 1826 and is now a popular spot for boating. There are several campsites. Cradle Mountain Wilderness Lodge lies on the northern boundary of the national park.

Although **Maria Island**, off the east coast, is not easily accessible it is well worth a visit. You can get there either by light aircraft or by passenger ferry from Triabunna. On arrival, it seems as if you have stepped into another world, for on Maria Island, no tourist vehicles are permitted. The island embraces magnificently coloured sandstone cliffs and is a refuge for over eighty species of birds. Forester kangaroos, emus and Cape Barren geese roam freely in this totally unspoiled landscape. Its intriguing history and historic buildings date back to the convict era of 1825 and provide a contrast

Cradle Mountain-Lake St Clair National Park

to the now peaceful surroundings.

Tasmania's largest national park is **Southwest National Park**, which has 605 213 hectares of mainly remote wilderness country. Here there are dolerite and quartzite capped mountains, sharp ridges and steep valleys left by glaciers; the dense forests are made up of giant mountain ash, eucalypts, ancient Huon pines, shrubs and limbs of the Antarctic beech, all covered with mosses, ferns and lichens and the pink-flowered climbing heath. Mountain climbers will find a challenge in Federation Peak, Mount Anne and Precipitous Bluff, while anglers will be kept busy with trout-fishing at Lakes Pedder and Gordon. A new bird hide at Melaleuca can be used in summer to observe the extremely rare orange-bellied parrot.

The 440 000 ha **Franklin–Lower Gordon Wild Rivers National Park** forms the central portion of Tasmania's World Heritage Area. The Franklin attracts wilderness adventurers from around the world to test its challenging rapids. Along the slightly more placid Gordon River are stands of 2000-year-old Huon pine. Unusual buttongrass vegetation growing right to the edge of the water stains it to the colour of tea. The Lyell Highway, the road link between Hobart and the west coast, runs through the park. A number of excellent short walks lead off the highway to rainforests and spectacular lookouts.

A two-hour drive from Hobart, through Geeveston to the south-east, brings visitors to the **Hartz Mountains National Park**. Most of the

area is over 600 metres in altitude with Hartz Peak being 1 255 metres high. There are basic facilities for the day visitor and no camping facilities, although camping is permitted. Bushwalking is popular, although all visitors are warned the area is subject to sudden storms, even in summer.

At the southern end of Flinders Island in Bass Strait is **Strzelecki National Park** (4215 ha). Famed for its exhilarating views from Mt Strzelecki's granite summit, the park also boasts pristine beaches and camping amongst she-oaks at Trousers Point.

In some of the many state reserves, limestone caves are a popular attraction. The cave interiors are dramatically lit to enhance the wonderland of limestone-derived calcite formations. The Hastings Caves, located 110 kilometres from Hobart, include a nearby thermal swimming-pool with a year-round warm temperature. Set in a fern glade, the pool is surrounded by lawns and picnic areas.

For further information on Tasmania's national parks, contact the Department of Parks, Wildlife and Heritage, 134 Macquarie Street, Hobart (GPO Box 44A, Hobart 7001); (002) 30 6285.

Scenic reserve at Mavista Falls. On North Bruny: Memorials to early navigators. Dennes Point beach on D'Entrecasteaux Channel. At Variety Bay, remains of convict-built church on private property near airstrip; conducted tours. **Tourist information:** Council Offices, Alonnah; (002) 93 1139. **Accommodation:** 1 hotel, 2 caravan/camping parks.
MAP REF. 477 M9, 477 M11

Buckland   Population under 200
A stained-glass window depicting the life of John the Baptist and dating back to the 14th century is in the church in this tiny township, 64 km north-east of Hobart. History links the window with Battle Abbey, England, which stands on the site of the Battle of Hastings. The abbey was sacked by Oliver Cromwell in the 17th century, but the window was hidden before it could be destroyed. Two centuries later it was given to Rev. T.H. Fox, Buckland's first rector, by the Marquis of Salisbury. It is now set into the east wall of the Church of St John the Baptist, which was built in 1846. Although the window has been damaged and restored several times in its long life, the original figure-work is intact. Also of interest is Ye Olde Buckland Inn, a 19th-century tavern and restaurant. **Accommodation:** Limited.
MAP REF. 475 N3, 477 O5

Burnie   Population 20 665
The rapid expansion of Burnie, now Tasmania's fourth largest town, is based on one of the state's largest industrial enterprises, Associated Pulp and Paper Mills Ltd. Situated on Emu Bay, 148 km west of Launceston, Burnie has a busy deepwater port, which serves the west coast mining centres. Other important industries include plants for the manufacture of titanium oxide pigments, dried milk, chocolate products and cheese. **Of interest:** Lactos cheese factory; tastings and sales. Tours of Associated Pulp and Paper Mills. Pioneer Village Museum, High St; reconstruction of Burnie's small tradesmen's shops at turn of century. Meals at restored Burnie Inn, town's oldest remaining building, re-erected in Burnie Park. Burnie's Athletic Carnival on New Year's Day features cycling and woodchopping. **In the area:** Local beauty spots include: on town's outskirts, Round Hill, for panoramic views; Fern Glade, 5 km west, for riverside walks and picnics; Emu Valley Rhododendron Gardens, 3 km south; Guide Falls at Ridgley, 17 km south; and 20 km south, Upper Natone Forest Reserve for picnics. Day tours to: Cradle Mountain, Gunns Plains, Leven Canyon and Fossil Cliffs, inland. Pieman River cruises. **Tourist information:** 48

Cattley St; (004) 34 6111. **Accommodation:** 4 hotels, 2 hotel/motels, 5 motels, 2 caravan/camping parks. **See also:** Scenic Island State.
MAP REF. 478 G5

Campbell Town   Population 867
Campbell Town, on the Midlands Hwy, 66 km south of Launceston, is a national centre for selling stud sheep. The area's links with the wool industry go back to the early 1820s, when Saxon merinos were introduced to the Macquarie Valley, west of the town. Timber and stud beef are also important primary industries. The town and the Elizabeth River were named by Governor Macquarie for his wife, the former Elizabeth Campbell. **Of interest:** National Trust classified buildings include: Balmoral Cottage (1840s); St Luke's Church (1839); The Grange (1840); Campbell Town Inn (1840); and St Michael's Roman Catholic Church (1857). Convict-built Red Bridge (1837). **In the area:** Evansville Game Park, 30 km east. Trout fishing in local rivers and lakes, particularly Lake Leake, 30 km south-east. **Accommodation:** 1 hotel.
MAP REF. 477 N1, 479 N11

Coles Bay   Population under 200
This beautiful unspoiled bay, 39 km south of Bicheno on the Freycinet Peninsula, is a good base for visitors to the 10 000 ha Freycinet National Park. **Of interest:** Park's pleasant beaches, crystal-clear waters and colourful heathlands make it ideal for swimming, fishing and beach and bushwalking. Abundant birdlife and variety of wildflowers, including 60 varieties of small ground orchid. Rock-climbing on the Hazards and nearby cliffs. Opportunities for water-skiing, skin-diving, canoeing and sailing. Charter boat trips to Schouten Island. Tours by

arrangement. **Tourist information:** Park Ranger; (002) 57 0107. **Accommodation:** Coles Bay, 1 motel, 2 caravan/camping parks. Friendly Beaches, camping area. **See also:** Tasmania's National Parks.
MAP REF. 477 R2, 479 R12

Cygnet   Population 832
The centre of a fruit-growing district, 54 km from Hobart, the town was originally named Port de Cygne (meaning Swan Port) by the French Admiral Bruni D'Entrecasteaux because of the number of swans in the bay. **Of interest:** Good beaches and boat-launching facilities at Verona Sands, Randalls Bay and Egg and Bacon Bay. Port Cygnet Fishing Carnival held in Mar. **In the area:** Boating, fishing, bushwalks and gem-fossicking. Winter Wood Winery, 10 km west; tastings and sales. At Gardners Bay, 8 km south: Tahune Woodturning; wildlife park with picnic/barbecue facilities. Unique Lymington lace agate sometimes found at Drip Beach, Lymington, 12 km south. **Tourist information:** Council Offices, Mary St; (002) 95 1217. **Accommodation:** 1 caravan/camping park.
MAP REF. 474 G11, 477 L9

Deddington   Population under 200
In 1830 artist John Glover arrived from England and bought land on the site of this little town, 37 km south-east of Launceston. He named his property Deddington after the village in the English Lake District where he had lived. **Of interest:** Deddington Chapel (1840), designed by Glover, classified by National Trust. John Glover's grave beside chapel. **Accommodation:** Limited.
MAP REF. 479 N8, 480 I12

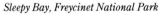
Sleepy Bay, Freycinet National Park

Deloraine
Population 1997

Scenic Deloraine, with Bass Strait to the north and the Great Western Tiers to the south, is an ideal base for exploring the many attractions of northern Tasmania. The surrounding rich countryside is used mainly for dairying and mixed farming. **Of interest:** Self-guiding Heritage Walk. Deloraine Folk Museum and Cider Bar, Emu Bay Rd; housed in Plough Inn, classified by National Trust. **In the area:** Tasmania Pottery, on Mole Creek Rd, 1 km west; displays and sales. Tasmanian Smokehouse, 10 km west; sales of gourmet fish. Tasmanian Wildlife Park, 18 km west; specially designed 'noctarium' for displaying nocturnal animals. Heidi Cheese Factory, Exton, 6 km east; tastings and sales. Scenic drives south to Liffey, Meander and Montana Falls; also to Central Highlands, through Golden Valley, to Great Lake, highest body of water in Australia. Excellent trout fishing on lake and in Mersey and Meander Rivers. **Tourist information:** Westchurch St; (003) 62 2046. **Accommodation:** 1 motel, 1 caravan/camping park. MAP REF. 479 J8

Derby
Population 202

Derby is a small tin-mining town on the Tasman Hwy, 34 km from Scottsdale in the north-east. In its heyday, tin-mining was a flourishing industry, but there has been a gradual swing to rural production, although tin is still worked. **Of interest:** Derby Tin Mine Museum, housed in old school (1890s), with tearooms; local history, gemstone and mineral displays, tin-panning demonstrations. Reconstructed 'town' surrounding museum consists of 7 original buildings from area: miner's cottage, newspaper office, mining assay office, butcher's shop, general store, blacksmith's shop and two cells from old Derby gaol. **Tourist information:** Tin Mine Museum, Main St; (003) 54 2262. **Accommodation:** Limited. MAP REF. 479 P5

Devonport
Population 22 645

As the terminal for a vehicular ferry from Melbourne, Devonport has become a busy industrial and agricultural-export town, as well as a major tourist centre. Devonport has its own airport, and is ideally suited as a visitor base for seeing scenic northern Tasmania. **Of interest:** Self-guiding leaflets from tourist centre. Showcase Gallery and Art Centre, Best St. Maritime Museum, Victoria Pde, The Bluff. Bramich's Early Motoring and Folk Museum, Don Rd; open by appointment. Taswegia, printery museum, Formby Rd. Tiagarra, Tasmanian Aboriginal Culture and Art Centre at Mersey Bluff, parklands

Abel Tasman ferry coming into the terminal at Devonport

and beach resort promontory at river mouth; Tasmanian Aboriginal rock carvings outside display area. Home Hill, Middle Rd; tours of home of former Prime Minister Joseph Lyons and Dame Enid Lyons. Serendipity Fun Park for children. **In the area:** Walking track from The Bluff to Don River Railway and Museum, at Don, 2 km west. Forth, 13 km west, has spring of pure water claimed to have medicinal qualities. Braddon's Lookout, near Forth, with panoramic view of coastline. Tasmanian Aboretium (45 ha) at Eugenana, 10 km south; picnic area and walking tracks. **Tourist information:** 18 Rooke St; (004) 24 1526. **Accommodation:** 4 hotels, 2 hotel/motels, 2 motels, 3 caravan/camping parks. **See also:** Scenic Island State. MAP REF. 478 I5

Dover
Population 394

This attractive fishing port, south of Hobart, was once a convict station. The original Commandant's Office still stands, but the cells, which are underground just up from the wharf, can no longer be seen. Quaint old cottages and English trees give the town an 'old-world' atmosphere. The three islands in the bay are called Faith, Hope and Charity. **Of interest:** Chartered fishing trips. Several old graves on Faith Island. Attractive scenery and unspoiled beaches make area ideal for bushwalking and swimming. Drivers who continue south should stock up here

on petrol and provisions. **In the area:** Tours of Tassal Atlantic Salmon Farm, Meads Creek, 20 km south. Southport, 21 km south, fishing port established in days of sealers and whalers; good fishing, swimming, surfing and bushwalking. Catamaran, 39 km south; most southerly town in Australia. Cockle Creek, further 2 km south, is start of extended South Coast Walking Track. **Accommodation:** 1 hotel, 1 caravan/camping park. MAP REF. 477 L10

Dunalley
Population 286

This prosperous fishing village stands on the narrow isthmus connecting the Forestier Peninsula to the rest of Tasmania. The Denison Canal, spanned by a swing bridge, provides access to the east coast for small vessels. **In the area:** Tasman Memorial, marking first landing by white men on 2 December 1642, to north-east, near Cape Paul Lamanon. **Accommodation:** 1 motel. MAP REF. 475 N7, 477 O7

Eaglehawk Neck
Population under 200

In convict days this narrow isthmus, which separates the Tasman from the Forestier Peninsula, was guarded by a line of ferocious tethered dogs. Soldiers and constables also stood guard, to ensure that no convicts escaped from the notorious convict settlement at Port Arthur. The only prisoners to escape did

SCENIC ISLAND STATE

Wherever your holiday journey in Tasmania takes you, you will be sure to see magnificent scenery and to have many fascinating experiences along the way. Most travellers start their Tasmanian holiday in the north, where they have either taken their car off the ferry or the fast catamaran from the mainland, or have hired a car or mobile home for the journey south.

Probably the best way to see what Tasmania has to offer is to take the 'circle route', with as many diversions along the way as time permits to see and explore scenic or historic highlights. Such a tour of the island, which is small enough to allow you to see most of it in a short space of time, will take you through some of the most fascinating country that Australia has to offer. The incomparable wilderness of the west coast, the towering mountains of the central

Chapel at Grindelwald, a Swiss-style village near Legana

district, the gentle pastoral landscapes of the Midlands, the lavish orchard country around Launceston and the Huon Valley, the snug beaches, bays and villages of the east coast, are all relatively accessible on good roads.

You will soon find that not everything about Tasmania is small. The trees are taller here than on the mainland, nurtured by the temperate climate (Tasmania has the world's tallest hardwood trees, some exceeding ninety metres); mountains vault to the skies from wild forest land. The great inland lakes in the mountains feed savage rivers, some of which harness the state's great hydro-electric schemes. The hills and valleys are harshly carved by the weather and become gentle only in the rolling pastoral lands of the Midlands and the north.

In this romantic landscape, more reminiscent of Scotland than Australia, are set the remnants of a rich past of convict and colonial life — the prisons, churches, cottages and court-houses, the barracks, mansions and homesteads from the earliest days of settlement.

From **Devonport**, the coast road west runs with the northern railway along the sea's edge, beneath the impressive cliffs that face Bass Strait. Along this road are the thriving towns of **Ulverstone**, **Burnie**, **Wynyard** and **Stanley**, and the striking headlands of Table Cape, Rocky Cape and the Nut. They are worth a special trip, as is a detour down the side road from **Penguin** to the peaceful mountain farmland of Gunns Plains and the Gunns Plains caves. The road from **Forth** into the vast wilderness areas of the magnificent Cradle Mountain–Lake St Clair National Park is also well worth a visit, but the turn-off to follow the circle route is at **Somerset**, from where you head south down the Murchison Highway through the rich farmlands towards the increasingly mountainous country of the west coast. An interesting diversion leads to **Corinna**, once a thriving town but now virtually abandoned, on the beautiful Pieman River, not far from its mouth. A launch trip from Corinna travels through deeply-cut river gorges west to the Indian Ocean.

GREAT CIRCLE ROUTE, TAS.

KING ISLAND

FLINDERS ISLAND

BASS STRAIT

CAPE BARREN ISLAND

Stanley
Marrawah
Wynyard · Bridport
Somerset · Burnie · George Town · Derby
Ulverstone · Devonport · Beaconsfield
Exeter · Scottsdale · St Helens
Deloraine · LAUNCESTON · St Marys
Cradle Valley
Rosebery · Avoca
Zeehan · Campbell Town · Bicheno
Queenstown · Derwent Bridge · Miena · Coles Bay
Strahan · Swansea
Oatlands
Bothwell
Melton Mowbray · Triabunna
Strathgordon · Orford
New Norfolk · Sorell
HOBART
Huonville · Port Arthur
Geeveston
Southport

SOUTHERN OCEAN

Great circle route
Other main roads
Other roads
Principal locations ●

0   25   50   70   100 km

N

Back on the main road, the mountain scenery is unique and quite spectacular. The towns here developed as a result of their mineral wealth. **Zeehan** now has only a small population, but at the turn of the century there were more than 10 000 inhabitants when tin-mining was at its height. Many buildings of those days still stand. The larger town of **Queenstown** has grown up around the Mount Lyell copper-mine, in a valley beneath bare, bleached hills, streaked and stained with the hues of minerals — chrome, purple, grey and pink. Nearby is **Strahan** on Macquarie Harbour, the only coastal town in the west. The harbour can be reached only by shallow-draught vessels through the notorious passage called Hell's Gates. Visitors can cruise through beautiful wilderness country along the Gordon River, past the ruins of the remote convict settlement on Sarah Island.

The road turns inland from these towns, avoiding the almost inaccessible south-west, and travels through the Franklin – Lower Gordon Wild Rivers National Park, across the Central Highlands past Lake St Clair and down the Derwent River valley through the town of **New Norfolk**, centre of the Tasmanian hop-growing industry. This valley, brilliantly coloured with foliage in autumn, is both of scenic and historical interest. It was settled in 1808, the site having been chosen by Governor Macquarie.

A detour from the Hobart road leads to the lovely old town of **Richmond**, one of the many historic towns off the Midlands Highway that are not visited if the circle route is followed. (Some of the others are **Ross, Oatlands, Campbell Town, Bothwell** and **Longford**, all set in the charming rolling countryside of the Midlands with their English trees framing or hiding the landowners' mansions.) Richmond is probably the best example, its old Georgian houses and cottages clustered together with its bridge, convict-built and the oldest freestone bridge still in use in Australia. The gaol predates Port Arthur as a penal settlement; two churches, a courthouse, a schoolhouse, a rectory, the hotel granary, a general store and a flour-mill were all built in the 1820s and 1830s.

Hobart, Australia's second oldest and most southerly city, is attractively sited on the Derwent River, with Mount Wellington looming above it. The port area at Salamanca Place, where the old bond stores and warehouses are sited, is a reminder of the days when the whaling-fleet and the timber-ships tied up at the wharf and sailors went out on the town. Battery Point with its barracks, workers' cottages and Arthur's Circus — its Georgian-style houses built around a circular green — is part of Hobart's early beginnings.

There are many fine public buildings in the city, which help it to retain something of the feeling of its colonial days. There is modern-day fun in Hobart, too, since the Wrest Point Hotel-Casino developed as Hobart's best-known entertainment complex.

In complete contrast, the grim but beautiful penal settlement of **Port Arthur** is not far from Hobart, on the Tasman Peninsula. Here, within the forbidding sandstone walls, visitors will feel something of the hopelessness and isolation of the thousands of convicts who passed through this settlement during its forty-seven years of existence.

South of Hobart is the scenic Huon Valley, particularly spectacular when the apple trees are in blossom. At the southern end of the route is Cockle Creek on Recherche Bay, where the South Coast walking track begins.

North on the circle route from Hobart the Tasman Highway traverses the east coast, a region which enjoys a mild and equable climate throughout most of the year and which has a number of attractive seaside resorts. Most are on sheltered inlets but within easy reach of surf beaches and fishing-grounds: towns like **Orford, Triabunna, Swansea, Bicheno, Scamander** and **St Helens**.

Off the Tasman Highway near Bicheno is the Freycinet National Park on the Freycinet Peninsula. There are many walking tracks through this park, which is dominated by the Hazards, a red-granite mountain range. Many varieties of the small ground orchid have been identified in the park and the birdlife is prolific.

The road cuts across the less-developed farming country of the north and goes west to **Launceston**, the northern capital of Tasmania, sixty-four kilometres from the north coast at the junction of the North Esk, South Esk and Tamar Rivers. It is a smaller, more provincial city than Hobart, set in pleasant hilly countryside, and makes an excellent base from which to explore the rich coastal plain of the Tamar Valley and the mountain country to the north of the island's central plateau. Cataract Gorge, historic Franklin House and Entally House, and the hydro-electric station at Duck Reach, built in 1895, are all within easy reach of Launceston.

On to Devonport, where this description of the circle route began. Many of Tasmania's magnificent national parks are not far from the circle route highway, and a close scrutiny of the map will lead to many other interesting diversions.

For further information, contact the Tasmanian Travel Centre, 80 Elizabeth St, Hobart; (002) 30 0250.

See also: Individual entries in A–Z listing; Tasmania's National Parks.

Strahan, on Macquarie Harbour

so by swimming. The town today, in complete contrast, is a pleasant fishing resort. A charter tuna fishing-fleet operates from Pirate's Bay. **In the area:** Four unusual natural features in Tasman Arch State Reserve, off Arthur Hwy—Tasman's Arch, Devil's Kitchen, Blowhole and Tessellated Pavement—are within 4 km east of town. Coastal walking track leads from Devil's Kitchen to Waterfall Bay and on to Fortescue Bay. Port Arthur convict settlement, 21 km south-west. **Accommodation:** 1 hotel, 1 motel. **See also:** Tasmania's Convict Past; Tours from Hobart.
MAP REF. 475 P9, 477 P8

Evandale   Population 723

This little township, 19 km from Launceston, has been proclaimed a historic village. Founded in 1829, some of its buildings date from as early as 1809. Originally it was named Collins Hill, but was renamed in 1836 in honour of Tasmania's first Surveyor-General, G. W. Evans. It remains unspoiled by progress and retains many buildings of historical and architectural significance. **Of interest:** Self-guiding Heritage Walk from Tourism and History Centre, High St. Also in High St: Solomon House (1836) offers Devonshire teas; St Andrew's Anglican (1871) and Uniting (1839) churches; Blenheim (1840s), stained-glass sales and inspection of workshop. Strickland's Gallery, Russell St; bronze castings and foundry inspection. Sunday market in Falls Park, Russell St. Village Fair and National Penny Farthing Championships held in Feb. **In the area:** Clarendon (1838), 8 km south near Nile; designed in grand manner and set in extensive formal gardens. Old inn at Nile also of historic interest. **Tourist information:** High St; (003) 91 8128. **Accommodation:** Limited. **See also:** Stately Homes.
MAP REF. 479 M8, 480 G11

Exeter   Population 344

In the midst of a large fruit-growing area, 24 km north-west of Launceston, Exeter serves the district surrounding it. **In the area:** To north-east, former river resorts of Gravelly Beach and Paper Beach. Walking track (5 km return) leads from Paper Beach to Supply River. Near (400 m) mouth of Supply River, ruins of first water-driven flour-mill in Tasmania, built 1825. Notley Fern Gorge, at Notley Hills, 11 km south; 10 ha rainforest reserve with picnic/barbecue areas. Brady's Lookout, rocky outcrop used by notorious bushranger Matthew Brady, in State Reserve, 5 km south-east. Monument to John Batman's ship *Rebecca*, in which he crossed Bass Strait to Yarra

River; ship was built at once busy shipyards at Rosevears, 6 km south-east. On Rosevears Dr, historic Rosevears Hotel, first licensed 1831; also Waterbird Haven, wetlands habitat with tree-top hide. Tastings and sales at 10 wineries in West Tamar wine-growing area. **Tourist information:** Tamar Visitors Centre, Main Rd; (003) 94 4454. **Accommodation:** 1 hotel. MAP REF. 479 L6, 480 D7

Fingal   Population 443

Fingal is situated in the Esk Valley, 21 km inland from St Marys on the South Esk River, and is the headquarters of the state's coal industry. The first payable gold in Tasmania was found in 1852 at The Nook, near Fingal. **Of interest:** Historic buildings include: St Joseph's Roman Catholic Church, Grey St. Masonic Lodge, Brown St. In Talbot St: St Peter's Church; Holder Bros. General Store; and Fingal Hotel, with collection of over 280 different brands of Scotch whisky. **In the area:** Mathinna, 27 km north, extensive forestry development area with waterfalls nearby. White Gum Forest Reserve at Evercreech, further 3 km, with 89 m white gum; picnic/barbecue areas and rainforest walking tracks. **Tourist information:** Fingal Valley Neighbourhood House, Talbot St; (003) 74 2344. **Accommodation:** Limited. **See also:** Stately Homes.
MAP REF. 479 P9

Franklin   Population 453

This timber-milling town, 45 km south-west of Hobart, was the site of the first settlement in the Huon district in 1804. It was named after Governor Sir John Franklin, who took up 259 ha on the

Devil's Kitchen, near Eaglehawk Neck

banks of the Huon River. Timber-milling has been an important local industry since the very early years. Orcharding and dairy farming are the other main industries. **Accommodation:** Limited. MAP REF. 474 F10, 477 L8

Geeveston   Population 753

This important timber town is the gateway to Tasmania's south-west World Heritage Area. **Of interest:** Esperance Forest and Heritage Centre, Church St; tourist complex incorporating Gateway to South-West (Huon Hwy), Hartz Gallery (wilderness art and craft) and 5 forest walks. **In the area:** Arve and Weld valleys west of town contain world's tallest (87 m) hardwood trees. Hartz Mountains National Park, 23 km south-west, off Arve Rd. Tahune Forest Reserve, 27 km northwest on Arve Rd; camping and recreation area. Cruises on Huon River. 4WD tours of south-west wilderness. **Tourist information:** Church St; (002) 97 1836. **Accommodation:** Limited.
MAP REF. 474 E11, 477 K9

George Town   Population 5315

Situated at the mouth of the River Tamar, George Town was first settled in 1811, when it was named for King George III. Today it is a flourishing commercial centre, due mainly to the Comalco plant at Bell Bay and other industrial developments in the area. It is also the home port of the Bass Strait fast *Sea Cat* catamaran service. **Of interest:** Self-guiding walk. Monument on Esplanade commemorates unintentional landing in 1804, when Lieut.–Col. William Paterson and his crew in HMS *Buffalo* ran aground during storm. Devonshire teas and lunches at The Grove (c. 1838). **In the area:** Inspections of Comalco plant at Bell Bay, 6 km south. At Hillwood, 24 km south; strawberry farm for pick-your-own-fruit. Ghost town of former gold-mining settlement at Lefroy, 10 km east; ruins, old diggings and cemetery. Pipers Brook wine-growing region, 33 km east; tastings and sales at several wineries. Low Head, 5 km north; surf beach and safe river beach; also Maritime Museum in Australia's oldest continuously used pilot station, first opened in 1803. Day trips and weekend cruises to Bass Strait islands on SS *Furneaux Explorer*. **Tourist information:** Main Rd; (003) 82 1700. **Accommodation:** 2 hotels, 1 hotel/motel, 1 motel. **See also:** Stately Homes.
MAP REF. 479 K5, 480 B4

Gladstone   Population under 200

The small township of Gladstone is one of the few communities in the far north-east that still relies on tin-mining. The district

STATELY HOMES

One of Tasmania's big attractions is its wealth of beautiful stately homes with a distinctly English air. You can dine in style in some, such as Prospect House in the historic township of **Richmond**, and stay in others.

Several of Tasmania's grand old mansions, such as Malahide and Killymoon, both on the Esk Highway near **Fingal**, are privately owned and cannot be inspected, but many of the state's finest homesteads are open daily to the public.

Superb Clarendon House, near **Nile**, and a short drive from Launceston, is probably Australia's grandest Georgian mansion. Completed in 1838 and owned by the National Trust, it has been meticulously restored and suitably furnished.

Three other stately homesteads within easy reach of **Launceston** are Franklin House, just six kilometres south; Entally House at **Hadspen**; and Brickendon in **Longford**.

Franklin House is another elegant Georgian mansion owned by the National Trust.

Charming Entally House, the most historic of the Trust houses, was built in 1819. Set in superb grounds, Entally has a greenhouse, chapel and coach-house also open for inspection.

Two-storeyed, shuttered Brickendon, with its graceful metal front porch, looks French, but long stretches of hawthorn hedges and many old chestnuts, oaks, ash and junipers make it seem part of an English landscape.

The Grove in **George Town**, north of Launceston, is another privately owned historic house open to visitors. Built in the 1820s, it has been painstakingly restored by the present owners, who dress in period costume to serve lunch and teas.

Privately owned, but operated by the Trust, the White House, in **Westbury**, near **Deloraine**, was built c. 1841 as a corner shop and residence. It stands on a corner of the town's Village Green and displays a fine collection of Staffordshire china.

Hobart has two historic homes open for inspection: the National Trust property Runnymede, in the suburb of **New Town**, and Narryna in **Battery Point**.

Graceful Runnymede, built c. 1836, has been restored and furnished by the Trust.

Narryna, a Georgian sandstone and brick townhouse with a walled courtyard, is set in an old-world garden shaded by elm trees. Also known as the Van Diemen's Land Memorial Folk Museum, it houses a significant collection of colonial artefacts.

The misleadingly named Old Colony Inn in **New Norfolk** serves lunches (with fresh trout as a specialty) and Devonshire teas. This beautiful old building set in delightful grounds has become one of Tasmania's most photographed tourist attractions. Despite its name, it was never used as an inn.

For further information, contact National Trust of Australia (Tasmania), 413 Hobart Rd, Franklin Village 7249; (003) 44 6233.

See also: Individual entries in A–Z listing.

Prospect House, Richmond

was once a thriving tin- and gold-mining area, with a colourful early history. Now many of these once-substantial townships are near-ghost towns or ghost towns. **In the area:** Geological formations in Gladstone–South Mt Cameron area. Boobyalla, old mining town, 20 km north-west. Pioneer, 20 km south-west; operating tin mine and water sports on artificial lake. Moorina, 30 km south-west; section of old cemetery contains graves of Chinese miners. Former tin-mining town of Weldborough, 37 km south-west, once headquarters for 900 Chinese miners. Mt William National Park, 25 km east; prolific flora and fauna and excellent beaches. Historic lighthouse at Eddystone Point, 35 km east. **Accommodation:** 1 hotel.
MAP REF. 479 Q4

Hadspen
Population 1089
The township of Hadspen, which was first settled in the early 1820s, has many historic buildings. **Of interest:** Row of Georgian buildings, including Red Feather Inn (c. 1844), old coaching station. Hadspen Gaol (c. 1840). Church of the Good Shepherd; building commenced in 1858, funded by Thomas Reibey, who after a dispute with the bishop, withdrew his support. Church was finally completed in 1961, almost 50 years after Reibey's death. Rutherglen Holiday Village and Wildlife Park. **In the area:** Entally House (1819), one of Tasmania's most famous historic homes, 1 km west on banks of South Esk River; magnificent collection of Regency furniture and fine silverware. **Accommodation:** 1 hotel/motel, 1 caravan/camping park. **See also:** Stately Homes.
MAP REF. 479 L8, 480 E10

Hamilton
Population 2480
A classified historic town in a rural setting, Hamilton has retained many of its colonial buildings. **Of interest:** Glen Clyde House (c. 1840), Grace St; award-winning craft gallery and tearooms. **In the area:** Meadowbank Lake, 10 km north-west; popular venue for picnics, boating and water-skiing, and trout fishing. **Tourist information:** Council Offices, Tarleton St; (002) 86 3202. **Accommodation:** 1 hotel.
MAP REF. 474 D2, 477 K5

Hastings
Population under 200
This small centre, about 100 km from Hobart on the Huon Hwy, attracts many tourists to its famous limestone caves, local gemstones and nearby scenic railway. **In the area:** Hastings Caves, 13 km north-west; regular guided tours of illuminated Newdegate Cave and swimming in

Picking apples, Huonville

thermal pool. Lune River, 2 km south, haven for gem collectors. Beyond river, 2 km further south, Ida Bay Scenic Railway; originally built to carry limestone, it now carries passengers 7 km to Deep Hole and back; picnic facilities at both ends of track. **Accommodation:** Limited. **See also:** Tours from Hobart.
MAP REF. 477 K10

Hawley Beach
Population under 200
This popular seaside area near Port Sorrell is well-known for its good fishing, excellent beaches and safe swimming. **Of interest:** Meals and accommodation at historic Hawley House (1878). **Accommodation:** Limited.
MAP REF. 479 J5

Huonville
Population 1305
Huonville is an important commercial centre serving the surrounding townships, and is the largest apple-producing centre in the area. In the early days the valuable softwood now known as Huon pine was discovered in the district. **Of interest:** Daily river cruises, over rapids, to Port Huon. Model Train World, Main Rd. **In the area:** Apple Museum at Grove, 6 km north-east. Scenic drives to western townships of Glen Huon, Judbury and Ranelagh, and east to Cygnet. Antique Motor Museum near Ranelagh, 5 km north-west. Model Miniature Village at Glen Huon, 8 km west. **Tourist information:** Huon River Jet Boats, Esplanade; (002) 64 1838.

Accommodation: 1 hotel. **See also:** Tours from Hobart.
MAP REF. 474 F9, 478 L8

Kettering
Population 318
This township on the Channel Hwy serves a large fruit-growing district. The Bruny Island ferry leaves several times daily from the terminal at Kettering, with extra services provided during holidays. **In the area:** Bruny Island. Oyster Cove Inn and marina, 6 km north-west. Pleasant walks in Snug Falls Track area, near township of Snug, 8 km north. Good swimming and boating at Coningham Beach nearby. Hill Farm Herbs, 15 km south at Middleton. Monument to French explorer Admiral Bruni D'Entrecasteaux at Gordon, 21 km south. **Accommodation:** 1 hotel.
MAP REF. 474 H13, 477 M9

Kingston – Blackmans Bay
Population 10 932
Kingston Beach, 12 km south of Hobart, was discovered by Scottish botanist Robert Brown in 1804. **Of interest:** Kingston Cultural Centre, Windsor St. Display at federal government's Antarctic research headquarters, Channel Hwy. **In the area:** Scenic drives south through Blackmans Bay, Tinderbox and Howden; magnificent views of Droughty Point and Bruny Island from Piersons Point. Small blowhole at Blackmans Bay, at reserve on Talone Rd; spectacular in stormy weather. Walking tracks in Snug Falls area. **Accommodation:** Limited.
MAP REF. 474 I9, 477 M8

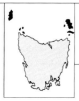

THE BASS STRAIT ISLANDS

King Island and Flinders Island, Tasmania's two main Bass Strait islands, are ideal holiday-spots for the adventurous. You can fish, swim, go bushwalking or skin-dive among the wrecks of the many ships that foundered off their shores last century. Each spring millions of muttonbirds make a spectacular sight as they fly in to nest in coastal rookeries.

King Island, at the western end of the strait, is a picturesque, rugged island with an unspoiled coastline of beautiful sandy beaches on the east and north coasts, contrasting with the forbidding cliffs of Seal Rocks and the lonely coast to the south. The lighthouse at Cape Wickham is the largest in Australia. Once famous for its seal population and now almost extinct sea-lions, the island's main industries today are scheelite mining and farming. King Island dairy and free-range beef and pork products have earned a reputation for their high quality. The unofficial capital is **Currie**, which has a kelp factory. Accom-

Cape Barren goose

modation includes a hotel, a motel, two guest-houses and several holiday flats. There is a penguin colony on the breakwater at Grassy Harbour.

Flinders Island is renowned for its excellent fishing, its magnificent granite mountains and its gemstones, including the Killiecrankie 'diamonds', actually a kind of topaz. Strzelecki National Park, near the civic centre,

Whitemark, provides challenging rock-climbing. The island is also popular with scuba-drivers, naturalists and photographers. Accommodation on the island includes two hotels, two guest-houses and several holiday flats. Flinders is one of more than fifty islands in the Furneaux Group that were once part of the land-bridge linking Tasmania with the mainland.

In the 1830s the few surviving Tasmanian Aborigines were settled near **Emita**, in an attempt to save them from extinction. All that remains of the settlement today is the graveyard and the chapel, Wybalenna, which has been restored by the National Trust.

Fishing is the main industry of the tiny community of **Lady Barron** to the south, a port village overlooking Franklin Sound and **Cape Barren Island**, the home of the protected Cape Barren goose.

For further information, contact: King Island Shoppe, Edward St, King Island, (004) 62 1666; and Council Offices, Davey St, Flinders Island, (003) 59 2131.

Latrobe   Population 2578

Situated on the Mersey River, 9 km southeast of Devonport, Latrobe was once a busy town with its own shipyards. Today it is the site of one of the biggest cycling carnivals in Australia, the Latrobe Wheel Race, held every Christmas. The Latrobe Bicycle Race Club was established in 1896. **Of interest:** Many early buildings and shop fronts dating from 1840s, including some with National Trust classifications. Self-guiding leaflet. Several renowned restaurants in Gilbert and Forth Sts. Court House Museum, Gilbert St; local history. Bell's Parade, picturesque reserve with picnic areas along riverbank. **In the area:** Historic homestead Frogmore, now host farm, 1 km south-west. **Tourist information:** Council Offices, Gilbert St; (004) 26 1041. **Accommodation:** 1 motel.
MAP REF. 478 I6

Launceston   Population 66 286

Although it is Tasmania's second largest city and a busy tourist centre, Launceston manages to retain a relaxed, friendly atmosphere. Nestling in hilly country

where the Tamar, North Esk and South Esk rivers meet, Launceston is also at the junction of four main highways and has direct air links with Melbourne and Hobart. It is sometimes known as the Garden City because of its beautiful parks and gardens. **Of interest:** St John and George Sts, Trustee Court and Prince's Square with its magnificent baroque fountain and fine surrounding buildings. Main shopping area around the Mall. Old Umbrella Shop, George St; unique 1860s shop preserved by National Trust. Penny Royal World, Paterson St, collection of buildings originally sited at Barton, near Cressy, and moved stone by stone to Launceston; complex includes accommodation, restaurants and tavern, museum, working watermill and corn-mill, and graceful windmill. It is linked by restored tramway to Penny Royal Gunpowder Mill at old Cataract quarry site; boat trips on artificial lake. Parks include: 5 ha City Park with small zoo and conservatory; Design Centre of Tasmania nearby displays contemporary art and craft; Royal Park, formal civic park fronting on to South Esk River; and Zig Zag Reserve, leading to Cataract Gorge area. Queen

Victoria Museum and Art Gallery, in Royal Park, with displays of Tasmania's mineral wealth, flora and fauna, Aboriginal and convict relics, early china and glassware, and colonial and modern art. *Lady Stelfox* departs from Ritchie's Mill Arts Centre, Bridge Rd, for cruises on lower reaches of Tamar. Guided tours of Boags Brewery, William St. Self-guiding walking tours; leaflets from tourist centre. Garden Festival held in Oct. **In the area:** One of Launceston's outstanding natural attractions, spectacular Cataract Gorge, 2 km west of city centre. Cataract Cliff Grounds Reserve, on north side of gorge; formal park with lawns, European trees, peacocks and licensed restaurant. Area linked to south side (swimming pool and kiosk) by scenic chair-lift and suspension bridge; delightful walks on both sides of gorge. Landscaping around Trevallyn Dam, 6 km west, makes attractive picnic spot. Nearby, Australia's only hang-gliding simulator. Waverley Woollen Mills, 5 km east; tours include inspection of historic collection of plant machinery, creating industry for which Launceston earned national reputation. Launceston Federal

Country Club Casino, 7 km south-west. Launceston Wildlife Sanctuary and Rhododendron Gardens, 8 km south-west; native and European fauna in natural surroundings. Three historic houses: Franklin House, 6 km south; Entally House, 13 km south-west at Hadspen; and Clarendon, near township of Nile, 28 km south-east: all National Trust properties. Grindelwald Holiday Resort, near Legana, 12 km north; Swiss-style village with chalets. St Matthew's Church, 15 km north at Windermere. Tamar Valley wineries, 50 km north/north-east, including St Matthias, Heemskerk, Rochecombe and Pipers Brook. Guided tours throughout northern Tasmania; details from tourist centre. **Tourist information:** Cnr St John and Paterson Sts; (003) 37 3111. **Accommodation:** 8 hotels, 9 hotel/motels, 12 motels, 1 caravan/camping park. **See also:** Fisherman's Paradise; Scenic Island State; Stately Homes.
MAP REF. 479 L7, 480 F9

Lilydale
Population 357

At the foot of Mt Arthur, 27 km from Launceston, the township of Lilydale has many nearby bush tracks and picnicspots. **In the area:** Lilydale Falls Reserve, 3 km north; two oak trees grown from acorns from Great Park at Windsor planted here on Coronation Day, 12 May 1937. Scenic walks to top of Mt Arthur (1187 m). Hollybank Forest Reserve, 5 km south at Underwood; picnic/barbecue areas. At Lalla, 4 km west: Lalla Market, at weekends; Lalla Gardens; Appleshed for local art and craft. Rhododendron nursery, on northern slopes of Brown Mountain. Bridestowe Lavender Farm, near Nabowla, 26 km north-east; sales of lavender products and tours in flowering season, Dec.–Jan. **Accommodation:** 1 hotel.
MAP REF. 479 M6, 480 G6

Longford
Population 2437

This quiet country town, 22 km south of Launceston, was first settled in 1813 when former settlers of Norfolk Island were given land grants in the area. Since then it has had three name changes, having previously been known as Norfolk Plains and Latour. Now classified as a historic town, it serves a rich agricultural district. The municipality of Longford carries the largest head of stock in the state. **Of interest:** Self-guiding leaflet on town and area. Many historic buildings, some convict-built. Christ Church (1839), Wellington St, noted for outstanding stained-glass window; also pioneer gravestones. Targa Tasmania held in Mar.; motor racing and classic and veteran car displays. Country Club Hotel, Wellington St,

with 'car in window'. **In the area:** Brickendon (1824), 2 km south; homestead built by William Archer and still owned by descendants. Longford Wildlife Park, 5 km north, conservation area for fallow deer and Australian fauna and flora; picnic/barbecue areas and man-made lake. Perth, 5 km north-east; historic buildings include: Eskleigh, Jolly Farmer Inn, Old Crown Inn and Leather Bottell Inn. At Cressy, 10 km south, Connorville sheep station, established by early settler, Roderic O'Connor, whose descendants still produce superfine wool there. **Tourist information:** Council Offices, Smith St; (003) 91 1303. **Accommodation:** 1 hotel, 1 caravan/camping park. **See also:** Stately Homes.
MAP REF. 479 L8, 480 E2

Mole Creek
Population 288

This town, 74 km south of Devonport, serves an important farming and forestry district. The unique Tasmanian leatherwood honey, made by bees from the blossom of the leatherwood tree, which grows only in the rainforests of the west coast of Tasmania, is produced here. Each summer, apiarists transport hives to the nearby leatherwood forests. **In the area:** Guided tours of fine limestone caves in state reserves: Marakoopa, 8 km west, and smaller, but still spectacular, King Solomon Cave, further 7 km west; glowworm display at Marakoopa. **Accommodation:** 1 hotel, 1 caravan/camping park.
MAP REF. 478 I8

New Norfolk
Population 6152

Mellow old buildings set among English trees and hop-fields dotted with oasthouses give this classified historic town a decidedly English look; the countryside has often been compared to that of Kent in England. On the Derwent River, 38 km north-west of Hobart, the town owes its name to the fact that displaced settlers from the abandoned Norfolk Island settlement were granted land in this area. Although the New Norfolk district produces a majority of the hops used by Australian breweries, the chief industry today is paper manufacture. **Of interest:** Self-guiding historic walk leaflet at Historical Centre in Council Offices. Old Colony Inn (c. 1835), Montague St; museum and tea-rooms. Oast House, Tynwald Park, Lyell Hwy; hops museum, art gallery and tea-rooms. St Matthew's Church of England (1823), reputedly oldest church still standing in Tasmania; craft centre in adjoining Close. Bush Inn (1815), Lyell Hwy; claims oldest licence in Commonwealth, although contested by Launceston Hotel. Jet boat rides on Derwent River rapids leave from Bush Inn. Hop Festival held in Mar. **In the area:** Tours of Australian Newsprint Mills at Boyer, 5 km east. Famous Salmon Ponds at Plenty, 11 km north-west; hatchery where first brown and rainbow trout in southern hemisphere were bred in 1864; also restaurant and museum. Mt Field National Park, with impressive Russell Falls, 40 km north-west.

Penny Royal Gunpowder Mill and Cataract Gorge, Launceston

Tourist information: Council Offices, Circle St; (002) 61 2777. **Accommodation:** 3 hotels, 1 motel, 1 caravan/camping park. **See also:** Rural Landscapes; Scenic Island State; Stately Homes; Tours from Hobart. MAP REF. 474 F5, 477 L6

Oatlands   Population 514
This classified historic town on the shores of Lake Dulverton, 84 km north of Hobart, attracts both lovers of history and anglers. It was named by Governor Macquarie in 1821 and surveyed in 1832. Many of the town's unique sandstone buildings were constructed in the 1830s and it is said that almost everyone lives in a historic house. **Of interest:** Convict-built court-house (1829), Campbell St. Holyrood House (1840), High St; restaurant and historic gardens. St Peter's Church of England (c. 1838), William St. Callington Flour Mill (1836), Mill Lane. Lake Dulverton Wildlife Sanctuary. **In the area:** Trout fishing on Lake Sorell, 29 km north-west, and adjoining Lake Crescent. **Tourist information:** Council Offices, 71 High St; (002) 54 1101.

Old flour mill, Oatlands

Accommodation: 1 hotel. **See also:** Rural Landscapes. MAP REF. 477 M3, 479 M13

Orford   Population 458
Views from this popular holiday resort at the estuary of the Prosser River, on the Tasman Hwy, are dominated by Maria Island National Park, which is 20 km offshore. **Of interest:** Bush walks, river and sea fishing, scuba-diving and golf. **In the area:** Beautiful 14th-century stained-glass window in Church of St John the Baptist at Buckland, 18 km south-west. Daily ferry service from Triabunna, 7 km north-east, to Maria Island. **Accommodation:** 2 hotel/motels, 1 motel, 1 caravan/ camping park. MAP REF. 475 O2, 477 P5

Penguin   Population 2801
The Dial Range rises over this quiet town, named after fairy penguins still found in rookeries nearby. **Of interest:** National Trust classified St Stephen's Church and

Uniting Church, Main St. Hiscutt Park with working Dutch windmill; tulips in season. Tours of penguin rookeries, Dec.–early Mar. Town Fiesta held in Nov. **In the area:** Magnificent view from summit of Mt Montgomery, 5 km south. Also south: Ferndean Wildlife Reserve (6 km); picnic spot with walking tracks. Pioneer Park at Riana (10 km). Pindari Deer Farm (15 km); deer handling demonstrations. Beltana Ostrich Farm, South Riana (20 km); guided tours and viewing of chicks, Oct.–Apr. Scenic drive south-east to Ulverstone via coast road. **Tourist information:** King Edward St, Ulverstone; (004) 25 5564. **Accommodation:** 1 hotel, 1 caravan park. MAP REF. 478 G5

Poatina   Population 213
This modern plateau town, south-west of Launceston, was built to house the construction team working on the hydro-electric power-station. **In the area:** Poatina underground power-station, 5 km west; guided tours. **Accommodation:** None. **See also:** Dams for Power. MAP REF. 479 L10

Pontville   Population 962
Much of the freestone used in Tasmania's old buildings was quarried near this classified historic township. Pontville was founded in 1830 and many of its early buildings remain. On the Midland Hwy, 27 km north of Hobart, it is the seat of local government for the Brighton Municipality. **Of interest:** Historic buildings on or adjacent to Midland Hwy include: St Mark's Church of England (1841); 'The Sheiling' behind church (built in 1819 and restored in 1953); old post office; Crown Inn; and 'The Row', thought to have been built in 1824 as soldiers' quarters and now restored. **In the area:** Townships nearby with interesting historic buildings: Bagdad, 8 km north; Kempton, 15 km north, beyond Badgad; Tea Tree, 5 km east; and Broadmarsh, 10 km west. **Tourist information:** Council Offices, Tivoli Rd, Gagebrook; (002) 63 0333. **Accommodation:** Limited. MAP REF: 474 I4, 477 M6

Port Sorell   Population 1173
Sheltered by hills, this well-established holiday resort at the estuary of the Rubicon River near Devonport has a mild climate. Named after Governor Sorell and established in 1822, it is the oldest township on the north-west coast. Unfortunately, many of its old buildings were destroyed by bushfires early this century, after it had been almost deserted for the thriving new port of Devonport. **Of interest:** Swimming, fishing, boating and

bushwalking. Views from Watch House Hill, once site of old gaol and now bowling-green. Asbestos Range National Park across estuary. **Accommodation:** 2 caravan/camping parks. **See also:** Tasmania's National Parks.
MAP REF. 479 J5

Queenstown   Population 3593

The discovery of gold and mineral resources in the Mt Lyell field last century led to the almost overnight emergence of the township of Queenstown. It is a town literally carved out of the mountains that tower starkly around it. Mining has been continuous in Queenstown since 1888, and the field has so far produced more than 670 000 tonnes of copper, 510 000 kg of silver and 20 000 kg of gold. The Mt Lyell Company, which employs most of the town's inhabitants, is engaged in a scheme to establish large-scale underground mining. The town has modern shops and facilities, but its wide streets, remaining historic buildings and unique setting give it an old mining-town flavour. In certain lights, multi-coloured boulders on the bare hillsides surrounding the town reflect the sun's rays and turn to amazing shades of pink and gold. Of interest: Guided tours of Mt Lyell Mine from Farmers Store, Driffield St, include viewing of mine workings and Mining Museum. Gallery Museum, cnr Sticht and Driffield Sts, depicts history of west coast in photographs and memorabilia. **In the area:** Spectacular views from Lyell Hwy as it climbs steeply out of town. Original (1833) Iron Blow gold-mine, off Lyell Hwy, at Gormanston, 6 km south-east. Ghost town of Linda, 9 km south-east. Mt Jukes Rd lookout, 7 km south-west; road leads to old mining settlement of Lynchford and Crotty Dam. Rafting on Franklin River. Mt Mullens and Franklin River scenic nature walk along old mining railway-line between Queenstown and Zeehan. **Tourist information:** RACT, 18 Orr St; (004) 71 1974. **Accommodation:** 3 hotels, 2 hotel/motels, 3 motels, 1 caravan/camping park. **See also:** Scenic Island State; Tasmania's West Coast.
MAP REF. 476 E1, 478 E11

Railton   Population 857

This substantial country town south of Devonport owes its existence to the Goliath Portland Cement Company, representing one of Tasmania's major industries. Raw materials are taken from a huge quarry on the site and carried by an overhead conveyor to the crusher. **In the area:** Scenic drive through area known as Sunnyside to Stoodley Forest Reserve, 14 km south; picnic/barbecue areas and walking tracks. **Accommodation:** Limited.
MAP REF. 478 I7

Darlington settlement, Maria Island

Richmond   Population 693

Charming Richmond, 26 km from Hobart, is one of the oldest and most important historic towns in Australia. The much-photographed Richmond Bridge is the oldest bridge in Australia (1823–25) and many of the town's buildings were constructed in the 1830s or even earlier. Some of these structures, including the bridge, were built by convicts under appallingly harsh conditions. Legend has it that the ghost of an overseer who was murdered by convicts still haunts the bridge. **Of interest:** Self-guiding leaflet of town and area. Old Richmond Gaol (1825), Bathurst St, one of Australia's best preserved convict prisons; guided tours. St John's (1837), St John's Circle; oldest Catholic church in Australia. St Luke's Anglican Church (1834–36), Torrens St; fine timber ceiling. General store and former post office (1832), Bridge St; oldest postal building in Australia. Georgian mansion Prospect House (1830s) off Hobart Rd, haunted by ghost of Mrs Buscombe; meals and accommodation. In Bridge St: galleries featuring local art and crafts include Saddler's Court (c. 1848), Peppercorn Gallery (c. 1850) and the Granary (c. 1829); restored Bridge Inn, one of town's oldest buildings, houses complex of shops. Village Store (1836), one of oldest general stores still operating in Tasmania. **In the area:** Scenic drive north through Campania (7 km) and Colebrook (19 km). **Tourist information:** Saddler's Court Gallery, 48 Bridge St; (002) 62 2132. **Accommodation:** 1 caravan/camping park. **See also:** Scenic Island State; Stately Homes; Tours from Hobart.
MAP REF. 475 J5, 477 N6

Ringarooma   Population 262

Farming and timber-milling support this north-eastern town, which dates back to the 1860s. **In the area:** Views of Ringarooma and surrounding towns from Mathinna Hill. Pleasant drives on New River Rd and Alberton Rd. Old Tin Mining Rd to Branxholm, 16 km north-east, gives glimpses of area as it was in days of early pioneers. **Accommodation:** Limited.
MAP REF. 479 O6

Rokeby   Population 3495

This old township on the eastern shore of the Derwent River was first settled in 1809. The first apples to be exported from Tasmania were grown here, as was the first wheat ever produced in Tasmania. Rokeby's rural character is now rapidly changing with the expansion of the Clarence Municipality. **Of interest:** Historic buildings include: Rokeby Court, Rokeby House and St Matthew's Church (1843). Some chairs in church's chancel were carved from wood from ship in Nelson's fleet; organ, brought from England in 1825 and first installed in what is now St David's Cathedral, Hobart, is still in use. **In the area:** To south, excellent surfing at Clifton Beach; boating and swimming at South Arm. **Tourist information:** Council Offices, 38 Bligh St, Rosny Park; (002) 44 0600. **Accommodation:** Limited.
MAP REF. 475 K7, 477 N7

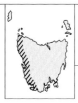

TASMANIA'S WEST COAST

The beautiful but inhospitable west coast, with its wild mountain ranges, lakes, rivers, eerie valleys and dense rainforests, is one of Tasmania's most fascinating regions. The majestic, untamed beauty of this coast is in complete contrast to the state's pretty pastures. The whole area has vast mineral wealth and a colourful mining history, reflected in its towns. The discovery of tin and copper in 1879 and 1883 started a rush to the west coast, booming at the turn of the century. Today **Queenstown**, the largest town, still depends almost entirely on the Mt Lyell copper mine, and the other main towns — Zeehan, Rosebery and Strahan — also owe their existence to mining.

It was not until 1932 that a rough road was pushed through the mountainous country between Queenstown and Hobart. Fortunately, modern road-making techniques have improved the situation and today west coast towns are linked by the Murchison, Zeehan and Waratah Highways, and the Lyell Highway (the original road to Hobart) has been brought up to modern standards. In fact, the flooding of Lake Bunbury has resulted in the re-routing of the highway, which now takes motorists around the lake itself, enhancing the spectacular entry to Queenstown. Driving round the west coast road circuit and seeing the superb mountain scenery and colourful towns of the area is an unforgettable experience. The only drawback is the area's exceptionally heavy rainfall, even in summer and autumn.

The little township of **Zeehan**, south-west of Rosebery, typifies the changing fortunes of mining towns. Following the rich silver-lead ore discoveries in 1882 its population swelled to 10 000 and the town boasted twenty-six hotels and the largest theatre in Australia, the Gaiety, where Dame Nellie Melba sang. Many of these fine buildings from the boom period can still be seen, including the Gaiety Theatre and the Grand Hotel. Zeehan's West Coast Pioneers Memorial Museum, housed in the former School of Mines, is a very popular tourist attraction.

One of the most spectacular views on any highway in Australia can be seen as you drive into Queenstown. As the narrow road winds down the steep slopes of Mt Owen, you can see the amazingly bare hills — tinged with pale pinks, purples, golds and greys — that surround the town. At the turn of the century, the trees from these hills were cut down to provide fuel for the copper smelters, and heavy rains eroded their topsoil, revealing the strangely hued rocks beneath.

The first European settlement of the west coast was established in 1821, when the most unruly convicts from Hobart were dispatched to establish a penitentiary on **Sarah Island** in Macquarie Harbour, and to work the valuable Huon pine forests around the Gordon and King Rivers. Sarah Island soon became a notorious prison and most of the unfortunate convicts who managed to escape died in the magnificent, but unyielding, surrounding bush. The horrors of that time are echoed in the name of the entrance to the harbour — Hell's Gates. Today the port of **Strahan** on Macquarie Harbour has thousands of visitors each year, all attracted to the spectacular Gordon River, one of Tasmania's largest and most remote wild rivers. Cruise boats make regular trips to Heritage Landing at the mouth of the river. On the return trip they stop along the way to allow visitors to see the old convict ruins on Sarah Island. Scenic flights depart from Strahan, to enable visitors to take in the beauty of more inaccessible areas. Another interesting trip from Strahan is to Ocean Beach, six kilometres from the town. This long, lonely stretch of beach, lashed by spectacular breakers, somehow typifies the magnificent wild west coast.

See also: Individual entries in A–Z listing.

The bare hills of Queenstown

Forest scene near Queenstown

Rosebery   Population 2102

Gold was discovered at Rosebery in 1893 in what is now called Rosebery Creek. Huge deposits of lead and zinc were also discovered in the area. Gold-mining has long since been abandoned and the town now owes its existence to the zinc mining company Pasminco-EZ. **In the area:** Williamsford, 7 km south, where ore is carried from mine to refinery by spectacular system of aerial buckets. Montezuma Falls, highest waterfall in state, 5 km west; accessible by 4WD or walking track. **Accommodation:** 1 hotel, 1 caravan/camping park. **See also:** Tasmania's West Coast.
MAP REF. 478 F.9

Ross   Population 283

One of the oldest and most beautiful bridges in Australia spans the Macquarie River at this historic township. The bridge was designed by colonial architect John Lee Archer and built by convicts in 1836. The convict stonemason Daniel Herbert who worked on the bridge received a free pardon in recognition for his fine carvings. Ross was established in 1812 as a military post for the protection of travellers who once stopped there to change coaches. Today it is still an important stopover on the Midland Hwy between Launceston and Hobart. The district is famous for its superfine wool. **Of interest:** Self-guiding leaflet on town and area. Tasmanian Wool Centre, Church St; highlights area's links with wool industry. Avenue of English trees in Church St complements historic buildings: Scotch Thistle Inn and Coach House, former coaching stop, now licensed restaurant; and old Ross General Store and Tea Room, with range of Tasmanian crafts and Devonshire teas. In Bridge St: old barracks building, restored by local National Trust. Street leads to Ross Bridge (floodlit at night). Ross Rodeo held in Nov. **In the area:** Some of the state's best trout-fishing lakes—Sorell, Crescent, Tooms and Leake—are within hour's drive of town. **Accommodation:** 1 hotel, 1 caravan/ camping park.
MAP REF. 477 N1, 479 N11

St Helens   Population 1149

This popular resort on the shores of Georges Bay is renowned for its crayfish and flounder. The largest town on Tasmania's east coast, it has three freezing works in or near the settlement to handle the catch of the crayfishing and scallop fleet based in its harbour. **Of interest:** Bayside beaches, ideal for swimming; coastal beaches for surfing. Charter boats for deep-sea fishing. Excellent fishing for bream on Scamander River. Many local restaurants specialise in fish dishes. St Helens History Room, Cecilia St; guided tours of town and district. **In the area:** Bushwalks to view varied birdlife and abundant wildflowers. Scamander, 19 km south; swimming and fishing. Binalong Bay, 11 km north-east; surf and rock fishing. Healey's Cheese Factory, at Pyengana, 28 km north-east; sales of cheeses. Several coastal reserves in district (known as Bay of Fires), with camping areas, offer good beach fishing. **Tourist information:** St Helens Secretariat, 20 Cecilia St; (003) 76 1329. **Accommodation:** 1 hotel, 1 hotel/motel, 1 motel, 2 caravan/ camping parks.
MAP REF. 479 R7

St Marys   Population 668

The position of this small township, at the junction of the Tasman Hwy and the Esk Main Rd, makes it a busy thoroughfare. At the headwaters of the South Esk River system, St Marys is about 10 km inland from the attractive east coast. **In the area:** Small coastal township of Falmouth, 14 km north-east; early settlement of historical interest with several convict-built structures and fine beaches, attractive rocky headlands and good fishing. Spectacular mountain and coast views to south through Elephant Pass. **Accommodation:** 1 hotel.
MAP REF. 479 Q8

Savage River   Population 1058

This township in the rugged west coast region serves the workers on the major Savage River iron-ore project, which has been financed by a consortium of American, Japanese and Australian interests. Ore deposits are formed into a slurry and pumped through an 85 km pipeline north to Port Latta on the coast, where they are pelletised and shipped to Japan. **Of interest:** Inspections of mine complex. **In the area:** Former gold-rush township of Corinna, 28 km south-west; good fishing, spectacular scenery and regular launch excursions on Arcadia II to Pieman Head. Old graves with Huon pine headstones are reminders of past. Luina, 21 km north-east; once important mining township with second largest tin mine in Australia. **Accommodation:** 1 hotel.
MAP REF. 478 D8

Ross Bridge

Scamander
Population 386

This well-developed resort town, midway between St Marys and St Helens, offers excellent sea and river fishing, and has good swimming beaches. **Of interest:** Scenic walks and drives via forestry roads through plantations. Scamander River, noted for bream fishing; trout in upper reaches. **In the area:** Beaches and lagoons at Beaumaris, 5 km north. **Accommodation:** 1 hotel/motel, 1 caravan/camping park.
MAP REF. 479 R8

Scottsdale
Population 1983

Scottsdale is the major town in Tasmania's north-east and serves some of the richest agricultural and forestry country on the island. A large food-processing factory specialises in the deep-freezing and dehydrating of vegetables grown in the district. **In the area:** Beach resort of Bridport, 23 km north. Bridestowe Lavender Farm near Nabowla, 13 km west; sales of lavender products and tours in flowering season, Dec.–Jan. Sideling Lookout, 16 km west. **Tourist information:** Rose's Travel, 11 Alfred St; (003) 52 2186. **Accommodation:** 2 hotels, 1 motel, 1 caravan/camping park.
MAP REF. 479 N5

Sheffield
Population 934

This town, 30 km south of Devonport, stands at the foothills of the Great Western Tiers, in one of the most scenically attractive areas in the state. Known as the Gateway to the Wilderness, Mt Roland is its outstanding natural feature. The town's economy is based on farming. **Of interest:** Community project: 23 murals on various buildings depict area's history. Kentish Museum, Main St; local history and hydro-electric exhibits. Daffodil Festival held in Sept. **In the area:** Lakes and dams of Mersey-Forth Power Development Scheme, 10 km west. Lake Barrington, created by scheme; major recreation area and international rowing venue. Devil's Gate Dam, 13 km west; spectacular scenery from viewing areas. Cradle Mountain National Park, 61 km southwest. **Tourist information:** Kentish Museum, 93 Main St; (004) 91 1861. **Accommodation:** 1 motel, 1 caravan/camping park.
MAP REF. 478 I7

Smithton
Population 3414

This substantial township is the administrative centre of Circular Head in the far north-west. It serves the most productive dairying and vegetable-growing area in the state, and also is the centre of one of Tasmania's most important forestry

FISHERMAN'S PARADISE

Fish are biting all year round in Tasmania, which is a fisherman's paradise by any standards. Tasmania is famous for three species of fish: trout in the fresh water, bream in the estuaries, and tuna off the coast.

One area alone contains hundreds of lakes and lagoons stocked with trout of world-class size. This is the inaccessible 'Land of Three Thousand Lakes'. You are more likely, however, to choose from the huge range of developed areas brimming with trout in the central highlands region, such as Great Lake, Bronte Lagoon, Lake Sorell and Arthurs Lake. Brumby Creek, just twenty-five kilometres from Launceston between Cressy and Poatina, is rapidly gaining a reputation as one of the great trout waters of Australia.

As the trout season closes in May, game fish begin to move down the mild east coast and fishermen start hauling in the big ones: bluefin tuna often weighing in at over forty-five kilograms. Then, as the bluefin leave in the midwinter months, schools of barracouta arrive in their thousands, and large Australian salmon schools return to the estuaries and along the shoreline.

In spring, one of the great sport-fish of Tasmania, the tasty silver bream, arrives in the river estuaries. Many anglers regard this as one of the best fighting fish for its size.

Of course, in late spring and early summer the whole island is an angler's dream. January and February are peak inland trout-fishing months, and from February to March schools of Australian salmon swim close to the shoreline of Tasmania's many river estuaries, providing exciting fishing for the angler using a silver flash lure from the beach or rocks.

For further information on licence requirements, fees, bag limits, seasons and regulations, contact the Inland Fisheries Commission, 127 Davey St, Hobart 7000; (002) 23 6622.

Trout fishing near Launceston

TASMANIA'S CONVICT PAST

Despite their grim history, the ruins of the infamous Port Arthur settlement are the greatest single tourist attraction in Tasmania. The fact that they were a place of isolated incarceration for more than 12 000 prisoners has been blurred by time but it is still possible, particularly in bleak weather, for the ruins to create something of the atmosphere of hopelessness and misery which existed there about 150 years ago.

Port Arthur is on the Tasman Peninsula, which extends from the Forestier Peninsula south-east of Hobart, screening Pitt Water and the Derwent estuary from the Tasman Sea. The whole area of both peninsulas is very beautiful, with sweeping pasture, timbered areas and a coastline of sheltered bays and towering cliffs. Many secondary roads and tracks and a host of secluded beauty spots make it an ideal place for bushwalking. Accommodation is varied and includes a motor-inn, caravan park and youth hostel.

Eaglehawk Neck is on the isthmus between the two peninsulas. In the

Port Arthur settlement

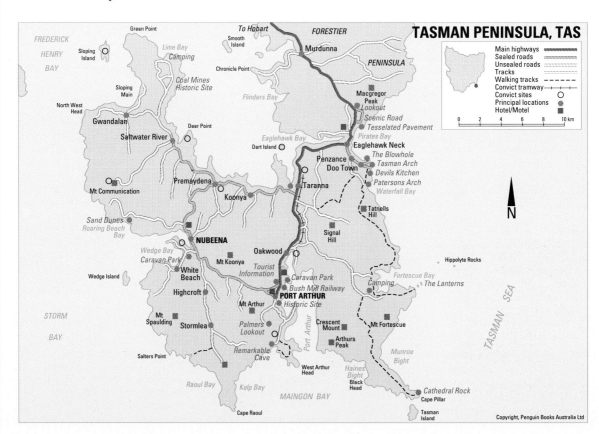

days of the penal colony, hounds were tethered in a tight line across the Neck to prevent escapes. The line was continually patrolled and guard posts were established in the nearby hills. No prisoner ever broke through this fearful barrier, although some did swim to freedom.

A major conservation project designed to conserve and maintain Port Arthur was completed in 1986. Among the buildings still standing are the church, penitentiary, guard tower, hospital and model prison. Buildings that have been restored include Exile Cottage, home of exiled Irish rebel William Smith O'Brien, the Commandant's House and the Junior Medical Officer's House. The partially restored lunatic asylum acts as a museum and visitor centre. Guided tours of the Government Gardens are conducted in spring.

The settlement was established by Governor Arthur in 1830 and although transportation ceased in 1853, it was not abandoned until 1877. Many buildings were demolished by contractors and others were badly damaged by a bushfire that swept through the peninsula in 1897. Today, nocturnal historical 'ghost tours' through the settlement are an unforgettable experience. The site is open daily; an entrance fee allows visitors access to over sixty buildings, ruins and sites. Free guided tours are conducted and Frank 'The Poet' recounts his experiences as a Port Arthur convict on audio tours.

In the middle of Port Arthur Bay stands the **Island of the Dead**, with its 1769 unnamed convict graves; 180 additional named graves mark the resting-places of free settlers, prison staff and the military. The ferry *Bundeena* makes regular trips to this unique island cemetery.

For further information, contact Port Arthur Historic Site, 'Clougha', Port Arthur 7182; (002) 50 2363.

Convict buildings

areas, with several large sawmills. Fishing is another important industry. **Of interest:** Fishing and boating on Duck River and at Duck Bay. Kauri Timber Company; tours by arrangement. Lookout tower on Tier Hill, at end of Massey St. **In the area:** Forestry Commission reserves throughout district for wide range of recreational activities. Allendale Gardens at Edith Creek, 13 km south; rainforest walks and Devonshire teas. Graveyard at ghost town of Balfour, 40 km south-west. Lacrum Dairy Farm at Mella, 6 km west; milking demonstrations, afternoon teas, cheese tastings and sales. Nearby Wombat Tarn has picnic/barbecue area, lookout, bushwalks, children's playground. Historic Van Diemen's Land Co. cattle and sheep property, Woolnorth, 40 km north-west, at tip of Cape Grim; tours from Smithton or Burnie. Possum Trot, at Redpa, 40 km south-west; woodcraft, native gardens and rainforest bushwalks. Excellent surfing at Marrawah, 50 km south-west. Seasonal scenic cruises on Arthur River, 70 km south. **Tourist information:** Council Offices, Goldie St; (004) 52 1265. **Accommodation:** 1 hotel, 1 motel. MAP REF. 478 C3

Somerset

Population part of Burnie

At the junction of the Bass and Waratah Hwys, Somerset has become a satellite town for Burnie, 6 km east. **In the area:** Scenic drive from town, south through Elliott to small rural settlement of Yolla, which serves surrounding rich pastoral country. **Tourist information:** 48 Cattley St, Burnie; (004) 34 6111. **Accommodation:** 1 hotel, 1 hotel/motel, 1 motel, 1 caravan/camping park. **See also:** Scenic Island State. MAP REF. 478 F5

Sorell

Population 2882

Named after Governor Sorell, this town is 27 km north-east of Hobart. Founded in 1821, it played an important part in early colonial history by providing most of the grain for the state from 1816 to 1860. It also provided grain for NSW for more than 20 years. The area is still an important agricultural district, specialising in fat lambs. **Of interest:** Historic Blue Bell Inn, Somerville St. In the area: Many Hobartians have holiday homes in extensive and popular beach area around Dodges Ferry and Carlton, 18 km south. **Tourist information:** Council Offices, 12 Somerville St; (002) 65 2201. **Accommodation:** Limited. MAP REF. 475 I5, 477 N6

Stanley

Population 588

This quaint little village, nestling under a huge rocky outcrop called 'the Nut', is steeped in history. It was the site for the headquarters of the Van Diemen's Land Company, set up in 1825 to cultivate land and breed high-quality sheep. Then its wharf handled whalers and sailing-ships. Today these are replaced by modern crayfish and shark-fishing fleets, but little else has changed. The birthplace of Australia's only Tasmanian prime minister, the Hon. J. A. Lyons, Stanley has been declared a historic town and in 1991 won the award as Tasmania's 'Premier Tourist Town'. **Of interest:** Chair-lift to top of the Nut (152 m). Historic buildings in wharf area: bluestone bond store, Wharf Rd; and former VDL Co. store, in Marine Park, designed by colonial architect John Lee Archer, who lived in township. Archer's own home, now Poet's Cottage, Alexander Tce, at base of the Nut; private residence, not open to public. Also in Alexander Tce, birthplace of J. A. Lyons, Lyons Cottage; open for inspection. Other historic buildings in Church St include: still licensed Union Hotel (1849), with its nest of cellars and narrow stairways; Commercial Hotel (1842), now private residence; and restored Plough Inn (1843); museum, Tasmanian handcrafts and tourist information. Next door, Discovery Centre Folk Museum and art gallery. Headstones in Burial Ground on Browns Rd, dating from 1828, include those on graves of John Lee Archer and explorer Henry Hellyer. Small colonies of fairy penguins near wharf and cemetery, and on Scenic Drive. **In the area:** Highfield (1835), headquarters of VDL Co., on Scenic Drive, 2 km north; family chapel and remains of servants' quarters nearby; two arched gates are all that remain of former deer park. Popular picnic area at Dip Falls, off highway, 40 km south-east, at Mawbanna. Pelletising plant of Savage River Mines at Port Latta, 20 km east, where ore is moved by conveyor to jetty for loading on to carriers. Self-guiding leaflet *Things to See and Do* in Circular Head area. Circular Head Arts Festival held in Sept. **Tourist information:** 35 Church St; (004) 58 1226. **Accommodation:** 1 motel, 1 caravan/camping park. **See also:** Scenic Island State. MAP REF. 478 D3

Strahan

Population 516

This pretty little port on Macquarie Harbour is the only town on Tasmania's forbidding west coast. Originally a Huon pine timber-milling town, its growth was boosted by the copper boom at the Mt Lyell mine. When the Strahan–Zeehan railway opened in 1892, it became a busy port. Today it handles freight to and from

DAMS FOR POWER

Tasmania has the largest hydro-electric power system in Australia, producing nearly ten per cent of the nation's electrical energy.

It is Tasmania's mighty highland rivers that produce the immense volume of water necessary for these extensive hydro-electric systems. The Derwent, Mersey, Forth and Gordon Rivers have already been harnessed for power production.

Stage one of the Gordon River power development involved four major dams, the creation of Lakes Gordon and Pedder, and an underground power-station. These lakes are liberally stocked with trout and have already become tourist attractions.

Continuing development to harness and use this massive water power has included the construction of four major dams – Murchison, Mackintosh, Bastyan and Lower Pieman – and the creation of four new lakes. A spectacular rockfill has created Lake Pieman on the Lower Pieman River and will supply water for the third and biggest power-station in the complex.

Driving between Hobart and Queenstown, you can see much of the Derwent power scheme, the most extensive of the hydro-electric developments, consisting of ten power-stations. The Derwent River rises in Lake St Clair, 738 metres above sea-level, and all but the last forty-four metres of its fall is utilised.

There are public viewing galleries at Tungatinah, Tarraleah, Liapootah and Trevallyn power-stations, and overnight accommodation is available at HEC chalets at Bronte Park, Tarraleah and Poatina.

The power developments on the Mersey and Forth Rivers, although producing only half the power of the Derwent scheme, are far more spectacular as the whole system lies within a very steep river valley. The scheme encompasses seven power-stations and rises at Lake Mackenzie, 1121 metres above sea-level. Day trips may be arranged at any north-west-coast tourist centre.

For further information on HEC public viewing areas, roads open to the public, guided tours and accommodation, contact the Hydro-electric Commission, 4–16 Elizabeth St, Hobart 7000; (002) 30 5533.

Water harnessed for power production

Queenstown and is used by crayfish, abalone and shark fishermen, but the use of the harbour is limited because of the formidable bar at Hell's Gates, the mouth of the harbour. **Of interest:** Excellent views of township and harbour from Water Tower Hill. On the Esplanade: self-guiding leaflets and historical collection at Visitors Centre; NPWS Wold Heritage display at Customs House; and colonial accommodation at stately Franklin Manor, built late last century. Mineral and gemstone museum, Inne St. Morrison's Mill, one of few remaining Huon pine sawmills. **In the area:** Botanical Creek Peoples Park and Hogarth Falls on outskirts of town; camping and picnic/barbecue areas. Surfing and trail rides at Ocean Beach, 6 km west; also mutton bird rookery. Picnic/barbecue areas and coastline views at Sand Dunes, 12 km north on Strahan–Zeehan Hwy. Cruises up Gordon River to Heritage Landing and infamous Sarah (or Settlement) Island, Tasmania's first and most brutal penal establishment. Cruises also across Macquarie Harbour to Hell's Gates. Strahan Wilderness 4WD tours following Old Abt Railway between Strahan and Queenstown. **Tourist information:** Visitors Centre, The Esplanade; (004) 71 7488. **Accommodation:** 2 hotels, 1 motel, 1 caravan/camping park. **See also:** Scenic Island State; Tasmania's West Coast. MAP REF. 476 D2, 478 D12

Swansea   Population 206

Swansea is a small town of historical interest nested on Great Oyster Bay, in the centre of Tasmania's east coast. It is the administrative centre of Glamorgan, the oldest rural municipality in Australia. The original council chambers (c. 1860) are still in use. **Of interest:** Self-guiding leaflet on town and area. In Franklin St: Bark Mill and East Coast Pioneer Museum (c. 1885); restored working displays and tearooms. Morris' General Store (1838), run by Morris family for over 100 years. Community Centre (c. 1860); museum with largest billiard-table in Australia. Schouten House (c. 1841), Bridge St; once Swansea Inn, now restaurant. **In the area:** Views from Duncombes Lookout, 3 km south. Spikey Beach, 7 km south; picnic area with excellent rock fishing. Mayfield Beach, 14 km south; safe swimming and popular fishing area. Walking track from camping area to Three Arch Bridge. **Tourist information:** Council Offices, Noyes St; (002) 57 8115. **Accommodation:** 1 hotel/motel, 1 motel, 1 caravan/camping park. MAP REF. 477 Q2, 479 Q12

Triabunna   Population 883

When Maria Island was a penal settlement, Triabunna, 86 km north-east of Hobart, was

The Nut, Stanley

a garrison town and whaling base. Today it is a fishing port, with an important export wood-chipping mill just south of the town. **Of interest:** On The Esplanade: Bicentennial Park with picnic/barbecue areas; National Trust-run Pioneer Park with machinery exhibits. Working Horse Museum, Vicary St. Daily ferry service to historic settlement of Darlington on Maria Island National Park. Charter fishing boats for hire. Local beaches for swimming, water-skiing and fishing. Tourist information: Council Offices, cnr Vicary and Henry Sts; (002) 57 3113. **Accommodation:** 1 hotel, 1 hotel/motel. **See also:** Tasmania's National Parks. MAP REF. 475 P1, 477 P4

Ulverstone   Population 10 055
Situated 19 km west of Devonport, near the mouth of the Leven River, Ulverstone is a well-equipped tourist centre. **Of interest:** On Beach Rd: Riverside Anzac Park, with children's adventure playground and picnic/barbecue areas; Fairway Park, with wild-fowl reserve and giant water-slide. Westella (1886), Westella Dr; art and crafts and tearooms. Weeda Copper, Eastland Dr; local handmade copperware. **In the area:** Extensive beaches east and west of town provide safe swimming areas for children. Good beach, river and estuary fishing. Tours of hop fields. Scenic views at Preston Falls, 19 km south. Guided tours

of Gunns Plains Caves, 24 km south-west. Walking tracks to viewing platform at Leven Canyon, 41 km south-west. **Tourist information:** King Edward St; (004) 25 5564. **Accommodation:** 2 hotels, 3 motels, 3 caravan/camping parks. **See also:** Scenic Island State. MAP REF. 478 H5

Waratah   Population 334
This lonely little settlement, set in mountain heathland 100 km north of Queenstown, was the site of the first mining boom in Tasmania. In 1900 it had a population of 2000 and Mount Bischoff was the richest tin mine in the world. The deposits were discovered in 1871 by James 'Philosopher' Smith, a colourful local character, and the mine closed in 1935, with dividends totalling 200 pounds for every one pound of original investment. Today the town is experiencing a revival of mining activity at nearby Que River. **Of interest:** Self-drive tour of town. In Smith St: Waratah Museum and Gift Shop; adjacent, Philosopher Smith's Hut, replica of miner's hut with audio historical commentary. Atheneum Hall (c. 1887), with portrait of Smith. St James' Anglican Church (1880), first church in Tasmania to be lit by hydro power. **In the area:** River and lake fishing. Mining townships of Luina, Savage River and fascinating former goldmining town of Corinna. Cruises on Pieman River. **Tourist information:**

Council Offices, Smith St; (004) 39 1231. **Accommodation:** 1 hotel, 1 caravan/camping park. **See also:** Tasmania's West Coast. MAP REF. 478 E7

Westbury   Population 1222
A village green gives this town, 16 km east of Deloraine, a decidedly English air. Situated on the Bass Hwy, Westbury was first surveyed in 1823 and laid out on a bold scale in 1828, and has several fine old colonial buildings. **Of interest:** Self-guiding leaflet on town and area. White House (c. 1841), Village Green, King St; displays of vintage cars, bicycles, wagons and dolls and toys in stable complex. On Bass Hwy: Gemstone and Mineral Display; Pearn's Steam World, display of old tractors, farm machinery and motor vehicles. Maypole Festival, with Morris dancing on Village Green, held in Nov. **In the area:** At Hagley, 5 km east: St Mary's Anglican Church, noted for fine east window, donated by Lady Dry, wife of Sir Richard Dry, Tasmania's first native-born premier. At Carrick, 10 km east: fine examples of Georgian and Victorian buildings. Liffey Falls, 25 km south; picnic/barbecue area and walking tracks. Trout fishing at Brushy Lagoon, 15 km north. **Tourist information:** Old Bakehouse, 52 William St; (003) 93 1140. **Accommodation:** 1 hotel. **See also:** Stately Homes. MAP REF. 479 K8, 480 B11

Lavender farms, north-east Tasmania

Wynyard   Population 4705

Situated within a short driving distance of many varied attractions, this small centre at the mouth of the Inglis River, west of Burnie, has become a well-developed tourist centre, offering a range of accommodation and sporting facilities. There are daily flights between the town's airport and Melbourne. The Wynyard municipality is a prosperous dairying and mixed-farming district and the town has a large, modern dairy factory. **Of interest:** Excellent trout, fly and sea fishing. Tulip Festival held in Oct. **In the area:** Oldest marsupial fossil in Australia found at Fossil Bluff, 7 km north. Panoramic views from Table Cape Lookout nearby. Boat Harbour, 11 km north-west; one of best beaches on coast. Good swimming and fishing at Sisters Beach, further 5 km north-west, within Rocky Cape National Park, 30 km north-west. **Tourist information:** Council Offices, Sanders St;

(004) 42 2221. **Accommodation:** 1 hotel, 1 motel, 1 caravan/camping park. **See also:** Scenic Island State; Tasmania's National Parks.
MAP REF. 478 F4

Zeehan   Population 1610

Named after one of Abel Tasman's ships, this former mining town has had a chequered history and is now a National Trust classified historic town. Situated 36 km north-west of Queenstown, silver-lead deposits were discovered here in 1882. By 1901, Zeehan had 26 hotels and a population of 10 000, making it Tasmania's third largest town. Just seven years later mining began to decline and Zeehan became a virtual ghost town. In the boom period between 1893 and 1908, 8 million dollars' worth of ore had been recovered. Now the town is again on an upward swing with the reopening of the Renison Bell tin mine. **Of interest:** Many 'boom'

buildings in Main St: Gaiety Theatre, Grand Hotel, ANZ Bank, St Luke's Church, post office and court house (now art gallery). West Coast Pioneers Memorial Museum; mineral, historical, geological and biological collections. Beside museum, unique display of steam locomotives and rail carriages used on west coast. **In the area:** Old mine workings at Dundas, 13 km east. Trial Harbour, 20 km west; popular fishing area. Unsealed roads to both areas often in poor condition; check before departure. Fishing and boating on Lake Pieman, 50 km north-west. Trout fishing on Henty River, 25 km south. **Tourist information:** West Coast Pioneers Memorial Museum, Main St; (004) 71 6225. **Accommodation:** 1 hotel, 1 hotel/motel, 1 motel, 1 caravan/camping park. **See also:** Scenic Island State; Tasmania's West Coast.
MAP REF. 478 D10

Maps of Tasmania

Location Map

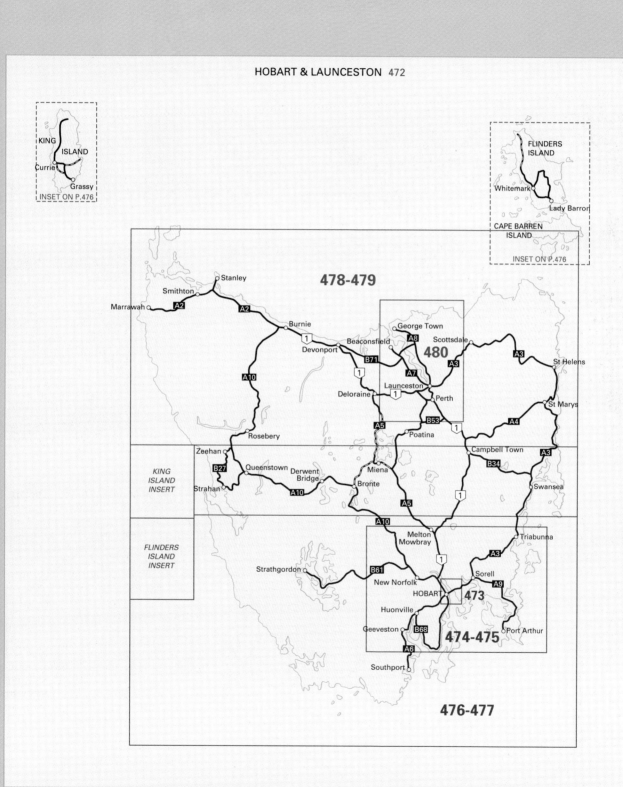

KING ISLAND
Currie
Grassy
INSET ON P.476

FLINDERS ISLAND
Whitemark
Lady Barron
CAPE BARREN ISLAND
INSET ON P.476

478-479

Stanley
Smithton
Marrawah
A2
A2
Burnie
1
Devonport
Beaconsfield
George Town
A8
Scottsdale
480
A3
St Helens
B71
A7
A10
1
Deloraine
Launceston
1
Perth
St Marys
A5
B53
Poatina
1
A4
Roseberv
Zeehan
Campbell Town
A3
KING ISLAND INSERT
B27
Queenstown
Derwent Bridge
Miena
B34
Strahan
A10
Bronte
Swansea
A5
FLINDERS ISLAND INSERT
A10
1
Melton Mowbray
Triabunna
A3
Strathgordon
B61
Sorell
A9
New Norfolk
473
HOBART
Huonville
Geeveston
B68
474-475
Port Arthur
A6
Southport

476-477

472 Hobart & Launceston

Hobart

North Hobart
West Hobart
City
Glebe
Queens Domain
Battery Point
Sullivans Cove

Holy Trinity Church
St. Andrews Pk
Elizabeth College
St. Marys Cathedral
St. Marys College
St. Virgils College
RACT Headquarters
Car Park
Criterion
State Library
Tas Travel Centre
Centrepoint Arcade
Ansett Car Park
St. Davids Cathedral
Hadleys Hotel
Franklin Square
Police Headquarters
Royal Hobart Hospital
City Hall
Market Pl
Sheraton Hotel Intl
Post Office
Town Hall
Museum and Art Gallery
Constitution Dock
Macquarie Wharf
Victoria Dock
Railway Goods Yard
Railway Depot
Naval Depot
Macquarie Point
Cenotaph
Olympic Swimming Pool
ABC
Aust Airlines
Parliament House
Parlt. Square
St. Davids Park
National Trust Information Office
Kellys Steps
Lenna Motor Inn
Princes Park
Runnymede
Salamanca
Castray Esplanade
Princes Wharf
Brooke St Pier
Bellerive
Ferry
CSIRO
Anglesea Barracks
Repat Hospital
Folk Museum (Narryna)
To Wren Point Hotel & Casino
Hobart Rivulet

Scale: 0 100 200 300 m
One-way Streets shown →

Streets: Arthur St, Burnett St, Murray St, Mary St, Tasma St, Elizabeth St, Church St, Argyle St, Campbell St, Brooker, Scott St, Glebe St, Short St, Aberdeen St, Edward St, Davies Av, Tasman Hwy, Paternoster St, Union St, Browne St, Devonshire St, Warwick St, Windsor Ct, Watkins Av, Harrington St, Brisbane St, Patrick St, Barrack St, Melville St, Faraday St, Cavell St, Bathurst St, Goulburn St, Molle St, Liverpool St, Collins St, Macquarie St, Davey St, Watchorn St, Victoria St, Salamanca, Sandy Bay, Gladstone, Montpelier, Morrison, Despard, Franklin, Market Pl, Dunn Pl, Sackville St, Sun St, Hunter St, Evans St, Elizabeth St Pier, Castray, Esplanade, Runnymede, South St, Kelly St, Arthur Circus, Hampton, Findlay St, James St, Stowell Av, Heathfield Av, Wilmot St, Hampden, Forest, Prospect Pl, Roberts St, Amelia St, Cann St, Hugos La, Frederick St, Ben St

Launceston

Inveresk
Launceston City
Trevallyn
West Launceston
East Launceston
Elphin

Ogilvie Park
Kings Wharf
River Tamar
West Tamar Hwy
North Esk
River
Victoria Bridge
Charles Street Bridge
Dry Dock
Town Point
Royal Park
Esk Brewery
City Park
Albert Hall
Car Park
Launceston Intl Hotel
Town Hall
Police HQ
Public Library
Civic Square
Post Office
Tas Travel Centre
Car Park Ansett
Yorktown Sq
Brisbane St Mall
Mall Quadrant
Aust. Airlines
RACT
Art Gallery & Museum
Cenotaph
Penny Royal World
Penny Royal Mills
Ritchies Mill
Lady Stelfox Cruises
Kings Park
Paterson Bridge
Kings Bridge
Cataract Gorge
Zig Zag Reserve
Walking Track
Trevallyn Res
Windmill Hill Reserve
Olympic Pool
N.T.C.A. Ground
Racecourse
St. Georges Square
StVincents Hospital
Princess Square
ABC
Sports Ground
To Launceston Gen. Hosp.

Scale: 0 100 200 300 m
One-way Streets shown →

Streets: Kings Wharf, Goderich St, Lindsay St, Taroona St, Cleaver, William St, St John St, George St, Tamar St, Esplanade, Willis St, Lawrence St, Innes St, Elphin Rd, Bifrons Ct, Lyttleton St, Abbott St, Clarence, Weymouth St, Fawkner St, Bathurst St, Charles St, Canal St, Cimitiere St, Cameron St, Wellington St, Brisbane St, Frederick St, Canning St, York St, Elizabeth St, Middle St, Margaret St, Paterson, Barrow St, Kingsway, Vincent St, Earl St, Adelaide St, Welman St, My Street, Stewart St, Arthur St, Spencer St, Scott St, Ann St, Hopkins St, Sanden, Hornsey St, High St, Phillip St, Shields St

See fold-out page for an explanation of the map symbols

COPYRIGHT, BP AUSTRALIA LTD

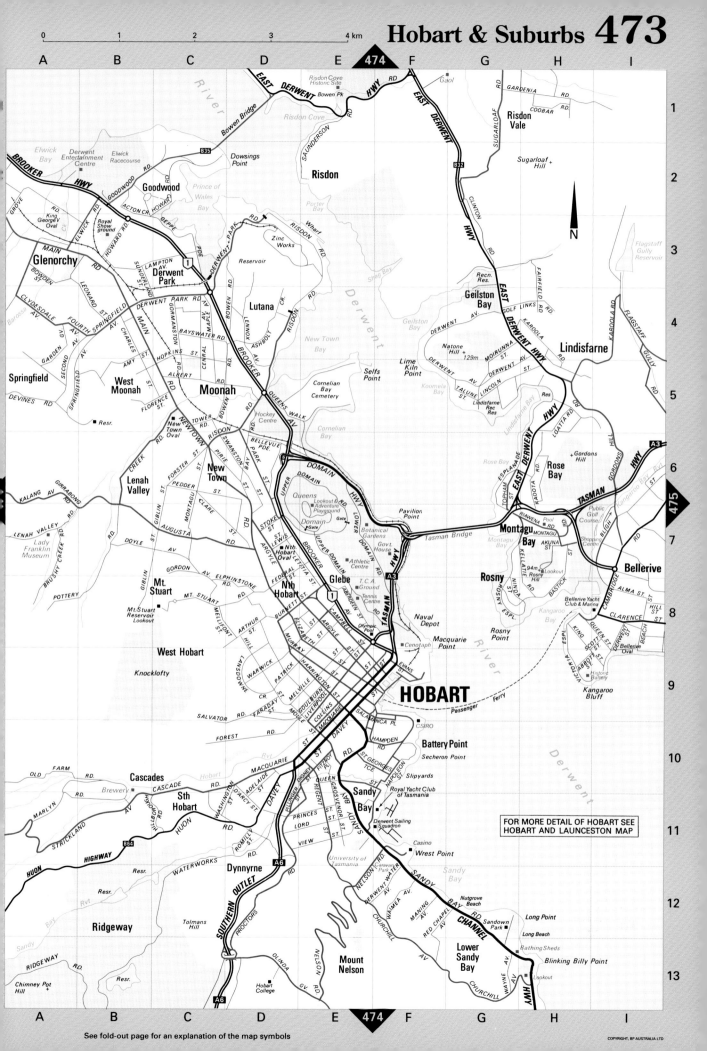

FOR MORE DETAIL OF HOBART SEE
HOBART AND LAUNCESTON MAP

See fold-out page for an explanation of the map symbols

A B C D E F G H I

477

1

2

3

4

5

476

6

7

8

9

10

11

12

13

Ouse
Cluny Power Stn.
A10
Lawrenny
Chiltern Hill
+ Mt. Clark
Black Tier + 775m
Melton Mowbray
Mt. Mercer 548m +
Repulse Power Stn.
Langloh
Hollow Tree
MIDLAND
Kempton
Yarlingt
Repulse
River Broad
Meadowbank Lake
8 Hamilton
3
8
5
Pelham
Espies Crag 667m
Weedons Fords
Hill
Huntingdon Tier 545m
5
Quoin Mt. 900m +
Dysart
13
LYELL
35
Mt. Spode 521m
Taylors Tier 640m +
8
HWY 1
34
Butlers Hill 670m +
Jones River
Mt. Bethune 508m +
A10
13
Meadowbank Power Station
13
Mt. Fenton
Elderslie
Bagdad
MT. FIELD NATIONAL PARK
Ellendale
Fentonbury
Russell River
8
HWY 4
Mangalore Tier
Mangalore
Mt. Field West
L. Webster
Mt. Field East + 1269m
Trout Farm
Derwent
5 Gretna
Broadmarsh
8
Crafts
2
Winton Hill
L. Seal
L. Nicholls
Westerway
B61
Karanja
Glenora
Rosegarland
Platform Peak
Cobbs Hill
11
Pontville
Lady Barron C.
National Park
33
11
3
Bushy Park
Macquarie Plains
Mt. Dromedary 989m +
Dromedary Upr.
8
5
Brighton
L. Belcher
L. Dobson
16
Russell Falls
6
A10 12
A10
Dromedary
6
Bridgewater
Wildlife Park
L. Belton
Mt. Mawson
Tyenna
B62
8 Plenty
Black Hills
Hayes
Paper Mill 11
A10 11
Granton
Cove Bay 239.
ANM Private Road
Fitzgerald
5
Park River
13
Salmon Ponds
Boyer
Magra
10
Claremont
Old Beach
GORDON RIVER RD
Barren Mt.
Maydena
Tyenna R.
Styx
Uxbridge
Moogara
13
HWY
4
5 32
New Norfolk
Sorell
3
Malbina
Molesworth
Mt. Faulkner 901m
Berriedale
Mt. Dire 448m
Risdon Histo
Humboldt
Feilton
Jet Cruise
Glenlusk
Bowen Bridge
21
Mt. Styx
Glen Fern
Lachlan
Glenorchy
Moonah
Mount Lloyd Leather Craft
Collins Cap
Collinsvale
Collins Cap + 1091m
New Town
Snowy Range
Lonnavale
Blue Hill 756m
Mountain River
Collins Bonnet + 1260m
Mt. Wellington + 1270m The Pinnacle
12
HOBART
10
Little Denison
Mt. Weld + 1338m
Mt. Misery 695m +
Crabtree
Mt. Montagu 1061m
Ferntree
B64
Ridgeway
37
A6
Weld River
Judbury
Lucaston
Car Museum
A6
3
Grove
Apple Museum
10
Longley Lower
11
Longley
Neika
Leslie Vale
HWY
10
10
Kingston
35
Ranelagh
15
Herring Back 747m
Sandfly
10
Boronia Hill
B68
Glen Huon
Apple Carver
8
Huonville
Kaoota
Nierinna
Margate
Howder
25
Irving Pan Ck.
HUON VALLEY
8
HUON
Boat Hire
6
Pelverata
Grey Mt. 827m
13
North West Bay
Snug
Tahune Forest Reserve
Huon
Woodstock
Cradoc
5
Franklin
B68
5
17
Kaoota
Coningham Snug Pt.
Huon River
Franklin Sth
Egg Id.
Oyster Cove
Castle Forbes Bay
A6
23
Glaziers Bay
7
Cygnet
20
Kettering
Roberts Hill 206m
Mt. Picton 1327m +
L. Picton
Port Huon
Cruise
Wattle Grove
Wattle Grove Upr.
Nicholls Tahune Rivt. Wildlife Pk.
Woodbridge
Geeveston
5
Cairns Bay
Petcheys Bay
15
Gardners Bay
Birchs Bay
Green I.
Arve River
Waratah Lookout
Waterloo
Lymington
13
CHANNEL
HARTZ MOUNTAINS NATIONAL PARK
Surges Bay
Tongatabu
Police Pt.
Garden Island Creek
Middleton
48
Simpson Pt.
Hartz Mt. + 1255m
Glendevie
SOUTH WEST NATIONAL PARK
Cracroft
Kermandi
Webb C.
Picton R.
Huon Pt.
Surveyors Bay
A6
Nine Pin Pt.
Garden Id.
Gordon Monument
14
D'Entrecasteaux
Simpsons Ba
Isthn

A B C D E F G H I

477

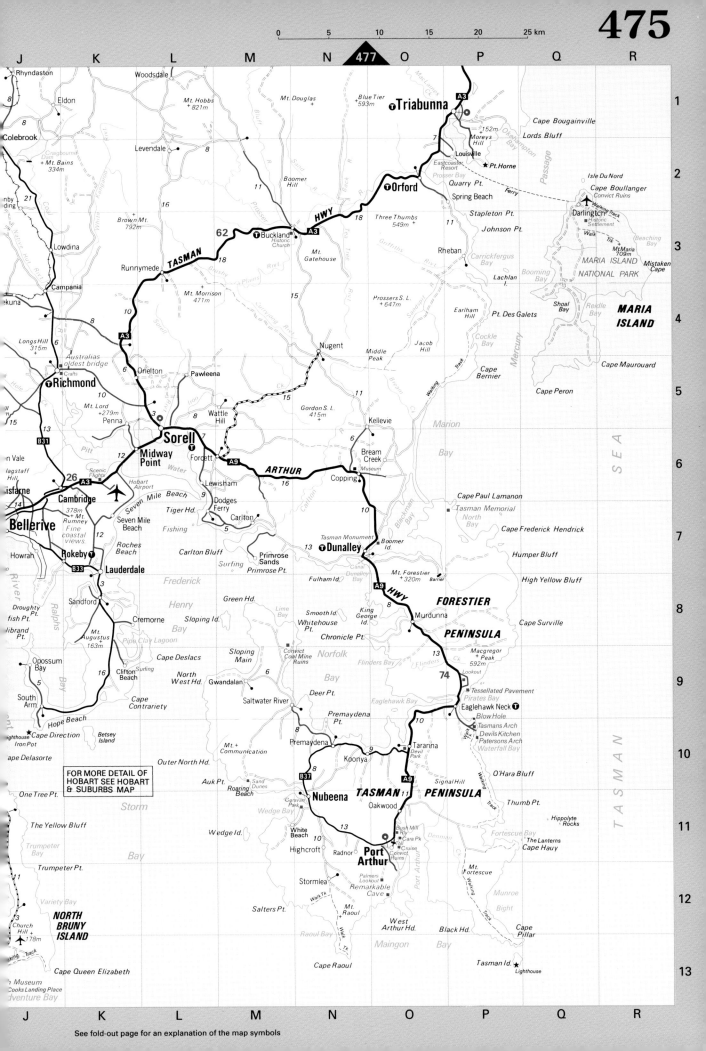

J   K   L   M   N   O   P   Q   R

Rhyndaston
Woodsdale
Eldon
Colebrook
Cape Bougainville
Lords Bluff
Mt. Hobbs
+821m
Mt. Douglas
+
Blue Tier
+593m
Triabunna
A3
Levendale
+152m
Moreys Hill
Okehampton Bay
Isle Du Nord
Cape Boullanger
Convict Ruins
Craigbourne
Dam
+ Mt. Bains
334m
21
Boomer
Hill
Eastcoaster
Resort
Louisville
Pt. Horne
Darlington
Historic
Settlement
Lowdina
11
Orford
Quarry Pt.
Spring Beach
Stapleton Pt.
Walk   Trk
Beaching
Bay
HWY
18
Three Thumbs
549m
Johnson Pt.
62
Buckland
Historic Church
A3
Runnymede
TASMAN
18
Mt.
Gatehouse
Rheban
Carrickfergus
Bay
MARIA ISLAND
Mt. Maria
709m
Mistaken
Cape
Campania
Mt. Morrison
471m
15
Prossers S. L.
+647m
Earlham
Hill
Lachlan
I.
Booming
Bay
NATIONAL PARK
MARIA
ISLAND
10
Nugent
Middle
Peak
Jacob
Hill
Cockle
Bay
Cape Bernier
Reidle
Bay
Shoal
Bay
Cape Maurouard
Longs Hill
315m
Australias
oldest bridge
6
Orielton
Pawleena
11
Cape Peron
SEA
Richmond
Crafts
10
3
Wattle
Hill
15
Gordon S. L.
415m
+
Kellevie
Marion
Bay
Mt. Lord
+279m
Penna
8
Sorell
6
Bream
Creek
Museum
Pitt
12
Midway
Point
Forcett
A9
ARTHUR
16
Copping
Cape Paul Lamanon
Tasman Memorial
North
Bay
Cape Frederick Hendrick
26
A3
Hobart
Airport
9
Lewisham
Dodges
Ferry
10
Humper Bluff
Cambridge
378m
+ Mt.
Rumney
Seven Mile Beach
Tiger Hd.
Carlton
5
Tasman Monument
Dunalley
13
Boomer
Id.
High Yellow Bluff
Bellerive
Fine
coastal
views.
Seven Mile
Beach
Fishing
Canal
Dunalley
Bay
Mt. Forestier
+320m
Barrier
Rokeby
12
Roches
Beach
Carlton Bluff
Surfing
Fulham Id.
A9
HWY
FORESTIER
Lauderdale
3
Frederick
Primrose
Sands
Primrose Pt.
8
Murdunna
Cape Surville
B33
Henry
Green Hd.
Lime
Bay
Smooth Id.
Whitehouse
King
George
Id.
PENINSULA
Sandford
Droughty
Pt.
fish Pt.
Cremorne
Sloping Id.
Bay
Chronicle Pt.
Macgregor
+ Peak
592m
Lookout
alibrand
Pt.
Mt.
Augustus
163m
Pipe Clay Lagoon
Cape Deslacs
Sloping
Main
Convict
Coal Mine
Ruins
Norfolk
Flinders Bay
Flinders
13
74
Tessellated Pavement
Pirates Bay
Opossum
Bay
16
Clifton
Beach
Surfing
North
West Hd.
Gwandalan
Bay
Deer Pt.
Eaglehawk Bay
Eaglehawk Neck
Blow Hole
South
Arm
5
Saltwater River
Premaydena
Pt.
10
Tasmans Arch
Devils Kitchen
Patersons Arch
Waterfall Bay
Hope Beach
Lighthouse
Cape Direction
Iron Pot
Betsey
Island
Outer North Hd.
Mt. +
Communication
Premaydena
9
Koonya
Taranna
Devil
Park
O'Hara Bluff
ape Delasorte
FOR MORE DETAIL OF
HOBART SEE HOBART
& SUBURBS MAP
Auk Pt.
Sand
Dunes
Roaring
Beach
B37
8
Signal Hill
One Tree Pt.
Storm
Caravan
Park
Wedge Bay
Nubeena
Oakwood
TASMAN
11
PENINSULA
Thumb Pt.
Hippolyte
Rocks
The Yellow Bluff
Wedge Id.
White Beach
10
13
Bush Mill
Rly
Cara Pk.
Toll
Cruise
Convict
Ruins
Denman
Fortescue Bay
The Lanterns
Cape Hauy
Trumpeter
Bay
Highcroft
Radnor
Port Arthur
Trumpeter Pt.
Stormlea
Palmers
Lookout
Remarkable
Cave
Mt.
Fortescue
Munroe
Bight
Cape Pillar
11
Variety Bay
Salters Pt.
Mt.
Raoul
West
Arthur Hd.
Black Hd.
NORTH BRUNY
ISLAND
Church
Hill +
178m
Walk
Tk
Walk
Maingon
Bay
Cape Queen Elizabeth
Cape Raoul
Tasman Id.
Lighthouse
Museum
Cooks Landing Place
dventure Bay

KING ISLAND

Cape Farewell — Cape Wickham
New Year Islands
Phoques Bay
Whistler Pt
Egg Lagoon
Yambacoona
Lavinia Pt
57 — Reekara
Loorana — Dairy Factory
Currie
Pegarah 26
Parenina
Sea Elephant
Naracoopa
Fraser Bluff
Sea Elephant Bay
29
Yarra Creek
Lymwood — Mine — Bold Head
Pearshape
Grassy
Surprise Bay
Stokes Pt

King Island
Flinders Island
Launceston
HOBART

0 — 10 kilometres

FLINDERS ISLAND

Inner Sister Id.
Bligh Pt.
Stanley Point
Palana
Killiecrankie
Cape Frankland
Leeka
29
FURNEAUX
Lughrata
Babel Id.
Marshall Bay
Emita Museum
Blue Rocks
Memana
Prime Seal Id.
Arthur Bay 19
Whitemark
Sellars Lagoon
Cameron Inlet
GROUP
East Kangaroo Id.
15 Ranga
Loccota
24
Lady Barron
Trousers Pt.
Mt. Chappell Id.
STRZELECKI NATL. PARK
Franklin Sound
Great Dog Id.
Vansittart Id.
Puncheon Pt.
Goose Id.
Anderson Id.
Badger Id.
Long Id.
Cape Barren Island
Cape Barren Island
Cape Barren
Kent Bay
Clarke Id.
Look Out Heads
Banks Strait

0 — 10 kilometres

478
A10
ZEEHAN HWY
L. Langdon
Mt. Sedgewick
Power Stn
Mt. Margaret
Badm?
Eldon Peak 1439m
Eldon Bluff 1357m
High Dome 1356m
CRADLE MT. LAKE ST.CLAIR
NAT. PK.
Mt Gould 1491m
Scenic walking tracks
+1147m
Lookout
Henty
Mt.Lyell Mine
Mt.Lyell
+1147m
1250m+
Mt Olympus 1447m
Queenstown
Gormanston
Linda
Lake Burbury (under const.)
Pyramid Mt.
Part of World Heritage Area
Mt Hugel 1307m
737m
Strahan
36
LYELL
Mt Owen
Lynchford
Mt Huxley
King River
Last Hill
LYELL HWY
Mt Rufus 1402m
6
Derwent Bridge
20 — 26
A10
Bro Pa
B24
Regatta Point
B27
Ocean Beach
Cape Sorell
Heils Gates
Walking Track
Mt. Jukes 1168m
Bubs Hill
Governor
81
71
Mt Gell 1439m
Mt Arrowsmith +981m
Mt King William I +1324m
Bron
Macquarie Harbour
King River Gorge
Gordon River
Mt Strahan 1031m
Mt Darwin 1144m
Mt Sorell
King River Power Development (under const.)
Mt Fincham
Part of World Heritage Area
Franklin
Frenchmans Cap 1443m
Mt King William II 1372m
Clark Dam
Butlers Gorge P.S.
Mt Hobhouse 1219m
16
21
Tar
Sloop Pt
Gorge Pt.
Cruise
Pillinger
Sarah Id. (Settlement Id.) Convict Ruins
Birthday Bay
Andrew
Forest Walk
Mt Lyne
Jane
FRANKLIN LOWER GORDON
WILD RIVERS
NATIONAL PARK
Erebus
Algonkian
Mt King William III 1158m
KING WILLIAM RANGE
Wylds Craig 1337m
Reeds Pk 1280m
Wayati
Liapoon
11
Derwent
Point Hibbs
Hibbs Bay
Maxwell
Mt Humboldt
PRINCE OF WALES RANGE
Clear Hill
Tim Shea
Spero Bay
Mt Discovery
Mt Lee 734m
Innes Peak
Sir John Falls
Gordon
Denison
Wings L.O.
Adamsfield
Old Mine
Lookout
Endeavour Bay
Sprent
Smith
Lake Gordon
Wanderer
793m
Mt Lewis
Olga
Gordon Power Station
13
Strathgordon
GORDON RIVER
McPartlan Pass
84
10
Mt M
Frodshams Pass
Lookout Forest Wal
High Rocky Point
Halls
Serpentine Dam
Mt Sorent 1058m
Lookout
40 Lookout
Mt Wedge 1146m
Mt Bowes
FRANKLAND RANGE
PEAK
35
Mt An 1425m
Nye Bay
Galin
Huboldt
Double Peak 1060m
Lake Pedder
Mt Solitary
Mt Eliza 1289m
Lake Judd
Low Rocky Pt
Elliott Bay
Lewis
SCOTTS RD.
Lookout
Scotts Peak Dam
Edgar Dam
SOUTHWEST
Mucahy Bay
Davey
Crossing
Walking Track
Mt Hayes
ARTHUR
Arthurs Plains
Track
Mt Hean 747m
RANGE
NATIONAL
Wreck Bay
Payne Bay
Spring
North
Bushy
Mt Ripple
Mt Norold
Mt Anne
Federation Pe 1224m
PARK
Pt.St.Vincent
Part of World Heritage Area
Port Davey
Bathurst Harbour
Mt Rugby 771m
Watts
SOUTHERN
Stephens Bay
Island Bay
800m
Mine
Mt Counsel
Ray
OCEAN
Window Pane Bay
Mt Melaleuca 595m
Cox Bight
Louisa
N
South West Cape
Ile Du C
Flat Witch I.
De Witt I.
MAATSUYKER GROUP
Maatsuyker I.

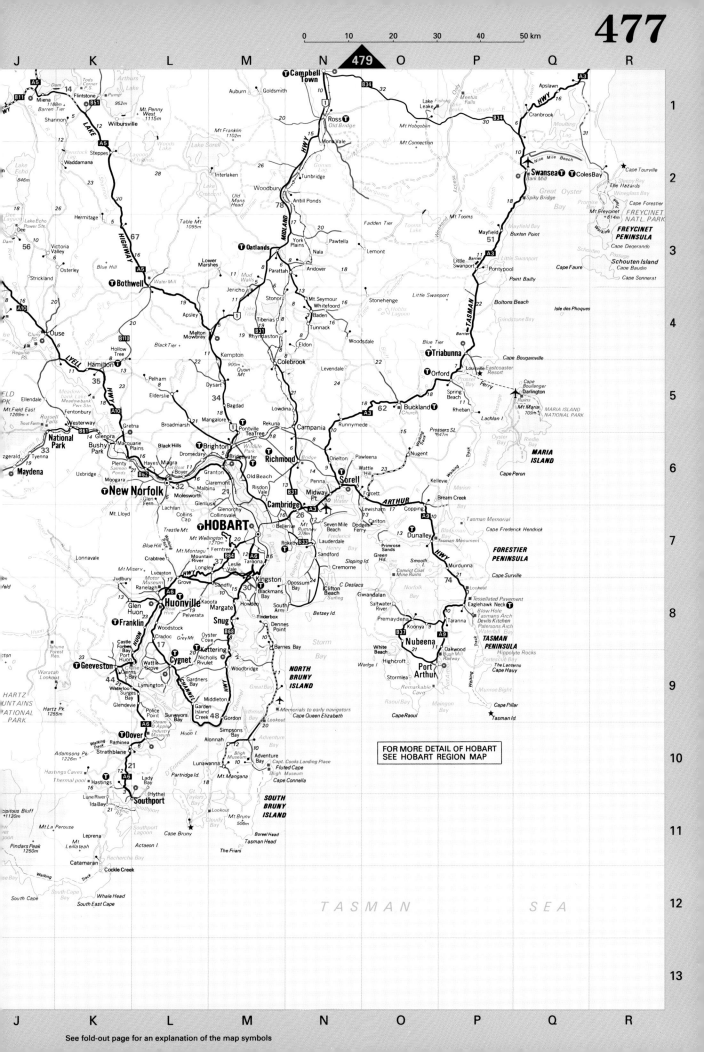

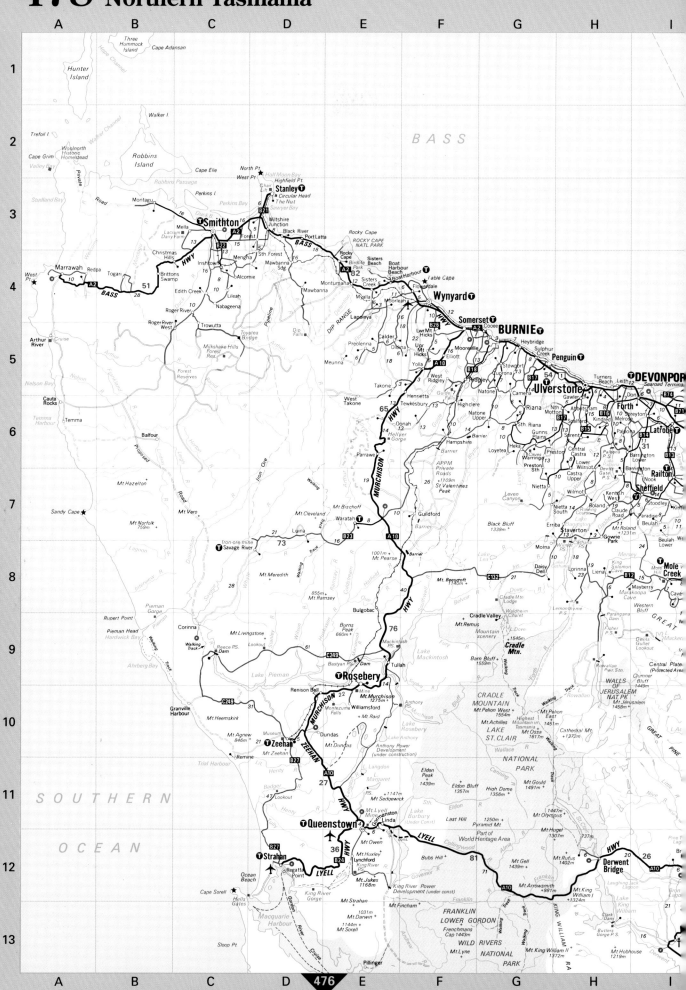

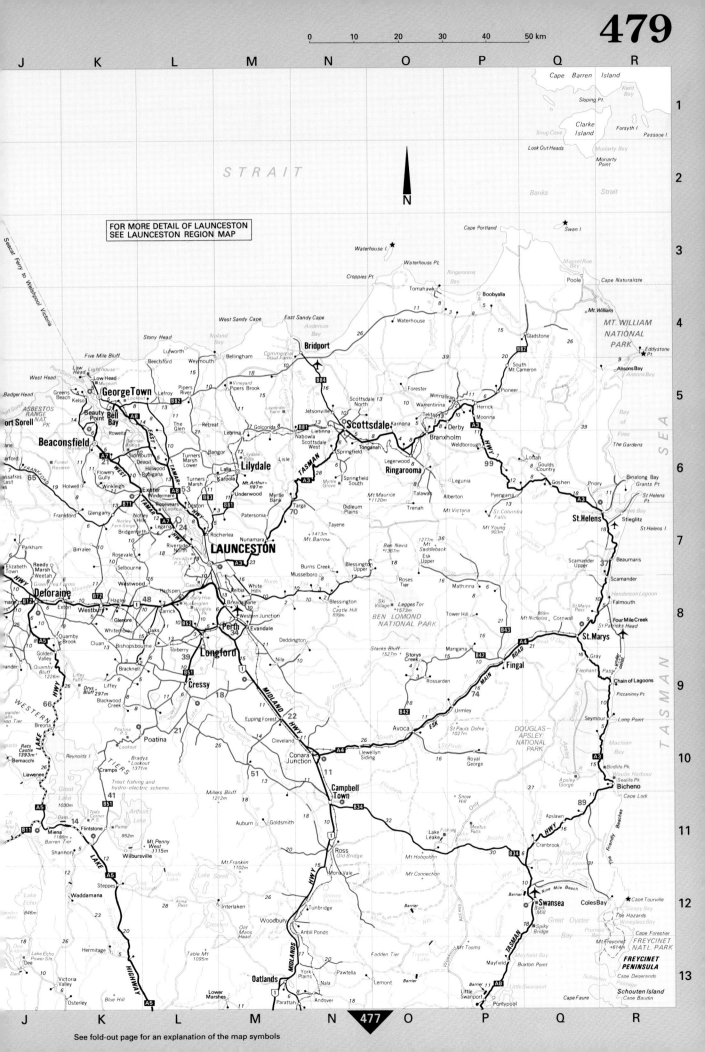

0   10   20   30   40   50 km

J   K   L   M   N   O   P   Q   R

1

2

STRAIT

N

Cape Barren Island

Kent Bay
Sloping Pt.
Snug Cove
Clarke Island
Forsyth I
Passage I.
Look Out Heads
Moriarty Bay
Moriarty Point

Banks   Strait

FOR MORE DETAIL OF LAUNCESTON
SEE LAUNCESTON REGION MAP

Waterhouse I.
Cape Portland
Swan I
Mt. William
MT. WILLIAM NATIONAL PARK
Eddystone Pt.

Waterhouse Pt.
Croppies Pt.
Mussel Roe Bay
Cape Naturaliste
Poole
Ringarooma Bay

Tomahawk
Boobyalla

West Sandy Cape
East Sandy Cape
Anderson Bay
Waterhouse
Gladstone
Ansons Bay
Ansons Bay

Stony Head
Noland Bay
Bellingham
Commercial Trout Farm
South Mt. Cameron
Pioneer

Five Mile Bluff
Weymouth
Bridport
Forester
Winnaleah
Herrick
Loffah

Low Head
Lighthouse
Beechford
Pipers River
Vineyard Pipers Brook
B84
Scottsdale North
Warrentinna
Telita
Moorina
HWY 99
Goulds Country
The Gardens
Bay of Fires

Low Head
George Town
Lefroy
Jetsonville
Karnona
Derby
Weldborough
Goshen

Badger Head
Greens Beach
Kelso
Lavender Farm
Scottsdale
Branxholm
A3

Port Sorell
ASBESTOS RANGE NAT. PK
Beauty Point
Bell Bay
A8
The Glen
Golconda
B61
Lietinna
Nabowla
Tonganah
Legerwood
Pyengana
Priory
Binalong Bay
Grants Pt.

Beaconsfield
A71
Sidmouth
Devoit
Hillwood
Robigana
Turners Marsh Lower
Lisle
Scottsdale West
Springfield
Ringarooma
Legunia
St Columba Falls
St Helens Pt.

Forest Reserve
Flowery Gully
Winkleigh
Exeter
Bangor
Lilydale
Myrtle Grove
Springfield South
Talawah
Alberton
St.Helens
St Helens I.

FRANKFORD 65
Holwell
Glenore
TAMAR HWY
Rosevears
Underwood
Mt Arthur 1187m
Targa
Didleum Plains
Trenah
Mt Victoria
St.Helens

Frankford
Glengarry
B71
Dilston
Patersonia
70
Mt Maurice 1120m
Mt Young 903m
Scamander Upper
Beaumaris

Parkham
Notley Fern Gorge
Legana
A7
Rocherlea
Nunamara
Tayene
Ben Nevis 1367m
Mt Saddleback Esk Upper
1277m 903m
37
Scamander

Birralee
Riverside North
Mt.Barrow 1413m
Burns Creek
Blessington Upper
Mathinna
Henderson Lagoon
Falmouth

Elizabeth Town
Reedy Marsh
Weetah
Rosevale
Selbourne
LAUNCESTON
A3 23
Musselboro
Roses Tier
Tower Hill
St Marys Pass
Four Mile Creek

HWY
Deloraine
B72
Hagley
Westwood
Hadspen
White Hills
Kelbia
Blessington
Ski Village
Legges Tor 1573m
869m
Mt Nicholas
Cornwall
St.Marys
St Patricks Head

Exton
Westbury
Carrick
Rutherglen
Breadalbane
Castle Hill 699m
BEN LOMOND NATIONAL PARK
B43
A4

Quamby Brook
Glenore
Whitemore
Oaks
Perth
34
Evandale
Deddington
Stacks Bluff 1527m
Mangana
B42
Fingal
Gray

Golden Valley
Quamby Bluff 1226m
Bishopsbourne
Toiberry
Longford
Nile
Storys Creek
Rossarden
MAIN ROAD 74
Elephant Pass

WESTERN 66
Liffey Falls
Bracknell
Cressy
B51
Blackwood Creek
Urmley
Avoca
ESK
St Pauls Dome 1027m
Royal George
Chain of Lagoons

Breona
Poatina P.S.
Epping Forest
Cleveland
B42
DOUGLAS-APSLEY NATIONAL PARK
A3
Long Point

Rats Castle 1393m
Bernacchi
Cramps
Bradys Lookout 1371m
Poatina
MIDLAND HWY
Conara Junction
Llewellyn Siding
St Pauls
Seymour

Liawenee
TIERS
Trout fishing and hydro-electric scheme.
Millers Bluff 1212m
Lookout
Campbell Town
B34
Waubs Harbour
Sealife Pk
Bicheno

A5
B51
Arthurs Lake
Auburn
Goldsmith
Snow Hill
Apsley Gorge
Birdlife Pk.
Cape Lodi

Miena
Flintstone
Tods Corner P.S.
Mt Penny West 1115m
Wilbursville
B34
Cranbrook
89
HWY

Shannon
952m
Ross Old Bridge
Mona Vale
Lake Leake
Meetus Falls
Nine Mile Beach

Waddamana
Steppes
Mt Franklin 1102m
Mt Hobgobbin
Mt Connection
Swansea
Coles Bay
Cape Tourville

Lake Echo
Wilbursville
Lake Sorell
Woodbury
Antill Ponds
Tunbridge
Barrier
Spiky Bridge
FREYCINET NATL. PARK

Hermitage
846m
Table Mt. 1095m
Fadden Tier
Mt Tooms
Mayfield
Buxton Point
Cape Forestier

Victoria Valley
Dee
Blue Hill
HIGHWAY
Oatlands
York Plains
Nala
Lemont
Little Swanport
FREYCINET PENINSULA

Osterley
Lower Marshes
Parattah
Andover
Pontypool
Cape Faure
Schouten Island
Cape Baudin

TASMAN SEA

J   K   L   M   N   O   P   Q   R

3

4

5

6

7

8

9

10

11

12

13

See fold-out page for an explanation of the map symbols

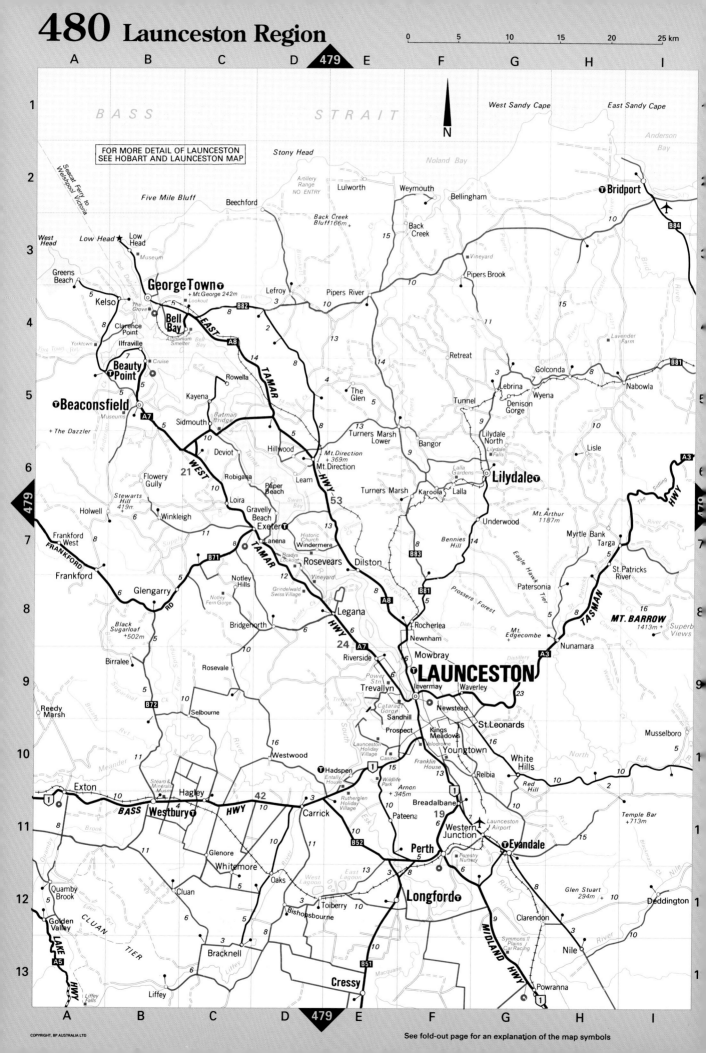

GAZETTEER OF PLACE NAMES

To enable the ready location of the place names that appear in this gazetteer, each is followed by a map page number and grid reference, and/or the text page number on which that place name occurs. A page number set in bold type indicates the main text entry for that place name.
Sale Vic. 209 R7, 220 B10, 178, 179, **184**
Sale — Place name **Vic.** — State
209 R7, 220 B10 — Sale appears on these map pages
178, 179 — Sale is mentioned on these pages **184** — Main entry for Sale.

The alphabetical order followed in the gazetteer is that of 'word-by-word', where all entries under one word are grouped together. Where a place name consists of more than one word, the order is governed by the first and then the second word. For example:
Green Bay
Green River
Greenbank
Greens Beach
Greenwood Forest
Greg Greg
Gregafell

Names beginning with Mc are indexed as Mac and those beginning with St, as Saint.
The following abbreviations and contractions are used in the gazetteer:
ACT — Australian Capital Territory
NSW — New South Wales
NT — Northern Territory
Qld — Queensland
SA — South Australia
St — Saint
Tas. — Tasmania
Vic.— Victoria
WA — Western Australia

Abbeyard Vic. 217 P10
Abbotsford NSW 96 I3
Abbotsford Vic. 194 I8, 141
Abbotsham Tas. 478 H6
Abercorn Qld 435 N6
Abercrombie NSW 109 E2, 110 F7
Aberdeen NSW 111 J1, 113 J13
Aberfeldy Vic. 209 O4
Aberglasslyn NSW 104 E2
Abermain NSW 104 D4, 111 L3
Abernethy NSW 104 D5
Abminga SA 270 I1, 357 L13
Acacia Creek NSW 428 C11
Acacia Plateau NSW 428 C11
Acacia Ridge Qld 422 H11
Acacia Store NT 352 E5
Acheron Vic. 209 K1, 217 K13, 218 F5, 150
Acton ACT 126 A11, 131 K2, 121
Adaminaby NSW 109 D8, 110 E13, **50**
Adamsfield Tas. 476 I6
Adamstown NSW 103 C8, 104 H5
Adamstown Heights NSW 103 B10
Adavale Qld 434 E7, 410
Addington Vic. 211 P2
Adelaide SA 259, 260, 262 G11, 266 I6, 223, **224–7**, 228, 229, 230–1, 235, 247, 251, 253, 257, 306
Adelaide Airport SA 260 B9, 262 F12
Adelaide Lead Vic. 213 P12
Adelaide River NT 352 E6, 332, **333**
Adelong NSW 109 B6, 110 C11, 117 R11, **50**
Adjungbilly NSW 109 C5, 110 D10
Admiralty Gulf Aboriginal Land WA 327 O1
Advancetown Qld 429 N7, 407
Adventure Bay Tas. 477 M10, 449
Agery SA 266 F3, 268 F12
Agnes Vic. 209 O11
Agnes Banks NSW 101 J5
Agnes Creek SA 270 G2
Agnes Water Qld 435 O5, 404, 417
Aileron NT 356 I5, **333**
Ailsa Vic. 212 I6
Ainslie ACT 129 M13, 131 M1
Aireys Inlet Vic. 205 C12, 208 C10, 150
Airlie Beach Qld 437 K9, **371**, 379, 383, 410, 413, 416
Airly Vic. 209 R7, 220 B9
Airport West Vic. 194 D3
Alanwick NSW 104 H3
Alawa NT 350 A1
Alawa Aboriginal Land Trust NT 353 K11
Alawoona SA 267 P5
Albacutya Vic. 212 G3, 174
Albany WA 321 N13, 324 G13, 275, **280**, 285, 287, 289, 298
Albany Creek Qld 420 F6, 414
Albert NSW 110 B2, 115 Q13, 117 Q2
Albert Park Vic. 193 B13, 140, 142
Alberton Qld 429 N1
Alberton Tas. 479 O6
Alberton Vic. 209 P11, 180, 191
Albion Qld 420 I12
Albion Vic. 208 F5
Albion Park NSW 107 F7
Albury NSW 110 A13, 117 P13, 217 R4, 219 B4, **50**, 53, 68, 182, 184, 190, 461
Alcomie Tas. 478 C4
Alderley Qld 420 G11, 441 D1
Aldersyde WA 319 L11

Aldgate SA 262 I13, 264 I1, 267 J7, 228
Aldinga SA 264 F5, 266 I8, **232**
Aldinga Beach SA 264 E5
Alectown NSW 110 D4
Alexander Heights WA 314 I2
Alexandra Vic. 209 K1, 217 K12, 218 F4, **150**
Alexandra Bridge WA 320 C8, 282
Alexandra Headland Qld 427 M10, 367, **405**
Alexandria NSW 97 M6
Alford SA 266 F1, 268 F10
Alfred Cove WA 316 F7
Alfred National Park Vic. 109 E13, 221 M6, 174
Algester Qld 422 I12
Alice NSW 113 O3
Alice Springs NT 357 J8, 359 M5, 241, 253, 329, 330, **333**, **337**, 336, 338, 339, 342, 344, 345
Allambee Vic. 209 M8
Allambie Heights NSW 99 O8
Allanby Vic. 212 H5
Allandale NSW 104 D3
Allandale Vic. 200 B7
Allans Flat Vic. 217 R6, 219 B6, 191
Allansford Vic. 211 K9, 190
Allanson WA 320 G4
Allawah NSW 117 L6
Allawah NSW 97 J12
Alleena NSW 110 A7, 117 P7
Allendale East SA 213 A7, 273 H12, 253
Allendale North SA 263 K1, 267 J3, 269 J12
Allenvale Vic. 205 A13, 174
Allies Creek Qld 435 N8
Alligator Creek Qld 436 H8, 414
Allora Qld 435 O11, **371**, 416
Alma SA 262 G1, 266 I3, 268 I12
Alma Vic. 213 P11
Almaden Qld 436 E4, 438 H13
Almonds Vic. 217 M5
Alonnah Tas. 477 M10
Aloomba Qld 439 G10
Alpha Qld 434 H3
Alpine NSW 107 B5
Alpine National Park Vic. 109 A10, 209 P2, 217 P12, 219 B11, 219 F9, 220 G1, 143, **158**, 175, 179
Alstonville NSW 113 Q3, **50**
Alton Qld 435 L11
Alton Downs SA 441 C8
Altona Vic. 194 B12, 208 F6
Alvie Vic. 211 P8, 162
Alyangula NT 353 O7
Amamoor Qld 426 G5
Ambania WA 322 C4
Ambleside SA 263 J13, 265 J1
Ambrose Qld 435 N4
Amby Qld 435 J8
Ambyne Vic. 221 J2
Amelup WA 321 O8
American River SA 266 F11, 239, 242
Amery WA 319 K4
Amherst Vic. 213 P12
Amity Point Qld 425 Q9, 385
Amoonguna NT 357 J8, 359 N6
Amosfield NSW 113 N2, 435 O12
Amphitheatre Vic. 211 O1, 213 O12
Anakie Qld 434 I3, 408
Anakie Vic. 205 D4, 208 C6, 167
Anakie Gorge Vic. 200 E13, 205 E3, 151, 167
Anarel NSW 100 A6

Ancona Vic. 217 L11, 218 G1
Andamooka SA 271 M9, 272 H1, 223, **232**, 241, 257
Anderson Vic. 209 J10
Ando NSW 109 E10
Andover Tas. 477 N3, 479 N13
Andrews SA 268 I9
Angahook – Lorne State Park Vic. 205 B11, 208 B10, 211 R11, 150, 174
Angas Plains SA 265 L6
Angaston SA 263 M4, 267 K4, 269 K13, 228, **232**
Angip Vic. 212 H5
Angle Park SA 260 C6, 227
Angle Vale SA 262 H7
Anglers Paradise Qld 429 P5
Anglers Rest Vic. 219 E11, 220 D2, 178
Anglesea Vic. 205 D11, 208 C9, **150**, 159, 180, 187
Angourie NSW 113 Q5, 92
Angurugu NT 353 O8
Angus Place NSW 100 B2
Angustown Vic. 216 H9, 183
Anindilyakwa Aboriginal Land Council NT 353 O8
Annandale NSW 97 K5
Annangrove NSW 101 M6
Annerley Qld 422 I5
Annuello Vic. 116 F10, 215 K7
Antechamber Bay SA 266 G11, 242
Antill Ponds Tas. 477 N2, 479 N12
Antwerp Vic. 212 G6, 171, 173
Anzac Village NSW 101 M10
Apamurra SA 263 O10, 267 K6
Apoinga SA 267 J2, 269 J11
Apollo Bay Vic. 211 Q12, 150, 180, 187
Appila SA 268 H6, 242
Appin NSW 107 E2, 109 I3, 111 J8
Appin Vic. 213 Q3, 216 A3
Apple Tree Creek Qld 435 P6, 385
Apple Tree Flat NSW 110 G3
Applecross WA 316 G5
Apslawn Tas. 477 Q1, 479 Q11
Apsley Tas. 477 L4
Apsley Vic. 212 B11, 273 I7
Araluen NSW 109 F7, 110 G12, 53, 77
Aramac Qld 434 F2, **371**
Aramara Qld 435 P7
Arana Hills Qld 420 D9
Aranda ACT 128 H13, 130 H1
Arapiles Vic. 212 F9, 177
Ararat Vic. 211 M1, 213 L13, 143, **150**, 156, 168, 186, 188
Aratula Qld 428 E5
Arcadia NSW 101 N5
Arcadia Vic. 216 I8
Arcadia Vale NSW 104 G8
Archdale Vic. 213 O10
Archer River Roadhouse Qld 438 E6
Archerfield Qld 422 H10
Ardath WA 319 O9
Ardeer Vic. 194 A7
Ardingly WA 322 D4
Ardlethan NSW 110 A8, 117 P8
Ardmona Vic. 216 I6
Ardmory Qld 424 F9
Ardno Vic. 210 C5
Ardross WA 316 G6
Ardrossan SA 266 F4, 268 F13, **232**
Areegra Vic. 213 J6
Areyonga NT 356 G9, 358 A9
Argalong NSW 109 C6, 110 D11

Bittern Vic. 199 M7, 208 H9
Black Hill NSW 104 G4
Black Hill SA 263 R8, 248
Black Hill Vic. 207 F4
Black Hills Tas. 474 F4
Black Mountain NSW 113 L7
Black Mountain Qld 426 I6
Black River Tas. 478 D3
Black Rock SA 268 I5, 271 O13
Black Rock Vic. 196 G11, 208 G6
Black Springs NSW 109 F1, 110 G6
Black Springs SA 267 J1, 269 J10
Black Swamp NSW 113 N3
Blackall Qld 434 F5, **373**
Blackalls Park NSW 104 G7
Blackbull Qld 440 G3
Blackburn Vic. 195 P9
Blackdown Tableland National Park Qld
   435 K4, 373, 408
Blackfellows Caves SA 273 G12
Blackheath NSW 100 E6, 109 G1, 110 I6,
   48, 72
Blackheath Vic. 212 I7
Blackmans Bay Tas. 474 I9, 477 M8, **458**
Blacksmiths NSW 104 H8
Blackville NSW 112 I11
Blackwall NSW 101 Q2
Blackwarry Vic. 209 P10
Blackwater Qld 435 K3, **373**, 408, 409
Blackwood SA 260 E12
Blackwood Vic. 200 F8, 208 D3, 151, 172, 174
Blackwood Creek Tas. 479 K9
Blackwood Ranges Vic. 200 F9
Bladensburg National Park Qld 434 C2,
   436 C13, 440 I12
Blair Athol Qld 434 I2, 436 I13, 386, 408
Blairgowrie Vic. 198 D8, 208 F9, 146
Blakehurst NSW 96 I13
Blakeville Vic. 200 E8, 208 C3
Blampied Vic. 200 C7, 208 B2
Blanchetown SA 267 M3, 269 M13, 256
Bland NSW 109 A2, 110 B7, 117 Q7
Blanket Flat NSW 109 E2, 110 F7
Blaxland NSW 100 I7
Blaxlands Ridge NSW 101 J3
Blayney NSW 110 F5, **54**
Bleak House Vic. 212 D6
Blenheim Qld 424 C12
Blessington Tas. 479 N8
Bletchley SA 265 L5
Blewitt Springs SA 264 G3
Bli Bli Qld 427 L9, 404
Blighty NSW 117 L12
Blinman SA 271 O10, **236**
Bloods Creek SA 357 L13
Bloomsbury Qld 437 K10
Blow Clear NSW 110 B6
Blowclear NSW 110 C4
Blue Gum Forest NSW 107 G1
Blue Lake National Park Qld 425 Q11,
   435 Q11, 385
Blue Mountains NSW 100 F5, 37, 45, 46, **48**, 49,
   59, 70, 72–3, 74
Blue Mountains National Park NSW 100 F5,
   109 H1, 110 I6, 48, **71**, 72
Bluff Beach SA 266 E6
Bluff Rock NSW 113 M4
Blyth SA 266 I1, 268 I10, 238
Boambee NSW 113 P7
Boara NSW 109 B3, 110 D8
Boat Harbour NSW 429 O10
Boat Harbour Tas. 478 E4, **448**, 470
Boatswain Point SA 273 D8
Bobadah NSW 115 O13, 117 O1
Bobbin Head NSW 99 J1, 83
Bobin NSW 113 N11
Bobinawarrah Vic. 217 O8
Bobs Creek Vic. 217 N11
Bochara Vic. 210 G5
Bodalla NSW 109 G8
Bodallin WA 319 R6, 324 H9
Boddington WA 318 H13, 320 H1, 324 F11
Bogan Gate NSW 110 C4, 117 R4
Bogangar NSW 429 R11
Bogantungan Qld 434 I3
Boggabilla NSW 112 I2, 435 M12
Boggabri NSW 112 H8, **54**
Bogolong NSW 109 B1, 110 D6, 117 R6
Bogong Vic. 219 C10
Bogong National Park Vic. 219 C11, 168, 176
Boho Vic. 217 L9
Boigbeat Vic. 213 L1, 215 L12
Boinka Vic. 214 E10
Boisdale Vic. 209 R6, 220 B8
Bokal WA 321 J4
Bolangum Vic. 213 L9
Bolgart WA 318 I5
Bolinda Vic. 201 J7, 208 F2
Bolivar SA 262 G9

Bolivia NSW 113 M4
Bollon Qld 434 I11
Bolong NSW 107 E11
Bolton Vic. 215 L8
Bolwarra NSW 104 F2
Bolwarra Vic. 210 F9
Bolwarrah Vic. 200 C9
Bomaderry NSW 107 D12, 109 H4, 110 I9, **80**
Bombala NSW 109 E11, 221 N2, **54-55**
Bombo NSW 107 G8, 109 I4, 111 J9
Bomera NSW 112 H11
Bonalbo NSW 113 O2
Bonang Vic. 109 C11, 221 K3, 178
Bonaparte Archipelago WA 327 M2
Bonbeach Vic. 197 L7
Bondi NSW 97 Q5, 41
Bondleigh SA 263 M13, 265 M1
Bonegilla Vic. 217 R5, 219 B5
Boneo Vic. 198 F9, 208 G10
Bongaree Qld 425 M4, 435 Q10, 385
Bonnells Bay NSW 104 F8
Bonnie Doon Vic. 217 L11, 218 H1, 150, 166
Bonnie Rock WA 319 P1, 323 P13, 324 G8
Bonnyrigg NSW 101 M9
Bonshaw NSW 113 L3, 435 N13
Bonville NSW 113 P7
Bonython ACT 132 G7
Booborowie SA 269 J9
Boobyalla Tas. 479 P4, 458
Boodarockin WA 319 R4
Boogardie WA 323 N1
Bookabie SA 270 F11
Bookaloo SA 268 D1, 271 M11, 272 I5
Bookar Vic. 211 M7
Bookara WA 322 B6
Booker Bay NSW 101 Q2
Bookham NSW 109 C4, 110 E9
Bool Lagoon SA 273 H8, **234**, 249
Boolading WA 320 I4
Boolaroo NSW 104 G6, 74
Boolarra Vic. 209 N9
Boolba Qld 435 J11
Boolboonda Qld 435 O6
Booleroo SA 268 H5, 251, 247, 257
Boolgun SA 267 N4, 269 N13
Booligal NSW 117 K6, 68
Boolite Vic. 213 K6
Booloumba Qld 426 G10
Boomahnoomoonah Vic. 217 M5
Boomi NSW 112 G2, 435 L12
Boomleera NT 352 F7
Boonah Qld 428 G5, 435 P11, **373**
Boonah Vic. 205 A11, 208 B10, 211 R10
Boonangar Qld 435 L12, 386
Boondall Qld 421 K6
Boonoo Boonoo NSW 113 N3
Boonoonar Vic. 214 H5
Booraan WA 319 P5
Booragoon WA 316 G7
Booral NSW 111 M2
Boorcan Vic. 211 M8
Boorhaman Vic. 217 N5
Boorindal NSW 115 N7
Boorolite Vic. 217 N12
Boorongie Vic. 214 I9
Booroobin Qld 426 H12
Booroopki Vic. 212 C10
Booroorban NSW 117 K10
Boorowa NSW 109 C3, 110 E8
Boors Plain SA 266 F2, 268 F11
Boort Vic. 213 P5, 216 A4, **157**
Boosey Vic. 217 L4
Bootenal WA 322 A5
Boothby SA 266 A1, 268 A10
Boowillia SA 266 H2, 268 H11
Booyal Qld 435 O6
Bopeechee SA 271 M7
Boppy Mount NSW 115 N11
Borallon Qld 424 G11
Boralma Vic. 217 O5
Borambil NSW 112 H12
Boraning WA 320 I2
Borden WA 321 P8, 324 G12
Border Ranges National Park NSW 113 P1,
   435 Q12, **71**, 73, 74, 79
Border Village SA 270 A11, 325 Q9, 307
Borderdale WA 321 M7
Bordertown SA 171, 212 A7, 267 Q13, 273 H4,
   171, **236**
Boree NSW 110 E4
Boree Creek NSW 117 O10
Boreen Point Qld 427 K4
Bornholm WA 321 M13
Boro NSW 109 F5, 110 G10
Boronia Vic. 202 A8, 218 A13
Boronia Park NSW 97 J1, 99 J12
Bororen Qld 435 O5
Borrika SA 267 N7
Borroloola NT 353 O12, 355 O2, **338**

Borung Vic. 213 P6, 216 A6
Boscabel WA 321 K5
Bostobrick NSW 113 O7
Bostock Creek Vic. 211 N9
Bostock Reservoir Vic. 200 D10, 208 C4
Boston Island SA 272 F12, 250
Botany NSW 97 N9
Botherling WA 319 J4
Bothwell Tas. 477 L3, 443, **448–9**, 455
Bouddi National Park NSW 101 R2, 64, 86
Boulder WA 325 J8, 275, 276, 292–3, **295–6**, 307
Boulia Qld 440 D13, 441 D2, **373**, 387
Boulka Vic. 214 I9
Boundain WA 321 L2
Boundary Bend Vic. 116 G9, 215 M6
Bourke NSW 115 M6, **55**
Bow NSW 112 I13
Bow Bridge WA 321 J12
Bowhill SA 267 M6
Bowden SA 259 B3
Bowelling WA 320 I4
Bowen Qld 437 J9, **373**, **377**
Bowen Hills Qld 420 I13, 422 I1, 363, 365
Bowen Mountain NSW 100 I5
Bowenfels NSW 100 C4
Bowenvale Vic. 213 P11, 175
Bowenville Qld 435 O10
Bower SA 267 L2, 269 L12
Boweya Vic. 217 M6
Bowgada WA 322 G7
Bowling Alley Point NSW 113 K10
Bowman Vic. 217 P7
Bowmans SA 266 H3, 268 H12
Bowna NSW 117 P13, 219 C4
Bowning NSW 109 D4, 110 E9
Bowral NSW 107 A6, 109 H3, 110 I8, 45, **55**
Bowraville NSW 113 O8, 75
Bowser Vic. 217 O6
Box Creek Qld 434 G8
Box Creek SA 271 K6
Box Hill Vic. 195 N9, 208 H5
Box Tank NSW 114 D13, 116 D2
Boxwood Vic. 217 L6
Boxwood Hill WA 321 R9, 324 H12
Boyankil Qld 429 P4
Boyanup WA 320 F4, 324 E12, 283
Boydtown NSW 109 F11, 221 P3, 52, 63
Boyeo Vic. 212 E6
Boyer Tas. 474 G5, 477 L6, 460
Boyerine WA 321 L4
Boyland Qld 429 M5
Boys Town Qld 429 K5
Boyup Brook WA 320 H6, 324 F12, **282**, 298
Bracalba Qld 424 I3
Bracken Ridge Qld 420 I5
Brackendale NSW 113 L10
Bracknell Tas. 479 K9, 480 C13
Bradbury SA 264 I2
Braddon ACT 126 H4, 131 L2
Bradford Vic. 213 R10, 216 B10
Bradvale Vic. 211 O5
Brady Creek SA 267 K2
Braefield NSW 113 J11
Braemar NSW 107 B6
Braeside Vic. 196 H7
Braidwood NSW 109 F6, 110 G11, **55**, 77, 124
Bramfield SA 272 D9, 240
Brampton Island Qld 437 L10, **382**, 401
Brandon Qld 436 I8
Brandsby Qld 441 H11
Branxholm Tas. 479 O6, **449**, 462
Branxholme Vic. 210 G6
Branxton NSW 104 C2, 111 K3
Brawlin NSW 109 B4, 110 C9
Bray Junction SA 273 E9
Bray Park NSW 429 P11
Bray Park Qld 420 E2
Braybrook Vic. 194 C8
Brays Creek NSW 429 M11
Breadalbane NSW 109 E4, 110 G9
Breadalbane Qld 441 D3
Breadalbane Tas. 479 M8, 480 F11
Break O'Day Vic. 201 P6, 218 B6
Breakfast Creek NSW 109 D2, 110 E7
Breakfast Creek* NSW 110 H3
Breakfast Creek Qld 421 J12, 362, 365
Breakwater Vic. 204 G13
Bream Creek Tas. 475 O6, 477 O6
Breamlea Vic. 205 F9, 208 D9, 187
Bredbo NSW 109 D8
Breelong NSW 112 E11
Breeza NSW 112 I10
Bremer Bay WA 324 H12, **282**
Brendale Qld 420 F4
Brentwood SA 266 E6, 272 I12, 248
Brentwood WA 316 H7
Breona Tas. 479 J10
Bretti NSW 113 M12
Brewarrina NSW 112 A6, 115 O6, **55**

Cathedral Rock Vic.   213 J13
Catherine Field NSW   101 K11, 56
Catherine Hill Bay NSW   104 G9
Cathkin Vic.   217 J12, 218 E3
Cathundral NSW   112 C12, 115 R12
Cattai NSW   101 L4, 91
Catumnal Vic.   213 P4
Caulfield Vic.   195 K13, 196 B11, 137
Cavan NSW   109 D5, 110 E10
Cave of Fishes Vic.   210 I1
Cave of Hands Vic.   210 I2
Caveat Vic.   201 R2, 217 J12, 218 D2, 191
Cavendish Vic.   210 H3
Caversham WA   315 P7
Caves Beach NSW   104 H8
Caveside Tas.   478 I8
Cawdor NSW   101 J12
Cawongla NSW   113 P2
Cecil Park NSW   101 L9
Cecil Plains Qld   435 N10, 414
Cedar Brush NSW   104 C10
Cedar Glen Qld   429 L9
Cedar Grove Qld   429 K3
Cedar Pocket Qld   426 H3
Ceduna SA   270 H12, 272 A6, **237**, 243, 306
Cement Creek Vic.   209 K4, 218 F11
Centennial Park NSW   97 O5, 46
Central Aboriginal Land WA   325 Q2, 327 Q12
Central Castra Tas.   478 H6
Central Mangrove NSW   104 C12
Central Tilba NSW   109 G9
Ceratodus Qld   435 N6
Ceres NSW   112 D13
Ceres Vic.   208 D8, 167
Cervantes WA   318 C1, 322 C13
Cessnock NSW   104 C5, 111 K3, 49, **57**
Chain Valley NSW   104 G9
Chain of Lagoons Tas.   479 R9
Chain of Ponds SA   263 J10
Chakola NSW   109 E8
Challambra Vic.   213 J6
Chambigne NSW   113 O5
Chandada SA   272 C7
Chandler Qld   423 P5
Chandler SA   270 G3
Chandler WA   319 P4
Chandlers Creek Vic.   109 E12, 221 M4
Channel Country Qld   440 C13, 441 E4, 373, **387**, 408, 416
Chapel Hill Qld   422 D4
Chapman ACT   130 D12
Chapple Vale Vic.   211 O11
Charam Vic.   212 E11
Charbon NSW   110 H4
Chardons Bridge Qld   429 M3
Charleroi Vic.   219 C6
Charleston SA   263 K11
Charlestown NSW   103 A13, 104 H6
Charleville Qld   434 G8, **379**, 387
Charley Creek Vic.   211 P11
Charleyong NSW   109 F6, 110 H11
Charlotte Pass NSW   109 C9, 63, 71, 72
Charlton NSW   115 O6
Charlton Vic.   213 N6, **161**
Charlwood Qld   428 F6
Charmhaven NSW   104 F10
Charnwood ACT   128 D6
Charters Towers Qld   436 G9, **379, 385**
Chatsbury NSW   109 F3, 110 H9
Chatswood NSW   99 L11
Chatsworth Qld   426 F2
Chatsworth Vic.   211 K6
Cheepie Qld   434 F8, 410
Cheesemans Creek NSW   110 E4
Cheethams Flats NSW   100 B5
Chelmer Qld   422 F6
Chelsea Vic.   197 L7, 208 H7
Cheltenham NSW   98 F8
Cheltenham SA   260 C6, 227
Cheltenham Vic.   196 G10
Chepstowe Vic.   211 O4
Chermside Qld   420 H8
Cherokee Vic.   207 I7
Cherry Gardens SA   264 H2
Cherry Tree Pool WA   321 L6
Cherrypool Vic.   212 H12
Cherryville SA   262 I11
Cheshunt Vic.   217 O10, 187
Chesney Vale Vic.   217 M7
Chester Hill NSW   96 C7
Chetwynd Vic.   210 D2, 212 D13
Cheviot Vic.   201 R4, 209 J1, 217 J13, 218 D4
Chewton Vic.   200 E2, 216 C11, 160
Chidlow WA   318 H8
Chifley ACT   130 H11
Chifley NSW   97 P10
Chifley WA   325 L9
Childers Qld   435 P6, **385**

Childers Vic.   209 M9, 191
Chillagoe Qld   436 E4, 438 G12, **385–6**, 401
Chillagoe – Mungana Caves National Parks Qld   436 D4, 438 F12, **374**, 385
Chillingham NSW   113 Q1, 429 N10
Chillingollah Vic.   215 M10
Chiltern Vic.   117 O13, 217 P5, 152, **161**, 188
Chiltern Hills Qld   441 G1
Chiltern State Park Vic.   217 P5, 159, 161
Chilwell Vic.   204 D11
Chinamans Wells SA   273 E9
Chinchilla Qld   435 M9, **386**
Chinderah NSW   113 R1, 429 R9
Chinkapook Vic.   116 F11, 215 L10
Chintin Vic.   201 K7, 208 F2
Chippendale NSW   94 A13
Chipping Norton NSW   96 A10, 49
Chirnside Park Vic.   202 C1
Chirrup Vic.   213 M5
Chisholm ACT   133 L6
Chiswick NSW   97 J3
Chittaway Point NSW   104 F12
Chittering WA   318 G6, 308
Chorregon Qld   434 C2, 436 C13
Chowerup WA   320 I8
Chowilla SA   116 A7
Christies Beach SA   264 F3, 228, 229, 250
Christmas Creek Qld   429 K8
Christmas Hills Tas.   478 C4
Christmas Hills Vic.   201 P10, 208 I4, 218 B10
Chudleigh Tas.   478 I8
Chullora NSW   96 E7
Church Land SA   267 L1, 269 L10
Church Point NSW   101 Q5
Churchill Qld   424 H12
Churchill Vic.   209 O9, 176
Churchill Island Vic.   199 Q12, 208 I10, 163, 170
Churchill National Park Vic.   196 F1, 208 I6
Churchlands WA   314 E10
Chute Vic.   211 O2, 213 O13
Cinnabar Qld   426 A2
City Beach WA   314 C10, 279
Clackline WA   318 I7, 304
Clairview Qld   437 L12
Clandulla NSW   110 H4
Clare Qld   436 I8
Clare SA   266 I1, 268 I10, **237–8**
Clare Valley SA   268 I10, 228, 231, 236–7, 240, 251, 253
Claremont Tas.   474 H6, 477 M6, 447
Claremont WA   316 E3, 318 F9, 279
Clarence NSW   100 D4
Clarence Point Tas.   480 B4
Clarence Town NSW   111 L3, 63
Clarendon NSW   101 K5
Clarendon Qld   424 F4
Clarendon SA   264 H2, 266 I7
Clarendon Tas.   480 G12
Clarendon Vic.   200 B11, 205 A1, 208 B4, 211 R4
Claretown Vic.   200 C9
Clareville Beach NSW   101 Q4
Clarke Island Tas.   479 Q1
Clarkefield Vic.   201 J8, 208 F3
Clarks Hill Vic.   200 B8
Claude Road Tas.   478 H7
Clay Wells SA   273 F9
Clayfield Qld   421 J11
Claymore WA   320 E6
Claypans SA   267 M6
Clayton Qld   435 P6
Clayton SA   265 K9
Clayton Vic.   196 E6
Clear Lake Vic.   212 F11
Clear Mountain Qld   420 A4
Clear Ridge NSW   110 B6
Cleary WA   319 M1, 323 M13
Cleland Conservation Park SA   260 G10, 227, 228, **235**
Clematis Vic.   202 G12
Clements Gap SA   268 G9
Clements Gap Conservation Park SA   268 G9
Clempton Park NSW   96 I8
Clermont Qld   434 I2, 436 I13, **386**, 408
Cleve SA   268 A10, 272 G10, **238**
Cleveland Qld   425 O11, 385, **386**, 410, 411
Cleveland Tas.   479 N10
Cliffordville WA   319 L12
Clifton NSW   107 G2
Clifton Qld   435 O1, **386**
Clifton Beach Qld   439 E5, 409
Clifton Beach Tas.   475 K9, 477 N8, 446, 462
Clifton Gardens NSW   97 O1, 99 O13
Clifton Springs Vic.   205 H7, 208 E8, 164
Clinton Centre SA   266 F3, 268 F12
Clinton Conservation Park SA   266 G3, 268 G12
Clintonvale Qld   435 O11
Clonbinane Vic.   201 N6, 208 H2, 216 H13
Cloncurry Qld   440 E8, **386**, 387, **388**, 400, 401, 404, 406, 415

Clontarf NSW   99 P11
Closeburn Qld   424 I8
Clothiers Creek NSW   429 Q11
Clouds Creek NSW   113 O6
Clovelly NSW   97 Q6, 41
Cloverdale WA   315 N13, 317 N2
Cluan Tas.   479 K8, 480 B12
Club Terrace Vic.   109 D12, 221 L6
Clumber Qld   428 E6
Clunes NSW   113 Q2
Clunes Vic.   208 A1, 211 Q1, 213 Q13, 216 A13, 154, 155–6, **161–2**
Clwydd NSW   100 D5
Clybucca NSW   113 P9
Clyburn NSW   96 D3
Clyde NSW   96 C3
Clyde Vic.   208 I8
Clydebank Vic.   220 C9
Clydesdale Vic.   200 C4, 208 C1, 213 R12, 216 B12
Coal Creek Qld   424 D5
Coal Point NSW   104 G7
Coalcliff NSW   107 G2
Coaldale NSW   113 P4
Coalstoun Lakes Qld   435 O7
Coalstoun Lakes National Park Qld   435 O7, 372
Coalville Vic.   209 N8, 176
Cobains Vic.   209 R7, 220 B10
Cobaki NSW   429 Q9
Cobar NSW   115 M10, **57**
Cobargo NSW   109 F9, 54
Cobark NSW   111 L1, 113 L12
Cobaw Vic.   200 I5, 208 E1, 216 E13
Cobbadah NSW   113 J7
Cobbannah Vic.   220 C6
Cobberas – Tingaringy National Park Vic.   109 B11, 219 H10, 220 H1, 160
Cobbitty NSW   101 J11
Cobbora NSW   112 F12
Cobden Vic.   211 M9, 160
Cobdogla SA   267 P3, 269 P12, 233
Cobera SA   267 P5
Cobourg Peninsula NT   352 G2, 345, 347
Cobram Vic.   117 M13, 217 K3, 51, **162**, 182, 191
Cobrico Vic.   211 M9
Cobungra Vic.   219 D12, 220 D3
Coburg Vic.   194 G5, 208 G5
Cocamba Vic.   215 L9
Cochranes Creek Vic.   213 P9
Cockaleechie SA   272 F11
Cockatoo Vic.   209 J6, 166
Cockburn SA   114 A13, 116 A1, 269 R2, 271 R12
Cockle Creek Tas.   477 K12, 453, 455
Cocklebiddy WA   325 O10, **284, 286**, 307
Coconut Grove NT   350 C6
Cocoparra National Park NSW   117 N7, 67
Cocoroc Vic.   208 E6
Codrington Vic.   210 H9
Coen Qld   438 E7, 395
Coffin Bay SA   272 E12, **238**, 243, 251
Coffin Bay National Park SA   272 D11, 235, 238, 251
Coffs Harbour NSW   113 P7, **57–8**
Coghills Creek Vic.   208 A2, 211 Q2
Cohuna Vic.   116 I12, 216 C2, **162**
Colac Vic.   211 P9, **162**, 190
Colac Colac Vic.   219 G5
Colbinabbin Vic.   216 F8
Coldstream Vic.   201 Q11, 208 I5, 218 C11, 145, 188
Coleambally NSW   117 M9, **58**
Colebrook Tas.   475 J1, 477 M5, 462
Coledale NSW   107 G3, 109 I3, 111 J8
Coleraine Vic.   210 F4, 161, **163**
Coles Bay Tas.   477 R2, 479 R12, 443, 450, **452**
Coles Beach Vic.   208 K9, 147
Coleyville Qld   428 F3
Colignan Vic.   214 I5
Colinroobie NSW   117 O8
Colinton NSW   109 E7
Colinton Qld   424 C1
Collarenebri NSW   112 E4
Collaroy NSW   99 Q6, 112 H12
Collector NSW   109 E5, 110 G10
College Park SA   259 H4
Collerina NSW   115 O5
Collgar WA   319 P7
Collie NSW   112 D11
Collie WA   320 G4, 324 F11, **286**
Collie Cardiff WA   320 G4
Collieburn WA   320 G4
Collingullie NSW   110 A10, 117 P10
Collins WA   320 G9
Collins Cap Tas.   474 G6, 477 L7
Collinsfield SA   268 H9
Collinsvale Tas.   474 H6, 477 M7
Collinsville Qld   437 J10, 377
Collombatti Rail NSW   113 O9
Colly Blue NSW   112 I10
Colmslie Qld   421 K13, 423 K1

Koppio SA   272 F11, 238, 251, 255
Koraleigh NSW   215 N9
Korbel WA   319 O7
Koriella Vic.   209 K1, 217 K12, 218 F3
Korobeit Vic.   200 F10, 208 D4
Koroit Vic.   211 J9, **171**
Korong Vale Vic.   213 P6
Koroop Vic.   213 R2, 216 B2
Korora NSW   113 P7, 58
Korralocking WA   319 M5
Korumburra Vic.   209 L10, 145, **171–2**, 173
Korunye SA   262 F5
Korweinguboora Vic.   200 D8
Korweinguboora Reservoir Vic.   208 C3
Kosciusko National Park NSW   109 C6, 110 D13, 219 I9, 220 I1, 37, **62–3, 71**, 72, 158, 163
Kotara NSW   103 A10
Kotara South NSW   103 A11
Kotta Vic.   216 E5
Kotupna Vic.   216 H5
Koumala Qld   437 L11
Kowanyama Aboriginal Community Qld   438 B10, 401
Kowat Vic.   221 M4
Koyuga Vic.   216 G5
Krambach NSW   111 N1, 113 N12
Kringin SA   267 Q7
Krongart SA   273 H10
Krowera Vic.   209 K10
Kudardup WA   320 C9
Kuender WA   321 Q2
Kukerin WA   321 O3, 324 G11, 290
Kulangoor Qld   427 K9
Kulgera NT   356 I12, **343**
Kulgera SA   270 G1, 241
Kulgun Qld   428 G4
Kulikup WA   320 I6, 282
Kulin WA   319 O12, **296**
Kulja WA   319 L1, 323 L13
Kulkami SA   267 O7
Kulkyne Vic.   214 I5
Kulnine Vic.   214 D3
Kulnura NSW   104 C11, 111 K5
Kulpara SA   266 G2, 268 G11
Kultpo SA   264 H4
Kultpo Colony SA   264 H5
Kulwin Vic.   116 F10, 215 J9
Kulyalling WA   319 K11
Kumarl WA   325 J11
Kumbarilla Qld   435 N10
Kumbia Qld   435 O9
Kumorna SA   267 O11, 273 F2
Kunama NSW   109 B6, 117 R12, 219 H1
Kunat Vic.   215 O12
Kundabung NSW   113 O10
Kungala NSW   113 P6
Kunghur NSW   113 Q1, 429 N13
Kunjin WA   319 N11
Kunkala Qld   424 F12
Kunlara SA   267 N5
Kunmunya Aboriginal Land WA   327 M3
Kununoppin WA   319 N4
Kununurra WA   327 R3, 289, **296**, 301, 310, 311
Kunwarara Qld   435 M2
Kuraby Qld   423 L12
Kuranda Qld   439 E6, 374, 378, 392, **399**, 403
Kureelpa Qld   427 J9
Kuridala Qld   440 E9, 388
Ku-ring-gai Chase National Park NSW   101 P4, 111 K6, 47, **70**, 83
Kurlana SA   267 O3
Kurmond NSW   101 J4
Kurnbrunin Vic.   212 F3
Kurnell NSW   97 O13, 47
Kurnwill Vic.   214 D5
Kurraca Vic.   213 P8
Kurrajong NSW   100 I4, 109 H1, 111 J6
Kurrajong East NSW   101 J3
Kurrajong Heights NSW   100 I4
Kurri Kurri NSW   104 E4, 111 L3
Kurting Vic.   213 Q8, 216 A8
Kurumbul Qld   113 J2, 435 M12
Kweda WA   319 L11
Kwelkan WA   319 O4
Kwinana WA   318 E10, 324 E10, **296**, 307
Kwobrup WA   321 O5
Kwolyin WA   319 N8
Kyabram Vic.   216 H6, 164, **172**, 182
Kyalite NSW   116 H10, 215 O8
Kyancutta SA   272 E8, 306
Kybeyan NSW   109 E9
Kybong Qld   426 H5
Kybunga SA   266 I2, 268 I11
Kybybolite SA   212 B11, 273 I7
Kydra NSW   109 E9
Kyeamba NSW   109 A6, 110 B11, 117 Q11
Kyeema Conservation Park SA   264 H5, 257
Kyeemagh NSW   97 L10

Kyndalyn Vic.   215 L6
Kyneton Vic.   200 G5, 208 D1, 216 D13, 160, 167, **172**
Kynuna Qld   436 A11, 440 G10, **399**
Kyogle NSW   113 P2, 435 Q12, **73**
Kyup Vic.   210 H4
Kyvalley Vic.   216 G6
Kywong NSW   117 O10

La Perouse NSW   97 O12
Laanecoorie Vic.   213 Q10, 216 A10
Laanecoorie Reservoir Vic.   216 A10, 163
Laang Vic.   211 L9
Labertouche Vic.   209 L7, 189
Labrador Qld   429 P5
Lachlan Tas.   474 F6, 477 L7
Lady Barron Tas.   476 B5, 459
Lady Bay Tas.   477 L10
Lady Elliot Island Qld   435 Q4, 377, 380, **381**
Lady Julia Percy Island Vic.   210 H10, 181
Lady Musgrave Island Qld   435 P4, 361, **375**, 377, **381**
Ladys Pass Vic.   216 F10
Ladysmith NSW   109 A5, 110 B10, 117 Q10
Laen Vic.   213 K7
Laggan NSW   109 F3, 110 G8, 61
Lagoon Pocket Qld   426 G4
Laguna NSW   104 A7
Lah Vic.   212 I5
Lah-Arum Vic.   212 I11
Laheys Creek NSW   112 F13
Laidley Qld   424 D12, **399**
Lake Albacutya Park Vic.   214 G13
Lake Albert SA   265 P11, 267 L10, 246
Lake Alexandrina SA   265 N7, 267 K9, 182, 223, 229, 237, 240, 246, 249
Lake Argyle WA   327 R4, 297, 301, 311, 332
Lake Barrine National Park Qld   439 E12, 371, 374, 417
Lake Barrington Tas.   479 H7, 465
Lake Bathurst NSW   109 F5, 110 G10
Lake Bellfield Vic.   213 J13, 167, 185
Lake Boga Vic.   116 H11, 215 P12, 171, 186
Lake Bolac Vic.   211 L, **172**
Lake Brown WA   319 P3
Lake Buloke Vic.   213 L6, 163, 189
Lake Burley Griffin ACT   127 E4, 130 L7, 119, 120–1
Lake Burragorang NSW   100 G11, 49
Lake Burrumbeet Vic.   211 P3, 152
Lake Cargelligo NSW   117 N5, **73**
Lake Charm Vic.   116 I12, 213 Q1, 215 Q13, 216 A1
Lake Clarendon Qld   424 C10, 399
Lake Clifton WA   318 E13, 320 E1
Lake Corangamite Vic.   211 O8, 158, 161
Lake Cowal NSW   117 Q5, 77, 90
Lake Cullulleraine Vic.   116 C8, 214 E3
Lake Dalrymple Qld   436 H10
Lake Dartmouth Vic.   219 E8, 186
Lake Dumbleyung WA   321 M4, 308
Lake Eacham Qld   439 E13, 371, 417
Lake Eacham National Park Qld   439 E12, 374
Lake Echo Tas.   479 J12, 449
Lake Eildon Vic.   218 H3, 150, 175
Lake Eppalock Vic.   216 E10, 157, 168
Lake Eucumbene NSW   109 C8, 50, 124
Lake Eyre SA   271 M5, 241, 387
Lake Eyre National Park SA   271 M5, 441 A12, 441 B12, **234–5**
Lake Frome SA   271 P10, 232
Lake Fyans Vic.   213 K12, 167, 185
Lake Gairdner SA   271 K11
Lake George NSW   109 E5, 110 G10, 124
Lake George SA   273 E9
Lake Gilles Conservation Park SA   271 L13, 235, 242, 257
Lake Ginninderra ACT   128 G10
Lake Goldsmith Vic.   211 O3, 152
Lake Gordon Tas.   476 H6, 447, 451, 468
Lake Grace WA   321 Q2, 324 H11, **296–7**
Lake Hindmarsh Vic.   212 F4, 169, 174, 177, 183, 189
Lake Hinds WA   318 I2
Lake Illawarra NSW   107 F6, 85, 89
Lake Jindabyne NSW   109 C9
Lake Kajarabie Qld   435 K11
Lake King WA   324 I11, **297**, 303
Lake Leake Tas.   477 O1, 479 O11, 452, 464
Lake Lonsdale Vic.   213 K11
Lake MacFarlane SA   268 B1
Lake Macleod WA   324 C1
Lake Macquarie NSW   104 G7, **73–4**, 80
Lake Marmal Vic.   213 O5
Lake Meering Vic.   213 Q3, 216 A3
Lake Menindee NSW   116 D2
Lake Moogerah Qld   428 E6, 373
Lake Mountain Vic.   209 L3, 165, 175
Lake Mulwala NSW   117 N13, 217 M4, 79, 135, 182, 183, 191
Lake Mundi Vic.   210 B4
Lake Pedder Tas.   476 H7, 443, 447, 451, 468

Lake Plains SA   265 M7
Lake Powell Vic.   215 L6
Lake Rowan Vic.   217 L6
Lake St Clair Tas.   476 H1, 451, 455, 468
Lake Samsonvale Qld   420 B1
Lake Sorell Tas.   479 L12, 461, 464, 465
Lake Tinaroo Qld   439 D1, 371, 401
Lake Torrens SA   268 E1, 271 N10, 232
Lake Tyers Vic.   220 G8, 171
Lake Tyers National Park Vic.   220 H8
Lake Victoria NSW   214 C1
Lake View NSW   104 G8
Lake View SA   268 H9
Lake Wallawalla Vic.   214 B3
Lake Wendouree Vic.   207 B5
Lakefield National Park Qld   438 G9, **374**, 388
Lakemba NSW   96 G8
Lakes Entrance Vic.   109 B13, 220 G8, 151, **172–3**, 179
Lakesland NSW   107 B1
Lal Lal Vic.   200 C11, 208 B4
Lalbert Vic.   116 G12, 213 N1, 215 N13
Lalbert Road Vic.   215 O12
Lalla Tas.   479 M6, 480 F6, 460
Lallat Vic.   213 K8
Lamb Island Qld   425 P12, 411
Lambton NSW   103 A6, 104 H5
Lameroo SA   267 P8, **245**
Lamington Qld   429 K9
Lamington National Park Qld   113 P1, 429 M9, 366, 368, 372, **376**
Lamplough Vic.   213 O12
Lancaster Vic.   216 H6
Lancefield Vic.   201 J5, 208 F1, 216 F13, **173**, 174
Lancelin WA   318 D4, 324 E9, 293, **297**
Landers Shoot Qld   427 J11
Landsborough Qld   427 K12, 367, **399**
Landsborough Vic.   213 M11
Landsdale WA   314 H2
Lane Cove NSW   99 K12, 41
Lanena Tas.   480 D7
Lang Lang Vic.   209 J8
Langford WA   317 N8
Langhorne Creek SA   265 M5, 267 K8, 255
Langi Kal Kal Vic.   211 O2
Langi Logan Vic.   211 M2
Langkoop Vic.   210 B1, 212 B12, 273 I8
Langley Vic.   200 G4, 216 E12
Langlo Crossing Qld   434 F8
Langloh Tas.   474 D1
Langshaw Qld   426 F4
Langville Vic.   213 Q3, 216 A3
Langwarrin Vic.   199 N1
Lankeys Creek NSW   109 A7, 117 Q12
Lannercost Qld   436 G6
Lansdowne NSW   96 B8, 113 N12
Lansvale NSW   96 A8
Lapoinya Tas.   478 E4
Lara Vic.   205 F5, 208 D7, 167
Lara Lake Vic.   205 F5, 208 D7
Larapinta Drive NT   358 G7
Laravale Qld   429 J7
Largs NSW   104 F2
Largs Bay SA   262 F10
Larpent Vic.   211 P9
Larrakeyah NT   351 O12
Larras Lee NSW   110 E4
Larrimah NT   352 I11, 354 I1, **343**
Lascelles Vic.   116 F12, 213 J1, 215 J13
Latham ACT   128 C8
Latham WA   322 H9, 324 F7
Latrobe Tas.   478 I6, **459**
Lauderdale Tas.   475 K7, 477 N7, 446
Laughtondale NSW   101 M2
Launceston Tas.   472, 479 L7, 480 F9, 443, 454, 455, 457, **459–60**
Launceston Airport Tas.   480 G11
Launching Place Vic.   209 J5, 218 E12
Laura Qld   436 E1, 438 G10, 388, 395
Laura SA   268 H7, 231, 240
Laurel Hill NSW   109 B7, 117 R12
Laurence Road NSW   113 P4
Laurieton NSW   113 O11, 56
Lauriston Vic.   200 F5, 208 D1, 216 D13
Lauriston Reservoir Vic.   200 F5, 208 D1, 216 D13, 172
Lavender Bay NSW   95 C10
Lavers Hill Vic.   211 O12, 150, 180
Laverton Vic.   208 F6
Laverton WA   325 K6, 292, **298**
Lavington NSW   117 P13, 217 R4, 219 B4
Lawes Qld   424 C11
Lawgi Qld   435 M5
Lawloit Vic.   212 D7
Lawn Hill National Park Qld   440 A5, 401, 406
Lawnton Qld   420 E2
Lawrence Vic.   200 A6, 208 B2, 211 R2, 213 Q13
Lawrenny Tas.   474 C1
Lawson NSW   100 G7, 109 H1, 110 I6

Narraport Vic.   213 M4
Narraweena NSW   99 P7
Narrawong Vic.   210 F9
Narrewillock Vic.   213 O5
Narridy SA   268 H8
Narrikup WA   321 M11, 301
Narrogin WA   321 K2, 324 G11, 285, **303**
Narromine NSW   110 D1, 112 D13, **80**
Narrung SA   265 N9, 267 K9, 247
Narrung Vic.   215 N7
Narwee NSW   96 G10
Narwinbi Aboriginal Land Trust NT   353 O12, 355 O2, 338
Naryilco Qld   441 H12
Nashdale NSW   110 F5
Nashville Qld   421 J3, 426 G3
Nathalia Vic.   117 L13, 216 H4, 178
Nathan Qld   423 J8, 363, 365
Natimuk Vic.   212 G9, 173, **177–8**
Native Valley SA   263 L13, 265 L1
Natone Upper Tas.   478 G6
Nattai NSW   109 H2, 110 I7
Nattai River NSW   100 H13
Natte Yallock Vic.   213 O11
Natural Arch National Park Qld   429 N9, 407
Natya Vic.   215 N8
Naval Base WA   318 F10
Navarre Vic.   213 M10
Navigators Vic.   200 B10
Nayook Vic.   209 L6, 164
N'Dhala Gorge National Park NT   357 K8, 359 R5, 335, 337, **345**
Neales Flat SA   267 K3, 269 K12
Neath NSW   104 D4
Nebo Qld   437 K11, **407**
Nectar Brook SA   268 F5
Nedlands WA   316 F3
Neds Corner Vic.   214 C2
Needilup WA   321 R7
Needles Tas.   479 J8
Neeralin Pool WA   321 L3
Neerim Junction Vic.   209 L6
Neerim South Vic.   209 L7, 164, 189
Neeworra NSW   112 F3, 435 K13
Neika Tas.   474 H8
Neilborough Vic.   216 C8
Neilrex NSW   112 F11
Nelia Qld   436 A10, 440 H8
Nelligen NSW   109 G7, 53
Nelshaby SA   268 G7
Nelson Vic.   210 C7, 160, 161, 181, 248
Nelson Bay NSW   111 M3, 78, **80**
Nelsons Plains NSW   104 H2
Nelungaloo NSW   110 C4, 117 R4
Nembudding WA   319 M5
Nerang Qld   429 O5, 366, **407**
Neranwood Qld   429 O7
Nerriga NSW   109 G5
Nerrigundah NSW   109 F8, 77
Nerrin Nerrin Vic.   211 M5
Nerrina Vic.   200 A9, 207 H3
Nerring Vic.   211 O3
Netherby Vic.   212 E5
Nethercote NSW   109 F11
Neuarpurr Vic.   212 B10, 273 I6
Neurea NSW   110 F3, 89
Neuroodla SA   268 G1
Neurum Qld   424 G2
Neusa Vale Qld   426 I3
Neutral Bay NSW   95 F7, 97 N1, 99 N13, 41
Nevertire NSW   112 C11, 115 R11
Neville NSW   109 E1, 110 F6
New Angledool NSW   112 C3, 115 R3, 435 J13
New Beith Qld   429 J2
New Brighton NSW   113 Q2, 429 R13
New England NSW   37, 51, **84**, 86, 87, 88
New England National Park NSW   113 N8, 51, **71**
New Farm Qld   419 H2, 423 J2, 365
New Farm Park Qld   423 J3, 365
New Farm Wharf Qld   423 J2
New Koreela NSW   428 C13
New Lambton NSW   103 B7
New Lambton Heights NSW   103 A7
New Mapoon Aboriginal Community Qld   438 C1
New Mollyann NSW   112 F11
New Norcia WA   318 G4, 324 F9, **303**
New Norfolk Tas.   474 F5, 477 L6, 443, 447, 449, 455, 457, **460–1**
New Residence SA   267 P4, 269 P13
New Town Tas.   473 C6, 474 I7, 446, 457
New Well SA   267 N4, 269 N13
Newborough Vic.   209 N8
Newbridge NSW   109 E1, 110 G6
Newbridge Vic.   213 Q9, 216 B9
Newburn WA   315 P12, 317 P1
Newbury Vic.   200 E7, 208 D2
Newcastle NSW   103, 104 I5, 111 L4, 37, 46, **80**, 329
Newcomb Vic.   204 H11

Newdegate WA   324 H11
Newell Qld   439 B1, 405
Newfield Vic.   211 M11
Newham Vic.   200 I6, 208 E2, 216 E13
Newhaven Vic.   199 Q13, 208 I10, 163, 170
Newington Vic.   207 C7
Newland SA   264 G10
Newland Head Conservation Park SA   266 I10
Newlands WA   320 F5
Newlyn Vic.   200 B7, 208 B2, 211 R2
Newman WA   326 I12, 297, **303**, 309
Newmarket Qld   420 H12
Newmerella Vic.   220 I7
Newminster WA   319 M12
Newnes NSW   110 I4
Newnes Junction NSW   100 D4
Newnham Tas.   480 F8
Newport Vic.   194 D10
Newport Beach NSW   101 Q5
Newry Vic.   209 Q6, 220 A8
Newrybar NSW   113 Q2
Newstead Qld   421 J13, 423 J1, 365
Newstead Tas.   480 F9
Newstead Vic.   200 C3, 213 R12, 216 B12, 161
Newton Boyd NSW   113 N5
Newtown NSW   97 L6, 101 K5
Newtown Vic.   204 C10, 167
Ngallo Vic.   214 B11, 267 R8
Ngapala SA   267 J2, 269 J11
Ngarkat Conservation Park SA   267 P10, 273 G1, 243, 245, 250
Ngukurr NT   353 L9
Nhill Vic.   212 E6, 171, **178**
Nhulunbuy NT   353 P4, 337, 339
Ni Ni Vic.   212 F6
Niagara Park NSW   104 E13
Niangala NSW   113 L10
Nicholls Rivulet Tas.   474 G11, 477 L9
Nicholson Vic.   220 F8
Nierinna Tas.   474 H9
Nietta Tas.   478 G7
Nightcap National Park NSW   113 Q2, 435 Q12, 74, 78
Nightcliff NT   350 B6
Nildottie SA   267 M5
Nile Tas.   479 M9, 480 H13, 456, 457, 460
Nillahcootie Vic.   217 M11
Nilma Vic.   209 L8
Nimbin NSW   113 Q2, 74
Nimmitabel NSW   109 E9
Ninda Vic.   215 K12
Ninderry Qld   427 L9
Nindigully Qld   112 F1, 435 K12
Nine Mile Vic.   213 O7
Ninety Mile Beach Vic.   220 C11, 135, 171, 172, 179, 180, 181, 184, 191
Ninnes SA   266 G2, 268 G11
Ninyeunook Vic.   213 O4
Nipan Qld   435 M5
Nippering WA   321 M3
Nirranda Vic.   211 L10
Nitmiluk (formerly Katherine Gorge) National Park NT   352 G8, 341, **345**
Noarlunga Centre SA   264 F3
Nobby Creek NSW   429 O10
Nobby Glen Qld   426 G6
Noble Park Vic.   196 G4
Nobles Nob NT   355 K10
Noccundra Qld   434 B11, 441 J10, 387
Nockatunga Qld   434 B10, 441 I10
Noggerup WA   320 G5
Noggojerring WA   318 I7
Nokarning WA   319 P6
Nollamara WA   314 H7
Nomans Lake WA   321 M1
Nonda Qld   436 B10, 440 H8
Nondiga Qld   426 C1
Nonedia SA   265 K3
Noojee Vic.   209 M6, 145, 164
Nookanellup WA   321 L6
Noonamah NT   352 E5, **345**
Noonbinna NSW   109 C1, 110 E6
Noondoo Qld   112 D1, 435 J12
Noora SA   116 A9, 214 A5, 267 Q4, 269 Q13
Nooramunga Vic.   217 L6
Noorat Vic.   211 M8, 160, 186
Noorinbee Vic.   221 M6
Noorlah Qld   437 K10
Noorongong Vic.   219 C6
Noosa Heads Qld   427 L6, 435 Q8, 367, 390, **407, 409**
Noosa National Park Qld   427 M6, **376**, 390, 407, 409
Noosaville Qld   427 L6, 390, 407, 409
Nora Creina Bay SA   273 E9
Noradjuha Vic.   212 G10
Norah Head NSW   104 G11, 111 L5, 87
Norahville NSW   104 G11
Noranda WA   315 K6

Nords Wharf NSW   104 G9
Norlane Vic.   204 D2, 167
Norman Park Qld   423 J3, 363
Normanby Qld   419 A1, 422 H2
Normanhurst NSW   98 F6
Normanton Qld   440 F3, 377, 388, 395, 398, 400, 401, **409**
Normanville SA   264 D8, 266 H9, 257
Normanville Vic.   213 P2, 216 A2
Nornakin WA   319 N10
Nornalup WA   321 J13, 287, 298
Norong Vic.   217 O5
Norpa WA   319 P7
Norseman WA   325 K10, 292, 297, **303**, 307
North Adelaide SA   259 D3, 225, 226, 227
North Arm Qld   427 K8
North Balgowlah NSW   99 O9
North Beach WA   314 C5, 318 F8
North Berry Jerry NSW   110 B9
North Blackwood Vic.   200 F7
North Bondi NSW   97 R5
North Bruny Island Tas.   477 M9, 452
North Canberra ACT   127 F3, 129 L12
North Curl Curl NSW   99 Q7
North Dandalup WA   318 F12, 305
North Deep Creek Qld   426 G1
North Fitzroy Vic.   194 H7, 140
North Fremantle WA   316 B7
North Geelong Vic.   204 D5, 167
North Haven NSW   113 O11, 56
North Hobart Tas.   472 B1, 473 D8, 446
North Lake WA   316 G10
North Manly NSW   99 P8
North Motton Tas.   478 H6
North Narrabeen NSW   99 P3
North Parramatta NSW   96 C1, 98 C12
North Perth WA   314 I11
North Riverside Tas.   480 E9
North Rocks NSW   98 C10
North Ryde NSW   98 I10
North Shields NSW   272 F12, 251
North Shore Vic.   204 F2
North Star NSW   112 I2, 435 M13
North Stradbroke Island Qld   424 Q10, **385**, 386
North Strathfield NSW   96 G4
North Sydney NSW   95 B7, 97 M2, 99 M13, 38
North West Aboriginal Land NT   356 D13
North West Cape WA   326 D10, 291, 309
Northam WA   318 I7, 324 F9, **303–4**, 308
Northampton WA   322 A2, 324 D6, **304**
Northbridge NSW   99 M11
Northbridge WA   313 D3, 278
Northcliffe WA   320 G11, 324 F13, **304**, 304
Northcote Vic.   194 I7
Northern Gully WA   322 B4
Northgate Qld   421 K9, 365
Northmead NSW   98 B11
Northville NSW   104 G6
Northwood Vic.   216 H11
Norton Summit SA   262 I11, 227, 229
Norval Vic.   211 L1, 213 L13
Norwell Qld   429 O2
Norwood SA   260 E8
Notley Hills Tas.   479 K7, 480 C8, 456
Notting WA   319 P11
Notting Hill Vic.   196 C6
Notts Well SA   267 M4, 269 M13
Nourlangie NT   352 H5
Nowa Nowa Vic.   220 G7, 172
Nowendoc NSW   113 L11
Nowie North Vic.   215 N10, 186
Nowingi Vic.   214 H5
Nowley NSW   112 F6
Nowra NSW   107 D12, 109 H5, 110 I10, **80**, 89
Nowra Hill NSW   109 H5, 110 I10
Nubba NSW   109 B3, 110 D8
Nubeena Tas.   475 N11, 477 O8
Nudgee Qld   421 L8
Nudgee Beach Qld   421 M6
Nugadong WA   322 I12
Nugent Tas.   475 N4, 477 O6
Nukarni WA   319 O5
Nulkaba NSW   104 C4
Nulla Vale Vic.   201 J4, 208 F1, 216 F12
Nullagine WA   326 I10, 299
Nullan Vic.   213 J7
Nullarbor SA   270 D11, 307
Nullarbor National Park SA   270 C11, 325 R9
Nullarbor Plain SA/WA   270 A9, 325 M8, 236, 243, 275, **306–7**
Nullawarre Vic.   211 L10
Nullawil Vic.   213 M3
Numbla Vale NSW   109 D10
Numbugga NSW   109 F10
Numbulwar NT   353 N8
Numeralla NSW   109 E8
Numinbah NSW   429 N10
Numinbah Valley Qld   429 N8, 368, 407

ACCIDENT ACTION

Those vital first moments
Treating an unconscious person

1. CLEAR AIRWAY
Lie victim on side and tilt head back.

2. CLEAR MOUTH
Quickly clear mouth, using fingers if necessary. If breathing, leave on side.

3. TILT
IF NOT BREATHING, place victim on back. Tilt head back. Support the jaw, keeping fingers away from neck.

4. BLOW
Kneel beside victim's head.
Place your widely open mouth over victim's slightly open mouth, sealing nostrils with your cheek. Blow until victim's chest rises.

5. LOOK, LISTEN
Watch chest fall. Listen for air escaping from mouth. Repeat steps 4 and 5, 15 times per minute.

6. RECOVERY POSITION
When breathing begins, place victim on side, head back, jaw supported, face pointing slightly towards ground.

NOTE: For an injured child, cover mouth and nose with your mouth. Blow until chest rises (20 times per minute).

7. IF UNCONSCIOUS
If victim is unconscious and trapped in the car, still tilt head back and support the jaw.

SEND SOMEONE FOR AN AMBULANCE.

DO NOT LEAVE AN UNCONSCIOUS PERSON.